# Environmental Protection, Law and Policy

Environmental law is shaped by the results of research in many different fields. Legal regulation and legal activities are supported and legitimated by the work of biologists, chemists, economists, engineers, geneticists and physicists, but also underpinned by cultural assumptions, the sources of which – philosophies, popular culture, ecological theories – are diverse and sometimes obscure, but arguably no less influential than those from the more traditional scientific domains. A full understanding of environmental problems requires students, practitioners and academics working within the discipline of environmental law, at whatever level, to engage with the concepts and methods employed by disciplines other than law.

This book explores environmental law from a range of perspectives, emphasising the policy world from which environmental law is drawn and nourished. It seeks to introduce students to a wide variety of non-legal material, whilst placing that material firmly in a legal context. A range of regulatory techniques is explored, through a close examination of both pollution control and land use. The highly complex nature of current environmental problems, demanding sophisticated and responsive legal controls, is illustrated by several in-depth case studies, including legal and policy analysis of the highly contested issues of genetically modified organisms and renewable energy projects.

**Jane Holder** is Reader at University College London.

**Maria Lee** is Senior Lecturer at King's College London. Both have published widely in environmental law.

# Environmental Protection, Law and Policy

Text and Materials

Second Edition

JANE HOLDER AND MARIA LEE

CAMBRIDGE
UNIVERSITY PRESS

CAMBRIDGE UNIVERSITY PRESS
Cambridge, New York, Melbourne, Madrid, Cape Town, Singapore, São Paulo, Delhi

Cambridge University Press
The Edinburgh Building, Cambridge CB2 8RU, UK

Published in the United States of America by Cambridge University Press, New York

www.cambridge.org
Information on this title: www.cambridge.org/9780521690263

First published 2007
Reprinted 2009

Printed in the United Kingdom at the University Press, Cambridge

*A catalogue record for this publication is available from the British Library*


ISBN  978-0-521-69026-3 paperback

For Sue Elworthy

# Contents

# Table of EU legislation

# Table of international conventions

# Table of legislation

# Table of cases

# Acknowledgements

Every attempt has been made to secure permission to reproduce copyright material in this title and grateful acknowledgement is made to the authors and publishers of all reproduced material. In particular, the publishers would like to acknowledge the following for granting permission to reproduce material from the sources set out below:

Carolyn Abbot, 'The Enforcement of Pollution Control Laws in England and Wales: A Case for Reform?' 22 *Environmental and Planning Law Journal* 68 (2005) pp. 70–3. Reprinted with permission by Sweet and Maxwell.

Carolyn Abbot, 'Environmental Command Regulation and its Enforcement' in Benjamin Richardson and Stepan Wood, *Environmental Law for Sustainability* (2006) pp. 61–4. Reprinted with permission by Hart Publishing.

William M. Adams, *Against Extinction: the Story of Conservation* (2004), p. 240. Reprinted with permission by Earthscan.

William M. Adams, *Future Nature: A Vision for Conservation* (2003) pp. 116–17, 117–18. Reprinted with permission by Earthscan.

John Alder, 'Environmental Assessment – the Inadequacies of Law' © J. Holder and Pauline Lane *et al.* (eds.), *Perspectives on the Environment: Interdisciplinary Research in Action* (1993) p. 61. Reprinted with permission by Ashgate.

Alexandra Aragao, 'The Impact of EC Environmental Law on Portuguese Law' in Richard Macrory (ed.), *Reflections on Thirty Years of EU Environmental Law: A High Level of Protection?* (2006) p. 507. Reprinted with the permission of Europa Law Publishing.

Barry Barton, 'Underlying Concepts and Theoretical Issues in Public Participation in Resources Development' in Donald Zillman, Alastair Lucas and George (Rock) Pring (eds.), *Human Rights in Natural Resource Development: Public Participation in the Sustainable Development of Mining and Energy*

*Resources* (2002), pp. 92–6. Reprinted with permission by Oxford University Press.

Wilfred Beckerman, '"Sustainable Development": Is it a Useful Concept?' (1994) 3 *Environmental Values* 191, pp. 191–206. Reprinted with permission from White Horse Press.

Derek Bell and Tim Gray, 'The Ambiguous Role of the Environment Agency in England and Wales' (2002) 11 *Environmental Politics* 76, pp. 83–4, 87–9. Routledge. Reprinted with permission of the publisher Taylor and Francis Ltd, http://tandf.co.uk/journals).

Derek Bell, Tim Gray and Claire Haggett, 'The "Social Gap" in Wind Farm Siting Decisions: Explanations and Policy Responses' (2005) 14(4) *Environmental Politics* pp. 460–74. Routledge. Reprinted with permission of the publisher Taylor and Francis Ltd, http://tandf.co.uk/journals).

Stuart Bell and Donald McGillivray, *Environmental Law* 6th edition (2005), p. 449. Reprinted with permission by Oxford University Press.

Thomas Bernauer, *Genes, Trade, and Regulation.* Princeton University Press. Reprinted by permission of Princeton University Press.

Julia Black, 'Decentring Regulation: Understanding the role of Regulation and Self-Regulation in a "Post-Regulatory" World' (2001) 54 *Current Legal Problems* 103, pp. 106–11, 125–7. Reprinted with permission by Oxford University Press.

Eric Bregman and Arthur Jacobson, 'Environmental Performance Review: Self-Regulation in Environmental Law' in Gunther Teubner, Lindsay Farmer and Declan Murphy (eds.), *Environmental Law and Ecological Responsibility: The Concept and Practice of Ecological Self-Organisation* (1994) p. 222. Reproduced by permission of John Wiley & Sons Limited.

Roger Brownsword, 'What the World Needs Now: Techno-Regulation, Human Rights and Human Dignity' in Roger Brownsword (ed.), *Global Governance and the Quest for Justice, Volume IV: Human Rights* (2004), pp. 208–9. Reprinted with permission by Hart Publishing.

Sir Robert Carnwath, 'Environmental Litigation – A Way Through the Maze?' (1999) 11 *Journal of Environmental Law* 3, p. 13. Reprinted with permission by Oxford University Press.

Liam Cashman, 'Environmental Impact Assessment: A Major Instrument for Achieving Integration' in Marco Onida (ed.), *Europe and the Environment: Legal*

*Essays in Honour of Ludwig Kramer* (2004), pp. 86–90. Reprinted with the permission of Europa Law Publishing.

Damian Chalmers, 'Inhabitants in the Field of EC Environmental Law' in Paul Craig and Grainne de Burca (eds.), *The Evolution of EU Law* (1999), pp. 672–84. Reprinted with permission by Oxford University Press.

Damian Chalmers, '"Food for Thought": Reconciling European Risks and Traditional Ways of Life' (2003) 66 *Modern Law Review* 532, pp. 538–9, 540–2. Reprinted with permission by Blackwell Publishing.

Aaron Cosbey, *Lessons Learned on Trade and Sustainable Development* (2004), p. 1. International Institute for Sustainable Development and International Centre for Trade and Sustainable Development. Reprinted with the permission of IISD and ICTSD.

Richard Cowell, 'Stretching the Limits: Environmental Compensation, Habitat Creation and Sustainable Development' (1997) 22 *Transactions of the Institute of British Geographers*, pp. 292–3. Reprinted with permission by Blackwell Publishing.

Sean Coyle and Karen Morrow, *The Philosophical Foundations of Environmental Law* (2004), pp. 167–8, 108–9. Reprinted with permission by Hart Publishing.

Cormac Cullinan, *Wild Law: A Manifesto for Earth Justice* (2003), pp. 32–3. Reprinted with permission by Green Books.

Barry Cullingworth and Vincent Nadin, *Town and Country Planning in Britain* 13th edition (2003), pp. 15, 77–8. Routledge. Reproduced by permission of Taylor and Francis Books UK.

D. Curtin, 'Women's Knowledge as Expert Knowledge: Indian Women and Ecodevelopment' in K. J. Warren (ed.), *Eco-feminism: Women, Nature and Culture* (1997), pp. 84 and 88. Reprinted with permission by Indiana University Press.

Herman E. Daly, 'On Wilfred Beckerman's Critique of Sustainable Development' (1995), *Environmental Values* 49, pp. 49–52. Reprinted with permission from White Horse Press.

Sara Dillon, *International Trade and Economic Law and the European Union* (2002), pp. 4–5, 11. Reprinted with permission by Hart Publishing.

Andrew Dobson, 'Biocentrism and Genetic Engineering' (1995) 4 *Environmental Values* 3, pp. 231–6. Reprinted with permission from White Horse Press.

Andrew Dobson, *Green Political Thought* (2000), pp. 62–8, 205. Routledge. Reproduced by permission of Taylor and Francis Books UK.

Andrew Dobson, *Citizenship and the Environment* (2003) pp. 1–8, 12–15, 146–56. Reprinted with permission by Oxford University Press.

John S. Dryzek, *The Politics of the Earth: Environmental Discourses* (1997), pp. 79–95, 117–18, 118–19. Reprinted with permission by Oxford University Press.

Paul Durman, 'Tract: Locke, Heidegger and Scruffy Hippies in Trees' in Allen Abramson and Dimitrios Theodossopoulous (eds.), *Land, Law and Environment: Mythical Land, Legal Boundaries* (2000) pp. 87–90. Reprinted with permission by Pluto Press.

Klaus Eder, 'Rationality in Environmental Discourse: A Cultural Approach', in W. Rudig (ed.), *Green Politics Three* (1995), p. 9. Reprinted with permission by Edinburgh University Press, www.eup.ed.ac.uk.

Susan Emmenegger and Axel Tschentscher, 'Taking Rights Seriously: The Long Way to Biocentrism in Environmental Law' (1994) 6 *Georgetown International Environmental Law* 545, pp. 545 and 552–68. © Georgetown International Environmental Law Review. Reprinted with the permission.

Neil Evernden, *The Social Creation of Nature* (Baltimore, John Hopkins, 1993) pp. 4–9. Reprinted with permission of The Johns Hopkins University Press.

Sanford E. Gaines, 'International Trade, Environmental Protection and Development as a Sustainable Development Triangle' (2002) 11 *Review of European Community & International Environmental Law* 259, pp. 263, 272–4. Reprinted with permission by Blackwell Publishing.

Sanford E. Gaines and Clíona Kimber, 'Redirecting Self-Regulation' (2001) 13 *Journal of Environmental Law* 157, p. 169. Reprinted with permission by Oxford University Press.

Kevin Gray, 'Equitable Property' (1994) 47 *Current Legal Problems* 157, pp. 194–8. Reprinted with permission by Oxford University Press.

David Hall, Michael Hebbert and Helmut Lusser, 'The Planning Background', in A. Blowers (ed.), *Planning for a Sustainable Environment* (1993) pp. 20–1. Reprinted with permission by Earthscan.

G. Hardin, 'The Tragedy of the Commons' (1968) 162 *Science* 1243, pp. 1244–5. Reprinted with the permission of the American Association for the Advancement of Science.

Carol Harlow, 'Public Law and Popular Justice' (2002) 65 *Modern Law Review* 1, pp. 8–14. Reprinted with permission by Blackwell Publishing.

David Hayes, 'Ozymandias on the Solway', from *Town and Country*, edited by Anthony Barnett and Roger Scruton (1998) pp. 46–7. Reprinted by permission of The Random House Group Ltd.

Patsy Healey, *Collaborative Planning* (1997), pp. 8–9, 33–4, 39–41, 47–8, 50–3. Reprinted with permission by Macmillan.

Patsy Healey and Tim Shaw, 'Changing Meanings of "Environment" in the British Planning System' (1994) 19 *Transactions of the Institute of British Geographers* 425, p. 431. Reprinted with permission by Blackwell Publishing.

Chris Hilson, *Regulating Pollution* (Oxford, Hart Publishing, 2000), p. 1. Reprinted with permission by Hart Publishing.

Chris Hilson, 'Greening Citizenship: Boundaries of Membership and the Environment' (2001) 13 *Journal of Environmental Law* 335, pp. 335–6. Reprinted with permission by Oxford University Press.

Chris Hilson, 'Planning Law and Public Perceptions of Risk: Evidence of Concern or Concern Based on Evidence' [2004] JPL 1638. Reprinted with permission by Sweet and Maxwell.

J. Holder, 'New Age: Rediscovering Natural Law' edited by M. D. A. Freeman, (2000) 53 *Current Legal Problems* pp. 151, 159–65. Reprinted with permission by Oxford University Press.

J. Holder, *Environmental Assessment: The Regulation of Decision Making* (2005) pp. 22–9, 60. Reprinted with permission by Oxford University Press.

Francis Jacobs, 'The Role of the European Court of Justice in the Protection of the Environment' (2006) 18 *Journal of Environmental Law* 185, pp. 192–3. Reprinted with permission by Oxford University Press.

Michael Jacobs, 'Sustainable Development as a Contested Concept', in Andrew Dobson (ed.), *Fairness and Futurity: Essays on Environmental Sustainability and Social Justice* (1999), pp. 22, 25–7. Reprinted with permission by Oxford University Press.

Robert A. Kagan and John T. Scholz, 'The "Criminology of the Corporation" and Regulatory Enforcement Strategies' in K. Hawkins and J. M. Thomas (eds.), *Enforcing Regulation* (1984), pp. 67–86. Reprinted with kind permission from the authors and Springer Science and Business Media.

Bettina Lange, 'From Boundary Drawing to Transitions: The Creation of Normativity under the EU Directive on Integrated Pollution Prevention and Control' (2002) 8 *European Law Journal* 246, pp. 259–60. Reprinted with permission by Blackwell Publishing.

Kathryn V. Last, 'Mechanisms for Environmental Regulation – a Study of Habitat Conservation', in Andrea Ross (ed.), *Environment and Regulation*, Hume Papers on Public Policy Vol. 8, No. 2 (2000), pp. 39–41. Reprinted with permission by Edinburgh University Press, www.eup.ed.ac.uk.

Maria Lee, *EU Environmental Law: Challenges, Change and Decision Making* (2005), pp. 47, 269–70. Reprinted with permission by Hart Publishing.

Maria Lee and Carolyn Abbot, 'The Usual Suspects? Public Participation Under the Aarhus Convention' (2003) 66 *Modern Law Review* 80, pp. 107–8. Reprinted with permission by Blackwell Publishing.

Jurgen H. Lefevere, 'Greenhouse Gas Emission Allowance Trading in the EU: A Background' 3 *Yearbook of European Environmental Law* 149, pp. 169, 162–3. Reprinted with permission by Oxford University Press.

Gertrude Lubbe-Wolff, 'Efficient Environmental Legislation – On Different Philosophies of Pollution Control in Europe' (2001) 13(1) *Journal of Environmental Law* 79, pp. 80–1, 84–7. Reprinted with permission by Oxford University Press.

Roy MacLaren, 'Integrating Environment and Labour in the World Trade Organization' © John J. Kirton and Michael J. Trebilcock, *Hard Choices, Soft Law* (2004). Reprinted with permission by Ashgate.

Richard Macrory, 'The Enforcement of Community Environmental Laws: Some Critical Issues' (1992) 29 *Common Market Law Review* 347, pp. 362–7. Reprinted with the permission of Wolters Kluwer.

Richard Macrory, 'Regulating in a Risky Environment' (2001) 54 *Current Legal Problems* 619, pp. 622–4, 630–1, 627–8. Reprinted with permission by Oxford University Press.

Richard Macrory and Sharon Turner, 'Participatory Rights, Transboundary Environmental Governance and EC Law' (2002) 39 *Common Market Law Review* 489, pp. 495–7. Reprinted with the permission of Wolters Kluwer.

Donald McGillivray (ed.), *Locality and Identity: Environmental Issues in Law and Society* pp. 60–1. © J. Holder and Donald McGillivray (1999). Reprinted with permission by Ashgate.

Donald McGillivray and John Wightman, 'Private Rights, Public Interest and the Environment', in Tim Hayward and John O'Neill (eds.), *Justice, Property and the Environment* (1997), p. 154. Reprinted with permission by Ashgate.

Alex Mehta and Keith Hawkins, 'Integrated Pollution Control and its Impact: Perspectives From Industry' (1998) 10 *Journal of Environmental Law* 61, pp. 65–8. Reprinted with permission by Oxford University Press.

Michele Micheletti, Andreas Follesdal and Dietland Stolle, 'Introduction' in Micheletti, Follesdal and Stolle (eds.), *Politics, Products and Markets: Exploring Political Consumerism Past and Present* (2004), pp. x–xv. Reprinted with permission byTransaction Press.

Chris Miller, 'Attributing "Priority" to Habitats' (1997) 6 *Environmental Values* 341, 348. Reprinted with permission from White Horse Press.

Karen Morrow, 'Public Participation in the Assessment of the Effects of Certain Plans and Programmes on the Environment' 4 *Yearbook of European Environmental Law* 49, pp. 54–7. Reprinted with permission by Oxford University Press.

François Ost, 'A Game Without Rules? The Ecological Self-Organisation of Firms', in Gunther Teubner, Lindsay Farmer and Declan Murphy (eds), *Environmental Law and Ecological Responsibility: The Concept and Practice of Ecological Self-Organisation* (1994), pp. 350–5. Reproduced by permission of John Wiley & Sons Limited.

Susan Owens and Richard Cowell, *Land and Limits: Interpreting Sustainability in the Planning Process* (Routledge, 2002), pp. 1–5, 52–3, 59–60, 121. Reproduced by permission of Taylor and Francis Books UK.

David Pearce and Edward B. Barbier, *Blueprint for a Sustainable Economy* (2000), pp. 2, 8. Reprinted with permission by Earthscan.

Mark Pennington, *Liberating the Land: The Case for Private Land-Use Planning* (2002), pp. 47–51. Reprinted with permission from Institute of Economic Affairs.

Oren Perez, *Ecological Sensitivity and Global Legal Pluralism: Rethinking the Trade and Environment Conflict* (2004), pp. 33–4. Reprinted with permission by Hart Publishing.

John Peterson and Elizabeth Bomberg, *Decision Making in the European Union* (1999), pp. 185–99. Reprinted with permission by Macmillan.

Lavanya Rajamani, 'From Stockholm to Johannesburg: The Anatomy of Dissonance in the International Environmental Dialogue' (2003) 12 *Review of European Community and International Environmental Law* 23, pp. 25–6, 30–1. Reprinted with permission by Blackwell Publishing.

Richard Rawlings, 'Engaged Elites, Citizen Action and Institutional Attitudes in Commission Enforcement' (2000) 6 *European Law Journal* 28, pp. 8–27. Reprinted with permission by Blackwell Publishing.

Christopher Rodgers, 'Agenda 2000: Land Use and the Environment: Towards a Theory of "Environmental" Property Rights', in J. Holder and C. Harrison (eds.) *Law and Geography* (2002), pp. 255–6. Reprinted with permission by Oxford University Press.

Andrea Ross-Robertson, 'Is the Environment Getting Squeezed Out of Sustainable Development?' (2003) *Public Law* 249, pp. 250, 251–3. Reprinted with permission by Sweet and Maxwell.

Wolfgang Sachs, *The Development Dictionary* (1992), pp. 28–9. Reprinted with permission from Zed Books.

Nicolas de Sadeleer, 'Habitat Conservation in EC Law: From Nature Sanctuaries to Ecological Networks' (2005) 5 *Yearbook of European Environmental Law*, pp. 251–2. Reprinted with permission by Oxford University Press.

Nicolas de Sadeleer, 'EC Law and Biodiversity', in Richard Macrory (ed.), *Reflections on 30 Years of EU Environmental Law* (Europa, 2006), pp. 351–2. Reprinted with the permission of Europa Law Publishing.

Mark Sagoff, 'Biotechnology And Agriculture: The Common Wisdom And Its Critics' (2001) 9 *Indiana Journal of Global Legal Studies* 13, pp. 13–18. Reprinted with permission by Indiana University Press.

Joanne Scott, 'Flexibility, "Proceduralization", and Environmental Governance in the EU' in Joanne Scott and Grainne de Búrca (eds), *Constitutional Change in the European Union* (2000), pp. 261–70. Reprinted with permission by Hart Publishing.

Joanne Scott, 'European Regulation of GMOs: Thinking about Judicial Review in the WTO' [2004] *Current Legal Problems* 117, pp. 118–19, 144–7. Reprinted with permission by Oxford University Press.

Joanne Scott and Jane Holder, 'Law and New Environmental Governance in the European Union', in Grainne de Búrca and Joanne Scott (eds.), *Law and New Governance in the EU and the US* (2006), p. 213. Reprinted with permission by Hart Publishing.

Karen Scott, 'Tilting at Offshore Windmills: Regulating Wind Farm Development within the Renewable Energy Zone' (2006) 18 *Journal of Environmental law* 89, pp. 117–18. Reprinted with permission by Oxford University Press.

Philip Selznick, 'Law in Context Revisited' (2003) 30 *Journal of Law and Society* 177, pp. 177–8. Reprinted with permission by Blackwell Publishing.

Gregory Shaffer, 'The World Trade Organisation under Challenge: Democracy and the Law and Politics of the WTO's Treatment of Trade and Environment Matters' (2001) 25 *Harvard Environmental Law Review* 1, pp. 62–74, footnotes omitted. Reprinted with the permission of the author and Harvard Law School.

Vandana Shiva, *Staying Alive: Women, Ecology and Development* (1989), pp. 22–3. Reprinted with permission from Zed Books.

G. Smith, *Deliberative Democracy and the Environment* (2003), pp. 1–5. Routledge. Reproduced by permission of Taylor and Francis Books UK.

Nicola Staeck, Tanja Malek and Hubert Heinelt, 'The Environmental Impact Assessment Directive' © Hubert Heinelt, Tanja Malek, Randall Smith and Annette E. Toller (eds.), *European Union Environment Policy and New Forms of Governance: A Study of the Implementation of the Environmental Impact Assessment Directive and the Eco-management and Audit Scheme Regulation in Three Member States* (2001), pp. 40–1. Reprinted with permission by Ashgate.

Mark Stallworthy, *Sustainability, Land Use and Environment: A Legal Analysis* (2002), pp. 100–2. Cavendish Publishing. Reprinted with permission by Taylor and Francis Books UK.

Jenny Steele, 'Participation and Deliberation in Environmental Law: Exploring a Problem-solving Approach' (2001) 21 *Oxford Journal of Legal Studies* 415, pp. 427–8, 437–8. Reprinted with permission by Oxford University Press.

Peter Strachan and David Lal, 'Wind Energy Policy, Planning and Management Practice in the UK: Hot Air or a Gathering Storm? (Routledge 2004) 38(5) *Regional Studies*, pp. 551–71, 553–4. Reprinted with permission by Taylor and Francis Books UK.

Cass R. Sunstein, *Risk and Reason: Safety, Law and the Environment* (2002) pp. 58–64, 291, 292–3, 294. Reprinted with permission from Cambridge University Press.

C. R. Sunstein, 'Beyond the Precautionary Principle' (2003) 151 *University of Pennsylvania Law Review* 1003, pp. 1003–8. Reprinted with permission from University of Pennsylvania and William S. Hein.

Peter Taylor, *Beyond Conservation: A Wildland Strategy* (2005), pp. 2–4. Reprinted with permission by Earthscan.

Riki Therivel, *Strategic Environmental Assessment in Action* (2004), pp. 14–16. Reprinted with permission by Earthscan.

Third Party Rights of Appeal, research project by Green Balance, Leigh Day and Co. Solicitors, John Popham and Michael Purdue (on behalf of CPRE, RSPB, WWF-UK, Civic Trust, Friends of the Earth, TCPA, ELF and ROOM), 2002, pp. 4–5. Reprinted with the permission of Green Balance.

Stephen Tindale and Chris Hewitt, 'Must the Poor Pay More? Sustainable, Development, Social Justice and Environmental Taxation' in A. Dobson (ed.), *Fairness and Futurity: Essays on Environmental Sustainability and Social Justice* (1999), pp. 234–8. Reprinted with permission by Oxford University Press.

David Toke, 'Will the Government Catch the Wind?' (2005) *Political Quarterly*, pp. 48, 50. Reprinted with permission by Blackwell Publishing.

Joseph H. H. Weiler, 'Epilogue: "Comitology" as Revolution – Infranationalism, Constitutionalism and Democracy', in Christian Joerges and Ellen Vos (eds.), *EU Committees: Social Regulation, Law and Politics* (1999), pp. 348–9. Reprinted with permission by Hart Publishing.

Hugh Wilkins, 'The Need for Subjectivity in Environmental Law' (2003) 23 EIA Rev 401, pp. 401–13. Reprinted with permission by Elsevier.

Rhiannon Williams, 'The European Commission and the Enforcement of Environmental Law: An Invidious Position' (1994) 14 *Yearbook of European Law* 351, pp. 353–4. Reprinted with permission by Oxford University Press.

Wouter Wils, 'Subsidiarity and EC Environmental Policy: Taking People's Concerns Seriously' (1994) *Journal of Environmental Law* 85–91, p. 89. Reprinted with permission by Oxford University Press.

World Commission on Environment and Development, *Our Common Future* (1987) (the 'Brundtland Report'), pp. 1–2, 4, 5, 43–5. Reprinted with permission by Oxford University Press.

B. Wynne, 'Uncertainty and Environmental Learning: Reconceiving Science and Policy in the Preventive Paradigm' (1992) 2 *Global Environmental Change* 111, pp. 114–24. Reprinted with permission by Elsevier.

S. Yearley, 'Green Ambivalence about Science: Legal-rational Authority and the Scientific Legitimation of a Social Movement' (1992) 43 *British Journal of Sociology* 511, pp. 514–30. Reprinted with permission by Blackwell Publishing.

# Preface

A book about environmental law fits remarkably well in the Law in Context series. Understanding environmental problems, even at a simple level, requires some appreciation of the concepts and methods employed by disciplines other than law. In turn, the law is shaped by the results of research in these different fields, with legal regulation and legal activities (for example standard setting, enforcement, prosecution) supported and legitimated by the work of biologists, chemists, economists, engineers, geneticists and physicists. As Dan Farber states, 'it has long been a cliché that environmental regulation operates on the frontier of science'.[1] But, importantly, environmental law is also underpinned by cultural assumptions, the sources of which – philosophies, popular culture, ecological theories – are diverse and sometimes obscure, but arguably no less influential than those from the more traditional scientific domains. A contextual approach to environmental law is therefore less a choice of research methodology, and more an imperative arising from the subject itself. The title of this book, *Environmental Protection, Law and Policy*, is a deliberate reflection of this, emphasising the political context, or policy world, from which environmental law is drawn and nourished, and also making clear that *law* is but one aspect of 'environmental protection'. Philip Selznick has highlighted these and other aspects of a law in context approach – not specifically with regard to environmental law, but many of his observations are highly pertinent to the approach that we have adopted in writing this book.

## Philip Selznick, 'Law in Context Revisited' (2003) 30 *Journal of Law and Society* 177, pp. 177–8

In law-and-society theory, the phrase 'law in context' points to the many ways legal norms and institutions are conditioned by culture and social organization. We see how legal rules and concepts, such as those affecting property, contract, and conceptions of justice, are animated and transformed by intellectual history; how much authority and self-confidence of legal institutions

---

[1] Daniel A. Farber, 'Building Bridges Over Troubled Waters: Eco-Pragmatism and the Environmental Prospect' (2003) *Minnesota Law Review* 851, p. 855.

depend on underlying realities of class and power; how legal rules fit into broader contexts of custom and morality. In short, we see law in and of society, adapting to its contours, giving direction to change. We learn that the legal order is far less autonomous, far less self-regulating and self-sufficient, than often portrayed by its leaders and apologists. This perspective encourages us to accept blurred boundaries between law and morality, law and tradition, law and economics, law and politics, law and culture. Accepting the reality of blurred boundaries leads to much puzzlement and controversy. Law loses some of its special dignity, and some jurisprudential questions cannot be avoided.

Selznick continues by explaining that engaging in socio-legal inquiry is bound to be more open-ended and controversial than when examining 'positive', or 'lawyers'', law – the intricate tapestry of legislation, judicial decisions and administrative regulations which traditionally makes up the stuff of legal argument and jurisprudential debate (p. 178). In looking beyond the already certified elements of positive law, the 'controversy may spill over into the political process, and even into the streets' (p. 179). An extensive inquiry such as this relies upon empirical research and is necessarily guided by a multi-disciplinary perspective.

To return to the 'law in context' approach that we have adopted, and taking a lead from its title, throughout this book we explore the relationship between law and policy, in the sense of understanding the initial, political, motivation for legislation, but also the continuing shaping of the policy process by law. We highlight that law remains highly receptive to the political and policy climate in which it is formed, and particularly to the dominant interests in an area. Our aim is to show up as a misconception the assumption of policy analysts that law is an output of the policy process, and that of lawyers that policy is merely a precursor to law, rather than a continuing influence in its implementation and enforcement. We use as a key example of the dynamic between law and policy the regulation of genetically modified organisms (GMOs): the eventual agreement of legislation on GMOs at European Union (EU) level[2] by no means resolved the complex and polarised debate on the acceptability of this technology; and controversy persists in the implementation of the legislation, particularly as the EU institutions and the Member States consider applications for the authorisation of GMOs. In the context of legal controls over land use, we consider the permeability of the categories 'law' and 'policy', for example the influence of legal disputes on the policy shift towards a presumption in favour of renewable energy developments,[3] and the creation of a hybrid form of law and policy ('binding policy') in the form of statements of community involvement in plan-making.[4] The following passage presents several further meanings of policy, some of which are highly politicised.

[2] See Ch. 5.    [3] See Ch. 17, p. 704.    [4] See Ch. 13, pp. 536-7.

### Patsy Healey, *Collaborative Planning: Shaping Places in Fragmented Societies* (Macmillan, 1997), pp. 215–16

The explicit concern with policy presupposes a governance activity which is directed at achieving some democratically acceptable public purpose, rather than particular private purposes or the domination of the powerful. A policy-driven approach to governance activity requires that policy objectives and strategies are articulated, and linked to programmes of action, judged by output and outcome criteria linked to the objectives ... A policy-driven approach helps to render the exercise of governance power in a society legitimate. Explicit policies become the reasons given by those exercising power on behalf of collectivities when asked why they did something. They become the basis for decision rules, and/or feed into processes of public argumentation about policies and actions. Policies thus help to make governments accountable. They may in addition be a valuable tool for managing government activities in efficient and effective ways ...

In this sense, policies are not only a mechanism to distance what governments do from merely a naked power play. They are also tools for influencing how governments organise themselves. It is here that the terms *administration* and *management* come in. In our complex and formally democratic societies, organizational arrangements develop to follow through programmes which 'politicians' decide upon. These presume some formal separation of the political arenas in which policies are debated and agreed and an administrative arena which delivers these policies. These arrangements are an amalgam of organizational structures, which formally specify competences and reporting responsibilities, and procedures, operating practices and cultures, which shape ways of thinking about how to do the job, and about the technique and ethics of government work. They become the operating routines of governance, with their accompanying modes of behaviour, or expressive *styles*.

Following this inclusive approach, in this book we consider 'policy' to include formal statements or guidance notes issued by government departments but also, in a looser sense, to mean those understandings and assumptions that frame political and legal decision making.

Part I of this book provides the general 'context' for the development of environmental law and policy, outlining a range of different approaches to environmental protection (science, economics, ecological theories, more 'popular' approaches) in Chapter 1. Because their regulation has had such a high profile in recent environmental debate (and protest), and because they highlight some contrasting approaches to the very idea of environmental protection, risk and nature, GMOs provide a more specific starting point from which to explore a range of contemporary challenges for environmental law; we devote Chapter 2 to introducing the dilemmas posed by agricultural biotechnology. In Chapter 3 we introduce the issue of public participation in decision making. In Part II we present the EU context of environmental law, and again use GMOs as an example of multi-level decision making in the EU (Chapter 5). Part III discusses the international context of environmental law, examining particularly sustainable development (Chapter 6) and the World Trade Organisation

(Chapter 7). Again, agricultural biotechnology provides a fitting example of some of the challenges facing modern environmental law, as regulation and democratic debate run up against international trade rules.

In keeping with a contextual approach, which demands a rounded and multifaceted view of socio-legal phenomena, in Part IV, discussing the development of pollution control measures in the UK and the EU, we continue to use case studies to illustrate how environmental protection is pursued – or not – through various regulatory approaches. Hence, after tracking the development of pollution controls in Chapter 8, in Chapter 9 on licensing we consider in detail the integrated pollution prevention and control regime. In Chapter 10 on implementation and enforcement, we study water protection, and in considering methods of regulation beyond the licence (Chapter 11) we outline the ways in which a number of legal regimes, including waste regulation, use a variety of traditional and 'alternative' approaches to environmental regulation. In Part V, which examines the legal control of land use, we provide a historical perspective on the development of land use controls in urban and countryside areas (Chapter 12). We then focus on planning controls (Chapter 13), environmental assessment (Chapter 14) and nature conservation (Chapters 15 and 16). A case study on wind farm development, a highly contested land use issue, provides an important insight into how these various areas of law and policy interrelate in a practical manner (Chapter 17).

The discipline of environmental law has undergone considerable changes over the decade since the first edition of this book was prepared. Lawyers are now far more comfortable looking beyond their discipline for the context of environmental law than were the pioneers of the 1980s, who, whilst often recognising and using non-legal materials, were busy building environmental law as a respected and autonomous discipline. The benefit of a sophisticated and greatly expanded literature in and around environmental law has made the writing of this edition a great pleasure, but has also meant that we have had to engage in a fairly fundamental re-orientation of the substantive content of the book. For example, the range of instruments referred to as 'alternative' approaches to regulation in the first edition are now considered part of the 'mainstream' regulatory toolbox. We have had to make sense of important pieces of legislation enacted since the first edition was published, including the Planning and Compensation Act 2004 and the Countryside and Rights of Way Act 2000, as well as much legislation from the EU. Also new are the case studies on GMOs and wind farm development, both of which provide analysis of the way in which law and policy interrelate and highlight the great complexity of environmental issues. Whilst the content has changed considerably since the first edition, however, this edition builds on the original ethos, and would not have been possible without that innovative and challenging approach. We both owe a great deal to Sue Elworthy for her unceasing intellectual generosity, as well as her friendship and support. We are also grateful to colleagues, reviewers and students for their thoughts on the first edition – as James Lovelock has said, 'Good criticism is like bathing in an ice cold sea. The sudden chill of immersion in what seems at first a hostile medium soon stirs the blood and shapes the senses.'[5]

The second edition of this book arose from our collaboration in teaching on the University of London's LLM course on Environmental Law and Policy. We have greatly benefited from this experience and indeed the structure of the book roughly follows the syllabus of the course. We would therefore like to thank all those who have taught on the course and have in many ways shaped and enriched it, and we are particularly grateful for the influence and support of Richard Macrory, Ludwig Krämer and Sue Elworthy. We would like especially to mention that Sue's inspirational teaching and comprehensive compilation of articles on ecological theories for that course provided the backbone to writing on this area in Chapter 1. We hope that the book reflects the intellectual fun and stimulation that we (and, we hope, our students) have enjoyed over many years, not least in preparing this book. We also very greatly appreciate the generosity of Carolyn Abbot, Sue Elworthy, Donald McGillivray and Joanne Scott for their advice on drafts of various (sometimes substantial!) parts of this book. William Twining has, as usual, been supportive and generous with his time and advice. And finally we are grateful to Natalie Cook, Linda Siegele and Robert Trigg for their excellent research assistance, and to Ian Johnson (Powergen Renewables) and Anne McCall (RSPB (Scotland)) for their help in compiling the case study on wind farm development.

One of our primary aims in this book has been to take some of the non-legal material that we think is crucial to the study of environmental law, and make that material both more accessible, and more obviously relevant, to law students. In putting this material into its legal setting, we have included some substantial extracts from primary legal materials. However, because of our particular focus, we have not always included lengthy passages from some of the key environmental law journals – although we have in many cases included articles from these journals in 'Further reading' Sections at the end of each chapter (which generally do not include work cited in the chapter). We have had the great privilege of reading some wonderful work, from which we have selected for this book. We should note that references and footnotes from extracts throughout are heavily edited (including extracts from cases and treaties).

Finally, Jane wishes to thank Donald McGillivray for continuing to provide inspiration, for helping to make writing, researching and day-to-day life an enjoyable and reflective experience and, very importantly, for sharing his library.

---

[5] James Lovelock, *The Ages of Gaia* (W. W. Norton, 1988), p. 31.

# Part I
# Introduction: Law in Context

# Preface to Part I

As we explained in the preface to this book, environmental law demands that we engage with the context within which the law is developed. In this Part, we locate modern environmental law within contemporary discourses about the environment, and begin to identify the boundaries and contours of the subject. In Chapter 1, we emphasise that the subject matter and content of environmental law has traditionally been set by a scientific agenda – what we refer to as the 'scientific paradigm'. We also discuss the prospects for a change in direction in environmental law, away from scientism, in order to embrace more wide-ranging values and concerns, including various ethical positions and philosophies about the relationship between humans and nature. This is a slightly unusual starting point for a book primarily, though not entirely, about environmental law. However, our teaching of the subject for many years has convinced us that a contextual and critical approach to studying this field of law cannot be sustained without questioning the dominance of a scientific approach, for example by considering different and opposing visions of human/nature relations. In addition, various tenets of ecological thinking are slowly influencing mainstream environmental law, leading us to ask about the prospect of this body of law shifting in a more radical direction. One important aspect of this is the now accepted need to broaden significantly and enhance 'real' public participation in environmental decision making, an issue taken up in Chapter 3. Chapter 2 on agricultural biotechnology (specifically genetically modified organisms or GMOs) both picks up on many of the debates and tensions introduced in Chapter 1, and, because this technology was the subject of an innovative 'public dialogue' in the UK in 2003, feeds into Chapter 3 on public participation.

Before embarking upon an account of the scientific paradigm and the main strands of ecological thinking which stand in opposition to this, the following provides a conceptual and temporal framework within which much of the following discussion and debate in Part I (and also the rest of the book) may be fitted. This takes the form of a generational analysis of *international* environmental law, and as such some of the key ideas and examples (especially 'sustainable development') will be developed in Part III of this book. However, this schema may be considered to apply more generally.

### Susan Emmenegger and Axel Tschentscher, 'Taking Nature's Rights Seriously: The Long Way to Biocentrism in Environmental Law' (1994) 6 *Georgetown International Environmental Law Review* 545, pp. 552–68

THE FIRST STAGE: ENVIRONMENTAL PROTECTION AS SELF-INTEREST OF THE PRESENT GENERATION

With the advent of international environmental law in the late 19th century, environmental protection based on humankind's immediate self-interest gave rise to the first wave of environmental instruments. A primary purpose pursued by those instruments was to maximise nature's resources in view of their exploitation. The need for protective measures became international whenever exploitation threatened natural resources beyond state borders, particularly in the case of high-sea fishing, whaling, and the hunting of migratory birds. Approaches to maximise resource exploitation have rightfully been assigned to the ethical perspective of utilitarianism exposing them to the general criticism and limitations commonly associated with utilitarian rationales. A second purpose pursued by first stage treaties was to ensure the physical and mental well-being of the population of the signatory states, especially in the light of the health hazards caused by extensive international pollution. This form of protection adds a human rights perspective to utilitarian rationales. Yet first stage instruments always retain their characteristic limitation as pure anthropocentrism, even though they extend beyond the principle of utility.

…

THE SECOND STAGE: ADDING THE INTERGENERATIONAL DIMENSION

An intergenerational dimension of environmental instruments builds the second stage in our main thesis of a step by step development. It adds complexity to international environmental law by going beyond the limited first stage scope of present generation provisions. As before, we can link this development to a theoretical background in environmental ethics.

1. Future Generations and Sustainability in the Treaties

A gradual shift of focus in the field of multi-lateral environmental instruments took place in the 1970s. As mentioned in the introductory sentences of this section, the development is not perfectly linear in chronological terms. All stages have fore-runners and late-bloomers. However, the increasing reference to the intergenerational dimension of the effort to protect the environment stated in environmental documents of that period allows ascribing the beginning of the second stage to this period.

The duty of the present generation to future generations to 'preserve the diversity and quality of our planet's life-sustaining environmental resources' mentioned in various international instruments has been termed an 'emerging norm of customary international law'.[1] Adding the intergenerational dimension signals a departure from the pure version of

---

[1] Antonio D'Amato, 'Do We Owe a Duty to Future Generations to Preserve the Global Environment?' (1990) 84 *American Journal of International Law* 190, p. 190.

anthropocentrism. Nevertheless, the approach of these treaties remains species chauvinistic: the protection of nature remains subordinated to the interests of humankind.

…

Thus, the intergenerational dimension offered by the future generations approach clearly remains within the boundaries of anthropocentrism. For 'sustainability' as the new term for future generations protection, the Rio Declaration explicitly states that 'Human beings are at the center of concerns for sustainable development', thereby formulating the core belief of anthropocentrism that humans are the measure of all things.

### THE THIRD STAGE: THE EMERGING NON-ANTHROPOCENTRIC PARADIGM AND NATURE'S OWN RIGHTS

#### 1. Intrinsic Value in the Treaties

The assertion of nature's intrinsic value made its entry into the law making process of multi-lateral environmental instruments only recently. By proclaiming that nature has a value which is independent of human interests, these multi-lateral instruments use a very different kind of argument and thereby express a paradigm shift in environmental law. The conceptual difference between recognizing non-anthropocentric value and evaluating all other kinds of anthropocentric values is best expressed in the following introductory sentence of the Biodiversity Convention: 'Conscious of the intrinsic value of biological diversity and of the ecological, genetic, social, economic, educational, cultural, recreational and aesthetic values of biological diversity and its components … we have agreed as follows: …'. This passage not only draws a clear line between intrinsic value of nature on the one hand, and all kinds of anthropocentric values on the other, but also puts non-anthropocentrism first, thereby emphasizing its importance as a new approach.

In this third phase the primary concern is identified as ecological survival, rather than human development and aspirations. The authors explain that environmental ethics beyond anthropocentrism can focus either on 'duties of humans towards nature', or on 'the original rights of nature' (as well as identifying problems with each approach), making clear that this last stage is not a monolithic ideal.

Even with the proviso that the evocative declarations of purpose and intent relied upon by the authors to support their generational thesis are a particular characteristic of international environmental law, in this book we identify law that expresses these various stages in other areas, sometimes simultaneously. The most obvious example of the 'first stage' (the protection of the environment for self-interested reasons) is the enactment of pollution controls at the height of the industrial revolution to protect public health and thus secure a healthy workforce, and to ensure a good supply of a particular natural resource, for example clean water for brewing and distilling.[2] We discuss the shift towards intergenerational concerns in law (the second evolutionary stage) in Chapter 6 on sustainable

---

[2] See Ch. 8.

development. Examples of a shift in environmental law to embrace the 'third stage' concerns about the intrinsic value of nature (or a shift to a type of 'ecological law') are undeniably less easy to find, and our general conclusion is that much of environmental law remains antithetical to ecological precepts. However, there are occasional moves towards a closer representation of ecological values, several examples of which we discuss in Chapter 1. Furthermore, an important aspect of ecological thinking, 'holism', is reinterpreted in law as the principle of integration, discussed especially in Chapter 4.[3]

As mentioned above, although Emenegger and Tschentscher's stages may coexist at a particular time, they also describe a rough chronology of events in environmental law. A difficulty is, as Carrie Menkel-Meadow puts it, how does one know when an evolutionary apogee has been reached?[4] Several attempts have been made to identify such shifts with regard to environmental law. Although in general the exercise of ascertaining the current developmental phase of environmental law is particularly popular in the United States,[5] Gerd Winter famously, in a prophetic article in the first issue of the *Journal of Environmental Law*,[6] identified four phases of environmental law: 'the circular economy' in which 'man uses nature while allowing her the material, spatial, and temporal possibilities necessary for self-regeneration';[7] 'the exploitation of nature by man', at which point law is oriented towards 'releasing the inventiveness and energy of the individual', with scant regard for environmental degradation;[8] the 'planned management of nature' in which environmental protection law begins to be put in place; and 'thinking about new solutions', in which traditional approaches to the control of environmental degradation are recognised as ineffective, and new legal solutions are sought. Again, these different stages can be identified in examples of environmental law throughout this book, particularly in Parts IV and V, which discuss evolving approaches to pollution control and land use regulation.

It must be admitted that so far we have been talking about 'the environment' as though it were axiomatic. However, the environment is not a given. People's perceptions of nature, the environment and harms are often very different, informed by upbringing, religion, ethnicity, art and literature, as well as by their professional perspectives. For example a landscape may be made up of physical forms and elements – water, soil, flora and fauna, and artificial objects such as roads and buildings, shaped by natural processes and human activities. But the landscape is also formed by the observer's viewpoint which is influenced by individuals' differing perspectives and experiences, for example how they relate a landscape to their cultural identity. Without denying that nature exists 'out

---

[3]  See also 'Ecological Law', Ch. 1, pp. 55–7.

[4]  'Is the Adversary System Really Dead?' (2004) 57 *Current Legal Problems* 85, with regard to the development of alternative dispute resolution.

[5]  See, for example, the papers arising from a symposium on twenty-five years of environmental regulation in the USA (1993–4) 27 *Loyola of Los Angeles Law Review*.

[6]  'The Four Phases of Environmental Law' (1989) 1 *Journal of Environmental Law* 38.

[7]  *Ibid.*, p. 38.     [8]  *Ibid.*, p. 39.

there', it should be recognised that nature is inseparable from human perception, and for this reason has been described by some theorists as a social construct as much as a physical reality. Neil Evernden, for example, accounts for the social creation of pollution as 'matter out of place', threatening to 'the social ideal of proper order'.

### Neil Evernden, *The Social Creation of Nature* (Johns Hopkins University Press, 1993), pp. 4–9

In his survey of the opinions of different sectors of British society, sociologist Stephen Cotgrove detected some interesting differences in the apprehension of environmental risk. Two of his categories showed wide divergence: the 'environmentalists' (composed of a sample drawn from membership lists of the Conservation Society and the Friends of the Earth), and the 'industrialists' (selected from *Business Who's Who* and *Who's Who of British Engineers*). As one would expect, the environmentalists perceived considerably more environmental danger than did the industrialists. But what is interesting is that the latter group does not seem to be deliberately acting in an irresponsible way, but rather seems not to perceive significant risk at all.

If pollution is regarded as a matter of empirical fact, it may seem odd that such disagreements can persist. But since pollution involves questions not only of concentrations but also of consequences, even 'hard' evidence is inevitably open to interpretation – hence the frequent spectacle of contradicting experts. Equally significant, however, is our tendency to treat pollution as a purely material phenomenon, a bias that tends to establish arbitrary boundaries to environmental debate.

We must bear in mind that the current understanding of pollution is just that: the current understanding. Yet there is no reason to limit the definition to physical abuse alone. The dictionary definition is much broader and entails 'uncleanness or impurity caused by contamination (physical or moral)'. Our attention to physical pollution may distract us from the fact that much of the debate is over the perception of moral pollution. For example, while voicing their opinions about how many parts per billion of a toxin are 'acceptable', both environmentalists and industrialists may be responding to a perceived instance of moral contamination. This emerges occasionally when one or other makes predictions about future consequences, or about what 'standard of living' ought to be protected. Environmentalists will assert that if the current action continues, our future well-being will be imperiled and our children will inherit a blighted planet. Cease, they say, and learn to live in a small-scale, cooperative society without the constant pressure for growth and transformation. Industrialists may reply that it is all very well for the impractical environmentalist to advocate such irresponsible action, but if their policies were ever to be put in place, our life-style would be in jeopardy, jobs would be lost, and food shortages would loom. To the environmentalists, what is at risk is the very possibility of leading a good life. To the industrialists, what is at risk is the very possibility of leading a good life. The debate, it appears, is actually about *what constitutes a good life*. The instance of physical pollution serves only as the means of persuasion, a staging ground for the underlying debate.

...

... Being able to determine the 'parts per billion' of a contaminant enables the environmentalist to argue that pollution has indeed occurred, and thus to infer that the entire *position* of the polluter is untenable – the polluter has clearly done something 'unnatural' and in so doing has placed nature, and ourselves, at risk. The polluter is condemned not only for a physical pollution but also, implicitly, for a moral pollution that is revealed by the physical pollution. Hence the highly charged emotional tone of much environmental debate: far more is at stake than the chemical composition of a river.

...

In public discussions of environmental affairs, ecology is frequently a rather loosely defined entity, often treated as the environmentalists' chief ally and occasionally even as a synonym for the natural environment. Indeed, the very plasticity of our concept of nature may be illustrated by the contrasting uses to which ecology is put. It is pressed into the service of a variety of social alternatives ... But exactly what is advocated is of less interest here than that ecology functions as the exemplar of the natural and the healthy, and in so doing seems to indicate to us how we might re-orient our lives. Indeed, ecology will inevitably be so used if our understanding of ecology includes the establishment of norms as part of its function.

...

So far I have spoken of the use of ecology only by those in support of social reform. There is, however, a much heavier reliance on ecology by those who defend the status quo. I speak of the use of ecology in such officially sanctioned activities as environmental impact assessment, wildlife management, and land reclamation. While these may be useful in the immediate support of environmental integrity, they constitute a use of ecology in the service of technological and bureaucratic intervention. There is a tacit expectation that some form of environmental engineering must emerge that will facilitate continued growth with a minimum of environmental backlash. Ecology is to help us anticipate difficulties, so that alternative technologies can be forged to circumvent them.

...

These are two contrasting interpretations of the function of ecology. Undoubtedly they are caricatures of actual attitudes and assumptions, but they serve to illustrate the possibility of alternative uses of ecology, the contemporary nature-explainer that we expect to be 'objective' and, of course, 'value neutral'. Persons with contrasting viewpoints can draw upon this discipline, one group regarding it as a revealer of the natural and proper, the other as a source of power and control (which it is natural to use). Each group believes its stance to be correct, and each expects endorsements from ecology.

The question of where 'nature' and, we might add, 'the environment' comes from leads us to the discussion in Chapter 1 about how law has come to express scientific understandings of the environment and risk, and how this is opposed by those adhering to various 'alternative' ecological theories about the 'proper' relationship between humans and nature. The accommodation of expert information with ecological, political or popular values, in recognition that the scientific expert can only ever offer a partial understanding of environmental problems and hence provide limited solutions, is very possibly the main dilemma currently facing environmental law. The tension this accommodation creates forms the focus of this first Part of the book and continues to inform our analysis throughout the rest of it.

# 1

# Environmental Law in Context

## 1 Introduction

Recent decades have seen questions of environmental protection become a significant issue for government, and part of mainstream public debate. Most jurisdictions now have government departments and independent agencies dedicated to environmental protection, as well as public interest groups committed to raising the profile of environmental issues. Whilst the need for environmental protection is virtually uncontroversial, however, the reasons for protecting the environment are rarely spelt out; in turn, and as foreshadowed in the Preface to this Part, the *meaning* of environmental protection, and the best way of achieving environmental protection, retain potential for real conflict.

### Graham Smith, *Deliberative Democracy and the Environment* (Routledge, 2003), pp. 1–3

Value conflict is at the heart of environmental politics. Decisions that affect the environment are typically multi-faceted: when reasoning about the non-human world, individuals and groups often find themselves pulled in contradictory directions, appealing to values that they find difficult to reconcile ...

The environmental movement itself can be understood as being born out of value conflict, a conflict with interests in society that did not recognise or give sufficient attention to environmental values. Greens have challenged the values associated with the idea of progress based on ever-increasing levels of economic growth on the grounds that it represents a failure to consider the full range of values that we associate with the environment.

But it is important to remember that the environmental movement itself is pluralistic in nature. So, for example, we find distinctions drawn between preservationists and conservationists, between ecologists and environmentalists, and between ecosocialists, social ecologists, ecofeminists, animal liberationists, bioregionalists, deep ecologists and advocates of environmental justice, to name but a few distinct positions. Different factions within the broad environmental movement draw on different conceptions of environmental values. The way in which different environmental and non-environmental values are prioritised at times places their proponents in conflict with one another. The classic example is the conflict that can emerge between conservationists and preservationists, 'often with that special degree of hostility reserved for former allies'.[1] Conservationists are typically concerned with ensuring sustainable yields of environmental resources for on-going human consumption; the preservationist ethic, in contrast, argues for the protection of areas from direct human interference, often on the grounds that aspects of the non-human world have intrinsic value. Again, the 'special degree of hostility' has famously been witnessed between social and deep ecologists. Murray Bookchin, the founder of social ecology, frequently rails against the 'mysticism' that he sees as prevalent within deep ecological thought.[2] As Kate Soper recognises: 'The ecology movement, when viewed as a whole, draws its force from a range of arguments whose ethical underpinnings are really quite divergent and difficult to reconcile.'[3]

If we take one of the most celebrated sites of environmental conflict – the world's rainforests – we can begin to appreciate the plurality of values associated with the non-human world. At an instrumental level, the rainforests have direct use for us in a number of ways. We value their role in climatic processes, acting as a carbon dioxide sink to secure basic ecological conditions for human existence and flourishing, and as a resource for timber, pharmaceutical and other products. Prudential appeals are frequently made to the scientific value of such unique ecosystems and the possible advancements in medical and scientific knowledge that could be gained from the study of the rich biodiversity. Using the language of justice, conflicting arguments have emerged about the rights of indigenous peoples to remain in the environment that has always provided the background for their form of life, and the rights of individual nations to self-determination in exploiting resources within their national territory. Appeals to justice have also focused on the rights of future generations, pulling judgements about the value of the rainforest in a different direction. Ethical considerations have been extended to the diversity of non-human entities that constitute the ecosystems of the rainforest. Not only is the very existence of such 'wild' places often constitutive of individuals' own sense of identity and understanding of the relation between human and non-human worlds, but their existence can be judged as significant in their own right.

A sophisticated body of environmental law has grown up as a response to the perceived demands of environmental protection. The proper role of environmental law is, however, much contested. Whilst it is far from unique in this respect, we should be aware that environmental law and policy develops in a context of competing, but often silenced, value judgments. Environmental law cannot be read in isolation; it is important to read environmental law critically, and in its context. In this chapter, we will therefore consider a number of frequent, but not always consistent, ways of viewing 'the environment' and environmental 'problems'. First, we present the dominant, scientific approach

---

[1] John Passmore, *Man's Responsibility for Nature* (Duckworth, 1980), p. 73.

[2] Murray Bookchin, 'Social Ecology versus Deep Ecology: A Challenge for the Ecology Movement' (1987) 4/5 *Green Perspectives*; *The Ecology of Freedom* (Black Rose, 1991).

[3] Kate Soper, *What is Nature?* (Blackwell, 1995), p. 254.

to assessing risk, since the views of expert biologists, chemists and geneticists about the probability of a particular risk, its prevalence and likely causal effects commonly provide the framework within which environmental problems are understood and debated, particularly by regulators and lawyers. In general this perspective results in a broadly instrumental approach that justifies a measure by reference to scientific observations of environmental harm, and some direct or assumed human interest in that harm. The natural sciences have a special role in identifying and explaining measures of environmental protection, and our definition of an environmental problem is often based on 'a distinctively scientific perception of the world'.[4] Because of the primacy of this approach we provide a (necessarily truncated) account of how science came to dominate, and define, the debate, particularly when compared to more instinctive, value-laden interpretations. In this context we also elaborate the increasingly important role of the precautionary principle, which is subject to many interpretations, but has the potential to bring a scepticism towards a rigid approach to scientific evidence into the legal process, whilst at the same time implying some degree of acceptance of the inevitability of scientific uncertainty.

Economics also frequently provides the justificatory basis of environmental protection, with some arguing that environmental problems are simply economic problems, the result of a failure to put the correct economic value on environmental 'goods'. Even without going this far, the tools of the economist increasingly dominate discussion of how, and how intensely, to protect the environment. In the first two sections of this chapter, we therefore find common ground between the scientific ('hard' science) and economic ('soft' science) foundations of environmental law and policy, and the bureaucratic techniques of risk assessment and cost benefit analysis that grow out of them. Very simplistically, these are approaches that see the environment as fundamentally capable of management, if only we can harness the appropriate expertise.

In contrast, the ethical basis for environmental measures is rarely explicit. Competing ethical approaches are discussed in section 5. Even if these ethical approaches are rarely openly engaged with, however, there is a growing recognition, discussed in section 3, that environmental decisions are not purely technical, but are fundamentally normative in nature, based on important political, moral, cultural, even religious values. This demands of environmental decision makers that they enter the political arena and engage in debate about 'what should be done'. There is a tension at the heart of environmental law and policy, between demands for expertise, and demands for popular engagement (see also Chapter 3). Agricultural biotechnology provides a case study of this tension in Chapter 2.

---

[4] Stephen Yearley, 'Green Ambivalence About Science: Legal–Rational Authority and the Scientific Legitimation of a Social Movement' (1992) 43 *British Journal of Sociology* 511, p. 512.

## 2 The scientific paradigm

### (a) The role of science

The natural sciences have a crucial input to contemporary environmental law. Many environmental problems cannot be perceived, let alone understood or addressed, without sophisticated scientific expertise: the depletion of stratospheric ozone, for example, was never likely to have been identified by simple intuition. And science is more than just a tool for the identification and resolution of environmental problems. Science has a central role in legitimating environmental law and policy: an appeal to the 'facts', as established by science, is used to pre-empt and undermine criticism. Although, as we shall see, there are inherent difficulties with relying on science in this area, the *apparent* objectivity and testability of science, seemingly above the fray of divided interests and political advantage, can be extremely attractive to politicians and to lawyers. The authority provided by an appeal to science extends of course to environmentalists.

### Stephen Yearley, 'Green Ambivalence About Science: Legal–Rational Authority and the Scientific Legitimation of a Social Movement' (1992) 43 *British Journal of Sociology* 511, pp. 514–30

IS SCIENCE AN IDEOLOGICAL FRIEND OF THE EARTH?

Despite the benefits, which ... flow from scientific conservation, many greens are uneasy about aligning themselves too closely with science. Such ambivalence about science stems in part from the role science and technology have played in bringing about our ecological problems. In some instances this connection is clear and direct. Humans invented the CFCs which are threatening the ozone layer. Technological advance allowed humans to develop nuclear power, which in turn has brought us persistent environmental problems, such as those associated with the calamitous explosion at Chernobyl in 1986. It was scientists who developed the pesticides which in the last three decades have contaminated our food and our wildlife. In such cases we can trace environmental problems directly to specific products of science and technology. There is also a more diffuse connection: present-day industrial society is inseparable from the pollution caused by motor vehicles, power generation and waste disposal. Many environmentalists are thus critical of technical progress and, at least, equivocal about science. Scientists may be viewed as active collaborators in our society's ecological destructiveness.

Additionally, greens may distrust science because of the particular activities of sections of the scientific establishment: on account, for example, of scientists' involvement in the development of nuclear power and weaponry or in the genetic engineering of food crops and domesticated animals. Equally, greens may just be repelled by cases of the deliberate harming or mistreatment of laboratory animals.

In the face of these inherent problems with the scientific legitimation of environmentalism, some of the ideologists of the movement have been attracted to versions of the green argument which are principally founded on non-scientific forms of authority. For example, it is possible to seek to underpin an ecological world view in conventionally religious or other spiritual ways. People can claim to gain a knowledge of nature's purposes and needs through this sort of inquiry … But in secular Western societies these appeals can exercise only a limited attraction and the principal form of legitimation in the leading environmental organizations remains that of scientific expertise.

…

### LEGAL–RATIONAL AUTHORITY AND THE SOCIOLOGY OF SCIENCE

Up to this point I have claimed that 'establishment' green groups embraced science early on and that there is evidence that – despite some ideological misgivings – the most radical groups are following suit. However, I wish to argue that the turn to science has been less straightforwardly beneficial than had been anticipated; in some respects the movement has even been confounded by science.

To understand the sociological implications of embracing science, we need to examine the special authority enjoyed by legal-rational forms of argument, an authority which has often been taken for granted by social scientists. Indeed, since social science itself appears to rest on this form of authority, to throw it into question might seem a self destructive pursuit. But in the last two decades there has been a re-assessment of this kind of authority among sociologists and philosophers of science who have studied decision making in what might be taken to be the temple of legal-rational thinking, natural science. What they have suggested is that the authority commonly associated with scientific beliefs is not as straightforward or as unequivocal as many people … appear to have assumed. These sociologists and philosophers have argued that the public, policy makers and more traditional philosophers of science have exaggerated the authority of science.

Characteristically, these analysts accepted an uncontentious definition of science … What is radical is not their definition of science but their insistence that scientists' judgments inevitably go beyond the evidence on which they are based, so that scientific authority cannot be justified by a simple appeal to its factual foundations … Second, these analysts of science argue that even facts themselves are provisional. Factual claims cannot be legitimated by an unquestionable appeal to observation. Observations may themselves be affected by scientists' assumptions or by their prior theoretical commitments.

…

### SCIENCE AS UNREELIABLE FRIEND – EMPIRICALLY

The first way in which science is an unreliable ally is a simply empirical one. Compared to social movements which appeal to an orthodoxy or to a charismatic leader, avowedly scientific movements face a number of pragmatic disadvantages. Scientists may not have an answer to every question. Similarly, they accept in principle that their knowledge is revocable and incomplete.

…

### SCIENCE AS UNRELIABLE FRIEND – EPISTEMOLOGY

Up to this point we have examined ways in which *in fact* science may be a less good friend than conservationists might anticipate. It may not provide the answers on occasions when it would be politic to have them … in some cases these deficiencies come close to endemic problems of scientific knowledge – to do with sciences as a way of knowing at all. Most nature conservationists would defend science as a form of knowledge by pointing to its observational basis and its methodic development. But … the observational basis is open to discrepant interpretations. As soon as there arise competing and plausible accounts of what the observational facts are, then the basis which appears so secure becomes itself problematic. The empirical and provisional basis of scientific knowledge – its apparent strength – can readily be re-formulated as an *uncertain* basis.

…

### CONCLUSION

To regard the green movement as profoundly anchored in science is surely correct. But, in practical terms, green campaigners have found it far harder to cash in on that scientific authority than might have been anticipated …

In part, the explanation is philosophical. Scientific knowledge is inherently open to revision; it is intrinsically provisional. Particularly at the forefront of science, it is always possible that the truth is at odds with scientists' current beliefs. Despite science's cognitive power, it cannot offer transcendental support for particular substantive propositions. Moreover, the green movement is dependent on extra-scientific, moral considerations. Scientific studies indicating that the whale populations are declining to non-sustainable levels may well offer good grounds for not whaling. But when (as now may be the case for minke whales) populations begin to recover, science does not suffice to say whether hunting should be resumed.

The explanation is also sociological. The profession and practice of science mean that the research which greens desire or need may not be done. The social composition of green groups may not afford them the scientific expertise they require. Governments, firms, unions – even campaigners – may be far from disinterested in the uses they make of scientific information. Finally, philosophical and sociological factors may overlap and interact. The social context of legal inquiries encourages the tendentious exploitation of science's epistemological weaknesses; media conventions about 'fairness' encourage broadcasters to give 'equal time' to competing views even if the scientific credentials of those views are far from equal.

Many of the tensions that Yearley identifies prefigure the discussions below on scientific uncertainty (pp. 18–31) and on the politics of environmental decision making (pp. 40–7 and Chapter 3). What Yearley identifies as 'ambivalence' on the part of public interest groups is equally identifiable in other parts of environmental policy making and law; the difficulty of reconciling broader grounds for decision making with the continuing centrality of science (and related technical processes such as risk assessment and cost benefit assessment) is a recurring theme in contemporary environmental regulation.

The legacy of the 'scientific paradigm' is a type of 'shallow' environmentalism, primarily concerned with the exhaustion of natural resources and the implications of this for humankind (akin to the 'second stage' of environmental law identified by Emmenegger and Tschentscher in the Preface to Part I

(pp. 2–3)). Shallow environmentalists advocate so-called 'environmental management' (including methods such as risk assessment) and place their faith in
technological advancement as a way out of environmental problems ('cleaning
up the earth'): the 'planned management of nature' according to Winter's
schema, also discussed in the Preface. Those adhering to ecological theories
(see below, pp. 47–57) critique this branch of environmentalism as little more
than a self-serving ideology legitimating the status quo – the 'business as usual'
scenario.

## (b)  Risk assessment and the environment

Closely related to the use of science in environmental law is the technical assessment of 'risk'. 'Risk' is a complex and profoundly political idea. Ulrich Beck has
developed a theory of 'risk society'[5] to reflect the centrality of risk to contemporary society. This thesis posits that it is no longer the production and distribution of *goods* that dominates political and private life (as it does when those
goods are scarce), but the distribution (and minimisation) of *bads*, of risks.
Beck argues that technological risks largely escape the traditional institutions of
representative democracy, pointing towards more radical and participatory
approaches. Even without going as far as Beck, it is easy to identify occasions on
which questions of 'risk' dominate political discourse and private anxiety:
climate change, bovine spongiform encephalopathy (BSE) in cattle, agricultural
and medical biotechnology, lower-key debates about food safety, air pollution,
water pollution, as well as Beck's primary example of nuclear technology, are all
political events.

Risk has, however, a technical aspect that fits very well into a scientific way of
viewing the world. Technical risk assessment, to simplify, involves the
identification of a hazard associated with a substance or activity, and the likelihood of that hazard's occurrence. The expertise of the risk assessor is increasingly central as environmental law becomes more pre-emptive, moving beyond
a series of reactions to harm after the event.

One factor that complicates discussion of risk is the now well-recognised
divergence between 'public perceptions' of risk and scientific analyses of risk.
Whilst some believe that this is evidence of public ignorance, and urge that
important and expensive matters of risk regulation be kept away from the 'irrational' public, and their representatives,[6] it is also increasingly accepted that at
least part of the divergence can be explained by a broader, but still rational,
approach to risk on the part of the public.[7] On the latter view, whilst experts

---

[5]  Ulrich Beck, *Risk Society: Towards a New Modernity* (Sage, 1992).
[6]  See, for example, Stephen Breyer, *Breaking the Vicious Circle: Toward Effective Risk Regulation*
(Harvard University Press, 1993).
[7]  See, for example, the discussion of the 'social dimension' of risk in Department of the
Environment, Food and Rural Affairs (DEFRA), *Guidelines for Environmental Risk Assessment
and Management* (available at www.defra.gov.uk/environment/risk), Ch. 3.

tend to focus on numbers (for example lives lost), the public perception of risk is multi-dimensional and qualitative, with particular hazards meaning different things to different people depending on underlying values and the context of the risk.[8] So, for example, the distribution of risk and benefit is relevant to the public, an unfamiliar risk may lead to greater concern than a familiar risk, a freely chosen risk is less worrying than one imposed from outside.[9] The fundamental disagreement is over whether people 'think poorly' about risk, or whether they assess risk according to a 'richer rationality' than the experts.

### Cass R. Sunstein, *Risk and Reason: Safety, Law and the Environment* (Cambridge University Press, 2002), pp. 59–64

There is much wisdom in the tradition [of 'richer rationality'], and indeed the 'richer rationality' view has started to become highly influential … And in some ways, it is clearly correct. The risks associated with voluntary activities (skiing, horseback riding) receive less public concern than statistically smaller risks from involuntary activities (food preservatives, pesticides, herbicides, certain forms of air pollution). But in the context of risks, I believe that the richer rationality claim is overstated. To be sure, some of these factors do justify special concern with some risks. But there is no 'rival rationality' in the minds of ordinary people.

… Media attention, for example, is a heuristic for determining whether the problem is serious. If people are especially concerned about risks that preoccupy the media, it is probably because what concerns the media is likely, other things being equal, to be worthy of concern. Especially in light of the availability heuristic and social influences, ordinary people, trying to reduce large risks, will naturally be concerned about hazards that are receiving attention from newspapers and television stations. The point helps explain why people have sometimes been excessively fearful of shark attacks, air travel, and new diseases. The same point also helps explain why different cultures, and different subcultures, are frightened of different things: They hear, from relevant media, different reports of what is dangerous.

Past history also works as a heuristic. What has happened before is a (rough) proxy for what will happen again. Sensible people who want to reduce large risks, and to ignore tiny ones, will care about history. Similar things can be said about trust. If people do not trust an institution's assurances, they are thinking that the risk is more serious than they are being told. Nor is any special puzzle posed by the fact that public concern is heightened when children and future generations are at risk. When this is so, more life-years are at stake, and in the case of future generations, more lives. Of course, people want to save more lives, and more life-years, rather than fewer. On all these counts, experts and ordinary people seem to be on exactly the same page – with the qualification that ordinary people sometimes use simplifying devices, such as media attention, to test whether a risk is really large or small.

---

[8]  *Ibid.*, para. 3.3.
[9]  See Chauncey Starr, 'Social Benefit Versus Technological Risk' (1969) *Science* 1232; Paul Slovic, *The Perception of Risk* (Earthscan, 2000).

But some of these factors do seem to suggest that people are not concerned only with numbers of lives at stake. For example, deaths that are particularly 'dreaded' may have aggravating characteristics, to which ordinary people are alert but which experts neglect. The notions of voluntariness and control may also be relevant insofar as they suggest that some risks are more freely run, and therefore deserving of less public concern.

Although accepting the basic legitimacy of these positions, Sunstein does 'question the claim that qualitative factors of this kind explain all or even much of people's disagreement with experts', arguing that 'experts are more likely to be right than are ordinary people'.

I believe that for most people, reactions to risks are a product of a rapid, largely intuitive assessment, not based on a careful sorting of the consequences of exposure. Of course that assessment depends in significant part on what concerns experts, the statistical magnitude of the risk at issue. A rough sense of the magnitude of the risk certainly plays a role in producing affect. And indeed nothing in the data is inconsistent with the possibility that people fear certain risks because they have a general impression that they are statistically large, and that this fear helps to explain their rankings. If so, people will naturally rank the risks they most fear as worse, on the qualitative dimensions, than risks that they fear least. Notice that on this view, people's rankings on the qualitative judgments are not the reason for their relative rankings of risk. On the contrary, their general impression of statistical magnitude is doing most of the work ...

Certainly it is puzzling to find that people treat as quite serious dangers that are microscopically small as a statistical matter, while risks that are statistically much larger are treated as 'just a part of life'. No doubt it is *possible* that people's judgments about risk severity are a product of some of the more qualitative considerations ... But it is also possible that an apparently rich judgment that a certain risk is severe, or not severe, depends not on well considered judgments of value, but instead on a rapid intuitive judgment, on a failure to see that tradeoffs are inevitably being made, on heuristic devices that are not well-adapted to the particular context, or instead on a range of confusing or confused ideas that people cannot fully articulate. When people say, for example, that the risk of nuclear power is very serious, they might be responding to their intense visceral concern. The affect associated with nuclear power is, for many people, quite negative, and that affect operates as a heuristic for a judgment of the seriousness of the risk.

As I have said, the affect, and the judgment, might well be based, at least in part, on (uninformed) statistical judgments about likely lives at risk and on people's failure to see (as they do in other contexts) that that risk is accompanied by a range of social benefits ...

A MIXED VERDICT

I have been claiming, not that qualitative factors are irrelevant to ordinary perceptions of risk, but that the same evidence said to support 'rival rationality' might reflect simple errors of fact ...

Where does this leave us? Many of the disagreements between experts and ordinary people stem from the fact that experts have more information and are also prepared to look at the benefits as well as the risks associated with controversial products and activities. To the extent that experts focus *only* on the number of lives at stake, they are genuinely obtuse. It is reasonable to devote special attention to dangers that are hard to avoid, or accompanied by special suffering, or faced principally by children. But there is no 'rival rationality' in taking these factors into account. On the positive side, what is needed is more empirical work to determine the extent to which ordinary risk perceptions are based on errors or instead on values. On the normative side, we need to think more clearly about the nature of concepts like 'dread', 'involuntary', and 'uncontrollable'. With respect to policy, what is needed is incorporation of people's values, to the extent that they can survive a process of reflection.

## (c) Scientific uncertainty and the precautionary principle

Attempting to rely on science (and related technical disciplines such as risk assessment) as a route through environmental decisions runs quickly into the barriers posed by the unavoidable uncertainty attached to scientific information. Once it is accepted and well known that science is uncertain, it becomes increasingly difficult to base decisions on 'the facts'. Some of the complexities of uncertainty are suggested in the extract from Yearley (pp. 12–14). Uncertainty goes much further than 'data gaps' to be filled by further research over time; far more profound questions about the nature of our knowledge are also implied.

### Brian Wynne, 'Uncertainty and Environmental Learning: Reconceiving Science and Policy in the Preventive Paradigm' (1992) 2 *Global Environmental Change* 111, pp. 114–24

In the first place, we can talk authentically about *risk* when the system behaviour is basically well known, and chances of different outcomes can be defined and quantified by structured analysis of mechanisms and probabilities.

Second, if we know the important system parameters but not the probability distributions, we can talk in terms of *uncertainties*. There are several sophisticated methods for estimating them and their effects on outcomes. These uncertainties are recognized, and explicitly included in analysis.

Third, a far more difficult problem is *ignorance*, which by definition escapes recognition. This is not so much a characteristic of knowledge itself as of the linkages between knowledge and commitments based on it – in effect, bets (technological, social, economic) on the completeness and validity of that knowledge.

Since this third distinction is conceptually more elusive, an example is justified. In the aftermath of the Chernobyl nuclear accident, in May 1986 a radioactive cloud passed over the UK. Heavy thunderstorms rained out radiocaesium deposits over upland areas, and, despite reassurances that there would be no lasting effects of the radioactive cloud, six weeks after the accident a sudden ban on hill sheep sales and slaughter was announced. Although this ban was expected to last only three weeks, because the radiocaesium was thought to be chemically immobilized in the soil once washed off vegetation, some hill farms in these areas of Cumbria and North Wales in particular, are still restricted six years later. The scientists made a spectacular mistake in predicting the behaviour of radiocaesium in the environment of interest. It was gradually learned that the reason for the mistake was that the original prediction had been based on the observed behaviour of caesium in alkaline clay soils, whereas those of the areas in question were acid peaty soils. It was assumed by the scientists – wrongly as it turned out – that the previously observed behaviour also prevailed in the conditions which existed in the hill areas. Thus, contrary to the confident expectations of the scientists, the elevated levels of radiocaesium in the sheep from these upland areas did not fall, and restrictions had to be extended indefinitely, severely damaging the credibility of the scientists and institutions concerned. Eventually it was realized that the chemical immobilization which had been assumed took place only in aluminosilicate clays, and that in the upland peaty acid soils caesium remains chemically mobile, hence available for root uptake and recycle via edible vegetation back into the food chain.

It is important to recognize that this highly public scientific mistake actually followed normal scientific practice. Scientists attempted to predict the behaviour of an agent (here radiocaesium) by extrapolating from its observed behaviour under certain conditions, making some inadvertent assumptions about the new conditions. When the new observations did not fit with expected behaviour, the models underlying the predictions were (eventually) re-examined. Through this, certain previously unnoticed but significant differences were identified, and the models were elaborated accordingly.

…

Thus ignorance is endemic to scientific knowledge, which has to reduce the framework of the known to that which is amenable to its own parochial methods and models. This only becomes a problem when (as is usual) scientific knowledge is misunderstood and is institutionalized in policy making as if this condition did not pervade all competent scientific knowledge. This institutionalized exaggeration of the scope and power of scientific knowledge creates a vacuum in which should exist a vital social discourse about the conditions and boundaries of scientific knowledge in relation to moral and social knowledge.

… social commitments are necessary to define the boundaries of, and to give coherence to, scientific knowledge – not only in the large but in quite specific ways. Whenever events expose the ignorance which always underlies scientific models used in public policy, the dominant response is invariably to focus on improving the scientific model. However, although this is important, it is not enough. A response of at least equal importance ought to examine critically the (often inflated) social commitments built over the existing knowledge, because it is here that ignorance and its corresponding risks are created. Indeterminacy exists in the open-ended question of whether knowledge is adapted to fit the mismatched realities of application situations, or whether those (technical and social) situations are reshaped to 'validate' the knowledge.

…

The extra concept of indeterminacy … introduces the idea that *contingent social behaviour* also has to be explicitly included in the analytical and prescriptive framework.

Wynne demonstrates that 'uncertainty' is both complex and inescapable. It extends not only to areas where more or better scientific information is required, but to the unpredictability of the real-life behaviour of human beings and eco-systems (indeterminacy), and to areas in which we simply 'don't know what it is that we don't know' (ignorance), and so cannot investigate it. As Wynne observes, the dangers of CFCs and DDT escaped investigation because the 'uncertainty along which the question of scientific proof for regulation was stretched was in each case the wrong question altogether, as we now know. For DDT, uncertainties were recognized only over acute toxicity; chronic toxicity was not even conceived of. For CFCs, the very property thought to bring low risk to biological species, long-term stability, meant it could reach the stratospheric ozone layer – but this was not even considered at that time.' We might add to these uncertainties the notion (developed further in Sections 4 and 5 below) that environmental concerns are not limited to the evaluation of harm, but also incorporate questions of value, for example as to distribution of burden and benefit or ethical questions.

The varied dimensions of uncertainty *should* make a real difference to the way we assess decision making in environmental law. The precautionary principle has emerged as a central tool for the management of pervasive uncertainty in environmental and public health policy, a recognition that decisions must be made in situations of uncertainty. The precise role and meaning of the precautionary principle remain uncertain and controversial; the literature is enormous, and the most that can be attempted here is to outline some of the main areas of disagreement. It is a good starting point to think about the legal role of a principle.

### Elizabeth Fisher, 'Precaution, Precaution Everywhere: Developing a "Common Understanding" of the Precautionary Principle in the European Community' (2002) 9 *Maastricht Journal of European and Comparative Law* 7, pp. 15–16

Much of the discussion concerning the precautionary principle has proceeded on the assumption that the principle is a 'bright line' autonomous rule that dictates a particular outcome in a certain set of circumstances. As such, the principle is understood as analogous to rules such as those that state that 'if you drive over 60 kmph you have broken the law and will be fined 100 euros'. Thus for example, McKinney and Hammer Hill describe it as placing a 'burden of proof of non-harm on anyone undertaking an environmental action whose consequences are unknown'.[10] Stone suggests that one interpretation of it 'commands an activity to be terminated' in a certain set of circumstances.[11] The problem with such a characterization is that, as Stone rightly points out, the preconditions are in no way determinate. Likewise, as others have noted, formulations that demand particular outcomes are neither logically possible nor particularly desirable in cases of scientific uncertainty. As such, as Cross states, the principle can be 'attacked as an uncertain decision rule'.[12]

Yet these critiques, by assuming the principle is a rule, proceed on the wrong basis and ignore a basic feature of the principle – that it is, in legal terms, a principle rather than a rule. Whilst the concept of 'principle' will vary depending on its jurisprudential and jurisdictional context, in all cases a principle is not an 'explicitly formulated' rule that is unchanging in its application. Rather its application is flexible and will depend on specific circumstances. Moreover, just as other principles do, it 'states a reason that argues in one direction, but does not necessitate a particular decision'.[13]

The definition of the precautionary principle found in the Rio Declaration is perhaps the most commonly cited: 'Where there are threats of serious or irreversible damage, lack of full scientific certainty shall not be used as a reason for postponing cost-effective measures to prevent environmental degradation.'[14] The Rio approach is often categorised as a *weak* approach to the precautionary principle, characterised by the need for serious or irreversible damage and the question of cost-effectiveness. The latter not only limits the space for precautionary action, but may even deny much of the radicalism of the precautionary principle, as it is precisely in situations of uncertainty that calculations of costs and benefits are most difficult. The weak approach to the precautionary principle can be contrasted with a *strong* version. This would provide that where there are threats to the environment or health, the proponent of an activity must prove its safety, without reference to costs and benefits. There are unavoidable difficulties with this approach: proof of 'no risk' is rarely if ever available, and a consistent refusal to innovate in the absence of such proof would lead to technological stagnation.[15]

A third, alternative, understanding of the precautionary principle would understand the principle as indicating a need to move beyond a technical

[10] William McKinney and J. Hammer Hill, 'Of Sustainability and Precaution: The Logical, Epistemological, and Moral Problems of the Precautionary Principle and Their Implications for Sustainable Development' (2000) 5 *Ethics and the Environment* 178.

[11] Christopher Stone, 'Is there a Precautionary Principle?' (2001) 31 *Environmental Law Reporter* 10790.

[12] Frank B. Cross, 'Paradoxical Perils of the Precautionary Principle' (1996) 53 *Washington and Lee Law Review* 859.

[13] Ronald Dworkin, *Taking Rights Seriously* (Duckworth, 1977), p. 26.

[14] *Declaration of the UN Conference on Environment and Development* (Rio Declaration), 3–14 June 1992, principle 15, see Ch. 6, p. 223.

[15] Giandomenico Majone, 'What Price Safety? The Precautionary Principle and its Policy Implications' (2002) 40 *Journal of Common Market Studies* 89.

approach to risk, bringing factors other than scientific and technical expertise into decision making fora, including more qualitative, and personal, experience.[16] As Elizabeth Fisher puts it, 'decision-makers cannot hide behind a façade of "facts" where no definitive factual basis exists. Such a façade not only bears little relation to reality but also results in inefficiency and a false form of accountability.'[17] This understanding of the precautionary principle points towards open decision making, and may even reinforce the move towards 'public participation' apparent in many areas of environmental law, as discussed in Chapter 3; the 'risk society' thesis discussed above (p. 15) also points towards more radical forms of participation, democratising technical decision making. This approach to the precautionary principle could have a profound impact on the way in which decisions are made. A recognition that the 'facts' are no longer a sure-fire response to those who disagree with the scientists also makes it harder to dismiss the factors that impact on public 'risk perception', discussed above (pp. 15–18): 'public scepticism and alarmism become a bit more understandable' once one recognises what a 'blunt instrument' many of the tools used by the risk assessor are.[18] And public disagreement between scientists further compounds this breakdown in the use of science to justify decisions.

The precautionary principle has received a great deal of attention at European Union (EU) level. Of a number of judicial decisions on the principle,[19] *Pfizer*[20] was the first very detailed and explicit analysis, and remains a significant decision on both the precautionary principle and the use of science by the EU institutions. Although the approach adopted by the Court of First Instance is evolving and not consistently applied in its full rigour, it is illustrative of how the courts will tackle problematic and disputed science. *Pfizer* arose out of the use of certain antibiotics in animal feed, in order to bring the animals to the appropriate weight for slaughter more quickly and with less feed. Concern about the possible development by bacteria of resistance to particular antibiotics, making the treatment of some

[16] Elizabeth Fisher, 'Is the Precautionary Principle Justiciable?' (2001) 13 *Journal of Environmental Law* 315. See also Nicholas de Sadeleer, *Environmental Principles: From Political Slogans to Legal Rules* (Oxford University Press, 2002), arguing that the principle *politicises* technical debates.

[17] Elizabeth Fisher, 'Precaution, Precaution Everywhere: Developing a "Common Understanding" of the Precautionary Principle in the European Community' (2002) 9 *Maastricht Journal of European and Comparative Law* 7, p. 9.

[18] John S. Dryzek, *The Politics of the Earth: Environmental Discourses* (Oxford University Press, 1997), p. 73.

[19] Although the precautionary principle was not explicitly invoked, the BSE saga raised many relevant issues: Case C-241/01 *National Farmers Union* v. *Secrétariat Général du Gouvernement* [2002] ECR I-907; Case C-1/00 *Commission* v. *France* [2001] ECR I-9989; Case C-180/96 *UK* v. *Commission* [1996] ECR I-3903. More recently, see Cases T-74/00, T-76/00 and T141/00 *Artegodan and Others* v. *Commission* [2002] ECR II-4945; Case T-392/02 *Solvay Pharmaceuticals BV* v. *Council* [2003] ECR II-4555.

[20] Case T-13/99 *Pfizer Animal Health SA* v. *Council* [2002] ECR II-3305; Case T-70/99 *Alpharma Inc.* v. *Council* [2002] ECR II-3495 was decided on the same day on an almost identical basis.

diseases by that antibiotic ineffective, has increased in recent years. The applicants sought annulment of a Regulation banning the use of certain antibiotics as additives in feedingstuffs.[21]

### Case T-13/99 *Pfizer Animal Health SA* v. *Council* [2002] ECR II-3305

139. It is appropriate to bear in mind that, as the Court of Justice and the Court of First Instance have held, where there is scientific uncertainty as to the existence or extent of risks to human health, the Community institutions may, by reason of the precautionary principle, take protective measures without having to wait until the reality and seriousness of those risks become fully apparent …

…

141. *A fortiori*, the Community institutions were not required, for the purpose of taking preventive action, to wait for the adverse effects of the use of the product as a growth promoter to materialise …

142. Thus, in a situation in which the precautionary principle is applied, which by definition coincides with a situation in which there is scientific uncertainty, a risk assessment cannot be required to provide the Community institutions with conclusive scientific evidence of the reality of the risk and the seriousness of the potential adverse effects were that risk to become a reality …

143. However, it is also clear … that a preventive measure cannot properly be based on a purely hypothetical approach to the risk, founded on mere conjecture which has not been scientifically verified …

144. Rather, it follows from the Community Courts' interpretation of the precautionary principle that a preventive measure may be taken only if the risk, although the reality and extent thereof have not been fully demonstrated by conclusive scientific evidence, appears nevertheless to be adequately backed up by the scientific data available at the time when the measure was taken.

…

160. … unless the precautionary principle is to be rendered nugatory, the fact that it is impossible to carry out a full scientific risk assessment does not prevent the competent public authority from taking preventive measures, at very short notice if necessary, when such measures appear essential given the level of risk to human health which the authority has deemed unacceptable for society.

161. In such a situation, the competent public authority must therefore weigh up its obligations and decide either to wait until the results of more detailed scientific research become available or to act on the basis of the scientific information available. Where measures for the protection of human health are concerned, the outcome of that balancing exercise will depend, account being taken of the particular circumstances of each individual case, on the level of risk which the authority deems unacceptable for society.

…

---

[21] Regulation 2821/98 banning the use of certain antibiotics as additives in feedingstuffs OJ 1998 L 351/4.

410. The Court considers that a cost/benefit analysis is a particular expression of the principle of proportionality in cases involving risk management.

…

456. The Court observes that the importance of the objective pursued by the contested regulation, i.e. the protection of human health, may justify adverse consequences, and even substantial adverse consequences, for certain traders … The protection of public health, which the contested regulation is intended to guarantee, must take precedence over economic considerations …

…

467. … Pfizer, … emphasise the fact that the ban on the use of antibiotics as growth promoters has significant adverse effects on the environment, which ought also to have been taken into account by the Community institutions. In their view, use of those products as additives allows waste from farming, such as nitrogen and phosphates, to be reduced and makes it unnecessary to use other additives based on zinc oxide, a heavy metal causing extensive pollution.

468. The Court notes *in limine* that the contested regulation is founded on a political choice, in respect of which the Community institutions were required to weigh up, on the one hand, maintaining, while awaiting further scientific studies, the authorisation of a product which primarily enables the agricultural sector to be more profitable and, on the other, banning the product for public health reasons.

469. As regards Pfizer's complaint that the institutions, when making their policy choice, did not carry out a cost/benefit analysis, it is apparent from the documents before the Court that an assessment of that kind was made in several of the reports by international bodies which had been submitted to the institutions during the procedure culminating in adoption of the contested regulation and which were examined by the Standing Committee …

…

471. … it is appropriate to begin by observing that public health, which the contested regulation is intended to protect, must take precedence over economic considerations …

472. Next, it is not disputed that use of antibiotics as growth promoters is not essential to meat production. Nor is it disputed that there were alternatives to that practice, even though, as Pfizer maintains, those alternatives make it essential to alter farming methods and may entail higher production costs and higher meat prices. However, there is nothing to suggest that the policy choice made by the institutions was unreasonable in that regard.

*Pfizer* is a complex decision. A number of (deceptively) straightforward observations about the precautionary principle in the EU might, however, be made in its wake. Most basically, the precautionary principle applies to the protection of public health (we know that it also applies more broadly,[22] particularly to environmental protection[23]) and this allows decisions to be taken in conditions

---

[22] *Artegodan.*    [23] Article 175 EC, see Ch. 4, p. 153.

of scientific uncertainty. A risk assessment is a necessary first step to any such decision, albeit one that cannot be expected to provide certainty. This brings us to the crucial question of when there is *sufficient* scientific evidence on a risk to bring into play the precautionary principle, and so to take action in the absence of certainty. The Court of First Instance (CFI) in *Pfizer* distinguishes between a 'purely hypothetical' approach to risk, and risk which is 'adequately backed up by the scientific data available at the time' (para. 144); but without examining quite how that distinction might be drawn. In the words of Advocate General Mischo, this distinction 'fully expresses all the tension inherent in applying the precautionary principle: on the one hand, a measure cannot be based on a purely hypothetical risk, yet, on the other hand, one cannot wait until the risk has been established with certainty';[24] he uses the language of 'plausible risk'.[25] In a subsequent decision on the control (by *national* authorities) of activities under EC nature conservation law, the European Court of Justice (ECJ) refers to 'reasonable scientific doubt' as the moment for *mandatory* application of the precautionary principle.[26] This is a far simpler (even simplistic, and of course the rub is in that 'reasonable') approach to the precautionary principle, possible in this case because the Court had no need to involve itself in the science at issue, or the use of that science.

Like risk assessment, cost benefit analysis (CBA) has a central, but somewhat ambiguous, role in the *Pfizer* decision. CBA is 'a particular expression of the principle of proportionality in cases involving risk management' (para. 410). It would be a matter of concern if the Court intends to replace the evaluative proportionality balancing exercise with a technical approach to CBA. The Court, however, seems most concerned to ensure a weighing up of the various options, a qualitative as much as a quantitative process (paras. 464–75).

Nor, according to *Pfizer*, can a decision seek 'zero risk' (para. 145). Whilst the phrase 'zero risk' is somewhat ambiguous (it might mean the attempt to reduce a clearly identified risk, such as the risk of lung disease from exposure to certain types of asbestos,[27] to zero), the CFI is concerned to reject any suggestion that positive proof of absolute safety might be required. In doing so, the CFI rejects the 'strong' approach to the precautionary principle and its associated difficulties (particularly technological stagnation), as had the European Commission in its *Communication on the Precautionary Principle*: measures based on the precautionary principle 'must not aim at zero risk, something which rarely exists'.[28]

---

[24] Case C-192/01 *Commission* v. *Denmark* [2003] ECR I-9693, para. 101.    [25] *Ibid.*, para. 102.

[26] Case C-127/02 *Landelijke Vereniging tot Behoud van de Waddenzee* v. *Staatssecretaris van Landbouw, Natuurbeheer en Visserij* [2005] 2 CMLR 31, para. 59. See Ch. 15, pp. 651–3.

[27] At World Trade Organisation (WTO) level, see *European Communities – Measures Affecting Asbestos and Asbestos Containing Products* WT/DS135/AB/R, 12 March 2001, para. 174. In the EU this is permissible, see C-121/00 *Hahn* [2002] ECR I-9193; *Solvay*.

[28] COM (2000) 1 final, p. 17.

Finally, whilst a 'strong' approach to the precautionary principle (requiring action to be taken on harm regardless of cost) is rarely found in official circles, *Pfizer* provides that the protection of public health should take priority over economic interests. In a subsequent case, the CFI refers to the precautionary principle as 'a general principle of Community law requiring the competent authorities to take appropriate measures to prevent specific potential risks to public health, safety and the environment, by giving precedence to the requirements related to the protection of those interests over economic interests'.[29] This provides potentially important 'cover' for protective regulatory decisions. However, not only is there a level of inconsistency, given the simultaneous emphasis on risk assessment and CBA; this approach may also rest on the type of oversimplification criticised in the next extract.

### Cass R. Sunstein, 'Beyond the Precautionary Principle' (2003) 151 *University of Pennsylvania Law Review* 1003, pp. 1003–8

I aim to challenge the precautionary principle here, not because it leads in bad directions, but because, read for all that it is worth, it leads in no direction at all. The principle threatens to be paralyzing, forbidding regulation, inaction, and every step in between. To explain this problem very briefly, the precautionary principle provides help only if we blind ourselves to many aspects of risk-related situations and focus on a narrow subset of what is at stake. A significant part of my discussion will be devoted to showing why this is so. I will also urge that the precautionary principle gives the (false) appearance of being workable only because of identifiable cognitive mechanisms, which lead people to have a narrow rather than wide viewscreen. With that narrow viewscreen, it is possible to ignore, or to neglect, some of the risks that are actually at stake. I emphasize that we have good reason to endorse the goals that motivate many people to endorse the precautionary principle. These goals include the importance of protecting health and the environment even from remote risks, the need to attend to unintended adverse effects of technological change, and the need to ensure that wealthy countries pay their fair share for environmental improvement and risk reduction. But the precautionary principle is a crude way of protecting these goals, which should be pursued directly …

…

The most serious problem with the strong version of the precautionary principle is that it offers no guidance – not that it is wrong, but that it forbids all courses of action, including inaction. To understand this point, it will be useful to anchor the discussion in some concrete problems:

1. One of the most controversial environmental issues faced in the first year of the Bush administration involved the regulation of arsenic. There is a serious dispute over the precise level of risks posed by low levels of arsenic in drinking water, but in the 'worst case' scenario, over one hundred lives might be lost each year as a result of the fifty parts per billion (ppb) standard that the Clinton administration sought to revise. At the same time, the proposed

---

[29] *Artegodan*, para. 184.

ten ppb standard would cost over two hundred million dollars each year, and it is possible that it would save as few as five lives annually.

2. Genetic modification of food has become a widespread practice. But the risks of that practice are not known with precision. Some people fear that genetic modification will result in serious ecological harm and large risks to human health.

3. Scientists are not in full accord about the dangers associated with global warming, but there is general agreement that global warming is in fact occurring. It is possible that global warming will produce, by 2100, a mean temperature increase of 4.5 degrees Celsius, that it will result in well over five trillion dollars in annual monetized costs, and that it will also produce a significant number of deaths from malaria. The Kyoto Protocol would require most industrialized nations to reduce greenhouse gas emissions to between ninety-two percent and ninety-four percent of 1990 levels.

4. Many people fear nuclear power on the grounds that nuclear power plants raise various health and safety issues, including some possibility of catastrophe. But if a nation does not rely on nuclear power, it might well rely instead on fossil fuels, and in particular on coal-fired power plants. Such plants create risks of their own, including risks associated with global warming. China, for example, has relied on nuclear energy in part as a way of reducing greenhouse gases and in part as a way of reducing other air pollution problems.

...

In these cases, what kind of guidance is provided by the precautionary principle? It is tempting to say, as is in fact standard, that the principle calls for strong controls on arsenic, on genetic engineering of food, on greenhouse gases, ... and on nuclear power. In all of these cases, there is a possibility of serious harms, and no authoritative scientific evidence suggests that the possibility is close to zero. If the burden of proof is on the proponent of the activity or process in question, the precautionary principle would seem to impose a burden of proof that cannot be met. Put to one side the question of whether the precautionary principle, understood to compel stringent regulation in these cases, is sensible. Let us ask a more fundamental question: Is that more stringent regulation therefore compelled by the precautionary principle?

The answer is that it is not. In some of these cases, it should be easy to see that, in its own way, stringent regulation would actually run afoul of the precautionary principle. The simplest reason is that such regulation might well deprive society of significant benefits, and for that reason produce a large number of deaths that otherwise would not occur. In some cases, regulation eliminates the 'opportunity benefits' of a process or activity, and thus causes preventable deaths. If this is so, regulation is hardly precautionary. The most familiar cases involve the 'drug lag', produced by a highly precautionary approach to the introduction of new medicines and drugs into the market. If a government takes such an approach, it might protect people against harms from inadequately tested drugs; but it will also prevent people from receiving potential benefits from those very drugs. Is it 'precautionary' to require extensive premarketing testing, or to do the opposite?

Or consider the case of genetic modification of food. Many people believe that a failure to allow genetic modification might well result in numerous deaths, and a small probability of many more. The reason is that genetic modification holds out the promise of producing food that is both cheaper and healthier – resulting, for example, in 'golden rice', which might have large benefits in developing countries. Now the point is not that genetic modification will definitely have those benefits or that the benefits of genetic modification outweigh the risks. The point is only that if the precautionary principle is taken in its strongest form, it is offended by regulation as well as by nonregulation …

Sometimes regulation would violate the precautionary principle because it would give rise to *substitute risks*, in the form of hazards that materialize, or are increased, as a result of regulation. Consider the case of nuclear power. It is reasonable to think that in light of current options, a ban on nuclear power will increase dependence on fossil fuels, which contribute to global warming. If so, such a ban would seem to run afoul of the precautionary principle. …

It is possible to go much further. A great deal of evidence suggests the possibility that an expensive regulation can have adverse effects on life and health. To be sure, both the phenomenon and the underlying mechanisms are disputed. It has been urged that a statistical life can be lost for every expenditure of $7.25 million, and one study suggests a cutoff point, for a loss of life per regulatory expenditure, of $15 million. A striking paper suggests that poor people are especially vulnerable to this effect – that a regulation that reduces wealth for the poorest twenty percent of the population will have twice as large a mortality effect as a regulation that reduces wealth for the wealthiest twenty percent. I do not mean to accept any particular amount here, or even to suggest that there has been an unambiguous demonstration of an association between mortality and regulatory expenditures. The only point is that reasonable people believe in that association. It follows that a multimillion-dollar expenditure for 'precaution' has – as a worst case scenario – significant adverse health effects, with an expenditure of $200 million leading to perhaps as many as thirty lives lost.

… the precautionary principle, taken for all that it is worth, is paralyzing: it stands as an obstacle to regulation and nonregulation, and to everything in between. To say this is not to say that the precautionary principle cannot be amended in a way that removes the problem. But once it is so amended, it is much less distinctive and increasingly resembles an effort to weigh the health benefits of regulation against the health costs, or even to measure benefits against costs.

Whilst Sunstein might be criticised for taking issue with a strong form of the precautionary principle that is seldom adhered to (even *Pfizer*, which requires that public health be prioritised, refers to the costs and benefits of regulatory options, and bars the search for 'zero risk'), his warning is pertinent. And in any event, we should be wary of any claim that there are simple answers to the difficult decisions we face in environmental law; the misuse of the precautionary principle could obscure the difficult value judgments to be made. Critics of the precautionary principle, including Sunstein, often discuss a 'strong' version of the precautionary principle because, they argue, a 'weak' version adds nothing to ordinary good decision making, which always takes scientific uncertainty into account. There is something in this: science never provides absolute certainty. However, the precautionary principle should at least avoid the routine misuse of uncertainty as a justification of non-action. And we could of course go much further, and argue that, rather than telling us what to do with the information from science, the precautionary principle should completely recast the ways in which public administration makes decisions, moving beyond a purely technical approach (see pp. 21–2).

The EU judiciary has discussed the potential role of the precautionary principle in good decision making in some detail. The English courts have been somewhat less forthcoming.

### R (on the application of Amvac Chemical UK Ltd) v. Secretary of State for the Environment, Food and Rural Affairs [2001] EWHC Admin 1011

1. The Claimant challenges a decision communicated on 4 August 2001 to suspend regulatory approvals for dichlorvos, a chemical used in pesticides.

…

65. The Claimant does not contend that the Defendants were necessarily under any duty to follow the precautionary principle. Essentially its case is that the Defendants purported to do so, but failed.

66. The precautionary principle, as defined at the 1992 Rio Conference on the Environment and Development, requires that:

> 'Where there are threats of serious or irreversible damage, lack of full scientific certainty should not be posed as a reason for postponing cost effective measures to prevent environmental degradation.'

67. It is self-evident that the principle itself, as stated above, would not assist the Claimant – rather the reverse. What the Claimant says is that if measures are to be taken in the absence of full scientific certainty, there must necessarily be a proper assessment of risk, since it would be absurd to take measures simply because the absence of any risk could not be completely excluded. Rarely is it possible to prove a negative.

…

73. In May 1999 the Department for Environment, Food and Rural Affairs, issued a Strategy on Sustainable Development entitled *A better quality of life*, with a foreword by the Prime Minister. Having referred to the precautionary principle, the document continues:

> 'The precautionary principle means that it is not acceptable just to say we can't be sure that serious damage will happen, so we'll do nothing to prevent it.
>
> 'Precaution is not just relevant to environmental damage – for example, chemicals which may affect wildlife may also affect human health.
>
> 'At the same time, precautionary action must be based on objective assessments of the costs and benefits of action. The principle does not mean that we only permit activities if we are sure that serious harm will not arise, or there is proof that the benefits outweigh all possible risks. That would severely hinder progress towards improvements in the quality of life.

'There are no hard and fast rules on when to take action: each case has to be considered carefully. We may decide that a particular risk is so serious that it is not worth living with. In other cases society will be prepared to live with a risk because of other benefits it brings. Transparency is essential: difficult decisions on precautionary action are most likely where there is reason to think that there may be a significant threat, but evidence is as yet lacking or inconclusive. Decisions should be reviewed to reflect better understanding of risk as more evidence becomes available.'

...

83. I have been referred to two cases in which the precautionary principle was considered. In *R* v. *Leicester City Council and others, ex parte Blackfordby and Boothorpe Action Group Ltd* [2000] JPL 1266, Richards J. referred at paragraphs 65 to 68 to a submission based on the precautionary principle 'briefly advanced and again plucked out of the air in the course of oral argument, that the decision was *Wednesbury* unreasonable in its application of the principle ...'. Richards J. said that it was difficult to see precisely how counsel relied on the principle, in the field of planning and waste management. In the end he held that it did not take the arguments any further. In *R (on the application of Murray)* v. *Derbyshire County Council,* 6 October 2000, Maurice Kay J. dealt with similar submissions in the same field of regulation. After a limited discussion of the principle, he held that the submission added nothing to a submission based on the relevant regulations and that in any event he was unable to find that there was a failure to have regard to the principle in any event.

84. I am prepared to accept that on a substantive challenge to a regulatory decision, it may in some fields of regulation be relevant to take into account the precautionary principle and, more important, its limitations. It may be relevant to refer to the principle in a substantive challenge in the field of pesticide approval. However, my very firm conclusion is that there is – at least so far – no settled, specific or identifiable mechanism of risk assessment in the field of pesticide approval that the Claimant is entitled to rely on as part of the 'precautionary principle', viewed as a separate basis for challenging a decision ...

86. In any event I do not consider that the Defendants or their advisory bodies purported in relation to the present decision to apply the precautionary principle as a term of art or any settled, specific or identifiable mechanism or methodology.

We might note that the precautionary principle in this case is argued by the industry party resisting regulation. We should not be surprised to see that the relatively powerful are best placed to use the law. But we can also see here the paradox that the precautionary principle can even refocus attention on the technical risk assessment, whilst simultaneously suggesting that the information from the risk assessment has inherent limitations. The tension between a technical risk assessment and the emphasis on the evaluative and the political is rather intense.

The flexibility of the precautionary principle, together with the restriction of judicial review to questions of process and illegality, rather than the merits or substance of a decision, mean that although the precautionary principle may protect certain decisions, it will rarely be used to strike down decisions, at EU or UK level. In the words of the CFI in *Pfizer*, when the Community institutions have a broad discretion to act, 'it is settled case-law that … review by the Community judicature of the substance of the relevant act must be confined to examining whether the exercise of such discretion is vitiated by a manifest error or a misuse of powers or whether the Community institutions clearly exceeded the bounds of their discretion' (para. 166). Nevertheless, this leaves some space for judicial intervention in interpreting and applying the precautionary principle,[30] and *Pfizer* demonstrates the willingness of the EU courts to assess the action of the EU institutions by reference to the precautionary principle.[31] English judges are decidedly reluctant to use the precautionary principle as a tool of judicial review,[32] but we might expect them to follow EC-level cases and get more involved over time. This is partly a question of the extent to which the EC legal approach to the precautionary principle binds the Member States, a far from straightforward question.[33] At the very least, the ECJ interprets EC legislation in such a way that it complies with environmental principles: cases such as *Standley* (below, p. 37) demonstrate how this interpretative role can extend into the national implementation of EC law;[34] similarly, *Waddenzee*[35] requires national courts to assess national implementation of nature conservation legislation by reference to its interpretation of the precautionary principle. This simplifies some complex and potentially important legal developments; we will revisit the role of the precautionary principle in allowing national bodies to justify derogating from free trade rules in Chapters 4 (EU) and 7 (WTO) below.

### (d) Accounting for the authority of science

Having asserted the influence of science on law making, and its limitations in the environmental field, we should try to account for the authority of science. It is well known that the scientific paradigm has roots that are deep in history, and steeped in religion. But the onset of the Enlightenment is considered to have most powerfully and persistently shaped attitudes to the natural world,[36] so that a 'domination of nature' thesis prevails. In the following, Holder explains the 'radical lawyer's conventional account of law's place in the Enlightenment project' (p. 165).

---

[30] See, for example, Michael Doherty, 'The Judicial Use of the Principles of EC Environmental Policy' (2000) 2 *Environmental Law Review* 251.    [31] See also, for example, *Artegodan*.

[32] See, for example, *R* v. *Secretary of State for Trade and Industry ex p Duddridge* [1996] Env LR 325 (CA); [1995] Env LR 151 (HC); Fisher, 'Is the Precautionary Principle Justiciable?'.

[33] See further Joanne Scott, 'The Precautionary Principle before the European Courts' in Richard Macrory (ed.), *Principles of European Environmental Law* (Europa Law Publishing, 2004).

[34] See also the decisions in Case C-6/99 *Greenpeace* v. *Ministère de l'Agriculture et de la Pêche* [2000] ECR I-1651; Case C-236/01 *Monsanto Agricoltura Italia SpA* v. *Presidenza del Consiglio dei Ministri* [2003] ECR I-8105.    [35] Above, n. 26. See further pp. 651–3

[36] David Harvey, *Justice, Nature and the Geography of Difference* (Blackwell, 1996), p. 123.

### Jane Holder, 'New Age: Rediscovering Natural Law' (2000) 53 *Current Legal Problems* 151, pp. 159–63

Concerns about the damaging effects of mankind's activities on the environment have led to considerable debate, reams of academic writings, policy proposals, and some legal measures to protect 'the environment'. But the very word 'environment' is a symptom of the malaise, meaning, as it does, that which surrounds, which 'environs us', which is apart from people. There is a school of thought that before the scientific revolution man's moral and physical relationship to nature was close and intimate; man and nature were locked into one interacting world. In the medieval cosmology, a 'Great Chain of Being' linked together all elements of the universe (living and non-living objects on earth, earthly creatures and heavenly beings) so that they were mutually dependent …

The scientific revolution challenged the medieval cosmology based on divine purpose and proposed a more mechanistic conception of nature, governed by mathematical laws which destroyed the symbolic meanings attached to plants, stones and animals … Descartes' reductionism – that animals and the human body as well as nature were machines which could be understood in terms of mathematics – was instrumental in forging this divide. In addressing whether man was distinguishable from the rest of nature, Descartes reasoned that thinking established the fact of human existence. Whereas matter was composed of primary, 'knowable' qualities, the mind was subjective and attributed secondary qualities to nature. This dualism of mind/matter and subject/object implied that nature was composed of reducible objects, metaphysically separated from man. 'Nature' came to be understood as a portion of the world, as one aspect of everything (and as a 'resource'), rather than, as previously understood, as 'an invisible medium through which each moved'.[37]

The empirical method of the later *philosophes* began with phenomenal experience – observation and analysis of data in such a way as to uncover universal principles or 'laws of nature', the emphasis being 'not on the diversity of forms but on the uniformity of laws'. These were the classical laws of physics – laws of gravity, and laws of motion. The accepted version of the Enlightenment is that the conception of nature as separate from man, as capable of being objectively observed, and 'laws of nature' understood, enabled man to exploit it more effectively than he had previously done. This assertion rests on a 'domination of nature' interpretation of, particularly, the Baconian creed that objective, scientific knowledge of the laws of nature meant that those laws could and should be used for man's benefit. The technocentric approach to environmental problems, enshrined in modern environmental law, may be, albeit simplistically, traced to the ascendancy of such ideas in this time.

The Enlightenment *philosophes* and Baconian science challenged the paradigm for medieval science, set by theology, but did not entirely override it. There was dissent, for example, from within the Enlightenment about the extent to which physical laws of nature might be understood by science and tamed. And medieval 'laws of nature' remained influential. The Chain of Being, for example, was restated by Locke in his *Essay Concerning*

---

[37] Neil Evernden, *The Social Creation of Nature* (Johns Hopkins University Press, 1993).

*Human Understanding* (1690) and it strongly resembled Darwin's 'Web of Life' which embodied a holistic approach to nature, albeit advancing the idea that there might be a grand design with mankind as the culmination of evolutionary progress. The Chain of Being also influenced the Romantic movement of the eighteenth and nineteenth centuries, particularly its strains of animism and pantheism. Like other so-called laws of nature, the Chain of Being was used by many in this period to justify inequality; equality was contrary to nature and to seek to change one's place was to thwart the 'laws of order'. But, the implications of a hierarchy within species, as well as between, meant that the Chain of Being was discarded by Methodists, slave trade abolitionists and Benthamites. The Romantic movement continued to seek the reenchantment of the natural world in the supposed unity of man and the land, as seen in the work of the Romantic poets in England, and the American (wilderness) transcendentalists. The emphasis was on being at one with the natural world to achieve a form of spiritual and inspirational 'self-realisation' or awareness, through poetry, hiking, art, and landscape gardening. Although taking an apparently benign form, appeals to the 'state of nature' were also functional, used particularly by the emerging middle classes to assert their natural rights against the remnants of the ecclesiastical order and to justify an economic programme of laissez faire, upheld by free market 'natural laws' of supply and demand. 'Laws of nature' were not merely a means by which the physical environment might be understood, they also became a sanction for unrestricted competition.

A further 'law of nature' was deduced by Malthus, as an antidote to the optimism of the Enlightenment (but which became a foundation for the tenets of capitalism which grew from it): population growth and the struggle for existence (of the *labouring* poor) places pressure on the means of subsistence, inevitably producing poverty, disease, famine and war. As a metaphor for the entrepreneurial values of competition, and the survival of the fittest in a struggle for existence, this Malthusian 'law of nature' was taken up by Darwin, amongst others. That economics and politics played a part in the understanding and acceptance of Malthus' 'law' may be seen in the rejection of ideas of struggle, and competition for limited space and resources in Russia, an expansive, sparsely populated land. A critical interpretation of 'natural limits' follows: scarcity is socially produced, rather than some externally imposed necessity or natural law. Nevertheless, Malthus' appeal to respect 'natural limits' has become the modern ecologist's holy grail, encouraged by Hardin's parable on the tragedy of the commons [pp. 35–6 below].

At this stage it is possible to identify the antecedents of the modern battleground over nature. Modern ecologists, stressing interdependence and adherence to 'laws of nature' or 'natural limits', draw upon the idea of a Chain of Being and Malthus' population principle, whereas the intellectual roots of the environmental technicists or modernisers stressing the ability of man to understand laws of nature through physics and mathematics and thus manage the environment are Cartesian dualism and Baconian science.

Hence the argument that the separation of man and nature engendered by the scientific method and its ideological consequences provided the conditions for the future exploitation of the physical environment, sanctioned by law. As

Fitzpatrick states: 'In the creation and maintenance of nature, as well as for its identity as liberal legality, law comes to depend on scientific, disciplinary administration.'[38]

At the core of the shallow environmentalism engendered by enlightenment science is acceptance of a narrow meaning of progress or development, at least compared to the ecologists' ideal that no one conception of progress should be privileged, but rather that there should be multiple readings and meanings of progress and development. It is this aspect of the critique of shallow environmentalism that leads to a powerful challenge to the globalisation of the western model of development or the 'westernisation' of the world, as discussed in the review of radical ecological theories, below (see Section 5).

## 3  Environment and economics

Discussions of appropriate levels of environmental protection have long been dominated by economic understandings of the environment. Environmental economics were first brought to the mainstream in the UK by the influential *Blueprint* report to government in the late 1980s.[39]

### David Pearce and Edward B. Barbier, *Blueprint for a Sustainable Economy* (Earthscan, 2000), p. 2

*The Original Themes of* Blueprint for a Green Economy
Environmental assets are important not just in themselves (so-called intrinsic value) but in economic terms, that is in terms of the economic services they provide.

Economic importance relates to the contribution that those assets make to human well-being.

Human well-being embraces everything that gives humans happiness and satisfaction. It is not confined to the satisfaction derived from material goods and services nor is the motive for being happy or satisfied confined to self-interest.

Economic value is most commonly revealed and observed in the market place.

But the contributions that environmental goods and services make to human well-being may or may not be channelled via functioning markets. In a great many cases, they are not. We say there are missing markets.

Economic importance can be demonstrated by placing monetary values on environmental assets and services, values which reflect human preferences, just as if there was a market. This is the process of non-market valuation.

…

---

[38] Peter Fitzpatrick, '"The Desperate Vacuum": Imperialism and Law in the Experience of the Enlightenment' (1989) 13 *Droit et Société* 350.

[39] David W. Pearce, Edward B. Barbier and Anil Markandya, *Blueprint for a Green Economy* (Earthscan, 1989).

Once we know an asset has economic importance, we can focus on the policies to conserve it. But policies are not effective unless they address the root cause of the problem, and those root causes often lie in the structure of the economic system. Hence economic solutions are required for environmental problems.

The *Blueprint* approach posits incomplete economic analysis as the root cause of environmental problems, and more complete economic analysis as the solution. Economics has some powerful and useful ways of expressing how contemporary societal arrangements systematically neglect environmental issues.

### Garrett Hardin, 'The Tragedy of the Commons' (1968) 162 *Science* 1243, pp. 1244-5

The tragedy of the commons develops in this way. Picture a pasture open to all. It is to be expected that each herdsman will try to keep as many cattle as possible on the commons. Such an arrangement may work reasonably satisfactorily for centuries because tribal wars, poaching, and disease keep the numbers of both man and beast well below the carrying capacity of the land. Finally, however, comes the day of reckoning, that is, the day when the long-desired goal of social stability becomes a reality. At this point, the inherent logic of the commons remorselessly generates tragedy.

As a rational being, each herdsman seeks to maximise his gain. Explicitly or implicitly, more or less consciously, he asks, 'What is the utility *to me* of adding one more animal to my herd?' This utility has one negative and one positive component.

1. The positive component is a function of the increment of one animal. Since the herdsman receives all the proceeds from the sale of the additional animal, the positive utility is nearly +1.

2. The negative component is a function of the additional overgrazing created by one more animal. Since, however, the effects of overgrazing are shared by all the herdsman, the negative utility for any particular herdsman is only a fraction of −1.

Adding together the component partial utilities, the rational herdsman concludes that the only sensible course for him to pursue is to add another animal to his herd. And another; and another ... But this is the conclusion reached by each and every rational herdsman sharing a commons. Therein is the tragedy. Each man is locked into a system that compels him to increase his herd without limit – in a world that is limited. Ruin is the destination toward which all men rush, each pursuing his own best interest in a society that believes in the freedom of the commons. Freedom in a commons brings ruin to all.

...

In a reverse way, the tragedy of the commons reappears in problems of pollution. Here it is not a question of taking something out of the commons, but of putting something in – sewage, or chemical, radioactive, and heat wastes into water; noxious and dangerous fumes into the air; and distracting and unpleasant advertising signs into the line of sight.

> The calculations of utility are much the same as before. The rational man finds that his share of the cost of the wastes he discharges into the commons is less than the cost of purifying his wastes before releasing them. Since this is true for everyone, we are locked into a system of 'fouling our own nest', so long as we behave only as independent, rational, free-enterprisers.
>
> The tragedy of the commons as a food basket is averted by private property, or something formally like it. But the air and waters surrounding us cannot readily be fenced, and so the tragedy of the commons as a cesspool must be prevented by different means, by coercive laws or taxing devices.

Although this thesis has been criticised for its detail, its general explanatory force is strong. Hardin's tragedy of the commons builds on the notion of 'externalities', a key concept in environmental law. Externalities are the costs of producing a product that are not reflected in the final cost of the product. Farmers whose crops die because of pollution, government or consumers who pay to clean up pollution, and communities which suffer the health effects of pollution, by bearing the costs of pollution, are all bearing the external costs of the economic enterprise creating the pollution. In an unregulated market, a factory does not have to pay for the use of the water or air, reducing the cost of production. This is not only intuitively unfair, but also inefficient, because the artificially low prices lead to over-production. Regulation is justified as an attempt to internalise externalities, bringing them within operating costs; the 'polluter pays principle' has become a core principle of environmental law, and whilst there is a certain amount of ambiguity as to the extent that the principle rests on economic efficiency as opposed to intuitive notions of justice (it is 'fair' that the polluter pays), it is most commonly justified and explained by reference to cost internalisation. As with the precautionary principle, the Rio Declaration provides a commonly cited approach: 'National authorities should endeavour to promote the internalization of environmental costs and the use of economic instruments, taking into account the approach that the polluter should, in principle, bear the cost of pollution, with due regard to the public interest and without distorting international trade and investment.'[40] The polluter pays principle should discipline governmental decision making in such a way as to prevent the bearing of environmental costs by the general public. The polluter pays principle is frequently called on as a justification of so-called 'market instruments' of regulation, discussed further in Chapter 11 below. The principle in no way, however, dictates the nature of a regulatory scheme. *Standley* involves a challenge by the applicants before the national court of the Nitrates Directive,[41] alleging that farmers were being required to 'pay' for 'pollution' caused by industry.

---

[40] Rio Declaration, para. 16.
[41] Directive 91/676/EC concerning the protection of waters against pollution caused by nitrates from agricultural sources OJ 1991 L 375/1.

### C-293/97 *R v. Secretary of State for the Environment, Transport and the Regions ex p Standley* [1999] ECR I-2603, Opinion of Advocate General Leger

92. There are two aspects to that principle.

93. It must be understood as requiring the person who causes the pollution, and that person alone, to bear not only the costs of remedying pollution, but also those arising from the implementation of a policy of prevention.

94. It can therefore be applied in different ways.

95. Thus, it may be applied either after the event or preventively before the harm occurs. In the latter case the point is to prevent a human activity from causing environmental harm. The legislation adopted for that purpose may establish a system for assessing the environmental effects of certain public and private projects ... Article 5 of the [Nitrates] Directive, which requires the Member States to put in place specific programmes involving, in particular, the prevention of any new water pollution caused or induced by nitrates from agricultural sources (for example, the construction of storage vessels for manure).

96. The polluter pays principle may equally apply after environmental harm has occurred. The person responsible for the harmful effects will then be required to make good or bear the cost of that harm ...

97. Finally, that principle may take one further form in which, in return for the payment of a charge, the polluter is authorised to carry out a polluting activity. That is the case with taxes paid by the users of fuels which cause air pollution.

98. In this case I consider, as stated above, that Article 5 of the Directive must be interpreted as requiring the Member States to impose on farmers only the cost of plant for the reduction or avoidance of the water pollution caused by nitrates for which farmers are responsible, to the exclusion of any other cost. That interpretation therefore complies strictly with the polluter pays principle.

This case not only demonstrates that the polluter pays principle can be implemented in a number of ways, but also that the courts are willing to assess EC legislation, and national implementation of that legislation, against the polluter pays principle (and presumably other environmental principles contained in Article 175 of the EC Treaty, discussed in Chapter 4 below).

## (a) Cost benefit analysis

One of the key bureaucratic tools to emerge out of the centrality of economics to environmental policy is cost benefit analysis (CBA). CBA, although often more flexible than this might suggest, basically involves a comparison of the economic costs and benefits of proposed regulations, projects or policies. In theory, and to simplify, only measures that are demonstrated to be efficient, that is to create more benefit than cost, are pursued: 'The basic rule is not to sanction anything where the costs exceed the benefits'; beyond that, 'we aim to choose the option that maximizes the difference between benefits and costs'.[42] Even if one disputes the suitability of 'efficiency' as a social goal,[43] information on costs and benefits of particular activities may nevertheless be useful when difficult decisions are to be made.

### Sunstein, *Risk and Reason*, p. 291

> . . . cost-benefit analysis emerges as a natural step, one that can help overcome many of the problems we face in assessing risks. The great virtue of cost-benefit analysis is that it promotes a better understanding of the actual consequences of regulation. When availability bias makes people excessively concerned with trivial risks, cost-benefit analysis is a useful corrective. When the public is becoming fearful of an imaginary danger, but neglecting real dangers in daily life, an effort to tabulate the costs and benefits can overcome both panic and neglect. When regulation actually increases the very risks that it is designed to reduce, an understanding of health–health tradeoffs can be a valuable corrective. I have urged that in attempting to clean the air, the Environmental Protection Agency should be as quantitative as possible. This is not because the numbers tell us nearly everything that we need to know, but because, without the numbers, we do not know nearly enough.

In principle, all manner of considerations can be incorporated into a CBA, not just goods that we familiarly value in money. And CBA need not be wholly quantitative, but can include *qualitative* assessments (e.g. by narrative description) of different options.[44] Putting a monetary value on the environment, however, is said to help environmental goods stand up to comparison with more immediate economic benefits. Calculating that value is of course difficult.

### Pearce and Barbier, *Blueprint for a Sustainable Economy*, p. 8

> The underlying value judgement in economics is that resources should be allocated according to what people want. This is the notion of consumer sovereignty or, as it might better be termed, individual sovereignty. These wants, or preferences, are revealed directly where there is a market place. People vote for a product by buying it. Some preferences are revealed in market places which do not appear, at first sight, to have much to do with the environment. For example, the housing market is about the demand and supply of houses. But houses are bundles of characteristics, and the environment surrounding the house is one such characteristic. So the demand for that environment is very likely to show up in the

---

[42] David Pearce and Edward B. Barbier, *Blueprint for a Sustainable Economy* (Earthscan, 2000), p. 54.

[43] See the different approaches in Laurence Tribe, 'Ways Not to Think About Plastic Trees: New Foundations for Environmental Law' (1974) 83 *Yale Law Journal* 1315; Mark Sagoff, *The Economy of the Earth: Philosophy, Law and the Environment* (Cambridge University Press, 1988); Ronald Dworkin, 'Is Wealth a Value?' (1980) 9 *Journal of Legal Studies* 191.

[44] See the economics review of genetically modified organisms (GMOs), Ch. 2, p. 79.

demand for houses. This is a form of indirect market. In many cases there may be no direct or indirect markets, so it is necessary to elicit preferences through hypothetical markets, for example by asking what people are willing to pay.

The motives for preferences can be varied and include:

- Pure self-interest: wanting something now;
- Future self-interest: wanting something to be conserved in case we wish to use it later;
- Altruism: wanting something to be conserved or made available because others want it;
- Bequest: a form of altruism, wanting something to be conserved so our children or future generations can use it;
- Existence: wanting something to be conserved even though we make no use of it now, nor intend to in the future. This motive will capture some of the intrinsic value of the environment since individuals may be judging what the environmental asset wants.

In principle, then we can measure preferences by what people are, or say they are, willing to pay. This willingness to pay is a measure of economic value.

CBA is a controversial tool of environmental protection at many different levels, and we will return to this in Section 4 below. At the very least, estimates of 'willingness to pay' are fraught with uncertainty; different approaches to the calculation can lead to vastly different results.[45] More fundamental concerns relate to the very exercise of 'pricing' environmental goods.

### Frank Ackerman and Lisa Heinzerling, *Priceless: On Knowing the Price of Everything and the Value of Nothing* (New Press, 2004), pp. 8–9

The basic problem with narrow economic analysis of health and environmental protection is that human life, health, and nature cannot be described meaningfully in monetary terms; they are priceless. When the question is whether to allow one person to hurt another, or to destroy a natural resource; when a life or a landscape cannot be replaced; when harms stretch out over decades or even generations; when outcomes are uncertain; when risks are shared or resources are used in common; when the people 'buying' harms have no relationship with the people actually harmed – then we are in the realm of the priceless, where market values tell us little about the social values at stake.

There are hard questions to be answered about protection of human health and the environment, and there are many useful insights about these questions from the field of economics. But there is no reason to think that the right answers will emerge from the strange process of assigning dollar values to human life, human health, and nature itself, and then crunching the numbers. Indeed, in pursuing this approach, formal cost-benefit analysis often hurts more than it helps: it muddies rather than clarifies fundamental clashes

---

[45] See, for example, the debated gains of improving visibility at the Grand Canyon: Mark Sagoff, 'Cows Are Better Than Condos, Or How Economists Help Solve Environmental Problems' (2003) 12 *Environmental Values* 449, p. 458; see also the extracts from Macrory, Ch. 11, pp. 423–5.

about values. By proceeding as if its own assumptions are scientific and by speaking a language all of its own, economic analysis too easily conceals the basic human questions that lie at its heart and excludes the voices of people untrained in the field. Again and again, economic theory gives us opaque and technical reasons to do the obviously wrong thing. Obscuring the fundamental issues with talk of wage premiums and protest votes ... , cost-benefit analysis promotes a deregulatory agenda under the cover of scientific objectivity.

To say that life, health, and nature are priceless is not to say that we should spend an infinite amount of money to protect them. Rather, it is to say that translating life, health, and nature into dollars is not a fruitful way of deciding how much protection to give them. A different way of thinking and deciding about them is required.

## 4  Beyond expertise: the political (and popular) dimension of environmental protection

The preceding two sections of this chapter have discussed two broad approaches to assessing environmental decisions, CBA and risk assessment. Such formal technical approaches to decision making are increasingly prevalent in environmental decision making.[46] The imposition of technical approaches to decision making is one attempt to enhance the accountability of decision making; we can see whether and how the particular technical approach has been followed by the administration.[47] Numerous examples of formalised approaches to risk assessment or CBA in government policy have appeared in recent years. The establishment of an Environment Agency in the UK put this on a statutory footing.[48]

### Environment Act 1995, s. 39

1. Each new Agency—
    (a) in considering whether or not to exercise any power conferred upon it by or under any enactment, or
    (b) in deciding the manner in which to exercise any such power, shall, unless and to the extent that it is unreasonable for it to do so in view of the nature or purpose of the power or in the circumstances of the particular case, take into account the likely costs and benefits of the exercise or non-exercise of the power or its exercise in the manner in question.

However, these formal technical approaches can risk a dilution and misplacement of accountability, by providing an apparently inevitable and objective technical

---

[46]  See for example Royal Commission on Environmental Pollution, Twenty-first Report, *Setting Environmental Standards*, Cm 4053 (1998).

[47]  Elizabeth Fisher, 'Drowning by Numbers: The Pursuit of Accountable Public Administration' (2000) 20 *Oxford Journal of Legal Studies* 109.

[48]  On the Environment Agency, see further Ch. 8, pp. 334–9.

'answer' to what is actually a rather complex and normative/political question. Accordingly, we see competing efforts to broaden the input into decision making, sometimes by enhancing public participation. It is only rarely now urged that environmental decisions should be taken on the basis solely of technical information, be that from the natural sciences, from risk assessment or from CBA. We could not explain this evolution by reference to a single event, but it is fair to say that the discovery of a link between bovine spongiform encephalopathy (BSE or 'mad cow disease') in cattle and new variant Creutzfeldt-Jakob Disease (vCJD) in human beings[49] led to a sea change in regulation in the UK and the EU. The UK government had focussed on the safety of beef in a way that tended to suggest that transmissibility of BSE to humans was not possible. The public reaction to the resulting crisis contributed to greater political awareness of the difficulties of risk regulation, and considerable political attention has since been paid to uncertainty in the scientific process, to public perceptions of risks and to public values that fall outside traditional scientific assessments. A number of official reports brought these developments into the mainstream,[50] and whilst the importance of science to the policy process is kept firmly in view, the trend is to emphasise a more open and participative approach to environmental decision making, and the significance of moral, social and ethical concerns alongside technical issues.

Sunstein writes from the United States, and 'celebrates technocracy'; nevertheless, he ultimately returns to the *political* context of environmental decision making.

### Sunstein, *Risk and Reason,* p. 294

In many ways, this book has been a celebration of the centrality of science and expertise to the law of risk. Indeed, I have attempted to defend a highly technocratic approach to risk regulation, and given reasons to be sharply sceptical of populism, at least in this domain of the law. But I have also offered two objections to a purely technocratic approach to risk reduction.

First, ours is a deliberative democracy in which reflective public judgment plays a large role. Where judgments of value are to be made, they should be made by the citizenry, not by experts. Some deaths are particularly bad, and these deserve unusual attention. It would indeed [be] obtuse to treat all risks as if they were the same, regardless of context and quality. People are right to insist that it matters whether a risk is voluntarily incurred. When it is especially easy to avoid certain risks, government should not spend a great deal of time and effort in response. People are also right to say that fair distribution of risk matters. Thus I have urged that as part of a cost-benefit analysis, it is important to know who would gain

---

[49] See generally Gavin Little, 'BSE and the Regulation of Risk' (2001) 64 *Modern Law Review* 730.

[50] Royal Commission on Environmental Pollution, above, n. 46; House of Lords Select Committee on Science and Technology, 3rd Report Session 2000–01, *Science and Society* HL 57; Cabinet Office, *Risk: Improving Government's Capacity to Handle Risk and Uncertainty* (2002).

and who would lose – and that government legitimately seeks to mimimize the burdens faced by the most disadvantaged members of society and to maximize the benefits that they receive.

...

Second, technocrats tend to ignore the fact that to work well, a regulatory system needs one thing above all – public support and confidence. This is so whether or not a lack of confidence would be fully rational. To the extent that government relies on statistical evidence alone, it is unlikely to promote its own goals. Partly this is because people will assess that evidence in light of their own motivations and their inevitably limited capacities. Regulators who are alert to the importance of both confidence and trust will do what they can to provide information in a way that is well-tailored to how people think about risk – and that tries to educate people when their usual ways of thinking lead them astray. In some circumstances, an understanding of how people think will lead government toward approaches that technocrats will not have on their viewscreen. We might say that good technocrats need to know not only economics and science but psychology as well.

In this extract, Sunstein's second objection to basing regulation on expert judgment *alone* is connected with the loss of public trust in science emanating from government (and industry); enhancing the openness of and participation in regulation is a very frequent prescription for such a loss of trust. Sunstein's first objection is essentially about the role of public values in decision making. A need to go beyond an isolated exercise of expertise rests fundamentally on the fact that environmental decisions can involve the most profound political questions and value judgments. They raise questions about the sort of world in which we want to live, and what we are prepared to pay for that world. Questions such as the ethical implications of new technology or development, or the appropriate role of government in social life, can only problematically and with great uncertainty and controversy be captured by technical analysis. Moreover, environmental regulation distributes burden and benefit, and distributional questions are at the heart of any ordinary approach to politics. Whilst economists are confident of their ability to measure ethical or distributional questions in monetary terms (or to add useful qualitative statements to a CBA), the political process seems better suited to capturing the nuances of environmental decisions. Experts, in whatever field, should have no monopoly on value judgments.

Just as values are necessarily implicated in environmental decision making, science cannot be successfully isolated from those values. The impossibility of undertaking wholly objective technical and scientific assessments is very broadly accepted. When assessments are made by practitioners of the natural sciences, or by risk assessors or economists, even in complete accord with the best professional practice, the values of the individual and the profession are likely to be imperceptibly introduced into the assessment process. Technical assessments are shaped by the values of the practitioners, and the judgments of the relevant profession.[51] Assumptions will be made at every stage of the process, the accuracy or appropriateness of which is likely to be debated: estimates of the effect of a low, but perhaps lengthy, human exposure to a particular pollutant may be made on the basis of high exposure of laboratory animals; predictions will rely on numerous techniques requiring the exercise of professional judgment. And epidemiological studies, statistical analyses of human populations that relate degree of exposure to a risk, have their critics: 'a good working definition of a catastrophe is an effect so large that even an epidemiological study can detect it'.[52]

### Sally Eden, 'Public Participation in Environmental Policy: Considering Scientific, Counter-Scientific and Non-Scientific Contributions' (1996) 5 *Public Understanding of Science* 183, p. 187

Perhaps the best (and best known) example of a global environmental issue influenced by science and brought to international policy attention is stratospheric ozone depletion, a problem derived from modernization (in this case, from new chemical compounds: chlorofluorocarbons or CFCs) and primarily constructed in terms of atmospheric chemistry: the observations are taken by a small number of specialists and then communicated to the public and other groups in the environmental debate. The globalized change is located in the results from teams like the British Antarctic Survey, not in the everyday experiences of members of the public. So, it is not too simplistic to say that without the science of atmospheric chemistry, we would not see any ozone problem. Moreover, science at first calculated out these ozone depletion measurements by regarding them as errors, only later to regard them as 'facts' once the techniques of measurement and its interpretation were (internally) changed, emphasizing science's hold on the identification of the 'problem':

> The debacle of the 'hole' in the ozone layer, undiscovered for so many years because its observers programmed their computer to ignore measurements that diverged too greatly from expected norms, notoriously proved how highly 'interpretive' such climatic experiments can be.[53]

The practitioners of the developing specialism of 'atmospheric chemistry' had to make judgments about the interpretation of their results. These judgments created room for new errors, here delaying discovery of the 'hole' in the ozone layer. Equally importantly, these judgments demonstrate how even the 'best' science involves the inevitable introduction of choices and values. The exercise of personal and professional judgment is crucial in day-to-day scientific activity, which in turn is crucial to environmental protection.

Judgment is also an essential element of the practice of CBA, at every stage from deciding whose costs and values count, that is the scope of the 'community

---

[51] See, for example, Sheila Jasanoff, *The Fifth Branch: Science Advisors as Policymakers* (Harvard University Press, 1990); Kristen Schrader-Frechette, *Risk and Rationality* (University of California Press, 1991).

[52] Dryzek, *Politics of the Earth*, p. 73 (quoting Aaron Wildavsky, *But is it True?* (Harvard University Press, 1995), p. 254, in turn quoting David Ozonoff).

[53] Andrew Ross, 'Is Global Culture Warming Up?' (1991) 28 *Social Text* 18.

of concern',[54] to interpreting the results. For example, a survey of 'willingness to pay' (that is what individuals would pay to keep an environmental resource) provides consistently lower figures than a survey of 'willingness to accept' (that is the sum that would be accepted as compensation for the destruction of a resource); deciding which question to ask in these circumstances is quite blatantly not a neutral task. And every effort of the economist to adjust a calculation to reflect value issues, such as distributional or ethical concerns, involves an incorporation of non-economic criteria and professional judgment that undermines the apparent objectivity and inevitability of the exercise.

Mark Sagoff provides a classic and powerful criticism of economic understandings of environmental problems and the associated rise of CBA.[55] In the process, he explores the *political* nature of environmental decision making, arguing that political value judgments, rather than economic calculations, are required to justify environmental decisions. It is not necessary to accept every part of Sagoff's approach to environmental politics to agree that 'political questions are not all economic',[56] or that environmental regulation should be the product of rational discussion and debate, rather than economic analysis alone. None of this is to say that technical analyses such as risk assessment or CBA cannot feed into that political process. And Cass Sunstein responds positively to the challenges, suggesting a range of ways in which the accepted limitations of CBA can be acknowledged through its practice.

### Sunstein, *Risk and Reason*, pp. 292–3

- The magnitude of costs and the magnitude of benefits are not all that matters. Distributional considerations are indeed relevant ...
- Cost-benefit analysis can give an illusion of precision, at least if existing knowledge does not permit us to specify benefits or costs. In these circumstances, the best approach is not to reject cost-benefit analysis, but to offer ranges, with a full appreciation of the possibility of uncertainty.
- Some people claim, rightly, that social goods are 'incommensurable', in the sense that we do not value all goods in the same way that we value money. A human life is not really equivalent to $6.1 million, or whatever economic amount we choose to spend to prevent a statistical death. Beaches and parks and wolves and seals are not reducible to their economic value. For this reason, cost-benefit analysis, of the sort that I have urged here, should include qualitative as well as quantitative descriptions of the consequences of regulation. We should not think that the monetary 'bottom line' is anything magical; it is simply a helpful input into the decision.

---

[54] Graham Smith, *Deliberative Democracy and the Environment* (Routledge, 2003), pp. 39–45; see also Chris Hilson, 'Greening Citizenship: Boundaries of Membership and the Environment' (2001) 13 *Journal of Environmental Law* 335, discussing different values for non-use value of a stretch of river, depending on whether all of the water company's customers were included, or just those within the affected catchment area.     [55] *The Economy of the Earth.*

[56] Sagoff, *The Economy of the Earth*, Ch. 2.

- Cost-benefit analysis does not respect 'intuitive toxicology', and for this reason it might seem to disregard people's sense of risk and danger. The point is correct, but it is no objection. Policy should ordinarily be rooted in evidence, not baseless fear or unwarranted optimism.
- Cost-benefit analysis might seem to treat human lives cavalierly, simply because it places a monetary value on statistical risks. But any government is required to assign some non-infinite value to statistical risks. It is best for government to be clear about what it is doing and why it is doing it. If the amounts are too low, then government is indeed treating lives cavalierly, and the amounts should be increased.
- Cost-benefit analysis might seem to give insufficient weight to the future and in particular to the interests of future generations. I have urged that a sensible cost-benefit analysis does indeed give weight to the future, though the selection of the appropriate discount rate raises many conundrums.
- Cost-benefit analysis might seem to be undemocratic, especially insofar as it allows policy to be set in large part by experts. I have argued that, on the contrary, cost-benefit analysis is an important tool for promoting democratic goals because it ensures that some account of the likely consequences of regulation will be placed before officials and the public at large. Experts are crucial to sensible policy simply because of their expertise. If public officials want to proceed even though the costs do not justify the benefits, they are permitted to do that, so long as they can generate a good reason for their decision.
- Cost-benefit analysis might be criticized insofar as it relies on private willingness to pay as the basis for calculating both costs and benefits. Sometimes people are poorly informed, and hence are willing to pay little for significant benefits. Sometimes people are unwilling to pay for certain goods simply because their preferences have adapted to the status quo, in which they face real deprivation. Sometimes private willingness to pay will understate benefits, if people are willing to pay more for a good if other people are going to be paying for them too. Poor people might have little willingness to pay simply because they have little ability to pay. In many contexts, these objections have force. There is no special magic in the idea of willingness to pay. I have suggested that government needs some numbers from which to begin its analysis, that private willingness to pay is a good start, but that government can depart from that number if the context shows a sensible reason to do so. Current practice shows considerable good sense on this count.
- Some people fear that, as a practical matter, cost-benefit analysis will simply paralyze government and prevent it from issuing regulations that would do more good than harm. If this is true, then the pragmatic argument for cost-benefit analysis has been defeated. Any effort to ensure cost-benefit balancing should ensure that it does not produce 'paralysis by analysis'. I have urged that the record suggests that cost-benefit balancing does not, in fact, produce paralysis.
- Cost-benefit analysis might be challenged as a form of centralized government planning, likely to overload government's ability to compile the necessary information. The objection too has much force, especially in light of the fact that government's own incentives are not always to be trusted. The simplest response to this objection relies on the absence of good alternatives.

It is increasingly clear that environmental questions are political questions in the broadest sense, and, as such, they need to be resolved by the political processes in place in any particular society. A dilemma is, however, posed by the simultaneous imperatives of *political* decision making that responds to public values, and the usefulness or even necessity of *technical* information in a world of hard choices. A very common governmental response to this dilemma is to institute a division between risk assessment, a *technical* exercise, and risk management, a *political* exercise. The extract from Sunstein, in providing space for explaining decisions that do not fit within the results of the CBA, recognises this distinction. The Royal Commission on Environmental Pollution have moved this debate beyond academia, providing practical routes by which a broader range of values might be fed into the process of standard setting.

### Royal Commission on Environmental Pollution, Twenty-first Report, *Setting Environmental Standards* Cm 4053 (1998), p. 122

8.51 We have noted previously that a failure to make a clear separation between policy and analysis (which, in the environmental field, has predominantly been scientific analysis) … has had a pernicious effect on trust in the quality and integrity of both expert advice and the decision taken. There are several reasons why a separation of the scientific assessment stage from the policy-making stage is essential. It is important that all the component analyses restrict themselves to setting out the information which will form the raw material of the decision, and do not attempt to displace that decision. Even in cases where the scientific assessment may appear to lead directly to the deliberative procedure from which a standard will emerge, there must always be some consideration of the practicality, cost, legality and morality of the decision, however intuitive this consideration may be in practice. Rigour and accountability are better served if these considerations are kept explicit and distinct.

…

8.53 The knowledge provided by any single discipline is never sufficient to determine the precise level of a standard. By recommending that a distinction be made between analysis and policy making, we are not saying that scientists and other analysts are not qualified to exercise practical judgement, nor that they should not do so. We are suggesting that they should make it clear when they are speaking as scientists (or whatever) and when they are exercising practical judgement.

This distinction is commonly regarded as good practice at UK and EU level.[57] According to *Pfizer*, when a Community institution seeks the opinion of a Community scientific advisor, it is not bound to accept the conclusions reached in that opinion, but to the extent that the Community institution disregards the opinion, 'it must provide specific reasons for its findings by comparison with those made in the opinion and its statement of reasons must explain why it is

---

[57] European Commission, *Communication on the Precautionary Principle* COM (2000) 1 final; DEFRA, *Guidelines for Environmental Risk Assessment.*

disregarding the latter. The statement of reasons must be of a scientific level at least commensurate with that of the opinion in question.'[58] Scientific advisors are denied the final word because whilst they are expert bodies, they have neither democratic legitimacy nor political responsibilities. Decisions on 'acceptable' risk are political. Along similar lines, when Community institutions are required to assess complex facts of a technical or scientific nature, they can only adopt a preventive measure without consulting the relevant EU-level scientific committee in 'exceptional situations', and where there are otherwise adequate guarantees of scientific objectivity.[59]

The recognition of the political significance of risk management is broadly welcome. However, the distinction between the technical and the political is not as clear cut as the dichotomy between risk assessment and risk management might suggest. In particular, the language assumes that the technical risk assessment is value free and neutral, whilst, as observed above, technical assessments are full of value judgments and are shaped by regulatory context.[60] There is a danger that entrenching the divisions between political decision makers and experts will leave the uncertainties and value judgments of the prior technical stage of risk assessment unexamined, although the emphasis generally seems to be on transparency at all stages. In addition, the late involvement of the policy makers means that they may be presented with very limited options; more generally, they may tend to prefer the scientific evidence in any event.

## 5 'Alternative' ways of viewing the world: ecological theories

A range of 'alternative' ecological theories fundamentally question the prevalence or hegemony of science (discussed above, pp. 12–15) in shaping environmental law, as well as many of the cultural assumptions which underpin it. Whilst the following discussion may appear to be largely theoretical in nature, it should also allow us to evaluate the prospects for greater approximation between environmental legislation and aspects of ecological thinking, and to consider the source of diverse 'voices' whose engagement in environmental decision making is increasingly sought, particularly those of women. A practical side also exists in that current 'environmental' debates, such as those over hunting, are clearly informed by ecological ideas about 'closeness to nature', as well as by animal rights arguments.

At the core of various branches of ecological thinking is the desire to eclipse the apparent divide between humans and nature and to encourage a sense of the 'common', to create a 'new enlightenment of ecological consciousness' or, in environmental terms, a holistic approach to environmental problems.

---

[58] *Pfizer*, para. 199.    [59] *Alpharma*, para. 213.

[60] Les Levidow and Claire Marris, 'Science and governance in Europe: lessons from the case of agricultural biotechnology' (2001) *Science and Public Policy* 350.

defining entirely new ecological practices',[67] deep ecology is not (unlike social ecology, discussed below) aimed at the disruption or reform of social and political structures and practices. Perhaps most trenchant criticism comes from feminists who question the centrality of the Self (or *autology*, the process of self-realisation) as ultimately inward-looking. As Val Plumwood tightly notes: 'It is ironic that a position claiming to be anti-anthropocentric should thus aim to reduce questions of the care and significance of nature to questions of the real-isation of the human self (or Self).'[68] The process of self-realisation is also cul-turally specific – the process of 'losing oneself in wilderness' tending to be described by North American ecologists (the 'mountain-men'). Most seriously, for Plumwood, deep ecology denies 'difference' and continues to conceive of nature in ways which reflect male domination, thus providing its own version of the rationalist account of self and species. She concludes that in many crucial respects, deep ecology does not present a very thoroughgoing alternative to extensions of mainstream ethics.

### Val Plumwood, *Feminism and the Mastery of Nature* (Routledge, 1993), p. 10

Although deep ecology contrasts with the mainstream in emphasising connections with the self and the continuity between humans and nature, there remain severe tensions between some forms of deep ecology and feminist perspectives. These forms have not satisfactorily identified the key elements in the traditional framework, or noted their connections with rationalism and the master identity. As a result they fail to reject adequately rationalist accounts of self, universalisation and the discarding of particular connections.

The analysis of human/nature and other dualisms ... has stressed the importance of affirming both difference and continuity, and of maintaining the balance between them. Respect for others involves acknowledging their distinctiveness and difference, and not trying to reduce or assimilate them to the human sphere. We need to acknowledge differ-ence as well as continuity to overcome dualism and to establish non-instrumentalising rela-tionships with nature, where both connection and otherness are the basis of interaction. The failure to affirm difference is characteristic of the colonising self which denies the other through the attempt to incorporate it into the empire of the self, and which is unable to expe-rience sameness without erasing difference.

### (b) Social ecology

Social ecology describes environmental problems as rooted in human relations rather than (as deep ecologists suggest) in human misunderstanding of their connection with the natural world. Murray Bookchin, for example, states that 'the domination of nature by man stems from the very real domination of

---

[67] Harvey, *Justice, Nature*, pp. 164–9.
[68] Val Plumwood, *Feminism and the Mastery of Nature* (Routledge, 1993), p. 11.

human by human'.[69] The exploitation of the earth is therefore another example of hierarchical and abusive relations in society.[70] For social ecologists, the 'solution' to environmental problems lies in fundamental social and political reform. Bookchin's 'ectopia', for example, envisages a decentralised society of 'ecocommunities' situated in local ecosystems, creating a federation of communes.[71] This is a radical approach, particularly in the sense that it is dismissive of action which falls short of wholesale social reform. For example, in *The Modern Crisis* (1986) Bookchin writes: 'This is not to say that measures to palliate the bad effects of the present economic system should not be taken, but that these should be seen for what they are: mere palliatives and not steps towards an ecological society' (p. 387). Social ecologists are also deeply sceptical about the spiritual dimension to deep ecology, dismissed as 'eco-la-la' by Bookchin. Social ecology remains, however, a deeply anthropocentric approach with, arguably, the focus firmly on society, rather than ecology.

### (c) Ecofeminism

Ecofeminist thinking is multifarious, and at least some of its strands have gained mainstream acceptability in international law documents, for example the Rio and Johannesburg Declarations on sustainable development.[72] Ecofeminists see women, particularly those in 'developing' countries, as more sensitive to the devastating ecological effects of human (male) domination of nature, and also as potentially responsible for environmental education of children. This aspect of ecofeminism rests on ideas of women being 'closer' to nature, but also, and less contentiously, on the commonplace activities and responsibilities of women: as well as bearing children, women are in many societies also responsible for feeding families and tilling the land. Strikingly, it is the tendency of traditional development schemes to elevate men and further marginalise women. Deane Curtin advances a more sophisticated variant of this thesis:

### Deane Curtin, 'Women's Knowledge as Expert Knowledge: Indian Women and Ecodevelopment' in Karen J. Warren (ed.), *Eco-feminism: Women, Nature and Culture* (Indiana University Press, 1997), pp. 84 and 88

Taking Women's Practices Seriously

… while women are not essentially more 'natural', closer to nature, than men and nature is no more female than male, the actual practices typically demanded of women involve

---

[69] Murray Bookchin, *Toward an Ecological Society* (Black Rose Books, 1980).
[70] On 'deep ecology' versus 'social ecology', see Peter Marshall, *Nature's Web: An Exploration of Ecological Thinking* (Simon and Schuster, 1992), Chs. 29 and 30.
[71] *Toward an Ecological Society*, pp. 426–7.    [72] Ch. 6, pp. 223 and 228.

mediation between culture and nature. We see this particularly in the material lives of Third World women farmers …

Women's work is the everyday work of translation between the needs of the environment and the needs of the human community.

Such depictions of a woman's 'proper' role create a dilemma: while such labor is often experienced by women as an oppressive demand, the environment and the human community cannot survive without it. Children's health and safety depend on regular access to clean water. Traditional medicine and safety depend on the biodiversity of an environment that can supply medicines as well as fuel, fodder and food. Caring labor holds together the family and the environment and is inherently interested in future generations. Third World development, therefore, is a feminist project. Its success requires the revaluation of women's caring labor.

The core idea of ecofeminism is that environmental problems are inextricably linked to the subordinate position of women in society: 'with the violation of nature is linked the violation and marginalisation of women, especially in the third world'.[73] But the feminist argument extends beyond the subjugation of women – 'phallocentrism and the exclusion of women's experience is a very good indicator of similar exclusions of other related subordinated groups, the undersides of the western web of dualisms'.[74] For this reason, ecofeminists identify a link between the domination of nature and discrimination against women, rooted in abstracted and universalist (Enlightenment) ways of thinking. The essence of this basic feminist position is captured by Vandana Shiva.

### Vandana Shiva, *Staying Alive: Women, Ecology and Development* (Zed Books, 1989), pp. 22–3

I characterise modern western patriarchy's special epistemological tradition of the 'scientific revolution' as 'reductionist' because it reduced the capacity of humans to know nature both by excluding other knowers and other ways of knowing, and it reduced the capacity of nature to creatively regenerate and renew itself by manipulating it as inert and fragmented matter. Reductionism has a set of distinctive characteristics which demarcates it from all other non-reductionist knowledge systems which it has subjugated and replaced. The basic ontological and epistemological assumptions of reductionism are based on homogeneity. It sees all systems as made up of the same basic constituents, discrete, unrelated and atomistic, and it assumes that all basic processes are mechanical. The mechanistic metaphors of reductionism have socially reconstituted nature and society. In contrast to the organic metaphors, in which concepts of order and power were based on interconnectedness and reciprocity, the metaphor of nature as a machine was based on the assumption of separability and manipulability. As Carolyn Merchant has remarked: 'In investigating the

---

[73] Vandana Shiva, *Staying Alive: Women, Ecology and Development* (Zed, 1989), p. 42.
[74] Plumwood, *Feminism and the Mastery of Nature*, p. 1.

roots of our current environmental dilemma and its connections to science, technology and the economy, we must re-examine the formation of a world-view and a science that, by reconceptualising reality as a machine, rather than a living organism, sanctioned the domination of both nature and women.' This domination is inherently violent, understood as the violation of integrity. Reductionist science is a source of violence against nature and women because it subjugates and dispossesses them of their full productivity, power and potential. The epistemological assumptions of reductionism are related to its ontological assumptions: uniformity allows the knowledge of parts of a system to be taken as knowledge of the whole. Separability allows context-free abstraction of knowledge and creates criteria of validity based on alienation and non-participation, then projected as 'objectivity'. 'Experts' and 'specialists' are thus projected as the only legitimate knowledge seekers and justifiers.

The various arguments outlined above are examples of the feminist critique of 'phallocentrism' in modern life. More positively, at the root of ecofeminist approaches is the pre-eminence of ideas of relationship and (specific) context, as opposed to masculine universalities and rationalities. Some ecofeminists call for more local, context-specific approaches to environmental ethics as opposed to a universalising, rationalist, logic: 'the expulsion of the master identity from the western construction of reason requires not the abandonment of reason itself, but an effort to install another, less hierarchical, more democratic, and plural identity in its place'.[75]

One manifestation of this is the deliberate development of an 'ethic of care' which aims to extend environmental ethics to include the (private) home-based concepts such as community, care and compassion to overcome the restrictiveness of instrumentalism of the public sphere. For Plumwood: 'motherhood and friendship represent perhaps the clearest examples of relational selfhood and an identity expressed in caring practices which treat the "other" non-instrumentally'.[76] She continues:

> Special relationships with, care for, or empathy with particular aspects of nature as experienced, rather than with nature as abstraction, are essential to provide a depth of concern. Under appropriate conditions, experience of and care and responsibility for particular animals, trees, rivers, places and ecosystems which are known well, are loved and are appropriately connected to the self, enhance rather than hinder a wider, more generalised concern for the global environment.[77]

That said, the process by which an ethics of care in the home and community translates to one of care for the environment is difficult, since it appears to involve even at a basic level the re-evaluation and realignment of relations of the public and private spheres, almost certainly requiring involvement by politics and law.

[75] *Ibid.*, p. 23.    [76] *Ibid.*, p. 18.    [77] *Ibid.*, p. 21.

## (d) Gaia theory

Each of the above theoretical and ethical approaches to environmental protection has identified the connections between nature and humans, rather than nature's 'otherness'. Gaia theory takes this to an extreme, delivering a supremely and simplistically holistic approach to life. Gaia (the name the ancient Greeks gave to the Earth Goddess) is the creation of James Lovelock, originally of his *Gaia: A New Look at Life on Earth* (1979),[78] in which he regards earth in its entirety, including species, rocks and atmosphere, as a single living organism. Whilst freely admitting that the idea that the earth is alive is at the outer bounds of scientific credibility, he draws his conception of Gaia within modern environmentalism by suggesting that some parts of the earth are 'vital organs' which if disturbed would cause the whole organism of the earth to malfunction. This is reminiscent of (but not synonymous with) a scientific understanding of the biosphere, 'the envelope of all life, i.e. the area of living matter … the biosphere can be regarded as the area of the Earth's crust occupied by transformers which convert cosmic radiation into effective terrestrial energy: electrical, chemical, mechanical, thermal, etc'.[79]

### James Lovelock, *The Ages of Gaia* (W. W. Norton, 1988), p. 19

The name of the living planet, Gaia, is not a synonym for the biosphere. The biosphere is defined as that part of the Earth where living things normally exist. Still less is Gaia the same as the biota, which is simply the collection of all individual living organisms. The biota and the biosphere taken together form part but not all of Gaia. Just as the shell is part of the snail, so the rocks, the air and the oceans are part of Gaia. Gaia, as we shall see, has continuity with the past back to the origins of life, and extends into the future as long as life persists. Gaia, as a total planetary being, has properties that are not necessarily discernible by just knowing individual species or populations of organisms living together.

In Lovelock's theory, it is for the living organisms on earth to control their environment to make it 'comfortable' for life. He, like many environmentalists, therefore questions the prevalence of three threats to Gaia: cars (carbon dioxide), chainsaws (cutting down forests for pasture) and cattle (intensive agriculture). More radically, he advocates the return to small, densely populated cities, with one third of the land reverting to woodland, and agricultural reform. Interestingly, Lovelock combines scientific and statistical insights (he relies upon 'models' in much of his work) with much thought and emotion about the interrelationship of 'man' and Gaia, concluding, obliquely '[T]here can be no prescription, no set of rules, for living within Gaia. For each of our different actions there are only consequences.'[80] Lovelock therefore informs his Gaia

---

[78] Oxford University Press.
[79] As described by Lovelock in *The Ages of Gaia* (W. W. Norton, 1988), p. 10.
[80] Lovelock, *Gaia: A New Look*, p. 140.

theory with contemporary environmental problems. His approach is, however, at times profoundly Eurocentric. His claim, for example, that the developing countries in the tropics pose the greatest threat to Gaia as compared to the industrialised North is criticised by environmentalists who understand development, particularly through western supported schemes, to be a symptom of the problem, rather than its cause. In particular the experience of environmentalists is precisely that urban, industrial man does not always 'put things right again' as Lovelock suggests.[81]

### (e) Ecological law?

The question remains whether the different ways of conceiving of the environment and environmental problems outlined above have infiltrated legal understandings and 'solutions', in other words whether law has shifted much beyond the 'first stage' anthropocentrism described by Emmenegger and Tschentscher (above, pp. 2–3), to valuing and protecting the intrinsic qualities of nature. At the apogee of legal–ecological thinking is Cormac Cullinan, a practising lawyer with radical views.

### Cormac Cullinan, *Wild Law: A Manifesto for Earth Justice* (Green Books, 2003), pp. 32–3

Firstly, the term 'wild law' cannot easily be snared within the strictures of a conventional legal definition. It is perhaps better understood as an approach to human governance, rather than as a branch of law or a collection of laws. It is more about ways of being and doing than the right thing to do.

Wild law expresses Earth jurisprudence. It recognises and embodies the qualities of the Earth system within which it exists. As an approach it seeks both to foster passionate and intimate connections between people and nature and to deepen our connection with the wild aspect of our own natures. It tends to focus more on relationships and on the processes by which they can be strengthened, than on end-points and 'things' like property. It protects wilderness and the freedom of communities of life to self-regulate. It aims to encourage creative diversity rather than to impose uniformity. Wild law opens spaces within which different and unconventional approaches can spring up, perhaps to flourish, perhaps to run their course and die.

Wild laws are laws that regulate humans in a manner that creates the freedom for all the members of the Earth Community to play a role in the continuing co-evolution of the planet. Where wild laws prevail, cultural and biological diversity, creativity and the freedom to play a creative role in the co-evolution of this planet will be found.

With a little practice you can start to recognise flashes of it even in our current legal and political systems. Wildness can be glimpsed in laws that reserve a certain amount of water

---

[81] *Ibid.*, p. 121.

to the river in order that it may flow healthily, and in international declarations that assert the inherent value of all living organisms and of biological diversity itself. It crops up in the recent amendment to the German constitution … which recognises that the state has a responsibility to protect animals as well as humans. Bills of rights that enshrine the right not to be unfairly discriminated against on the basis of ethnicity, nationality, gender, age or sexual preference also reflect elements of wild law in so far as they protect spaces within which human diversity can flourish.

Sometimes it is easier to identify what is not wild law. For example, laws that define seeds and genes as the property of someone and which prohibit farmers from saving seeds to plant next season's crop, deny wildness … the purpose behind these laws is incompatible with the purpose of wild law.

In their book, *Law and Ecology*,[82] Brooks, Jones and Virginia adopt a less spiritual tone. They consider that, especially since the mid 1980s, ecological thinking has played an important role in US endangered species legislation, national parks planning, coastal zone management and forestry management, and that, even in legal areas more resistant to ecology such as the Clean Air Act and Clean Water Act, recent amendments incorporate ecological notions. They highlight the influence of an ecosystem approach in recognising the cumulative effects of pollution and development, and in amending time frames, such as for environmental impact assessment and other aspects of development controls.

Closer to home, William Howarth considers that at least in the area of water protection, purely human-centred objectives for the quality of environmental media have been superseded, or at least supplemented, by the need for diversity of species and ecosystems to be maintained *for their own sake*. Howarth defines ecological quality standards as follows:

> a statement of the minimum acceptable state of ecosystems and their biological components, with a corresponding legal obligation that no deterioration below that standards should be permissible. Hence, for flora, fauna and habitats, ecological quality standards are intended to serve as a mandatory baseline for minimal levels of diversity and abundance, specified quantitatively for each component, and backed by legal obligations to ensure their realisation.[83]

He considers that the furthest point presently reached in the progression towards ecological quality standards lies in the EC Water Framework Directive. Whereas previous attempts to legislate for water quality at Community level have focussed upon physical and chemical aspects, the Directive takes an ambitious step beyond this in seeking to characterise water quality on explicit and precise ecological terms which form part of the 'good status' requirement for

---

[82] Richard Brooks, Ross Jones and Ross Virginia, *Law and Ecology: The Rise of the Ecosystem Regime* (Ashgate, 2002), pp. 390–2.

[83] William Howarth, 'The Progression Towards Ecological Quality Standards' (2006) 18 *Journal of Environmental Law* 3.

surface waters within its scope. Although lauded, there are some difficulties with using such standards, for example the dynamic character of ecosystems and the elusiveness of identifying, measuring and realising what is to count as a 'satisfactory' ecological state.[84]

In conclusion, these are early days in the creation of a body of ecological law which approaches environmental problems in a fundamentally different way from that used hitherto. As Brooks, Jones and Virginia state from their experience as 'ecological lawyers': 'Despite the deep insights of ecology and the comprehensive perspective that it yields, many environmental scientists continue to pursue a reductive scientific approach which fails to yield any central vision of our world. Meanwhile, traditional legal scholars continue to accept uncritically the given legal categories which ignore the gradual knitting together of new webs of law within ecosystem regimes.'[85]

## 6 Conclusions

The reliance of environmental law on science is part of a larger picture of modern law being born from and sustained by scientific rationality. This has created difficulties for environmentalists seeking to justify action on the basis of scientific 'fact', whilst also embracing alternative rationalities as a way of understanding human behaviour towards the environment.

### Klaus Eder, 'Rationality in Environmental Discourse: A Cultural Approach' in Wolfgang Rudig (ed.), *Green Politics Three* (Edinburgh University Press, 1995), p. 9

The environmentalist discourse presents a paradox: it is based upon 'hard facts' about nature, namely damage to the natural environment, and it has also undermined the belief in 'hard facts', the unspoken authority of expert knowledge. There is nothing more 'factual' than environmental problems – yet the discourse on facts has shown that we have to grapple with contradictory factual certainties in the state of the environment. The debate in environmental discourse does not concern only what should be done when we are confronted with the 'hard facts' of damage to the environment. Facts are also contested.

This has repercussions for the way environmental issues are communicated in public discourse. Traditional public discourse has taken facts for granted and engaged in the struggle over which normative (moral or legal) principles to apply in a situation where facts were given. Public discourse on environmental issues differs in that it has extended communication of norms to communication of facts. This in turn increases the discourse's paradoxical structure. Experts have to tell us what the facts are – yet they produce contradictory evidence. Ultimately then the facts are the result of a debate; in the literal sense of the word, they are socially constructed.

---

[84] *Ibid.*     [85] Brooks, Jones and Virginia, *Law and Ecology*, p. 391.

The changed relationship between science and society, through the communication of arguments and ideas about threats to the environment (particularly via the precautionary principle), is for John Gillot and Majit Kumar a symptom of a broader rejection of science by society, and with it 'the project of progress'.[86] Whilst the precautionary principle is highly dependent on scientific disciplines, and especially on risk assessment, it arguably allows space for the entry of alternative perspectives and even for a 'retreat from science', at least according to the more radical interpretations of the principle. The persistent tension between scientific fact and socially constructed values, identified and commented upon throughout this chapter, clearly has important repercussions for environmental law, and the governance of decision making. In the context of the regulation of GMOs in EU environmental law, Maria Lee points out the subtleties involved in arguing for one approach or the other, and points towards their possible reconciliation in policy making.

### Maria Lee, *EU Environmental Law: Challenges, Change and Decision Making* (Hart, 2005), pp. 269–70

Notwithstanding acknowledgement of public values, the temptation for final decision-makers to seek refuge (rather than enlightenment) in scientific or technical discourse such as risk assessment or cost benefit analysis is great. The legal barriers to basing decisions on factors that do not fit within a technical analysis also remain powerful. These circumstances simply enhance the urgent need to ensure that rhetoric of public participation in EC environmental policy is not simply used to sidestep genuine public engagement. However, just as a purely technical approach to decision-making would be radically incomplete, so abandoning the tools provided by risk assessment and economics, let alone the natural sciences, would be absurd. The challenge is to ensure that technical information is used in a way that informs, rather than usurps, political decision-making. The discomfort provoked by expressly political decision-making is legitimate, not least precisely *because* of the value-laden and interest-ridden nature of the decisions. Allowing the apparent objectivity, neutrality and external testability of decisions rationalised on a technical or scientific basis to be overtaken by 'values' leaves decision open to protectionism, self-interest, inefficiency and simple error. It should be recalled at this point that technical and scientific opinion rarely if ever actually imbue decisions with the inevitability that is craved, but may on the contrary simply obscure the real nature of the decision. The point is not that public opinion should be followed (even if public opinion were ever so monolithic that it realistically could be), but that it should be heard and addressed. This involves both seeking general information on the opinions of the public and attempting to examine the values and reasons behind these opinions.

A broad range of contemporary environmental and ecological thinking opposes the prevailing scientific model of conceiving environmental degradation, with various explanations for environmental problems, and prescriptions for living.

---

[86]  John Gillot and Majit Kumar, *Science and the Retreat from Reason* (Merlin Press, 1995), p. 7.

The discussion of agricultural biotechnology in the next chapter illustrates the types of appeal made to the different approaches to the environment surveyed in this chapter. One of the logical, but difficult, responses to the tension between technical and popular decision making is to allow greater 'public participation', including participation by environmental interest groups, in environmental decision making, allowing alternative expertise and information on public values into the process. We return to the trend towards public participation in environmental decision making, particularly in Chapter 3, but also throughout the rest of the book.[87]

## 7 Further reading

This chapter embraces entire disciplines, comprising an enormous literature that we have only touched on.

There is a huge literature on the precautionary principle, and on science in environmental law. For anybody unconvinced by the principle, Giandomenico Majone, 'What Price Safety? The Precautionary Principle and its Policy Implications' (2002) *Journal of Common Market Studies* 89, provides a sceptical approach. John Gillot and Majit Kumar, *Science and the Retreat from Reason* (Merlin Press, 1995) is very worthwhile reading for a, now intellectually unfashionable, defence of the scientific method.

Elizabeth Fisher has written a number of important pieces on risk and science in law: in addition to the work cited in this chapter, see for example 'Risk and Environmental Law: A Beginner's Guide', in Benjamin J. Richardson and Stepan Wood (eds.), *Environmental Law and Sustainability* (Hart Publishing, 2006). Veerle Heyvaert, 'Guidance Without Constraint: Assessing the Impact of the Precautionary Principle on the European Community's Chemicals Policy' (2006) 6 *Yearbook of European Environmental Law* 27, examines whether the precautionary principle has had any practical effect in a particular policy context. In 'The Precautionary Principle Before the European Courts' (in Richard Macrory (ed.), *Principles of European Environmental Law* (Europa Law, 2004)), Joanne Scott considers the impact of the WTO on the European Courts' case law on precaution. Finally, see Mike Fentuck, 'Precautionary Maybe, but What's the Principle? The Precautionary Principle, the Regulation of Risk, and the Public Domain' (2005) *Journal of Law and Society* 371, evaluating the extent to which the precautionary principle may play a part in reasserting the values of the public domain in the face of powerful private interests. Michael Doherty, 'Hard Cases and Environmental Principles: An Aid to Interpretation?' (2003) 3 *Yearbook of European Environmental Law* 57, examines the potential jurisprudential role of environmental principles generally.

Mark Sagoff is associated with a sceptical approach to cost benefit analysis, which he submits to a powerful critique in *The Economy of the Earth: Philosophy, Law and the Environment* (Cambridge University Press, 1988). In *Price, Principle and the Environment* (Cambridge University Press, 2004), he develops the argument that cost benefit analysis cannot substitute for political debate, but outlines also useful economic contributions.

---

[87] See, for example, discussion of public participation in planning decisions (Ch. 13, pp. 530–45) and environmental assessment (Ch. 14, pp. 557–60, 583–6)

On the nature/law relationship, a challenging but worthwhile read is David Delaney's *Law and Nature* (Cambridge University Press, 2003). An edited collection by Robert Elliot, *Environmental Ethics* (Oxford University Press, 1995), includes several fine chapters. An interesting and comprehensive collection from the United States is edited by Susan Hanna, Carl Folke, and Karl-Goran Maler, *Rights to Nature: Ecological, Economic, Cultural, and Political Principles of Institutions for the Environment* (Island Press, 1996). On policy making we recommend Mikael Stenmark, *Environmental Ethics and Policy Making* (Ashgate, 2002), which offers a complex map of environmental ethics. *Environmental Values*, edited by Linda Kalof and Terre Satterfield (Earthscan, 2005), is designed to get readers 'up to speed' on the key determinants of environmental values debates.

The most recent writing on Gaia theory is James Lovelock's *The Revenge of Gaia* (Allen Lane, 2006), in which he relates his theory more closely to climate change.

On the development of environmental law as a discipline, we particularly recommend Richard Lazarus' *The Making of Environmental Law* (University of Chicago, 2004). This is a beautifully written, thoughtful, book. Lazarus (with Oliver Houck) has also edited an intriguing 'behind the scenes' look at key environmental law cases, *Environmental Law Stories* (Foundation Press, 2005).

# 2

# Genetically Modified Organisms:
# Introducing a Dilemma

## 1 Introduction

In the previous chapter we outlined a range of different approaches to environmental protection. The case of regulating agricultural biotechnology tends to highlight these contrasting approaches in a single policy context, in particular the potential for conflict between 'scientific' and 'popular' or non-expert forms of deliberation and decision making. We explore throughout this book the legal and policy dynamics of this area of regulation, beginning in this chapter with an introduction to the many ethical and practical dilemmas posed by genetically modified organisms (GMOs).

Biotechnology is variously perceived as the most frightening or most promising scientific development of the twentieth century; agricultural biotechnology has proved an extraordinarily fraught topic for environmental regulators over recent years.

### Thomas Bernauer, *Genes, Trade, and Regulation: The Seeds of Conflict in Food Biotechnology* (Princeton University Press, 2003), pp. 22–3

WHAT IS AGRICULTURAL BIOTECHNOLOGY?

In the 19th century, an Augustinian monk from Central Europe, Gregor Mendel, claimed that the traits of living organisms were inherited. Only in the 1950s to 1970s, however, did scientists discover the chemical and physical properties of 'genes', the key elements in the process of inheritance. They found that a molecule called DNA (deoxyribonucleic acid) contains the information that controls the synthesis of enzymes and other proteins, which in turn are responsible for the basic metabolic processes of all cells. DNA thus encodes genetic information in cells. A gene is a particular DNA sequence. The total set of genes of an organism (the genome) is organized into chromosomes within the cell nucleus. The development of a single cell into a living organism is determined by the genetic information of the cell and by the interaction of genes and gene products with environmental conditions.

Rapid scientific progress since the discovery of DNA has created unprecedented opportunities in plant and animal breeding. Traditional breeding was (and still is) based on swapping and manipulating genes by crossing plants or animals, with the aim of improving productivity, quality, or performance. While in traditional breeding thousands of genes with unknown functions are swapped in a rather haphazard fashion, genetic engineering allows for more controlled transfer of one or a few specific genes with known functions from one organism to another, and also across different species (e.g., from bacteria to corn).

Typically, one or more genes with known effects are spliced with a promoter, a regulator, and a tag. They are then inserted into an organism that includes 10,000–30,000 genes (e.g., a plant cell) by means of an agrobacterium, a so-called shotgun, or protoplast injection. Marker genetic material (a tag) and a genome are used to establish which cells have absorbed the transferred genetic material. The outcome of this transformation (called 'event') depends on the components of the genetic material and the place where the novel DNA is inserted. The cell that has absorbed the inserted DNA is cultivated into a plant or animal that expresses the properties encoded in the inserted genetic material. The purpose of traditional breeding and genetic engineering is the same, namely to produce new plant or animal varieties by manipulating genetic information. Yet, genetic engineering, primarily in the form of recombinant DNA techniques, can produce new plant or animal varieties that would be impossible to produce with traditional breeding methods.

For example, Bt corn, a genetically engineered corn variety, produces toxins originally produced by a soil bacterium, *Bacillus thuringiensis* (Bt). This toxin kills some insects (notably, the European corn borer), while leaving other insects unaffected. Similarly, Bt cotton is genetically modified to control budworms and bollworms. Glyphosate-resistant soybeans include a modified growth-regulating enzyme. This enzyme is immune to glyphosate, a herbicide that inactivates the enzymes in most plants and thus kills them. Weed control with glyphosate tends to be cheaper and more convenient for farmers than weed control with other herbicides.

Some characterise the development of genetic modification as a small step in the development of agriculture; others as a watershed in human intervention in nature. The description above suggests that GM technology can be qualitatively different from centuries of genetic manipulation through selective breeding: not only is biotechnology much more immediate than traditional breeding, but no barriers are posed by sexual compatibility; breeding would never, for example, lead to the presence of genes from the Bt bacterium in corn, or the genetic material that prevents the blood of certain fish freezing at very low temperatures in soft fruit. This distinction is reflected in the EC legislative definition of a genetically modified organism: '"genetically modified organism (GMO)" means an organism, with the exception of human beings, in which the genetic material has been altered in a way that does not occur naturally by mating and/or natural recombination'.[1] GMOs have required

---

[1] Directive 2001/18/EC on the deliberate release into the environment of genetically modified organisms OJ 2001 L 106/1, Art. 2(2).

authorisation, on a case by case basis, before they can be marketed in the European Union (EU) since 1990. Following an initially low-key introduction and consumption of GM food (particularly labelled GM tomato paste), the late 1990s saw high-profile campaigns against GM food around the EU, including in the UK. Food retailers and processors responded to what they saw as consumer demand and began to undertake that their products did not contain GM material. The regulators were also pushed into action. Between 1998 and 2004 no new authorisations were granted at EU level (we discuss the EU authorisation process in Chapter 5), and a number of Member States introduced measures barring market access to GMOs that had already been authorised. The EU essentially abandoned its regulatory framework for GMOs, introducing a de facto 'moratorium' on the marketing of GMOs in the EU. Whatever one's view on the technology, this constituted a remarkable, indeed unprecedented, breakdown in the EU legal framework. Whilst the UK did not formally support the moratorium, the government reached an agreement with the industry body (SCIMAC, the Supply Chain Initiative on Modified Agricultural Crops) that there would be no commercial cultivation of GM crops in the UK pending completion of certain scientific trials (discussed below, pp. 77–9). This UK 'moratorium' had a specifically scientific starting point, and, as a temporary decision pending the completion of further scientific investigation, fits well with certain legal approaches to the precautionary principle.[2]

The postponement of commercialisation of GMOs at both UK and EU level provided time for public discussion of the issues. At EU level, much effort was put into creating a new, more acceptable, regulatory framework for GMOs, which we will discuss in detail in Chapter 5. The UK in the meantime engaged in an elaborate and ambitious consultation process, which will be discussed below. First in this chapter, we will provide an overview of the main arguments that divide those in favour of the further development of agricultural biotechnology, and those who resist. The debate over GMOs is heated not only in respect of the appropriate role of GMOs in agriculture, but even as to the very questions that need to be asked.[3] The concerns might be divided into three main categories: environmental; health; and 'other', ethical, socio-economic and political concerns. These clearly overlap, for example with respect to ethical questions around harming the environment or the health of farmers. But for the purposes of discussion, and for the purposes of the legislation we will discuss in later chapters, the division is useful, and takes us back to the question of the political/normative versus technical/expert nature of environmental disputes, introduced in Chapter 1.

[2] See Ch. 7 below (pp. 286–300); also European Commission, *Communication on the Precautionary Principle* COM (2000) 1 final.

[3] Julia Black, 'Regulation as Facilitation: Negotiating the Genetic Revolution' (1998) 61 *Modern Law Review* 621.

## 2 Environmental concerns

The possible negative environmental impacts of GMOs are disputed, but provoke considerable concern. This section can only give a flavour of the issues.[4] The spectre of 'superweeds', for example, has received a great deal of attention. This would involve the modified gene entering the natural environment, for example by cross-pollination of the GM crop with wild relatives, or as a volunteer (a crop that self-seeds and persists outside of the field environment). If the genetic modification of this new 'weed' allows it to withstand herbicides, the effectiveness of weed control techniques is compromised. Genetic modification to withstand pests, frosts or drought could allow the GM weeds to out-compete native wild plants, with attendant reductions in overall biodiversity. GM technology also threatens to intensify problems with which we are familiar from conventional industrial-scale farming. The 'clean' fields promised by some GMOs, free of weeds and pests, have an obvious impact on farmland biodiversity. There are also indications that crops modified to kill particular pests may be toxic to certain non-target species. Herbicide-tolerant crops, modified to allow for constant exposure to certain herbicides, or crops modified constantly to express a pesticide, threaten to speed up the development of pesticide and herbicide resistance, and make such resistance more difficult to control. Any reduced effectiveness of the Bt pesticide, a naturally occurring microbial pesticide, could have diffuse and particularly important environmental effects, by depriving organic farmers of one of their few acceptable 'last resort' pesticides. Less directly, GM technology is thought likely to encourage agricultural intensification and the increase in mono-cultures, arguably more vulnerable to pests and disease, raising food security issues as well as environmental problems.

## 3 Human health concerns

Again, the existence of risks to human health from the cultivation or consumption of GMOs is much disputed. Concerns include the possibility that the modified gene will get into cells in the human gut, provoking new diseases; unanticipated nutritional differences between GM and non-GM food, with widespread effects on public health; the possibility of allergic reactions to a particular GM food, or to the pollen of GM crops.[5] The possibility that GM crops not suitable for human consumption will enter the human food chain is also a real concern. Because of concerns about allergenicity, 'starlink' maize was approved in the USA only for use as animal feed, and explicitly not for human

---

[4] See the discussion in Soil Association, *Seeds of Doubt* (Soil Association, 2003).

[5] Stephen Nottingham, *Eat your Genes: How Genetically Modified Food is Entering Our Diet* (Zed Books, 1998), p. 92, discusses the case of soybeans modified to make them more nutritious, using a gene from the brazil nut that coded for methionine, one of the few nutrients that soybeans lack. The process also transferred a major food allergen from nuts to soybeans.

consumption. When starlink maize was discovered in the human food chain, there was an outcry, mass withdrawals of products from the market and enormous associated costs.[6] If 'biopharming', the technique that involves modifying crops to grow the raw materials for industrial or pharmaceutical processes, becomes commercially viable and widespread, the concern that unwanted material will enter the human food chain can only intensify.

## 4 'Other' issues

The concern about harm to human health or the environment revolves around disputed or unavailable evidence on the 'risk' posed by GMOs. GMOs also provoke a complex range of ethical, political and socio-economic concerns; it is not just about 'risk' in a technical sense. So, for example, GM crops are likely to have a serious impact on the socio-economics of existing farming methods. The nature of the technology (for example the resources required for research and development) may enhance corporate control of the food sector, provoking associated food security issues. Increasing the level of technology in farming may also exacerbate the difficulties faced by small producers, including subsistence farmers. EU rural communities are familiar with the social and environmental problems attendant on abandonment of the land, but the socio-economic impacts on developing countries are likely to be particularly intense. With widespread commercial growing of GMOs, GM material will become pervasive, and its presence in many other crops and foodstuffs will be virtually impossible to avoid. Farmers who wish to market their produce as being free of GMOs, particularly organic farmers, may face real difficulties; this question of 'coexistence' will be discussed further in Chapters 5 and 9 (the latter in the context of liability for harm).

Perhaps the most worrying issue that does not fit easily into the 'risk/safety' questions of environment or human health protection, at least on the approach to risk assessment taken in the EU and UK, is the uncertainty of the evidence. Applying Brian Wynne's categorisation of 'uncertainties' discussed in Chapter 1 (pp. 18–20), along with data gaps, we have difficulties of both 'indeterminacy' and 'ignorance': GMOs are released into unpredictable and infinitely variable real-world social and ecological systems; and the prospect of harm that we have not yet even thought of also looms rather large in this area. The 'precautionary principle', claimed as a key justificatory element of the regulation of GMOs, does not address all of these concerns, at least as interpreted in the EU, where regulation cannot tackle 'hypothetical' risk or seek 'zero' risk (pp. 22–31). It is true that, as a matter of fact, society does not generally demand proof of no risk; if we had, the world would be a very different, and arguably poorer, place. Nevertheless, the GM example highlights the inflexibility of denying the very possibility

---

[6] See Rebecca Bratspies, 'Myths of Voluntary Compliance: Lessons from the Starlink Corn Fiasco' (2003) 27 *William and Mary Environmental Law and Policy Review* 591.

of public debate about the 'acceptability' of 'hypothetical' risk, particularly if the social benefits to set against the unknowns are also largely hypothetical.

The ethical objections that might be taken to agricultural biotechnology are varied, and in most cases would overlap with questions of safety: for example the ethical acceptability of risk to the environment or the health of producers. The most obvious free-standing ethical issue is a 'biocentric' ethical position concerned about unacceptable interference with nature. This may seem slightly esoteric in the context of the more concrete and immediate issues raised above, but one does see hints of this in some rather unlikely places. Parts of the UK popular press, for example, have branded GM food 'frankenfood'.[7] Whilst this has been widely dismissed as scare-mongering and unhelpful, the reference to the Frankenstein story may reflect an instinctive anxiety about punishment for human temerity. The Nuffield Council on Bioethics has discussed the ethical implications of GM crops in an accessible, if not uncontroversial, manner. Many of the issues discussed in the following extract resonate with the different approaches to environmental protection in Chapter 1.

### Nuffield Council on Bioethics, *Genetically Modified Crops: The Ethical and Social Issues* (Nuffield Council on Bioethics, 1999), www.nuffieldbioethics.org/

1.39 The concern that GM crops transgress natural barriers raises a question: how does nature set boundaries and why is their transgression wrong? Anthropologists have explored this question in discussing ideas of pollution. Some critics of GM crops talk of cross-pollination from GM crops as 'pollution'. The concept of pollution has been said by some anthropologists to refer to illicit boundary-crossings, and they have thought that all cultures seem to have some conception of pollution because all cultures have some conception of 'things in the wrong place'. Sometimes the undesirability of pollution has a simple practical explanation. Grit in the oil will wreck the engine. Coal dust in the air will give us black lung. Not all sorts of wrongness have an easy explanation of that kind. Racism is an extreme, though widespread, symptom of the desire for purity. Indeed, many of the yearnings for 'natural purity' have little or no justification. Tribes that kill twins at birth appear to do so out of a sense that human beings are rightly born singletons and that only animals have multiple births, but they seem to take these drastic measures without much thought about exactly what would go wrong if they did not do so. Is it possible that some of the fear of GM crops is of the same sort?

1.40 The 'natural/unnatural' distinction is one of which few practising scientists can make much sense. Whatever occurs, whether in a field or a test tube, occurs as the result of natural processes, and can, in principle, be explained in terms of natural science. When human abilities to transform the world are limited, the distinction between nature and artifice seems fairly clear. It has often made better sense to accommodate ourselves to the forces of nature than to fight them. Is a plant acceptably natural or 'organic' if it has been successively bred to have a particular gene complement, but unnatural and not 'organic' if precisely the same

---

[7] The *Daily Mail* in particular picked up this language.

gene complement has been arrived at through laboratory processes? We can see no reason in ethics to draw a distinction.

### Taboos and moral conservatism

1.41 If the point of drawing a line between the natural and the unnatural is to provide a sort of comfort in our dealings with the world, what is the source of that comfort, and how far can we do without it? Two answers to that question may be borrowed, one from Mary Douglas, the other from Martin Heidegger. The anthropologist Mary Douglas is one of the few writers to treat pollution and taboos entirely seriously but from a secular point of view. Her view of taboos is that they are reflections of attachments and cleavages in society. The Jewish prohibition on eating pork was a way of imposing order on a disordered world. Pigs have cloven hooves but do not ruminate; they were viewed as anomalous and therefore potentially dangerous.

1.42 This is, of course, speculative but, whatever the cause of taboos, the question then arises as to whether taboos should be given up whenever they are inconvenient. The 'defence' of taboo is complicated because it comes in two different layers which are not easy to separate. Societies with well-entrenched taboos are said to be happy, culturally coherent and religiously harmonious. Attempts to modernise such belief systems may cause more misery than good. This is the defence of moral conservatism in general. It infuriates rationalists and progressives, because it denies that there are overwhelming gains to be made by throwing out what progressives and rationalists regard as superstitions. Conservatives reply that they agree that we pay a price for conserving the moral environment. There are things we could do but do not do, and maybe some of them would have good effects. We need not deny that progress is progress when we decide not to pay the price of it, because that price is too high.

1.43 There is a further defence of a morally conservative view of the environment to be considered. It stems from the notoriously difficult philosopher, Heidegger, but its appeal is wide. His idea is that the world possesses a meaning that we can only understand if we approach the world in a receptive mode, in the way the poet, the artist or the traditional peasant does, not in an 'industrial' way. On Heidegger's view, technology is a moral disaster. We become manipulators of things and lose touch with their sense. It does not follow that no use of the natural world is permissible or worthwhile, but many are not. All forms of industrialised agriculture are culturally impoverishing and GM crops would be another step further down an already disastrous road. This may be so, but there seems little justification in banning GM crops on these grounds when the rest of society travels so substantially in the direction Heidegger opposed.

1.44 The thought that animates many people when they object to the unnaturalness of one or another way of treating plants is that some relations with the world take the form of harmonious, satisfying, emotionally fulfilling interactions, and others amount to assaults on the world. Certainly, some of the case for organic farming seems to rest on that thought. Someone who holds that view can accept much of the sceptic's reminder that what we call 'nature' is for the most part the result of old technologies. The world bears many traces of what humanity has done to it in the past. The critic will think that some have gone with the grain of nature and some against it.

1.45 One view is that there is more to our interaction with the physical world than techni-cal manipulation of it. That view does something to explain why some environmentalists would want an environmental audit to include a dimension that the most scrupulous and well-informed scientific inquest into the physical risks posed by the introduction of GM crops would lack. If new crops change the appearance of the environment, alter the wildlife in the terrain, demand new working habits and so on, they impose a kind of cost not easily captured by the usual cost/benefit analysis. We may doubt whether there is much prospect of living perfectly harmoniously with nature, no matter what form of agriculture we practice.

...

8.8 The most complicated ethical considerations have been those implicated in the concern that genetic engineering is 'unnatural'. Since most human behaviour is in various senses 'unnatural', and does not arouse moral comment, the line between those unnatural activities that do not cause unease and those that do is hard to draw. Maize is everywhere very differ-ent from its wild ancestor; is Bt maize unnatural in a different and morally deplorable way? It is, of course, true that the presence of Bt will have some tendency to encourage immuni-ties in insects that would not otherwise have developed them. But using Bt insecticides as sprays will also have that effect, and such sprays are used by organic farmers. Breeding insect resistance in crops by conventional means will also encourage the development of immunities in insect pests. In short, it is the *deleterious consequences* of our farming techniques to our environment and human health, not their 'unnatural' character that should preoccupy us.

8.9 'Naturalness' and 'unnaturalness' are part of a spectrum. At one end of the scale, some modifications of the plants that are now being achieved by genetic modification might also have been achieved over time by conventional means of plant breeding; indeed, this has recently occurred. It would be hard to object to such a modification as a matter of principle as being 'unnatural', since it would only be using a new and presumably more efficient means of achieving a result that could have been achieved by conventional, more 'natural' means. Other plant modifications currently being developed probably could not have been achieved by more conventional means, but their effects in terms of increased yield or improved pest or herbicide tolerance are still not very dissimilar to the kind of changes that have been achieved over time by conventional methods. At the farther end of the spectrum are possible modifications such as putting copies of animal genes into plants. Some of these would be truly novel and unachievable by conventional breeding. Such modifications are felt by some to be 'unnatural'. We ourselves, however, can find no clear dividing line on the spec-trum which would provide in advance a generally agreed barrier for defining what types of genetic modification of plants are unacceptable because they are unnatural.

The fundamental basis for the dismissal of the ethical concerns around biotech-nology can be seen in the Nuffield Council's essentially instrumental approach to the technology:

1.51 We think that the general welfare of affected peoples largely determines the ethical acceptability of GM crops. In concrete terms, this means that their potential advantages are a matter of cheaper, more secure and less environmentally damaging food supplies, and their disadvantages, any risk to human health and environmental damage they may pose. GM foods raise issues of the right of consumers to choose what to consume and of the costs these rights may impose on producers and consumers alike. The way that the costs and benefits of agricultural technologies fall on the citizens of well-off and poor societies respectively raises questions of justice, as well as difficult issues of how policy makers can steer technological change so that it does good to those who most need it. We think that the decision about what is unnatural cannot be one for public policy, but that the freedom of choice of consumers must embrace the ability to refuse what they reject as 'unnatural' products. We do not believe GM crops will necessarily increase monoculture and conclude that there are no ethical objections to GM food other than any direct or indirect risk to human health or the environment.

The Nuffield Council's approach is unlikely to be persuasive to those who reject entirely such weighing of costs and benefits, because of a fundamental objection to GMOs, however safe and beneficial they may turn out to be. The following extract considers a similarly fundamental approach in respect of *medical* biotechnology.

### Roger Brownsword, 'What the World Needs Now: Techno-Regulation, Human Rights and Human Dignity' in Roger Brownsword (ed.), *Global Governance and the Quest for Justice, Volume IV: Human Rights* (Hart, 2005), pp. 208–9

When we turn to biotechnology, however, Fukuyama sees a far more insidious and earth-shaking threat. What exactly is wrong with the biotechnologically engineered and pharma-cologically controlled world depicted by Huxley? According to Fukuyama,[8] the A grade answer runs along the following lines:

> [T]he people in *Brave New World* may be healthy and happy, but they have ceased to be human beings. They no longer struggle, aspire, love, feel pain, make difficult moral choices, have families, or do any of the things that we traditionally associate with being human. They no longer have the characteristics that give us *human dignity*.

This is not to say that biotechnology offers no benefits for human health and well-being. However, Fukuyama's point is that our deepest concerns about biotechnology cannot be captured by a utilitarian calculation. Thus:

> While it is legitimate to worry about unintended consequences and unforeseen costs, the deepest fear that people express about [bio]technology is not a utilitarian one at all. It is rather a fear that, in the end, biotechnology will cause us in some way to lose our humanity – that is, some essential quality that has always underpinned our sense of who we are and where we are going …

---

[8] Francis Fukuyama, *Our Posthuman Future: Consequences of the Biotechnology Revolution* (Profile Books, 2002).

Brownsword calls this focus on human dignity regardless of costs and benefits (or, importantly for medical biotechnology, perhaps less so in the current context, consent) a 'dignitarian' approach. Whilst the issues are different, and perhaps clearer, with respect to developments such as human cloning or stem cell research, there are parallels with agricultural biotechnology. In particular, some ecological approaches will see the natural world as fundamentally compromised by biotechnology, such that no level of human benefit could counter such compromise. The Nuffield Council's instrumental approach is arguably a reflection of the dominant approach to ethical questions in contemporary society, and does not respond to this concern. However, this 'fundamentalist' objection to agricultural biotechnology is almost by definition unreceptive to any argument. Andrew Dobson takes a more nuanced approach, requiring questions of biocentric value to enter into assessments of the utility of the technology, but without precluding the development of biotechnology.

### Andrew Dobson, 'Biocentrism and Genetic Engineering' (1995) 4 *Environmental Values* 3, pp. 231–6

Before making any specific remarks about the environmental-ethical implications of genetic engineering, it is worth making one general one. Environmental ethics itself is part of the response to what is widely regarded as an environmental crisis. The dimensions of that crisis are well-known: globally, we are confronted by ozone depletion and global warming; more locally, communities suffer from deforestation, desertification, acid rain, eutrophication of rivers and lakes and so on. The reasons given for environmental degradation of this sort sometimes seem as numerous as the commentators who give them. Some environmental ethicists, though, have made a specific pitch for the problems associated with the way we *regard* the non-human natural world. Deep-ecological thinking has become an extremely complex and often arcane affair, but the general idea advanced is that we misunderstand our place in the scheme of things. On this view, our unwarranted adoption of a position of mastery with respect to the non-human natural world leads to practices that threaten its integrity as a sustainer of human and non-human life.

The general point, then, is that deep ecologists are likely to take up a *prima facie* position against genetic engineering precisely because it is a technology that expresses the very world view that they consider causes all the trouble: one of human mastery of the non-human natural world. The point, they say, is to develop practices and habits of mind that are an expression of membership, rather than domination, of the non-human natural world. From this point of view the ethical argument over genetic engineering is nothing less than an argument about what our relationship with the rest of the biotic (and abiotic) community should be. Peter Bunyard and Fern Morgan-Grenville express this in the following way: 'Biotechnology [by which they mean genetic engineering] is the most extreme instance of the modern, anthropocentric desire that we become "masters and possessors of nature". The biotechnology debate has to do with the kind of beings we wish to be and the kind of world in which we wish to live.'[9]

---

[9] Peter Bunyard and Fern Morgan-Grenville, *The Green Alternative* (Methuen, 1987).

In similar vein Bill McKibben opposes genetic engineering pretty much wholesale because of the counter-productive effects it has on our relationship with the non-human natural world.[10] In his view we need to retain a sense of the 'natural' in order to counteract our potentially lethal Promethean tendencies. He believes that the (increasingly vestigial) sense of wonder we experience when confronted by natural processes, and which he feels acts like the amber colour in a traffic light, giving us pause for thought before pressing on (or stopping altogether), is in danger of being wiped out by genetic engineering.

…

Biocentric views of genetic engineering derive from two main sources. First, genetic engineering is held to constitute a practice that expresses a human will to domination of the non-human natural world. This, they will say, is inappropriate in the context of a global environmental crisis part of whose cause, at least, is the very habits and practices of which genetic engineering is such a sophisticated example. Second, biocentrics find value in beings and collections of beings whom we do not normally regard as members of the moral community. From this point of view, and to the extent that genetic engineering interferes with the moral considerability of an individual's *telos*, or with a species, it is held in *prima facie* suspicion by biocentrics.

There seem to be two principal ways to go from here. First, this *prima facie* suspicion can be turned into wholesale opposition to all forms of genetic engineering, on the grounds that its practice is immoral from the perspectives outlined above. Such a view, though, has two possible defects. The first is that the biological descriptions upon which the moral case are based are themselves questionable. There are biologists who will claim that the notion that species are morally considerable cannot be true because species do not, as such, exist.

The second is that such wholesale rejection pays too little mind to the potentially beneficial consequences of some forms of genetic engineering, and I would like to explore this objection in rather more detail. On this reading, a case-by-case examination is appropriate in which the guideline questions would be *what* is being done to *whom* (or to what), and *why*. Biocentrics might merely demand in this context that the moral considerability of species (to the extent that it is believed that there is such a thing) be taken into account as a further factor in the decision-making process. They would probably be happy, in this case, with a stewardship-type formulation such as that suggested by Alan Holland: that genetic engineering should be conducted 'in a manner compatible with the continuing existence of the biosphere viewed as a community'.[11]

This consequentialist dimension seems an appropriate one for biocentrics to take into account: the fields of application of genetic engineering are many and varied, and it is unhelpful to take an uncompromisingly prohibitive view of its practice. In the context of medicine, for example, the uses to which genetic engineering can be put are multiple, and the list can sometimes read as a succession of nails being banged into the coffin of those who would seek to restrict genetic engineering experimentation. How could anyone refuse to

---

[10]  Bill McKibben, *The End of Nature* (Penguin, 1990).

[11]  Alan Holland, 'The Biotic Community: A Philosophical Critique of Genetic Engineering' in Peter Wheale and Ruth McNally (eds.), *The Bio-Revolution: Cornucopia or Pandora's Box?* (Pluto Press, 1990), p. 232.

endorse something with such potential for improving human health? Applications range from the production of larger quantities of insulin than would be available without genetic engineering, through the manufacture of vaccines for (for example) malaria, dengue fever and leprosy, to the possible treatment of genetically-based human disorders.

As far as agriculture is concerned, genetic engineering has sometimes been hailed as the cutting edge of the second 'green revolution': the application of scientific and industrial techniques to the problem of growing more food, more effectively in ever smaller spaces. In this case, genetic manipulation takes the place of artificial pesticides, herbicides, fungicides and fertilisers. There is, for example, the possibility of creating cereal crops with built-in herbicide or pesticide resistance, or of developing plants that are capable of 'fixing' air-borne nitrogen, thus doing away with the need to use ever greater quantities of nitrogen-rich artificial fertiliser which have uncertain but potentially environmentally damaging effects if used over long periods of time.

…

Again, much of the opposition to genetic engineering comes from the environmental movement, while its supporters will point out the irony of this given that genetic engineering has the potential to deal with environmental problems. Most obviously, micro-organisms with the ability to degrade toxic waste can be cultured and then put to work on the dispersal of (for example) oil slicks. Similarly, environmentalists' concerns over water scarcity could be made redundant with the creation of drought-resistant plants. More generally, genetic engineering could be read as undermining many of the positions environmentalists adopt on environmental protection because whatever we do to the environment can be rectified or modified by genetic manipulation. In this respect genetic engineering turns out to be the ultimate 'technological fix': 'Environmentalists … may lose important utilitarian or prudential arguments for protecting natural ecosystems [with advances in genetic engineering]. These arguments become harder and harder to defend as we find cheap technological substitutes for nature's gifts.'[12]

Determining the legitimacy of genetic engineering, then, becomes a question of weighing up the claims of moral agents and objects within these various fields of application. In these contexts most people will agree on the legitimacy of the genetic engineering of microbes with a view to dispersing oil slicks, on the grounds that the value of microbes and of the ecosystems into which they are delivered are outweighed by the good that will be done. Likewise, we might reach the conclusion that genetic engineering can be carried out on an animal without altering its *telos* in unacceptable ways, and for sufficiently good reason.

## 5 The benefits of GM technology

The above extract from Dobson outlines some of the claimed benefits of GM technology. Supporters of GM technology, like the critics, focus on environmental and health issues. Hoped-for environmental benefits from

---

12  Mark Sagoff, 'Biotechnology and the Environment: What is at Risk' (1988) *Agriculture and Human Values* Summer, p. 29.

GM technology include the possibility of modifying a crop to need less nitrogen or phosphate, reducing reliance on fertilisers. There is also discussion of the possibility of modifying crops to address the health problems of the wealthy world (for example obesity, diabetes, cancer), or the use of GM crops for the production of pharmaceutical products, 'bio-pharming'. These sorts of benefits will bring the possible costs of *rejecting* GM crops to the centre of debate. The promised benefits of agricultural biotechnology that are perhaps most difficult to dismiss out of hand are those that look to the improvements of yield of subsistence crops in poor countries where underproduction and hunger are pressing.

### Nuffield Council, *Genetically Modified Crops*

4.3 If we value the ethic of 'to each according to need' (or in the alternative, believe that the poorest possess a 'right to survive', given feasible efforts on their own part and a global capacity to feed them), then the introduction of GM crops on a large scale would be a moral imperative. This is because GM crops are expected to produce more food, or more employment income for those who need it most urgently. 'More food for the hungry', unlike 'tomatoes with longer shelf-life', is a strong ethical counterweight to set against the concerns of the opponents of GM crops.

4.4 However, ordinary notions of justice or fairness are challenged by the present distribution of research effort, GM seed marketing and field trials which are dominated by a small group of leading agrochemical and seed multinational companies. In contrast, the Green Revolution[13] was largely due to public-sector research. Most of the companies' effort goes into reducing costs in capital-intensive farming in developed countries. Research on staples mostly involves varieties used for animal food. Only a small proportion of effort goes into what is most needed in less developed countries: cheap, labour-intensive, robust and high-yielding staples for human food. Inevitably, the companies respond mostly to the demands of the market. So it is unlikely that this state of affairs will change in the near future unless like-minded governments step in and act on explicitly market-correcting moral principles – financing or stimulating an orientation of GM research towards the needs of the hungry.

These most compelling arguments against restricting GM technology will quickly lose their moral weight if progress is not made. The slow emergence of GMOs that will feed the hungry or save the environment also reinforces the centrality of trust as a difficulty for regulators of GMOs.[14] High levels of public scepticism about technological innovation in agriculture should not be surprising given the recent history of food crises and scandals in the EU, and awareness of the very powerful commercial imperatives pushing the industry. Even

---

[13] The increase in agricultural production between the 1930s and 1960s, because of improved agricultural technologies (footnote added).

[14] Apparently a significant factor in the UK: see *GM Nation? The Findings of a Public Debate* (2003), available at www.gmnation.org, extracted in Ch. 5, pp. 195–6.

the most commonly cited example of the promise of GM, 'golden rice', is not without its critics. Golden rice is modified to contain higher levels of beta carotene, which converts into vitamin A. This is said to be capable of saving around 120 million children from the childhood diseases and blindness to which vitamin A deficiency contributes among children with diets heavily dependent on rice. Critics claim, however, that the distribution of vitamin A pills, together with education, could reduce vitamin A deficiency at much lower cost.[15] Moreover, many deny even the possibility that GMOs are the solution to hunger. The argument that poverty, inequality and lack of access to land, not lack of food, causes hunger was powerfully, and famously, made by Amartya Sen in the 1980s,[16] and applies equally to a GM age.

### Mark Sagoff, 'Biotechnology and Agriculture: The Common Wisdom And Its Critics' (2001) 9 *Indiana Journal of Global Legal Studies* 13, pp. 13–18

When I was a child, my mother implored me to eat everything on my plate because 'people are starving in Africa'. The non sequitur was apparent, even to me. The amount of food children in wealthy countries waste has little or no effect on the amount children in poorer nations have to eat. Industrial economies produce vast farm surpluses. In spite of these surpluses, many of the world's poor will go to bed hungry. Food shortages arise because of failures in distribution, not in production. This is the common wisdom many analysts accept.

If this common wisdom is correct, agricultural biotechnology will affect industrial economies and peasant economies differently. In many industrial economies, for example, in the United States and in Europe, three chronic problems plague agriculture: glut, glut, and more glut. Even without the benefit of biotechnology, farm commodities flood markets and drive prices below costs – leading to trade wars as European, Australian, Canadian, and South American producers compete for buyers. Bailouts, payments for not growing crops, and export subsidies have been hallmarks of farm policy.

…..

Let me begin with the common wisdom about the elasticity of farm production. According to conventional economics, farm production and automobile production rise and fall for exactly the same reason: market demand. Farmers can, and will, plant and harvest as much as they can sell. As Nobel laureate Amartya Sen wrote in 1994, 'food output is being held back by a lack of effective demand in the market' rather than by ecological constraints on production.[17] In other words, food is not scarce, but demand is, since many people are too poor or powerless to purchase food, even at historically low prices.

---

[15] See the discussion in Thomas Bernauer, *Genes, Trade, and Regulation: The Seeds of Conflict in Food Biotechnology* (Princeton University Press, 2003).

[16] See, for example, Amartya Sen, *Poverty and Famine: An Essay on Entitlement and Deprivation* (Clarendon Press, 1981).

[17] Amartya Sen, 'The Population Delusion' *New York Review of Books*, 22 Sept. 1994, p. 62.

*Look Who's a Malthusian Now*

Many environmentalists – especially those who warn society about ecological limits to economic growth – bristle at the idea that the cause of famine lies in the shortage not of supply but of effective demand. These environmentalists adopt the Malthusian position that famines are inevitable because population growth will always outstrip agricultural production. On this view, famines arise because of the intransigence of nature, not because of the injustice of society; in other words, if populations grow, famines are inevitable, since they result from the paucity of resources, not from the inability of the poorest people to get access to them. To proponents of this view, genetic engineering offers only a false promise of throwing back nature's limits – a promise that cannot be redeemed because nature's limits cannot be altered. In this vein, ecologist Paul Ehrlich has denounced the 'hope that development can greatly increase the size of the economic pie and pull many more people out of poverty'. This hope is 'basically a humane idea', Ehrlich has written, 'made insane by the constraints nature places on human activities'.[18]

Since environmentalists have for so long associated themselves with 'the limits to growth', one might think that critics of agricultural biotechnology, since they generally adopt a 'green' ideology, would scoff at the hope that biotechnology might help feed the world's growing population. Actually, this is not the case. Those who oppose the application of genetic engineering in agriculture concede its power to push back the natural barriers that constrain yields, for example, by increasing the efficiency of photosynthesis ... How can Malthusians plausibly argue that genetic engineering cannot achieve these breakthroughs? Only those well versed in the technology itself can speak to its possibilities, and they are full of optimism.

The advent of genetic engineering, along with other technological advances, has led many environmentalists to downplay the old Malthusian arguments about the limits to growth. Critics of agricultural biotechnology – though overwhelmingly identifying themselves with environmental causes – do not endorse the old Malthusian ideology. Instead, they agree with Sen that the causes of famine are to be found in social and economic relationships, not in nature ... The problem, these critics contend, is that big corporations, while patenting genetic information, have no incentive to share or use it in ways to benefit the poorest of the poor.

Who, then, defends the Malthusian position that fixes the blame for famine on the limits of nature rather than on the injustices of society? In fact, it is free-marketeers associated with corporate interests ... who invoke Malthusian reasons for promoting agricultural biotechnology in order to throw back nature's constraints ...

This amusing do-si-do should not go unremarked. Agricultural biotechnology has pried environmentalism apart from Malthusianism. That biotechnology can substitute for nature, extend nature, and overcome natural boundaries has become obvious; the power of genetic engineering is too plain to deny. Thus, Malthusian fears serve only to buttress the case for biotechnology, because if nature were the cause of famine, biotechnology would be the cure.

---

[18] Paul R. Ehrlich and Anne H. Ehrlich, *The Population Explosion* (Simon and Schuster, 1990).

> For this kind of reason, proponents of biotechnology find Malthusian arguments to be con-
> genial. Critics of biotechnology, in contrast, reject Malthusian arguments that in their view
> no longer serve to support the cause of environmentalism, if they ever did. These critics
> identify the cause of hunger in distribution, not production. If the problem lies with social,
> political, and economic relationships – in injustice rather than in scarcity – then biotechnol-
> ogy is not relevant.

Sagoff's ascription of Malthusian / 'limits to growth' motivations to greens across the board may be rather too absolute; as we have seen, the basis of environmental consciousness is much more difficult than that to pin down. We will also see in later chapters that certain strands of environmentalism were 'pried apart' from Malthus well before the advent of biotechnology (particularly by proponents of sustainable development: Chapter 6). And even those who understand hunger to be a problem of underproduction rather than distribution may baulk at yet another 'technical fix' to social and environmental problems: the success of modern agriculture in terms of production has come at environmental and social cost, and from an ecological perspective, biotechnology is looking to symptoms rather than cause: at best a short-term solution.[19]

Nevertheless, Sagoff's discussion of Malthus brings out again the fundamental nature of the disputes over GM technology (and indeed other environmental debates): the very nature of the problem is disputed. Moreover, the benefits of GMOs are as heavily debated, and remain in many cases as intangible or uncertain, as the risks.

## 6 Consultation and beyond in the UK

Whatever one's views on the technology, it should be clear that a diverse range of concerns is raised by the prospect of widespread GM agriculture. As such, agricultural biotechnology challenges established ways of decision making: in particular neither the 'scientific paradigm', nor the economic approaches discussed in Chapter 1, will readily *hear*, let alone respond to, the full range of debate. Recognising, at least in principle, the breadth and complexity of the concerns, the UK government undertook in 2003 an interesting experiment in public participation in decision making. The 'public dialogue' over the future of agricultural biotechnology in the UK had three strands: a scientific review, an economic review, and a public consultation on 'other' issues. We will not examine each exercise in detail here, but the way this 'dialogue' attempts to collect information based on different ways of understanding the world illuminates some of the main themes of this chapter.

---

[19] See also the discussion of 'environmental limits' in Ch. 6, pp. 250–6.

## (a) Science and GMOs

The Science Review was set up to consider the current state of the science behind GM issues, including clarifying the state of knowledge and areas of uncertainty, basing its conclusions on pre-existing work. One of the key findings of the Review (at least as far as government was concerned) was the conclusion that 'GM is not a single homogeneous technology', and so blanket judgments cannot be made. The Review examined a number of common concerns about GM crops and, in the words of the Secretary of State:

> reported **no** verifiable ill-effects from extensive human and animal consumption of products from GM crops over 7 years, and it concluded too that current GM crops were very unlikely either to invade the countryside or to be toxic to wildlife. The most important environmental issue identfied was indeed the effect on farmland wildlife which was the subject of our extensive trials – the largest carried out in the world.[20]

The trials referred to by the Secretary of State were the 'Farm Scale Evaluations' (FSEs), carried out as part of an agreement between government and industry to postpone commercialisation of GMOs in the UK; the industry undertook that there would be no commercial cultivation of GM crops in the UK until the FSEs were complete. The FSEs are scientific studies of particular GM crops at the farm level, addressing the biodiversity impact of GMOs, rather than food or feed safety. Whilst not strictly part of the 'science review', the results of the FSEs became available around the same time, and are a nice case study of the controversies that surround scientific endeavour in this field.

### Environmental Audit Committee, Second Report of Session 2003–4, *GM Foods – Evaluating the Farm Scale Trials* HC 90–I.

#### The results

6. In short, the FSE results on the first three crops showed that GMHT [genetically modified herbicide tolerant] spring-sown oilseed rape and GMHT beet, with their associated herbicide regimes, resulted in lower levels of field biodiversity than was the case for their conventional counterparts managed conventionally. The opposite was the case for GMHT forage maize with its herbicide regime which resulted in greater levels of field biodiversity than was the case for its conventional equivalent, conventionally managed. These results were widely held to be both consistent and clear within the parameters of the design and operation of the trials. While there is of course a direct link between GMHT crops and their particular herbicide and management regime, these trials were an assessment of the impact upon biodiversity of that herbicide under its particular regime, and not of the GMHT crop itself. Moreover, the trials were very narrow in their remit: they were intended only to provide benchmark assessments of

---

[20]  Secretary of State's Statement on GM Policy, 9 March 2004, available at www.defra.gov.uk/corporate/ministers/statements/mb040309.htm.

biodiversity in four conventional crops against which GMHT varieties could be measured. **The benchmark against which GMHT crops were measured was not ambitious, since biodiversity in conventional crops has suffered greatly over the last half-century**.

. . .

47. Atrazine is a very powerful broad spectrum residual herbicide. Various groups, including Friends of the Earth, have for a number of years been opposed to its use on the grounds of its potent effect upon biodiversity and its possible threat to human health. Opposition to the use of this herbicide was not just a UK issue: it led to moves in Europe in the late 1990s which culminated late in 2003 with an EU agreement to phase out its use by April 2005. In the UK, one of the conventional crops on which it is predominantly used is forage maize. Consequently, when the FSEs were set up, GMHT forage maize crops (for which the herbicide was Bayer's 'Liberty', glufosinate ammonium) were to be grown and compared against conventional forage maize crops on 75% of which atrazine was to be used. This predominant use of atrazine was certainly reflective of the then current herbicide regime for forage maize.

48. The use of atrazine on the non-GM forage maize crop was the focus of the most widespread criticism of the FSEs that we came across. Even bodies happy with every other element of the trials were unhappy about the fact that the conventional benchmark for GMHT maize was largely an atrazine-dosed crop. Since atrazine was such a devastatingly efficient herbicide, almost any other herbicide used, however potent, might still appear beneficial when in comparison. As Dr Brian Johnson of English Nature put it to us: 'atrazine turns a maize field from what was once a diverse grass field … into a wildlife desert. It is really ground zero as far as wildlife is concerned. It is not surprising that a herbicide-tolerant system is better for biodiversity.' Effectively, it could be argued that given the predominant use of atrazine in the conventional forage maize crop, GMHT forage maize had too easy a time of it in the FSEs.

49. The phasing out and replacement of atrazine casts serious doubt on the value of the forage maize trial results. Since any predominant successor herbicide to atrazine may be less potent than atrazine and consequently may have reduced harm on biodiversity, indeed less harm than 'Liberty' has on biodiversity in the GMHT crop, the level of biodiversity that will in future be found in conventional forage maize crops may be higher than it is at present. In other words, while the atrazine benchmark is valid for an agronomy in which atrazine is used, it is not valid for the agronomy in which GMHT forage maize, if commercially licensed, will be grown.

It is clear that GM crops will compare more favourably with conventional intensive farming than with less intensive or organic farming. Even without getting into the rights and wrongs of the particular comparators for GMOs, the FSEs illustrate the degree of professional judgment involved in the risk assessment. The 'norm' is assumed to be heavily industrialised farming, and although in this case the 'norm' was in principle controllable by government as well as scientists, this implies a value judgment about the 'acceptable' level of environmental harm associated with farming. However, the outcry that met the assessment also illustrates how crucial transparency of scientific assessment is; the judgments implicit in the trial, and the possible alternatives, were at least brought into the open. The question of comparators also highlights a serious unevenness in regulation, apparent also in other areas of environmental law: conventional agriculture has very significant adverse environmental effects, but is neither regulated nor debated as intensely as agricultural biotechnology.

### (b) Economics and GMOs

The economic review of GM crops was carried out by the government's Strategy Unit, and the intention was that it analyse the costs and benefits of GMOs in the UK. The prominence given to economics in environmental policy creates concern that important uncertainties and value judgments will be hidden from view behind a display of apparently inevitable numbers. In this case, the report emphasises the limited evidence and data on which it is based, and makes 'no attempt to provide a single "net present value" of total costs and benefits; neither has the study attempted to make policy recommendations'.[21] Instead, it paints a complex picture that emphasises the difficulty of the political judgments to be made. It resorts predominantly to assessing the pros and cons of different regulatory approaches, setting out results based on five possible 'scenarios' for the future of GM agriculture in the UK,[22] which incorporate varying public attitudes and varying regulatory regimes, and consider the possibility of 'shocks and surprises'.[23] The government apparently found it rather difficult to summarise the nuances of the report, but concluded that 'the GM crops currently available offer only some small and limited benefits to UK farmers, but that future developments in GM crops could potentially offer benefits of greater value and significance even in the United Kingdom'.[24]

### (c) The public debate

The most common and long-standing method of involving the public in decision making in the UK is a process of written consultation. Both the science and the economics review were subject to public consultation, but by their very nature were likely to attract only experts in the field. Nor would this form of involvement necessarily involve interaction between participants.

More general public consultation took the form of a nationwide, government-sponsored but 'arm's-length', public debate on the future commercialisation of GM crops. The public debate on GMOs went under the strange title of *GM Nation?*, and reported in September 2003. It arose out of a recommendation by

---

[21] Cabinet Office, *Field Work: Weighing up the Costs and Benefits of GM Crops*, available at www.strategy.gov.uk/work_areas/gm_crops/index.asp, para. 1.5.4.    [22] *Ibid.*, Ch. 4.

[23] These include 'shocks' unrelated to GMOs such as an oil price shock (which could alter the economics of energy crops), and shocks internal to GMOs, for example the identification of an unexpected environmental impact.    [24] Secretary of of State's Statement on GM Policy.

the Agriculture and Environment Biotechnology Commission (AEBC), set up in 2000 to advise government on the social and ethical issues relating to developments in biotechnology.

### Agriculture and Environment Biotechnology Committee, *Crops on Trial* (2001), www.aebc.gov.uk

21. We believe that robust public policies and regulatory frameworks for GM crops need to expose, respect and embrace the differences of view which exist, rather than bury them. The appropriate development of GM technology has suffered as a result of the lack of opportunity for serious debate about the full range of potential implications of GM agriculture, on the basis of clear understandings of what is involved, away from concern that has been promoted by campaigning elements of the media. There have been public protests around the [farm scale evaluations]. At some sites hostility – either local or more widely orchestrated – has led to farmers and their families being threatened and crops and farm equipment being damaged.

22. We believe that the Government must now encourage comprehensive public discussion of the ecological and ethical – including socio-economic – issues which have arisen. Time is needed for people to overcome differences of language and explore the extent of their shared understandings, and above all there is a need to include those who have felt themselves to be excluded and hence to have no control over events.

*GM Nation?* was not a mini-referendum, both in the sense that it was not determinative of the result, and in the sense that it was not to be aggregative of pre-existing interests. Instead, *qualitative* information on what the public thinks about GMOs was to feed into UK government decision making. *GM Nation?* was a self-consciously deliberative and inclusive exercise.[25] 'Deliberation' is a complex political notion, discussed further in Chapter 3, but basically it involves a form of decision making that revolves around rational argument, including the provision of reasons that are capable of recognition as 'reasons' by others who disagree. Deliberation assumes that values can be transformed by deliberation, by contrast with the pre-formed and static private interests elicited in simpler consultation exercises. The core activity of *GM Nation?* was a series of public meetings around the country, including a small number of high-profile regional events together with a larger number of smaller local meetings. Attendees were encouraged to listen and engage with other opinions, as well as put forward their own views. The *GM Nation?* process allowed for discussion of the 'other' issues around GMOs, as well as allowing lay discussion of

---

[25] Its record in both of those respects is, however, mixed. The Understanding Risk Team from the University of East Anglia carried out a formal evaluation of *GM Nation?*: Understanding Risk Team (Tom Horlick-Jones *et al.*), *A Deliberative Future? An Independent Evaluation of the* GM Nation? *Public Debate about the Possible Commercialisation of Transgenic Crops in Britain, 2003* Understanding Risk Working Paper 04–02 (Centre for Environmental Risk, University of East Anglia, 2004).

scientific and economic issues. Deliberation need not include the general public (experts can deliberate), but the intention was that *GM Nation?* would reach beyond 'activists' in the area, and allow the lay public to participate. The evidence, however, suggests that the participants were more negative about GMOs than the general population,[26] which inevitably leads to questions about how their views should be fed into policy making. Nevertheless, *GM Nation?* clarified to some degree the nature of 'public concern' about GMOs.

Perhaps the simplest observation to be drawn from *GM Nation?* is that 'Among the participants in the debate there are many more people who are cautious, suspicious or outrightly hostile about GM crops than there are supportive towards them' (para. 41). Perhaps more interestingly for the current context, 'the public do not view GM as purely a scientific, or environmental, or economic, or political or ethical issue. All of these aspects are important to them' (para. 42 (emphasis omitted)). This illustrates nicely the complexity of public opinion on agricultural biotechnology: one of the striking aspects of the factors raised by the participants is that 'there are so many of them'. For the sake of completeness, seven 'key messages' were identified:

- People are generally uneasy about GM
- The more people engage in GM issues, the harder their attitudes and more intense their concerns
- There is little support for early commercialisation
- There is widespread mistrust of government and multi-national companies
- There is a broad desire to know more and for further research to be done
- Developing countries have special interests
- The debate was welcomed and valued

## (d) The public dialogue on GMOs: the response

The three strands of the 'public dialogue' attempted to find room for the open consideration of economics, science and 'other' areas. There was an effort to ensure that all groups and perspectives could have a say in decision making. In the early days of concern around GMOs, a scientific logic was the only acceptable framework of debate, and any public concern that did not fit in that framework was easily dismissed as irrational. That is clearly no longer the case. The debate also brings into the process a range of information that would be difficult to locate in a single bureaucracy – including external information on the economics and the science, and, more strikingly, information on public views.

---

[26] *Ibid.* To avoid the exclusion of a 'silent majority', the public meetings were supplemented by 'focus groups' in which participants selected to represent the general population discussed similar issues, as a form of 'control'. Whilst the official report of *GM Nation?* saw no significant differences between these two strands of the debate, the Understanding Risk Team were more concerned.

*GM Nation?* was clearly flawed in many important respects (as well as concerns about inclusiveness, we might note discussion of the confidence with which some of the final report's conclusions were drawn[27]) but it was also quite remarkably ambitious and far-reaching. This is the first such debate on the development of scientific and technological innovations in the UK, where decisions have historically been far more secretive. The government response to the three strands of the dialogue is in the following terms:

### Department for Environment, Food and Rural Affairs (DEFRA), *The GM Dialogue: Government Response*, 9 March 2004, pp. 12–13

4.3 We take public concern very seriously, and we recognise the need to address the people's legitimate anxieties about GM crops. But having weighed up all the evidence, we have concluded that we should continue to assess each GM crop on an individual case-by-case basis. This is also consistent with the way other applications of GM technology, such as veterinary and human medicines, are regulated in the EU.

4.4 This Government is committed to evidence-based policy-making, and the scientific evidence supports neither an outright ban on nor a blanket acceptance of all GM crops (nor does the European regulatory regime allow for an outright ban). The results of the Farm-Scale Evaluations demonstrate very clearly that each crop is different, and each must be considered on its own merits.

The government is at least rhetorically responsive to a very wide range of concerns about GMOs. Government accepts that people are 'generally uneasy', and that there is 'little public support for early commercialisation';[28] it acknowledges the 'complex range of issues and concerns' that shape people's views on biotechnology,[29] emphasising the legitimacy of issues going beyond technical assessments of risk to health or the environment. The response to the debate does turn very quickly, however, to the commitment to 'evidence-based policy-making', concluding that the existing case-by-case approach is the right one.[30] As it goes through 'each of the concerns raised in the public debate', the focus is on responding to those concerns by reference to the rigorous safety and approval processes in the regulation, and to opinions provided by expert bodies, including the Science Review and the Economics Review, but also the report of the Nuffield Council on Biotechnology discussed above (pp. 66–9). In spite of best efforts, the government seems to prefer evidence from the 'experts' when all else is said and done.

We should also recall that the agreement between the industry body and the UK government not to pursue commercial planting of GMOs for a period was

---

[27] *Ibid.* The level of government funding of the debate, and its timing (it wound up before the Farm Scale Evaluations were completed) were also criticised.

[28] DEFRA, *The GM Dialogue: Government Response*, 9 March 2004, available at www.defra.gov.uk/Environment/gm/Crops/debate/index.htm, Executive Summary, para. 7.

[29] Ch. 3, para. 3.1.    [30] Executive Summary, para. 11.

subject to completion of the Farm Scale Evaluations. At this point, the UK government had to take action in respect of certain applications in the pipeline. The
UK government was willing to approve only the crop that came out of the FSEs
favourably (this was the crop compared with a conventional crop using
atrazine). Interestingly, however, this GM maize will not be grown in the UK in
spite of approval; Bayer Crop Science stopped pursuing commercialisation of
its GM maize in the UK, because of 'a number of constraints on this conditional
approval before the commercial cultivation of GM forage maize can proceed in
the UK'.[31] Whether the response from Bayer was anticipated by government is
something for the conspiracy theorists. However, this should remind us that if
only a narrow range of reasons are deemed to be permissible, and government
is clearly here trying to base its decisions on 'sound science', we may get an
explanation of a decision that fails to provide any genuine accountability.

Moreover, the UK government is subject to considerable constraints in its
decision making on GMOs. Authorisation of GMOs is ultimately a decision
taken for the whole EU on the basis of qualified majority voting by the Member
States, as will be discussed in Chapter 5 below. The UK is simply one state of
twenty-seven. There is a significant disconnection between the participation
mechanism at the national policy level, and case by case authorisation at EU
level. And the EU is itself subject to pressure in respect of international trade
rules. The USA, Argentina and Canada initiated a dispute over EU GMO regulation before the World Trade Organisation in 2003, discussed in Chapter 7
below.

## 7 Conclusions

The importance of technical contributions to environmental decisions, including for current purposes the natural sciences and specialist bureaucratic techniques such as risk assessment and cost benefit analysis, is undeniable. There is,
however, an increasing recognition that environmental decisions are not purely
technical, but are based on important political values. A very common response
to this recognition is to urge deliberation among decision makers, together with
broad public involvement in environmental decision making.

The profound tension that exists between the technical and the more evaluative approaches to environmental law is a theme that will recur throughout this
book. *GM Nation?* was an experiment in incorporating a range of different perspectives on a topic that historically would have been subject to closed and
'expert' fora of decision making. However, quite what should be done with
the information received is problematic. Evidence from an apparently neutral,
objective elite is very attractive to politicians faced with polarised public opinion
and controversial evidence. And the law no less than the politicians tends to prefer
the apparent objectivity of science or economics: *Pfizer* (Chapter 1, pp. 30–1)

---

[31] Bayer CropScience Press Release, 31 March 2004.

is one indication of that, an issue we will revisit in Chapter 5. We should also note that the Environmental Protection Act 1990 provides that the purpose of legislation on GMOs is to ensure 'that all appropriate measures are taken to avoid damage to the environment which may arise from escape or release from human control of genetically modified organisms'.[32] In a decision in which an organic farmer successfully challenged a decision to allow a trial planting of a GM crop near his farm, the Court of Appeal nevertheless held that the Minister had no power to order the destruction of the crop: 'the only power the Minister has to require destruction of the crop before flowering is that provided by section 111(10). But that power can only be properly exercised in pursuance of the 1990 Act purposes – i.e. with regard to considerations of health and safety and the protection of the environment.'[33] This gives some indication of how the narrow legal basis for a decision might limit the range of considerations taken into account by a decision maker, discounting the nuances of public concern on GMOs.

## 8 Further reading

More readings on GMOs may be found following Chapters 5 and 8.

For an insight into GMOs from the perspective of some of the debates outlined in Chapter 1, see Jane Holder, 'New Age: Rediscovering Natural Law' (2000) 53 *Current Legal Problems* 151.

Julia Black, 'Regulation as Facilitation: Negotiating the Genetic Revolution' (1998) 61 *Modern Law Review* 621, emphasises the difficulties of regulating in this area, looking to the role of the regulator as facilitator rather than director.

There are some useful websites in this fast-changing and highly controversial area. The UK government website is useful, and contains links to the GM dialogue: www.defra.gov.uk/environment/gm/index.htm. For a more polemical website, see www.genewatch.org/.

---

[32] Environmental Protection Act 1990, s. 106(1), as amended by Genetically Modified Organisms (Deliberate Release) Regulations 2002, regulation 3(2).

[33] *R* v. *Secretary of State for the Environment and MAFF, ex parte Watson* [1999] Env LR 310, p. 319.

**3**

# Public Participation in Environmental Decision Making

## 1 Introduction

Recent decades have seen the emergence of a very widespread consensus that 'public participation' is a crucial element of good and democratically legitimate environmental decision making. Consensus around public participation can be seen at every level, international, regional, national and local. In Chapter 1, we discussed the public *values* inherent in an environmental decision, which mean that 'experts' have no monopoly on judgment. Public participation in decision making is very often put forward as a way through the tension between technical and popular input into decisions, and has become a conventional element of any discussion of 'good governance' for the environment. In the words of Sherry Arnstein, 'The idea of citizen participation is a little like eating spinach: no one is against it in principle because it is good for you.'[1] Notwithstanding agreement on its desirability, however, the precise meaning of 'public participation' remains unclear. We might include the most basic form of political participation, voting in elections; this can be contrasted with highly visible unofficial forms of participation, such as mass public demonstrations, protests and civil disobedience. Sherry Arnstein's famous 'ladder' of citizen participation considers different levels of participation between these two possibilities.[2]

### Sherry R. Arnstein, 'A Ladder of Citizen Participation' (1969) 36 *Journal of American Planning Association* 216, p. 217

The bottom rungs of the ladder are (1) *Manipulation* and (2) *Therapy*. These two rungs describe levels of 'non-participation' that have been contrived by some to substitute for genuine participation. Their real objective is not to enable people to participate in planning or conducting programs, but to enable powerholders to 'educate' or 'cure' the participants. Rungs 3 and 4 progress to levels of 'tokenism' that allow the have-nots to hear and to have a voice: (3) *Informing* and (4) *Consultation*. When they are proffered by powerholders as the total extent of participation, citizens may indeed hear and be heard. But under these

---

[1] Sherry R. Arnstein, 'A Ladder of Citizen Participation' (1969) 36 *Journal of American Planning Association* 216, p. 216.

[2] Consider also how this 'ladder' applies in the planning system, Ch. 13.

conditions they lack the power to insure that their views will be *heeded* by the powerful. When participation is restricted to these levels, there is no followthrough, no 'muscle', hence no assurance of changing the status quo. Rung (5) *Placation* is simply a higher level tokenism because the ground rules allow have-nots to advise, but retain for the powerholders the continued right to decide.

Further up the ladder are levels of citizen power with increasing degrees of decision-making clout. Citizens can enter into a (6) *Partnership* that enables them to negotiate and engage in trade-offs with traditional powerholders. At the topmost rungs, (7) *Delegated Power* and (8) *Citizen Control*, have-not citizens obtain the majority of decision-making seats, or full managerial power.

Obviously, the eight-rung ladder is a simplification, but it helps to illustrate the point that so many have missed – that there are significant gradations of citizen participation. Knowing these gradations makes it possible to cut through the hyperbole to understand the increasingly strident demands for participation from the have-nots as well as the gamut of confusing responses from the powerholders.

It is difficult to pin down a meaning of public participation for all purposes. For current purposes, rather than attempt the thankless task of defining public participation, we take an approach to public participation that looks beyond basic political participation through periodic elections, and involves the three different elements:

- *access to environmental information*, without which any further opportunities for public participation are meaningless;
- tautologously, *public participation* in environmental decision making, which could range from (4) upwards on Arnstein's ladder;
- *access to justice*, addressing the potential for judicial or other dispute resolution or review in respect of an environmental decision.

These three elements of public participation are the three 'pillars' of the high-profile Aarhus Convention, the *Convention on Access to Information, Public Participation in Decision-making and Access to Justice in Environmental Matters* (1998).[3] The Aarhus Convention is the most significant international innovation in this area, and in order to put some flesh on the bones of the current enthusiasm for public participation, its provisions are be discussed in some detail in this chapter: in sections 3, 4 and 5 we examine each of the three pillars of the Aarhus Convention in turn. Rather than examining UK implementation of these pillars, we consider the Convention's embrace by the European Union (EU): ratification 'is a political priority for the Commission'.[4] Binding and enforceable European Community (EC) law has the potential to give the

---

[3]  Available at www.unece.org/env/pp/welcome.html.

[4]  European Commission, *Proposal for a Directive of the European Parliament and the Council Providing for Public Participation in Respect of the Drawing Up of Certain Plans and Programmes*

Aarhus Convention real teeth in the Member States. And although the Aarhus Convention is widely accepted, the detail of participatory arrangements remain controversial, going rather deeply into national democratic arrangements and administrative processes. However, the fact that every Member State of the EU has signed the Aarhus Convention gives Commission proposals on public participation considerable political weight.

Whilst increased participation in environmental decision making is largely welcome, it should not be considered uncritically, and in section 6, we outline some of the main difficulties inherent in a move to public participation. We begin by examining the main rationales for public participation.

## 2 The attractions of public participation

'Public participation' has a firm place in the political and legal mainstream, and is capable of appealing to very different understandings of what is wrong with environmental regulation. Simply put, broader involvement in decision making can be approached from two main perspectives: a *process* perspective and a *substantive* perspective. The latter, an 'instrumental' approach to public participation, rests on arguments that public participation improves the outcome of decision making processes. The former considers participation to be valuable in itself, and this can merge into discussion of the procedural or democratic legitimacy of decision making processes. This division is of course a simplification, albeit useful for illustrative purposes. The two categories overlap, and if, as discussed in Chapter 1, it is accepted that environmental decisions rest on values as well as expertise, taking those decisions without democratic involvement (of course this leaves open a range of options) is untenable in terms of *either* a good decision *or* a good process.

## (a) The process rationale for public participation

The 'process' approach to public participation is often aligned with 'democratic' principles. Although this tells us nothing specific about what participation might involve, beyond perhaps periodic voting in elections, it is a powerful claim.

### John S. Dryzek, *The Politics of the Earth: Environmental Discourses* (Oxford University Press, 1997), pp. 84–5

Ours is a democratic age; it is decidedly unfashionable for anyone, anywhere in the world to proclaim themselves to be anything but a democrat. Francis Fukuyama recently declared that we have arrived at the 'end of history', where there are no plausible global competitors to

*Relating to the Environment and Amending Council Directives 85/337/EEC and 96/61/EC* COM (2000) 839, p. 3.

the basic ideology of liberal democracy in a capitalist economic context.[5] Even military dictators take pains to argue that they are just stabilizing the situation so that democracy can be restored or attained in the fullness of time (of course, they also find ways of making that time a very long one). Thus it is increasingly easy to proclaim one's faith in democracy, just as it is increasingly hard to proclaim one's faith in bureaucracy and administrative rationalism … administration is not necessarily very popular as an ideal; rather, it is just what a lot of people, and a lot of institutions, actually end up doing. Even the people doing it rarely admit to liking it. Democracy is different; everyone wants to be a democrat. Whether they truly are democrats is a different question, made harder to answer by the sheer variety of meanings and models of democracy.

Public participation has the potential to mitigate a range of concerns about the democratic condition of environmental decision making. The relationship between democracy and 'green' politics has historically been difficult:[6] the belief in environmental cataclysm that propels some ecological politics can make authoritarian rule seem like the only realistic solution. Some form of democracy is now largely accepted as the only way of making good and legitimate environmental decisions, but the openness to different values that is normally associated with representative democracy runs into difficulties when faced with a single set of acceptable (environmental) ends. Some respond to this by arguing that environmental constraints should be a part of liberal democracies, much as human rights constraints are.[7] In addition, various 'participative' or 'deliberative' alternatives or supplements to representative democracy have become very influential in the effort to reconcile 'green' thought and democracy. Whilst green outcomes cannot be guaranteed, wide participation in political debate is seen as an important way of allowing the expression of green values,[8] and of ensuring that environmental issues receive attention alongside other priorities.

More prosaically, real-world environmental decisions are frequently taken by a non-majoritarian body, an environmental agency of some description. And yet, as discussed in Chapter 1 (especially pp. 40–7), controversial decisions cannot rest solely on that expertise: value judgments are necessary, perhaps to fill gaps in knowledge, to determine 'acceptable' levels of safety, to distribute the costs and benefits of regulation, to decide on the ethical acceptability of a new technology, to decide between fundamentally divided interests, to decide what 'counts' as an environmental problem or an environmental solution. Rules of openness and involvement are frequently used as a way to mediate between the

---

[5]  Francis Fukuyama, 'The End of History?' [1989] *National Interest* 3; *The End of History and the Last Man* (Free Press, 1992).

[6]  See, however, Andrew Dobson, *Green Political Thought* (Routledge, 2000), pp. 114–24.

[7]  See, for example, the contributions to Brian Doherty and Marius de Geus (eds.), *Democracy and Green Political Thought – Sustainability, Rights and Citizenship* (Routledge, 1996).

[8]  Graham Smith, *Deliberative Democracy and the Environment* (Routledge, 2003).

inescapably political nature of environmental decisions and the delegation of those decisions to unelected experts. This approach to public participation manifests itself in different ways, but is perhaps most familiar from developments in American administrative law in the 1960s.

### Barry Barton, 'Underlying Concepts and Theoretical Issues in Public Participation in Resources Development' in Donald Zillman, Alastair Lucas and George (Rock) Pring (eds.), *Human Rights in Natural Resource Development: Public Participation in the Sustainable Development of Mining and Energy Resources* (Oxford University Press, 2002), pp. 92-6

Much of our public thinking about public participation comes from American pluralist theory. How much it affected American environmental law was explained, and criticized, by Richard Stewart in 1975.[9] The traditional model of administrative law concerned itself with confining regulators to their statutory jurisdiction and ensuring that they exercised their discretion in the ways that the legislature had intended. It controlled the intrusion of government into private affairs; a classically liberal, rule-of-law objective. It conceived of the agency as a mere 'transmission belt' for implementing legislative directives in particular cases, and the court's function was to cabin or contain the agency to the directives that the legislature has issued. This model had to be supplemented by the expertise model in order to accommodate the broad discretionary authority vested in agencies by the New Deal legislation of the 1930s. The courts did not attack that legislation with the traditional kind of judicial review, but, reacting in part to the Administrative Procedure Act of 1946, made new requirements for agency fact base, procedures, and reasoning; and made new use of statements of legislative purpose. The expertise model involved acceptance and judicial supervision of a degree of rational elitism.

In the 1960s, these models came under attack. There were important rights that were not being protected, for instance in the fields of welfare, schools, and prisons. Pluralist political analysis attacked the possibility of an objective basis for social choice, an objective 'public interest'. The exercise of agency discretion was characterized as a process of adjusting the competing claims of various private interests affected by agency policy. Traditionally, that function had been allocated to the legislature. The pluralist view that this was now the function of administrative agencies was widely adopted, and affected legal decision-making considerably. The courts shifted the focus of judicial review so that its dominant purpose was no longer the prevention of unauthorized intrusions on private autonomy, but the assurance of fair representation for all affected interests in the exercise of the legislative power delegated to agencies. The new focus accepted that there could be no ascertainable public interest; legislation and agency decisions simply reflected the compromises struck between competing interest groups ... The obligation to consider all choices and all affected interests found its apotheosis in the judicial implementation of the

---

[9]  Richard Stewart, 'The Reformation of American Administrative Law' (1975) 88 *Harvard Law Review* 1660.

National Environmental Policy Act. But in fact virtually every environmental statute passed in the USA from the 1960s onward contained citizen participation provisions. Administrative law was becoming interest representation.

Stewart criticized this change. It was not self-evident which interests were to be represented, or how. Lawyers and others seeking to represent the 'public interest' are selective and self-interested. Costs and delay would be a problem. It was not clear that agency decisions would be of better quality, no matter what criteria were used. Nor was it clear what standards of judicial review the courts could usefully impose for interest representation purposes. He argued that interest representation could better be achieved by explicitly political mechanisms, such as the popular election of agency officials or legislation requiring the agency to be composed of representatives of different interests. But neither such mechanisms nor a new administrative law could provide a surrogate political process. Nor could they conceal the absence of any broad agreement on appropriate social goals.

How much public participation has pluralist origins comes through clearly in Stewart's account, an account that has dated well. Also clear is the uneasy relationship between the pluralist theory of decision-making and the expertise or rational elitist theory. So too is pluralism's rationale for participation procedures; they are the arena for conflict and trade-off between the competing interests that make up society. The sum of their interests is as close as we can get to any general concept of the public interest. Representation of interests provides all necessary legitimacy and accuracy for agency decisions; the right answer is whatever the calculus of interests says it is. Agencies need not have views of their own. Stewart's critique is valuable where it challenges pluralist assumptions that at first sight seem entirely reasonable, and where it focuses specifically on the law's role in resources and environmental decision-making. To what extent is public participation law being asked to shoulder the burden of balancing interests and values in society that properly should be carried by the legislature?

Nonetheless, the value to environmentalists of pluralism-inspired public participation is also part of the record. Studies show that citizens can restructure power relationships involved in agency decision-making. Pluralist participation is not biased like the rational elitist, or synoptic, model. It has been a great improvement over the days when environmentalists had no say over the disposition of natural resources ...

...

Participatory democracy has been the hallmark of a number of progressive movements, including the environmental movement. The main challenge it faces is to find realistic ways of organizing effective participation in larger groups or political communities.

Without going into the complexities of pluralist theories, this approach to public participation sees it as a form of competition, or sometimes compromise, between the fixed preferences of different interest groups, for example compromise between environmental interest groups and industry. This is a familiar understanding of many established 'consultation' processes. A crucial concept in environmental law, which goes much further, is 'deliberation'.

Deliberative theories often assume that deliberation takes place within existing decision making institutions (Parliament, committees), but deliberation can extend to broader 'public' participation, discussed in this chapter.

### Jenny Steele, 'Participation and Deliberation in Environmental Law: Exploring a Problem-solving Approach' (2001) 21 *Oxford Journal of Legal Studies* 415, pp. 427–8

Real definitions of deliberation are thin on the ground, despite the frequency with which the term is used ... the precise meaning of deliberation is hotly contested. For example, should deliberation only include reasoned arguments, or can it include emotional appeals and rhetoric? Should there be a bar on attempts to coerce an audience? How is the line between coercion and persuasion to be drawn?

In its review of democratic decision-making with regard to risk, the National Research Council of America (NRC) begins the glossary entry for deliberation by describing it as 'Any process for communication and for raising and collectively considering issues.'[10] It continues by stating that 'In deliberation, people discuss, ponder, exchange observations and views, reflect upon information and judgments concerning matters of mutual interest, and attempt to persuade each other.' The NRC review can be taken as an excellent example of a worked through account of the way that deliberation can be made the focal point of real problem-solving processes.

... It should be noted that the description of deliberation encapsulated above is oriented to *collective* discussion. That is to say, although any decision-maker might be able to reflect upon and ponder a broad range of information (and therefore in a sense be loosely referred to as 'deliberating'), deliberation is assumed to involve a collective process. Deliberation is not just about decision-making which 'takes account of' all perspectives, but (ideally) it includes all perspectives in the process itself. Citizens therefore are deliberators; they are not simply called on to inform those with greater expertise in decision-making. There is a crucial difference between this sort of active deliberation by citizens, and expert decision-making on the basis of a broad range of evidence. The idea that citizens have the capacity, through deliberating, to amend their views and expectations is as important here as it is for the liberal models of legitimacy. A certain amount of experience suggests that citizens may indeed be more inclined to revise and alter their views if they are asked to work towards solutions, than if they are simply given an opportunity to speak.

### Dryzek, *The Politics of the Earth*, pp. 94–5

Democratic pragmatism involves talk and written communication, not just strategizing and power-plays, and such communication works best when it is couched in the language of the public interest, rather than private interests. Steven Kelman believes that such talk is not

---

[10]  National Research Council of America, *Understanding Risk* (1996).

cheap, and that people actually internalize public interest motivations.[11] Adolf Gundersen applies this sort of analysis to public deliberation about environmental affairs.[12] Deliberation is necessary for democratic pragmatism to work. Problem solving in democratic pragmatism, recall, is never a matter of individuals acting in isolation or under command from anyone else. Instead, problems always get discussed. Gundersen believes that the very act of discussion or deliberation about issues activates a commitment to environmental values, or, more precisely, 'collective, holistic, and long term thinking'. Long-term thinking might even extend to the wellbeing of future generations, who cannot of course participate directly in current debates ...

The idea that participation in democratic settings activates environmental values is shared by the environmental philosopher Mark Sagoff.[13] Sagoff believes that every individual has two kinds of preferences: as a consumer and as a citizen. These preferences may point in quite different directions for the same individual. His running example concerns the Mineral King Valley in California's Sierra Nevadas, where the Walt Disney Corporation wanted to build a ski resort. Confronting his students with this possibility, it turns out that many of them would enjoy visiting such a resort to ski and enjoy the après-ski nightlife. Few had any interest in backpacking into the existing Mineral King wilderness. But when asked whether they would favor construction of the resort, none did. The answer is that while as consumers they would love to ski there, as citizens they object to wilderness destruction. The implication is that citizen preferences are more concerned with collective, community-oriented values, as opposed to the selfish materialism of consumer values. While one might dispute the degree to which such public-spirited motivation pervades real-world liberal democratic politics, Sagoff's critique of economic reasoning and market rationality as applied to environmental policy is devastating. He also deploys his argument to excuse some of his more disgusting personal habits, notably driving a car that leaks oil everywhere which sports an 'ecology now' bumper sticker (p. 53). The sticker proclaims his citizen preferences, the oil slick under his car his consumer preferences. The citizen in him would like the government to crack down on the consumer in him.

It is not necessary here to go too far into the detail of competing deliberative theories. At the risk of over-simplifying, perhaps the seminal material on deliberation is found in the work of Jürgen Habermas.[14] Reference to his 'communitarian' critique of the 'liberal' view of public life takes us beyond individual (liberal) *rights*, to questions of citizens' duties and the development of public values. This adds an important dimension to 'rights' of public participation in

---

[11]  Steven Kelman, *Making Public Policy: A Hopeful View of American Government* (Basic Books, 1987).

[12]  Adolf Gundersen, *The Environmental Promise of Democratic Deliberation* (University of Wisconsin Press, 1995).

[13]  Mark Sagoff, *The Economy of the Earth: Philosophy, Law and the Environment* (Cambridge University Press, 1988).

[14]  Especially Jürgen Habermas, *Between Facts and Norms: Contributions to a Discourse Theory of Law and Democracy* (MIT Press, 1996). We should also note here the American tradition of civic republicanism, represented in this book particularly by Mark Sagoff.

the environmental sphere. It reminds us that 'deliberation' should be contrasted with models that use 'consultation' primarily to provide information for decision makers. Deliberation moves beyond competition, bargaining and compromise between different interests. As well as bringing public values to the attention of decision makers, 'deliberation' assumes that the political process shapes and determines those values, which emerge from debate and discussion. Values are developed through reason and reflection, unlike pre-formed private preferences or interests. This is potentially progressive, with real attractions from an environmental perspective. Whether public-serving, selfless processes are in fact possible is, not surprisingly, controversial.[15]

### (b) The substantive rationale for public participation

The 'substantive' rationale for public participation focusses on the quality of the outcome of decision making, on substance. The type of public participation remains undetermined, and can be limited to traditional representative democracy, or extended to consultation processes and beyond.

### Dryzek, *The Politics of the Earth*, pp. 84–92

In this chapter I will treat democracy not as a set of institutions (elections, parliaments, parties, etc.), but rather as a way of apprehending problems. I will be concerned with democracy as a problem-solving discourse, which means it is reconciled to the basic status quo of liberal capitalism. Other discourses of democracy do exist, some of which challenge this status quo, advocating for example radical participatory alternatives to established institutions ... for the moment it is appropriate to focus on what I call democratic pragmatism, which involves more or less democratic problem solving constrained by the structural status quo. For this is indeed the version of democracy which dominates today's world, especially after the revolutions of 1989 destroyed the credibility of some Marxist alternatives.

Democratic pragmatism may be characterized in terms of interactive problem solving within the basic institutional structure of liberal capitalist democracy. The word 'pragmatism' can have two connotations here, both of which I intend. The first is the way the word is used in everyday language, as signifying a practical, realistic orientation to the world, the opposite of starry-eyed idealism.[16] The second refers to a school of thought in philosophy, associated with names such as William James, Charles Peirce, and John Dewey. To these pragmatist philosophers, life is mostly about solving problems in a world full of uncertainty. The most rational approach to problem solving, in life as in science, involves learning through experimentation. For problems of any degree of complexity, the relevant knowledge cannot be centralized in the hands of any individual or any administrative state structure. Thus problem solving should be a flexible

---

[15] See, for example, Cass R. Sunstein, 'Deliberative Trouble? Why Groups Go To Extremes' (2000) 110 *Yale Law Journal* 71; Damian Chalmers, 'The Reconstitution of European Public Spheres' (2003) 9 *European Law Journal* 127.

[16] One connotation I do not intend is that pragmatism is anti-theoretical. Pragmatists still have to think! [Footnote in original.]

process involving many voices, and cooperation across a plurality of perspectives. As long as this plurality is achieved, there is no need for more widespread public participation in problem solving. So the degree of democratic participation with which pragmatists are happy corresponds roughly to the limited amount found in existing liberal democracies, and this is why there is an essential congruence between the demands of rationality in social problems and democratic values, a happy coincidence indeed!

Pragmatist philosophy has recently received an explicit environmental twist with the arrival of 'environmental pragmatism', which takes its bearings from philosophical debates in the field of environmental ethics. Environmental pragmatism does battle with all attempts to propose moral absolutes to guide environmental affairs, which are treated instead as ripe for tentative problem-solving efforts in which a plurality of moral perspectives is always relevant ...

It should be emphasized that democratic pragmatism does not have to proceed within the formal institutional structure of liberal democracy; that is, it does not have to involve debate in legislatures. This style of problem solving can also be found within administrative structures, in negotiations between parties to a legal dispute, in international negotiations, in informal networks, and elsewhere.

...

Democratic pragmatism describes an orientation to governing in its entirety ... This orientation stresses interactive problem solving involving participants from both within government and outside it. Such interaction can occur in the context of committee meetings, legislative debate, hearings, public addresses, legal disputes, rule-making, project development, media investigations, and policy implementation and enforcement; it can involve lobbying, arguing, advising, strategizing, bargaining, informing, publishing, exposing, deceiving, image-building, insulting, and questioning. In this light, the real stuff of liberal democratic government is not to be found in constitutions and formal divisions of responsibility. Rather, it is to be found in interactions that are only loosely constrained by formal rules. Quiet conversations in the bar may matter as much as speeches to parliament.

Public participation is thought to have the potential to improve the quality of decisions in a number of ways. At its simplest, providing the decision maker with information from a wide range of participants increases the information available, allowing access to otherwise dispersed expertise.

### Steele, 'Participation and Deliberation in Environmental Law', pp. 437–8

There are a number of things which citizens might offer to the decision-making process. One of these can be summarised as 'situated knowledge'. Those who are closest to a problem and its effects may in certain respects have derived a greater understanding of that problem than those ordinarily required to resolve it. This might be expected to be the case with citizens who can be referred to as 'affected parties' – the people who will feel the effects of environmental problems most closely. However, other groups may provide the opposite and complementary virtue, of breadth of reflection. These could be referred to as 'interested' parties. 'Interested' parties are often those who have reflected broadly about a particular set of problems, such as conservation or biodiversity, including non-governmental action groups such as environmental groups. So 'interested' and 'affected' parties are important components of the deliberating group, with almost opposing virtues to offer.

Furthermore, it is argued that dissenting views should be carefully considered where any claim to 'knowledge' is asserted, particularly in an area where there are many uncertainties. Scientific claims are increasingly debated in the public realm, and citizens are supposedly more able to gain access to information on the basis of which knowledge-claims can be asserted and questioned. It has been argued that civil society is thus increasingly well informed, and citizens increasingly aware that the claims of science are disputable. There is some difficulty with this claim, not least that scientific claims could equally well be seen as becoming increasingly closely associated with the industries which promote development, as those industries pay for more of the research. One suggestion here is that the public through its very scepticism and willingness to question scientific claims, may provide important decision-making resources in respect of information, where those with responsibility for decisions choose to recognise this.

The range of potential 'solutions' may also be extended by opening deliberation to citizens. This is partly, again, because those closest to a problem may be able to see potential solutions which would be overlooked by those who are more remote. This could be especially valuable where decisions are to be taken which are likely to have a strong local impact. But solutions may also be imagined by 'interested groups', as defined above, which look across categories of problem and decision and beyond the interests of the parties who have most to gain from the easiest solutions. In other words, interested groups might extend the parameters of the imagined or tabled solutions. If the question is about the right kind of transport, the answer may prove to be about increased local facilities and both reduced transport time, and reduced social inequality, for example. This is an answer which was not envisaged in the framing of the question. Discursiveness is therefore important.

Finally, it has already been argued at a number of points above that citizens have a crucial role in providing judgements as to 'value'. How to value elements of environmental issues, including the effects of risk (chance) and long-term or non-human effects, is a constant theme of environmental decision-making, and provides one of the most important reasons for suggesting that citizen involvement is particularly significant. No matter how great the expertise applied to a particular problem, risk acceptability is a matter of opinion. Experts are frequently bewildered by the public's response to remote and uncertain risks in particular. While there is no doubt some scope for the kind of 'public education programme' which sets out to 'help' us to put such risks in perspective (a distinctly top-down activity), it is a mistake to think that a 'science' of risk-taking can in any sense exclude value. Strong reactions to remote risks need not be irrational, but might reflect strong views either about the content of the risk (what is risked), or about the value of what is to be *gained* from the risk-taking – for example, is it agreed that nuclear power, or genetically-modified crops, have great advantages to be weighed against their risks, as is urged? On many recent occasions, strong expressions of public opinion have been felt after the event of decision-making, especially as regards health and other toxic effects. Early involvement is often urged not only to improve decision-making, but occasionally also to temper the public response.

Jenny Steele argues that participation should go beyond the eliciting of information, to deliberation between citizens. She argues that deliberation, as well as contributing to the legitimacy of decisions, can contribute to problem solving, hence that deliberation has substantive as well as process rationales.

The *substantive* approach to public participation involves better decisions, but also better outcomes, following the decisions. This has extra resonance in environmental law, given the necessary public involvement in solutions. For example, any progressive effort to address the contemporary 'waste mountain' requires public participation in separating waste for reuse and recycling and reducing waste production. It is often suggested that implementation may be enhanced by participation in setting policy, creating a sense of ownership and responsibility that encourages thoughtful environmental behaviour. Similarly, communities will need to host waste management facilities. Public participation on the role, siting and regulation of these facilities may contribute to their acceptability. In a slightly different vein, regulation scholars often see third party involvement and transparency as a way to keep regulators on the straight and narrow, again potentially improving outcomes.[17] Aspects of public participation, especially access to information, might have a similar effect on industry, which makes its environmental decisions knowing that their impact will be made public.

If public participation in environmental decisions is justified by instrumental criteria, its effectiveness should be susceptible to testing by outcome. This is not likely to be straightforward. Testing the quality of decisions assumes first of all that there is some level of consensus as to the objectives of any decision, and so what constitutes a good outcome. Even if the aim of the decision is simply the most environmentally benign outcome, there may be legitimate disagreement about what environmental protection requires. Trade-offs within environmental protection are common, and different ideas of what would be prioritised by 'true' environmental protection would lead to different measurements of 'good' decisions. So, for example, wind-generated energy might reduce the negative environmental effects of fossil fuels, but wind turbines can have negative effects on landscape and bird populations. Nor does hindsight necessarily make judgment of even uncontroversial objectives a great deal easier: a bad outcome does not necessarily mean that a decision was wrong; the question of 'acceptable' risk is only marginally less controversial retrospectively than prospectively.[18] Moreover, a 'good' decision will inevitably incorporate other facets of the public interest alongside environmental protection. The quality of any particular decision is a normative question, rather than a simple empirical inquiry. Revisiting and re-assessing decisions and the ways in which they were reached is an important part of environmental learning, but is likely to be contentious.

---

[17] See, for example, Ian Ayres and John Braithwaite, *Responsive Regulation* (Oxford University Press, 1992).

[18] Jenny Steele, 'Participation and Deliberation in Environmental Law: Exploring a Problem-solving Approach' (2001) 21 *Oxford Journal of Legal Studies* 415.

## (c) The Aarhus Convention

Public participation responds to diverse concerns about the quality and legitimacy of environmental decision making, and its aims in particular cases are rarely fully spelt out. The different arguments in favour of increasing participation are rather persuasive, perhaps particularly when considered cumulatively. Nor are they mutually exclusive: the complex, normative and political nature of environmental decisions means that public involvement at some level (representative democracy may suffice) is a necessary component of *both* good *and* legitimate decisions. However, the more specific purposes of public participation may be important in some cases. In particular, if it is convincingly established that participation does not improve outcomes, participation becomes dispensable from a purely substantive approach to its desirability. The costs and time required for adequate public participation (resources that might otherwise be more directly put into environmental protection) mean that the benefits of public participation would need to be clear. A substantive rationale for public participation might also suggest more limited public involvement than a process ambition, as it would tend to concentrate on the articulate and well-informed, those most able to help decision makers. For as long as environmental issues receive 'special' treatment relative to other government decisions, and notwithstanding certain distinctive elements to 'environmental democracy' (above, p. 88), it seems likely that the substantive claims will be foremost.

The Aarhus Convention is the most detailed and far-reaching international development in public participation to date, with forty signatories, including the EU and all its Member States.[19] The Aarhus Convention is a Treaty of the United Nations Economic Commission for Europe (UNECE), one of five United Nations regional commissions, but is open to *any* member of the United Nations.[20]

The Aarhus Convention rests on a basic expectation of extensive involvement in environmental decision making at all levels. It is, however, ambiguous in its objectives, with the recitals recognising diverse, although related, motivations.

### Aarhus Convention

The Parties to this Convention,
*Recalling* principle 1 of the Stockholm Declaration on the Human Environment,
*Recalling* also principle 10 of the Rio Declaration on Environment and Development,[21]
...

*Recognizing* also that every person has the right to live in an environment adequate to his or her health and well-being, and the duty, both individually and in association with others, to protect and improve the environment for the benefit of present and future generations,

---

[19] September 2006, see www.unece.org/env/pp/ctreaty.htm.    [20] Article 17(3).    [21] See Ch. 6.

*Considering* that, to be able to assert this right and observe this duty, citizens must have access to information, be entitled to participate in decision-making and have access to justice in environmental matters, and acknowledging in this regard that citizens may need assistance in order to exercise their rights,

*Recognizing* that, in the field of the environment, improved access to information and public participation in decision-making enhance the quality and the implementation of decisions, contribute to public awareness of environmental issues, give the public the opportunity to express its concerns and enable public authorities to take due account of such concerns,

*Aiming* thereby to further the accountability of and transparency in decision-making and to strengthen public support for decisions on the environment,

*Recognizing* the desirability of transparency in all branches of government and inviting legislative bodies to implement the principles of this Convention in their proceedings,

*Recognizing* also that the public needs to be aware of the procedures for participation in environmental decision-making, have free access to them and know how to use them,

*Recognizing* further the importance of the respective roles that individual citizens, non-governmental organizations and the private sector can play in environmental protection,

*Desiring* to promote environmental education to further the understanding of the environment and sustainable development and to encourage widespread public awareness of, and participation in, decisions affecting the environment and sustainable development,

*Noting*, in this context, the importance of making use of the media and of electronic or other, future forms of communication,

*Recognizing* the importance of fully integrating environmental considerations in governmental decision-making and the consequent need for public authorities to be in possession of accurate, comprehensive and up-to-date environmental information,

*Acknowledging* that public authorities hold environmental information in the public interest,

*Concerned* that effective judicial mechanisms should be accessible to the public, including organizations, so that its legitimate interests are protected and the law is enforced,

*Noting* the importance of adequate product information being provided to consumers to enable them to make informed environmental choices,

*Recognizing* the concern of the public about the deliberate release of genetically modified organisms into the environment and the need for increased transparency and greater public participation in decision-making in this field,

*Convinced* that the implementation of this Convention will contribute to strengthening democracy in the region of the United Nations Economic Commission for Europe (ECE),

...

Have agreed as follows:

**Article 1**

**OBJECTIVE**

In order to contribute to the protection of the right of every person of present and future generations to live in an environment adequate to his or her health and well-being, each Party shall guarantee the rights of access to information, public participation in decision-making, and access to justice in environmental matters in accordance with the provisions of this Convention.

Although the Aarhus Convention has mixed motives, perhaps the clearest and strongest link is with improving environmental protection. The pursuit of a 'better' decision *simpliciter* leaves the level of environmental protection open-ended, but in the Aarhus Convention, the understanding seems to be that public participation actually leads to more environmentally benign decisions. As discussed above, this is not a straightforward objective, given competing conceptions of 'the' environment and necessary trade-offs between different forms of environmental harm and benefit, as well as the background of scientific uncertainty. And it is by no means clear that general public involvement will prioritise long-term environmental protection over short-term economic benefits. Whilst the popular image is of public enthusiasm moving ahead of resistant experts and policy makers, climate change was until recently one example of concerned scientists faced with an unconcerned or resigned population. Public participation cuts both ways. The involvement of environmental interest groups is probably crucial in any effort to use participation to enhance levels of environmental protection, and indeed the distinct role for environmental interest groups is perhaps the most significant innovation of the Convention.

### Aarhus Convention, Art. 2

4. 'The public' means one or more natural or legal persons, and, in accordance with national legislation or practice, their associations, organizations or groups;
5. 'The public concerned' means the public affected or likely to be affected by, or having an interest in, the environmental decision-making; for the purposes of this definition, non-governmental organizations promoting environmental protection and meeting any requirements under national law shall be deemed to have an interest.

The Aarhus Convention pays little heed to mechanisms by which the more 'ordinary' public might be involved in decisions, which is likely to require much thought and effort in many cases. The contribution of the Aarhus Convention to 'strengthening democracy' (in the final recital – above, p. 98) in any familiar sense depends largely on national practice towards individual members of the public.

Article 1 of the Aarhus Convention draws links between human rights and public participation. Placing environmental issues on the solid foundations of individual rights is a long-standing objective of many environmentalists. As both an anthropocentric and an individualistic concept, however, the ability of human rights *directly* to protect either the collective good in the environment, or the environment itself, is open to question. Putting in place substantive rights to environmental quality is anyway problematic, and in particular the definition of environmental quality involves difficult questions of prioritisation between different environmental goods, and between environmental protection and other public goods. As a result, it is now reasonably familiar to see human rights in the environmental field focussing on procedural rights,[22] and the Aarhus Convention fits this pattern. The matching of 'rights' with 'duties', as in the recitals to the Aarhus Convention, is also particularly appropriate in the environmental sphere, where individual choices can have a significant impact on outcomes. In this respect, the rights in the Aarhus Convention have the potential to enhance active environmental citizenship, enabling both contribution to public debate, and environmentally responsible private decisions. Talk of rights in the Aarhus Convention seems to be mainly a substantive claim on participation: the rights are an instrument by which to enhance environmental quality.

### (d) Why participation?

This section has attempted to draw out some of the possible (and usually unstated) justifications or objectives of public participation in environmental decision making. We have by no means exhausted the possibilities. For example, in Chapters 9 and 11, we will discuss reflexive regulation, an approach to environmental regulation that relies on the stimulation of information production and disclosure, as in the Aarhus Convention. And deliberative theories beyond the environmental sphere emphasise the 'consciousness raising' aspects of public involvement, the stimulation of a strong public forum; in an environmental context, there may be an expectation that the general public will become more environmentally aware.

We should conclude by noting that the EU has embraced the rhetoric of participation in environmental law with much enthusiasm; the rationales for public participation discussed here have added resonance at that level. So, for example, public participation is perceived to add legitimacy to decision making, and to provide a connection with the European peoples at a time of great concern about the 'democratic deficit' in the EU. And the 'implementation deficit' (see Chapter 10, p. 403) in EC environmental law emphasises the substantive appeal of public participation in decision making; the instrumental benefits of third parties in ensuring the effectiveness of the law has very deep roots in EU law: 'the vigilance of individuals concerned to protect their rights' was appropriated to the supervision of the national application of EC law in the EEC's early days.[23] Whilst these roots are concerned with litigation, an instrumental understanding of the role of the 'people' extends relatively easily into access to information and public participation, allowing outsiders to monitor and influence regulators and regulated.

---

[22] See, for example, one of the seminal decisions of the European Court of Human Rights in the environmental sphere, *Guerra* v. *Italy* (1998) 26 EHRR 357, which linked the provision of information with the right to a private and family life; access to information is also linked with the right to life, see *Öneryildiz* v. *Turkey* (2005) 41 EHRR 20.

[23] Case 26/62 *Van Gend en Loos* [1963] ECR 1, p. 13.

In the following three sections of this chapter we examine the three 'access principles' found in the Aarhus Convention in turn: access to information, public participation and access to justice.

## 3. Access to environmental information

Access to information is a crucial element of a democratic society, a precondition of basic rights to vote or to free speech, and certainly of any form of participation in decision making. In the UK, rights of access to information were pioneered in the environmental arena. Access to environmental information was introduced (following an EC directive) when government was still suffused by an expectation of secrecy; even now, after the Freedom of Information Act 2000, environmental information is subject to more generous access arrangements than other information under the Environmental Information Regulations.[24] In these circumstances, we should think carefully about the role of access to information in this area in particular. Access to environmental information is the necessary starting point for any public involvement in decisions. It is also the basis of formal (for example private prosecution or civil claims) enforcement opportunities enjoyed by the public; informally, open access to information can embarrass both polluters and public regulators, contributing to environmental probity. There is also frequently an educational, awareness-raising element to access to environmental information, for example in the positive promotion of environmentally more benign choices, such as energy saving or waste reduction measures.

Access to information is the 'hardest' and most detailed element of the Aarhus Convention, contained in Articles 4 and 5.

### Aarhus Convention, Art. 4

1. Each Party shall ensure that, subject to the following paragraphs of this article, public authorities, in response to a request for environmental information, make such information available to the public, within the framework of national legislation, including, where requested and subject to subparagraph (b) below, copies of the actual documentation containing or comprising such information:

   (a) Without an interest having to be stated;

   (b) In the form requested unless:

      (i) It is reasonable for the public authority to make it available in another form, in which case reasons shall be given for making it available in that form; or

      (ii) The information is already publicly available in another form.

2. The environmental information referred to in paragraph 1 above shall be made available as soon as possible and at the latest within one month after the request has been submitted, unless the volume and the complexity of the information justify an extension of this period up to two months after the request. The applicant shall be informed of any extension and of the reasons justifying it.

---

[24] SI 2004 No. 3391.

EC Access to Environmental Information Directive 2003/04 (the 'Directive')[25] implements the Aarhus Convention in respect of rights to information held by public authorities in the Member States, replacing an earlier directive on the subject. This Directive, like the Aarhus Convention, provides a basic right of access to 'environmental information' held by a 'public authority', without an interest having to be stated. For as long as 'environmental information' is subject to greater transparency than other government information, its definition is of considerable practical importance.

### Aarhus Convention, Art. 2

3. 'Environmental information' means any information in written, visual, aural, electronic or any other material form on:

    (a)   The state of elements of the environment, such as air and atmosphere, water, soil, land, landscape and natural sites, biological diversity and its components, including genetically modified organisms, and the interaction among these elements;

    (b)   Factors, such as substances, energy, noise and radiation, and activities or measures, including administrative measures, environmental agreements, policies, legislation, plans and programmes, affecting or likely to affect the elements of the environment within the scope of subparagraph (a) above, and cost-benefit and other economic analyses and assumptions used in environmental decision-making;

    (c)   The state of human health and safety, conditions of human life, cultural sites and built structures, inasmuch as they are or may be affected by the state of the elements of the environment or, through these elements, by the factors, activities or measures referred to in subparagraph (b) above.

This is a broad definition. For example, it recognises the importance of administrative techniques of environmental decision making, allowing a potentially important insight into the rationales for a decision; and the inclusion of 'environmental agreements' is a potentially crucial transparency component to the increasingly important 'voluntary approach' in environmental policy (discussed in Chapter 11, pp. 437–51). The EC definition of 'environmental information' had to be expanded by the new Directive, in spite of an already broad interpretation by the European Court of Justice (ECJ).[26] It now follows the Aarhus Convention very closely; the language is slightly more expansive in places, including for example explicit reference to 'contamination of the food chain' as an element of 'environmental information'.[27]

As one would expect, the Aarhus Convention contains a number of exceptions to rights of access to environmental information.

---

[25] Directive 2003/04/EC on public access to environmental information OJ 2003 L 41/26.

[26] Case C-321/96 *Mecklenburg* v. *Kreiss Pinneberg der Landrat* [1998] ECR I-3809.

[27] Overturning in this respect Case C-316/01 *Glawischnig* v. *Bundeskanzler* [2003] ECR I-5995 on the 1990 Directive.

## Aarhus Convention, Art. 4

3. A request for environmental information may be refused if:

    (a) The public authority to which the request is addressed does not hold the environmental information requested;

    (b) The request is manifestly unreasonable or formulated in too general a manner; or

    (c) The request concerns material in the course of completion or concerns internal communications of public authorities where such an exemption is provided for in national law or customary practice, taking into account the public interest served by disclosure.

4. A request for environmental information may be refused if the disclosure would adversely affect:

    (a) The confidentiality of the proceedings of public authorities, where such confidentiality is provided for under national law;

    (b) International relations, national defence or public security;

    (c) The course of justice, the ability of a person to receive a fair trial or the ability of a public authority to conduct an enquiry of a criminal or disciplinary nature;

    (d) The confidentiality of commercial and industrial information, where such confidentiality is protected by law in order to protect a legitimate economic interest. Within this framework, information on emissions which is relevant for the protection of the environment shall be disclosed;

    (e) Intellectual property rights;

    (f) The confidentiality of personal data and/or files relating to a natural person where that person has not consented to the disclosure of the information to the public, where such confidentiality is provided for in national law;

    (g) The interests of a third party which has supplied the information requested without that party being under or capable of being put under a legal obligation to do so, and where that party does not consent to the release of the material; or

    (h) The environment to which the information relates, such as the breeding sites of rare species.

The aforementioned grounds for refusal shall be interpreted in a restrictive way, taking into account the public interest served by disclosure and taking into account whether the information requested relates to emissions into the environment.

5. Where a public authority does not hold the environmental information requested, this public authority shall, as promptly as possible, inform the applicant of the public authority to which it believes it is possible to apply for the information requested or transfer the request to that authority and inform the applicant accordingly.

6. Each Party shall ensure that, if information exempted from disclosure under paragraphs 3(c) and 4 above can be separated out without prejudice to the confidentiality of the information exempted, public authorities make available the remainder of the environmental information that has been requested.

7. A refusal of a request shall be in writing if the request was in writing or the applicant so requests. A refusal shall state the reasons for the refusal and give information on access to

the review procedure provided for in accordance with article 9. The refusal shall be made as soon as possible and at the latest within one month, unless the complexity of the information justifies an extension of this period up to two months after the request. The applicant shall be informed of any extension and of the reasons justifying it.

Whilst exceptions are to be expected, the use of exceptions is constrained by the language of the Convention, most obviously by the final paragraph of Art. 4(4). A blanket approach to exceptions would be at least beyond the 'spirit' of the Convention, and there is an obligation to engage in some sort of consideration of the pros and cons of disclosure and confidentiality: exceptions to access are provided not for convenience, but to protect genuinely competing public interests. Again, the Directive follows the Convention closely, with similar categories of exception, all to be interpreted restrictively, and in each case 'the public interest served by disclosure shall be weighed against the interest served by the refusal' (Art. 4(2)). We might note that the UK goes further in this 'proportionality'-type approach to exceptions. The exceptions apply only if 'in all the circumstances of the case, the public interest in maintaining the exception outweighs the public interest in disclosing the information' (Regulation 12(1)(b)); there is also an explicit presumption in favour of disclosure (Regulation 12(2)).

The special treatment of information relating to emissions under Art. 4(4)(d) and the final paragraph of Art. 4(4) may reflect the fact that emissions lose 'their proprietary character' once they are emitted into the environment;[28] there is probably also greater public concern around emissions. This approach to emissions pre-empts any claim, for example, that information on emissions from a chimney or into water would breach 'commercial confidentiality' by allowing competitors to work out what the facility is doing. Going a little further than the Aarhus Convention, the Directive *prohibits* refusal of a request for information relating to emissions into the environment not only in respect of commercial confidentiality, but also in the case of exceptions providing for the confidentiality of the proceedings of public authorities, personal data protection, information provided voluntarily, and protection of the environment to which the information relates (Art. 4(2)). The Directive is simultaneously narrower than the Aarhus Convention, however, containing no obligation to take into account the fact that the information relates to emissions with respect to other exceptions.

As well as the formal exceptions to access, the practicalities of access can limit the actual transparency of information. The Aarhus Convention requires the parties to 'endeavour' to ensure that officials and authorities 'assist and provide guidance to the public in seeking access to information'; and to 'promote environmental education and environmental awareness among the public, especially on how to obtain access to information, to participate in decision-making and to

---

[28] Stephen Stec and Susan Casey-Lefkowitz, *The Aarhus Convention: An Implementation Guide* (United Nations / Economic Commission for Europe, 2000), p. 60.

obtain access to justice in environmental matters' (Art. 3(3)). Charging for access is the most obvious limit to apparently 'open' information, but requests for access clearly have the potential to create considerable administrative cost.

### Aarhus Convention, Art. 4

8. Each Party may allow its public authorities to make a charge for supplying information, but such charge shall not exceed a reasonable amount. Public authorities intending to make such a charge for supplying information shall make available to applicants a schedule of charges which may be levied, indicating the circumstances in which they may be levied or waived and when the supply of information is conditional on the advance payment of such a charge.

Quite what constitutes a 'reasonable amount' is open to question. The full costs of complying with a request for information, taking into account, for example, staff time, could be very high. The ECJ has taken a purposive approach to the question of 'a reasonable cost' ('reasonable amount' in the new Directive):[29]

47 As the Advocate General observed … the purpose of the directive is to confer a right on individuals which assures them freedom of access to information on the environment and to make information effectively available to any natural or legal person at his request, without his or her having to prove an interest. Consequently, any interpretation of what constitutes 'a reasonable cost' of the directive which may have the result that persons are dissuaded from seeking to obtain information or which may restrict their right of access to information must be rejected.

More specifically, 'reasonable' does not authorise Member States to charge 'the entire amount of the costs, in particular indirect ones, actually incurred for the State budget in conducting an information search'.

A more subtle limitation on access to information is in its presentation, for example the presentation of information in a way that only a specialist can understand, or buried in a mass of raw data. Article 4 of the Aarhus Convention is silent on the presentation of information, although when the Convention turns to public participation on particular activities, it goes a little further, as we will see (p. 112). The Directive provides that information has to be 'up to date, accurate and comparable' (Art. 8), but again makes little comment on the presentation of requested information.

The Aarhus Convention as a whole, but most obviously in its information provisions, is centred around public authorities. No right of access is provided in respect of information held by private parties, although Art. 5 contains certain obligations on public authorities to collect information from private parties, as well as provisions on voluntary information disclosure by private parties through management systems and labelling (see Chapter 11,

---

[29] Case C-217/97 *Commission* v. *Germany* [1999] ECR I-5087.

pp. 437–51). Restricting mandatory access to publicly held information is a significant, albeit quite common, limitation on legal rights of access to information, complicated by the changing nature of public responsibilities.

### Aarhus Convention, Art. 2

2. 'Public authority' means:

    (a)  Government at national, regional and other level;

    (b)  Natural or legal persons performing public administrative functions under national law, including specific duties, activities or services in relation to the environment;

    (c)  Any other natural or legal persons having public responsibilities or functions, or providing public services, in relation to the environment, under the control of a body or person falling within subparagraphs (a) or (b) above;

    (d)  The institutions of any regional economic integration organization referred to in article 17 which is a Party to this Convention.

This definition does not include bodies or institutions acting in a judicial or legislative capacity.

As well as government bodies, environmental regulatory agencies are brought clearly within the framework of the Aarhus Convention, avoiding a very obvious gap in rights of access to environmental information. The shift of information to the private sector with the privatisation of formerly governmental activities, for example water and drainage services or power provision, is more difficult. There are genuine variations in a society's conception of what constitutes a 'public' function. Paragraph (c) attempts to ensure that privatisation does not 'take public services or activities out of the realm of public involvement, information and participation'.[30] The EC legislation follows this broad approach.

### Directive 2003/04/EC on public access to environmental information OJ 2003 L 41/26, Art. 2

2. 'Public authority' shall mean:

(a) government or other public administration, including public advisory bodies, at national, regional or local level;

(b) any natural or legal person performing public administrative functions under national law, including specific duties, activities or services in relation to the environment; and

(c) any natural or legal person having public responsibilities or functions, or providing public services, relating to the environment under the control of a body or person falling within (a) or (b).

Member States may provide that this definition shall not include bodies or institutions when acting in a judicial or legislative capacity.

---

[30]  Stec and Casey-Lefkowitz, *The Aarhus Convention*, p. 32.

A broad interpretation of 'public responsibilities or functions' and 'public services' could extend information obligations to bodies such as privatised utilities, or even waste collectors, particularly given the high level of government authority over these sorts of operations. The precise application of access to environmental information is still to be explored.

### Clíona Kimber, 'Understanding Access to Environmental Information: The European Experience' in Tim Jewell and Jenny Steele (eds.), *Law in Environmental Decision Making* (Clarendon Press, 1998), p. 148

... much information held or generated by purely private bodies is not subject to the access to information legislation. This includes information on manufacturing processes, products, or procedures; surveys; reports commissioned or produced by private bodies; any information or results stemming from research and development activities, together with internal communications about proposed decisions or future directions; and a whole range of private records and documents, with the exception of information which private bodies are legally obliged to supply to public or regulatory bodies.

The result is that the many enabling, facilitating, and informing functions which access to information could perform, will not be achieved where decision-making might involve or could benefit from access to these categories of information, and can only be achieved to the much more limited extent with regard to the activities and decisions of these private bodies.

The Directive imposes obligations of access to environmental information on the Member States, but Art. 2(2)(d) of the Aarhus Convention applies its provisions to the EU institutions. This has proved more challenging. The diplomatic origins of international law-making show themselves in the EU's gradual and ongoing move from a culture of secrecy to formal legal obligations of access to Community documents. The value of 'transparency' is recognised by Treaty (Art. 255 EC), and given increasing attention by the EC judiciary, which even uses the language of fundamental rights in respect of access to information.[31] Rules on public access to documents were laid down by Regulation 1049/2001,[32] which provides a right of access, within specified time limits, to documents of the institutions. In order both to implement the Aarhus Convention, and to achieve consistency with Member State obligations in respect of access to environmental information, the Commission proposed that the Regulation be adjusted in respect of 'environmental information',[33] the definition of which for

---

[31]  See, for example, Case C-58/94 *Netherlands* v. *Council* [1996] ECR I-2169.

[32]  Regulation 1049/2001/EC regarding public access to European Parliament, Council and Commission documents OJ 2001 L 145/43.

[33]  European Commission, *Proposal For A Regulation of the European Parliament and of the Council on the Application of the Provisions of the Aarhus Convention on Access to Information, Public Participation in Decision-making and Access to Justice in Environmental Matters to EC Institutions and Bodies* COM (2003) 622 final.

these purposes closely follows the broad approach taken in the Aarhus Convention.[34] The main inconsistency between Regulation and Convention is in the exceptions.

### Regulation 1049/2001/EC regarding public access to European Parliament, Council and Commission documents OJ 2001 L 145/43, Art. 4

1. The institutions shall refuse access to a document where disclosure would undermine the protection of:
   - (a) the public interest as regards:
     - – public security,
     - – defence and military matters,
     - – international relations,
     - – the financial, monetary or economic policy of the Community or a Member State;
   - (b) privacy and the integrity of the individual, in particular in accordance with Community legislation regarding the protection of personal data.

2. The institutions shall refuse access to a document where disclosure would undermine the protection of:
   - – commercial interests of a natural or legal person, including intellectual property,
   - – court proceedings and legal advice,
   - – the purpose of inspections, investigations and audits,

unless there is an overriding public interest in disclosure.

3. Access to a document, drawn up by an institution for internal use or received by an institution, which relates to a matter where the decision has not been taken by the institution, shall be refused if disclosure of the document would seriously undermine the institution's decision-making process, unless there is an overriding public interest in disclosure.

Access to a document containing opinions for internal use as part of deliberations and preliminary consultations within the institution concerned shall be refused even after the decision has been taken if disclosure of the document would seriously undermine the institution's decision-making process, unless there is an overriding public interest in disclosure.

4. As regards third-party documents, the institution shall consult the third party with a view to assessing whether an exception in paragraph 1 or 2 is applicable, unless it is clear that the document shall or shall not be disclosed.

5. A Member State may request the institution not to disclose a document originating from that Member State without its prior agreement.

6. If only parts of the requested document are covered by any of the exceptions, the remaining parts of the document shall be released.

7. The exceptions as laid down in paragraphs 1 to 3 shall only apply for the period during which protection is justified on the basis of the content of the document. The exceptions may apply for a maximum period of 30 years. In the case of documents covered by the exceptions relating to privacy or commercial interests and in the case of sensitive documents, the exceptions may, if necessary, continue to apply after this period.

---

[34] Article 2(1)(e).

These exceptions go beyond the Aarhus Convention in a number of ways. First and most generally, there is no explicit obligation to interpret the exceptions in a restrictive way, although the courts have provided for restrictive interpretation of exceptions.[35] Second, there is no special treatment in respect of emissions. Third, the Aarhus Convention simply contains no exception relating to 'financial, monetary or economic policy'. On a slightly different note, the exception in Art. 4(4)(h) of the Aarhus Convention, aimed at protecting the environment, is not included. And finally, the unlimited nature of the exception in para. 5 is not in line with the Aarhus Convention. The intention of this exception seems to be to allow Member States to maintain their national rules on access to information, avoiding the subversion of the national position through EC law. Given that all Member States have commitments to the Aarhus Convention, not to mention obligations on access to environmental information under EC legislation, the restriction should not cause any practical problems in an environmental context. The Regulation on implementation of the Aarhus Convention at EU level amends Art. 4 of Regulation 1049/2001, and should be compared with Art. 4 of the Aarhus Convention (p. 103):[36]

### Article 6

1. As regards Article 4(2), first and third indents … with the exception of investigations, in particular those concerning possible infringements of Community law, an overriding public interest in disclosure shall be deemed to exist where the information requested relates to emissions into the environment. As regards the other exceptions set out in Article 4 … the grounds for refusal shall be interpreted in a restrictive way, taking into account the public interest served by disclosure and whether the information requested relates to emissions into the environment.
2. In addition to the exceptions set out in Article 4 … Community institutions and bodies may refuse access to environmental information where disclosure of the information would adversely affect the protection of the environment to which the information relates, such as the breeding sites of rare species.

Moving on from the right of access to existing information provided by Art. 4 of the Aarhus Convention, Art. 5 imposes duties on public authorities actively to collect and disseminate environmental information. This requires the establishment of systems to ensure that public authorities possess adequate information, something that is clearly important in any progressive environmental policy. The obligation to disseminate, presenting information to the public rather than requiring them to know what to ask for, is similarly progressive.

[35] See, for example, Case T-211/00 *Kuijer* v. *Council* [2002] ECR II-485; Joined Cases C-74/98 and 189/98P *Netherlands and Van der Wal* v. *Commission* [2002] ECR I-1.
[36] Regulation 1367/2006/EC on the application of the provisions of the Aarhus Convention on access to information, public participation in decision-making and access to justice in environmental matters to community institutions and bodies OJ 2006 L 264/13.

Article 5 of the Aarhus Convention contains 'emergency' provisions on the information to be made available where there is an 'imminent threat to human health or the environment' (Art. 5(1)(c)). A range of information, including legislation, policies, plans and programmes, and other information 'to the extent that the availability of such information in this form would facilitate the application of national law implementing this Convention', is to be made 'progressively' available 'in electronic databases which are easily accessible to the public through public telecommunications networks'. Article 5 also requires the production of 'reports on the state of the environment' (Art. 5(3)(a)), which are to include information on 'the quality of the environment and information on pressures on the environment'. Article 5(7) requires the publication of the background of certain environmental decision making, specifically 'the facts and analyses of facts' that the public authority 'considers relevant and important in framing major environmental policy proposals' (Art. 5(7)(a)). Information on dealings with the public on the Convention rights must be made available (Art. 5(7)(b)), as must 'information on the performance of public functions or the provision of public services relating to the environment by government at all levels' (Art. 5(7)(c)). And finally, the Aarhus Convention, 'where appropriate', also requires parties to establish 'a coherent, nationwide system of pollution inventories or registers' (Art. 5(9)). Before any general right of access to environmental information existed, access to environmental information in the UK had developed in an ad hoc way, through obligations in particular pieces of legislation to maintain registers of authorisations, and perhaps conditions and actual emissions; the Aarhus Convention indicates the need for a more consistent and formal basis.

## 4 Public participation in environmental decision making

The Aarhus Convention provides for public participation in decision making at three stages: 'decisions on specific activities' (Art. 6); 'plans, programmes and policies relating to the environment' (Art. 7); and 'the preparation of executive regulations and/or generally applicable legally binding normative instruments' (Art. 8).

We will begin with the first of these three stages, decisions permitting certain activities listed in Annex I of the Convention (for example activities within the 'mineral industry', 'chemical installations' and 'waste management'), or other activities 'which may have a significant effect on the environment' (Art. 6(1)).

### Aarhus Convention, Art. 6

2. The public concerned shall be informed, either by public notice or individually as appropriate, early in an environmental decision-making procedure, and in an adequate, timely and effective manner, inter alia, of:
    (a)  The proposed activity and the application on which a decision will be taken;
    (b)  The nature of possible decisions or the draft decision;

(c)  The public authority responsible for making the decision;

(d)  The envisaged procedure, including, as and when this information can be provided:

  (i)  The commencement of the procedure;

  (ii)  The opportunities for the public to participate;

  (iii)  The time and venue of any envisaged public hearing;

  (iv)  An indication of the public authority from which relevant information can be obtained and where the relevant information has been deposited for examination by the public;

  (v)  An indication of the relevant public authority or any other official body to which comments or questions can be submitted and of the time schedule for transmittal of comments or questions; and

  (vi)  An indication of what environmental information relevant to the proposed activity is available; and

(e)  The fact that the activity is subject to a national or transboundary environmental impact assessment procedure.

3. The public participation procedures shall include reasonable time-frames for the different phases, allowing sufficient time for informing the public in accordance with paragraph 2 above and for the public to prepare and participate effectively during the environmental decision-making.

4. Each Party shall provide for early public participation, when all options are open and effective public participation can take place.

5. Each Party should, where appropriate, encourage prospective applicants to identify the public concerned, to enter into discussions, and to provide information regarding the objectives of their application before applying for a permit.

…

7. Procedures for public participation shall allow the public to submit, in writing or, as appropriate, at a public hearing or inquiry with the applicant, any comments, information, analyses or opinions that it considers relevant to the proposed activity.

8. Each Party shall ensure that in the decision due account is taken of the outcome of the public participation.

9. Each Party shall ensure that, when the decision has been taken by the public authority, the public is promptly informed of the decision in accordance with the appropriate procedures. Each Party shall make accessible to the public the text of the decision along with the reasons and considerations on which the decision is based.

10. Each Party shall ensure that, when a public authority reconsiders or updates the operating conditions for an activity referred to in paragraph 1, the provisions of paragraphs 2 to 9 of this article are applied mutatis mutandis, and where appropriate.

11. Each Party shall, within the framework of its national law, apply, to the extent feasible and appropriate, provisions of this article to decisions on whether to permit the deliberate release of genetically modified organisms into the environment.


Article 6 provides a fairly detailed framework for public participation. It picks up on what are now reasonably well-established arrangements for environmental assessment in various jurisdictions, and emphasises their participatory elements. In the EU, Art. 6 of the Aarhus Convention has been implemented through amendment of environmental impact assessment (EIA) and integrated pollution prevention and control, discussed in Chapters 14 and 9 respectively. Both pieces of legislation provide an authorisation process for certain activities (broadly consistent with those listed in Annex I of the Aarhus Convention; EIA also covers projects likely to have a significant effect on the environment), and public participation feeds into that process.

The Aarhus Convention does not require signatories to take a particularly challenging approach to public participation. Article 6(7) is the backbone of public participation, and whilst Parties can go further, this is easily satisfied by familiar written consultation mechanisms. There is no suggestion of more active 'deliberative' processes. Article 6(5) is possibly more demanding, but not mandatory.

We mentioned above the absence of detail on the presentation of environmental information under the first pillar of the Aarhus Convention.

### Aarhus Convention, Art. 6

6. Each Party shall require the competent public authorities to give the public concerned access for examination, upon request where so required under national law, free of charge and as soon as it becomes available, to all information relevant to the decision-making referred to in this article that is available at the time of the public participation procedure, without prejudice to the right of Parties to refuse to disclose certain information in accordance with article 4, paragraphs 3 and 4. The relevant information shall include at least, and without prejudice to the provisions of article 4:

 (a) A description of the site and the physical and technical characteristics of the proposed activity, including an estimate of the expected residues and emissions;

 (b) A description of the significant effects of the proposed activity on the environment;

 (c) A description of the measures envisaged to prevent and/or reduce the effects, including emissions;

 (d) A non-technical summary of the above;

 (e) An outline of the main alternatives studied by the applicant; and

 (f) In accordance with national legislation, the main reports and advice issued to the public authority at the time when the public concerned shall be informed in accordance with paragraph 2 above.

Information is never neutral, and the drafting of the non-technical summary in particular increases concern that a process of information provision could be manipulated. However, the obligation to provide information in an accessible form is potentially important, especially if the lay public are to be meaningfully involved.

Public participation on specific projects or activities would not on its own allow full engagement with environmental decision making. Notwithstanding

Art. 6(4), by this late stage of a process participants may be reduced to the role of objectors, reactive to developers' proposals. Public participation in the planning framework that precedes proposals for specific projects or activities should allow a more proactive stance, and more constructive engagement. In particular, a broader range of issues arises at the earlier stage. So, for example, looking at proposals for a particular road building project or waste incinerator is likely to be limited to questions of siting and possibly the detail of operation: the relative role of rail versus road, or of waste minimisation versus waste disposal may be the real issues of concern. Article 7 of the Aarhus Convention attempts to minimise the mismatch between the issues at stake and the issues open for discussion

### Aarhus Convention, Art. 7

Each Party shall make appropriate practical and/or other provisions for the public to participate during the preparation of plans and programmes relating to the environment, within a transparent and fair framework, having provided the necessary information to the public. Within this framework, article 6, paragraphs 3, 4 and 8, shall be applied. The public which may participate shall be identified by the relevant public authority, taking into account the objectives of this Convention.

In the EU, public consultation on plans and programmes is addressed primarily through the strategic environmental assessment (SEA) Directive,[37] which again will be discussed in Chapter 14, pp. 599–601. For current purposes, however, the obligation on the public authority to identify the 'public which may participate' raises obvious concerns about the extent of institutional control over 'public' participation: in particular, familiar and predictable groups may be favoured, and groups with challenging ecological viewpoints could easily be excluded as unhelpful or unconstructive. Nevertheless, in these cases of more strategic decision making, some thought does need to be paid to whose views should be actively sought. The complexity of public participation increases as the scale of the decision expands, and so as one moves further from individual projects, interest intensifies as specific outcomes (the waste incinerator, the airport extension) get closer. So, for example, whilst consultation on the future of waste management is not likely to engage the lay public, interest is sure to be quickened by a leaflet through the letterbox explaining proposals to build a waste incinerator down the road. Public participation should not, from the government perspective, be a passive exercise.

---

[37] Directive 2001/42/EC on the assessment of the effects of certain plans and programmes on the environment OJ 2001 L 197/30. Other directives, for example Directive 2000/60/EC establishing a framework for Community action in the field of water policy OJ 2000 L 327/1, also contain 'planning' provisions including public participation.

The Regulation for the implementation of the Aarhus Convention at EU level provides for:

> early and effective opportunities for the public to participate during the preparation, modification or review of plans or programmes relating to the environment when all options are still open. In particular, where the Commission prepares a proposal for such a plan or programme which is submitted to other Community institutions or bodies for decision, it shall provide for public participation at that preparatory stage. (Art. 9(1))

There is an obligation to take 'due account of the outcome of the public participation', along with a reason-giving requirement (Art. 9(5)).

This Regulation applies only to plans and programmes. The assumption seems to be that decisions in respect of particular activities and projects will not be made at EU level.[38] Certain plans or programmes are excluded from the provision, including financial or budget plans or programmes. Covered plans and programmes are those:

> (i)   which are subject to preparation and, as appropriate, adoption by a Community institution or body; and
>
> (ii)  which are required under legislative, regulatory or administrative provisions; and
>
> (iii) which contribute to, or are likely to have significant effects on, the achievement of the objectives of Community environmental policy, such as laid down in the Sixth Community Environment Action Programme, or in any subsequent general environmental action programme.
>
> General environmental action programmes shall also be considered as plans and programmes relating to the environment. (Art. 2(1)(e))

The Aarhus Convention's provisions on 'policies' are much less demanding than those on 'plans and programmes': 'To the extent appropriate, each Party shall endeavour to provide opportunities for public participation in the preparation of policies relating to the environment' (Art. 7). Rather than leading to legal amendment, this will continue to be a question of ad hoc involvement, as for example in the *GM Nation?* debate, discussed in Chapter 2, which incidentally demonstrates how very demanding such an exercise is. The Aarhus Convention is still less rigorous in respect of 'executive regulations and other generally applicable legally binding rules': Art. 8 requires parties to 'strive to promote effective public participation at an appropriate stage, and while options are still open'.

## 5. Access to justice in environmental matters

The third pillar of the Aarhus Convention imposes obligations in respect of 'access to justice'.

---

[38] Although note EU-level authorisation of genetically modified organisms (GMOs), Ch. 5. The negotiation of the Aarhus Convention's provisions on GMOs was controversial: authorisation of GMOs is not found in Annex 1, but see Art. 6(11), p. 111.

### Carol Harlow, 'Public Law and Popular Justice' (2002) 65 *Modern Law Review* 1, pp. 8–14

The most important strand in forming the modern public interest action is probably the access-to-justice movement. Though its origins are much older, the access-to-justice movement gained momentum in the heady days of the 1970s and has never entirely lost its force. Radical lawyers, practising first in the US and later in Britain, noted with dismay the gaps left unfilled by legal aid systems and saw the inadequacy of legal services as a serious omission in the provision of the welfare state. The strong ideology of community lawyering, manifested in the setting up of community law centres, was important in building a strong bias towards *collective* legal action. This propensity first underlies the representative action, next entices the representative to set in place the opportunity for public interest actions and finally, results in the claim to undertake litigation in their own name.

...

Three further justifications [in addition to 'responsiveness to the client' (users of courts)] are commonly advanced for public interest actions. The first, most commonly advanced by practitioners, is that representative actions are 'efficient', by which is meant that the case will be better presented and easier to adjudicate. As already suggested, this explanation is defective, since it entirely passes over the key question of whether the case should come to court in the first place; in other words, justiciability is assumed ... The second sees the public interest action as an aspect of globalisation, imported with the human rights movement from the practice of international courts and institutions ...

...

Perhaps the strongest theoretical justification for public interest action lies in theories of pluralist and participatory democracy, of the type associated with the name of Robert Dahl. Dahl has spoken of a society in which 'the demos is fully inclusive and where it exercises final control over the agenda of decisions'.[39] As a consequence, high priority is accorded to direct participation in civil society by the citizenry, which operates not only through the constricted medium of political parties but also through a plurality of interest groups. But while it is very widely accepted that campaigning groups play an important part in the political process, this does not necessarily imply a right greater than that of individuals to invoke the law. In the United States, where the policy-making role of the Supreme Court had long been recognised, the idea of interest representation in the courtroom was easily digested during the 1970s and used by radical lawyers to buttress their claims for access to justice for the under-privileged. Widened standing also allowed for the protection of intangible interest, notably the environment, not covered by traditional standing rights. This is the reasoning of Richard Stewart's famous article on the reform of American administrative law. There is a clear link between a democratic right to participate in policy- and rule-making; the right to go to court to protect that right; and the right to participate in the court's decision.

[39] Robert A. Dahl, *Dilemmas of Pluralist Democracy, Autonomy versus Control* (Yale University Press, 1982).

Access to justice has three main elements: 'standing', or *locus standi*, which determines who has formal rights to go to court; more practical questions as to the resources needed to bring an action; and the remedies ('justice') actually provided. The Aarhus Convention has relatively little to say on the final two issues: access to justice under the Convention 'shall provide adequate and effective remedies, including injunctive relief as appropriate, and be fair, equitable, timely and not prohibitively expensive' (Art. 9(4)). The striking limitation on remedies in the UK is in respect of interim relief. If interim relief is not available, for example to prevent a development on ecologically valuable land, the environmental damage may be done even if environmental arguments are eventually successful in court. The grant of interim relief is often subject to the provision by the applicant of financial guarantees, in order to compensate the party submitting to the interim relief if the applicant is ultimately unsuccessful. This is particularly problematic in the environmental field, given the stretched resources of environmental interest groups. For example, in the *Lappel Bank* case,[40] although the ultimate decision would have protected the environmental resource at issue (an internationally important wetland), in the absence of interim relief the site had been destroyed by the time of the decision. A Privy Council decision in respect of an alleged failure to carry out an appropriate environmental assessment of a new dam in Belize brings out some of the main issues, and is an indication of the discretion enjoyed by the courts.

### *Belize Alliance of Conservation Non-Governmental Organisations* v. *Department of the Environment (Interim Injunction)* [2003] 1 WLR 2839

*Lord Walker of Gestingthorpe*

1  Belize is bordered on the north by the Yucatan province of Mexico, on the east by the sea, and on the south and west by Guatemala. In the centre of the country are the Maya Mountains. Their north-western slopes give on to the Macal and Raspaculo river valleys, partly in the Chiquibul National Park. Much of this area is rainforest virtually unaffected by the impact of human activity since the age of the Mayas, about 500 years ago. The area is rich in rare fauna and flora; the mammals (variously classified as vulnerable, threatened or endangered) include jaguars, ocelots, pumas, and tapirs; there is also a rare form of crocodile; the birds include scarlet macaws. The area also contains a number of Mayan sites of great archaeological interest.

2  Belize is not a rich country. Tourism (and especially what is sometimes called eco-tourism) is important to its economy, so that Belize has an economic (as well as a cultural) interest in the preservation of these precious and fragile natural resources. However Belize has an energy problem. Part of its electricity supply is imported from Mexico. Domestic consumers pay exceptionally high rates for electricity. Demand for electricity is growing. Power cuts occur from time to time. There is therefore a public interest in increasing the country's

---

[40]  Case C-44/95 *R* v. *Secretary of State for the Environment, ex parte RSPB* (*Lappel Bank*) [1996] ECR I-3805.

hydroelectric generating capacity, and the Macal River Upstream Storage Facility ('MRUSF') project aims to do that by the construction of a dam and associated works at Chalillo, upstream from the villages of Cristo Rey and the town of San Ignacio.

...

38 In *R* v. *Inspectorate of Pollution, ex parte Greenpeace Ltd* [1994] 1 WLR 570 ... a campaigning organisation was challenging an official decision which, if stayed, would have adverse financial implications for a commercial company (British Nuclear Fuels plc) which was not a party to the proceedings. Brooke J had refused a stay and the Court of Appeal upheld this decision. Glidewell LJ said, at p 574:

> 'At the hearing before Brooke J no offer was made by Greenpeace to give an undertaking as to damages suffered by BNFL should they suffer any; the sort of undertaking that would normally be required if an interlocutory injunction were to be granted. ... '

...

... Some observations of Lord Jauncey of Tullichettle in *R* v. *Secretary of State for the Environment, ex parte RSPB* [*Lappel Bank*] [1997] Env LR 431, 440 are also consistent with the view that an undertaking in damages should normally be required, even in a public law case with environmental implications, if the commercial interests of a third party are engaged.

39 Both sides rightly submitted that (because the range of public law cases is so wide) the court has a wide discretion to take the course which seems most likely to produce a just result (or to put the matter less ambitiously, to minimise the risk of an unjust result). In the context Mr Clayton referred to the well-known decision of the Court of Appeal in *Allen* v. *Jambo Holdings Ltd* [1980] 1 WLR 1252, which has had the result that in England a very large class of litigants (that is, legally assisted persons) are as a matter of course excepted from the need to give a cross-undertaking in damages. However their Lordships (without casting any doubt on the practice initiated by that case) do not think that it can be taken too far. The court is never exempted from the duty to do its best, on interlocutory applications with far-reaching financial implications, to minimise the risk of injustice. In *Allen* v. *Jambo Holdings Ltd* Lord Denning MR said, at p 1257: 'I do not see why a poor plaintiff should be denied a *Mareva* injunction just because he is poor, whereas a rich plaintiff would get it.' On the facts of that case, that was an appropriate comment. But there may be cases where the risk of serious and uncompensated detriment to the defendant cannot be ignored ...

*Arguable case*

40 ... their Lordships have to form some view of the strength or weakness of BACONGO's [Belize Alliance of Conservation Non-Governmental Organisations'] case. That is particularly important where, as here, the grant of an injunction would cause the respondents significant financial loss, and no undertaking in damages has been offered.

...

44 Mr Clayton submitted that BACONGO has a strong case on appeal ... Mr Fitzgerald pointed to the largely concurrent conclusions of Conteh CJ and the Court of Appeal, and described BACONGO's case as risible. Their Lordships certainly do not accept that BACONGO's case is risible. This is a matter of great public concern, involving as it does competition between two

very important public interests. But despite the skill with which Mr Clayton developed his case in the limited time available, it does not appear to their Lordships to be a strong case on which to seek, without an undertaking in damages, an injunction which would halt a major construction project for four months.

### Balance of risk of injustice

45 The dam site is already a very busy construction site. Access roads have been built, large numbers of trees have been felled, and the abutments of the dam have been constructed. If no injunction is granted, the work (restricted by the wet season) will continue until the appeal hearing in December. It will then be further advanced, and the total expenditure incurred will be proportionately greater. But if BACONGO succeeds on appeal, it will be for the Board hearing the appeal to determine what significance (if any) to give to the fact that the work will have been in progress for about six months rather than about two months …

…

47 Their Lordships have concluded that the grant of an injunction at this stage would entail a greater risk of ultimate injustice than its refusal. This dispute cannot fairly be described as a clash between public and private interests. Although BECOL is in the private sector, it is very closely associated in this matter with the government of Belize … and there are public interests of real importance on both sides of the argument. Both courts below have, although for rather different reasons, rejected BACONGO's challenge to the project. Their reasoning and conclusions have not been shown to have been ill-founded. In their Lordships' view this is not a case in which, in the absence of an undertaking in damages, it would be right to halt a major project which is of real importance to the economy of Belize.

If the provision of interim remedies provokes genuine dilemmas of competing justices, the cost of litigation is even more difficult: litigation is frequently not pursued, even in a good case, simply because it would be financially crippling. There are again competing justices – the fear that too easy and risk-free litigation will prejudice innocent defendants. Parties are required under the Aarhus Convention to 'consider the establishment of appropriate assistance mechanisms to remove or reduce financial and other barriers to access to justice' (Art. 9(5)). The funding of litigation is however an extraordinarily sensitive topic, going deep into national welfare states and national legal systems.

The Aarhus Convention has rather more useful things to say on standing. Traditional liberal legal systems have relied on the assertion of individual interests and rights. This rarely captures the collective and diffuse nature of harm to environmental interests: although environmental harms can affect individuals disproportionately or particularly seriously, issues such as chronic air pollution or loss of biodiversity affect large numbers of people in not readily perceptible ways.

The first two paragraphs of the Aarhus Convention's access to justice pillar use access to justice to guarantee the other two pillars.

### Aarhus Convention, Art. 9

1. Each Party shall, within the framework of its national legislation, ensure that any person who considers that his or her request for information under article 4 has been ignored, wrongfully refused, whether in part or in full, inadequately answered, or otherwise not dealt with in accordance with the provisions of that article, has access to a review procedure before a court of law or another independent and impartial body established by law.

In the circumstances where a Party provides for such a review by a court of law, it shall ensure that such a person also has access to an expeditious procedure established by law that is free of charge or inexpensive for reconsideration by a public authority or review by an independent and impartial body other than a court of law. Final decisions under this paragraph 1 shall be binding on the public authority holding the information. Reasons shall be stated in writing, at least where access to information is refused under this paragraph.

The requirement for administrative (as well as judicial) review of access to environmental information is a recognition of the limitations of formal, expensive court proceedings. This innovation is contained also in the EU Directive on access to environmental information, which provides that Member States must provide a procedure under which the act or omission can be 'reconsidered' by the same or another public authority, or 'reviewed administratively by an independent and impartial body established by law', with the possibility for final decisions to be made by a court 'or another independent and impartial body established by law'.[41]

Article 9(2) of the Aarhus Convention provides for review of an 'act or omission subject to the provisions of article 6'. As discussed above (p. 112), the rules on public participation provided by Art. 6 are implemented primarily through amendments to integrated pollution prevention and control and EIA (Chapters 9 and 14); in an effort to pre-empt narrow rules of standing in the Member States, EC legislation has introduced access to justice provisions to these pieces of legislation.

More general provisions on standing in environmental matters are found in Art. 9(3): ' … each Party shall ensure that, where they meet the criteria, if any, laid down in its national law, members of the public have access to administrative or judicial procedures to challenge acts and omissions by private persons and public authorities which contravene provisions of its national law relating to the environment'. This suggests that it is desirable to allow members of the public to take action against both private polluters and public regulators, but access to justice is

---

[41] Article 6. In the UK, the Environmental Information Regulations provide for three tiers of review: internal representation and reconsideration (reg 11); appeal to the Information Commissioner, followed by the Information Tribunal (reg 18). There is then the final possibility of judicial review before the High Court.

strictly limited by reference to national law. We will concentrate on EU-level judicial review here. Because standing has been notoriously restrictive at this level (more so than in English law), it illustrates some of the key issues very nicely.

Article 230 EC provides for claims against the Community institutions. The Member States and institutions are 'privileged' applicants, with absolute access. Ordinary private litigants have a more difficult task.

### EC Treaty, Art. 230

Any natural or legal person may … institute proceedings against a decision addressed to that person or against a decision which, although in the form of a regulation or a decision addressed to another person, is of direct and individual concern to the former.

The interpretation by the European Court of Justice of 'direct and individual concern' excludes most litigation over diffuse interests, paradigmatically environmental protection. 'Direct concern' requires that the Community measure directly affects the legal situation of the litigant, and leaves no discretion to those who have the task of implementing it. More problematically, 'individual concern' has been interpreted as requiring the measure to affect the applicant's position by reason of certain attributes peculiar to it, or by reason of a factual situation which differentiates it from all other persons and distinguishes it individually.[42] The *Greenpeace* case classically illustrates how restrictive this is.[43] Greenpeace, together with local individuals and local groups, attempted to challenge a Commission decision to grant funding to Spain for the construction of two power stations, arguing breach of environmental law. The ECJ applied the conservative interpretation of 'individual concern' outlined above. Greenpeace was denied standing because the members it claimed to represent lacked standing: none of the local residents was affected in a way that distinguished them from 'all the people who live or pursue an activity in the areas concerned'.

Two recent cases for a brief period re-opened the question of 'individual concern'; only for the ECJ ultimately to reaffirm the status quo. *Unión de Pequeños Agricultores (UPA)*[44] involved a challenge to a regulation on the common organisation of the market in oils and fats. In *Jégo-Quéré*,[45] a fishing company applied to the Court for the annulment of provisions requiring certain fishing vessels to use nets with a minimum mesh size. In *UPA*, the Court of First Instance (CFI) held the application to be manifestly inadmissible on the ground that the members of the association were not individually concerned by the provisions of the regulation. Advocate General Jacobs, on appeal to the ECJ, took a more liberal approach to standing, and usefully reviewed the main arguments.

---

[42]  Case 25/62 *Plaumann* v. *Commission* [1962] ECR 207.
[43]  Case T-585/93 *Stichting Greenpeace Council* v. *Commission* [1995] ECR II-2205; Case C-321/95P *Stichting Greenpeace Council* v. *Commission* [1998] ECR I-1651.
[44]  Case C-50/00P *Unión de Pequeños Agricultores* v. *Council* [2002] ECR I-6677.
[45]  Case T-177/01 *Jégo-Quéré et Cie SA* v. *Commission* [2002] ECR II-2365.

### Case C-50/00P *Unión de Pequeños Agricultores* v. *Council* [2002] ECR I-6677, Opinion of Advocate General Jacobs

37. I agree with UPA that the case-law on the *locus standi* of individual applicants is problematic. As I shall suggest below, the fact that an individual cannot (in most cases) challenge directly a measure which adversely affects him, if it is a measure of general application, seems unacceptable for, essentially, two reasons. First, the fourth paragraph of Article 230 EC must be interpreted in such a way that it complies with the principle of effective judicial protection. Proceedings before national courts do not, however, always provide effective judicial protection of individual applicants and may, in some cases, provide no legal protection whatsoever. Secondly, the Court's case-law on the interpretation of the fourth paragraph of Article 230 EC encourages individual applicants to bring issues of validity of Community measures indirectly before the Court of Justice via the national courts. Proceedings brought directly before the Court of First Instance are however more appropriate for determining issues of validity than proceedings before the Court of Justice pursuant to Article 234 EC [the preliminary ruling procedure], and less liable to cause legal uncertainty for individuals and the Community institutions. In addition to those points, it may be argued that the Court's restrictive attitude towards individual applicants is anomalous in the light of its case-law on other aspects of judicial review and recent developments in the administrative laws of the Member States.

*Proceedings before national courts may not provide effective judicial protection of individual applicants*

38. As is common ground in the present case, the case-law of the Court of Justice acknowledges the principle that an individual who considers himself wronged by a measure which deprives him of a right or advantage under Community law must have access to a remedy against that measure and be able to obtain complete judicial protection.

39. That principle is, as the Court has repeatedly stated, grounded in the constitutional traditions common to the Member States and in Articles 6 and 13 of the European Convention on Human Rights. Moreover, the Charter of fundamental rights of the European Union, while itself not legally binding, proclaims a generally recognised principle in stating in Article 47 that '[e]veryone whose rights and freedoms guaranteed by the law of the Union are violated has the right to an effective remedy before a tribunal'.

40. In my view, proceedings before national courts are not, however, capable of guaranteeing that individuals seeking to challenge the validity of Community measures are granted fully effective judicial protection.

41. It may be recalled, first of all, that the national courts are not competent to declare measures of Community law invalid ...

42. ... Access to the Court of Justice via Article 234 EC is however not a remedy available to individual applicants as a matter of right. National courts may refuse to refer questions, and although courts of last instance are obliged to refer under the third paragraph of Article 234 EC, appeals within the national judicial systems are liable to entail long delays which may themselves be incompatible with the principle of effective judicial protection and with the need for legal certainty. National courts – even at the highest level – might also err in their

preliminary assessment of the validity of general Community measures and decline to refer questions of validity to the Court of Justice on that basis. Moreover, where a reference is made, it is in principle for the national court to formulate the questions to be answered by the Court of Justice. Individual applicants might thus find their claims redefined by the questions referred. Questions formulated by national courts might, for example, limit the range of Community measures which an applicant has sought to challenge or the grounds of invalidity on which he has sought to rely.

43. Thirdly, it may be difficult, and in some cases perhaps impossible, for individual applicants to challenge Community measures which – as appears to be the case for the contested regulation – do not require any acts of implementation by national authorities. In that situation, there may be no measure which is capable of forming the basis of an action before national courts. The fact that an individual affected by a Community measure might, in some instances, be able to bring the validity of a Community measure before the national courts by violating the rules laid down by the measures and rely on the invalidity of those rules as a defence in criminal or civil proceedings directed against him does not offer the individual an adequate means of judicial protection. Individuals clearly cannot be required to breach the law in order to gain access to justice.

44. Finally, compared to a direct action before the Court of First Instance, proceedings before the national courts present serious disadvantages for individual applicants. Proceedings in the national courts, with the additional stage of a reference under Article 234 EC, are likely to involve substantial extra delays and costs. The potential for delay inherent in proceedings brought before domestic courts, with the possibility of appeals within the national system, makes it likely that interim measures will be necessary in many cases. However, although national courts have jurisdiction to suspend a national measure based on a Community measure or otherwise to grant interim relief pending a ruling from the Court of Justice, the exercise of that jurisdiction is subject to a number of conditions and is – despite the Court's attempts to provide guidance as to the application of those conditions – to some extent dependent on the discretion of national courts. In any event, interim measures awarded by a national court would be confined to the Member State in question, and applicants might therefore have to bring proceedings in more than one Member State. That would, given the possibility of conflicting decisions by courts in different Member States, prejudice the uniform application of Community law, and in extreme cases could totally subvert it.

…

45. I consider, moreover, that proceedings before the Court of First Instance under Article 230 EC are generally more appropriate for determining issues of validity than reference proceedings under Article 234 EC.

46. The procedure is more appropriate because the institution which adopted the impugned measure is a party to the proceedings from beginning to end and because a direct action involves a full exchange of pleadings, as opposed to a single round of observations followed by oral observations before the Court. The availability of interim relief under Articles 242 and 243 EC, effective in all Member States, is also a major advantage for individual applicants and for the uniformity of Community law.

47. Moreover, where a direct action is brought, the public is informed of the existence of the action by means of a notice published in the Official Journal and third parties may, if they are able to establish a sufficient interest, intervene ...

48. Of even greater importance is the point that it is manifestly desirable for reasons of legal certainty that challenges to the validity of Community acts be brought as soon as possible after their adoption. While direct actions must be brought within the time-limit of two months laid down in the fifth paragraph of Article 230 EC, the validity of Community measures may, in principle, be questioned before the national courts at any point in time ...

...

50. I do not agree with UPA, however, that it follows from that conclusion that an applicant who is not individually concerned within the meaning of the fourth paragraph of Article 230 EC, as that provision has hitherto been interpreted in the case-law, should be granted standing to challenge a regulation where an examination of the particular case reveals that the applicant would otherwise be denied effective judicial protection.

51. First, there is – as the Commission points out – no support for that suggestion in the wording of the fourth paragraph of Article 230 EC ...

52. Secondly, the Treaty confers upon the Community judicature the task of ruling on the interpretation and validity of Community law; it is – as the Court of Justice has repeatedly stated – not competent to rule on the interpretation and validity of national law. For the Community judicature to examine, on a case-by-case basis, the existence in national law of procedures and remedies enabling individual applicants to challenge Community measures would in my view come perilously close to taking on a role not conferred by the Treaty. Moreover, the Community judicature is not well placed to carry out what may in some cases be a complex and time-consuming inquiry into the details of national procedural law. That point is illustrated by the present case where the parties disagree on the applicant's position in Spanish law and where it is difficult, perhaps impossible, to determine on the basis of the information in the file and the arguments presented at the hearing whether the applicant has an alternative remedy in national law.

53. Thirdly, to accept that *locus standi* under the fourth paragraph of Article 230 EC may depend on national law – which is likely to differ as between Member States and to develop over time – would inevitably lead to inequality and a loss of legal certainty in an area of law already marked by considerable complexity ...

...

59. The key to the problem of judicial protection against unlawful Community acts lies therefore, in my view, in the notion of individual concern laid down in the fourth paragraph of Article 230 EC. There are no compelling reasons to read into that notion a requirement that an individual applicant seeking to challenge a general measure must be differentiated from all others affected by it in the same way as an addressee. On that reading, the greater the number of persons affected by a measure the less likely it is that judicial review under the fourth paragraph of Article 230 EC will be made available. The fact that a measure adversely affects a large number of individuals, causing wide-spread rather than limited harm, provides however to my mind a positive reason for accepting a direct challenge by one or more of those individuals.

60. In my opinion, it should therefore be accepted that a person is to be regarded as individually concerned by a Community measure where, by reason of his particular circumstances, the measure has, or is liable to have, a substantial adverse effect on his interests.

*Advantages of the suggested interpretation of the notion of individual concern*

61. A development along those lines of the case-law on the interpretation of Article 230 EC would have several very substantial advantages.

62. First, ... it seems the only way to avoid what may in some cases be a total lack of judicial protection – a *déni de justice.*

63. Secondly, the suggested interpretation of the notion of individual concern would considerably improve judicial protection. By laying down a more generous test for standing for individual applicants than that adopted by the Court in the existing case-law, it would not only ensure that individual applicants who are directly and adversely affected by Community measures are never left without a judicial remedy; it would also allow issues of validity of general measures to be addressed in the context of the procedure which is best suited to resolving them, and in which effective interim relief is available.

64. Thirdly, it would also have the great advantage of providing clarity to a body of case-law which has often, and rightly in my view, been criticised for its complexity and lack of coherence, and which may make it difficult for practitioners to advise in what court to take proceedings, or even lead them to take parallel proceedings in the national courts and the Court of First Instance.

65. Fourthly, by ruling that individual applicants are individually concerned by general measures which affect them adversely, the Court of Justice would encourage the use of direct actions to resolve issues of validity, thus limiting the number of challenges raised via Article 234 EC. That would, as explained above, be beneficial for legal certainty and the uniform application of Community law ...

66. A point of equal, or even greater, importance is that the interpretation of Article 230 EC which I propose would shift the emphasis of judicial review from questions of admissibility to questions of substance. While it may be accepted that the Community legislative process should be protected against undue judicial intervention, such protection can be more properly achieved by the application of substantive standards of judicial review which allow the institutions an appropriate 'margin of appreciation' in the exercise of their powers than by the application of strict rules on admissibility which have the effect of 'blindly' excluding applicants without consideration of the merits of the arguments they put forward.

67. Finally, the suggested interpretation of the notion of individual concern would remove a number of anomalies in the Court's case-law on judicial review. The most important anomalies arise from the fact that the Court has adopted different approaches to the notion of individual concern and to other provisions of Article 173 of the EEC Treaty (now, after amendment, Article 230 EC).

...

75. First, it may be acknowledged that the wording of Article 230 EC sets certain limits which must be respected. All individual applicants do not have standing to challenge all Community acts. However, I do not accept the proposition that the wording of the fourth paragraph of Article 230 EC excludes the Court from re-considering its case-law on individual concern. It

is clear, and cannot be stressed too strongly, that the notion of individual concern is capable of carrying a number of different interpretations, and that when choosing between those interpretations the Court may take account of the purpose of Article 230 EC and the principle of effective judicial protection for individual applicants. In any event, the Court's case-law in other areas acknowledges that an evolutionary interpretation of Article 230 EC is needed in order to fill procedural gaps in the system of remedies laid down by the Treaty and ensure that the scope of judicial protection is extended in response to the growth in the powers of the Community institutions. While that case-law acknowledges that it may even be necessary to depart from the wording of the Treaty to provide effective judicial protection, the Court is not required to take such a step in the present case, since the interpretation I propose is wholly compatible with the wording of the Treaty.

…

77 … To insulate potentially unlawful measures from judicial scrutiny can rarely, if ever, be justified on grounds of administrative or legislative efficiency. That is true in particular where limitations on standing may lead to a complete denial of justice for particular individuals …

…

79 Third, I am not convinced that a relaxation of the requirements for individual concern would result in a deluge of cases which would overwhelm the judicial machinery. There is no record of that having happened in those legal systems, inside and outside the European Union, which have in recent years progressively relaxed their requirements for standing. The instigation of proceedings by an individual pursuant to Article 230 EC is moreover subject to a number of conditions. In addition to individual concern, applicants are required to show direct concern, and actions must be brought within a time-limit of two months. While those conditions have played only a limited role in the case-law in the past, their importance would almost certainly increase in response to a relaxation of the requirement of individual concern. It may be thought that a relaxation of the requirements for standing would therefore result in an increase in the number of applications under the fourth paragraph of Article 230 EC which, though appreciable, would not be insuperable.

This Opinion clearly influenced the Court of First Instance when it made its subsequent decision in *Jégo-Quéré*. The CFI, however, provides a slightly different reinterpretation of 'individual concern' (see para. 60 of the Advocate General's Opinion). According to the CFI, an applicant is individually concerned: 'if the measure in question affects his legal position, in a manner which is both definite and immediate, by restricting his rights or by imposing obligations on him. The number and the position of other persons who are likewise affected by the measure, or who may be so, are of no relevance in that regard' (para. 51).

The intention in both cases was clearly to liberalise standing, and thus individuals would be better able to challenge environmentally harmful decisions. Individuals, however, are not the most obvious litigants in cases of diffuse environmental harm, and the extent to which environmental interest groups would benefit depends upon accepting that they hold rights and interests in the required sense, or alternatively could rely upon the rights or interests of their members.

Notwithstanding the Advocate General's detailed critique of the ECJ's restrictive approach, in *UPA* the Court confirmed its long-standing case law. The ECJ held that it is for the Member States to ensure that there is access to a domestic court (from which a preliminary reference can be made to the ECJ) and that further change would require amendment of the Treaty. In a subsequent case, the European Environmental Bureau (EEB) and other public interest groups challenged the reauthorisation of paraquat, a pesticide. The CFI refused standing to the applicants, citing the cases above.

### T-94/04 *European Environmental Bureau* v. *Commission*, 28 November 2005

48 ... applicants who, as in the present case, are not the addressees of an act may not claim that they are individually concerned by it unless it affects them by reason of certain attributes peculiar to them, or by reason of a factual situation which differentiates them from all other persons and distinguishes them individually in the same way as the addressee of the act would be ...

...

50 ... the applicants claim, first, that they are especially affected by that act due to the serious adverse effects it has on protection of the environment and workers' health, in the form of a setback in the protection of those interests ...

...

53 ... it is clear that [the provisions of the challenged act] affect them in their objective capacity as entities active in the protection of the environment or workers' health, or even as holders of property rights, in the same manner as any other person in the same situation.
54 It is apparent from the case-law that that capacity is not by itself sufficient to establish that the applicants are individually concerned by the contested act ...
55 It follows from the foregoing that the alleged serious adverse effects the contested act has on the applicants' interests and property rights do not establish that they are individually concerned by the contested act.
56 Second, the applicants claim that [they] have special advisory status with the European institutions, ... and that, in accordance with the stated goal in their statutes, some of the applicants specifically requested the Commission not to include paraquat in Annex I to Directive 91/414.
57 ... the fact that a person participates, in one way or another, in the process leading to the adoption of a Community act does not distinguish him individually in relation to the act in question unless the relevant Community legislation has laid down specific procedural guarantees for such a person ...
59 ... Community law, as it now stands, does not provide for standing to bring a class action before the Community courts, as envisaged by the applicants in the present case.
60 Fourth, the applicants maintain that effective judicial protection, as enshrined in Articles 6 and 13 of the ECHR, which is applicable to the Community institutions pursuant to Article 6(2) EU, means that the present action must be declared admissible because, first, proceedings

brought before national courts would be lengthy, complex and costly and, second, those courts are not able to rule on the questions raised in the present proceedings.

61 The Court of Justice has held [in *UPA*] that the right to effective judicial protection is one of the general principles of law stemming from the constitutional traditions common to the Member States and that that right has also been enshrined in Articles 6 and 13 of the ECHR ...

62 In the same judgment, the Court of Justice stated that by Article 230 EC and Article 241 EC, on the one hand, and by Article 234 EC, on the other, the EC Treaty has established a complete system of legal remedies and procedures designed to ensure judicial review of the legality of acts of the institutions, and has entrusted such review to the Community courts. Under that system, where natural or legal persons cannot, by reason of the conditions for admissibility laid down in the fourth paragraph of Article 230 EC, directly challenge Community measures of general application, they are able, depending on the case, either indirectly to plead the invalidity of such acts before the Community courts under Article 241 EC or to do so before the national courts and ask them, since they have no jurisdiction themselves to declare those measures invalid, to make a reference to the Court of Justice for a preliminary ruling on validity ...

63 Lastly, it is apparent from the case-law that the admissibility of an action for annulment before the Community courts does not depend on whether there is a remedy before a national court enabling the validity of the act being challenged to be examined ...

64 It follows that, according to the approach taken in the case-law of the Court of Justice, the argument relating to effective judicial protection put forward by the applicants is not in itself sufficient to justify the admissibility of their action

65 Fifthly, the applicants maintain that their action must be declared admissible by virtue of the principle of equality of arms. Suffice it to note that it is apparent from the case-law that the mere fact that an applicant is affected by an act in a manner opposite to that in which a person entitled to bring an action for annulment of that act is affected is not sufficient to confer standing on that applicant ... In those circumstances, even if the intervener did have standing to bring an action for annulment of the contested act, as the applicants maintain, that fact alone would not establish that the applicants meet the requirement of being individually concerned by the contested act or exempt them from having to prove that they meet that requirement.

That is not quite the end of the story. The Regulation for the implementation of the Aarhus Convention at EU level attempts to enhance the standing of environmental interest groups. Environmental interest groups[46] are given the right to ask a Community institution or body to review internally an administrative act or omission; Art. 12 then provides that 'the non-governmental organisation which made the request for internal review pursuant to Article 10 may institute

---

[46] Article 11 requires 'an independent non-profit making legal person', which has 'the primary stated objective of promoting environmental protection in the context of environmental law', which has existed for more than two years, and is actively pursuing that objective. The subject matter of the request must be covered by its objective and activities.

proceedings before the Court of Justice in accordance with the relevant provisions of the Treaty'. This is designed to open up standing only to environmental interest groups. Whilst this might be justified narrowly by referring to the Aarhus Convention, the complaints of inequality are not difficult to imagine. It is also a ruse – a clever ruse, but the ECJ has said that Treaty amendment (not secondary legislation) is necessary to amend Art. 230. It is not a foregone conclusion that review of the reconsidered decision will open up review of the initial, contested decision. The EEB in the above case argued that the statement of reasons in the Commission's *proposal* for this Regulation was relevant to the admissibility of its claim. Whilst the precise issue of the application of the Regulation is not considered, the CFI 'notes, first, that the principles governing the hierarchy of norms ... preclude secondary legislation from conferring standing on individuals who do not meet the requirements of the fourth paragraph of Article 230 EC'. The statement of reasons in the Commission's proposal 'does not release [the applicants] from having to show that they are individually concerned by the contested act. Moreover, even if the applicants were acknowledged as qualified entities for the purposes of the Aarhus Regulation Proposal, it is clear that they have not put forward any reason why that status would lead to the conclusion that they are individually concerned by the contested act' (paras. 67–8). How the Community Courts will approach the actual Regulation now it has been passed remains to be seen.

There is undoubtedly an assumption in the Aarhus Convention that broad standing is desirable, and restricted access to justice is certainly in tension with the *spirit* of the Convention. Whilst not strictly a question of 'access to justice', disputes under the Convention are revealing: unusually for international environmental law (although less so in human rights treaties) the compliance mechanism under the Aarhus Convention may be triggered by a member of the public, as well as a state Party. Whatever its 'spirit', however, the 'letter' of the Aarhus Convention is limited on access to justice, deferring to national law. This may reflect the fact that access to justice is often the most sensitive of the access principles, evoking concern that excessive litigation will lead to a focus on procedures at the expense of effectiveness, tying up resources better spent on other regulatory activity. Carol Harlow, in the article at the beginning of this section (p. 115), expresses concern that the involvement of interest groups in litigation politicises the judicial process: 'If we allow the campaigning style of politics to invade the legal process, we may end by undermining the very qualities of certainty, finality and especially independence for which the legal process is esteemed' (p. 2).

## 6 The challenges of public participation

Public participation in environmental decision making is on the whole a welcome development. Genuine dilemmas are, however, raised by any claimed move to more participatory (rather than representative) forms of democracy.

The prime concern must be that, paradoxically, 'participation' might actually enhance *exclusion*.

Creating institutions and situations in which meaningful public participation or deliberation can take place is the greatest challenge for those who advocate enhanced public participation in environmental decision making. We should be aware of who is allowed or willing to participate, and how the grounds of the debate might work to exclude some ideas and some people. Exclusion can be direct, by explicitly restricting access to the forum, for example by inviting only certain 'sensible' environmental groups, or only those physically affected by a particular development, to provide information or take part in debate. There are less obvious forms of exclusion. The institutions in which debate takes place may be physically remote or otherwise poorly accessible by those who lack insider knowledge – think, for example, of the obscurity of much EU decision making. The nature of the debate may also serve to marginalise certain positions: debates framed in overwhelmingly technical or scientific terms could limit the discussion to competing experts. It is not unusual to see limitations placed on what counts as 'legitimate' reasoning in environmental debate: most obviously, a narrow approach to 'sound science' or economic efficiency can mean that other concerns are dismissed as 'irrational' or 'NIMBYism' ('not in my back yard'). The terms of the debate on GMOs, for example, until relatively recently took this line. The Aarhus Convention demonstrates very little concern with the mechanics of public participation or with the possible exclusion of the poorly educated or poorly organised.

The real emphasis in the Aarhus Convention is on the involvement of environmental interest groups, and it seems to be assumed that they automatically have the capacity to engage in meaningful participation. If no attention is given to this issue, however, only larger, well-resourced environmental interest groups will be empowered, with dangers of capture and exclusion. And the funding of environmental interest groups, as happens, for example, at EU level,[47] is an important but far from simple solution. It exacerbates concerns that already exist about the 'taming' of public interest groups by their involvement in official processes, which 'could be envisaged as a process of enrolment into unarticulated dominant discourses and traditional networks of power'.[48]

Although the involvement of public interest groups potentially provides a forum for citizen participation,[49] the uncertain role of the more general public under the Aarhus Convention calls into question the process-focussed objectives

[47] Decision 466/2002 laying down a Community action programme promoting non-governmental organisations primarily active in the field of environmental protection OJ 2002 L 75/1.

[48] Sue Weldon and Brian Wynne, *Assessing Debate and Participative Technology Assessment (ADAPTA) Project No. Bio-CT98–0318 Annex No 6. The UK National Report* (Centre for the Study of Environmental Change, Lancaster University, January 2001), p. 17.

[49] See Deirdre Curtin, 'Private Interest *Representation* or Civil Society *Deliberation*? A Contemporary Dilemma for European Union Governance' (2003) 12 *Social and Legal Studies* 55.

of public participation, particularly when elected representatives, with a more multi-faceted conception of the public interest, make the final decision. Environmental interest groups are not representatives of the 'public', or even the 'public interest'. The following extract discusses the role of environmental interest groups at an international level, but similar questions arise with respect to domestic 'participation'.

### Karen Morrow, 'Public Participation in the Assessment of the Effects of Certain Plans and Programmes on the Environment' (2004) 4 *Yearbook of European Environmental Law* 49, pp. 54–7

Favourable views of NGO participation are usually based on the notion that such groups are 'acting as the identifiable voices of broad segments of civil society', importing the notion of the desirability of their playing a representative or at least quasi-representative role …

The employment of NGOs as a form of proxy for the general public leads to a view of public participation that, while workable and certainly convenient, is, at the same time, inevitably reductionist and potentially problematic. It is arguable that the incorporation of NGOs as players in international environmental law and policy allows IGOs [international governmental organisations] and states to take a useful shortcut to some sort of democratic credibility at comparatively little financial cost and less effort. It allows them to pay lip service to the ideals of public participation without having to tackle the difficulty of getting the public in its broader guise to engage with the decision-making processes in question …

The proxy role accorded to NGOs in international environmental law does, however, give significant cause for concern as, by employing this subtly bastardized version of public participation, its whole character is in fact altered from a notional mechanism of participative democracy to a practical alternative form of representative democracy. This proves problematic in its own right as, once NGOs reach a certain critical mass, they cease to be organs of participative democracy and become *de facto* representative in their function – but without an electoral mandate. This means that they must seek their legitimacy by other means, for example through their expertise. These arguments may also serve to justify the quasi-representative role of NGOs in international environmental law. An alternative lens through which to view the 'representative' function of NGOs can be found in regarding them not as representatives of individual members of the public in the same way as an elected politician, but instead as representatives of otherwise inadequately covered interests. In this way the quasi-representative role of NGOs could be viewed as complementary to that of mainstream representative democracy rather than inimical to it …

…

… NGOs certainly have a great deal to contribute to decision-making processes, bringing new or additional voices to the fore, providing alternatives to the dominant official version of the public interest. Even more significantly, NGOs can bring considerable and varied expertise to the decision-making process and this is augmented by their ability to exploit established networks to add breadth and depth to their input. The ability of NGOs to make linkages across geographical, political, and hierarchical barriers and their (albeit flawed) ability to give voice to otherwise poorly or even unrepresented interests, such as those of the planet or future generations, places them in a good position to augment traditional state and IGO inputs into law and policy-making processes ...

There is an additional caveat that should be kept in mind when considering NGOs as the prime harbingers of public participation in international environmental law and policy, in the form of the danger of NGOs becoming the new technocracy, squeezing out less officially sanctioned forms of public participation. Favoured status for certain NGOs may even push less favoured NGOs out of the arena. The net result is the creation of a new type of decision-making 'closed shop', as cut off from outside influence as that which it replaced. This is a very real danger given the convenience and benefits that accrue to IGOs and NGOs in their interactions with one another.

The Aarhus Convention actually says little about public participation at an international level, simply requiring Parties to 'promote' the application of the principles in the Convention 'in international environmental decision-making processes and within the framework of international organizations in matters relating to the environment' (Art. 3(7)). The Aarhus Convention is most concerned with the role of environmental interest groups *domestically*. And interest groups are likely also to dominate here, particularly in more strategic decision making: the effect of plans and programmes, for example a national or regional 'waste strategy', on individuals is not readily perceived; nor is it likely to be obvious to individuals what they can contribute.

Whilst there are real concerns about the likely dominance of interest groups (rather than the 'public' more generally), we should be clear: industry and business groups are always likely to have a say in decision making, and the presence of environmental interest groups provides a useful counterbalance. A recognition of the 'public interest' in the environment could also balance the common willingness of courts and administrators to align the *economic* benefit of a development with the more general 'public interest'. This leads to another caveat, however. Disparity of resources makes it difficult for environmental interest groups to exert the same influence as industry on decision making: 'in the face of the expertise that business interests are able to mobilise, NGOs can find themselves breathless, lacking real weight in the decisions taken by the bodies in which they participate'.[50] Environmental interest groups always have to be cautious that their limited involvement does not simply disguise the continued dominance of economic interests.[51]

In this chapter we have touched on international, EU and domestic arrangements for public participation. One further form of exclusion is in the frequent mismatch between the level of participation and the level of decision. For example, the UK held an ambitious, if flawed, process of public participation over policy on agricultural biotechnology in 2003, discussed in Chapter 2,

---

[50] Luigi Pellizzoni, 'Responsibility and Environmental Governance' (2004) 13 *Environmental Politics* 541, p. 559.     [51] See also the extract from Peterson and Bomberg: Ch. 4, pp. 146–8.

pp. 79–81. The results of this sort of innovative and exciting public debate are, however, difficult to feed into EU-level decision making on GMOs (Chapter 5); and their role in international trade rules (Chapter 7) is still more problematic. Public participation at EU or international level cannot compensate for this gap, if only because it is associated more or less entirely with pan-European or international interest groups. The reality of public participation as decision making communities expand geographically is a huge dilemma. And GMOs are by no means an isolated example. Siting waste incinerators in the UK, for example, has been contentious over recent years. It is subject to local public participation under planning law and EIA. However, this local participation takes place in the context of a decision taken at EU level to reduce the amount of waste going to landfill, which is bound to divert at least some waste to incineration.[52]

And finally, there are legitimate concerns about the time and expense of procedural rights. The tension between public participation and reasonably swift and decisive regulation is acute, and environmental interest groups should be particularly concerned that making regulatory activity more difficult may simply strengthen the status quo. And if public participation does successfully introduce a plurality of perspectives into decision making, one result could be unduly complex solutions, which attempt to incorporate incompatible positions. However, to argue that environmental decisions can be made well without some breadth of involvement involves a mistaken understanding of environmental issues, which are rarely one-dimensional technical decisions. And whilst a balance needs to be achieved, the inevitable involvement of industry suggests that environmental interest groups have an important contribution to make to decision making.

## 7 Conclusions

Public participation is an important theme in contemporary environmental decision making at all levels. The language at least is now very well established, and governments and business seem to have lost much of their fear of the development. Putting in place functioning institutions for meaningful public involvement is, however, if anything an even more daunting challenge. *GM Nation?*, discussed in Chapter 2, should remind us that reaching the 'grass roots' is difficult, as is overcoming the appeal of elite, disinterested 'expert' advice. Nevertheless, the mainstream acceptance that public participation is an important part of environmental decision making is to be welcomed, subject to some important reservations.

---

[52]  See the discussion in Maria Lee, 'Public Participation, Procedure and Democratic Deficit in EC Environmental Law' (2002) 3 *Yearbook of European Environmental Law* 193.

### Maria Lee and Carolyn Abbot, 'The Usual Suspects? Public Participation Under the Aarhus Convention' (2003) 66 *Modern Law Review* 80, pp. 107-8

A serious limitation of the Aarhus Convention, which reflects a more general failure in the movement towards participation, is the lack of engagement with the real nature of participation. Public participation is potentially a very radical innovation, and even in its more modest guises, challenges not only expertise based administrative decision-making, but also the appropriate role and the legitimacy of representative democracy. There is little sign that these challenges are recognised, as a problem or an opportunity.

Concern about public cynicism and disillusionment with traditional mechanisms of representative democracy probably encourages attempts to organise more direct participation, but it is far from a straightforward solution. Whatever the benefits of multiple perspectives on environmental problems, moves to participation suffer from a failure to consider the quality of the process. If public participation 'simply holds a mirror up to the pattern of power in the community; if the rich and well-organized are heard, while the poor and minorities are weakly represented',[53] the wisdom of devaluing or at least de-emphasising the institutions of representative democracy must be doubted. Whilst we must not be naïve about the real-life weaknesses of representative democracy or expert decision-making on environmental issues, this question of power is central to how public participation works. A move to participation needs to be informed by an awareness of the existing distribution of power and how participation will affect that power. We need to think about who (or what, perhaps the environment really is the winner) benefits most from the practical manifestation of public participation. International discussions of public participation often emphasise traditionally marginalised groups for special inclusion in public participation mechanisms – 'indigenous peoples, local communities, women, youth', as well as NGOs.[54] Whatever the problems and ambiguities in that list, it is notable that the Aarhus Convention makes no comparable attempt to broaden participation. The real emphasis in the Aarhus Convention is on the involvement of NGOs. Since industry involvement is not likely to wither away (and we would not suggest that it should), the involvement of NGOs in environmental regulation provides an important balance. However, we should always be aware of the dangers of claiming that NGOs 'represent' anybody, and of the possibility that a small (even if larger than before) number of participants will wrap up important decisions. More generalised public participation of course faces real obstacles. There has been provision for public participation in planning law for over three decades, but it is still dominated by professional planners, statutory consultees such as the Environment Agency, and

---

[53] Barry Barton, 'Underlying Concepts and Theoretical Issues in Public Participation in Resources Development' in Donald Zillman, Alastair Lucas and George (Rock) Pring (eds.), *Human Rights in Natural Resource Development: Public Participation in the Sustainable Development of Mining and Energy Resources* (Oxford University Press, 2002), p. 109.

[54] George R. Pring and Susan Y. Noé, 'The Emerging International Law of Public Participation Affecting Global Mining, Energy and Resources Development' in Zillman *et al.*, *Human Rights*, p. 59.

organised special interest groups, rather than the general public. The Aarhus Convention does not address this phenomenon, and given low levels of participation in even the most basic form of political participation at a local level – voting –[55] we perhaps should not be too optimistic about change.

Whatever the pros and cons, addressing questions of public participation at the international or EU level should perhaps be more controversial than it has been: 'Public participation is a matter of a nation's legal, political and administrative arrangements, and therefore closer to the heart of national sovereignty than many other issues in international environmental law. How a nation wishes to conduct its public affairs is a very political matter.'[56] International conventions, including the Aarhus Convention, typically use vague language, are deferent to national law and custom, and are in any event subject to only weak enforcement. The way in which the signature of the Aarhus Convention by all Member States and the EU has allowed discussion of the legitimacy of EC legal intervention in this area to be sidestepped, or at least delayed, is far more important than its direct legal impact. And in a mutually reinforcing circle, the EC law in turn gives real teeth to the Convention.

## 8  Further reading

For detailed legal analysis in this area, see Robert McCracken and Gregory Jones, 'The Aarhus Convention' [2003] *Journal of Planning and Environmental Law* 802, analysing the Convention in terms of a 'shift from a paternalistic to a participatory approach to environmental decision making', and Jonas Ebbesson, 'The Notion of Public Participation in International Environmental Law' (1997) 8 *Yearbook of International Environmental Law* 51, which considers the move to public participation in international environmental law. Philip Coppel, 'Environmental Information: The New Regime' [2005] *Journal of Planning and Environmental Law* 12, is a very useful review of the regime for access to environmental information in the UK.

There is a large literature on the use (and abuse) of 'public participation' and 'civil society' at EU level. The special issue of the *European Law Journal* (8(2002)1) devoted to new approaches to governance has some very useful papers in various contexts, including, but also going beyond, environmental law.

The Aarhus Convention website provides information on the implementation of the Convention: www.unece.org/env/pp/welcome.html.

---

[55]  Turn-out was about 28 per cent in local elections in England and Wales in 1999 and 2000; see House of Commons Public Administration Select Committee, Session 2000–1 Sixth Report, *Innovations in Citizen Participation in Government*, para. 12.

[56]  Barton, 'Underlying Concepts and Theoretical Issues'.

# Part II
# The EU Context

---

# Preface to Part II

In this Part of the book we embed environmental law and policy in a European context. This context is made up of a complex of European law and policy-making institutions and adjudication and enforcement bodies. The relationship between European Union (EU) law and policy in this context is highly intricate and politically charged (both at the EU and Member State levels) such that the line between non-binding legal instruments and areas of policy 'hardened' up over time to create firm obligations is at times difficult to draw. Key principles (for example precaution) also appear to straddle the law–policy divide: although their legal nature is somewhat uncertain, they do feature in the European Community (EC) Treaty's Title on the Environment, and the Court of First Instance (CFI) and the European Court of Justice (ECJ) have been prepared to assess the actions of both the EU institutions[1] and the Member States[2] by reference to them. The status of 'principles', and the absence of a hard definition, both makes them important policy guidance and suggests that they are not likely to play a very strong role in judicial review. A sense of the complexity of the institutional arrangements, and the relationship between law and policy, is provided by Damian Chalmers.

### Damian Chalmers, 'Inhabitants in the Field of EC Environmental Law' in Paul Craig and Grainne de Búrca (eds.), *The Evolution of EU Law* (Oxford University Press, 1999), pp. 672–84

The assumption at the heart of the [EU's Fifth Environmental] Action Programme of collaboration is a heuristic one of a shared vision of society. It does not sit easily with pluralistic theories which see the political process as a form of elite competition or social theories which emphasize social fragmentation and cultural diversity. The 1990s have departed from this vision by, first, witnessing change in the habits of pre-existing actors in the field in a manner

---

[1] For example Case T-13/99 *Pfizer Animal Health SA v. Council* [2002] ECR II-3305, see Ch. 1, pp. 23–5.

[2] See, for example, C-293/97 *R v. Secretary of State for the Environment, Transport and the Regions ex p. Standley* [1999] ECR I-2603, Ch. 1, p. 37. See also Case C-127/02 *Landelijke Vereniging tot Behoud van de Waddenzee v. Staatssecretaris van Landbouw, Natuurbeheer en Visserij* [2005] 2 CMLR 31, Ch. 15, pp. 651–3.

whereby EC environmental law has become a field of forces – something to be vied over, with each actor seeking to imprint its vision/interpretation on EC environmental law.

Many national governments have thus become more antagonistic to the development of EC environmental law. Part of this resulted from the wider legitimacy crisis affecting the European Union. There were also reasons specific to the field which brought about this change. EC environmental law had begun to challenge the symbolic capital enjoyed by national governments over their territories in a variety of ways. Traditionally, the poor application of EC environmental law had resulted in dissonant national interests finding voice in the policy process not at the law-making stage but at the stage of implementation. The Commission threatened to foreclose this option at the end of the 1980s ...

Secondly, there was the 1990 Commission proposal to place a tax on carbon dioxide emissions. While not the first environmental tax to be proposed by the Community, it was by some way the broadest. This had important symbolic implications. Tax-raising powers have traditionally been bound up with state-building, in that the submission to fiscal obligations they place on a populace suggests the construction of a unitary territory with the central authorities presenting themselves as a 'fount of sovereignty'.

Thirdly, EC environmental law was beginning to create a space between the state and its citizens within national territories. The Directive on Environmental Impact Assessment, in particular, created new political structures and forms of engagement by granting the public concerned the right to be informed and the opportunity to express an opinion on developments covered by the Directive. This intruded directly on the political praxis of a state's own subjects within that state's territory and Member States' traditional ability to control that praxis.

...

The second feature of the 1990s was an increase in the number of actors participating in the EC environmental legal field. This has resulted in the field becoming more fragmented and disparate, with its becoming increasingly difficult for any actor to acquire sufficient capital to exercise a hegemony over the field.

There has thus been a burgeoning of the public sphere in Brussels as NGOs have sought to expand their influence ...

Industry has also intervened more directly in EC environmental law rather than through the mediation of national administrators ...

The increased number of NGOs and industries which participate in the Brussels processes have made these 'groupings' less and less homogenous. The structures, interests, and contacts of the NGOs vary considerably. Correspondingly, industrial interests are often competing rather than convergent with strong national rivalries often persisting. One finds, furthermore, that NGOs and industry are not always in opposition.

...

The final group of actors who have emerged strongly on the field are scientists. Science is perceived as enjoying a monopoly over the detection, identification, and solution of most environmental problems. Scientists and scientific communities have therefore always enjoyed considerable symbolic and informational capital in this field. The trans-national nature of scientific discourse has facilitated EC governance by rooting regulation around concepts which are blind to national structures. In addition, the reductionist, neutralizing, universalizing language of science allows bureaucrats to engage in a discrete process of systematization, classification, and differentiation autonomous from wider social or cultural considerations.

In the 1970s and 1980s policy-making was science-based, but it was confined by the predominant regulatory style of pollution control. Such a style acknowledged that damage to the environment was being perpetrated, but sought to limit it in a socially or politically acceptable way. Many of the standards developed were often the result of pork-barrelling within the Council with little clear external rationale behind the thresholds finally adopted.

...

The development of judicially enforceable norms; the establishment of formal, horizontal structures of communication between the national administrations of Member States, between national administrations and private parties, and between private parties; the administration and implementation of EC environmental policies or policies into which EC environmental considerations have been integrated have all resulted in EC environmental law being used in a multiplying number of arenas. A variety of examples come to mind. NGOs have sought to use the EC Courts to annul Community policies and acts of the EC institutions. They have also sought to use the Court and, with more success, the Ombudsman to challenge national policies. Both industry and NGOs are increasingly using national courts to pursue their own interests. Environmental norms are increasingly having to be administered by a large number of ministries or state agencies. Local authorities are having to consider questions of EC environmental law in the exercise of their duties, *inter alia* in the fields of planning, air pollution, and waste. Private parties are increasingly using EC environmental law to gain voice in these proceedings ... The wider diversity of venues within which there is an interest in EC environmental law is likely to be the central influence on the field in the years to come, and conclusions can only be drawn tentatively.

The first consequence is that barriers to entry to the field have been reduced. Many of the institutions mentioned in the preceding paragraph are more accessible and have a presence for local actors which is not possessed by EC institutions ...

...

Fragmentation within the field benefits the increasing number of 'non-national' actors who are present on the field. These are operators whose horizons, internal systems of organization, and communication are not bounded, significantly, by national administrative structures. The increase in venues to use EC environmental law allows them to arbitrage between arenas – to engage in multiple lobbying, judicial politics in a variety of jurisdictions, internal interpretation, and application of norms across a variety of jurisdictions. For them the concepts of 'supranational' and 'infranational' have little resonance as they seek to acquire capital in any arena within which the opportunity presents itself.

The field is, finally, likely to become increasingly polydimensional in nature. Systems of integration and co-operation may emerge which are not in any sense hierarchical but which create EC environmental law as surely as legislation from Brussels. Codes of conduct between industries is one example. Internal standards of operation of multi-national enterprises is another. This need not be merely non-statal activity but may also develop from interstatal developments. The regulation establishing the European Environment Agency also sets up an observation network (EIONET), one component of which requires that 'national focus points' be set up which pass information onto the Agency and other members of the network. More normatively, a network of national environmental agencies was established in 1992, now called the EU Network for the Implementation and Enforcement of Environmental Law (IMPEL), which considers questions of enforcement and implementation of EC environmental law.

The various 'inhabitants' of EU environmental law identified by Chalmers are faced with many different environmental problems on a grand scale. Various reports on the state of the environment have been compiled by the EU institutions, including by the European Environment Agency (EEA), a primarily information-gathering (rather than enforcement or standard-setting) organisation. These suggest that environmental improvements have occurred in the case of certain environmental media and sectors, but that there remain areas of serious concern, a prognosis echoed by the European Commission as a background to its policy plans set out in its *Sixth Environmental Action Programme*.[3]

### European Commission, *Sixth Environmental Action Programme, Environment 2010: Our Future, Our Choice* COM (2001) 31 final, pp. 2–3

Despite the improvements on some fronts, we continue to face a number of persistent problems. Of particular concern are climate change, the loss of biodiversity and natural habitats, soil loss and degradation, increased waste volumes, the build-up of chemicals in the environment, noise and certain air and water pollutants. We also face a number of emerging issues such as pollutants that affect the functioning of our hormone systems. Forecasts suggest that, with current policies and socio-economic trends, many of the pressures that give rise to these problems, such as transport, energy use, tourist activities, land-take for infrastructure, etc., will worsen over the coming decade.

The third assessment report of the EEA, *European Environment*, confirms the trend that whilst some areas have improved in terms of environmental quality, these improvements are balanced by degeneration in others.[4] The Agency relies upon quantitative assessment methods, referred to as 'facts and figures'. However, this methodological approach does not prevent the Agency in the third report from advocating particular regulatory approaches.

There is still a heavy emphasis on the use of traditional regulatory instruments in specific areas to deal with environmental issues. Environmental impacts caused by economic

---

[3] See Ch. 4, pp. 149–51.

[4] This report now forms part of a more general report published by the European Environment Agency, *The European Environment: State and Outlook* (EEA, 2005). See particularly the 'executive summary', pp. 16 ff. The third report differs in geographical coverage from the previous reports by addressing also central Asia and the whole of the Russian Federation.

developments and general patterns of production and consumption are typically not taken into account. Other instruments, such as economic instruments and voluntary agreements, which are more appropriate tools to deal with such impacts are being developed in the EU, but have as yet not been used to any large degree across the European region ... A better balance of policy action – between regulatory measures to deal with specific environmental problems and the use of economic and other instruments to deal with the environmental impacts of sectoral activities – will be indispensable for the transition towards sustainable development. (pp. 7–8)

This draws the report beyond a purely 'state of the environment' remit and towards the realm of instrument choice and policy making.[5] As observed by Damian Chalmers, there is a 'premium on information' in the EU system:

A claim to prove a new form of environmental damage or a causal connection between certain activities and environmental damage has significant policy implications. As Shapiro observes a finding that vehicle emissions are responsible for 90 per cent of air pollution in a given area is a powerful form of agenda-setting which imposes an imperative to act.[6] The European Environment Agency has by its own admission found it increasingly difficult to divorce itself from policy-making. Reference is being made to its work in policy-making. Actors are using its information to refine their views on particular policies. (p. 684)

In this latest report there is clearly some acknowledgement of the part played by EU policies in the creation, or exacerbation, of the 'environmental crisis' described. As well as the oblique references to the environmental impact of 'continuing economic growth', the Agency states that, at the Johannesburg World Summit on Sustainable Development, 'the role of Europe as the originator of several of the world's environmental problems was highlighted. European cooperation can therefore, if there is the political will, play a major role in attaining global progress towards sustainability' (p. 8). On the other hand, environmental improvements are in part attributed by the Agency to the shift *away* from centrally planned economies, to market economies such as those currently in existence in the Member States of the Union.

### EEA, *Europe's Environment: The Third Assessment (Summary)* (EEA, 2003), pp. 6–7

The last decade of the 20th century saw substantial changes in economic terms in Europe. Under conditions of steady economic growth throughout most of the period, western Europe continued to move from an agricultural and manufacturing base towards a more service oriented society. Central and eastern Europe saw transition to a market economy coupled

---

[5]  See Ch. 4, section 3 (c), on environmental governance and regulatory change.

[6]  Martin Shapiro, 'The Problem of Independent Agencies in the United States and the European Union' (1997) 4 *Journal of European Public Policy* 276, p. 285.

with the political process of accession to the European Union. In the twelve countries of eastern Europe, Caucasus, and central Asia (EECCA), there was a slower transition to a market economy, but nonetheless radical departures from the previously centrally planned economies.

These developments have resulted in overall reductions in emissions of greenhouse gases, and, in central and eastern Europe and EECCA, reduced pressure on water resources from agriculture and industry and lower diffuse emissions from agriculture to the ground and air. In central and eastern Europe and EECCA, economic restructuring was also the major driving force behind the observed reductions in emissions of air pollutants.

On the negative side, land abandonment due to economic restructuring in central and eastern Europe and EECCA is threatening biodiversity. Furthermore, economic growth is making the achievement of individual burden-sharing targets for greenhouse gas emissions challenging for many western Europe countries. Urban development and transport infrastructure is stealing soil and fragmenting habitats in many places across the region. Overfishing is threatening marine natural resources.

This works to detract attention from the contribution of capitalist economies to environmental problems. The following provides a forceful reminder of the original, and still prevalent, economic aims of the Community (in this case in the context of the regional policy of the European Union – an area fraught with difficulties from an environmental perspective[7]) albeit that these economic aims are now being pursued in conjunction with the Union's environmental policy. The author argues that there has been (perhaps until now) little reflection on the part played by the EU in worsening the state of the environment in Europe, and beyond.

### David Wood, 'Challenging the Ethos of the European Union: A Green Perspective on European Union Policies and Programmes for Rural Development and the Environment' in Jane Holder and Donald McGillivray (eds.), *Locality and Identity: Environmental Issues in Law and Society* (Ashgate, 1999), pp. 60–1

The European Union is a capitalist organisation. This point is almost too obvious to state, yet it seems all too often ignored that as such it reflects the ideology, law and policy characteristic of capitalist industrialism. Its ethos is to make the European Union a strong and competitive economic power on world markets.[8] With respect to rural areas, European Union Commissioner, Padraig Flynn, has stated that the aim of policy is 'integration of European Union areas into the rapidly globalizing world economy'.

---

[7] See, in particular, Joanne Scott, *Development Dilemmas in the European Community: Rethinking Regional Development Policy* (Open University Press, 1995).

[8] Commission of the European Communities, *Agenda 2000 – Volume 1: For a Stronger and Wider Union* (1997).

At the same time, the EU tries to mitigate the worst effects of those markets on its population. This mitigation is carried out both by direct aid (such as the Structural Funds) and protectionist tariffs (in the Common Agricultural Policy), but also by continually aiming to increase production and consumption (the throughput of energy) overall with the aim of raising the poorest along with the rich. Because this requires ever increasing resources and ever more capacious sinks for wastes, it is unsustainable.

...

But the EU refuses to take any direct responsibility for the way in which it operates, referring to the rationale behind policy with phrases like 'the Union will have to adjust to the continued process of globalization'.[9] This implies that the market is beyond control and that Europe is merely following an inevitable economic tide. In fact the European Community is a key player in the growth of the global free market, and the EU remains one of the three regions (the 'triads') vital to its dominance. This attitude is part of the political ideology of globalisation and results in particular policy choices with very specific kinds of results in terms of environmental destruction and income and quality-of-life disparity at global and local levels. It also involves the deliberate and anti-democratic ceding of the already limited popular mandate of the EU to unelected, unaccountable, yet extraordinarily biased global bodies like the [World Trade Organisation] which operate largely in the interests of the transnational corporations.

There is clearly great potential for conflict between the type of economic 'progress' advanced by the Union and the movement for environmental protection (especially when considering the rapid transformation of rural areas in order that they may 'catch up' with richer parts of the EU). Nevertheless, from very unpromising beginnings, a firm legal basis for environmental policy has been achieved. Environmental protection policy now exists in a considerably advanced legal form, as witnessed by the symbolic strength of the commitment to 'sustainable development' in Art. 2 of the EC Treaty, the creation of a legal base for legislation in the EC Treaty,[10] and hundreds of pieces of European legislation (mainly Directives) enacted to pursue this policy. We still question whether, overall, this development might be considered as a sophisticated legal exercise in 'mitigation' for the worst excesses of the economic policies of the Union.

With this question in mind, in Chapter 4 we address the EU's competence to legislate for environmental protection by setting out the present state of environmental law and policy. We then locate this state of affairs in a simplified evolutionary framework of phases of environmental law and policy, culminating in the limited acknowledgement of environmental 'rights' in the broader process of constitutional reform. Also in Chapter 4 we show up both the potential for integration of environmental protection with other policy objectives, and the retention of serious policy conflicts, in the context of the EU's conduct of trade.

[9] *Ibid.*, p. 8.     [10] Articles 174, 175 and 176, see Ch. 4, pp. 151–4.

We exemplify many of the problems of operating a multi-level (national, local, regional (EU) and global) decision making process with a case study on the EU's regulation of genetically modified organisms (GMOs) in Chapter 5. The regulation of GMOs provokes intense public concern, has significant trade implications (as directly involving goods, traded both within and beyond the EU) and is subject to inconsistent national approaches.

The aim of this Part is not to give a comprehensive account of substantive areas of EU environmental law. We provide an account of trade law and policy of the Union (Chapter 4) and an outline of the law and policy relating to GMOs (Chapter 5). Several other chapters examine substantive EU environmental law: pollution controls (Chapter 9), eco-labelling and eco-auditing (Chapter 11), environmental assessment (Chapter 14) and nature conservation, including reform of the EU's Common Agricultural Policy (Chapters 15 and 16). We do not aim to give an account of the reception of EU environmental law in the Member States; implementation and enforcement are discussed in Chapter 10.

# 4

# The Development and State of EU Environmental Law and Policy

## 1 Introduction

The EU is currently engaged in far-reaching regulatory activity over a broad range of areas relating to environmental protection, many of which are not confined to the borders of Europe – pollution control, nature conservation and biodiversity, town and country planning, waste (including the 'end of life' of some products), ozone depletion, regulation of genetically modified organisms (GMOs), protection of endangered species and rainforests, and climate change. This accretion of environmental law has been a key trend in the European Community (EC) since the early 1970s, when the (then) European Economic Community (EEC) pledged in its First Environmental Action Programme (1973) primarily to enact legislation to combat existing pollution. This was a significant goal, but of only marginal importance when compared to the overriding aims of the European body politic at that time, which was concerned with fostering economic growth and competition in the Community by the establishment of a common market. Nevertheless, during its relatively short history, the environmental law of the EC[1] has deployed the full scope of available legal instruments and regulatory techniques over a wide range of policy areas. Importantly, EC environmental law has also operated as a testing ground for principles (particularly subsidiarity and integration) and regulatory techniques (most notably environmental impact assessment (EIA)) before they have been applied to the core areas of Community policy. This process has resulted in the slow absorption of environmental protection as an objective of policy making into the more mainstream policy areas of Community activity, headlined by the following commitment set out in Art. 2 of the EC Treaty:

> The Community shall have as its task, by establishing a common market and an economic and monetary union and by implementing common policies or activities ... to promote throughout the Community a harmonious, balanced and sustainable development of

[1] In strict terms, the environmental law of the European Union (EU) is part of *EC* law, because its legal base is provided by the EC Treaty (this forms one of the three 'pillars' of the European Union). However, the political and intergovernmental construct of the European Union is highly important in policy making terms.

economic activities, a high level of employment and of social protection, equality between men and women, sustainable and non inflationary growth, a high degree of competitiveness and convergence of economic performance, a high level of protection and improvement of the quality of the environment, the raising of the standard of living and quality of life, and economic and social cohesion and solidarity among member states.

This statement of the Community's tasks suggests that environmental protection is, if not central to Community activities and policy objectives, at least in line with the *Community's* conception of sustainable development. This is reinforced by the 'integration principle', found in Art. 6 of the EC Treaty: 'Environmental protection requirements must be integrated into the definition and implementation of the Community policies and activities referred to in Article 3, in particular with a view to promoting sustainable development.' However, even though procedural mechanisms such as impact assessment (which forms the subject of Chapter 14) have been applied to help achieve the 'mainstreaming' of environmental protection, there remain many examples of serious policy conflicts between environment-related concerns and Community policy on agriculture, fisheries, competition, transport, energy, regional development, and trade, to name but a few. We introduce some trade / environmental protection issues later in this chapter (pp. 171–84) and extend this analysis in Chapters 5 and 7. As we discuss further below (pp. 164–70), these examples of 'disintegration' suggest that the process of incorporating environmental protection concerns into the core of Community (and Union) decision making processes is far from complete, and has not yet generated the expected results in terms of more sustainable policy and law making.

### European Environment Agency (EEA), *Europe's Environment: The Third Assessment (Summary)* (EEA, 2003), pp. 58–9

Integration initiatives at the EU level have so far had only a minor impact on the more fundamental problems to be addressed. The EU integration process has lacked urgency and has yet to have a significant impact on sectoral policy-making. At the Member State level, few strategies are yet beyond the stage of formulation, and few have yet clearly demonstrated positive outcomes. Integration in central and eastern Europe is at an even earlier stage, although there are some positive examples emerging. EECCA countries [countries of eastern Europe, Caucasus and central Asia] are aware of the requirements of integration but do not generally have the administrative capacity or other resources to carry forward initiatives for drafting strategies and plans, far less for their implementation. There is however no uniformity within the blocks [of Member States] as to progress in formulating and implementing integration strategies.

In this chapter we first outline current law and policy, including an analysis of the complexity of the policy making process (section 2). We locate present law and policy in an evolutionary framework which has been simplified to present major shifts in policy as four main phases (section 3). The key determinants of the state of EU environmental law have been the need to overcome concerns about the competence of the Union to act in this area and, as these concerns have abated, the EU's integration of environmental protection concerns into other policy areas – the process of 'mainstreaming'. A key concern of this section is the development of specific decision making procedures by the EU in an attempt to cope with the unique difficulties presented by environmental governance on a supranational level. These include in particular the expression and accommodation of (expert and lay) assessments of risk via participation in decision making processes at different levels, and the promulgation of fitting regulatory instruments, illustrated by way of a case study on the EU regulation of GMOs in Chapter 5. As mentioned above in relation to the integration of different policy areas, a central concern of the current chapter is the move towards reconciling trade and environmental protection. We consider this issue in terms of trade between Member States (i.e. what Scott refers to as the 'internal market perspective' on 'trade and the environment'[2]), driven forward (in the most part) by the European Court of Justice (ECJ), and that between the EU and the rest of the world (the 'external market perspective'). The disciplines of international trade law, and their potential effect on environmental protection, are discussed further in Chapter 7.

## 2  Current EU environmental law and policy

### (a)  Environmental policy

The environmental policy of the EU is the outcome of a distinctive and evolving process which reflects tensions which arise during that process between the many interests of the Member States, scientific advisers, campaigning groups, and policy makers. As John Peterson and Elizabeth Bomberg state: 'Environmental policy is one of the EU's most diverse and crowded policy realms, populated by a staggering array of actors and interests.'[3] This mix of influences and interests, operating at different levels, is illustrated clearly by the case of multi-level decision making in respect of the release and labelling of GMOs (the subject of Chapter 5). More generally, the policy process has been analysed at two main levels: the *systemic* level – intra- and inter-institutional bargaining within and between the Council, Commission and the European Parliament – and the *sub-systemic* level, which is made up of 'messy networks'.

[2] Joanne Scott, *EC Environmental Law* (Longmans, 1998), p. 64.
[3] John Peterson and Elizabeth Bomberg, *Decision Making in the European Union* (Macmillan, 1999), p. 173.

### John Peterson and Elizabeth Bomberg, *Decision Making in the European Union* (Macmillan, 1999), pp. 185–99

*The Systemic Level: Intra- and Interinstitutional Bargaining*

Decisions taken at the highest political levels have determined the overall framework for making environmental policy …

At the systemic level, bargaining on the Council is marked by attempts to accommodate diverse environmental interests. QMV [qualified majority voting] is the dominant form of voting on the Environment Council and this rule informs bargaining on most (non-fiscal) environmental matters by encouraging coalition building between leaders or laggard Member States. 'Fence sitters', committed to neither camp, occupy an enviable bargaining position. Their ability to deliver decisive votes under QMV gives them strength well beyond their size or voting weight. However, there are no fixed coalitions on environmental policy. Allies on issues, say, of water quality legislation often oppose one another on issues related to biotechnology or nuclear energy.

Fundamental differences in environmental preferences mean that it is often easy to end up with clear winners and losers on the Council. In the EU's consensual system, enormous efforts are made to ensure that no one comes out a clear loser. A variety of tools for consensus building are deployed. Laggards are often allowed exemptions or extended periods in which to comply with legislation …

…

In short, environmental decision-making is not simply a process which reflects dominant coalitions of Member States (leader or laggard) pushing their own national style of regulation. National concerns are 'displaced' onto a higher level, but in the process become mediated by institutional bargaining between the Council, Commission and, increasingly, the EP [European Parliament]. In environmental policy the institutional balance of power is constantly shifting, and decisions rules are manipulated in the struggle. Three institutional factors are particularly important in determining how policies are set: the increase in 'veto players', the growth in the EP's power and the Commission's enduring role as agenda-setter.

Previous to the SEA [Single European Act], the setting of environmental policy was dominated by the bilateral relationship between the Council and the Commission. The policy-making process provided little formal access through which 'third' actors such as the EP, or oppositional groups, could exert influence. The number of 'veto players' – actors whose agreement is required for a change in policy – was small. The SEA expanded the use of QMV in nearly all sectors related to the internal market (including much environmental policy). The SEA's introduction of the cooperation procedure also increased the powers of the EP, in which environmental concerns tended to be better represented than in other institutions. Under co-operation, the EP had a second chance to table amendments and bargain. The EP's more robust role affected decision making on a range of legislation. The best known example is the 1989 auto emissions directive in which the EP was able to force the Council to accept standards well above those preferred by most EU Member States.

The EP's influence over policy setting decisions increased with the enactment of the Maastricht Treaty. The new co-decision procedure gave the EP the right to veto legislation related to environmental strategy, consumer protection and public health … In particular, the co-decision required much greater sensitivity on the part of the Commission to the policy aspirations of the EP … By extending co-decision to virtually all non-fiscal environmental measures, the Amsterdam Treaty further enhanced Parliament's bargaining power.

…

Although both Member States and the EP participate in setting the environmental agenda, the main initiator remains the Commission. The precise origins of its ideas are usually unclear, but its formal prerogatives give it obvious agenda-setting powers vis-à-vis the Council: 'The Council can instruct the Commission to prepare a text, but cannot command its contents' …

…

The Commission's power of initiative is critical because the content of early drafts is essential in shaping the final text. But the Commission is not a monolithic actor. First, the services or Directorates-General feature fierce rivalries, particularly in environmental matters … Fragmentation and rivalry within the Commission are more acute in the environmental field than in other sectors. Most environmental issues cross over several policy areas and Directorates-General. Extensive discussions must take place within the Commission itself to determine which policies should be allocated to which Directorates. To illustrate the point, the Commission's formulation of EU climate policy (including energy efficiency measures and a carbon/energy tax) initially involved 10 separate DGs. Ambiguity concerning 'ownership' of policy means that the content of environmental proposals often reflects turf battles and competing agendas … In sum, the Commission retains important powers to set environmental policy, but the influence of DG XI [now DG environment] is highly circumscribed. Moreover, the Commission must share its power to set policy not only with the Council but, increasingly, with the EP, whose influence in environmental policy has expanded steadily.

*The Sub-systemic level: Messy Networks*

One of the most conspicuous features of environmental decision-making is the influence of a wide array of non-institutional members and interests, particularly in the early 'shaping' stages. In addition to national and EU officials, the formulation of environmental policy usually brings together scientific experts, business interest groups and environmental non-governmental organisations (NGOs). The crowded nature of the environmental policy-making process means that policy-shaping usually takes place within loose 'issue networks'. These issue networks often feature a range of actors who have radically different views of the policy problem as well as the desired outcomes. Memberships change frequently and sometimes dramatically when new issues arise or as they are transformed. Environmental policy networks are messier than most.

Technical expertise is an important entry card to most policy networks, but the role of scientific and technical expertise is especially important in environmental policy …

The importance of such experts stems from the highly technical character of environmental policy and the Commission's dependence on a wide variety of sources for information. The European Environmental Agency (EEA), which came into operation in 1993, can provide the Commission with comparable information at the European level on the state of the environment. But the EEA's limited resources, as well as its independence from the Commission, accentuates the Commission's need for additional outside experts. Given the restricted size of its permanent staff, DG XI depends on experts and officials on secondment from national capitals, other EU institutions, private organisations and foundations.

The dense web of expert committees and technical working groups which prepare dossiers allows allied groups of specialised technicians or technocrats – epistemic communities – opportunities to control the policy agenda. In the formulation of climate change policy, for instance, the Council set up working groups to prepare dossiers and keep ministers well informed, but these groups were soon dominated by scientific experts …

In addition to ostensibly neutral actors [scientists/'experts'], more overtly political actors seek to forward the aims of their members by combining resources, and sharing information within advocacy coalitions. Made up of largely lobbyists and politicians, as opposed to the technocrats who dominate the epistemic communities, advocacy coalitions span the EU's institutions and compete for control of networks shaping environmental policy …

…

Yet it is easy to exaggerate the pluralist character of environmental policy issue networks. Compared to other sectors, environmental policy networks are relatively accessible, but openness should not be confused with equal influence. Clearly, resource imbalances occur within even fairly accessible networks. For instance, a senior Commission official responsible for waste management policy insisted that, for DG XI, apart from contacts with national administrations, '90 per cent of the contacts are with trade and industry' …

…

The environment marks an especially dynamic policy area in the EU. Unlike more entrenched policy areas such as agriculture, patterns of EU decision-making in the environmental arena are still relatively new and fluid. The open and experimental character of decision-making on environmental policy has several broad implications. It means that there is no single pattern to environmental decision-making. Not only does decision-making reflect the diverse goals and means of 15 [now 27] Member States, it also reflects a set of institutional rules with its own form and logic. Finally, decision-making reflects the *informal* politics of bargaining and resource exchange across and within loose issue networks.

The lack of established patterns means that outputs (environmental legislation) remain unpredictable. Legislative outputs reflect bargaining and resource exchange among Member States, institutions, and a wide variety of public and private actors who often disagree about the nature of the problem as well as the solution. Certain features of environmental decision-making – its crowded pattern of interest representation and reliance on varying, sometimes conflicting, scientific advice – can result in policies which are difficult to follow and harder to implement. The most oft cited example is water quality, but other cases, such as the packaging waste directive, reveal EU regulations that are rich in incongruities and ambiguities. In environmental policy, the complex bargaining required to reach decisions can produce results that are as tortured as the decision-making process itself.

This assessment of the policy making process in the EU raises many important issues, but nevertheless presents a simplistic picture of law as an 'output' of the policy process. In reality, the relationship between law and policy is more complex: the policy process is shaped by law, and law remains highly receptive to the political and policy climate in which it is formed, and particularly to the dominant interests in an area (see Preface, pp. xv–xviii). An example is the eventual agreement of legislation on GMOs, discussed in Chapter 5 below, which failed to resolve the complex and polarised debate on the acceptability of this particular technology. This controversy persists in the implementation of the legislation, that is in the consideration of applications for authorisation of GMOs by the EU institutions and the Member States. It is also important to note that Peterson and Bomberg's analysis above is drawn from the pre-enlargement European Union. In practice, an EU of twenty-seven Member States, with differing environmental problems and economic priorities, will further complicate and diversify policy making processes, even following 'structured dialogue' on environmental issues at a high level between the new members and the Commission, and the Commission's production of a 'road map' for the approximation of environmental law and policy in the accession states.

Turning to one *formal* product of the policy making process, a statement of the objectives of Community environmental law and plans for future legislation are found in six Environmental Action Programmes that in formal terms constitute the Community's environmental policy, the first from 1973 and the most recent (the sixth) from 2001. This last Programme differs from previous plans in its emphasis upon the action that must be taken at national, regional and local levels, as well as the more familiar concern with legislative activity at the EU level.

### European Commission, Sixth Environmental Action Programme, *Environment 2010: Our Future, Our Choice* COM (2001) 31 final, pp. 12–13

Nature of the Programme

This new Programme establishes the environmental objectives for the next 10 years and beyond and sets out the actions that need to be taken over the coming 5 to 10 years to achieve these objectives. Whilst the Programme focuses on actions and commitments that need to be made at the Community level, it also identifies actions and responsibilities that need to be addressed at the national, regional and local levels and in the different economic sectors. In selecting these actions, full account is taken of the need for the highest possible level of harmonisation and approximation of laws to ensure the functioning of the internal market. This includes a limited number of Thematic Strategies (which may include a range of instruments from proposals for legislation for adoption by the European Parliament and the Council of Ministers through to dissemination of information) in areas where only a package of coordinated measures will yield results …

The conclusions of the Global Assessment [of the Fifth Environmental Action Programme] and the reports on the state and trends of the environment lead to the programme's focus on the following priority issues, that have been grouped under four main headings:

    (i)   tackling climate change;

    (ii)  nature and bio-diversity – protecting a unique resource;

    (iii) environment and health;

    (iv) ensuring the sustainable management of resources and wastes.

…

### A STRATEGIC APPROACH TO MEETING OUR ENVIRONMENTAL OBJECTIVES

Environmental legislation is and will remain an important pillar of the Community's approach to achieving its environmental objectives and one of the strategic priorities for the coming decade is to tackle the significant implementation failures we face in a number of areas.

However, meeting the challenges of today's environmental problems requires that we look beyond a strictly legislative approach and that we take a more strategic approach to inducing the necessary changes in our production and consumption patterns. We need to make the best use of a whole range of instruments and measures to influence decisions made by business, consumers, citizens and policy planners in other areas, for example at the local level when making land-use planning and management decisions.

Thus, this Programme proposes five priority avenues of strategic action to help us meet our environmental objectives. The first is to improve the implementation of existing legislation. The second aims at integrating environmental concerns into the decisions taken under other policies. The third focuses on finding new ways of working closer with the market via businesses and consumers. The fourth involves empowering people as private citizens and helping them to change behaviour. Finally, the fifth aims at encouraging better land-use planning and management decisions.

The legal status of action programmes such as this is relatively weak, at least as interpreted by the ECJ which has held that the Fifth Environmental Action Programme did not lay down any legal rules of a mandatory nature but provided merely a framework for defining and implementing Community environmental policy.[4] Even in policy terms, the programmes are not definitive, since there are examples of policy being formulated outside the strict remit of the programmes. In addition the programmes tend to offer a bland portrayal of the state of environmental policy and forecasted legislation, with conflicts and compromises made between the different interests in the Commission often glossed over. So, for example, one of the 'actions' required in the Sixth Environmental Action Programme is the 'Reinforcement of controls on

---

[4]  Case C-142/95P *Associazione agricoltori della provincia di Rovigo and Others* v. *Commission* [1996] ECR I-6669.

monitoring, labelling and traceability of GMOs', which neatly side-steps the dispute over the appropriate role of genetically modified organisms in EU agriculture. The Programme goes no way towards resolving the dilemmas raised by GMOs, discussed in Chapters 2 and 5, but assumes that conventional risk assessment plus labelling (and consumer choice) addresses all of the doubts:

> Whilst the use of modern biotechnology, including the release of genetically modified organisms into the environment, may offer potential benefits for reducing pollution and for biodiversity, the potential long-term risks, particularly to biodiversity, should not be overlooked. The Community has legislation that controls the placing of these products on the market, which require assessment of the potential risks to human health and the environment. This legislation is being reinforced through the introduction of mandatory monitoring as well as labelling and traceability at every stage of the placing of the market. (p. 37)

In summary, at any one time the policy framework in which the EU, and particularly the European Commission, operates is far more contingent, complex and varied than that represented by the various action programmes (as indicated by the analysis of the various inter-institutional and non-governmental influences on the policy making process, discussed above).[5]

## (b) Legislative framework

Title XIX of the EC Treaty (reproduced below) provides the current legal basis for the EC's action relating to the environment. It describes the limits of the Community's competence in this area. The Title is the product of several revisions of the EC Treaty, and also reflects the transfer of provisions (on integration and subsidiarity) into the more mainstream parts of the EC Treaty concerned with setting out the overriding principles of the Community. As mentioned above, the commitment to integrated policy making is now contained in Art. 6 EC and, as it is tied to the concept of sustainable development, should apply more generally to policy making. The principle of subsidiarity, first introduced into the Environment Title as Art. 130r(4) EC, was elevated to a general principle of Community constitutional law by the Treaty on European Union and is now found in Art. 5(2) EC:

> In areas which do not fall within its exclusive competence, the Community shall take action, in accordance with the principle of subsidiarity, only if and insofar as the objectives of the proposed action cannot be sufficiently achieved by the Member States and can therefore,

---

[5] On the role of non-governmental organisations in shaping environmental law, see Peter Newell and Wynne Grant, 'Environmental NGOs and EU Environmental Law' [2000] 1 *Yearbook of European Environmental Law* 225, and Peter Bombay, 'The Role of NGOs in International Environmental Conferences and Agreements: Some Important Features' (2001) 10 *European Environmental Law Review* 228.

by reason of the scale or effects of the proposed action, be better achieved by the Community.

We will discuss below the development of a firm legal basis for EC environmental law and policy (pp. 158–64). Subsidiarity's high political (if not legal) profile means that the resolution of debate on whether the EC can take action *at all* simply moves attention to whether it *should* in any particular case: the justifications for EC environmental law discussed below (physical, economic and 'psychic' spillovers, pp. 158–69) reappear in the context of subsidiarity.

## Title XIX Environment

### Article 174 (ex Article 130r)

1. Community policy on the environment shall contribute to pursuit of the following objectives:

- preserving, protecting and improving the quality of the environment;
- protecting human health;
- prudent and rational utilisation of natural resources;
- promoting measures at international level to deal with regional or worldwide environmental problems.

2. Community policy on the environment shall aim at a high level of protection taking into account the diversity of situations in the various regions of the Community. It shall be based on the precautionary principle and on the principles that preventive action should be taken, that environmental damage should as a priority be rectified at source and that the polluter should pay.

In this context, harmonisation measures, answering environmental protection requirements shall include, where appropriate, a safeguard clause allowing Member States to take provisional measures, for non-economic reasons, subject to a Community inspection procedure.

3. In preparing its policy on the environment, the Community shall take account of:

- available scientific and technical data;
- environmental conditions in the various regions of the Community;
- the potential benefits and costs of action or lack of action;
- the economic and social development of its regions.

4. Within their respective spheres of competence, the Community and the Member States shall cooperate with third countries and with the competent international organisations. The arrangements for Community cooperation may be the subject of agreements between the Community and the third parties concerned, which shall be negotiated and concluded in accordance with Article 300.

The previous sub-paragraph shall be without prejudice to Member States' competence to negotiate in international bodies and to conclude international agreements.

### Article 175 (ex Article 130s) (as amended by the Treaty of Nice)

1. The Council, acting in accordance with the procedure referred to in Article 251 [the 'co-decision' procedure] and after consulting the Economic and Social Committee and the Committee of the Regions, shall decide what action is to be taken by the Community in order to achieve the objectives referred to in Article 174.

2. By way of derogation from the decision making procedure provided for in paragraph 1 and without prejudice to Article 95, the Council, acting unanimously on a proposal from the Commission and after consulting the European Parliament, the Economic and Social Committee and the Committee of the Regions, shall adopt:

    (a)   provisions primarily of a fiscal nature;

    (b)   measures affecting:

        – town and country planning;

        – quantitative management of water resources or affecting, directly or indirectly, the availability of those resources;

        – land use, with the exception of waste management;

    (c)   measures significantly affecting a Member State's choice between different energy sources and the general structure of its energy supply.

The Council may, under the conditions laid down in the first subparagraph, define those matters referred to in this paragraph on which decisions are to be taken by a qualified majority.

3. In other areas, general action programmes, setting out priority objectives to be attained shall be adopted by the Council, acting in accordance with the procedure referred to in Article 251 and after consulting the Economic and Social Committee and the Committee of the Regions.

    The Council, acting under the terms of paragraph 1 or paragraph 2 according to the case, shall adopt the measures necessary for the implementation of these programmes.

4. Without prejudice to certain measures of a Community nature, the Member States shall finance and implement the environment policy.

5. Without prejudice to the principle that the polluter should pay, if a measure based on the provisions of paragraph 1 involves costs deemed disproportionate for the public authorities of a Member State, the Council shall, in the act adopting that measure, lay down appropriate provisions in the form of:

        – temporary derogations, and/or

        – financial support from the Cohesion Fund set up pursuant to Article 161.

### Article 176 (ex Article 130t)

The protective measures adopted pursuant to Article 175 shall not prevent any Member State from maintaining or introducing more stringent protective measures. Such measures must be compatible with this Treaty. They shall be notified to the Commission.

Note the hierarchy implicit in Art. 174, with policy objectives described in the first paragraph of the Article, followed by a list of principles in the second paragraph, and finally, policy considerations (para. 3). The Title appeals to several guiding principles – the precautionary principle, and the principles that preventive action should be taken, that environmental damage should as a priority be rectified at source and that the polluter should pay. Of these, we discuss the precautionary and polluter pays principles in Chapter 1 (pp. 18–31 and 36–7). The Title carves out several policy areas destined for unanimous voting in the Council. This is a concession to Member State sensitivity about certain areas of environmental concern which are also highly politically sensitive (for example energy policy) or which touch upon Member States' concerns about the preservation of sovereignty because of their potential effect upon autonomy over the physical territory of the state (such as town and country planning). Finally, the legislative motivation for this Title is clearly not harmonisation of standards for the purposes of encouraging the movement of goods and services, but is instead the imposition of high standards of environmental protection. This is reinforced by the terms of Art. 176. This provides the conditions for 'two speeds' of environmental regulation in Europe – 'standard' provisions adopted under Art. 175, and more stringent measures under Art. 176. The following extract is taken from a preliminary reference to the ECJ in which German measures on waste were found to be more stringent than the Landfill Directive[6] in a number of respects: for example, the Directive requires Member States to reduce the amount of certain wastes going to landfill by a specified proportion, by dates; the German legislation requires *lower* amounts by *earlier* dates.

### Case C-6/03 *Deponiezweckverband Eiterköpfe* v. *Land Rheinland-Pfalz* [2005] ECR I-2753

27 The first point to be noted is that the Community rules do not seek to effect complete harmonisation in the area of the environment. Even though Article 174 EC refers to certain Community objectives to be attained, Article 176 EC allows the Member States to introduce more stringent protective measures ... Article 176 EC makes such measures subject only to the conditions that they should be compatible with the Treaty and that they should be notified to the Commission.

...

41 ... the thresholds and tests contained in a measure of domestic law such as that at issue in the main proceedings follow the same policy of protecting the environment as the Directive does. Inasmuch as such a regulation imposes requirements stricter than those of that Directive, it constitutes a more stringent protective measure for the purposes of Article 176 EC.

...

57 By its second question, the national court in substance asks the Court whether measures of national law such as those at issue in the main proceedings are compatible with the Community law principle of proportionality.

...

---

[6] Directive 99/31/EC on the landfill of waste OJ 1999 L 182/1.

61 It is clear from the broad logic of Article 176 EC that, in adopting stricter measures, Member States still exercise powers governed by Community law, given that such measures must in any case be compatible with the Treaty. Nevertheless, it falls to the Member States to define the extent of the protection to be achieved.

62 In that context, in so far as it is a matter of ensuring that the minimum requirements laid down by the Directive are enforced, the Community principle of proportionality demands that measures of domestic law should be appropriate and necessary in relation to the objectives pursued.

63 In contrast, and inasmuch as other provisions of the Treaty are not involved, that principle is no longer applicable so far as concerns more stringent protective measures of domestic law adopted by virtue of Article 176 EC and going beyond the minimum requirements laid down by the Directive.

64 As a result, the reply to the second question has to be that the Community-law principle of proportionality is not applicable so far as concerns more stringent protective measures of domestic law adopted by virtue of Article 176 EC and going beyond the minimum requirements laid down by a Community directive in the sphere of the environment, inasmuch as other provisions of the Treaty are not involved.

This is only helpful up to a point: the more challenging question is the extent to which 'other provisions of the Treaty' (particularly on the free movement of goods (below, pp. 171–82), but also, for example, competition law) are indeed involved.

## 3 An evolutionary framework: four phases

As mentioned above, the development of environmental law in the EU is a relatively recent legal phenomenon. This development falls roughly into four phases. The first phase may be judged to have taken place roughly between 1957 (the inception of the EEC) and 1972 when the United Nations Conference on the Human Environment took place in Stockholm. This resulted in the EEC's First Action Programme on the Environment despite there being no explicit mention of 'environment' in the EEC Treaty. This phase is also characterised by several incidental developments aimed primarily at harmonising trade restrictions, but having environmental effects. The second phase (1973–86) sees the rapid development of environmental legislation, culminating in the grounding of law and policy in a Title on the Environment in the EC Treaty (Art. 130r–t), inserted by the Single European Act 1987. As a consequence, the output of environmental legislation expands considerably, but mostly to complete the single market. In the following years (1987–93), there are residual struggles over the competence of the EC to legislate for environmental protection played out in the context of cases concerned with establishing, or challenging, the 'correct' legal base of a measure. From the time of the signing of the Maastricht Treaty (The Treaty on European Union) (1993 onwards), the Community (and wider

Union) has been seeking to establish more firmly the conditions for *environmental governance*, particularly by expanding the range of regulatory instruments available (notably economic and more 'flexible' instruments) and pursuing shared responsibility for environmental protection amongst a range of legal and policy actors, and on several different levels (often simultaneously). More recently (entering a fourth phase, which may be dated from 1998 – the date of the Aarhus Convention), the environmental law of the EU may also be characterised by attempts to constitutionalise its legal basis, clarify the nature of environmental rights in EU law, and secure access to environmental justice. To date, however, it may still be said that the environment remains marginal to the main constitutional project of the Union.

We now turn to each of these phases in greater detail, outlining in particular the sometimes competing rationales for intervention by the Community in environmental matters, and the clear and decisive role of the ECJ in progressing the legitimacy of the EC's competence in this area.

## (a) First phase: recognising the need for action

In 1951, France, Germany, Italy, Belgium, the Netherlands and Luxembourg signed the Treaty of Paris which brought into existence the European Steel and Coal Community (ECSC) at the start of 1952. The aim of this Treaty was to develop and supervise the production of steel and coal by building a single market in these within the structure of an international organisation. In 1957 the six participating Member States signed two Treaties of Rome, creating the European Atomic Community (Euratom) and the European Economic Community (EEC). The effect of the creation of these three Communities was a single, unrestricted Western European market in potential pollutants – steel, iron, coal, and nuclear materials, as well as other 'goods'. The aims of the Communities were not solely economic: the preamble to the Treaty of Rome (EEC Treaty) stated that its signatories were 'resolved by thus pooling their resources to preserve and strengthen peace and liberty'. Nevertheless, the immediate goal of the EEC was to achieve four fundamental 'freedoms' with the ultimate aim of untrammelled economic activity: the free movement of goods, capital, services and people. These freedoms were expressed in Art. 3 of the Treaty of Rome which consequently listed the EEC's activities as including the elimination of trade restrictions (customs duties and quotas) by establishing a common market, and the abolition of obstacles to the free movement of persons, services and capital between Member States. A legal system for ensuring that competition within the EEC was not distorted (and was to be encouraged) was to be set up, and common policy making in the spheres of agriculture, transport and fisheries was envisaged. More broadly, Art. 3h of the original Treaty of Rome referred to 'the approximation of the laws of the Member States to the extent required for the proper functioning of the common market'. A common customs tariff and a common commercial policy towards third countries was also to be established. The EEC Treaty created procedures whereby legislation could be adopted in pursuance of these activities by the Commission, the Assembly (which became the European Parliament after 1979) and the Council, the supervision and enforcement of which was entrusted to the ECJ.

Clearly, at this stage in its development, the EEC had made no commitment to environmental protection. It was not until the 1972 United Nations Stockholm Conference on the Human Environment, convened following a General Assembly Resolution in 1968, that the impetus for international environmental measures gathered speed as an expression of concern for the state of the environment. In particular the conference highlighted the problem of acid rain, which was leading to the death of large tracts of forest in Scandinavia and Germany. One of the Community's original tasks (Art. 2 EEC Treaty) was to promote throughout the Community a harmonious development of economic activities, and a continuous and balanced expansion. But at the Paris Summit in 1972, which followed the Stockholm conference, the heads of state or government (acting as the European Council) declared that this focus was incorrect: 'economic expansion is not an end in itself. Rather, its aim is to reduce disparities in living conditions and to improve the quality and standard of living.' In particular, attention was to be paid to non-material values and wealth and to environmental protection. At the Paris Summit, the conference organisers noted that: 'Man is both creature and moulder of his environment ... a stage has been reached where ... man has acquired the power to transform his environment ... on an unprecedented scale. Both aspects of man's environment, the natural and the man made, are essential to his well being ... even the right to life itself', and that 'the protection and improvement of the human environment is a major issue which affects the well being of people and economic development throughout the world; it is the earnest desire of people in the whole world and the duty of government'.[7]

The 'Paris Declaration' followed: a communiqué issued by the heads of state or of governments of the countries of the Community at their meeting later in 1972, in which was included the guidance that: 'as befits the genius of Europe, particular attention will be given to intangible values and to protecting the environment so that progress may really be put to the service of mankind'. The leaders of the Member States emphasised the importance of and need for a Community environmental policy. To this end they invited the Community institutions to establish, before 31 July 1973, a programme of action setting out the responsibilities incumbent on Europe. This first *Action Programme for the Environment*[8] – a political declaration which

---

[7] On this and other rationales for early EU environmental policy, see Stuart Bell and Donald McGillivray, *Environmental Law* (Oxford University Press, 6th edn, 2005), pp. 195–6.

[8] OJ 1973 C 112/1.

provided the policy framework for EC action over the next four years – had as its broad-ranging objects: to prevent, reduce and as far as possible eliminate pollution and nuisances; to maintain a satisfactory ecological balance and ensure the protection of the biosphere; to ensure the sound management of and avoid any exploitation of resources or of nature which cause significant damage to the ecological balance; to ensure that more account is taken of environmental aspects in town planning and land use; to seek common solutions to environmental problems with States outside the Community, and also international organisations.

In the absence of a legislative foundation in the EEC Treaty on which to base this new area of Community activity, the European Commission relied upon a dynamic interpretation of the Treaty which gives 'the constant improvement of the living and working conditions of their peoples' as one of the Community's essential objectives. The Commission also relied upon Art. 2 of the Treaty which declares the Community's tasks as promoting 'harmonious development', 'increased stability' and 'raising the standard of living through the establishment of a common market and a programme of approximating Member States' economic policies'. In this respect, early environmental policy corresponded to the Community's social policy, an alliance justified on the basis of the affinity between environmental quality and social concerns such as public health and the condition of the working environment.

### (b) Second phase: establishing a firm legal base

Moving beyond this initial policy declaration in the First Environmental Action Programme, competence to legislate on environmental matters, in the absence of any explicit Treaty provisions at the time, was mainly assumed on economic grounds. A Council declaration on the adoption of the First Environmental Action Programme stated that the establishment of the common market could not be realised without an effective campaign against pollution and nuisance and an improvement in the quality of life and protection of the environment.

In particular, the free movement of goods might be inhibited by Member States' differing product and process regulations set for 'environmental' reasons, and so be capable of hindering competition in the Community. This economic or 'functional spillover' argument was used to explain Community intervention in the case of early legislation designed to reduce the occurrence of economic externalities but which also had the effect of protection of the environment, such as Directive 67/548/EEC on the classification, packaging and labelling of dangerous substances.[9] This explanation for intervention corresponded almost exactly with an existing legal base for legislation – Art. 100 of the EEC Treaty. This provision gave the Council power 'to issue directives for

---

[9] OJ 1967 L 196/1.

the approximation of such laws, regulations or administrative provisions of the Member States as directly affect the establishment or functioning of the common market'. Under such a legal base the Drinking Water Directive 80/778/EEC[10] was enacted with the following rationale: 'disparity between provisions … in the various Member States relating to the quality of water for human consumption may create differences in the *conditions of competition* and, as a result, directly affect the *operation of the common market*'.

A further, and possibly competing, explanation for Community intervention was provided by the frequently transboundary nature of environmental impacts, as highlighted by the growing political philosophy of the environmental movement. For example the need to protect *migratory* birds (as the common heritage of the Community) provided an apposite lesson in the need for common, cross-border, action at the Community level. This further justification for environmental law – physical transnational externalities – or 'physical spillover' did not, at this stage, find specific expression in the EEC Treaty. Rather, it was artificially accommodated within the expansive remit of Art. 235 which provided: 'If action by the Community should prove necessary to attain, in the course of the operation of the common market, one of the objectives of the Community and this Treaty has not provided the necessary powers, the Council shall, acting unanimously on a proposal from the Commission and after consulting the European Parliament, take the appropriate measures.'

In this formative period of environmental law several 'environmental' measures were adopted on the basis of both Art. 100 and Art. 235, for example the Environmental Impact Assessment Directive (see Chapter 14).[11] The preamble to the Wild Birds Directive (Directive 79/404/EEC[12]) clearly encompasses both economic and 'environmental' rationales – 'Whereas the species of wild birds naturally occurring in the European territory of the member states are mainly migratory species; whereas such species constitute a *common heritage* and whereas effective bird protection is typically a *trans-frontier environment problem* entailing common responsibilities [emphasis added]', and, less obviously, given the relatively small impact on intra-Community trade of the hunting of wild birds:

> Whereas the conservation of the species of wild birds naturally occurring in the European territory of the member states is necessary to attain, within the operation of the common market, of the community's objectives regarding the improvement of living conditions, *a harmonious development of economic activities throughout the community* and a continuous and balanced expansion, but the necessary specific powers to act have not been provided for in the treaty [emphasis added].

Thinking more imaginatively, economic and physical spillovers do not provide the only justifications for Community action in the cause of environmental

---

[10] OJ 1980 L 229/11.     [11] Directive 85/337/EEC, OJ 1985 L 175/40.
[12] See further Ch. 15, pp. 627–34.

protection. Wils, for example, suggests that concerns about practices that take place in other EC countries may provide a 'psychic' justification for legislative intervention at the Community level. Although writing many years ago, the arguments that he advances are roughly in line with contemporary thinking about the expansion of standing rules for judicial review, particularly that the 'direct and individual concern' test in the case of challenging *Community* action is too restrictive in an age of transnational, and global, environmental concern (see further Chapter 3, pp. 119–28). They also resonate with the discussion of environmental values in Chapter 1 (pp. 40–7).

### Wouter Wils, 'Subsidiarity and EC Environmental Policy: Taking People's Concerns Seriously' (1994) 5 *Journal of Environmental Law* 85–91, p. 89

Whereas physical and economic spill-overs appear in any discussion on subsidiarity and environmental policy, *psychic* spill-overs are usually overlooked. This third type of spill-overs touches upon the essence and specificity of environmental policy, though. This policy is driven by people's concerns about the environment. For many people (all those who are 'really' environmentally sensitive), these concerns transcend physical proximity and economic relevance, relating directly to the integrity of nature and the well-being of various living creatures. Many people have strong feelings about whaling, the hunting of elephants, the destruction of the rain forest and the killing of seals, even if they are unlikely ever to see a whale, elephant or seal in the wild or to visit the rain forest, and independently of any other physical or economic relationship. Many people in Denmark or the Netherlands are affected by the hunting and trapping of birds in France even if these birds are not migratory, and irrespective of any touristic interest. Similarly, a large number of EU citizens in various Member States are appalled by bullfighting in Spain, and would derive satisfaction from a ban.

To recap, prior to 1986 (i.e., in the first two phases of environmental law in the EEC) two articles of the Treaty of Rome were used for 'environmental' Directives and Regulations: Art. 100 and Art. 235 EEC. Thus while, on grounds of economic spillover, Art. 100 EEC could be used, Art. 235 was used only once it was accepted that there were non-economic reasons why an economic Community should legislate in this area. So, although there are some Directives which we now call 'environmental' which were adopted before 1986, these were adopted on the basis of Art. 100, or a combination of Arts. 100 and 235. The most obvious reason that the Community was able to develop such a considerable body of environmental legislation, often under uncertain, or unrealistic, legal bases, was that the promotion of an environmental policy was by the common consent of all the Member States (unanimous voting in the Council was required under both legal bases) and encouraged by the Commission and Parliament and, importantly, by the Court of Justice. For example, in a relatively early case, Case 91/79 *Commission* v. *Italy*,[13] the ECJ strongly confirmed that

---

[13] [1980] ECR 1099.

economic concerns are capable of justifying environmental measures taken by the Community, providing crucial judicial support for the use of this rationale in the environmental sphere: 'Provisions which are made necessary by considerations relating to the environment and health may be a burden upon undertakings to which they apply and if there is no harmonisation of national provisions on the matter, competition may be appreciably distorted' (p. 1106). This development was not without its critics. For example, the UK's House of Lords Select Committee on the European Communities expressed the view that national pollution control does not directly affect the functioning of the common market; such control merely affects, and is one of the many factors which affect, the cost of production of a commodity.[14] In its strong support of environmental protection policy in Case 240/83 *Procureur de la République* v. *Association de Défense Des Brûleurs D'huiles Usagées (ADBHU)*,[15] the Court of Justice took on its critics. Its trump card was to present the Community's environmental policy as concerned with far more than the functioning of the common market. In a radical reading of the Treaty with, it must be said, little textual support, the Court considered that a European environmental policy was necessary to protect an 'essential objective' of the Community – environmental protection.

The *ADBHU* case grew out of a reference from a French court concerning Council Directive 75/439/EEC on the disposal of waste oils.[16] Articles 2–4 of the Directive required Member States to take the measures necessary to ensure the safe collection and disposal of waste oils, preferably by recycling. Article 5 provided that if the aims of those Articles could not be met, then 'Member States shall take the necessary measures to ensure that one or more undertakings carry out the collection and/or disposal of the products offered to them by the appropriate authorities.' Article 6 provided that 'any undertaking which disposes of waste oils must obtain a permit'. The French decree that implemented the Directive divided France into zones and authorised waste oil collectors and disposers to operate on a zone-by-zone basis. The French court asked the ECJ whether Art. 5 and 6 were in conformity with the Treaty.

### Case 240/83, *Procureur de la République* v. *Association de Défense Des Brûleurs D'huiles Usagées* [1985] ECR 531 (emphasis added)

9. The national court asks whether the system of permits is compatible with the principle of free trade, free movement of goods and freedom of competition, but does not elaborate further. In that connection it should be borne in mind that the principles of free movement of goods and freedom of competition, together with freedom of trade as a fundamental right, are general principles of Community law of which the Court ensures

---

[14] House of Lords Select Committee on the European Communities, Second Report Session 1978–9, *Approximation of Laws Under Article 100 of the Treaty of Rome: Environmental Problems of the Treaty of Rome* HL 131, p. 199.     [15] [1985] ECR 531.     [16] OJ 1975 L 194/23.

observance. The above-mentioned principles of the directive should therefore be reviewed in the light of those principles.

…

12. In the first place it should be observed that the principle of freedom of trade is not to be viewed in absolute terms but is subject to certain limits justified by the objectives of general interest pursued by the Community provided that the rights in question are not substantially impaired.

13. There is no reason to conclude that the directive has exceeded those limits. *The directive must be seen in the perspective of environmental protection, which is one of the Community's essential objectives.* It is evident, particularly from the third and seventh recitals in the preamble to the directive, that any legislation dealing with the disposal of waste oils must be designed to protect the environment from the harmful effects caused by the discharge, deposit or treatment of such products. It is also evident from the provisions of the directive as a whole that care has been taken to ensure that the principles of proportionality and non-discrimination will be served if certain restrictions should prove necessary. In particular, Article 5 of the directive permits the creation of a system of zoning 'where the aims defined in Articles 2, 3, and 4 cannot otherwise be achieved'.

This judgment meant that, even before a specific environmental title existed in the Treaty, the legitimacy of a body of environmental law was accepted, both as a matter of economic and transboundary concern, and as a matter that the Court should have regard to (and possibly even give priority to) when faced with a clash between the Community's 'essential objectives'.

An explicit legal base for the Community's environmental law and policy was provided shortly after the *ADBHU* judgment, in the form of Title VII on the Environment (Arts. 130r, s and t) inserted by Art. 25 of the Single European Act 1986. The Title gave legislative effect to the arguments of the Court in that case and reaffirmed the Community's de facto competence in environmental matters. This meant that in the majority of circumstances the EC could dispense with the need to find an economic rationale for environmental legislation. But an economic nexus of sorts remained. The Single European Act was concerned with environmental protection primarily because of the likely distorting effects of national environmental laws on the achievement of the internal market, and the prospect of environmental harm caused by increased transport, industrial restructuring and enhanced economic growth associated with this. Environmental policy, alongside social policy, therefore came to be regarded as a flanking policy to complement the internal market.

Moreover, one of the central features of the Single European Act was the introduction of Art. 100a on the establishment and functioning of the internal market into the EEC Treaty, which, with Arts. 130r–t (the legal base for specifically environmental measures) meant that two potential (and competing) legal bases for environmental action existed. Apart from dealing with different (though clearly related) subject matter, the key differences between these bases lay in the voting requirements for the Council and the participation of the European Parliament which they established; Art. 130t required a unanimous vote in Council and more limited participation in the legislative process by the Parliament, compared with qualified majority voting in Council under Art. 100a, and 'cooperation' between the Council and Parliament in law-making. In the years following the Single European Act, these differences led to inter-institutional struggles about the respective competence, involvement and influence of the Council, Commission and European Parliament in the legislative process relating to environmental matters, centred around questions about the correct legal base for a measure. The question of the rationale for legislation relating to environmental protection – economic or 'purely environmental' spillovers – therefore became imbued with political significance.[17]

In terms of the substance of the Single European Act, it is particularly important that, even at this early stage, environmental considerations were required 'to be a component of the Community's other policies' (Art. 130r(2)) (particularly given the environmental damage likely to ensue from economic expansion envisaged by the Single European Act). This requirement was to be developed later into the more broadly applicable integration principle of later Treaty revisions, discussed further below (pp. 164–70). The concept of subsidiarity (Art. 130r(4)) in the environmental field was also introduced at this point, providing an important indicator of the Member States trying to restrict, in certain ways, the further development of uniform environmental legislation. It is also the first legislative expression of what is now referred to as flexibility.[18]

The specific legal base for environmental activity on the part of the Community was confirmed, and strengthened to some degree, by the Treaty on European Union. Notably, environmental protection entered the Treaty as a fundamental objective of the Community, but the reference in the EC Treaty to 'sustainable and non-inflationary growth respecting the environment'[19] was generally considered a fundamental, and problematic, misreading of the concept of sustainable development. The Treaty of Amsterdam (1997) sought to remedy this: the objectives of the Community came to include the promotion of 'balanced and sustainable development of economic activities' and

---

[17] See Case C-300/89 *Commission* v. *Council* [1991] ECR 2867 (Titanium Dioxide) in which the political ramifications for the Parliament of a choice of legal base were not lost in the ECJ's judgment. For a different, 'centre of gravity', approach by the Court, see Case C-155/91 *Commission* v. *Council* [1993] ECR I-936 (Waste Framework Directive) and Case C-187/93 *Parliament* v. *Council* [1994] ECR I-2857 (transfrontier movement of hazardous waste). See also Joined Cases C-164/97 and C-165/97 *European Parliament* v. *Council* [1999] ECR I-1139 (forest regulations). For the implications in practice of the choice of legal base, see the passage of the Waste Electrical and Electronic Products Directive (the so-called 'WEE' Directive) – in which different aspects of the proposal were founded on different legal bases. More recently, see Case C-281/01 *Commission* v. *Council* [2002] I-12049 ('Energy Star Agreement').

[18] See discussion of the 'third developmental phase', below, pp. 164–70.

[19] Article 2 EC, as amended by the Treaty on European Union.

### Julia Hertin and Frans Berkhout, 'Ecological Modernisation and EU Environmental Policy Integration', Science and Technology Policy Research Unit Working Paper No. 72 (2001), pp. 5–6

First, environmental interests and polluter interest tend to be asymmetric. Polluter interests are usually concentrated and driven by strong economic motives and often represented by well-established advocacy groups with good access to the political system. In contrast, environmental interests tend to be more dispersed, long term and less well represented. The rise of civil society environmental organisations is not regarded as having compensated for this imbalance. Environmental ministries have historically a low status and conflicts between government agencies tend to be dominated by strong sectoral departments.

Second, the institutional separation between sector and environmental policies means that environmental departments tend to be involved during the later stages of sectoral policy formulation where environmental concerns are often reflected as costs and restrictions. This perception of environmental policy as a burden weakens its position further. Third, opposing interests of environmental and sectoral departments are often 'resolved' through bargains that satisfy the interests of both agencies but are highly inefficient. Either contradictory policies are implemented in parallel or costly end of pipe technologies are added to a controversial project to make it acceptable for environmental departments. In short, the critique argues that the environmental policy formulation process has been dominated by opposing interests between environmental and sector departments which have led to an insufficiently high level of environmental protection at high cost. A shift from remedial to anticipatory policies is seen to depend on the integration of environmental concerns across the whole range of government policy.

Advocates of policy reform have argued that this 'additivity' needs to be replaced by a process of integration. Rather than a 'layering' of new environmental demands on top of existing policy processes, environmental considerations should be embedded at the heart of policy-making routines ...

Where the protection of natural resources is seen mainly as a source of additional costs, environmental policy involves a strong conflict of interest between environmental and sectoral departments ... This configuration of assumptions and organisation structure will tend to lead to 'additive' environmental measures, reinforcing the conflict between environmental and sectoral departments, and probably imposing additional costs on all parties.

In contrast, when environmental protection and economic development are perceived as potentially compatible aims, relationships between environmental and sectoral ministries can be expected to be more cooperative. Environmental policy could then take the form of a joint problem-solving process, which is more likely to result in policy measures that encourage integrated technological or structural responses. These are usually seen to be more cost-efficient, or even profitable ('no regret' measures). The option of win-win solutions is likely to allow sectoral departments to take a constructive position in negotiations, thus improving the cooperation between the departments.

We argue that this idea of self-reinforcing cycles ... underlies the critique of 'additive' environmental policy expressed by advocates of ecological modernisation. From this perspective, the main objective of environmental policy integration is to enable environmental policy-making to shift from a traditional antagonistic model to a new cooperative model. The analytical and discourse perspectives of ecological modernisation provide the interpretive backdrop for this shift.

In the European Union, the legislative, rather than philosophical, basis for the process of integration is provided for by Art. 6 EC: 'Environmental protection requirements must be integrated into the definition and implementation of the Community policies and activities referred to in Article 3, in particular with a view to promoting sustainable development.'

Since Art. 3 includes a long and wide-ranging list of policies and activities (common commercial policy, internal market, agriculture and fisheries, transport, energy, competition, development cooperation and the free movement of goods, persons, services and capital, and so on) there is the potential for significant policy integration. The 'Cardiff process' was a political initiative of the European Council in 1998 to kick-start the process of policy integration by requesting different Council committees to prepare strategies and programmes aimed at integrating environmental considerations into their policy areas, starting with energy, transport and agriculture. The process now embraces further sectors (enterprise, research, internal market, development cooperation, fisheries, structural funds, trade, and economic and financial affairs), all of which have adopted integration strategies. However, as Hertin and Berkhout go on to observe, the barriers to environmental policy integration are deep-rooted. The European Commission, like most governments, is described as having developed a strongly vertical and segmented structure of Directorates-General (DGs), co-ordinated through strong centralised political control. This means that the integration process runs counter to many accepted axioms of the organisation of public administration (p. 6), rendering the principle of integration more a 'rhetorical reference point' than a realistic political and policy strategy. This is quite apart from questions about the enforceability, or 'justiciability', of the principle.[25] Examples of the failure of integrative strategies are discussed throughout this book.[26] The reality of entrenched interests (at Community level *and* national level), so clearly identified by David Wood,[27] is recognised by the European Commission in its 'stocktaking' of the Cardiff process:

> The processes set in place over the past few years have led to environmental improvements in several sectors. However, the pace of progress towards further environmental integration would be boosted if all sectors implemented commitments made over the past five years.

[25] See Martin Hession and Richard Macrory, 'The Legal Duty of Environmental Integration: Commitment and Obligation or Enforceable Right?' in Tim O'Riordan and Heather Voisey (eds.), *The Transition to Sustainability: The Politics of Agenda 21 in Europe* (Earthscan, 1998).

[26] On trade and the environment, see below, pp. 171–84, for further discussion of 'disintegration' decisions, see Ch. 16, which considers the impact of an environmental agenda on agricultural policy, pp. 680–91. On the integration of pollution controls, see Ch. 9, pp. 354–7.

[27] See Preface to Part II, pp. 140–1.

This will be a difficult process: as many of the 'low hanging fruits' of integration have already been picked, future efforts to reverse persisting unsustainable trends will need to focus increasingly on structural reforms, which may generate tensions with established interest groups in the sectors concerned. In addition, action at national level is needed to deliver on the commitments made at the Union level, as in many areas Community competence is limited.[28]

Part of the problem in securing integrated policy making has been in finding a suitable mechanism by which different policy areas may be fully integrated, particularly since the bilateral production of discussion papers on various themes (for example the environmental implications of agriculture[29]) by the relevant directorates appears not to have resulted in policy making processes capable of reaching beyond the policy areas involved. For this reason the Commission has seen fit to expand the remit of environmental assessment to allow for an assessment of *multiple* policy areas when drawing up legislative proposals and policy. This enlarged form of assessment, referred to as 'impact' or 'sustainability' assessment, as yet only applies to the Commission's *internal* law and policy making processes (although there are indications that it will be required of Member States in the future). It is at present a sign of the Commission's adherence to the broad concerns and values of sustainable development as the 'central objective of all sectors and policies', and is designed to ensure that 'careful assessment of the full effects of a policy proposal must include estimates of its economic, environmental, and social impacts inside and outside the EU'.[30] In practical terms the Commission must initially conduct an assessment of *all* policy options and legislative proposals to identify possible options and sectors affected. Of these preliminary impact assessments, the potentially most significant proposals and policies will then be subject to a further round of more detailed and extended impact assessment, the test for which is whether the proposal will result in substantial economic, environmental and/or social impacts on a specific sector or several sectors. The assessments flagged up by DG Environment as currently having most relevance, and on which work has already begun, are policies on the tobacco and sugar regimes, and the sustainability of European tourism. DG Environment is responsible for or closely involved (with other DGs) with the conduct and compilation of these and almost every other extended impact assessment, the assessment process thereby offering an opportunity to include environmental factors and criteria in previously disparate policy areas. This development, perhaps more than any other, suggests that doubts about the legitimacy of environmental policy as a core area of activity of the EU have been overcome. Indeed, requiring environmental concerns to be addressed in a whole range of policy areas (in line with sustainable

---

[28] European Commission, *Integrating Environmental Considerations into other Policy Areas*, p. 3.
[29] European Commission, *Indicators for the Integration of Environmental Concerns into the Common Agricultural Policy* COM (2000) 20 final.
[30] European Commission, *Proposal for an EU Sustainable Development Strategy* COM (2001) 264.

development) has provided a template for integrated policy making more generally. Furthermore, this expanded form of environmental assessment, now applied to all internal Commission policy making activity, shows that this instrument of environmental policy has strongly influenced the style, process, and possibly also the content of policy making. In a very real sense, then, environmental policy has been subjected to a process of mainstreaming, and thus applies to a more general sweep of policy making, due mainly to the perceived need to integrate environmental concerns into all EU activities and policies (on this development, see further Chapter 14, pp. 601–4).

This development is one of the subjects of a Commission Communication (or working document) which aims to assess progress in integrating environmental considerations into other policy areas, described as a 'stocktaking exercise'. True to this description, the Commission provides for each sector (energy, agriculture, transport and so on) a list of strategies, programmes and legislation designed to achieve the integration of environmental considerations. Common to assessments of several of the sectors is the recommendation to use flexible, market-based, instruments to promote environmental protection (these form the subject of Chapter 11). The close relationship between securing integrated policy making and broadening the range of legal instruments is elaborated by the Commission below. This extract from the Commission's working document also highlights the increasing significance of more participative approaches to law and policy making, as an important part of the process of policy integration.

### European Commission, *Integrating Environmental Considerations into other Policy Areas – a Stocktaking of the Cardiff Process* COM (2004) 394 final, pp. 35–6 (emphasis in the original)

... there is a need to develop innovative **instruments and approaches that can actively foster environmental integration while minimising economic and social costs**. Legislation, while remaining one of the main means of achieving environmental objectives, needs to be complemented in the most cost-effective way, while taking full account of economic and social considerations. As indicated in the EU Sustainable Development Strategy and the Sixth Environmental Action Programme, measures that lead to the **internalisation of environmental costs** offer one of the fastest routes for integration as a successful internalisation means that price signals would reflect the real environmental costs, thus informing the decisions of both economic operators and policy makers in the concerned sectors. This internalisation of costs is facilitated by the use of market-based instruments to promote environmental objectives as illustrated by the recently adopted emissions trading scheme,[31] or the directive on the taxation of energy products. There are many advantages to the use of market-based instruments. As flexible mechanisms, they allow sectoral actors to develop cost-effective approaches to reducing environmental impacts. By internalising environmental costs, they can

[31] See Ch. 11, pp. 428–32.

lead to changes in behaviour. Yet, competence in this field principally lies with the Member States and the full deployment of some market-based instruments at Community level suffers from this situation, as exemplified by the time needed to adopt measures in the area of taxation.[32]

Other instruments that are designed to contribute to environmental integration include the **thematic strategies** foreseen in the 6th Environmental Action Programme (soils, marine, air quality; resources; waste and recycling; urban; pesticides) and the Strategy on environment and health. These strategies exemplify the Commission's new integrated approach to policy-making in the environmental field. They are being developed with the full consideration of stakeholders and the involvement of the concerned policy sectors, so as to promote environmental integration and policy convergence. The strategies will set out clear quantifiable targets and, where possible, promote the use of market-based instruments. They provide a test bed for innovative approaches.

The full implementation ... of the **Extended Impact Assessments**, as part of the Better Regulation package and in the context of the Sustainable Development Strategy will allow spill-overs from one policy area to another or synergies to be identified and addressed, hence facilitating the identification and negotiation of trade-offs. Experience so far has confirmed that, properly used, extended impact assessments could be a powerful instrument for promoting environmental integration while ensuring that due account is taken of the economic and social dimensions of sustainable development.

...

**Raising awareness** of environmental problems and solutions available may sensitise the public and decision makers to the need to further environmental integration. Information can also be used to promote stakeholder participation for better environmental policy making and encourage changes in behaviour.

### (d) Fourth phase: constitutionalism

The Community legal order has been subject to a process of confirming and further elaborating its constitutional basis, through the drafting of a Treaty Establishing a Constitution for Europe. The ratification of the Treaty by Member States has been 'derailed' by negative referenda, but the plan had been to replace the existing EU Treaties and merge the EU and the European Community, creating one Union. The Constitutional Treaty would have given formal legal status to the Charter of Fundamental Rights by incorporating the Charter into the Treaty, whereas currently its legal standing is uncertain. There is also some further elaboration of the Union's objectives, some of which have environmental implications. For example, reference is made for the first time to the contribution of the Union to 'free and fair trade' (Art. I-3(4)) – a

---

[32] Note the need for a unanimous vote in Council in the case of measures on taxation: Art. 175(2) EC.

subject we explore further immediately below – alongside the reproduction of the more familiar objectives of contributing to 'the sustainable development of the Earth' (Art. I-3(4)) and 'the sustainable development of Europe … with a high level of protection and improvement of the quality of the environment' (Art. I-3(3)). The key change for environmental law and policy would have been the relocation (some say demotion) of the principle of integration from the 'head' of the Treaty (Art. 6 of Part I 'Principles' of the EC Treaty) to Art. III-119 of Part III 'The Policies and Functioning of the Union' of the Constitutional Treaty. This positioning, nevertheless, would mean that the principle of integrating environmental considerations would apply to *all* Union policies and activities, for example defence, and external relations. A strengthened integration principle also forms the basis for the main environmental entry in the Charter of Fundamental Rights of the Union, found in Art. II-97, which states: 'A high level of environmental protection and the improvement of the quality of the environment must be integrated into the policies of the Union and ensured in accordance with the principle of sustainable development.' This apart, there was little progress for an environmental agenda. Most notably the opportunity was not taken to refer to environmental *rights* in the Charter, which jars with its strong declaration of a variety of social and economic rights.

Given that the current shape of environmental policy has been greatly influenced by the 'constitutionalising' force of the ECJ (first seen in *ADBHU*, above, pp. 161–2), it is interesting that environmental protection remained, in the Draft Constitutional Treaty, an underdeveloped area in terms of the attribution of rights and duties (even more so in earlier, much-criticised drafts of the Constitution). Environmental law and policy has, in other words, entered the constitutional vocabulary of the EU, but the implications of this have not yet been followed through in terms of any entrenchment or even elaboration of environmental rights.

## 4 'Free and fair trade'? Trade/environment dilemmas and the EU

'Free and fair trade' is listed as one of the EU's objectives in its Treaty Establishing a Constitution for Europe.

### Article I-3(4)

In its relations with the wider world, the Union shall uphold and promote its values and interests. It shall contribute to peace, security, the sustainable development of the Earth, solidarity and mutual respect among peoples, free and fair trade, eradication of poverty and protection of human rights and in particular the rights of the child, as well as to strict observance and to development of international law, including respect for the principles of the United Nations Charter.

Although in political terms, the Draft Constitution is in abeyance, this provides an important indicator of the changing priorities of the Union – very few of these objectives featured in the original Rome Treaty. The use of the phrase 'free and fair' is, of course, a highly presentational appropriation of the word 'fair', which currently carries great weight in progressive social and environmental debate (and is usually cited in opposition to 'free trade', for example 'the free trade versus fair trade debate'[33]). That 'fair' has been linked to 'free' in relation to the EU's description of its preferred trade policy creates what some consider to be an oxymoron, but it also signifies that the Union has taken on board broad concerns about the inequities and injustices created by its involvement in, and furthering of, global free trade patterns. The linkage is nevertheless used by the Union in a vague and aspirational manner, suggesting that it is far from being translated into a fuller and more radical programme for countering the social and environmental problems which flow from increased and globalised trade. A first step requires at the very least a more precise sense of what 'fair' means in the context of trade relations between Member States and between the Union and the rest of the world.

The Union's history as a leading free trade organisation is very strong. As we discussed above (p. 156), at a very basic level the EU was initially developed to create a single trading bloc (the common market) capable of competing with the United States and the emerging Asian markets and thus to encourage economic regeneration in the unstable post-war period. This economic basis was recognised to be a simple starting point; the political and social equality dimensions of the EU were important motivations for its formation but were (perhaps deliberately) obscured in its early development. The free trade in goods between the states of the EU (one of the four 'freedoms' – see p. 173) has been hugely significant in terms of shaping the economies and cultures of the Member States, but it has also brought heavy environmental costs – increased manufacturing, packaging, transportation (and discarding) of goods, producing a range of pollutants and wastes, and supported by the massive development of infrastructure in the form of roads, ports and airports. Levied against these environmental burdens, the claim that EC environmental law is capable of countering the worst effects of the market appears very weak. However, the greater level of recognition (at popular and legal levels) of the environmental costs of free trade within the EU and between the EU and the rest of the world has produced numerous complex and engaging legal dilemmas, which the ECJ and the World Trade Organisation (WTO) have attempted to resolve, or at least to make some sense of. Rather than a detailed examination of the voluminous

[33] Miguel Poiares Maduro, 'Is There Any Such Thing as Free or Fair Trade? A Constitutional Analysis of the Impact of International Trade on the European Social Model' in Grainne de Burca and Joanne Scott (eds.), *The EU and the WTO: Legal and Constitutional Issues* (Hart, 2003), p. 257.

case law (which can be sought in the works referenced in the 'Further reading' section of this chapter), in this section we consider the background to these trade/environment dilemmas, and some of the main legal turning points. In line with other works we divide this introductory analysis of the EU's trade/environment dilemmas into internal and external dimensions, although this is inevitably a conceptual rather than realistic distinction – after all, imported products from outside the EU enter into free circulation in the single market on crossing any Member State's borders. A more detailed examination of why trade law raises dilemmas for environmental protection, and their treatment by *international* trade law, can be found in Chapter 7; EU regulation of GMOs, discussed in Chapter 5, provides a rather unhappy context for the consideration of certain trade-related issues, including an example of the EU's attempt to reach an accommodation between trade and the environment in the form of the so-called 'environmental guarantee' (Arts. 95(4) and 95(5)EC – pp. 206–7).

The idea that the EU's law and policy on trade is rooted primarily in an economic motive – the creation of a free market functioning within a capitalist economy – is emphasised by Ian Ward in his critique of the Union: 'the primary reason that the European Community exists is to make money'.[34] He identifies in particular the paradox that such economic conditions seem to rely upon 'lots of legal regulation and lots and lots of laws' (p. 134), exactly of the type traditionally favoured by European bureaucracy, and reflected in the EC Treaty and numerous pieces of secondary legislation.

### Ian Ward, *A Critical Introduction to European Law* (Butterworths, 2nd edn, 2003), pp. 138–9, 170–2

The free market lay at the centre of the Treaty of Rome. The sentiments which lay behind it can still be found in article 2, which waxes lyrically about the need for the Community to 'promote' a 'harmonious, balanced and sustainable development of economic activities', as well as 'a high degree of competitiveness and convergence of economic performance', and article 14 which affirms that the

> internal market shall comprise an area without internal frontiers in which the free movement of goods, persons, services and capital is ensured in accordance with the provisions of this Treaty.

These four 'freedoms' are the heartbeat of the common market, and have been the subject of considerable legal reinforcement. Much of the rest of the Treaty was devoted to fleshing out further the nature of the market and its 'freedoms'. Articles 23–31, or Title I of the Community Treaty, describe the free movement of goods, including the remnants of the original Customs Union enacted in the Rome Treaty, whilst articles 39–60, presently comprising Title III, establish the primary legislation for the free movement of persons, capital and services.

---

[34] Ian Ward, *A Critical Introduction to European Law* (Butterworths, 2nd edn, 2003), p. 134.

We examine the provisions of the Treaty concerning the free movement of goods from an environmental perspective below (pp. 176–82). Ian Ward continues by reviewing the general law relating to the free movement of goods (as well as other, and related, aspects of Community law in sectors such as agriculture, competition policy and regional policy) and reaches broad and striking conclusions about the nature of democracy and decision making in the common market. Ward makes a claim for the opening up of decisions about the market similar to those which have been forcefully made for participation in environmental decision making (as discussed in Chapter 3).

> But, perhaps, the deepest problem lies at the very heart of the notion of a 'free market'. For, whilst the 'common' market might be 'free' in the economic sense, it is certainly not free in the political or ethical sense. Joseph Weiler rightly observes that the 'culture of the Market' describes a 'highly politicised choice of ethos, of ideology and of political culture'.[35] Francis Snyder reaches a similar conclusion, emphasising that the four 'freedoms' which underpin the law of the European 'market' carry a very particular ideological baggage, one that polarises economic power and marginalises alternative conceptions of redistribution. In other words, the common market, like any other, favours certain individuals and interests over others and, being unregulated, provides no instruments with which to restore the balance. Economic freedom in the 'new' Europe has come at the price of political freedom.[36]
>
> The experience of the European 'common' market has, then, reinforced the reality that no market is really 'free', but rather the reflexive instrument of various interest groups, amongst which the consumer is usually the weakest and the larger corporation is invariably the strongest. Between these two mismatched competitors, the institutions of the European Union, including national institutions, are supposed to ensure fair play. In reality, however, the Commission has never made the slightest effort to hide its lust for business.
>
> The statistics are telling. Brussels has become the Shangri-La of big business. Over two hundred of the largest transnational corporations have permanent offices in Brussels, from which over ten thousand lobbyists ply their trade, acting in the words of one recent commentary 'as a replacement for the citizen-based constituency that the Community lacks'. Over three thousand lobbyists flutter around the European Parliament alone.[37] The Union is awash with business groupings, many of which are peopled not only by representatives of business, but also by members of the Commission. The largest, such as the European Roundtable of Industrialists (ERT), pride themselves on their capacity to pick up a phone and chat to a head of state or a Director General of the Commission …

---

[35] Joseph Weiler, 'Problems of Legitimacy in Post 1992 Europe' (1991) 46 *Aussenwissenschaft* 411, p. 430.

[36] Francis Snyder, *New Directions in European Community Law* (Weidenfeld and Nicholson, 1990), pp. 24–6, 35–42, 49–56.

[37] Belen Balanya, Ann Doherty, Olivier Holderman, Adam Ma'arit and Eric Wesselius, *Europe Inc: Regional and Global Restructuring and the Rise of Corporate Power* (Pluto, 2000), pp. 3–5.

> ... The main driving force behind the common market should be those who work in it and shop in it, whilst the main driving force behind the Union should be its citizens. To the extent to which public concerns regarding various aspects of the market, such as the environment and advances in biotechnology, are swept aside is depressing ... The case for democracy in the common market is every bit as pressing as it is for democracy in the Union itself.

A more balanced picture of the EU's motivations or 'driving forces' is drawn by Sara Dillon in her account of the Union's place within international trade. She compares the 'multi-dimensional entity' of the Union, expressing diverse public interest ideologies and providing protection for a range of rights other than 'the right to free trade', with the more monolithic objectives pursued by the WTO in the absence of any public interest dimension. She stresses a great awareness on the part of the 'drafters of the European project' and particularly the ECJ that 'the EU is not simply about economics' and that it is quite possible 'that the central economic requirements, necessary for integration, have had as their main purpose the preservation of non-economic values'.[38]

### Sara Dillon, *International Trade and Economic Law and the European Union* (Hart, 2002), pp. 4–5, 11

The EU, for all its deficiencies, has had an actual response: it can claim at least to have delivered peace and stability, a high level of social and environmental protection, as well as economic rights and freedoms. The EU legal system also early on created an alternative route to influence for citizens, bypassing the national state; the EU was able to marshal resentments against individual Member States held by citizens of those states. Concrete requirements emanating from the EC, such as equal pay for equal work, made sense as obvious benefits available from the centre ...

As to justifications for the WTO's new powers (as of 1995) justifications are thinner on the ground, and tend to be without content that can be recognised and understood by persons outside economics, transnational business, or trade law studies ...

There *is* no public interest dimension to WTO; at best the WTO bodies (the panels and Appellate Body) can decide, or not, that a national public interest measure with restrictive trade effects is consistent with WTO law ... The EU by contrast, is a multi-dimensional political and economic project, with binding law in many areas of concern to the non-economic aspects of life. This multi-dimensional quality acts as a recognition that economic integration in and of itself creates dangers for social and other protections developed over time within the confines of the nation state. It is part of the logic of economic integration that economic and social losers may be created; it is also apparent that the 'race to the bottom' in terms of regulatory structures is a natural product of integration across national borders. It is plain that there was an acute awareness among the drafters of the modern European project that economic integration posed dangers to protections that had been developed at national level; hence the requirement that prior to accession, candidate countries would

---

[38] Sara Dillon, *International Trade and Economic Law and the European Union* (Hart, 2002), p. 3.

> receive funding to bring their economies up to a certain standard (cohesion); and also that they would create a broad range of legislation that would qualify them for membership …
>
> …
>
> The framers of the original EC system were acutely aware that economic integration was a means to an end: peace through overcoming the impulse towards economic rivalry. The war and peace dimension, and the grand assumption that politics would not only follow but also inform economics, has allowed for the development of EC law in such diverse areas as labour protection, social equality, consumer and environmental protection, and lately human rights more explicitly. The European system was able to create a direct link between citizens and the Community institutions; in many and complex areas, the benefits on offer from the Community could surpass those available from the nation (member) state.

As Dillon puts it, the EU is a quite different legal and political entity from the WTO, but 'the EU as a whole is now faced and faced dramatically with the problem of how to configure itself within the WTO' (p. 2), an issue we return to when considering the external dimension of EU trade (pp. 182–4, and Chapter 7).

## (a) Internal trade

Adherence to free market principles, even when coupled with protections and rights in other areas, habitually throws up ethical and welfare problems. A graphic illustration of this was raised by the campaign which took place in the mid 1990s to ban live exports of animals from Britain to other Member States – in particular calves destined to be raised in crates to satisfy the trade in veal meat. An important feature of the campaign was that European Union law on the free movement of such live 'goods' was subject to far greater and more critical scrutiny than previously, as were the larger issues of the desirability and functioning of the single market. Litigation determined that the prior regulation of this issue at EU level prevented the introduction of trade restrictions in the UK.[39] Although this might not be considered an 'environmental' dilemma as such, it offers a good example of the complex dynamic when different actors take different views on what might reasonably justify restrictions on trade. We examine examples of trade restrictions imposed by Member States for reasons more overtly concerning environmental protection below, and particularly trace the response of the European courts to such action.

A starting point to any discussion of free movement of goods, as a vital aspect of the EU's free trade policy, is Art. 23 of the EC Treaty which, as Ian Ward notes, in a very real sense 'describes the original purpose of the Community' (p. 144): 'The Community shall be based upon a customs

---

[39] *R v. MAFF, ex parte Compassion in World Farming* [1998] ECR I-1251. More generally, see Rhoda McLeod, 'Calf Exports at Brightlingsea' [1998] 51 *Parliamentary Affairs* 345.

union which shall cover all trade in goods and which shall involve the prohibition between Member States of customs duties on imports and exports and of all charges having equivalent effect, and the adoption of a common customs tariff in their relation with third countries.' This provision, though brief, sought initially to establish a single trading area within the (then) EEC, reinforced by the erection of an agreed tariff in respect of goods coming from or going to 'third countries'. Although an expansive body of case law has grown up around this article, especially relating to the meaning of 'charges having equivalent effect', the achievement of the purpose underlying this Article was relatively straightforward, with very few Member States imposing customs duties after the end of the transitional period in 1969, though rather more seeking to circumvent this provision by the application of supposed internal 'taxes'. Greater difficulties, particularly from an environmental point of view, have arisen from the working of a second set of articles which are aimed at securing the free movement of goods (Arts. 28–30). Article 28 EC prohibits 'quantitative restrictions on imports' (such as quotas) and 'all measures having equivalent effect' – which can include, for example, product standards – and Art. 29 prohibits similar restrictions on exports. Article 30 provides Member States with a list of justifiable reasons for restrictions on the movement of goods.

## Article 30

The provisions of Articles 28 and 29 shall not preclude prohibitions or restrictions on imports or exports or goods in transit justified on the grounds of public morality, public policy or public security; the protection of health and life of humans, animals or plants; the protection of national treasures possessing artistic, historic or archaeological value; or the protection of industrial and commercial property. Such prohibitions or restrictions shall not, however, constitute a means of arbitrary discrimination or disguised restriction on trade between Member States.

This Article has remained practically unchanged since the Rome Treaty was signed in 1957; it therefore reflects the moral and legal concerns of that time, and ignores the significance of social movements such as consumer protection and environmental protection. Instead, legal recognition of these emerging policy areas has come from the ECJ in the form of its development of a non-exhaustive category of justifications which act as a judicial supplement to Art. 30 EC.[40] The breakthrough for the recognition of environmental protection as an objective capable legitimately of hampering trade between Member States came with the Court's judgment in Case 302/86 *Commission* v. *Denmark* ('Danish Bottles').[41]

---

[40] Case 120/78 *Rewe-Zentrale AG* v. *Bundesmonopolverwaltung für Branntwein (Cassis de Dijon)* [1979] ECR 649.    [41] [1988] ECR 4607.

In 1981 Denmark introduced legislation for beer and soft drinks containers requiring that they be marketed only in returnable containers, approved by the Danish authorities. The laudable aim of the legislation was to encourage the widespread return of bottles. However, this inevitably imposed a burden upon manufacturers of soft drinks and beer in other Member States who wished to sell their products in Denmark. In 1984, Denmark amended its legislation to allow producers to 'test the market' using 'non-approved' containers, but only up to 3,000 hectolitres per producer per year, and so long as a deposit-and-return scheme for bottles was established. In practice these national rules represented an extension of the territorial scope of Danish environmental law, because the rules affected the bottling of drinks in other Member States. The European Commission brought enforcement proceedings against Denmark (now Art. 226 EC) on the basis of its apparent infringement of the Treaty's provisions for the free movement of goods (now Art. 28 EC). The Court followed closely its reasoning in *ADBHU* (above, pp. 161–2) that the protection of the environment is 'one of the Community's essential objectives' (para. 13), which may as such justify certain limitations of the principle of the free movement of goods. It therefore held the protection of the environment to be a 'mandatory requirement' (or imperative of the state) which may limit the application of Art. 28 of the Treaty.

The Court then applied the principle of proportionality to the Danish measures. The requirement that the containers be returnable was found to be acceptable: the obligation to establish a deposit-and-return system for empty containers was 'an indispensable element of a system intended to ensure the re-use of containers and therefore appears necessary to achieve the aims pursued by the contested rules. That being so, the restrictions which it imposes on the free movement of goods cannot be regarded as a disproportionate system' (para. 13). However, the requirement that containers be 'approved' was addressed differently; the Court considered that the limitation on the *quantity* of products which may be marketed by importers in non-approved containers *was* disproportionate to the environmental protection objectives being pursued (para. 21).

The great importance of the case is that the Court acknowledged the existence (for the first time) of a 'mandatory requirement' relating to environmental protection. The Danish deposit-and-return scheme was considered necessary to satisfy this requirement, but the rule requiring the use of *approved* containers was not. In terms of environmental protection the difference between these is vital: a deposit-and-return scheme using approved, and therefore pretty much uniform, bottles encourages the rinsing out and refilling of bottles (using relatively little energy), whereas the use of non-approved (variously shaped) bottles, even in the context of a deposit-and-return scheme, is more likely to lead to the recycling (crushing and reconstituting) of bottles, involving large inputs of energy. In this case, the Court found the Danish pursuit of a particular standard of environmental protection to be acceptable. But the basis on which the Court determined exactly what *level* of environmental protection should be achieved by the Danish has been questioned. Why not a higher standard (i.e. one requiring the use of *approved* containers)? A great deal of discretion on this point was accorded to the Court by its application of the proportionality test. Joanne Scott warns that in cases such as *Danish Bottles*, the Court appears to arrive at a decision about the proportionality measures intuitively, but that, just as worryingly, it may also approach proportionality as a form of cost benefit analysis (p. 70; see also Chapter 1, pp. 37–40). In the following passage, she discusses the relationship between the proportionality test and the precautionary principle, both of which are concerned with the nature of 'appropriate action'.

### Joanne Scott, *EC Environmental Law* (Longmans, 1998), pp. 69–72

Proportionality proper speaks, on the one hand, to the intensity of a measure in terms of the degree of restraint of trade which it implies and, on the other, to the degree of protection which it is capable of achieving. It demands a balancing of one against the other … Balancing the intensity of the restriction against the intensity of the benefit, [in Danish Bottles] the Court found that the measure [relating to the limited quantity of drinks to be sold in non-approved containers] was 'disproportionate to the objective pursued'. Consequently, a measure may be strictly necessary to achieve that 'extra inch' in terms of environmental protection; nonetheless in the absence of a reasonable relationship between the extra restriction on trade implied by the measure, and the extra protection achieved, such rules will be sacrificed in the name of proportionality. Proportionality, however, should be viewed as art not science. It demands not only a necessarily subjective assessment of the degree of environmental worth attaching to Member State action, and of the costs associated with this in terms of market fragmentation, but also a balancing of competing, and arguably incommensurable, goals (integration and environment). Intensely value-laden, Member States must be permitted a wide margin of appreciation.

Such language of necessity, proportionality and alternative means sounds, or ought to sound, warning bells in the minds of environmental lawyers. It appears to be predicated upon a naïve faith in the revelationary potential of science, and an assumption of knowledge, pertaining especially to the existence, magnitude and origins of environmental risk. In the absence of certainty, regarding, for example, the causal relationship between certain substances and their alleged effects, and/or the intensity of the risk associated with a given activity, it is not at all apparent that attempts to apply these principles will be meaningful at all. How, in the face of scientific uncertainty, can the necessity or sufficiency of a measure be authoritatively assessed? How, in the face of conflicting evidence as to the magnitude of environmental risk, might the proportionality of a measure be evaluated?

…

In the area of public health the Court has demonstrated a willingness to adopt a broadly precautionary approach. What remains unclear is whether this approach is to apply regardless of the intensity of the putative risk arising. The subject of numerous, often inconsistent, formulations in international law, the precautionary principle is thought by many to apply only in the face of a threat of 'serious' or 'irreversible' damage. In the area of public health which 'ranks first among the property or interests protected by Article 36'[42] [now Article 30], every risk may properly be characterised as serious, even when it attaches only to a small number of particularly vulnerable and sensitive consumers. Hence in this area the Court, unsurprisingly, appears to have adopted a liberal conception of risk and to have defined broadly the scope of application of the precautionary principle. To what extent it would be prepared to adopt a comparable approach in the face of insufficient, or less than conclusive, evidence of environmental risk remains, for the present, a matter of speculation.

Scott is of course writing prior to the Court's judgments in *Pfizer* (Chapter 1, pp. 23–4) and *Waddenzee* (Chapter 15, pp. 651–3), both of which provide examples of the Court's application of the precautionary principle in different contexts – use of antibiotics in animal feed, and nature conservation, respectively. In Case C-41/02 *Dutch Vitamins*,[43] the precautionary principle (and the proportionality principle) is applied in the context of a Member State prohibition on the addition of vitamins to food (*Pfizer* concerned Community measures, and *Waddenzee* the national application of a Directive). The Netherlands argued (unsuccessfully) that the prohibition was necessary because the consumption of excess quantities of certain vitamins is dangerous. In a familiar formula, the ECJ accepted that: 'a Member State may, in accordance with the precautionary principle, take protective measures without having to wait until the existence and gravity of those risks become fully apparent, ... However, the risk assessment cannot be based on purely hypothetical considerations' (para. 52).

In *Danish Bottles* the Court added to an existing category of mandatory requirements or 'state imperatives' which included consumer protection,[44] and the protection of social and cultural life[45] (subject, of course, to the principle of proportionality). These form alternative justifications to those found in the very restricted list in Art. 36 EC. Since *Danish Bottles*, the Court has continued to be confronted with cases centred upon Member State restrictions on trade, ostensibly for environmental protection reasons,[46] and stimulating much critique and comment.[47] Francis Jacobs, a former Advocate General at

---

[42]  Case 104/75 *De Peijper* [1976] ECR 613, para. 16.

[43]  *Commission* v. *Netherlands* [2004] ECR I-11375; see also the discussion in Damien Chalmers, Christos Hadjiemmanuil, Giorgio Monti and Adam Tomkins, *European Union Law: Texts and Materials* (Cambridge University Press, 2006).     [44]  In *Cassis de Dijon*.

[45]  Cases 60 and 61/84 *Cinetheque SA* v. *Fédération Nationale des Cinémas Français* [1985] ECR 2605.

[46]  Including, most notably, Case C-2/90 *Commission* v. *Belgium* (*'Wallonian Waste'*) [1992] ECR I-4431, Case C-379/98 *PreussenElektra AG* [2001] ECR I-2099, Case C-67/97 *Ditlev Bluhme* (*'Danish Bees'*) [1998] ECR I-8033 and Case 169/89 *Criminal Proceedings against Gourmetterie van den Burg (Red Grouse)* [1990] ECR I-2143.

[47]  See, in particular, Scott, *EC Environmental Law*, Ch. 4, and case commentaries by Ludwig Krämer in the first edition of his *Casebook on European Environmental Law* (Sweet and Maxwell, 1993).

the ECJ, has argued that the Court has been notably generous to domestic environmental measures. One of the limitations on the use of 'mandatory requirements', as compared with the use of Art. 36, is that in principle the mandatory requirements doctrine only applies to measures that are applicable to domestic and imported products without distinction (are non-discriminatory); examining a number of cases,[48] Jacobs argues that the Court avoids this question of non-discrimination, or adopts tortuous reasoning to find a measure non-discriminatory, enabling the Court simply to assess whether the measure is justified for environmental reasons. Whilst Jacobs is critical of the Court's failure to provide a solid conceptual base for this development, and the consequent increase in legal uncertainty (and, of course, from an environmental perspective, this makes backtracking all too easy), he refers to 'the laudable enthusiasm of the ECJ to assess measures aiming at the protection of the environment favourably … Environmental protection aims should indeed be given the greatest weight, and it may indeed be desirable that even directly discriminatory measures should be capable of justification on grounds of environmental protection.'[49]

### Francis Jacobs, 'The Role of the European Court of Justice in the Protection of the Environment' (2006) 18 *Journal of Environmental Law* 185, pp. 192–3

In my opinion in *PreussenElektra* [in which German measures favouring renewable energy were held not to be incompatible with Art. 28], I suggested two possible reasons that could be invoked in favour of a more flexible approach in respect specifically of the mandatory requirement of environmental protection.

I referred in the first place to the amendments to the Treaties agreed in Amsterdam, which show a heightened concern for the environment (even though Article 30 EC itself was not amended to include environmental protection as a ground for exceptions to the free movement of goods), in particular, Article 6 EC which, as its wording shows, is not merely programmatic but imposes legal obligations; it provides that the requirements of environmental protection must be integrated into the definition and implementation of all policies and activities of the Community. From this new legal framework, it follows that special account must be taken of environmental concerns in interpreting the Treaty provisions on the free movement of goods.

In the same vein, I also argued that harm to the environment, even where it does not immediately threaten, as it often does, the health and life of humans, animals and plants protected by Article 30 EC, may pose a more substantial, if longer term, threat to the ecosystem as a whole.

---

[48] Especially '*Wallonian Waste*'; Case C-203/96 *Dusseldorp BV* [1998] ECR I-4075; Case C-389/96 *Aher-Waggon* [1998] ECR I-4473; *PreussenElektra*.

[49] Francis Jacobs, 'The Role of the European Court of Justice in the Protection of the Environment' (2006) 18 *Journal of Environmental Law* 185, p. 192.

> It would be hard to justify, in these circumstances, giving a lesser degree of protection to the environment than to the interests recognised in trade treaties concluded many decades ago and taken over into the text of Article 30 EC, itself unchanged since it was adopted in 1957. Legal rules, and especially treaty provisions which of their nature are more difficult to amend, should be interpreted, as far as possible, as a living and evolving text that needs to be adapted to a changing context. ...
>
> The second reason I suggested for distinguishing environmental protection from all other mandatory requirements was that to hold that environmental measures could be justified only where they are applicable without distinction would risk defeating the very purpose of the measures. National measures for the protection of the environment are inherently liable to differentiate on the basis of the nature and origin of the cause of harm and are therefore liable to be found discriminatory, precisely because they are based on such accepted principles as that according to which environmental damage should, as a priority, be rectified at source [Art. 174(2) EC]. Where such measures necessarily have a discriminatory impact of that kind, the possibility that they may be justified should not be excluded.

Whilst the EU's environmental impact remains troublesome (and of course the mere *threat* of legal action could inhibit Member State action), Jacobs' analysis at least identifies efforts at reconciliation between trade disciplines and environmental protection. This area of law is far from settled though. For example, better appreciation of environmental threats by the Member States suggests that they may attempt more far-reaching trade restrictions and assertions of sovereignty, not because of the characteristics of the products concerned, per se, but because of, for example, the 'air miles' that they have travelled to reach the receiving member state. The practical meaning of the EU's linkage of 'fair trade' with 'free trade' is up for debate: for instance, concerns about carbon emissions produced in the course of transporting goods may be relevant in recognition of the uneven distribution of the effects of climate change.

### (b) External trade

One of the solutions to any negative impact of trade rules (and increased trade) on environmental protection is to introduce EU-level regulation, and many examples of this strategy are discussed in this book. However, the EU as environmental regulator runs up against very similar problems in respect of *international* rules on trade as do Member States at EU level. The operation of these trade rules, and the ways in which dispute settlement bodies have accommodated (or not) environmental issues, are discussed in Chapter 7. The EU, situated in a global market, is as subject to global forces as nation states, with significant, and sometimes grave, environmental consequences; as well as legal obligations, the competitive pressures of a global market may also negatively influence regulation.

Increasingly, as Joanne Scott notes,[50] EU environmental law cannot be viewed in isolation from WTO law. A number of trade disputes involving EU environmental or public health measures will be discussed in Chapter 7. One area arguably showing the significant impact of the WTO on EU measures is the regulation of GMOs. As we discuss in Chapter 5, the EU has a complex system of regulation for GMOs, requiring both prior authorisation and labelling. Certain of the EU's trade partners are concerned about the trade-restrictive effects of this regulation, and it is likely that it will find itself before the WTO dispute settlement bodies in time. Whilst the EU is taking a strong stand on its right to regulate in this area, the legislation can be read as evidencing a concern to stay within the WTO disciplines; in particular, there is a highly scientifically constrained approach to the question of authorisation of GMOs, and much effort at explaining and justifying other elements of the regulatory process.

We should also note that the EU moratorium on authorisation of GMOs (Chapter 2, p. 63) has already been challenged before the WTO, and, as discussed in Chapter 7, has been found to fall foul of certain WTO agreements, with little attention paid to the enormous public sensitivity of the issue. Perhaps more difficult in the long term, the WTO Panel also found that Member State safeguard measures violated the WTO agreements, stating that these measures were not based on a risk assessment as required. Importantly, however, the new regulation was not considered, and the moratorium is (supposedly) over. Nevertheless, again, it is possible to see the shadow of the WTO in the highly controversial circumstances surrounding the end of the moratorium: the Commission was legally able to recommence the authorisation process, in the teeth of profound disagreement between the Member States (and between it and the Member States), without fully acknowledging or addressing public and political antipathy to this resumption of the process (Chapter 5, p. 201).

This WTO law 'spillover' in EC environmental law and EC law more generally[51] has (constitutional) limits, most obviously those imposed by the ECJ's refusal to recognise the direct applicability of the WTO agreements (in striking similarity to the stance adopted by some Member States in the early days of the Community with regard to recognising the direct effect of provisions of EC law). Recalling that there is no public interest dimension to the WTO, Dillon questions 'how can a court charged with the protection and vindication of all parts of the Treaty be expected to lead the charge in the full and total embrace of a GATT/WTO law that might well threaten many aspects of the full European "project"?'[52] However, the legal status of the WTO agreement is of less significance to the political bodies of the EU: the rules are binding, and have

---

[50] *EC Environmental Law*, Ch. 5, p. 86.
[51] On this 'spillover', see Grainne de Búrca and Joanne Scott, 'The Impact of the WTO on EU Decision-making' in de Burca and Scott (eds.), *The EU and the WTO: Legal and Constitutional Issues* (Hart, 2001).        [52] Dillon, *International Trade and Economic Law*, p. 9.

considerable political as well as legal strength. We see this reflected in both the assertion by the EU of its own right to regulate, and its undoubted efforts to stay within WTO rulings.

## 5 Conclusions

This chapter has examined the evolution of the EU's involvement in environmental protection. From inauspicious beginnings, a remarkably extensive legislative framework has been put in place. It has not been our intention to study the substantive detail of that legislation. Rather, we have examined the emergence of a clear legal framework and sometimes elaborate administrative and governance systems for the development and implementation of a legislative backbone for environmental protection. We will study this further in the next chapter, as we look at decision making processes for GMOs. We have also introduced aspects of the complex (and potentially destructive) relationship between trade and environmental protection which, perhaps better than most areas, sums up the nature of the contradictory forces and policy areas in the EU. We continue this theme in Chapters 5 and 7.

In spite of facing a remarkable range of challenges, not least the dominance of 'market' thinking, even within environmental policy, and the legacy of the development of this policy as a 'flanking policy', the vigour of EC environmental law remains apparently undaunted: 'the union constitutes a very "productive" and maturing system of public policy-making'.[53] Damian Chalmers describes EC environmental law as 'a bundle of paradoxes':

> Whilst the need for common legislation is far from clear, there is widespread consensus among both policy-makers and wider public that there should be common norms. There is extensive legislation in the field but EC environmental law is poorly applied and the European environment continues to degrade at a rate which exceeds even the Community's own targets. Despite all these paradoxes, EC environmental law continues to be used and its status upgraded.[54]

## 6 Further reading

Ludwig Krämer's contribution to EC environmental law – in practice and academia – is unparalleled. His distinguished career in the Legal Service of DG Environment has richly informed his numerous books and articles. The two editions of his *Casebooks on European Environmental Law* (Sweet and Maxwell, 1993, and Hart, 2002) make very good companions; *EC Environmental Law* (Sweet and Maxwell, 2003) has now entered its fifth edition. The collection of essays written in honour of his career, edited by Marco

---

[53] Jeremy Richardson, 'Policy-making in the EU: Interests, Ideas and Garbage Cans of Primeval Soup' in Jeremy Richardson (ed.), *European Union: Power and Policy-making* (Routledge, 1996), p. x.

[54] Damian Chalmers, 'Inhabitants in the Field of EC Environmental Law' in Paul Craig and Grainne de Búrca (eds.), *The Evolution of EU Law* (Oxford University Press, 1999), p. 653.

Onida, *Europe and the Environment: Legal Essays in Honour of Ludwig Krämer* (Europa, 2004), is an accomplished and broad-ranging work.

Jan Jans' *European Environmental Law* (Europa, 2nd edn, 2000) provides detailed and useful analysis of a broad range of EU environmental law. Joanne Scott's *EC Environmental Law* (Longmans, 1998) broke new ground, being a succinct, theoretically informed *and* readable book on key issues in the area. Its analysis holds up and still works to alert the reader to the underlying problems with 'new' governance techniques. In *EU Environmental Law: Challenges, Change and Decision-Making* (Hart, 2004), Maria Lee takes up some of the key criticisms of ('new' and 'old') regulatory activity in the EU, and provides a picture of the complexity of modern regulation.

Richard Macrory (ed.), *Reflections on 30 years of EU Environmental Law: A High Level of Protection?* (Europa, 2006) encourages an important 'stock taking' exercise in particular fields of EU environmental law, with insights from individual Member States.

Gerd Winter's 'Constitutionalizing Environmental Protection in the European Union' [2002] 2 *Yearbook of European Environmental Law* 67 discusses the 'constitutional' potential of environmental law before the drafting of the Constitutional Treaty. Jan Jans' edited collection, *The European Convention and the Future of European Environmental Law* (Europa, 2003), represents a 'state of the art' project on the subject. A number of articles consider the development of EC environmental law from inauspicious beginnings: Donald McGillivray and Jane Holder, 'Locating EC Environmental Law' [2001] 2 *Yearbook of European Law* 139, and Yoichiro Usui, 'Evolving Environmental Norms in the European Union' (2003) 9 *European Law Journal* 9, each takes interesting (and challenging) approaches to this development, the former asking questions about the extent to which EC law has moved towards 'ecological' law, so drawing links with Chapter 1.

The collection edited by Grainne de Búrca and Joanne Scott, *The EU and the WTO: Legal and Constitutional Issues* (Hart, 2001), explores many of the facets of the relationship between the EU and the WTO. A detailed and analytically rich study of the place of Europe in international trade is provided by Sara Dillon in *International Trade and Economic Law and the European Union* (Hart, 2002).

The key institutional website in this area is the Commission's DG Environment website, http://europa.eu.int/comm/environment/index_en.htm; the European Environmental Law Service, at www.eel.nl, contains updates and links to cases and legislation, as well as dossiers on particular subjects.

# 5

## Multi-Level Decision Making: The EU and GMOs

### 1 Introduction

The regulation of genetically modified organisms (GMOs) has a rather fraught history in the European Union (EU), becoming embroiled in the profound political, ethical and social choices implied by the technology. As discussed in Chapter 2, the regulation of GMOs at EU level fell into disarray in 1998. Intense public concern about GMOs, coupled with an inappropriately technical and ultimately centralised decision making process, led to a moratorium on authorisations from 1998. Rather than seeking either to enforce the existing legislation, or to regularise the moratorium, the EU institutions put intensive efforts into negotiating a new legislative framework for the regulation of GMOs. The ideal sought was the creation of a system that would respond more effectively to public concern, whilst simultaneously allowing in principle the possibility of widespread GM agriculture in the EU. The effort to compromise between 'pro' and 'anti' GM sentiments (and the success of this compromise is still to be seen) led to the negotiation of politically contentious and legally complex legislation – the subject of this chapter.

The regulation of GMOs in the EU involves, in most cases, and certainly the most controversial cases, a centralised, Community-level decision on whether particular GMOs should be marketed in the EU. Once the decision has been taken, it applies throughout the EU: free movement of goods applies. In many respects the centralised authorisation procedure is rather unusual in EC environmental law. Most environmental permitting decisions are taken at the national or local level, subject to an EC legal framework for the decision. Despite the unusual form of the procedure, however, the regulation of GMOs illustrates a number of the typical characteristics of EU decision making on matters of risk much more generally. In particular, it illustrates the some-times elaborate divisions of responsibility at EU level, both *vertically*, that is between Member States and the centre, and *horizontally*, between scientific and political decision makers. This involves discussion both of the famous comitology committees at EU level, and, given the continued political pressure on Member States to regulate on this issue, the ability of Member States to step back from an EU-level decision on a unilateral basis. The general arrangements for GMOs post-authorisation, as well as indicating the difficulty of arranging national and central responsibilities in controversial areas, bring out the centrality of the market and the consumer in EU politics.

The new regime for GMOs has two main elements: a requirement for authorisation of every GMO marketed and/or released in the EU; and an obligation to label GMOs. These obligations attempt to respond to the wide range of concerns identified in Chapter 2: human health concerns, environmental concerns and 'other', political, socio-economic and ethical concerns; in certain respects, they fall short. We concentrate on Regulation 1829/2003 on Genetically Modified Food and Feed (the 'Food and Feed Regulation'),[1] although it is important also to observe the relationship between this sectoral or 'vertical' Regulation (applying to food and (animal) feed only) and the 'horizontal' Directive applying to *all* GMOs, that is Directive 2001/18 on the Deliberate Release into the Environment of Genetically Modified Organisms (the 'Deliberate Release Directive').[2] There are also several subsidiary instruments.[3]

This chapter is divided into two main parts: a risk regulation section, which addresses the authorisation of GMOs; and a 'co-existence' section, which addresses control of GMOs post-authorisation. First, we should introduce the two main pieces of legislation.

## Deliberate Release Directive

*Article 1*

**Objective**

In accordance with the precautionary principle, the objective of this Directive is to approximate the laws, regulations and administrative provisions of the Member States and to protect human health and the environment when:

– carrying out the deliberate release into the environment of genetically modified organisms for any other purposes than placing on the market within the Community [e.g. experimental releases of GMOs].

– placing on the market genetically modified organisms as or in products within the Community [i.e. all marketing applications, including those that involve a 'deliberate release' of GMOs].

---

[1] OJ 2003 L 268/1. Prior to this regulation, GM food was covered by Regulation 258/97 concerning Novel Foods and Novel Food Ingredients OJ 1997 L 43/1.    [2] OJ 2001 L 106/1.

[3] Especially Regulation 1830/2003 concerning the Traceability and Labelling of Genetically Modified Organisms and the Traceability of Food and Feed Products Produced from Genetically Modified Organisms OJ 2003 L 268/24; Regulation 1946/2003 on Transboundary Movements of Genetically Modified Organisms OJ 2003 L 287.

*Article 4*
**General Obligations**
1. Member States shall, in accordance with the precautionary principle, ensure that all appropriate measures are taken to avoid adverse effects on human health and the environment which might arise from the deliberate release or the placing on the market of GMOs. GMOs may only be deliberately released or placed on the market in conformity with Part B [experimental releases] or Part C [marketing] respectively.

...

3. Member States and where appropriate the Commission shall ensure that potential adverse effects on human health and the environment, which may occur directly or indirectly through gene transfer from GMOs to other organisms, are accurately assessed on a case-by-case basis ...

## Food and Feed Regulation

*Article 1*
**Objective**
The objective of this Regulation, in accordance with the general principles laid down in Regulation (EC) No 178/2002 [the general Food Safety Regulation], is to:
(a) provide the basis for ensuring a high level of protection of human life and health, animal health and welfare, environment and consumer interests in relation to genetically modified food and feed, whilst ensuring the effective functioning of the internal market;
(b) lay down Community procedures for the authorisation and supervision of genetically modified food and feed;
(c) lay down provisions for the labelling of genetically modified food and feed.

*Article 4*
**Requirements**
1. Food [covered by this legislation] must not:
   (a) have adverse effects on human health, animal health or the environment;
   (b) mislead the consumer;
   (c) differ from food which it is intended to replace to such an extent that its normal consumption would be nutritionally disadvantageous for the consumer.

Both pieces of legislation focus primarily on avoiding any risk posed by GMOs to human health or the environment, rather than on 'other' (political, ethical, socio-economic) concerns, although the Food and Feed Regulation has somewhat broader objectives, in particular including reference to consumer interests. Both pieces of legislation are intimately concerned with the internal market, and are based, *inter alia*, on Art. 95 EC, one of the key internal market provisions.

The regulatory system revolves around the case by case examination of GMOs, requiring the party seeking to market a GMO to apply for authorisation. The two pieces of legislation overlap. Article 3(1) of the Food and Feed Regulation provides that it applies to:

(a)  GMOs for food use;
(b)  food containing or consisting of GMOs;
(c)  food produced from or containing ingredients produced from GMOs.[4]

The Deliberate Release Directive applies to GMOs that are placed on the market as or in products (Art. 1). Any GMOs intended for placing on the market *and* food or feed use fall under *both* Art. 1 of the Deliberate Release Directive *and* Art. 3(1)(a) or (b) of the Food and Feed Regulation (para. (c) covers processed food, which it is assumed does not contain a 'viable' GMO). This overlap applies to many current commercial applications of biotechnology suitable for the EU. Rather than applying for separate authorisations under each piece of legislation, a single application can be made under the Food and Feed Regulation, but incorporating the *environmental risk assessment* from the Deliberate Release Directive when there is a 'deliberate release' (e.g. a crop is planted). The Deliberate Release Directive is not currently much used for stand-alone commercial applications, although this is likely to change quickly as the technology develops; GM cotton, for example, is already very widely used globally.

## 2  Risk regulation and GMOs: the authorisation process

In its effort to tread a path between the divergent views on GMOs, the new regulatory framework puts in place a complex procedural framework to ensure the rigorous and thorough risk analysis of GMOs.

Article 5 of the Food and Feed Regulation sets out the initial process for applying for authorisation: the application is made to 'the national competent authority of a Member State', which 'shall inform without delay the European Food Safety Authority' (the Authority). The Authority in turn informs the other Member States and the Commission of the application, and makes the application available to them. It also makes the summary of the dossier provided by the applicant available to the public.

Article 6 requires the Authority to give an opinion on the application:

> 3. In order to prepare its opinion the Authority:
> > (a)  shall verify that the particulars and documents submitted by the applicant are in accordance with Article 5 and examine whether the food complies with the criteria referred to in Article 4(1) [above, p. 188];
> > (b)  may ask the appropriate food assessment body of a Member State to carry out a safety assessment of the food … ;

---

[4]  Provisions on animal feed are very similar.

(c)   may ask a competent authority designated in accordance with Article 4 of Directive 2001/18/EC to carry out an environmental risk assessment; however, if the application concerns GMOs to be used as seeds or other plant-propagating material, the Authority shall ask a national competent authority to carry out the environmental risk assessment;

...

4. In the case of GMOs or food containing or consisting of GMOs, the environmental safety requirements referred to in Directive 2001/18/EC shall apply to the evaluation to ensure that all appropriate measures are taken to prevent the adverse effects on human and animal health and the environment which might arise from the deliberate release of GMOs. During evaluation of requests for the placing on the market of products consisting of or containing GMOs, the national competent authority within the meaning of Directive 2001/18/EC designated by each Member State for this purpose shall be consulted by the Authority. The competent authorities shall have three months after the date of receiving the request within which to make their opinion known.

...

6. The Authority shall forward its opinion to the Commission, the Member States and the applicant, including a report describing its assessment of the food and stating the reasons for its opinion and the information on which this opinion is based, including the opinions of the competent authorities when consulted in accordance with paragraph 4.

7. The Authority ... shall make its opinion public, after deletion of any information identified as confidential in accordance with Article 30 of this Regulation. The public may make comments to the Commission within 30 days from such publication.

The EU has a reasonably well-established division in risk analysis, between a *technical* process of risk assessment and a *political* process of risk management. As discussed in Chapter 1 (pp. 46–7), this division is not clear cut or uncontroversial. Not least, it implies that the science can be isolated from value judgments, which are made later in time by a different set of decision makers, whilst in practice, professional and personal values are likely imperceptibly to form part of the scientific process. Nevertheless, this division between risk assessment and risk management is followed in the regulation of GMOs, and is a useful framework for discussion here. Article 6 above deals with the *technical*, risk assessment stage of decision making.

With respect to the division of risk assessment responsibilities between the centre and the Member States, the Authority plays a central role in the risk assessment, whilst the role of the national competent authorities is rather limited. By contrast, under the law that applied to GMOs before the creation of the Authority in 2002, and even now in respect of GMOs without food or feed implications (e.g. cotton, to which the Deliberate Release Directive alone applies), the entire responsibility rests with national authorities: only if there is disagreement between national authorities is a centralised process invoked, and that is a political (not technical) process, essentially the same 'comitology' process as discussed below (pp. 192–8). The more centralised process now seeks to overcome the reluctance of the Member States to accept each other's risk assessments, which made progress in authorisation under the old law impossible. Whilst the Deliberate Release Directive retains decentralised risk assessment, it provides detailed obligations on the *content* of that decentralised environmental risk assessment.

To return to risk assessment under the Food and Feed Regulation, notwithstanding the existence of the Authority, national risk assessors are actually far from excluded. When there is an actual GMO (so not in respect of processed GMOs), national competent authorities must be consulted (Art. 6(4), p. 190), and if the GMO is a seed, a national competent authority actually carries out the risk assessment (Art. 6(3)(c), p. 190). As well as providing an opening for any distinctive national risk assessment concerns, this provides a crucial opening for a specifically *environmental* perspective on decision making; the Authority's primary responsibility and expertise is food safety, rather than environmental safety. In cases to which the Deliberate Release Directive does not apply (processed food), the Authority *may* request a risk assessment from a national body (Art. 6(3)(b) and (c), pp. 190–1).

The status and role of the national involvement in risk assessment is not explained in the legislation. Article 6(6) (above, p. 190) imposes reason-giving and publicity obligations, suggesting that national concerns will not be easily ignored. The precise relationship between the centre and the Member State, however, remains to be played out. Even beyond the wording of the Food and Feed Regulation, the nature of the Authority raises novel questions about 'transnational governance'.

### Damian Chalmers, ' "Food for Thought": Reconciling European Risks and Traditional Ways of Life' (2003) 66 *Modern Law Review* 532, pp. 538–9

With regard to the Authority's institutional make-up, it is impossible to locate it along any conventional national-supranational continuum. It is rather a *transnational governance regime* which cuts across national/supranational and public/private distinctions, and which both guides and is accountable to scientific communities, national food authorities and civic society. As these networks inform its constitution, it cannot be seen as something starkly autonomous from them, but something that both contributes to their constitution and is constituted by them. This dialectic is reflected in the Authority's composite organs.

The Management Board is the political guardian of the Authority. It is to ensure that the Authority carries out its mission and to adopt the Authority's programme for each year as well as a revisable multi-annual programme in a manner consistent with EC legislative and policy priorities in food safety. Composed of a representative of the Commission plus 14 independent members the body is intended to be an interlocutor for different societal interests rather than a representative of national interests. There is therefore no requirement of national representation, but there must be representatives, instead, of consumers and other interests in the food chain. The next apex of the triangle are the Scientific Committee and permanent Scientific Panels. These are the engine room of the Authority and are made up of independent scientific experts. They issue scientific opinions and organise public hearings. The bulk of the opinions are provided by the eight specialised Scientific Panels, whilst the Committee is responsible for ensuring consistency of procedures and working methods between the different Panels, and for issues that cut across Panels. The final body is the Advisory Forum, which comprises representatives of the national food authorities or their equivalents. It advises on the work programme of the Authority and constitutes a mechanism for cooperation, networking and exchange of information between these and the Authority. More specifically, it also acts to prevent duplication of scientific studies and to resolve differences where there is a divergence between the scientific opinion of the Authority and that of a national authority. Whilst being the closest to a national representative institution, its stake is that of national regulatory interests rather than governmental or industrial ones.

The Authority's opinion on the application goes to all Member States and the Commission, and is also made public (Art. 6(7)). The next stage of the process shifts to *political* risk management. This involves deciding what should be done about the information provided by the Authority in its risk assessment. To this end, the public has also had the opportunity to 'make comments' under Article 6(7).

It will be recalled from the discussion in Chapter 1 (pp. 40–7) that a key element of risk management is to decide what level of risk is 'acceptable'. The legislation to some degree pre-empts this: the basis for the decision under the Food and Feed Regulation includes the proviso that GM food must not 'have adverse effects on human health, animal health or the environment' (Art. 4(1)(a)). However, this presumably does not require proof by an applicant of absolute safety, or proof that there is no 'hypothetical risk'.

### Case T-13/99 *Pfizer Animal Health SA* v. *Council* [2002] ECR II-3305, para. 145[5]

As Pfizer has rightly pointed out, the taking of measures, even preventive ones, on the basis of a purely hypothetical risk is particularly inappropriate in a matter such as the one at issue here. The parties do not dispute that in such matters a zero risk does not exist, since it is not possible to prove scientifically that there is no current or future risk associated with the addition of antibiotics to feedingstuffs.

When explaining its proposals on GM food and feed for the benefit of its WTO partners, the Commission has expressed the view that a 'zero risk' approach is not appropriate in the field of GMOs.

[5] For the background to this case, see Ch. 1, pp. 22–4.

### Response from the Commission to Comments submitted by WTO Members under Either or Both G/TBT/N/EEC/6 and G/SPS/n/EEC/149, 26 July 2002, p. 12

The proposed Regulation did not intend to impose an absolute 'no risk' standard for genetically modified food and feed, but only a standard that can meet the high level of protection required by the EC Treaty (e.g. Article 95, paragraph 3). The applicants should not be required, therefore, to demonstrate the absence of any unknown risk for human health, animal health or the environment.[6]

Nevertheless, the legislation clearly prohibits adverse effects, a requirement that, especially coupled with the precautionary principle,[7] could be enormously restrictive. Given that virtually any agricultural activity could be said to have an adverse effect on the environment, it is likely that an element of 'acceptability' will be introduced to make this provision workable.

The decision on every application is made on the basis of 'a draft of the decision' provided by the Commission to a committee (Art. 7), one of the famous comitology committees. 'Comitology' committees are composed of Member State representatives, and supervise powers of implementation delegated to the Commission in legislation. Comitology involves one of a number of different procedures, ranging from consultation with an 'advisory committee', to the submission of a proposal to a 'regulatory committee',[8] as in the case of GMOs. The 'regulatory' committee makes a decision on the Commission's draft by qualified majority voting. If the committee approves the draft, the Commission adopts it. If not, the draft is submitted to Council, and so becomes a high-level political decision. Under Art. 5(6) of the Comitology Decision:

The Council may, where appropriate in view of any such position, act by qualified majority on the proposal, within a period to be laid down in each basic instrument but which shall in no case exceed three months from the date of referral to the Council. If within that period the Council has indicated by qualified majority that it opposes the proposal, the Commission shall re-examine it. It may submit an amended proposal to the Council, re-submit its proposal or present a legislative proposal on the basis of the Treaty. If on the expiry of that period the

---

[6] Note that the wording was changed between the Commission proposal (COM (2001) 425 final) referred to here and the final legislation; the proposal had said that GM food must not 'present a risk for human health or the environment'.

[7] The Deliberate Release Directive is explicitly based on the precautionary principle (Recital 8); although the Food and Feed Regulation does not explicitly mention it, the precautionary principle is one of the 'general principles of food law' in the EU: Regulation 178/2002 Laying Down the General Principles and Requirements of Food Law OJ 2002 L 31/1, Art. 7.

[8] Council Decision 1999/468 laying down the procedures for the exercise of implementing powers conferred on the Commission OJ 1999 L 184/23, Art. 5. Note Council Decision of 17 July 2006 OJ 2006 L 200/11, providing 'regulatory procedure with scrutiny', a further procedure which enhances the role of the European Parliament.

Council has neither adopted the proposed implementing act nor indicated its opposition to the proposal for implementing measures, the proposed implementing act shall be adopted by the Commission.

It is not unusual for comitology committees, as political bodies, to be involved (with the Commission) in the *risk management* decisions reserved for political bodies in the EU's 'structured approach' to risk analysis. This is clearly the case with GMOs, which, as discussed in Chapter 2, raise a number of interesting political questions. Although the decision is a political one, however, comitology committees are generally made up of national *technical* experts. The danger that the common (technical) perspective of the participants could weaken any understanding of the problems at issue as political is widely recognised.

### Joseph H. Weiler, 'Epilogue: "Comitology" as Revolution – Infranationalism, Constitutionalism and Democracy' in Christian Joerges and Ellen Vos (eds.), *EU Committees: Social Regulation, Law and Politics* (Hart, 1999), pp. 348–9

It is possible that the committee members themselves ... are frequently unaware of the profound political and moral choices involved in their determinations and of their shared biases. This would be especially likely in a group of persons who share common world-views and a common vocabulary and where, as a result, moral premises are presumed but not discussed. Though scientific analysis can predict how many people will die as a result of adopting this or that safety standard, it cannot determine whether the risk is worth taking or not worth taking. This is a political choice even if at times it is inextricably linked with the scientific data. The biases of the actors in this mixed scientific/political agenda would be crucial.

And of course, in the current context of GMOs, scientific analysis lacks the tools even to 'predict' harm to the level assumed in this extract, enhancing the opportunity for political or professional judgments to enter the process. Moreover, although deemed political, decisions made through comitology are rarely subject to national parliamentary scrutiny, and to a large degree evade the close attention of the European Parliament[9] and the general public, including the media.[10] Decisions under comitology can even evade systematic *Council* control: in most cases, comitology committees agree with the Commission, and so the decision never reaches the higher levels. Only if the regulatory committee does not agree with the Commission proposal is it passed to Council. The Council can accept or reject the Commission pro-

[9]  Which is informed in order to check whether the Commission is exceeding its power, Art. 5(4)(5). The Parliament has blocking powers under the 2006 Decision, but that will not apply to the authorisation procedure.

[10]  See, generally, the contributions to Christian Joerges and Ellen Vos (eds.), *EU Committees: Social Regulation, Law and Politics* (Hart, 1999).

posal by qualified majority voting. However, if, as is perfectly possible in a contentious area, the Council is unable to muster a qualified majority in *either* direction, the decision is in the hands of the Commission. This has the advantage of avoiding regulatory impasse, but the very cases in which it is impossible to reach a qualified majority in either direction are those in which sensitive political and national issues are at stake. The authorisation of GMOs is precisely the sort of controversial decision in which the Council will find it difficult to muster a qualified majority vote in either direction, such that national and political involvement in the final decision on GMOs is undermined by disagreement. The restarting of authorisations for GMOs in 2004 depended on Commission decisions in the face of Member State inability to reach a qualified majority in either direction.[11]

Even if the national governments collectively in Council do manage to assert authority over the final decisions on GMOs, by reaching a qualified majority, each Member State is one of twenty-seven. The UK's preferred national policy on GMOs is accordingly diluted at the risk management as well as the risk assessment stages of decision making (even whilst its impact on the policies of other Member States is increased, compared to a purely national approach). We should recall at this point the complexity of the views on genetic modification, brought out by the 'key messages' of *GM Nation?*, the UK public debate on GMOs discussed in Chapter 2 (pp. 76–83).

### 'GM Nation? The Findings of the Public Debate' (September 2003), pp. 6–8, www.gmnation.org

#### 1. People are generally uneasy about GM

Across the different elements of the debate, participants expressed unease about GM. They were uneasy not only about issues directly related to GM technology (is GM food safe to eat? What will GM crops do [to] the environment?) but about a range of broader social and political issues. The mood ranged from caution and doubt, through suspicion and scepticism, to hostility and rejection. Despite the range of expression, among people who chose to take an active part in the debate these attitudes far outweighed any degree of support or enthusiasm for GM ...

...

#### 3. There is little support for early commercialisation

There is little support for the early commercialisation of GM crops. Among active participants in the debate just over half never want to see GM crops grown in the United Kingdom under any circumstances. Almost all the remainder want at least one new condition to be satisfied before this happens.

...

[11] With the authorisation of Syngenta's Bt11 sweetcorn on 19 May 2004; see the Commission's GMO webpages, http://europa.eu.int/comm/food/food/biotechnology/authorisation/index_en.htm.

### *4. There is widespread mistrust of government and multi-national companies*

Alongside arguments over the potential risks and benefits of GM itself, [the debate] … highlighted a series of political issues, manifested in a strong and wide degree of suspicion about the motives, intentions and behaviour of those taking decisions about GM – especially government and multi-national companies. Such suspicion is commonly expressed as a lack of trust. Here, mistrust of government applies both to government in general and in particular and expresses itself through several avenues. One is the suspicion that the government has already taken a decision about GM: the debate was only a camouflage and its results would be ignored … The GM debate also reflects a weakening of faith in the ability or even the will of any government to defend the interest of the general public … The debate also highlighted unease over the perceived power of the multi-national companies which promote GM technology, and of such companies in general. People believe that these companies are motivated overwhelmingly by profit rather than meeting society's needs, and that they have the power to make their interests prevail over the wider public interest, both at home and throughout global society. Even when people acknowledge potential benefits of GM technology, they are doubtful that GM companies will actually deliver them.

Public opinion is complex and nuanced, and, of course, nor are the economics and science of GM straightforward. It would hardly be surprising to discover different nuances and complexities around the EU. The reflection of such subtleties through the European Food Safety Authority's responsibility for risk assessment, or in the comitology process, is problematic, and certainly very far from transparent to national publics. Nor is the dilution of responsiveness to national public opinion likely to be fully compensated by participation at the EU level. The legislation allows comments to be made to the Commission, but makes no effort to encourage rather than allow participation, and imposes no explicit obligation on the Commission to take public comments into account.

Not surprisingly in these circumstances, and notwithstanding the application of the law on free movement of goods, a number of Member States have undertaken unilateral action to prevent the use of EU-authorised GMOs in their territory. A Member State seeking to derogate from EU law in this way has a number of options. As discussed in Chapter 4 (pp. 153–5), Art. 176 provides for more stringent protection; Art. 95 (below, pp. 206–7) provides a so-called 'environmental guarantee' for Member States; and EC legislation (including the GMO regulation) frequently provides 'safeguard' clauses for Member States. All of these options are subject to strict legal control. A taste of the difficulties of applying free movement laws to GMOs can be seen in the saga around safeguard action taken by the Member States. The safeguard clause in the Deliberate Release Directive (see below, pp. 203–4 for the safeguard clause under the Food and Feed Regulation) allows the provisional restriction of use and/or sale of a GMO by a Member State where 'new or additional information' affecting the environmental risk assessment process, or the 'reassessment of existing information on the basis of new or additional scientific knowledge', gives the Member State 'detailed grounds for considering that a GMO ... constitutes a risk to human health or the environment' (Art. 23). The safeguard clause has been invoked on a number of occasions.[12] The scientific evidence provided by the Member States was submitted to EU Scientific Committee(s), which in each case determined that there was no new evidence which would justify overturning the original authorisation decision. However, because of the extreme sensitivity of safeguard measures, there is an element of EU-level *political* control in this area, by the subjection of safeguard measures to comitology. In June 2005, the Council reached a qualified majority against Commission proposals to lift eight bans invoked by five Member States. This is a further example of the pressure that efforts to regulate GMOs are placing on the EU institutions and basic principles of EU law. Something of a quandary remains: it will be recalled (Chapter 4, p. 183) that the WTO has held that certain Member State safeguard measures breach the WTO agreements. In order to comply with WTO law, just as in EC law, Member States will need to base their bans on a risk assessment.

One final issue needs to be considered with respect to the risk management decision, and that is the basis on which that decision can be made. Recall that concern around GMOs falls into the category of risk to the environment, risk to human health, and a complex range of political, ethical and social issues. Whilst scientifically evidenced 'risk' has always been the point of most environmental regulation, these latter, more ephemeral debates fit with difficulty into 'risk' regulation. According to Art. 7, the Commission's draft decision is drawn up 'taking into account the opinion of the Authority, any relevant provisions of Community law and other legitimate factors relevant to the matter under consideration'. The nature of these other legitimate factors is not pursued in any detail in the Food and Feed Regulation, although 'It is recognised that, in some cases, scientific risk assessment alone cannot provide all the information on which a risk management decision should be based, and that other legitimate factors relevant to the matter under consideration may be taken in to account' (Recital 32). The general Food Safety Regulation goes further, recognising 'that scientific risk assessment alone cannot, in some cases, provide all the information on which a risk management decision should be based, and that other factors relevant to the matter under consideration should legitimately be taken into account including societal, economic, traditional, ethical and environmental factors and the feasibility of controls' (Recital 19).

It is clear that danger to health or the environment that is scientifically established can be addressed through the authorisation process. In principle, a wide range of the political, ethical and socio-economic concerns discussed in Chapter 2 could also enter into the authorisation process for GMOs through the incorporation of 'other legitimate factors'. The introduction of this phrase

---

[12] Also under the legislation predating the Deliberate Release Directive.

is an enormously significant and progressive legal development: under the law applied until 1998, the authorisation process was predicated on a wholly technical approach. Even under the 2001 Deliberate Release Directive, although there is space for consultation of an ethics committee and of the public, it is far from obvious how the information received feeds into the authorisation decision, which concentrates on a technical approach to environmental and health risk. By contrast, under Art. 7 of the Food and Feed Regulation, the only legal constraint on the Commission seems to be that it provide reasons for any disagreement with the Authority's opinion.

However, the legal and political context of decision making suggests that explicitly going beyond the science (rather than finding a scientific justification for a political decision), and explicitly basing decisions on 'other legitimate factors', for example ethical or socio-economic concerns, will at best face significant barriers. Most importantly, and as discussed in Chapter 1 (pp. 22–5), the Community judiciary tends to prioritise scientific information; secondly, the justificatory role of science is equally attractive to politicians; and finally, the decision on authorisation must fit within the purposes of the legislation.

## (a) The judiciary and science

### Case T-13/99 Pfizer, para. 199

To the extent to which the Community institution opts to disregard the [scientific] opinion, it must provide specific reasons for its findings by comparison with those made in the opinion and its statement of reasons must explain why it is disregarding the latter. The statement of reasons must be of a scientific level at least commensurate with that of the opinion in question. In such a case, the institution may take as its basis either a supplementary opinion from the same committee of experts or other evidence, whose probative value is at least commensurate with that of the opinion concerned.

There is a clear judicial preference for the apparent objectivity and certainty provided by scientific information, over the more evaluative and more obviously manipulable political concerns provoked by GMOs; whilst the Court of the First Instance (CFI) allows for alternative sources of science, the Authority is the key player in producing that preferred information.

### Chalmers, '"Food for Thought"', pp. 540–2

Whilst the Regulation anticipates that the Authority will have no direct regulatory authority, it anticipates that it will, however, have considerable normative authority, so that its rulings will nevertheless structure individual and institutional choices on food safety within the European Union.

...

... The Authority is merely one element in Regulation 178/2002/EC which provides a new basic food law for the EC. The overarching principles of this new regime are that food law should seek to achieve a high level of protection of human health and life, and that in order to achieve this food law should, in principle, be based on risk analysis. This bestows indirect legal effects upon the Authority's opinions. For, often, the actual content of the obligations imposed on institutional actors to meet these objectives is heavily influenced by its opinions ...

*EC Institutions* are required to take the Authority's opinions into account, as these are to provide the scientific basis for the drafting and adoption of Community measures ...

This duty is set out explicitly in the Commission's proposal for a Regulation on genetically modified food and feed, where an opinion of the Authority is a procedural pre-condition for any Commission authorisation. The recent *Pfizer Animal Health* judgment has, however, established this duty as a more general one of EC law.

...

... Yet is this simply a hollow procedural process or must the authorities follow the opinion? The Commission has stated that it will take into consideration not 'only science, but also many other matters for example economic, societal, traditional, ethical or environmental factors, as well as the feasibility of controls.' In *Pfizer Animal Health* a more constraining test was adopted. The Standing Committee on Animal Nutrition (SCAN) was consulted, but its advice that there was insufficient evidence to ban the drug was rejected. The CFI held this was legal because two conditions were met. The Council relied upon other scientific evidence of equivalent probative value and gave reasons for why it departed from SCAN's opinion. Whilst Pfizer lost, therefore, the judgment imposed constraints on the EC decision-maker, which allows it to depart from [the Authority's] opinions in only those exceptional circumstances where equivalent scientific evidence can be found and a justification for using it provided.

...

The food safety decision-making processes suggest a particular relationship between knowledge and policy. An institutional division is made in which the Authority is responsible only for the promulgation of knowledge, but policy-makers are required to justify themselves in the light of the knowledge it presents. It is thus a system of politics that not only privileges a particular form of knowledge, but also locates an authoritative source for that knowledge. It allows the Authority to generate a set of expectations about food safety, which enable law-making, by providing a justification for it, but which also act as a point of critique and review of food law and policy.

Because the *Pfizer* decision was made in a legislative context that did not refer to 'other legitimate factors', it presumably would not be directly applied to decisions made under the Food and Feed Regulation. However, the judicial risk 'philosophy' that it suggests could prove hard to resist.

### (b) Politics and science

In any event, politicians are also likely to prefer to find support in science, both because they are fully aware of the need to justify these decisions before WTO partners at some stage (Chapter 4, pp. 182–4, Chapter 7), and also because the appearance of neutrality, objectivity and inevitability that science can some-times enjoy exerts a powerful influence. Rationalising decisions on the basis of political choices will remain difficult. The Authority is sheltered from the political hurly-burly by its status as an independent and purely scientific body, which reinforces the appeal and apparent objectivity of its views. The separate consideration of 'other legitimate concerns' may even further marginalise political decision making.

### Les Levidow and Claire Marris, 'Science and Governance in Europe: Lessons from the Case of Agricultural Biotechnology' [2001] *Science and Public Policy* 345, p. 349

Such practices relegate 'extra-scientific' concerns to a subjective realm; they are thereby assumed to be evaluated differently by various individuals or groups, according to their vested interests or values. Such concerns are contrasted to objective scientific facts, which are assumed to be amenable to consensus.

By systematically distinguishing 'other concerns' from 'science', official discourses further reinforce the notion that science itself is value-free and neutral. Such a distinction dismisses public suspicions about the hidden values inherent in science itself. Ultimately, it also means that these 'extra-scientific' factors are still considered to be of secondary importance compared to 'scientific fact'.

### (c) The purposes of the legislation

And finally, it is also of course the case that decisions made under the GMO legislation must fit within the purposes of that legislation.

### Joanne Scott, 'European Regulation of GMOs: Thinking about Judicial Review in the WTO' (2004) 57 *Current Legal Problems* 117, pp. 118–19

European Union law identifies the objectives which may legitimately be pursued by the system of prior approval. The range of objectives is somewhat expanded in the GM Food and Feed Regulation. Alongside the critical internal market objective, this is concerned not only with the protection of human life/health and the environment, but also with animal health and welfare and 'consumer interests in relation to genetically modified food or feed'. Though expanded, the range of underlying objectives nonetheless remains finite. No authorisation shall be granted or refused other than on the grounds set out in the Regulation. The paradigm for prior approval is fixed and closed. Viewpoints which cannot be accommodated within this paradigm will be excluded, and voices which do not resonate within this paradigm will not be heard. To take an example, there is provision in the GM Food and Feed Regulation for consultation with the European Group on Ethics in Science and New Technologies. Yet, other than to the extent that ethical concerns may be packaged as integral to the attainment of the above objec-tives, their place in prior approval is not clear. Similarly, it is for the European Commission to draw up a draft of the authorization decision in respect of GM food or feed. In so doing, it shall take account not only of the opinion of the European Food Safety Authority (EFSA), but also of 'other legitimate factors relevant to the matter under consideration'. In view of the strictures above – requiring that no authorisation be granted or refused other than on the grounds set out in the Regulation – the place of 'legitimate concerns' not integrally connected to the closed list of stated objectives remains, at best, uncertain.

The need to fit the authorisation decision within the dynamics of the regulation, whilst still uncertain in its implications, takes us back to the dominant questions of human and animal health and environmental protection. This in turn takes us back to the need for scientific justifications, although it might be noted that in a context where regulation pursues predominantly public health objectives, 'the restoration of consumer confidence can in such circumstances also be an important objective which may justify even substantial economic consequences for certain traders'.[13]

### (d) The authorisation process

To conclude, the authorisation process for GMOs in the EU is decidedly complex, with a delicate balancing between central and national authority and between politics and science. Whether it will be enough to hold together the EU-wide regulation of GMOs remains to be seen – the Member States are still struggling to work together on this issue, and the political controversy is still intense. The early authorisations in 2004 to 2006 relied on Commission action in the face of Member States' inability to agree. This is not particularly indicative of a robust and effective system; in fact the somewhat grim determination of the Commission may even indicate just the opposite. And, of course, Council could vote *against* a Commission draft, in which case the Commission will no longer be able to push approvals through.[14]

The legislation discussed in this section, negotiated during the 'moratorium' from 1998, introduces two very important changes to the 'old' legislation. First, the process for risk assessment is much more rigorous, and more centralised. Secondly, the legitimacy of 'other legitimate factors' than science in the decision making process is a potentially significant opening up of decision making. However, there are considerable barriers, legal and political, to the development of that concession, which in any event applies only to food and feed. These barriers suggest that the legislation will continue to focus on formal 'risk' to the environment and health, sidelining the more political concerns identified in Chapter 2.

[13] Case T-13/99 *Pfizer Animal Health SA* v. *Council* [2002] ECR II-3305, para. 462.
[14] The 24 July 2005 Environment Council did find a qualified majority against Commission proposals on a number of national safeguard measures under the Deliberate Release Directive, which the Commission had proposed *rejecting*.

## 3  Co-existence and the EU's 'market citizen'

EU regulation of GMOs is not limited to risk regulation through the authorisation process. One of the objectives of the EU's GMO regulation is to provide a 'high level of protection of … consumer interests',[15] and the primary tool for this is mandatory labelling of GMOs.

### Food and Feed Regulation

Article 12

1. This Section shall apply to foods which are to be delivered as such to the final consumer or mass caterers in the Community and which:

    (a)   contain or consist of GMOs; or

    (b)   are produced from or contain ingredients produced from GMOs.

2. This Section shall not apply to foods containing material which contains, consists of or is produced from GMOs in a proportion no higher than 0,9 per cent of the food ingredients considered individually or food consisting of a single ingredient, provided that this presence is adventitious or technically unavoidable.

3. In order to establish that the presence of this material is adventitious or technically unavoidable, operators must be in a position to supply evidence to satisfy the competent authorities that they have taken appropriate steps to avoid the presence of such material.

There are at least *two major gaps* in the obligation to label GMOs. First of all, the exception set out above: 'adventitious' presence of GMOs up to 0.9 per cent need not be labelled. We will return to this, but should note that if GM agriculture is to proceed, some tolerance is necessary to deal with mixture of GM and non-GM material. Total isolation of GM material is largely accepted to be impossible, and some mixing will inevitably take place by means including natural cross-pollination by wind or insects, the survival of GM 'volunteer' plants, mixing by farm machinery, or in storage, distribution or processing.

The second gap in the labelling obligations is the exclusion of GM food produced 'with' GMOs:

This Regulation should cover food and feed produced 'from' a GMO but not food and feed 'with' a GMO. The determining criterion is whether or not material derived from the genetically modified source material is present in the food or in the feed. Processing aids which are only used during the food or feed production process are not covered by the definition of food or feed and, therefore, are not included in the scope of this Regulation. Nor are food and feed which are manufactured with the help of a genetically modified processing aid included in the scope of this Regulation. Thus, products obtained from animals fed with genetically modified feed or treated with the genetically modified medicinal products will be subject neither to the authorisation requirements nor to the labelling requirements referred to in the Regulation. (Recital 16)

---

[15]  Regulation 1830/2003, Art. 1.

Hence, consumers will not know if their milk, eggs or meat is produced from animals reared on GM feed. Note also that labelling obligations for non-food or feed GMOs (for example cotton, flowers, tobacco) are contained in a separate regulation,[16] according to which processed GMOs are excluded from the labelling obligations – the 'produced from' limb (Art. 12(1)(b), p. 202) is absent. This means that, for example, imported clothes produced from GM cotton are not subject to mandatory labelling.

Labelling is to 'contribute to promoting the right of consumers to information', as well as enabling the consumer 'to make an informed choice' (Recital 17). The question of consumer choice between organic, conventional and GM products depends crucially on the ability of those three forms of agriculture to 'co-exist'. The starting point on co-existence in the EU is the assertion that co-existence is needed; no one form of agriculture should be allowed to crowd out the others. 'Co-existence' measures are designed to keep to a minimum the levels of presence of GM in non-GM products and/or to minimise associated problems. The Commission has produced a (non-binding) Recommendation and guidelines on the subject, which set out 'an open-ended catalogue' of possible co-existence measures,[17] including things like the use of separation distances between crops, buffer zones, coordination of crop rotation and pollination times between farms, along with measures such as using separate machinery for GM and non-GM crops, and careful management of volunteers and other weeds. Whilst not guaranteeing the absence of gene flow, these measures can be designed to minimise its extent; particularly combined with labelling thresholds, many of the problems raised by co-existence can be avoided. However, the regulation of co-existence is the responsibility of the Member States; the Food and Feed Regulation introduces a new Art. 26a into the Deliberate Release Directive:

1. Member States may take appropriate measures to avoid the unintended presence of GMOs in other products
2. The Commission shall gather and coordinate information based on studies at Community and National level, observe the developments regarding coexistence in the Member States and, on the basis of the information and observations, develop guidelines on the coexistence of genetically modified, conventional and organic crops.

This is fairly open language, and in theory leaves the way clear for distinctive national approaches, whereby national farming practices and preferences could be protected, and quite different balances between different forms of farming could exist around the EU. This is significant because, of course, any GMO granted authorisation under the legislation is subject to rules on the free movement of goods; the harmonised system of risk analysis of GMOs leaves little

---

[16] Regulation 1830/2003.

[17] Commission Recommendation 2003/556 on guidelines for the development of national strategies and best practices to ensure the coexistence of genetically modified crops with conventional and organic farming OJ 2003 L 189/36, para. 3.

flexibility for Member States. A very narrowly drawn 'safeguard clause' in the Food and Feed Regulation operates only if it is 'evident'[18] that there is 'a serious risk to human health, animal health or the environment', and only if the centralised bodies do not act.[19]

In an effort to get around rules on free movement, some urge Member States to limit GM agriculture to the greatest extent possible through the regulation of co-existence. The apparent national flexibility on this subject is, however, placed in a restrictive legal and policy framework. Quite what is meant by 'appropriate measures' must be the crucial question in assessing the legitimacy of national measures for co-existence. 'Appropriate measures' must at least be consistent with the regulatory framework and objectives, not to mention basic EU law. The Commission certainly has a very restrictive approach to what is permissible. It is keen to avoid any question of GM-free zones, emphasising the small scale of co-existence measures.

### Commission Recommendation 2003/556 on guidelines for the development of national strategies and best practices to ensure the coexistence of genetically modified crops with conventional and organic farming OJ 2003 L 189/36

*2.1.5. Appropriate scale*

While considering all the options available, priority should be given to farm-specific management measures and to measures aimed at coordination between neighbouring farms. Measures of a regional dimension could be considered. Such measures should apply only to specific crops whose cultivation would be incompatible with ensuring coexistence, and their geographical scale should be as limited as possible. Region-wide measures should only be considered if sufficient levels of purity cannot be achieved by other means. They will need to be justified for each crop and product type (e.g. seed versus crop production) separately.

Perhaps the most important element of the Commission's recommendation is that it clearly sees co-existence as a purely *economic* issue, on the basis that any environmental or health issues related to co-existence should have been dealt with in the authorisation process (Recitals 4 and 5). If co-existence is an economic issue, purity is irrelevant for as long as impurity has no economic impact, that is as long as the market accepts impurity. This brings the legislative thresholds for mandatory labelling of GMOs and for seed purity centre-stage: if it is impossible to distinguish (through labelling) between products with and without GM material, there can be no market preference one way or another.

---

[18] A high standard of evidence seems to be implied. The European Court of Justice's (ECJ's) willingness to interpret safeguard clauses in accordance with the precautionary principle should, however, be noted: see Case C-236/01 *Monsanto Agricoltura Italia SpA* v. *Presidenza del Consiglio dei Ministri* [2003] ECR I-8105; Case C-6/99 *Greenpeace* v. *Ministère de l'Agriculture et de la Pêche* [2000] ECR I-1651.

[19] Food and Feed Regulation, Art. 34, which cross-refers to the General Food Safety Regulation.

The co-existence guidelines are defined by reference to 'legal obligations for labelling and/or purity standards' (Recital 3), and assume that the thresholds set in the legislation are entirely unproblematic. The Commission's language even suggests that it would be illegitimate for a Member State to apply mandatory regulatory measures aiming below that threshold: 'Measures for coexistence should be efficient and cost-effective, and proportionate. They shall not go beyond what is necessary in order to ensure that adventitious traces of GMOs stay below the tolerance thresholds set out in Community legislation' (para. 2.1.4). Arguably, this changes the purpose of the thresholds set out in the legislation, which are no longer a pragmatic response to exceptional cases of contamination, but an aspiration, a limitation of regulatory action. Similarly, recall that reliance on the 0.9 per cent threshold under Art. 12 is limited by the obligation to establish that 'appropriate steps to avoid the presence of such material' have been taken. This suggests that to avoid labelling obligations, the efforts of the producer must aim to avoid GMOs entirely; and possibly even that 0.9 per cent will be deemed to be acceptable only on an extraordinary and exceptional basis, in respect of particular 'contaminated' batches of a product. However, one might equally assume that meeting a national regulatory author- ity's instructions on co-existence would constitute 'appropriate steps'. The Commission's approach could amount to defining appropriate steps to avoid contamination by reference to co-existence requirements *themselves* defined by reference to the thresholds, depriving the requirement to take 'appropriate steps' of much of its restrictive value. The Commission is not of course the ultimate interpreter of statutory language – its approach to the labelling thresholds could be challenged politically or before the Court.[20]

Regardless of the labelling thresholds set in the legislation, a regulatory policy of purity, or something approaching purity, is simply not envisaged by the Commission. Many producers, most obviously organic producers but also conventional farmers seeking to comply with more stringent requirements of purchasers such as supermarkets, will want to go beyond 0.9 per cent, and even to tolerate no GM material in products (in practice this means looking to a 0.1 per cent 'surrogate zero' presence of GMOs, as this is the lowest level for which testing is reasonably reliable). It appears that any effort of the Member States to support such endeavours by regulation will be considered unlawful by the Commission. If GM agriculture becomes widespread, however, it will be difficult for producers to aim below 0.9 per cent without regulatory assistance.[21] The organic sector in the UK currently operates to a tolerance threshold as close to zero as is measurable, a policy that may not survive

[20] It would be difficult for an environmental interest group to challenge this approach directly: see the discussion of 'standing', Ch. 3, pp. 120–8; it is possible, however, that a Member State will wish to challenge this approach, either in a direct application for judicial review or as a defence to an action brought by the Commission under Art. 226.

[21] Voluntary agreements between landowners bear much of the burden of delivering lower levels of GM contamination according to the Commission. The main drawback of this approach is clearly that any individual landowner can scupper the plan.

widespread commercialisation of GMOs in the circumstances envisaged by the Commission, which assumes that the 0.9 per cent threshold applies to organics and seems also to think that any effort of the Member States to assist the organic sector to go further by introducing mandatory regulation goes beyond the scope of lawful measures.[22] We might go so far as to say that this implies a backdoor redefinition of organic by the Commission.

The effort of Austria to seek to protect its organic farming sector under the 'environmental guarantee' in Art. 95(5) of the Treaty provides an indication of the problems. Article 95(5) provides a route for the introduction of national measures to an area subject to harmonised Community law, if those measures are necessary to protect the environment. The measures must be notified to the Commission, which can accept or reject them.

## Article 95 EC

4. If, after the adoption by the Council or by the Commission of a harmonisation measure, a Member State deems it necessary to maintain national provisions on grounds of major needs referred to in Article 30, or relating to the protection of the environment or the working environment, it shall notify the Commission of these provisions as well as the grounds for maintaining them.

5. Moreover, without prejudice to paragraph 4, if, after the adoption by the Council or by the Commission of a harmonisation measure, a Member State deems it necessary to introduce national provisions based on new scientific evidence relating to the protection of the environment or the working environment on grounds of a problem specific to that Member State arising after the adoption of the harmonisation measure, it shall notify the Commission of the envisaged provisions as well as the grounds for introducing them.

6. The Commission shall, within six months of the notifications as referred to in paragraphs 4 and 5, approve or reject the national provisions involved after having verified whether or not they are a means of arbitrary discrimination or a disguised restriction on trade between Member States and whether or not they shall constitute an obstacle to the functioning of the internal market.

The Austrian measures, although designed primarily to protect organic agriculture, were claimed by Austria also to protect conventional agriculture and biodiversity. The Commission rejected Austria's measures for a variety of reasons,[23] of which the most pertinent are set out below.

---

[22] EC legislation sets minimum standards for the accreditation of organic produce by authorised certification bodies: Regulation 2092/1991 on organic production of agricultural products OJ 1998 L 198/1; organic certification bodies (such as the Soil Association in the UK) can require their members to go beyond the minimum regulatory standards. GMOs cannot be *used* in organic agriculture. The commission has proposed amendments to Regulation 2092/91, clarifying that products labelled as containing GMOs cannot also be labelled as organic, COM (2005) 671 final.

[23] The Upper Austrian region and Austria unsuccessfully appealed this decision: [2005] ECR II-4005.

### Commission Decision 2003/653 Relating to National Provisions on Banning The Use of Genetically Modified Organisms in the Region of Upper Austria OJ 2003 L 230/34

66. Moreover, the Austrian authorities have not provided any new scientific evidence, which specifically concerns the protection of the environment or the working environment.

67. It therefore appears that Austrian concerns about coexistence relate more to a socio-economic problem than to the protection of the environment or the working environment. Again, this assessment is confirmed by the [Authority], which opinion states: 'No evidence was presented in the report to show that coexistence is an environmental or human health risk issue. [The Authority] was not asked by the Commission to comment on the management of coexistence of genetically modified and non-genetically modified crops, but the Panel recognised that it is an important agricultural issue.'

68. On this basis, and in line with the definition of coexistence contained in its Recommendation on the issue, the Commission therefore considers that the concerns relating to coexistence raised by Austria cannot be specifically regarded as protection of the environment or the working environment within the meaning of Article 95(5) of the EC Treaty.

69. The Commission also considers that any measure for coexistence, to be introduced on a regional basis, in the context of economic risk should be proportionate. In accordance with the new Article 26(a) of Directive 2001/18/EC and the Commission Recommendation of coexistence, such measures would have to take account of (i) specific crop-type, (ii) specific crop use and (iii) if sufficient levels of purity cannot be achieved by other means.

And yet despite its assertion that co-existence is an economic rather than an environmental issue, the Commission elsewhere accepts that organic farming is a form of farming that delivers 'public goods' as well as a market issue. In these circumstances, it seems reductive to define co-existence as a purely economic issue.

### Commission Staff Working Document, European Action Plan for Organic Food and Farming, SEC (2004) 739, s. 1.4

In designing a global policy concept for organic farming the dual societal role of organic farming should be recognised.

1. Organic farming is a method for producing food products, which created a specific market for organic food products and consumers willing to buy those products, usually at a higher price. From this point of view, organic farming is financed by the consumers who reap the benefit of it, i.e. the food products of their choice. From this angle, the development of organic farming is governed by market rules.

2. Organic farming is known to deliver public goods, primarily environmental benefits, but also public health, social and rural development and animal welfare. The emphasis here is rather on the land management carried out by organic farmers. The public goods so delivered can be financed by public means. Seen from this angle, the development of organic farming is a policy choice, mainly on environmental policy grounds.

The intimately connected labelling, co-existence and consumer choice elements of the GMO regime supplement the authorisation process, in an effort to respond to the full range of public concerns about GMOs. The consumer has in fact been remarkably powerful in the GM saga so far, with many European food retailers and processors rejecting GM materials in response to their understanding of consumer demand. This is one of those areas in which the 'green consumer', to be further discussed in Chapter 11, has had a significant role.

However, the reliance on consumer choice to 'sweep up' public concern about GMOs beyond the protection of the environment or human or animal health (and so beyond scientific risk assessment) may be optimistic. Most obviously, a turn to consumer choice assumes that the choices available are meaningful. The consistency of thresholds with the consumer choice rhetoric is at best problematic, the GM-free 'consumer choice' being in all practical senses abandoned. Similarly, save for voluntary labelling, consumers will not know whether their food derives from animals fed with GM feed (above, pp. 202–3), restricting the potential to exercise ethical choices over the form of agriculture one wishes to support. And of course not all operate equally in the market: the poor in particular are excluded, as are those outside the jurisdiction. Even if we look at the most privileged consumers, it is not difficult to envisage a policy of aggressive pricing and marketing overcoming consumer rejection of GMOs, or at least creating consumer resignation in the face of the apparently inevitable.

Finally, one might be concerned that the 'market citizen' in the EU is fundamentally individualised, with individual rights and largely economic functions.[24] Many consumers coming together can have a collective impact, and are capable of exerting a serious influence on producers, but short-term choices in the market may not provide a full account of political values. So, for example, even an informed, active, empowered consumer concerned not just with his/her own impact on the environment, but with the *overall* environmental impact or risk of GMOs, may be unprepared to bear the cost of avoiding GMOs because of the perceived limited impact of individual action. The discussion in Chapter 3, pp. 92–3, of the distinction between 'preferences' and 'values' is pertinent here. The limitations of economising and individualising political and collective questions are significant.

## 4 Conclusions

The regulation of GMOs demonstrates a great deal about governance arrangements at EU level, and in more general terms is instructive as to how regulators go about making decisions in areas of great public controversy. We see in GMO regulation a familiar tension between politics and science in decision making, alongside a tension between central and national responsibilities.

---

[24] Michelle Everson, 'The Legacy of the Market Citizen' in Jo Shaw and Gillian More (eds.), *New Legal Dynamics of the European Union* (Oxford University Press, 1996).

Equally importantly for current purposes, the study of GMOs also illustrates elements of the 'four phases' of environmental law, a useful reminder that a shift to 'new approaches' by no means entails an abandonment of the old[25] (and in this respect, discussion of GMOs prefigures certain discussions to come in later chapters[26]). The regulation of GMOs rests fundamentally on the most traditional of the tools at the disposal of the environmental regulator: the authorisation, or licence. This, together with the expert-led approach to risk assessment that we see in the authorisation procedure for GMOs, is the legal mechanism on which EU legislators (and indeed environmental legislators around the globe) relied when they first turned their attention to environmental problems. At the same time, however, GMO regulation is in tune with the development at EU level of more sophisticated notions of environmental governance. So the legislation concentrates on the provision of a rigorous procedure for the regulation of GMOs, as much as on substantive environmental standards. Allied to this focus on procedure is the recognition that some opening for public involvement is a necessary component of good and legitimate decision making. Although the legal commitment to public participation is rather low-key in this area compared to certain other recent legal developments (see particularly Chapter 3), this reflects an important shift of approach to decision making on risk. We can also glimpse a new age of environmental regulation in the emphasis on markets as a tool of regulation, here in the delegation of controversial political and ethical choices to individual consumers. Perhaps more controversially, GMOs even indicate the continuing potential for debate over the relative roles of the centre and the Member States in regulation. In summary, agricultural biotechnology has been an extraordinarily fraught issue for the EU, and there are as yet no guarantees as to the stability of the regulatory regime. Whether the emphasis on central control will turn out to be a mixed blessing for the development of the EU, at a time of increased public scepticism about the legitimacy and effectiveness of its regulation, is something that time will tell.

## 5 Further reading

Tamara Hervey in 'Regulation of Genetically Modified Products in a Multi-level System of Governance: Science or Citizens?' (2001) 10 *Review of European Community and International Environmental Law* 321 discusses a particularly notorious case in which, because of the operation of comitology at the time, the Commission was able to authorise a GMO in the teeth of vociferous objections from a number of Member States and the European Parliament, and the positive approval of only one Member State in Council. Whilst some of the more acute difficulties that she identifies in this article have been ameliorated, the basic concern that the legislation focuses unduly on technical elements remains valid.

[25] There is much discussion of the EU's move from rigid substantive environmental standards in Directives towards more flexible approaches: see Ch. 9.

[26] Particularly the use of licensing (Ch. 9) and market instruments of environmental regulation (Ch. 11).

There is now a considerable literature on the 'new' legislation. By contrast with this chapter, Sara Poli, 'The Overhaul of the European Legislation on GMOs, Genetically Modified Food and Feed: Mission Accomplished. What Now?' [2004] *Maastricht Journal of European and Comparative Law* 13, argues that the new legislation has the potential to address adequately the concerns about GMOs. See also Maria Lee, *EU Environmental Law: Challenges, Change and Decision-Making* (Hart, 2004), Ch. 9.

One of the tasks of the GMO case study in this book is to illustrate the complexity of science/politics interactions in environmental law and policy; one of its tasks in this chapter has been to illustrate how sensitive the allocation of regulatory responsibility between EU and national levels can be: Estelle Brosset, 'The Prior Authorisation Procedure Adopted for the Deliberate Release into the Environment of Genetically Modified Organisms: The Complexities of Balancing Community and National Competences' (2004) 10 *European Law Journal* 555, and Theofanis Christoforou, 'The Regulation of Genetically Modified Organisms in the European Union: The Interplay of Science, Law and Politics' (2004) 41 *Common Market Law Review* 637, provide different approaches to these themes.

European Commission information on GMOs is spread over a number of websites, but information on the legislation and links can be found at http://ec.europa.eu/environment/biotechnology/index_en.htm.

# Part III

# The International Context

## Preface to Part III

This is not a book about international law. However, to ignore the global dimension to contemporary environmental law would be almost wilfully misleading. In this Part, rather than attempting to describe and analyse international environmental law and international decision making processes,[1] we focus on two issues in the international arena that are of particular salience for domestic and European environmental lawyers: the evolution of the concept of 'sustainable development' and the relationship between international trade rules and environmental protection.

International action to protect the environment rests on the commonplace reality that environmental problems respect no borders: pollution travels, and the degradation of certain environmental resources, such as the rainforests or atmospheric ozone, have immediate and more indirect global impacts. And just as environmental problems are increasingly global, so is a global solution increasingly necessary: one state's response to climate change, for example, is meaningless in isolation.

### World Commission on Environment and Development, *Our Common Future* (Oxford University Press, 1987), pp. 4–5 (The Brundtland Report)

Until recently, the planet was a large world in which human activities and their effects were neatly compartmentalized within nations, within sectors (energy, agriculture, trade), and within broad areas of concern (environmental, economic, social). These compartments have begun to dissolve. This applies in particular to the various global 'crises' that have seized public concern, particularly over the past decade. These are not separate crises: an environmental crisis, a development crisis, an energy crisis. They are all one.

...

A mainspring of economic growth is new technology, and while this technology offers the potential for slowing the dangerously rapid consumption of finite resources, it also entails high risks, including new forms of pollution and the introduction to the planet of new variations of life forms that could change evolutionary pathways. Meanwhile, the industries

---

[1] For a detailed discussion of international environmental law, see, for example, Patricia Birnie and Alan Boyle, *International Law and the Environment* (Oxford University Press, 2002).

most heavily reliant on environmental resources and most heavily polluting are growing most rapidly in the developing world, where there is both more urgency for growth and less capacity to minimize damaging side effects.

These related changes have locked the global economy and global ecology together in new ways. We have in the past been concerned about the impacts of economic growth upon the environment. We are now forced to concern ourselves with the impacts of ecological stress – degradation of soils, water regimes, atmosphere, and forests – upon our economic prospects. We have in the more recent past been forced to face up to a sharp increase in economic interdependence among nations. We are now forced to accustom ourselves to an accelerating ecological interdependence among nations. Ecology and economy are becoming ever more interwoven – locally, regionally, nationally, and globally – into a seamless net of causes and effects.

Impoverishing the local resource base can impoverish wider areas: Deforestation by highland farmers causes flooding on lowland farms; factory pollution robs local fishermen of their catch. Such grim local cycles now operate nationally and regionally. Dryland degradation sends environmental refugees in their millions across national borders. Deforestation in Latin America and Asia is causing more floods, and more destructive floods, in downhill, downstream nations. Acid precipitation and nuclear fallout have spread across the borders of Europe. Similar phenomena are emerging on a global scale, such as global warming and loss of ozone. Internationally traded hazardous chemicals entering foods are themselves internationally traded. In the next century, the environmental pressure causing population movements may increase sharply, while barriers to that movement may be even firmer than they are now.

The identification of global environmental problems, and the need for common responses, has led to institutional developments since the early 1970s. First, some existing multi-lateral institutions, such as the United Nations (UN) organs and more recently the World Trade Organisation (WTO), have had to take new problems into account. Second, we have also seen the establishment of multi-lateral environmental institutions, most significantly the United Nations Environment Programme (UNEP). UNEP was established in 1972 as a subsidiary organ of the UN General Assembly, to work as a 'catalyst' for environmental activities within the UN system. Third, 'multi-lateral environmental agreements' (MEAs) in particular sectors, such as those on ozone-depleting substances, create institutional arrangements such as a conference or a meeting of the parties, and a secretariat, as well as specialist subsidiary bodies. This ad hoc approach to international intervention in environmental problems inevitably leads to concerns about fragmentation, overlap, and the lack of 'voice' for the environment, particularly compared to economically focussed bodies such as the WTO. There is some support for a global environmental body, a World Environmental Organisation, to provide greater coherence and speed, and a higher profile, in respect of international action on the environment.[2] However, whilst the imperative of a

---

[2]  See the discussion in Julie Ayling, 'Serving Many Voices: Progressing Calls for an International Environmental Organisation' (1997) 9 *Journal of Environmental Law* 243.

global approach to environmental problems is almost too obvious to require justification, real questions of legitimacy are raised by the pursuit of global environmental regulation. International obligations are conventionally justified by reference to state consent. And yet basing environmental obligations on the 'specific' consent of states, and accordingly on unanimity, has very obvious limitations: action can be blocked or reduced to the lowest common denominator. But if specific consent to particular treaty obligations is increasingly problematic and complex in international law (most obviously, consent by whom, on whose behalf?), more 'general consent' to a system of regulation not based on unanimity is enormously ambitious.

### Daniel Bodansky, 'The Legitimacy of International Governance: A Coming Challenge for International Environmental Law?' (1999) 93 *American Journal of International Law* 596, p. 623

The process of globalization has put mounting strains on the state system. Environmental problems are increasingly escaping the control of individual states and international institutions have often been too weak to step into the breach. The result has been a 'decision-making deficit', an erosion in the ability of government to address environmental problems effectively. In the long run, overcoming this deficit will require stronger international institutions and decision-making mechanisms. But, as the case of the European Union illustrates, the stronger the institution, the greater the concern about its legitimacy. Unless the issue of legitimacy is addressed, it is likely to act as a drag on the development and effectiveness of international environmental regimes.

Many factors can contribute to or detract from a regime's legitimacy. Legitimacy is a matter not of all or nothing, but of more or less. Authority should be exercised in accordance with law and principle (legal legitimacy). The decision-making mechanisms should be transparent and give people an opportunity to participate (participatory legitimacy). Furthermore, decisions should be based on the best scientific expertise (expert legitimacy). But these are minimum conditions. They contribute to legitimacy (and their absence undermines it), but by themselves do not provide a firm basis for legitimacy. They do not address the central problem, which is how decisions should be made when consensus cannot be reached – by whom, using what voting rule, and with what safeguards.

Calls for global environmental institutions with binding decision-making powers are usually criticised as utopian. This is perhaps too mild a criticism. The term 'utopian' carries the connotation of desirable; the criticism suggests that global institutions with real power would be a good thing, if only states would agree. But this is by no means clear, given the lack of a strong theory of legitimacy. In the absence of a global community, the one compelling candidate, democracy, does not provide an answer. And, at the moment, we lack any persuasive alternative.

Whilst 'globalisation' (at least in the sense of international action) has very obvious attractions in the environmental field, many are unconvinced that its current reach is benign, either for the environment, or for those living in poverty, on whose behalf globalisation (especially global trade) is increasingly invoked. The following extract addresses the need to think about the distribution of power and resources when we think about the impact of globalisation.

### Andrew Dobson, *Citizenship and the Environment* (Oxford University Press, 2003), pp. 12–15

'Political communities', Held writes 'are enmeshed and entrenched in complex structures of overlapping forces, processes and movements'.[3] It is easy to overdo the complexity and especially easy to overdo the overlapping. Compare the Held view with the following from the Indian environmentalist Vandana Shiva:

> The 'global' in the dominant discourse is the political space in which a particular dominant local seeks global control, and frees itself of local, national and international restraints. The global does not represent the universal human interest, it represents a particular local and parochial interest which has been globalized through the scope of its reach. The seven most powerful countries, the G-7, dictate global affairs, but the interests that guide them remain narrow, local and parochial.[4]

Held talks … of the blurring of boundaries between domestic and global affairs. Shiva's point is that not everyone touched by this blurring experiences it in the same way. Held tells us that 'the effects of distant events can be highly significant and even the most local developments can come to have enormous global consequences'. Shiva's crucial corrective is that only the 'local development' of countries or other agencies with globalizing possibilities have global consequences. She puts it like this:

> The notion of 'global' facilitates this skewed view of a common future. The construction of the global environment narrows the South's options while increasing the North's. Through its global reach, the North exists in the South, but the South exists only within itself, since it has not global reach. Thus the South can *only* exist locally, while only the North exists globally.[5]

Globalization is, on this reading, an asymmetrical process in which not only its fruits are divided up unequally, but also in which the very possibility of 'being global' is unbalanced. It is not that Held's position is incompatible with Shiva's corrective, but that *beginning* with asymmetry rather than *adding it on* makes a considerable difference to the political prescriptions that follow the description …

…

… to describe the movement of 'trade, investment, finance [and] culture' in terms of 'networks' and 'flows' as Held does, is in effect to misdescribe them in the same way that to describe the relationship between master and slave as 'interdependent' is to misdescribe it. As an example of the way the global terms of negotiation are skewed, consider the manner in which the World Trade Organization (WTO) operates. The WTO denies skewing because, it says, the organization's decisions are taken by consensus. This is much more

---

[3] David Held, 'Globalization, Corporate Practice and Cosmopolitan Social Standards' [2002] *Contemporary Political Theory* 59, p. 61.

[4] Vandana Shiva, 'The Greening of Global Reach' in Gearoid O. Thuatail, Simon Davey and Paul Routledge (eds.), *The Geopolitics Reader* (Routledge, 1998).    [5] *Ibid.*, p. 233.

equitable than a simple majority system of voting, says the WTO, since even the smallest and least powerful participant in negotiations can oppose an agreement through using what is effectively the power of veto. The reality, though, is somewhat different: consensus decision-making only works in the way the WTO suggests when all participants are equally powerful. As the WTO itself recognizes, though, 'not every country has the same bargaining power'. In cases where governments refuse to come on board, the WTO continues by saying, rather darkly, that 'reluctant countries are persuaded by being offered something in return'. The key orienting question here is: in a world of asymmetrical globalization, what can be offered to countries that already have most of what they want? What can one offer the present United States, for example, if it refuses to play ball with everyone else? The answer, in effect, is nothing. Pre-eminently powerful countries do not have to think in terms of bargaining, or partnerships. In sum, to describe the WTO as if it were a 'node' in a 'network' of multi-lateral 'flows' of 'trade, investment, and finance' is to speak of globalization in terms of characteristics that we might *want* it to possess, rather than those it actually *does* possess.

This focus upon asymmetrical power relationships and their implications for decision making provides an important conceptual context for the chapters that follow in this Part. In Chapter 6 we examine a key international legal and policy concept, sustainable development. Sustainable development emerged in the international arena as a way through the impasse brought about by a perception that environmental protection and economic development for the world's poorest people are conflicting objectives. Sustainable development is an example of a concept, developed primarily at an international level, which has gained widespread support at all levels and has been applied to a range of policy areas;[6] we also look at its UK implementation in Chapter 6. Whatever the attractions of global cooperation in the pursuit of social objectives, global cooperation is currently most developed in areas in which the dominant discourse is one of economic growth and profit. In Chapter 7 we discuss the World Trade Organisation from a perspective concerned with both the relationship between trade rules and environmental protection, and the role of trade in sustainable development, especially in addressing extremes of global poverty.

[6] Including planning, see Ch. 13.

# 6

## Sustainable Development: Quality of Life and the Future

### 1 Introduction

'Sustainable development' has been an enormously influential concept in environmental law since at least the early 1980s. The World Commission on Environment and Development published the seminal work on sustainable development, *Our Common Future* (more commonly known as the 'Brundtland Report', after its chair) in 1987.[1] The Brundtland Report has been built on at an international level, most prominently by the United Nations Convention on Environment and Development (the famous Rio Earth Conference) in 1992, and more recently by the 2002 World Summit on Sustainable Development in Johannesburg.[2] Sustainable development is now extraordinarily widely accepted and supported across the world. We begin this chapter by discussing the evolution of sustainable development through international law. The most widely quoted 'definition' of sustainable development comes from the Brundtland Report, according to which sustainable development is development that 'meets the needs of the present without compromising the ability of future generations to meet their own needs' (pp. 8 and 43). The Johannesburg *Declaration on Sustainable Development* provides an alternative in its reference to 'the interdependent and mutually reinforcing pillars of sustainable development – economic development, social development and environmental protection' (para. 5), although this three-pillared approach is an evolution of earlier approaches, rather than a break with the past.

Sustainable development has clearly entered the political and academic mainstream, and those interested in environmental law cannot afford to ignore questions of sustainable development. Sustainable development is, however, not without its environmental critics.

---

[1] World Commission on Environment and Development, *Our Common Future* (Oxford University Press, 1987) (The Brundtland Report).    [2] www.un.org/events/wssd/.

### Michael Jacobs, 'Sustainable Development as a Contested Concept' in Andrew Dobson (ed.), *Fairness and Futurity: Essays on Environmental Sustainability and Social Justice* (Oxford University Press, 1999), p. 22

Amongst those participating in environmental debates three forms of resistance are discernible. The first is frustration or irritation, usually expressed from a policy-technocratic standpoint. Sustainable development is never properly *defined*, it is protested; everybody seems to think it means something different. How can the term be adopted as a policy objective unless its meaning is clarified and agreed upon?

The second form of resistance is outright rejection. Not all environmentalists have endorsed the concept of sustainable development. Politically, its most outspoken opposition comes from those we might call 'ultra-greens'. For them, the fuzziness of its meaning is integral to its purpose. Sustainable development is a smokescreen put up by business and development interests to obscure the conflicts between ecological integrity and economic growth, and between the interests of the rich North and poor South. Acceptance of the concept by environmental groups is a mistake, it is argued: a fatal co-option into technocratic 'global management' sideshows designed not to disturb the fundamental processes of capitalist exploitation.

The third form of resistance comes from those we might call 'cultural critics', principally within academia. The argument here is that the discourse of sustainable development represents an inappropriate response to the 'environmental problematic'. It derives from the same cultural sources – modernism, scientific positivism and realism, technocratic social democracy – as the problems it is trying to address.[3] Despite good intentions, its inability to understand or reflect recent cultural changes in industrial societies leaves its programme liable to failure.

In this chapter, we do not attempt to provide a definition or single acceptable approach to sustainable development. Instead, we consider the various elements of sustainable development (in Section 3), by reference particularly to the international law documents. In Section 4 we move on to discussing the place of sustainable development in the UK.

In Section 5 we discuss what divides sustainable development from the belief that environmental questions impose absolute 'limits to growth'. One of the attractions of sustainable development has always been its assertion that economic growth and environmental protection need not be incompatible, flatly contradicting the understanding of the world held by those who assert the existence of 'limits'. Returning to a familiar theme (from Chapter 1, especially), in Section 6 we consider the *normative* nature of sustainable development, that is whether decisions in sustainable development can be discussed as technical matters, or only politically, as value judgments. Jacobs, for example, in the paper from which the passage above is taken, identifies enormous value in the concept of sustainable development, partly *because* the lack of fixed meaning means that

---

[3] See also the discussion in Ch. 1 above, pp. 47–57.

sharply conflicting groups and interests are using the 'same language and endorsing the same nominal objective, that of sustainable development' (p. 22). Along similar lines, and responding to those who criticise the difficulty of pinning down a 'definition' of sustainable development, John Dryzek rejects the position of those that suggest that the 'proliferation' of definitions of sustainable development render it unhelpful or damaging.

### John S. Dryzek, *The Politics of the Earth: Environmental Discourses* (Oxford University Press, 1997), p. 125

Does this variety of meanings mean we should dismiss sustainable development as a mere slogan, an empty vessel that can be filled with whatever one likes? Not at all. For it is not unusual for important concepts to be contested politically. Think, for example, of the word 'democracy', which has at least as many meanings and definitions as does sustainable development. Part of what makes democracy interesting is this very contestation over its essence. Democracy is doubly interesting because just about everyone who matters in today's political world claims to believe in it. The parallels with sustainable development are quite precise. Just as democracy is the only game in town when it comes to political organization, so sustainable development is emerging as the main game (though not quite the only game) when it comes to environmental affairs, at least global ones.

## 2 The evolution of sustainable development in international law

An unabashedly anthropocentric concept (see also the extract from Emmenegger and Tschentscher in the Preface to Part I, pp. 2–3), sustainable development attempts to reconcile human objectives that might otherwise be thought to compete. Its origins are usually identified in the Stockholm conference of 1972,[4] which sought to emphasise links between human development and environmental protection. It was the 1987 Brundtland Report, however, that really captured the imagination. This Report from a United Nations (UN) commission is best viewed in its international context. It explored the possibility of reconciling demands for development from developing countries with demands for environmental protection, primarily from rich industrialised countries.[5] The 'no-growth' response to environmental degradation had been rejected, especially by developing countries. And tension around the injustice of leaving human beings in abject poverty in order to protect the environment was compounded by, and drew attention to, a similar tension (less easily justified) within wealthy nations: 'the compulsion to drive up the GNP had turned many into cheerful enemies of nature'.[6] Arguably the greatest success of

---

[4] Declaration of the UN Conference on the Human Environment, Stockholm, 1972.
[5] See the discussion in Lavanya Rajamani, 'From Stockholm to Johannesburg: The Anatomy of Dissonance in the International Environmental Dialogue' (2003) 12 *Review of European Community and International Environmental Law* 23.
[6] Wolfgang Sachs, *The Development Dictionary* (Zed Books, 1992), p. 28.

the Brundtland Report was to bring many formerly opposing positions, particularly growth / environmental protection, into agreement around the same ideas. It is an extraordinarily optimistic piece of work.

### Brundtland Report, pp. 1–2

In the middle of the 20th century, we saw our planet from space for the first time. Historians may eventually find that this vision had a greater impact on thought than did the Copernican revolution of the 16th century, which upset the human self-image by revealing that the Earth is not the centre of the universe. From space, we see a small and fragile ball dominated not by human activity and edifice but by a pattern of clouds, oceans, greenery, and soils. Humanity's inability to fit its doings into that pattern is changing planetary systems, fundamentally. Many such changes are accompanied by life-threatening hazards. This new reality, from which there is no escape, must be recognized – and managed.

Fortunately, this new reality coincides with more positive developments new to this century. We can move information and goods faster around the globe than ever before; we can produce more food and more goods with less investment of resources; our technology and science gives us at least the potential to look deeper into and better understand natural systems. From space, we can see and study the Earth as an organism whose health depends on the health of all its parts. We have the power to reconcile human affairs with natural laws and to thrive in the process. In this our cultural and spiritual heritages can reinforce our economic interests and survival imperatives.

This Commission believes that people can build a future that is more prosperous, more just, and more secure. Our report, *Our Common Future*, is not a prediction of ever increasing environmental decay, poverty, and hardship in an ever more polluted world among ever decreasing resources. We see instead the possibility for a new era of economic growth, one that must be based on policies that sustain and expand the environmental resource base. And we believe such growth to be absolutely essential to relieve the great poverty that is deepening in much of the developing world.

But the Commission's hope for the future is conditional on decisive political action now to begin managing environmental resources to ensure both sustainable human progress and human survival. We are not forecasting a future; we are serving a notice – an urgent notice based on the latest and best scientific evidence – that the time has come to take the decisions needed to secure the resources to sustain this and coming generations. We do not offer a detailed blueprint for action, but instead a pathway by which the peoples of the world may enlarge their spheres of co-operation.

The major legal contribution to sustainable development following Stockholm and Brundtland came at the Rio conference in 1992. This conference produced several important legal outputs, including the United Nations Framework Convention on Climate Change, the United Nations Convention on Biological Diversity, and 'Agenda 21', which provided detail on the implementation of sustainable development, monitored by the United Nations Commission on

Sustainable Development. For current purposes, its most significant agreement was the Rio *Declaration on Environment and Development.* The Rio Declaration sets out many of the enduring features of sustainable development, including some of the key environmental principles that underlie environmental law,[7] as well as the instruments to be deployed to achieve sustainable development.[8]

## UN Declaration on Environment and Development, Rio de Janeiro, 1992 (the Rio Declaration)

The United Nations Conference on Environment and Development,

Having met at Rio de Janeiro from 3 to 14 June 1992,

Reaffirming the Declaration of the United Nations Conference on the Human Environment, adopted at Stockholm on 16 June 1972, and seeking to build upon it,

With the goal of establishing a new and equitable global partnership through the creation of new levels of cooperation among States, key sectors of societies and people,

Working towards international agreements which respect the interests of all and protect the integrity of the global environmental and developmental system,

Recognizing the integral and interdependent nature of the Earth, our home,

Proclaims that:

Principle 1

Human beings are at the centre of concerns for sustainable development. They are entitled to a healthy and productive life in harmony with nature.

Principle 2

States have, in accordance with the Charter of the United Nations and the principles of international law, the sovereign right to exploit their own resources pursuant to their own environmental and developmental policies, and the responsibility to ensure that activities within their jurisdiction or control do not cause damage to the environment of other States or of areas beyond the limits of national jurisdiction.

Principle 3

The right to development must be fulfilled so as to equitably meet developmental and environmental needs of present and future generations.

Principle 4

In order to achieve sustainable development, environmental protection shall constitute an integral part of the development process and cannot be considered in isolation from it.

Principle 5

All States and all people shall cooperate in the essential task of eradicating poverty as an indispensable requirement for sustainable development, in order to decrease the disparities in standards of living and better meet the needs of the majority of the people of the world.

---

[7] Especially Principle 15 on the precautionary principle (Ch. 1, pp. 18–31), and Principle 16 on the polluter pays principle (Ch. 1, pp. 36–7).

[8] Especially Principle 17 on environmental assessment, on which see Ch. 14.

Principle 6

The special situation and needs of developing countries, particularly the least developed and those most environmentally vulnerable, shall be given special priority. International actions in the field of environment and development should also address the interests and needs of all countries.

Principle 7

States shall cooperate in a spirit of global partnership to conserve, protect and restore the health and integrity of the Earth's ecosystem. In view of the different contributions to global environmental degradation, States have common but differentiated responsibilities. The developed countries acknowledge the responsibility that they bear in the international pursuit of sustainable development in view of the pressures their societies place on the global environment and of the technologies and financial resources they command.

Principle 8

To achieve sustainable development and a higher quality of life for all people, States should reduce and eliminate unsustainable patterns of production and consumption and promote appropriate demographic policies.

Principle 9

States should cooperate to strengthen endogenous capacity-building for sustainable development by improving scientific understanding through exchanges of scientific and technological knowledge, and by enhancing the development, adaptation, diffusion and transfer of technologies, including new and innovative technologies.

Principle 10

Environmental issues are best handled with the participation of all concerned citizens, at the relevant level. At the national level, each individual shall have appropriate access to information concerning the environment that is held by public authorities, including information on hazardous materials and activities in their communities, and the opportunity to participate in decision-making processes. States shall facilitate and encourage public awareness and participation by making information widely available. Effective access to judicial and administrative proceedings, including redress and remedy, shall be provided.

Principle 11

States shall enact effective environmental legislation. Environmental standards, management objectives and priorities should reflect the environmental and developmental context to which they apply. Standards applied by some countries may be inappropriate and of unwarranted economic and social cost to other countries, in particular developing countries.

Principle 12

States should cooperate to promote a supportive and open international economic system that would lead to economic growth and sustainable development in all countries, to better address the problems of environmental degradation. Trade policy measures for environmental purposes should not constitute a means of arbitrary or unjustifiable discrimination or a disguised restriction on international trade. Unilateral actions to deal with environmental challenges outside the jurisdiction of the importing country should be

avoided. Environmental measures addressing transboundary or global environmental problems should, as far as possible, be based on an international consensus.

Principle 13

States shall develop national law regarding liability and compensation for the victims of
pollution and other environmental damage. States shall also cooperate in an expeditious and
more determined manner to develop further international law regarding liability and
compensation for adverse effects of environmental damage caused by activities within their
jurisdiction or control to areas beyond their jurisdiction.

Principle 14

States should effectively cooperate to discourage or prevent the relocation and transfer to
other States of any activities and substances that cause severe environmental degradation
or are found to be harmful to human health.

Principle 15

In order to protect the environment, the precautionary approach shall be widely applied by
States according to their capabilities. Where there are threats of serious or irreversible
damage, lack of full scientific certainty shall not be used as a reason for postponing cost-
effective measures to prevent environmental degradation.

Principle 16

National authorities should endeavour to promote the internalization of environmental costs
and the use of economic instruments, taking into account the approach that the polluter
should, in principle, bear the cost of pollution, with due regard to the public interest and
without distorting international trade and investment.

Principle 17

Environmental impact assessment, as a national instrument, shall be undertaken for
proposed activities that are likely to have a significant adverse impact on the environment
and are subject to a decision of a competent national authority.

Principle 18

States shall immediately notify other States of any natural disasters or other emergencies
that are likely to produce sudden harmful effects on the environment of those States. Every
effort shall be made by the international community to help States so afflicted.

Principle 19

States shall provide prior and timely notification and relevant information to
potentially affected States on activities that may have a significant adverse transboundary environmental effect and shall consult with those States at an early stage and in
good faith.

Principle 20

Women have a vital role in environmental management and development. Their full participation is therefore essential to achieve sustainable development.[9]

Principle 21

The creativity, ideals and courage of the youth of the world should be mobilized to forge
a global partnership in order to achieve sustainable development and ensure a better
future for all.

---

[9]  See the discussion of eco-feminism in Ch. 1, pp. 51–3.

Principle 22

Indigenous people and their communities and other local communities have a vital role in environmental management and development because of their knowledge and traditional practices. States should recognize and duly support their identity, culture and interests and enable their effective participation in the achievement of sustainable development.

Principle 23

The environment and natural resources of people under oppression, domination and occupation shall be protected.

Principle 24

Warfare is inherently destructive of sustainable development. States shall therefore respect international law providing protection for the environment in times of armed conflict and cooperate in its further development, as necessary.

Principle 25

Peace, development and environmental protection are interdependent and indivisible.

Principle 26

States shall resolve all their environmental disputes peacefully and by appropriate means in accordance with the Charter of the United Nations.

Principle 27

States and people shall cooperate in good faith and in a spirit of partnership in the fulfilment of the principles embodied in this Declaration and in the further development of international law in the field of sustainable development.

## Lavanya Rajamani, 'From Stockholm to Johannesburg: The Anatomy of Dissonance in the International Environmental Dialogue' (2003) 12 *Review of European Community and International Environmental Law* 23, pp. 25–6

Despite the altered emphasis in the title [the 'Earth Charter' had been preferred by most industrialised countries], the old conflicts between the developing and industrial countries re-surfaced at UNCED [United Nations Conference on Environment and Development, Rio] in 1992. There was little consensus on the real environmental issues, the significance of the terms 'environment' and 'development', and indeed the nature of the 'environment – development' interaction. While the industrial countries sought progress on climate change, biodiversity, forest loss and fishery issues, the developing countries pushed for market access, trade, technology transfer, development assistance and capacity building. While the industrial countries sought to place global environmental issues on the agenda, perceived as a consequence of affluence, the developing countries sought to emphasize local issues, perceived as intimately linked to poverty. The values and issues promoted by the developing countries in the international environmental arena speak to their belief that the principal aim of an international environmental regime should be *intra-generational equity*, which would entail that the development needs of the developing countries receive priority in any effort to promote a better global environment. The values promoted by the industrial countries, and the interests they espouse, speak to their belief that the *regulation of trans-boundary pollution* and the *environmental ethic* should be central to the international environmental agenda. The term *environmental ethic* refers to the existence of wide-ranging responsibilities stemming from the premise of an interconnected world within which actions of individuals or groups in one place are liable to generate repercussions elsewhere.

The issue of blame was also a bone of contention between developing and industrial countries. While the industrial world inclined toward sourcing global environmental degradation to population growth in the developing world, the developing world sought to source it to consumption levels in the industrial world.

Notwithstanding the clear conflict of values and priorities between the developing countries and the industrial ones, at Rio a fragile consensus developed once again around the marginally better articulated, although still inchoate, concept of 'sustainable development'. 'Sustainable development', as a concept, acquired a rhetorical power and promise that essentially had something for everyone. Developing countries could see it encompass their demand for intra-generational equity, and the industrial countries could see it include their desire to control trans-boundary pollution and promote an environmental ethic. The resulting Rio Declaration is a delicate balance between the interests of the developing and industrial countries. This balance is reflected in two sets of key principles. They are, on the one hand, the precautionary approach and the polluter-pays principle and, on the other, the right to development, poverty alleviation and the recognition of common but differentiated responsibilities.

Although in Rio, as in Stockholm, the compromise revolved around the recognition that environmental protection was not necessarily incompatible with development, in its tone and intent, the Rio Declaration is considered qualitatively different from the Stockholm Declaration. Indeed, the UNCED was heralded as a 'paradigm shift' from international environmental law to the international law of sustainable development, and as signifying a 'new international ecological order'.[10] This paradigm shift can be traced to the increasing currency of the development rhetoric, as well as the heightened mobilization of developing country coalitions in the lead up to UNCED.

The Johannesburg conference in 2002, the World Summit on Sustainable Development, was supposed to provide for the implementation of the goals agreed at Rio, putting in place a range of concrete measures, including instruments to address poverty and environmental degradation. The negotiation was painful, with preparatory committees over two years making worryingly little progress. There were two main official outputs of the Johannesburg summit, the political declaration – the Johannesburg Declaration on Sustainable Development – and the Johannesburg Plan of Implementation.

[10] Jan Pronk, 'A New International Ecological Order' (1991) 14 *Internationale Spectator* 728.

## Johannesburg Declaration on Sustainable Development, Johannesburg 2002 From our origins to the future

1. We, the representatives of the peoples of the world, assembled at the World Summit on Sustainable Development in Johannesburg, South Africa, from 2 to 4 September 2002, reaffirm our commitment to sustainable development.

2. We commit ourselves to building a humane, equitable and caring global society, cognizant of the need for human dignity for all.

3. At the beginning of this Summit, the children of the world spoke to us in a simple yet clear voice that the future belongs to them, and accordingly challenged all of us to ensure that through our actions they will inherit a world free of the indignity and indecency occasioned by poverty, environmental degradation and patterns of unsustainable development.

4. As part of our response to these children, who represent our collective future, all of us, coming from every corner of the world, informed by different life experiences, are united and moved by a deeply felt sense that we urgently need to create a new and brighter world of hope.

5. Accordingly, we assume a collective responsibility to advance and strengthen the interdependent and mutually reinforcing pillars of sustainable development – economic development, social development and environmental protection – at the local, national, regional and global levels.

6. From this continent, the cradle of humanity, we declare, through the Plan of Implementation of the World Summit on Sustainable Development and the present Declaration, our responsibility to one another, to the greater community of life and to our children.

7. Recognizing that humankind is at a crossroads, we have united in a common resolve to make a determined effort to respond positively to the need to produce a practical and visible plan to bring about poverty eradication and human development.

### From Stockholm to Rio de Janeiro to Johannesburg

8. Thirty years ago, in Stockholm, we agreed on the urgent need to respond to the problem of environmental deterioration. Ten years ago, at the United Nations Conference on Environment and Development, held in Rio de Janeiro, we agreed that the protection of the environment and social and economic development are fundamental to sustainable development, based on the Rio Principles. To achieve such development, we adopted the global programme entitled Agenda 21 and the Rio Declaration on Environment and Development, to which we reaffirm our commitment. The Rio Conference was a significant milestone that set a new agenda for sustainable development.

9. Between Rio and Johannesburg, the world's nations have met in several major conferences under the auspices of the United Nations, including the International Conference on Financing for Development, as well as the Doha Ministerial Conference. These conferences defined for the world a comprehensive vision for the future of humanity.

10. At the Johannesburg Summit, we have achieved much in bringing together a rich tapestry of peoples and views in a constructive search for a common path towards a world that

respects and implements the vision of sustainable development. The Johannesburg Summit has also confirmed that significant progress has been made towards achieving a global consensus and partnership among all the people of our planet.

### The challenges we face

11. We recognize that poverty eradication, changing consumption and production patterns and protecting and managing the natural resource base for economic and social development are overarching objectives of and essential requirements for sustainable development.

12. The deep fault line that divides human society between the rich and the poor and the ever-increasing gap between the developed and developing worlds pose a major threat to global prosperity, security and stability.

13. The global environment continues to suffer. Loss of biodiversity continues, fish stocks continue to be depleted, desertification claims more and more fertile land, the adverse effects of climate change are already evident, natural disasters are more frequent and more devastating, and developing countries more vulnerable, and air, water and marine pollution continue to rob millions of a decent life.

14. Globalization has added a new dimension to these challenges. The rapid integration of markets, mobility of capital and significant increases in investment flows around the world have opened new challenges and opportunities for the pursuit of sustainable development. But the benefits and costs of globalization are unevenly distributed, with developing countries facing special difficulties in meeting this challenge

15. We risk the entrenchment of these global disparities and unless we act in a manner that fundamentally changes their lives the poor of the world may lose confidence in their representatives and the democratic systems to which we remain committed, seeing their representatives as nothing more than sounding brass or tinkling cymbals.

### Our commitment to sustainable development

16. We are determined to ensure that our rich diversity, which is our collective strength, will be used for constructive partnership for change and for the achievement of the common goal of sustainable development.

17. Recognizing the importance of building human solidarity, we urge the promotion of dialogue and cooperation among the world's civilizations and peoples, irrespective of race, disabilities, religion, language, culture or tradition.

18. We welcome the focus of the Johannesburg Summit on the indivisibility of human dignity and are resolved, through decisions on targets, timetables and partnerships, to speedily increase access to such basic requirements as clean water, sanitation, adequate shelter, energy, health care, food security and the protection of biodiversity. At the same time, we will work together to help one another gain access to financial resources, benefit from the opening of markets, ensure capacity building, use modern technology to bring about development and make sure that there is technology transfer, human resource development, education and training to banish underdevelopment forever.

19. We reaffirm our pledge to place particular focus on, and give priority attention to, the fight against the worldwide conditions that pose severe threats to the sustainable development of our people, which include: chronic hunger; malnutrition; foreign occupation; armed

conflict; illicit drug problems; organized crime; corruption; natural disasters; illicit arms trafficking; trafficking in persons; terrorism; intolerance and incitement to racial, ethnic, religious and other hatreds; xenophobia; and endemic, communicable and chronic diseases, in particular HIV/AIDS, malaria and tuberculosis.

20. We are committed to ensuring that women's empowerment, emancipation and gender equality are integrated in all the activities encompassed within Agenda 21, the Millennium development goals and the Plan of Implementation of the Summit.

21. We recognize the reality that global society has the means and is endowed with the resources to address the challenges of poverty eradication and sustainable development confronting all humanity. Together, we will take extra steps to ensure that these available resources are used to the benefit of humanity.

22. In this regard, to contribute to the achievement of our development goals and targets, we urge developed countries that have not done so to make concrete efforts towards the internationally agreed levels of official development assistance.

23. We welcome and support the emergence of stronger regional groupings and alliances, such as the New Partnership for Africa's Development, to promote regional cooperation, improved international cooperation and sustainable development.

24. We shall continue to pay special attention to the developmental needs of small island developing States and the least developed countries.

25. We reaffirm the vital role of the indigenous peoples in sustainable development.

26. We recognize that sustainable development requires a long-term perspective and broad-based participation in policy formulation, decision-making and implementation at all levels. As social partners, we will continue to work for stable partnerships with all major groups, respecting the independent, important roles of each of them.

27. We agree that in pursuit of its legitimate activities the private sector, including both large and small companies, has a duty to contribute to the evolution of equitable and sustainable communities and societies.

28. We also agree to provide assistance to increase income-generating employment opportunities, taking into account the Declaration on Fundamental Principles and Rights at Work of the International Labour Organization.

29. We agree that there is a need for private sector corporations to enforce corporate accountability, which should take place within a transparent and stable regulatory environment.

30. We undertake to strengthen and improve governance at all levels for the effective implementation of Agenda 21, the Millennium development goals and the Plan of Implementation of the Summit.

### Multilateralism is the future

31. To achieve our goals of sustainable development, we need more effective, democratic and accountable international and multi-lateral institutions.

32. We reaffirm our commitment to the principles and purposes of the Charter of the United Nations and international law, as well as to the strengthening of multilateralism. We support the leadership role of the United Nations as the most universal and representative organization in the world, which is best placed to promote sustainable development.

33. We further commit ourselves to monitor progress at regular intervals towards the achievement of our sustainable development goals and objectives.

**Making it happen!**

34. We are in agreement that this must be an inclusive process, involving all the major groups and Governments that participated in the historic Johannesburg Summit.

35. We commit ourselves to act together, united by a common determination to save our planet, promote human development and achieve universal prosperity and peace.

36. We commit ourselves to the Plan of Implementation of the World Summit on Sustainable Development and to expediting the achievement of the time-bound, socio-economic and environmental targets contained therein.

37. From the African continent, the cradle of humankind, we solemnly pledge to the peoples of the world and the generations that will surely inherit this Earth that we are determined to ensure that our collective hope for sustainable development is realized.

Notwithstanding the platitudinous (sometimes downright strange) language resulting from the search for international consensus, this political declaration confirms a number of key commitments from Rio. This confirmation of existing principles turned out to be hard fought, and was by no means a foregone conclusion.[11]

As well as the two official outputs (we return to the Plan of Implementation below, pp. 240–3), the use of 'partnership initiatives' for the implementation of sustainable development objectives was agreed at Johannesburg. These are voluntary agreements between government, industry and civil society in the field of sustainable development. Over 300 agreements had been registered with the UN Commission on Sustainable Development by 2005.[12] Registered partnerships should be 'new' and should 'add concrete value to the implementation process of global agreements related to sustainable development'.[13] A majority of the partnerships registered with the Commission secretariat were launched at or around the time of the World Summit on Sustainable Development.

Two rather different examples in the field of water are the 'Global Rainwater Harvesting Collective'[14] and the 'EU Water Initiative: Water for Life'.[15] The Johannesburg Plan of Implementation includes a target of halving the proportion of the world's people without access to safe drinking water, along with other water-related objectives. The Global Rainwater Harvesting Collective

---

[11] See Marc Pallemaerts, 'International Law and Sustainable Development: Any Progress in Johannesburg?' (2003) 12 *Review of European Community and International Environmental Law* 1.     [12] See www.un.org/esa/sustdev/partnerships/partnerships.htm.

[13] Commission on Sustainable Development, Twelfth Session, 14–30 April 2004, *Partnerships for Sustainable Development*, Report of the Secretary, para. 20.

[14] http://webapps01.un.org/dsd/partnerships/public/partnerships/1101.html.

[15] http://webapps01.un.org/dsd/partnerships/public/partnerships/843.html#gen_info

involves a number of developing-country governments, plus private and public interest organisations, in the provision of drinking water to schools around the world through roof top 'rain water harvesting'. Water for Life involves the European Union (EU) and its Member State governments, together with a number of private sector organisations (for example Thames Water and Vivendi) and public interest groups (for example Tearfund), with the intention of providing 'a platform for strategic partnerships' to contribute to the meeting of targets relating to clean drinking water and sanitation. The following objectives are outlined:

- Reinforce political will and commitment to action
- Make water governance effective and build institutional capacity
- Improve co-ordination and cooperation
- Increase the efficiency of existing EU aid flows

This latter agreement in particular indicates the central role of the private sector in Johannesburg, which is highly controversial (see also below, pp. 241–2). Partnership agreements have received something of a mixed reception.[16] Positively, they seek engagement with the private sector as an innovative way to reach solutions, and, if individual projects are successful, that will make a significant difference to many people. Others are concerned that partnership agreements may shift the emphasis too far from government, 'privatising' sustainable development and deflecting attention from the failure of governments to agree and achieve meaningful action, as well as allowing corporations superficially to 'greenwash' their corporate image without meaningful change. Although partnership agreements are not supposed to be 'a substitute for government responsibilities and commitments', but are supposed to strengthen implementation,[17] the diffusion of responsibility can deflect attention from more traditional, mandatory implementation.

In fact, the Johannesburg Summit as a whole received a lukewarm response. On the positive side, the reaffirmation of key Rio principles and commitments, together with some new commitments and implementation measures, may have reinvigorated international cooperation on sustainable development. And this occurred at a time of high-profile difficulties for international cooperation: in particular, the war in Iraq had led to international divisions, and there was considerable disquiet about the withdrawal of the United States from the Kyoto Protocol to the United Nations Framework Convention on Climate Change. There was also, however, widespread criticism of the Summit: Friends of the

---

[16] See the discussion in Iva von Frantzius, 'World Summit on Sustainable Development Johannesburg 2002: A Critical Analysis and Assessment of the Outcomes' (2004) 13 *Environmental Politics* 467; Charlotte Streck, 'The World Summit on Sustainable Development: Partnerships as New Tools in Environmental Governance' (2002) 13 *Yearbook of International Environmental Law* 63.

[17] Commission on Sustainable Development, *Partnerships for Sustainable Development*, para. 1.

Earth, for example, criticised the absence of targets, and the failure to provide for the institutional arrangements and legal frameworks[18] necessary for practical action. They even expressed their 'dismay' at hearing the Summit described as a great success by government: 'Given the scale of the challenges now facing the planet, and the dire warnings issued by (for example) the United Nations Environment Programme before the WSSD [World Summit on Sustainable Development] it is difficult to see how any government could regard the Summit as anything other than a disappointment.'[19]

## 3 The elements of sustainable development

Rather than seek to provide a 'definition' of sustainable development, or to choose between competing approaches, in this section we will examine some of the main elements of sustainable development.

### (a) The future and sustainable development

The inclusion of the long-term future in policy debate has been a distinguishing feature of sustainable development since the Brundtland Report's 'definition' of sustainable development as development that 'meets the needs of the present without compromising the ability of future generations to meet their own needs' (see above, p. 217). This aspiration of inter-generational equity is conceptually difficult. At its most basic, the implication is that *something* must be 'sustained' for future generations; quite what, is of course the difficult question. For our purposes, although economic growth (particularly in the alleviation of desperate poverty) and the development of robust political institutions[20] will make a significant contribution to the ability of future generations 'to meet their own needs', a reference to the long-term future also brings environmental concerns to the centre of political debate. Environmental degradation is a very obvious way of limiting the options of future generations.

Deciding what should be sustained, and determining whether development is 'sustainable' in any particular case, are questions that have long been dominated by economists. When economists consider what should be sustained, they turn to 'capital', one of the fundamental conceptual tools of their discipline. By the attribution of a monetary value to a whole range of marketed and non-marketed 'goods' (including a clean environment), 'capital' allows an economic assessment of measures affecting those goods. This

---

[18] Pallemaerts, 'International Law and Sustainable Development', discusses the limited role for international law in Johannesburg.

[19] Environmental Audit Committee, Twelfth Report of Session 2002–3, *World Summit on Sustainable Development 2002 – From Rhetoric to Reality*, HC 98-I, para. 24.

[20] Wilfred Beckerman and Joanna Pasek, *Justice, Posterity, and the Environment* (Oxford University Press, 2001).

method has been highly contentious. As we discussed in Chapter 1, pp. 39–40, an economic approach to environmental protection is subject to disputed and unpredictable methods of calculation, and some would say that it is simply incapable of capturing the public values or ethical perspectives inherent in sustainable development.

Even within the economic debate on sustainable development, some serious disputes arise, particularly over the relative role of different forms of 'capital'. 'Capital' includes 'natural' capital, 'physical' capital and 'human' capital, including technology, works of art and factories as well as forest, fossil fuels and an intact ozone layer. These 'definitions' of different types of capital, and particularly what counts as 'natural capital', are as disputed as any other aspect of sustainable development, but do allow the different positions to be further explored.

### David Pearce and Edward B. Barbier, *Blueprint for a Sustainable Economy* (Earthscan, 2000), pp. 23–4

In *Blueprint 1* we noted that economists are generally split into two camps over the special role of natural capital and sustainable development. The main disagreement between these two perspectives is whether natural capital has a unique or essential role in sustaining human welfare, and thus whether special compensation rules are required to ensure that future generations are not made worse off by natural capital depletion today. These two contrasting views are now generally referred to as weak sustainability versus strong sustainability.

According to the weak sustainability view, there is essentially no inherent difference between natural and other forms of capital, and hence the same optimal depletion rules ought to apply to both. As long as the natural capital that is being depleted is replaced with even more valuable physical and human capital, then the value of the aggregate stock – comprising both human, physical and the remaining natural capital – is increasing over time. Maintaining and enhancing the total stock of all capital alone is sufficient to attain sustainable development.

In contrast, proponents of the strong sustainability view argue that physical or human capital cannot substitute for all the environmental resources comprising the natural capital stock, or all of the ecological services performed by nature. Essentially, this view questions whether, on the one hand, human and physical capital, and on the other, natural capital, effectively comprise a single homogeneous total capital stock. Uncertainty over many environmental values, in particular the value that future generations may place on increasingly scarce natural resources and ecological services, further limits our ability to determine whether we can adequately compensate future generations for irreversible losses in essential natural capital today.

The economists' enthusiasm for sustainable development has not, however, been universal. Beckerman argues that 'strong' sustainability is 'morally repugnant', but that 'weak' sustainability adds nothing of interest to normal welfare economics.

### Wilfred Beckerman, ' "Sustainable Development": Is it a Useful Concept?' (1994) 3 *Environmental Values* 191, pp. 191–206

During the last few years the fashionable concept in environmental discourse has been 'sustainable development'. It has spawned a vast literature and has strengthened the arm of empire builders in many research institutes, Universities, national and international bureaucracies and statistical offices. Environmental pressure groups present the concept of sustainable development as an important new contribution to the environmental debate. It is claimed that it brings new insights into the way that concern for the environment and the interests of future generations should be taken into account in policy analysis. But in fact it only muddles the issues …

It seems high time, therefore, for somebody to spell out why, if the Emperor of Sustainable Development has any clothes at all, they are pretty threadbare. In this article I maintain that 'sustainable development' has been defined in such a way as to be either morally repugnant or logically redundant. It is true that, in the past, economic policy has tended to ignore environmental issues, particularly those having very long run consequences. It is right, therefore, that they should now be given proper place in the conduct of policy. But this can be done without elevating sustainability to the status of some over-riding criterion of policy. After all I am sure that the reader can easily think of innumerable human activities that are highly desirable, but, alas, not indefinitely sustainable!

…

Over the past few years innumerable definitions of sustainable development have been proposed. But one can identify a clear trend in them. At the beginning, sustainability was interpreted as a requirement to preserve intact the environment as we find it today in all its forms. The Brundtland report, for example, stated that 'The loss of plant and animal species can greatly limit the options of future generations; so sustainable development requires the conservation of plant and animal species'.

But, one might ask, how far does the Brundtland report's injunction to conserve plant and animal species really go? Is one supposed to preserve all of them? And at what price? Is one supposed to mount a large operation, at astronomic cost, to ensure the survival of every known and unknown species on the grounds that it might give pleasure to future generations, or that it might turn out, in 100 years time, to have medicinal properties? About 98 percent of all the species that have ever existed are believed to have become extinct, but most people do not suffer any great sense of loss as a result. How many people lose sleep because it is no longer possible to see a live Dinosaur?

Clearly, such an absolutist concept of 'sustainable development' is morally repugnant. Given the acute poverty and environmental degradation in which a large part of the world's population live, one could not justify using up vast resources in an attempt to preserve from extinction, say, every one of the several million species of beetles that exist

…

As it soon became obvious that the 'strong' concept of sustainable development was morally repugnant, as well as totally impracticable, many environmentalists shifted their ground. A new version of the concept was adopted, known in the literature as 'weak' sustainability. This allows for some natural resources to be run down as long as adequate compensation is provided by increases in other resources, perhaps even in the form of man made capital. But what constitutes adequate compensation? How many more schools or hospitals or houses or factories or machines are required to compensate for using up of some mineral resources or forests or clean atmosphere? The answer, it turned out, was that the acceptability of the substitution had to be judged by its contribution to sustaining human welfare.

This is clear from one of the latest definitions provided by David Pearce, who is the author of numerous works on sustainability. His definition is that '"Sustainability" therefore implies something about maintaining the level of human well-being so that it might improve but at least never declines (or, not more than temporarily, anyway). Interpreted this way, sustainable development becomes equivalent to some requirement that well-being does not decline through time.'[21]

The first important feature of this definition is that it is couched in terms of maintaining 'well-being', not in terms of maintaining the level of consumption or GNP [gross national product], or even in terms of maintaining intact the overall stock of natural capital, a condition that is found in many definitions of sustainable development including one to which David Pearce had earlier subscribed, (though in collaboration with two other authors who clearly had a bad influence on him). This implies, for example, that sustainable development could include the replacement of natural capital by man-made capital, provided the increase in the latter compensated future generations for any fall in their welfare that might have been caused by the depletion of natural capital. In other words, it allows for substitutability between different forms of natural capital and man-made capital, provided that, on balance, there is no decline in welfare.

But this amounts to selling a crucial pass in any struggle to preserve the independent usefulness of the concept of sustainability. For if the choice between preserving natural capital and adding to (or preserving) man-made capital depends on which makes the greatest contribution to welfare the concept of sustainable development becomes redundant. In the attempt to rid the original 'strong' concept of sustainable development of its most obvious weaknesses the baby has been thrown out with the bath water. For it appears now that what society should aim at is not 'sustainability', but the maximisation of welfare. In other words, it should pursue the old-fashioned economist's concept of 'optimality'.

...

... when one is concerned with optimality for society as a whole ... account has to be taken of distributional considerations. This applies whether one is maximising welfare of society at any moment of time or maximising welfare over some time period. Making due allowance for distributional considerations means that when we are seeking to maximise total social welfare at any point of time we will be concerned with the manner in which the total consumption of society is distributed amongst the population at the point in time in question – e.g. how equally, or justly (which may not be the same thing) it is distributed. And if we are seeking to maximise welfare over time whilst making allowance for distributional considerations we would be concerned with the distribution of

[21]  David Pearce, *Economic Values and the Natural World* (Earthscan, 1993).

consumption over time – e.g. how equally, or justly, consumption is distributed between different generations.

Both procedures fit easily into welfare economics. Environmentalists may not be aware of the fact that it has long been conventional to include distributional considerations into the concept of economic welfare – which is a component of total welfare – that one seeks to maximise …

Welfare can also be defined to include considerations of social justice and freedom, and so on. Of course, the more widely one draws the net of welfare to include such variables the greater the difficulty in making them all commensurate with each other. It is true that this makes it more difficult to define exactly what is meant by the 'maximisation' operation. But the same difficulty is encountered by any proposition to the effect that 'welfare' (or 'well-being') had declined in any specific time period.

### Herman E. Daly, 'On Wilfred Beckerman's Critique of Sustainable Development' (1995)4 *Environmental Values* 49, pp. 49–52

Beckerman's discussion of sustainable development provides some useful clarifications, and a good occasion for making a few more. Since I advocate what he calls the 'sustainability as constraint' position, I will move straight to it, and begin with the dilemma in which he claims to have placed those like me:

> The advocates of sustainable development as a constraint, therefore, face a dilemma. Either they stick to 'strong' sustainability, which is logical, but requires subscribing to a morally repugnant and totally impractical objective, or they switch to some welfare-based concept of sustainability, in which case they are advocating a concept that appears to be redundant and unable to qualify as a logical constraint on welfare maximisation.

I advocate strong sustainability, thereby receiving Beckerman's blessing in the realm of logic but provoking his righteous indignation in the realms of morality and practicality. Consequently I will focus on a reply to those charges. But first, I must congratulate him for his effective demolition of 'weak sustainability'. I hope he has more success than I have had in converting the many environmental economists who still cling to it.

Beckerman's concept of strong sustainability, however, is one made up by himself in order to serve as a straw man. In the literature, weak sustainability assumes that manmade and natural capital are basically substitutes. He got that right. Strong sustainability assumes that manmade and natural capital are basically complements. Beckerman completely missed that one. He thinks strong sustainability means that no species could ever go extinct, nor any nonrenewable resource should ever be taken from the ground, no matter how many people are starving. I have referred to that concept as 'absurdly strong sustainability' in order to dismiss it, so as to focus on the relevant issue: namely are manmade and natural capital substitutes or complements? That is really what is at issue between strong and weak sustainability.

…

The complementarity of manmade and natural capital is made obvious at a concrete and commonsense level by asking: what good is a saw-mill without a forest; a fishing boat without populations of fish; a refinery without petroleum deposits; an irrigated farm without an aquifer or river? We have long recognised the complementarity between public infrastructure and private capital – what good is a car or truck without roads to drive on? ... we can take the concept of natural capital even further and distinguish between endosomatic (within-skin) and exosomatic (outside-skin) natural capital. We can then ask, what good is the private endosomatic capital of our lungs and respiratory system without the public exosomatic capital of green plants that take up our carbon dioxide in the short run, while in the long run replenishing the enormous atmospheric stock of oxygen and keeping the atmosphere at the proper mix of gases – i.e. the mix to which our respiratory system is adapted and therefore complementary.

We discussed in Chapter 1 the tendency for economic analysis to dominate environmental decision making (pp. 34–8). We also noted some significant concerns about this phenomenon, including the practical and conceptual difficulties of calculating the economic value of elements of the environment, political concerns that value judgments are hidden by economic practices and language, as well as more far-reaching concerns about the ability of economic analysis to capture environmental values in any meaningful way. These concerns multiply in the presence of sustainable development, a more extensive objective than environmental protection. In Section 6, we will discuss the dangers of viewing sustainable development as a technical objective, sheltered from values and debate (pp. 256–62).

Alternative approaches to 'measuring' the implementation of sustainable development attempt to assess the point at which the environment collapses, and so literally cannot 'sustain' something into the future. What that 'something' might be is the hidden value judgment (different human activities, habitats, species, natural spaces – see also Dobson, below, pp. 258–61). This approach to 'sustainability' involves the development of techniques to assess the 'thresholds' or 'carrying capacity' of elements of the environment, essentially requiring a scientific assessment of the burden that natural resources can bear. These approaches look at the role of the natural world in providing us with resources (such as food or fuels), with services (such as climate regulation or water purification, as well as less concrete services such as aesthetic gratification) and with the assimilation of waste materials.

### Brundtland Report, pp. 45–6

Economic growth and development obviously involve changes in the physical ecosystem. Every ecosystem everywhere cannot be preserved intact. A forest may be depleted in one part of a watershed and extended elsewhere, which is not a bad thing if the exploitation has been planned and the effects on soil erosion rates, water regimes, and genetic losses have been taken into account. In general, renewable resources like forests and fish stocks need not be depleted provided the rate of use is within the limits of regeneration and natural growth. But most renewable resources are part of a complex and interlinked ecosystem, and maximum sustainable yield must be defined after taking into account system-wide effects of exploitation.

As for non-renewable resources, like fossil fuels and minerals, their use reduces the stock available for future generations. But this does not mean that such resources should not be used. In general the rate of depletion should take into account the criticality of that resource, the availability of technologies for minimizing depletion, and the likelihood of substitutes being available. Thus land should not be degraded beyond reasonable recovery. With minerals and fossil fuels, the rate of depletion and the emphasis on recycling and economy of use should be calibrated to ensure that the resource does not run out before acceptable substitutes are available. Sustainable development requires that the rate of depletion of non-renewable resources should foreclose as few future options as possible.

As well as tending to obscure the values implicit in the assessment, the technical approaches to sustainability often reduce sustainable development to an environmental question, and concentrate on the importance of sustainability in the simple sense of making something last, rather than on competing interpretations of what makes for a 'good life'. This takes us again to the central question of the normative versus the technical nature of sustainable development, discussed below in Section 6.

## (b) The 'three pillars' and global poverty

The Johannesburg Summit has put a new emphasis on a 'three-pillared' approach to sustainable development, which seems to be emerging as a new international 'definition'.[22] The dominance of the Brundtland Report's definition of sustainable development (development that 'meets the needs of the present without compromising the ability of future generations to meet their own needs') until recently involved addressing the needs of the future through the filter of environmental protection, and the needs of the present through the filter of economic growth. This downplays questions of justice or equity within current generations, including the urgent needs of the presently poor. Counterintuitively, political acknowledgement of the interests of future generations proved easier than political acknowledgement of the needs of present generations. Things have changed in Johannesburg, which emphasises social and economic development over environmental protection.

The very long-term future is rather downplayed in the Johannesburg Declaration (above, pp. 226–9), which contains only rather conventional references to 'children' as representatives of the future, and to the need for a

---

[22] The three-limbed approach appears in UK and EU documents, in some cases predating the Johannesburg Summit.

'long-term perspective' to decision making.[23] Bringing the very long term into political debate had been one of the features of sustainable development pointing towards environmental protection. The downplaying of 'futurity' is surely a cause for concern, but can also be interpreted as a function of the increasingly self-evident nature of environmental harm. Michael Jacobs has argued (in a UK context) that the rhetoric of the 'future' is no longer as prevalent simply because it is no longer necessary. Environmental damage is already sufficiently bad to demand action: 'Even global warming, the ultimate of "future" issues, appears already to be happening, if we are to believe the climatologists' interpretation of the last few years' weather.'[24] Environmental protection is, however, also distinctly downplayed in the Johannesburg documents.

### Rajamani, 'From Stockholm to Johannesburg', p. 31

On the environmental protection front, the international community agreed to: 'encourage and promote' the establishment of a framework of programmes to accelerate the shift towards sustainable consumption and production (para. 15); 'substantially increase' the global share of renewable energy sources (para. 20(e)); 'aim' to use and produce chemicals in ways that do not lead to significant adverse effects on human health and the environment (para. 23); maintain or restore, where possible, by 2015 depleted fish stocks to levels that can produce the maximum sustainable yield (para. 31(a)); and achieve by 2010 a significant reduction in the current rate of loss of biodiversity (para. 44).

   Although the targets on fish stocks and biodiversity are significant, they are the only concrete commitments in the environmental arena. The language within which the remaining commitments are couched leaves little room for optimism that the commitments will be implemented or that countries will be held accountable if they are not. The text on energy contains no global target for the use of renewable energy. It includes hydro energy and does not exclude nuclear energy, throwing into question the purported environmental benefits of this provision (para. 20(e)).

Within the sustainable development rubric, environmental protection has to compete with other desirable social objectives. At Johannesburg, the question of social and economic development came out from the shadows, arguably sidelining questions of environmental protection. The objective of eradicating extreme poverty is absolutely central to the outputs from Johannesburg. Indeed, although powerful states sometimes try not to notice, ending poverty was a crucial element of sustainable development in the Brundtland Report: 'widespread poverty is no longer inevitable. Poverty is not only an evil in itself … A world in which poverty is endemic will always be prone to ecological and other catastrophes' (p. 8).

---

[23]  Principles 3, 4, 6, 26.
[24]  Michael Jacobs, *Environmental Modernisation: The New Labour Agenda* (Fabian Society, 1999), p. 3.

### Rajamani, 'From Stockholm to Johannesburg', pp. 30–1

On the social and economic development front, the international community agreed at the WSSD [World Summit on Sustainable Development] to: establish a world solidarity fund to eradicate poverty; halve by the year 2015 the proportion of people without access to basic sanitation; improve health literacy by 2010; and support African countries in implementing food security strategies and New Partnership for Africa's Development (NEPAD) objectives on access to energy. In addition, the international community reiterated numerous goals contained in the Millennium Development Goals, General Assembly Resolutions and other international agreements on reducing global hunger, improving the lives of slum dwellers, reducing infant and child mortality rates, reducing HIV prevalence among the youth, and ensuring gender-sensitive access to education. These commitments, in particular to establish the World Solidarity Fund and accept a target on sanitation, are arguably the more significant of the WSSD outcomes.

The link between environmental protection and poverty eradication is made on the basis that the poor generally suffer most from environmental degradation, being more likely to live in environmentally degraded areas and to rely directly on environmental resources (forests, soil, climate) for food, shelter and warmth. Even in highly privileged countries such as the UK, there seems to be a link between poverty and environmental degradation: there is Environment Agency research to the effect that poorer communities tend to suffer the worst air quality.[25] Poor nations are also less able to protect their people from the effects of environmental degradation, such as flooding. And just as the poor suffer from environmental degradation, the desperately poor may degrade the environment in search of survival. Whilst the two-way link between poverty and environmental degradation may be clear at the extremes, it is certainly not necessarily the case that increasing wealth will inevitably enhance environmental protection.

### Wolfgang Sachs, *The Development Dictionary* (Zed Books, 1992), p. 29

… environmentalism was regarded as inimical to the alleviation of poverty throughout the 1970s. The claim to be able to abolish poverty, however, has been – and still is – the single most important pretension of the development ideology, in particular after its enthronement as the official No. 1 priority after Robert McNamara's World Bank speech at Nairobi in 1973. Poverty was long regarded as unrelated to environmental degradation, which was attributed to the impact of industrial man; the world's poor entered the equation only as future claimants to an industrial lifestyle. But with spreading deforestation

---

[25] Cited in UK Government, *Securing the Future: Delivering UK Sustainable Development Strategy,* Cm 6467 (2005) p. 95: 'the most deprived wards experience higher concentrations of pollution that harm human health. People in deprived wards are exposed to 41% higher concentrations of nitrogen dioxide than those people living in average wards.'

and desertification all over the world, the poor were quickly identified as agents of destruction and became the targets of campaigns to promote 'environmental conscious-ness'. Once blaming the victim had entered the professional consensus, the old recipe could also be offered for meeting the new disaster: since growth was supposed to remove poverty, the environment could only be protected through a new era of growth. As the Brundtland Report puts it: 'Poverty reduces people's capacity to use resources in a sus-tainable manner; it intensifies pressure on the environment … A necessary but not suffi-cient condition for the elimination of absolute poverty is a relatively rapid rise in per capita incomes in the Third World.' The way was thus cleared for the marriage between 'envi-ronment' and 'development': the newcomer could be welcomed to the old-established family.

'No development without sustainability; no sustainability without development' is the formula which establishes the newly formed bond. 'Development' emerges rejuve-nated from this liaison, the ailing concept gaining another lease on life. This is nothing less than the repeat of a proven ruse: every time in the last 30 years when the destruc-tive effects of development were recognized, the concept was stretched in such a way as to include both injury and therapy. For example, when it became obvious, around 1970, that the pursuit of development actually intensified poverty, the notion of 'equi-table development' was invented so as to reconcile the irreconcilable: the creation of poverty with the abolition of poverty. In the same vein, the Brundtland Report incorporated concern for the environment into the concept of development by erecting 'sustainable development' as the conceptual roof for both violating and healing the environment.

The commitment to halve poverty, however, is one of the few firm commit-ments emerging from the Johannesburg Summit. It is radical, measurable and ambitious – if falling short of 'making poverty history'.

## Johannesburg Plan of Implementation

7. Eradicating poverty is the greatest global challenge facing the world today and an indis-pensable requirement for sustainable development, particularly for developing countries. Although each country has the primary responsibility for its own sustainable development and poverty eradication and the role of national policies and development strategies cannot be overemphasized, concerted and concrete measures are required at all levels to enable developing countries to achieve their sustainable development goals as related to the inter-nationally agreed poverty-related targets and goals, including those contained in Agenda 21, the relevant outcomes of other United Nations conferences and the United Nations Millennium Declaration. This would include actions at all levels to:

(a) Halve, by the year 2015, the proportion of the world's people whose income is less than 1 dollar a day and the proportion of people who suffer from hunger and, by the same date, to halve the proportion of people without access to safe drink-ing water.

This commitment was not new in Johannesburg, but a reaffirmation of the Millennium Development Goals.[26] Whilst we would not wish to understate the importance or desirability of this commitment, its pre-existence raises at least two questions: first, whether this re-commitment could ever really be used as 'proof' of the Summit's success; and secondly, whether sustainable development is playing any distinctive role here (or is this just development by another name?). Moreover, of all those 'good things' implied by sustainable development, the objective of ending poverty might be expected to force a dramatic rethinking of the global distribution of power and resources. However, the mechanisms put forward in Johannesburg on the whole fit into dominant perspectives on how the world should function. International trade is crucial, as discussed in the following chapter; as is private investment: Johannesburg emphasises the role of 'foreign direct investment' as 'the primary engine of development'.[27] Simply by way of example, one of the key proposals for the provision of safe drinking water and sanitation is the development of 'innovative financing and partnership mechanisms'.[28] This is likely to involve a leading role for transnational corporations in developing infrastructure: the positive link between private corporations and social and economic development for the world's very poorest people is, however, by no means self-evident.

Perhaps more importantly than the emphasis on the private sector, *redistribution* receives very little attention in Johannesburg, overall economic growth being the main path to development.[29] Emphasising growth over redistribution not only allows the rich and powerful to avoid rethinking their role in the world, but also denies any notion that the natural environment might impose limits on economic growth (discussed further below, pp. 250–6). By contrast, it is 'quite obvious' not only to green radicals, but also to 'responsible' parliamentary committees, that 'over the last millennium economic growth while it has contributed substantially to social progress has also resulted in huge negative impacts on the environment'.[30]

Redistribution is not entirely absent from Johannesburg. The well-established principle of 'common but differentiated responsibilities'[31] implies some relatively

---

[26] General Assembly of the United Nations, *Millenium Declaration* (2000).

[27] John W. Foster, 'The Role of Non-Governmental Organisations and Social Movements in Developing Countries' in John J. Kirton and Michael J. Trebilcock (eds.), *Hard Choices, Soft Law: Voluntary Standards in Global Trade, Environment and Social Governance* (Ashgate, 2004), p. 205, discussing the Monterrey Financing for Development Conference, 2002.

[28] Johannesburg Plan of Implementation, para. 8 (f). See also the discussion of partnerships, pp. 229–30.

[29] This is also apparent in the Brundtland Report. See also Ch. 4 above, p. 163 – the original appearance of sustainable development in the EC Treaty was as 'sustainable *growth*', not sustainable development.

[30] Environmental Audit Committee, 13th Report Session 2003–4, *The Sustainable Development Strategy: Illusion or Reality?* HC 624-I, para. 26.

[31] *Rio Declaration*, Principle 7, confirmed in the Johannesburg Plan of Implementation, for example paras. 2 and 75.

modest indirect redistribution, recognising that the costs of environmental protection or sustainable development should be attributed in a way that reflects a state's ability to respond to problems, as well as different contributions to harm. Even common but differentiated responsibility proved controversial at Johannesburg, however, with developing and developed countries arguing for different understandings of the concept. The status quo was, however, ultimately retained.[32]

Vestiges of more traditional redistribution from the wealthy to the poor are found in Johannesburg, including debt relief and cancellation. The wording of the Johannesburg Plan of Implementation is frequently vague and lacking in compulsion, full of undertakings to 'strengthen', 'promote' and 'encourage', but even in this context the language relating to debt relief is strikingly ambivalent.

### Johannesburg Plan of Implementation

89. Reduce unsustainable debt burden through such actions as debt relief and, as appropriate, debt cancellation and other innovative mechanisms geared to comprehensively address the debt problems of developing countries, in particular the poorest and most heavily indebted ones. Therefore, debt relief measures should, where appropriate, be pursued vigorously and expeditiously, including within the Paris and London Clubs and other relevant forums, in order to contribute to debt sustainability and facilitate sustainable development, while recognizing that debtors and creditors must share responsibility for preventing and resolving unsustainable debt situations, and that external debt relief can play a key role in liberating resources that can then be directed towards activities consistent with attaining sustainable growth and development.

Provision is also made for the direct funding of development through a 'world solidarity fund to eradicate poverty and to promote social and human development in the developing countries'. However, the Plan of Implementation stresses 'the voluntary nature of the contributions', as well as the 'encouragement' of 'the role of the private sector and individual citizens relative to Governments in funding the endeavours' (para. 7(b)). A commitment to Official Development Assistance (ODA) is perhaps the clearest commitment to redistribution in Johannesburg.

### Johannesburg Plan of Implementation

85. Recognize that a substantial increase in official development assistance and other resources will be required if developing countries are to achieve the internationally agreed development goals and objectives, including those contained in the Millennium Declaration. To build support for official development assistance, we will cooperate to further improve

---

[32] See Rajamani, 'From Stockholm to Johannesburg'; Lee Kimball, Franz X. Perrez and Jacob Werksman, 'The Results of the World Summit on Sustainable Development: Targets, Institutions and Trade Implications' (2002) 13 *Yearbook of International Environmental Law* 3.

policies and development strategies, both nationally and internationally, to enhance aid effectiveness, with actions to

   (a)  Make available the increased commitments in official development assistance announced by several developed countries at the International Conference on Financing for Development. Urge the developed countries that have not done so to make concrete efforts towards the target of 0.7 per cent of gross national product as official development assistance to developing countries.

Again, however, this is a restatement of an earlier commitment, here already made at Rio.[33] In itself, that is not a problem, but we might note that the target was not reached in the ten years between Rio and Johannesburg. And although there has recently been more optimism about tackling poverty than for many years, and progress is possible, there seems to be no real expectation that the 0.7 per cent objective will be met any time soon.[34]

## 4 The implementation of sustainable development: the UK

Sustainable development has had a significant impact on, at least, the presentation of environmental policy and law in the UK. Its introduction into legislation was fairly slow, appearing as part of the 'principal aim' of the Environment Agency set up by the Environment Act 1995, as discussed in Chapter 8, p. 335. Whilst this might be interpreted as an injunction on an explicitly *environmental* body to look beyond environmental protection, to the other elements of sustainable development, similar statutory duties apply beyond the specifically environmental sector.[35] For example, as discussed in Chapter 13, pp. 505–13, sustainable development is also an objective of bodies carrying out planning functions under the Planning and Compulsory Purchase Act 2004. Sustainable development first entered official policy documents far earlier than it found its place in legislation. The more radical implications of the concept were not, however, clearly grasped.

### Andrea Ross-Robertson, 'Is the Environment Getting Squeezed Out of Sustainable Development?' [2003] *Public Law* 249, p. 250

Despite a heavy reliance on the Brundtland definition, throughout the 1990s sustainable development was largely defined as a trade-off between economic development and environmental protection. In its 1990 White Paper, *This Common Inheritance – Britain's*

---

[33]  Agenda 21, Ch. 33, para. 13. For discussion of the 'reaffirmation' of previous commitments at Johannesburg, see Kimball *et al.*, 'The Results of the World Summit on Sustainable Development'.

[34]  Figures for the EU can be found in European Commission, *Report on the Millennium Development Goals 2000–2004* (2004).

[35]  See also, for example, the statutory duty in Water Act 2003, s. 35. Note that the government intends to publish guidance on these statutory duties: see UK Government, *Securing the Future*, p. 156.

*Environmental Strategy*, the Conservative Government claimed that '[t]here is, therefore, no contradiction in arguing for both economic growth and for environmental good sense. The challenge is to integrate the two.' Sustainable development is used cautiously in the document, appearing in Chapter 4 and interpreted as simply balancing economic prosperity against environmental concern. 'The Government therefore supports the principle of sustainable development ... To achieve sustainable development requires the full integration of environmental considerations into economic policy decisions.' Any reference to social considerations is made only in relation to how the standard of living in developing countries will improve with both increased economic growth and a clean environment.

In 1994, the country's first sustainable development strategy retained the same bilateral approach: '[m]ost societies aspire to achieve economic development to secure rising standards of living both for themselves and for future generations. They also seek to protect and enhance their environment now and for their children. Reconciling these two aspirations is at the heart of sustainable development.'[36]

The strategy mentions social issues only as a by-product of sustainable development or where they are linked to the notion of stewardship or shared responsibility such as increased public access to information and public participation.

The 1999 strategy for sustainable development, *A Better Quality of Life*,[37] moves on to the three-pillared approach to sustainable development.[38] Sustainable development was co-opted by environmentalists for a long time, leading to at least a perception of domination by the concerns of the wealthy, at the expense of the poor. The centrality of poverty eradication to sustainable development should remind us more generally that other desirable or necessary social objectives exist alongside environmental protection. At the national level, questions of desperate poverty are less acute than at the global level, but other elements of social justice may be just as compelling. However, the three-pillared approach creates its own challenges.

### Ross-Robertson, 'Is the Environment Getting Squeezed Out of Sustainable Development?', pp. 251–2

Some environmentalists have argued that sustainable development even in its narrowest 'economy v environment' form provides governments with a clear exit clause with respect to environmental issues. They argue the balancing is fictitious and the economy will always win. Any solution aimed at resolving harm to the environment which has perceived adverse effects on the economy will be held to be unsustainable.

---

[36] UK Government, *Sustainable Development – the UK Strategy*, Cm 2426 (1994) para. 3.1.
[37] UK Government, *A Better Quality Of Life – A Strategy for Sustainable Development for the United Kingdom*, Cm 4345 (1999), para.1.2.
[38] Sometimes presented as the four aims of economic and social progress, protection of the environment and use of natural resources (in the three-limbed approach, natural resources and environmental protection are a single 'pillar').

> Sustainable development is a contradiction in terms, in that growth and environmental protection are enemies. Because the earth has finite resources, it is impossible to achieve growth, social justice and environmental benefits simultaneously ... Poverty can therefore be reduced and the environment improved only if the rich accept lower living standards. This is consistent with the 'deep' ecology ethic. Similarly the goals of free trade cannot be harmonized with those of environmental protection. One must be at the expense of the other so that compromise is called for.[39]

Others, the author included, have tended to argue that sustainable development provides an opportunity for the environmental effects of a policy or project to be considered early in the decision-making process and not simply bolted on at a later stage. Environmental issues are considered at the same time as the social and economic effects of a given decision.

But, lately one has to question whether this is genuinely happening – especially now that the environment has to compete with social objectives as well as economic ones in the sustainable development process.

...

Implementing this 'three pronged' approach to sustainable development is a formidable task. Sustainable development can no longer simply be a concern of environment departments, agencies and interest groups and needs to be understood and implemented in a variety of contexts by a variety of bodies. Put another way, the sustainable development agenda is one of several 'crosscutting' policy objectives currently being tackled by the UK Government that require co-operation among many government and non-government actors. In order to embrace sustainable development, individual departments and agencies must reassess their objectives and priorities and in many instances alter the way they operate. This needs to be supported by strong leadership from the centre. The result is that the public sector must change the way it operates to meet these new objectives. In particular, 'departmentalism' is to be replaced by co-operation, 'joined up' thinking and more central control.

The breadth of concerns to be addressed in any particular decision should remind us of the principle of 'integration' discussed in Chapter 4, pp. 164–70, and found in Art. 6 of the EC Treaty, which is intimately related to sustainable development. As at EU level, the UK government has developed a number of institutional mechanisms for encouraging integration of sustainable development (or environmental) issues.[40] So a Cabinet Committee on the Environment and Sustainable Development should take these issues to the highest level of government; an expert Sustainable Development Unit within the Department of Environment, Food and Rural Affairs can provide advice

---

[39] As explained in John Alder and David Wilkinson, *Environmental Law and Ethics* (Macmillan, 1999), p. 141.

[40] See Andrea Ross, 'UK Approach to Delivering Sustainable Development in Government: A Case Study in Joined-Up Working' (2005) 17 *Journal of Environmental Law* 27.

and guidance; the Sustainable Development Commission, a non-departmental public body, is supposed to act as the government's independent advisor and 'critical friend' on sustainable development.[41] The House of Commons Environmental Audit Committee is in place as a tool of accountability of government to Parliament on sustainable development issues. The effectiveness of these efforts at integration is often criticised,[42] and even government has recognised the difficulty: 'although the 1999 strategy stressed that these objectives had to be pursued at the same time, in practice, different agencies focused on those one or two most relevant to them. So a new purpose is needed to show how government will integrate these aims and evolve sustainable development policy.'[43] Tools are being developed to allow for the assessment of a decision's impact on all three limbs of sustainable development, for example the EU's 'sustainability assessment', discussed in Chapter 14, pp. 601–4. These tools build on experience with environmental impact assessment, as well as administrative techniques such as regulatory impact assessments and equal opportunities assessments. The aim is to integrate the three limbs of sustainable development.[44] We should recall the potential environmental benefits of an integrated approach, and the limitations of seeing environmental protection as a 'special interest' to be 'bolted on' at the end of policy making. Nevertheless, the danger remains that environmental concerns, which have always had difficulty competing with short-term economic gain, might be further disadvantaged in the more expansive 'three-pillared' approach to sustainable development.

In 2005, the UK government produced, following a long period of consultation, its new Sustainable Development Strategy, *Securing the Future: Delivering UK Sustainable Development Strategy*. The newly defined 'purpose' of sustainable development continues to concentrate on the broad 'quality of life' issues raised in the 1999 Strategy; whether 'quality of life' really captures the full range or depth of sustainable development (particularly in respect of those distant in time or space) is open to question.

### UK Government, *Securing the Future: Delivering UK Sustainable Development Strategy*, Cm 6467 (2005), p. 16

The goal of sustainable development is to enable all people throughout the world to satisfy their basic needs and enjoy a better quality of life, without compromising the quality of life of future generations.

For the UK Government and the Devolved Administrations, that goal will be pursued in an integrated way through a sustainable, innovative and productive economy that delivers high levels of employment; and a just society that promotes social inclusion, sustainable

---

[41] UK Government, *Securing the Future*, p. 154.

[42] See, for example, Andrea Ross-Robertson, 'Is the Environment Getting Squeezed Out of Sustainable Development?' [2003] *Public Law* 249; Environmental Audit Committee, *The Sustainable Development Strategy*.    [43] UK Government, *Securing the Future*, p. 15.

[44] See the discussion in Ross, 'UK Approach to Delivering Sustainable Development'.

communities and personal wellbeing. This will be done in ways that protect and enhance the physical and natural environment, and use resources and energy as efficiently as possible.

Government must promote a clear understanding of, and commitment to, sustainable development so that all people can contribute to the overall goal through their individual decisions.

Similar objectives will inform all our international endeavours, with the UK actively promoting multi-lateral and sustainable solutions to today's most pressing environmental, economic and social problems. There is a clear obligation on more prosperous nations both to put their own house in order, and to support other countries in the transition towards a more equitable and sustainable world.

The 'three pillars' are all in place. There has, however, been some response to criticisms that the earlier Strategy placed insufficient emphasis on environmental protection. The Environmental Audit Committee had, for example, argued strongly that 'it is no longer appropriate simply to consider environmental objectives as an adjunct to social and economic objectives' and that the new Strategy 'should have a primarily environmental focus'.[45] The Strategy does not go quite that far, but one of its 'five principles' is 'living within environmental limits', a subject to which we will return (pp. 250–6). The other four principles are more tangentially environmental: ensuring a strong, healthy and just society; achieving a sustainable economy; promoting good governance; and using sound science responsibly.[46] 'Priority areas' also emphasise environmental issues.

### UK Government, *Securing the Future*, p. 17

As a result of the consultation the priority areas for immediate action, shared across the UK, are:

**Sustainable Consumption and Production** – Sustainable consumption and production is about achieving more with less. This means not only looking at how goods and services are produced, but also the impacts of products and materials across their whole lifecycle and building on people's awareness of social and environmental concerns. This includes reducing the inefficient use of resources which are a drag on the economy, so helping boost business competitiveness and to break the link between economic growth and environmental degradation.

**Climate Change and Energy** – The effects of a changing climate can already be seen. Temperatures and sea levels are rising, ice and snow cover are declining, and the consequences could be catastrophic for the natural world and society. Scientific evidence points to the release of greenhouse gases, such as carbon dioxide and methane, into the atmosphere

---

[45] Environmental Audit Committee, *The Sustainable Development Strategy*, foreword.

[46] At p. 16. Note that the 'sound science' principle requires account to be taken of scientific uncertainty (through the precautionary principle) as well as public attitudes and values.

by human activity as the primary cause of climatic change. We will seek to secure a profound change in the way we generate and use energy, and in other activities that release these gases. At the same time we must prepare for the climate change that cannot now be avoided. We must set a good example and will encourage others to follow it.

**Natural Resource Protection and Environmental Enhancement** – Natural resources are vital to our existence and that of communities throughout the world. We need a better understanding of environmental limits, environmental enhancement and recovery where the environment is most degraded to ensure a decent environment for everyone, and a more integrated policy framework.

**Sustainable Communities** – Our aim is to create sustainable communities that embody the principles of sustainable development at the local level. This will involve working to give communities more power and say in the decisions that affect them; and working in partnership at the right level to get things done. The UK uses the same principles of engagement, partnership, and programmes of aid in order to tackle poverty and environmental degradation and to ensure good governance in overseas communities. These priorities for action within the UK will also help to shape the way the UK works internationally, in ensuring that our objectives and activities are aligned with international goals.

The Strategy suggests at least a rhetorical shift back to environmental questions within sustainable development in the UK. One of the key tools for the measurement of sustainable development has been the use of 'indicators' by government. The 1999 Strategy had 147 indicators, with 15 'headline' indicators.[47] The government sees 'some merit' in the large set of indicators, although 'in practice it was difficult to determine overall progress and the majority of indicators were also monitored elsewhere', whilst the headline indicators were used extensively, 'but could only provide a broad overview' (p. 167). There are more fundamental difficulties with indicators.

### Andrew Dobson, *Citizenship and the Environment* (Oxford University Press, 2003), p. 150

One of [the British Government's 2002] objectives is 'maintaining high and stable levels of economic growth and employment', and one of its indicators in this regard is 'GDP and GDP per head'. Another of its objectives is 'effective protection of the environment', and one measure of this is 'rivers of good or fair quality'. Now these two objectives, both of which

---

[47] Economic Output (GDP and GDP per head); Investment: Total and social investment relative to GDP; Employment (Proportion of people of working age who are in work); Poverty (Indicators of success in tackling poverty and social exclusion); Education (Qualifications at age 19); Health (Expected years of healthy life); Housing (Households living in non-decent housing); Level of crime; Climate change (Emissions of greenhouse gases); Air quality (Days when air pollution is moderate or higher); Road traffic; River water quality (Chemical and biological river quality); Wildlife (Populations of wild birds); Land use (New homes built on previously developed land); Waste.

are intended to be compatible parts of a general framework, might uncharitably be regarded as competing rather than compatible versions of what 'improvement' means. This becomes especially apparent when we see that Gross Domestic Product (GDP) is an extremely blunt instrument for determining the health of an economy. GDP, as environmentalists never tire of pointing out, is a measure of *every* activity carried out in an economy – including clearing up environmental damage once it has occurred. There is the possibility, then, that an event which pulls down one sustainable development indicator – a discharge of effluent into a river, for example – will register as a bonus on another (the increased economic activity associated with cleaning up the mess). At the very least, then, there are mixed messages as far as the British government's view of 'improvement' in the context of sustainable development is concerned.

The 2002 Strategy develops the sustainable development indicators. Neither the fifteen headline indicators that preceded it, nor the indicators in the 2005 Strategy, prioritise environmental protection over the other elements of sustainable development, but a number of the indicators can broadly be termed 'environmental'. Whilst indicators should be very effective at allowing a full consideration of all elements of sustainable development, we can still see the potential for conflict or contradiction in the 20 UK Framework Indicators.[48]

- Greenhouse gas emissions
- Resource use
- Waste
- Bird populations
- Fish stocks
- Ecological impacts of air pollution
- River quality
- Economic output
- Active community participation (informal and formal volunteering at least once a month)
- Crime
- Employment
- Workless households
- Childhood poverty
- Pensioner poverty
- Education
- Health inequality
- Mobility

[48] There are now 68 indicators, including the 20 UK Framework Indicators. The division between the UK Government Strategy and UK Framework indicators reflects devolution in the UK: the UK Framework Indicators apply across the UK, including the devolved administrations; the UK Government Strategy applies in England, and on non-devolved matters (such as international relations) to the whole of the UK.

- Social justice
- Environmental equality
- Wellbeing

## 5  Sustainable development and environmental limits

As we have discussed, sustainable development aims at the reconciliation of different, but desirable, social objectives, the range of which has expanded as the place of sustainable development in the political lexicon has become more secure. Over the very long term, and at the extremes, it is probably true that social, economic and environmental objectives can only be achieved hand in hand. At the day-to-day level, however, trade-offs must be made. Whilst discussion of sustainable development rarely explicitly denies the existence of conflict between desirable objectives, the overall direction of sustainable development is to try to smooth them away – at least rhetorically, if it is not possible practically. Some would say that the reconciliation of the three pillars of sustainable development is pure wishful thinking; it is certainly something of 'an act of faith'.[49] The evolution of sustainable development as discussed here provides an alternative to the idea that the natural environment sets *absolute* limits on (economic) growth. The 'limits to growth' thesis became popular in the 1970s, entering the political mainstream as the oil crisis made clear the dependence of economic growth on at least certain natural resources. The following extract from Dobson highlights a number of factors that divide sustainable development from the 'limits' thesis. Dobson distinguishes between 'ecologism', which 'holds that a sustainable and fulfilling existence presupposes radical changes in our relationship with the non-human natural world, and in our mode of social and political life' and 'environmentalism', which 'argues for a managerial approach to environmental problems, secure in the belief that they can be solved without fundamental changes in present values or patterns of production and consumption'.[50]

### Andrew Dobson, *Green Political Thought* (Routledge, 2000), pp. 62–8

Amid the welter of enthusiasm for lead-free petrol and green consumerism it is often forgotten that a foundation-stone of radical green politics is the belief that our finite Earth places limits on industrial growth ...

... Greens have all along been confronted with rebuffs to their belief in limits to growth, and as their responses to these criticisms have developed it has become easier to identify what they are prepared to jettison in the thesis and what they feel the need to defend.

It turns out that there are three principal thoughts related to the limits to growth thesis that have come to be of prime importance to the radical green position. They are, first, that

---

[49] Environmental Audit Committee, *The Sustainable Development Strategy*, para. 26.
[50] Andrew Dobson, *Green Political Thought* (Routledge, 2000), p. 2.

technological solutions (broadly understood; i.e. solutions formulated within the bounds of present economic, social and political practices) will not in themselves bring about a sustainable society; second, that the rapid rates of growth aimed for (and often achieved) by industrialized and industrializing societies have an exponential character, which means that dangers stored up over a relatively long period of time can very suddenly have a catastrophic effect; and third, that the *interaction* of problems caused by growth means that such problems cannot be dealt with in isolation – i.e. solving one problem does not solve the rest, and may even exacerbate them. These three notions will be discussed in more detail very shortly, but first (principally for the uninitiated) the strategy and conclusions of the original *Limits to Growth* report ought briefly to be noted. The description and assessments that follow are primarily based on the 1974 report, although I have included references from the 1992 sequel where it seems appropriate. In one or two of these cases it is the sense of the two reports that is identical, rather than the quoted words.

The researchers pointed to what they describe as '5 trends of global concern': 'accelerating industrialisation, rapid population growth, widespread malnutrition, depletion of nonrenewable resources, and a deteriorating environment'.[51] They then created a computerized world model of the variables associated with these areas of concern, i.e. industrial output per capita, population, food per capita, resources and pollution; and programmed the computer to produce pictures of various future states of affairs given changes in these variables. From the very beginning it was understood that such modelling would be rough and ready, and the Club of Rome (the name given to the informal association of scientists, researchers, industrialists, etc., that carried out the research) anticipated later criticisms of inaccuracy and incompleteness by admitting that the model was 'imperfect, oversimplified and unfinished'.[52] From our perspective, the important point to make is that greens have generally been unperturbed by criticisms of the detail of the various limits to growth reports, and have rather relied upon the general principles and conclusions of these reports.

The first computer run, then, assumed 'no major change in the physical, economic, or social relationships that have historically governed the development of the world system'.[53] This, in other words, was a run in which business carried on as usual. In this case the limits to growth were reached 'because of nonrenewable resource depletion'.[54] Next, the group programmed a run in which the resource depletion problem was 'solved' by assuming a doubling in the amount of resources economically available. In this case collapse occurred again, but this time because of the pollution brought about by the spurt in industrialization caused by the availability of new resources. The group concluded that 'Apparently the economic impetus such resource availability provides must be accompanied by curbs on pollution if a collapse of the world system is to be avoided.'[55] Consequently, the next computer run involved not only a doubling of resources but also a series of technological strategies to

[51]  Donella H. Meadows, Dennis L. Meadows, Jorgen Randers and William W. Behrens III, *The Limits to Growth* (Pan, 1972), p. 21.

[52]  *Ibid.*; and Donella H. Meadows, Dennis L. Meadows and Jorgen Randers, *Beyond the Limits: Global Collapse or a Sustainable Future* (Earthscan, 1992), p. 105.

[53]  Meadows *et al.*, *The Limits*, p. 124; Meadows *et al.*, *Beyond the Limits*, p. 132.

[54]  Meadows *et al.*, *The Limits*, p. 125; Meadows *et al.*, *Beyond the Limits*, p. 132.

[55]  Meadows *et al.*, *The Limits*, p. 133; Meadows *et al.*, *Beyond the Limits*, p. 134.

reduce the level of pollution to one quarter of its pre-1970 level.[56] This time the limit to growth are reached because of a food shortage produced by pressure on arable land owing to its being taken for 'urban-industrial use'.[57]

And so the experiment progresses, with the world model programmed each time to deal with the immediate cause of the previous collapse. Eventually all sectors have technological responses filled in:

> The model system is producing nuclear power, recycling resources, and mining the most remote reserves; withholding as many pollutants as possible; pushing yields from the land to undreamed-of heights; and producing only children who are actively wanted by their parents.[58]

Even this does not solve the problem of overshoot and collapse:

> The result is still an end to growth before the year 2100 [2050 in the 1992 report, p. 174]. In this case growth is stopped by three simultaneous crises. Overuse of land leads to erosion, and food production drops. Resources are severely depleted by a prosperous world population (but not as prosperous as the present [1970] US population). Pollution rises, drops then rises again dramatically, causing a further decrease in food production and a sudden rise in the death rate.[59]

and the next sentence of the group's conclusion on the computer's final run helps distance environmentalism from ecologism and provides the intellectual springboard for radical green political strategy: 'The application of technological solutions alone has prolonged the period of population and industrial growth, but it has not removed the ultimate limits to that growth.'[60] In the words of the 1992 report, 'This is a society that is using its increased technical capacity to maintain growth, while the growth eventually undermines the effects of these technologies.'[61]

This, then, brings us to the first of the three notions associated with the limits to growth thesis that I suggested above are essential to the theory and practice of political ecology: that technological solutions cannot provide a way out of the impasse of the impossibility of aspiring to infinite growth in a finite system.

...

So if the sustainable society is not, on the face of it, going to be full of environment-friendly technological wizardry, what *will* it be like? ... if the green movement believes technological solutions to the limits to growth problem to be impossible, then it will have to argue for more profound changes in social thought and practice changes in human values and ideas of morality. These changes will involve accommodating social practices to the limits that surround them, and abandoning the Promethean (in this context, technological) attempt to overcome them. It is in this kind of respect, once again, that the dark-green sustainable society is different from the environmentalist one, and why the latter can sit only uncomfortably with the former. All of this is a result of the idea that technological solutions can have 'no impact on the *essential* problem, which is exponential growth in a finite and complex system'.[62]

---

[56] Meadows *et al.*, *The Limits*, p. 136; Meadows *et al.*, *Beyond the Limits*, p. 168.
[57] Meadows *et al.*, *The Limits*, p. 137; Meadows *et al.*, *Beyond the Limits*, p. 168.
[58] Meadows *et al.*, *The Limits*, p. 141; Meadows *et al.*, *Beyond the Limits*, p. 174.
[59] Meadows *et al.*, *The Limits* p. 141.      [60] *Ibid.*      [61] Meadows *et al.*, *Beyond the Limits*, p. 174.
[62] Meadows *et al.*, *The Limits*, p. 45.

And this is the second notion that political ecologists have rescued from the debate over limits to growth, making it central to their argument as to why present industrial practices are unsustainable: the idea of exponential growth. Meadows *et al.* claim that all of the five elements in the Club of Rome's world model experience exponential growth, and explain that 'A quantity exhibits *exponential* growth when it increases by a constant percentage of the whole in a constant time period.'[63] In quantitative terms this is easily demonstrated by placing rice grains on the squares of a chess board, with one on the first square, two on the second, four on the third, sixteen on the fourth, and so on. The numbers build up very fast, and while the twenty-first square will be covered with over 100,000 grains of rice, the fortieth will require about 1 million million.[64]

The central point is that such growth is deceptive in that it produces large numbers very quickly. Translated to the arena of industrial production, resource depletion and pollution, what seems an innocuous rate of use and waste disposal can quickly produce dangerously low quantities of available resources and dangerously high levels of pollution. Greens often point to the staggeringly rapid growth in industrial production this century and ask the (increasingly less rhetorical) question: 'Can this be sustained?' Thus, Irvine and Ponton note that 'In a mere blink on the timescale of human evolution, industrial society has been depleting and impairing Earth's "supply system" at a phenomenal rate', and that 'Americans, for example, have used more minerals and fossil fuels during the past half-century than all the other peoples of the world throughout human history.'[65]

Greens believe, simply, that present rates of resource extraction and use – a '3 per cent growth rate implies doubling the rate of production and consumption every twenty-five years'[66] – and the production of waste and pollution necessarily associated with them, are unsustainable. They further believe that the nature of the rate of growth produces a false sense of complacency: what appears to be a safe situation now can very quickly turn into an unsafe one. A relevant French riddle for schoolchildren goes like this:

> Suppose you own a pond on which a water lily is growing. The lily plant doubles in size each day. If the lily were allowed to grow unchecked, it would completely cover the pond in 30 days, choking off the other forms of life in the water. For a long time the lily plant seems small, and so you decide not to worry about cutting it back until it covers half the pond. On what day will that be? On the twenty-ninth day, of course. You have one day to save your pond.[67]

...

The third and final aspect of the limits to growth thesis that has become central to the radical green position is that of the interrelationship of the problems with which we are confronted. It should already have become clear from the description of the Club of Rome's computer runs that solving one problem does not necessarily mean solving the rest, and our refusal to confront the complexity of the global system and to draw the right conclusions

[63] *Ibid.*, p. 27; emphasis in original.    [64] *Ibid.*, p. 29; Meadows *et al.*, *Beyond the Limits*, p. 18.
[65] Sandy Irvine and Alec Ponton, *A Green Manifesto: Policies for a Green Future* (Macdonald Optima, 1988), pp. 24–5.    [66] Paul Ekins (ed.), *The Living Economy* (Routledge, 1986), p. 9.
[67] Meadows *et al.*, *The Limits.* p. 29; Meadows *et al.*, *Beyond the Limits*, p. 18.

for action (or inaction) from it is why most greens believe our attempts to deal with environmental degradation, in particular, to be insensitively inadequate. 'What matters', write Irvine and Ponton, 'is not any particular limit, which might be overcome, but the total interaction of constraints, and costs'.[68] Change in one element means change in the others: nuclear power might contribute to solving problems of acid rain but it still contributes to global warming, and chemical fertilizers help us grow more food but simultaneously poison the water courses.

...

So radical greens read off three principal features of the limits to growth message and subscribe to them and their implications wholeheartedly: technological solutions cannot help realize the impossible dream of infinite growth in a finite system; the exponential nature of that growth both underpins its unsustainability and suggests that the limits to growth may become visible rather quicker than we might think; and the immense complexity of the global system leads greens to suggest that our present attempts to deal with environmental problems are both clumsy and superficial.

At the root of all this, of course, is the most profound belief of all: that there *are* limits to growth.

Sustainable development is ambivalent, or even suspicious, about the concept of limits. The Brundtland Report is a good example, accepting the existence of limits, but challenging them in the same breath:

The concept of sustainable development does imply limits – not absolute limits but limitations imposed by the present state of technology and social organization on environmental resources and by the ability of the biosphere to absorb the effects of human activities. But technology and social organization can be both managed and improved to make way for a new era of economic growth. (p. 8)

This is far removed from the 'deep green' approach to limits discussed by Dobson. Similarly, the Brundtland Report says: 'The accumulation of knowledge and the development of technology can enhance the carrying capacity of the resource base. But ultimate limits there are, and sustainability requires that long before these are reached, the world must ensure equitable access to the constrained resource and reorient technological efforts to relieve the pressure' (p. 45). This implies a slightly more challenging approach to limits, but still assumes the ultimate success of human ingenuity. The ambivalence towards limits is also apparent in the approach of the Brundtland Report to 'needs'. Although the 'overriding priority' is said to be 'the essential needs of the world's poor' (p. 43), the Brundtland Report quickly moves on to much broader questions of 'aspiration'.

---

[68] Irvine and Ponton, *A Green Manifesto*, p. 13.

### Brundtland Report, pp. 43–4

The satisfaction of human needs and aspirations is the major objective of development. The essential needs of vast numbers of people in developing countries – for food, clothing, shelter, jobs – are not being met, and beyond their basic needs these people have legitimate aspirations for an improved quality of life. A world in which poverty and inequity are endemic will always be prone to ecological and other crises. Sustainable development requires meeting the basic needs of all and extending to all the opportunity to satisfy their aspirations for a better life.

Aspirations beyond the satisfaction of basic needs are surely legitimate, and to deny them from the comfort of a British university would be desperate hypocrisy. However, resistance to the redistribution of resource use from the wealthy world (discussed above, pp. 241–2) means that this is not necessarily consistent with environmental protection. Eliding needs and wants downplays limits; and of course the Johannesburg approach to sustainable development not only fails to define needs, but even downplays the relevance of needs, preferring to focus on the 'three-pillared' approach to sustainable development.

Whilst concentrating on 'quality of life' rather than 'needs', one of the UK government's five guiding principles for sustainable development is 'living within environmental limits'.

### UK Government, *Securing the Future*, p. 100

Environmental limits are the level at which the environment is unable to accommodate a particular activity or rate of activities without sustaining unacceptable or irreversible change.

There is evidence that this is already occurring in many places, the commercial extinction of the Newfoundland cod fisheries being a notable example. Decisions that involve the sustainable use of natural resources need to take proper account of these limits so that suitable management measures can be put in place.

- **The Government will collate existing research and identify shortfalls in understanding about where environmental limits exist, and where they are being exceeded. We will then conduct a strategic assessment of future research needs in all policy areas** [emphasis in original].

This comes closer to accepting that limits may ultimately have to be respected. The government response to limits is, however, to identify limits through scientific endeavour, and then put in place 'suitable management measures'. There is some faith in 'technical fixes', and no notion either that environmental problems may be inter-related or that they may be unresponsive to human brilliance. Moreover, the apparently scientific approach to identifying limits hides a pivotal value judgment ('unacceptable' change).

assert that sustainable development is a locus for discussion. The moral authority provided by sustainable development cuts both ways, and can be appropriated by powerful interests; some would argue that that is precisely what happened in Johannesburg.

In this respect, the pattern of contestation identified by Jacobs should be noted. He suggests that the radical and mainstream approaches to sustainable development differ along four main faultlines: the degree of environmental protection required; the importance of 'equity';[71] the role of public participation; and the scope of the subject matter. Jacobs suggests that a radical, challenging approach to sustainable development will tend to argue for higher levels of environmental protection, a central role for equity and public participation, and for a broad scope to the subject matter covered by sustainable development; whilst a 'business as usual' approach would take the opposite perspective. The boundaries seem to have moved in recent years, as formerly radical perspectives are rapidly incorporated into something approaching a 'business as usual' approach to sustainable development. So whilst the level of environmental protection remains controversial along the parameters suggested by Jacobs, equity has transformed itself into 'social development' and been co-opted by the mainstream; public participation no longer holds the fear for the mainstream that it perhaps once did; and the dominant view puts a mass of detailed policy into the rubric of sustainable development. Perhaps this is an indication that the radicals have won; it is however far too soon to be sure that the radicals have not already lost.

The final issue to bear in mind when we turn to a normative, flexible account of sustainable development is the possibility that there will be a disjunction between rhetoric and reality. This is already familiar from the discussion of the government response to public debate on GMOs in Chapter 2 (pp. 81–3), where there was a rhetorical acceptance of the normative and broadly based nature of the decision, but a real difficulty in actually moving beyond the technical material.

### Dobson, *Citizenship and the Environment*, pp. 146–56

I confess surprise that there is still a debate as to whether environmental sustainability is a matter of norms or of scientific determination. Most readers of this book will likely agree with me that sustainability is a normative notion and will therefore wonder at my devoting a section of this chapter to arguing that it is. Has not this been conclusively established? Well, my experiences talking formally and informally to the policy community suggest that no, it has not – or at least not in the systematic and internalized way that would make a difference to policy formulation … The litmus test, I have found, is how people react to the term 'threshold'. This is a key term in sustainability debates, where a threshold refers to the borderline between a sustainable and an unsustainable state of affairs. Time and again I am told in these fora that thresholds are most appropriately

---

[71] This covers the issues discussed under the Johannesburg heading of 'social development'; the different terminology may suggest that Johannesburg has a less challenging understanding of this element of sustainable development than Jacobs.

determined by natural scientists because they possess the investigative tools and knowledges required to determine them most accurately. One small question, though, is sufficient to unsettle this cosy consensus: a threshold for whom or for what? Scientists will only
be able to tell us that practice P is likely to push us over a threshold once we have told
him/her to whom or to what the threshold applies (human beings or parakeets?), and this
cannot be determined by science alone. Different degrees of human intervention in an
ecosystem will have different impacts on the biotic and abiotic elements in that system. It
might be thought that the question of which of these elements 'matter', and therefore
which of them should be preserved or otherwise sustained, can only be answered by
scientific investigation. But deciding which elements 'matter' is itself a normative as well
as a scientific affair.

...

Barry's[72] point is that arguments against fungibility and in favour of the preservation of
natural capital are usually couched in terms of the impossibility of fungibility; the idea, that
is, that natural capital is simply *not* permanently and systematically replaceable by man-
made substitutes. While this may be true, says Barry, it misses the normative point. The key
thing he argues, is that even if we accept the possibility of fungibility we might not accept
its desirability. The content of sustainability's X, in other words, cannot be determined by the
'facts' alone.

It would be wrong to think that the policy-making community is driven by a naïve commitment to fact- and science-based solutions to defining sustainability, however. In Britain,
at least, the various government departments, commissions, and committees most closely
connected with these debates are showing welcome signs of grappling with the difficulties
that recognition of the normative nature of sustainability brings in its train. The best that can
be said, though, is that messages in this context are still mixed: the normative nature of sustainability is regarded as an annoying feature that just has to be dealt with, rather than its
central and defining characteristic.

...

Perhaps the best way to substantiate my claim that an awareness of the normative nature
of sustainability in policy-making circles has yet to be converted into a principled and
integrated feature of the decision-making process, is to show how values come into the
process too late. Governments around the world grapple with the problem of 'environmental standards', and with just how to determine what these standards should be. There is an
understandable desire to base standards on 'objective criteria', and the British government
constantly refers to 'evidence-based policy making' as a shorthand for such criteria.[73] But
the real question, of course, is what are to count as criteria in the first place. Of course
scientific testimony will count, but bearing in mind everything we have said about the
irreducibly normative nature of sustainability, should not values be captured and offered as
evidence too?

Sometimes government seems to be aware of the need to allow values to count as
evidence. I referred earlier to the UK government's list of sustainable development objectives

[72] Brian Barry, *Sustainability and Intergenerational Justice* (Sage, 1999), p. 102.
[73] Department of Environment, Food and Rural Affairs *The Government's Response to the Royal
Commission on Environmental Pollution's 21st Report* (2000), pp. 1, 5.

… I pointed out that there are likely to be tensions between these objectives, and it is important to see that these tensions cannot be resolved solely through the application of science. The British government seems to recognize as much:

> The Government believes that the need for integrated thinking, which is at the heart of sustainable development, will lead to better environmental standard-setting. As the Royal Commission[74] points out, 'there is much debate about the relative weight that should be placed on the different elements within the overall balance sustainable development is intended to achieve'. Such debate will continue. But thinking in terms of sustainable development can help to define priorities, build consensus and identify opportunities for multiple benefits.[75]

The idea of 'relative weight' acknowledges the tensions between the four objectives, and the reference to 'debate' suggests something other than decision by scientific fiat. The apparent official determination to regard values as evidence is even clearer in the following:

> In launching its report, the Royal Commission said that a new approach was needed such that 'as well as drawing on rigorous and dispassionate analysis, there must be a greater sensitivity to people's values. It must recognise that scientific assessments, and analyses of technology, economics and risk, must inform policy decisions, but cannot pre-empt them. Setting a standard or target is not only a scientific or technical matter, but also a practical judgement which has to be made in the light of all the relevant factors. People's values must be taken into account from the earliest stages of defining the problem and framing the questions that need to be addressed'. The Government fully endorses this conclusion.[76]

Reading passages like this, one could be forgiven for thinking that government and its advisers had fully grasped the normative dimension of sustainability and was determined to factor it into decision-making as far as the setting of environmental standards is concerned. And just in case some cynics remain unconvinced, DEFRA underscores the importance of taking values into account when setting agendas and when framing the very questions to be asked:

> Values have to play a part not only in the synthesis, but also – as the Commission recognise – in deciding what constitutes a 'problem', and in framing the questions for analysis. The Government agrees that better ways need to be found to articulate people's values. As part of the Modernising Government agenda it has established a People's Panel to give one indication of the way individuals perceive certain issues. As part of the reform of the regulatory system for genetically modified organisms the Government is setting up an Agriculture and Environment Biotechnology Commission which will consider not only scientific but also ethical and social questions raised by genetically-modified organisms.[77]

It would be churlish to try to argue that all this is not a massive improvement on the belief that the nature of sustainability can be determined in scientific laboratories. But there are signs that the transformation is not quite complete. One sign is the reference to the

---

[74] Royal Commission on Environmental Pollution, Twenty-first Report, *Setting Environmental Standards*, Cm 4053 (1998).

[75] DEFRA, *The Government's Response to the Royal Commission on Environmental Pollution's 21st Report*, p. 15.    [76] *Ibid.*, p. 21.    [77] *Ibid.*, p. 27.

'articulation' of people's values in the last quotation. Environmentalists have long argued that forums for discussing these matters should allow for the development of people's values as well as their articulation. There may be more values present in the case, in other words, than those articulated in any given forum. Other signs come more explicitly from the selfsame document from which I have been quoting. Commenting on the need to determine which bits of the environment are most in need of protection, for example, DEFRA writes that:

> Environmental standard setting cannot aim to protect every bit of the environment for ever. But the Government aims to prevent further overall deterioration, and to secure enhancements that contribute to an overall improvement in quality of life. Environmental capital techniques, which help us understand which aspects of the environment are important, and why, can be useful aids to some types of environmental decision making.[78]

The reference to 'environmental capital techniques' here is a nod in the direction of the idea of 'natural capital', according to which … some of the 'services' provided by nature cannot be adequately delivered by human-made substitutes. These, in other words, are the 'aspects of the environment [that] are important' for policy-making purposes.

It is not the difficulty of determining just where the line ought to be drawn on which I want to comment here, but the idea of referring to the environment in terms of 'capital' at all. In earlier quotations from this key DEFRA document we have seen a laudable determination to 'get values in' as early as possible – at the point of the very framing of the question indeed. Referring to the environment in terms of 'capital', though, violates this rule of thumb. Brian Barry is surely right to say that:

> 'Capital' is a term that is inherently located within economic discourse. A mountain is, in the first instance, just a mountain. To bring it under the category of 'capital' – of any kind – is to look it in a certain light, as an economic asset of some description. But if I want to insist that we should leave future generations mountains that have not been strip-mined, quarried, despoiled by ski-slopes, or otherwise tampered with to make somebody a profit, my point will be better made by eschewing talk about 'capital' altogether.[79]

There is of course no such thing as an entirely value-free language in which to discuss the X of sustainability (or anything else for that matter), but 'capital' is surely one of the more obviously loaded categories available to us. While a tomato may be regarded as capital in that it can be bought and sold, its value can be expressed in other ways too (it has a nice smell, you can write poems about it, and so on). A thorough-going application of the rule to get values in at the earliest opportunity would have led to some commentary, at least, on the implications of using 'capital' to describe the environment.

The normative nature of sustainable development is largely accepted at the rhetorical level, and the use of sustainable development as a framework within which different social objectives should receive serious consideration is perhaps

---

[78] *Ibid.*, p. 18.    [79] Barry, *Sustainability*, p. 103.

its most valuable function. The above examples are simply intended to illustrate that a constant battle is being fought over the meaning of sustainable development in any particular case.

## 7 Conclusions

A number of key developments in environmental law over recent years can be fitted directly within the framework of sustainable development. One is the development of an enthusiasm for 'market' or 'economic' instruments, discussed in Chapter 11 below; another is the development of public participation in the environmental field, discussed in Chapter 3, in which respect we should note the reference to public participation in both the Rio (Principle 10) and the Johannesburg (para. 26) Declarations, as well as the implication of 'bottom up' decision making in the 'social pillar' of sustainable development.

Sustainable development has been an immensely powerful idea. Its initial strength was in bringing together development and the environment, overcoming impasse at an international level, and allowing progress on both the environmental protection and the development agendas. A similar reconciliation occurred within industrialised countries, leading to the early understanding of sustainable development as an economy/environment issue. Sustainable development sought win–win solutions, measures of environmental protection that not only would not harm, but would even benefit, the economy, and vice versa. Even if one doubts the wisdom of forcing environmental protection to rationalise its existence within an economic framework, the positioning of environmental degradation as threatening economic growth, as well as vice versa, was at least likely to capture attention.

From a perspective previously dominated by the environment/economy framework, the question of global poverty reasserted itself with a vengeance at Johannesburg. This leads to considerable concern about the sidelining of environmental protection, a concern matched at national level – if environmental protection loses its independent status as a policy objective, and is entirely subsumed within sustainable development, the future of environmental protection could be compromised.

From a 'development' perspective, the question of poverty received a great deal of attention at Johannesburg, but whether the practice will match the rhetoric is still to be seen. The dreadful impact of the Indian Ocean tsunami in December 2004 provoked an unprecedented response from the public of wealthy countries, and large sums were donated to relief efforts. This hint to governments that their publics have greater compassion than might otherwise be thought coincided with the high priority being given to poverty eradication (particularly in Africa) in the UK in 2005. Both Chancellor and Prime Minister asserted the need for greater generosity towards African countries, in trade, in direct aid and in debt relief – a rare example of (more or less) open discussion of redistribution in UK politics. The 'Commission for

Africa'[80] had been set up by the British Prime Minister to provide advice on development in time for the UK's 2005 presidencies of the EU Council and the G8 ('Group of Eight', informal meetings of the world's richest countries on mainly economic issues). This received enormous public attention, in the UK at least. Whilst the output of the G8 was disappointing, mainly pointing to future negotiations (for example within the WTO), these issues are at least on the agenda.

## 8 Further reading

A range of stimulating approaches to some of the dilemmas and conflicts in what we would now call the 'social' pillar of sustainable development can be found in the collection edited by Andrew Dobson, *Fairness and Futurity: Essays on Environmental Sustainability and Social Justice* (Oxford University Press, 1999). The Brundtland Report is the seminal work on sustainable development, and still worth reading. For a highly critical account of Johannesburg, see Neil Middleton and Phil O'Keefe, *Rio Plus Ten: Politics, Poverty and the Environment* (Pluto Press, 2003).

Andrea Ross, 'UK Approach to Delivering Sustainable Development in Government: A Case Study in Joined-Up Working' (2005) 17 *Journal of Environmental Law* 27, is a very useful analysis of the UK approach to implementing sustainable development.

The UN website on sustainable development can be used to follow practical projects: www.un.org/esa/sustdev/index.html.

---

[80]  www.commissionforafrica.org/.

# 'Globalisation' and International Trade

## 1 Introduction: the international trading system

Environmental law is often described as a still 'young' discipline, and the law of sustainable development is barely in its infancy. Trade law has deeper foundations. The General Agreement on Tariffs and Trade (GATT) came into effect in 1947, when 'environment' simply did not exist as a policy issue. As environment and sustainable development entered the political radar screen in the 1970s, the United Nations (UN) was seen as a more appropriate forum for their international development than the GATT. The societal and environmental relevance of trade rules has only slowly become clear, and environmental concern is being accommodated within those rules even more slowly.

Environmental lawyers often approach trade as a threat to environmental protection. Trade rules can constrain the autonomy of states (or the European Union (EU)) to set standards pursuing social objectives such as public health or environmental protection; and even when states join together in treaties promoting environmental protection, the relationship between core trade law and those 'multi-lateral environmental agreements' (MEAs) is uncertain. And the effects of trade liberalisation go beyond regulatory effects: transport of goods around the world has obvious environmental implications. And 'free trade' promises greater production and consumption – all things being equal, increasing pollution and resource use.

Far from being presented as a threat, however, international trade liberalisation is now widely presented as a solution to the most pressing elements of the sustainable development conundrum. And if in the past sustainable development was seen in terms of economy (trade) / environment, the question of trade and development (economic and social, including poverty eradication in the world's poorest countries – see Chapter 6) is increasingly central. The paradigm case for making trade–environment–development links is perhaps agriculture. This is a sector in which developing countries have a competitive advantage, but agricultural subsidies in developed countries mean that the products of developing countries are unable to compete fairly on either domestic or international markets, whilst subsidies linked to production simultaneously exacerbate the environmental damage caused by intensive agriculture. Or trade–environment–development objectives could be simultaneously pursued by using technology to reduce waste among industries in developing countries, benefiting the environment and saving money on inputs, so improving trade competitiveness. If trade is to make a serious contribution to the objectives of sustainable development, however, we should look beyond these more obvious 'win–win' solutions. And even these possibilities are problematic. In the case of reducing waste, technological and financial constraints in poorer states pose a major barrier to progress.[1] Agricultural reform faces significant vested interests, and promises economic dislocation for some groups in developed countries. Moreover, the still tentative efforts of developed countries to shift subsidies from production to environmentally sensitive farming may address the environmental harm, without necessarily opening up markets. Mutual reinforcement within the 'sustainable development triangle'[2] is to some extent coincidental.

Whilst the World Trade Organisation (WTO) is far from the only manifestation of 'globalisation', or the only international organisation operating to an economic agenda,[3] it has such a central and revealing role in the law of international trade that it will be the main subject of discussion here. The WTO was the result of the agreement of GATT II in 1994, and now has over 140 members, including the major economic powers of the EU, Japan and the United States, as well as many developing countries, including China and India. The GATT (1947) remains the central treaty on international trade, but the WTO agreements crucially put in place a far more rigorous, quasi-judicial dispute resolution and implementation process, unprecedented in international law.[4] A complaint by one WTO member against another leads first to a period of consultation, and, in the absence of resolution, a 'panel' is then established to hear the dispute. The panel's decision is subject to appeal on points of law before the WTO Appellate Body. Failure to implement a decision of the WTO's Dispute Settlement Body (which formally adopts the Appellate Body or Panel reports) entitles the complaining party to compensation or to 'suspend concessions' in response.[5] By contrast with these powerful dispute settlement procedures, the WTO has no formal rule making powers, which remain with the state. The rules of the WTO are found in the GATT, and associated agreements such as the Sanitary and Phyto-Sanitary (SPS) Agreement

---

[1] See Aaron Cosbey, *Lessons Learned on Trade and Sustainable Development* (International Institute for Sustainable Development and International Centre for Trade and Sustainable Development, 2004), www.ecolomics-international.org/gova_trade_knowl_netw_lessons_learned_iisd_ictsd_aaron_cosbey_2004.pdf for interesting examples.

[2] Sanford E. Gaines, 'International Trade, Environmental Protection and Development as a Sustainable Development Triangle' (2002) 11 *Review of European Community & International Environmental Law* 259.

[3] See the discussion in Oren Perez, *Ecological Sensitivity and Global Legal Pluralism: Rethinking the Trade and Environment Conflict* (Hart, 2004).

[4] WTO, *Understanding on Rules and Procedures Governing the Settlement of Disputes* (1994).

[5] The process is detailed, see Arts. 21 and 22.

discussed further below. However, the WTO provides the 'forum for negotiations' of further trade rules,[6] in periodic 'ministerial conferences' (often referred to as trade 'rounds').

This chapter provides an introduction to international trade law as it relates to environmental protection, and more broadly to the objective of sustainable development. We discuss not only the main legal issues, but also the hugely sensitive context of the 'sustainable development triangle'. As elsewhere in this book, genetically modified organisms (GMOs) provide a useful case study. In 2003, the USA, Canada and Argentina invoked the WTO dispute settlement procedure against the European Community (EC) (the *EC-biotech* dispute[7]), in respect of, first, the general 'moratorium' on GMOs (see Chapter 5); second, the failure to make decisions in respect of a number of specified products; and third, Member State bans (safeguard measures) on GMOs previously authorised at EU level. The Panel decision was published on 29 September 2006. The Panel did not rule on a number of issues raised by the complainants, but found that in all three challenged categories, the EC had violated the SPS Agreement, as discussed below. The EU has not appealed to the Appellate Body against the Panel's ruling,[8] but even this may not be the end of the saga: assuming that it does eventually function effectively, the new GMO regime (discussed in Chapter 5) could raise novel and significant questions about WTO law,[9] both in respect of refusals of authorisation, and in respect of onerous regulatory requirements that apply to GMOs but not other products, including obligations to apply for authorisation, to keep records and to label GMOs. Importantly, the *EC-biotech* Panel did not consider either the legitimacy of requiring pre-marketing approval of GMOs, or the legitimacy of the new EU regulatory system for GMOs.

## 2 The promise of trade: Johannesburg and sustainable development

In Chapter 6 we observed that the Johannesburg Summit on Sustainable Development presents trade as a tool of sustainable development. This is not a new approach: trade also received attention in Rio[10] and in the Brundtland Report.[11] The relationship between trade and the environment, predominantly

---

[6] Agreement Establishing the World Trade Organisation, Art. III.2.

[7] *European Communities – Measures Affecting the Approval and Marketing of Biotech Products*, DS291, 292, 293.

[8] Reports can be found at www.wto.org by following the link through 'disputes' by subject (GMOs).

[9] There is a considerable literature on the subject. See, for example, Joanne Scott, 'The European Regulation of GMOs and the WTO' (2003) *Columbia Journal of European Law* 213; Robert Howse and Petros C. Mavroidis, 'Europe's Evolving Regulatory Strategy for GMOs – The Issue of Consistency with WTO Law: of Kine and Brine' (2000) 24 *Fordham International Law Journal* 317.

[10] Declaration of the UN Conference on Environment and Development, Rio de Janeiro, 1992, Principle 12: see Ch. 6, pp. 221–4.

[11] World Commission on Environment and Development, *Our Common Future* (Oxford University Press, 1987).

from the perspective of developed nations, is discussed in section 3 below. Here, we outline some of the issues around trade and development, more specifically the sustainable development objectives that demand the eradication of poverty. We should recall here the discussion in Chapter 6 (pp. 241–2) of the reluctance of developed countries to contemplate significant redistribution of resources as a way to end poverty: 'trade not aid', whatever its merits, is consistent with this reluctance. Trade purports to offer economic growth for poor nations. To complete the sustainable development triangle, it then has to be assumed that the resources of developing countries will reach the point at which populations are able and willing to turn to progressive social and environmental policies. There is, however, no necessary or automatic connection between trade / global economic growth and the relief of poverty / environmental protection. Even if one acknowledges the potential benefits of trade, 'the promise that the wealth-generating benefits of market-driven international economic systems can help alleviate grinding poverty comes with the danger that those same unconstrained market forces will perpetuate and even exacerbate economic inequalities and environmental harms that are socially unacceptable and environmentally unsustainable'.[12]

Big promises have been made, most recently in the Johannesburg Plan of Implementation. Chapter V, 'Sustainable Development in a Globalising World', and Chapter X, 'Means of Implementation', contain the key provisions on trade, but do not add significantly to commitments made in the 2001 Doha Declaration.[13] The fourth WTO Ministerial conference was held in Doha, Qatar, in 2001, and was dominated by development issues.[14] The promise of trade is set out in the Declaration:

1. The multi-lateral trading system embodied in the World Trade Organization has contributed significantly to economic growth, development and employment throughout the past fifty years. We are determined, particularly in the light of the global economic slowdown, to maintain the process of reform and liberalization of trade policies, thus ensuring that the system plays its full part in promoting recovery, growth and development. We therefore strongly reaffirm the principles and objectives set out in the Marrakesh Agreement Establishing the World Trade Organization, and pledge to reject the use of protectionism.

2. International trade can play a major role in the promotion of economic development and the alleviation of poverty. We recognize the need for all our peoples to benefit from the increased opportunities and welfare gains that the multi-lateral trading system generates. The majority of WTO members are developing countries. We seek to place their needs and interests at the heart of the Work Programme adopted in this Declaration. Recalling the Preamble to the Marrakesh Agreement, we shall continue

---

[12] Gaines, 'International Trade', p. 260.

[13] Doha WTO Ministerial 2001: Ministerial Declaration, Wt/Min(01)/Dec/1, 20 November 2001. Also the Monterrey Consensus of the International Conference on Financing for Development (2002).

[14] Surya Subedi, 'The Road from Doha: The Issues for the Development Round of the WTO and the Future of International Trade' (2003) 52 *International and Comparative Law Quarterly* 425.

to make positive efforts designed to ensure that developing countries, and especially the least-developed among them, secure a share in the growth of world
trade commensurate with the needs of their economic development. In this
context, enhanced market access, balanced rules, and well targeted, sustainably
financed technical assistance and capacity-building programmes have important
roles to play.

Doha provided a 'Work Programme', to be filled in by subsequent negotiation.
Topics to be addressed include agriculture (the 'long term objective' is
to establish 'a fair and market-oriented trading system through a programme
of fundamental reform encompassing strengthened rules and specific
commitments on support and protection in order to correct and prevent
restrictions and distortions in world agricultural markets' (para. 13));
the enhancement of 'the capacity of the multi-lateral trading system to
contribute to a durable solution to the problem of external indebtedness of
developing and least-developed countries' (para. 36); technical cooperation
and capacity building; and special and differential treatment for developing
countries. Many of Doha's development objectives are in aspirational language, and progress remains slow.[15] Agriculture, for example, the area to
which developing countries attach perhaps most importance, is still described
as 'the most distorted sector' in the WTO's 2005 annual report.[16] If promises
are not kept, nobody should be surprised by dissatisfaction with global trade
regimes.

### Sylvia Ostry, 'The Future of the World Trading System: Beyond Doha' in John J. Kirton and Michael J. Trebilcock (eds.), *Hard Choices, Soft Law: Voluntary Standards in Global Trade, Environment and Social Governance* (Ashgate, 2004), pp. 274–5

In writings on antiglobalisation two words appear with striking frequency: alienation and
anomie. The first term is borrowed from Marx and is essentially a moral critique of capitalism. Marx argued that because labour becomes a commodity, the worker loses all power to
control the processes by which decisions are made that affect his or her life. Anomie, first
used by the French sociologist Emile Durkheim at the beginning of the twentieth century,
stresses the individual's sense of powerlessness and the loss of social cohesion. When
anomie is confined to a small number, they can form groups – alienated from the rest of
society but unified among themselves. The anarchists and the neo-fascists provide good
examples. But if widely dispersed groups can unite around one theme – say feminism or
environmentalism – that is a qualitatively different phenomenon. And if divergent groups

---

[15] Progress can be followed on the WTO website, www.wto.org/english/tratop_e/dda_e/dda_e.htm.
Progress stalled in 2006.
[16] *Overview of Developments in the International Trading Environment*, Annual Report by the
Director-General (World Trade Organization, 2005).

with divergent objectives can, by means of the internet, unite around one theme, say, anti-corporate globalisation, that could produce a quantum change.

Alienation and anomie are useful concepts in explaining the rise of the antiglobalisation movement. The disjuncture between the goals of free trade – rising living standards for all – and the distributional impact, especially between rich and poor countries, is taken as evidence (not accurate, to be sure) that the WTO does not deliver. Unfortunately, this view was reinforced by overzealous proponents of free trade that unleashed unrealistic expectations. If Nirvana is promised but not delivered, it is bound to provoke cries of Armageddon from the disapproving and the disappointed. In many developing countries, this anger and disappointment are threatening already fragile democracies. Moreover, increasing inequality both within and, especially, among countries has been highlighted by the media and used effectively by many NGOs. The figures are stunning, and many are quoted. And it is not just poverty that marks the increasing marginalisation of the poorest. There is also disease – and not only AIDS but also ebola, malaria, and drug-resistant bacterial infections …

But, of course, freer trade did not create the growing inequality in economic social conditions, nor will blocking trade cure these problems. *Au contraire*. Something far more complex would be needed in terms of policy co-ordination (including compensating the losers), and since that seems improbable at present, it is easier for politicians to yield to the temptation of promising simple solutions.

Using trade to achieve sustainable development objectives is even more problematic when one adds the third (environmental) pillar to the economic and social pillars. Whilst it would be wrong to characterise developing (or indeed developed) countries as homogeneous either individually or collectively, there is something of a north/south divide on the proper place for environmental protection.

### Sanford E. Gaines, 'International Trade, Environmental Protection and Development as a Sustainable Development Triangle' (2002) 11 *Review of European Community & International Environmental Law* 259, p. 263

The points of tension in the trade–environment–development policy triangle are readily apparent. Environmentalists and many others in Northern civil society, observing that world environmental conditions are worsening as trade has become more open, tend to frame the post-Rio trade policy debate not as 'trade and sustainable development' but as 'trade and environment', because they see the lack of explicit consideration of environmental values in trade policy to be the main deviation from sustainable development. The sharpest grievance of the developing South, in contrast, has been that the world trade system is not yet liberal enough, denying them the poverty-reducing and developmental benefits of free access to the markets of the North. Moreover, the developmental potential of liberalized trade has not been realized because of deep problems, scarcely yet addressed, of administrative capacity, obsolete technology and low levels of foreign investment in and official assistance to the least developed of the developing countries. For this reason, many developing countries share many environmentalists' scepticism of 'sustainable development' as a mantra, but for the opposite reason – because they think it ignores developmental needs. Even in the late stages of preparations for the WSSD [World Summit on Sustainable Development (Johannesburg)], this divergence of views prevented consensus on any express incorporation of environmental or developmental considerations into world trade rules.

Active steps must be taken to ensure that the relationship between trade and sustainable development is positive: even for those who agree in principle that trade is the solution, much remains to be done in practice. Others, of course, doubt that change is possible.

## 3 Trade and the environment

### (a) The main issues

### Oren Perez, *Ecological Sensitivity and Global Legal Pluralism: Rethinking the Trade and Environment Conflict* (Hart, 2004), pp. 33–4

The trade–environment problem can be examined through several perspectives. The first perspective looks at the way in which international trade influences the *domestic environment* of the trading parties; the second examines the way in which trade affects *transboundary ecological problems*. The third perspective examines the linkage between transnational trade and the *'global commons'* (eg, the ozone layer, fish stocks, Antarctica, etc). The economic literature has tackled the question of the environmental impact of trade liberalisation by distinguishing between four causal effects or paths. The *scale* effect measures the ecological impact of the expansion in scale of production, which is likely to occur with the transition to an open trading regime. Ceteris paribus, the scale effect is likely to prove damaging to the environment: if production and/or consumption of a good is pollutive, an expansion in the global output of that good is likely to lead to greater environmental degradation. The *composition* effect examines the change in the composition of industry, which is triggered by the process of trade liberalisation, as countries *specialise* in sectors in which they enjoy a comparative advantage. Whether the ecological impact of this change is positive or negative depends on the nature of the specialisation (ie whether it is geared toward more or less pollution-intensive sectors). Environmentalists have raised, in this context, the pollution havens hypothesis, which argues that free trade will increase industrial pollution in developing countries through the migration of dirty industries from developed countries (with stricter environmental regulations) into developing countries.

   Third, the *technological* effect examines how the technological changes, which usually accompany the process of trade liberalisation, could influence the environment. It is usually assumed that these (trade-induced) technological changes should, overall, be beneficial to the environment, whether by introducing cleaner production methods, or through improved recycling or waste treatment methods. This hypothesis is supported by two different arguments. First a nation with a liberal trade policy should have greater access to foreign 'environmental' technologies. Second, the transition to an open market is usually associated with an increase in individual incomes, which, in turn should generate a greater demand for 'environmental goods', such as clean air and uncontaminated water (generating steeper demand for 'clean technology'). Finally, the *regulatory effect* examines the way in which trade liberalisation affects local environmental standards. In this context one can distinguish between two contradictory trends. On the one hand the anticipated increase in average income, as well as deeper exposure to foreign regulatory methods, is likely to lead to increase in the demand for environmental control, pushing the government to adopt stricter environmental regulations. On the other hand, the 'race to the bottom' hypothesis ... suggests that free trade may induce a process by which countries will lower their environmental standards in order to gain competitive advantage.

The role of trade in sustainable development is of course in part an empirical question – is trade contributing to environmental protection and poverty eradication?

### Aaron Cosbey, *Lessons Learned on Trade and Sustainable Development* (International Institute for Sustainable Development and International Centre for Trade and Sustainable Development, 2004), p. 1

Is trade good or bad for the environment? It is a mark of how far we have come in the debates on trade and environment, trade and sustainable development, that this question will be widely recognized as silly. The answer is no, trade is not good for the environment, nor is it bad for the environment. The actual relationship is too complex to be described by such general truisms. Trade, and trade liberalization, can in some cases be good for the environment, and in other cases bad, or (frequently) both at once. The final impacts in any given country will depend on the sector's economic characteristics – both domestically and abroad –, the domestic institutions for managing trade and investment, the strength of ancillary institutions such as regimes for environmental management, the details of the liberalizing agreement, and so on.

The role of trade in sustainable development can never, however, be an exclusively empirical question: the data gaps, the scientific uncertainty, the values inherent in the empirical enquiry, the values underpinning what counts as success, all prevent that. Views on the extent to which trade can, or should, contribute to sustainable development are also the product of ideological divisions. Some environmentalists will see environmental problems (and problems of poverty) as requiring a fundamental break with existing social and economic arrangements; others see such problems as simpler (albeit complex) pragmatic dilemmas, to which solutions must be sought within existing institutions, through the better management of resources.[17]

For lawyers, the trade–environment debate usually manifests itself through restrictions that may be imposed by international trade rules on measures taken domestically to protect the environment, either within the jurisdiction or externally. WTO law has moved beyond border measures such as tariffs and quantitative restricts on imports/exports, to look at the trade impact of domestic regulation. This raises similar questions as at the EU level (Chapter 4, pp. 171–82), although the WTO and the EU are very different creatures, and of course WTO rules also impact on regulation *by* the EU. Next, we discuss the reach of the WTO into domestic regulation, and then consider the difficulty that arises when states, rather than putting in place independent domestic regulation, join together in an MEA.

### (b) The legal regime: domestic measures

In this section we examine some of the central legal questions on trade and the environment, through the WTO Appellate Body's approach to a small number of trade disputes, as well as the *EC-biotech* Panel report. First in this section, we will outline the basic GATT provisions, including the possibility for exceptions and the vexed question of whether products are alike for the purposes of the discrimination disciplines of WTO rules (e.g., is GM soya 'like' conventional soya?); we then examine the WTO approach to science and risk.

### (i) The basic provisions

Very basically, the GATT imposes a non-discrimination framework that requires (subject to certain exceptions) that all imports from WTO members be treated no less favourably than imports from other members (the 'most favoured nation' principle, found in Art. I) and that all imported products be treated no less favourably than domestic 'like' products (the 'national treatment' principle, found in Art. III). If a regulatory measure falls foul of these basic GATT principles, attention turns to whether the measure can be excepted from censure under Art. XX.

#### General Agreement on Tariffs and Trade, Art. XX

*General Exceptions*
Subject to the requirement that such measures are not applied in a manner which would constitute a means of arbitrary or unjustifiable discrimination between countries where the same conditions prevail, or a disguised restriction on international trade, nothing in this

---

[17] Recall also Dobson's contrast between 'ecologism' and 'environmentalism', in Ch. 6, p. 250. See also Perez, *Ecological Sensitivity*, pp. 13–14, for detailed discussion of the divisions over the role of trade.

Agreement shall be construed to prevent the adoption or enforcement by any Member of measures:

...

    (b)  necessary to protect human, animal or plant life or health;

...

    (g)  relating to the conservation of exhaustible natural resources if such measures are made effective in conjunction with restrictions on domestic production or consumption;

Article XX(b) was considered in detail by the Appellate Body in the *Asbestos* dispute, which concerned a complaint from Canada about a French ban on asbestos products. Relying on scientific evidence that asbestos is harmful to human health, the Appellate Body confirmed the Panel's decision that the French measure protects human life or health under Art. XX(b) (para. 62). The key legal question was the 'necessity' of the measure: would a less restrictive approach (controlling use of asbestos rather than banning it) protect human life and health?

### EC – Measures Affecting Asbestos and Asbestos-Containing Products WT/DS135/AB/R, 12 March 2001

168 ... it is undisputed that WTO Members have the right to determine the level of protection of health that they consider appropriate in a given situation. France has determined, and the Panel accepted, that the chosen level of health protection by France is a 'halt' to the spread of *asbestos*-related health risks. By prohibiting all forms of amphibole asbestos, and by severely restricting the use of chrysotile asbestos, the measure at issue is clearly designed and apt to achieve that level of health protection. Our conclusion is not altered by the fact that PCG fibres [the alternatives to asbestos] might pose a risk to health. The scientific evidence before the Panel indicated that the risk posed by the PCG fibres is, in any case, *less* than the risk posed by chrysotile asbestos fibres, although that evidence did *not* indicate that the risk posed by PCG fibres is non-existent. Accordingly, it seems to us perfectly legitimate for a Member to seek to halt the spread of a highly risky product while allowing the use of a less risky product in its place ...

...

172 ... In this case, the objective pursued by the measure is the preservation of human life and health through the elimination, or reduction, of the well-known, and life-threatening, health risks posed by asbestos fibres. The value pursued is both vital and important in the highest degree. The remaining question, then, is whether there is an alternative measure that would achieve the same end and that is less restrictive of trade than a prohibition.

173. Canada asserts that 'controlled use' represents a 'reasonably available' measure that would serve the same end. The issue is, thus, whether France could reasonably be expected to employ 'controlled use' practices to achieve its chosen level of health protection – a halt in the spread of asbestos-related health risks.

174. In our view, France could not reasonably be expected to employ *any* alternative measure if that measure would involve a continuation of the very risk that the Decree seeks to 'halt'. Such an alternative measure would, in effect, prevent France from achieving its chosen level of health protection. On the basis of the scientific evidence before it, the Panel found that, in general, the efficacy of 'controlled use' remains to be demonstrated. Moreover, even in cases where 'controlled use' practices are applied 'with greater certainty', the scientific evidence suggests that the level of exposure can, in some circumstances, still be high enough for there to be a 'significant residual risk of developing asbestos-related diseases'. The Panel found too that the efficacy of 'controlled use' is particularly doubtful for the building industry and for DIY enthusiasts, which are the most important users of cement-based products containing chrysotile asbestos. Given these factual findings by the Panel, we believe that 'controlled use' would not allow France to achieve its chosen level of health protection by halting the spread of asbestos-related health risks. 'Controlled use' would, thus, not be an alternative measure that would achieve the end sought by France.

Turning now to the exception in Art. XX(g), one of the occasions on which the WTO Appellate Body showed greatest willingness to consider the environmental implications of trade decisions (thus with significance beyond Art. XX(g)) was in its Report on the *Shrimp/Turtle* dispute. Worrying numbers of sea turtles, including endangered species, are captured and drowned annually in shrimp trawl nets. The USA had introduced restrictions on the import of shrimp, in an effort to reduce turtle mortality. The measures were complex, but essentially demanded that shrimp be fished using 'turtle excluder devices' (TEDs).

### United States – Import Prohibition of Certain Shrimp and Shrimp Products WT/DS58/AB/R, 12 October 1998

128 … Textually, Article XX(g) is *not* limited to the conservation of 'mineral' or 'non-living' natural resources. The complainants' principal argument is rooted in the notion that 'living' natural resources are 'renewable' and therefore cannot be 'exhaustible' natural resources. We do not believe that 'exhaustible' natural resources and 'renewable' natural resources are mutually exclusive. One lesson that modern biological sciences teach us is that living species, though, in principle, capable of reproduction and, in that sense, 'renewable', are in certain circumstances indeed susceptible of depletion, exhaustion and extinction, frequently because of human activities. Living resources are just as 'finite' as petroleum, iron ore and other non-living resources.

129. The words of Article XX(g), 'exhaustible natural resources', were actually crafted more than 50 years ago. They must be read by a treaty interpreter in the light of contemporary concerns of the community of nations about the protection and conservation of the environment. While Article XX was not modified in the Uruguay Round, the preamble attached to the *WTO Agreement* shows that the signatories to that Agreement were, in 1994, fully aware of the importance and legitimacy of environmental protection as a goal of national and international policy. The preamble of the *WTO Agreement* – which informs not only the

GATT 1994, but also the other covered agreements – explicitly acknowledges 'the objective of *sustainable development'* ...

...

132. We turn next to the issue of whether the living natural resources sought to be conserved by the measure are 'exhaustible' under Article XX(g). That this element is present in respect of the five species of sea turtles here involved appears to be conceded by all the participants and third participants in this case. The exhaustibility of sea turtles would in fact have been very difficult to controvert since all of the seven recognized species of sea turtles are today listed in Appendix 1 of the Convention on International Trade in Endangered Species of Wild Fauna and Flora ('CITES'). The list in Appendix 1 includes 'all species *threatened with extinction* which are or may be affected by trade'. (emphasis added)

133. Finally, we observe that sea turtles are highly migratory animals, passing in and out of waters subject to the rights of jurisdiction of various coastal states and the high seas ...
The sea turtle species here at stake, i.e., covered by Section 609 [the disputed US measure], are all known to occur in waters over which the United States exercises jurisdiction ... We do not pass upon the question of whether there is an implied jurisdictional limitation in Article XX(g), and if so, the nature or extent of that limitation. We note only that in the specific circumstances of the case before us, there is a sufficient nexus between the migratory and endangered marine populations involved and the United States for purposes of Article XX(g).

134. For all the foregoing reasons, we find that the sea turtles here involved constitute 'exhaustible natural resources' for purposes of Article XX(g) of the GATT 1994.

...

147. Although provisionally justified under Article XX(g), Section 609, if it is ultimately to be justified as an exception under Article XX, must also satisfy the requirements of the introductory clauses – the 'chapeau' – of Article XX ...

...

150. We commence the second tier of our analysis with an examination of the ordinary meaning of the words of the chapeau. The precise language of the chapeau requires that a measure not be applied in a manner which would constitute a means of 'arbitrary or unjustifiable discrimination between countries where the same conditions prevail' or a 'disguised restriction on international trade'. There are three standards contained in the chapeau: first, arbitrary discrimination between countries where the same conditions prevail; second, unjustifiable discrimination between countries where the same conditions prevail; and third, a disguised restriction on international trade ...

...

156. Turning then to the chapeau of Article XX, we consider that it embodies the recognition on the part of WTO Members of the need to maintain a balance of rights and obligations between the right of a Member to invoke one or another of the exceptions of Article XX, specified in paragraphs (a) to (j), on the one hand, and the substantive rights of the other Members under the GATT 1994, on the other hand. Exercise by one Member of its right to invoke an exception, such as Article XX(g), if abused or misused, will, to that extent, erode or render naught the substantive treaty rights in, for example, Article XI:1, of other Members. Similarly, because the GATT 1994 itself makes available the exceptions of Article XX, in recognition of

the legitimate nature of the policies and interests there embodied, the right to invoke one of those exceptions is not to be rendered illusory. The same concept may be expressed from a slightly different angle of vision, thus, a balance must be struck between the *right* of a Member to invoke an exception under Article XX and the *duty* of that same Member to respect the treaty rights of the other Members. To permit one Member to abuse or misuse its right to invoke an exception would be effectively to allow that Member to degrade its own treaty obligations as well as to devalue the treaty rights of other Members. If the abuse or misuse is sufficiently grave or extensive, the Member, in effect, reduces its treaty obligation to a merely facultative one and dissolves its juridical character, and, in so doing, negates altogether the treaty rights of other Members. The chapeau was installed at the head of the list of 'General Exceptions' in Article XX to prevent such far-reaching consequences.

157. In our view, the language of the chapeau makes clear that each of the exceptions in paragraphs (a) to (j) of Article XX is a *limited and conditional* exception from the sub-stantive obligations contained in the other provisions of the GATT 1994, that is to say, the ultimate availability of the exception is subject to the compliance by the invoking Member with the requirements of the chapeau …

158. The chapeau of Article XX is, in fact, but one expression of the principle of good faith. This principle, at once a general principle of law and a general principle of international law, controls the exercise of rights by states …

…

163. The actual *application* of the [US] measure … *requires* other WTO Members to adopt a regulatory program that is not merely *comparable*, but rather *essentially the same*, as that applied to the United States shrimp trawl vessels. Thus, the effect of the application of Section 609 is to establish a rigid and unbending standard by which United States officials determine whether or not countries will be certified, thus granting or refusing other countries the right to export shrimp to the United States …

164. We understand that the United States also applies a uniform standard throughout its territory, regardless of the particular conditions existing in certain parts of the country. The United States requires the use of approved TEDs at all times by domestic, commercial shrimp trawl vessels operating in waters where there is any likelihood that they may interact with sea turtles, regardless of the actual incidence of sea turtles in those waters, the species of those sea turtles, or other differences or disparities that may exist in different parts of the United States. It may be quite acceptable for a government, in adopting and implementing a domestic policy, to adopt a single standard applicable to all its citizens throughout that country. However, it is not acceptable, in international trade relations, for one WTO Member to use an economic embargo to *require* other Members to adopt essentially the same com-prehensive regulatory program, to achieve a certain policy goal, as that in force within that Member's territory, *without* taking into consideration different conditions which may occur in the territories of those other Members.

165. Furthermore, when this dispute was before the Panel and before us, the United States did not permit imports of shrimp harvested by commercial shrimp trawl vessels using TEDs [turtle excluder devices] comparable in effectiveness to those required in the United States if those shrimp originated in waters of countries not certified under Section 609. In other words, *shrimp caught using methods identical to those employed in the United States* have

been excluded from the United States market solely because they have been caught in waters of *countries that have not been certified by the United States*. The resulting situation is difficult to reconcile with the declared policy objective of protecting and conserving sea turtles. This suggests to us that this measure, in its application, is more concerned with effectively influencing WTO Members to adopt essentially the same comprehensive regulatory regime as that applied by the United States to its domestic shrimp trawlers, even though many of those Members may be differently situated. We believe that discrimination results not only when countries in which the same conditions prevail are differently treated, but also when the application of the measure at issue does not allow for any inquiry into the appropriateness of the regulatory program for the conditions prevailing in those exporting countries.

166. Another aspect of the application of Section 609 that bears heavily in any appraisal of justifiable or unjustifiable discrimination is the failure of the United States to engage the appellees, as well as other Members exporting shrimp to the United States, in serious, across-the-board negotiations with the objective of concluding bilateral or multi-lateral agreements for the protection and conservation of sea turtles, before enforcing the import prohibition against the shrimp exports of those other Members ...

167. *A propos* this failure to have prior consistent recourse to diplomacy as an instrument of environmental protection policy, which produces discriminatory impacts on countries exporting shrimp to the United States with which no international agreements are reached or even seriously attempted, a number of points must be made ...

...

168 ... the protection and conservation of highly migratory species of sea turtles, that is, the very policy objective of the measure, demands concerted and cooperative efforts on the part of the many countries whose waters are traversed in the course of recurrent sea turtle migrations. The need for, and the appropriateness of, such efforts have been recognized in the WTO itself as well as in a significant number of other international instruments and declarations ...

...

172. Clearly, the United States negotiated seriously with some, but not with other Members (including the appellees), that export shrimp to the United States. The effect is plainly discriminatory and, in our view, unjustifiable ... The unilateral character of the application of Section 609 heightens the disruptive and discriminatory influence of the import prohibition and underscores its unjustifiability.

...

181. The certification processes followed by the United States ... appear to be singularly informal and casual, and to be conducted in a manner such that these processes could result in the negation of rights of Members. There appears to be no way that exporting Members can be certain whether the terms ... are being applied in a fair and just manner by the appropriate governmental agencies of the United States. It appears to us that, effectively, exporting Members applying for certification whose applications are rejected are denied basic fairness and due process, and are discriminated against, *vis-à-vis* those Members which are granted certification.

...

184. We find, accordingly, that the United States measure is applied in a manner which amounts to a means not just of 'unjustifiable discrimination', but also of 'arbitrary discrimination' between countries where the same conditions prevail, contrary to the requirements of the chapeau of Article XX. The measure, therefore, is not entitled to the justifying protection of Article XX of the GATT 1994 ...

185. In reaching these conclusions, we wish to underscore what we have *not* decided in this appeal. We have *not* decided that the protection and preservation of the environment is of no significance to the Members of the WTO. Clearly, it is. We have *not* decided that the sovereign nations that are Members of the WTO cannot adopt effective measures to protect endangered species, such as sea turtles. Clearly, they can and should. And we have *not* decided that sovereign states should not act together bilaterally, plurilaterally or multilaterally, either within the WTO or in other international fora, to protect endangered species or to otherwise protect the environment. Clearly, they should and do.

186. What we *have* decided in this appeal is simply this: although the measure of the United States in dispute in this appeal serves an environmental objective that is recognized as legitimate under paragraph (g) of Article XX of the GATT 1994, this measure has been applied by the United States in a manner which constitutes arbitrary and unjustifiable discrimination between Members of the WTO, contrary to the requirements of the chapeau of Article XX.

In *Shrimp/Turtle*, the Appellate Body set forth an interpretation of Art. XX that differed importantly from earlier interpretations. It concluded that Art. XX(g) could, 'in principle, provide a legal basis for unilateral trade measures to protect the global environment, in this case endangered species of sea turtles, even where directed against other countries' policies'.[18] The parts of the 'global environment' that measures can be directed at was left open, but here there was a sufficient connection between the USA and the resources it sought to protect (para. 133). *Shrimp/Turtle* more generally provided the Appellate Body with the opportunity to demonstrate a level of sensitivity to environmental concerns (as in *Asbestos* it would to health and safety concerns), albeit whilst in this case condemning the measure before it (essentially because the USA had failed to comply with minimum procedural demands set out in the Report (paras. 163–81)). This has been broadly welcomed. Nevertheless, the welcome, even from those who seek greater environmental sensitivity in international trade rules, has not been universal. Sanford Gaines has a range of concerns, but his particular concern about the Appellate Body's categorisation of the US policy as 'rigid and unbending' (para. 163) resonates with some of the material we will be discussing in Part IV on modes of regulation.

[18] Robert Howse, 'From Politics to Technocracy – and Back Again: The Fate of the Multi-lateral Trading Regime' (2002) 96 *American Journal of International Law* 94, p. 111.

### Sanford E. Gaines, 'The WTO's Reading of the GATT Article XX Chapeau: A Disguised Restriction On Environmental Measures' (2001) 22 *University of Pennsylvania Journal of International Economic Law* 739, pp. 799–803

Domestically, the United States chose a command-and-control approach to sea turtle conservation, the uniform requirement to use TEDs. This policy choice was dictated by several factors. First, technical experts had devised a rather simple technological fix to a complicated problem, so a technology-based standard was an obvious choice. Moreover, there were no competing technologies, and the evidence available then, since confirmed by further studies, showed that the TEDs were very effective. Second, the decline in sea turtle populations was severe, so there was an urgent need to implement responsive measures as rapidly as possible. Third, an effective turtle conservation program required near-universal compliance. Voluntary and economic incentive approaches rarely yield either rapid or comprehensive changes in behavior. Fourth, the TEDs requirement was more reliable, much easier to enforce, and interfered less with fishing operations than any alternative for sea turtle protection, such as restricted areas or reduced tow times.

...

The simplistic policy to require TEDs in all countries, though deemed 'unjustifiable' by the Appellate Body, looks eminently justifiable when viewed from the environmental policy perspective. It exemplifies the common practice of applying a technological solution uniformly across many countries or regions or actors. To insist, as the Appellate Body does, that environmental policies or technology standards should permit variation according to physical and economic conditions that differ from place to place or firm to firm exalts theoretical elegance over practical responses to political and administrative difficulties in environmental regulation. In an ideal world where all interests operate from a position of perfect information, tailor-made regulations to fit precisely each firm's or each nation's unique situation would clearly be preferable to a one-size-fits all uniform standard across diverse situations. But our information about the state of the environment and the effectiveness of environmental controls is very imperfect, and there is a limit to how many 'tailors' the public sector can employ to take the precise measure of each regulation. In the real world, therefore, uniform standards are a staple of environmental regulation. They are relatively simple and transparent, easy for regulators to apply and for the regulated community to understand. And they usually get the basic job done efficiently ... They continue to be the norm, not the exception, in most fields of environmental regulation. This is as much true of international environmental regulation as it is of domestic regimes. From this perspective, the degree of 'coercion' involved in the TED-only policy requires a more thorough and thoughtful analysis than appears in Shrimp-Turtle.

A deeper problem revealed by the weaknesses in the Appellate Body's handling of this issue is that the WTO simply has no capacity for such analysis. In dealing with a dispute like Shrimp-Turtle, the lack of environmental expertise within the WTO becomes a serious weakness. The missing expertise is not merely one of scientific understanding. That can be remedied by resort to expert consultants; the panel in the Shrimp-Turtle case used, and the

Appellate Body benefited from, an international group of experts on sea turtles. What is missing and what hired scientific experts cannot transfer to the WTO, is a deeper, intuitive comprehension of environmental policy that comes only with experience. A group of veteran trade experts dealing only sporadically with environmental cases can never develop a robust capacity to judge these policy issues.

Whilst *Shrimp/Turtle* made progress on the GATT environmental exceptions, another environmentally important, and controversial, issue was not challenged. As stated above (p. 272), under the GATT, less favourable treatment of 'like' products is prima facie not permissible, whilst, if products are not alike, one would not necessarily expect them to be treated in similar ways. This appears in various parts of the GATT and associated agreements. The starting point for determining whether products are alike is the *Tuna/Dolphin* dispute.[19] The USA had sought to reduce dolphin death in tuna fisheries by prohibiting the import of tuna from countries that did not require the use of 'dolphin friendly' fishing methods. This decision established that the 'likeness' of products must be assessed on the basis of the characteristic of the product itself, rather than the way it is made – in the jargon, 'process and production methods' (PPMs). A trade measure distinguishing between domestic and imported goods on the basis of the way they are harvested (e.g. in a 'dolphin friendly' manner or not) constitutes different treatment for 'like products', and so is prima facie unlawful, requiring exception under Art. XX. However, establishing whether products are alike is not a simple mechanical exercise, and the narrow approach has been subject to considerable criticism, both in respect of its effect (the environmental impact of a product is very often in the way it is made, rather than in its physical characteristics once manufactured), and in respect of the legal reasoning that led to the conclusion.[20]

The subject of 'like' products will be one of the more difficult legal questions in respect of eventual WTO treatment of EU regulation of GMOs[21] (albeit not considered in the *EC-biotech* Panel Report). A range of obligations apply to imports of GMOs, which do not apply to conventional counterparts. Even whether GM maize differs from conventional maize will be controversial; foods 'containing or consisting of' GMOs, similarly. The application of the EC legislation to products produced *from* GMOs is more clearly concerned with PPMs, as there need be no GM material in the actual product to which the legislation

---

[19] *United States Restrictions on Imports of Tuna* (1992) 30 ILM 1598 (*Tuna/Dolphin* I); *United States Restrictions on Imports of Tuna* (1994) 33 ILM 839 (*Tuna/Dolphin* II). These reports were never adopted by the GATT membership. Before 1994 and the WTO Dispute Settlement Understanding, panel rulings had to be adopted before they became binding; adoption now is automatic unless the WTO membership votes unanimously to block the adoption.

[20] Robert Howse and Donald Regan, 'The Product/Process Distinction – An Illusory Basis for Disciplining "Unilateralism" in Trade Policy' (2000) 11 *European Journal of International Law* 249; for criticism, see John H. Jackson, 'Comments on the Shrimp/Turtle and the Product/Process Distinction' (2000) 11 *European Journal of International Law* 303.

[21] Scott, 'European Regulation of GMOs'.

is applied. Although PPMs were not at issue, the question of 'like' products has been reopened by the Appellate Body Report in *Asbestos*.

### *Asbestos*

99. As products that are in a competitive relationship in the marketplace could be affected through treatment of *imports* 'less favourable' than the treatment accorded to *domestic* products, it follows that the word 'like' in Article III:4 is to be interpreted to apply to products that are in such a competitive relationship. Thus, a determination of 'likeness' under Article III:4 is, fundamentally, a determination about the nature and extent of a competitive relationship between and among products. In saying this, we are mindful that there is a spectrum of degrees of 'competitiveness' or 'substitutability' of products in the marketplace, and that it is difficult, if not impossible, in the abstract, to indicate precisely where on this spectrum the word 'like' in Article III:4 of the GATT 1994 falls. We are not saying that *all* products which are in *some* competitive relationship are 'like products' under Article III:4. In ruling on the measure at issue, we also do not attempt to define the precise scope of the word 'like' in Article III:4 …

…

113. The European Communities argues that the inquiry into the physical properties of products must include a consideration of the risks posed by the product to human health. In examining the physical properties of the product at issue in this dispute, the Panel found that 'it was not appropriate to apply the "risk" criterion proposed by the EC'. The Panel said that to do so 'would largely nullify the effect of Article XX(b)' of the GATT 1994. In reviewing this finding by the Panel, we note that neither the text of Article III:4 nor the practice of panels and the Appellate Body suggest that any evidence should be excluded *a priori* from a panel's examination of 'likeness'. Moreover, as we have said, in examining the 'likeness' of products, panels must evaluate *all* of the relevant evidence. We are very much of the view that evidence relating to the health risks associated with a product may be pertinent in an examination of 'likeness' under Article III:4 of the GATT 1994. We do not, however, consider that the evidence relating to the health risks associated with chrysotile asbestos fibres need be examined under a *separate* criterion, because we believe that this evidence can be evaluated under the existing criteria of physical properties, and of consumers' tastes and habits, to which we will come below.

114. Panels must examine fully the physical properties of products. In particular, panels must examine those physical properties of products that are likely to influence the competitive relationship between products in the marketplace. In the case of chrysotile asbestos fibres, their molecular structure, chemical composition, and fibrillation capacity are important because the microscopic particles and filaments of chrysotile asbestos fibres are carcinogenic in humans, following inhalation … This carcinogenicity, or toxicity, constitutes, as we see it, a defining aspect of the physical properties of chrysotile asbestos fibres. The evidence indicates that PCG [an alternative to asbestos] fibres, in contrast, do not share these properties, at least to the same extent. We do not see how this highly significant physical difference *cannot* be a consideration in examining the physical properties of a product as part of a determination of 'likeness' under Article III:4 of the GATT 1994.

This Report makes no mention of process and production methods (PPMs), but arguably, by suggesting a broader approach to 'like products' in the future,[22] makes way for a reassessment of the issue. Indeed, it arguably moves towards the position of those who criticise the more traditional *Tuna/Dolphin* approach on the basis that 'in the context of a discussion of discrimination, what "like" standardly means is something like "not differing in any way which justifies different treatment"'.[23] In any event, the reference to 'consumer tastes and habits' in *Asbestos* is potentially important. Returning to any future considera-tion of GMO regulation, the distinctions drawn by consumers (or the public more generally?) between GM and non-GM products, whilst no doubt difficult to establish and possibly open to manipulation, could be a powerful way of distinguishing between products for the purposes of regulation. The *EC-biotech* Panel did not consider the question of 'likeness'. The following, taken from a third party brief submitted to the Panel by a group of academics specialising in the study of science, technology and society, suggests a flexible approach.

### Lawrence Busch, Robin Grove-White, Sheila Jasanoff, David Winickoff and Brian Wynne, *Amicus Curiae Brief Submitted to the Dispute Settlement Panel of the World Trade Organization in the Case of EC: Measures Affecting the Approval and Marketing of Biotech Products*, http://csec.lancs.ac.uk/wtoamicus/index.htm, pp. 27–9

#### a. 'Properties, nature and qualities'

GMO and non-GMO products differ in 'Properties, Nature, Qualities' as the WTO has defined them. In the *Hormones* case, the Appellate Body held that there might be a range of reasons why risks inherent in nature in the absence of any human intervention might call for a lower level of protection than risks produced or exacerbated by human intervention. Breeding agri-cultural products using recombinant DNA (rDNA) techniques can be said to introduce at least four categorical and qualitative differences between GM and conventionally bred products:

1. Adaptive traits can be leap-frogged over vast phylogenetic distances to form radically new combinations of competitive features;

2. Sexual reproduction and traditional breeding are largely limited to exchanges of alleles (which are variants of genes), and exchanges typically demand substitutions and adaptive trade offs and compromises, but with rDNA this class of exchange-based trade-offs can be circumvented;

3. Sexual reproduction and traditional breeding cannot normally reprogram the large frac-tion of genomes that are functionally homozygous. But rDNA holds the potential to repro-gram fundamentally important genetic programs that are normally protected against change;

4. Transgenes often have unusual genetic side effects, apparently when a host organism's editing and buffering systems do not recognize them and cannot correct or control them properly.

---

[22] *Ibid.*      [23] Howse and Regan, 'Product/Process Distinction', pp. 260–1.

Such differences pose special challenges for risk regulation. In the words of trade scholars Howse and Mavroidis,

> genetic engineering removes or alters many restraints or controls that limit variation in nature, resulting in a vast potential expansion of variants and the speed at which they occur. Reliance on long-acquired general knowledge of the properties of non-genetically modified foods might be reasonable given the EU's level of protection, whereas a requirement that specific investigation be undertaken with respect to GMOs may also be reasonable, given the same level of protection, in light of the greater degree of uncertainty and relative speed at which new organisms with unknown risk properties relative to specific ecosystems can be created.[24]

**b. 'Consumer attitudes and perception'**

The case for finding a difference between GM and non-GM foodstuffs is even stronger when one considers the outpouring of consumer activity on behalf of such differentiation, both in Europe and the United States. In the EU, publics have shown strong resistance to using GM products. They have determined, after ample public information and debate, that GM crops and foods should require special regulatory treatment.

The health impact of asbestos is clearly relevant to the likeness of products, but the Report is ambiguous as to whether it is relevant in its own right or because of its impact on the market.[25] Both health impact and market impact were better established in the *Asbestos* dispute than they might be in future cases. *Asbestos* addresses consumer differentiation around a product notorious for its carcinogenic properties. Consumer views of GMOs may rest on broader public values and on complex uncertainties as much as on scientific evidence, and this takes us into rather different territory.

### (ii) Science and risk in the WTO

The GATT is no longer the sole consideration in trade and environment disputes, and, especially when we consider health impacts, we should look also at the 1994 SPS Agreement. Whilst providing certain incentives for reliance on internationally agreed standards (pp. 312–13, below), the SPS Agreement confirms that members of the WTO may set their own standards for sanitary and phytosanitary protection (protection of animal, plant or human life and health, and targeting of other damage caused by pests). This autonomy is subject to conditions, to be discussed below. The SPS Agreement deepens and extends the reach of the WTO into domestic regulation of health and safety issues. The Agreement on Technical Barriers to Trade (the TBT Agreement), entered into at the same time as the SPS Agreement, applies basic 'like treatment' and 'most favoured nation' principles to 'technical regulations and

---

[24] Howse and Mavroidis, 'Evolving Regulatory Strategy for GMOs'.

[25] The Appellate Body hints that health risks which do not affect consumer tastes and habits may not enter into the consideration of 'like' products, see para. 122.

standards'.[26] Like the SPS Agreement, it is a complex document, but the Appellate Body has so far had little opportunity to discuss it.[27]

Both Agreements have the potential to be significant in environmental disputes. Here we will concentrate on the SPS Agreement, which brings out nicely some of the issues we focus on in this book: in particular, it is through this Agreement that the WTO most directly addresses the question of the role of science in decision making on public health (raising very similar issues to environmental decision making, discussed in detail in Chapters 1 and 3).

All three of the contested elements of the EU approach to GMOs (see p. 266, above) between 1998 and 2003 were found by the *EC-biotech* Panel to fall under the SPS Agreement. 'SPS' measures, and hence the scope of the Agreement, are defined broadly by the Panel; importantly, for example, an environmental objective does not exclude the application of the SPS Agreement to the extent that an environmental measure aims to protect animals or plants (or presumably humans) (para. 7.203). Each challenged element was found to have violated the Agreement. We will return to the Panel's treatment of national safeguard measures, but begin with the general de facto moratorium, which was characterised as a 'procedural decision to delay final substantive approval decisions', rather than a substantive decision; a similar approach was taken to the application of the moratorium to individual GMOs. As such, the moratorium was not considered under the provisions of the SPS Agreement dealing with risk assessment, to which we turn below. However, the Panel determined that the moratorium breached the requirement in Annex C (necessary under Art. 8), that procedures be 'undertaken and completed without undue delay'.

### *EC - Measures affecting Biotech products* DS291, 292, 293, 26 September 2006

7.1496 ... what matters is whether there is a legitimate reason, or justification, for a given delay, not the length of a delay as such. Accordingly, if a Member causes a relatively short, but unjustifiable delay, we do not consider that the mere fact that the delay is relatively short would, or should, preclude a panel from finding that it is 'undue'. Similarly, we do not consider that a demonstration that a particular approval procedure has been delayed by,

---

[26] A Technical Regulation is a 'Document which lays down product characteristics or their related processes and production methods, including the applicable administrative provisions, with which compliance is mandatory. It may also include or deal exclusively with terminology, symbols, packaging, marking or labeling requirements as they apply to a product, process or production method.' A Standard is a 'Document approved by a recognized body, that provides, for common and repeated use, rules, guidelines or characteristics for products or related processes and production methods, with which compliance is not mandatory. It may also include or deal exclusively with terminology, symbols, packaging, marking or labeling requirements as they apply to a product, process or production method.' Annex I.

[27] See *European Communities – Trade Description of Sardines* WT/DS231/AB/R, 26 September 2002.

say, two years would always and necessarily be sufficient to establish that the relevant procedure has been 'unduly' delayed. Having said this, we note that a lengthy delay for which no adequate explanation is provided might in some circumstances permit the inference that the delay is 'undue'.

7.1497 In our view, a determination of whether a particular approval procedure has been undertaken and/or completed 'without undue delay' must be made on a case-by-case basis, taking account of relevant facts and circumstances. We therefore consider that it would be neither possible nor useful to attempt to define the reasons which would render a given delay 'undue', and those which would not render it 'undue'. Nevertheless, it may be noted that a Member is not legally responsible for delays which are not attributable to it ...

7.1498 ... we view Annex C(1)(a), first clause, essentially as a good faith obligation requiring Members to proceed with their approval procedures as promptly as possible, taking account of the need to check and ensure the fulfilment of their relevant SPS requirements ...

The Panel held that the moratorium did constitute an undue delay. It rejected the EC's argument that its need for legislation on labelling and traceability justified the delay whilst such measures were passed. The EC also attempted to justify the delay by arguing that there was no 'moratorium', but rather that because 'the underlying science is still in a great state of flux, it has chosen to apply a prudent and precautionary approach to identifying, assessing and managing risks to human health and the environment' (para. 7.1514). This question of the impact of problematic scientific evidence goes to the heart of the EC's defence of its position on GMOs. The Panel rejected this approach:

7.1526 ... evolving science, scientific complexity and uncertainty, and limited available scientific information or data are not, in and of themselves, grounds for delaying substantive approval decisions, and ... the SPS Agreement does not envisage that Members in such cases defer making substantive SPS decisions. Indeed, even in cases where relevant scientific evidence does not permit the performance of a risk assessment, the SPS Agreement envisages that Members take substantive SPS decisions. Certainly, such factors as evolving science and limited availability of scientific evidence affect the confidence which Members can have in the results of their assessments. But they do not inherently affect a Member's ability to reach substantive decisions on an application, particularly since a Member may take account of such factors in reaching substantive decisions.

7.1527 ... It is important to note in this regard that the SPS Agreement nowhere states that substantive decisions on applications need to give a straight yes or no answer to applicants. Members may in principle grant time-limited approvals or approvals subject to other appropriate conditions. Alternatively, they may in principle decide to reject an application subject to the possibility of a review of that decision if and when relevant circumstances change. Relevant circumstances could include the state of scientific knowledge. Thus, there is no reason to consider that our interpretation of Annex C(1)(a), first clause, would prejudice Members' ability to take differentiated, proportionate action to protect human health and/or the environment from potential risks arising from GMOs or GMO-derived products.

Importantly, however, the Panel emphasised that it is not saying 'that it would under no circumstances be justifiable … to delay the completion of approval procedures by imposing a general moratorium on final approvals of biotech products. We consider that there may conceivably be circumstances where this could be justifiable' (para. 7.1525). Those circumstances may include in certain cases the consideration of new scientific evidence that conflicts with available scientific evidence and which is directly relevant to *all* biotech products subject to a pre-marketing approval requirement.

Whilst the EC's defence of its 'moratorium' did raise numerous questions around the scientific complexity of the products at issue, the Panel did not dwell on the issue of science and risk assessment at this point. These topics are, however, at the heart of the SPS Agreement.

## SPS Agreement

*Article 2*
*Basic Rights and Obligations*
1. Members have the right to take sanitary and phytosanitary measures necessary for the protection of human, animal or plant life or health, provided that such measures are not inconsistent with the provisions of this Agreement.
2. Members shall ensure that any sanitary or phytosanitary measure is applied only to the extent necessary to protect human, animal or plant life or health, is based on scientific principles and is not maintained without sufficient scientific evidence, except as provided for in paragraph 7 of Article 5.
3. Members shall ensure that their sanitary and phytosanitary measures do not arbitrarily or unjustifiably discriminate between Members where identical or similar conditions prevail, including between their own territory and that of other Members. Sanitary and phytosanitary measures shall not be applied in a manner which would constitute a disguised restriction on international trade.
4. Sanitary or phytosanitary measures which conform to the relevant provisions of this Agreement shall be presumed to be in accordance with the obligations of the Members under the provisions of GATT 1994 which relate to the use of sanitary or phytosanitary measures, in particular the provisions of Article XX(b).

…

*Article 5*
*Assessment of Risk and Determination of the Appropriate Level of Sanitary or Phytosanitary Protection*
1. Members shall ensure that their sanitary or phytosanitary measures are based on an assessment, as appropriate to the circumstances, of the risks to human, animal or plant life

or health, taking into account risk assessment techniques developed by the relevant international organizations.

2. In the assessment of risks, Members shall take into account available scientific evidence; relevant processes and production methods; relevant inspection, sampling and testing methods; prevalence of specific diseases or pests; existence of pest- or disease-free areas; relevant ecological and environmental conditions; and quarantine or other treatment.

3. In assessing the risk to animal or plant life or health and determining the measure to be applied for achieving the appropriate level of sanitary or phytosanitary protection from such risk, Members shall take into account as relevant economic factors: the potential damage in terms of loss of production or sales in the event of the entry, establishment or spread of a pest or disease; the costs of control or eradication in the territory of the importing Member; and the relative cost-effectiveness of alternative approaches to limiting risks.

4. Members should, when determining the appropriate level of sanitary or phytosanitary protection, take into account the objective of minimizing negative trade effects.

5. With the objective of achieving consistency in the application of the concept of appropriate level of sanitary or phytosanitary protection against risks to human life or health, or to animal and plant life or health, each Member shall avoid arbitrary or unjustifiable distinctions in the levels it considers to be appropriate in different situations, if such distinctions result in discrimination or a disguised restriction on international trade. Members shall cooperate in the Committee, in accordance with paragraphs 1, 2 and 3 of Article 12, to develop guidelines to further the practical implementation of this provision. In developing the guidelines, the Committee shall take into account all relevant factors, including the exceptional character of human health risks to which people voluntarily expose themselves.

6. Without prejudice to paragraph 2 of Article 3, when establishing or maintaining sanitary or phytosanitary measures to achieve the appropriate level of sanitary or phytosanitary protection, Members shall ensure that such measures are not more trade-restrictive than required to achieve their appropriate level of sanitary or phytosanitary protection, taking into account technical and economic feasibility.

7. In cases where relevant scientific evidence is insufficient, a Member may provisionally adopt sanitary or phytosanitary measures on the basis of available pertinent information, including that from the relevant international organizations as well as from sanitary or phytosanitary measures applied by other Members. In such circumstances, Members shall seek to obtain the additional information necessary for a more objective assessment of risk and review the sanitary or phytosanitary measure accordingly within a reasonable period of time.

The *Beef Hormones* dispute is perhaps the best-known SPS decision, and although it has now been joined by other cases with slightly different emphases, it remains instructive of the WTO approach to scientific justification of regulatory measures.

### *Beef Hormones, EC Measures Concerning Meat and Meat Products*
### WT/DS26/AB/R, WT/DS48/AB/R, 16 January 1998

177 ... The requirements of a risk assessment under Article 5.1, as well as of 'sufficient scientific evidence' under Article 2.2, are essential for the maintenance of the delicate and carefully negotiated balance in the *SPS Agreement* between the shared, but sometimes competing, interests of promoting international trade and of protecting the life and health of human beings ...

...

178. We turn to the appeal of European Communities from the Panel's conclusion that, by maintaining SPS measures which are not based on a risk assessment, the European Communities acted inconsistently with the requirements contained in Article 5.1 of the *SPS Agreement*.

...

180. At the outset, two preliminary considerations need to be brought out ... Article 2.2 informs Article 5.1: the elements that define the basis obligation set out in Article 2.2 impart meaning to Article 5.1.

181. The second preliminary consideration relates to the Panel's effort to distinguish between 'risk assessment' and 'risk management'. The Panel observed that an assessment of risk is, at least with respect to risks to human life and health, a 'scientific' examination of data and factual studies; it is not, in the view of the Panel, a 'policy' exercise involving social value judgments made by political bodies. The Panel describes the latter as 'non-scientific' and as pertaining to 'risk management' rather than to 'risk assessment'. We must stress, in this connection, that Article 5 and Annex A of the *SPS Agreement* speak of 'risk assessment' only and that the term 'risk management' is not to be found either in Article 5 or in any other provision of the *SPS Agreement*. Thus, the Panel's distinction, which it apparently employs to achieve or support what appears to be a restrictive notion of risk assessment, has no textual basis. The fundamental rule of treaty interpretation requires a treaty interpreter to read and interpret the words actually used by the agreement under examination, and not words which the interpreter may feel should have been used.

...

186 ... We agree with the Panel that ... theoretical uncertainty is not the kind of risk which, under Article 5.1, is to be assessed. In another part of its Reports, however, the Panel appeared to be using the term 'scientifically identified risk' to prescribe implicitly that a certain *magnitude* or threshold level of risk be demonstrated in a risk assessment if an SPS measure based thereon is to be regarded as consistent with Article 5.1. To the extent that the Panel purported to require a risk assessment to establish a minimum magnitude of risk, we must note that imposition of such a quantitative requirement finds no basis in the *SPS Agreement*. A panel is authorized only to determine whether a given SPS measure is 'based on' a risk assessment. As will be elaborated below, this means that a panel has to determine whether an SPS measure is sufficiently supported or reasonably warranted by the risk assessment.

...

187. Article 5.2 of the *SPS Agreement* provides an indication of the factors that should be taken into account in the assessment of risk ... The listing in Article 5.2 begins with 'available scientific evidence'; this, however, is only the beginning. We note in this connection that the Panel states that, for purposes of the EC measures in dispute, a risk assessment required by Article 5.1 is 'a *scientific* process aimed at establishing the *scientific* basis for the sanitary measure a Member intends to take'. To the extent that the Panel intended to refer to a process characterized by systematic, disciplined and objective enquiry and analysis, that is, a mode of studying and sorting out facts and opinions, the Panel's statement is unexceptionable. However, to the extent that the Panel purports to exclude from the scope of a risk assessment in the sense of Article 5.1, all matters not susceptible of quantitative analysis by the empirical or experimental laboratory methods commonly associated with the physical sciences, we believe that the Panel is in error. Some of the kinds of factors listed in Article 5.2 such as 'relevant processes and production methods' and 'relevant inspection, sampling and testing methods' are not necessarily or wholly susceptible of investigation according to laboratory methods of, for example, biochemistry or pharmacology. Furthermore, there is nothing to indicate that the listing of factors that may be taken into account in a risk assessment of Article 5.2 was intended to be a closed list. It is essential to bear in mind that the risk that is to be evaluated in a risk assessment under Article 5.1 is not only risk ascertainable in a science laboratory operating under strictly controlled conditions, but also risk in human societies as they actually exist, in other words, the actual potential for adverse effects on human health in the real world where people live and work and die.

189 ... We believe that 'based on' is appropriately taken to refer to a certain *objective relationship* between two elements, that is to say, to an *objective situation* that persists and is observable between an SPS measure and a risk assessment ...

190. Article 5.1 does not insist that a Member that adopts a sanitary measure shall have carried out its own risk assessment. It only requires that the SPS measures be 'based on an assessment, as appropriate for the circumstances ...'. The SPS measure might well find its objective justification in a risk assessment carried out by another Member, or an international organization ...

191. In the course of demanding evidence that EC authorities actually 'took into account' certain scientific studies, the Panel refers to the preambles of the EC Directives here involved. The Panel notes that such preambles did not mention any of the scientific studies referred to by the European Communities in the panel proceedings. Preambles of legislative or quasi-legislative acts and administrative regulations commonly fulfil requirements of the internal legal orders of WTO Members. Such preambles are certainly not required by the *SPS Agreement*; they are not normally used to demonstrate that a Member has complied with its obligations under international agreements. The absence of any mention of scientific studies in the preliminary sections of the EC Directive does not, therefore, prove anything so far as the present case is concerned.

193. We consider that, in principle, the Panel's approach examining the scientific conclusions implicit in the SPS measure under consideration and the scientific conclusion yielded by a risk assessment is a useful approach. The relationship between those two sets of conclusions is certainly relevant; they cannot, however, be assigned relevance to the exclusion of

everything else. We believe that Article 5.1, when contextually read as it should be, in conjunction with and as informed by Article 2.2 of the *SPS Agreement*, requires that the results of the risk assessment must sufficiently warrant – that is to say, reasonably support – the SPS measure at stake. The requirement that an SPS measure be 'based on' a risk assessment is a substantive requirement that there be a rational relationship between the measure and the risk assessment.

194. We do not believe that a risk assessment has to come to a monolithic conclusion that coincides with the scientific conclusion or view implicit in the SPS measure. The risk assessment could set out both the prevailing view representing the 'mainstream' of scientific opinion, as well as the opinions of scientists taking a divergent view. Article 5.1 does not require that the risk assessment must necessarily embody only the view of a majority of the relevant scientific community. In some cases, the very existence of divergent views presented by qualified scientists who have investigated the particular issue at hand may indicate a state of scientific uncertainty. Sometimes the divergence may indicate a roughly equal balance of scientific opinion, which may itself be a form of scientific uncertainty. In most cases, responsible and representative governments tend to base their legislative and administrative measures on 'mainstream' scientific opinion. In other cases, equally responsible and representative governments may act in good faith on the basis of what, at a given time, may be a divergent opinion coming from qualified and respected sources. By itself, this does not necessarily signal the absence of a reasonable relationship between the SPS measure and the risk assessment, especially where the risk involved is life-threatening in character and is perceived to constitute a clear and imminent threat to public health and safety. Determination of the presence or absence of that relationship can only be done on a case-to-case basis, after account is taken of all considerations rationally bearing upon the issue of potential adverse health effects.

...

205 ... It should be recalled that Article 5.2 states that in the assessment of risks, Members shall take into account, in addition to 'available scientific evidence', 'relevant processes and production methods; [and] relevant inspection, sampling and testing methods'. We note also that Article 8 requires Members to 'observe the provisions of Annex C in the operation of control, inspection and approval procedures ...'. The footnote in Annex C states that 'control, inspection and approval procedures include, *inter alia*, procedures for sampling, testing and certification'. We consider that this language is amply sufficient to authorize the taking into account of risks arising from failure to comply with the requirements of good veterinary practice in the administration of hormones for growth promotion purposes, as well as risks arising from difficulties of control, inspection and enforcement of the requirements of good veterinary practice.

206. Most, if not all, of the scientific studies referred to by the European Communities, in respect of the five hormones involved here, concluded that their use for growth promotion purposes is 'safe', if the hormones are administered in accordance with the requirements of good veterinary practice. Where the condition of observance of good veterinary practice ... is *not* followed, the logical inference is that the use of such hormones for growth promotion purposes may or may not be 'safe'. The *SPS Agreement* requires assessment of the potential for adverse effects on human health arising from the presence of contaminants and toxins in food. We consider that the object and purpose of the *SPS Agreement* justify the

examination and evaluation of all such risks for human health whatever their precise and immediate origin may be. We do not mean to suggest that risks arising from potential abuse in the administration of controlled substances and from control problems need to be, or should be, evaluated by risk assessors in each and every case. When and if risks of these types do in fact arise, risk assessors may examine and evaluate them. Clearly, the necessity or propriety of examination and evaluation of such risks would have to be addressed on a case-by-case basis.

207. The question that arises, therefore, is whether the European Communities did, in fact, submit a risk assessment demonstrating and evaluating the existence and level of risk arising in the present case from abusive use of hormones and the difficulties of control of the administration of hormones for growth promotion purposes, within the United States and Canada as exporting countries, and at the frontiers of the European Communities as an importing country. Here, we must agree with the finding of the Panel that the European Communities in fact restricted itself to pointing out the condition of administration of hormones 'in accordance with good practice' 'without further providing an assessment of the potential adverse effects related to non compliance with such practice' …

208. In the absence of any other relevant documentation, we find that the European Communities did not actually proceed to an assessment, within the meaning of Articles 5.1 and 5.2, of the risks arising from the failure of observance of good veterinary practice combined with problems of control of the use of hormones for growth promotion purposes. The absence of such a risk assessment, when considered in conjunction with the conclusion actually reached by most, if not all, of the scientific studies relating to the other aspects of risk noted earlier, leads us to the conclusion that no risk assessment that reasonably supports or warrants the import prohibition embodied in the EC Directives was furnished to the Panel. We affirm, therefore, the ultimate conclusion of the Panel that the EC import prohibition is not based on a risk assessment within the meaning of Articles 5.1 and 5.2 of the *SPS Agreement* and is, therefore, inconsistent with the requirements of Article 5.1.

*Beef Hormones* is the key reference point for establishing the scientific framework within which the WTO regime operates. Verdicts on *Beef Hormones* have been mixed,[28] and indeed it attempts a very fine balance between relying on the 'objectivity' of science to police trade protectionism, and respect for domestic regulatory decisions. There are significant openings in the Report for a nuanced approach to risk regulation: the evaluation of likelihood or probability need not lead to a quantitative evaluation (para. 186); the evidence does not have to be 'monolithic' (para. 194), so measures can be taken when opinions diverge or are

[28] See, for example, Robert Howse, 'Democracy, Science and Free Trade: Risk Regulation on Trial at the World Trade Organisation' (2000) 98 *Michigan Law Review* 2329; Joanne Scott, 'On Kith and Kine: Trade and Environment in the EU and WTO' in Joseph H. H. Weiler (ed.), *The EU, WTO and NAFTA: Towards a Common Law of International Trade* (Oxford University Press, 2000); Vern R. Walker, 'Keeping the WTO from Becoming the "World Trans-Science Organization": Scientific Uncertainty, Science Policy, and Factfinding in the Growth Hormones Dispute' (1998) 31 *Cornell International Law Journal* 251.

uncertain; indeterminacy of effects is acknowledged, by reference to effects in the 'real world' (para. 188), rather than in the laboratory; and a strict distinction between risk assessment and risk management is rejected (para. 181), avoiding narrowing down the exercise required under the Agreement.

Notwithstanding the broad approach to the language of the Agreement, the mandatory nature of scientific risk assessment (directed to the measure at issue[29]), and the willingness of the Appellate Body to examine the detail of risk assessments relied on by members, are inescapable. Nor is there any sophisticated analysis of the limitations of science in risk regulation, which are especially compelling in respect of the *low* risks from long exposure at issue in *Beef Hormones*. If anything, these concerns are reinforced by more recent disputes. The 'rational relationship' between risk assessment and measure has been fleshed out, and it has become clear that the *possibility* of harm is not a sufficient basis for protective measures: likelihood or probability has to be evaluated, and '*some* evaluation of the likelihood or probability' does not suffice.[30] And apparently the absence of a relationship between measures taken and risk assessment can in appropriate cases be demonstrated by a 'clear disproportion' between 'negligible' risk and measure taken.[31] This proportionality type review could, if pursued, allow the WTO (and science) very far into the assessment of domestic risk regulation. It may raise some questions about the confirmation in *Asbestos* that a WTO member may choose to reduce a risk to zero (para. 168 – above, p. 273), and take measures accordingly.[32] Proportionality review suggests that this will be legitimate only if the measure and risk are in tandem – so the nature of the risk is serious (as in *Asbestos*), or the measures are not.

The extent to which the precautionary principle (Chapter 1, pp. 18–31) softens an assumption that only the 'facts', scientifically established, can justify trade measures is a question left unanswered by *Beef Hormones*. A version of the precautionary principle can be found in Art. 5.7 of the SPS Agreement (p. 287), although *Beef Hormones* indicates that this may not 'exhaust' the relevance of the precautionary principle.

### *Beef Hormones*

123. The status of the precautionary principle in international law continues to be the subject of debate among academics, law practitioners, regulators and judges. The precautionary principle is regarded by some as having crystallized into a general principle of customary international *environmental* law. Whether it has been widely accepted by Members

---

[29] *Australia – Measures Affecting Importation of Salmon* WT/DS18/AB/R, 20 October 1998; *Japan – Measures Affecting the Importation of Apples* WT/DS245/AB/R, 26 November 2003.

[30] *Salmon*, paras. 123–4.

[31] *Japan – Apples*, paras. 163–8. The appropriate approach depends on the particular case – see especially para. 164.

[32] Although *Asbestos* is a dispute under the GATT, not the SPS Agreement.

as a principle of *general* or *customary international law* appears less than clear. We consider, however, that it is unnecessary, and probably imprudent, for the Appellate Body in this appeal to take a position on this important, but abstract, question ... the precautionary principle, at least outside the field of international environmental law, still awaits authoritative formulation.

124. It appears to us important, nevertheless, to note some aspects of the relationship of the precautionary principle to the *SPS Agreement*. First, the principle has not been written into the *SPS Agreement* as a ground for justifying SPS measures that are otherwise inconsistent with the obligations of Members set out in particular provisions of that Agreement. Secondly, the precautionary principle indeed finds reflection in Article 5.7 of the *SPS Agreement*. We agree, at the same time, with the European Communities, that there is no need to assume that Article 5.7 exhausts the relevance of a precautionary principle. It is reflected also in the sixth paragraph of the preamble and in Article 3.3. These explicitly recognize the right of members to establish their own appropriate level of sanitary protection, which level may be higher (i.e., more cautious) than that implied in existing international standards, guidelines and recommendations. Thirdly, a panel charged with determining, for instance, whether 'sufficient scientific evidence' exists to warrant the maintenance by a Member of a particular SPS measure may, of course, and should, bear in mind that responsible, representative governments commonly act from perspectives of prudence and precaution where risks of irreversible, e.g. life-terminating, damage to human health are concerned. Lastly, however, the precautionary principle does not, by itself, and without a clear textual directive to that effect, relieve a panel from the duty of applying the normal (i.e. customary international law) principles of treaty interpretation in reading the provisions of the *SPS Agreement*.

If the precautionary principle were a recognised principle of international law, it would have to be taken into account in the interpretation of international treaties, including the GATT and the SPS Agreement, regardless of Art. 5.7. After citing precisely these two paragraphs of *Beef Hormones*, the Panel in *EC-biotech* observes that 'the legal debate over whether the precautionary principle constitutes a recognized principle of general or customary international law is still ongoing' (para. 7.88):

> Since the legal status of the precautionary principle remains unsettled, like the Appellate Body before us, we consider that prudence suggests that we not attempt to resolve this complex issue, particularly if it is not necessary to do so. Our analysis below makes clear that for the purposes of disposing of the legal claims before us, we need not take a position on whether or not the precautionary principle is a recognized principle of general or customary international law. Therefore, we refrain from expressing a view on this issue. (para. 7.89)

The Appellate Body has, however, considered Art. 5.7 since *Beef Hormones*. *Japan – Apples* was a dispute over requirements and prohibitions imposed by Japan on the importation of apples from the United States, designed to prevent the entry into Japan of the 'fire blight' pest.

## *Japan – Measures Affecting the Importation of Apples*
## WT/DS245/AB/R, 26 November 2003

176. In *Japan – Agricultural Products II* [below, p. 295], the Appellate Body stated that Article 5.7 sets out four requirements that must be satisfied in order to adopt and maintain a provisional phytosanitary measure. These requirements are:

(i)   the measure is imposed in respect of a situation where 'relevant scientific evidence is insufficient';

(ii)  the measure is adopted 'on the basis of available pertinent information';

(iii) the Member which adopted the measure 'seek[s] to obtain the additional information necessary for a more objective assessment of risk'; and

(iv)  the Member which adopted the measure 'review[s] the ... measure accordingly within a reasonable period of time'.

These four requirements are 'clearly cumulative in nature'; as the Appellate Body said in *Japan – Agricultural Products II*, '[w]henever *one* of these four requirements is not met, the measure at issue is inconsistent with Article 5.7'.

...

179 ... The first requirement of Article 5.7 is that there must be insufficient scientific evidence. When a panel reviews a measure claimed by a Member to be provisional, that panel must assess whether 'relevant scientific evidence is insufficient'. This evaluation must be carried out, not in the abstract, but in the light of a particular inquiry ...

...

182. These findings of fact by the Panel suggest that the body of available scientific evidence permitted, in quantitative and qualitative terms, the performance of an assessment of risks, as required under Article 5.1 and as defined in Annex A to the *SPS Agreement*, with respect to the risk of transmission of fire blight through apple fruit exported from the United States to Japan. In particular, according to these findings of fact by the Panel, the body of available scientific evidence would allow '[t]he evaluation of the likelihood of entry, establishment or spread' of fire blight in Japan through apples exported from the United States. Accordingly, in the light of the findings of fact made by the Panel, we conclude that, with respect to the risk of transmission of fire blight through apple fruit exported from the United States to Japan ('normally', mature, symptomless apples), the 'relevant scientific evidence' is not 'insufficient' within the meaning of Article 5.7.

...

183 ... Japan draws a distinction between 'new uncertainty' and 'unresolved uncertainty', arguing that both fall within Article 5.7. According to Japan, 'new uncertainty' arises when a new risk is identified; Japan argues that the Panel's characterization that 'little, or no, reliable evidence was available on the subject matter at issue' is relevant to a situation of 'new uncertainty'. We understand that Japan defines 'unresolved uncertainty' as uncertainty that the scientific evidence is not able to resolve, despite accumulated scientific evidence ...

184. We disagree with Japan. The application of Article 5.7 is triggered not by the existence of scientific uncertainty, but rather by the insufficiency of scientific evidence. The text of Article 5.7 is clear: it refers to 'cases where relevant scientific evidence is insufficient', not to 'scientific uncertainty'. The two concepts are not interchangeable. Therefore, we are unable to endorse Japan's approach of interpreting Article 5.7 through the prism of 'scientific uncertainty'.

185. We also find no basis for Japan's argument that the Panel's interpretation of Article 5.7 is too narrow for the reason that it excludes cases where the quantity of evidence on a phytosanitary question is 'more than little', but the available scientific evidence has not resolved the question. The Panel's statement that Article 5.7 is intended to address 'situations where little, or no, reliable evidence was available on the subject matter at issue', refers to the availability of *reliable* evidence. We do not read the Panel's interpretation as excluding cases where the available evidence is more than minimal in quantity, but has not led to reliable or conclusive results.

This passage considers especially the first of the four cumulative requirements set out in para. 176, a subject considered also in *EC-biotech* (below, pp. 296–300). The provisional nature of precautionary measures arises in the third and fourth criteria, and is discussed in an earlier dispute. In this case, Japan had required importers to establish the efficacy of quarantine treatment for each variety of certain agricultural products.

### *Japan – Measures Affecting Agricultural Products* WT/DS76/AB/R, 22 February 1999

92 … Article 5.7 states that the additional information is to be sought in order to allow the Member to conduct 'a more objective assessment of risk'. Therefore, the information sought must be germane to conducting such a risk assessment, i.e., the evaluation of the likelihood of entry, establishment or spread of, *in casu*, a pest, according to the SPS measures which might be applied. We note that the Panel found that the information collected by Japan does not 'examine the appropriateness' of the SPS measure at issue and does not address the core issue as to whether 'varietal characteristics cause a divergency in quarantine efficacy'. In the light of this finding, we agree with the Panel that Japan did not seek to obtain the additional information necessary for a more objective risk assessment.

93. The second part of the second sentence of Article 5.7 stipulates that the Member adopting a provisional SPS measure shall 'review the … measure accordingly within a reasonable period of time'. In our view, what constitutes a 'reasonable period of time' has to be established on a case-by-case basis and depends on the specific circumstances of each case, including the difficulty of obtaining the additional information necessary for the review *and* the characteristics of the provisional SPS measure. In the present case, the Panel found that collecting the necessary additional information would be relatively easy. Although the obligation 'to review' the varietal testing requirement has only been in existence since 1 January 1995, we agree with the Panel that Japan has not reviewed its varietal testing requirement 'within a reasonable period of time'.

Notwithstanding the openness of elements of the system under decisions like *Beef Hormones*, when one considers the dilemmas discussed in Chapter 1 above (pp. 18–31), the Appellate Body has so far taken a narrow approach to the precautionary principle, ignoring the complexity and nature of scientific uncertainties. Although 'insufficiency' has qualitative as well as quantitative aspects, and as such looks rather similar to 'uncertainty', the Appellate Body's denial that 'uncertainty' is even the issue suggests an expectation that *more* or *better* ('sufficient') science will ultimately fill in the gaps and establish the 'facts'. The tension between the *limitations* of science and its *necessity* seems to disappear. This concern is reinforced by the approach of the *EC-biotech* Panel. The closest examination of risk and science in *EC-biotech* takes place in the context of national safeguard measures. Once a GMO has been approved for Community-wide marketing, Member States ordinarily may not restrict trade in, or use of, that product. Under the 2001 Directive,[33] a Member State can provisionally restrict or prohibit a GMO where 'as a result of new or additional information made available since the date of the consent and affecting the environmental risk assessment or reassessment of existing information on the basis of new or additional scientific knowledge', a Member State has 'detailed grounds for considering that a GMO as or in a product ... constitutes a risk to human health or the environment'. Safeguard measures are supposed to be provisional, pending full assessment at EC level: the Commission and other Member States must be informed of a safeguard measure, and the Commission (through the 'comitology' process, so with the assistance of a regulatory committee and the backstop of a Council decision: see Chapter 5, pp. 193–6) must take a decision with respect to that measure, leading to either the modification of the Community-wide marketing approval, or the termination of the safeguard measure.

The Panel dealt with each of the challenged safeguard measures individually. It found that safeguard measures taken by some Member States were inconsistent with the obligation that SPS measures be 'based on' risk assessment (Art. 5.1 – above, p. 286). The following is just one example of the Panel's approach, in respect of the Panel's treatment of the Austrian safeguard measure prohibiting T25 maize. Austria was arguing that the safeguard measure aimed at the protection of the environment and human health.

> 7.3042 The Hoppichler study [Concepts of GMO-Free Environmentally Sensitive Areas] focuses on the protection of environmentally-sensitive areas. Based on the evidence submitted to us, we understand that Austria is seeking to prevent the cultivation and other uses of GMOs on its territory due to possible long-term ecological risks associated with GMOs, particularly in fragile areas. In addition, the study argues that 'multiple releases and the marketing of GMOs are irreversible processes, and ... products of organic agriculture will also contain GMOs even if they are produced strictly on the basis of organic guidelines'.

[33] Directive 2001/18 on the Deliberate Release into the Environment of Genetically Modified Organisms and Repealing Council Directive 90/220/EEC OJ 2001 L 106/1.

7.3043 In considering the Hoppichler study, we recall that the Commission requested the SCP [EU level Scientific Committee for Plants] to analyse the information provided by Austria, including the aforementioned study, in order to determine whether this information may '- constitute relevant scientific evidence, which would cause the SCP to consider that this product constitutes a risk to human health and the environment'. In response, the SCP prepared an opinion which notes that the Hoppichler study 'does not contain any new scientific information which is relevant to the original scientific risk assessment that [the SCP] published in 1998. Rather the document contains arguments for the establishment of GMO-free environmentally-sensitive areas and summarises surveyed opinions of people who may be confronted professionally with any environmental effects of the release of GMOs.' We understand this statement to indicate that the SCP did not view this study as a risk assessment.

7.3044 We also note that the Hoppichler study does not indicate relative probability of the potential risks it identifies, but rather makes reference to possibilities of risks or simply to the inability to determine probabilities. For example, the document states that 'there are possibilities of direct risks which can be assessed within some limits according to the status of science and technology'. In addition, the study cites two analyses regarding environmental risk assessment of releasing GMOs. A quote from the first analysis indicates that 'the ecological impact of transgenic grasses may be pervasive' (emphasis added). The second analysis is said to demonstrate that 'the contamination of natural gene pools through synthetic genes is incalculable in principle in predictive risk assessment'. This statement highlights the lack of estimated risk associated with gene flow from GMOs.

7.3045 Regarding these references to possibilities of risks, we recall that the Appellate Body in Australia – Salmon stated that:

> '[I]t is not sufficient that a risk assessment conclude that there is a possibility of entry, establishment or spread of diseases and associated biological and economic consequences. A proper risk assessment of this type must evaluate the "likelihood" i.e., the "probability", of entry, establishment or spread of diseases and associated biological and economic consequences.'

7.3046 Given the lack of evaluation of likelihood in the Hoppichler study, we consider that the study does not meet the definition of a risk assessment as provided in Annex A(4), and therefore does not constitute a risk assessment within the meaning of Annex A(4) and Article 5.1.

7.3047 We now turn to determine whether any of the relevant documents relied on by Austria contains a risk assessment with regard to Austria's concerns over the development of antibiotic resistance and allergenicity and toxicity ... to the extent Austria's measure is applied to address such concerns, it falls within the scope of Annex A(1)(b) the SPS Agreement. The second clause of Annex A(4) to the SPS Agreement provides the following definition for the 'risk assessment' to be carried out for measures which have purposes falling within the scope of Annex A(1)(b):

> 'Risk assessment: ... the evaluation of the potential for adverse effects on human or animal health arising from the presence of additives, contaminants, toxins or disease causing organisms in food, beverages or feedstuffs.'

7.3048  We note that, unlike for the definition of risk assessment contained in the first clause of Annex A(4), WTO jurisprudence provides little guidance on the meaning of key concepts contained in the definition provided in the second clause. The Appellate Body merely observed in this respect that the first clause is substantially different from the second clause, and that the second clause requires 'only' the evaluation of the 'potential' for adverse effects on human or animal health arising from the presence of certain substances in foods, whereas the first clause requires an evaluation of the 'likelihood' of entry, establishment or spread of a pest or disease and of the associated biological and economic consequences. We note that the dictionary defines the term 'potential' as 'the possibility of something happening ... in the future'.

7.3049  In this context, one relevant document to be examined is the Austrian study on toxicology and allergology of biotech products of March 2003 ... The objective of the study was to investigate risk assessment practices for food derived from biotech plants, and to make proposals to 'concretise and standardise the toxicological and allergological risk assessment'. We consider that this study evaluates risk assessment procedures, and not the potential for adverse effects on human or animal health arising from the consumption of specific foods containing or consisting of GMOs. We therefore think that the March 2003 study does not meet the definition of a risk assessment as provided in Annex A(4).

So the information relied on by Austria was held by the Panel *not* to be a risk assessment for the purposes of the SPS Agreement. There were, however, risk assessments available for the GMOs subject to safeguard measures by the various Member States: the risk assessments carried out by the national competent authority or relevant EU committee in respect of the initial application for marketing (see Chapter 5, pp. 189–92), or the subsequent EU-level consideration of the safeguard measures. Although each of these was used to justify authorising the GMO in question, the Panel did consider whether they could also be used to justify a restriction on marketing.

### EC-biotech

7.3060  Where a given risk assessment sets out a divergent opinion and this opinion comes from qualified and respected sources, it can be reasonably said that an SPS measure which reflects the divergent opinion is 'based on' the risk assessment in question in as much as the divergent opinion is expressed in that risk assessment. In contrast, where a given risk assessment sets out a single opinion, it cannot be reasonably said that an SPS measure is 'based on' *that* risk assessment if the relevant SPS measure reflects a divergent opinion which is not expressed in the risk assessment in question. *Ex hypothesi*, the opinion expressed in that risk assessment would not 'sufficiently warrant', or 'reasonably support', the SPS measure taken.

7.3061  In the case of the Austrian safeguard measure, the European Communities asserts that new scientific information became available and that this new information justified Austria's differing assessment of the risks. Even assuming this were the case, however, this would not alter the fact that we are unaware of any divergent opinions expressed in the risk assessments ... Therefore, it would be clear that, on the date of establishment of this Panel, Austria's safeguard measure would not have been based on these existing risk assessments, but on its own modified version of these assessments, namely, its divergent assessment.

7.3062 Even if the alleged divergent assessment by Austria in a number of respects did not depart from the existing risk assessments, Austria's safeguard measure could not, for that reason alone, be considered to be based on these risk assessments if these assessments reached a different overall conclusion. To be clear, we are not suggesting that Members cannot rely in part on an existing risk assessment which sets out a single opinion. But to the extent they disagree with some or all of the conclusions contained in such an assessment, it would in our view be necessary for Members to explain, by reference to the existing assessment, how and why they assess the risks differently, and to provide their revised or supplemental assessment of the risks ...

7.3063 ... The second argument of the European Communities is ... that the same risk assessment can 'sufficiently warrant', or 'reasonably support', more than one type of SPS measure, or, as the European Communities puts it, one and the same risk assessment may justify 'divergent responses by equally responsible and representative governments'.

7.3064 As a general matter, the Panel agrees with the European Communities that a particular risk assessment might conceivably serve as a basis for different types of SPS measures. Indeed, there may be a range of measures that may be rationally related to a given risk assessment, at least in cases where a risk is determined to exist. In the present case, the risk assessments conducted by the lead [competent authority] and by the SCP with regard to T25 maize were favourable. These assessments concluded that there was no evidence that T25 maize presents any greater risk to human health or the environment than its conventional (non-biotech) counterpart. Yet, the safeguard measure which Austria allegedly adopted on the basis of these risk assessments provides for a complete prohibition of the product. In our view, the favourable findings of the risk assessments in question do not naturally lead to the conclusion that what is arguably the strictest type of SPS measure, *i.e.*, a complete prohibition, was warranted in Austria's case to protect human health and the environment. To the contrary, these findings strongly suggest that this type of measure was not sufficiently warranted.

7.3065 The European Communities asserts that each of the safeguard measures at issue in this dispute is based on the precautionary principle. We would agree that the fact that a Member has decided to follow a precautionary approach could have a bearing on a panel's assessment of whether an SPS measure is 'based on' a risk assessment as required by Article 5.1. We consider that if there are factors which affect scientists' level of confidence in a risk assessment they have carried out, a Member may in principle take this into account in determining the measure to be applied for achieving its appropriate level of protection from risks. Thus, there may conceivably be cases where a Member which follows a precautionary approach, and which confronts a risk assessment that identifies uncertainties or constraints, would be justified in applying (i) an SPS measure even though another Member might not decide to apply any SPS measure on the basis of the same risk assessment, or (ii) an SPS measure which is stricter than the SPS measure applied by another Member to address the same risk. However, even if a Member follows a precautionary approach, its SPS measures need to be 'based on' (*i.e.*, 'sufficiently warranted' or 'reasonably supported' by) a risk assessment. Or, to put it another way, such an approach needs to be applied in a manner consistent with the requirements of Article 5.1.

7.3066  In the case of Austria's safeguard measure on T25 maize, the European Communities has not identified possible uncertainties or constraints in the risk assessments in question, much less explained why, in view of any such uncertainties or constraints, Austria's prohibition is warranted by the relevant risk assessments. Therefore, the European Communities' argument about the precautionary approach does not persuade us that Austria's safeguard measure is 'sufficiently warranted' by the favourable risk assessments which were performed with regard to T25 maize. In other words, if Austria's safeguard measure reflects a precautionary approach, we consider, based on the evidence before us, that Austria did not implement that approach in a manner consistent with the requirements of Article 5.1.

Having found the safeguard measures to be incompatible with Art. 5.1, the Panel turned to Art. 5.7; if they were compatible with Art. 5.7, Art. 5.1 would not apply. The EU-level positive risk assessments, however, further prevented the reliance on Art. 5.7 to justify the safeguard measures. The main concern here was the question of the 'sufficiency' of the scientific evidence; only if available scientific evidence is 'insufficient' can Art. 5.7 come into play. The Panel rejected the EC argument that 'in assessing the sufficiency of relevant scientific evidence, regard must be had to the protection goals pursued by legislators' (para. 7.3224); it held that the sufficiency of the science was assessed solely by the ability to perform a risk assessment under Art. 5. The reference by the Appellate Body in *Japan – Apples* to the use of the available scientific evidence to perform an 'adequate' assessment of risks refers to whether it meets the standard and definition in the SPS Agreement, rather than one which is 'adequate for the purposes of the legislator' (para. 7.3226). In the case of Austria, the Panel reiterated that the original EC-level assessments and the assessments delivered after the adoption of the safeguard measures are risk assessments within the meaning of the SPS Agreement:

In the light of this, we agree with the Complaining Parties that the SCP's review assessment of T25 maize, and the SCP's original assessment of T25 maize (which, as noted, was confirmed by the SCP's review assessment), serves to demonstrate that at the time of adoption of the Austrian safeguard measure, the body of available scientific evidence permitted the performance of a risk assessment as required under Article 5.1 and as defined in Annex A(4). We consider, therefore, that the Complaining Parties have established a presumption that Austria's safeguard measure was imposed in respect of a situation where relevant scientific evidence was not insufficient. This presumption has not been effectively rebutted by the European Communities. (para. 7.3251)

Whilst, as ever, the lengthy Report leaves plenty of scope for debate and interpretation, overall the *EC-biotech* approach is suggestive of a narrowing of flexibility relative to *Beef Hormones*. The WTO system's demand for scientific justification of regulation is designed to ensure the objectivity of measures that affect trade. Any attempt to remove political judgment from decisions on risk is, however, futile. The greatest danger is that as politicians and regulators are encouraged to shape their decisions around science, transparency is reduced as the real reasons for a decision are hidden from view.

It is possible to offer a much more ambitious interpretation of the approach to science within the WTO system. Busch *et al.* in their amicus brief on the subject argue that the state of the science on GMOs is such that the EU measures have the necessary scientific basis to comply with WTO disciplines. In this respect, they argue first that the 'science of GMOs is low certainty, low consensus' (by contrast with, e.g., asbestos), and that the 'more uncertainty and the less consensus in the knowledge, the broader the range of "appropriate levels" of food safety protection and regulations that should be deemed rational', and the greater the role of public participation; secondly, that 'risk assessment of GMOs is an evolving technical practice', and so 'no single form of risk assessment can incorporate all the known or potential risks'; and thirdly, that 'risk assessment of GMOs should be locally based', because impact on biodiversity will vary within and between jurisdictions, depending on the eco-system at issue (pp. 22–3). The following passage addresses the demand in Art. 5 of the SPS Agreement for risk assessment.

### Busch *et al.*, *Amicus Curiae Brief*, pp. 23–6

#### 1. Regulatory and scientific developments in the EU

The circumstances surrounding the alleged EU and EU member-state moratoria suggest that these 'measures' – if they are deemed to be measures – were appropriately based on the risk assessment procedures being implemented during this period of fluid scientific and regulatory development. [The Panel did not assess the moratorium against the substantive provisions of the SPS Agreement – above, pp. 286-7.] The sequence of interactions among the public, expert, and official spheres during the alleged EU 'moratorium' has contributed not only to a greater understanding of GM risk parameters, but also the clarification of important gaps in knowledge. Therefore, notwithstanding its unplanned character and the fact that the so-called moratorium *preceded*, in part at least, conclusive confirmation of the empirical substance of knowledge gaps – the alleged 'moratorium' itself was *'based on'* an assessment meeting the criteria of Article 5.1.

#### 2. Risk assessment under the SPS permits qualitative factors

...

#### 3. Risk embedded in the social system

The SPS Agreement text uses the word 'risk' a number of times without specifically defining it. However, the Appellate Body has stated that risk should be 'not only risk ascertainable in a science laboratory operating under strictly controlled conditions, but also *risk in human societies as they actually exist*, in other words, the actual potential for adverse effects on human health in the real world where people live and work and die' (emphasis added). In other words, Member States are encouraged to consider how risk arises within patterns of human behavior and practice in societies. This point needs to be factored into evaluations of the adequacy of risk assessments.

Risks are always created and distributed in social systems, including the organizations and institutions that are supposed to control the risky activity. As a consequence, the magnitude of a physical risk is, *inter alia*, a direct function of qualities and characteristics of the social relations and processes within those systems. This canonical finding from the social studies of risk has been borne out in recent cases. For instance, the official report on the Columbia space shuttle accident recognized the important role of NASA's history, culture, and organizational realities. Indeed, the sources of risk *within the organizational structure* of the space program were emphasized as the investigation proceeded.

The Chernobyl disaster demonstrated to risk assessors that the risks associated with nuclear power could no longer be evaluated outside the political and organizational structures in which they operate. Experiences with BSE further illustrate how physical risk should not be viewed in isolation. Similarly, it is now widely agreed that the risks of chemical pesticides cannot be adequately assessed without knowledge of how agribusiness, farmers, food producers, and consumers will use the pesticides and the products containing pesticide residues.

### 4. The role of public deliberation in risk assessment

We have already stated above how expert committees within the United States regulatory system have emphasized public participation and stakeholder deliberation as central components of successful risk-based decisionmaking. The SPS case law can and should be read to support this view, especially in the context of low certainty, low consensus knowledge of risks.

The Appellate Body's conclusion that risk formulation should address 'real world' situations in which people live, work and die – i.e., in sites of human practice and social systems – carries an important corollary: inclusion of these public voices as a component of 'risk assessment'. Scientific risk assessment often presumes radically simplified contexts of production in which complex organizational and behavioral factors are not fully accounted for. This provides rational support for giving greater practical standing to public knowledge and attitudes in risk assessment, so that real world factors in their variety and complexity can be adequately considered.

Relevant public knowledge may include varieties of practical expertise, as well as everyday experience of how formal rules and regulatory norms are implemented in practice. Neglect or non-recognition of such knowledge in risk assessment is not only a threat to analytic rigor and validity, but also adversely influences public attitudes to risk and trust in technology management.

### 5. Retaining democratic elements in regulatory process

Public consultations on GMOs have been essential in contributing to the identification of risks as they arise in real world contexts. The need for public consultation on GMOs has been implicitly acknowledged in both the US and the EU, though perhaps not expressly articulated as such. Important changes of focus in EU and US risk assessment policy have been the result of public controversy and sometimes accidental recognition of new risk questions, rather than the result of a supposedly determinate scientific process. To find that planned public consultations were not appropriately a component of risk assessments would be to undermine important democratic elements in the regulatory processes of Member States.

There are frequent mismatches between official risk assessment and public attitudes with respect to the framing of the risk issues to be addressed, but evidence indicates that public consultation is not antithetical to science. It is striking that when scientific review is allowed to range more freely in a domain like GM crops and foods, as in the 2003 UK GM Science Review,[34] which was not confined to case-by-case regulatory decisionmaking, the collective expert identification of areas of scientific uncertainty and concern converged with expressed public concern over such matters as unknown environmental and health consequences. These results underscore the importance of public review in securing robust and legitimate assessment of uncertainties.

The Panel, perhaps not surprisingly, takes a rather different approach to risk in the context of GMOs. We await with interest any decisions of the WTO Dispute Settlement Bodies on the operation of the new regulatory regime.

### (c) The legal regime: multi-lateral environmental agreements

The relationship between MEAs and WTO law is unclear. Whilst reports such as *Shrimp/Turtle* suggest a certain prioritisation of multi-lateral solutions to environmental protection (above, pp. 277–8), a direct conflict between an MEA and WTO rules is likely to be problematic. Dispute settlement arrangements under MEAs are nothing like as powerful as within the WTO. Any dispute is likely to find itself before the WTO dispute settlement bodies.

And environmental agreements often do contain or purport to allow trade restrictive measures, ranging from straightforward bans to labelling obligations. For example, the 'advance informed agreement' provisions of the Cartagena Protocol on Biosafety may be argued in any future dispute over the EU's new GMO regime. The Cartagena Protocol was agreed under the auspices of the UN Convention on Biological Diversity. 'Advance informed agreement' from the importing country is required for transnational transfers of 'Living Modified Organisms' (LMOs). For current purposes, 'LMO' has a similar definition to 'GMO' in EU law, but the choice of wording reflects the exclusion from the Cartagena Protocol of the 'non-living' products of GMOs, a subject to which we will return below (p. 305). The objective of the Protocol is set out in Art. 1 as follows:

In accordance with the precautionary approach contained in Principle 15 of the Rio Declaration on Environment and Development, the objective of this Protocol is to contribute to ensuring an adequate level of protection in the field of the safe transfer, handling and use of living

---

[34] See Ch. 2.

modified organisms resulting from modern biotechnology that may have adverse effects on the conservation and sustainable use of biological diversity, taking also into account risks to human health, and specifically focusing on transboundary movements.

Article 7 applies the advance informed agreement procedure to 'the first intentional transboundary movement of living modified organisms for intentional introduction into the environment of the Party of import'. The advance informed agreement procedure assumes that imports can be blocked. Scientific risk assessment is the starting point for decision making on import. Decisions on advanced informed agreement have to be taken in accordance with Art. 15,[35] as follows:

> 1. Risk assessments undertaken pursuant to this Protocol shall be carried out in a scientifically sound manner, in accordance with Annex III and taking into account recognized risk assessment techniques. Such risk assessments shall be based, at a minimum, on information provided in accordance with Article 8 [information required on notification] and other available scientific evidence in order to identify and evaluate the possible adverse effects of living modified organisms on the conservation and sustainable use of biological diversity, taking also into account risks to human health.

The Protocol's version of the precautionary principle is contained in Art. 10:[36]

> 6. Lack of scientific certainty due to insufficient relevant scientific information and knowledge regarding the extent of the potential adverse effects of a living modified organism on the conservation and sustainable use of biological diversity in the Party of import, taking also into account risks to human health, shall not prevent that Party from taking a decision, as appropriate, with regard to the import of the living modified organism in question … in order to avoid or minimize such potential adverse effects.

Unlike Art. 5.7 of the SP Agreement (above, p. 287), there is no suggestion here of provisionality, and the reference is to the 'uncertainty' as well as 'insufficiency' of scientific knowledge. However, as well as being inconsistent with the SPS Agreement, the Cartagena Protocol is also internally ambiguous,[37] referring in Art. 1 to Principle 15 of the Rio Declaration, but without reference to the Rio Declaration's limitations of 'serious and irreversible damage' and cost-effectiveness.[38] The precautionary principle is of course extremely difficult to pin down, and gaps could simply be filled in by reference to the SPS Agreement and/or the Rio Declaration. However, on its face the Cartagena Protocol seems to profess less faith in the ultimate ability of science to resolve uncertainty than other formulations, suggesting a more evaluative approach to the precautionary principle, and an understanding that the 'facts' cannot justify a decision if the 'facts' cannot be established.[39] Along similar lines, the

---

[35] Article 10.     [36] Article 11 for GMOs not intended for deliberate release.
[37] Scott, 'European Regulation of GMOs'.     [38] Chapter 7, p. 223.

Cartagena Protocol moves beyond a purely scientific approach to decision making in Art. 26:

> 1. The Parties, in reaching a decision on import under this Protocol or under its domestic measures implementing the Protocol, may take into account, consistent with their international obligations, socio-economic considerations arising from the impact of living modified organisms on the conservation and sustainable use of biological diversity, especially with regard to the value of biological diversity to indigenous and local communities.

This does not expand the basis for a decision very far, but is nevertheless significant, and backed up by the support in the Cartagena Protocol for the involvement of the public in decision making[40] (again, there is no explicit reference to public participation in the Sanitary and Phytosanitary Agreement).

The application of the Cartagena Protocol to the EU's authorisation process for GMOs, especially the possible relevance of political evaluations moving beyond the limited scientific evidence, could make a significant difference to its legitimacy. The 'advance informed agreement' provisions would, however, cover only a small part of the EU's regime. Advance informed agreement applies only to the 'intentional introduction into the environment' of living modified organisms ('deliberate release' in EU parlance). Living modified organisms intended for direct use as food or feed or for processing are not subject to advance informed agreement. Instead, under Art. 11(4), 'A Party may take a decision on the import of living modified organisms intended for direct use as food or feed, or for processing, under its domestic regulatory framework that is consistent with the objective of this Protocol.' Provision is made for risk assessment[41] and the operation of the precautionary principle, and information on decisions must be provided to a 'Bio-Safety Clearing House'. More drastically, unlike the EU regime (Chapter 5), the Protocol does not apply *at all* to food and feed produced 'from' GMOs/LMOs (i.e. processed food), but just to the living modified organism itself. Nor does the Cartagena Protocol consider labelling and associated obligations in any detail.[42] So even if it were to apply, the Cartagena Protocol would not provide anything like a complete set of answers to the EU regulatory scheme.

The place of the Cartagena Protocol in a trade dispute is by no means certain. The preamble to the Cartagena Protocol takes an ambiguous position that reflects tensions in negotiation, stating both that the Protocol does not imply 'a change in the rights and obligations of a Party under any existing international agreements', and also that this comment 'is not intended to subordinate this Protocol to other international agreements'. Whilst every effort will probably be made to interpret the Cartagena Protocol consistently with the GATT, or as argued by the EC in *EC-biotech* 'that the Protocol's provisions on precaution and risk assessment inform the meaning and effect of the relevant provisions of

[39] Chapter 1, p. 22.    [40] Article 23(2).
[41] This is part of the information that must be provided by importers under Annex II.
[42] Applicants are required to provide information on labelling.

the WTO agreements' (para. 7.55), there are genuine differences. And even if (controversially) an MEA 'trumps' trade rules between states which are party to both, the USA is not a party to the Cartagena Protocol. In its *EC-biotech* report, the Panel concluded that: 'In view of the fact that several WTO Members, including the Complaining Parties to this dispute, are not parties to the *Biosafety Protocol*, we do not agree … that we are required to take into account the *Biosafety Protocol* in interpreting the multi-lateral WTO agreements at issue' (para. 7.92). The decision is very restrictive of the use of MEAs. Moreover, although it found itself not *bound* to consider the Protocol, the Panel was free to consider it if it wished to do so; it declined with little explanation.

## 4 Reconstructing world trade?

The WTO, and indeed 'globalisation' more generally, have been the subject of furious, and sometimes violent, dissent in recent years.

### Corporate Watch, Magazine Issue 9, Autumn 1999, *The Road to Seattle*, available at www.corporatewatch.org.uk/

In a few short years the WTO has transformed the nature of the global economy, striking down labour standards and environmental legislation as it creates an ever more frenzied environment for global trade, forcing all countries to lower standards in a world wide race to the bottom. And behind the closed doors of the conference centres the grey suits, representing the 134 member nations of the WTO, will be thrashing out plans to de-regulate even more of the world economy.

This campaigning view of the WTO at a moment in time exemplifies a particular type of public attention paid to global trade rules. Corporate Watch predicted that 'Seattle will explode with protests', and they were not too far wrong. Protests during the WTO's third ministerial conference in Seattle in 1999 were so intense that the conference's opening ceremony was cancelled, a state of emergency declared and a curfew imposed.[43] Whilst north–south divides in the conference hall were perhaps central, the protests contributed to the failure of the Summit to meet its objective of agreeing an agenda for a new trade round. The protests in Seattle became the pivotal moment in a much broader 'anti-globalisation' movement. Regular protests at later international meetings have ended for sure the benign neglect that had formerly characterised public interest in the affairs of global economic bodies.

Anti-globalisation protests are often criticised and belittled for the lack of a coherent agenda for change. However, Corporate Watch captures some core concerns: that global trade rules drive down social standards, including environmental standards; that the WTO is biased in favour of corporations (grey suits); and that it is unaccountable and anonymous (grey suits, closed

---

[43]   See Perez, *Ecological Sensitivity*, pp. 1–7.

doors). For current purposes we need to examine two different, but probably related, points: how to make WTO rules more sensitive to environmental protection; and the 'democratic deficit' at international level. We will consider three possible responses to perceived failures of the WTO: enhanced participation in decision making; greater 'integration' of environmental objectives into decision making on trade;[44] and finally, two diametrically opposed 'solutions' to the dilemma of setting environmental standards within a trade regime – either greater deference to domestic measures, or a greater willingness to use international environmental standards in trade law.

## (a) Participation in decision making

The anti-globalisation protests are a grass roots, chaotic and intermittently influential approach to public involvement in decision making. They inevitably, however, turn attention to more formalised routes for public participation. Oversight of WTO rule making by Parliaments, nationally or through transnational arrangements, is one possibility that is explored to different extents and with varying levels of enthusiasm in different jurisdictions.[45] Perhaps more discussed is the possible contribution of public interest groups to WTO decision making. Whilst the 'public' is still largely excluded, and there is still no direct external scrutiny or influence of trade negotiations, there have been some developments in this area since Seattle, for example in the improvement of WTO websites, on which a large number of documents can be found; there are also formal meetings between non-governmental organisations and the WTO secretariat.

In efforts to open up decision making, the role of environmental interest groups in trade/environment dispute settlement becomes important. In *Shrimp/Turtle*, three environmental interest groups had presented briefs to the Panel hearing the dispute. The Panel stated that accepting non-requested information from non-governmental sources would be 'incompatible' with the provisions of the Dispute Settlement Understanding, but allowed a party to the dispute to put forward the briefs as part of its own submissions to the Panel. The Appellate Body overturned the Panel's interpretation of the Dispute Settlement Understanding, confirming that whilst 'only Members who are parties to a dispute, or who have notified their interest in becoming third parties in such a dispute to the [Dispute Settlement Body], have a *legal right* to make submissions to, and have a *legal right* to have those submissions considered by, a panel' (para. 144), the panel 'has the discretionary authority either to accept and consider or to reject information and advice submitted to it, *whether requested by a panel or not*' (para. 151).

---

[44] See the discussion of the 'integration principle' in Ch. 4, pp. 164–70.
[45] Gregory Shaffer, 'Parliamentary Oversight of WTO Rule-making: The Political, Normative, and Practical Contexts' (2004) 7 *Journal of International Economic Law* 629.

Outsider submissions can bring an otherwise excluded perspective into decision making, creating what has been called 'a small space for the display of "critical public reason" … a green public sphere within the WTO',[46] as well as potentially providing a link between citizens and decision makers. We might see the submission of briefs as a tool towards the 'integration' of environmental matters (and sustainable development) into trade disputes. However, the role of public interest groups in WTO decision making (in political or dispute resolution bodies) is not without its difficulties. In Chapter 3 we noted some possible reservations about privileging public interest group involvement in decision making. Particularly pertinent here, however, is the ambiguity of who or what environmental interest groups are supposed to 'represent', as well as the danger that the admission of environmental interest groups (but their lack of influence) is misused to legitimise 'business as usual'. The normal dilemmas of interest group involvement are exacerbated in the context of international trade by the 'Northern' origins of most international environmental interest groups.

### Gregory Shaffer, 'The World Trade Organisation under Challenge: Democracy and the Law and Politics of the WTO's Treatment of Trade and Environment Matters' (2001) 25 *Harvard Environmental Law Review* 1, pp. 62–74

Not all NGOs [non-governmental organisations], however, have advocated adopting a stakeholder model of WTO governance. The model has been primarily advocated by environmental groups in the United States and Europe, because southern NGOs, although sometimes large in number, are short on resources and typically localist in orientation. They thus recognize the northern NGOs' advantage in international fora. Just as all states are not equal, all NGOs are not equal. Northern NGOs have more funding, are located closer to WTO offices in Geneva, are more likely to finance international networks, and have greater indirect access to information from their state representatives. Southern NGOs have less access, in part because southern governments themselves have difficulty monitoring all developments in the WTO. One London-based environmental NGO, the Foundation for International Environmental Law and Development ("FIELD"), even negotiated a deal with a developing country, Sierra Leone, to represent it before the CTE [Committee on Trade and Environment]. Sierra Leone, beset by violent civil conflict, did not have the resources or the priority to represent its 'stakeholder' interests before the CTE. A northern NGO, though with serious conflicts of interest, offered to do so in its stead. FIELD supported the cost of attending and reporting in meetings in exchange for direct access to CTE meetings.

In short, northern NGOs are much better positioned than southern NGOs and southern trading interests to have their views heard at the international level. Given scarce resources,

---

[46] Robyn Eckersley, 'A Green Public Sphere in the WTO: The *Amicus Curiae* Interventions in the Trans-Atlantic Biotech Dispute' (2005) *Ecolomic Policy and Law Journal of Trade and Environment Studies*, www.ecolomics-international.org, p. 3.

southern states even question the appropriateness of the WTO sending NGO delegates to Geneva for symposia when those resources could be spent on water purification, nutrition, education, and disease control projects in developing countries. While some northern commentators may condescendingly counter that the alternative use of funds will not go to social services, but to line the pockets of southern elite, the fact remains that international NGO conferences remain more of a prerogative of northern governments and constituencies.

Information comes at a price. Northern environmental NGOs such as Greenpeace and WWF [Worldwide Fund for Nature], have multi-million-dollar budgets that they use to address environmental matters. Some of their budgets exceed that of the WTO itself. They can channel more resources toward CTE negotiations than the vast majority of WTO members. Northern NGOs publish glossy magazines, circulate statements and pamphlets, coordinate lobbying campaigns, call press conferences, take out full page ads in major publications such as the New York Times, and, more recently, submit amicus briefs to WTO dispute settlement panels.

...

In these information campaigns, northern environmental NGOs do not represent the environmental perspective. Rather, the term 'environment' has vastly different meanings to a northern public than to stakeholders in developing countries. In developing countries, it is much more difficult to separate the notion of the 'environment' from that of 'development' because people's livelihoods are more intimately connected on a day-to-day basis with the environment. Developing country stakeholders are thus much less likely to adhere to a preservationist perspective of environmental protection when their lives and livelihoods are directly at stake.

While northern environmental NGOs may be internationalist in orientation and more likely than the WTO Secretariat to represent the 'trees', they do not represent a 'global civil society'. They have a specifically northern perspective, and often, even more specifically, an Anglo-Saxon one. Their representatives were raised and educated in the North. Almost all of their funding comes from contributors from the North. They obtain their financing by focusing on issues that strike the northern public's imagination, in particular animal rights and species preservation issues ...

Southern states and southern NGOs thus distrust demands for greater WTO transparency when 'transparency' means greater access for private groups to WTO decision-making. Southern interests are wary that this form of transparency will merely permit northern NGOs to better exploit the media to pressure state delegates, the WTO Secretariat, and WTO dispute settlement panelists to take their views into account and thereby advance northern ends. Southern delegates fear precisely these 'constructivist' aspects of the stakeholder model. As a developing country consultant to WWF (India) states, 'there is an urgent need to contest the anti-environment image of the WTO so assiduously disseminated by northern academics and environment groups' pursuant to their 'dual strategy' of pressuring WTO dispute settlement bodies through critiques and amicus curiae briefs, on the one hand, and pressuring northern governments to include trade-environment issues in the next round of WTO negotiations, on the other.

NGOs from the United States and Europe are already relatively powerful in affecting WTO agendas and outcomes precisely because they can work with and through the WTO's most powerful members. They simply lobby and otherwise pressure their national representatives. Developing countries question whether a stakeholder model would, in fact, exacerbate this disequilibrium. While communitarian and civic republican models may work relatively better at the local level, they are much more problematic at the international level where numbers, complexity, and inequality of access to information and decision-makers increase.

The resistance of developing countries is likely to prevent more formal rights of participation for environmental interest groups in the near future. It has been suggested, however, that there is greater common ground between northern environmental interest groups and southern states than there used to be – the prime examples being common approaches to the trade treatment of agriculture and certain intellectual property rights.[47] Nevertheless, Shaffer's basic observations on the arrangements of power and influence are convincing for as long as this common ground is simply occasional and expedient.

The approach of the Appellate Body to third party briefs in *Asbestos* is a more general taste of the controversy. The Appellate Body invited outsiders to apply to submit a brief on the dispute, the first time such formal procedures had been offered. However, following the expression of disquiet by some members, the Appellate Body denied leave to all of the applications, without giving reasons.[48] Similarly, in *EC-biotech*, the Panel accepted three briefs (including Busch *et al.* p. 282), but, with no further explanation in spite of the sensitivity of the subject, stated that 'in rendering our decision, we did not find it necessary to take the *amicus curiae* briefs into account' (para. 7.11).

## (b) Environmental integration

One of the aims of greater inclusion of environmental interest groups is to enhance awareness of and sensitivity towards the environmental impact of trade – more generally, a greater integration of environmental interests into economic decision making. Environmental reform of the WTO's rules in a manner requiring a more focused assessment of the relative impacts of different trade measures (something like sustainability assessment) is potentially more powerful. Indeed, without *some* sort of institutional arrangements to this effect, the promise that trade will contribute to sustainable development looks a little empty. However, there is no systematic expectation that the environmental or developmental impacts of trade decisions will be assessed, and as we saw in *Shrimp/Turtle* (para. 129, p. 274), whilst 'sustainable development' was inserted

---

[47] Michael Mason, 'Representing Transnational Environmental Interests: New Opportunities for Non-Governmental Organisation Access within the World Trade Organisation?' (2004) 13 *Environmental Politics* 566.

[48] See Marie-Claire Cordonnier-Segger and Markus W. Gehring, 'The WTO and Precaution: Sustainable Development Implications of the WTO Asbestos Dispute' (2003) 15 *Journal of Environmental Law* 289, pp. 317–19.

into the GATT preamble in 1994 (at the time of the creation of the WTO), it is not legally binding.

Although the interpretive role of the Appellate Body could be influential, integration of environmental concerns is best sought in the political bodies of the WTO. The Committee on Trade and Environment was convened in 1994 to address issues regarding the relationship between environment and trade at a political level,[49] but, certainly in terms of proposing legal amendments to WTO rules, has made little progress.

### Urs P. Thomas, 'Trade and the Environment: Stuck in a Political Impasse at the WTO after the Doha and Cancun Ministerial Conferences' (2004) 4 *Global Environmental Politics* 9, p. 10

Disagreements among WTO members over trade and environment policies are always present in spite of the fact that the mandate of the organization's Committee on Trade and Environment (CTE) is very constrained and seems to favor the protection of commercial inter-ests over sustainable development objectives. The latter are mentioned in the WTO legal text, but do not appear in any legally binding paragraphs. The CTE in fact after nearly ten years of existence has still not formulated any recommendations to the WTO General Council or a min-isterial conference. There is no space here for an in-depth discussion of these tensions, but an explanation indirectly provided by Shaffer[50] seems to me convincing: he found that the widespread assumption that the CTE was created in order to allow the WTO to address environmental concerns and to integrate them into trade law cannot be substantiated by the results of his research into the CTE's origins. He concludes, to the contrary, that it was established to protect trade concerns from potential environmental incursions 'in reaction to the perception of environmental groups' growing success in promoting environmental regulation'.

### (c) Environmental standards: domestic or international?

One response to the allegedly negative environmental impact of trade rules is to put in place strong and enforceable international environmental standards. Existing development in that direction can be found in the full range of MEAs. The rather weak status of MEAs within the international trade regime, together with their painful negotiation, dependence on voluntary adherence, and fre-quently weak enforcement, are obvious limitations when compared with the strength of the WTO system. However, the serious legitimacy problems that would be raised by a very powerful international environmental organisation were briefly considered in the Preface to this Part (pp. 213–15). The frequently diverging interests of developing and developed countries are likely also to prevent progress in this direction.

---

[49] For detailed discussion, see Gregory Shaffer, 'The World Trade Organisation under Challenge: Democracy and the Law and Politics of the WTO's Treatment of Trade and Environment Matters' (2001) 25 *Harvard Environmental Law Review* 1.     [50] *Ibid.*

Nevertheless, the potential for a greater role for international standardisation is clear in the language of the SPS Agreement and the TBT Agreement.[54]

The diametrically opposite 'solution' to the problems of environmental protection in a trade context is to allow greater autonomy to domestic decision makers, with greater deference from the dispute settlement bodies. The Reports outlined above begin to frame the Appellate Body's approach. In the following, Joanne Scott looks at the possibility of allowing members to 'justify restrictions on the basis that the protective measures in question are necessary precisely, and conceivably exclusively, because the public considers them to be so' (p. 144).

### Joanne Scott, 'European Regulation of GMOs: Thinking about Judicial Review in the WTO' (2004) 57 *Current Legal Problems* 117, pp. 144–7

The objections to any such suggestion spring readily to mind. The objections are so numerous and so intense that it may be misconceived to even contemplate travelling down this road. Public opinion is harder to ascertain than it is to manipulate. Adept at the strategic framing of issues, Members may contrive to achieve results which merely shroud their choices in the garb of democracy. Public opinion is rarely uniform and less often static. Even where policies do, unequivocally, command public support, these may rest upon assumptions which are ignorant or prejudiced. To this list, one must add arguments about the nature of a properly functioning democracy. Even for those for whom democracy is essentially a procedural ideal, the ideal tends to add up to more than the mere, uncritical, aggregation of ill-informed public preferences.

...

The dispute settlement bodies will be called upon to delimit, in a manner which may be universally applied – in states which are (deliberative) democracies and in states which are not – the circumstances in which additional latitude is to be granted to Members to respond to public opinion, even when in so doing the Member in question will fall foul of the 'normal' benchmarks for review ...

...

Perhaps then the challenge for the WTO in relation to public opinion is not to exclude it as uncompromisingly irrelevant, but to instantiate with care the conditions according to which its entry into the justification equation may be mediated. Such conditions must be such that the WTO neither foists internal democracy on reluctant Member States, nor undermines it in its wide variety of prevailing guises. Most obviously, any such conditions would be concerned with the nature of the evidence required to substantiate claims relating to public opinion. Equally though, additional safeguards could be introduced. These could relate to transparency, both in terms of the fact of reliance upon public opinion as an element in the defence, and in terms of the evidential record upon which this element rests. Any such safeguards might, moreover, acknowledge the

---

[54] Scott, 'International Trade and Environmental Governance', argues that the Appellate Body could find itself a legitimate and important role if it took a more proactive approach to the procedural legitimacy of standards.

peculiarly volatile and contingent nature of public opinion. Thus, measures which purport to rest upon this, might reasonably be required to be regarded as provisional, to be revisited on a regular basis in order to verify the continuing validity of their evidential base. Additional positive obligations could be incurred by states as preconditions for recourse to a public-opinion style defence … Such preconditions might oblige states to explore and to communicate, proactively and vigorously, the costs and benefits of its regulatory stance rooted in public opinion. Awareness of costs should extend not only to those endured within the territory of the regulating state, but also to external costs and to the manner and consequences of their distribution. To the extent that Members choose to fall back on arguments from public opinion to justify their regulatory choices, such Members might reasonably be expected to incur a duty to seek to stimulate informed and critical reflection on the part of the fearful or objecting public. To the extent that Members are passive in the face of public opinion which is not demonstrated to be rooted in those forms of rationality which resonate in the WTO, the 'necessity' of their measures may be open to doubt.

If the challenge posed by public opinion is complex, it is not one which can or should be avoided. There are problems on both sides of the line. Problems confront those who favour responsiveness and those who do not.

The Appellate Body has avoided commenting in detail on the appropriate response of democratic institutions to domestic demands, although para. 124 (above, p. 293) of *Beef Hormones* suggests that it is not entirely blind to the issue. There are genuine concerns that excessive derogations would undermine trade rules, reducing the benefits of trade, and most likely benefiting the most powerful: the constraints of law are a response to 'might is right'. Whilst any country can be on either side in a trade dispute, the spectre of 'green protectionism' is particularly real for developing countries. Domestic measures of environmental protection are not necessarily or always consistent with the 'development' objectives of sustainable development, whatever the rhetoric. There is considerable potential that setting up a response to public opinion as a legitimate basis for trade measures will open up space for abuse, and increased trade protectionism. However, science is also a problematic method of distinguishing legitimate from illegitimate trade measures in this sort of uncertain and value-ridden area: may states '[a]dept at the strategic framing of issues' not 'shroud their choices in the garb' of *science* as readily as that of democracy? Whilst the EC argued in *EC-biotech* that the extremely problematic science, which was 'in flux', was a justification of its 'moratorium', the public and political *response* to that difficult science, which was arguably the real explanation for the delay, was largely undiscussed in the Panel report. Politics cannot realistically be ignored, and the amicus brief on GMOs above (pp. 301–3) indicates that a more sophisticated and nuanced approach could be fitted within the WTO disciplines.[55]

---

[55] Also Howse and Mavroidis, 'Europe's Evolving Regulatory Strategy for GMOs'.

## 5 Conclusions

In this chapter we have attempted to provide a very brief introduction to the rules of the WTO, whilst setting them in the context of both their claimed *contribution* to sustainable development, and their perceived *challenges* for environmental protection. The GMO dispute illustrates how the themes of environmental regulation at domestic and EU level are reflected at the global level: the tension between expertise and public participation; the role of public concern in decision making; the complexity of scientific uncertainty; and the question of competing public values, particularly if one considers the claimed benefits of agricultural biotechnology as a way to 'feed the world'. The profoundly political and normative nature of decisions on the application of trade rules is unavoidable.

### Gaines, 'International Trade, Environmental Protection and Development', pp. 272–4

A candid assessment of the last 10 years of trade, environment and development policy must conclude that for all the advances in analysis and understanding across disciplinary boundaries, the decade-old observation of a Nobel-laureate economist still applies:

> [w]hile many nice things can be said about liberalizing and thus increasing trade, the structure of trade, as we know it at present, is a curse from the perspective of sustainable development.[56]

The fault, though, does not lie exclusively, or even primarily, with trade officials and trade policy. Liberal trade rules merely create the opportunity for businesses around the world to engage in the exchange of goods and in the selection of efficient locations for production and services. What goods are produced where and what services are provided where are influenced not by trade policy, but by the economic, social, cultural and geographical conditions of each country, and the economic and social policies of national governments.

In several important cases – removing agricultural and resource extraction and fisheries subsidies are the most prominent examples – trade policy reform could make a contribution to reform of trade structure. But even this option is fraught with difficulty in the current climate of negotiations …

In any case, trade policy reform by itself cannot move economic systems and patterns of trade onto the sustainable development path. We come back, in the final analysis, to the third side of the policy triangle, trade and development. As David Runnalls of the International Institute for Sustainable Development put it:

> the efforts to bridge the gaps [between the Northern environmental agenda and the Southern development agenda] through the so called 'Rio bargain' have been a failure.

---

[56] Tryve Haavelmo and Stein Hansen, 'On the Strategy of Trying to Reduce Economic Inequality by Expanding the Scale of Human Activity' in Robert Goodland, Herman Daly, Salah el Serafy and Bernd von Droste (eds.), *Environmentally Sustainable Economic Development: Building on Brundtland* (UNESCO, 1991).

A major factor in that failure has been the insistence by the North that trade should replace aid as the main vehicle for transferring economic resources to the South, without attending adequately to the other conditions, such as debt repayments, local governance capacity and deteriorating environmental conditions in developing countries, which must also be adjusted if the resource flows of trade are to promote development on a sustainable basis ...

The more that Northern reformers insist on the right to apply trade-based or trade-affecting environmental measures like eco-labels oriented to developed country concerns, packaging requirements that discourage low-cost materials like Indian jute, and, at the extreme, the right to ban products from the richest markets if they are made in an allegedly environment-harming manner, the deeper the suspicion among governments and peoples of the South that their developmental aspirations, which cannot be realized without the effective opportunity to trade with the North, will be frustrated in the name of environmental protection. Policies and means must be found to bridge the gap with a new North–South bargain that builds the still missing foundations for sustainable development in the South and which radically redesigns the economic superstructures in the North to make them sustainable as well.

...

Such an ambitious agenda has political and social, as well as economic, dimensions. The economist Amartya Sen, noting that the Bretton Woods institutions, including the GATT, have helped with trade and development but not with distributional equity, concludes that:

> [t]he debate, rather, is about the inequality of power, for which there is much less tolerance now than in the world that emerged at the end of the Second World War.[57]

The United Nations Development Programme defines the challenge in similar terms. It states that:

> [t]he challenge of globalization in the new century is not to stop the expansion of global markets. The challenge is to find the rules and institutions for stronger governance – local, national, regional and global – to preserve the advantages of global markets and competition, but to provide enough space for human, community and environmental resources to ensure that globalization works for people – not just for profits.[58]

Such a challenge is staggering in its complexity. For the WTO to play a constructive role in working towards it will require new institutional systems to enhance the strength and legitimacy of the organization. But political analysts, observing that 'the lack of intermediating politicians is the most serious "democratic deficit" of ... the WTO in particular', have only admittedly 'utopian' solutions to offer.[59]

... the 'new deal' proposal builds from an inescapable truth that governments seem slowly to be coming to accept: only with sincere, sustained and effective attention to development can environmental considerations become integral and accepted elements of development and trade for South and North alike, and only in that way can international trade be restructured to become a blessing rather than a curse for sustainable development.

---

[57] Amartya Sen, 'Global Doubts', Harvard Commencement Address (2000).

[58] United Nations Development Programme, *Human Development Report* (1999), p. 2.

[59] Robert Keohane and Joseph S. Nye Jr, 'Between Centralization and Fragmentation: The Club Model of Multi-lateral Cooperation and Problems of Democratic Legitimacy', KSG Working Paper 01/004.

## 6 Further reading

The law of the WTO is a huge, evolving and fascinating topic, and we have only been able to scratch the surface. We have referred to a great deal of useful work in this chapter. For a broader introduction to the WTO, see Michael J. Trebilcock and Robert Howse, *The Regulation of International Trade* (Routledge, 2004). Gerd Winter, 'The GATT and Environmental Protection: Problems of Construction' (2003) 15 *Journal of Environmental Law* 113, examines the Appellate Body's approach to some of the key trade/environment dilemmas. Joanne Scott has written a number of thought-provoking and readable articles on some of the themes in this chapter: on GMOs, see 'The European Regulation of GMOs and the WTO' [2003] *Columbia Journal of European Law* 213.

Key institutional websites include www.wto.org/ and www.biodiv.org/biosafety/ (for the Cartagena Protocol). Some interesting research papers examining the balance between economic and ecological objectives can be found at www.ecolomics-international.org/.

# Part IV
# Mechanisms of Regulation I: Pollution Control

---

# Preface to Part IV

In this Part we examine a range of different approaches to regulating for environmental protection. Rudimentary forms of regulation were developed in response to the pollution problems of industrialisation, and these provided the template for modern environmental regulation. In Chapter 8 we discuss both the Victorian origins of pollution control measures, and the development of the modern institutional architecture of pollution control. From the late 1960s, in response to the public and political attention turned to environmental matters, governments developed elaborate administrative systems and public law measures to control environmental degradation. Direct regulation by a government body was seen in many cases as the only rational government response to environmental degradation at this time – that a government response was required went almost without saying. It is this sort of direct government regulation, for example through a licensing regime backed up by criminal penalties, that most people have in mind when they think of 'regulation'. The precise meaning of 'regulation' is, however, more problematic.

### Chris Hilson, *Regulating Pollution* (Hart, 2000), p. 1

Regulation is an elastic concept. At its broadest, the term is used to refer to any governmental rules which seek to organise or control behaviour. On this view, traditional criminal laws on theft and so on might be regarded as regulation. However, this definition is too broad in the context of ... pollution control. A somewhat narrower focus sees regulation as a 'sustained and focused control exercised by a public agency over activities that are valued by a community'.[1] The emphasis on 'valued activity' has the advantage of including most pollution regulation (where, for example, manufacturing industry is a valued activity), but excluding traditional criminal law (theft not being a valued activity). However, it has the disadvantage of excluding some non-valued activities that are covered by pollution regulation (for example the deliberate fly-tipping of waste by individuals), and may also include some non-regulatory activities such as fraud (where business is valued but fraud is not). Similarly, while the emphasis on 'sustained and focused control' captures

---

[1] Philip Selznick, 'Focusing Organisational Research on Regulation' in Roger Noll (ed.), *Regulatory Policy and the Social Sciences* (University of California Press, 1985), p. 363.

the essence of the continuing relationship found in most industrial pollution, pollution regulation also includes control of 'one-off' activities (fly-tipping again). And finally, the definition, in stressing the role of 'public agencies' also excludes self-regulation, which is an alternative means of delivering regulatory goals. A more appropriate definition – and one which is sufficiently broad to encompass European regulation – may therefore be: control exercised by a non-police body over the activities of individuals, firms or Member States in order to achieve defined goals; or control by firms of their own activities to achieve such goals.

The main topic of Chapter 9 is licensing as a form of environmental regulation. As well as outlining the place of this traditional and still dominant form of environmental regulation, we will examine in depth the system of Integrated Pollution Prevention and Control (IPPC), put in place by European Community (EC) law, but overlaid upon an existing national system of Integrated Pollution Control. IPPC illustrates the ways in which the 'licence' can adapt to some of the emerging limitations of traditional regulation, and become a more subtle form of regulation than critics might suggest. We will touch here on the use of direct regulation to exercise an *indirect* influence on the behaviour of regulators and regulatees, both by allowing and encouraging external scrutiny, and by changing processes for decision making within the organisation. This theme of indirect influence, however, will be picked up in more detail in Chapter 11. From the 1980s, arguably as part of the challenge to the accepted role of government that went with the 'Thatcherite' or 'Reaganite' economic 'revolutions', traditional forms of regulation came under real pressure. The stark dichotomy set up at that time between the 'pro-' and the 'anti-' regulation 'camps' was to a large degree empty political rhetoric. However, it stimulated an important debate about the best (or least harmful) ways of regulating for environmental protection, and this debate remains lively. In Chapter 11 we look in detail at the regulatory approaches that have emerged as alternatives or supplements to the 'traditional' tool of the licence (including taxation, emissions allowance trading, labelling), and will conclude by examining the diversity of instruments relied on in waste regulation. The licence remains at the heart of much environmental regulation, but other instruments are increasingly important, particularly as part of an effort to forge a productive alliance between economic progress and environmental protection. By contrast with this enthusiasm for 'alternative' regulatory instruments, however, we should note that in certain areas, notably the designation of land for special protection (see Chapter 15), there has been a significant swing *towards* the use of traditional 'command and control' methods of regulation, away from a more voluntary (and undeniably lenient) approach.

Before we turn to 'alternative' forms of regulation in Chapter 11, in Chapter 10 we examine questions of enforcement and implementation of environmental law. Putting legislation in place is only the first step in achieving environmental objectives. Using water pollution as an example, we examine the typical dilemmas that arise in the enforcement of a licensing regime. We also examine implementation of EC environmental law, which raises some distinctive issues of implementation; however, because the responsibility for implementation and enforcement of EC environmental law is ultimately with the Member State, the domestic and European Union levels are intimately related.

# 8

# The Institutional Architecture of Pollution Control

## 1 Introduction

Pollution has long been a concern of government, property owners and citizens, and law has been laid down in response for centuries. But Britain was the first country to industrialise, and, by the mid nineteenth century, the effects of pollution were no longer limited by the scale of polluting activities and the size of cities. Cities began to swell, London becoming 'the murky, modern Babylon', Manchester 'a Babel built of brick', its warehouses 'Babylonian monuments'.[1] In the next section of this chapter we outline the development of a legal response to polluting activities in the nineteenth century.

If the nineteenth century can be usefully identified as marking the beginning of a focussed response to pollution control, the late 1960s are generally identified as the beginning of a focussed and conscious *environmental* awareness, moving (at least in principle) beyond the Victorian concern with private property and public health. The modern era of environmental law is usually dated from the early 1970s. 'Environmental' law, however, is part of a slow historical process, not a sudden development. The early measures of pollution control reflected the ad hoc nature of the public pressures that stimulated their development, which were primarily focussed on the protection of property and public health. Towards the end of the 1960s, a more self-consciously and recognisably 'environmental' awareness developed among the public, and that demanded a more focussed government response. The change of awareness is attributed to a range of factors. These include changes to our sense of space through technological development (easier transport and communications bring the distant closer, and the observation of the minute makes visible previously unnoticed pollution); economic growth and prosperity arguably turned attention to non-material values; environmental 'incidents', such as the death of 144 people (mainly children) when waste from a coal mine collapsed onto a school in Aberfan in 1966, and the oil tanker spill from the Torre Canyon off Land's End in 1967, focussed attention on environmental degradation; and the

---

[1] Mark Giroud, *Cities and People: A Social and Architectural History* (Yale University Press, 1985), p. 343.

development of nuclear power provided an outlet for more general fears of environmental destruction. The image of the earth from space remains the iconic visual stimulant of a new environmental consciousness.

### Richard J. Lazarus, *The Making of Environmental Law* (University of Chicago Press, 2004), pp. 56–7

Space exploration in the 1950s and 1960s, commencing first with satellites and then manned spacecraft, expanded horizons and seemed to open up new frontiers. But the ultimate human psychological effect of the first photographs of Earth from the lunar orbiters in 1966 and the first manned flight to the surface of the Moon in 1969 was far different.

The Earth on which life depended seemed more, not less, fragile after these events. By expanding our horizons, we appeared smaller, more vulnerable, and less secure than ever before. It was, of course, hardly news that humankind resided on a planet travelling through space, but those first photographs from space drove home that reality in a way that was both exhilarating and unsettling. The Earth thereafter was frequently characterised as a 'space-ship' and as a 'lifeboat'. Soon after the first walk on the moon, author C. P. Snow captured well the sentiment in an essay in *Look* magazine.

> The solar system is dead, apart from our world; and the distances to any other system are so gigantic that it would take the entire history of mankind from paleolithic man to the present day to traverse – at the speed of Apollo 11 – the distance to the nearest star. So that the frontier is closed. We can explore a few lumps in our system, and that is the end … As a result of supreme technological skill and heroism, we are faced not with the infinite but with the immovable limits.[2]

Scientific advances and technological change also combined in unanticipated ways to make the world seem smaller, less autonomous, less exclusive, and less secure.

An emerging environmental consciousness fitted well into the 'counter-cultural' movements of the late 1960s, including student protests in 1968, which revolved around issues including nuclear energy, the Vietnam war and (especially in the United States) civil rights. Environmental protest, like the development of pollution control, had a history, but again, had a more recognisably environmental quality than nineteenth-century protest around issues such as the health of the urban working classes, or the survival of salmon fisheries. Environmentalism is the element of 1960s protest most swiftly accommodated by the mainstream, arguably because it was (wrongly, as we now know) perceived to be a relatively simple problem, and less challenging to the social and economic status quo than other elements of the counter-cultural movements.[3]

---

[2]  C. P. Snow, 'The Moon Landing' *Look* 26 August 1969.

[3]  Richard J. Lazarus, *The Making of Environmental Law* (University of Chicago Press, 2004); John Dryzek, David Downes, Christian Hunold, David Schlosberg, and Hans-Kristian Hernes, *Green States and Social Movements: Environmentalism in the United States, United Kingdom, Germany, and Norway* (Oxford University Press, 2003).

Following a review of the fragmented origins of governmental control of environmental pollution, in this chapter we examine a number of aspects of the contemporary institutional architecture of pollution control.

## 2  The historical context of pollution control

As early as the first quarter of the nineteenth century the environmental effects of intense economic activity became apparent in the form of polluted air, and blackened and effluvial rivers. The concomitant growth of cities led to outbreaks of epidemic diseases, such as cholera.

### Sean Coyle and Karen Morrow, *The Philosophical Foundations of Environmental Law* (Hart, 2004), pp. 108–9

… it was only with the advent of the Industrial Revolution and its side effects that state intervention in environmental matters in a more specific sense fully emerged. Principally important among these effects were urbanisation and pollution. In the eighteenth century, industrial activity was characterised by fairly dispersed domestic outworking. The Industrial Revolution first harnessed water power, resulting in the concentration of manufacturing activity in relatively small-scale and topographically confined factories. Later, the advent of steam power largely freed industry from physical constraints of location and of scale, and facilitated the concentration of factories in cities. The environmental pollution that was the inevitable by-product of industrial activity was experienced on a greater scale and in a more complex and concentrated form, than ever before.

By the nineteenth century, industry was characterised by labour-intensiveness and the growth across the country of large conurbations. Some settlements expanded with unprecedented rapidity whilst others, so-called 'shock towns', grew from nothing. In both, sanitary conditions deteriorated rapidly with disastrous effect. Epidemics of typhoid and cholera were commonplace; and even in the absence of particular crises, infant mortality was high and adult life expectancy was low in the urban populations. Social reformers began to latch on to the need to exercise deliberate control over the urban environment in order to tackle the atrocious living conditions of the urban poor. The reforms which eventually resulted from such initiatives, although obviously anthropocentric in their intention, also generated incidental benefit for the environment as they focused on cleaning up the surroundings of urban dwellers.

Legal regulation of the environment began as a series of attempts at the reconciliation of diverse groups of interests: a body of principles concerning property rights grew up around the resolution of clashes between private users, between private owners and commercial industrial interests, and between private or commercial interests and collective goals and interests. The conceptual framework which emerged from these cases would embody a set of principles essentially different from the utilitarian ideas which had developed in the eighteenth century. Property came to be seen as bounded *in principle* (rather than exclusively on the basis of *interests*). The principles involved often related (roughly speaking) to conceptions of harm and well-being; yet the courts articulated such conceptions in terms of the notion of 'natural use': the extent of an owner's entitlement to use property in his own way was conceived as depending on the nature of the environment over which rights are exercised. From these ideas would emerge a juridical framework in which property rights are restricted and shaped according to goals and interests essentially un-utilitarian in nature. The body of case-law which developed during the eighteenth and nineteenth centuries, and the legislative regimes which followed, would embody a moral context for property, in which proprietary rights are thought of as being hemmed in by countervailing moral ideas and needs.

Initially, however, environmental legislation was closely and explicitly associated with human welfare, with Parliament and the courts only willing to interfere in private property rights where necessary for securing important social benefits. Yet developments in legislation, as much as in the patterns of common law thinking which evolved to deal with nuisance claims, sometimes exceeded a purely instrumental approach to environmental protection. The evolution of legal responses to environmental problems ... reveals a body of thought of increasing sophistication: the impact of human activity upon the natural environment is seen as constituting, not merely a conflict between individual rights and collective interests, but a complex moral problem invoking notions of value and responsibility which cannot be fully articulated within a framework of interpersonal rights and duties. The resulting picture is one of a complex body of thought which exceeds the bounds of the positivistic and utilitarian assumptions most closely associated with interventionist legislation.

A whole range of industrial activity generated both national income and pollution – chemical production, mining, metal industries, building and engineering, as well as secondary sectors such as the manufacture of domestic goods and distilling. Early attempts to reduce air pollution from the release of hydrochloric acid gas from chemical works, by wide dispersal of the noxious fumes from remarkably high chimney 'stalks', were unsuccessful: the cold, wet fumes rapidly descended to the ground where they inflicted greater harm over a wider area. The following report, concerned specifically with the depreciation of the value of agricultural land, gives a picture of the immensity of the environmental harm.

### Report of the Select Committee of the House of Lords, *Injury from Noxious Vapours* BPP 14 (HMSO, 1862), pp. v–viii

It is difficult to exaggerate the amount of injury to the adjoining district, which in some instances is caused by the neighbourhood of these works. The pungent vapour is perceptible, in certain states of the atmosphere, at the distance of five or six miles: and its effects, within a radius of one or two miles, are fearful. Trees appear to suffer the most: 'they lose their leaves; the top branches begin to decay; afterwards the bark becomes discoloured and hardened; when very much affected it adheres to the tree and the tree is ultimately killed'. The same witness, describing the neighbourhood of St Helens, where there are numerous works of this description says: 'It is one scene of desolation. You might look around for a mile, and not see a tree with any foliage on whatever. I do not mean to say there are not individual trees within a mile of St Helens that have any foliage on; but I do not think there is a tree within a mile of St Helens that possesses half its natural vigour; and I should think that three-fourths of the trees are totally dead.'

...

Other witnesses speak to the destruction of trees, by hundreds, in successive years, from the effects of the vapours. Farms recently well wooded, and with hedges in good condition, have neither tree nor hedge left alive; whole fields of corn are destroyed in a single night, especially when the vapour falls upon them while in bloom; orchards and gardens, of which there were great numbers in the neighbourhood of St Helens, have not a fruit tree alive; pastures are so deteriorated that graziers refuse to place stock upon them; and some of the witnesses have attributed to the poisonous nature of the grass the fact that their sheep and cattle have cast their young in considerable numbers.

The mining industry also had deleterious effects, leading to severe water pollution, arising from the discharge of solid matter during coal washing, from tin and zinc mines which clogged flowing streams and from the emission of other poisonous, noxious solid or liquid waste from the mines. The perceived need to balance such losses with the economic advantages of a healthy mining industry comes out clearly from the following.

### Royal Commission on Salmon Fisheries, *Report on Fisheries in England and Wales* BPP 2768 (HMSO, 1861), pp. 15–16

The most striking case of contamination of waters is by the efflux from mines. For example rivers form a junction as they fall into the sea at Aberystwyth and since machinery is employed at Goginan lead mines to make the crushing process more effectual a total extinction of animal life has taken place in the waters of the surrounding rivers. Furthermore, it has been proved beyond doubt that not only the fish in these rivers, but animals grazing on their banks, cows, pigs, horses and poultry, had been poisoned, not so much by drinking the water as by eating the grass which in times of floods had been covered by the infected waters ... In Cornwall which is peculiarly mineral country, the salmon fisheries may be said to have been virtually destroyed by the mines.

The first question is thus whether it is possible to reconcile the interests of mines and fisheries, either by diverting mine water or by rendering it by mechanical or chemical means innoxious to the fish. Secondly, if this cannot be done at least not without an expense which would be unreasonable or prohibitory and if, consequently it becomes necessary to elect between conflicting interests. The comparative extent of industry and capital invested in the respective undertakings form an important ingredient in the consideration of this question.

On grounds of superior public importance it may be considered that established mineral undertakings of great value ought not to be interfered with, although the consequences of their working may be to destroy the fish in those rivers into which they drain.

The functions of central government are usually divided up between different 'departments', with a Secretary of State at the head of each. The Department of the Environment was set up in 1970, taking on the environmental responsibilities of a number of bodies, especially the Ministry of Housing and Local Government. It was not a department concerned only, or even primarily, with environmental protection; in particular, its responsibilities for local government, including local government finances (and the notorious 'poll tax' in the 1990s), tended to absorb considerable political and administrative resources. The environment was an area of 'low politics' at this time:

> Environmentalism was not seen as crucial to the nation's performance and it did not arouse political contention. The major political parties paid little attention to environmental issues and they were not seen as matters of mainstream concern for central government. They were therefore pushed away from the political centre to devolved structures of administration. Even when the Department of Environment was created in 1970, environmental protection was only one relatively small part of its functions. Many environmental issues remained outside its remit. The DoE was thus regarded by environmentalists as a department *of* the environment and not *for* the environment.[14]

With the election of a Labour government in 1997, a new Department of the Environment, Transport and the Regions (DETR) was created. This was a department with resources and political influence, with a political heavyweight, John Prescott the Deputy Prime Minister, at the helm. Transport had come to be seen as a major environmental problem, particularly with the high visibility of the 'road protests' of the 1980s and early 1990s, during which there was relatively broad support for those taking direct action (particularly by occupying land designated for road building) against the environmental impact of road building. The creation of the DETR was both a symbolic gesture and an effort to put transport firmly within the environmental policy context; we should note, however, that transport had been part of the remit of the original Department of the Environment until 1974.

After the 2001 election, the government created another new department, the Department of the Environment, Food and Rural Affairs (DEFRA). DEFRA took over the responsibilities of the former Ministry of Agriculture, Fisheries and Food (MAFF), as well as the 'environmental' elements of the former DETR. Just as transport had been a 'hot' environmental topic in the early 1990s, so was agriculture now. Farmers had gone from being seen as the 'stewards' of the countryside to, in many cases, despoilers of nature (we discuss the 'fall from grace' in Chapter 12, pp. 501–2). Gradual environmental degradation of agricultural land had recently been dramatised by the mass culls of animals and the burning of carcasses in the open air following both the crisis around the

---

[14]  Philip Lowe and Stephen Ward, 'Themes and Issues in National Environmental Policy' in Philip Lowe and Stephen Ward (eds.), *British Environmental Policy and Europe* (Routledge, 1998), p. 7.

discovery of a link between BSE in cattle and Creutzfeldt-Jakob Disease (CJD) in humans in the 1990s and the outbreak of foot and mouth disease immediately before the 2001 election. MAFF had been very severely criticised for some time, perceived as a promoter rather than a regulator of farming. Creating DEFRA was a significant symbolic and practical response to the failures of MAFF,[15] as well as arguably a recognition of the environmental impact of farming. DEFRA also indicates a new emphasis on rural affairs within government, responding to a perceived 'crisis in the countryside', arising out of dramatic events like foot and mouth disease, as well as the decline in farm incomes and problems of rural crime, transport and poverty, not to mention political conflict over legislation to ban hunting with hounds.[16]

There are some concerns with the new DEFRA structure. Reinforcing the image of 'environmental' issues as 'countryside' issues ('bunnies and bloody farmers'[17]), rather than urban, global or simply everybody's issues, would be a major backward step. And because agriculture is a physically much larger part of government than environmental protection, its staff and responsibilities dwarf the environmental elements of the Department. Some environmental interest groups express concern that environmental issues are being marginalised within government, and 'distanced from the big decisions'.[18] Land use planning (although not nature conservation) went to the Office of the Deputy Prime Minister (ODPM) along with regional government, and transport went to the new Department for Transport.[19] Whilst the DETR had been considered too large and unwieldy, the loss of planning in particular suggests additional challenges for the development of a coherent approach to environmental protection. The ODPM was superseded by the Department of Communities and Local Government (DCLG) in May 2006 and its planning responsibilities transferred accordingly. The DCLG has an instantly more recognisable portfolio than the ODPM, suggesting that the succession has more to do with presentation politics than a search for coherence in government administration relating to environmental protection.

One of the major difficulties faced by environmental departments worldwide is that their responsibilities cut across those of the more powerful sectors of government: energy, industry, transport, agriculture most obviously, but arguably right across government. The arrangement of government departments can only achieve so much in the way of spreading environmental consciousness through different areas of policy; an effective integration of environmental

[15] See Allan McConnell and Alastair Stark, 'Foot-and-Mouth 2001: The Politics of Crisis Management' (2002) 55 *Parliamentary Affairs* 664.    [16] Hunting Act 2004.

[17] The Director of Friends of the Earth, quoted in Environmental Audit Committee, 1st Report 2001–2, *Departmental Responsibilities for Sustainable Development* HC 326, para. 13.

[18] House of Commons Select Committee on Environment, Food and Rural Affairs, 10th Report Session 2001–2, *The Role of DEFRA* HC 991, paras. 9–10.

[19] Briefly, a Department of Transport, Local Government and the Regions (DTLR) was created, whose responsibilities were subsequently divided primarily between the Department for Transport and the ODPM.

protection across all policy areas is much more demanding. In Chapter 6 we outlined some of the procedural measures being taken in this respect (pp. 243–50). There is a very long way to go.

## 4 The Environment Agency

Whilst central government has the main policy role in the environmental field, most of the actual administration of environmental regulation, for example the issuing and monitoring of permits and the provision of environmental information to the public, is carried out by an independent Environment Agency.

In the next chapter, we discuss the slow move from the piecemeal response to environmental problems discussed above, focussing on specific industries and environmental media separately, towards the integration of pollution regulation. The fragmentation of regulation was reflected in a bewildering array of agencies responsible for administering environmental regulation, dealing with different environmental media or different sources of pollution. By the 1990s, Her Majesty's Inspectorate of Pollution (HMIP, the successor to the Alkali Inspectorate, which at the time had been an innovative response to pollution problems) controlled large industrial polluters; local authorities considered air pollution from smaller sources; the National Rivers Authority regulated water; and local authority Waste Regulation Authorities regulated solid waste. This plethora of regulators not only prevented an integrated approach to pollution control, but was potentially inefficient, and could easily lead to confused public accountability (who should the public turn to when things go wrong?).

The Environment Act 1995 brought HMIP, the National Rivers Authority, waste regulatory authorities and many other local authority responsibilities (in fact, in total, eighty-six bodies) together as a single 'Environment Agency' in England and Wales (there is a separate Scottish Environmental Protection Agency, with slightly different powers). Local authorities retain a range of responsibilities: as well as the major responsibility in land use planning, discussed in Part V below, these include some industrial air pollution, statutory nuisances and some contaminated land issues.

Historically, the environmental arena could be characterised as one of 'devolved fragmentation': 'The organisation and implementation of environmental policies has tended to be devolved to local authorities, quangos and semi-independent inspectorates. Local government historically accumulated a range of environmental responsibilities based on the conviction that environmental issues were best dealt with locally.'[20] The Environment Agency is a centralising development, moving powers from local authorities to a national body. It does, however, operate from a number of regional offices, and has a

[20] Lowe and Ward, 'Themes and Issues in National Environmental Policy', p. 7.

number of regional consultative bodies. A degree of centralisation had also been inherent in the creation of the nineteenth-century pollution control bodies, but the more pronounced centralisation of the Environment Agency responds to concern about the competence and commitment of local bodies in this area, as well as the obligation on central government to ensure compliance with EC law.[21]

The Environment Agency is primarily a pollution control agency, although it does have other responsibilities (notably flood defence). It responds to approaches for permits under various pollution control regimes, and monitors and enforces the law; we will return to these responsibilities in Chapters 10–12. The statutory aim of the Environment Agency puts sustainable development centre stage.

### Environment Act 1995, s. 4

1. It shall be the principal aim of the Agency (subject to and in accordance with the provisions of this Act or any other enactment and taking into account any likely costs) in discharging its functions so to protect or enhance the environment, taken as a whole, as to make the contribution towards attaining the objective of achieving sustainable development mentioned in subsection (3) below.

2. The Ministers shall from time to time give guidance to the Agency with respect to objectives which they consider it appropriate for the Agency to pursue in the discharge of its functions.

3. The guidance given under subsection (2) above must include guidance with respect to the contribution which, having regard to the Agency's responsibilities and resources, the Ministers consider it appropriate for the Agency to make, by the discharge of its functions, towards attaining the objective of achieving sustainable development.

4. In discharging its functions, the Agency shall have regard to guidance given under this section.

### House of Commons Select Committee on Environment, Transport and Regional Affairs, 6th Report of Session 1999–2000, *The Environment Agency* HC 34-I

19. The Agency's failure to set out a clear role for itself and a vision of what it is aiming to achieve has compromised not only its operational effectiveness but also its ability to influence public debate and Government environmental and sustainable development policy. As a result, the Agency is currently 'punching below its weight'. We were unconvinced, for example, by the Agency's explanations of why it had not taken a strong public line on genetically modified organisms. This issue has been arguably the most high-profile environmental concern in recent months: it seems to us that to argue, as the Chairman of the Agency

---

[21] See Richard Macrory, 'The Environment and Constitutional Change' in Robert Hazell (ed.), *Constitutional Futures* (Oxford University Press, 1999).

did, that 'we have a very limited view because our statutory remit is very limited' is an abne-gation of its central statutory responsibilities to protect the environment and to contribute to the promotion of sustainable development. We find it difficult to believe that, with its knowl-edge of environmental media, the Agency has nothing useful to say on the subject of GMOs, and its stance compares unfavourably with that of English Nature, which has taken a much more active line.

20. Furthermore, the examples which we were given of areas in which the Agency has been influential were, for the most part, hardly high-profile. Groundwater monitoring, the introduction of integrated pollution prevention and control, and agricultural waste are important issues and ones on which we were very pleased to hear that the Agency had been influential, but the Agency's work on these issues has been very much 'behind the scenes'. Even on climate change, cited by the Chairman of the Agency as a controversial issue on which the Agency had put forward 'a strong set of views', we feel that the Agency has been following the debate, not leading it. ... **The Agency needs to recognise that if progress is to be made towards sustainable development, then it will need to be more active. The matter cannot be left solely to central government policy and voluntary initiatives**.

...

22. The Environment Agency has a large number of highly trained staff and is a substantial repository of expertise. **As an important advisor to Government on environmental issues, we would like to see the Agency engage more vigorously in public debate and raise its profile on matters of importance where protection and enhancement of the environment and sustainable development are concerned. Clearly, the Agency must conduct itself in accordance with Government policy, but it should also play an important role in influ-encing that policy as it is formed. The phrase used by the Deputy Prime Minister of the Environment Agency's fellow NDPB [Non-Departmental Public Body], the Countryside Agency, was that it should be a 'champion' for the countryside. The Environment Agency should become a 'champion' of the environment, and of sustainable development** [emphasis in original].

The Environment Agency is not, however, an environmental pressure group, and should not become one; whilst its responsibility is towards environmental protection, it can legitimately be expected to be taking into account other elements of the public interest. To borrow from a slightly different context: 'It surely is bad for regulators to believe that "what's good for General Motors is good for America"; but it is also undesirable for regula-tors to believe that "what's bad for General Motors is of no consequence to America".'[22] Further, not only are there multiple interpretations of 'envi-ronmental protection', and accordingly very different versions of what it means to be a 'champion of the environment', but s. 4 puts environmental

---

[22] Toni Makkai and John Braithwaite, 'In and Out of the Revolving Door: Making Sense of Regulatory Capture' (1995) 1 *Journal of Public Policy* 61.

protection and enhancement firmly in the context of sustainable development. A 'champion of the environment' is not the same thing as a 'champion
of sustainable development'. Sustainable development is a complex and
multifaceted objective, not limited to the pursuit of environmental protection (Chapter 6). The Agency's 'principal aim' is anyway constrained in
a number of ways. Most obviously, it is obliged to 'have regard to' government
guidance in respect of its contribution to sustainable development. The
government approach to sustainable development has changed a great deal
since 1995, in particular through increased emphasis on the social 'pillar' of
sustainable development (in addition to environmental and economic
'pillars').

The principal aim is further constrained by reference to other legislation,
and the Environment Act itself. Section 5 provides, for example, that the
Agency's pollution control powers are exercisable 'for the purpose of preventing or minimising, or remedying or mitigating the effects of, pollution of
the environment'. Section 7 imposes 'general environmental and recreational
duties': outside of 'pollution control functions', powers will be exercised so as
'to further the conservation and enhancement of natural beauty and the conservation of flora, fauna and geological or physiographical features of special
interest'; when the Agency is exercising its pollution control functions there
is a duty only 'to have regard to the desirability of conserving and enhancing
natural beauty and of conserving flora, fauna and geological or physiographical features of special interest'. Always preventing pollution or always
furthering conservation may well be the role of a champion of the environment, but not necessarily of the Environment Agency, which is responsible for authorising pollution, with one eye to commercial imperatives. Along
these lines, s. 4 contains an obligation to take costs into account, firmed up
in s. 39:

1. Each new Agency—
    (a) in considering whether or not to exercise any power conferred upon it by or under
        any enactment, or
    (b) in deciding the manner in which to exercise any such power, shall, unless and to
        the extent that it is unreasonable for it to do so in view of the nature or purpose
        of the power or in the circumstances of the particular case, take into account the
        likely costs and benefits of the exercise or non-exercise of the power or its exer-
        cise in the manner in question.
2. The duty imposed upon a new Agency by subsection (1) above does not affect its obligation, nevertheless, to discharge any duties, comply with any requirements, or pursue any
objectives, imposed upon or given to it otherwise than under this section.

The proper role of cost benefit analysis in regulatory decisions is controversial,
as discussed in Chapter 1 above (pp. 37–40). The obligation to carry out a cost

benefit analysis is softened in s. 39 by the question of reasonableness, and the obligation to comply with *duties* in any event.

We would not want to suggest that the constraints on the principal aim are inconsistent with the pursuit of sustainable development, just that it is not a simple or pure aim to 'champion'. Notwithstanding the difficulties, the Environment Agency agrees with the Select Committee's conclusions (above, pp. 335–6) on this issue.[23] It has set out its 'Environmental Vision', in which 'people enjoy a rich, healthy and diverse environment, now and in the future. Air, land and water are cleaner, wildlife flourishes, resources are used more wisely and everyone enjoys a better quality of life.'[24] Whilst this sort of platitude is perhaps to be expected, the document in which the 'vision' is set out in more detail does discuss certain environmental priorities. It also seems to rest on an understanding that environmental protection (rather than, for example, economic or social issues) is at the heart of the Environment Agency's self-definition, although as part of the 'quality of life' framework familiar from the government's approach to sustainable development.[25] The desire to balance environmental protection with other social, especially economic, objectives, so obvious in the nineteenth-century development of pollution control, persists into the Environment Agency's 'vision'.

Finally, we turn to the complicated relationship between the Environment Agency and government. One of the benefits of an 'independent' agency is that it can exercise its expertise sheltered from the short-term political pressures of government. An independent expert Environment Agency could, however, deflect attention from the difficult value and distributional implications of environmental regulation. The profoundly open character of the Environment Agency's statutory 'aim' emphasises the extent of the Environment Agency's discretion. The balance between independence and accountability is a tough one. It is partly addressed by obligations of transparency and public involvement in licensing and other decision making (see especially Chapter 9), alongside voluntary initiatives such as opening up Environment Agency board meetings to the general public. The Environment Agency is also accountable to Parliament and government. As well as the obligation to have regard to guidance on sustainable development under s. 4 above, s. 40 *requires* the Environment Agency to *comply with* 'directions of a general or specific character' from a minister. It is not then ultimately independent, although in most day to day activities it does have considerable independence. The Select Committee on Environment, Transport and Regional Affairs report above (pp. 335–6) criticised the Agency's failure to assert greater independence from government.

---

[23] Environment, Transport and Regional Affairs Committee, Third Special Report 1999–2000, *Response from the Environment Agency to the Sixth Report of the Committee: The Environment Agency* HC 870, para. 3.

[24] This can be found on the Environment Agency website www.environment-agency.gov.uk/.

[25] Chapter 6, pp. 246–7.

### Derek Bell and Tim Gray, 'The Ambiguous Role of the Environment Agency in England and Wales' (2002) 11 *Environmental Politics* 76, pp. 83–4

First, how is the Agency's credibility affected by its relationship with Government? If the Agency is to have public respect and support as an impartial guardian of the environment it must not be dependent on government. It is a fundamental principle of environmental governance that there should be 'independence of regulation both from those who are licensed and from governments that might interfere'.[26] However, if the Agency is independent, it may be more prone to 'capture' either by industry or by environmental pressure groups. It may also find itself excluded from the policy process and treated as an 'outsider' pressure group. Being seen as either 'captured' or 'excluded' may be worse for its credibility with some of its stakeholders than being seen as dependent upon government. Ideally, the Agency needs the strength (and the resources) to assert its independence from government and from its other external stakeholders (especially industry) while ensuring that it has a key role in the policy process.

Second, what should be the Agency's role in the policy process? The Select Committee describes the Agency as 'an important advisor to Government on environmental issues'. But what kind of adviser should it be? The Committee's suggestion that it 'should become a "champion" of the environment, and of sustainable development' certainly implies that it should do more than provide the government with statistical information on the state of the environment or technical information on pollution control methods …

Third, how and to whom should the Agency be accountable? If the Agency asserts its independence from government to increase its credibility as an impartial guardian of the environment and to fulfil the role in the policy process assigned to it by the Select Committee, it would be less accountable to the democratic process.

## 5 Advisory bodies

A range of bodies provide advice to government on environmental strategy and detail. Perhaps the most prominent policy advisor is the Royal Commission on Environmental Pollution (RCEP), established in 1970. This is a permanent standing committee, rather than one of the ad hoc Royal Commissions established to look into specific events or issues (such as those looking into pollution problems in the nineteenth century). Its advice is usually in the form of detailed reports, which are the outcome of major studies and carry considerable authority. We look at a number of RCEP reports in this book.

Parliamentary select committees provide another forum for the discussion of environmental policy. Ministers are directly accountable to Parliament through Parliamentary questions and debates. Specialist select committees, composed of members of the House of Commons or the House of Lords, are in place to

---

[26] Timothy O'Riordan and Albert Weale, *Greening the Machinery of Government* (Greenpeace, 1992), 2.11.

enhance Parliamentary scrutiny. They take evidence from outsiders and produce detailed reports on issues selected for investigation. The Commons has select committees shadowing each government department (so the work of the Committee on Environment, Food and Rural Affairs is most relevant for environmental lawyers). In addition, the Environmental Audit Committee scrutinises the environmental and sustainable development performance of government more generally.

## 6 An environmental court?

There has been considerable discussion in recent years of the need for a specialist environmental court to complete the institutional architecture. Distinguishing the 'environmental' from the non-environmental would be difficult, but broadly one could envisage a jurisdiction embracing judicial review on environmental matters, tort and property litigation in environmental matters, criminal cases and appeals. The justification of such a special jurisdiction rests on the distinctive characteristics of environmental law discussed in this book, including technical and scientific complexity, wide-ranging and sophisticated underlying principles, and a difficult legislative framework based on a range of sources including EC and international law. Environmental litigation is also classically 'polycentric', with knock-on implications far beyond the issues directly before the court, and accordingly wide-ranging public interests.[27] A perception of 'environmental myopia'[28] on the part of judges reinforces arguments for an environmental court, as does the increased emphasis on 'access to justice' as a fundamental part of environmental protection (see Chapter 3, pp. 114–28).

### Sir Robert Carnwath, 'Environmental Litigation – A Way Through the Maze?' (1999) 11 *Journal of Environmental Law* 3, p. 13

I am sure ... that one obstacle to the development of coherent principles through the courts is the lack of a unified structure for dealing with environmental cases. I have long argued the advantages of bringing the various jurisdictions relating to planning and environmental law within a single environmental court ...

In his Lord Morris Memorial Lecture in October last year, Lord Woolf referred to the parallel of the Environmental Court in New South Wales and said:

> I have long been in favour of a one-stop emporium. A court centre where environmental, criminal and civil issues can be resolved. Where the need for judges to have the benefit of technical assessors is recognised. A situation where the divide between inspectors who conduct inquiries and judges who sit in courts is bridged. A situation where an appropriate team of decision makers can be deployed depending on the nature of the dispute.

---

[27] Lon Fuller, 'The Forms and Limits of Adjudication' (1978) 92 *Harvard Law Review* 353.
[28] Lord Woolf, 'Are the Judiciary Environmentally Myopic?' (1992) 4 *Journal of Environmental Law* 1.

He thought that the inquiries system would be 'renovated through a stronger relationship between the court and inspectors'. Earlier in the same paper he recognised the role of 'public spirited individuals and bodies' in enforcing environmental law. He suggested that there should be a Director of Civil Proceedings, or similar agency, to whom the public should complain and who could take action on the public's behalf.

Although the fuller environmental court may, as Lord Justice Carnwath suggests, be 'an idea whose time will come', it is not currently finding favour with government. Such an expensive and disruptive change demands a firm rationale, with a clearer distinction between 'environmental' litigation and other politically, scientifically and legally difficult areas. The precise role of the court would also need to be clarified: it would not be appropriate for an environmental court to act (to borrow a phrase) as a 'champion' of the environment.

It may be that more modest proposals to rationalise environmental appeals into a single tribunal will be more successful.[29] Currently, appeals under environmental legislation (for example in respect of refusal of a licence, or the imposition of conditions or the issuing of an enforcement order) go to one of a range of bodies (magistrates', county or high court, Secretary of State, planning inspectors) and are available on a range of grounds from a full revisiting of the case on the merits to a check only on procedural propriety. Rationalising the forum of appeal would allow the grounds for appeal to be reconsidered, including the possibility of enhancing the rights of third parties to appeal against the *grant* of a licence. Third parties generally have no opportunity to challenge a decision other than through judicial review, but there has been considerable debate recently over the adequacy of this approach, particularly in the wake of the Aarhus Convention (Chapter 3).

## 7 The role of the modern common law

This is not the place for a lengthy discussion of the law of tort; there are many texts available for that purpose.[30] Tort, however, continues to play a role, albeit marginal, in environmental protection. There is something of a 'back to the future' flavour to discussion of tort by environmental lawyers at the moment. As we discuss below (Chapter 11), the limitations of traditional regulatory approaches to pollution have turned attention to the role of private property and the role of economic incentives in environmental protection. This could extend to a tort law obligation to pay damages in respect of environmental

---

[29] See RCEP, 23rd Report, *Environmental Planning*, Cm 5459 (2002); Richard Macrory and Michael Woods, *Modernising Environmental Justice: Regulation and the Role of an Environmental Tribunal* (2003), available at www.ucl.ac.uk/laws/environment/publications/index.shtml?pub_reports.

[30] See, for example, Mark Lunney and Ken Oliphant, *Tort Law: Text and Materials* (Oxford University Press, 2003).

harm. The instrumental employment of tort in the pursuit of environmental improvement, however, suffers from the same limitations as it always has (p. 330, above), most fundamentally the concentration on property rights. Environmental protection may be effected through the protection of property rights, but only ever incidentally. Private law will act only to protect the individualised, self-interested claim;[31] tort can even inhibit an appreciation that environmental damage is harmful to a wider public interest, rather than simply being a number of discrete individual difficulties.

The law of negligence, which emerged clearly as a free-standing tort only in the 1930s,[32] was not an obvious response to pollution at the height of the industrial revolution. It still plays a very minor role in the environmental arena for two main reasons. First, its understanding of property damage, focusing most readily (although not necessarily exclusively) on 'broken' property, is less useful than the 'interference' approach in private nuisance (p. 329, above) in a pollution context. Secondly, the requirement to prove 'fault' (negligence) is a serious limitation compared with private nuisance: pollution is a daily consequence of activities carried out by operators working well within the boundaries of the 'reasonable person' test in negligence.

Negligence is, however, potentially more helpful in its extension of tort to personal injury, not addressed by private nuisance. The main limitation here is in the requirement to establish causation. Disease, as opposed to traumatic injury, is the normal consequence of environmental degradation, and establishing causation of disease is notoriously difficult – the intuitive link between, for example, a car accident and a broken arm is missing between lung disease and traffic pollution. A large amount of complex case law governs causation, but the basic position is simple: it is for the claimant to prove, on the balance of probabilities, that the defendant's negligence (rather than background factors) caused, or materially contributed to, his or her disease.[33]

As well as practical barriers to successful litigation, which could be addressed, however, there are again more fundamental concerns. It is simply unrealistic to re-frame environmental damage in terms of a relationship between, for example, the large number of individuals who breathe polluted air and the large number of individual air polluters, groups that will in any event overlap. There is a danger that overrelying on tort encourages a basic misapprehension of the nature of environmental harm.

Private nuisance and *Rylands* v. *Fletcher*, therefore, continue to dominate the arena of 'environmental torts'. After an extremely quiet few decades, a number of cases have reached the highest courts in recent years.

---

[31] See Jenny Steele, 'Private Law and the Environment: Nuisance in Context' (1995) 15 *Legal Studies* 236, p. 237.    [32] *Donoghue* v. *Stevenson* [1932] AC 562.

[33] *Fairchild* v. *Glenhaven Funeral Services* [2002] 3 WLR 89 relaxes rules on causation by requiring the claimant in certain circumstances to establish only that the defendant materially contributed to the *risk* of disease, rather than to the disease itself. Whilst the precise scope of *Fairchild* is not yet clear, it is narrowly applied.

In *Hunter* v. *Canary Wharf*,[34] the House of Lords confirmed in the strongest terms that private nuisance is a tort against land, not people, and so that only those with an interest in land can bring an action. This approach has, however, been under some pressure, particularly from a human rights perspective, specifically the right to respect of private and family life and the home under Art. 8 of the European Convention on Human Rights. Article 8 has been interpreted to embrace the effects of severe pollution.[35] When nuisance is used instrumentally to assert rights to respect for the home and family life from nuisance-type situations such as severe pollution, the property limitation makes little sense. The High Court declined in 2002 to strike out a private nuisance claim by non-owning children, on the basis that it is arguable that the common law should be extended in this respect to comply with Art. 8 of the Convention.[36] However, the continued validity of *Hunter* has recently been confirmed by the House of Lords in *Transco plc.* v. *Stockport MBC*,[37] albeit that human rights issues were not raised by that case. The position is likely to be subject to further litigation before it is finally settled.

The property focus of private nuisance is most immediately challenged by the human rights perspective. This, however, continues to rely on individual rights to protect the common good, and environmental protection is only an incidental result. A more fundamental restructuring of the tools of private law to accommodate the need to protect *common* property has also been discussed, for example in Gray's radicalisation of the trust, an ancient legal tool. Gray argues that there is increasing evidence on all sides that we are slowly recognising some concept of social trust in relation to the natural environment.

### Kevin Gray, 'Equitable Property' (1994) 47 *Current Legal Problems* 157, pp. 194–8

In more recent years a number of related factors have conduced in the United States to a gathering recognition of the general social stake in property. It has even become possible to suggest that all rights of land ownership should be commuted forthwith to 'socially derived privileges' of use. Indeed, with the proliferation of zoning law and the remorseless intrusion of regulation following the National Environmental Policy Act 1969, the fee simple estate in land may already have been stripped back to a mere usufructuary title heavily conditioned by the public interest. Such developments are readily understood as exemplifying a 'principle of stewardship, under which ownership or possession of land is viewed as a trust, with attendant obligations to future generations as well as to the present'.[38] The steady infiltration of this notion of stewardship inevitably impresses on land tenure a range of social obligations which effectively create a public beneficial entitlement in respect of ecologically critical assets. Meanwhile the advent of this new civic property in strategic environmental

---

[34] [1997] AC 655.     [35] *Lopez Ostra* v. *Spain* (1995) 20 EHRR 277.
[36] *McKenna* v. *British Aluminium Limited* [2002] Env LR 30.     [37] [2003] 3 WLR 1467.
[38] L. K. Caldwell, 'Rights of Ownership or Rights of Use? The Need for a New Conceptual Basis for Land Use Policy' (1973–4) 15 *William and Mary Law Review* 759, p. 766.

resources merges quite harmoniously with other contemporary American social and intellectual themes. The community-oriented aspect of the new environmental property confirms and complements the insights of the ecofeminist movement and also blends easily with the communitarian vision of property advanced in much recent economic and philosophic theory. Additional intellectual sustenance for the current socialisation of property relationships can be derived from the modern rediscovery of the 'land ethic' first proposed by Aldo Leopold over four decades ago.[39] Leopold's call for the adoption of a cooperative 'land ethic' was aimed at enlarging 'the boundaries of the community to include soils, waters, plants, and animals, or collectively: the land'. For Leopold it had become imperative to bring about 'the extension of the social conscience from people to land'.

...

... It has suddenly become realistic to envisage the creation of a 'new property' which consists, not of individual private property rights, but of 'new collective private property rights' in respect of the common pool resources of the natural land base.[40]

...

The advantages conferred by this trust model may be substantial indeed. For the first time it becomes meaningful to claim on behalf of the citizenry a 'property' interest comprising enforceable access to such inherent public goods as clean air, unpolluted rivers and seaways, ozone regeneration, recreational enjoyment of wild country, and the sustainable development of land and marine areas. The moral parameters which have come to delimit the exclusory dimension of 'property' thus go some way towards converting green politics into relatively good communitarian law.[41] The environmental trust also generates rather less tangible – though perhaps ultimately more important – public benefits. The equitable property conferred by the new trust includes shared rights of access to the regenerative socialising dimensions of public environmental goods.

Gray acknowledges, however, that 'there will remain some who cannot, even in their wildest dreams, envisage such "equitable property" vested in the community'.

Moving on to *Rylands* v. *Fletcher*, the House of Lords decision in *Cambridge Water Co. Ltd* v. *Eastern Counties Leather plc*[42] involved a claim by a provider of drinking water in respect of contamination of its borehole with a solvent (PCE) used in the defendant's leather treatment business. The solvent was spilled over a number of years and seeped into the aquifer feeding the borehole some distance away. Given that mandatory standards on the maximum permissible levels of the solvent in drinking water had been introduced by regulation, once the contamination had been discovered, Cambridge Water had to find an alternative water source. The House of Lords confirmed that the rule in *Rylands*

---

[39] Aldo Leopold, *A Sand County Almanac* (Ballantíne Books, 1968) (see Ch. 1, pp. 48–9).
[40] Robert H. Nelson, 'Private Rights to Government Actions: How Modern Property Rights Evolve' [1986] *University of Illinois Law Review* 361, p. 373.
[41] Kevin Gray, 'Property in Thin Air' [1991] *Cambridge Law Journal* 252, p. 297.
[42] [1994] 2 AC 264.

v. *Fletcher* is simply one part of the law of private nuisance, applying to one-off events rather than ongoing activities. Given the private property roots of private nuisance, this implies a property focus for *Rylands* actions. It also means that, as in private nuisance, the harm must be reasonably foreseeable; in this case it was not: 'at the time when the PCE was brought onto ECL's [Eastern Counties Leather's] land, and indeed when it was used in the tanning process there, nobody at ECL could reasonably have foreseen the resultant damage which occurred at CWC's [Cambridge Water Company's] borehole at Sawston' (p. 306). Whilst foreseeability should not be equated with 'fault' or 'negligence', this does make some inroads into the nature of the strict liability imposed by *Rylands* v. *Fletcher*.

> ... as a general rule, it is more appropriate for strict liability in respect of operations of high risk to be imposed by Parliament, than by the courts. If such liability is imposed by statute, the relevant activities can be identified, and those concerned can know where they stand. Furthermore, statute can where appropriate lay down precise criteria establishing the incidence and scope of such liability. It is of particular relevance that the present case is concerned with environmental pollution. The protection and preservation of the environment is now perceived as being of crucial importance to the future of mankind; and public bodies, both national and international, are taking significant steps towards the establishment of legislation which will promote the protection of the environment, and make the polluter pay for damage to the environment for which he is responsible – as can be seen from the WHO [World Health Organisation], EEC, and national regulations to which I have previously referred. But it does not follow from these developments that a common law principle, such as the rule in *Rylands* v. *Fletcher*, should be developed or rendered more strict to provide for liability in respect of such pollution. On the contrary, given that so much well-informed and carefully structured legislation is now being put in place for this purpose, there is less need for the courts to develop a common law principle to achieve the same end, and indeed it may well be undesirable that they should do so. (p. 305)

And indeed, certain hazardous industries, for example the civilian nuclear industry, have been made subject to strict liability for harm by statute.[43] Lord Goff's excursus into the question of 'natural use', which as discussed above (p. 329) had traditionally been a major barrier for plaintiffs, provided a more optimistic future for *Rylands*.

### *Cambridge Water Co. Ltd* v. *Eastern Counties Leather plc* [1994] 2 AC 264, pp. 307–9

*Lord Goff*: The judge [in this case] held that it was a natural use. He said:
> 'In my judgment, in considering whether the storage of organochlorines as an adjunct to a manufacturing process is a non-natural use of land, I must consider whether that storage created special risks for adjacent occupiers and whether the activity was for

---

[43] Nuclear Installations Act 1965.

the general benefit of the community. It seems to me inevitable that I must consider the magnitude of the storage and the geographical area in which it takes place in answering the question. Sawston is properly described as an industrial village, and the creation of employment is clearly for the benefit of that community. I do not believe that I can enter upon an assessment of the point on a scale of desirability that the manufacture of wash leathers comes, and I content myself with holding that this storage in this place is a natural use of land.'

It is a commonplace that this particular exception to liability under the rule has developed and changed over the years ... the concept of natural use, in the sense of ordinary use, has been extended to embrace a wide variety of uses, including not only domestic uses but also recreational uses and even some industrial uses.

...

Fortunately, I do not think it is necessary for the purposes of the present case to attempt any redefinition of the concept of natural or ordinary use. This is because I am satisfied that the storage of chemicals in substantial quantities, and their use in the manner employed at ECL's [Eastern Counties Leather's] premises, cannot fall within the exception. For the purpose of testing the point, let it be assumed that ECL was well aware of the possibility that PCE, if it escaped, could indeed cause damage, for example by contaminating any water with which it became mixed so as to render that water undrinkable by human beings. I cannot think that it would be right in such circumstances to exempt ECL from liability under the rule in *Rylands* v. *Fletcher* on the ground that the use was natural or ordinary. The mere fact that the use is common in the tanning industry cannot, in my opinion, be enough to bring the use within the exception, nor the fact that Sawston contains a small industrial community which is worthy of encouragement or support. Indeed I feel bound to say that the storage of substantial quantities of chemicals on industrial premises should be regarded as an almost classic case of non-natural use; and I find it very difficult to think that it should be thought objectionable to impose strict liability for damage caused in the event of their escape. It may well be that, now that it is recognised that foreseeability of harm of the relevant type is a prerequisite of liability in damages under the rule, the courts may feel less pressure to extend the concept of natural use to circumstances such as those in the present case; and in due course it may become easier to control this exception, and to ensure that it has a more recognisable basis of principle. For these reasons, I would not hold that ECL should be exempt from liability on the basis of the exception of natural use.

This suggests that the question of natural use will no longer be the barrier it once was in litigation against industrial enterprises; the more recent decision in *Transco plc* v. *Stockport MBC*, however, suggests otherwise. The defendants in this case supplied water to a multi-storey block of flats, through a pipe of sufficient capacity to supply sixty-six dwellings. Without negligence, the pipe leading to the flats failed, allowing water to escape and percolate into an embankment that supported Transco's gas main, causing the embankment to collapse, and leaving the gas main exposed and unsupported. This is not an environmental case, but has significant environmental implications, suggesting that non-natural use remains a major restriction on liability. The House of Lords stated that the defendant's use of land must pose an 'extraordinary risk to neighbouring property' (para. 103) and must be 'extraordinary and unusual ... quite out of the ordinary in the place and at the time' (para. 308); 'the criterion of exceptional risk must be taken seriously and creates a high threshold for a claimant to surmount' (para. 49). Although there is no suggestion that the *Cambridge Water* approach to industrial premises is to be rejected, the two decisions sit rather uncomfortably together.

In one sense, the approach to natural use is simply an element of the law of tort that puts up barriers for certain claimants, and is not a specifically *environmental* issue. It is suggestive, however, of the persistence of the nineteenth-century judiciary's tendency to link the development of industry with the public benefit of a strong local and national economy. In emphasising this link the Victorian common law courts provided a forum in which the costs and benefits of industrial activity could be weighed. They therefore played an important part in legitimating polluting industrial activity. In *Transco* the House of Lords resists sounding the death knell for *Rylands* v. *Fletcher*, expressly confirming that the tort has a role in the twenty-first century; it simultaneously, however, restricts that role to the most extreme cases.

The depth and breadth of the pragmatic and more fundamental limitations to the environmental use of the common law led from the nineteenth century to an ever greater reliance on the apparatus of the state for environmental protection. The limitations of government intervention, however, have led to an investigation of how to stimulate the regulated parties themselves, and outsiders, to act as environmental regulators. We will explore some of these ideas in Chapter 11 below, but part of this movement has been to reinvestigate the use of civil liability. Donald McGillivray and John Wightman argue that private litigation can be a way to provide 'a means of privately initiated (ie, unofficial) challenges to official definitions of the public interest'.[44]

### Donald McGillivray and John Wightman, 'Private Rights, Public Interest and the Environment' in Tim Hayward and John O'Neill (eds.), *Justice, Property and the Environment* (Ashgate, 1997), p. 154

How can we begin to justify the use of private law to argue for a definition of the public interest which is at odds with that reached by a public authority? Our case for a role for private law in shaping conceptions of the public interest rests on its potential to counteract regulatory failure by providing an institutional means of opening the substance of regulatory decisions to scrutiny. The model of environmental decision making we envisage is pluralist in the sense that the official decision sanctioned by public law would not necessarily be the

---

[44] Donald McGillivray and John Wightman, 'Private Rights, Public Interest and the Environment' in Tim Hayward and John O' Neill (eds.), *Justice, Property and the Environment* (Ashgate, 1997), p. 144.

final word on the legality of an activity. Individuals and groups could privately initiate legal proceedings in which it would be possible to challenge not only the infringement of private interests, but also the regulator's view of where the public interest lay.

In a world of perfect regulation, such institutionalised second guessing would be indefensibly irrational. But given the various modes of regulatory failure – which apply to the identification of public as much as the treatment of private interests – an institutional pluralism is, we argue, defensible. Thus it is possible to regard the whole legal response to environmental issues as comprising not just the regulatory view, buttressed by its official status, but also the outrider of unofficial legal action. In this pluralist view, private law takes its place alongside other legal mechanisms, notably private prosecutions and applications for judicial review, which are unofficial since the initiation of legal proceedings is not controlled by regulatory agencies or other parts of the state. This way of seeing unofficial legal action places emphasis not just on the outome of litigation, but on the more indirect effects of legal action in raising the visibility of an issue, in turn leading to more rigorous scrutiny.

As well as a closer look at the common law, the possibility of fundamental statutory intervention in tort has been raised. So, for example, there have been proposals at EU level to ease the burdens faced by claimants in an 'environmental' type case, particularly by changing the requirements on causation and introducing strict liability,[45] and also by moving beyond the property limitation in tort law by allowing environmental interest groups to bring tort type action in respect of genuinely 'environmental' harm on somebody else's property, putting damages to environmental restoration. These difficult and controversial proposals were dropped in favour of a far more modest scheme allowing regulators to force polluters in particular circumstances to remedy environmental harm;[46] civil liability tools are borrowed by administrative lawyers.

The EC legislation on environmental liability does not address what must be the most striking land use conflict at the beginning of the twenty-first century, between genetically modified (GM) and organic farming (see Chapter 2). If GM crops are grown near the same or similar organic crops, some GM presence in the organic crop is inevitable, because of cross-pollination, spilled seeds and shared machinery. This puts organic farmers at risk of losing their organic status. It is far from clear how private nuisance or *Rylands* v. *Fletcher* might be applied in litigation. The application of the locality test (is GM farming something to be expected in an agricultural locality?), non-natural use (the 'naturalness' of GM farming is subject to wildly differing views) and reasonable use (especially given the prior authorisation of the GM crop) are not capable of certain prediction simply on the basis of the case law.[47] On the contrary, they are inevitably value-driven and contentious decisions. One of the nineteenth-century doctrinal

---

[45] European Commission, *White Paper on Environmental Liability* COM (2000) 66 final.

[46] Directive 2004/35 on environmental liability with regard to the prevention and remedying of environmental damage OJ 2004 L 143/56.

[47] See Maria Lee, 'Regulatory Solutions for GMOs in Europe: The Problem of Liability' [2003] *Journal of Environmental Law and Practice* 311.

limitations on private nuisance was the condition that interference with a plaintiff's 'sensitive use' of land would not provide a basis for a nuisance claim: 'it would ... be wrong to say that the doing something not in itself noxious is a nuisance because it does harm to some particular trade in the adjoining property, although it would not prejudicially affect any ordinary trade carried on there, and does not interfere with the ordinary enjoyment of life'.[48] The Court of Appeal has suggested (*obiter*) that organic crops may be 'special or specially sensitive crops'.[49] Sensitive use, however, seems not to have survived the twentieth century, being replaced by 'an analysis of the demands of reasonableness in [the] particular case'.[50] This simply reinforces how very open the legal framework for resolving such land use disputes is. We are again cast on an ad hoc balancing exercise, as in the nineteenth century. The courts were reluctant then to put barriers in the way of technological development, and we might speculate that they would still be so now.

There seems to be rather limited potential for using the common law courts to reopen regulatory decisions (as urged in the passage from McGillivray and Wightman – above, pp. 347–8 on GMOs. And yet liability is an important part of GMO regulation:

> If the overall regulation ultimately in place is to be at all transparent, the liability position needs to be reasonably predictable. And that applies whether the outcome is a liability regime that is designed to shelter the industry in the interests of innovation, or one that is designed to expose the industry to liability. Who bears the risk of ill effect is anyway a deeply political question, inextricably linked with the overall regulatory regime, and a question that should be addressed within that context.[51]

The civil law has, however, been more effectively used *by* the biotech industry, against campaigning groups opposed to agricultural biotechnology who uprooted GM crops that were being grown experimentally in the UK in the late 1990s. Genetix Snowball was the main such group:

> There is a desperate need for citizens to slam on the brakes of this runaway experiment before it's too late. In the face of all responsibility being waived by those in a position to wield it, the responsibility falls on each one of us. We are therefore inviting people to join together to take nonviolent action by safely pulling up genetically engineered crops; to carry out their action openly and to inform the local Environment Agency of the location of the contaminated plants so that they can be destroyed safely without causing any further harm. In the spirit of democracy we are asking people who take part in the genetiX snowball to be prepared to take the consequences of their nonviolent action. We call on those who have embarked on this genetix experiment to stop. We call on those who have allowed it to happen

---

[48] *Robinson* v. *Kilvert* (1888) 41 ChD 88, at p. 94, *per* Cotton LJ.

[49] *R* v. *Secretary of State for the Environment and MAFF, ex parte Watson* [1999] Env LR 310, p. 323.

[50] *Network Rail Infrastructure* v. *Morris (Soundstar)* [2004] Env LR 41, para. 36, *per* Buxton LJ.

[51] Lee, 'Regulatory Solutions for GMOs in Europe', pp. 313–14.

to do at least five years of checking on whether we really need genetically engineered crops and if so, whether they are really safe to grow.[52]

Monsanto successfully applied for injunctions to prevent any trespass to land or goods, the courts roundly rejecting arguments that the protestors' actions were capable of a defence of justification in the public interest:

> The defendants are frustrated that they have been unable to change government policy by the strengths of their arguments. It is the breaking of the law, with its potential for martyrdom, which affords far better publicity than any other … It seems to be implicit in GXS' [Genetix Snowball's] method of operating that they cannot attract sufficient attention to their cause without breaking the law. It would in my judgment be an astonishing proposition if the law were to recognise this as justification for law breaking. Many people have strong views about what they perceive to be dangerous or unacceptable; in some cases their perceptions are widely shared, in others not; they try and influence government into making illegal and criminal their particular object of dislike or fear. There are campaigns against disposal of nuclear waste, smoking, alcohol, motorcars, abortion, experiments on animals, hunting, the use of animal skins for clothing, to mention but a few.[53]

To have a defence, 'the danger must be immediate and obvious and … a reasonable person would conclude that there was no alternative to the act of trespass'. We might note, however, that the date of the extract from the Genetix Snowball website above is 1998, a time when it was extraordinarily difficult to have any argument on GMOs that did not fall in a narrowly scientific framework heard by decision makers. Allowing a breadth of perspectives into political debate is crucial.

## 8 Conclusions

During the nineteenth century two tiers of control developed in response to the considerable problems of pollution from industrial and associated activities: the common law of private nuisance and statutory regimes. The common law is inherently reactive to problems of pollution; in the nineteenth century, the legislature was similarly reactive. Significantly, the legislature did not countenance the idea of *preventive* legal controls. In a report on the disposal of liquid wastes from manufacturing processes, the Royal Commission on Sewage Disposal considered representations that the law should be altered so that every person who proposes to set up works might be required to give notice to the sanitary authority or Rivers Board specifying the steps to be taken to prevent liquid refuse from becoming polluting, and that any person failing to give notice or commencing to discharge liquid refuse after his proposals have been disapproved, should incur a penalty. The Commission rejected the representations, believing

---

[52] www.fraw.org.uk/gs/handbook/acclaim.htm.
[53] *Monsanto* v. *Tilly* [2000] Env LR 313, Stuart Smith LJ, para. 25.

that the suggested procedures might involve needless interference with manufactures. It was not until the Alkali Etc Works Regulation Act 1906, in respect of air pollution, that legislation introduced a system of prior authorisation for 'scheduled processes'. These sorts of preventive measures are, however, the familiar bedrock of contemporary environmental legislation. They are now even old-fashioned; more forward-looking approaches to environmental law concentrate on efforts to move beyond the preventive approach to an increasingly precautionary and pro-active approach. After discussing the contemporary use of the environmental licence or permit and its enforcement in Chapters 9 and 10, in Chapter 11 we turn to the tendency in modern environmental law to look beyond the licence, to more subtle methods of regulatory control.

## 9  Further reading

More detail on the historical development of pollution control can be found in the first edition of this book, Sue Elworthy and Jane Holder, *Environmental Protection* (Butterworths, 1997). Sean Coyle and Karen Morrow's *The Philosophical Foundations of Environmental Law* (Hart, 2004) provides an intellectual history of environmental law, focussing on property, rights and nature. Ben Pontin, 'Tort Law and Victorian Government Growth: The Historiographical Significance of Tort in the Shadow of Chemical Pollution and Factory Safety Regulation' (1998) 18 *Oxford Journal of Legal Studies* 661, examines the role of tort during the evolution of regulation in the nineteenth century.

In John Harman, 'Environmental Regulation in the 21st Century' (2004) 6 *Environmental Law Review* 141, the Chairman of the Environment Agency discusses the Agency's 'Vision' and how it will respond to 21st-century challenges.

John Lowry and Rod Edmunds (eds.), *Environmental Protection and the Common Law* (Hart, 2000), contains a number of interesting papers on the role of the common law in environmental protection.

and, where it is not, to minimize them in order to achieve a high level of protection for the environment as a whole;

9. Whereas this Directive establishes a general framework for integrated pollution prevention and control; whereas it lays down the measures necessary to implement integrated pollution prevention and control in order to achieve a high level of protection for the environment as a whole; whereas application of the principle of sustainable development will be promoted by an integrated approach to pollution control.

Environmental lawyers in the UK were first introduced to the concept of 'integration' in a 1976 Report from the Royal Commission on Environmental Pollution (RCEP) which, looking beyond its remit of 'air pollution', advocated a more holistic approach to pollution control.

### RCEP, Fifth Report, *Air Pollution Control: An Integrated Approach* Cmnd 6371 (1976)

263. The three principal forms of pollution – of air, water and land – are often very closely linked. In order to reduce atmospheric pollution, gases or dusts may be trapped in a spray of water or washed out of filters. This leaves polluted water, which if not discharged to a sewer or direct to a river or the sea can be piped into a lagoon to settle and dry out, leaving a solid waste disposal problem. The pollutant may even go full circle by blowing off the lagoon as a dust. Other examples of the possible transference of pollution include water seeping through refuse tips, smoke from the incineration of rubbish or sludge, and pollution of land where sewage sludge containing heavy metals is used as a fertiliser.

In the absence of immediate government warmth to its ideas, the Royal Commission twelve years later devoted a Report to the concept of 'Best Practicable Environmental Option' (BPEO):

A BPEO is the outcome of a systematic consultative and decision-making procedure which emphasises the protection and conservation of the environment across land, air and water. The BPEO procedure establishes, for a given set of objectives, the option that provides the most benefit or least damage to the environment as a whole, at acceptable cost, in the long term as well as in the short term.[6]

This work on 'integration' was finally picked up in the Environmental Protection Act 1990, which introduced a system of 'integrated pollution control' (IPC). Authorisation was required for specified industrial activities, and there was an obligation to use 'best available techniques not entailing excessive cost' (BATNEEC) for the purpose of 'minimising the pollution which may be caused to the environment taken as a whole by the releases having regard to the best practicable environmental option available' (s. 7(2) and (7)).

---

[6] RCEP, Twelfth Report, *Best Practicable Environmental Option* Cm 310 (1988).

As explained above, this chapter examines the IPPC Directive, which is implemented into English law and practice through the Pollution Prevention and Control Act 1999 and detailed associated regulations, and administered by the Environment Agency (in the main – local authorities retain some responsibility). For current purposes, it suffices to view the European Union's (EU's) IPPC as a replacement of IPC. In any event, whilst IPPC and IPC make different detailed arrangements for environmental protection, they are both also broader, and broadly similar, approaches to regulating in a more integrated way. They do, however, differ in some respects: for example, IPPC embraces a greater number of installations than IPC; it is concerned with a broader range of 'environmental impacts' (IPC concentrates on emissions); and although it takes an integrated approach to the environmental media, IPPC makes no mention of BPEO.

Although the integration of pollution control, and the holistic approach to the environment that it implies, is an important component of broader efforts to integrate environmental protection into other policy areas, in turn an important part of sustainable development, IPPC only weakly reflects the concept of integration found in Art. 6 of the EC Treaty (Chapter 4 above, pp. 164–70). Rather than attempting to integrate environmental considerations into other policy areas, IPPC is specifically about integrating different parts of environmental regulation.[7] And gaps remain even in this respect: e.g., there is no consideration of the environmental impact of any resulting product, nor of its transportation. The list of 'General principles governing the basic obligations of the operator' is, however, reasonably far-reaching:

> Member States shall take the necessary measures to provide that the competent authorities ensure that installations are operated in such a way that:
> (a)  all the appropriate preventive measures are taken against pollution, in particular through application of the best available techniques;
> (b)  no significant pollution is caused;
> (c)  waste production is avoided ...; where waste is produced, it is recovered or, where that is technically and economically impossible, it is disposed of while avoiding or reducing any impact on the environment;
> (d)  energy is used efficiently;
> (e)  the necessary measures are taken to prevent accidents and limit their consequences;
> (f)  the necessary measures are taken upon definitive cessation of activities to avoid any pollution risk and return the site of operation to a satisfactory state.
> For the purposes of compliance with this Article, it shall be sufficient if Member States ensure that the competent authorities take account of the general principles set out in this Article when they determine the conditions of the permit. (Art. 3)

---

[7] The Directive does not require a single agency, but does require the application procedure and conditions to be 'fully coordinated': Art. 7.

## 3 Flexibility and decentralisation in the IPPC directive

In sectors from waste to water, EC law requires the direct regulation of polluting activities. As suggested in the introduction to this chapter, direct regulation has been under considerable pressure in recent years. And if that applies even at the domestic level, the role of the EU is potentially highly controversial. The caricature of command and control offered above (p. 352), applying uniform inflexible standards, regardless of circumstances, is particularly damaging at EU level. It ignores the enormous variety and complexity of environmental and industrial conditions across the EU, and contributes to the efforts of 'Euro-sceptics' to paint the EU as an inefficient and burdensome bureaucracy.

### Richard Macrory and Sharon Turner, 'Participatory Rights, Transboundary Environmental Governance and EC Law' (2002) 39 *Common Market Law Review* 489, pp. 495–7

Transboundary externalities or spillovers – both physical and economic – were traditionally asserted as the factors that justified the first period of Community intervention in the field of environmental governance. From the point of view of physical externalities, it had long been evident that activities within one State had the capacity to have a negative impact on the environmental quality within neighbouring and more distant States. In addition, the danger of a regulatory 'race to the bottom' between Member States, and the threat to the level competitive playing field underpinning the common market project, provided a powerful economic rationale for centralizing legislative action on the environment at Community level. The compelling nature of these arguments enabled Community environmental law to develop rapidly during the 1970s and 1980s, but the legislation that emerged tended to be based on conventional approaches towards regulation, and was better suited towards controlling point sources of pollution rather than dealing with diffuse sources or influencing longer term resource and consumption trends. Community legislation on the environment favoured the imposition of specific minimum emission standards or quality objectives for the Community as a whole, leaving Member States with little substantive discretion when implementing these standards. In particular, Member States had very little flexibility in terms of taking local environmental conditions into account when implementing EC environmental Directives; similarly, they retained little discretion in terms of the policy instruments that could be used to achieve implementation. By the early 1990s there were growing concerns that the Community's apparently inflexible approach to regulation across several spheres – including the environment – posed a threat to the achievement of competitiveness and employment goals. The Fifth Environmental Action Programme responded to the pressure for deregulation by supporting a more flexible approach to environmental regulation.

The discussion concerning the impact of subsidiarity in the context of EC environmental law has been going on for many years. Recent legislative developments suggest that this principle, together with the pressure for deregulation in the environmental context, have stimulated the development of a new generation of Community legislation on the environment, which avoids setting detailed emission standards and limit values, and instead establishes a framework of objectives that confers considerable substantive discretion on Member States in implementing these goals.

Perhaps the most distinctive and interesting feature of the IPPC Directive is its embodiment of the phenomenon of increased flexibility and decentralisation in EC environmental law.[8] In the manner outlined by Macrory and Turner, the Directive offers considerable flexibility to regulators in the Member States, emphasising the importance of local conditions and costs, allowing regulators to respond to varying environmental and economic conditions, as well as moving decisions 'closer to the people'.

At the heart of the flexibility and decentralisation of IPPC is the concept of 'best available techniques' (BAT). The permissible emissions for each installation are set by reference to what could be achieved by BAT. In principle, the Member State determines BAT, which is defined at some length, although in a very open-ended way, in the Directive.

### Directive 1996/61 concerning integrated pollution prevention and control OJ 1996 L 257/26

Article 2

11. 'best available techniques' shall mean the most effective and advanced stage in the development of activities and their methods of operation which indicate the practical suitability of particular techniques for providing in principle the basis for emission limit values designed to prevent and, where that is not practicable, generally to reduce emissions and the impact on the environment as a whole:
– 'techniques' shall include both the technology used and the way in which the installation is designed, built, maintained, operated and decommissioned,
– 'available' techniques shall mean those developed on a scale which allows implementation in the relevant industrial sector, under economically and technically viable conditions, taking into consideration the costs and advantages, whether or not the techniques are used or produced inside the Member State in question, as long as they are reasonably accessible to the operator,
– 'best' shall mean most effective in achieving a high general level of protection of the environment as a whole.
In determining the best available techniques, special consideration should be given to the items listed in Annex IV;

...

---

[8] Joanne Scott, 'Flexibility, "Proceduralization", and Environmental Governance in the EU' in Joanne Scott and Grainne de Búrca (eds.), *Constitutional Change in the European Union* (Hart, 2000).

ANNEX IV

Considerations to be taken into account generally or in specific cases when determining best available techniques, as defined in Article 2(11), bearing in mind the likely costs and benefits of a measure and the principles of precaution and prevention:

1. the use of low-waste technology;
2. the use of less hazardous substances;
3. the furthering of recovery and recycling of substances generated and used in the process and of waste, where appropriate;
4. comparable processes, facilities or methods of operation which have been tried with success on an industrial scale;
5. technological advances and changes in scientific knowledge and understanding;
6. the nature, effects and volume of the emissions concerned;
7. the commissioning dates for new or existing installations;
8. the length of time needed to introduce the best available technique;
9. the consumption and nature of raw materials (including water) used in the process and their energy efficiency;
10. the need to prevent or reduce to a minimum the overall impact of the emissions on the environment and the risks to it;
11. the need to prevent accidents and to minimize the consequences for the environment;
12. the information published by the Commission pursuant to Article 16 (2) or by international organisations.

## Joanne Scott, 'Flexibility, "Proceduralization", and Environmental Governance in the EU' in Joanne Scott and Grainne de Búrca (eds.), *Constitutional Change in the European Union* (Hart, 2000), pp. 261–70

This concept of BAT represents the core of Member State obligations under the IPPC Directive. It provides a framework within which they are to exercise their regulatory discretion, and constitutes the principal, though by no means the exclusive, source of substantive flexibility in the implementation of the directive.

The concept of BAT is profoundly open-ended and is characterised by ambiguity and uncertainty. It is predicated upon recourse to a wide range of economic, technical and technological considerations, as well as upon cost-benefit and (practical) feasibility concerns. Not only are such considerations themselves barely defined, but the status and role of the various factors, and the relationship between them, is far from clear. Thus, for example, while 'costs and advantages' are to be taken 'into consideration' in assessing the 'availability' of the relevant industrial techniques, the Directive does not seek to constrain Member States in their measurement and/or assessment of the relevant costs and benefits, or establish a threshold according to which 'excessive' is to be defined in the cost/benefit stakes. Similarly, and equally nebulously, Annex IV lays down a range of factors to be taken 'into account generally or in specific cases' in defining BAT, 'bearing in mind the likely costs and benefits of a measure and the principles of precaution and prevention'. Methodologically open-ended, and normatively weak, the concept of BAT tactfully blends a range of regulatory approaches and priorities, generating a hybrid form apparently acceptable to all by virtue of its exaggerated flexibility.

The substantive flexibility which inheres in the concept of BAT, and hence the indeterminacy of the performance standards to be derived therefrom, highlights the salience of the implementation phase in the environmental governance equation in the EU, and the importance of the siting of political authority for implementation. Implementation clearly involves the exercise of substantial discretion and, in the case of BAT, a choice between competing and contested environmental methodologies and assessment techniques. Hence one of the most crucial questions arising is who is to put flesh on the bare BAT bones ...

...

In so far as the IPPC Directive rests upon Member State flexibility in implementation, it implies a decentralisation of responsibility for environmental decision-making. The nature of the decentralisation which it promotes will depend in part upon the level of government at which BAT is to be articulated, be it national, regional or local. This issue will have important implications for the degree of differentiation of standards which will be tolerated in the implementation of the Directive, and hence the decentralisation theme is closely tied to that of flexibility ... The extent to which Member States enjoy flexibility in identifying the governmental authority with responsibility for defining BAT will be crucially important in clarifying the limits to flexibility and differentiation within the framework of the IPPC Directive.

Responsibility for determining the outcome of permit applications, and for attaching conditions to permits granted, lies with the 'competent authority or authorities' designated by the relevant Member State. It is these authorities which are to be responsible for carrying out the obligations arising from this Directive. Member States enjoy considerable autonomy in establishing or identifying such authorities, and attempts to restrict that autonomy have conspicuously failed. It is thus conceivable, and in practice inevitable, that such authorities will be situated at a variety of different levels of government, in the different Member States. In some cases regional and local bodies will be endowed with responsibility in this respect. Thus, and this is the crucial question in clarifying the nature of the decentralisation achieved by the Directive, if it is assumed that it is for these authorities to bring their own conception of BAT to bear, then it is equally fair to assume that within any one Member State, a variety of conceptions of BAT will emerge for any given industrial sector. This would then imply the emergence of different standards for different undertakings within a given Member State, and consequently differentiation within as well as between states.

### European Commission, *On the Road to Sustainable Production: Progress in Implementing Council Directive 96/61/EC Concerning Integrated Pollution Prevention and Control* COM (2003) 354 final

#### 5.2. The definition of 'best available techniques'

...

BAT can actually vary from one plant to another because costs and benefits can obviously vary. The fact that costs and benefits are elements in the definition of BAT also means that

BAT inevitably is a balance between different environmental impacts and associated costs. Therefore, techniques may very well be better than BAT in terms of their overall environmental performance or for one particular environmental aspect.

The definition of BAT requires that the technique is developed on a scale that allows implementation in the sector. The evidence to support a technique as BAT can come from one or more plants applying the technique somewhere in the world. In some rare cases, even pilot projects can provide a sufficient basis.

It is expected that process-integrated measures will generally have a positive or more or less neutral impact on the profitability of enterprises. 'End-of-pipe' measures, on the other hand, often have a negative short-term impact on profitability. It is inevitable that some BAT will not have any payback at all, but their societal benefits outweigh the costs incurred by the operator, in keeping with the polluter pays principle.

The determination of BAT involves an assessment of the estimated net costs of implementing a technique in relation to the environmental benefits achieved through its implementation. A second economic test relates to whether the technique can be introduced in the relevant sector under economically viable conditions. This affordability test can only be legitimately applied on a European sectoral level, not to individual installations. If the techniques are considered too expensive for the sector as a whole, then they are not BAT. However, by taking the sector and not the individual installation as a basis for this test, there can be no perverse effect whereby installations in a difficult financial situation are allowed to continue to pollute because they cannot afford to take the required measures.

## 4 Standard setting in environmental regulation

One crucial aspect of environmental regulation in all its forms, but most obviously and most centrally in direct regulation, is the setting of standards; of which BAT is one form.

'Standard' in its narrowest sense is 'a legally enforceable numerical limit', but can include various non-mandatory criteria, and need not be numerical. Standards may be set and enforced by government or they may 'carry authority for other reasons, especially the scientific eminence or market power of those who set them'.[9] The RCEP understands an environmental standard 'to be any judgment about the acceptability of environmental modifications resulting from human activities' that is both 'formally stated after some consideration and intended to apply generally to a defined class of cases' and 'because of its relationship to certain sanctions, rewards or values … can be expected to exert an influence, direct or indirect, on activities that affect the environment'.[10]

---

[9] RCEP, Twenty-first Report, *Setting Environmental Standards*, Cm 4053 (1998), para. 1.15.
[10] *Ibid.*, para. 1.16.

### Gertrude Lubbe-Wolff, 'Efficient Environmental Legislation – On Different Philosophies of Pollution Control in Europe' (2001) 13 *Journal of Environmental Law* 79, pp. 80–1

Trying to classify different possible modes of regulating pollution by way of command and control, we can distinguish three different approaches:

1. technical prescriptions
2. emission standards
3. quality standards

*Technical prescriptions* are norms which make the use of certain technologies obligatory. For instance, rules requiring that power plant fumes be cleaned by wet scrubbing or that coalescence filters be used for the treatment of certain effluents would belong to that category.

*Emission standards* are rules that specify the pollutant amounts which may be released from specific installations. The numerical definitions of these amounts, that is, the relevant emission limit values, can be framed for instance as concentration values, freight values, reduction values (defining in per cent the degree to which pollutants must be removed from effluent air or water), or per-production-unit values.

…

*Quality standards*, finally, are standards relating to the quality of the environmental media into which emissions are released, i.e. to the quality of ambient air or of rivers, lakes, ground waters or coastal waters into which effluent waters are discharged. These standards are usually framed as limit values for the concentration of a pollutant in the relevant medium.

The terminology by which standards are described varies, and we could make the division one between 'quality' standards (also target, ambient or receptor standards), and 'source-related' standards (technical or emission standards), as well as product standards, which regulate the impact of the manufactured product.[11]

Article 2 of the IPPC Directive provides definitions:

5. 'emission' shall mean the direct or indirect release of substances, vibrations, heat or noise from individual or diffuse sources in the installation into the air, water or land;

6. 'emission limit values' shall mean the mass, expressed in terms of certain specific parameters, concentration and/or level of an emission, which may not be exceeded during one or more periods of time …

The emission limit values for substances shall normally apply at the point where the emissions leave the installation, any dilution being disregarded when determining them …;

7. 'environmental quality standard' shall mean the set of requirements which must be fulfilled at a given time by a given environment or particular part thereof, as set out in Community legislation.

---

[11] See Carolyn Abbot, 'Environmental Command Regulation' in Benjamin Richardson and Stepan Wood (eds.), *Environmental Laws for Sustainability* (Hart, 2006), pp. 66–9.

Distinctive national approaches to regulation can be identified. The UK historically preferred an 'absorb and disperse' approach to pollution, relying on the features of its island geography, with fast flowing rivers and prevailing westerly winds, to avoid local effects. The reliance on target standards (and the export of pollution) has been under pressure as EC environmental law, influenced by those Member States that prefer emission standards, becomes more significant. The UK has also had to formalise its target standards, which had previously been relegated to 'the realm of shadow mechanisms such as circulars or technical notes'.[12] In 1991, Richard Macrory observed the '[f]undamental changes' taking place on this question, predicting 'a new era of legal formalism in relation to pollution standards and objectives'.[13] Equally, what has been described as the 'deep and politically painful Europeanization of national policy' has forced the UK to take steps to exert greater influence on EU environmental policy.[14]

### Lubbe-Wolff, 'Efficient Environmental Legislation', pp. 84–7

Following the usual characterisation, according to which the German regulatory philosophy is technically or emission-oriented, one might expect to find only emission standards and no quality standards in German environmental law. However, this is not true. Apart from the fact that Germany, as well as other EC Member States, observes a number of quality standards prescribed by European environmental law, such standards have always been an element of Germany's domestic environmental law.

It is characteristic of the German regulatory approach that it combines emission standards and quality standards in a cumulative manner ... Both are equally binding, and binding independently of each other. This means that an installation will have to observe the relevant emission standards regardless of whether or not this is necessary to prevent a transgression of the relevant quality standards. On the other hand, a new installation will not be permitted if permitting it would lead to a transgression of quality standards, irrespective of whether the emissions of the installation are in line with the relevant emission standards or not. In other words, where a new installation might lead to a transgression of quality standards, operating it will only be permitted if emissions can be reduced beyond the BAT standard to such an extent that no such transgression will ensue. Likewise, where ambient air or water quality deteriorates and drops below existing quality standards, existing installations will face administrative orders changing the original conditions of their permits to the effect that emissions will have to be reduced below the level of existing normative emission standards. So the German regulatory philosophy is called emission-oriented not because it is disinterested in quality standards, but because it insists on the binding force of general emission standards, irrespective of whether or not compliance with them is a prerequisite for the attainment of quality objectives.

---

[12]   Richard Macrory, 'Environmental Law: Shifting Discretions and the New Formalism' in Owen Lomas (ed.), *Frontiers of Environmental Law* (Chancery Law Publishing, 1991), p. 17.

[13]   *Ibid.*, p. 15.

[14]   Andrew Jordan, 'The United Kingdom: From Policy "Taking" to Policy "Shaping"' in Andrew Jordan and Duncan Liefferink (eds.), *Environmental Policy in Europe* (Routledge, 2004), p. 205.

By contrast, the British philosophy – at least as it is expressed in European environmental policy – is called quality-oriented not because it opposes any emission standards (which it does not), but because it tends to assign to them a subordinate, merely instrumental role in relation to quality standards. According to the British philosophy, European emission standards should be binding … only in so far as observing them is necessary to secure attainment of the relevant quality standards …

Now what about the thesis that the quality-oriented British approach is more efficient than the emission-oriented German approach because it renounces any establishment of ways and means that are unnecessary for the attainment of the ultimate, quality-oriented regulatory goal? The starting point of this argument, i.e. the idea that any kind of intervention should be as goal-oriented as possible, is certainly reasonable. The problem is that the goals presented as relevant by the quality-oriented philosophy capture only part of the environmental quality situation that we ought to be interested in. The quality standards used in environmental regulation usually refer to the quality of environmental media (air, water, or, less frequently, soil) in the immediate vicinity of the source of pollution concerned. However, keeping ambient air or water quality constantly below a certain quality standard in spite of continuous polluting activities is possible only because the greater part of the pollutants is usually transported elsewhere. Air pollutants, for instance, may to some extent be chemically dissolved in the vicinity of the polluting source, but most of them will usually be blown away by the wind, carried to higher layers of the atmosphere or washed down into the soil or into rivers, lakes or oceans by rain, and in the course of time, they will accumulate in these deposits. A quality approach which takes into account only the quality of the immediate environment of the polluting source (or of parts of it) neglects all these more far-reaching effects.

Of course, it is possible to think of quality-oriented regulatory approaches that would take a broader range of effects into account. The Directive on dangerous substances discharged into the aquatic environment can be taken as an example. According to this directive, discharges of certain substances require a permit which fixes emission limit values in line with normative emission limit values to be set by the EC council on the basis of BAT (Articles 3 and 6 I). In addition, however, the council is to formulate quality objectives for the substances in question (Article 6 II), and the relevant emission limit values may be disregarded in permitting releases if the Member State can show that the entire geographical area affected by the releases keeps to the quality objectives. However, this still implies a highly selective consideration of qualitative effects. Let us look at the example of a release of dangerous pollutants from a chemical plant located in Frankfurt on the river Main (which flows into the Rhine). According to the directive, Frankfurt authorities would be entitled to depart from BAT-based European emission limit values, that is, to allow higher emissions in the relevant permit, if it can be shown that from the point of release to the estuary of the Rhine, water quality is (and will, in spite of the release, remain) in line with the relevant quality objectives. This is certainly preferable to making the binding force of emission limit values dependent only on the quality of the River Main just below the point of release, but it is still far from taking into account all the relevant qualitative impacts. An all-encompassing qualitative approach would also have to consider water quality in the seas, the quality of soils in the flood areas of the Main and Rhine, the quality of sediments from the Main to the Arctic Sea, and so on. Obviously, even if quality objectives existed concerning all these aspects, securing compliance with them cannot reasonably be left to the design of individual permits by water authorities in Frankfurt.

At any rate, the idea of a comprehensive quality approach is mere theory. The quality approach favoured by Great Britain on the European stage is more restrictive in that it takes into account only a very small segment of the relevant quality situation. It is goal-oriented only with respect to this very small segment, i.e. with respect to ambient air or water quality, at the cost of neglecting qualitative effects produced outside its area of interest by way of transport, deposition and accumulation.

Of course, the German approach does not *directly* control such distant and accumulative effects, either. For example, permit requirements for a power plant in Lower Saxony do not depend on the degree of soil acidification in Sweden or the state of the ozone layer above the North Pole. But at least, impacts on Sweden and the ozone layer are reduced by a policy of *minimising* pollution, i.e. by setting strict emission limit values which are generally applicable as a minimum standard, irrespective of whether or not they are necessitated by quality demands in Lower Saxony or Germany as a whole. This is the policy which Germany would like to see generalised on the European level, a policy that cannot properly be described as less efficient than the quality-oriented approach favoured by Great Britain. The emission-oriented approach is indeed the more expensive one since it holds up emission standards in cases where the quality-oriented approach does not, but we get something in return for the additional expense, namely more consideration for aspects of environmental quality which the so-called quality-oriented approach chooses not to consider at all.

Christian Hey observes that the IPPC Directive 'represents a compromise between the British environmental quality and the German emission control approach', but that 'Part of this compromise is, however, that the conflict between the two approaches is shifted to the technical level.' He looks particularly at the definition of 'BAT'.

### Christian Hey, *Towards Balancing Participation* (European Environmental Bureau, 2000), p. 10

The comprehensive definition with numerous qualifying comments raises more questions than actual clarification. In particular the definition of 'available' significantly limits the level of environmental policy demands. Through the conditions for commercial justifiability and the cost/benefit relationship, the British philosophy orientated towards local environmental conditions has again crept in. In this way the level of environmental policy demands becomes itself the subject of a political confrontation in forums set up for the clarification of technical questions. Some member states and the industries involved expect a diffuse result from the information exchange process[15] with a large range of recommended techniques and emission limits. The environmental orientated interested parties on the other hand expect an ambitious European standard for innovative techniques.

---

[15] The information exchange process under the Directive leads to the drawing up of 'BAT reference notes', pp. 369–73 below, footnote added.

Because it relies on a variety of standards, IPPC makes for a nice case study on what form environmental standards can take, and therefore also the variety within direct regulation; whether the compromise makes for a predictable regulatory structure is another matter.

The BAT standard is a 'technology based standard'. The permits granted by regulators must include:

> emission limit values for pollutants, in particular, those listed in Annex III, likely to be emitted from the installation concerned in significant quantities, having regard to their nature and their potential to transfer pollution from one medium to another (water, air and land). If necessary, the permit shall include appropriate requirements ensuring protection of the soil and ground water and measures concerning the management of waste generated by the installation. Where appropriate, limit values may be supplemented or replaced by equivalent parameters or technical measures. (Art. 9(3))

These limit values:

> shall be based on the best available techniques, without prescribing the use of any technique or specific technology, but taking into account the technical characteristics of the installation concerned, its geographical location and the local environmental conditions. In all circumstances, the conditions of the permit shall contain provisions on the minimization of long-distance or transboundary pollution and ensure a high level of protection for the environment as a whole. (Art. 9(4))

This extends BAT's flexibility from the realm of the regulator to that of the regulated. A BAT-type standard, which aims for pollution control that keeps up with technological development, could be filled out by telling an operator to comply with specified techniques or procedures; instead, under IPPC, operators must meet the level of emissions achievable through BAT. Regulated installations will often simply use whatever technique is BAT, and in most cases there will be no reason to do otherwise; but operators are able to choose their own method of implementation. This allows for innovation and experimentation within the regulated installation, building in an incentive for operators to discover cheaper or better ways of achieving regulatory objectives. BAT is also a dynamic standard, capable of evolving as techniques and conditions change. This is inherent in the definition of BAT, but reinforced in the Directive by the obligation to 'ensure that the competent authority follows or is informed of developments in best available techniques' (Art. 11), and the obligation to update licences even in the absence of changes to processes (Art. 13).

BAT is, however, not the end of the story on standards. First of all, any 'quality' standard set out in other legislation must be met, regardless of whether this means going *beyond* BAT in any particular case: 'Where an environmental quality standard requires stricter conditions than those achievable by the use of the best available techniques, additional measures shall in particular be required in the permit, without prejudice to other measures which might be taken to comply with environmental quality standards' (Art. 10). Quality standards are generally more flexible than emissions standards, and so they provide a level of reassurance on environmental quality in the context of decentralisation, without intruding too deeply into the principle of flexibility. However, a quality standard for a particular environmental medium and for a particular pollutant inevitably compromises the principle of integration: the 'environment as a whole' analysis no longer applies. And, returning to Lubbe-Wolff's discussion above, the quality standards do not prevent or dissuade from the export of pollution; yet this question of cross-border pollution has always been perhaps the most fundamental justification for EC environmental standard setting. Article 9(4), however, requires permits to provide conditions on the 'minimization of long-distance or transboundary pollution'; obligations of public participation (pp. 377–8) also at least bring transboundary issues to the regulator's attention.

Secondly, Art. 18 of the IPPC Directive contains a more complex proviso that centrally set emission standards may take priority over BAT:

> 1. Acting on a proposal from the Commission, the Council will set emission limit values, in accordance with the procedures laid down in the Treaty, for:
> - the categories of installations listed in Annex I ...,
>   and
> - the polluting substances referred to in Annex III, for which the need for Community action has been identified, on the basis, in particular, of the exchange of information provided for in Article 16.

The identification of BAT is one way to articulate appropriate emission limits. Article 18 provides a backstop of central control if national decision making is found wanting in this respect (or if other legislation sets emission standards). The Directive does not identify the circumstances in which a Community 'need' arises. Joanne Scott discusses the Commission's explanation of its initial proposal for the Directive:

> there 'may' be no need for such action where broadly comparable limits are set across the Community, and where the effect on competitiveness (of such differences as do emerge) is minimal. 'Where, however, standards are very different, so affecting competitiveness, future proposals under the framework of this Directive are much more likely in order to ensure the effective functioning of the internal market.'[16]

An economic basis for EU environmental regulation is nothing new: a common basis of environmental regulation before the Single European Act, and a primary reference point in the subsidiarity debate subsequently (i.e., justifying Community action), has been *economic* rather than environmental (see Chapter 4, pp. 158–64).

---

[16] Scott, 'Flexibility, "Proceduralization", and Environmental Governance', p. 267.

### European Commission, *On the Road to Sustainable Production*, p. 23

… to some extent, Community-wide limit values undermine both the decentralised and the integrated approach of the Directive, since they restrict the possibility for the competent authority to make pragmatic and environmentally- and economically-justified trade-off decisions. For example, if a limit value corresponding to the lowest achievable emission level of dioxins in steel-making is set, this might cause installations to lower their scrap recycling rates (they would be forced to reject more scrap that could be contaminated) or to significantly increase their carbon dioxide emissions (dioxin reduction measures are not energy-efficient).

When weighing different environmental objectives against each other, and considering the costs of the various options, the most sensible decision is very often influenced by the local situation at each site. Therefore, Community-wide limit values should only be introduced where they are necessary.

If, on the other hand, it becomes clear that in one or more Member States the authorities systematically set emission limit values that are too lenient and not based on BAT, it may be necessary to introduce additional Community emission limit values.

Before moving on from the question of standard-setting, we should note that the IPPC Directive allows for 'general binding rules' to be set: 'Without prejudice to the obligation to implement a permit procedure pursuant to this Directive, Member States may prescribe certain requirements for certain categories of installations in general binding rules instead of including them in individual permit conditions, provided that an integrated approach and an equivalent high level of environmental protection as a whole are ensured.'[17] This allows the Member States to restrict the discretion of their regulators to take account of local conditions in setting permits, as well as providing the possibility of reducing the administrative burden carried by the regulator.[18] This idea that flexibility is for the benefit of the Member State (rather than a burden for the Member State, or a benefit for sub-national decision makers) tells us a great deal about the Community institutions' understanding of 'subsidiarity'.

## 5  Soft harmonisation and flexibility

The backstop of centralised (quality or emission) standards is not the only limitation on substantive flexibility in IPPC. In law, decisions on 'BAT' are left to the national level, and decisions on how to achieve the emissions possible through BAT are left to the regulated party. Just as regulated parties will very often simply use BAT, the flexibility for the regulator may sometimes be more apparent than real, because of what the Commission approvingly refers

---

[17] Article 9(8).
[18] See Ray Purdy, *Implementation, Flexibility and the IPPC Directive: A Legal Analysis* (University College London, 2002).

to as 'soft harmonisation'.[19] Article 16(2) of the IPPC Directive provides for information exchange: 'The Commission shall organize an exchange of information between Member States and the industries concerned on best available techniques, associated monitoring, and developments in them. Every three years the Commission shall publish the results of the exchanges of information.'

This banal-looking provision has been radically interpreted by the Commission. It has delegated information responsibilities to the European IPPC Bureau, based in Seville, which on the basis of the 'information exchange' drafts a 'BAT reference note' (BREF) for different industries or sectors, published by the Commission. BREFs are not legally binding, but simply one factor for consideration under Annex IV (above, p. 360). The Commission acknowledges that BREFs cannot be the sole consideration, particularly because of the need to consider local conditions, but it expects them to be a 'key tool' for authorities in the permitting process, regardless of their legal status. It also anticipates that operators will refer to BREFs in preparing applications, as will the public and environmental interest groups in monitoring performance.[20] The 'Sevilla process' is described by the Commission as 'a key driver for improved environmental performance' as well as 'a highly cost-effective activity, as, in its absence, each Member State would be required to do a corresponding identification/determination of BAT'.[21]

IPPC imposes on the Member States a technically and politically challenging permitting process, and the scientific authority provided by the BREF is likely to be an attractive way of justifying decisions on BAT (see the discussion of scientific authority in Chapters 1 and 5, pp. 199–200), particularly in Member States with limited resources to devote to environmental regulation.

The authority of BREFs is not problematic in itself, and 'in each Member State some unique best available techniques exist',[22] suggesting that at least in nationally important sectors, BREFs are not blindly followed. It may however lessen the local responsiveness of the permitting process in many cases. The influence of BREFs means that the way in which they are drafted is crucial: their voluntary nature should not deflect questions of procedural legitimacy. The balance between industry and environmental representation in the 'information exchange' process leading to the BREF is crucial. Only industry and Member States are mentioned in the Directive, so the practice, which includes outsiders, is already more inclusive than the law. The concern is less that environmental interests will be explicitly and deliberately excluded, more that they will be unable to match the resources available to competing interests.

---

[19] European Commission, *On the Road to Sustainable Production: Progress in Implementing Council Directive 96/61/EC Concerning Integrated Pollution Prevention and Control* COM (2003) 354 final, p. 7.     [20] *Ibid.*, Ch. 6.     [21] *Ibid.*

[22] *Ibid.*, para. 6.2. This observation preceded the 2004 enlargement.

### Hey, *Towards Balancing Participation*, pp. 10–11

Institutionally, the process of information exchange takes place at several levels. For the clarification of political and strategic questions, an 'Information Exchange Forum' (IEF) has been set up that comprises representatives from the member states, industrial umbrella organisations, the European Commission and the European Environmental Bureau.[23] The actual exchange of information takes place at the level of the technical working groups. The composition of these technical-working groups is formally pluralistic and informally selective. Formally experts from environmental groups are invited in the same way as experts from the respective sectors of industry. In reality, however, the European Environmental Bureau (EEB) only achieves partial staffing of the technical working groups with experts, as the work is on a voluntary basis and the EEB and its members lack the resources to pay the customary market fees for experts. Since 1999 the EEB has however set up a limited budget for experts from the general EU support …

The infrastructure for the information exchange process is provided by the European IPPC Bureau (EIPPCB) in Seville. This supports an office with one expert per sector who prepares draft reports based on the information provided and the results of the expert's own research. As the process of information exchange is generally under-financed, the EIPPCB is dependent on support from the member states. It can be seen that some member states have recognised the strategic role of the specialists in the EIPPCB and dispatch such to Seville. With the dispatch of experts, countries with ambitious environmental policy have the opportunity to influence the quality of the BREFS. Representatives of the member states, partially from the ministry for the environment and partially from the ministry for economic affairs, are also involved in the information exchange process. An important role as moderator is mostly also played by the representative from the European Commission. From the side of industry, there are reports of, in some cases, dozens of participants from the affected sector. The affected branches of industry are investing in some cases considerable resources in influencing the process. In this way they demonstrate a willingness to co-operate, however they are also not deterred from making strong threats to stop the work. The exchange of information process is thus pluralistic, however in actual fact between unequally equipped partners. The balance of the interests represented in each case is rather random and depends on the ability of the involved interested parties in the affected industrial sector to mobilise support.

… The information exchange process does not include any formal conflict resolution and decision mechanisms. This deficit can be traced to the unrealistic conception of the information exchange process as a purely technical data collection process. In general, the informal consensus principle is adopted, that is, in effect, a majority rule. If, under these conditions, it is nevertheless not possible to reach agreement, compromise rules are applied: The reference values for emissions based on BAT are, e.g., the result of the mean of that which the experts consider possible … Finally there is the option of recording differing opinions in a footnote. Sometimes the EIPPC Bureau also further worsens the figure in agreement with the affected industries. This, however, not unusually triggers political conflicts.

---

[23] A pan-European federation of environmental interest groups, *www.eeb.org*, footnote added.

Political conflicts at the working group level can also be resolved at the IEF level, which, however, also does not have a formal decision procedure. At this level negotiations are more along the lines of the principle of informal pressure to agree, the rule of 'no sustained opposition'. The Commission and the EIPPCB often have a pivotal role in identifying and determining what they consider as 'consensus'.

As the Commission publishes the results of the information exchange in the EU Official Journal, formally it has a political recall facility that it, however, does not in reality consider using – the Commission does not want to endanger the overall process.

The process thus takes place under conditions of high time pressure, significant shortage of resources for the representatives of public interests, an informal pressure to agree, and in an institutional vacuum that does not include any adequate rules for a balanced representation of interests and allocation conflicts. The formally reasonable offer to the environmental groups of participation thus changes into an informally rather unreasonable institutional framework.

Issues of representation matter most if what goes on at the Seville meetings is interest representation (and hence negotiation and compromise) rather than fact finding, or even disinterested deliberation in the public interest. Joanne Scott takes a positive perspective on the potential of BREFs, suggesting (cautiously, and acknowledging that the process 'may be as easily conceived in terms of pluralist bargaining') that the technical working groups may be a 'candidate for deliberative democracy'. 'Multi-level and multi-actor in nature, these groups, in principle, transcend the technocratic elitism of Commission implementation committees, and operate on a basis which is supposed to be more transparent.'[24] Lange's subsequent empirical investigation, however, suggests a form of interest bargaining rather than deliberation.[25]

### Bettina Lange, 'From Boundary Drawing to Transitions: The Creation of Normativity under the EU Directive on Integrated Pollution Prevention and Control' (2002) 8 *European Law Journal* 246, pp. 259–60

In the political discourse, arguments about what constitutes BAT were based on the actors' expression of their own interests or what they perceived as other actors' interests in the BREF-writing process. Various overlaps between industries', Member States' and environmental NGOs' interests occurred. For example, sometimes industry perceived Member States' representatives as expressing a 'regulatory interest'. But at times Member States perceived their interests as close to industry's interests, for example, if a particular sector covered by a BREF was a key industrial sector in a Member State. Furthermore some Member States sent as representatives for their state staff from an industry, not an environmental ministry to TWG [Technical Working Group] and IEF [Information Exchange Forum] meetings. Other Member States which already had high environmental standards in place saw the BREF-writing exercise and particular BAT standards which they advocated also as an opportunity

---

[24] Scott, 'Flexibility, "Proceduralization", and Environmental Governance', p. 272.
[25] See also the passages from Hey, pp. 366 and 371.

to support the competitiveness of their industries. Similarly, within an EU-wide industry association different members could have different views on what constituted BAT depending on
what Member State they came from.

Actors' views on BAT could be informed by a range of interests. For example, Germany
argued that BAT should not just involve a description of a particular technology but should
also include reference to associated emission values that could be achieved by the techniques considered as BAT. On the one hand this was based on the idea that a BAT definition
should be very specific. On the other hand this was also an expression of Germany's interest to minimise work and hence cost involved in the implementation of the IPPC Directive.
This would be facilitated by moulding a definition of BAT to the already existing emission
limit value based regime of environmental regulation in Germany.

Reference to interests in BAT definitions could be sometimes very explicit. For example,
one participant in a second TWG meeting referred to 'political pressures' to treat a particular
type of combustion plant covered by the BREF in the same way as waste incineration plants
...

The recognition in the political discourse that interests influenced what became defined
as BAT also meant that information was perceived as containing subjective elements. For
example, the source of information could affect its content ... Furthermore in the political
discourse figures for emission limits of a particular technology would not just be accepted as
a 'fact', even if they were presented as that by the BREF-author or other participants in the
BREF-writing process. Instead they would be open to critical scrutiny on the basis of the interests of the various actors.

For current purposes, the main concern is the under-representation of environmental protection interests in BREF drafting.[26] The likelihood that resource-
intensive negotiations on BREF will be dominated by larger and wealthier
Member States adds a further dimension to this question of inclusion. The
Commission notes that 'in general the contributions of German and Dutch
experts are particularly significant', and expresses its 'gratitude' to German and
UK administrations for seconding national experts to 'author' BREFs.[27] We might
also expect greater participation by the larger and wealthier sections of industry.
The risk of exclusion therefore extends beyond environmental interests.

## 6 Proceduralisation

Although there are limits on substantive decentralisation, the Member States
have considerable flexibility in their implementation of the IPPC Directive. This
flexibility is 'procedurally constrained',[28] balanced by procedural obligations,[29]

---

[26] The Commission states that the 'contribution made by the industries concerned is usually the
most comprehensive information that the Commission receives': *On the Road to Sustainable
Production*, p. 17.    [27] *Ibid.*
[28] Scott, 'Flexibility, "Proceduralization", and Environmental Governance'.
[29] Scott, *ibid.*; Richard Macrory and Sharon Turner, 'Participatory Rights, Transboundary
Environmental Governance and EC Law' (2002) 39 *Common Market Law Review* 489.

designed both to allow outsiders to keep national regulators (and regulated parties) on the environmental straight and narrow, and to stimulate reflection and learning.

## (a) Reflexive law?

Certain aspects of 'proceduralisation' in the Directive fit nicely with theories of 'reflexive law'.[30] We will return to this in Chapter 11, but briefly, rather than dictating the objectives to be achieved, or principles to be followed, reflexive law provides structures for self-reflection and self-criticism. The objective is to create regulators and regulatees that think critically about their environmental performance, and learn from experience. The IPPC Directive's mechanisms are supposed to encourage institutions to learn, to revisit decisions, and to absorb new information, giving an indication of how direct regulation can attempt to exercise less direct influence over decision making, by changing the *culture* within which decisions are taken.

So, for example, the obligation in Art. 6 to provide a wide range of information in the permit application expands the information basis for a decision. It also, however, enables proper thought to be given by all parties to matters including 'the raw and auxiliary materials, other substances and the energy used in or generated by the installation', 'measures for the prevention and recovery of waste' and 'the main alternatives, if any, studied by the applicant in outline'.[31] The information-exchange mechanisms in the Directive, including the Sevilla process, are also part of this indirect approach to stimulating reflexivity, as is the obligation on the Commission to produce 'Reports on the implementation of this Directive and its effectiveness compared with other Community environmental instruments' (Art. 16(3)). Obligations periodically to reconsider permits, even where there is no significant change to the operation (as would be more conventional) add to the proposition that IPPC stimulates 'learning':[32]

> 1. Member States shall take the necessary measures to ensure that competent authorities periodically reconsider and, where necessary, update permit conditions.
> 2. The reconsideration shall be undertaken in any event where:
>    – the pollution caused by the installation is of such significance that the existing emission limit values of the permit need to be revised or new such values need to be included in the permit,

---

[30] Scott, 'Flexibility, "Proceduralization", and Environmental Governance'.

[31] Second, seventh and tenth indents. The final indent is added by Directive 2003/05 providing for public participation in respect of the drawing up of certain plans and programmes relating to the environment and amending with regard to public participation and access to justice Council Directives 85/337/EEC and 96/61/EC OJ 2003 L 156/17.

[32] Article 13. This can be contrasted with the position under environmental impact assessment: Ch. 14, although see the discussion of 'living assessments', pp. 604–7.

- substantial changes in the best available techniques make it possible to reduce emissions significantly without imposing excessive costs,
- the operational safety of the process or activity requires other techniques to be used,
- new provisions of Community or national legislation so dictate.

### (b) Public participation

The most significant procedural obligations in the IPPC Directive relate to public participation. The public participation is intimately related with the decentralisation in the IPPC Directive: participation at the local level (as implied by the IPPC Directive) is only meaningful if local decision makers have some discretion; in turn, it is hoped, public participation will prevent regulators discounting their environmental responsibilities.

The IPPC Directive expands public access to environmental information. Information in the application must be made available to the public, as must a copy of the permit, and the 'results of monitoring of releases as required under the permit conditions' (Art. 15(2)). The obligation on the Commission to publish 'an inventory of the principal emissions and sources responsible' every three years has been filled out by the European Pollutant Emission Register (EPER),[33] providing internet registers of emissions under IPPC. As well as providing registers in local offices, the Environment Agency provides a website that allows local emissions to be checked by entering a postcode.[34] This active dissemination of environmental information allows local people and environmental interest groups to monitor the performance of polluters and regulators. They can monitor and put pressure on these bodies, who in turn (reflexively) make their decisions in full awareness that information is available to the public.

Whilst participation arrangements are long-standing in UK planning and land use, pollution control was traditionally seen as a technical matter, suitable for confidential negotiation between regulator and regulated. In the UK, consultation provisions have been gradually introduced over several decades. The original IPPC Directive was undemanding on public participation, but the 2003 Participation Directive amends the IPPC Directive,[35] and provides that 'the public concerned are given early and effective opportunities to participate' in permitting procedures. It clarifies the legitimacy of environmental interest group involvement, by incorporating the Aarhus Convention definitions of the 'public' and the 'public concerned' (see above, p. 99). And importantly, 'the reasons and considerations on which the decision is based,

---

[33] Commission Decision 2000/479 on the implementation of a European pollutant emission register (EPER) according to Art. 15 of Council Directive 96/61/EC concerning Integrated Pollution Prevention and Control (IPPC) OJ 2000 L 192/36.

[34] www2.environment-agency.gov.uk/epr/?lang=_e&lang=_e.

[35] Directive 2003/35/EC providing for public participation in respect of the drawing up of certain plans and programmes relating to the environment OJ 2003 L 156/17.

Transboundary consultation in IPPC implies an extension of the issues considered by decision makers. As with any form of public participation, different rationales are possible. Most basically, transboundary consultation provides information on cross-border effects, meaning that there is no export of environmental harm in ignorance. More fundamentally, and if we think about the 'learning' involved in reflexive law, it could contribute to a cultural change in national administrations, ending the definition of 'relevance' by reference to national borders. Transboundary consultation has an important political dimension.

### Chris Hilson, 'Greening Citizenship: Boundaries of Membership and the Environment' (2001) 13 *Journal of Environmental Law* 335, pp. 335–6

In political terms, citizenship concerns a number of key issues. First, there is the question of the *object* of citizenship. Historically, of course, the objects of citizenship have been states. Second, there is the issue of *membership* or defining the relevant subjects of citizenship. Here, it is a matter of deciding who falls within the relevant political community and who are outsiders. Traditionally, only citizen insiders would have been entitled to *participate* in various ways in the political process – in particular through voting. And again, only those who were insiders would have been granted common *rights* as against the state or polity and may also have been under certain obligations or *duties* in relation to their community. Finally, there is an affective or *identity* element to citizenship, which involves citizens feeling an affiliation or identity with the relevant political community.

Traditionally, citizenship has been bound-up, territorially with the state in terms of both membership and identity. Only citizens of a state could receive the benefits (rights and participation) and burdens (duties) of membership. And, at least where state and nation coincided, one's identity was partly shaped by the state. In democratic terms, states were regarded as sovereign, which meant that citizen preferences in that state were supreme: no regard had to be taken of interests from other states. However, with globalisation, there are increased trade, environmental and cultural interdependencies between states which make such traditional models of citizenship and democracy unsustainable. Sovereignty, as in the EU, is increasingly 'pooled', which means that a state's citizens lose out on the ability to be in sole charge of their own policy decisions, but in return get a say (albeit typically indirect) in the affairs of other states. Functional governance has, to a significant extent, been unbundled from territory. *Government* of the nation state, where functional tasks (such as environmental policy) are coincidental with territory and identity gives rise to multi-level *governance*, where territory, functional tasks and identity are increasingly disconnected. The features of citizenship have thus also become multi-level in nature: membership is multiple and therefore rights, participation and identity can all be enforced, practised or felt, respectively, at different levels.

And finally, the amendments to the IPPC Directive also address the third 'pillar' of the Aarhus Convention: access to justice. Article 9(2) of the

Aarhus Convention provides for review of an 'act or omission subject to the provisions of article 6', which includes IPPC decisions (see Chapter 3, p. 119).

*Article 15a*

Access to justice

Member States shall ensure that, in accordance with the relevant national legal system, members of the public concerned:

   (a)  having a sufficient interest, or alternatively,

   (b)  maintaining the impairment of a right, where administrative procedural law of a Member State requires this as a precondition;

have access to a review procedure before a court of law or another independent and impartial body established by law to challenge the substantive or procedural legality of decisions, acts or omissions subject to the public participation provisions of this Directive.

Member States shall determine at what stage the decisions, acts or omissions may be challenged.

What constitutes a sufficient interest and impairment of a right shall be determined by the Member States, consistently with the objective of giving the public concerned wide access to justice. To this end, the interest of any nongovernmental organisation meeting the requirements referred to in Article 2(14) shall be deemed sufficient for the purpose of subparagraph (a) of this Article. Such organisations shall also be deemed to have rights capable of being impaired for the purpose of subparagraph (b) of this Article.

The provisions of this Article shall not exclude the possibility of a preliminary review procedure before an administrative authority and shall not affect the requirement of exhaustion of administrative review procedures prior to recourse to judicial review procedures, where such a requirement exists under national law.

Any such procedure shall be fair, equitable, timely and not prohibitively expensive.

In order to further the effectiveness of the provisions of this Article, Member States shall ensure that practical information is made available to the public on access to administrative and judicial review procedures.

This is an effort to pre-empt narrow rules of standing in the Member States, in particular enhancing the standing of environmental interest groups. Standing has been relatively unproblematic in the UK for some time, and the government is satisfied that existing judicial review procedures satisfy both Aarhus and the Directive.[40] Whilst that is probably uncontroversial in respect of standing, the *practical* barriers to access to justice are more difficult – judicial review is expensive, sometimes prohibitively so. However, whilst the affordability of judicial review is fairly intractable, it is surprising that the UK government has not made more of the possibility of less expensive *administrative* or *internal* review,[41] which is an option under Art. 15a, although not required.

---

[40]  See DEFRA, *Public Participation Directive Consultation Paper*, 28 January 2005.

[41]  As it has in the Environmental Information Regulations 2004 (SI 2004 No. 3391).

## 7 Conclusions

Licensing remains the core activity of environmental regulation. It has a very long and sometimes ignoble history, but we hope that this chapter gives some indication of how far licensing has come. The 'resurrection' of the licence may be seen in the current regime for the designation of land for special protection established by the Countryside and Rights of Way Act 2000 (Chapter 15, pp. 625–6).

The integration of pollution control was a crucial step in the development of a coherent approach to environmental protection, even if true 'integration' remains some way off. And by allowing, at least in principle, flexibility to both regulators and regulated parties, IPPC responds to criticisms of the efficiency and effectiveness of 'command and control', as we discuss in more detail in Chapter 11 below. This is enhanced by a number of contemporary 'alternative' features in IPPC which attempt to influence the self-regulatory capacities of regulated institutions (including national regulators).[42] Because this is an EC Directive, these mechanisms apply to regulators as well as regulatees. The IPPC Directive not only allows national command and control regulators to respond to criticisms of their role, but responds to pressures (especially subsidiarity pressures) at the EU level. It 'commands' the national regulator, but lightly. However, whilst the move to greater flexibility in environmental substance is an important development in EC environmental law, it would be wrong to give the impression that the EC legislator has renounced detail; highly detailed environmental legislation is still passed.[43]

## 8 Further reading

Of the extensive literature on command and control (and its critics), see in particular Robert Baldwin and Martin Cave, *Understanding Regulation: Theory, Strategy and Practice* (Oxford University Press, 1999), Chapters 4 and 6; Chris Hilson, *Regulating Pollution* (Hart, 2000), Chapter 6; and Joanne Scott, *EC Environmental Law* (Longmans, 1998), Chapters 2 and 3. Neil Emmot and Nigel Haigh, 'Integrated Pollution Prevention and Control: UK and EC Approaches and Possible Next Steps' [1996] *Journal of Environmental Law* 301, discuss the move from IPC to IPPC in some detail.

---

[42]  It will be useful to set these mechanisms against the discussion of reflexive regulation in Ch. 11, pp. 435–7.
[43]  For example some of the criteria on the management of landfill in Directive 99/31 on the landfill of waste OJ 1999 L 182/1.

# 10

# Enforcement and Implementation of Environmental Regulation

## 1 Introduction

This chapter examines a phenomenon 'so ubiquitous that we take it for granted: something that is legally mandated fails to happen. Deadlines are missed, standards are ignored or fudged, enforcement misfires.'[1] Simply putting the law in place does not lead by straight cause and effect to an improved or protected environment. Policy analysts and lawyers can misconceive the relationship between law and policy in the environmental arena, either seeing law as an 'output' of the policy process, or seeing policy as a precursor to law. This is nowhere clearer than in implementation and enforcement; policy decisions exercise a continuing and profound influence on the relationship between 'law on the books' and 'law on the ground'.

Enforcement is what happens when regulated bodies fall short of full compliance with environmental law, but the question of 'compliance' is not straightforward. The definition of compliance is rarely obvious, but will be subject to discretion: think, for example, of the discussion of 'best practicable means' in Chapter 9 (pp. 359–62), and of the values inherent in much technical activity in Chapter 1 (pp. 40–7). In addition, it is rare in environmental law for there to be a moment at which compliance can be said to be 'complete': 'The state of compliance is continuously changing. New companies are created and others go out of business, new technology or industries are introduced, markets shift, operational practices change and regulatory provisions are amended or updated.'[2] Enforcement action is no more automatic than is compliance. Enforcement requires resources and ingenuity from regulatee and regulator, such that seeking full compliance will not always be the 'best' solution. The economists talk of 'optimal compliance', where the costs of compliance (including enforcement costs) do not exceed the benefits achieved. More intuitively, we can see that resources will sometimes be better put into other (environmental) endeavours.

---

[1] Daniel A. Farber, 'Taking Slippage Seriously: Noncompliance and Creative Compliance in Environmental Law' (1999) 23 *Harvard Environmental Law Review* 297, p. 299.
[2] Christopher Demmke, 'Towards Effective Environmental Regulation: Innovative Approaches in Implementing and Enforcing European Environmental Law and Policy', Jean Monnet Working Paper 5/01, available at www.jeanmonnetprogram.org/papers/, p. 5.

In this chapter, we examine first the regulatory enforcement context in England and Wales, using water as a case study. Enforcement of environmental law is in most cases the responsibility of the Environment Agency, although local authorities retain many responsibilities, especially in land use. Enforcement rests fundamentally on criminal law, which is able in theory to provide symbolic moral condemnation, deterrence and punishment. There is, however, a range of alternative or supplementary enforcement tools. We then turn to implementation of European Community (EC) environmental law. Member States are responsible for implementing EC environmental law, and so the discussion of national enforcement should be central to reform in this area. EC environmental law also, however, raises a number of distinctive issues. Again, some examples are drawn from the field of water pollution.

## 2 National enforcement of environmental law

Enforcement of environmental law in the UK relies heavily on the existence of criminal law, but criminal law is rarely the first resort of regulators; negotiation is usually the starting point, and administrative rather than criminal sanctions have real attractions. We will begin this section by setting out the typical structure of environmental criminal law, using the example of water pollution. We then examine the Environment Agency's discretion in enforcement, before turning to the adequacy of sanctions in this area: the fine is rather a blunt instrument for dealing with breaches of environmental regulation. Finally, we consider administrative alternatives to criminal law.

This section concentrates on the consequences of a known breach; monitoring and inspection are equally important elements of enforcement. The Environment Agency has wide powers of entry and inspection. It also relies heavily on self-reporting; permits generally include conditions on self-monitoring and an obligation to inform the Environment Agency of breaches of conditions.

### (a) The criminal law: the principal water pollution offence

Important case law on environmental crime has emerged out of the principal water pollution offence in the Water Resources Act 1991:

> Section 85
> (1) A person contravenes this section if he causes or knowingly permits any poisonous, noxious or polluting matter or any solid waste matter to enter any controlled waters.
> ...
> (6) Subject to the following provisions of this Chapter, a person who contravenes this section or the conditions of any consent given under this Chapter for the purposes of this section shall be guilty of an offence.

Section 85 provides a reasonably common 'pattern' for environmental offences, with a general offence (s. 85(1)), applicable whether or not a permit has been breached (and indeed whether or not such a permit is available), and a separate offence of failing to comply with the conditions of a permit (s. 85(6)). Section 88 then introduces a defence 'in respect of authorised discharges', that is those that are within the terms of a licence.

The offence in Art. 85(1) has been very broadly interpreted by the courts. For example, 'poisonous, noxious or polluting' matter does not require the prosecutor to prove that harm has been caused by the pollution (likelihood or capability of causing harm is sufficient), or that water quality standards have been breached.[3] And 'controlled waters' is broadly defined, for example including water that has overflowed its course.[4] There are two ways to commit the offence: 'knowingly permitting' or 'causing'. The former 'involves a failure to prevent the pollution, which failure, however, must be accompanied by knowledge';[5] it is rarely prosecuted, presumably because it requires proof of *mens rea* (knowledge), and because 'causing' has been interpreted so broadly by the courts, as we shall now see.

In the next case, the defendant maintained a diesel tank in a yard which drained directly into the river. The tank's tap had no lock, and was opened by a 'person unknown', whom the Crown Court found could have been 'a malicious intruder, an aggrieved visitor or an upset local person', but could also have been an employee. The contents of the tank ran into the yard and into the river. The defendant argued that if the evidence was consistent with the tap having been opened by a stranger, the company should have been acquitted.

### *Environment Agency* v. *Empress Car Co. (Abertillery) Ltd* [1998] Env LR 396, pp. 400–10

*Lord Hoffmann*

Putting the matter shortly, if the charge is 'causing', the prosecution must prove that the pollution was caused by something which the defendant did, rather than merely failed to prevent. It is, however, very important to notice that this requirement is not because of anything inherent in the notion of 'causing'. It is because of the structure of the subsection which imposes liability under two separate heads: the first limb simply for doing something which causes the pollution and the second for knowingly failing to prevent the pollution. The notion of causing is present in both limbs: under the first limb, what the defendant did must have caused the pollution and under the second limb, his omission must have caused it. The distinction in section 85(1) between acts and omissions is entirely due to the fact that Parliament has added the requirement of knowledge when the cause of the pollution is an omission. Liability under the first limb, without proof of knowledge, therefore requires that the defendant must have done something.

…

---

[3] *Environment Agency* v. *Express Dairies* [2005] Env LR 7; *R* v. *Dovermoss Ltd* [1995] Env LR 258.
[4] *Dovermoss.*
[5] *Alphacell Ltd* v. *Woodward* [1972] AC 824, p. 834.

The courts have repeatedly said that the notion of 'causing' is one of common sense. So in *Alphacell Ltd* v. *Woodward* [1972] AC 824 at 847 Lord Salmon said: 'what or who has caused a certain event to occur is essentially a practical question of fact which can best be answered by ordinary common sense rather than by abstract metaphysical theory'.

I doubt whether the use of abstract metaphysical theory has ever had much serious support and I certainly agree that the notion of causation should not be overcomplicated. Neither, however, should it be oversimplified. In the *Alphacell* case, at page 834, Lord Wilberforce said in similar vein:

'In my opinion, "causing" here must be given a common sense meaning and I deprecate the introduction of refinements, such as cause causans, effective cause or novus actus. There may be difficulties where acts of third persons or natural forces are concerned …'.

The last concession was prudently made, because it is of course the causal significance of acts of third parties (as in this case) or natural forces that gives rise to almost all the problems about the notion of 'causing' and drives judges to take refuge in metaphor or Latin. I therefore propose to concentrate upon the way common sense notions of causation treat the intervention of third parties or natural forces. The principles involved are not complicated or difficult to understand, but they do in my opinion call for some explanation. It is remarkable how many cases there are under this Act in which justices have attempted to apply common sense and found themselves reversed by the Divisional Court for error of law. More guidance is, I think, necessary.

The first point to emphasise is that common sense answers to questions of causation will differ according to the purpose for which the question is asked. Questions of causation often arise for the purpose of attributing responsibility to someone, for example, so as to blame him for something which has happened or to make him guilty of an offence or liable in damages. In such cases, the answer will depend upon the rule by which responsibility is being attributed. Take, for example, the case of the man who forgets to take the radio out of his car and during the night someone breaks the quarterlight, enters the car and steals it. What caused the damage? If the thief is on trial, so that the question is whether he is criminally responsible, then obviously the answer is that he caused the damage. It is no answer for him to say that it was caused by the owner carelessly leaving the radio inside. On the other hand, the owner's wife, irritated at the third such occurrence in a year, might well say that it was his fault. In the context of an inquiry into the owner's blameworthiness under a non-legal, common sense duty to take reasonable care of one's own possessions, one would say that his carelessness caused the loss of the radio.

Not only may there be different answers to questions about causation when attributing responsibility to different people under different rules (in the above example, criminal responsibility of the thief, common sense responsibility of the owner) but there may be different answers when attributing responsibility to different people under the same rule.

…

What, therefore, is the nature of the duty imposed by section 85(1)? Does it include responsibility for acts of third parties or natural events and, if so, for any such acts or only some of them? This is a question of statutory construction, having regard to the policy of the Act. It is immediately clear that the liability imposed by the subsection is strict: it does not require *mens rea* in the sense of intention or negligence. Strict liability is imposed in the interests of protecting controlled waters from pollution …

Clearly, therefore, the fact that a deliberate act of a third party caused the pollution does not in itself mean that the defendant's creation of a situation in which the third party could so act did not also cause the pollution for the purposes of section 85(1).

…

While liability under section 85(1) is strict and therefore includes liability for certain deliberate acts of third parties and (by parity of reasoning) natural events, it is not an absolute liability in the sense that all that has to be shown is that the polluting matter escaped from the defendant's land, irrespective of how this happened. It must still be possible to say that the defendant caused the pollution. Take, for example, the lagoons of effluent in *Price* v. *Cromack* [1975] 1 WLR 988. They leaked effluent into the river and I have said that in my view the justices were entitled to hold that the pollution had been caused by the defendant maintaining leaky lagoons. But suppose that they emptied into the river because a wall had been breached by a bomb planted by terrorists. I think it would be very difficult to say, as a matter of common sense, that the defendant had caused the pollution. On what principle, therefore, will some acts of third parties (or natural events) negative causal connection for the purposes of section 85(1) and others not?

In *Alphacell* v. *Woodward* [1972] AC 824, Lord Salmon, as I have mentioned, suggested that the difference might depend upon whether the act of a third party or natural event was foreseeable or not …

…

In the sense in which the concept of foreseeability is normally used, namely as an ingredient in the tort of negligence, in the form of the question: ought the defendant reasonably to have foreseen what happened, I do not think that it is relevant. Liability under section 85(1) is not based on negligence; it is strict …

The true common sense distinction is, in my view, between acts and events which, although not necessarily foreseeable in the particular case, are in the generality a normal and familiar fact of life, and acts or events which are abnormal and extraordinary. Of course an act or event which is in general terms a normal fact of life may also have been foreseeable in the circumstances of the particular case, but the latter is not necessary for the purposes of liability. There is nothing extraordinary or abnormal about leaky pipes or lagoons as such: these things happen, even if the particular defendant could not reasonably have foreseen that it would happen to him. There is nothing unusual about people putting unlawful substances into the sewage system and the same, regrettably, is true about ordinary vandalism. So when these things happen, one does not say: that was an extraordinary coincidence, which negatived the causal connection between the original act of accumulating the polluting substance and its escape. In the context of section 85(1), the defendant's accumulation has still caused the pollution. On the other hand, the example I gave of the terrorist attack would be something so unusual that one would not regard the defendant's conduct as having caused the escape at all.

### Carolyn Abbot, 'The Enforcement of Pollution Control Laws in England and Wales: A Case for Reform?' (2005) 22 *Environmental and Planning Law Journal* 68, pp. 70–1

The merits and defects of imposing criminal liability in the absence of mens rea are well rehearsed. Some commentators posit that strict liability crimes run contrary to the central tenet of criminal law: the punishment of the morally blameworthy. They focus particularly on the perceived unfairness of such laws in their application to individuals. Others argue that due to the nature of environmental harm, a strict approach to liability is justified. By reducing the burden on regulators to secure a successful prosecution and lessening the procedural costs associated with criminal litigation, environmental offenders, whose actions should be punished in the public interest, will receive the full force of the criminal law. This is particularly so in the case of corporate entities who 'wield such power (in terms of economic resources and influence), that there is no social unfairness in holding them to higher standards than individuals when it comes to criminal liability – so long as fair warning is given, since companies are run by individuals'.[6] ... the Environment Agency's Enforcement Policy responds to the harshness of strict liability by stating that the blameworthiness of the defendant is a factor in determining the most appropriate enforcement action. And in sentencing offenders, the culpability of the defendant is an important aggravating factor.

Prosecutions for environmental offences are generally brought against companies, but the ability to prosecute individuals can be equally important, concentrating the mind more effectively than corporate liability.

### Water Resources Act 1991, s. 217

(1) Where a body corporate is guilty of an offence under this Act and that offence is proved to have been committed with the consent or connivance of, or to be attributable to any neglect on the part of, any director, manager, secretary or other similar officer of the body corporate or any person who was purporting to act in any such capacity, then he, as well as the body corporate, shall be guilty of that offence and shall be liable to be proceeded against and punished accordingly.

...

(3) ... where the commission by any person of an offence under the water pollution provisions of this Act is due to the act or default of some other person, that other person may be charged with and convicted of the offence.

This possibility is infrequently pursued.[7] According to the Environment Agency, it is most appropriate 'where it can be shown that the offence was

---

[6] Andrew Ashworth, *Principles of Criminal Law* (Oxford University Press, 2003), pp. 166–7.

[7] *Express Dairies* involved a s. 217 prosecution against the owner of land: in this case the 'act or default' was in failing to undertake a proper risk assessment of the activities carried out on the property (the delivery of milk).

committed with their consent, was due to their neglect or they "turned a blind eye" to the offence or the circumstances leading to it'.[8]

## (b) Discretion in enforcement

The Environment Agency enjoys considerable discretion as to what action to take in respect of breaches of environmental law, and prosecution is by no means automatic. There is a long-standing debate about the best approach to enforcement of environmental law. The main distinction is drawn between 'compliance' approaches, where the environmental regulator seeks to work with a polluter and improve performance, and 'deterrence' approaches, where the full force of the law is brought to bear on polluters.[9] It is generally accepted that the Environment Agency operates a 'compliance' approach to enforcement.

### Abbot, 'The Enforcement of Pollution Control Laws', pp. 71–3

The Environment Agency's enforcement strategy reflects the compliance-based model of enforcement. Under a compliance strategy, regulators will try to negotiate with and persuade the regulated community to comply with their legislative obligations. Under this model, formal enforcement mechanisms such as criminal prosecution and licence revocation are seen more as a 'last resort' and often signify a breakdown in communication between the two parties. Compared with deterrence or sanctioning enforcement strategies, under which regulators will detect and punish violations, using prosecutions and other legal sanctions as routine enforcement mechanisms, a compliance strategy is arguably a more cost-effective system. Formal enforcement action, particularly criminal prosecution is a costly exercise for public regulators. The Environment Agency, like most other regulatory authorities, is notoriously understaffed and under-resourced and resource issues will hugely influence its choice of enforcement strategy.

In the 1980s a number of legal scholars undertook empirical studies of environmental enforcement activities in the UK. During this time, environmental agencies adopted a predominantly compliance-based enforcement strategy with great value being placed on the importance of maintaining a good relationship with regulated entities. In general, officers most frequently coaxed compliance by using informal enforcement mechanisms such as verbal warnings. But where these tactics failed, they would have recourse to increasingly formal and punitive methods including the serving of administrative notices, licence suspension and criminal prosecution …

Since this time, the enforcement approach in the UK has become more legalistic and contentious: there has been 'a discernible shift away from the informal, cooperative approach to enforcement'.[10] Recent policy statements in the Environment Agency's corporate publications

---

[8] Environment Agency, *Enforcement and Prosecution Policy* (1998).

[9] See, for example, Keith Hawkins, *Environment and Enforcement; Regulation and the Social Definition of Pollution* (Clarendon, 1984); Bridget M. Hutter, *The Reasonable Arm of the Law? The Law Enforcement Procedures of Environmental Health Officers* (Clarendon, 1988).

[10] Stuart Bell and Donald McGillivray, *Environmental Law* (Blackstones, 5th edn, 2000), p. 243.

indicate a greater reliance on a deterrence style of enforcement, particularly in the application of the law to directors and other company managers. For example, in the Agency's Spotlight on Business Environmental Performance 2000, it was stressed that 'directors of businesses must recognise that they are personally responsible for complying with the law'. During 2003, 11 company directors were convicted and fined.[11]

...

To say, however, that the Environment Agency has adopted a deterrence-based approach across the board would be misleading. Firstly, prosecution numbers are still very low in comparison with the proliferation of pollution incidents that occur. For example, in 1999–2000, 17,592 waste incidents were investigated by the Agency, but only 342 offenders were prosecuted. And as regards water pollution offences under the *Water Resources Act 1991*, 246 prosecutions resulted from the investigation of 14,417 substantiated pollution incidents. But there is little doubt that the Environment Agency is increasingly prosecuting environmental offenders.

There are several possible explanations for this. Firstly, one could point to the fact that as there has been a steady increase in the level of fines imposed by the courts on environmental offenders, criminal prosecution becomes a more effective and efficient enforcement mechanism. But where fines are very low compared with the profits generated from harmful activities, their deterrence value (and therefore the impact of prosecution) is limited. Secondly, the Agency, which is funded partly by central government grants, has seen its grant-in-aid from the Department for Environment, Food and Rural Affairs (DEFRA) rise from approximately £100.1 million in 1998/99 to £117.4 million in 2003/04.[12] The Agency has therefore been able to fund more inspections and more enforcement. In addition, there has been a change in cultural attitudes to environmental harm with pollution now being seen as morally unacceptable as opposed to an acceptable by-product of industry. This, fuelled by the increase in public interest in environmental accidents, could also help to explain the rise in prosecutions.

## Derek Bell and Tim Gray, 'The Ambiguous Role of the Environment Agency in England and Wales' (2002) 11 *Environmental Politics* 76, pp. 87–9

Clearly, the Agency's stakeholders have different perceptions of its regulatory style: operators see it as too confrontational; environmentalists see it as too co-operative. Five factors might explain these differences in perception. First, different Agency organs use different regulatory styles in response to their different circumstances. For example, IPPC (Integrated Pollution Prevention and Control) inspectors 'usually work face to face with senior corporate executives or specialists in environmental management' whereas 'waste regulation is often akin to street policing – unannounced spot checks, detective work and surveillance of those

---

[11]  Environment Agency, *Spotlight on Business Environmental Performance in 2003* (2004), pp. 1 and 5.

[12]  Note more recent concern about cuts and 'efficiency savings': House of Commons Environmental Audit Committee, 2nd Report of Session 2004–5, *Corporate Environmental Crime* HC 136, footnote added.

suspected of illegal dumping of waste'.[13] We might reasonably expect the Agency to adopt different regulatory styles in such different circumstances.

Second, differences in perception of the Agency's regulatory style may simply reflect stakeholders' different interests. The community or environmental group that does not get its way is likely to be suspicious of the Agency's motives, while the company forced to comply with costly regulations or 'named and shamed' for its poor performance is likely to view the Agency as confrontational. Third, criticising the Agency's regulatory style may be a conscious attempt by different political actors to advance their own agenda.

Fourth, it may be that the Agency is intermittently and inconsistently confrontational and co-operative. This might be due to the Agency's lack of a vision and the consequent absence of an organising principle for regulation. Finally, it may be that the Agency is 'simultaneously' confrontational *and* co-operative. Fineman has suggested that the Agency engages in 'sabre rattling' to sustain a 'separatory myth'.[14] In other words, there is collusion with industry (or 'mutual capture'), but to maintain confidence in the 'impartiality and independence of the regulator' the Agency needs to proceed '*as if* regulator and regulated are separate'.[15] If Fineman is right, the adoption of a confrontational regulatory style is (consciously or unconsciously) intended to 'keep up appearances' while co-operation is the inevitable product of informal networks and mutual resource-dependence between the Agency and the companies it regulates. However, this strategy risks the alienation of both industrial and environmental stakeholders.

If the Agency is to improve its standing in the eyes of its stakeholders it needs carefully to consider its regulatory style and find ways of institutionalising that style, from board level to 'street-level'. Three issues seem especially relevant to the Agency's deliberations. First, would it consider itself a successful regulator if it ensured that the companies it regulates complied with the minimum standards set by legislation or is it seriously committed to encouraging and inspiring operators to go beyond minimum requirements? If the Agency's aim were to encourage operators to exceed minimum requirements rather than merely achieve them, a confrontational style would seem to be less appropriate because the main threat that backs a confrontational approach is legal action but that threat is not available if operators are already meeting legal requirements. Given that the Agency's general duty to promote the environment and sustainable development suggests that as a regulator it should aim to encourage operators to exceed minimum requirements, it seems to have some grounds for preferring a more co-operative regulatory style.

Second, is the Agency's role 'to "prevent" industry from doing things' or 'to "enable" industry to operate'?[16] ...

Third, how dependent is the Agency on the co-operation of industry to achieve its aims? Insofar as the Agency needs industry's co-operation, a confrontational regulatory style may be less effective than a co-operative style. The Agency's level of dependence on the companies it regulates will be a function of its 'resources' and its 'needs'. For

---

[13]   Stephen Fineman, 'Street-level Bureaucrats and the Social Construction of Environmental Control' (1998) 19 *Organisation Studies* 953, p. 955.

[14]   *Ibid.*, pp. 963, 971.     [15]   *Ibid.*, p. 971.

[16]   *Memorandum by Cleanaway Ltd Submitted to the Environment Subcommittee of the Environment, Transport and Regional Affairs Committee* (2000).

example, if the Agency needs detailed technical data about pollution control technology being used by the companies it regulates, it has little option but to rely on the
companies to provide it. However, its level of dependence might be decreased if either
it has quick and effective legal means of forcing compliance with requests for information (for example, fast-track prosecutions, high fines) or it has less need for that
information (for example, it adopts a 'hands-off', less technically prescriptive approach to
regulation leaving it to companies to find the best means of achieving their emissions
targets).

As suggested in the above passages, a number of advantages are quite convincingly claimed for a compliance approach. In addition to cost effectiveness and
the maintenance of relationships over the long term, we should recall the reality
of environmental crime. Routine and relatively minor breaches of regulation
are in principle criminal: often environmental offences are strict liability and
require no evidence of environmental harm. However, 'the adoption of strict
liability does not expedite formal enforcement of the law, for taking advantage
of strict liability is regarded as being "unreasonable"'.[17] We should also expect
the Environment Agency to select prosecutions that they will win, not least for
symbolic value.[18] An immediately confrontational approach may be counter-
productive in a more fundamental sense.

### Robert A. Kagan and John T. Scholz, 'The "Criminology of the Corporation" and Regulatory Enforcement Strategies' in Keith Hawkins and John M. Thomas (eds.), *Enforcing Regulation* (Kluwer-Nijhoff Publishing, 1984), pp. 67–86

Stated most simply, the three images and the corresponding theories of noncompliance are
as follows:

In the first image, business firms are pictured as *amoral calculators*. Motivated entirely
by profit-seeking, they carefully and competently assess opportunities and risks. They
disobey the law when the anticipated fine and probability of being caught are small in
relation to the profits to be garnered through disobedience. Non-compliance stems
from *economic calculation*.

The second image pictures the business firm as a political *citizen*, ordinarily inclined to
comply with the law, partly because of belief in the rule of law, partly as a matter of
long-term self-interest. That commitment, however, is contingent. Business managers
have strong views as to proper public policy and business conduct. At least some law
breaking stems from *principled disagreement* with regulations or orders they regard as
arbitrary or unreasonable.

In the third image, the business firm is seen as inclined to obey the law but as
a potentially fallible or *organisationally incompetent* entity. Many violations of regulations are attributed to *organisational failure* – corporate managers fail to oversee

---

[17] Hawkins, *Environment and Enforcement.*     [18] *Ibid.*

subordinates adequately, to calculate risks intelligently, to establish organisational mechanisms that keep all operatives abreast of and attentive to the growing dictates of the law.

Each of these images and theories of deviant behavior suggests a somewhat different regulatory enforcement strategy.

If regulated businesses are seen as keen-eyed *amoral calculators*, the regulatory agency should emphasize aggressive inspection of all firms and promptly impose severe legal penalties for any violations, lest the firm be tempted to try to 'get away with more'. The goal, in short, is *deterrence*. The governmental inspector, accordingly, should be a strict *policeman*, indifferent to businessmen's manipulative excuses.

If regulated business firms are viewed as *political citizens*, responding to the perceived reasonableness or unreasonableness of regulatory orders, the regulatory inspectors should be, in many cases, not a strict policeman but more of a *politician*. He should be concerned with *persuading* the regulated firm of the rationality of the regulation in question ...

If regulated business firms are thought to be prone to *incompetence* and regulatory violations due to organisational failures, the regulatory inspector should serve in large part as a *consultant*. His responsibility would be to analyze informational gaps and organisational weaknesses in the regulated firm, and to *educate* businessmen concerning feasible technologies and management systems that would best ensure compliance in the future.

...

One implication of the diverse sources of noncompliance is that indiscriminate reliance on any single theory of noncompliance is likely to be wrong, and when translated into an enforcement strategy, it is likely to be counterproductive. To treat every firm as an amoral calculator, whereby any deviation from specific regulatory rules is met by legal penalties, burdens the economy with unnecessary costs. It also breeds legal and political opposition on the part of good corporate citizens who are offended by being forced to meet unreasonable requirements and by the perceived injustice of punishment pursuant to legalistic rule application. Conversely, if regulators were always to act as responsive politicians or consultants, and always withhold penalties, in hopes of convincing or teaching the company to do 'the right thing', the amoral calculators will take advantage of their flexibility. The relevant question, therefore, both from the standpoint of explanatory or predictive theory and from the standpoint of regulatory strategy, is not which theory to use, but *when* each is likely to be appropriate.

Going back to the Environment Agency's 'style', Richard Macrory and Michael Woods suggest that 'there has been a tendency to follow the compliance approach, although more recently, so-called "responsive regulation" has become an influential alternative'.[19] Ian Ayres and John Braithwaite developed

---

[19]  Richard Macrory and Michael Woods, *Environmental Civil Penalties: A More Proportionate Response to Regulatory Breach* (2004), available at www.ucl.ac.uk/laws/environment/civil-penalty/, para. 2.13.

what has become the very influential theory of 'responsive regulation' in 1992. Responsive regulation relies on an 'enforcement pyramid', according to which regulators will begin with attempts 'to coax compliance by persuasion', escalating gradually up the pyramid, through warning letters and financial penalties, to the most coercive approaches.[20] Like Kagan and Scholz above, Ayres and Braithwaite see a range of motivations and capacities in offenders. Regulation has to be flexible and dynamic to respond to these different factors, and operate to 'protect us against knaves while leaving space for nurturing of civic virtue'.[21] Crucially, the regulator must have a range of sanctions at its disposal: 'regulatory agencies are often best able to secure compliance when they are benign big guns. That is, regulators will be more able to speak softly when they carry big sticks (and crucially, a hierarchy of lesser sanctions).'[22]

Whilst in principle flexible enforcement seems to be the most sensible approach for environmental regulators, questions inevitably arise about the accountability of regulators. Rather than taking a compliance approach, they may be inefficient, incompetent, poorly resourced or corrupt; they may have been 'captured' by the parties they are supposed to regulate; there may be discrimination in favour of (mainly) 'white collar' criminals. The exercise of enforcement discretion has traditionally been wholly sheltered from public scrutiny, although improved rights of access to environmental information now ameliorate the position somewhat. So, for example, the 'pollution control register' under the Water Resources Act 1991 makes available consents and their conditions as well as monitoring information.[23] This means that many possible breaches can be identified, even if regulatory negotiations remain confidential. Private prosecution is usually available in the UK, and although resource considerations mean that it is rarely used, it can shame regulators into action.

The Environment Agency does face criticism for using the full force of the law too rarely, and bringing too few prosecutions. Access to information provides some accountability. This is supplemented by the Environment Agency's policy on enforcement, which at least allows an open debate on overall policy, even if individual decisions in routine cases remain in the shadows. The Environment Agency states that the 'purpose of enforcement is to ensure that preventative or remedial action is taken to protect the environment or to secure compliance with a regulatory system',[24] and that the principles of '**proportionality** in the application of the law and in securing compliance; **consistency** of approach; **transparency** about how the Agency operates and what those regulated may expect from the Agency; and **targeting** of enforcement action' underlie its policy.[25]

---

[20] Ian Ayres and John Braithwaite, *Responsive Regulation: Transcending the Deregulation Debate* (Oxford University Press, 1992), pp. 35–6.

[21] *Ibid.*, p. 53.    [22] *Ibid.*, p. 19.    [23] Water Resources Act 1991, s. 190.

[24] Environment Agency, *Enforcement and Prosecution Policy*, para. 6.    [25] *Ibid.*, para. 9.

### Environment Agency, *Enforcement and Prosecution Policy* (1998)

#### Targeting

16. Targeting means making sure that regulatory effort is directed primarily towards those whose activities give rise to or risk of serious environmental damage, where the risks are least well controlled or against deliberate or organised crime. Action will be primarily focused on lawbreakers or those directly responsible for the risk and who are best placed to control it.

…

18. In the case of regulated industries, management actions are important. Repeated incidents or breaches of regulatory requirements which are related may be an indication of an unwillingness to change behaviour, or an inability to achieve sufficient control and may require a review of the regulatory requirements, the actions of the Operator and additional investment. A relatively low hazard site or activity poorly managed has potential for greater risk to the environment than a higher hazard site or activity where proper control measures are in place. There are, however, high hazard sites (for example, nuclear installations, some major chemical plants or some waste disposal facilities) which will receive regular visits so that the Agency can be sure that remote risks continue to be effectively managed.

More specifically on the use of prosecution, 'the criminal process … aims to punish wrongdoing, to avoid a recurrence and to act as a deterrent to others'.[26]

### Environment Agency, *Enforcement and Prosecution Policy*

#### Sufficiency of Evidence

21. A prosecution will not be commenced or continued by the Agency unless it is satisfied that there is sufficient, admissible and reliable evidence that the offence has been committed and that there is a realistic prospect of conviction. If the case does not pass this evidential test, it will not go ahead, no matter how important or serious it may be. Where there is sufficient evidence, a prosecution will not be commenced or continued by the Agency unless it is in the public interest to do so. Public interest factors that can affect the decision to prosecute usually depend on the seriousness of the offence or the circumstances of the offender.

#### Public Interest Factors

22. The Agency will consider the following factors in deciding whether or not to prosecute:
  - **environmental effect** of the offence,
  - **foreseeability** of the offence or the circumstances leading to it,
  - **intent** of the offender, individually and/or corporately,
  - **history** of offending,
  - **attitude** of the offender,
  - **deterrent effect** of a prosecution, on the offender and others,
  - **personal circumstances** of the offender

---

[26] *Ibid.*, para. 19.

23. The factors are not exhaustive and those which apply will depend on the particular circumstances of each case. Deciding on the public interest is not simply a matter of adding up the number of factors on each side …

…

**Presumption of Prosecution**

28. Where there is sufficient evidence, the Agency will normally prosecute in any of the following circumstances:-

**incidents or breaches which have significant consequences for the environment or which have the potential for such consequences**. The Agency takes seriously such incidents or breaches.

**carrying out operations without a relevant licence**. It is a pre-requisite to successful regulation that those required to be regulated come within the appropriate licensing system.

**excessive or persistent breaches of regulatory requirements** in relation to the same licence or site.

**failure to comply or to comply adequately with formal remedial requirements**. It is unacceptable to ignore remedial requirements and unfair to those who do take action to comply.

**reckless disregard for management or quality standards**. It is in the interests of all that irresponsible operators are brought into compliance or cease operations.

**failure to supply information without reasonable excuse or knowingly or recklessly supplying false or misleading information**. It is essential that lawful requests for information by the Agency are complied with and that accurate information is always supplied to enable informed regulation to be exercised.

**obstruction of Agency staff** in carrying out their powers. The Agency regards the obstruction of, or assaults on, its staff while lawfully carrying out their duties as a serious matter.

**impersonating Agency staff**. The Agency regards impersonation of staff, for example, in order to gain access to premises wrongfully, as a serious matter.

## (c) Sanctions: fines and beyond

The award of light punishment by the courts is a very understandable reason for the Agency being slow to prosecute. Indeed, the House of Commons Environmental Audit Committee has said that 'it is remarkable that prosecuting bodies have the determination to prosecute as many cases as they do. Justice must often appear to be a lottery, and a lottery that costs the authority pursuing the case more than it is likely to receive in costs and more than the offender is likely to receive in terms of any fine.'[27] One of the major challenges for criminal environmental law is that defendants are frequently corporations, with 'no soul to damn, no body to kick':[28] a company cannot be imprisoned. And whilst custodial sentences are in principle available against individuals who commit

---

[27] House of Commons Environmental Audit Committee, Sixth Report of Session 2003–4, *Environmental Crime and the Courts* HC 126, para. 28.

[28] John C. Coffee Jr, '"No Soul to Damn, No Body To Kick": An Unscandalised Enquiry into the Problem of Corporate Punishment' (1981) 79 *Michigan Law Review* 386.

environmental crimes, they are only rarely used,[29] deemed too harsh a penalty.[30] The following case involved an appeal against sentence for illegally dumping 2,000 lorry tyres, and the Court of Appeal sets out some of the considerations around imposing a custodial sentence.

### *R* v. *O'Brien and Enkel* [2000] Env LR 653, pp. 655–6

*Goldring J*

In our view, this case is at the lower end of the scale. The appellants became involved in the offences because they saw a chance of making a quick profit. It is clear to us that they could not have believed that they were entitled to dump the tyres as they did. Having said that, there are some features that need to be taken into account when deciding the appropriate sentence on the facts of this case. Although unsightly, the tyres were not dangerous. There was no long-term effect on the environment. The fact that a licence was not required simply to store them suggests that lack of danger. It is difficult in the circumstances to see how they could be described, as they were by the judge in sentencing, as a nuisance. There were not here repeated breaches. It may be the appellants thought they could in due course dispose of the tyres to farmers, although we are a little sceptical about that. Neither has a conviction for an offence of this sort. In the final analysis, albeit at the last moment, they pleaded guilty. It is also the case that they were not the only ones who were involved in these offences. In our view, this case does not pass the custody threshold. The justice of the case would have been met by a fine or a community service order.

The most common sanction, in this context of corporate offenders and a reluctance to imprison, is the fine, which fails to rise to the challenge of environmental protection in a number of ways. Most obviously, 'fines are too low'.[31]

However, even huge fines would not solve the problem of deterrence. Fines are ineffective against companies with enormous resources, and those with very few. In the latter case, because there is no alternative sanction such as imprisonment, fines only deter up to solvency – once the company has run out of funds, no further punishment or deterrence is available. In the former case, a fine that 'hurts' would have to be so large that it seems either absurd or unfair. For example, Esso were fined a 'staggering' $2 million in Australia for breach of health and safety legislation: 'but considering that the company earns approximately $2 million per day from its Bass Strait operations, the fine could be described as derisory'.[32] High fines can also have negative social impacts, an even more acute problem with a public sector defendant.

---

[29] For a case in which a custodial sentence was imposed, see *R* v. *Garrett* [1997] 1 Cr App R 109.

[30] See, for example, Environmental Audit Committee, *Environmental Crime*: 'The use of custodial sentences at all for environmental crime is rare and probably should remain that way' (para. 30).    [31] *Ibid.*, para. 29.

[32] Carolyn Abbot, 'Regulatory Enforcement of Pollution Control Laws: The Australian Experience' (2005) 17 *Journal of Environmental Law* 161, p. 171.

The next extract involves an appeal against the £4 million fine awarded against a defendant that had pleaded guilty to the water pollution offence in s. 85(1), but simply because of the strict liability nature of the offence, and without accepting fault of any kind. The case arose out of the grounding of the tanker *Sea Empress* sailing into Milford Haven, and the resulting serious spill of oil. The pilot guiding the tanker was employed by Milford Haven Port Authority, and had made serious errors.

### *R* v. *Milford Haven Port Authority* [2000] Env LR 632, Court of Appeal, pp. 635–48

*The Lord Chief Justice*

The area around Milford Haven is a beautiful, remote, environmentally sensitive area particularly sought after by bird watchers, fishermen, walkers, holiday makers and lovers of secluded countryside. It contains a national park, nature and marine nature reserves, many sites of special scientific interest, special protection areas and special areas of conservation. There has for many years been a port at Milford Haven and in recent years a major oil terminal serving several refineries. The port and its associated facilities are a major source of employment and economic activity in the area. But entering the Haven for large vessels such as oil tankers poses a number of navigational problems and risks. In particular the West Channel, which Sea Empress was entering, is narrow; the underwater contours of the Channel give rise to potential dangers; and the Channel itself is affected by significant tide patterns and flows. The weather pattern includes south-westerly gales and storms, particularly in the winter months. The entrance therefore requires careful navigation by a sufficiently trained and experienced pilot. But the passage of vessels into and out of the port is an everyday event all the year round.

…

The culpability of the Port Authority would have been very much greater had it pleaded guilty or been convicted on any basis other than one of strict liability. It is, however, important to bear prominently in mind a countervailing consideration. Parliament creates an offence of strict liability because it regards the doing or not doing of a particular thing as itself so undesirable as to merit the imposition of criminal punishment on anyone who does or does not do that thing irrespective of that party's knowledge, state of mind, belief or intention. This involves a departure from the prevailing canons of the criminal law because of the importance which is attached to achieving the result which Parliament seeks to achieve. The present case affords a very good example. The danger of oil pollution is so potentially devastating, so far-reaching and so costly to rectify that Parliament attaches a criminal penalty to breach of section 85 even where no lack of care or due diligence is shown … So although the Port Authority is fully entitled to rely strongly on its relative lack of culpability – and its position would be very much more vulnerable if it were unable so to rely – it cannot reasonably hope to escape a very substantial financial penalty when its commission of an offence against the section has such serious results.

… It would be quite wrong to suggest – and counsel for the Port Authority does not suggest – that public bodies are immune from appropriate criminal penalties because they have no shareholders and the directors are not in receipt of handsome annual bonuses. The policy of Parliament would be frustrated if such a notion were to gain currency. But in fixing the amount of a fine it is proper for the judge to take all the facts of the case into account ... The judge has to consider how any financial penalty will be paid. If a very substantial financial penalty will inhibit the proper performance by a statutory body of the public function that it has been set up to perform, that is not something to be disregarded ...

...

It is plain that, in order to meet the fine and because of the other expenses to which it has been put by this disaster, the Port Authority has cut back on expenditure and attempted to retrench. This has provoked a letter from the Pembrokeshire County Council dated March 6, 2000, and written with specific reference to this appeal. In the penultimate paragraph of that letter written by the Chief Executive of the County Council it is said:

> 'The Council considers that Pembrokeshire has had to suffer twice from the impact of the Sea Empress. The economic damage and the associated negative publicity of the oil spill itself was a disaster, the fine and curtailment of investment plans by the Port Authority has worsened the situation at a time when the County needs additional support.'

The Pembrokeshire County Council is not of course responsible for assessing the appropriate level of fine, but it does represent a body of citizens who might well have been expected to wish a severe penalty to be inflicted on a body regarded as responsible for violating its environment in this way.

We fully appreciate the judge's reasons for regarding this as a very serious case calling for a substantial penalty. He was rightly anxious to make clear that offences of this kind on this scale come high in the scale of seriousness. But we conclude that he did fall into error in failing to give effect to the agreed basis of the Port Authority's plea of guilty, in failing to give full credit for its plea of guilty, and in failing to consider the possible impact of a £4 million fine on the Port Authority's ability to perform its public functions. We also conclude (although largely on the basis of material which was not before the judge) that he took much too rosy a view of the Port Authority's financial position and prospects.

We are satisfied that in the result the fine imposed was in all the circumstances manifestly excessive. That leaves us with the difficult task of substituting what we consider an appropriate fine. It must be at a level which recognises the seriousness of such disasters and the need to ensure the highest levels of vigilance. But it should not be such as to cripple the Port Authority's business and blight the economy of Pembrokeshire. We conclude that, in the light of all the circumstances now known to us, an appropriate fine is one of £750,000.

The Court of Appeal in this case does not lay down any general guidance for environmental sentencing, although it sets out relevant factors for consideration in each case.[33] It is clear that the Court of Appeal is concerned about the

---

[33] The Court of Appeal had a statutory duty (s. 80(2) Crime and Disorder Act 1998) to consider framing guidelines, following the provision by the Sentencing Advisory Panel of advice on environmental crime in 2000. The Court of Appeal determined that it could not 'usefully do more than draw attention to the factors relevant to sentence which we have already briefly alluded to': p. 670.

potential of fines to rebound on the innocent: here local residents and employees, but also shareholders, or consumers. None of these 'innocent' groups should gain an advantage from illegal acts, but it remains a real issue that the negative social side-effects of a genuinely deterrent financial penalty could be excessive.

As well as the formal sanction, the negative publicity associated with criminal conviction is an important informal consequence of conviction.

### Alex Mehta and Keith Hawkins, 'Integrated Pollution Control and its Impact: Perspectives From Industry' (1998) 10 *Journal of Environmental Law* 61, pp. 65–8

It seems reasonable to suggest that the days of companies consciously polluting the environment for purely financial motives (because it is cheaper to pay a fine than the costs of compliance) may well be disappearing. Indeed, most managers interviewed agreed with the principle of IPC [Integrated Pollution Control] and with the broad aims of pollution control in general. Many also mentioned a strong sense of moral and legal obligation supporting compliant behaviour. No manager thought the IPC regime represented an unreasonable or in some sense illegitimate intrusion by the law. Therefore, it is probably reasonable to assume that while the pursuit of profit remains the primary concern of business, for most people in business the protection of the environment has become an important corporate priority.

... In general, most Big firms could be regarded as 'political citizens',[34] whilst many Small firms could be described as 'incompetent'. Central to the distinction lie differences in company knowledge of environmental law and resources available for compliance. This means, in effect, that firms of different size not only have different reasons to comply, but also different capacities to comply.

Furthermore, despite their differences, both types also fear the threat of prosecution, a matter which plays a significant role in motivating firms to meet IPC. Compliance takes place, as earlier studies of regulation have argued, in the context of the ultimate threat of prosecution which is suspended in the great majority of cases while the inspector monitors progress towards what he or she may deem to be an acceptable level of compliance. In other words, in keeping with conciliatory styles of law enforcement, firms always keep one eye on the regulator's benign 'big gun'. However, while both Big and Small firms may be intimidated, they fear different aspects of prosecution ...

...

Big firms were intensely concerned about the public and political consequences of transgression. Being squarely in the public eye they thought that news of their transgressions which would come to light if they were ever prosecuted (regardless of whether or not they were formally punished) would seriously stain their corporate image. This assault on their reputation could have repercussions for sales and income and cause their insurance premiums to rise. Moreover, it was suggested that being labelled as an environmental transgressor might deter other companies from trading with them ...

---

[34] In this study, firms employing 1 to 499 people are termed 'Small', those employing 500 to more than 10,000 are termed 'Big'.

At this point it should be stressed that these sentiments are only beliefs. It is immaterial whether such consequences in fact flow from prosecution. What is more important is that managers believe they do. Indeed, publicity about a significant number of environmental offences in various parts of the world does not seem to have affected Shell's standing as a leading oil producer (neither, for that matter, has its involvement with the brutal military regime in Nigeria). But one might speculate that a company seen as responsible for an environmental catastrophe in the UK might suffer a sharp drop in domestic sales, and it may be that such a 'worst-case' scenario is what most managers have at the back of their minds. Hence, as is often the case in regulation, what is important is not whether this publicity-threat link works in reality, but that firms *believe* that it does.

Enforcement officials are aware of these concerns, and play on them to their advantage. As one HMIP Inspector stated:

> Pollution is no longer an ambiguous issue – it's become very emotive. Everyone we deal with has families, and no company wants to be associated with poisoning children. We play on malignancy a great deal.

The result is that many Big firms feel compelled to comply with IPC requirements because they cannot take the risk of their carefully cultivated (and expensive) consumer image being exposed to the uncompromising stare of the media. The bargaining chips held by environmental regulators are the threat of prosecution coupled with exposure to the glare of harmful publicity, which suggests that they enjoy an effective power that exceeds the fines that might be imposed upon a conviction for a violation of IPC requirements.

…

… Small firms could generally be classed as incompetent, in Kagan and Scholz' terms. Many agreed with the general aims of IPC but few knew how to put them into practice without assistance. Their ignorance of IPC requirements was compounded by their lack of resources. Being largely impoverished and operating on only marginal returns, Small companies were motivated to comply particularly because they feared the financial costs of prosecution itself. In contrast to Big operators many were less sensitive to bad publicity since their corporate images were seldom prestigious or well known. Moreover, such firms were also less able to recognise and appreciate the benefits of IPC largely because they lacked the skills and money to research how investment in IPC compliance might assist their firm more generally. Some Small firms not only relied heavily upon the Inspectorate for assistance but also treated HMIP inspectors with great respect. Not surprisingly, such firms were rather easily intimidated into compliance.

In England and Wales, the publicity associated with conviction is enhanced by the Environment Agency's use of websites and press releases. This informal approach can be contrasted with the powers of, for example, the Australian courts to make 'adverse publicity orders', essentially requiring the defendant to purchase advertising of its conviction;[35] government is

---

[35] Carolyn Abbot, 'The Enforcement of Pollution Control Laws in England and Wales: A Case for Reform?' (2005) 22 *Environmental and Planning Law Journal* 68.

considering the introduction of 'publicity orders' as a sentencing option for the criminal courts in the UK.[36]

The courts are not limited to fines. Environmental remediation carried out by the prosecutor is within the discretion of English courts to award costs;[37] courts can also order offenders to clean up pollution under specific environmental statutes[38] (see also the discussion of 'compensation' in Chapter 16). We should perhaps consider also more imaginative possibilities, such as 'environmental community service' by a corporation. However, we should bear in mind that the courts have not shown themselves eager to use the full range of penalties already at their disposal: it is generally recognised that magistrates lack experience of environmental crime (relative to more run-of-the-mill crimes), and there may still be a perception that environmental crime is 'different' from ordinary crime.

### (d) Alternatives to the criminal law

The threat of criminal prosecution is an important part of ensuring compliance. And yet, the low likelihood of prosecution reduces the strength of this threat.[39] A combination of inadequate sanctions and the heavy resource burden of prosecution reduces likelihood, and so deterrence.

The Environment Agency does not face a simple choice between prosecution and negotiation, having a number of administrative responses at its disposal. It has the power to revoke or suspend a licence, which has low costs and allows a quick response to problems. However, it has extremely serious consequences, shutting down an installation and probably depriving individuals of their livelihood. This 'corporate capital punishment'[40] seems, not surprisingly, to be little used.[41] The Environment Agency can also issue other forms of 'administrative notice', including enforcement notices and works notices (to prevent or remedy a breach), and prohibition notices (where there is an imminent risk of serious environmental damage).[42] It is perhaps more surprising that these are not more heavily used. The Environment Agency can also carry out remedial works and seek to recover the costs in a civil (rather than criminal) case. Again, though, bringing the action has resource implications.

Some options available elsewhere, however, are not currently available in England and Wales. So, for example, agencies in Australia can require companies to carry out an environmental audit of their operations, 'especially useful

---

[36] Richard Macrory, *Regulatory Justice: Making Sanctions Effective* (Cabinet Office, 2006) recommends that government consider introducing 'publicity orders'. The Cabinet Office has accepted all of the recommendations of the Macrory review.

[37] Prosecution of Offences Act 1985.

[38] For example Environmental Protection Act 1990, s. 26.

[39] This intuitive conclusion is also supported by economic analysis, see Anthony Ogus and Carolyn Abbot, 'Sanctions for Pollution: Do We Have the Right Regime?' (2002) 14 *Journal of Environmental Law* 283.     [40] Ayres and Braithwaite, *Responsive Regulation*, p. 53.

[41] See the statistics in Ogus and Abbot, 'Sanctions for Pollution'.

[42] For example Environmental Protection Act 1990, s. 13 and 14.

when applied to "environmental laggards"'.[43] There is now growing support for the introduction of civil penalties to supplement the criminal law in certain areas of regulation; the Cabinet Office in 2006 accepted recommendations that government consider introducing schemes to allow 'monetary administrative penalties' to be imposed by regulators in particular circumstances.[44] The following passage discusses the principles behind such an innovation.

### Richard Macrory and Michael Woods, *Environmental Civil Penalties: A More Proportionate Response to Regulatory Breach*, available at www.ucl.ac.uk/laws/environment/civil-penalty/

2.18 Civil penalties have been described as a 'hybrid' form of sanction, lying between the criminal and civil law, which can address harm caused to the public in general, though being similar in other respects to criminal fines. Civil penalties can be used to achieve a number of results: retribution; social condemnation; specific deterrence; general deterrence; the protection of third parties; and the payment of compensation or reparation. Civil penalties therefore appear more closely aligned with criminal fines than private law civil damages, in particular because they retain a punitive element, even if their purpose is more focussed on deterrence.

2.19 Civil penalties can be distinguished from 'administrative' or 'fixed' penalties, which are imposed more mechanically by a regulator, without the discretion available for assessing the amount of a civil penalty ... A civil penalty can perhaps therefore be defined as a discretionary monetary sum which is imposed flexibly under the civil law rather than the criminal law, in order to achieve deterrence and reparation.

...

7.3 The current approach to regulatory compliance, premised as it is on the threat of criminal prosecution, does not seem to adequately accommodate the type of environmental regulatory breach which calls for a more proportionate response, in terms of the moral condemnation applied; the financial penalty imposed; or the level of the procedural safeguards needed. This historically based approach seems unnecessarily dogmatic when trying to establish a modern system of environmental regulation. It is unsatisfactory, not only for regulators who therefore lack the flexibility needed to operate efficiently and cost effectively, and for the regulated parties who may resent the strict moral condemnation associated with criminal prosecution, but also for the public whose growing interest in the protection of the environment is not as well served as it could be.

...

7.5 ... the current regulatory system, with its inappropriate overreliance on prosecution, does not provide the flexibility, fairness or moral accuracy to achieve optimal compliance and therefore the adequate protection and conservation of the environment. But what benefits might the use of civil penalties bring?

...

---

[43] Abbot, 'Regulatory Enforcement', p. 169.        [44] Macrory, *Regulatory Justice*.

### Benefits from Environmental Civil Penalties

7.9 Civil penalties could also enhance the use of non-criminal sanctions such as warning letters and enforcement notices, by providing a more 'hard hitting' but not overly harsh means of further recourse in the event of continued non-compliance with a licence or a statutory prohibition. They would reduce the need for regulators to 'bluff' regarding their intention to bring criminal proceedings, when they are not perhaps in a position to do so because of evidential difficulties. Civil penalties would also provide a more viable alternative to either the revocation of a licence (which can risk the regulator having to pay compensation), or the regulator carrying out remedial work under an enforcement notice (which requires the regulator to then recover its costs).

7.10 Through this more tempered regulatory approach, improved compliance and reduced resistance to regulatory action could be anticipated on the part of the regulated, through the removal of inappropriate prosecutions for less serious offences … It could also be anticipated that potential offenders would be less likely to risk non-compliance based on the knowledge that the regulator would be better equipped to take enforcement action without having to resort to criminal proceedings. Civil penalties would therefore fit well with the 'compliance' approach to regulation used in the UK, by avoiding the need for more severe enforcement action which might damage ongoing relationships between the regulator and the regulated.

7.11 The ability to recover or 'recapture' the costs of damage to the environment would also allow for the better internalisation of the costs of environmental damage in accordance with the polluter-pays principle … There are certainly dangers in allowing regulatory agencies to use the funds obtained for their own purposes. However, if properly directed and open to review (perhaps by an independent body), the hypothecation of penalty funds could achieve the improved restoration of environmental damage, without causing any serious risk of conflict of interest on the part of the regulatory agency.

### Some Practical Considerations

7.12 It is also apparent from the use of civil penalties in other areas of regulation, that they need not replace criminal sanctions, but can be used as mutually supportive alternatives dependent on the particular circumstances arising …

7.13 In terms of implementation, the difference between civil and fixed penalties should be borne in mind, especially as there is currently greater use of the latter in this country. Whilst fixed penalties can perhaps more readily avoid the theoretical and practical concerns which flow from a regulator having discretion in assessing and applying a penalty, they cannot therefore adequately accommodate matters of mitigation or aggravation, which is key if the penalties imposed are to be set at more than a nominal amount. It follows that for any civil penalty regime, it is vital for there to be a suitable means of appeal in order to allow the independent review of the regulator's discretion.

There are of course concerns about the use of civil penalties. Perhaps the greatest is the absence of the procedural protections for defendants that would be a matter of course in a criminal trial. Although appeal procedures go some way to fixing that (as with 'corporate capital punishment'), and there is less stigma than with a criminal conviction, there remains a risk that those who have committed no wrong will pay the penalty rather than the costs associated with an appeal.[45] From the precisely opposite perspective, others argue that civil penalties will inappropriately diminish the stigma and moral disapproval attached to pollution. There has traditionally been some moral ambivalence around the criminality of breaches of environmental law, but that is now less the case. It is important that civil penalties are reserved for appropriate cases, and that prosecution remains available. This brings us back to the accountability of regulators, who exercise important discretion within necessarily broad statutory constraints.

## 3 Implementation of EC environmental law

EC environmental law suffers from a rather notorious 'implementation deficit', and a great deal of attention is being paid to improving the situation. It is, however, far from straightforward. There are many reasons for a Member State's failure properly to implement EC environmental law, not always readily identifiable in particular cases, and the appropriate response varies accordingly. In this section we first consider the Commission's role as 'guardian' of the treaties before turning to examine some of the actions taken to improve implementation.

### (a) The Commission as guardian of the treaties

#### EC Treaty

Article 211

In order to ensure the proper functioning and development of the common market, the Commission shall:

— ensure that the provisions of this Treaty and the measures taken by the institutions pursuant thereto are applied,

...

Article 226

If the Commission considers that a Member State has failed to fulfil an obligation under this Treaty, it shall deliver a reasoned opinion on the matter after giving the State concerned the opportunity to submit its observations.

If the State concerned does not comply with the opinion within the period laid down by the Commission, the latter may bring the matter before the Court of Justice.

---

[45] Abbot, 'The Enforcement of Pollution Control Laws'. Macrory and Woods suggest that procedural safeguards would satisfy Human Rights Act concerns (para. 7–12).

A number of challenges arise in the enforcement of Community environmental law, many of which apply throughout EC law, but often with added weight in the environmental arena.

The first challenge faced by the Commission is in identifying failure to implement. 'Implementation' implies not just *formal* implementation of Directives into national law, but also the far more difficult task of *practical* application, that is ensuring that environmental obligations or standards of environmental quality or performance are in place on the ground.[46] Monitoring the formal implementation of Directives, which may require a sophisticated understanding of national law, can be problematic, although the Commission is assisted by obligations to report on implementation measures.[47] Monitoring the *practical* application of the law, where national legislation correctly transposes EC law, is even more challenging. Breach can show itself in a number of ways: the regulator may not require licences in a pattern of cases, or in any individual case; it may not ensure compliance with permits, again generally or in a single case; substantive environmental standards as to water or air quality may be missed in the Member State. The Commission can take action against 'the conduct of a Member State's authorities with regard to particular specifically identified situations', or also with regard to 'a general practice', a more systemic failure.[48] Identifying and confirming a suspected practical breach is complex, and may well require the exercise of considerable expert judgment.

### Richard Macrory, 'The Enforcement of Community Environmental Laws: Some Critical Issues' (1992) 29 *Common Market Law Review* 347, pp. 362–7

In the environmental sector, the Commission has no express powers to assist its investigation of the kind it has been granted in the competition field. There are as yet no Community environmental inspectors, working alongside national enforcement officers, although the idea has been mooted in the past, and may yet surface again …

Against this background, the Commission has been peculiarly dependent on its own complaint system to enable it to be alerted to possible infringements in practice …

A number of criticisms can be made about the current system. It means that the Commission is, initially at any rate, playing a largely reactive role to the type of issues and subject matter raised; its stated commitment to investigate every complaint received, while a laudable goal of an administration exercising enforcement powers, leaves little room for strategic decision-making, especially given the current limited man-power involved. When the numbers of complaints are broken down on a country by country basis, it is clear that there are considerable disparities, which reveal as much about a country's tradition of

---

[46] See, for example, Case C-337/89 *Commission* v. *UK* [1992] ECR I-6103.

[47] Directive 91/692 standardizing and rationalizing reports on the implementation of certain directives relating to the environment OJ 1992 L 377/48.

[48] Case C-494/01 *Commission* v. *Ireland* [2005] ECR I-3331, para. 27.

environmental activism and political protest as they do about the state of implementation of Community law ...

...

A further concern of present procedures is the extent to which the Commission may be dependent on a Member State's cooperation in complying with the Commission's initial requests for information following the lodging of a complaint. An absolute refusal to respond may result in the Member State being threatened with infringement proceedings for failure to comply with its duty to assist the Commission in its tasks under Article 5 [now 10] of the EEC Treaty. But the provision of poor or incomplete information by the Member States poses peculiar difficulties for the Commission, and while in some cases site visits have been undertaken or consultants' reports commissioned, the current system is hardly geared to this type of intensive investigative work, although it may be required.

The reliance on a system of complaints from third parties not only raises questions of coherence, but also emphasises questions of accountability. Accountability for the Commission's exercise of discretion has improved a little in recent years. The Commission has set itself time limits for making decisions on complaints, and provides certain basic information to complainants on steps taken, including notice of a decision to close a case.[49] The Commission also publishes enforcement decisions on the internet, although not documents such as correspondence.[50] Because complainants are such a crucial part of the process in respect of environmental law, disenchantment with Commission enforcement would be particularly problematic here. The role of the complainant is, however, very much as a 'resource' to the Commission, and the Commission has traditionally been 'aloof and unresponsive' to complainants.[51] Moreover, the Art. 226 process is, for the complainant, 'a judicial "no-go" area'.[52] The complainant lacks standing, and the European courts consistently emphasise the breadth of the discretion enjoyed by the Commission.[53]

### Richard Rawlings, 'Engaged Elites, Citizen Action and Institutional Attitudes in Commission Enforcement' (2000) 6 *European Law Journal* 28, pp. 8–28

According to the case law, the enforcement procedure involves a power on the part of the Commission to consider the most appropriate means and time-limits for the purposes of putting an end to an infringement. To this end, the classic model of international procedure envisages a dialogue and mutual accommodation with the Member State. The aim is not the

---

[49] European Commission, *Communication on Relations with the Complainant in Respect of Infringements of Community Law* COM (2002) 141 final.

[50] The Commission claims an exception to the right of access under Art. 4(2) Regulation 1049/2001 regarding public access to European Parliament, Council and Commission documents OJ 2001 L145/43 – see Ch. 3, pp. 108–9.

[51] Richard Rawlings, 'Engaged Elites, Citizen Action and Institutional Attitudes in Commission Enforcement' (2000) 6 *European Law Journal* 28, p. 25.     [52] *Ibid.*, p. 12.

[53] See, for example, Case T-191/99 *Petrie* v. *Commission* [2001] ECR II-3677.

protection of the individual but to obtain compliance. Complaints are merely a 'source of information for detecting problems'. This aspect of enforcement proceedings is appropriately analysed in terms of a series of familiar concepts in administrative justice.

Thus, the 'decision-making chain' is elongated, and so generates many opportunities and incentives for negotiation and settlement. Take the pre-pre-litigation procedure that the Commission has created: an administrative graft onto the formal legal framework. Nothing better illustrates the twin themes of informality and confidentiality, the aim, in the case of a valid complaint, being to achieve some form of quiet accommodation with the Member State. Then, there is the formal 'administrative phase', inaugurated by the 'Article 226 letter' or formal request to the Member State to submit observations. The scope for protracted nego-tiation is demonstrated, the Commission having adopted the norm of a year in which to decide whether or not to close a file. The next stage, the concretising of the dispute via the obligation on the Commission to give a reasoned opinion, is also identified as hybrid in char-acter. Recording the infringement and defining the issues serve not only to prepare the way for court action but also to establish the parameters of a possible final settlement. It is a long-established practice for the Commission to bargain proactively at this stage by means of suggestions of what action would be appropriate to end an infringement. Last but not least, the classic design of maximising the opportunities for voluntary compliance is demon-strated at the 'judicial phase' of referral to the Court. The 'enormous discretionary power to do nothing' is, to this effect, famously underwritten by the Treaty.

…

Infringement proceedings on the classic model are a brilliant illustration of regulation operating 'in the shadow of the law'. Court proceedings are thus seen as a sanction of last resort against which compliance is sought through negotiation, bargaining and threats. Attention correctly focuses on the 'hidden jurisprudence' of the Commission and not merely on the (judicial) 'tip of the iceberg'. So, too, the Commission has consistently emphasised the need to preserve the co-operative model of decision-making that is typified by regula-tory bargaining, and with it the close and fluid workings of its closed relationships with the Member States as 'the Guardian of the Treaties'. Mutual trust or confidence is a notion that has been repeatedly invoked.

It is not surprising to learn that the Commission has clung tenaciously to the élite model of regulatory bargaining. Considerations of institutional self-interest inevitably play a significant role in the operation of the procedure: for which the closed, informal model is such a useful vehicle. Viewed in a positive light, the Commission can seek, via 'test-casing', to establish basic principles and 'play for rules', that is itself to structure the framework for bargaining. The potential for integrating enforcement action with the Commission's other activities, most obvi-ously its agenda-setting role, is highlighted. Then, there is the space left for political consid-erations, the hallmark of 'international procedure' and so a recurrent theme especially in the older accounts of the process. At best, the Commission has been able to steer clear of certain highly sensitive areas, as shown by its policy of non-enforcement in respect of the activities of the national court systems. At worst, it is seen in individual cases effectively to have sur-rendered in the face of the political intransigence of, or organised defiance in, a Member State.

Selective enforcement is a basic element of a good enforcement policy and the Commission is no exception. Reference need only be made to the 'black hole' that is non-compliance in the Union, that is the systemic but elusive quality of the phenomenon, and to the limited resources available, even supposing that the Commission were run properly. The criticism is the familiar one of a failure to specify clear and appropriate criteria which structure and confine the selective exercise of enforcement powers. To anticipate an argument, only recently has the Commission begun to articulate a policy in this field. A typical consequence in individual cases is the complaint that the Commission has somehow been 'got at' by the Member State: a popular manifestation of the theory of 'agency capture'. Again, attention naturally focuses on some prime output of the strong discretionary model: the differential rates of compliance among Member States, or that which is tendentiously described in terms of 'the usual suspects' or 'north-south gradient'. Whither the uniform application that is stated *ad nauseam* as a basic principle of Community law?

At European Union (EU) level, questions of accountability raised by Commission discretion are compounded by the very immediate question of potential conflict between the political and legal roles of the Commission.

### Rhiannon Williams, 'The European Commission and the Enforcement of Environmental Law: An Invidious Position' (1994) 14 *Yearbook of European Law* 351, pp. 353–4

All decisions on whether to commence, continue, or close infringement proceedings are taken by the Commissioners. These are the same men and women who, sitting in the same forum, take a host of overtly political decisions, for example: whether to make certain proposals, and if so in what form; who is to be appointed to certain posts; what view to take on certain opinions of the European Parliament; and whether to revise proposals, and, if so, how. In the political arena, it is taken for granted that, in the play off of certain proposals against others, compromises will be made. This is entirely proper. In the enforcement arena, however, it would be entirely improper were such compromises to be made in order to achieve political benefit. Enforcement would cease to be impartial, and the Commission would be unable to ensure its compliance with the first indent of Article 155 of the EC Treaty [now 211].

...

Quite apart from the dangers posed to just and effective law enforcement, it is unfair for each Commissioner to be placed in a situation where the temptation may continually arise (whether as a result of pressure from Member States or otherwise) to compromise enforcement in order to gain the support of a recalcitrant Member State for the adoption or issue of a legal measure, particularly one brought forward within his or her portfolio. It is similarly unfair to the Commissioners if such an improper compromise can be publicly perceived to have been made in circumstances where a difficult decision not to commence infringement proceedings has been taken independently of irrelevant political factors.

... there are no procedural safeguards in place which could effectively minimize the scope for improper political influence of deliberations on matters of enforcement ...

...

The perception alone that inappropriate considerations appear to influence the outcome of legal proceedings (whether or not they do so) brings the system into disrepute and distrust.

48. In the light of that particular factor, it is conceivable that the defendant Member State might manage significantly to increase the extent of its implementation of the Directive but not to implement it fully in the short term. If the amount of the penalty payment were to stay the same it would continue to be due in its entirety for as long as the Member State concerned had not achieved complete implementation of the Directive.

…

50. In order for the penalty payment to be appropriate to the particular circumstances of the case and proportionate to the breach which has been found, the amount must take account of progress made by the defendant Member State in complying with the judgment in *Commission* v. *Spain*. To that end it is necessary to require that Member State to pay annually an amount calculated according to the percentage of bathing areas in Spanish inshore waters which do not yet conform to the mandatory values laid down under the Directive.

…

52. As regards the amount of the fine, the basic criteria which must be taken into account are, in principle, the duration of the infringement, its degree of seriousness and the ability of the Member State to pay …

53. With regard to the duration of the infringement, it must be acknowledged that compliance with the judgment in *Commission* v. *Spain* by the Member State concerned is difficult to achieve in a short time. In this case such compliance presupposes detection of the problems, drawing up plans of action and implementing those plans. In that context, account must amongst other things be taken of the fact that the Community directives on public procurement require, inter alia, that the specifications be drawn up exhaustively before the public procurement procedure is initiated and they cannot be amended subsequently. Furthermore, the directives require the awarding authorities to comply with certain time-limits which may not be reduced, and they strictly limit the possibility of urgent procedures.

54. Having regard to those considerations, it must be concluded that the coefficient of 2 (on a scale of 1 to 3) proposed by the Commission to reflect the duration of the infringement is too harsh in this case and that a coefficient of 1.5 is more appropriate.

…

57. It must further be observed that the purpose of bringing bathing water into conformity with the limit values of the Directive is to protect public health and the environment. In so far as the breach found at paragraph 35 of this judgment can endanger human health and damage the environment it is clearly of significance.

58. Having regard to those factors, the coefficient of 4 (on a scale of 1 to 20) proposed by the Commission seems adequately to reflect the seriousness of the infringement.

59. The Commission's proposal to multiply a basic amount by a coefficient of 11.4 based on the gross domestic product of the Kingdom of Spain and on the number of votes it has in the Council is an appropriate way of reflecting that Member State's ability to pay, while keeping the variation between Member States within a reasonable range (see *Commission* v. *Greece*, paragraph 88).

## (b) Reform

Improving rates of implementation is a powerful driver of EU environmental policy at the moment. This may be having some effect: the Commission is certainly of the view that 'Implementation of EU environmental law by Member States has improved in recent years', as evidenced by falling numbers of complaints.[59] Failure to implement remains a serious issue, and is complex, not likely to respond to a single solution. In particular, changing the approach to Art. 226–8 would be inadequate. This section will consider, first, changes to EU-level practice, and secondly, reform of national implementation.

### (i) EU-level reform: enforcement

The most radical proposal is that enforcement of EC environmental law should be taken out of the hands of Member States and Commission, and given to a powerful independent agency, 'equipped with environmental (and possibly other) inspectors with appropriate powers (akin to those of the competition officials who have powers of search and seizure)',[60] able to take action directly against polluters or recalcitrant authorities. This would be politically unthinkable at the moment, removing one of the Commission's most important responsibilities, and transferring national sovereignty upwards to the EU level. The European Environment Agency is rather toothless in respect of powers of enforcement, although its ability to influence policy (including enforcement) by its control of information should not be discounted[61] – for example, simply highlighting relative levels of water pollution in different areas creates a level of political pressure towards compliance/enforcement. In any event, reliance on national administrations (and habits, cultures and relationships) is a strength as well as a weakness of EC environmental regulation, given the extent to which compliance is embedded in its social context. There are less extreme options around enforcement, particularly enhancing Commission investigation powers and resources, or removing enforcement against the Member States (rather than polluters) from the Commission in favour of an independent agency (which could simply be a separate division of the Commission). This would neutralise some of the concerns about political manipulation of Art. 226, but would simply shift the forum for the exercise of discretion; new temptations (needs) for negotiation would arise.

Radical change is a distant prospect. In the meantime, the Commission is reforming its internal procedure. As well as the enhanced transparency mentioned

---

[59] Commission Staff Working Paper, *Sixth Annual Survey on the Implementation and Enforcement of Community Environmental Law* (2004), SEC(2005) 1055, p. 1.

[60] Rhiannon Williams, 'The European Commission and the Enforcement of Environmental Law: An Invidious Position' (1994) 14 *Yearbook of European Law* 351, p. 398.

[61] Brian Wynne and Claire Waterton, 'Public Information on the Environment: The Role of the European Environment Agency' in Philippe Lowe and Stephen Ward (eds.), *British Environmental Policy and Europe* (Routledge, 1998).

above (p. 405), there is apparently (how closely this policy is followed is open to question[62]) a clearer setting of priorities for enforcement. Elizabeth Hattan has discussed the priorities set out in an important 1996 report from the Commission,[63] and more recent unofficial policy. The Commission emphasises that failures to put the law in place correctly are priority cases. The later policy also emphasises the importance of practical implementation breaches that relate to the establishment of infrastructure or which reflect deeper conformity issues. Most cases of practical implementation are, however, left to the Member States. Hattan considers this de-centralised approach to be 'more consistent with the principles of good governance and subsidiarity', and capable of providing 'a more responsive and flexible approach'.[64] It does, however, raise very acutely the capacity and willingness of Member States to implement, to which we will now turn.

### (ii)  National reform: implementation

### Commission Staff Working Paper, *Sixth Annual Survey on the Implementation and Enforcement of Community Environmental Law* (2004), SEC(2005) 1055, pp. 6–8

With infringement proceedings, the Commission aims to improve Member States' compliance with EU environmental law in order to provide citizens with a high level of environmental protection. However, infringement proceedings pursuant to Articles 226 and 228 of the Treaty are not the only way to ensure proper implementation of EU environmental law. Good implementation requires a range of complementary approaches under which the Commission strives to be proactive and prevent infringements occurring in the first place.

Proactive initiatives include the production of guidelines and interpretative texts to help Member States understand the Commission's view as to how certain directives or certain provisions should be best implemented on the ground. They also include multi-lateral discussions in technical committees, contributions to expert seminars and bilateral contacts between the Commission and the Member States in the course of package meetings with Member States … Coordinated use of Community funds can also help …

Secondly, the Commission is trying to be as systematic as possible in checking compliance. In some sectors, reports play a key role – for instance, annual reports on bathing water quality. In others, the Commission collects and analyses key data, such as the rate of progress in installing waste-water treatment facilities. Major studies have been launched to check the completeness and accuracy of national implementing legislation …

Finally, where problems are identified, the Commission is seeking to be as strategic, coordinated and effective as possible in its interventions – for example, through the development of implementation plans for key sectors. These put the emphasis on achieving the main implementation goals. The Commission is also making it clear that it favours constructive

---

[62]  Elizabeth Hattan, 'The Implementation of EU Environmental Law' (2003) 15 *Journal of Environmental Law* 271.

[63]  European Commission, *Implementing Community Environmental Law* COM (96) 500.

[64]  Hattan, 'Implementation of EU Environmental Law', p. 287.

engagement with Member States – that is, where Member States are willing to take steps to resolve problems, the Commission will provide them with all the assistance it can.

Information exchange between implementing authorities is also a tool for improving implementation. Since its inception in 1992, the informal EU network for the Implementation of Environmental Law (IMPEL), consisting of the Commission and the Member States, has been a key instrument in discussing the practical application of existing legislation.

There is also a need to improve transparency and awareness on the state of implementation of EU environmental legislation. To this end, this Sixth Annual Survey includes a Scoreboard, which details the comparative implementation record of each Member State in each sector of the environment.

Responsibility for ensuring compliance with EC environmental legislation rests ultimately with the Member States, who enjoy a broad discretion on mechanisms of enforcement. It makes sense, then, for the Commission to try to address implementation by looking closely at the Member States. The initiatives can be divided into three, overlapping categories: information strategies; privatising enforcement; and empowering national regulators.

Information is used at EU and national level. At EU level, the Commission provides advice and assistance to Member States, and the IMPEL network, referred to in the previous passage, is an informal network of national environmental inspectorates that examines and reports on implementation issues, encouraging institutions to learn from each other. The 'name and shame' approach of the 'scoreboard' is a more punitive approach. At the national level, rights of access to environmental information (see Chapter 3, pp. 101–7) are also explicable in part on this basis, allowing private monitoring of polluter and regulator. This overlaps with the question of 'privatising' enforcement. If a Member State fails to comply with rules on the free movement of goods, importing enterprises have every incentive not just to provide information to the Commission, but also in many cases to litigate in the national courts. Environmental interest groups are the obvious candidates for intervention in environmental cases, but they may have inadequate resources; not only can litigation be costly, but the investigation of breaches can be very resource-intensive. Whilst the EU has not intervened in the resource issue, the 'access principles' (Chapter 3 above) are an effort to empower environmental interest groups at the national level, particularly regarding access to environmental information, but also via initiatives such as the access to justice provisions in the Integrated Pollution Prevention and Control (IPPC) Directive (Chapter 9, p. 379). These are attempts to reduce the sometimes formidable legal barriers faced in the private monitoring of EC environmental law.

Direct effect is the doctrine through which EC law can be applied by national courts even if a Member State has failed to implement. Direct effect has traditionally been problematic in the environmental arena, particularly because of the idea that 'rights' have to be enjoyed by the litigant (*individual* rights can be hard to find in environmental Directives) and also because of the rule against 'hori-zontal' direct effect of Directives (i.e. direct effect only applies against an emana-tion of the state, not against a private party).[65] This traditional approach to direct effect is, however, no longer at the heart of the application of incorrectly imple-mented EC law by national courts. A line of case law now confirms that if a Community measure imposes a clear obligation on a Member State, national courts must be able to use that provision to review the legality of the Member State's exercise of discretion,[66] removing the emphasis on 'rights'. As for effects against private third parties (horizontal direct effect), 'mere adverse repercus-sions' are acceptable, although imposing 'direct obligations' (the difference is hardly obvious) on a third party is not permissible.[67] The changing focus means that the main legal barrier to private action against regulators[68] in national courts is standing, pre-empted in particular Directives, including IPPC, environmental impact assessment and environmental liability. In spite of these ameliorations of the position of those seeking to apply EC environmental law against the state in the national courts, we should note that courts are generally only willing to inter-fere with administrative discretion in the most egregious cases. And the absence of direct financial interest in implementation, coupled with the resource demands of litigation, remains a disincentive to litigation relative to other areas of EC law. Commission enforcement is then still crucial.

And finally, there are efforts to go directly to the capacity of the national regulators. So, for example, a Recommendation on minimum criteria for envi-ronmental inspections is a 'soft law' instrument that seeks to improve the performance of national regulators by defining minimum criteria for environ-mental inspections.[69] There have also been two initiatives to make criminal sanctions available nationally for breaches of EC environmental law.[70]

This is old hat for UK lawyers, who are beginning to look beyond criminal law, but would be a big step for Member States that do not traditionally criminalise the corporation. Another general tool can be found in the Environ-mental Liability Directive, which requires the Member States to put in place an

---

[65] For a reminder of the basic rules of direct effect, see Paul Craig and Grainne de Búrca, *EU Law* (Oxford University Press, 2003), Ch. 5.

[66] See, especially, Case C-72/95 *Aanemersebedrijf PK Kraaijeveld BV* v. *Gedeputeerde Staten van Zuid-Holland* [1996] ECR I-5403.

[67] Case C-201/02 *The Queen on the application of Wells* v. *Secretary of State for Transport, Local Government and the Regions* [2004] 1 CMLR 31.

[68] EC law does not provide for actions directly against polluters, although that had been mooted in early versions of Directive 2004/35 on environmental liability with regard to the prevention and remedying of environmental damage OJ 2004 L 143/56.

[69] Recommendation 2001/331/EC OJ 2001 L 118/41.

[70] European Commission, *Proposal for a Directive on the Protection of the Environment through Criminal Law* COM (2001) 139 final, amended COM (2002) 544 final; Council Framework Decision 2003/80/JHA on the protection of the environment through criminal law OJ 2003 L 29/55. Following a major institutional dispute, in Case C-176/03 *Commission* v. *Council* the ECJ annulled the Council framework decision under the Treaty on European Union as encroaching upon the powers of the Community under the EC Treaty. In the process, the Court highlighted once more the central place of environmental protection in the EC Treaty.

administrative scheme under which regulators are able to require polluters to finance the restoration of environmental damage.[71] And we might note the obligation to 'name and shame' and impose a fixed penalty in respect of any breach of the EU's emissions trading scheme (Chapter 11, pp. 428–32).[72]

## 4 Conclusions

It is a mistake to think that putting the law in place is the end of a process, or the solution to a problem; it is just the beginning. Indeed when we look at the persuasion and negotiation that goes on in regulation, the language of 'command and control' begins to look 'ironic': 'This is a rhetorical accomplishment which has no real basis, as very little commanding and controlling actually goes on in the implementation of environmental regulations.'[73]

And yet being 'tough' with polluters is only one part of the solution. Regulators need a range of options. Considerable attention is now being paid to enhancing the tools available to regulators (and courts), and it is possible that there will be reform. An impressive body of scholarship on regulatory enforcement emphasises the importance of regulatory discretion. Discretion, however, raises a dilemma around accountability. One of the functions of the 'access principles' discussed in Chapter 3 above is to provide some scrutiny of regulators. They also allow for additional scrutiny of polluters, supplementing Environment Agency enforcement with political, if not always legal, pressure.

These observations about the use of discretion apply equally at EU level; whether this delicate and *sui generis* type of 'enforcement' would benefit from additional sanctions is a different matter. However, the Commission should take account of the practicalities of national enforcement in its own action, and resist the temptation to encourage strict and inflexible enforcement. EC legislation is taking some modest steps towards enhancing the tools available to national regulators. The steps are rightly modest, because of the incremental constitutional change this suggests, with respect to the relationship between the EU and regulators.

## 5 Further reading

For an account of 'creative' approaches to environmental sentencing, see Carolyn Abbot, 'Regulatory Enforcement of Pollution Control Laws: The Australian Experience' (2005) 17 *Journal of Environmental Law* 161. Chris Hilson, *Regulating Pollution: A UK and EC Perspective* (Hart, 2000), Chs. 7 and 8, and Maria Lee, *EU Environmental Law: Challenges, Change and Decision-Making* (Hart, 2005), Ch. 3, provide more discussion of domestic and EU implementation issues. Bettina Lange, 'Compliance Construction

---

[71] Directive 2004/35.

[72] Directive 2003/87 establishing a scheme for greenhouse gas emission allowance trading within the Community and amending Council Directive 96/61/EC OJ 2003 L 275/32.

[73] John S. Dryzek, *The Politics of the Earth: Environmental Discourses* (Oxford University Press, 1997), p. 82.

in the Context of Environmental Regulation' (1999) 8 *Social and Legal Studies* 549, brings out the complexity of the very concept of compliance in an environmental context. Richard Macrory, *Regulatory Justice: Making Sanctions Effective* (Cabinet Office, 2006), reviews the limitations of the UK's traditional approach to regulatory enforcement, and makes a number of important recommendations for change.

# 11

## Regulatory Techniques: Beyond Licensing

### 1 Introduction: 'Command and control'?

As we have discussed in earlier chapters, 'command and control' regulation is subject to very considerable pressure from a number of directions. Gunther Teubner refers to this as the 'crisis of the interventionist state'.[1] In an environmental context, John Dryzek discusses a 'crisis of administrative rationalism'.[2]

> **John S. Dryzek, *The Politics of the Earth: Environmental Discourses* (Oxford University Press, 1997), pp. 79–83**
>
> #### Administrative Rationalism in Crisis
>
> Among those who have recently reflected upon administrative rationalism in an environmental context, increasingly few have done so in order to defend or advance it. Part of this is due to the association with bureaucracy: it is hard to find anyone who actually likes bureaucracy (recall that even Max Weber did not welcome the bureaucratic world whose arrival he announced; indeed, he described it as an 'iron cage', a 'polar night of icy darkness and hardness'). It is more common to find bureaucracy defended as necessary rather than attractive. Still, a discourse can soldier on without reflective defenders – indeed, particular discourses may persist precisely because nobody at all is reflecting on them, whether in attack or defense. Unfortunately for administrative rationalism, it is meeting with reflection, much of which turns out to be very critical.
>
> Prosaic and uninspirational though it might be, administrative rationalism could always sustain itself so long as it delivered the goods. In an environmental context, that would mean cleaner air and waters, fewer toxins circulating in the human environment, an environmentally secure future, improving aesthetic standards in city, suburb, countryside, and wilderness, more securely protected ecosystems and species. But the administrative state's performance on these standards has been called into question. This questioning can often be put under the heading of 'implementation deficit' – a substantial gap between what

---

[1] Gunther Teubner, 'Substantive and Reflexive Elements in Modern Law' (1983) 17 *Law and Society Review* 241, p. 267.

[2] Administrative rationalism being an attempt 'to organize scientific and technical expertise into bureaucratic hierarchy in the service of the state': John S. Dryzek, *The Politics of the Earth: Environmental Discourses* (Oxford University Press, 1997), p. 73.

legislation and high-level executive decisions declare will be achieved and what is actually achieved at street level in terms of attainment of environmental standards ...

More generally, the administrative state may be running out of steam in the environmental arena, or experiencing diminishing returns to effort. This would accord with experience in other policy areas such as crime, public health, industrial development, and education. It is relatively easy to achieve substantial initial gains, because the relatively easy and most visible problems will be attacked first. It is very hard to show sustained improvement on any dimension once these initial gains have been made (though occasionally a technological breakthrough may allow more substantial change) ...

What lies at the root of these apparent problems in administrative rationalism as an orientation to environmental affairs? To begin with, administrative rationalism implies hierarchy based on expertise, with both power and knowledge centralized at the apex of the administrative hierarchy. Those at the apex are assumed to know better than those at subordinate levels, so as to be able to assign tasks and coordinate operations. But problems of any degree of complexity defy such centralization: nobody can possibly know enough about the various dimensions of an issue such as acid rain, global climate change, ozone depletion, or the interacting cocktail of urban air pollutants, not to mention the social and economic aspects of these issues, to sit with any confidence at any such apex. As the philosophers Karl Popper[3] and F. A. von Hayek[4] have argued at length (though never in the context of environmental problems), the relevant human knowledge is dispersed and fragmentary. The closed, hierarchical style of administrative rationalism simply has no way to aggregate these pieces of information in intelligent fashion. Popper's solution is the give and take of liberal democracy; Hayek's is the market. Popper's critique is especially devastating because it is rooted in a model of science, which is for Popper the exemplary human problem-solving activity. To Popper, the hallmark of the scientific community is not authority based on expertise, but free, open, and equal criticism and test of the conjectures of scientists by other scientists. Just as hierarchy and deference to expertise can only obstruct scientific problem solving, so it can only obstruct problem solving in policy and politics.

...

As if all these difficulties confronting administrative rationalists were not enough, the liberal capitalist context in which administration must operate – and which, as a problem-solving discourse, administrative rationalism cannot call into question – can be quite debilitating. The first concern of all states operating in a market context must be to secure the confidence of actual and potential investors. If they make such investors unhappy, for example by putting costly anti-pollution laws and regulations into place, then the likely result is disinvestment and capital flights to locales more hospitable to business interests. Disinvestment means economic recession and unpopularity of the government in the eyes of the voters; it also means falling tax revenues to finance whatever it is that governments want to do. These constraints are exacerbated in the emerging era of free trade and capital mobility across national boundaries. If I am correct in postulating diminishing returns to effort

---

[3] Karl Popper, *The Open Society and Its Enemies* (Routledge and Kegan Paul, 1966).
[4] F. A. von Hayek, *Law, Legislation and Liberty: The Political Economy of a Free People* (University of Chicago Press, 1979).

in environmental administration, then in the early days this was not a problem, because demonstrable improvements in environmental quality could be achieved at little cost to business. But as diminishing returns set in, each increment of environmental improvement becomes more costly to achieve.

...

For better or for worse, administrative rationalism has clearly had substantial impact in the environmental arena. Today it may be running out of steam and facing crisis, but its past achievement should not be forgotten. The countries of the developed world have an environment which is cleaner, safer, and more aesthetically pleasing than it would have been without the last thirty years of administrative rationalism. This evaluation does not mean that administrative rationalism was the most effective conceivable response to environmental crisis, or even an adequate one. Nor are past achievements any guarantee of future success.

This general concern that regulation is 'running out of steam' is widespread, particularly in respect of new or persistent problems. Climate change, for example, is extremely complex environmentally, and tackling it has enormous economic and social implications. Although a number of gases contribute to climate change, carbon dioxide is the major culprit, and addressing our reliance on carbon, particularly fossil fuels, implicates an extraordinary range of industrial, agricultural, transport and consumption activities. As well as doubts about the ability of direct regulation to effect meaningful change across such an expanse of daily life, the extent and depth of the changes envisaged emphasise the need for the least intrusive and most cost effective action. The acceptance that anthropogenic climate change was a problem more or less coincided with the arrival of new regulatory instruments in the mainstream; it is not, however, just new problems that challenge direct regulation. The problem of waste has always been with us, and, again because of its broad and deep implications, invites an approach that goes beyond licensing; we discuss the use of diverse regulatory instruments to regulate waste in the final section of this chapter.

Criticisms of command and control come from many different perspectives. In the following passage, Julia Black looks at limitations of government regulation generally, but the 'aspects' of the problem that she discusses apply perfectly to the environmental sphere.

### Julia Black, 'Decentring Regulation: Understanding the Role of Regulation and Self-Regulation in a "Post-Regulatory" World' (2001) 54 *Current Legal Problems* 103, pp. 106–11

The first aspect is complexity. Complexity refers both to causal complexity, and to the complexity of interactions between actors in society ... There is a recognition that social problems are the result of various interacting factors, not all of which may be known, the nature and relevance of which changes over time, and the interaction between which will be only imperfectly understood. Attention is also drawn in more conceptual writings to the dynamic interactions between actors and/or systems, and to the operations of forces which produce a constant tension between stability and change within a system (loosely defined). Those interactions are themselves complex and intricate, and actors are diverse in their goals, intentions, purposes, norms and powers.

The second aspect is the fragmentation, and construction, of knowledge. This is sometimes referred to simply as the information asymmetry between regulator and regulated: that government cannot know as much about industry as industry does about itself. Phrased in those terms, the problem is familiar and well recognized. In the decentred understanding of regulation, however, the information problem is more complex. For unlike the traditional analysis, it does not assume that any one actor has all the information necessary to solve social problems: it is not a question of industry having, government needing. Rather, no single actor has all the knowledge required to solve complex, diverse, and dynamic problems, and no single actor has the overview necessary to employ all the instruments needed to make regulation effective. The problem can be more radically framed. That is, that not only is knowledge fragmented but that information is socially constructed: there are no such things as 'objective' social truths …

The third aspect is fragmentation of the exercise of power and control. This is the recognition that government does not have a monopoly on the exercise of power and control, rather that is fragmented between social actors and between actors and the state. The regulatory systems existing within social spheres are just as important to social ordering, if not more so, as the formal ordering of the state. Regulation occurs in many locations, in many fora: 'regulation in many rooms'.

The fragmentation of the exercise of power and control entails the fourth aspect of the decentred understanding of regulation: a recognition of the autonomy of social actors. Autonomy is not used in the sense of freedom from interference by government, but in the sense that actors will continue to develop or act in their own way in the absence of intervention. Regulation therefore cannot take the behaviour of those being regulated as a constant …

The fifth aspect of the decentred understanding of regulation is the existence and complexity of interactions and interdependencies between social actors, and between social actors and government in the process of regulation. This is both a descriptive and a normative claim. Descriptively, the observation is that regulation is a two-way, or three- or four-way process, between all those involved in the regulatory process, and particularly between regulator and regulatee in the implementation of regulation … the dynamic of the relationship embraced in the new understanding of regulation is that interdependencies and interreactions exist between government and social actors. Further, it is not the case that society has needs (problems) and government has capacities (solutions). Rather each should be seen as having both problems (needs) and solutions (capacities), and as being mutually dependent on each other for their resolution and use. These interactions and interdependencies should not be presumed to be contained within national territorial borders: analyses of globalization emphasize that they may extend well beyond them.

> The claim that governance and regulation are the product of interactions and interdependencies leads into a sixth aspect of the decentred understanding of regulation. That is the collapse of the public/private distinction in socio-political terms, and a rethinking of the role of formal authority in governance and regulation. In the decentred understanding of regulation, regulation happens in the absence of formal legal sanction – it is the product of interactions, not of the exercise of the formal, constitutionally recognized authority of government …
>
> So complexity, fragmentation and construction of knowledge, fragmentation of the exercise of power and control, autonomy, interactions and interdependence, and the collapse of the public/private distinction: all are elements of the composite 'decentred understanding' of regulation. Together they suggest a diagnosis of regulatory failure which is based on the dynamics, complexity, and diversity of economic and social life, and in the inherent ungovernability of social actors, systems and networks. They are accompanied by the final, seventh aspect of the new understanding of regulation, and that is the set of normative propositions as to the regulatory strategies that should be adopted.
>
> The hallmarks of the regulatory strategies advocated are that they are hybrid (combining governmental and non-governmental actors), multi-faceted (using a number of different strategies simultaneously or sequentially), and indirect.

It is, then, widely accepted that direct regulation has certain limitations, and that other forms of intervention need to be explored. Of many possible examples, in this chapter we examine first economic instruments (especially tax and tradable permits). We then outline ideas of 'reflexive' law, looking closely at the European Union's (EU's) Environmental Management and Audit Scheme (EMAS). The 'green consumer' takes a central place in many discussions of alternative approaches to environmental protection, and we will discuss this in Section 4. Finally, we look briefly at the range of regulatory mechanisms employed in efforts to tackle our 'waste mountain'.

## 2 Economic instruments

Command and control regulation is frequently criticised for inefficiency. There are two senses to 'inefficiency', either of which might apply: a measure is inefficient if it costs more than the (environmental) benefit it reaps; or if it is more costly than alternative ways of reaching the same objective. As far as regulators (funded out of the public purse) are concerned, direct regulation is resource-intensive throughout the process: gathering information, setting standards, monitoring and then enforcing these standards. And from the regulated party's perspective, variable 'marginal abatement costs' mean that some firms will reduce pollution very cheaply, whilst others will find it more costly, depending on things like the age, location or scale of the plant. Requiring the same environmental performance across the sector may not be the most efficient way of reducing overall levels of pollution. One possible response to poor efficiency, and also to certain questions of effectiveness, is the 'intelligent deployment of market mechanisms to achieve public ends'.[5]

In Chapter 1 (pp. 34–6) we discussed the key economic metaphors of the 'tragedy of the commons' and 'externalities'. Extreme 'free market environmentalists' take the tragedy of the commons rather literally, and urge the privatisation of environmental goods (species, air, water), giving 'owners' incentives to manage them properly, and to take legal action against outsiders who cause damage. This has not really gained ground in the UK or EU,[6] and faces major practical difficulties in respect of mobile and intangible environmental goods, such as air, not to mention the social and political questions inherent in mass privatisation.

By the more modest tactic of placing a cost on pollution, or a benefit on abatement, other economic instruments can be designed to respond to criticisms of direct regulation. Because they put a price on pollution (or a benefit on abatement) right down to zero, they create a constant incentive to reduce pollution, by contrast with direct regulation and its generally fixed environmental standards. By leaving decisions to the regulated party, they harness the knowledge and information of the regulated industry. And they allow marginal abatement costs to be taken into account by regulated parties: rational polluters will only reduce pollution for as long as polluting (including the cost of the economic instrument) costs more than abatement.

Whilst economic instruments now have reasonably broad support across the environmental spectrum, they first became influential among those most resistant to government intervention in industry. Economic instruments were seen as a form of 'de-regulation'. This fails to account for the degree of state intervention required to correct the failure or absence of markets, but those who mistrust government would still argue that the market, built on many small uncontrolled decisions, is a more legitimate way of influencing social behaviour than direct regulation.

## (a) Green taxes

The 'green tax' is the archetypal economic instrument. Environmental taxes are designed to put a price on either emissions from, or inputs to, a process. In our discussion of waste, below, we consider the UK landfill tax (pp. 454–5); here we examine the main features of green taxation.

Environmental taxes have at least three possible objectives, which are not always clearly distinguished. The aim could be to internalise all of the external

---

[5] John S. Dryzek, *The Politics of the Earth: Environmental Discourses* (Oxford University Press, 1997), p. 102.

[6] Although the use of English tort law by angling groups to clean up rivers is a very commonly cited example of the benefits of a property approach: see *Pride of Derby* v. *British Celanese* [1952] Ch. 149.

costs of an activity (Chapter 1, pp. 34–6), correcting market failure. If the economic incentive successfully internalises all environmental externalities, pollution ceases to be economically worthwhile at the 'efficient' level of pollution, that is the level at which the total social cost of pollution meets the total social cost of abatement. The precise calculation of externalities, however, depends on uncertain and controversial economic valuations of predicted or actual environmental impacts, uncertain in their turn.

### Richard Macrory, 'Regulating in a Risky Environment' (2001) 54 *Current Legal Problems* 619, pp. 622–4

… it seems unlikely that we will ever succeed in measuring environmental costs with such a degree of precision that they can be imposed on relevant economic actors in a way that will allow us to rely upon market forces alone. Two recent examples illustrate the difficulties involved. In 1997 Andrew Stirling of Sussex University collated over thirty studies published between 1979 and 1995 estimating in monetary terms the environmental externalities of modern coal-fired power stations.[7] The results of individual studies were often expressed in extremely precise terms and with considerable confidence, but when presented collectively the variations were so immense as to throw doubt on their validity as a policy tool: values on the lowest estimates were less than 4/100 of a cent per kilowatt hour with the highest around $20 per kilowatt hour, a factor of more than fifty thousand. Deriving a workable and acceptable set of fiscal instruments to internalize such an uncertain range of costs would have proved near impossible, or have involved so many political choices as to undermine the intellectual grounding of the exercise.

The second example concerns transport. In its 18th Report on Transport the Royal Commission on Environmental Pollution attempted to estimate the external costs imposed by transport in the United Kingdom. Some costs, such as property costs, were quantifiable with a reasonable degree of certainty. Others, such as global warming, are based on arguable assumptions, and in any event contain an enormous range of uncertainty. When considering damage from transport in the form of, say, visual intrusion, loss of habitats, and severance of communities, the Commission, rightly in my view, eventually concluded that the methodologies were so suspect that any numerical figures would not produce useful results. Instead, it was felt preferable to start with a judgment of the environmental goals one wished to secure, and then to consider the most cost-effective ways of achieving them. This does not mean that an exercise in estimating external costs in general terms is without value. In that case it provided a broad-scale picture of the extent of external damage imposed by transport, and highlighted substantial discrepancies between the costs paid by private motorists and heavy goods vehicles. But it also revealed the enormous difficulties facing those who wished to internalize external costs. If motorists were prepared to pay such costs, did it then follow that all was well with the market-based approach and that society should accept that consequential environmental damage was being paid for?

---

[7] Andrew Stirling, 'Limits to the Value of External Costs' (1997) 25 *Energy Policy* 517.

Secondly, taxes might be used to influence behaviour, in an effort to achieve a particular level of environmental protection at least cost. This is also, however, problematic at the practical level. Whether a tax will change behaviour depends on uncertain and uncontrollable factors, including the elasticity of demand, the availability of substitutes, and the profits or economic efficiency of firms, as well as the level of the tax. It also assumes that the regulated all behave like rational economic calculators; when they do not, different approaches (including but not limited to direct regulation) may be preferable; when they do, monitoring and enforcement strategies will need serious attention. In the following extract, Richard Macrory considers possible approaches to reducing greenhouse gas ($CO_2$) emissions from road transport, which requires the reduction of fuel consumption.

## Macrory, 'Regulating in a Risky Environment', pp. 630–1

Faced with such a challenge, what is the most appropriate policy response? As the [Royal Commission on Environmental Pollution] noted, without policy intervention, improved design of the scale required would not come by itself:

> It is unlikely to be applied in practice unless government provides appropriate signals to influence decisions by manufacturers and the behaviour of the general public as purchasers and drivers.

Regulatory instruments in the form of mandatory efficiency standards represents one form of policy mechanism …

The Commission, however, was eventually persuaded that the use of economic instruments, in the form of an annual fuel escalator, might achieve the same effect, sending a sustained signal to car manufacturers to introduce greatly increased efficiencies. Such an escalator was introduced by the government, but when the Commission revisited the subject of transport in 1997 and again in its 2000 report on Energy it was apparent that while there had been some reductions of $CO_2$ emissions from the average new car, there had been no reduction in overall fuel consumption. Improvements in engine efficiency had been more than offset by increased sales of larger vehicles (including four-wheel-drive vehicles) and increases in vehicle weights. At the same time the intended price signals of the fuel escalator tax had been weakened by fluctuations in the price of crude oil, with prices at the pump failing to match increases in the tax. The sudden escalation in crude oil prices revealed the political vulnerability of the escalator, and the Chancellor of the Exchequer announced its abandonment in November 1999 stating that any future fuel duty increases would be determined on a budget-by-budget basis. A striking feature of the initial political response to fuel demonstrations was the failure to justify the fuel escalator as a policy instrument for improving efficiency. Instead it was presented as an important source of government income for sectors such as education or health which would otherwise have to be raised from other forms of taxation.

In a 1996 study on European political responses to climate change Professor Tim O'Riordan described the then emerging fuel prices escalator as a 'real piece of policy innovation'. Yet he was also sufficiently perspicacious to note that:

> The test will come in the political determination to continue the increase, year in and year out, and the manner in which the additional revenue is spent.[8]

The demise of the fuel escalator demonstrates the potential vulnerability of relying solely on an economic instrument as a means of securing policy goals, whatever the underlying theory. Its intended effect lacked precision, its impact was subject to many external economic forces outside the control of government, and its original purpose could be easily forgotten and overtaken by the attractions of its value to government as a revenue stream. In comparison to the sorry saga of the fuel escalator, one may conclude that direct regulation in the form of mandatory efficiency standards with sufficient advance notice to manufacturers would have had a greater effect on achieving key policy goals.

This also touches on the third possible aim of environmental taxation, after internalising or incentivising, which is to raise revenue. 'Hypothecation', that is reserving tax revenues for particular purposes, would allow revenue to be raised for environmental projects. Hypothecation on a grand scale is unusual in the UK, strongly resisted by the Treasury.[9] Hypothecation is not possible if environmental taxation is designed to be 'fiscally neutral', that is offset by a reduction in other taxes: the opportunity to reduce tax on social 'goods' such as employment is one of the major attractions of taxing social 'bads' such as pollution. Moreover, if a tax's primary purpose is revenue raising, it cannot really be called an environmental tax. The environmental objective of changing behaviour conflicts with the objective of raising revenue; as behaviour changes in an environmentally beneficial direction, revenue falls. Although there are difficulties with each of these three rationales for environmental taxation, pragmatically taxation can be used roughly to approximate some of the relevant externalities and simply to make pollution more expensive, incentivising environmental protection and innovation;[10] and efforts should be made to avoid allowing revenue raising to take centre stage. There are strong reasons for continuing to experiment in taxation as a policy tool. One further concern, however, is the 'regressive' nature of environmental taxation. Progressive taxation is, simply put, taxation that redistributes wealth from the richer to the poorer; regressive taxation is the opposite.

---

[8] Tim O'Riordan and Jill Jager (eds.), *Politics of Climate Change* (Routledge, 1996), p. 249.

[9] Andrew Jordan *et al.*, 'Policy Innovation or "Muddling Through"? "New" Environmental Policy Instruments in the United Kingdom' (2003) 12 *Environmental Politics* 179.

[10] Anthony Ogus, 'Nudging and Rectifying: The Use of Fiscal Instruments for Regulatory Purposes' (1999) 19 *Legal Studies* 245.

### Stephen Tindale and Chris Hewitt, 'Must the Poor Pay More? Sustainable Development, Social Justice and Environmental Taxation' in Andrew Dobson (ed.), *Fairness and Futurity: Essays on Environmental Sustainability and Social Justice* (Oxford University Press, 1999), pp. 236–8

There are, however, different ways of looking at progressivity and regressivity. One way, the theoretical approach, is to look at the incidence of taxation. An income tax is more progressive than a sales tax. A second, more practical way is to look at what the government proposes to do with the revenues. A package in which the government levies income tax and uses the revenue to subsidize opera tickets is *less* progressive than a package in which the government levies a sales tax and uses the revenue to pay welfare benefits to the poor. (The most regressive approach is to tax poor people and use the receipts to subsidize the opera – this is called the National Lottery.)

...

Environmental taxes have been criticized by some on the Left as 'rationing by price'. This is a strange statement. In a market economy, that is how most goods and services are apportioned. There are some things, like health and education, which should be outside the market – free at the point of use. But none of the candidates for environmental taxation, except perhaps domestic energy taxation, come into this category. Road use is currently free, but food is 'rationed by price'. What is the more essential? Genuine rationing – rationing by coupon – would be more equitable. It would also be politically impossible, and in any case not ideal. If the coupons were tradable, the rich would end up with them anyway, though the poor would have more money from the sale of their coupons. A non-tradable system would simply drive trading underground.

Current environmental patterns are highly inequitable, with poor households suffering more from pollution, local environmental degradation, and so on. One has to ask, therefore, whether environmental taxation is more regressive than inaction. The answer of course, is that sometimes it is, sometimes it is not. It all depends on the nature of the tax. The blanket assertion that environmental taxation is regressive therefore oversimplifies the picture. Cuts in government expenditure or a failure to act to protect the environment may be even more regressive. The distributional impact of green taxes should be assessed on a case-by-case basis.

Some environmental taxes will fall on business – taxes on toxic emissions, for example – so the regressive impact will be limited. An increase in business costs is likely to be mildly regressive if it feeds through into higher prices to the consumer, but a tax reform which redistributes rather than increases business taxes is likely to have a broadly neutral impact on prices. Other environmental taxes will fall indirectly on individuals, but can be collected through a progressive mechanism. An example is a landfill tax, which will increase the cost to local authorities of disposing of municipal waste (although most of the impact will be on the industrial sector). The local authority will be able to recoup its costs through local taxation, be it property- or income-based. Unfortunately, in the UK local taxation is itself not very progressive, but this need not be the case. Alternatively, if the tax is levied centrally, central government could choose to use some of the revenue to increase its support revenues to local authorities. Nevertheless, there are legitimate concerns about the impact of some green taxes.

Tindale and Hewitt argue that determining whether a tax is regressive requires concrete information on what is paid and received, and by whom. Unless care is taken, environmental taxation may well be regressive; if care is taken, for example through compensatory measures, it need not be. Distributive equity is particularly important when we take a sustainable development perspective (Chapter 6). Sustainable development thinking generally encourages the use of economic instruments, because the need to reconcile economic and environmental objectives demands efficient action that does not harm economic development. But if environmental taxation is regressive, the social 'pillar' of sustainable development becomes problematic. However, direct regulation also has distributive implications.

### Tindale and Hewitt, 'Must the Poor Pay More?', pp. 234–5

But the notion that environmental regulation avoids the problem is mistaken. It is impossible to say in the abstract whether taxation or regulation is the more regressive: it all depends on the issue. Minimum efficiency standards might increase the price of consumer durables, which would hurt the poor more than the rich. Higher standards of drinking-water have undoubtedly caused suffering among low-income households, since the cost of meeting them is passed on to consumers via water bills. In a market economy, the burden of both taxation and regulation tends to fall on the customer. And this, from an environmental perspective, is as it should be. It is the consumers who create the demand for a product who are the true polluters, not the manufacturers who meet that demand. It is the consumers who should pay.

In any case, most commentators accept that taxation and regulation have to be used in harness. Consider the case of transport. Let us assume that we want to tackle pollution and urban congestion. The options available are taxes or road-pricing, minimum fuel efficiency standards, mandatory pollution controls on vehicles, and traffic bans … higher taxes will be progressive across the population as a whole (since the poor cannot afford cars). But regressive among car-drivers. Banning cars in urban areas would in a sense be more equitable – though if taxis were allowed it could be said to discriminate against those unable to afford taxi fares. Efficiency standards and pollution controls could also be said to be even-handed in their impact (although if, as the car manufacturers claim, they will make vehicles more expensive there will be a regressive impact at the point of purchase). So should one reject taxation and opt instead for these regulations? The answer is that one should not – one should go for *both* taxation and regulation, because they are not really equivalent at all. Traffic-free city centres are greatly to be desired, but much of the traffic will then be displaced into the suburbs. Greater fuel efficiency and stricter emissions standards are similarly to be welcomed, but without policies which manage demand for transport their impact will be overwhelmed by increases in vehicle numbers – as is predicted to happen with catalytic converters. To say that environmental regulation is less regressive than taxation is like saying that the government health warning on cigarette packets is less regressive than tobacco taxes: it may be true, but it is not very relevant, since the one will not be effective without the other.

There is perhaps less of a clear distinction between economic instruments and 'command and control' than we might think. Economic instruments very often rely on the existence of more traditional forms of state regulation in the background; Lefevere even describes emissions trading as 'command and control *plus*', demanding 'even stronger government intervention and control, in particular in relation to the monitoring of emissions, and high non-compliance sanctions'. He argues that, rather than constituting a break with command and control, the 'true value of market-based instruments lies in building flexibility, cost effectiveness, and incentive for technology development into existing command and control-type regimes'.[22]

Fourth, the 'invisible hand' of the market place could operate to hide the political nature of the decisions being taken. Take the example of the (very likely) inability of environmental interest groups to compete economically with industry in emissions trading: the market is a very blunt instrument through which to weigh relative social goods, and political debate may be preferable. Market instruments move decisions into the private realm, reducing opportunities for public discussion and for collective decision making. In theory, the overall objectives of environmental policy are set by public debate (for example the 'cap' in emissions allowance trading, the objective of a tax), and the economic instrument is simply a tool of implementation. Nevertheless, democratic control of that process becomes difficult.[23] And yet again, the technical nature of the debate (here in economic terms) can exclude the lay public and exclude from open discussion the inevitable value judgments being made.

### Dryzek, *The Politics of the Earth*, pp. 117–18

To get at the real reasons for resistance to economic rationalism we need to treat it as a discourse rather than just a set of proposals for policies and institutions. Recall that the basic agents and motives recognized by economic rationalism treat people only as *homo economicus* consumers and producers. There are no citizens in economic rationalism ... Mark Sagoff points out that all individuals have both consumer preferences and citizen preferences, and ... these may point in different directions.[24] As a consumer I may want to make use of freeways to get to work more quickly, as a citizen I may demonstrate against construction of the freeways because they destroy communities and natural areas. As Sagoff argues, we normally put our citizen preferences first. But economic rationalists count only consumer preferences, and so citizens count for nothing. This is not a world likely to please environmental citizen activists which is why environmentalists have often opposed economic rationalist schemes, without always being able to explain exactly why ...

Such opposition, again often unarticulated, may also arise as a result of the way economic rationalism treats or, rather, does not treat the environment. Recall that in economic

[22] Lefevere, 'Greenhouse Gas Emission Allowance Trading', p. 154.
[23] Rehbinder, 'Market-Based Incentives'.
[24] Mark Sagoff, *The Economy of the Earth: Philosophy, Law and the Environment* (Cambridge University Press, 1988).

rationalist discourse, the environment exists only as a medium for the effects of some human actions on other humans, and as a source of inputs for the socio-economic machine. Thus it has no intrinsic value, and chunks of it can be bought or sold at will, depending only on the most profitable human use. When it comes to pollution, economic rationalism attaches no stigma: rights to pollute are just like any other commodity, to be bought or sold ... this failure to stigmatize pollution in moral terms makes many environmentalists uneasy. Goodin compares this selling of pieces of the environment by governments to the selling of indulgences by the medieval Catholic Church.[25] In both cases, individuals can have their sins forgiven if they can afford to pay. But just as places in heaven were not the church's to sell (only for God or St Peter to decide), so pieces of the environment are not government's to sell. Martin Luther and opponents of green taxes have more in common than they might think.

In short, no matter how attractive economic prescriptions may be in instrumental terms, even to committed environmentalists, they help constitute a discourse, and a world, which those according higher priority to citizenship, democratic and ecological values find unattractive.

This addresses also our final objection to economic instruments, the absence of any moral condemnation of pollution. Economic instruments institute fees, not fines: 'Payment of a fee exempts the behaviour for which the fee was paid from being classified as morally wrong.'[26] However, this does not particularly distinguish economic instruments from ordinary permits, which similarly provide permission to pollute, but the fee is absent or differently calculated.[27] The distinction is perhaps in the inability of economic instruments to stigmatise pollution over 'acceptable' levels.

## 3 'Reflexive' law

We introduced the idea of reflexive law in Chapter 9 (pp. 374–5).

### Eric W. Orts, 'Reflexive Environmental Law' (1995) 89 *Northwestern University Law Review* 1227, p. 1232

Reflexive law gets its name from being self-referential in two respects. First, it is a self-critical legal theory. A theory of reflexive law emphasizes the limits of law in the face of complexity. The complexity of society and its problems diminishes the capacity of law to direct social change in a specified or detailed manner. Second, a theory of reflexive law proposes an alternative approach to law reform. It focuses on enhancing self-referential capacities of social systems and institutions outside the legal system, rather than direct intervention of the legal system itself through agencies, highly detailed statutes, or delegation of great power to courts.

[25] Robert E. Goodin, 'Selling Environmental Indulgences' (1994) 47 *Kyklos* 573.
[26] Lefevere, 'Greenhouse Gas Emission Allowance Trading', p. 167.     [27] *Ibid.*

A fundamental element of reflexive law for environmental lawyers is about engendering responsibility within polluting organisations (and individuals, and regulators). In this respect the economic instruments discussed in the last section (although they engender economic thinking rather than a culture of environmental protection) and the consumer mechanisms discussed in the next are highly pertinent, as are elements of the IPPC regime and environmental assessment (Chapters 9 and 14, respectively). Reflexive law has an elaborate theoretical underpinning,[28] but some relatively straightforward ideas bring out its appeal for the environmental sphere. Although in the article from which the following extract is taken Julia Black goes beyond reflexivity in a theoretically pure sense, reflexive law is a response to the sorts of problems outlined in the passage from the same article in the introduction to this chapter (pp. 419–21).

### Black, 'Decentring Regulation', pp. 125–7

The decentred understanding of regulation, in recognizing the multiple locations of regulation, and the interdependencies and interactions of government and social actors, emphasizes that 'governments could never govern if people were not self-governing'.[29] One of its central insights is that social systems are steerable from the outside or from within only if the system itself can make use of its major component systems to effect correcting action, and each component is only reliable if it can keep its variability within bounds, ie it is self-regulating …

The normative aspect of the new understanding of regulation is that intervention in the self-regulation of social actors … has to be indirect. It has to harness that self-regulatory capacity but ensure that it is used for public policy ends, by adjusting, balancing, structuring, facilitating, enabling, negotiating, but never directly telling and never directly trying to control.

How these self-regulating capacities are in fact harnessed is now the current topic of debate. The instruments that governments have at their disposal remain the same: financial, legal and informational (the carrot, the stick, and the sermon).[30] It is the way that they are used that is significant. So the tools of the policy-maker include the usual financial ones of subsidies, loans, grants, incentives, public procurement policies; the 'new' aspect (and one could debate the extent to which it is empirically 'new') is the explicit recognition of these devices, not as budgetary devices but as regulatory ones. Similarly with information: the 'decentred' regulatory strategies emphasize a larger and more strategic role for information and its explicit recognition as a regulatory tool.

---

[28] See especially the work of Gunther Teubner, including 'Substantive and Reflexive Elements in Modern Law'.

[29] Andrew Dunsire, 'Modes of Governance' in Jan Kooiman (ed.), *Modern Governance: New Government–Society Interactions* (Sage Publications, 1993).

[30] Johan de Bruijn and Ernst Heuvelhof, 'Policy Instruments for Steering Autopoietic Actors' in Roeland in t'Veld, Linze Schaap, Catrien J. A. M. Termeer and Marc J. W. Van Twist (eds.), *Autopoiesis and Configuration Theory: New Approaches to Societal Steering* (Kluwer, 1991).

A bigger shift is required in the use of law, for here the prescription is to move away from 'regulatory law' to reflexive, 'procedural', or 'post-regulatory' law. 'Regulatory law' set substantive standards; 'reflexive' or 'procedural' law sets procedures. These procedures should be aimed at improving the reflexivity of systems and their responsiveness to their environments, and so the co-ordination or integration of perspectives between different social actors or systems, often summed up in the term 'democratization'. They could also be procedures which aid reflexivity by, for example, building feedback mechanisms, for the generation and dissemination of information and knowledge, for the risk-management of an institution.

These sorts of questions have been reflected in discussions of 'environmental governance', which scrutinise the choice of policy instrument by regulators, to contribute to efforts to harness diverse decision makers, public and private, in diverse fora. This form of governance debate has been particularly prominent at EU level (on which, see Chapter 4, pp. 164–70). In this section we will concentrate on the EU's EMAS. Environmental management systems are intended to encourage self-critical reflection on environmental performance, and active engagement with environmental impacts. EMAS is an entirely voluntary system to which an organisation can choose to commit itself.[31]

### (a) The EU's Environmental Management and Audit Scheme (EMAS)

### Regulation 761/2001 allowing voluntary participation by organisations in a community eco-management and audit scheme (EMAS) OJ 2001 L 114/1

Article 1

The eco-management and audit scheme and its objectives

1. A Community eco-management and audit scheme allowing voluntary participation by organisations, hereafter referred to as 'EMAS', is hereby established for the evaluation and improvement of the environmental performance of organisations and the provision of relevant information to the public and other interested parties.

2. The objective of EMAS shall be to promote continual improvements in the environmental performance of organisations by:

(a) the establishment and implementation of environmental management systems by organisations as described in Annex I;

(b) the systematic, objective and periodic evaluation of the performance of such systems as described in Annex I;

---

[31] There are other systems available, the main alternative being the international standard, ISO14001: www.iso14000-iso14001-environmental-management.com/. This does not go as far as EMAS in publicity, legal compliance or independent verification.

(c) the provision of information on environmental performance and an open dialogue with the public and other interested parties;

(d) the active involvement of employees in the organisation and appropriate initial and advanced training that makes active participation in the tasks referred to under (a) possible. Where they so request, any employee representatives shall also be involved.

EMAS is primarily about procedure rather than environmental substance. However, although actually achieving the 'continual improvement in the environmental performance' is not a condition of registration, it does direct attention to substance. It is defined as: 'the process of enhancing, year by year, the measurable results of the environmental management system related to an organisation's management of its significant environmental aspects, based on its environmental policy, objectives and targets; the enhancing of the results need not take place in all spheres of activity simultaneously' (Art. 2(b)).

Assessing environmental improvement is inevitably controversial, requiring judgments about environmental priorities and trade-offs that cannot be made on a purely technical basis. A less ambiguous element of substance is introduced by the obligation of compliance with environmental law (Art. 10):[32] the Environment Agency has stated that it will use its powers 'to suspend companies from their EMAS registration when they break the law', in accordance with their enforcement and prosecution policy.[33] Again, this is likely to be a matter of judgment in every case: breaches of environmental law are relatively routine, and this sanction will not be the 'first resort' of regulators (see Chapter 10); it does, however, enhance the range of sanctions available to regulators.[34]

Article 3

Participation in EMAS

1. EMAS shall be open to the participation of any organisation dedicated to improving its overall environmental performance.

2. In order for an organisation to be registered under EMAS it shall:

(a) Conduct an environmental review of its activities, products and services in accordance with Annex VII addressing the issues contained in Annex VI and, in the light of the results of that review, implement an environmental management system covering all the requirements referred to in Annex I, in particular the compliance with the relevant environmental legislation.

...

[32] Also detailed in the Annexes.

[33] Environment Agency, *Environmental Management Systems: Position Statement*, available at www.environment-agency.gov.uk/business/444251/466235/548723/.

[34] Note that Alex Mehta and Keith Hawkins, 'Integrated Pollution Control and its Impact: Perspectives From Industry' (1998) 10 *Journal of Environmental Law* 61 (above, pp. 398–9), found that EMAS was an incentive for regulatory compliance for the firms in their study.

(b) carry out, or cause to be carried out, environmental auditing in accordance with the requirements set out in Annex II. The audits shall be designed to assess the environmental performance of the organisation;

(c) prepare, in accordance with Annex III, point 3.2, an environmental statement. The statement shall pay particular attention to the results achieved by an organisation against its environmental objectives and targets and the requirement of continuing to improve its environmental performance, and shall consider the information needs of relevant interested parties;

(d) have the environmental review, if appropriate, management system, audit procedure and environmental statement examined to verify that they meet the relevant requirements of this Regulation and have the environmental statement validated by the environmental verifier to ensure it meets the requirements of Annex III;

(e) forward the validated environmental statement to the competent body of the Member State in which the organisation seeking registration is located and, after registration, make it publicly available.

3. In order for an organisation to maintain registration to EMAS it shall:

(a) have the environmental management system and audit programme verified in accordance with the requirements of Annex V, point 5.6;

(b) forward the yearly necessary validated updates of its environmental statement to the competent body and make them publicly available. Deviations from the frequency with which updates shall be performed can be made under circumstances laid down in Commission guidance adopted in accordance with the procedure laid down in Article 14(2), in particular for small organisations and small enterprises ... and when there is no operational change in the environmental management system.

So, starting with an environmental review (Art. 3(2)(a)), an environmental management system should be put in place (Art. 3(2)(a)), followed by internal audits (Art. 3(2)(b)); an environmental statement is prepared (Art. 3(2)(c)); and the whole lot is 'verified'. Standards are determined to a considerable degree by private 'verifiers', accredited under a national system, which must 'guarantee their independence and neutrality in the execution of their tasks' (Art. 4). The verifier is contracted by the registered organisation to carry out the verification, leading to inevitable concerns about the rigour with which they will challenge their polluting 'customers'. The environmental statement is submitted to the competent authority – in the UK, the Institute of Environmental Management and Assessment[35] – followed by yearly updates. Under Art. 6(1), registration follows, provided that the competent body

- has received a validated environmental statement and
- has received a completed form, which includes at least the minimum information set out in Annex VIII, from the organisation and
- has received any registration fee that may be payable under Article 16 and

---

[35] See www.emas.org.uk/aboutemas/mainframe.htm.

- is satisfied, on the basis of evidence received, and in particular through inquiries made at the competent enforcement authority regarding the compliance of the organisation with the relevant environmental legislation, that the organisation meets all the requirements of this Regulation.

Failure to submit the necessary material annually can lead to an organisation's suspension or deletion from the register, as can any evidence, including information of regulatory breach from the Environment Agency, leading to the conclusion that the organisation is no longer complying with the conditions of registration (Art. 6(3)(4)).

The detail of the procedural obligations under EMAS is found in lengthy annexes. Annex I sets out the requirements for the all-important environmental management system. One of its requirements is that 'top management' define an 'environmental policy' and review it at intervals. The organisation must ensure that the policy:

(a) is appropriate to the nature, scale and environmental impacts of its activities, products and services;
(b) includes a commitment to continual improvement and prevention of pollution;
(c) includes a commitment to comply with relevant environmental legislation and regulations, and with other requirements to which the organisation subscribes;
(d) provides the framework for setting and reviewing environmental objectives and targets;
(e) is documented, implemented and maintained and communicated to all employees;
(f) is available to the public.

Annex I requires objectives and targets to be set in the environmental management system, as well as programmes for meeting them. Implementation measures have to include training and awareness for employees, and the proper allocation of responsibilities. There have to be measures for emergencies, for routine monitoring and corrections, and everything has to be documented. Annex I lists four issues that must be addressed: legal compliance; performance (against the environmental aspects set out in Annex VI); external communication and relations; and employee involvement.

An organisation must consider, under Annex VI, 'all environmental aspects of its activities, products and services'. 'Environmental aspects' are wide-ranging, direct and indirect. Direct aspects include emissions, waste, noise, transport and effects on biodiversity; indirect aspects include the environmental performance and practices of contractors. 'Significance' of impact determines whether the environmental aspects should be used for setting objectives and targets: 'It is the responsibility of the organisation to define criteria for assessing the significance of the environmental aspects of its activities, products and services, to determine which have a significant environmental impact. The criteria developed by an organisation shall be comprehensive, capable of independent checking, reproducible and made publicly available.'[36] Some examples are provided, including 'views of interested parties' and 'those activities of the organisation with the most significant environmental costs, and environmental benefits'.

The environmental statement is the most public element of EMAS.

> Annex III
>
> 3.1 The aim of the environmental statement is to provide environmental information to the public and other interested parties regarding the environmental impact and performance and the continual improvement of environmental performance of the organisation. It is also a vehicle to address the concerns of interested parties … Environmental information shall be presented in a clear and coherent manner in printed form for those who have no other means of obtaining this information. Upon its first registration and every three years thereafter, the organisation is required to make available the information detailed under point 3.2 in a consolidated printed version.
>
> …
>
> 3.2
>
> …
>
> (a) a clear and unambiguous description of the organisation registering under EMAS and a summary of its activities, products and services and its relationship to any parent organisations as appropriate;
>
> (b) the environmental policy and a brief description of the environmental management system of the organisation;
>
> (c) a description of all the significant direct and indirect environmental aspects which result in significant environmental impacts of the organisation and an explanation of the nature of the impacts as related to these aspects (Annex VI);
>
> (d) a description of the environmental objectives and targets in relation to the significant environmental aspects and impacts;
>
> (e) a summary of the data available on the performance of the organisation against its environmental objectives and targets with respect to its significant environmental impacts. The summary may include figures on pollutant emissions, waste generation, consumption of raw material, energy and water, noise as well as other aspects indicated in Annex VI. The data should allow for year-by-year comparison to assess the development of the environmental performance of the organisation;
>
> (f) other factors regarding environmental performance including performance against legal provisions with respect to their significant environmental impacts;
>
> (g) the name and accreditation number of the environmental verifier and the date of validation.

The extension of information provision beyond obligations on public authorities, to voluntary commitments by the private sector, is an important part of EMAS. The influence of third parties is supposed to encourage

---

[36] Annex VI, para. 6.4.

environmentally beneficial behaviour. However, whilst EMAS has many supporters, there are difficulties with the very philosophy of 'voluntary' environmental commitments.

### François Ost, 'A Game Without Rules? The Ecological Self-Organisation of Firms' in Gunther Teubner, Lindsay Farmer and Declan Murphy (eds.), *Environmental Law and Ecological Responsibility* (Wiley, 1994), pp. 352–5

#### Eco-audit and eco-label: right to know or power to seduce?

Two regulations of the Council of the European Communities ... one for a 'Community Environmental Audit Scheme' (eco-audit), the other for a 'Community System of Ecological Labelling' (eco-labelling) [discussed below, pp. 448–51], further illustrate the political will to increase firms' self-responsibility in the area of environmental protection. These two texts are, moreover, part of a line of preventive action aimed at reducing nuisances at source, by rational planning of production and the promotion of clean technologies and products. In both cases, the point is to make the policy pursued by the firm in these areas more transparent, make the public aware of the efforts being made and to award the most efficient firms with a sort of good conduct certificate that they would be authorised to use in their publicity campaigns. The public's supposed preference for products and firms with that distinction would then, through the flexible play of the law of supply and demand on the market, lead to the repayment of investments made and to the launching of a general campaign in favour of the most environment-friendly technologies.

Positive as these prospects are, we propose, however, to put a few critical questions in connection with them, inspired by the same concerns as have guided us up to now. Should one, for instance, favour a system of deliberate self-commitment by certain firms in sectors they have chosen, or instead one of respect by *all* firms for *legal* obligations? Are the procedures for awarding the eco-label and doing the eco-audit of a sufficiently adversary nature? Do they give guarantees of independence and impartiality? Is the publicity that seems to be the real objective of both schemes inspired by a genuine concern for public information, or does it derive more from a media message? In other words, is the game one where the cards are on the table, or is it instead related to a game like poker where all moves, including bluffs and cheating, are permitted?

... First the eco-audit. This is a tool for the firm's environmental administration, consisting in the systematic, periodic, objective evaluation of its policy, programme and equipment in the sphere. In addition to better information for the public and authorities, it is expected to bring a steady improvement in the performance of firms. Among these aims there is also that of respect for the various legal regulations ...

This system will not, however, be of general application. It is planned to reserve it to firms that deliberately commit themselves to it ...

...

What is one to think of this system? It will first of all be noted that, following the logic of self-responsibility, it has a purely voluntary foundation. Firms conform to it if they want to ... They are to develop an internal system of environment protection 'in accordance with their own needs and choices'. It will be agreed that this is to push the logic of 'self' very far. One would, however, have no objections if it were established that this sort of scheme is, as the Preamble says, a complement to and not a substitute for the general legal obligations. If it means doing more than the law and better, then so much the better; if on the contrary the point is the *ad hoc* negotiation of the application of obligatory texts, with the state sometimes 'buying' conformity in the form of reductions in charges or of loans, it is clear that this sort of scheme would be unacceptable ... Is our criticism misplaced because the text explicitly rules out this hypothesis? Certainly the most flagrant abuses are unlikely; it is not unrealistic, by contrast, to fear that this scheme of self-responsibilization will gradually, in a climate of euphoric deregulation, replace the normative framework that is both binding and general. In that case, would we not see a growing differentiation between a few very efficient enterprises, at the cutting edge of research in terms of clean technology, and the bulk of the industrial sector whose polluting activities would scarcely be censured any longer? Moreover, how is one to guarantee that the bound measures by 'clean' firms would be maintained once they had acquired a dominant market share or ecology has gone out of fashion – especially since in the meantime the present binding mechanism would have been weakened? Here too, then, it is important for progress in the direction of self-responsibility to be accompanied by corresponding progress in the direction of defining general, binding normative objectives ...

Our second question relates to the nature of the publicity attached to the audit ...

...

Many precautions have certainly been taken to guarantee the objectivity of the information contained in the audit report and the outside auditors have the specific mission of ensuring the reliability of these documents. One cannot, however, avoid the impression that the real *raison d'être* of the text is the concern to reinforce the firm's image. In these circumstances, this 'licence to seduce' ought not to be a substitute for a much more fundamental legal institution, namely the citizen's 'right to know' ... Starting from the idea that the environmental game is at least as much conflictual as co-operative, we admit our preference for this logic of 'cards on the table' information over the publicity system of the audit. The regulation on ecological labelling leads us to a similar conclusion.

EMAS is, as discussed by Ost, expressly 'without prejudice' to community or national law (Art. 10). However: 'Member States should consider how registration under EMAS in accordance with this Regulation may be taken into account in the implementation and enforcement of environmental legislation in order to avoid unnecessary duplication of effort by both organisations and competent enforcement authorities' (Art. 10(2)). This suggests that, in some circumstances, EMAS could take the place of official (in the UK, Environment Agency) enforcement.

### Environment Agency, *Environmental Management Systems: Position Statement*, available at www.environment-agency.gov.uk/business/444251/466235/548723/

... there are widely recognised concerns about the ability of EMSs [environmental management systems] to secure good environmental performance, and particularly compliance with environmental legislation.

We believe legal compliance and good environmental performance are fundamental requirements of an EMS. We formally recognise EMSs certified by UKAS [UK Accreditation Service]-accredited bodies in our risk-based approach to regulation through the OPRA (Operator and Pollution Risk Appraisal) [one of the ways in which the Agency targets monitoring and inspection]. This is because our studies prove that the documentation of an EMS makes it quicker and easier for us to regulate a site or company.

There are still a number of unanswered questions in relation to EMSs. Studies suggest that sites with EMSs don't necessarily provide better compliance with permit conditions, have fewer incidents or better general environmental performance than those that do not have EMSs. However, the scope of a site EMS will often address issues that go beyond regulatory requirements. It may be that by introducing an EMS, a site's environmental performance will improve at a faster rate than if it does not implement one. Further work is needed to understand these issues better.

...

Government guidance to the Environment Agency states that it should 'take account of robust EMSs, in particular the Eco-Management and Audit Scheme (EMAS) and ISO 14001'. It also says that our objectives shall be 'to develop in conjunction with government a risk-based, proportionate, consistent, efficient and cost-effective approach to the regulatory process'. We are consultee for all EMAS applications in England and Wales, and can prevent a company registering if it is not complying with environmental legislation. We can have a company suspended from the EMAS register if it subsequently breaches legislation. We have a role in maintaining public confidence in formal EMSs by working with Government, business and the certification industry to highlight weaknesses in this process and to maintain and improve standards.

...

We take account of site EMSs through our OPRA scheme. Firms with a recognised EMS are awarded additional points in the OPRA scoring system. EMAS receives the highest number of points, followed by ISO 14001 and then companies' own in-house systems.

Our regulatory approach at any site will always be informed by the observed standards of environmental protection and management, including permit breaches, incidents and complaints from the public.

The Environment Agency is cautious. Relying heavily on EMAS for enforcement would pass considerable power to private verifiers. The Environment Agency does 'not believe there is sufficient consistency in approach between the various certification bodies [verifiers] or that enough of them pay adequate attention to compliance with legislation in their reviews of site performance'.[37] But 'regulatory control' is one of the incentives to participate in EMAS: 'Organisations should be encouraged to participate in EMAS on a voluntary basis and may gain added value in terms of regulatory control, cost savings and public image' (Recital 9).

Of the other two 'incentives', the promise of improved 'public image' is not too controversial, although we should recall that it may become the 'licence to seduce' (above, p. 443). Membership of EMAS entitles an organisation to use the EMAS logo, to signal environmental commitment to the public, investors and customers.[38] The promise of 'cost savings' assumes that good systems will lead to win-win solutions such as reducing waste of expensive inputs, and that regulatory compliance is rendered less costly by focussed consideration.

A voluntary scheme requires good levels of participation for any chance of success. In September 2004, there were 65 EMAS registered companies in the UK, and 4,019 registered sites in Europe.[39] Article 11 of the Regulation requires Member States to 'promote organisations' participation in EMAS' and 'in particular, [to] consider the need to ensure the participation of small and medium-sized enterprises', which have historically low levels of participation.[40] Information and technical support, including assistance with identifying 'significant environmental impacts', as well as 'reasonable registration fees' are the main tools of promotion, as well as considering how EMAS could be taken into account when setting criteria for public procurement policies.

EMAS is open to 'any organisation'. Sanford Gaines and Clíona Kimber argue that tools of reflexive law have been misdirected in their focus on large industrial concerns, and would be more suitably applied to, for example, public or voluntary organisations, individuals and landowning.

### Sanford E. Gaines and Clíona Kimber, 'Redirecting Self-Regulation' (2001) 13 *Journal of Environmental Law* 157, p. 169

… in the reflexive approach, final decisions are always the province of the regulated entities. The capacity of industry to learn good environmental behaviour by engaging in an examination of its conscience and internalising environmental values is thus central to the arguments of those who advocate reflexive environmental law. In any self-regulation regime, however, the 'self' needs a frame of reference for deciding what regulation to impose on itself. For environmental protection, that frame of reference is necessarily external to the firm because the natural environment is external. 'The ecological problem … is omnipresent, but is nowhere at

---

[37] Environment Agency, *Environmental Management Systems*.
[38] The logo is not designed to be used on the labels of products.
[39] Environment Agency, *Environmental Management Systems*.
[40] See also Mehta and Hawkins, 'Integrated Pollution Control and its Impact'; small companies were less aware of EMAS.

home'.[41] Reflexive theorists would nevertheless have the self-regulating entity construct its own conception of its role in society. Even for highly capable and responsible industrial enterprises, we are sceptical about their ability to cut themselves loose from their central focus on profit-making and engage in objectively valid self-examination and social-learning.

EMAS addresses two closely related objectives: turning attention within the firm to environmental protection; and providing environmental information to the public. A similar (again voluntary) approach to extending information provision into the private sector can be found in 'eco-labelling'.[42]

## 4 Green consumers?

Seeking to adjust patterns of consumption to reduce environmental impact is in principle a far-reaching response to environmental degradation brought about, directly and indirectly, by the consumption of goods and services. Economic instruments, such as taxes and subsidies, can be used to alter the price of goods, and give environmentally benign goods an advantage (or reduce any disadvantage). But an important strand of market thinking on environmental protection relies on the 'green consumer', who consciously and conscientiously purchases on environmental grounds.

### Michele Micheletti, Andreas Follesdal and Dietland Stolle, 'Introduction' in Micheletti, Follesdal and Stolle (eds.), *Politics, Products and Markets: Exploring Political Consumerism Past and Present* (Transaction Publishers, 2004), pp. x–xv

Why politicise the market? In some instances, the market becomes a site for politics when people are disassociated from political life. Earlier in history, people who were not part of the demos of political life often chose the market as an arena for politics. These people were without full citizenship rights and political voice. They were disembedded from politics. They fought against marginalization, colonization, and the repercussions of enslavement in one of the few arenas available for the oppressed and invisible: the market. Their aspirations for full citizenship and a good life for themselves, their community, and their nation urged them to partake in signing a new social contract based on civil, political, social, and economic rights of full citizenship that were embedded in democratically regulated structures of political life.

...

Use of the market as a political tool is not, however, reserved for the oppressed. Empowered and embedded people use their purchasing choices to criticize the policies and

---

[41] Leonnie Breunung and Joachim Nocke, 'Environmental Officers: A Viable Concept for Ecological Management?' in Gunther Teubner, Lindsay Farmer and Declan Murphy (eds.), *Environmental Law and Ecological Responsibility: The Concept and Practice of Ecological Self-Organisation* (John Wiley, 1994).

[42] Note that the Aarhus Convention requires parties to 'encourage' both eco-labelling and eco-auditing: Art. 5, see Ch. 3.

practices of corporations in their own and other countries in situations where strong government regulation in domestic and export settings is absent. Political consumer activists use the market to communicate their disapproval with other countries. They boycott goods from countries that violate the human rights of their own citizens and call on their states to use the market-based tools at hand to sanction these countries economically. The export market has frequently been chosen as their site for international politics because no other arena is really open for them to affect these foreign causes ...

...

The influence of markets is a central issue of politics in the twenty-first century. The asymmetrical balance between economics and politics, with market actors taking initiatives that formally belonged to the regulatory prerogative of the state, and the state as unable to develop itself more globally, has led to serious problems of political responsibility-taking nationally and world-wide ... Worried, conscientious people use the marketplace to vent their frustration, take responsibility concerning global injustices, and as a way of initiating discussions and standard-setting for global economic regulation ...

A final important cause for the politicisation of the market is the ever-increasing importance of consumer goods and consumption in the world today. This relationship of dependence triggers politicised market action in several ways. One view argues that the struggle between consumerism and citizenship, between market values of competition and political values of solidarity, politicizes the market and privatizes and commercializes politics. The market must, therefore, be politicized to liberate people from the dominance of consumer society. It is argued that citizens lured by the babbles of logotypes become slaves of mass customised lifestyle fashion, some even willing to kill for high-status brand goods. Thus, consumer society's transformation of citizens into manipulated, passive buyers of goods must be checked through market-based political action as well as political regulation.

A second view of ever-increasing consumption acknowledges our dependence on market consumer goods but does not see it as necessarily detrimental to democracy. This dependence is really a relationship of power that can be changed through collective action. The market becomes politicised when it is used to change the power balance between producers and consumers. Many scholars see shopping as embodying this struggle for power and consider consumer choices as infused with citizenship characteristics. Some scholars go so far as to consider consumers the primary agents of democracy in the world today. They analyze how citizens, and particularly young people, attempt to balance promotion of their personal identity and lifestyle through consumer choice with their commitment to global ethical issues. Their interpersonal, private struggle has, in much the same way as earlier efforts, spilled over into a search for arenas for political action. Thus, the market becomes politicised as a site for action and ethics ...

A third view points to the shift from industrial society to postmodern society for politicizing the market. Among other things, this shift implies the increasing importance of consumption over production for the creation of political identity. Consumption as an organising relation in its own right supplements and may even come to replace production, class position, and occupation as the hub of public identity, authority, and political controversy. Here the argument is that once consumption becomes a potentially powerful steering mechanism, the market becomes a site for politics and ethics.

Because the environmental qualities of a product are generally not apparent at the time of purchase, producers make 'green claims' to appeal to the green consumer. The environmental aspects of the product (the sustainability of the forest, or the dolphin-friendliness of the tuna) cannot be verified by the purchaser even after purchase, making these products what economists call 'credence goods'. The integrity of the information provided is crucial. Misleading or downright inaccurate information is one potential problem, and of course we are all familiar with the power of advertising to distract without actually lying. Here we will consider the move to more standardised systems of green claims, which try to control the quality of information. Standardised 'eco-labels' abound: including 'organic', sustainable forest certification, energy labels, as well as a range of eco-labels that apply across sectors. The UK does not support a general national eco-label, but the EC Eco-Label Regulation applies in the UK.[43] Like EMAS, it is entirely voluntary. Producers of goods or services can apply to the relevant national competent authority (the Department of the Environment, Food and Rural Affairs (DEFRA) in the UK) for a label that allows them to demonstrate to consumers the environmental qualities of their goods.

> Article 1
>
> Objectives and principles
>
> 1. The objective of the Community eco-label award scheme (hereafter referred to as the Scheme) is to promote products which have the potential to reduce negative environmental impacts, as compared with the other products in the same product group, thus contributing to the efficient use of resources and a high level of environmental protection. This objective shall be pursued through the provision of guidance and accurate, non-deceptive and scientifically based information to consumers on such products.
>
> For the purpose of this Regulation:
>
> — the term 'product' is taken to include any goods or services,
> — the term 'consumer' is taken to include professional purchasers.
>
> 2. The environmental impacts shall be identified on the basis of examination of the interactions of products with the environment, including the use of energy and natural resources, during the life cycle of the product.

The eco-label applies by 'product group', meaning 'any goods or services which serve similar purposes and are equivalent in terms of use and consumer perception' (Art. 2(1)), excluding products classified as 'very toxic, toxic, dangerous to the environment, carcinogenic, toxic for reproduction, or mutagenic', and goods manufactured by processes 'which are likely to significantly harm man and/or the environment, or in their normal application could be harmful to the consumer'. Nor does it apply to food, drink, pharmaceuticals or medical devices.

---

[43] Regulation 1980/2000/EC on a revised Community eco-label award scheme OJ 2000 L 237/1.

2. In order to be included in this Scheme, a product group must fulfil the following conditions:

(a) it shall represent a significant volume of sales and trade in the internal market;

(b) it shall involve, at one or more stages of the product's life, a significant environmental impact on a global or regional scale and/or of a general nature;

(c) it shall present a significant potential for effecting environmental improvements through consumer choice as well as an incentive to manufacturers or service providers to seek a competitive advantage by offering products which qualify for the eco-label; and

(d) a significant part of its sales volume shall be sold for final consumption or use.

The eco-label can be awarded to products available in the Community, which comply with the 'essential environmental requirements' set out in Art. 3:

1. The eco-label may be awarded to a product possessing characteristics which enable to contribute significantly to improvements in relation to key environmental aspects, which are linked to the objectives and principles set out in Article 1 …

2. The following provisions shall apply:

(a) in evaluating the comparative improvements, consideration shall be given to the net environmental balance between the environmental benefits and burdens, including health and safety aspects, associated with the adaptations throughout the various life stages of the products being considered. The evaluation shall also take into account the possible environmental benefits related to the utilisation of the products considered;

(b) the key environmental aspects shall be determined by identifying the categories of environmental impact where the product under examination provides the most significant contribution from a life-cycle perspective, and among such aspects the ones for which a significant potential for improvement exists;

(c) the pre-production stage of the life-cycle of goods includes extraction or the production and processing of raw materials and energy production. Those aspects shall be taken into account, as far as is technically feasible.

A very full range of information should be taken into account in considering whether a product will be awarded an eco-label. There will inevitably be difficult trade-offs and balances. These trade-offs, and relative performance in different areas, will not be reflected on the label, which works on a simple yes/no basis.[44] The Regulation only sets out the broad criteria for the award of an eco-label. Detailed requirements are developed by the EC Eco-Labelling Board (Art. 6), which is composed of Member State competent authorities, plus a 'consultation forum', which should comprise: 'a balanced participation of all relevant interested parties concerned with that product group, such as industry and service providers, including SMEs [small and medium sized enterprises], crafts and their business organisations, trade unions, traders, retailers, importers, environmental protection groups and consumer organisations' (Art. 15).

---

[44] The Commission's proposal for a 'graded' approach, awarding 1–3 flowers, was rejected: see Ludwig Krämer, 'European Community Eco-Labelling in Transition' (2000) 1 *Yearbook of European Environmental Law* 123.

The success of a scheme such as this depends not only on the existence of 'green' consumers, but also on take-up by industry and consumer awareness of the label, neither of which is particularly high in this case. Many 'green claims' continue to be made under non-standardised systems. We should also recall Ost's warning about the 'licence to seduce' (p. 443, above); this controlled, top down approach to political consumption contrasts with the more spontaneous consumer-led approach discussed in the extract from Micheletti *et al.* above (pp. 446–7), and the line between information provision and marketing in eco-labelling is a delicate one. Modern economies rely on growth, and the environmental benefits of individual purchases are likely to be quickly overtaken by increase in consumption. Indeed, the very idea of green consumption avoids fundamental questions about the relationship between environmental degradation and consumption, and whether particular products are necessary at all.

### Andrew Dobson, *Green Political Thought* (Routledge, 2000), p. 205

Porritt refers, for example, to [Friends of the Earth's] highly successful campaign to encourage producers to phase out the use of chlorofluorocarbons in aerosols. He noted that by the end of 1989 only some 5 or 10 per cent of aerosols would use CFCs, compared with nearly three-quarters just a year or so earlier. This, as he writes, is 'All good stuff – a small, incremental step towards a safer environment.' Then he asks: 'But does it actually bring us anywhere nearer sustainability?'[45] And, of course, this is the point – eradicating CFCs from aerosols is a respectable green achievement, but is it a radical one?
Porritt himself observes:

> Various deep Greens (including members of the Green Party) were quick to castigate Friends of the Earth for not campaigning against aerosols in general, inasmuch as they are indisputably unnecessary, wasteful and far from environmentally benign even if they don't use CFCs. Such critics suggested (and who can blame them?) that by campaigning for CFC-free aerosols, we were in fact condoning, if not positively promoting, self-indulgence, vanity, and wholly unsustainable patterns of consumption.

The EU eco-label ranks products within product groups, so it discounts not only the 'no consumption' option, but also less damaging alternative products.

Other limitations to 'green consumerism' as a form of environmental protection are equally severe. As we have discussed elsewhere (especially Chapter 1, pp. 40–7), the reflection of environmental values through economic choices is difficult if not impossible; political debate would allow a much more complete recognition of the nature of environmental concerns. The participation engendered by consumption decisions might be broad and immedi-

---

[45] In Felix Dodds (ed.), *Into the 21st Century* (Green Print, 1988), pp. 200–1.

ate, but it is both superficial, and limited to those with the financial and social means to participate in the market. It is also largely (not inevitably, see Micheletti *et al.* above, pp. 446–7) limited to individual participation on essentially collective issues. The consumer choice rhetoric surrounding the EU's regulation of genetically modified organisms (GMOs) (Chapter 5, pp. 202–8) is belied not only by the holes in the mandatory labelling scheme, but also by these more profound limitations of green consumerism. More positively, a focus on consumption can be part of efforts to engender a sense of individual responsibility for environmental degradation, taking the reflexive approach to an individual level, raising awareness and stimulating debate and cooperation. Green consumerism can stimulate external scrutiny (and even sanctioning) of private actions when state action falls short.

## 5 The example of waste: diversity in regulation

The intention of this section is not to provide a comprehensive description of waste management regulation. Instead, we hope briefly to illustrate how one particular environmental sector engages a range of regulatory techniques. Waste disposal was the first part of the waste cycle to be regulated, because of its clear and immediate polluting impact. Waste disposal can also, however, be indicative of a failure to use resources effectively. Properly addressing the environmental impacts of waste requires attention to be paid to the production and the destination of waste, as well as its disposal. This implicates enormous numbers of individuals and activities, which can only problematically be tackled by direct regulation. The waste hierarchy, which requires priority to be given to waste reduction, then reuse, recycling and recovery (usually meaning energy recovery by incineration of waste), with waste disposal at the bottom of the hierarchy, is supposed to underpin UK (and EU) waste policy.[46] The UK has begun to take the waste hierarchy seriously only recently, and the challenge now is to change patterns of waste production and use. Part of the reason for the sudden awakening to the hierarchy in the UK was the passage of the EC Landfill Directive,[47] which requires less waste to be disposed of in landfill. Landfill emits methane, a major greenhouse gas, creates local nuisances and water and soil contamination, with potentially damaging effects on human health. More fundamentally, as a relatively cheap form of disposal (because environmental externalities are ignored), it reduces incentives to avoid waste, or to make beneficial use of waste. This section attempts to give a flavour of the range of measures called on to change patterns of behaviour in this area.

---

[46] Department of the Environment, Transport and the Regions (DETR), *National Waste Strategy 2000*, Cm 4693 (2000); Directive 75/442 on Waste OJ 1975 L 194/39, amended by Directive 1991/156 OJ 1991 L 078/32, Art. 3.

[47] Directive 1999/31 on the landfill of waste OJ 1999 L 182/1.

### Andrew Dobson, *Citizenship and the Environment* (Oxford University Press, 2003), pp. 1–4, 7–8

There is a European Union directive that calls for deep cuts in the amount of household waste sent to landfill sites in Britain – currently about 1400 of them. 'The EU Landfill Directive requires the UK to reduce the volume of biodegradable municipal waste sent to landfill by 2010, with further reductions in 2013 and 2020. Failure to meet these targets could result in fines of up to £180 million per year.'[48] This leaves the British government with the tricky task of working out how best to wean the public and its institutions off the habit of throwing stuff away. Downing Street has a Strategy Unit charged with suggesting answers to such questions, and in November 2001 Margaret Beckett, Secretary of State for the Environment, Food and Rural Affairs, announced a 'Strategy Unit Waste Study' to be completed within a year. The Unit's proposals shed interesting light on the prevailing view of how to get people to do environmentally beneficial things when their inclination is not to do them.

The report notes that household waste is growing at 3 per cent annually – faster than GDP – and the authors wonder why. The answer offered is that 'there are few financial incentives in place for either industry or householder to seek alternatives to landfill'. With this premise established, the solution to the problem is obvious and the report predictably recommends 'Greater freedom for local authorities to develop new financial incentives for householders to reduce and recycle their waste. Householders currently pay the same Council Tax no matter how much waste they produce or whether they recycle or not. This means that they have no incentive to manage their waste in more sustainable ways.' A concrete suggestion floated over the summer of 2002 was to charge people for taking over-quota sacks of rubbish away – say £1.00 (E0.6) per sack or £5.00 (E3.0) per month.

From one point of view the logic is impeccable: people will want to avoid paying the rubbish tax and so will reduce the amount of waste they throw away. The proposal is rooted in the 'self-interested rational actor' model of human motivation, according to which people do things either for some gain or to avoid some harm to themselves. Critics of the proposed scheme immediately pointed out that this model contains the seeds of its own demise. People uncommitted to the idea behind the scheme will take the line of least resistance in a way entirely consistent with the model of behaviour on which the scheme depends, but entirely at odds with its desired outcomes. As a *Guardian* newspaper leader pointed out, 'Rather than pay up, the public are likely to vote with their cars and take their rubbish and dump it on the pavement, in the countryside or in someone else's backyard' (12 July 2002).

Supporters of the financial incentive routes to sustainability will claim, though, that it works, and that there is plenty of evidence to prove it. They will point, for example, to the road-pricing scheme that has been operating in a part of the ancient English city of Durham for the past few months (I write in January 2003). It costs £2.00 (E1.20) to take your car into the square at the top of the city, and it was hoped that this would cut traffic by 50 per cent

---

[48] Strategy Unit, *Waste Not, Want Not* (Cabinet Office, 2002), p. 9.

within a year. In fact it has been cut by 90 per cent in just a few months. This is success beyond the planners' wildest dreams. Imagine, though, that the scheme was withdrawn tomorrow. No doubt some people would continue to take the bus into town, or to cycle or walk, having seen what a difference there is between a square empty of cars and one that is filled with them. But the Italian experience of car-less city days suggests that when cars are allowed back in, people fire up their engines and drive into town. The chances are that traffic levels would return to their pre-fine levels within a few weeks or months. The 'success' of the Durham scheme, then, is bought at the cost of the signal failure to make anything other than a superficial impression on people's habits and practices. The change in behaviour lasts only as long as the incentives or disincentives are in place – and these are inevitably subject to the vagaries of fashion, experiment, and the direction of the political wind that happens to be blowing at the time.

At no point in this debate was an alternative approach canvassed, admirably captured in the following from Ludwig Beckman:

> the fact that the sustainability of the consumerist and individualist lifestyle is put in question undoubtedly raises a whole range of questions about how to reconstruct our society. What new economic and political institutions are needed? What regulations and set of incentives are necessary in order to redirect patterns of behaviour in sustainable directions?
>
> However, the question of sustainable behaviour cannot be reduced to a discussion about balancing carrots and sticks. The citizen that sorts her garbage or that prefers ecological goods will often do this because she feels committed to ecological values and ends. The citizen may not, that is, act in sustainable ways solely out of economic or practical incentives: people sometimes choose to do good for other reasons than fear (of punishment or loss) or desire (for economic rewards or social status). People sometimes do good because they want to be virtuous.[49]
>
> … Financial penalties invite attempts to get around them, as in the temptation to purchase means of making number plates illegible to cameras as cars enter the Congestion Charging Zone in the centre of London. Consumers react to superficial signals without caring about, understanding, or being committed to the underlying rationale for the incentives to which they respond. Ecological citizens, on the other hand, would harbour a commitment to the principles and would 'do good' because it is the right thing to do.
>
> …
>
> … There are no guarantees anywhere, of course, but democracy might be given a little shove towards sustainability by getting environmental concern in at the ground level. People are the 'raw material' of the democratic process and what they think and do makes a difference to the process's outcomes – if we do not believe that, then why endorse democratic procedures in the first place? My view is that ecological citizens will make democracies more responsive to sustainability demands than consumers charged a pound, a euro, a dollar or 100 yen to have an extra bag of rubbish taken away.

---

[49] Ludwig Beckman, 'Virtue, Sustainability and Liberal Values' in John Barry and Marcel Wissenburg (eds.), *Sustaining Liberal Democracy: Ecological Challenges and Opportunities* (Palgrave, 2001).

## (a) Waste management licensing

The roots of waste regulation lie in an obligation on those who handle waste to seek a waste management licence.

### Environmental Protection Act 1990, s. 33

1. ... a person shall not—

    (a) deposit controlled waste, or knowingly cause[50] or knowingly permit controlled waste to be deposited in or on any land unless a waste management licence authorising the deposit is in force and the deposit is in accordance with the licence;

    (b) treat, keep or dispose of controlled waste, or knowingly cause or knowingly permit controlled waste to be treated, kept or disposed of-

    (i) in or on any land, or
    (ii) by means of any mobile plant,

    except under and in accordance with a waste management licence;

    (c) treat, keep or dispose of controlled waste in a manner likely to cause pollution of the environment or harm to human health.

The 'duty of care' in s. 34 reinforces the criminal offences in this section by placing a responsibility (enforceable through criminal law) on those who hold waste (other than householders and their own waste) to prevent contravention of s. 33. This minimises the temptation to pass waste to the cheapest disposer, wilfully blind to the possibility that it will be disposed of unlawfully. Under s. 36(3) an application for a licence will be rejected if necessary for the purpose of preventing pollution of the environment, harm to human health, or serious detriment to the amenities of the locality.

Licensing attempts to mitigate the harm caused by waste during treatment, but would be difficult to apply to waste production (although the IPPC Directive takes waste production into account, as could mandatory product standards: see Chapter 9). It is this question of waste production, or at least its beneficial use after production, that underlies the instruments discussed below; however, every one of these measures relies on the fact of government regulation of the sites that manage waste.

## (b) Reducing landfill: taxing and trading

The landfill tax applies by weight to waste deposited in landfill (with a lower rate for 'inert' waste, which does not contribute to methane emissions or the leachate that pollutes ground water). It is designed to be fiscally neutral, offset by reductions in employers' national insurance contributions. The landfill

---

[50] Note the introduction of *mens rea*, by contrast with s. 85 Water Resources Act 1991 – see Ch. 10, pp. 382–7. The 'deposit or treat' offence is strict liability.

tax credit scheme allows a limited degree of hypothecation: operators can contribute up to 20 per cent of their liability to 'environmental bodies' who can fund certain environmental projects, the operators claiming back up to 90 per cent of donations.

### Macrory, 'Regulating in a Risky Environment', pp. 627–8

The policy intention behind the landfill tax, namely to increase the cost of landfill so that other waste disposal methods including minimization, recycling, and incineration became more economically attractive options, is environmentally persuasive. Yet markets behave in unpredictable ways. The cost of landfill did indeed rise considerably, but also led to a substantial diversion of waste to other destinations which were not included in the preferred options: increased fly-tipping, and more seriously the substantial diversion to, and possible abuse of, various forms of disposal exempted under current regulations. As the ENDS report noted:

> Within months of the landfill tax taking effect in 1996, reports came rolling in that golf courses and farms had become prime destinations for the disposal of construction and demolition waste.[51]

A government-commissioned report suggested that landfilling of inert wastes had fallen from around 66 million tonnes before the introduction of the tax to about 30 million tonnes in 2000. The Environment Agency itself was hampered in effective supervision, partly because its revenue streams in relation to waste derived from charges on licensed landfills, and it is only recently that the government is seriously addressing the need to tighten up the exempted routes. A key lesson from the saga was the danger of assuming that a market instrument by itself could achieve desired policy goals. Without a powerful and adequately enforced regulatory framework, unexpected consequences can arise. This of course is particularly the case when dealing with an issue such as waste which generally has negative economic value for producers, and where the cheapest diversion route will have a powerful attraction. In that context economic instruments need to be supportive rather than substitutive of regulation.

> Whether the landfill tax by itself, even against a background of strengthened regulation against undesired diversion, would have had the desired outcome of reducing landfill is difficult to judge. What is now clearly going to have a far more substantial impact on shifting the hierarchy of waste management options is the European Community Landfill Directive, which came into force in July 2001, and which imposes direct bans on overall quantities of waste going to landfill over the next decade or so. The Landfill Directive represents a form of command and control instrument, albeit one at supra-national level.

A modest 'allowance trading' scheme now supports this ambiguous effort through the landfill tax to divert waste. Waste disposal authorities (WDAs)[52]

---

[51] Environmental Data Services (ENDS) Report, 'Inertia over Inert Waste Embarrasses Ministers and Agency' (2000) 303 END Report 22.

[52] WDAs are within local authorities, and are responsible for arranging for the disposal of waste in their area: Environmental Protection Act (EPA) 1990, s. 51.

receive an allowance by weight for the landfill of 'biodegradable municipal waste' (the waste targeted under the Landfill Directive), and those allowances are tradable.[53] This is a resort to a direct system of control (limits on the amount of waste landfilled), made more palatable by the option of trading, which allows reductions to take place where they are most straightforward.

### (c) Recycling obligations

The Landfill Directive does not dictate how the waste diverted from landfill is to be dealt with. The preference would be for less waste to be produced, and then for re-use, followed by recycling. Government is concentrating direct legal measures on recycling, and aims to increase the recycling of household waste, to at least 30 per cent by 2010 and 33 per cent by 2015.[54]

The Household Waste Recycling Act 2003 requires every waste collection authority (WCA),[55] by 31 December 2010, to arrange for the collection of 'at least two types of recyclable waste together or individually separated from the rest of the household waste', unless 'the cost of doing so would be unreasonably high', or 'comparable alternative arrangements are available'.[56] This combines direct regulation of the authority with the provision of *opportunities* for positive action by the public. It is a fairly modest scheme, and the most surprising thing is perhaps that it has not been in place for years. Moreover, there is no obligation actually to recycle the collected materials, although according to DEFRA, 'it would be difficult … to justify the waste of resources that not recycling the collected materials would represent in light of both the investment in collection infrastructure and the value of the recyclates themselves'; nor does the Act make any demands in respect of levels of householder participation, although again, 'in the interests of value for money and requirements to improve rates of recycling and composting … all measures to encourage householder participation' should be considered.[57] Measures discussed by DEFRA include 'rewarding' householders in cash or kind for reducing waste or increasing recycling (variable charges for waste collection would require amendment of the Environmental Protection Act 1990) and 'intensive education' schemes.[58]

'Producer responsibility' legislation, mainly originating in EC law (with measures on packaging waste, waste electrical and electronic goods and batteries)

---

[53] Waste and Emissions Trading Act 2003.

[54] DETR, *National Waste Strategy 2000*; Strategy Unit, *Waste Not, Want Not*, has more ambitious targets; for details of the review of the waste strategy, see www.defra.gov.uk/environment/waste/strategy/review/index.htm.

[55] WCAs are part of local authorities and are responsible for arranging for the free-of-charge collection of household waste in their area (EPA, s. 45); actual collection is often delegated to a private operator.    [56] EPA 1990, new s. 45A.

[57] DEFRA, *Guidance for Waste Collection Authorities on the Household Waste Recycling Act 2003* (2005).    [58] http://www.defra.gov.uk/environment/waste/localauth/encourage.htm.

contains more direct recycling obligations. Producer responsibility extends the responsibility of producers through the life cycle of a product to the waste phase. Those who make the products have to retrieve a certain proportion of the waste that they turn into at the end of their life (or pay someone else to do so), and manage it as required. Producer responsibility works both as an economic instrument and as reflexive regulation. Price signals should affect the nature and amount of waste produced and encourage innovation, and there should be greater awareness and consideration of the product's waste phase during the manufacture of that product. Producer responsibility legislation also imposes good old-fashioned obligations as to quantity of waste that must be recycled. So, for example, the EC End-of-Life Vehicles Directive requires Member States to 'take the necessary measures to ensure' certain recovery and recycling targets.[59]

Even if waste reduction and recycling improves enormously, the Landfill Directive will divert waste from landfill to incineration in the UK. We might question whether this is a good use of social resources (inching waste slowly up the hierarchy is demanding enormous efforts), but it also raises practical and political problems around participation. Waste incinerators are not welcome neighbours: the label 'waste' is said to carry considerable stigma, and there is intense public concern about the impact of incinerators upon human health; the unfamiliarity of the technology and the fact that large-scale incinerators are likely to accept waste from outside the local area both exacerbate public concern. Every new incinerator will be subjected to public consultation through the application for planning permission (probably with environmental impact assessment), and often also the integrated pollution prevention and control regime. Consultation, however, takes place after one significant option (continuing with landfill) has been taken out of the equation. Public participation is essentially limited to the siting of facilities, by which point questions such as the appropriate balance between landfill, incineration, recycling, re-use and reduction are not readily addressed. This is where more strategic environmental decision making may prove useful (Chapter 14, pp. 597–601 below). There are earlier opportunities for public participation on waste management. The National Waste Strategy[60] was drafted following a very lengthy period of consultation, and that feeds into local and regional plans, also subject to public participation under planning legislation. Consultation, however, has not led to improved local acceptability of incinerators. One of the major problems is the different publics (local householder; local, national or pan-European environmental interest groups; the waste industry, again individually, nationally or supra-nationally) involved at the different stages; and of course the EU-level decision to restrict landfill was never likely to involve the communities hosting waste facilities. The Landfill Directive is indicative of the gaps in participation

[59] Directive 2000/53 on end-of-life vehicles OJ 2000 L 269/34, Art. 7(2).
[60] DETR, *National Waste Strategy 2000*.

that can emerge when decisions are taken at different levels of government. It arguably also raises serious questions about the real commitment of the EU institutions to public participation, beyond the rhetoric.

And the final 'tool' used in encouraging recycling (and indeed reduction and re-use) is public information, informing the public of the importance of these issues, as well as of opportunities for action. This is clearly important, even if it needs to be more deeply ingrained for the sort of ecological citizenship that Dobson discusses above (pp. 252–3).

## 6 Conclusions

The field of regulation has become politically contentious and theoretically complex over recent years. Direct regulation can take many forms, with greater and lesser degrees of flexibility, and incorporating elements of indirect persuasion and influence (Chapter 9). There are, however, important truths in the criticisms of command and control, and there are limitations to the permit as a tool of regulation. Alternative mechanisms, alternative fora and alternative participants have important roles to play. Each alternative brings its own limitations and new concerns, and it is vital that each case is assessed on its merits. We might also ask what role remains for government, or for representative democracy, in the reflexive/self-regulatory/decentred world?

### Black, 'Decentring Regulation', p. 145

That shift from hierarchies to heterarchies implies a different role for the state, one of mediator, facilitator, enabler, and for the skills of diplomats rather than bureaucrats. But it is suggested that the hierarchy of state–society will be difficult to dismantle in some ways, notwithstanding the empirical claims that the state has been displaced from the centre by developments at the global and mezzo level. This is for two reasons, first, because states still have the monopoly on the legitimate use of coercion and the authority to make binding law. There will always be the potential that those powers will be used. Secondly, because in democratic countries, at least, governments are elected in the expectation that they will act to resolve collective problems – it is hard to explain to complaining electors that governments cannot in fact perform that function and that the problem is being remitted back for consideration. There is an expectation that the state will perform its public responsibility as guardian of the 'public interest' (however that may be defined). Given those two factors, it is suggested, a truly horizontal relationship between government and others is unlikely to be possible. Hierarchy will always lurk behind heterarchy, and negotiations will always be in its shadow.

And finally, one vital issue lurking behind the discussion in this chapter is the question of environmental limits.[61] Whilst it is apparently acceptable to require a certain proportion of 'end of life' mobile telephones to be recycled,[62]

---

[61] Ch. 6, pp. 250–6.
[62] Directive 2002/96/EC on waste electrical and electronic equipment OJ 2003 L 37/24.

questioning the need for mobile telephones (or computers, or refrigerators), or even questioning their speed of obsolescence, is somehow beyond the pale in an economy built on growth. As long as we can pay, and as long as we follow processes, it seems that environmental degradation need never be squarely faced.

## 7 Further reading

*Public Administration* (2003) 81 (3) contains a special 'European Forum' on 'new' policy instruments in the EU, including material on environmental regulation; *Environmental Politics* (2003) 12 (1) is another special issue, on '"New" Instruments of Environmental Governance?: National Experiences and Prospects', again with some interesting articles, including Andrew Jordan et al, 'Policy Innovation or "Muddling Through"? "New" Environmental Policy Instruments in the United Kingdom'.

The edited collection by Richard L. Revesz, Philippe Sands and Richard B. Stewart, *Environmental Law, The Economy and Sustainable Development* (Cambridge University Press, 2000), contains a number of interesting papers on the key issues arising in the use of economic instruments. More specifically, Ludwig Krämer, 'European Community Eco-Labelling in Transition' (2000) 1 *Yearbook of European Environmental Law* 123, discusses the development of the 2000 regulations on eco-labelling.

Waste regulation is a huge topic: for a much more thorough review of waste management law, see Stuart Bell and Donald McGillivray, *Environmental Law* (Oxford University Press, 6th edn, 2005), Ch. 15.

# Part V
# Mechanisms of Regulation II: Controls Over Land Use and Development

## Preface to Part V

In the preceding Part on regulatory mechanisms we examined the evolution of legal responses to industrial pollution. We observed that although the licence remains at the heart of much environmental regulation, other instruments have become increasingly important. This deployment of a range of instruments is an expression of sustainable development, particularly ideas about extending responsibility for environmental protection to various agencies, individuals and companies. In this Part we similarly explore the range of legal techniques employed in environmental regulation, but in the markedly different context of controls over land use and development. In Chapter 12 we discuss the history of land use controls, before turning in Chapters 13 to 16 to specific areas of current law and policy relating to land use, followed by a contemporary case study on wind farm development in Chapter 17. We emphasise that the focus of this Part of the book is the environmental protection aspects of land use controls, with the objective of exploring the regulatory *techniques* employed.[1]

The licence remains the 'instrument of choice' in town and country planning (discussed in Chapter 13). In contrast, the controls employed to regulate the use of land in ecologically sensitive areas have been more diverse, and generally of a voluntary nature. The key example of this type of control is the management agreement. This form of regulation, commonly used in the case of land designated for special protection (discussed in Chapter 15), tends to support self-regulatory and voluntary approaches to regulation. However, following the enactment of the Countryside and Rights of Way Act 2000, these agreements were embedded within a licensing system involving more precisely defined duties, and enforcement procedures, thus bringing them more in line with more traditional 'command and control'-type mechanisms (of the sort identified in the context of pollution control in Chapter 9). In this example, then, we see a sophisticated combining of different regulatory approaches. In terms of the range of regulatory techniques, we also consider environmental assessment, which is integral to both planning law and nature conservation law (Chapter 14),

---

[1] A broader and more detailed view of the various subject areas in this Part may be found in Stuart Bell and Donald McGillivray, *Environmental Law* (Oxford University Press, 6th edn, 2005), Chs. 13, 14 and 21.

and has forged links between these previously separately controlled areas. This is because at a very simple level environmental assessment may inform planners and decision makers (by expert opinion and lay views) about the likely environmental effects of land development, including the consequences for the ecological interests of the site.

Through an analysis of this procedural instrument we return to several major themes pursued throughout this book. The first is the participation of the public in decision making.[2] Throughout this book we have highlighted the need for balance between lay and expert views in decision making. In the context of the case study on wind farm development (Chapter 17), we also explore one difficult consequence of enhancing opportunities for the public to play a part in planning decisions on siting wind farms – the so-called 'social gap' by which general public approval for this form of energy generation is not translated into support for individual projects at the local level.[3] This suggests that there are clear limits to the correlation between public participation and environmental protection.

The second theme is the influence of international and EU law on national provisions, by which international obligations, filtered through the EU's law-making procedures, are applied in the national context. This leads to a characteristic layering of environmental law which is particularly notable in the case of the law relating to environmental assessment (discussed in Chapter 14) and nature conservation (Chapter 15).

A further key theme is integration,[4] an important element of which is policy integration in decision making about land use and development. We discuss this as a valuable consequence of the currency of sustainable development in law and policy,[5] as recognised by Mark Stallworthy in the following extract which also highlights the potential breadth of planning.

### Mark Stallworthy, *Sustainability, Land Use and the Environment: A Legal Analysis* (Cavendish, 2002), pp. 100–2

#### The scope of plannning

… The traditional land use concerns of planning can be described as generally including 'the need to protect public health, to prevent unplanned (physical) development, to protect nature as a refuge from modern life, to provide for the public interest, to manage the environment, and to find a fair balance between competing demands'. The boundaries between planning and environmental protection are at times hard to distinguish. This is inevitable, given that planning 'is implicitly environmental in the sense that its *raison d'être* is to regulate our immediate surroundings, allowing for a rational allocation of land uses among

---

[2] See Ch. 3 on public participation.

[3] As identified by Derek Bell, Tim Gray and Claire Haggett, 'The "Social Gap" in Wind Farm Siting Decisions: Explanations and Policy Responses' (2005) 14 *Environmental Policy* 460.

[4] See Ch. 8 on the making of an integrated institutional architecture of pollution control.

[5] For a detailed analysis of sustainable development, see Ch. 6.

competing demands. It can also influence "hard" issues like air quality, water pollution and the siting of hazardous installations which attract a narrower sense of the term.' Planning can be a proactive policy tool, which likewise can be seen as having an ideological role, Rydin referring to its seeking 'a more acceptable pattern of use of our built and natural environment' thereby 'easing the pain' of a postmodern, fragmented, flexible economy.[6] It also has a conservational role, especially in respect of 'the broad structures within which we live, work and exist'.[7] The potential range of the planning process is such that it can claim an inclusiveness that is not apparent in other areas of the policy process. Thus an argument for the role of planning is that it is not the main means of expression of policy integration. As Steeley has put it, 'there are not enough good models of the relationships between things: economics, culture, space and causality models each having drawbacks, it was necessary to seek a way of integrating these models to help strategically plan the city as the basic unit of management'.[8]

However, the dominance of national policy making within the planning regime has traditionally tended to downplay the aspirational, or integrative, aspect of planning, in favour of an emphasis upon the physical land use implications, guardedly extended by reference to locational and amenity elements. The system in many respects has also been called upon to promote growth, to the extent even of the ordinary planning process being withdrawn or severely modified. This has meant that planning has not provided a consistent, land use-focused platform for a more integrated policy process. Instead, beset by constraints and isolated by discrete policy powers vested elsewhere, it has often appeared to be failing, as for instance in terms of the deficiencies in securing appropriate housing provision and transport infrastructure, and responding to urban and rural deprivation ... The plain and obvious truth, however, is that land use planning cannot be isolated from a vast range of public policy questions. The expectation that planning can work without a broader policy integration emphasis has been made possible by a combination of insistence upon the sanctity of market forces and a central dominance of policy issues ... it must be hoped that sustainable development objectives can offer a suitable platform for a more open and integrated process.

The sustainability discourse indeed suggests that a more expansive approach can be justified. Certainly, notions of sustainable development can readily be assimilated into an integrated perspective of planning. Its remit has been described to extend to environmental objectives, which include 'the redistribution of resources to disadvantaged inner city groups; the longevity of the built stock; the conservation of wildlife; or the encouragement of urban development. A composite goal – such as sustainable development – may guide the planning process. The common strand is the focus on the use of the built and natural environment, and strategies which can alter that use.' The modern environmental agenda, and the wider implications of land use decisions, regionally, nationally and globally, has the potential to bring about a change in planning priorities. Owens has pointed to the gradual injection of broader concerns 'exemplified by global warming and the consumption of non-renewable

---

[6] Yvonne Rydin, *Urban and Environmental Planning in the UK* (Macmillan, 1998), pp. 351–2.
[7] *Ibid.*, p. 353.     [8] Royal Commission on Environmental Pollution, Seminar, 2000.

resources' such as transport and pollution, although in 1994 she was unable to assert with any confidence that there had been more than a little practical impact.[9]

The role of planning has thus been circumscribed in one key respect, for it is concerned mainly with the locus of development activity, rather than questioning development viability. Though traditionally implicit, the central idea underlying planning is that it addresses the instabilities caused by the market system, including threats caused to both natural and built environments and the overexploitation and underutilisation of resources. Planning therefore operates at a crucial interface of market activities and public regulatory controls. The balance between the two shifts over time and the scope of planning as a regulatory response 'at any particular time will relate to the currently accepted limits of the public sector's role in devising strategies for the physical environment. It is important to recognise that as social and economic change occurs, the areas shaded by the planning umbrella will alter.'[10] Operating in the context of market forces, and in pursuit of its role 'to regulate, stimulate and impose order and structure', planning has features of an ideological nature, as well as addressing practical issues of land value. Seen thus, at its most proactive, it can be said to have a redistributional impact in addressing the externalities of economic activity; with dual tasks relating to negative externalities, by seeking to protect areas and communities against adverse consequences, and positive externalities, by seeking to divert resources into preferred land uses and facilities.

The idea of the planning 'umbrella', casting its shade over a varying number of policy areas, is a striking description of planning dealing with multiple contemporary problems, and explains why planning has been only periodically concerned with environmental protection, generally as other objectives, such as economic regeneration and advancement, recede. (The key episodes of environmental concern in planning policy, as reflected in law, are highlighted in Chapter 12, pp. 475–502.) Whilst noting the increasing ability of the planning system to take on board matters of nature conservation, we also suggest a fundamental flaw in the process of integration via environmental assessment – the current lack of any form of post-assessment monitoring means a divide still exists between the initial issues of the siting of development (planning controls) and operational issues (pollution controls).

As mentioned above, in this Part we stress the integration of different policy areas and, in line with this, the increasingly integrated nature of legal controls over land use and development. But for the purpose of analysis we divide the law and policy relating to town planning, environmental assessment, and nature conservation through countryside designations and other methods ('beyond designation') into individual chapters (Chapters 13, 14, 15 and 16 respectively), preceded by a chapter on the historical context of these areas of law. That these legal and policy areas interrelate and are conflated in practice is made clear by the

---

[9] Susan Owens, 'Land, Limits and Sustainability: A Conceptual Framework and some Dilemmas for the Planning System' (1994) 19 *Transactions of the Institute of British Geographers* 439.

[10] Rydin, *Urban and Environmental Planning*.

case study on wind farm development in Chapter 17. This provides a good example of the close relationship between environmental protection, and law and policy on land use and development. The case study highlights the problem of siting wind farms, particularly the resistance to national policy guidance on renewable energy by local communities likely to be affected in some way by such developments, the great difficulty of assessing the ecological effects of wind farms, as well as a more general evaluation of their negative and positive effects on the environment. It also suggests the unifying potential of environmental assessment, with the assessment procedure acting as a conduit for a 'one-stop shop' application for development consent in place of the current 'system' of multiple applications for a range of licences, each invoking several different assessment procedures. The siting of wind farms also suggests an important role for strategic environmental assessment; hitherto there has been little coordination of decisions about applications to develop wind farms, nor overall assessment of the environmental impact of off- and onshore wind farms as a sector. We include in Chapter 17 part of one of the first strategic environmental assessments for the future development of this sector in the United Kingdom (as well as a critique of the methodologies adopted in this) (pp. 723–9).

Over the following chapters, and through analysis of the case study, a picture of the complexity of legal controls over land is built up, as well as the potential for their further integration (although we have also discussed these issues in the context of the classic land use conflict between 'biotech' and 'organic' farming methods (discussed in Chapters 2, 5 and 8)). This legal picture can only hint at the complexity of land itself. Land can be seen in many different ways and how the law follows these alternatives, either (to adopt a dualist approach) as 'an object with use-value' or 'as a symbol with meaning',[11] is of real importance. The starkness of these alternative conceptions of land is expressed in the case study on wind farm development in Chapter 17, but is also nicely illustrated by Paul Durman's reflection on the protest against the expansion of Manchester airport ('The Campaign Against Runway Two') in which he describes the limitations of using law to reach beyond the economic value attributed to land by developers so as to protect more intangible values and relationships with the land.[12] The protesters' conception of the land (with which the author is sympathetic) is akin to Leopold's land ethic – that 'Land … is not merely soil'[13] (on the land ethic, see Chapter 1, p. 48), except that the following story of the direct action engaged in to protect the land concentrates on the social community of the protest sites – the Cliff Richard, River Rats, Flywood, Jimi Hendrix, Wild Garlic and Zion Tree camps – as much as the biotic community under threat.

[11] Allen Abramson, 'Mythical Land, Legal Boundaries: Wondering about Landscape and Other Tracts' in Allen Abramson amd Dimitrios Theodossopoulous (eds.), *Land, Law and Environment: Mythical Land, Legal Boundaries* (Pluto Press, 2000), p. 2.

[12] This is the familiar issue of economic values imperfectly reflecting more intangible environmental qualities, as previously discussed in Ch. 1, pp. 34–40. For a discussion of conflicts over land in a planning rather than theoretical context, see Ch. 13, pp. 508–9.

[13] Aldo Leopold, *A Sand County Almanac* (Ballantine Books, 1968), p. 253.

### Paul Durman, 'Tract: Locke, Heidegger and Scruffy Hippies in Trees' in Allen Abramson and Dimitrios Theodossopoulous (eds.), *Land, Law and Environment: Mythical Land, Legal Boundaries* (Pluto Press, 2000), pp. 87–90

BACK TO THE PROTEST SITE

To the airport the land stands as an economic resource, as a potential for profit. It is a resource to be used in the expansion of the airport's business, a defined tract of land abstractly represented by a project, as well as existing physically. It is signified as an economic entity that both facilitates development and resists it. Through the application of the airport's project, the land is transformed into the required physical base for the airport's operation. Such a land, defined in those narrow, instrumental terms, resists human action upon it as much as effort is required to 'develop' it. It must be transformed from its current state to the state required for its effective use. Physically this requires the filling of the Bollin Valley with several thousand tons of rubble and the levelling of a number of farmhouses …

The land then is conceived of as a means of economic production and dominance. The revenue gained by its use is the motivator for this particular use of the land and the means of enframing the land in question. It not only drives the project, but it also determines the way in which the land is apprehended. The land is to be utilised in the achievement of this project, which is presented to the local population as a desirable one in terms of jobs and the economic wealth it will provide. The goods gained by building the airport more than offset the goods lost in its construction. The goods lost, in this case, are the ability to enjoy the valley, the loss of farm land, some destruction of the local flora and fauna, the peace and quiet of the residents of the area, and the decreased air quality and so forth. This is the basis on which the Manchester Airport Authority enframes the issue of the development as well as the land utilised. In the case of a strict cost-benefit analysis, this latter category of goods lost should also have a price attached to them. It is here that the enframement of development reaches the limits of legal experience. In other words, the law has never been challenged to provide a mechanism by which the worth of such 'goods' is valued.

    …

For the protesters, the defence of the land was not merely a legal or an intellectual issue. An intense emotional engagement was consequent on the commitment of many of the protesters to defend the land. Their engagement led to polar opposition: their proposed scheme of protest was not merely reforming – it did not seek to negotiate an accommodation with the Runway Two project. This does not mean that the other protagonists in this conflict did not themselves develop intense relationships as a result of it. What characterises the difference between the protesters and the developers is the direction of their concerns. The form of engagement that the agents of development had with the land was concerned primarily with the land as it was coopted, and represented within an economic and technological enterprise. The very land that held these divergent meanings is now transformed into a different place from which passenger jets will shuttle people to and from Manchester.

However it is theorised (Durman refers to Locke and Heidegger in seeking to understand the positions in this dispute), this land was vitally important to the protesters, to the extent that they were prepared to be arrested for the sake of its protection from development. This example of 'intuited nature' goes far beyond a concern with pollution or resource consumption, making clear that 'spiritual, aesthetic and intrinsic qualities of the non-human world … are so often central to conflicts over the use and development of land'.[14] This case – some might say 'battle' – precisely illustrates the issues which underlie many legal disputes about land use and development. However, the polarised nature of this debate contrasts with wind farm projects (discussed in Chapter 17). For example, it is rarely the case that the environmental consequences of such projects are so clear cut; particularly the impact on landscape, which may differ widely depending upon the scale used to determine their effects, as well as individuals' subjective views about nature and the built environment. For example, the proposed wind farm development on the Isle of Lewis (flagged up as likely to be one of Europe's largest wind farms) has also divided environmental groups, with the Royal Society for the Protection of Birds vehemently opposed to the development because of the likely (as they see it) loss of valuable habitats for birds and other wildlife (see Chapter 17, pp. 735–42).

We will return to the case of wind farm development as a modern land use dilemma in Chapter 17, but we begin with the historical context of land use controls in Chapter 12, in which we draw parallels between some of the ideas which have informed the development of planning policy, such as amenity and self-sufficiency, and the modern form of sustainable development. This and later chapters also reveal the way political and cultural contexts have shaped the legal boundaries within which land use and development takes place, as seen particularly in the case of renewable energy projects.

[14] Susan Owens and Richard Cowell, *Land and Limits: Interpreting Sustainability in the Planning Process* (Routledge, 2003), p. 3.

# 12

## Historical context of land use and development controls

### 1 Introduction

In this chapter we present the historical context of land use and development controls which, with those controls over industrial activities discussed in Chapter 8, constituted early environmental regulation. We include not just town planning but also controls over use and development in rural areas, and we trace the roots of the different legal treatment accorded to these: the licence in the case of town planning, and the dependence upon voluntary (and undeniably more lenient) mechanisms such as payments as part of management agreements in the case of countryside designations. The modern forms of these controls are then discussed in Chapter 13 on planning and environmental protection and Chapters 15 and 16 on nature conservation and biodiversity.

In keeping with our emphasis upon the influence of sustainable development upon environmental law, in Section 2 ('Origins') we highlight the continuity between the utopian and social movements which informed early town planning (and which tended to pursue a formative type of 'sustainability') and the challenges to this ethos during particular periods in planning's history in which economic regeneration and progress were more singularly advanced. The developmental phases outlined in Section 3 of this chapter – early planning law, the post-war land settlement, enhancing participation, entrepreneurial planning, and planning and sustainable development – provide a basic chronological framework and analytical markers for Chapters 13–17 concerning more current law and policy relating to land use (Chapter 13 on planning and environmental protection, Chapter 14 on environmental assessment, Chapters 15 and 16 on conservation and biodiversity, and Chapter 17 on wind farm development and environmental conflicts). We should note that although we present these stages as an evolutionary progression of land use and development controls, in practice the planning system simultaneously maintains as objectives the priorities of each phase – public health, participation, economic growth and regeneration, environmental protection, and landscape. The weight attributed to each cumulative objective by decision makers is influenced by the prevailing policy and legal framework of a particular time. In this context, the ability of the planning system to absorb new policy preoccupations and development conditions flexibly means that planning has proved amply capable of transforming its traditional concern with environmental protection into an all-embracing expression of sustainable development.

## 2 Origins

### (a) Public health and 'amenity'

The roots of land use and development controls lie predominantly in the public health movement of the second half of the nineteenth century with its concerns for the, usually urban, community's health, the removal of nuisances and sanitation (as we discuss in Chapter 8, pp. 325–31). To achieve these objectives, local authorities were given powers to make and enforce by-laws for controlling street widths, and the height, structure and layout of buildings. Edwin Chadwick's Public Health Act 1848 provided for the registration of lodging houses and requirements for water supply, drains and the provision of water closets. The legal provisions were strong and prescriptive.

Pragmatic though his health reforms were, Chadwick was as much an idealist as the utopian thinkers who were his contemporaries. His general concern was with the dignity of humans – particularly when they were diseased and dying. The public health movement, headed by Chadwick, challenged the prevailing ethos of the sanctity of the landowners' rights to develop and use property as and how they desired. The conflict which arose between proprietorial rights and local government powers to regulate the use and development of land is seen clearly in *Cooper* v. *Wandsworth Board of Works* in which the plaintiff had failed to give notice of building works to Wandsworth Board of Works as required under the Local Management Act 1855, thus denying the Board the opportunity of directing the plaintiff developer as to how to build sewerage and drainage systems. In this case the 'public interest' is aligned with the plaintiff's individual and proprietorial rights. This judicial approach to the task of mediating between the interests of the general public and the individual landowner has informed modern planning law.

### *Cooper* v. *Wandsworth Board of Works* (1863) 143 ER 414

*Erle, C. J.*: I am of the opinion that this rule ought to be discharged. This was an action of trespass by the plaintiff against the Wandsworth district board, for pulling down and demolishing his house; and the ground of defence that has been put forward by the defendants has been under the 76th section of the Local Management Act, 18 & 19 Vict. c. 120. By the part of the section which applies to this case, it is enacted that, before any person shall begin to build a new house, he shall give seven days' notice to the district board of his intention to build; and it provides at the end that, in default of such notice it shall be lawful for the district board to demolish the house. The district board here say that no notice was given by the plaintiff of his intention to build the house in question, wherefore they demolished it. The contention on the part of the plaintiff has been that, although the words of the statute, taken in their literal sense, without any qualification at all, would create a justification for the act which the district board has done, the powers granted by the statute are subject to a qualification which has been repeatedly recognised, that no man is to be deprived of his property without his having an opportunity of being heard. The evidence here shews that the plaintiff and the district board have not been quite on amicable terms. Be that as it may, the district board say that no notice was given and that consequently they had a right to proceed to demolish the house without delay, and without notice to the party whose house was to be pulled down, and without giving him the opportunity of shewing any reason why the board should delay. I think that the power which is granted by the 76th section is subject to the qualification suggested. It is a power carrying with it enormous consequences. The house in question was built only to a certain extent. But the power claimed would apply to a complete house. It would apply to a house of any value and completed to any extent; and it seems to me to be a power which may be exercised most perniciously, and that the limitation which we are going to put upon it is one which is required by a due consideration for the public interest.

## (b) Utopianism and the garden city movement

The roots of land use controls might lie mainly in the public health movement, but utopian and socialist thinkers were also influential in planning experiments such as the creation of the 'industrial paradise' at Bourneville and the building of garden cities, both of which had an impact on the course of planning. Such experiments advocated not just interference with property rights, as was the case with much public health legislation, but a radical rethinking of property ownership and organisation of space, sometimes along utopian lines.

Ideas of 'the environment' have a rich heritage in utopian writing. A common strand is that the control of land use and the appurtenances of the land – fruits, animals, soil – is to be achieved by wide-scale social reform rather than by individual legal mechanisms. These social reforms centre upon the common ownership and equal distribution of land, and the relationship of man to the natural world. The ties between society and the environment were perceived by utopian thinkers to be very strong; a deeply *social* notion of the environment prevailed.

An idea of the environment as utopia can be traced to the ideas of Thomas Spence in the eighteenth century. For Spence, land and liberty were fundamental rights, neither of which could exist without the other. In his *Rights of Man*, he wrote 'the country of any people in a native state is properly their common, in which each of them has an equal property, with free liberty to sustain himself and connexions with the animals, fruits and other products thereof'. Spence

which we are all striving: the spontaneous movement of the people from the crowded and unhealthy cities to the bosom of our kindly mother earth.

...

An estate of 6,000 acres was to be bought at a cost of £40 an acre, or £240,000. The estate was to be held in trust, 'first, as a security for the debenture-holders, and secondly, in trust for the people of Garden City'. A town was to be built near the centre of the estate to occupy about 1,000 acres. In the centre was to be a park in which were placed the public buildings, and around the park a great arcade containing shops etc. The population of the town was to be 30,000. The building plots were to be of an average size of 20 by 130 feet. There were to be common gardens and cooperative kitchens. On the outer ring of the town were to be factories, warehouses, etc. fronting on a circular railway. The agricultural estate of 5,000 acres was to be properly developed for agricultural purposes as part of the scheme, and the population of this belt was taken at 2,000.

The entire revenue of the town was to be derived from ground rents, which were considered to be amply sufficient (a) to pay the interest on the money with which the estate is purchased, (b) to provide a sinking fund for the purpose of paying off the principal, (c) to construct and maintain all such works as are usually constructed and maintained by municipal and other local authorities out of rates compulsorily levied, and (d) after redemption of debentures to provide a large surplus for other purposes, such as old-age pensions or insurance against accident and sickness.

Howard's idealistic principles and theories on the garden city were put into practice first in Letchworth, an estate near Hitchin in Hertfordshire which was purchased from fifteen different owners in 1903 by the First Garden City Company. The planning of the town was carried out by the First Garden City Company by means of its powers as sole owner of the Estate, and not by the local authority under the powers of the Town Planning Acts. However, the Urban District Council had a voice in the Town Plan, deposited with the Council by the Company. This plan laid out the defining use, character and density of buildings; the Company agreed not to depart from the provisions of the plan without first consulting the Council. The establishment of Letchworth Garden City was followed by the purchase of a second estate at Welwyn, also in Hertfordshire, and the foundation of Welwyn Garden City. These garden cities, which still exist, were part of Howard's plan to create a cluster of such cities and eventually to rebuild London itself. There was some disappointment with the realisation of Howard's plans; the planned nature of the towns meant that they lacked a certain energy and character. And their building stopped far short of redirecting the geography and development of London.

Howard's utopian vision of combining town and country, thus alleviating the 'crowded, ill-ventilated, unplanned, unwieldy, unhealthy cities', and establishing conditions for the creation and distribution of new forms of wealth, followed Thomas Spence's utopian writings of the eighteenth century. However, his vision of the garden city had a distinctly contemporary feel, reflecting the ideals of ethical principles in industry, as well as self-government and self-sufficiency. As his biographer describes, in Howard's plans there was something for every kind of idealist: 'self-realisation to please the individualist, and a communal venture which pleased the socialist'.[4]

## 3 Phases of development of controls over land

### (a) Early planning law

As we highlighted in the Preface to this Part, planning is all-encompassing – from drains to 'designing' nature. But the progression from the early, rudimentary controls of the nineteenth century to the modern system of planning sees an expansion in the scale of issues tackled – from individual buildings, to local 'schemes' and, finally, regional and even national policy on land use. Early planning legislation had as at least one of its goals the provision of a healthier environment in the sense of a concern with amenity rather than environmental protection per se. But even 'amenity' was at this time combined with the predominantly local concerns of nuisances and sanitation. The Housing, Town Planning, Etc Act 1909 is generally referred to as the first Planning Act. Ebenezer Howard's physical planning ideals, such as low-density housing, were applied to new urban development by this Act.

The rationale and main provisions of the Act have been critically scrutinised.

### Barry Cullingworth and Vincent Nadin, *Town and Country Planning in Britain* (Routledge, 13th edn, 2003), p. 15

THE FIRST PLANNING ACT

The movement for the extension of sanitary policy into town planning was uniting diverse interests. These were nicely summarised by John Burns, President of the Local Government Board when he introduced the first legislation bearing the term 'town planning' – the Housing, Town Planning, Etc Act 1909:

> The object of the bill is to provide a domestic condition for the people in which their physical health, their morals, their character and their whole social condition can be improved by what we hope to secure in this bill. The bill aims in broad outline at, and hopes to secure, the home healthy, the house beautiful, the town pleasant, the city dignified and the suburb salubrious.

The new powers provided by the Act were for the preparation of 'schemes' by local authorities for controlling the development of new housing areas. Though novel, these powers were logically a simple extension of the existing ones. It is significant that this first legislative acceptance of town planning came in an Act dealing with health and housing. And,

---

[4] McFadyen, *Sir Ebenezer Howard*, p. 38.

as Ashworth has pointed out, the gradual development and the accumulated experience of public health and housing facilitated a general acceptance of the principles of town planning:

> Housing reform had gradually been conceived in terms of larger and larger units. Torrens' Act (Artizans and Labourers Dwellings Act 1868) had made a beginning with individual houses; Cross's Act (Artizans and Labourers Dwellings Improvement Act 1875) had introduced an element of town planning by concerning itself with the reconstruction of insanitary areas; the framing of bylaws in accordance with the Public Health Act 1875 had accustomed local authorities to the imposition of at least a minimum of regulation on new building, and such a measure as the London Building Act 1894 brought into the scope of public control the formation and widening of streets, the lines of buildings' frontage, the extent of open space around buildings, and the height of buildings. Town planning was therefore not altogether a leap in the dark, but could be represented as a logical extension, in accordance with changing aims and conditions, of earlier legislation concerned with housing and public health.[5]

The centrality of amenity to planning (both in the past and in contemporary planning) has been much commented upon. The following passage makes clear the continuity of ideas in the planning system: in this case between amenity and sustainable development.

### Denzil Millichap, 'Law, Myth and Community: A Reinterpretation of Planning's Justification and Rationale' (1995) 10 *Planning Perspectives* 279, pp. 279–80

'Amenity' and *The Housing, Town Planning &c Act 1909*

The first planning Act, The Housing, Town Planning &c Act 1909 ('the 1909 Act'), was a landmark in the development of the UK planning system. This was the first time that the word 'planning' had been used in legislation. The term 'amenity' was another key element. The legislation offered public authorities the powers to regulate certain types of development for 'planning' and 'amenity' reasons. Earlier legislation on land-use and development had not attempted to regulate land-use on the basis of amenity. This incorporation of the term 'amenity' into the first modern piece of planning legislation reflected the pioneering work of those advocating a broader approach to land-use control. So the concept reflected the efforts of planning pioneers of the era to move on from the 'sanitation'-based approach of the public health version of regulation, to an approach that also encompassed amenity. Such a concern for wider aspects of land-use control still informs much of current planning practice. 'Amenity' is still a term found in the planning legislation. It is arguably a concept that links the most recent concerns for sustainable development with that first planning legislation ... What is more relevant in terms of the concepts, ideology and cultural trappings

---

[5] W. Ashworth, *The Genesis of Modern British Town Planning* (Routledge, 1954), p. 181.

of planning in its infancy is that the key role to be played by the term 'amenity' was not lost on those supporting the passage of the legislation through Parliament ...

'Amenity' is thus not only a core statutory term, it is also a rallying cry to those in the vanguard of planning. It was meant to go beyond the rather drab and sterile urban environment which the focus on 'public health' had produced. Regulatory control was also to take as a central aim a new dimension of urban life – beauty: 'amenity' encapsulated that approach.

Although 'amenity' was a central term in the 1909 Act, it was left undefined. One understanding of this is that since the Act sought to regulate the development of land, and had such a bearing on landowners, the legislature thought it best not to prescribe a restrictive, legal meaning which might jeopardise cooperation between landowners and the local authorities charged with creating 'schemes' for residential development.[6]

The 1909 Act was followed by the Housing, Town Planning Act 1919 and the Town and Country Planning Act 1932, both of which required that all borough and urban districts prepare schemes to regulate *general* land use. In theory the schemes led to the zoning of land for particular uses such as residential or industrial. Developers did not have to apply for planning permission but, should the development fail to conform to the scheme, the planning authority could require that the owner remove or alter the development (without compensation). In practice, a number of difficulties arose with the administration of the planning schemes. By 1942, only 5 per cent of England and 1 per cent of Wales was subject to development schemes; large country districts, towns and cities were not covered by a scheme at all. Of those which were drawn up, most merely ratified existing trends of development because a more radical reappraisal of sites for development would have involved the planning authority in paying out compensation to landowners for restrictions or prohibitions on development which most authorities could ill afford. The schemes therefore placed few restrictions on developers. The system of paying compensation for loss of development rights was changed radically in the post-war reassessment of the planning system, representing a fundamental shift away from protecting property ownership and the associated right to develop land, in favour of a growing call for land nationalisation as the only way to secure development in the 'common good'.[7]

This recognition of the need to protect land from development is fairly recent. As Kathryn Last explains, a reversal in enlightenment thinking (on rationalist, enlightenment thought and the environment: see Chapter 1, pp. 31–4)

---

[6] Denzil Millichap, 'Law, Myth and Community: A Reinterpretation of Planning's Justification and Rationale' (1995) 10 *Planning Perspectives* 279, pp. 280–1.

[7] Dennis Hardy and Colin Ward, *Areadia for All: The Legacy of a Makeshift Landscape* (Mansell, 1984), p. 49.

was required before the state intervened in the use and development of land for the purpose of conservation (that is for purposes other than the protection of human health and property in urban settings).

### Kathryn V. Last, 'Mechanisms for Environmental Regulation – a Study of Habitat Conservation' in Andrea Ross (ed.), *Environment and Regulation* (2000): 8 (2) *Hume Papers on Public Policy*, pp. 39–41

#### Recognition of the need to conserve habitats: the establishment of private sanctuaries

Whereas steps had been taken to protect individual animal and bird species by the end of the nineteenth century, state intervention for habitat conservation came relatively late in Britain. The reasons for this were many and varied although it was in part a consequence of the greater emotional neutrality of the subject matter. This was due to the absence of the element of cruelty that was so crucial in providing the impetus for species protection. Rather it was the influence of science, concern about excessive collecting and a change in the concept of the balance of nature that were to prove instrumental in the impetus for habitat conservation.

In particular, the growth of the science of ecology had an important impact: 'At first everything was concentrated on preserving rare or distinctive plants and animals ... with the development of ecology as a science, the overriding need to protect the habitat of the individual species became more apparent'.[8] The conservation of habitats therefore assumed importance as an essential component of the regime for the protection of species.

The importance of conserving habitats was reinforced by a changing perception of the balance of nature. During the eighteenth century this concept connoted 'a robust, preordained system of checks and balances which ensured permanency and continuity in nature. By the end of the nineteenth century it conveyed the notion of a delicate and intricate equilibrium, easily disrupted and highly sensitive to human interference.'[9] There was a 'reversal of the rationalist, progressive outlook deriving from the Enlightenment which, with its confidence in the perfectability of all things, had looked always to the improvement of nature and society through the exercise of human reason'.[10] Actions that had previously been considered as advantageous and for the 'improvement' of nature were now classified as destructive and necessitating control.

Coupled with the industrial revolution, the consequence of this re-evaluation of the concept of nature was that man came to be seen as a major force in nature's destruction. When the rarity of nature and its vulnerability to man's interference was realised, the Victorians and Edwardians adopted a preservationist approach.

The concerns about habitat destruction were, however, essentially anthropocentric. Nature's vulnerability was an issue because of the value of nature to humans. The purpose of habitat conservation was therefore fairly restricted. Conservation was advocated in order

---

[8]  John Sheail, *Nature in Trust: The History of Nature Conservation in Great Britain* (Blackie, 1976), p. 196.

[9]  Phillip Lowe, 'Values and Institutions in the History of British Nature Conservation' in A. Warren and F. Goldsmith (eds.), *Conservation in Perspective* (John Wiley, 1983), p. 337.

[10]  Phillip Lowe and Jane Goyder, *Environmental Groups in Politics* (George Allen and Unwin, 1983), p.19.

to restrict damage to habitats by collecting and thus assist the preservation of individual species considered beneficial to humans.

Because there was no government policy on habitat conservation and thus no state intervention in these matters, the task of achieving these objectives was taken on by voluntary organisations concerned with wildlife protection. The prevailing ideology of these groups was that of letting nature alone because of the view that it was direct interference that caused damage. Thus, they established 'sanctuaries', the safety of which lay in the exercise of ordinary property rights which could be used to control access to a site and its management. Any unauthorised interference such as the damaging of plants, which are considered to belong to the owner of the soil upon which they are growing,[11] would be actionable at common law.

However, many naturalists were sceptical of the value of such reserves. Because the safety of these reserves lay in the exercise of ordinary property rights, they suffered from a number of limitations.[12] In particular, in Scotland this approach was inappropriate for the protection of wild birds and animals because they are *res nullius* and therefore belong to no one. Furthermore, it was believed that the cost of acquiring and guarding the land would be prohibitive, and that the act of making a reserve would attract the attention of collectors. There was also concern 'at the random way in which potential reserves were acquired, with apparently little regard for the national significance of their plants and animals'.[13] This was in part due to the organisations responsible for acquiring such sites. By 1910 the National Trust had acquired thirteen sites but 'site selection was haphazard, always secondary to the acquisition of buildings'. This led to the establishment in 1912 of the Society for the Promotion of Nature Reserves whose objectives were 'to preserve for posterity as a national possession some part of our native land, its fauna, flora and geological features'. It concentrated on encouraging other groups to purchase and manage nature reserves rather than doing this themselves.

Nature reserves were therefore considered to be a subsidiary and very expensive means of supplementing legislation to protect species against cruelty and over-collecting; they were merely a stop-gap measure because 'convictions and stringent penalties would soon make watchers redundant and sanctuaries irrelevant to wildlife protection'.[14]

Thus by the start of the twentieth century there was only a handful of such reserves and these were largely restricted to England.

## (b) The post-war land settlement and the great divide between urban planning and countryside controls

Radical developments in the control of land use followed the end of the Second World War. There was at this time a newly acquired confidence to tackle long-standing social and economic problems, and town planning formed part of this

---

[11] See, for example, *Burns* v. *Fleming* (1880) 8 R 226 and *Stewart* v. *Stewart's Exrs* (1761) Mor. 5436 in Scottish law, and *Stukeley* v. *Butler* (1615) Hob 168 in English law.
[12] These are well illustrated by the RSPB's first reserve, which had to be abandoned when development on neighbouring land destroyed its natural interest.
[13] Sheail, *Nature in Trust*, p. 60.   [14] *Ibid.*, p. 55.

idea of regeneration, creating a strand of planning since referred to as 'welfarist-utilitarianism'.[15] The 1944 White Paper, *The Control of Land Use*, sets the changes in a climate of social idealism and draws upon the utilitarian, but also utopian, heritage of planning.

### White Paper, *The Control of Land Use*, Cmd 6537 (HMSO, 1944)

Provision for the right use of land, in accordance with a considered policy, is an essential requirement of the government's programme of postwar reconstruction. New houses, whether of permanent or emergency construction; the new layout of areas devastated by reason of age or bad living conditions; the new schools which will be required under the Education Bill now before Parliament; the balanced distribution of industry which the government's recently published proposals for maintaining employment envisage; the requirements of sound nutrition and of a healthy and well-balanced agriculture; the preservation of land for national parks and forests, and the assurance to the people of enjoyment of the sea and countryside in times of leisure; a new and safer highway system better adapted to modern industrial and other needs; the proper provision of airfields – all these related parts of a single reconstruction programme involve the use of land, and it is essential that their various claims on land should be so harmonised as to ensure for the people of this country the greatest possible measure of individual well-being and national prosperity.

The Town and Country Planning Act 1947 was essential to the post-war nationalisation programmes and attempts to rebuild devastated areas. The 1947 Act considerably strengthened the state's control over the use and development of privately owned land by making all development subject to prior authorisation by the local authority. In addition, development plans were to be prepared in every area in the country. These were to outline the way in which each area was to be developed or preserved and thereby guide the authority in its decision making on individual applications for development consent. As well as having regard to these 'development plans', the authority was to have regard to 'any other material considerations' in making decisions about planning permission. Through the 1947 Act all development values in land were nationalised. This meant that compensation for loss of development rights was to be paid once and for all, after which the grant of development consent was to be decided on the basis of 'good planning principles'. The refusal of planning permission for development was therefore no longer compensatable. In addition, a development charge was imposed upon development value accruing to land by virtue of a grant of planning permission; although significant, this was short-lived.[16]

---

[15] Patsy Healey and Tim Shaw, 'Changing Meanings of "Environment" in the British Planning System' (1994) 19 *Transactions of the Institute of British Geographers* 425, p. 427.

[16] The system of charging for development was repealed by the Town and Country Planning Act 1952; see further Malcolm Grant, *Urban Planning Law* (Sweet and Maxwell, 1982), pp. 18–27. See also recent proposals for a 'housing land tax' to share windfall gains that are made when land is sold off for housebuilding ('Land Tax will Target Housebuilders' Profits'): *Independent*, 20.9.05.

The main provisions of the 1947 Act have been re-enacted in the Town and Country Planning Acts of 1968, 1971 and 1990, and were overhauled in 2004 (on the current planning system, see Chapter 13).

The main theme of the 1947 Act was economic regeneration. However, a link with the 1909 Act (discussed above) existed in the retention of the 'amenity' term and more broadly in the notion that public bodies had wide powers over land use and development. Landowners' economic interests were seriously affected by the 1947 Act, leading to litigation which examined the rights of landowners in the post-war planning system.[17]

In this early development of planning controls we see a powerful combination of social forces, economic plans and welfarist ideals. The legal apparatus for bringing about a pleasant city, salubrious suburbs and healthy environs, primarily the development scheme, was built on the bedrock of powers granted to local authorities for basic public health requirements. Even in this early period of land use controls, we already see the ability of the planning system to reflect the concerns of the time and to 'deliver the goods' in terms of public health and economic regeneration. Environmental protection had yet to be developed fully as one such concern, although the emphasis on amenity foreshadows this. Further common concerns include notions of the 'public interest' and 'community rights and duties'.

Having discussed public health and early planning legislation from the point of view of interfering with predominantly urban landowners' rights in the 'public interest', we now turn to the legal controls developed to protect the countryside from development, the evolution of which took place against a background of debate about the proper role of farming, and the appropriate scope of planning controls. Most importantly, these controls evolved separately from those applied to urban areas, which, as discussed above, centred originally upon a zoning system, supplanted later by a licensing system for development and change of use. This division of controls between town and country originates in the Report of the Committee on Land Utilisation in Rural Areas (the Scott Report) (1943). The Committee had a wide brief to review physical, social and economic development in the countryside. The Report came out strongly with the view that prosperous farming was essential for the whole country, for aesthetic and social reasons as well as for food production, and advocated a stewardship (and self-regulating) role for farmers, rather than the extension into the countryside of the existing 'urban' planning controls. Interestingly, the Scott Report includes a dissenting opinion given by Professor S. R. Dennison, in which he advocates that farmers be paid for *conservation* rather than for working the land (the basic premise of the current conservation regime, as discussed in Chapter 15). His minority report is usually overlooked but shows much foresight in predicting the social and environmental problems that have been caused by the favoured, and largely unregulated, position of

[17] See further analysis of this case law by Millichap, 'Law, Myth and Community', pp. 284–5.

farming (encouraged by the majority's opinion) and the main legal technique developed to resolve such problems, the voluntary management schemes provided for in ss. 28 and 29 of the Wildlife and Countryside Act 1981 and s. 95 of the Water Resources Act 1991. Until recently,[18] these schemes compensated farmers for loss of exploitation rights and profits forgone. Professor Dennison also recommended that planning controls be extended to the use and development of land in countryside areas (which effectively foreshadows the Royal Commission for Environmental Pollution's remarkably similar recommendations in this area, discussed below, pp. 501–2, and in Chapter 15 on conservation and biodiversity, pp. 625–6).

## *Scott Report* of the Committee on Land Utilisation in Rural Areas, 1941–2, Cmd 6378 (HMSO, 1943)

160. *The Preservation of Amenities.*– We regard the countryside as the heritage of the whole nation and, furthermore, we consider that the citizens of this country are the custodians of a heritage they share with all those of British descent and that it is a duty incumbent upon the nation to take proper care of that which it thus holds in trust.

In large part the beauties of Britain are man-made. Left to themselves the fields would quickly revert to thickets of shrub and brambles interrupted by bogs choked with reeds and rushes. The British countryside to-day owes its characteristic features to the fact that it has been used – in other words it has been farmed. The countryside cannot be 'preserved' (though its peculiar value to the nation can be); it must be farmed if it is to retain those features which give it distinctive charm and character. For this reason neither the farmer nor the forester can be regarded as simply members of an industry or on the same footing with those in other great industries. In addition to their function of producing food and timber from the land, farmers and foresters are unconsciously the nation's landscape gardeners, a privilege which they share with landowners.

    ...

### Minority Report by Professor SR Dennison

III THE PRESERVATION OF AMENITIES

41. The view of the Majority is that the beauties of the countryside depend essentially on agriculture, and the extension of this view is that anything which is hurtful to agriculture helps to destroy those beauties: thus (paragraph 160) 'the countryside cannot be "preserved" (though its peculiar value to the nation can be); it must be farmed if it is to retain those features which give it distinctive charm and character.' ...

42. Now if it were indeed true that amenities depended thus closely on agriculture, there might be a case for the extension and protection of agriculture and the limitation of any construction which would be harmful to it. This would not rest on economic grounds, for it would

---

[18]  See Ch. 15.

involve a considerable cost to the whole community. It would rest on the deliberate choice of the community to retain amenities at the expense of lower material standards of life; in this event, the cost should not fall on the agricultural worker more than on other members of the community – he should be paid in respect of his function as a landscape gardener and not as an agriculturalist. The cost would certainly be very great, and it is doubtful whether such beauty would be a luxury which we could afford; our standards of living are not so high that there would be a margin sufficient to allow it.

43. The question is, however, in fact one of degree. This is for two reasons. First, the area likely to be covered by new construction, even though there were widespread dispersal of congested cities, is but a small part of the total of agricultural land. Thus (taking the figures quoted in paragraphs 8 and 88 of the Majority Report) in the twelve years up to 1939, the average annual use of land for building and general construction amounted to 0.15 per cent of the agricultural acreage. Even if this were doubled, the rate of destruction of beauty would not be very formidable.

44. It is, however, one purpose of planning to prevent new construction from destroying beauty, so that even this relatively small amount of encroachment on the countryside need not involve a comparable loss of amenity. There are areas in the country where it would be generally agreed that construction should be severely restricted, if not completely prevented, and intelligent and comprehensive control would ensure that such areas would be left unspoilt. While construction might thereby be kept entirely away from certain areas, there would still be left the major part of the countryside, and here planning control should make it possible to reduce to a minimum any sacrifice of amenity.

...

50. The solution must lie in more comprehensive planning control. Not only is it necessary to prevent the spoliation of a particular piece of beauty (such as may occur through bad design or siting, or, indeed, in some cases by the intrusion of any construction), but it is also necessary that new construction should be so ordered as to give the best possible conditions for those who are to live in the new communities. It is in this way that a new beauty can be created – not, it is true, the beauty of a purely rural countryside (though much of that will remain), but a beauty with a greater social significance, enjoyed by many more than now have that privilege.

...

75. [Minority] *Recommendations*

(1) All land in the countryside should be included in planning schemes, and no interests of national importance should be excluded from the aims of planning.

(2) While particular planning schemes will certainly involve preservation of much land in agricultural use, it should not be accepted as a *necessary principle* that construction in the countryside must be prevented in order to maintain agriculture, to preserve rural communities, or to preserve amenities.

(3) The introduction of industry into the countryside, under effective planning control, could be of considerable benefit to rural communities; rather than preventing such development, some measure of it should be encouraged as part of the dispersal of existing concentrations.

(4) The needs of agriculture (including the protection of good quality land) should be met through the normal machinery of planning schemes, and not given any prior rights. They would be met, without undue hindrance to development, if the agricultural user were given opportunity to show why change of use of a particular piece of land should not be allowed.

Professor Dennison's argument for 'more comprehensive planning control' was not heeded: the Town and Country Planning Act 1947 excluded farming and forestry activities from the definition of 'development',[19] thus granting farming and forestry a pre-emptive claim over uses of rural land and making clear that the modern system of town and country planning would not place restrictions on farmers. The split between the 'countryside' activities of agriculture and forestry and all other types of development, fostered by the majority opinion of the Scott Report, therefore became settled in planning law and led to the evolution of different legal techniques for environmental protection in urban and countryside areas. The esteem in which farming was held by the majority of the Committee and their general approach towards farming is implicit also in the Agriculture Act 1947 which set up the conditions for considerable post-war expansion of farming. The general objectives of agriculture were given in s. 1:

> promoting and maintaining ... a stable and efficient agricultural industry capable of producing such part of the nation's food and other agricultural produce as in the national interest it is desirable to produce in the United Kingdom, and of producing it at minimum prices consistently with proper remuneration and living conditions for farmers and workers in agriculture and an adequate return on capital invested in the industry.

The two 1947 Acts were complementary: the Town and Country Planning Act 1947 ensured security of land use for agriculture and unhampered agricultural development; the Agriculture Act 1947 achieved security of investment in farming.

This period also saw the designation of countryside areas for the purpose of nature conservation. This grew out of a strategy evolved by voluntary organisations for the protection of common lands for recreational purposes.[20] The Ministry of Town and Country Planning in the Labour government set up the Wildlife Conservation Special Committee, chaired by the biologist Sir Julian Huxley, to consider setting up National Parks. The Report of the Huxley Committee articulates the aesthetic, recreational and educational

---

[19] See definition of 'development' in s. 55 Town and Country Planning Act 1990 and, particularly, the exclusion of agricultural and forestry activities from this definition in s. 55(e).     [20] Stuart Ball and Simon Bell, *Environmental Law* (Blackstone, 1991), p. 342.

benefits of having nature reserves, with a distinctly anthropocentric tone.[21] Whilst the Committee was cautious to extend the rationale for such reserves beyond that of scientific representativeness – 'the most valuable and interesting sites' – this directly informed the National Parks and Access to the Countryside Act 1949, which was aimed at protecting areas of 'special interest' (s. 15). Such an approach is now considered responsible for the fragmentation of controls for conservation, leading to calls for a more comprehensive network of sites protected for sound ecological reasons, rather than for their representativeness.[22]

The Scottish Wild Life Conservation Committee was appointed in 1946, under the chairmanship of Professor James Ritchie, to consider, and advise the Scottish National Parks Committee upon, the steps which should be taken to conserve wildlife in Scotland.[23] The Huxley and the Ritchie Committees liaised closely: as the Huxley Committee remarked 'Plants and animals do not recognise political borders, and although there are features peculiar to Scotland, there are many sites which take an essential place in any balanced scheme for the conservation of wild life on the continuous land mass of Great Britain, and which are necessary complements to sites recommended on the English side of the Border.'[24] The recommendations of the two Reports were largely enacted in the National Parks and Access to the Countryside Act 1949.

It is worth noting that under s. 23 of the National Parks and Access to the Countryside Act 1949 (see below), SSSIs were merely important sites that were on a list for the benefit of the scientific community. Though the local planning authority was informed of sites in its area, quite often the landowner or occupier of a site would not know that it was on the list, nor indeed of the existence of the list. It follows that landowners and occupiers were, at this date, under no legal obligation to protect the sites. Local planning departments would consult the Nature Conservancy before determining an application for planning permission for development, but, as we discussed above, agriculture and forestry were excluded from the remit of the Town and Country Planning Act 1947, making the legal regime for protecting these sites extremely weak.[25]

---

[21] See discussion on the possible shift from anthropocentrism to biocentrism as developmental phases of environmental law in the Preface to this book, pp. 2–3.

[22] This is perhaps even more the case with the Sites of Special Scientific Interest (SSSI) designation, on which see Ch. 15, pp. 618–24.

[23] *Nature Reserves in Scotland: Final Report by the Scottish National Parks Committee and the Scottish Wild Life Conservation Committee*, Dept of Health for Scotland Cmd 7814 (HMSO, 1949).        [24] Huxley Report, para. 91.

[25] On the changes brought by the Countryside and Rights of Way Act 2000, see Ch. 15 (pp. 625–6); on the consideration of matters of conservation in the planning system through environmental assessment, see Ch. 15 (pp. 649–53), and in planning policy statements, see Ch. 13 (pp. 676–7). See also the coupling of conservation and agriculture in agri-environmental measures in Ch. 16 (pp. 680–91).

## National Parks and Access to the Countryside Act 1949

PART III

NATURE CONSERVATION

15. In this Part of this Act the expression 'nature reserve' means land managed for the purpose–

(a) of providing, under suitable conditions and control, special opportunities for the study of, and research into, matters relating to the fauna and flora of Great Britain and the physical conditions in which they live, and for the study of geological and physiographical features of special interest in the area, or

(b) of preserving flora, fauna or geological or physiographical features of special interest in the area, or for both of these purposes.

16. (1) The Nature Conservancy may enter into an agreement with every owner, lessee and occupier of any land, being land as to which it appears to the Conservancy expedient in the national interest that it should be managed as a nature reserve, for securing that it shall be so managed.

(2) Any such agreement may impose such restrictions as may be expedient for the purposes of the agreement on the exercise of rights over the land by the persons who can be bound by the agreement.

(3) Any such agreement–

(a) may provide for the management of the land in such manner, the carrying out thereon of such work and the doing thereon of such other things as may be expedient for the purposes of the agreement;

(b) may provide for any of the matters mentioned in the last foregoing paragraph being carried out, or for the cost thereof being defrayed, either by the said owner or other persons, or by the Conservancy, or partly in one way and partly in another;

(c) may contain such other provisions as to the making of payments by the Conservancy, and in particular for the payment by them of compensation for the effect of the restrictions mentioned in the last foregoing subsection, as may be specified in the agreement.

...

[s. 18 powers to enter into management agreements with owners]

[s. 19 requirement to make Declarations that areas are nature reserves]

20. (1) The Nature Conservancy may, as respects land which is being managed as a nature reserve under an agreement entered into with them [under powers given in s. 18] or land held by them which is being managed as a nature reserve, make byelaws for the protection of the reserve:

> Provided that byelaws under this section shall not have effect as respects any land in a reserve unless a declaration under the last foregoing section is in force declaring that the land is being managed as a nature reserve and notice of the declaration has been published in pursuance of that section.

(2) Without prejudice to the generality of the last foregoing subsection, byelaws under this section–

    (a)   may provide for prohibiting or restricting the entry into, or movement within, nature reserves of persons, vehicles, boats or animals;

    (b)   may prohibit or restrict the killing, taking, molesting or disturbance of living creatures of any description in a nature reserve, the taking, destruction or disturbance of eggs of any such creature, the taking of, or interference with, vegetation of any description in a nature reserve, or the doing of anything therein which will interfere with the soil or damage any object in the reserve;

    (c)   may prohibit or restrict the shooting of birds or of birds of any description within such area surrounding or adjoining a nature reserve (whether the area be of land or of sea) as appears to the Nature Conservancy requisite for the protection of the reserve;

    (d)   may contain provisions prohibiting the depositing of rubbish and the leaving of litter in a nature reserve;

    (e)   may prohibit or restrict, or provide for prohibiting or restricting, the lighting of fires in a nature reserve, or the doing of anything likely to cause a fire in a nature reserve;

    (f)   may provide for the issue, on such terms and subject to such conditions as may be specified in the byelaws, of permits authorising entry into a nature reserve or the doing of anything therein which would otherwise be unlawful, whether under the byelaws or otherwise;

    (g)   may be made so as to relate either to the whole or to any part of the reserve or, in the case of byelaws made under paragraph (c) of this subsection, of any such surrounding or adjoining area as is mentioned in that paragraph, and may make different provisions for different parts thereof:

…

23. Where the Nature Conservancy are of opinion that any area of land, not being land for the time being managed as a nature reserve, is of special interest by reasons of its flora, fauna or geological or physiographical features, it shall be the duty of the Conservancy to notify that fact to the [local planning authority, originally] in whose area the land is situated.

### (c) Enhancing participation

As explained above (pp. 475–6), early planning legislation required borough and urban districts to prepare 'schemes' to regulate land use. These schemes, setting out particular uses such as residential or industrial for stretches of land, were the precursors to the requirement in the 1947 Act that development plans be prepared for each area. These plans were to guide decisions about whether to grant or refuse applications for planning permission. However, development planning was criticised for being too detailed and subject to delays. The system was altered by the Town and Country Planning Act 1968 which introduced a two-tier system of structure (strategic) and local (more detailed) plans. In 1969 the Committee on Public Participation in Planning published its report, *People and Planning*. The Committee was established to 'consider and report on the best methods, including publicity, of securing the participation of the public at the formative stage in the making of development plans for their area'. The Report told of their concerns about the scope of public participation in the democratic process of plan-making.

### Committee on Public Participation in Planning (the 'Skeffington Committee'), *People and Planning* (HMSO, 1969)

10. The advantages that flow from involvement of the public have been recognised by several local planning authorities whose work has, to some extent, anticipated the requirements of the Town and Country Planning Act 1968. That being so, it may be asked why there has been so little to show from past efforts and why, generally, the public has made so little impact on the content of plans. The reasons vary from place to place; but two general points emerge. They are:

(i)   First, most authorities have been far more successful in informing the public than in involving them. Publicity – the first step – is comparatively easy. To secure effective participation is more difficult.

(ii)  Secondly, some of the authorities who have made intensive efforts to publicise their proposals have done so when those proposals were almost cut and dried. At that stage, those who have prepared the plan are deeply committed to it. There is a strong disinclination to alter proposals which have been taken so far; but from the public's point of view, the opportunity to comment has come so late that it can only be an opportunity to object. The authority are then regarded more as an antagonist than as the representative of the community and what was started in good will has ended in acrimony.

11. Where information comes too late and without preliminary public discussion there is the likelihood of frustration and hostility. It may be that the plan produced is the one best suited to the needs of the community but the reasons for decisions do not emerge, nor are people told why superficially attractive alternatives have been put aside. The failure to communicate has meant that the preparation of a plan, instead of being a bridge between the authority and the public, has become a barrier, reinforcing the separation that springs up so easily between the 'them' of the authority and the 'us' of the public.

Following the recommendations of the Skeffington Committee, the Town and Country Planning Act 1971 was designed to increase rights of participation in plan-making, for example by the local planning authority holding a special, less formal variety of public inquiry, with pre-publicity and people given the opportunity to make representations. The recommendations of the Committee demonstrate the longevity of concerns about making participation effective, originating well before the Aarhus Convention made public participation in environmental decision making an imperative of environmental law and policy.[26] Importantly, Mark Stallworthy considers that it is this 'participatory base' of planning which, together with the growing emphasis on development planning and the emergence of a regional framework, suggests that appropriate planning structures can be put in place to bring about the array of changes required to achieve sustainable development, especially in urban living,[27] as discussed further below (pp. 530–45). Note, however, the distinct lack of synthesis between local views in decision making and environmental protection in the case of some renewable energy projects, the 'social gap', discussed further in Chapter 17.

## (d) Entrepreneurial planning

Notwithstanding the enhanced place for public participation in plan-making, the status of the development plan was progressively weakened in a period of 'entrepreneurial planning' or 'marketized utilitarianism'[28] which held currency in the 1980s. This planning policy formed part of the Conservative government's aim of 'releasing enterprise' or, as stated in a 1985 White Paper, 'Lifting the Burden' on business to bring about local economic regeneration. It included giving a greater priority to the right to develop land and, simultaneously, alleviating many of the legal and financial constraints imposed on development by the planning system. The Department of the Environment Circular 22/80, *Development Control: Policy and Practice* (1980), provides a very good example of this policy:

> The planning system should play a helpful part in rebuilding the economy. Development control must avoid placing unjustified obstacles in the way of any development especially if it is for industry, commerce, housing or any other purpose relevant to the economic regeneration of the country … Local planning authorities are asked therefore always to grant planning permission, having regard to all material considerations, unless there are sound and clear cut reasons for refusal.

This guidance was applied most clearly to housing projects: local authorities were required to undertake studies with the house building industry to ensure that sufficient land for private house building was allocated to meet the needs of the industry. Draft circulars mooted the withdrawal of green belt status from pockets of open land surrounded by existing housing development and the release of undeveloped land for house building. Similar policy was applied to road and airport projects.

In line with the policy aim of entrepreneurial planning, the Department of the Environment in 1988 stated that there should be a presumption in favour

---

[26] See Ch. 3.
[27] Mark Stallworthy, *Sustainability, Land Use and Environment: A Legal Analysis* (Cavendish, 2002), p. 217.    [28] Healey and Shaw, 'Changing Meanings of "Environment"', p. 427.

of development. This meant that planning consent for development projects was only to be refused by a local planning authority if the project was likely to 'cause demonstrable harm to interests of acknowledged importance'.

### Department of the Environment, Planning Policy Guidance Note 1, *General Policy and Principles* (HMSO, 1988)

15 … the planning system fails in its function whenever it prevents, inhibits or delays development which can reasonably be permitted. There is always a presumption in favour of allowing applications for development, having regard to all material considerations, *unless that development would cause demonstrable harm to interests of acknowledged importance* (emphasis added).

This presumption in favour of development, coupled with a host of deregulatory measures, radically changed the character of planning. The development plan was relegated in status to a material consideration on a par with any other. As a consequence of this policy, planning permission was often granted by the Secretary of State on appeal, even in cases in which the proposed project was in conflict with the relevant development plan at the local level. The planning system became 'appeal-led' rather than predominantly 'plan-led', with policy issues decided on a project-by-project basis rather than in relation to an overall planning framework. This had important environmental consequences, primarily because the statutory right of appeal was reserved for potential developers, who had been *refused* planning permission, rather than for those *opposing* development.[29]

'Stages' of law and policy are rarely self-contained and isolated, and the phenomenon of 'entrepreneurial' planning was not without certain countervailing tendencies. A significant and surprising change to the status of the development plan was prompted by an Opposition amendment to the Planning and Compensation Bill which called for the local planning authority to have *primary* regard to the development plan. The resulting provision (s. 26 of the Planning and Compensation Act 1991 which inserted s. 54A into the Town and Country Planning Act 1990) was actually more far-reaching than the original Opposition amendment and was considered at the time to amount to a volte-face on policy on the status of the development plan.

### Section 54A Status of development plans

Where, in making any determination under the Planning Acts, regard is to be had to the development plan, the determination shall be made in accordance with the plan unless material considerations indicate otherwise.

---

[29] On the limitations of the statutory right of appeal, see Ch. 13, p. 519.

This section was designed to be read in conjunction with s. 70 of the 1990 Act:

### Section 70 Determination of applications: general considerations

(1) Where an application is made to a local planning authority for planning permission –
    (a) subject to sections 91 and 92, they may grant planning permission, either unconditionally or subject to such conditions as they think fit; or
    (b) they may refuse planning permission.
(2) In dealing with such an application the authority shall have regard to the provisions of the development plan, so far as material to the application, and to any other material considerations.

This interplay of ss. 54A and 70 is particularly significant when read in the light of ss. 12(3A), 31(3) and 36(3) of the 1990 Act, which required that certain environmental policies be included in unitary development, structure, and local plans, respectively. Section 31(3) is as follows (the wording is very similar in each case):

s 31. (3) The policies shall … include policies in respect of –
(a) the conservation of the natural beauty and amenity of the land;
(b) the improvement of the physical environment; and
(c) the management of traffic.

The change in policy, manifested in s. 54A, arose because the government was concerned about discontent in some quarters, particularly among planners, caused by the rise in successful appeals to the Secretary of State in which approved planning policy was ignored. This practice was seen to undermine the development plan process which, after all, provides the main democratic input into the planning system. The increase in the number of appeals also placed the Department of the Environment under strain. A possible further factor was that environmental considerations had now to be accommodated by the government, following pressure to fulfil obligations arising from international and European Community law. The planning system presented a suitable legal mechanism with which to achieve this accommodation. However, this could not be achieved without greater emphasis on plan making and the tempering of policies of deregulation and 'lifting the burden'. In 1987 the Planning Minister, William Waldegrave, had given a speech warning that government policy did not mean that development plan policies would be given little weight. In May 1991, during the final stages of the progress of the Planning and Compensation Bill through Parliament, the Minister reiterated this policy: 'We have always regarded the development plan as important although Circular 14/85 appeared to downgrade it by referring to it as only one of the material considerations. Those days are well behind us. Today's debate should leave no doubt as to the importance of the plan-led approach.'

This change of policy back to 'planning' as well as 'markets' in the 1990s emphasises and reacts to the extent to which development had been market-led in the 1980s. To summarise, ideas about encouraging enterprise dominated planning policy in the 1980s and were played out in the law relating to the role of the development plan in decision making: the relegation of the development plan in policy indicating a move away from a 'planned' system of controls to one more sensitive to developers' needs and inevitably more ad hoc. Although described above as a developmental phase of controls over land, the period of entrepreneurial planning may more accurately be seen as a formal *withdrawal* of planning controls in certain areas. This policy reached its nadir in the Docklands 'regeneration' project which, whilst unleashing a huge amount of investment and producing development on an unprecedented scale, came also to be defined by the suspension of regular planning procedures (neatly dubbed a 'planning holiday'), particularly the imposition of conditions on the construction of major projects such as Canary Wharf.[30] This suggests that, rather than planning addressing the instabilities and mediating the excesses of a market-led economic system, as Mark Stallworthy has noted it is capable of doing,[31] in this period of encouraging enterprise, key elements and procedures of the planning system were disbanded, in the furtherance of market forces.

The various changes in law and policy outlined above brought about incremental centralisation of the planning system, even in the face of central government's rhetoric of deregulation. Stuart Bell and Donald McGillivray review this administrative, and political, shift and relate it to a concern with resolving competing land uses in the wider public interest, in favour of pursuing particular objectives. This provides a foundation for the recent modelling of the planning system as an integrated framework for resolving policy conflicts, which we discuss in Chapter 13, pp. 522–30.

### Stuart Bell and Donald McGillivray, *Environmental Law* (Oxford University Press, 6th edn, 2005), p. 449

#### Centralisation and decentralisation

In the 1980s the planning system became far more centralized, in two main senses: more decisions were taken at a central level and central policy pervaded every decision even at local level. One effect was to shift power from local government to central government; another to increase the areas of conflict between the two levels. But, interestingly, at the same time the system became in a way *less* centralized. This was because the changes in policy were designed to increase the role of the market at the expense of the State, and to make the system more developer-led. The system moved away from the direct promotion of wider social, economic and environmental objectives; reflecting the shift from public to

---

[30]  One possibility is that the lack of planning controls made inevitable the later nuisance actions in *Hunter* v. *Canary Wharf* [2003] 3 WLR 1467.

[31]  Stallworthy, *Sustainability, Land Use and Environment*, p. 101.

private development, it became more concerned with resolving a myriad of competing land uses in the wider public interest.

The 1990s also saw a mix of centralising and decentralising tendencies. The Secretary of State no longer had to approve all development plans and a presumption in favour of development in accordance with such plans was introduced. But the activity of land use planning became even less contentious politically. There were no longer the same debates about the purposes of planning as there were up to the 1980s, and so less need to impose government policy on appeal. However, the importance of central government rose because planning policy contained ever more prescriptive 'guidance', more in the form of rules for local authorities to follow than best practice to be commended. Increasingly, this prescriptive guidance shaped development plans, although in terms of content the emphasis was on facilitating private development.

In the light of evidence that suggests that in areas of discretion, the main influence on the formation of local planning officers' judgment is overwhelmingly central government guidance, this can be seen as a further centralizing step. In the 1990s the focus also shifted to the propriety of the planning system, and government guidance effectively put an onus on elected members to justify decisions taken against the advice of officers' written reports.

An important event in this phase of entrepreneurial planning was the implementation in the United Kingdom (admittedly with some initial reluctance, and thus legislative gaps) of the EC's Directive on environmental impact assessment (the EIA Directive) from 1988, which we discuss more fully in Chapter 14, pp. 568–97. The nub of this Directive was the requirement upon potential developers (be they public or private) to assess and describe the environmental impacts of their proposed development. The imposition of this type of procedural burden was directly in opposition to the 'lifting the burden' policy pursued by the Conservative government in planning policy at this time because it led to constraints being placed upon enterprise, as well as not inconsiderable costs for developers in terms of time and money.[32] This, the first major incursion of the European Union (EU) into the Member States' land use and development control systems, signified in the UK at least that the role of planning in environmental protection was no longer a latent force in planning policy. However, this alone failed to balance the political weight of 'marketized utilitarianism', as described by Patsy Healey and Tim Shaw below. Rather, the 'U-turn' in government policy on the role and content of development plans (above, pp. 490–2) and a move towards sustainable development in planning, and other policy areas, was caused by 'the adverse development and congestion consequences of the economic boom and slump [of the 1980s], coupled with the strength of generalised public support for the new environmental agenda'.[33] as well as international influences.

---

[32] For example, EIA procedures were also used as delay mechanisms by protesters, as in the case of the Twyford Down and Newbury protests. See Jane Holder, *Environmental Assessment: The Regulation of Decision Making* (Oxford University Press, 2004), Ch. 6.

[33] Healey and Shaw, 'Changing Meanings of "Environment"', p. 431.

**Patsy Healey and Tim Shaw, 'Changing Meanings of "Environment" in the British Planning System' (1994) 19 *Transactions of the Institute of British Geographers* 425, p. 431**

The 1980s thus saw dramatic swings in government attitudes to planning and to environmental questions. These first impeded and then accelerated the development of appropriate responses to the new environmental agenda by local authorities and the planning profession. The development of approaches to active environmental management was curtailed at the start of the decade. Instead, a narrow utilitarianism was promoted which treated the environment as a collection of tradable assets or commodities. During the mid-1980s, the value of such 'environmental quality' assets in relation to economic development strategy was increasingly appreciated. It was only late in the decade that the environmental sustainability debate was recognized and, with the exception of a few pioneers, the biospheric and resource conservation dimensions of the environmental agenda were largely neglected unless part of traditional agendas.

One explanation for these swings in policy attention and discursive formulation can be found in the hope and ultimate failure of the strategy of promoting a market-led approach to the amount, location and form of development. This served not only to undermine property development markets in themselves, it also activated a wide-ranging political backlash as the costs of such an approach to development management came to be widely appreciated. But beyond this narrow concern, the 'environmental turn' in British policy debate in the late 1980s reflects a belated appreciation among policy elites of the supranational and global dimensions of the environmental debate.[34] It was therefore not until the early 1990s that the operationalisation of the environmental sustainability agenda within the planning system really began.

## (e) Planning and sustainable development

In the Preface to this Part, we remarked upon the importance of the planning system for environmental protection, because of its control, through a sophisticated licensing system, of the location of sources of pollution and the location of the recipients of pollution (people), of the depositing of wastes and the allocation and use of natural resources such as minerals and aggregates, as well as of determining the type and sites of transport (see pp. 462–3). The licence, required before any 'development' or change of use (as defined in planning legislation[35]) takes place, instills an inherently pre-emptive, and potentially preventive, approach to potentially damaging developments and activities.[36] Put simply, by granting planning permission for any new development, planning authorities are in effect also sanctioning a new source of waste and pollution.

[34]  See Ch. 13.    [35]  Section 55 Town and Country Planning Act 1990. See, further, Ch. 13, pp. 513–14.    [36]  This point is elaborated in Ch. 13, pp. 506–7.

The relevance of planning controls for air pollution was closely examined by the Royal Commission on Environmental Pollution in its Fifth Report in 1976. In conducting its research, the Commission had refused to restrict itself to its formal remit – air pollution – and instead looked beyond pollution control to the roots of the problem in the planning system, thereby forging a more integrated way of conceiving environmental problems than hitherto.[37]

### Royal Commission on Environmental Pollution, Fifth Report, *Air Pollution Control: An Integrated Approach*, Cmnd 6371 (HMSO, 1976), p. 91

323. We have seen many examples during our study of the connection between pollution problems and planning. In most cases where pollution causes acute local problems, polluting industry is close to houses, shops or hospitals, or industry is so densely concentrated that the total pollution is unacceptable. Often these situations result from decisions taken many years ago when the development control was rudimentary and then, as now, many factors apart from pollution had to be taken into account. In a small industrialised country these situations are sometimes unavoidable. We have, however, seen cases where new housing development is still being allowed too close to polluting industry, or new polluting industry is allowed too close to houses. Here again, the decisions allowing these developments were not necessarily wrong, though they may lead to pollution problems in the future which will be difficult to resolve. Public expectations on environmental quality will no doubt continue to rise.

The specific roles which may be played by planning in *controlling* air pollution were listed by Christopher Wood in his work on the preventative function of planning.

### Christopher Wood, *Planning Pollution Prevention: A Comparison of Siting Controls Over Air Pollution In Great Britain and the United States of America* (Manchester University Press, 1989), pp. 26–7

The role of land use controls

The land use planning agencies or authorities exert control at most stages in the pollution process but their most powerful potential contribution is in determining the nature of new development and redevelopment. Because pollution originates as waste from production and consumption activities, one of the key variables in pollution control – the geographical point at which additional waste is created – is determined once the location of these activities has been established. Therefore, because of their control over land use, planning agencies exercise an important influence on the spatial origin of wastes and consequently upon pollution

---

[37] The product of this form of inquiry was the recommendation that BPEO (Best Practicable Environmental Option) be the central consideration in authorising sources of pollution. See further Ch. 9, p. 356.

levels and their distribution. These agencies are undoubtedly the principal controlling authorities in deciding the location of the pollution process, whether they recognise their position or not.

Control over the location of the pollution source is much more fundamental than other types of planning control over the pollution process. The new locations at which power is generated and at which goods are produced, and hence the location at which the associated wastes arise, are largely determined by grant or refusal of land use planning permits.

The locations at which products are used can be directly controlled by planning authorities. Apart from allocating land for the consumption of goods (e.g. residential areas) agencies have at least a voice in the determination of new road alignments (and also possess some indirect control over these … ) [In sanctioning] types of seemingly relatively non-polluting development (such as sports stadia, commercial buildings and shopping centres) agencies are permitting so called *indirect* pollution sources to arise as the large numbers of motor vehicles travelling to and from them will emit significant quantities of air pollutants. Land use planning authorities can exert some direct control over the treatment of various wastes emitted from stationary sources by, for example, insisting upon particular air pollution emission levels (ie, requiring technical controls) or by specifying discharge height or by demanding certain building types for containment of pollutants.

The place at which the waste matter is disposed of is generally determined once a development is approved, although the precise location (and height) of, for example, a new chimney stack associated with the development may be subject to planning approval. Planning authorities have some control over waste diffusion, apart from the specification of stack heights or locations. They may, for example, insist on buffer zones and/or planting to remove pollutants from the atmosphere.

Land use planning agencies have a crucial role in controlling the damage arising from the resulting pollution, since they control the nature and location of receptors. In other words, apart from protecting the environment around a proposed new source of pollution, authorities can control damage from an existing source of pollution by determining the nature of new developments close to it. This may be achieved either through the granting or withholding of land use permits (eg, refusal of housing close to an oil refinery) or by the attachment of conditions (eg, that a school building be constructed so as to be separated from a major air pollution source by its playing fields).

It must be stressed that there are two stages in the planning process, the preparation of a plan and its implementation in the form of decisions on the use of specific areas of land. While all the controls mentioned above can be exercised in the absence of an overall land use plan, the potential role of the land use planner in ameliorating air pollution is not restricted either to attempting to ensure that the best anticipatory controls are imposed when development is permitted or to preventing such development. Rather, it extends to planning the future use of land to reduce air pollution by the preparation of implementable plans.

One final role must be mentioned. Apart from their controls at different stages in the pollution process, land use planning agencies are in a unique position – as a focus for consultation on both plan making and land use decision-taking – to play a central co-ordinating role in the control of pollution.

As we discussed in the context of the previous evolutionary stages, the town planning system embraces a more diverse range of objectives than solely environmental protection, including urban regeneration, affordable housing and industrial and commercial development. A crucial point is that environmental protection is just one 'material consideration' amongst many others.

### Royal Commission on Environmental Pollution, *Air Pollution Control*, p. 93

The need for cooperation

334. Pollution is only one of the factors which need to be taken into account in planning decisions and in many situations there will be other factors which have to be given equal or higher priority. There may be pressures on a local authority to improve housing or local employment opportunities, or an authority may wish, for example, to put derelict land into use. While this is not strictly a planning consideration, a local authority may also wish to secure the rate revenue from a major development. As always, there is the need to balance conflicting requirements.

335. Our concern is not that pollution is not always given top priority; it is that it is often dealt with inadequately, and sometimes forgotten altogether in the planning process. In part this stems from lack of guidance and advice. Planning officers and committees are not often pollution experts and they are necessarily dependent on advice on pollution matters. Such advice is not always available but even when it is, it is not always sought. We have seen evidence of lack of consultation between planning officers and those responsible for air pollution control, whether the latter are Environmental Health Officers of the local authorities concerned or of neighbouring authorities or the Alkali Inspectorate.

In this Report, the Royal Commission expressed a general concern that matters of pollution were not dealt with adequately in the planning process. The Commission considered that in most of those cases where pollution caused acute problems, industry was located close by, and recommended that consultation to establish the pollution implications of proposals become common practice. There was some acceptance of the Royal Commission's recommendation by professional planning bodies. For example, in 1976, the Royal Town Planning Institute acknowledged the role of what was then known as the ecological movement in the general reassessment taking place of the objectives of planning. Over the following years, planning authorities and inquiry inspectors showed a greater readiness to cite particular forms of pollution such as noise, odour and air pollutants rather than rely on vague phrases such as 'prejudicial to amenity' in order to defend refusals of consent for environmentally unacceptable development. The planning system was recognised as offering an opportunity to anticipate and forestall environmental harm by refusing development consent or by separating incompatible land uses. In addition, green belt policies continued to perform a containment function and to protect land from development. However, the extent to which planning controls could be used to intervene further to prevent pollution was limited by government policy which stated that planning conditions should not be used to deal with problems which are the subject of controls under separate environmental legislation and that planning conditions are considered unnecessary where they duplicate pollution controls. Planning has since trodden carefully in imposing controls in the form of conditions and obligations in areas in which other statutory controls exist. This separation in practice of planning from pollution controls is one effect of the creation of special laws, institutions and procedures for dealing with pollution, minerals extraction, industrial development and transport. It is another example of the sectoral approach to environmental protection which provided the context for the development of pollution controls, discussed in Chapter 8. Some of the consequences of this approach are outlined in the following sharp critique of the planning system's track record on protecting the environment.

### David Hall, Michael Hebbert and Helmut Lusser, 'The Planning Background' in Andrew Blowers (ed.), *Planning for a Sustainable Environment* (Earthscan, 1993), pp. 20–1

THE LIMITATIONS OF PLANNING

How has the postwar planning system performed from an environmental point of view? In practice, it has been an effective instrument for achieving the policy objectives of the 1940s, particularly the demarcation of built-up areas from the countryside and the designation and protection of national parks, landscape areas, and nature reserves.

But it has been far less successful in responding to new kinds of environmental concern. Once established as a regular branch of government at central and local levels, land-use planning became set in its ways. Its place in the scheme of government was assured but circumscribed. It was not allowed to trespass on the preserve of agricultural policy, which has an exceptionally tight political nexus with the farm supply, farming and food industries. So the town and country planning system has protected the rural land resource from building development but not from some of the uglier side-effects of agribusiness.

The same applies to the control of noise, noxious emissions and wastes from manufacturing and extractive industry. The planning system set up by the 1947 Act had the potential to place local authorities in a key role in the control of industrial pollution. It gave them powers to determine the nature, as well as the location of development; a statutory responsibility to consult and co-ordinate (with pollution control agencies) in plan-making and development control; and an ability, through positive planning, to coordinate environmental improvement on a broad scale.

But this 'comprehensive range of techniques … for pollution control', as Christopher Wood describes it,[38] was largely left unused. Wood analyses the reasons why: inadequate training,

---

[38] Chris Wood, *Town Planning and Pollution Control* (Manchester University Press, 1976).

poor information, lack of central guidance, professional jealousies, and the fear – explored particularly in Blowers' study of pollution and planning in the brickfields[39] – that a tightening of local planning controls would lead to local job losses. There was also an important institutional factor. Industrial pollution control was the domain of the Alkali Inspectorate, now Her Majesty's Inspectorate of Pollution.

Hall, Hebbert and Lusser continue to examine the limited role of the planning system in curbing the wasteful transport of people and goods through structuring the provision of infrastructure.

Looking at much postwar development with the benefit of hindsight, we can see how town planning was forced astray in its response to rapidly rising car ownership and road transport. Effort was put into well-engineered new roads encompassing traffic-free precincts with concrete underpasses while neglecting the inequitable distribution of the car by class and age, as well as its heavy material demands and destructive environmental effects.

Even before the period of entrepreneurial planning had waned, and well before Hall, Hebbert and Lusser's lament that planning had created 'the worst of all worlds', one sees a radical reassertion and expansion of the role of planning in environmental protection, in the direction of the principle of sustainable development. Planning's broad scope and ability to adopt and accommodate often conflicting objectives and policies were recognised as allowing for the interaction of a number of key sectors responsible for compromising environmental quality – especially transport, housing and energy – to be addressed in the light of sustainable development, whilst also continuing to satisfy demands for economic development.

This expansion of planning's role was motivated by the World Commission on Environment and Development's Report, *Our Common Future* (1987),[40] the United Kingdom's response to which was set out in a White Paper on the environment, *This Common Inheritance.*[41] This identified the planning system as a particularly suitable forum for 'implementing' the principle, and triggered more detailed policy initiatives. For example, Planning Policy Guidance Note 1, *General Policy and Principles* (1992), which sets out the key elements of the government's philosophy on the planning system, charged planning with 'the objective of ensuring that development and growth are sustainable'.

In respect of legal process, the explicit recognition of the positive role of planning in sustainable development was strengthened by a swing back in favour of a plan-led planning system, directed by the insertion of s. 54A into the Town and Country Planning Act 1990. As discussed above (pp. 490–1), this 'return

---

[39] Andrew Blowers, *Something in the Air: Corporate Power and the Environment* (Harper and Row, 1984).     [40] See Ch. 6.

[41] HM Government, *This Common Inheritance*, Cm 1200 (HMSO, 1990).

to plans' (as opposed to the presumption in favour of granting planning permission) provided an opportunity for environmental protection to be translated into planning policy. This is illustrated by the requirement to include environmental policies in unitary development, structure and local plans.[42] Section 54A is a legal indication that, if environmental considerations are involved in an applicable development plan, they may be capable of constituting legitimate reasons for the refusal of planning permission. In practice, though, the impact of s. 54A was as much political as legal.[43]

The policy of achieving sustainable development through the planning system builds upon a more traditional role of stewardship and combines it with a public interest objective which developed out of the public health movement of the nineteenth century (above, pp. 470–5). But, more often than not, the argument that the planning system's role in regulating the use and development of land offers a vehicle for the achievement of sustainable development is set out in terms of its ability to accommodate and mediate conflicting objectives in plan-making, its 'conflict resolution' procedures of appeal and review,[44] and the opportunities offered for public participation. Potentially more difficult for the planning system to achieve is real engagement with the moral dimension of sustainable development – 'the value placed on environmental qualities and relationships with the natural world'.[45] This might, for example, mean encompassing more radical aspects of sustainable development which demand fundamental changes in lifestyle, and confronting resistance to unpopular siting decisions for renewable energy projects such as wind farms (Chapter 17). Less radical (or more shallow) approaches adopted by the planning system in response to moral questions about the value of the environment have produced a range of techniques designed to offset damaging development, such as planning obligations ('green gains') and 'compensation banking' (Chapter 16, pp. 677–80).

A vital starting point in realising the moral force of sustainable development in the planning system is to determine what more specific objectives might be embraced by this concept, a process embarked upon by the Royal Commission on Environmental Pollution, in its Twenty-third Report, *Environmental Planning*[46] (albeit some fifteen years after the Brundtland Report[47] was published): 'Para. 19 We recommend that the town and country planning system should be given a statutory purpose and that, rather than use the term "sustainable development", an appropriate purpose would be "to facilitate the achievement of legitimate economic and social goals whilst

---

[42] Sections 12(3A), 31(3) and 36(3) of the 1990 Act.

[43] A conclusion reached after a review of sometimes conflicting case law in this area, explored in greater detail in the first edition of this book (Sue Elworthy and Jane Holder, *Environmental Protection* (1997), pp. 254–61).

[44] Healey and Shaw, 'Changing Meanings of "Environment"', p. 426.     [45] *Ibid.*

[46] Cm 5459 (HMSO, 2002).     [47] *Our Common Future* (Oxford University Press, 1987). See Ch. 6.

ensuring that the quality of the environment is safeguarded and, wherever appropriate, enhanced".'

In the following chapters we return to many of the Commission's recommendations, but it is particularly significant in the light of the developmental phases of planning outlined above that the Commission discusses bringing agricultural and forestry developments within the scope of 'environmental planning' (an enlarged conception of planning, embracing land uses beyond those covered by the definition of 'development' in the Town and Country Planning Act 1990), and thereby potentially closing the gap between town and country land use and development controls that has endured since the post-war land settlement, and from which the use of different legal techniques originates. Such a move towards integrated legal controls would be an important response to sustainable development.

### Royal Commission on Environmental Pollution, Twenty-third Report, *Environmental Planning*, Cm 5459 (HMSO, 2002), paras. 9.36–9.42

ROLE OF TOWN AND COUNTRY PLANNING IN THE COUNTRYSIDE

9.36 Farming and forestry operations were expressly excluded from the definition of 'development' in the Town and Country Planning Acts. As they are very important forms of land use, and as they continue to have potential to cause significant environmental damage, we have considered whether this is an anomaly that ought to be ended … In their evidence to us the National Farmers Union argued that protection of many features of the rural environment, such as semi-natural habitats, is more likely to be achieved through encouraging land managers to apply more environmentally sensitive management methods (either traditional ones or more modern equivalents devised to achieve the same outcomes), rather than simple prohibition. Advice, financial incentives, or cross-compliance may therefore be equally, or more, effective than direct regulation. A further argument is that local authority planning departments are already under heavy pressure and currently lack the expertise to deal with agriculture and forestry.

9.37 We do not regard these arguments as necessarily conclusive in the longer term. However, a new form of control over potentially damaging agricultural operations is being introduced … We have concluded that experience ought to be gained of that regime before further consideration is given to requiring planning permission for changes in agricultural land use. We recommend that in the meantime other measures are introduced to improve the protection of the rural environment; in particular, there should be action to encourage the adoption of farm plans.[48]

This last recommendation on the compilation of 'farm plans' aims to bring agriculture (traditional farming as well as diversification projects) within the

---

[48] On farming, see further Ch. 16.

ambit of spatial planning for ostensibly environmental reasons. The Report of the Commission continues by recommending measures to restrict the special status of agricultural activities on land, whilst forestry activities are deemed to be in a different position because its grant schemes operate as controls on planting.[49] Interestingly, the Commission goes on to note that the licensing system currently in operation to protect hedgerows provides a good example of the possibility of controlling agricultural activities by the local planning authority, since it was previously an area governed by voluntary agreements and financial inducements, such as those we present as 'regulatory techniques beyond licensing' in Chapter 11.

## 4 Conclusions

Controls over the use and development of land in Britain, including the modern system of town planning, are the product of a mix of social and political forces, which had in common a desire to fashion or impose order on nature and chaotic urban areas in the cause of creating the conditions for a better, healthier, society. In this mix we can identify utopian and socialist thought, and the pragmatism and idealism of zealous public health reformers and popular social movements and groups. These influences were then combined with the opportunities and conditions for regeneration which followed the Second World War. The effects of the developing land use controls were not always benign. Planning offered a powerful means by which law defined what is meant by 'amenity', and the 'public benefit'. By containing the radicalism of popular social movements, the planning system ordered living and working patterns and conditions, and relations between individuals and communities. The strength and prescriptiveness of planning controls was softened by references to planning serving the public interest or common good.

The utopian influence on planning controls is seen clearly in the building of garden cities. The idealistic emphasis of the garden city movement on land as the source of wealth, on cooperation and community, has had an impact on the principles and practice of town planning beyond the confines of Letchworth and Welwyn, and can be seen in the modern town planning system in terms of the role that planning is expected to perform in protecting the environment, particularly its contribution to achieving sustainable development.[50] This is not surprising since some of the ideas and principles which informed the

---

[49] Although this factor created difficulties with the implementation of the EIA Directive, on which see Ch. 14. Note also the difficulties arising from wind farm development being located upon land owned by the Forestry Commission.

[50] See Denzil Millichap, 'Sustainability: A Long Established Concern of Planning' (1993) *Journal of Planning and Environmental Law* 111, for a discussion of the fundamental similarity between the concerns of sustainability and those of planning from the Victorian era onwards.

building of garden cities and new towns also helped develop the town planning movement. The nomenclature of the movement is significant: the Garden City Association became the Garden City and Town Planning Association in 1908 and the Town and Country Planning Association in 1932. There is also a sense of continuity of purpose and content of law; references in the early planning legislation to 'amenity' and the 'public interest' are made in the later Planning Acts. Recent environmental concerns have also led to proposals to revive the system of charging for development,[51] as introduced by the 1947 Act. An implicit form of this might be seen in the present use of planning contributions.[52]

During industrialisation, we see the social and physical 'construction' of the town and countryside – in relation to each other and also in opposition. The garden city idealists attempted to break down this division so as to create a 'marriage' of the town and country. It is telling that the separation of legal controls over land use and development in rural and urban areas, settled in the Town and Country Planning Act 1947, may still be seen in the modern town planning and countryside designations regimes. This continues to militate against an integrated approach to environmental protection, although, as we discuss in Chapter 15, some progress has been made to appreciate the effects of development on biodiversity, as recommended by the Royal Commission on Environmental Pollution in its Twenty-third Report on *Environmental Planning*.

The key point is that the planning system has undergone a considerable expansion of its objectives and thus its remit since the first Planning Act in 1909 sought to impose rudimentary controls over development through the prior approval of planning schemes. Its role in environmental protection has broadened far beyond questions of preventing and controlling pollution, to encompass sustainable development as an objective. A corollary of this expanded role is the enlargement of the scale of its concerns, a key example of which is the production of energy from renewable sources, as discussed more fully in Chapter 17.

## 5 Further reading

The implications of a shift towards sustainable development in planning are the subject of *Planning for a Sustainable Development*, edited by Andy Blowers on behalf of the Town and Country Planning Association (Earthscan, 1994), containing chapters on sustainable energy policy, and regional planning. Chris Miller's collection, *Planning and Environmental Protection* (Hart, 2001), also moves beyond a focus on land to consider (with the use of short case studies) issues of energy, waste, water and transport. See also Winter's 'Planning and Sustainability: An Examination of the Role of the Planning

---

[51] See Ch. 13.     [52] See Ch. 16, pp. 677–80.

System as an Instrument for the Delivery of Sustainable Development' (1994) *Journal of Planning Law* 883. The divide between the town and country in terms of land use and development controls is one of the subjects of the collection *Town and Country*, edited by Anthony Barnett and Roger Scruton (Jonathan Cape, 1998). This retains a sustainability focus (with chapters on urban futures, food and animals), but also offers a poetic treatment of such issues as light pollution and the 'unofficial' countryside.

# Planning and Environmental Protection

## 1 Introduction

In the previous chapter we introduced the idea that environmental protection and the regulation of land use and development are indivisible, through a historical account of legal controls and policies relating to land. The focus of this chapter is the significance for environmental protection of the current body of law and policy which provides the foundations of the planning system. In keeping with two of the main themes of this book – the move towards 'integration' (both of legal controls and of the consideration of environmental protection within a broader sweep of policy concerns), and enhancing participation in decision making – we analyse in particular the introduction of a system of integrated spatial planning by the Planning and Compulsory Purchase Act (PCPA) 2004 (pp. 522–9) and the apparent consensus in planning theory and policy on enhancing participation (pp. 530–45). We consider the strides that have been taken to open up decision making beyond the confines of expert opinion, so as to include local knowledge, and a range of viewpoints about landscape and the relative values of competing objectives. We also explore the implications for participation of the move towards spatial planning which will enlarge, but undeniably complicate, planning agendas.

It might now be a truism that the planning system is of vital importance to environmental protection, but a refinement of this, as described by Robin Grove-White, is that the system exercises a powerful influence on the distinctive (formal and legalistic) form in which environmental issues have emerged in a British context, not simply because of the regulatory constraints the system has provided, but also because of the 'cultural' framing created by the discourse and idioms of town and country planning law.[1] According to Grove-White, these have helped to shape the forms in which environmental tensions have been conceptualised and have found public expression. An example of this tendency is the ascendancy of the principle of sustainable development in

[1] Robin Grove-White, 'Land Use Law and the Environment' (1991) 18 *Journal of Law and Society*, Special Issue on 'Law, Policy and the Environment' 32, p. 32.

planning. This has become the main influence on policy for the regulation of land use and development, but also more generally, with the result that a greater range of issues and policy areas is now considered legitimately to fall within the ambit of the planning system.[2] This has had practical effects, such as the introduction by the Planning and Compulsory Purchase Act 2004 of regional spatial strategies which are concerned with a far broader range of issues than previously was the case. In other words, just as planning is socially significant beyond its formal sphere of influence, so it also picks up on broader social influences. The important shift from 'town planning' to integrated spatial planning that the 2004 Act has brought about was trenchantly argued for by the Royal Commission on Environmental Pollution in its report on *Environmental Planning* (2002), in recognition that the process of integration, now familiar in pollution control (see Chapter 9), is necessary also in regulating land use and development.

### Royal Commission on Environmental Pollution (RCEP), *Environmental Planning*, Cm 5459 (2002), paras. 1.5–1.9

THE CASE FOR ENVIRONMENTAL PLANNING

...

1.5   For over 50 years, the function of town and country planning in protecting and improving the environment has been largely implicit. Planning policies have also pursued economic and social objectives, and at times have placed relatively little emphasis on environmental considerations. Nevertheless, town and country planning has been a major force protecting the UK environment. Without it, urban and rural areas would now be less attractive. It has provided the traditional forum for thinking strategically about the future of particular areas. It is the arena in which many environmental controversies have been fought out.

1.6   The regulation and planning of land use is not something that can be considered in isolation. The ways in which land is used are linked to environmental change on many different scales. Air quality, the water cycle, biological diversity, transport, and energy production and use are also spatially related, and to significant extents policies in those fields depend for their success on decisions about land use. Equally, the management and condition of land are much influenced by other policies, and by other statutory and non-statutory regimes, as well as by town and country planning.

1.7   A quarter of a century ago, the Commission devoted part of one of its reports to the relationship between pollution control and town and country planning.[3] Since then a great deal has changed. In belated responses to that report's recommendations, the legislation

---

[2]  On this point, review the extract from Mark Stallworthy, *Sustainability, Land Use and the Environment: A Legal Analysis* (Cavendish, 2002), in the Preface to Part V, pp. 462–4. For a discussion of the range of topics which are now considered to fall within the sustainable development rubric, see Ch. 6.

[3]  Fifth Report, *Air Pollution Control: An Integrated Approach*, Cmnd 6371 (1976).

and organisation for controlling pollution in Britain have been transformed.[4] The nature of environmental concerns has changed radically.[5] There is now a much better understanding of the complexity of the environment and the interconnections between its different aspects. It has been realised that objectives to protect or improve particular aspects of the environment may sometimes come into conflict with each other, as well as with economic and social objectives.

1.8 Adopting sustainable development as a formal aim has created a new context for environmental policy and regulation. Major challenges lie ahead in achieving environmental sustainability. The question is, whether meeting those challenges requires radical reform or progressive adaptation of existing institutions.

1.9 A survey we commissioned of other developed countries found significant common trends in the organisation of environmental responsibilities. The importance of clear strategic direction has been increasingly recognised. There is also a general concern to establish more integrated systems of administration, often with an emphasis on making these simpler and clearer in order to facilitate a greater degree of public participation. Those findings confirmed us in the view that it was time to look again at the roles and relationships of key public bodies with environmental responsibilities, and to do so on a broader basis than the Commission's 1976 report which was primarily concerned with air pollution.

As mentioned above, the broader scope of their inquiry led the Commission to recommend the introduction of integrated spatial strategies which take account of all spatially related activities and aspects of environmental capacity.

10.3. Two themes running through this report have been the need for a much closer relationship between land use planning and other aspects of environmental policy, and the need to recognise the interdependence of urban and rural areas. We suggested … that these requirements can best be met by a system of planning which is strategic and spatial.

10.4. We have concluded that such a system needs to be based on a new form of integrated spatial strategy which will embrace economic, social and environmental objectives. We agree with the government that a rationalisation and streamlining of present planning procedures is required. Our concept of an 'integrated spatial strategy' … is much wider than the town and country planning system and we envisage a much more complete incorporation of environmental factors into the policy process. In referring to strategies as 'integrated' we do not imply that economic, social and environmental objectives can

---

[4] Through the introduction of integrated pollution control in the Environmental Protection Act 1990 (Ch. 9) and the establishment in 1996 of the Environment Agency and the Scottish Environment Protection Agency (Ch. 8). It is worth noting that in this respect there has been a speedy adoption of the RCEP's recommendations for a planning system based upon an integrated spatial strategy; this compares with the fourteen-year gap between the RCEP's Fifth Report and the development of a system of integrated pollution control.

[5] The Commission discussed the changing nature of environmental concerns and some of the implications of this in its Twenty-first Report, *Setting Environmental Standards*, Cm 4053 (1998), paras. 1.11–1.13.

ever be reconciled completely. What integrated spatial strategies will provide is a much more effective mechanism for bringing together considerations of economic and social objectives and environmental constraints. Only in that way can the crucial issues be identified, and sometimes difficult choices made, on the basis of adequate information and a full review of the options.

The Royal Commission adopts sustainable development as the organising idea behind planning reform. Susan Owens (a member of the Royal Commission) and Richard Cowell similarly adopt this premise, but identify the central paradox that, notwithstanding the impact of sustainable development as an influential idea, conflict over land use remains as ubiquitous and intense as ever. Note particularly the references to tackling modern, global, environmental dilemmas, such as climate change, through local planning. We return to this issue in the case study on wind farm development in Chapter 17.

### Susan Owens and Richard Cowell, *Land and Limits: Interpreting Sustainability in the Planning Process* (Routledge, 2002), pp. 1–5

OLD CONFLICTS AND NEW IDEAS

Conflict over the use of land often seems ubiquitous. As we write, there are many examples to choose from in Britain, but a few will suffice to illustrate the range of issues at stake. In Berkshire, a major company wishes to build its new headquarters in a controversial green field location. Opponents raise the spectre of congestion and pollution and claim that the development would make a mockery of government planning guidelines seeking to reduce car dependency. The local authority, alarmed at the prospect of a major employer going elsewhere, and influenced by the company's 'green transport' plan, grants planning permission after 'acrimonious' debate. In Scotland, development interests propose a funicular railway to carry increasing numbers of tourists into the Cairngorms, the UK's most significant mountain plateau, justifying the project – and around £12 million in public assistance – as a boon to the local economy. Environmentalists fear the impact of more visitors in a remote and ecologically vulnerable landscape. Planning permission is granted, but the decision, along with the case for public finance, is then subjected to challenges from environmental groups and a National Audit office review. At the other end of the country, plans for a by-pass that would bisect the renowned water meadows of the cathedral city of Salisbury run into deep controversy, undiminished by a public inquiry and a recommendation that the project should not go ahead. The government's advisory bodies on landscape and nature conservation, consulted about ways of mitigating the impacts of the new road, agree that no measures could effectively do so; the scheme is returned to the drawing board …

Many characteristics of these conflicts would have been familiar to Roy Gregory, whose classic book, *The Price of Amenity: Five Studies in Conservation and Government* (Macmillan, 1971), explored some of the great planning controversies of the 1960s: the claims of growth and jobs set against concerns for less tangible environmental qualities; conflicts between different sets of public and private goals; and issues of distributive justice.

Much has also changed. Whereas Gregory charted conflicts over projects promoted by nationalised industries 'in the public interest', the cases above centre upon more complex mixes of private and public development in the context of a more internationalised economy. The nature of environmental concerns has also shifted dramatically, with 'amenity' stretched to include invisible but potentially global threats, such as climate change and loss of biodiversity. What is most striking, however, is the persistent emergence of conflict over the use and development of land, apparently at odds with the more positive, less adversarial future for environmental politics heralded by widespread commitments to sustainable development.

...

Part of the difficulty is that changes in land use are linked to environmental change through a multiplicity of direct, indirect, sometimes cumulative and often uncertain effects. These links operate at different scales and have economic, legal and political dimensions: conflicts arise between multiple rights and jurisdictions, which ecological science alone can rarely if ever resolve. Interactions between neighbouring land uses have focused the minds of scholars for centuries, as 'nuisances' of noise, odour or pollution have spilled beyond properties and sites. Later came the recognition that impacts can cross national boundaries, as, for example, when land-use decisions in one country influence air or water quality in another. In the twenty-first century, 'the issue of global climate change makes all nations neighbours' as, one might add, do other transnational concerns in which land use is deeply implicated, such as loss of biodiversity. In many instances, the growth of global agreements and international organisations concerned with environmental issues has modified traditional assertions of national sovereignty over land resources, already weakened by the effects of ecological and economic processes operating beyond state or local control. In the case of the Cairngorm funicular project, for example, environmental objectors were able to point to the international significance of the summit habitats and the risks posed to mountain plant and bird communities by global warming. But internationalisation presents strong countervailing forces: communities can be reluctant to subject mobile economic resources to restrictive land-use policies.

We return to many of the points raised by Owens and Cowell, particularly the reform of the planning system in order to underpin economic development. The case study on wind farm development discussed in detail in Chapter 17 also points to the complex mix of private investment in 'public interest' projects such as these. It is important to note, however, that many of the planning disputes cited above arose because of the lack of a *strategic* overview of the demands on land *and its limits* (their book being published before even the adoption of the Directive on Strategic Environmental Assessment (SEA)[6]). As we discuss further below (pp. 522–30), the recent introduction of integrated spatial planning aims to provide this broader perspective. To provide the legal and policy context within which we discuss the process of integration and enhanced

---

[6] On the SEA Directive, which provides for a limited form of environmental assessment of plans and programmes, see Ch. 14, pp. 599–601.

participation in planning,[7] we first outline the main elements of the planning system having relevance for environmental protection. In particular we discuss the key controls and obligations imposed by the planning system, primarily the obligation to apply for planning permission before carrying out any 'development' and, implicitly, to make this development acceptable in social and environmental terms. In the process we consider how decisions on individual applications are made by local authorities and the Secretary of State, and in particular how these decisions are increasingly influenced by environmental protection considerations, frequently redrawn as 'sustainable development criteria'.

## 2  Elements of the planning system

Owens and Cowell use just a few examples to exemplify the great range of planning disputes – on different scales, and with the potential to create different, and in some cases uncertain, environmental impacts. Nevertheless, it remains the case that the core regulatory instrument of the planning system is the licence, for the development of land or a material change of use of land, the granting of which is primarily the responsibility of local planning authorities, with the possibility of an appeal (in the case of the refusal of planning permission) to the Secretary of State. Local decision making about individual applications for planning permission is strongly guided by development plans (formulated at the local level) and by central planning policy issued by the Department of Communities and Local Government (DCLG) (the successor to the Office of the Deputy Prime Minister (ODPM), see Chapter 8, p. 333). The long-standing centrality of the licence accounts for the stability of the planning system, as reflected in the barely changed central provisions of the Town and Country Planning Act (TCPA) 1990 (which hail from the Town and Country Planning Act 1947, discussed in the previous chapter, pp. 480–1). The licensing system also provides the pre-emptive or preventive nature of the planning system; a refusal of planning permission providing the ultimate example of precautionary action, alongside screening development and controlling the location of polluting development.[8]

The operation of a licensing system marks out the application of the familiar 'direct' approach to environmental regulation, discussed above in relation to the  development of pollution controls in Chapter 9. Other instruments have been introduced, or have evolved, to introduce some flexibility into this approach, most notably planning contributions (previously known as planning obligations, planning agreements and, more pejoratively, planning 'gain').

---

[7] For a more detailed and complete account of the planning system from an environmental perspective, see Stuart Bell and Donald McGillivray, *Environmental Law* (Oxford University Press, 6th edn, 2005), Ch. 13.

[8] On the precautionary character of planning, see William Walton, Andrea Ross-Robertson and Jeremy Rowan-Robinson, 'The Precautionary Principle and the UK Planning System' (1995) 7 *Environmental Law and Management* 35.

This mechanism has previously taken the form of a negotiated contract which allowed for some negotiation and persuasion (sometimes of the 'heavy-handed' variety) between the developer and planning authority about what community benefits (for example, the provision of playgrounds or 'affordable housing') might accompany an application for planning permission, but was also open to the critique of operating as a form of 'cheque book planning'. Planning contributions (now provided for by s. 46 of the Planning and Compulsory Purchase Act 2004), whilst still providing an opportunity for benefits (in cash or kind) to be given by the developer, are in the main to be determined in advance and set out in development plans. This promises to allow for greater transparency in determining what contributions are in the public interest. Contributions, in the form of environmental mitigation, such as attempting to compensate for lost habitats, are likely to continue to have particular relevance for environmental protection, but remain controversial from an ecological point of view. As Bell and McGillivray state, 'the use of planning contributions to provide for environmental benefits, or at least to prevent net environmental losses, raises important questions about valuation of the environment, perhaps also the "polluter pays principle", and wider questions about sustainable development in planning'.[9] We further discuss the implications of planning contributions for conservation interests in Chapter 16 (pp. 677–80).

## (a) Planning policy

As Jeremy Pike has noted, PPGs (Planning Policy Guidance Notes) and PPSs (Policy Planning Statements) (which will supersede PPGs) 'tell all of those who may have an interest in the planning process (no doubt the government describes them, currently, as "stakeholders") not so much what will be built where, but what values will carry weight in the decision as to what will be built where, and indeed what "values" the Secretary of State – in effect the government – will consider to be relevant or irrelevant, in planning decisions'.[10] Planning Policy Statement 1 sets out 'the overarching planning policies on the delivery of sustainable development through the planning system'. The statement must be taken into account by planning bodies in their preparation of various development plans which provide frameworks for decision making (see further below, p. 518), and by local planning authorities when considering individual applications for planning permission. Such policy statements are not legally binding, although they do constitute material, or relevant, considerations for decision makers. In short the statements provide a means by which central government policy influences day-to-day decision making at the local level.

[9] Bell and McGillivray, *Environmental Law*, p. 491.
[10] Jeremy Pike, 'PPS 1, and the Government's new Planning Policy Documents' (2005) 7 *Environmental Law Review* 273.

### ODPM (now succeeded by the Department of Communities and Local Government (DCLG)), Planning Policy Statement 1, *Delivering Sustainable Development* (HMSO, 2005)

KEY PRINCIPLES

13. The following key principles should be applied to ensure that development plans and decisions taken on planning applications contribute to the delivery of sustainable development:

(i) Development plans should ensure that sustainable development is pursued in an integrated manner, in line with the principles of sustainable development set out in the UK strategy. Regional planning bodies and local planning authorities should ensure that development plans promote outcomes in which environmental, economic and social objectives are achieved together over time.

(ii) Regional planning bodies and local planning authorities should ensure that development plans contribute to global sustainability by addressing the causes and potential impacts of climate change – through policies which reduce energy use, reduce emissions (for example, by encouraging patterns of development which reduce the need to travel by private car, or reduce the impact of moving freight), promote the development of renewable energy resources, and take climate change impacts into account in the location and design of development

(iii) A spatial planning approach should be at the heart of planning for sustainable development [see further below, pp. 522–30].

(iv) Planning policies should promote high quality inclusive design in the layout of new developments and individual buildings in terms of function and impact, not just for the short term but over the lifetime of the development. Development which fails to take the opportunities available for improving the character and quality of an area should not be accepted.

(v) Development plans should also contain clear, comprehensive and inclusive access policies – in terms of both location and external physical access. Such policies should consider people's diverse needs and aim to break down unnecessary barriers and exclusions in a manner that benefits the entire community.

(vi) Community involvement is an essential element in delivering sustainable development and creating sustainable and safe communities. In developing the vision for their areas, planning authorities should ensure that communities are able to contribute to ideas about how that vision can be achieved, have the opportunity to participate in the vision, strategy and specific plan policies, and to be involved in development proposals.

A raft of other policy statements seeks to carry these principles into specific policy areas (see, for example, PPS 9 on nature conservation (discussed in Chapter 16, p. 676) and PPS 22 on renewable energy (discussed in Chapter 17, pp. 705–8)).

PPS 1 adopts a fairly anodyne description of sustainable development. The RCEP supports the development of a clearer and more specific purpose for planning policy and legislation: 'We recommend that the town and country planning system should be given a statutory purpose and that, rather than use the term "sustainable development", an appropriate purpose would be to "facilitate the achievement of legitimate economic and social goals whilst ensuring that the quality of the environment is safeguarded and, wherever appropriate, enhanced".'[11] The Commission further suggests that this statutory purpose for the planning system be reinforced in legislation by the stipulation of key aspects of the environment and natural resources as material considerations which should be taken into account in considering all planning applications.[12]

### (b) Scope of town and country planning

Wendy Le-Las has usefully pointed out that 'the scope of the planning system defies rationality; it is a matter of convention born of historical accident … many of the activities which are damaging to wildlife [and the wider environment] do not fall within its sphere of influence'.[13] In formal terms, its scope is set out in the definition of 'development' in s. 55 of the 1990 Act (as amended by the Planning and Compulsory Purchase Act 2004) as making a physical change or a 'material' change in the existing use of any buildings or land.

> Meaning of 'development' and 'new development'
>
> 55.-(1) Subject to the following provisions of this section, in this Act, except where the context otherwise requires, 'development' means the carrying out of building, engineering, mining or other operations in, on, over or under land, or the making of any material change in the use of any buildings or other land.
>
> (1A) For the purposes of this Act 'building operations' includes –
>> (a)  demolition of buildings;
>> (b)  rebuilding;
>> (c)  structural alterations of or additions to buildings; and
>> (d)  other operations normally undertaken by a person carrying on business as a builder.
>
> (2) The following operations or uses of land shall not be taken for the purposes of this Act to involve development of the land–
>> (a)  the carrying out for the maintenance, improvement or other alteration of any building of works which–
>>> (i)  affect only the interior of the building, or
>>> (ii)  do not materially affect the external appearance of the building and are not works for making good war damage or works begun after December 5, 1968 for the alteration of a building by providing additional space in it underground;

---

[11]  RCEP, *Environmental Planning*, Cm 5459 (2002) para. 8.33.     [12]  *Ibid.*, para. 8.36.

[13]  Wendy Le-Las, 'Biodiversity in the Planning System' in Nicholas Herbert-Young (ed.), *Law, Policy and Development in the Rural Environment* (University of Wales Press, 1999), p. 81.

(b)  the carrying out on land within the boundaries of a road by a highway authority of any works required for the maintenance or improvement of the road;

(c)  the carrying out by a local authority or statutory undertakers of any works for the purpose of inspecting, repairing or renewing any sewers, mains, pipes, cables or other apparatus, including the breaking open of any street or other land for that purpose;

(d)  the use of any buildings or other land within the curtilage of a dwellinghouse for any purpose incidental to the enjoyment of the dwellinghouse as such;

(e)  the use of any land for the purposes of agriculture or forestry (including afforestation) and the use for any of those purposes of any building occupied together with land so used;

(f)  in the case of buildings or other land which are used for a purpose of any class specified in an order made by the Secretary of State under this section, the use of the buildings or other land or, subject to the provisions of the order, of any part of the buildings or the other land, for any purpose of the same class;

(g)  the demolition of any description of building specified in a direction given by the Secretary of State to local planning authorities generally or to a particular local planning authority.

The inclusion of 'material change in the *use* of any buildings or other land' as development for the purposes of the 1990 Act is unique to British planning law and makes for a category of development beyond *physical* changes to land to be controlled. There are also several exemptions from this definition of development set out in this section of the 1990 Act. See, in particular, the exemption under 55(2)(e) for 'the use of any land for the purposes of agriculture or forestry (including afforestation) and the use for any of these purposes of any building occupied together with land so used'. The historical roots of this exemption are discussed in Chapter 12, pp. 479–89, and its consequences in terms of the complex implementation of the EIA Directive are considered in Chapters 16, pp. 681–2. In addition, two statutory instruments make a number of further exemptions. The Town and Country Planning (Use Class) Order 1987[14] excludes a variety of use changes from the definition of development. For example, a change of use of a building or other land is deemed not to fall within the definition of a 'material change in the use of any buildings or other land' if they fall within the same 'class' in the statutory instrument, and are thus considered to have approximately the same social, amenity and environmental effects. The second instrument, the Town and Country Planning (General Permitted Development) Order 1995,[15] automatically grants planning permission ('permitted development rights') for a large number of activities. For example, in most instances, planning permission is not required for development deemed to be minor, for development carried out by a range of public services, or development related to certain 'favoured' activities such as agriculture and forestry.

---

[14]  SI 1987 No. 764.     [15]  SI 1995 No. 418.

## (c) Applications for planning permission

In dealing with an application for planning permission, s. 70(2)[16] of the Town and Country Planning Act 1990 provides that the local planning authority must have *regard* to the provisions of the relevant development plans (discussed further below), and to 'any other material considerations'. The authority may grant planning permission either unconditionally or subject to such conditions as it thinks fit, or refuse planning permission (section 70(1) of the 1990 Act). Prima facie, this section confers considerable discretion on the local planning authority. The 'material' or relevant considerations referred to might include circulars and PPG Notes, both of which are now being replaced by Planning Policy Statements (above). Importantly, representations made by third parties, or interested members of the public or local groups, should also be taken into account. The political and legal emphasis on public participation has meant that planning procedures, particularly involving major developments, now frequently include lengthy consultation exercises. In addition, since 1988, information arising from the environmental assessment process is also a material consideration of the local planning authority,[17] as we discuss further in the next chapter.

The key consideration for the local planning authority (and the Secretary of State on appeal or when s/he 'calls in' a planning application (below, pp. 518–19)) will be the terms of the relevant development plan. Planning permission is to be determined in line with that plan unless 'material considerations' indicate otherwise, as provided by s. 38(6) Planning and Compulsory Purchase Act 2004 (almost identical wording was used in s. 54A of the 1990 Act, as we discussed in the previous chapter, pp. 490–1).

## S. 38 Development Plan

(6) If regard is to be had to the development plan for the purpose of any determination to be made under the planning Acts the determination must be made in accordance with the plan unless material considerations indicate otherwise.

This section requires that particular 'weight' be given to development plan policies, and is tantamount to a statutory presumption in favour of the development plan. But this does not *necessarily* mean that the plan will always be followed. There is also a view that the most recent guidance implicitly confers greater discretion upon planning authorities and the Secretary of State when they are attributing weight to different material considerations in their planning decisions.[18]

---

[16] See reproduction of s. 70 and comment, Ch. 12, p. 491.

[17] This requirement is now governed by Town and Country Planning (Environmental Impact Assessment) (England and Wales) Regulations 1999 (SI 1999 No. 293).

[18] See Stuart Bell and Donald McGillivray's interpretation of ODPM, *The Planning System: General Principles* (2005), para. 10, in *Environmental Law*, p. 478.

## (d) Inter-relationship between planning and pollution controls

As mentioned above, when deciding upon an individual application for planning permission, the local planning authority may grant planning permission either unconditionally or subject to such conditions as it thinks fit, or refuse planning permission (s. 70(1) of the 1990 Act). Such conditions may clearly be imposed to regulate land use having environmental implications, for example to ensure decontamination of soil or the removal of chemicals, and to ensure proper reinstatement of land after the use. But the expansion of matters over which the planning authority now legitimately exercises control raises questions about the legitimate scope of these controls, for example to limit and render harmless emissions. In addition to conforming with policy guidance,[19] conditions designed to secure environmental protection objectives must fulfil certain tests established by the courts.[20] The use of conditions (or even a refusal of planning permission) to control the level of emissions from a proposed development is particularly problematic because such an enhanced role for planning authorities creates the possibility of planning overlapping with existing pollution controls.

The opportunities for this are seen in *Gateshead Metropolitan Borough Council v. Secretary of State for the Environment and Northumbrian Water Group*[21] which raises the issue of the extent to which the functions and efficiency of Her Majesty's Inspectorate of Pollution (HMIP, now subsumed in the Environment Agency, as discussed in Chapter 8, pp. 334–9) may legitimately be taken into account by the Secretary of State in the context of an appeal for planning permission. The Secretary of State granted planning permission for a clinical waste incinerator near Gateshead. The Inspector appointed to hear the appeal had recommended that permission be refused. One of the issues which was taken into account by the Inspector was the local public's fear that dioxins emitted from the site would be harmful (on taking into account the public perception of risks, see further below, pp. 542–5). The Secretary of State concluded that this issue could be satisfactorily addressed as part of the Integrated Pollution Control authorisation procedure (now replaced by the Integrated Pollution and Prevention Control regime, on which see further Chapter 9). That decision was challenged by the local planning authority on the ground that the planning system and Integrated Pollution Control were so closely linked that it would be unreasonable to grant planning permission without knowing if emissions could be adequately controlled under the Integrated Pollution Control authorisation. The High Court, confirmed by the Court of Appeal, decided that although the two statutory requirements overlapped, the extent of the overlap would vary on every occasion. Sullivan J held that 'just as the environmental impact of such emissions is a material planning consideration, so also is the existence of a stringent regime under the Environmental Protection Act 1990 for preventing or mitigating that impact

[19] ODPM, PPS 23, *Planning and Pollution Control* (ODPM, 2004).
[20] *Newbury District Council* v. *Secretary of State for the Environment* [1981] AC 578. For discussion, see Barry Cullingworth and Vincent Nadin, *Town and Country Planning in the UK* (Routledge, 13th edn, 2003), pp. 135–6.   [21] [1995] Env LR 36.

and for rendering any emissions harmless' (p. 44). This reasoning makes clear that, in appropriate cases, misgivings by the local planning authority about a project's effect upon the environment may be resolved by imposing conditions in the *pollution control* authorisation process and so need not be addressed at the planning stage. The trust placed in the operation of that system of pollution control by Sullivan J, and endorsed by the Court of Appeal,[22] circumscribes the means by which planning controls might *prevent* environmental pollution by refusing planning permission. Local planning authorities can still refuse planning permission on the grounds of harm to the environment, but they must adduce certain evidence of that harm. This is a countervailing approach to the precautionary principle, which ostensibly guides policy making.[23]

The Secretary of State's argument for the 'separation' of planning from pollution issues, accepted by the Court of Appeal, derives from confidence that HMIP was achieving many of the aims of Part I of the Environmental Protection Act 1990. However, at the time that the case was heard, the most comprehensive study on the effectiveness of the Integrated Pollution Control (IPC) regime, *Integrated Pollution Control: The First Three Years* (1994), reported that HMIP had not ensured a real commitment to the key concepts of environmental protection underlying the 1990 Act. This suggests, contrary to the Secretary of State's view in *Gateshead*, that the local planning authority was right to be concerned with the 'operational' element of facilities that were under the control of the Inspectorate. Although this case and the report on the workings of the (then) IPC system have been overtaken by other developments in pollution control (see Chapter 9 in which we discuss Integrated Pollution Prevention and Control), the fact remains that more comprehensive control of damaging activities might be brought about by explicitly linking pollution control procedures with the planning system, for example by requiring a single assessment to fulfil authorising activities under both the Integrated Pollution Prevention and Control regime and the planning system (as recommended by the Royal Commission on Environmental Pollution in their report on *Environmental Planning*[24]). To some extent, the Environmental Impact Assessment (EIA) regime is capable of fulfilling this function, particularly if this includes post-assessment monitoring, by which conditions can be amended in the light of the realisation of the environmental effects of a project (as we discuss further in the following chapter, pp. 604–7).

In summary, there is a fine line between achieving greater congruence between the planning system and pollution control systems to achieve mitigation of adverse environmental effects, and guarding against unnecessary overlaps. In *Gateshead* the Court of Appeal declined to overturn the Secretary of State's decision as a matter of law, but that does not mean that alternative results would not have been acceptable. Cases heard after *Gateshead* affirm that the

[22] *Gateshead.*     [23] See, for example, PPS 23, para. 6.

[24] Para. 5.24: 'We recommend that pollution control authorisation and planning permission for industrial plants should be obtained through a single open process involving a common environmental statement and, where appropriate, a joint public inquiry.'

existence of specialist pollution control agencies is no more than a material consideration for the planning authority to weigh in the balance.[25] Planning Policy
Statement 23, *Planning and Pollution*, continues to follow closely the judgment
in *Gateshead*, in effect dissuading planning authorities from imposing conditions and negotiating planning agreements to achieve mitigation which go
beyond regulating the physical use of the land to the detailed characteristics of
industrial processes, and thus highlighting the dynamic relationship between
policy-making and the courts.

### ODPM, Planning Policy Statement 23, *Planning and Pollution Control* (HMSO, 2004)

8. Any consideration of the quality of land, air or water and potential impacts arising
from development, possibly leading to an impact on health, is capable of being
a material planning consideration, in so far as it arises or may arise from any land
use.

9. [Reiterates the government's policy framework for planning in PPS 1 (see above, p.
512).]

10. The planning and pollution control systems are separate but complementary.
Pollution control is concerned with preventing pollution through the use of measures
to prohibit or limit the release of substances to the environment from different
sources to the lowest practicable level. It also ensures that ambient air and water
quality meet standards that guard against impacts to the environment and human
health. The planning system controls the development and use of land in the public
interest. It plays an important role in determining the location of development which
may give rise to pollution, either directly or from traffic generated, and in ensuring
that other developments are, as far as possible, not affected by major existing, or
potential sources of pollution. The planning system should focus on whether the
development itself is an acceptable use of the land, and the impacts of these uses,
rather than the control of processes or emissions themselves. Planning authorities
should work on the assumption that the relevant pollution control regime will be
properly applied and enforced. They should act to complement but not seek to duplicate it.

### (e) The decision: reasons, appeals and enforcement

To return to the procedures for granting a licence for development or change
of use of land, whether they grant or refuse development consent, the local planning authority and the Secretary of State must give reasons for their decision.[26]
The legal status of this requirement is uncertain, for example whether a failure to

---

[25] *R* v. *Bolton Metropolitan Council ex parte Kirkman* [1998] Env LR 719.
[26] This requirement appears to be an implicit part of the appeal regime.

provide reasons renders the decision void.[27] Appeals are at present handled by a specialist Planning Inspectorate. 'Transferred' appeals may be recovered (or 'called in') on request by the Secretary of State, in order that s/he make the final decision in the case of a particular application. Looking to enforcement, the 1990 Act provides that a local planning authority may issue an enforcement notice where it appears both that there has been a breach of planning control *and* that it is expedient to do so.[28] If at the end of the period for compliance the breach continues, the landowner is in breach of the notice and may be prosecuted in a magistrates' court.

It is highly significant that only the *applicant* has a statutory right of appeal to the Secretary of State (or to the Planning Decision Committee of the Welsh Assembly) against a *refusal* of planning permission,[29] or if the authority has failed to determine the application within the prescribed period. There is no third party[30] right of appeal against a *grant* of planning permission, in spite of strong arguments to the contrary. This means that third parties such as neighbours or local amenity groups are limited to a judicial review action against the local authority as a means of challenging such a decision,[31] but this is a more limited course of action, amounting to a review of the procedures by which a decision was reached, rather than the merits of the decision itself.

### RCEP, *Environmental Planning*

5.41 The Aarhus Convention[32] contains important provisions concerning rights of appeal against decisions of public authorities to permit a range of specified projects and activities. Article 9 requires that members of the public with a sufficient interest, or maintaining that a right conferred by the Convention has been impaired, shall 'have access to a review procedure before a court of law and/or another independent and impartial body established by law, to challenge the substantive and procedural legality of such decisions. Non-governmental organisations promoting environmental interests are to be deemed to have sufficient interest in this context.' Some may argue ... that existing procedures in the UK, most notably the availability of judicial review, fulfil these requirements. The Aarhus Convention does not directly require a right of appeal for third parties, but we have concerns that existing arrangements for the involvement of objectors in the decision-making process may not be consistent with the spirit and objectives of the Convention.

---

[27] Note that in the case of decision making subject to environmental assessment, the requirement that reasons be given is more closely defined (see Ch. 14, p. 591); in addition, see requirement to give reasons in environmental decision making in the Aarhus Convention, Art. 6(9), reproduced in Ch. 3, p. 111.    [28] See s. 172 TCPA 1990.    [29] Section 78 TCPA 1990.

[30] The 'first party' in development control in planning is the applicant for planning permission and the 'second party' is the local authority. 'Third parties' are anyone else with a view on a planning application, whether they have a direct interest (e.g. as owner of the land for which the application is submitted) or a personal interest (e.g. as a neighbour) or a wider interest (e.g. as a parish council or interest group).    [31] Section 288 TCPA 1990.

[32] See Ch. 3.

chapter, p. 491. The presumption in favour of the development plan contained in s. 54A of the 1990 Act (pp. 490–1) had the potential to strengthen further the environmental dimension of plan-making. Through these various requirements, the focus of planning shifted more clearly to environmental protection, but this continued to be refracted through a limited conception of 'land use', as Patsy Healey notes:

> The British approach to spatial planning is [also] distinctive both in its centrist and its functional sectionalism. This too reflects a general characteristic of British governance. It allows national philosophies about land policy and spatial organisation to be driven across local practices. For example, spatial planning in Britain since the 1970s has been forced by central government policy and practice into a narrow remit of 'land use matters' only. This is a deliberate attempt to narrow down the potential range of interests in land development and spatial organisation issues and to avoid straying into the remits of other government departments. In other countries where municipal governments have much greater powers, spatial planning is integrated with social, economic and environmental policy practices at the municipal level, for example, Sweden.[43]

The limited nature of traditional planning systems has also been highlighted by developments at the European Union (EU) level, such as the European Spatial Development Perspective (1999)[44] which sought to raise awareness of the significance of spatial development trends for achieving the EU's objectives and to promote policy integration across different sectors of activity, coupled with the fact that other Member States are increasingly establishing more strategic planning frameworks and spatial plans.[45] Cullingworth and Nadin put these developments into a European *and* global context:

### Barry Cullingworth and Vincent Nadin, *Town and Country Planning in the UK* (Routledge, 13th edn, 2003), pp. 77–8

#### The Rationale for Planning at the European Scale

The EU is driven by the goals of economic competitiveness, social cohesion and balanced development of economic activities among its regions, and, since the adoption of the Amsterdam Treaty in 1999, sustainable development. These objectives have an obvious spatial dimension. The main obstacle to meeting them are the great disparities in wealth, jobs, investment, and access to services across Europe. Indeed, recent evidence suggests that despite the actions of the EU, some disparities (especially between the north and the south) are widening, and that economic and political forces will ensure that they continue to do so.

---

[43] Patsy Healey, *Collaborative Planning: Shaping Places in Fragmented Societies* (Macmillan, 1997), p. 75.

[44] Committee on Spatial Development, European Spatial Development Perspective (ESDP) (1999) which aims to promote coherence of the development strategies of the Member States by coordinating the spatial aspects of the EC's sectoral policies.

[45] See D. G. Regio, *Compendium of EU Spatial Planning Systems and Policies.* Discussed by Cullingworth and Nadin, *Town and Country Planning in the UK*, pp. 85–6.

The growing economic and social integration of European nations and regions in the context of globalisation is having a profound effect on spatial development patterns. Significant elements of economic activity together with political and cultural relations are effectively becoming globalised and independent of nation-states. Locational decisions are now more likely to ignore regional and national boundaries. The extent and depth of globalisation are disputed, but it is widely accepted that it has specific implications for changing patterns of spatial development. Of particular note in the European context are increased spatial concentration of economic activity and the central role of global and regional cities; intensified competition between cities across national boundaries; the corresponding polarisation of economic prosperity; and the negative environmental consequences. Major development schemes have effects which often go well beyond national borders. In sum, the transboundary interdependencies of spatial development are now much stronger than they once were.

These effects are reinforced by Community policies, especially in the fields of regional policy, transport, environment, and agriculture, though their implications for spatial developments are not always explicitly considered in the policy-making process. Spatial planning and state regulation in other spheres play a significant role in addressing these trends, by maximising the competitive position and growth potential of major urban areas while attempting to ensure that, at best, patterns of growth are sustainable and, at worst, the negative impacts are ameliorated.

Cullingworth and Nadin use the structural funds as a case in point since the key objectives of the funds – to assist regions 'lagging behind' in development and to target economic and social conversion of areas facing structural difficulties – have a strong spatial dimension through investment in infrastructure and decisions about the most appropriate locations for development assistance. For this reason, Member States have been strongly 'encouraged' to work cooperatively on spatial planning as a means of coordinating the spatial impacts of sectoral policies, whilst promoting sustainable forms of development. More generally, Cullingworth and Nadin note that there has been a dramatic increase in spatial planning activities that cut across national borders and involve European institutions – transport, telecommunications, energy infrastructures, the Common Agricultural Policy, waste, nature conservation, environmental assessment and urban policy. They suggest that this involvement raises questions about the assignment of competences for spatial planning, asking 'Will spatial planning be yet another step in the continuing process of transfer of powers from the member states to the Community?' (p. 80).[46]

It is important also to see the integration of policy areas through spatial planning as having implications for *enhancing* public participation in planning. This

[46] Although note that town and country planning is subject to unanimous voting in Council (Art. 175(2)(b) EC).

in turn is likely to raise expectation: 'By raising the stakes of planning to embrace more users and by giving an enhanced voice to various groups in society, the audience for planning at the local and regional levels will raise expectations and optimism about what planning is there to do and who it serves. Whether practitioners are ready or not for this pressure is an aside; it is going to happen.'[47]

## (b) 'Bringing in' space:[48] reform of the planning system

The radical changes brought about by the 2004 Act were strongly influenced by the Twenty-third Report of the Royal Commission on Environmental Pollution (as discussed in the Introduction to this chapter). The Commission's recommendation to establish an integrated spatial strategy went far beyond the more conservative proposals included in the government's Green Paper on planning[49] which had been criticised for emphasising improvement of the speed and predictability of the planning system in order to satisfy business interests. Significantly, both of these remain important objectives for the new system, inevitably producing tensions with other objectives, such as public participation in planning decisions.

To recall, prior to its reform under the Planning and Compulsory Purchase Act 2004, 'a plethora of partial, overlapping, and often inconsistent plans produced by various bodies'[50] was a key feature of the planning system. This plethora included structure plans usually prepared by county councils on matters of strategic importance (housing, transport, environmental issues) and more detailed, geographically specific, local plans drawn up and adopted by district councils, but often having incomplete coverage, and merely reproducing policies derived from other plans. The 2004 Act sweeps away this system by abolishing structure plans and providing instead for a simplified hierarchy of plans and documents, with a regional spatial strategy at its apex. This regional strategy document will for the time being consist of existing regional planning guidance prepared by the Secretary of State, put on a statutory footing by Part I of the Act[51] as a way of giving greater effect to national policy guidance. Thereafter, the regional spatial strategies will be revised by Regional Planning Bodies, made up predominantly of members of county councils or local planning authorities, but with final decisions about policy resting with the Secretary of State. This is a good example of the hardening of existing policy, in the form of planning guidance, by enhancing its legal status. At the local level, in place of structure and local plans, a number of local development documents (as part of a local development

---

[47] Mark Tewdwr-Jones, 'Spatial Planning, Practices and Cultures' [2004] *Journal of Planning and Environmental Law* 560, p. 562.

[48] A phrase taken from Healey, *Collaborative Planning*, p. 34.

[49] DTLR, *Planning: Delivering a Fundamental Change*.

[50] RCEP, *Environmental Planning*, para. 12.     [51] Section 1(1) and (2) PCPA.

scheme[52]) will be prepared by the local planning authority, including minerals and waste development plans adopted by county councils. Together, these set out the policies of a local planning authority with respect to development and use of land. As a whole, though, the emphasis on spatial planning encourages the integration of policies on land use and development with other policies – housing, health, biodiversity, transport, culture, energy, education – set out in supplementary planning documents. The idea is that this will influence a balance to be struck between competing land uses, having regard to the overall principle of sustainable development. The full extent of the process of policy integration is not quite clear at this stage. William Howarth suggests, for example, that river basin management plans, prepared for the purpose of the Water Framework Directive, should also form part of the portfolio of local development documents, making up part of the local development scheme for an area.[53]

There is no specific mention of environmental considerations in the new statutory provisions. Rather, the requirement for structure and local plans policies to include policies on conservation, the improvement of the physical environment, and traffic management are now seemingly absorbed in a new duty in s. 39 of the 2004 Act. This requires plans to be prepared with the objective of contributing to the achievement of sustainable development. Sustainable development is not defined, but, in exercising this duty, regard must be had to the national policies and advice of the Secretary of State and the National Assembly of Wales. In addition, when revising the regional spatial strategy, the regional planning body must carry out a sustainability appraisal of its proposals.[54] This is now a familiar procedural mechanism, which, with regulatory impact assessment, is in line with the requirements of the Directive on strategic environmental assessment.[55]

---

[52] Under the 2004 Act, each local authority will adopt a local development framework (LDF). The contents of the LDF are set out in the local development scheme (LDS) which also proposes a timetable for their adoption and review. The documents in the scheme are referred to as local development documents (LDD). These are made up of: (i) development plan documents (DPDs) which form part of the development plan – according to reg. 7 Town and Country Planning (Local Development) England Regulations 2004, SI 2004 No. 2204, these include core strategies, area action plans and any other document which includes a site allocation policy; (ii) a statement of community involvement; (iii) an adopted proposals map (which might be a DPD); (iv) a submitted proposals map; and (v) other documents which will be supplementary planning documents. County councils will prepare minerals and waste development schemes and a suite of documents on these topics in a similar form to a local development scheme. See further Richard Harwood, 'Planning and Compulsory Purchase Act 2004 – How the Government Takes Control of Planning Policy' (2005) *Environmental Law Review* 124.

[53] Directive 2000/60/EC OJ 2000 L 327/1. See William Howarth, 'Environmental Assessment under the Water Framework Directive' in Jane Holder and Christopher Campbell-Holt (eds.), *Taking Stock of Environmental Assessment: Law, Policy and Practice* (Cavendish Routledge, 2007); see also William Upton, 'Planning Reform: The Requirement to Replace Supplementary Planning Guidance with Supplementary Planning Documents' [2005] *Journal of Planning Law* 34.

[54] Section 5(3). See parallel provision in the case of local development documents, s. 19 PCPA 2004.    [55] Directive 2001/42/EC. See further Ch. 14, pp. 599–601.

The broadening out of the plan-making process to include, for example, financial, resource, managerial and non-land use issues within the local development scheme raises a presumption that planning will become 'a core component in the delivery of sustainable development'.[56] Tewdwr-Jones lists the principles of spatial planning in these terms, notably integration and participation.[57]

### Tewdwr-Jones, 'Spatial Planning, Practices and Cultures', p. 563

The principles of spatial planning may be viewed as:

- broad ranging, concerning the assessment of the spatial dimensions of various activities and sectors, and interactions between them;
- visionary, by opening up planning to a range of participants and by relating processes of planning policy-making to notions of place;
- integrating, through the bringing together of both spatial issues relating to the development and use of land, and the users of planning;
- deliverable, applying strategy to programmes for action, through proactive processes, involving coordination and choreography between different overlapping sectors and resources; and
- participative, where planning is a facilitator and dependent on new forms of partnerships and engagement with a range of bodies, stakeholders, businesses and communities.

Such integration, or 'coordination and choreography' to use his terms, is more likely to take place predominantly at the national, rather than local, level precisely because, as Bell and McGillivray note, the importance of national policy in determining the content of regional spatial strategies (as required by s. 5(3)(a) of the 2004 Act) means that disputes over the content of these are likely to arise between government departments, 'to be thrashed out as matters of politics rather than law'.[58]

In summary, the expansion of the scope of the planning system was necessary to give effect to the meaning of sustainable development, but there are some costs. The pressure on planners will be great – as Mark Tewdwr-Jones colourfully puts it: 'Planners will have to be as adept as choreographers within increasingly complex, multi-layered and multi-dimensional planning activities within processes that require jargon-free language and excellent communication with a range of partners simultaneously.'[59] And, although many different sites of activity and policy are being brought within the 'umbrella' of planning, greater control of local policy is being exercised by the centre, in the shape of the Secretary of State. A rigid hierarchy of policy is in place,[60] maintained through the requirement in s. 24(1) of the 2004 Act that local development

---

[56] Tewdwr-Jones, 'Spatial Planning, Practices and Cultures', at p. 563.
[57] See further Ch. 6.     [58] Bell and McGillivray, *Environmental Law*, p. 457.
[59] Tewdwr-Jones, 'Spatial Planning, Practices and Cultures', p. 567.
[60] Harwood, 'Planning and Compulsory Purchase Act 2004'.

documents are in general conformity with the relevant regional spatial strategy, or 'the London plan'[61] (previously the general conformity rule applied only between structure and local plans). Within the overall structure of the 2004 Act this exerts a centralising force on the planning system, and is described as bringing about a fundamental change in the constitutional relationship between local and central government.[62] Such changes are at odds with moves to enhance local democracy through public participation, and are bound to revive the tensions between local and central control of land use which characterised the period of entrepreneurial planning in the 1980s and early 1990s (see previous chapter, pp. 489–94), and which are already a hallmark of planning disputes on wind farm development (as we discuss in Chapter 17, pp. 709–10). The following briefing comments on these 'dangers', and defends the old regime of structure and local plans, in the hands of local government.

### CPRE, *Planning to Deliver: A Briefing on the Government's Planning Reforms* (CPRE, 2002), p. 1

Strategic Planning

The abolition of county Structure Plans will create a dangerously wide gap between the new Regional Spatial Strategies and planning at the local level through new Local Development Frameworks. Structure Plans cover an area large enough to be strategic, yet small enough to allow sufficiently detailed consideration of major development issues and secure significant public identification. Their absence will make strategic planning for housing provision, for example, far less accountable and remove important opportunities for community involvement. Depriving county and unitary councils of a leading role in sub-regional planning will lead to a damaging loss of irreplaceable expertise and risk a breakdown in public consensus over strategic planning decisions. It will also make it much harder to achieve effective integration between spatial strategies and detailed transport policies contained in Local Transport Plans prepared by counties and unitary authorities. It is essential to good planning that the benefits of Structure Plans are retained in the new arrangements. The Government's commitment to a statutory role for country councils in regional planning is welcome, but not enough. Counties' statutory role needs to involve responsibility for formal decision-making on strengthened sub-regional chapters of Regional Spatial Strategies, as well as the provision of technical advice.

Interestingly, this caution focuses upon the loss of 'expertise', as much as any difficulties likely to be faced by lay participants in the plan-making process, particularly their need to master a large number of documents, covering different policy areas. We continue by discussing the implications of the move towards integrated spatial planning for public participation, within a broader analysis of the arguments for inclusive decision making, or 'collaboration', in planning.

---

[61] London continues to have a Spatial Development Strategy, prepared by the Mayor of London, under the Greater London Authority Act 1999.
[62] Harwood, 'Planning and Compulsory Purchase Act 2004'.

## 4 Public participation in planning

### (a) The argument for enhanced public participation

Public participation has long been entrenched in planning law and policy, with carefully demarcated opportunities for interested individuals and groups to make representations – considered to be 'material considerations' for the purpose of determining an application for planning permission under s. 70 of the Town and Country Planning Act 1990 – and to contribute to plan making.[63] As discussed in the last chapter (p. 488), the effectiveness of participation was scrutinised by the Skeffington Committee in 1969, which led to important changes in plan making.[64] A statement of community involvement must now be made in the case of preparing both the regional spatial strategy and the local development documents,[65] thus providing a procedural safeguard (rather than substantive rights) as discussed further below, pp. 536–8. However, when applying Sherry Arnstein's 'ladder' of citizen participation to the planning system, the experience (at the plan-making stage and at inquiry) remains generally one of 'informing and consultation': citizens may indeed hear and be heard, but under these conditions they lack the power to ensure that their views will be *heeded* by the powerful. As Arnstein describes, 'When participation is restricted to these levels, there is no follow-through, no "muscle", hence no assurance of changing the status quo.'[66] In recent years the methods and patterns of participation in the planning system have been held up as inadequate in the light of the wholesale adoption of sustainable development as a way of reconciling social, economic and environmental concerns through *democratic involvement*. This has resulted in a reappraisal and reinvigoration of the debate on participation.

Heading this reappraisal is Patsy Healey's work on producing a more consensual system of decision making known as 'collaborative planning', a label which has become a term of art in planning circles. Healey's argument for a particularly rich form of participation with the potential to reconstitute an active public realm extending beyond the confines of land use is a practical expression of the theoretical work underpinning moves in favour of public participation (or as Healey puts it the 'unravelling' of modernity, with its notion of the autonomous individual and materialist forms of science). Drawing upon the

---

[63] Via an 'examination in public' in the case of structure plans, and a local planning inquiry for local plans. Note that under the 2004 Act, the Secretary of State may still decide that an examination in public of a draft revision of a regional spatial strategy should be held (s. 8 PCPA).

[64] Note also the enhanced effectiveness of participation to arise ('by default') from the swing back to a plan-led system following the insertion of s. 54A into the Town and Country Planning Act 1990, on which see Ch. 12, pp. 490–1.     [65]     S. 6 and s. 18 PCPA, respectively.

[66] Sherry R. Arnstein, 'A Ladder of Citizen Participation' (1969) 36 *Journal of American Planning Association* 216, p. 217. For discussion of this 'ladder', see Ch. 3, pp. 85–6.

social theories developed by Anthony Giddens[67] and Jürgen Habermas,[68] she applies to planning the idea that social interaction and communicative networks create intellectual and social capital. This can usefully inform decision making, foster mutual learning and expand debate about land use *beyond* the confines of expert knowledge, so as to include types of local, intuitive and subjective knowledge, such as 'tacit know-how, practical "commonsense reason" and appeals to moral or ethical claims that are *not* open to scientific measurement and quantification'.[69] Whilst appearing to be a simple extrapolation of division between expert and lay knowledge, discussed in Chapter 1, pp. 40–7, as also discussed in Chapter 1, she holds that the claim to objectivity made by planning 'experts' is seriously limited; in practice both members of the public and planning officers express subjective value judgments in their decision making. This has led to collaborative planning being described as an attack on 'rational' decision making.[70]

Healey draws upon Giddens' theory of structuration – that we live within culturally bound structures of rules and resources, and that in reviewing and remaking these rules we also change ourselves and culture. She interprets the significance of this for planning.

### Patsy Healey, *Collaborative Planning: Shaping Places in Fragmented Societies* (Macmillan, 1997) (sources as marked)

Typically, we live in multiple webs, each with their cultures, that is modes of thought and systems of meaning and valuing. As active agents and in the social situations of the relations within which we live, we construct our own sense of identity. Thus we may well experience the clash of culture within ourselves, and within the nodes of our relational webs, in the workplace, the household, the bar, the sports club, the community group …

Understood in this way, living with cultural difference is not something that is alien or new. We have been doing it all the time with more or less success. Negotiating among diverse thoughtworlds is part of our daily life experience … [W]e manage to 'live with difference' and to challenge and even change the culturally blind. Through this experience, we mould new cultural referents, for ourselves, those we relate with and, more broadly, the abstract structures which support our lives. We are active agents in a culturally dynamic world. We are thus accustomed to making cultures as we live within them.

If this is so, then it is possible to imagine that, through the attempt to recognise and respect our cultural differences – that is, the different systems of meaning which are layered over each other in the array of claims for attention in thinking about local environments – we have the potential to 'make sense together', to arrive at a conception which works for

---

[67] *Consequences of Modernity* (Polity Press, 1990).

[68] *The Theory of Communicative Action, Vol. I: Reason and the Rationalisation of Society* (Polity Press, 1984).

[69] Mark Pennington, *Liberating the Land: The Case for Private Land-Use Planning* (Institute of Economic Affairs, 2002), pp. 47–51, p. 30.     [70] *Ibid.*, p. 30.

other provisions for the public to participate during the preparation of plans and programmes relating to the environment, within a transparent and fair framework, having provided the necessary information to the public'.[83] Having reviewed the various opportunities for participation by individuals and interest groups, Purdue concludes that the obligations for public participation in planning represent a high point of public participation in environmental plans and strategies and appear to comply with the requirements of Article 7 of the Convention,[84] a judgment he does not extend to the participation procedures for the national waste strategy and national air quality strategy.

### (c) Participation in practice

In contrast to the affirmation provided by Purdue, Anna Davies' empirical study, from a social geography perspective, of perceptions of planning practice (based on interviews with participants at Parents' Associations, Women's Institutes, and sporting and social clubs in south Bedfordshire) suggests that there are significant gaps between the theory and practice of participation, and between political rhetoric and the 'realpolitik' or real rationality of planning processes.[85]

### Anna R. Davies, 'Hidden or Hiding? Public Perceptions of Participation in the Planning System' (2001) 72 *Town Planning Review* 193, p. 212

In contrast to the aims and hopes of politicians, communicative planning theorists and many planners, members of focus groups in this research did not see the participation opportunities in planning as a forum in which to engage in dialogue about their locality and its future development. In many cases there remains a lack of awareness of the formal access they can have to decision making in planning, but even when this knowledge exists, or is provided, there is scepticism about the efficacy of participating. The problem of non-participation then is more than one of 'process' that can be resolved simply by providing access through new channels of participation. Specific locational histories will share public–institutional relations and diverse communities within places will experience those relations in very different ways. Even innovative deliberative forums (such as citizen juries, visioning exercises and focus groups) work within wider structures of political relations and themselves replicate, reconstruct and reproduce patterns of power at a variety of scales. As noted by Owens:

> genuine engagement of, and with, the public remains a profound challenge, not least because it requires that people have the capacity to act as informed citizens at a time when the crucial interrelated components of this process – knowledge, capacity and citizenship – are all subject to critical interpretation and renegotiation.[86]

---

[83] Article 7 Aarhus Convention. See also Principle 10 of the Rio Declaration (1992) on access to information on the environment and the opportunity to participate in decision making.

[84] Purdue, 'An Overview of the Law'.

[85] Anna R. Davies, 'Hidden or Hiding? Public Perceptions of Participation in the Planning System' (2001) 72 *Town Planning Review* 193.

[86] Susan Owens, 'Engaging the Publics: Information and Deliberation in Environmental Policy' (2000) 32 *Environment and Planning A.*, pp. 1141–8.

On one level the recent Government statements on participation do acknowledge public perceptions of a democratic deficit in local government, including planning, but the solutions remain solidly process-oriented. The difficult issues such as how different scales of government will interact, how different knowledges become legitimised and what types of rationalities underpin decision-making are subsumed under technical preoccupations with process. In the terms of Habermasian communicative theory, there is too much emphasis on programmes for action (processes) and not enough consideration of the construction of arenas (spaces) in which those actions can be formulated. The public voices – particularly their perceptions and understandings of political negotiations, decision-making and participation opportunities in planning – are being neglected. As a result the recent rhetoric calling for enhanced participation may be interpreted by the public as nothing more than a mere gloss over existing and persisting structures of power. … [I]t must be made very clear that while planning aims to protect what we 'as a society' value, the process of planning itself is also centrally about the mediation of power and interests.

Owens and Cowell see more reasons for optimism whilst, fundamentally, reaching the same conclusion as Davies about the importance of economic structures in determining the effectiveness of participation.

### Owens and Cowell, *Land and Limits*, pp. 59–60

Whatever the rationale, it has been widely assumed that new forums are needed if the acknowledged difficulties of meaningful participation are to be overcome. It is worth reflecting, therefore, on the adequacy, or otherwise, of established statutory arrangements for public involvement. Broadly speaking, attempts to engage the public – or at least a wider public – in plan making, through the usual methods of consultation drafts, exhibitions, public meetings and inquiries, have enjoyed only limited success. Among the most prominent grounds for this verdict have been the persistent failure to reach certain groups (often those who are socially disadvantaged) and the tendency for exercises to be ritualistic, offering the 'shadow rather than the substance' of participation. Even so, it would be misleading to imply that traditional arrangements have been wholly without effect. On the contrary, the apertures for 'public' involvement prised open over the years have admitted previously excluded interests, particularly environmental coalitions, edging the policy process in a more pluralist direction. Public inquiries, for example, have brought together diverse groups and individuals, raised the profile of important issues and provided a forum for evidence, argument and critical challenge. Although the reality falls a long way short of deliberative ideals, individual developments have been subjected to strong and effective challenges at inquiry, and successive challenges have contributed, in some instances, to a process of policy learning and change. In effect, procedures intended to give local people some right to be heard have been used in lieu of a wider deliberative process in the polity as a whole; we see this clearly in the context of the roads programme, and of minerals policy … Opportunities for participation have been promoted and defended by critics of government policy essentially for this reason, while development interests have persistently called for the 'streamlining' of the planning process, and for the remit of inquiries to be confined to local issues of siting, design and impact management. If the *status quo* often proves resistant to challenge, and public involvement seems ritualistic, this might be attributable not to procedural shortcomings but to wide structural commitments to particular patterns of growth.

Despite their criticisms of the way that participation is currently working, the researchers and lawyers above all seem to be working within a consensus that seeks to enhance participation – 'a new hegemony in planning theory'.[87] In marked contrast, Mark Pennington takes a blow at both collaborative planning and the moves towards a more integrated planning system, by seeing these two reforms as related and, together, flawed (unlike Healey who views these developments as mutually reinforcing and positive). Pennington's views are informed by his central thesis that management of land use is regulated too closely by government, leading him to advocate a radical departure from the current planning system, a private system of land use control in which, for example, local recreation and amenity companies would hold development rights collectively. Note that he places great importance on 'pricing mechanisms' and the 'usable' results of participation (as opposed to the more nebulous conception of 'social learning').

### Mark Pennington, *Liberating the Land: The Case for Private Land-Use Planning* (Institute of Economic Affairs, 2002), pp. 47–51

Planning without prices: incremental planning

…

In areas such as development control, the allocation of housing land and the siting of major infrastructure projects, such as roads and airports, there has been a legacy of dis-coordination between the various government agencies concerned. In the case of housing land allocations, for example, inter-agency conflicts are standard fare. There are frequent political battles between DEFRA and individual planning authorities with regard to the number of new housing developments to be permitted within particular counties and districts. It is common for local authorities to ignore the recommendations of DEFRA[88] inspectors and to set their own (usually much lower) housing land allocations, only to have the relevant plans 'called in' by the Secretary of State. Similar inter-agency conflicts occur at the local level, where the disputes between different district authorities and between counties and districts over the location of new housing and other major developments amount to little more than a game of inter-agency 'pass the parcel'.

---

[87]  Mark Tewdwr-Jones and Phillip Allmendinger, 'Deconstructing Communicative Rationality: A Critique of Habermasian Collaborative Planning' (1998) 30 *Environment and Planning A.*, 1975. See this article for a sharp critique of collaborative planning.

[88]  Department of Environment, Food and Rural Affairs, the planning responsibilities of which were transferred to the Office of the Deputy Prime Minister (ODPM), which is now succeeded by the Department of Communities and Local Government (DCLG).

It is precisely this lack of coordination which results in the frequent calls for a more 'joined up' or 'integrated' planning system and an end to the 'disjointed incrementalism' of the existing regime.

...

Whilst it must surely be accepted that participatory procedures may generate more information than purely 'expert-centred' modes of decision, there are a number of problems with the assumption that a participatory, democratic planning system can deliver an appropriately 'integrated' set of land-use decisions.

First, to suggest that *because* social and environmental systems are 'holistically' related entities they must be managed on a similarly 'holistic' or 'joined up' basis is a complete *non sequitur.* From a Hayekian perspective it is precisely *because* these systems are *complexly* related entities that *conscious* social planning is problematic. Advocates of participatory planning appear to be suggesting that fundamental epistemological problems could somehow be solved if only all the relevant 'stakeholders', in their multiple social and economic roles, could be gathered together in some sort of grand committee meeting to discuss the issues in hand (a logistical impossibility in itself). As both Hayek's work and recent developments in chaos and complexity theory suggest, however, it is because of the magnitude of the interrelations between the many components that make up a complex economy that they may not be grasped synoptically by a group of minds engaged in such a discussion.[89]

The logistical problems of participatory planning are revealed when one examines the institutional mechanisms that are advocated. It is never suggested that all or even a majority of the relevant populations will be involved in the requisite plan-making. Instead, the devices proposed include 'citizens' juries', 'community workshops' or 'focus groups' – small groups of citizens randomly selected from the populations concerned. When involved in the making of strategic plans and other 'integrated land-use policies', such groups are to make more comprehensible the complex interrelationships that permeate urban and regional economies, which are held to be beyond the comprehension of professional technocracy. For the reasons outlined above, such claims seem questionable. How, for example, are the members of citizens' juries to learn reflexively about the quality of their decisions when there is no equivalent of the profit-and-loss account and the constant feedback (positive and negative) provided by a set of relative prices which can 'test' the quality of the choices made? Similarly, how are voters to make meaningful judgements on the performance of such processes if the actors concerned are attempting to engage in a process that may be beyond *anybody's* comprehension? One might ask *why* the population in general should feel the sense of empowerment that is often claimed. It is far from clear why the multitude of people, who cannot for logistical reasons be involved, should feel any more 'empowered' than they might feel under the rule of technocratic procedures.

Given that 'the environment' is *not* an all-or-nothing good, but a bundle of *different* goods, it is hard to see how even relatively simple communication/co-ordination problems could be

---

[89]  F. A. Hayek, 'The Theory of Complex Phenomena' in *Studies in Philosophy, Politics and Economics* (Routledge, 1976).

adequately addressed by the participatory planning approach. To learn, for example, that some members of a citizens' jury would prefer that fewer green field sites be allocated for house-building, whilst others are prepared to tolerate the further loss of such sites, is to learn very little at all. How few is fewer? How do the environmental costs of building houses vary from one green-field site to another? For what combination of purposes are green-field sites to be used? Such questions will, of course, be multiplied many times over when the choice is between the vast array of potential land uses that make up a complex economy, the myriad possible combinations of such uses and the complexity of their environmental consequences. In short, without the information provided by a set of market-generated *relative prices* it will be difficult for participants in other than the crudest form, to communicate their values to each other, and hence find ways of 'integrating' these values with those of their fellows.

Here, Pennington makes several impassioned objections to the present direction of planning policy towards integration *and* enhanced participation, from the political perspective of liberating the planning system from government and agency regulation. His approach might be criticised for being crudely reduction-ist; as we discussed in Chapter 1 (pp. 37–40), not all values can be priced. But he is right to challenge the general direction that planning is taking, at least to the extent that planners are being asked to give effect to the conflicting objectives of speedier decision making *and* enhanced public participation. Added to these policy objectives is also environmental protection, now recast as one component of the broader concept of sustainable development. The situation is reminiscent of McAuslan's ideologies of planning,[90] but with his original schema replaced with the following set of assumptions and perspectives – private interest (speed, predictability), public interest (community involvement) and a less well-defined 'environmental' interest absorbed within sustainable development. The extent to which there is a correlation between these objectives, particularly between enhanced public involvement in planning decisions and environmental pro-tection, is difficult to determine at the best of times, but the potential for tension between these objectives is especially marked in several cases of wind farm development, discussed in Chapter 17.

## (d) Public perceptions of risk as material considerations

An important practical issue arising from enhanced public participation in the planning system is the weight to be given to public *perceptions* of risk, particu-larly where there is scientific uncertainty about the effects on the environment or human health. In particular, much controversy and litigation in this respect

---

[90] Patrick McAuslan, *Ideologies of Planning* (Pergamon Press, 1980), p. 7. McAuslan originally describes the ideologies of planning as follows: firstly, that the law exists and should be used to protect private property and its institutions; this may be called the traditional common law approach to the role of law. Secondly, the law exists and should be used to advance the public interest, if necessary against the interests of private property; this may be called the orthodox public administration and planning approach to the role of law. Thirdly, the law exists and

has arisen in recent years over proposals to build telecommunication masts. As we discussed in the context of the regulation of genetically modified organisms (GMOs) (Chapter 2), there is some danger in denying the public the opportunity to debate the 'acceptability' of risk or the 'hypothetical' risk of various developments, thus instituting an instrumental approach to technology. In the context of the planning system, perceptions of risk may be heightened because of the locational issues involved, for example the proximity of a mobile phone mast to school buildings. As with the 'public dialogue' over the future of agricultural biotechnology, discussed in Chapter 2, pp. 76–83, these perceptions, as advanced in planning procedures and reviewed by the courts, reflect different ways of understanding the world. Chris Hilson divides judicial reaction to popular perceptions of risk from telecommunication masts into opposing 'camps', and suggests that such an approach can probably be generalised across all environmental risk cases.

### Chris Hilson, 'Planning Law and Public Perceptions of Risk: Evidence of Concern or Concern Based on Evidence' [2004] *Journal of Planning and Environmental Law* 1638, p. 1638

If majority scientific opinion has stated that a proposed incinerator's emissions are safe, or that a proposed mobile phone mast poses no risk to human health – but local residents nevertheless continue to perceive that there is a risk – should planning authorities be able to deny planning consent based on this public concern? In basic terms, there is a battle between what one might term the 'rationalists' and the 'populists'. The former believe that public decisions should be based on objective and rational science and see no place for what they regard as subjective and irrational public fears. The latter, in contrast, point to the uncertainties surrounding science and modern technology; they believe that public perceptions of risk exhibit an alternative rationality and reflect values which ought to be taken into account in the democratic planning process.

As we discussed above, s. 70(2) of the Town and Country Planning Act 1990 states that, in determining a planning application, planning authorities 'shall have regard to the provisions of the development plan, so far as material to the application, and to any other material considerations'. Chris Hilson poses the question 'whether public concern is – as rationalists would contend – only a material planning consideration which planning authorities must take into account if it is objectively justified. Or is public perception of risk a material consideration which must be taken into account (albeit with planning authorities deciding what weight to give it) even if objectively unjustified, as populists would have it?' (p. 1639). He explains that the higher English courts have not been consistent on the matter. In *Gateshead*, discussed above, pp. 516–18,

should be used to advance the cause of public participation against both the orthodox public administration approach to the public interest and the common law approach of the overriding importance of private property; this may be called the radical or populist approach to the role of law.

Glidewell LJ (with whom Hoffmann and Hobhouse LJJ agreed) adopted a rationalist stance in stating that: 'Public concern is, of course … a material consideration … But, if in the end that public concern is not justified, it cannot be conclusive. If it were, no industrial development – indeed very little development of any kind – would ever be permitted' (p. 95). In contrast, in *Newport*, which involved public perception of risk from a proposed chemical waste treatment plant, Aldous LJ stated that perceived fears, even though they were not soundly based upon scientific or logical fact, were a relevant planning consideration and, further, that 'a perceived fear by the public can in appropriate (perhaps rare) occasions be a reason for refusing planning permission'.[91] As Hilson puts it, 'we are therefore left with the situation where we have two conflicting Court of Appeal decisions, *Gateshead* and *Newport*, the former representing a rationalist position and the latter a populist one' (p. 1640).

For Hilson, at issue is the legal status of Planning Policy Guidance Note 8 on telecommunications which addresses the issue of public concern. He notes in particular the apparent contradiction between the following paragraphs from this guidance note.

> 29. Health considerations and public concern can in principle be material considerations in determining applications for planning permission and prior approval. Whether such matters are material in a particular case is ultimately a matter for the courts. It is for the decision-maker (usually the local planning authority) to determine what weight to attach to such considerations in any particular case.
>
> 30. However, it is the Government's firm view that the planning system is not the place for determining health safeguards. It remains central Government's responsibility to decide what measures are necessary to protect public health. In the Government's view, if a proposed mobile phone base station meets the ICNIRP (International Commission on Non-Ionising Radiation) guidelines for public exposure it should not be necessary for a local planning authority, in processing an application for planning permission or prior approval, to consider further the health aspects and concerns about them.[92]

Having reviewed this guidance, Chris Hilson then discusses in detail a new generation of cases, locating each within the opposing camps.[93] He concludes:

> tensions remain within the case law between rationalist and populist perspectives. One line of case law states that public perceptions of risk cannot be conclusive unless they are objectively justified. The other states that public fears or concerns, even if they go against the scientific grain, can justify the refusal of planning permission. However, the gap between the two should not be overstated. Under a strict rationalist approach, planning authorities are entitled to ignore completely public perceptions of risk that are not objectively justified.

---

[91] *Newport CBC* v. *Secretary of State for Wales* [1998] JPL 377, p. 384.

[92] PPG 8, *Telecommunications*, paras. 29–30.

[93] See, in particular, *Trevett* v. *Secretary of State for Transport, Local Government and the Regions and Others* [2002] EWHC Admin 2696, labelled a 'populist' decision, and *T Mobile (UK) Ltd* v. *First Secretary of State* [2004] EWHC Admin 1713, deemed to be a more 'rationalist' judgment.

However, even under more populist decisions such as *Trevett* [2002] EWHC Admin 2696 – while they cannot ignore them entirely, planning authorities are, it seems, entitled to have regard to the extent to which the perceived health risks are objectively justified in deciding what weight to attribute to them. Even within the populist camp, the circumstances in which public concern will justify a refusal of planning permission are thus likely to be rare. Taking mobile phone masts as a specific example, such circumstances might include: where a suitable, alternative site which would have raised less in the way of public concern, was not included; where the developers have failed to self-certify that the International Commission on Non-Ionising Radiation (ICNIRP) standards have been complied with; and where public concern provides an additional support for a refusal which is predominantly on other grounds such as visual amenity. It is difficult to see how those in the rationalist camp could possibly disagree with public concern being taken into account in these circumstances, even if it is not objectively justified.

A further issue raised by the Independent Expert Group on Mobile Phones (the Stewart Report (2000)), discussed by Ray Kemp,[94] is that even though people's health may not be at risk from the radiation emitted from base stations, the threats to amenity and property values, coupled with frustration with the exclusion and disempowerment created by the planning process, can have negative effects on people's health and well-being:[95]

Although it seems highly unlikely that the low levels of RF (radio frequency) radiation from base stations would have significant, direct adverse effects on health, the possibility of harm from exposures insufficient to cause important heating of tissues cannot yet be ruled out with confidence. Furthermore, the anxieties that some people feel when this uncertainty is ignored can *in themselves* affect their well-being [emphasis added].[96]

The Independent Group recommended that a precautionary approach should be adopted by planning bodies until further scientific information is available and that the subject of siting phone masts should continue to be reviewed.

## 5 Conclusions

Several policy strands currently exist in planning, some of which are pulling in a different direction: speed and predictability; enhanced localised participation; and sustainable development. The expression of a mix of different objectives (or less formally articulated ideologies) is not unfamiliar in planning, as Healey has noted:

The planning tradition is a curious one, built up through a mixture of evangelism, formal institutional practice, scientific knowledge and, increasingly, academic development. It represents a continual effort to interrelate conceptions of the qualities and social dynamics of places with

---

[94] Ray Kemp, 'Perceived Risk as a Material Consideration: The Case of Telecom Development' [2003] *Journal of Planning and Environmental Law* 13, p. 16.
[95] The Stewart Report, para. 6.45.     [96] *Ibid.*, para. 6.44.

notions of the social processes of 'shaping places'. As John Friedmann[97] has repeatedly pointed out, it oscillates in its emphasis between a radical, transformative intention, and a role in maintaining the way cities function and governance works. This leads to an ambiguous relation to the social context of planning work. (p. 7)

The current primacy of sustainable development in planning may be explained by this familiar ability of planning to accommodate competing objectives by having regard to different policy areas in plan making and when making determinations about the grant of planning permission. By including local plans on a wide range of policy areas in the local development plan portfolio, the spatial planning system introduced by the 2004 Act formally extends the scope of the town and country planning system beyond land use and development, to all policy areas having spatial impacts. The expectation is that planners and members of the public and interest groups may thereby better appreciate the inter-relation and 'knock-on' effects of different policy areas and make judgments about land use and development in the light of these. The legislation and implementing regulations are now in place, but there is still some uncertainty about the nature and influence of the supplementary documents on policy areas other than land use. However, even at this stage it is quite clear that the reform of the system to introduce broad, spatial, considerations to plan making is a conceptual leap in planning law and policy, akin to that taken in environmental law with the onset of the system of integrated pollution control in 1990.[98] We conclude that the law and policy relating to land is now defined by a new developmental phase of integrated spatial planning, to add to those discussed in the previous chapter, pp. 494–8.

The inclusion of a range of policy areas looks set to extend further the range of legal instruments used in the planning system because policy areas such as transport, energy and waste tend to be shaped by social and cultural factors which are not easily controlled by licensing regimes. The continuing use and strengthening of economic incentives in the form of the new provisions for 'planning contributions', discussed above, pp. 510–11, provide an example of this. We further locate this form of instrument in the context of nature conservation in Chapter 16, pp. 677–80.

We are also increasingly seeing the use of procedural mechanisms, such as the statement of community involvement, sustainability appraisal, and environmental assessment (incorporating environmental impact assessment and strategic environmental assessment) in planning. In particular, environmental assessment provides a mechanism for integration between different regulatory regimes, most obviously planning and pollution control, as well as providing additional avenues for public participation. This suggests that an integration of

---

[97] John Friedmann, *Retracking America* (Anchor Press, 1973) and *Planning in the Public Domain* (Princeton University Press, 1987).

[98] See, for example, Michael Purdue, 'Integrated Pollution Control: A Coming of Age of Environmental Law?' (1991) 54 *Modern Law Review* 534.

*legal controls* is taking place, alongside the process of policy integration in decision making. We discuss these aspects of environmental assessment further in the next chapter.

## 6 Further reading

An invaluable starting point is Sweet and Maxwell's *Encyclopedia of Planning* (looseleaf, updated monthly), which includes annotated legislation and policy documents. Quite simply the best book on British planning is Barry Cullingworth and Vincent Nadin, *Town and Country Planning in the UK* (Routledge, 2003), now in its thirteenth edition. This combines detailed attention to planning policy with broad overviews of political and legal developments and a remarkably useful index of official publications. In a similar style, Barry Cullingworth's *Planning in the USA* provides useful points of comparison with the British planning system (Routledge, 1997). Yvonne Rydin's *Urban and Environmental Planning in the UK* (Macmillan, 2003) provides an accessible account of the major historical phases, and the theoretical, economic and political influences on planning (including from the European Union), creating a book which skilfully combines theory and practice. Mark Pennington's *Planning and the Political Market: Public Choice and the Politics of Government Failure* (Athlone Press, 2000) is a radical reinterpretation of the British town and country planning system from a public-choice perspective and provides a close critique of 'collaborative planning'.

On participation in planning, see John Forester, *The Deliberative Practitioner: Encouraging Participatory Planning Processes* (MIT, 2000), which combines theory and practice on participation and is written using stories to illustrate examples of practical deliberation. Also relevant are the discussions on 'Deliberative Democracy' (by James Meadowcroft) and 'Civic Environmentalism' (by John DeWitt) in *Environmental Governance Reconsidered*, edited by Robert Durant, Daniel Fiorino and Rosemary O'Leary (MIT, 2004). On the issue of weight to be attributed to the public's perception of risk, see Neil Stanley's article, 'Public Concern: The Decision-Makers' Dilemma' [1998] *Journal of Planning and Environmental Law* 919. Finally, James Simmie's collection of papers on a seemingly intractable planning problem, *Planning London* (UCL Press, 1994), analyses from a land use perspective many of the areas now brought within the scope of the planning system, such as employment, transport and housing.

# 14

## Environmental Assessment

### 1 Introduction

In this chapter we consider a different technique of environmental protection from those discussed so far: environmental assessment. As a *procedural* requirement that the likely effects of policies, plans and projects be taken into account before authorisation is granted, environmental assessment is strikingly different from substantive and prescriptive measures, which have until recently made up the bulk of modern environmental law. A type of assessment now pervades most environmental decision making. The *form* of environmental assessment has also been appropriated for use in areas which are not usually defined as 'environmental', for example in determining the likely impact (in social and economic terms) of a piece of proposed legislation, or the possible effects of changes to family structures.

The remarkable evolution of *environmental* assessment as a foundation for decision making reflects many of the developments in environmental law that we have discussed throughout this book – the development of integrated and preventive methods of control, the fostering of responsibility (or stewardship) for the environment, and the growing acceptance of the validity of pre-emptive or even precautionary measures. Environmental assessment also increasingly provides a vehicle for enhancing public participation in environmental decision making. The hopeful expectation is that this encourages some qualitative comment on the suitability of particular projects or policies capable of supporting, balancing or even countering scientific information about possible effects on the environment which has traditionally made up the bulk of information fed into decision making procedures as we discuss in Chapter 1, pp. 12–34. This movement in favour of public participation has been interpreted as a triumph of participatory democracy over the technocentric roots of environmental assessment, a point we return to when considering the evolution of environmental assessment in the form of the Environmental Impact Assessment (EIA) Directive in the European Union (EU) (pp. 568–97).

In terms of land use, environmental assessment provides a conceptual and practical bridge between pollution controls, which made up the subject of Part IV, and controls over the use and development of land, considered in

Chapter 13. As such it is an important practical example of the realisation of the principle of integration. We particularly discuss the place of environmental assessment in the planning system and the implications of this, for both planning procedures and the future evolution of environmental assessment. Whilst the potential role of planning in protecting the environment might be realised through the use of environmental assessment, as we discuss in this chapter the technique is also capable of being used by developers or policy makers to publicise and seek legitimacy for certain projects and policies. We consider that opportunities exist for the environmental assessment process to operate in favour of the proponent of a project, whether public or private. In this respect we refer specifically to the case of the Kentish Flats wind farm project, the environmental statement for which was used, in part, to present 'The Need for the Project' (see pp. 563–7).

Environmental assessment has undergone a considerable expansion of its remit – from development projects (environmental impact assessment) to plans, programmes and policies (strategic environmental assessment). This reflects an expansion of the scale of concerns in environmental law so that the measure of environmental planning now extends far beyond the confines of an individual parcel of property, and the traditional conception of geographical boundaries in law. This has taken place in stages: in early planning law the focus of regulation, the unit of planning, was the building which, as we outlined in Chapter 12, was made subject to quite precise and onerous building regulations in order to ensure rudimentary sanitation. The later requirement that local plans be drawn up which embraced broader concerns and allowed for regulation on a larger, though still local, scale extended the purview of planning (see pp. 470–9). Contemporary environmental assessment has further enlarged the scale of concerns by requiring the cumulative impacts of development, and alternative sites for development, to be taken into account as relevant or material considerations in decision making.

There is now a legal base, not just for project-based environmental assessment (the EU's EIA Directive)[1], but more wide-ranging assessment of plans and programmes (though, notably, not policy) in the form of the Directive on Strategic Environmental Assessment (the SEA Directive).[2] In this chapter we follow this progression, considering first environmental impact assessment by focussing upon the EIA Directive, and then the SEA Directive. In these legislative contexts we examine the margins of discretion available to Member States, the nature of the outcome of decision making procedures governed by environmental assessment (a key question being whether this procedural

---

[1] Directive 85/337/EEC on the assessment of the effects of certain public and private projects on the environment OJ/1985/L 175/40 as amended.

[2] Directive 2001/42/EC on the assessment of the effects of certain plans and programmes on the environment OJ 2001 L 197/30 (see Appendix III) and the Draft Protocol on Strategic Environmental Assessment to the Convention on Environmental Impact Assessment in a Transboundary Context, Kiev, May 2003 (Appendix V).

mechanism has influenced the *substance* of decision making), as well as the practical problem of how to secure public participation, particularly in the difficult case of 'revived permissions' (see pp. 587–90). We also consider the suitability of environmental assessment, particularly strategic environmental assessment, as a means of putting into effect the concept of sustainable development.

The logical conclusion of this widespread use of assessment is a form of 'sustainability analysis' which, as its name suggests, significantly broadens out the scope of assessment to take in social and economic, as well as environmental, factors (below, pp. 601–4). Although clearly in line with the demands of sustainable development, this form of assessment provides a procedure by which environmental protection issues may be weighted, and possibly traded-off, against social and economic factors. We finish by exploring a number of future paths for environmental assessment – the development of post-assessment monitoring and the digitalisation (and free distribution) of environmental information collected in the course of the environmental assessment process.

First, though, we explore the underlying premises of environmental assessment and the concept of environmental assessment as a legal technique which occupies the regulatory ground between 'command and control' approaches and more indirect forms of regulation such as negotiated agreements, financial incentives and management systems.

## 2 The positive idea of environmental assessment: changing the conditions and nature of decision making

As mentioned above, environmental assessment is a means of drawing together expert and public opinion of a project's or policy's environmental effects and ensuring that this information is taken into account by decision makers *before* a decision is made. The conceptual premise of environmental assessment is that introducing information about the effects of development into a decision making process encourages an informed choice to be made between environmental and other objectives, possibly resulting in less environmentally harmful decisions. Changing the rules governing the generation and use of knowledge in this way is thought also to change the intellectual and political culture of decision making so that decision makers become generally more aware of the environmental consequences of their decisions. As Liam Cashman puts it, environmental assessment is engaged in 'directing change',[3] or reorienting decision making towards more environmentally favourable outcomes.

---

[3] Liam Cashman, 'Environmental Impact Assessment: A Major Instrument in Environmental Integration' in Marco Onida (ed.), *Europe and the Environment: Legal Essays in Honour of Ludwig Krämer* (Europa, 2004), p. 90.

This conceptual basis of environmental assessment relies upon a set of presumptions that the causes and effects of harm can be predicted and that the significance of these effects can be measured. This idea of accurate prediction can be traced to the development in the eighteenth century of methods of collection, measurement and analysis in the fields of time measurement, astrological observation, anatomy, navigation, chemical substance analysis and mathematics, all of which took place in the scientific and intellectual climate of the Enlightenment. The impetus for the development of each of these areas was the idea of nature as observable, which was itself an idea based on dualism – a belief in the fundamental separation between man and nature, mind and matter, subject and object. The claim of accurate prediction which underlies environmental assessment, and other methods of evaluation, is frequently challenged because it is now recognised that the effects of change on complex ecological systems are not well understood. For example pollutants might accumulate, inter-relate and react in ways which are not easily foreseeable or capable of being accurately 'modelled'. That said, the (albeit imperfect) predictive element of environmental assessment also means that it is capable of operating as a precautionary measure because it encourages the consideration of the likely environmental effects of a project or policy in advance of these going ahead. The *ratio legis* for environmental assessment is therefore firmly rooted in risk assessment and risk avoidance. This emphasis on risk assessment underlines that, although governed by law, environmental assessment is an archetypal interdisciplinary technique: it relies upon diverse scientific methods – ecological science, botany, engineering – but its main purpose is to contribute to what are essentially political planning procedures.

## (a) Environmental assessment as a regulatory technique

### (i) Procedure/self-regulation

Environmental assessment possesses several key regulatory characteristics, the primary one of which is that it is procedural in nature, setting requirements for the style and structure of decision making, rather than containing specific standards. The element of legal control is broadly indirect: environmental assessment provides a conduit by which information may enter decision making procedures, but, in theory at least, it will not determine the outcomes of these procedures. This means that, should an environmental assessment establish that significant environmental harm will ensue from a particular development or project, this will be taken into account, but will not necessarily lead to a refusal of development consent for a project, or a policy being abandoned.

As a procedural mechanism, environmental assessment may be considered a response to some of the inadequacies identified with sectoral and direct, or 'command and control', forms of regulation (Chapter 11, pp. 417–21), which have frequently sought to achieve some prior specified standard. But neither does environmental assessment fall easily into the category of 'alternative' or

and individuals.[4] We consider these arguments and the future development of environmental assessment to facilitate this below (pp. 604–8). In the following extract Bregman and Jacobson discuss the opportunities for institutionalised coordination between 'regulated entities' (developers – whether public or private), regulators and 'regulatory beneficiaries' representing the public or public interest via the mechanism of environmental performance review.

### Eric Bregman and Arthur Jacobson, 'Environmental Performance Review: Self-Regulation in Environmental Law' in Gunther Teubner, Lindsey Farmer and Declan Murphy (eds.), *Environmental Law and Ecological Responsibility: The Concept and Practice of Ecological Self-Organisation* (Wiley, 1994), pp. 227–30

The environmental review process constitutes self-regulation in that the regulated entity has input into and participation in determining the scope, methodology, and standards for defining impacts, and mitigation. It is of utmost importance that the regulated entity initiates project proposals, and typically it is also responsible for environmental data gathering, analysis and presentation. As in self-audits, the regulated entity is responsible for providing information to the government. Trusting data-gathering to regulated entities alters the balance of power between regulatory and regulated entities in favour of the regulated entities. Involvement of the regulator 'on the ground floor' of a project also alters the balance of power, this time in favour of the regulator.

Environmental review clarifies the fact that regulatory beneficiaries play a role in self-regulation too. The only difference between regulatory beneficiaries and regulated entities is that regulation, in formal terms, does not purport to regulate the behaviour of regulatory beneficiaries, even though their behavior may be affected, often by legal compulsion. Regulatory beneficiaries may play as active a role in environmental review as regulated entities, sometimes even sharing the task of formulation of project proposals.

…

Environmental review can be looked at as forcing the co-ordination of interests: the government, regulated entities, and regulatory beneficiaries must go through the stipulated processes which force them to interact and co-ordinate their interests with respect to a proposed action. While courts are reluctant to substitute their judgment for the results of that co-ordination, they are not at all slow to intervene where the co-ordination process is flawed or incomplete. The environmental review process is a matrix, the purpose of which is to co-ordinate these interests.

The process is futile, however, if the government does not pay attention to the input it receives, or fails to look at concerns which are otherwise brought to its attention. In consequence, the courts have evolved the 'hard look' doctrine, which holds that a necessary part of the process is that government takes a 'hard look' at the relevant environmental issues

---

[4]  Daniel Farber, 'Bringing Environmental Assessment into the Digital Age' in Jane Holder and Christopher Campbell-Holt (eds.), *Taking Stock of Environmental Assessment Law, Policy and Practice* (Cavendish Routledge, 2007).

before taking action. Sloppily applied, this can blur the line between courts imposing their own substantive views as to the desirability of a particular government action and the enforcing of the process of coordinating the various interests concerned. In principle, though, it should not.

The environmental assessment form and the EIS [Environmental Impact Statement] appear to be completely novel legal devices. Nowhere else, in our understanding, does the regulated entity tell the regulator what the problem is and how to solve it, with the regulatory beneficiaries looking over everyone's shoulder and also giving their opinion as to the nature of the problem and appropriate solutions.

The EIS provides the material for a case law development, reminiscent of the role played by written opinions in common law. Agency decisions that would otherwise be protected by 'informality' are subject to review by the courts of whether their actions were arbitrary or capricious. The process goes further than common law, which focusses on adjusting rights between individual private parties as regulated entities and as regulatory beneficiaries. It needs also to be said that it shares with common law the fact that the process itself can be burdensome, time-consuming and expensive, and sometimes out of proportion to the ultimate benefits.

This account gives a good idea of the complexity of environmental assessment in terms of the interests – public and private – that are at stake and which are seemingly coordinated in the course of the assessment process. This coordination takes place particularly by giving the public the opportunity to comment on the developer's presentation of the likely effects of a project and thus 'formulate a public interest, that is informed by and is an expression of private interests', as Bregman and Jacobson put it. It is exactly the novelty and complexity of environmental assessment as a regulatory form (combined with some political intransigence) that is responsible for the difficulties which have arisen in the United Kingdom (as well as elsewhere) in implementing environmental impact assessment procedures developed by the European Union.[5]

Academics have clearly tried to typify the regulatory character of environmental assessment. This task is complicated by the fact that the procedure is commonly embedded within more traditional regulatory regimes such as the development consent (licensing) procedure for land use (discussed in Chapters 12 and 13). In this context, for example, an environmental impact assessment procedure must be conducted when certain projects (those with the greatest propensity to result in environmental damage) are the subject of an application for development consent. If an assessment is not carried out in such circumstances, any subsequent grant of development consent will be invalid. In settings such as this, the transformative and 'subversive' potential of environmental assessment has provided fertile ground for deep-rooted clashes with the

---

[5] See, e.g., the cases of 'revived permissions', below, pp. 587–90, as discussed in greater detail by Jane Holder, *Environmental Assessment: The Regulation of Decision Making* (Oxford University Press, 2004), Ch. 2.

defining characteristics of English legal culture – deference to discretion exercised by 'professionals' and government bodies, protection of private rights and semantic textual analysis – of the kind described by John Alder in an important paper written in the early 1990s on the implementation of the EIA Directive.[6]

Whilst John Alder presented environmental assessment procedures as originally posing a considerable challenge to legal culture as narrowly defined, the judicial branch of the legal system has now more fully accommodated the demands of environmental assessment procedures, particularly in terms of upholding rights of participation (as we discuss further below, pp. 583–7). Environmental assessment now permeates many other legal and quasi-legal arenas such as planning departments, central government policy making units, and even the work of the European Commission's directorates-general (on which, see below, pp. 601–4), by governing the way in which policy is framed and decisions are made. This incursion into policy and decision making (brought about when formal environmental assessment rules were introduced in the United Kingdom in 1988 in order to implement the EC's EIA Directive) was at first inimical to the policy presumption in favour of development and freedom of action which prevailed in the entrepreneurial period of planning (see Chapter 12, pp. 489–94), but has now generally altered the climate of decision making within and beyond land use planning, in favour of taking into account the effects of development on the environment, even in cases in which environmental assessment rules do not strictly apply.

## (ii) Anticipation/integration

In terms of its regulatory character, environmental assessment is also an inherently pre-emptive or anticipatory procedure, providing information about potential impacts *before* a final decision is taken (most commonly at the authorisation stage of planning procedures). This offers the possibility of imposing conditions about the siting of development and the mitigation of harmful environmental effects before harm occurs. If the environmental assessment procedure is not followed, as well as any subsequent grant of planning permission being invalid, enforcement action may be taken even though harm to the environment may not have arisen. The anticipatory control exercised by environmental assessment relies upon it requiring the developer to demonstrate that a proposed project is acceptable in environmental terms at the planning stage and, if that is not the case, to set out the ways in which negative effects will be mitigated, and/or losses compensated for. Any such duty on the developer to take account of the environmental effects of a proposal not only interferes with the 'right to develop', mentioned above, but also encourages a general perception of development as potentially environmentally harmful. This type of

---

[6] John Alder, 'Environmental Assessment – The Inadequacies of Law' in Jane Holder, Pauline Lane, Kevin Anderson and Ute Collier (eds.), *Perspectives on the Environment: Interdisciplinary Research in Action* (Avebury, 1993).

control contrasts markedly with forms of regulation which specify environmental quality standards or emission limits and which, typically, can only be enforced *after* the standard has been infringed or the limit exceeded and, commonly, after a harmful incident has occurred.

A related characteristic of environmental assessment as a form of regulation is that, in theory at least, it encourages an awareness of pollutants moving between environmental media by establishing procedures for integrated policy and decision making. This was novel to the United Kingdom's regulatory approach until the establishment of the Integrated Pollution Control in 1990 (see Chapter 8, pp. 356–7). The general approach had been to control pollution by industrial sector, as with the Alkali Acts, or by environmental medium, for example the Rivers (Prevention of Pollution) Act 1951. When pollution problems are approached in this manner – as problems of air, water or land – the solution is usually to move the pollutant to the least-protected parts of the environment. In contrast, integrated systems of pollution control potentially allow alternative processes and products to be judged in the light of all the possible paths or cycles of pollutants in the environment. Environmental harm might therefore be prevented by identifying possible changes to be made to the products or processes at an early stage in the authorisation procedure, thus reinforcing the element of anticipatory control. The EIA Directive provides a good example of the integrated nature of environmental assessment: Art. 3 requires the identification, description and assessment of the direct and indirect effects of a project on 'human beings, fauna and flora, soil, water, air, climate and the landscape, material assets and the cultural heritage' and, importantly, the interaction between these various factors.

As well as advancing a form of integrated pollution control by generally requiring a *cross-media* assessment of likely environmental harm (the similarities between Integrated Pollution Prevention and Control and EIA are well acknowledged[7]), in strategic forms of environmental assessment this integrated assessment is further extended to take into account various policy sectors and their inter-relation (the *cross-policy* effects). As we discuss below, this expansion introduces greater complexity into the process, particularly in terms of securing public participation, but it also brings environmental assessment closer to the idea of sustainable development.

### (iii) Participatory democracy and protest

In explicitly providing for some form of (initially limited) public participation in environmental decision making, the EIA Directive has been considered the first important example of EU-derived 'environmental rights legislation'.[8] Damian Chalmers, for example, argues that in adopting the EIA Directive the

---

[7] See, e.g., United Kingdom Environmental Law Association (UKELA), *Overlaps in the Requirements for Environmental Assessment* (UKELA, 1993).

[8] Cashman, 'Environmental Impact Assessment', p. 66.

European Community (EC) created a space between the state and its citizens in national territories.[9] Within this space the Directive established new political structures and forms of engagement by granting the public a formal right to be informed and the opportunity to express an opinion on the desirability in environmental terms of the developments covered by the Directive, and this intruded directly on the Member States' traditional ability to control political decision making. This view is predicated upon an optimistic idea of the transformative potential of environmental assessment, particularly in terms of delivering a form of local democracy in decision making.

The practice of environmental assessment is somewhat different. For example, we have presented environmental assessment as an inherently interdisciplinary exercise. However, this does not necessarily mean that a range of values and viewpoints are fully represented by the environmental assessment process. In terms of information gathering, the tendency is to rely upon eliciting quantitative information about the 'baseline' or existing environmental condition of a site and then use modelling techniques to extrapolate from this, producing what has been described as 'cold analysis'.[10] In particular, the developer's environmental statement tends to present this information in an objective, scientific manner, often with very little space for a range of (conflicting) opinions, which effectively masks the subjective opinions and values inevitably held by developers, consultants and scientists working on the assessment process. The gap between the ideal and practical experience of participation (as well as the current lack of opportunity for third parties to contest decisions in the planning system, discussed in Chapter 13, pp. 518–21) is bound to produce dissatisfaction amongst participants of environmental assessment processes. The question is whether a fundamentally technicist approach to decision making, reflected in the environmental assessment process, is capable of being overcome. Hugh Wilkins, for example, considers that the expression of more subjective views, or 'warmer analysis', is possible, and indeed necessary as a matter of furthering sustainable development, and, furthermore, that subjectivity is an inevitable element of the assessment process.

### Hugh Wilkins, 'The Need for Subjectivity in Environmental Law' (2003) 23 *EIA Review* 401, pp. 401–13

The values of the people engaged in an environmental impact assessment (EIA) play a significant role in its results due to the considerable subjective decision making upon which EIA is based. From screening projects to final decision making, discretion has a prominent role in determining the methodological and practical results of the process. Moreover, the central role of prediction in EIA makes subjectivity unavoidable due to politicised evaluations,

---

[9]  Damian Chalmers, 'Inhabitants in the Field of EC Environmental Law' in Paul Craig and Grainne de Búrca (eds.), *The Evolution of EU Law* (Oxford University Press, 1999), p. 673.
[10]  Jonathan Wiener, 'Better Regulation' (2006) 59 *Current Legal Problems*.

narrow boundary setting, data gaps and simplified assumptions. The attitudes and values of the actors involved in the process are critical to determining the results achieved …

The subjective element in EIA aids rather than hinders the process. If the main purposes of conducting an EIA are to advance sustainable development and to encourage legitimate decision making through the use of transparency and public participation, then subjectivity and predictive inaccuracy are not problems, but elements to promote and engage the process itself. A satisfactory decision at the end of the specific EIA is not the only goal of the process. As a forum in which the public, proponents and regulators deliberate on the design and implementation of development plans, the creation of discourse around the pertinent issues at stake is also an important result. The discourse that is nurtured through EIA influences the values people hold regarding the environment and their communities. It promotes the development of values that foster greater personal and social responsibility and has the capacity to increase the importance of long-term environmental considerations in decision making. Through subjectivity accompanied by public participation and discourse, EIA can produce more environmentally sustainable assessment decisions. Thus the legitimacy of EIA should not only be judged based on its assessment qualities, but rather on its potential to achieve the goals of sustainable development.

…

To effectively address long-term and community issues, people must understand environmental problems through social learning and support the mechanisms used to address these problems. The strengths of EIA as such a mechanism lie in its qualities of public participation, transparency, promotion of discourse, social learning and transformation of values. The degree to which these strengths are recognised depends on the willingness of proponents, regulators and the public to cooperate and assert the necessary efforts to achieve results that can have beneficial long-term effects. Effective public deliberation and decision-making will only occur where social conditions and institutional arrangements foster the public use of reason allowing free and open dialogue. EIA can provide these conditions. For an EIA system to facilitate free and open dialogue and promote discourse and sustainable development, the process must reflect local and cultural attitudes to decision making, be sensitive to the attitudes and opinions of the people potentially affected by the project, address the needs of future generations and provide a forum for social learning. Provided that these conditions are met, EIA can assist in promoting community decisions and understandings and over time may affect the values held by individuals as they are exposed to new experiences and beliefs. However, changes in values do not occur overnight. They require continual discourses to develop and evolve beyond the short timeframe of an EIA. EIA provides a rare starting point.

As Wilkins describes, securing cultural change or changing the values held by people is a long-term process. Those participating in environmental assessment procedures as a means of challenging a particular development are likely to be disappointed in the short term because, as we discuss further below (pp. 563–7), environmental assessment is equally capable of giving developers the opportunity to present their proposed project in favourable terms. That said, environmental assessment may also provide an avenue for popular protest, particularly because long delays can result from an environmental assessment process being required in cases in which it should have been carried out but was not. This describes the strategic use of environmental assessment as highlighted by several *causes célèbres* of the British environmental movement, including Twyford Down and Newbury, both of which featured litigation with environmental assessment at the core.[11] Such high-profile cases are now more infrequent because most major developers are only too aware of their obligations under environmental assessment law, and increasingly use the participatory and consultative elements of the environmental assessment process as opportunities to iron out in advance any areas which are likely to be particularly controversial to a local community, perhaps by their offering a package of 'environmental compensation'.

### (b) Operationalising sustainable development via environmental assessment

The regulatory characteristics of environmental assessment described above – encouraging environmental responsibility on the part of developers through various self-regulatory mechanisms (especially the compilation of an environmental statement), seeking cross-media and cross-policy integration, and furthering participatory democracy – all suggest that the instrument is a practical manifestation of the principle of sustainable development (see Chapter 6). This was clearly recognised by the World Commission on Environment and Development in the Brundtland Report which considered the environmental assessment of projects and policies as a means to achieve sustainable industrial development, alongside the use of economic instruments.[12] This role was also identified by the international community in the Rio Declaration (1992) which followed the Brundtland Report: 'Environmental Impact Assessment as a national instrument shall be undertaken for proposed activities that are likely to have a significant adverse impact on the environment and are subject to a decision of a competent national authority.'[13]

The International Court of Justice has since reinforced the role of environmental assessment in operationalising sustainable development, as seen particularly in the context of a case brought before it by New Zealand requesting that the Court examine the situation of France conducting a series of

[11] See *Twyford Parish Council* v. *Secretary of State for Transport* (1992) 4 JEL 273, and the clutch of cases on the Newbury by-pass: *Secretary of State for Transport* v. *Haughian* (CA) unreported 27.2.1996, *Goillon*, unreported 12.2.1996, and *Secretary of State for Transport* v. *Fillingham* [1997] Env LR 73. On these cases, see further Holder, *Environmental Assessment*, pp. 222–6.

[12] World Commission on Environment and Development, *Our Common Future* (Oxford University Press, 1987), pp. 221–4.

[13] United Nations Declaration on Environment and Development (Rio Declaration) 31 ILM 874 (1992), Principle 17.

underground nuclear tests in the Pacific Atolls. New Zealand challenged France's decision to resume these tests on the ground that France was under an obligation in customary international law to conduct an environmental impact assessment of the potential effects of this on the marine environment before carrying out the tests.[14] In a series of *dissenting* judgments (the majority of the Court took a conservative and legalistic approach to the request, distinguishing between atmospheric and underground nuclear tests), environmental assessment was closely associated with the achievement of both sustainable development and the precautionary principle. In particular, Judge Weeramantry describes the 'principle' of environmental assessment as gathering sufficient strength and international acceptance to justify the court taking notice of it. Judge Palmer pays particular attention to the role of environmental assessment in risk analysis, without which the paradigm of sustainable development could not be achieved.

The linking of environmental assessment with sustainable development in this manner has had the important effect of expanding the scope of forms of assessment. Originally environmental assessment was considered to assist mainly with pollution control (though also habitat and landscape concerns) through informing decisions about siting industrial development, and thus performing a technicist function in environmental law. It is now recognised as having a far broader role in influencing decision makers to take account of the *quality* of development and its effects upon the conservation of natural resources, as well of course as still influencing the location of development. In the European Union this expansion of environmental assessment fits well with the adoption of sustainable development as a guiding principle, informing the formation and fulfilment of all policies pursued by the Union,[15] not just those with an environmental purview. Since sustainable development is predicated upon integrating environmental considerations in decision making in exactly the manner supposedly achieved by environmental assessment instruments, this suggests some inevitability about the remit of environmental assessment being further extended (as sustainability analysis) and it similarly being placed at the centre of policy making, as we discuss further below (pp. 601–4).

As well as relating environmental assessment and sustainable development through aspects of regulatory theory, ecological science offers further reasons for this apparent alliance.

---

[14] *New Zealand* v. *France* ICJ, 22 September 1995.

[15] Article 2 EC Treaty, as amended, states: 'The Community shall have as its task, by establishing a common market and an economic and monetary union and by implementing common policies or activities … to promote throughout the Community a harmonious and balanced sustainable development of economic activities … a high level of protection and improvement of the quality of the environment'. Article 2 Treaty on European Union similarly states that the Union shall 'promote economic and social progress to achieve balanced and sustainable development'.

## Holder, *Environmental Assessment*, p. 60

The association of environmental assessment with the ideas of ecological modernisation and sustainable development may be further explained by the influence of ecological science, and the changing paradigms within the discipline.[16] Early environmental assessment was held up as an example of 'ecological science in action', synthesised with law in the United States' National Environmental Policy Act (NEPA) 1969. The conception of ecology at the time of this enactment was one based upon the dominant paradigm of homeostasis or equilibrium between organisms and the environment – a 'balance of nature' – which could be maintained only by resistance to change.[17] Although not prescribing a particular environmental standard, environmental assessment was a culturally significant evocation of the importance of such ecological concerns in decision making, so that the fairly strict environmental assessment requirements contained within the 1969 Act (alongside the development of nature reserves, biodiversity preservation strategies, and the setting of emission standards) suggest the absorption of some of this thinking into environmental law. In the meantime, the equilibrium paradigm underwent a revolution, with the result that ecological science now stresses change and instability of ecosystems, and no longer upholds as ideal the withdrawal of humankind from nature. This 'New Ecology' recognises instead the inevitability of interactions between humans and the natural environment,[18] and thus the management of ecosystems, rather than their preservation, or restoration. The reformed perspective of ecology inevitably informed the evolution of the political concept of sustainable development by providing a scientific basis for it, and the associated drive for the integration of environmental factors in all decision making. Bosselman and Tarlock sum this up: 'Environmentalism's initial objective was to make environmental quality a relative quality to be considered. This battle has now largely been won and the movement's focus has shifted to the assured comprehensive and long-term integration, if not dominance, of this perspective in all resource decision making.'[19] A triumvirate of law, ecology, and politics therefore acted to reconceive environmental assessment as a legal expression of sustainable development, particularly giving practical effect to the more integrative aspects of this concept, so that environmental concerns are taken into account in decision making, but do not (by design) necessarily predominate.

There are clearly strong links between the principle of sustainable development and environmental assessment, particularly so in the case of strategic environmental assessment of policy, plans and programmes (discussed further below, pp. 597–601) which also holds promise as a way of expressing the potentially more radical aspects of sustainable development which might otherwise be suppressed.

---

[16] Fred P. Bosselman and A. Dan Tarlock, 'The Influence of Ecological Science on American Law' (1994) *Chicago-Kent Law Review* 847.     [17] *Ibid.*, p. 866.

[18] This paradigm shift is attributed to several ecologists: Bill MacKibben, *The End of Nature* (Random House, 1989); Daniel B. Botkin, *Discordant Harmonies: A New Ecology for the Twenty-First Century* (Oxford University Press, 1990).

[19] Bosselman and Tarlock, 'The Influence of Ecological Science', p. 872.

### Susan Owens and Richard Cowell, *Land and Limits: Interpreting Sustainability in the Planning Process* (Routledge, 2002), pp. 52–3

Defining and Defending Approaches to Planning for Sustainability

How, then, might we characterise the relationship between environmental assessment and sustainable development? To the extent that it raises the profile of environmental considerations and encourages greener growth there is evidence that assessment makes development 'more sustainable', at least in the weaker sense. More significantly perhaps, in as much as it provides for the more open scrutiny of proposals, environmental assessment has the potential to stimulate learning within and between different groups and to provoke deliberation about what sustainable development should mean. Indeed these might be among the more useful effects of assessment procedures. Rarely, however, has this deliberative or critical framework been highly developed, either in the appraisal of individual applications or plans, or in the institutional arrangements that govern assessment and planning systems alike. SEA [strategic environmental assessment] has particularly interesting implications in this context. In exposing the environmental consequences of wider policies and plans, it might aid those who favour stronger conceptions of sustainability, but for this very reason it is more obviously challenging to the *status quo*. Little surprise, then, that governments have approached strategic assessment with caution, or that they have moved to extend coverage to economic and social issues, potentially neutralising any environmental threat to dominant modes of development.

An important implication of this discussion is that environmental assessment can mobilise different conceptions of sustainability, depending upon the context within which it is applied and what precisely is asked of the technique. The question 'what are the likely impacts of this project, and how can they be mitigated at acceptable cost?' is framed quite differently from one that asks 'what are the environmental implications of alternative ways of meeting this (social or economic) policy objective, and are these implications acceptable?' In the second context, environmental assessment, at the strategic level in particular, could assist in defining environmental capacities. At least it is hard to see how judgments about capacity could be arrived at without an assessment of sorts, or how this process could promote stronger conceptions of sustainability unless serious and irreversible impacts could be deemed unacceptable.

### (c) The 'power to seduce': the Kentish Flats wind farm

The previous discussion suggests that there is much to be gained from environmental assessment in terms of achieving the objectives of sustainable development, at least when looking at the 'big picture' of global environmental politics. Looking more precisely at the *content* of environmental statements, produced by developers who are often eager to present their proposals in a favourable light, gives us reason to adopt a more critical stance. This is because the environmental assessment process is capable of facilitating the balancing (or impression of balancing) of competing interests, rather than securing absolute environmental protection, in a manner which similarly underlies the conceptual inconsistency at the heart of sustainable development – can development ever be sustainable? From this perspective, making developers responsible for reporting the predicted outcomes of development in the form of an environmental statement might confer some type of ecological responsibility or instill them with a degree of environmental forethought, but it also provides them with an opportunity to present the project with an environmental 'gloss'. In such circumstances, the blurring of the line between public and private interests or 'logics', as Ost describes these, becomes important in terms of creating for the developer a 'power to seduce'.[20]

### François Ost, 'A Game Without Rules? The Ecological Self-Organisation of Firms' in Teubner, Farmer and Murphy (eds.), *Environmental Law and Ecological Responsibility*, p. 351

On the one hand there is the logic of 'publicity' with the accent on the public's 'right to information' and the independence of the author of the study whose task is conceived in terms of a 'public service'. On the other, a 'private' logic prevails with the emphasis on the promoter's freedom of enterprise. In this case the procedure is simplified to the extreme and the task of the author takes the form of an enterprise contract. The impact study will then appear as either an additional legal formality to be completed by the entrepreneur or promoter along the obstacle course leading him to secure all the necessary administrative organisation for his project, or else more or less as publicity, intended to calm the broader public's apprehensions and attract the favours of political decision makers. In the first case, by contrast, the study, whose impartiality will be guaranteed, ought to permit both substantive improvements to the project in terms of protection of the environment, or its banning should the balance sheet turn out too negative for ecosystems …

…

In the complex game set up between private interests and public institutions in the framework of our advanced capitalist states, the impact study ought to appear as a phase of relative scientific objectivity, guaranteed by some political impartiality. If the study is the outcome of the responsibility of firms alone, we cannot be sure that this aspect of relative externality has yet been guaranteed.

A practical example of the environmental statement as 'seduction' was produced to support an application for development consent for a wind farm off the north Kent coast (on wind farm policy more generally, see Chapter 17,

---

[20] François Ost, 'A Game Without Rules? The Ecological Self-Organisation of Firms' in Gunther Teubner, Lindsey Farmer and Declan Murphy (eds.), *Environmental Law and Ecological Responsibility: The Concept and Practice of Ecological Self-Organisation* (Wiley, 1994), p. 353.

pp. 699–709). When Global Renewable Energy Partners sought to develop the wind farm, consisting of thirty turbines about 8 km out to sea, an environmental impact assessment was required because, as an 'installation for the harnessing of wind power for energy production (wind farms)', the project exceeded thresholds set in Regulations[21] which implement the EIA Directive. The non-technical summary of the developer's environmental statement detailed 'The Need for the Project'. The language of 'balance' and 'environmental benefits' was also employed by the developer in this document, as well as references to the project contributing to 'the development of a new offshore industry', a point discussed further in Chapter 17. In strict terms, the environmental statement should detail only the predicted (positive and negative) impacts of the proposed project on the environment, including judgments about their significance. The 'balancing' of competing interests should take place when it is being decided whether or not to authorise the development – a decision which should be taken by elected and accountable representatives, as part of a political process. The pre-empting of the decision making process by the developer's statement in this manner risks diluting important information about the environmental effects of the development in a broader assessment of its potential social, economic, and even human health, benefits.

### Global Renewable Energy Partners, *Kentish Flats Environmental Statement* (2002) Non-technical summary and selected paragraphs from the main body of the Statement

Non-technical summary
The Kentish Flats offshore windfarm reflects the need to find alternatives to conventional electricity generation (e.g. oil, gas, nuclear). This is largely stimulated by the global need to reduce the emissions of greenhouse gases in relation to the issue of climate change in ensuring a cleaner, more sustainable future.

...

The Kentish Flats project is one of a first round of 18 offshore developments and will have a significant role to play in helping to achieve the Government targets in relation to climate change and the commitments of the Kyoto Protocol. The Kentish Flats project alone will displace an estimated 8.7 million tonnes of carbon dioxide over its proposed 20 year life time, compared to conventional fossil fuel generation.

...

---

[21] Town and Country Planning (Assessment of Environmental Effects) Regulations 1999 (SI 1999 No. 293) (the EIA Regulations 1999) Sch. 2(3)(i) in cases in which the development involves the installation of more than 2 turbines; or the hub height of any turbine or height of any other structure exceeds 15 metres. Electricity Works (Environmental Impact Assessment) (England and Wales) Regulations 2000 (SI 2000 No. 1927). On the authorisation of wind farms, see further Ch. 17.

1.2. THE IMPACTS OF THE KENTISH FLATS WIND FARM AS A SOURCE OF
RENEWABLE ENERGY

8.2.1 Background

...

In the case of wind farms, the actual development itself provides a wide range of environmental benefits, nationally and globally, because of its important contribution to reducing the emission of greenhouse gases. This in turn brings with it a range of social benefits which are not always associated with development such as cleaner air, potentially healthier populations, reduced risk from sea level rise or climate change and a more sustainable and renewable source of energy generation, as well as the more normal benefits of development such as employment opportunities.

Therefore, in assessing the relative environmental impacts of an offshore wind farm scheme, it is necessary to try to attach a significance of some of these potential benefits of the scheme in order to provide the desired balance of cost against benefit which is at the heart of the EIA process.

This approach is, in fact, embodied in some of the guidance available on the EIA of wind farm development generally and offshore wind farms specifically ...

... Greenpeace in their 2000 report 'North Sea Offshore Wind – A Powerhouse for Europe; Technical Possibilities and Ecological Considerations', identify the need to consider the positive effects on the global environment (e.g. climate) as part of the site specific EIA process.

The following sections provide an overview of these potential environmental benefits arising from the Kentish Flats offshore wind farm and its contribution to the development of a new offshore industry. Greater detail on the economic and social aspects of the development, including details on employment benefits and the economic rating of the potential environmental impacts are presented [elsewhere in the report].

...

**8.2.6 Summary of Positive Impacts of the Kentish Flats as a Source of Renewable Energy**
In summary, the Kentish Flats development will have a number of tangible positive impacts which may be summarised as follows:

- the displacement of up to 8,736,760 tonnes of $CO_2$ over the project life time. Equivalent to almost 6.0% of annual UK $CO_2$ emissions in 1998.
- the supply of clean, renewable sustainable electricity to an equivalent of 100,304 homes.
- a quantifiable and useable contribution to the diversity and security of energy supply.
- a major step in meeting local, regional and national Government policy with regard to energy supply, renewable energy and greenhouse gas emission reductions.
- an important contribution to the vision of sustainable development.
- an important step in the development of a major new UK offshore industry with associated employment opportunities.

The developer further used its preparation of the environmental statement to underline the 'Need For' this particular project by presenting only limited site-specific 'project alternatives'. Taking a broader view of possible alternatives, energy conservation measures and other forms of renewable energy should have been considered under this heading. The consideration of a 'do-nothing' alternative is not strictly required by the EIA Directive but this might usefully have formed part of the statement (and is required by the SEA Directive, discussed below, pp. 599–601).

A more serious variant of the 'power to seduce' is the occurrence of 'pseudo-EIAs'. These are assessments carried out with the single objective of getting a project cleared, irrespective of the true environmental costs. This has been identified as particularly a feature of large infrastructure projects in developing countries, and upon which possibly millions of pounds of foreign investment and aid depend.[22]

## 3 Environmental impact assessment

Having presented the various regulatory dimensions of environmental assessment in an abstract manner, we now consider the specific legislative forms that environmental assessment has taken, paying most attention to EIA, as the longest-standing approach in the European Union (EU), from which other forms of assessment have evolved.

One of the earliest environmental assessment regimes was introduced in 1969 in the United States in the context of a legislative declaration of objectives of environmental policy, which included the co-existence of man and nature in 'productive harmony'. It is a mark of the idealism of the generation of policy makers responsible for this Act that environmental assessment was considered to be a key means of achieving such goals. NEPA required federal agencies (not private developers) formally to document how they considered the environment when making decisions to authorise projects and pursue policies, and to make this information available to the public. Indeed, this last aspect of the Act was considered to reflect a 'populist' argument that public disclosure would lead to political accountability that would compel agencies to curb their most environmentally destructive practices.[23] Federal agencies are still required to include a detailed environmental impact statement in every recommendation or report on proposals for legislation and other major public developments and actions *significantly* affecting the quality of the human environment, including policy decisions. This regime established a template for many other environmental assessment regimes introduced

---

[22] See Prasad Modak and Asit Biswas (eds.), *Environmental Impact Assessment for Developing Countries* (Heinemann, 1999), pp. 240–1, cited in Oren Perez, 'Using Private–Public Linkages to Regulate Environmental Conflicts' (2002) 29 *Journal of Law and Society* 77, p. 94.

[23] Bradley C. Karkkainen, 'Toward a Smarter NEPA: Monitoring and Managing Government's Environmental Performance' (2002) *Columbia Law Review* 903, p. 913.

by international organisations such as the Organisation for Economic Cooperation and Development, the United Nations Environment Programme and the World Health Organisation.

## (a) EIA directive

The operation of environmental assessment procedures in the United States, and the recommended use of the technique by international organisations, stimulated interest in environmental assessment in Europe. Although the idea of a European form of assessment was accepted in principle, in practice the development of an instrument on environmental assessment was compromised by political concerns and interests at the state level, as Ludwig Krämer describes. His insider's account (as a long-serving Commission official) of the period prior to the adoption of the EIA Directive goes a long way to explain the diluted, complex and ambiguous nature of the finished 'product', as well as the many difficulties with its implementation, as experienced by both Member States and the European Commission. In particular, the large degree of discretion reserved for Member States in terms of the type and quantity of projects covered is a direct consequence of the political and territorial sensitivity of the adopting states. We further discuss the nature of discretion under the EIA Directive below (pp. 590–7).

### Ludwig Krämer, 'The Development of Environmental Assessments at the Level of the European Union' in Jane Holder and Donald McGillivray *Taking Stock of Environmental Assessment: Law, Policy and Practice* (Routledge Cavendish, 2007)

Environmental assessments were, at EU level, first announced in 1977, when the European Commission, inspired by legislation in the United States and in France and by a failed attempt in Germany to introduce such assessments, declared that it examined the possibility of proposing legislation, in order to systematically examine the incidences of certain plans and projects on the environment. Having discussed 23 internal draft texts, it made a proposal in 1980 for a directive on the environmental impact assessment of certain public and private projects.

Within the EC Member States, the principle of environmental assessment was hardly contested in general: experts and public opinion agreed that there should be such an assessment, wherever possible, as it was accepted that the environment was fragile. Objections rather came from the different national or regional, general or sectoral administrations that were afraid of losing the power which the monopoly over planning and permitting procedures gave them. Apart from this general aspect, detailed problems influenced the evolution of the discussion. Thus, for example, the *Netherlands* were keen on seeing plans and programmes that affected the environment, also included in the legislative proposal, but met the stiff opposition of the majority of Member States which wanted the field of application of the directive as narrow as possible and limited to projects only. *Denmark* planned to bridge the Oeresund between Denmark and Sweden and did not wish to have an environmental interference in its decision-making process; for that reason, it insisted that projects which had been adopted by Parliamentary decisions in Denmark, should not be covered by the directive. *France* wanted in particular nuclear installations to be excluded from the future legislation. Furthermore, it insisted that in cases, where a project had effects in another Member State, the planning administration should only be allowed to make contacts with the (central) government of that other Member State, but not directly with the citizens of the other Member States; also this attitude was influenced by its nuclear policy. The *United Kingdom* government did not consider it appropriate to legislate at European level, contrary to the opinion of the influential House of Lords. *Germany* was afraid that its existing administrative system which was based on strong administrative permitting procedures, could be affected by the requirement of an environmental impact assessment with public participation.

The Directive was adopted in 1985, after five years of protracted bargaining among Member States. The joint venture of national administrations and the requirement of unanimous decisions led to reducing the Directive's field of application, but in particular to the fixing of the principle of impact assessment, but then leaving a large discretion to the administrations with regard to the details of the procedure, the forms of consultation and the follow up of the impact assessment.

Nicola Staeck, Tanja Malek and Hubert Heinelt have additionally explained that the United States provided the impetus for a particular, idealist, vision of participation in a European form of assessment, whereby third parties, whether individuals, environmental groups or other relevant agencies, might usefully and easily confront both planning authorities and developers with objections and suggestions for better solutions. The idea was that such a high level of participation would foster broad public acceptance of the final decisions.[24] However, they describe that this idealism soon gave way to the traditionally more dominant technocentric approach to decision making so that the EIA Directive was reconceived as a means of securing a better, more *expert* basis for decisions. Note that the authors were writing prior to the adoption in 2003 of the Directive on participation which has since strengthened the EIA Directive's provision for public participation,[25] in line with the Aarhus Convention (see Chapter 3). This aspect of the EIA Directive's development provides a very clear

---

[24]  Nicola Staeck, Tanja Malek and Hubert Heinelt, 'The Environmental Impact Assessment Directive' in Hubert Heinelt, Tanja Malek, Randall Smith and Annette E. Toller (eds.), *European Union Environment Policy and New Forms of Governance: A Study of the Implementation of the Environmental Impact Assessment Directive and the Eco-management and Audit Scheme Regulation in Three Member States* (Ashgate, 2001), p. 33.

[25]  Directive 2003/35/EC providing for public participation in respect of the Drawing up of Certain Plans and Programmes relating to the Environment and Amending with regard to Public Participation and Access to Justice Directives 85/337/EEC and 96/61/EC OJ 2003 L 156/17, discussed further below, pp. 583–6.

example of the apparent dichotomy between expert scientific opinion and the inclusion of a broader range of opinion and values in decision making, discussed more fully in Chapters 1 (pp. 40–7) and 3 and, in the context of planning decisions, in Chapter 13 (pp. 530–45).

### Nicola Staeck, Tanja Malek and Hubert Heinelt, 'The Environmental Impact Assessment Directive' in Hubert Heinelt, Tanja Malek, Randall Smith and Annette E. Toller (eds), *European Union Environment Policy and New Forms of Governance: A Study of the Implementation of the Environmental Impact Assessment Directive and the Eco-management and Audit Scheme Regulation in Three Member States* (Ashgate, 2001), pp. 40–1

#### Between Participatory Democracy and Technocratic Paradigm – The Preframing of Environmental Impact Assessment

...

In the USA there had been and still is an influential discourse community which views the successes of environmental impact assessments in terms of negotiation and debate and participatory processes whereby the perceptions of problems, codes of conduct and individual values can change and perhaps converge. Environmental impact assessments are seen as capable of opening up the prospect of environmental democracy, or, in more general terms, an encouragement of participatory democracy.

Although the participatory dimension within the European EIA debate has played an important role as in the US, nevertheless in Europe the conceptualisation of the EIA Directive has been influenced as much by a technocratic paradigm: 'The technocratic paradigm of EIA is usually linked to a particular view of society's decision making processes: that these are, or should be, comprehensively rational. That is, the view that such processes are, at least ideally devoted to objectively investigating the effects of alternative courses of action and selecting that which has the greatest net benefits for society'.[26] This technocratic paradigm which influenced the EC directive, can be seen to be the consequence of the dominance of development planning ideas in Europe during the early stages of discussion about EIA … [D]evelopment planning was at that time influenced by beliefs in the ability to address social planning issues rationally and to control the implementation of strategies. The planning process was rational as long as it was based on sufficient information, pursued non-contradictory goals and controlled implementation … [T]his could be called the godfather model of planning. It implied a situation where an almighty omniscient being could create a new world by making a clean sweep.

This planning model has been questioned both in terms of its practical implementation as well as in scholarly debate over the last twenty years as both practical experience and scientific findings have shown that it is impossible to collect sufficient information relevant to decision making, given the level of social complexities and interdependencies.

---

[26] John Formby, 'The Politics of Environmental Impact Assessment' (1990) 8 *Impact Assessment Bulletin* 191, p. 191.

> Furthermore, it is difficult to pursue non-contradictory aims and to implement programmes without considering the inevitable conflict of interests and values in the environmental sector.
>
> Nevertheless, this approach is still widely followed both in practice and in the policy debate, not least in relation to environmental impact assessment …

The EIA Directive was the product of the first attempt of the European Community to influence Member States' planning systems. It was highly controversial because the Community had no obvious competence in this area and, by definition, a sovereign state controls its own land which carries great cultural significance. The EIA Directive was superimposed upon existing national or 'indigenous' methods of scrutinising the environmental effects of a development. This illustrates well the inter-relationship and integration of multiple layers of law. A process of exchanging information between Member States' forms of environmental assessment (following the implementation of the EIA Directive) and the EU's model has been a useful one, with information about the Member States' experiences (particularly examples of inadequate implementation) forming the basis for revisions to the EIA Directive in 1997.[27] The preamble to the EIA Directive shows that it was adopted as a means to fulfil many different functions, in accordance with several environmental principles. Article 3 of the Directive sets out the scope of the assessment process.

### Directive 85/337/EEC on the assessment of the effects of certain public and private projects on the environment OJ 1985 L 175/40 as amended by Directive 97/11/EC OJ 1997 L 73/5 and Directive 2003/35/EC on participation OJ 2003 L 156/17 (consolidated version) preamble, Articles 1 and 3

Whereas Council Directive 85/337/EEC of 27 June 1985 on the assessment of the effects of certain public and private projects on the environment aims at providing the competent authorities with relevant information to enable them to take a decision on a specific project in full knowledge of the project's likely significant impact on the environment; whereas the assessment procedure is a fundamental instrument of environmental policy as defined by Article 130r(2) [now Article 174(2) of the Treaty] and of the Fifth Community Programme of Policy and Action in relation to the environment and sustainable development;

Whereas, pursuant to Article 130r(2) of the Treaty, Community policy on the environment is based on the precautionary principle and on the principle that the preventive action should be taken, that environmental damage should as a priority be rectified at source and that the polluter should pay;

…

---

[27] Directive 97/11/EC amending Directive 85/337/EEC OJ 1985 L 73/5.

Whereas projects for which an assessment is required should be subject to a requirement for development consent; whereas the assessment should be carried out before such consent is granted;

Whereas it is desirable to strengthen the provisions concerning environmental impact assessment in a transboundary context to take account of developments at international level;

### Article 1
This Directive shall apply to the assessment of the environmental effects of those public and private projects which are likely to have significant effects on the environment.

...

### Article 3
The environmental impact assessment shall identify, describe and assess in an appropriate manner, in the light of each individual case and in accordance with Articles 4 to 11 [see below], the direct and indirect effects of a project on the following factors:
- human beings, fauna and flora;
- soil, water, air, climate and the landscape;
- material assets and the cultural heritage;
- the interaction between the factors mentioned in the first, second and third indents.

## (b)  Assessment procedure under the EIA directive

On analysing environmental assessment in general, Bregman and Jacobson have commented that 'impact analysis is simple in theory, complex in application'.[28] Such sentiments apply particularly to the environmental assessment procedure as set out in the EIA Directive. This is mainly because the Directive confers a great deal of discretion on decision makers about whether or not to apply the assessment procedure to particular projects, as we discuss further below. But it is also a product of an ambiguity at the heart of the Directive about what actually constitutes an environmental assessment for the purpose of this instrument. Whilst it is reasonably clear that information provided by the developer in the form of an environmental statement is not tantamount to the full assessment procedure envisaged by the Directive (it merely contributes to this), the Directive is vague about the exact nature of this assessment, for example whether there should be a written account of the assessment process, who should undertake this, and whether it should be subject to some form of judicial review. These areas of uncertainty are possibly an unavoidable aspect of procedural mechanisms such as EIA because their aim, to provide an adaptable framework for decision making in a range of different contexts, is a complex

---

[28] Eric Bregman and Arthur Jacobson, 'Environmental Performance Review: Self-Regulation in Environmental Law' in Teubner, Farmer and Murphy (eds.), *Environmental Law and Ecological Responsibility*, p. 224.

and difficult one, particularly when compared to a 'command and control' mechanism requiring compliance with quantified environmental quality standards or emission limits in the case of a specific environmental medium.

### (i) Screening: the selection of projects for environmental assessment

The first stage of the environmental assessment process, commonly referred to as 'screening', involves differentiating between projects that should be made subject to a full environmental assessment process on the basis of the likelihood of significant effects occurring if the project goes ahead and those which are unlikely to have significant adverse effects on the environment and can be treated in an ordinary way in the course of development consent procedures. The central provisions governing the application of the EIA Directive to the projects listed in Annex I and Annex II to the Directive are Articles 2 and 4.

#### Article 2

1. Member States shall adopt all measures necessary to ensure that, before consent is given, projects likely to have significant effects on the environment by virtue, *inter alia*, of their nature, size or location are made subject to a requirement for development consent and an assessment with regard to their effect. These projects are defined in Article 4.

2. The environmental impact assessment may be integrated into the existing procedures for consent to projects in the Member States, or, failing this, into other procedures or into procedures to be established to comply with the aims of this Directive.

   ...

#### Article 4

1. Subject to Article 2 (3), projects listed in Annex I shall be made subject to an assessment in accordance with Article 5 to 10.

2. Subject to Article 2 (3), for projects listed in Annex II, the Member States shall determine through:
   (a) a case-by-case examination
   or
   (b) thresholds or criteria set by the Member State
   whether the project shall be made subject to an assessment in accordance with Articles 5 to 10.
   Member States may decide to apply both procedures referred to in (a) and (b).

3. When a case-by-case examination is carried out or thresholds or criteria are set for the purpose of paragraph 2, the relevant selection criteria set out in Annex III shall be taken into account.

4. Member States shall ensure that the determination made by the competent authorities under paragraph 2 is made available to the public.

Major projects listed in Annex I, including power stations, refineries, motorways and major roads, *must* always be subject to prior environmental assessment

(Article 4(1)). For those projects listed under Annex II (including pig or poultry farming units, mineral extraction, food manufacture, tanneries and paper manufacturing), there must be an environmental assessment only where Member States consider that their characteristics so require (Art. 4(2)). This means that a project listed under Annex II does not automatically have to have an environmental assessment. The question of whether an assessment is required or not depends on whether a project is judged by the Member States to have 'significant effects on the environment' by virtue, *inter alia*, of its nature, size and location (Art. 2). Member States may prescribe more explicit thresholds and criteria to determine 'significance' and therefore which of the projects falling under Annex II are to be subject to an assessment (Art. 4(2)). Following research which found that the number of environmental assessments being conducted each year varied widely across the Member States (a couple of hundred in the UK, 5,500 in France, a dozen or so in Denmark and Portugal),[29] an annex was added to the EIA Directive which more carefully specifies the circumstances in which the assessment procedures set out in the Directive applied to certain projects.

ANNEX III

SELECTION CRITERIA REFERRED TO IN ARTICLE 4(3)

1. Characteristics of projects
The characteristics of projects must be considered having regard, in particular to:
– the size of the project,
– the cumulation with other projects,
– the use of natural resources,
– the production of waste,
– pollution and nuisances,
– the risk of accidents, having regard in particular to substances or technologies used.

2. Location of projects
The environmental sensitivity of geographical areas likely to be affected by projects must be considered, having regard, in particular, to:
– the existing land use,
– the relative abundance, quality and regenerative capacity of natural resources in the area,
– the absorption capacity of the natural environment, paying particular attention to the following areas:

     (a)  wetlands;
     (b)  coastal zones;
     (c)  mountain and forest areas;
     (d)  nature reserves and parks;

[29]  European Commission, *Report from the Commission on the Implementation of Directive 85/337/EEC* (CEC, 1993).

(e) areas classified or protected under Member States' legislation; special protected areas designated by Member States pursuant to Directive 79/409/EEC and 92/43/EEC;[30]

(f) areas in which the environmental quality standards laid down in Community legislation have already been exceeded;

(g) densely populated areas;

(h) landscapes of historical, cultural or archaeological significance.

3. Characteristics of the potential impact

The potential significant effects of projects must be considered in relation to criteria set out under 1 and 2 above, and having regard in particular to:

- the extent of the impact (geographical area and size of the affected population),
- the transfrontier nature of the impact,
- the probability of the impact,
- the duration, frequency and reversibility of the impact.

The core judgment which must be made by the competent authorities (in most cases local planning authorities) remains whether a project listed in Annex II is likely to have *significant* effects upon the environment. The criteria in Annex III are designed to help the authorities ascertain this. The difficulty is that 'significance' is not easily defined. As a judge noted with some frustration, 'significant effect lies somewhere in between "not trivial" and "momentous"'.[31] Judgments about significance may, for example, involve considering the state of the receiving environment and predicting the intensity of the likely impacts, or analysing what level of change to the environment is acceptable to a community. A finding of significance may also be influenced by the likely reaction of the decision maker and by the degree of public, or media, furore,[32] in other words by qualitative as well as more quantifiable criteria. As Barry Sadler comments: 'In the final analysis, recognise that the evaluation of significance is subjective, contingent upon values, and dependent upon the environmental and community context. Often scientists evaluate significance differently. The intrusion of wider public concerns and social values is inescapable and contentions will remain even with well-defined criteria and a structured approach.'[33]

The use of significance as the ultimate test for determining the application of the assessment procedure confers considerable discretion on Member States when they are setting thresholds or criteria to guide decision making on this

---

[30] On these designations, see Ch. 15, pp. 627–30 and 634-6.

[31] Judge Friendly, as quoted by Eric Orts, 'Reflexive Environmental Law' (1995) 89 *Northwestern University Law Review* 1227, p. 1272.

[32] Andrew Gilpin, *Environmental Impact Assessment: Cutting Edge for the Twenty-First Century* (Cambridge University Press, 1995), pp. 6–7. On significance, see further Holder, *Environmental Assessment*, Ch. 4, esp. pp. 102–4.

[33] Barry Sadler, *Environmental Assessment in a Changing World: Evaluating Practice to Improve Performance*, Final Report of the International Study of the Effectiveness of Environmental Assessment and Canadian Environmental Assessment Agency (Ottawa, 1996), p. 13.

subject, and upon decision makers when determining whether a particular project should be subject to assessment on a case-by-case basis. The European Court of Justice has now circumscribed this discretion so that Member States are unable to exempt in advance whole classes of projects listed in Annex II unless unusual circumstances apply.[34] This was most fully set out by the Court in its judgment in *Kraaijeveld*, a case brought by a company seeking to challenge the approval of flood relief works to the Merwede dyke without an environmental impact assessment being carried out (the works would have prevented Kraaijeveld from having access to waterways which it needed to carry out its shipping business). Dutch implementing legislation for the EIA Directive had fixed thresholds for this type of project at such a level that in practice all projects relating to dykes were exempted in advance from the requirement to conduct an environmental assessment. The judgment is also important because it gives a strong sense of the Court's approval of the broad purpose of the Directive.

### Case C-72/95 *Aannemersbedrijf P. K. Kraaijeveld BV* v. *Gedeputeerde Staten van Zuid-Holland* [1996] ECR I-5403

48. It should be noted that Article 2(1) of the directive refers to Article 4 for the definition of projects which must undergo an assessment of their effects. Article 4(2) allows Member States a certain discretion, since it states that projects of the classes listed in Annex II are to be subject to an assessment 'where Member States consider that their characteristics so require' and that, to that end, Member States may *inter alia* specify certain types of projects as being subject to an assessment or may establish the criteria or thresholds necessary to determine which projects are to be subject to an assessment.

49. The interpretation put forward by the Commission – namely that the existence of specifications, criteria and thresholds does not remove the need for an actual examination of each project in order to verify that it fulfils the criteria of Article 2(1) – would deprive Article 4(2) of any point. A Member State would have no interest in fixing specifications, thresholds and criteria if, in any case, every project had to undergo an individual examination with respect to the criteria in Article 2(1).

50. However, although the second paragraph of Article 4(2) of the directive confers on Member States a measure of discretion to specify certain types of projects which will be subject to an assessment or to establish the criteria or thresholds applicable, the limits of that discretion are to be found in the obligation set out in Article 2(1) that projects likely, by virtue inter alia of their nature, size or location, to have significant effects on the environment are to be subject to an impact assessment.

51. Thus, ruling on the legislation of a Member State in terms of which certain entire classes of projects included in Annex II were excluded from the obligation of an impact assessment, the Court held in its judgment … in Case C-133/94 *Commission* v. *Belgium* [1996]

---

[34] Such circumstances are when all projects, viewed as a whole, are regarded as not being likely to have significant effects on the environment, as set out in para. 53 of the Court's judgment in Case C-72/95 *Kraaijeveld* [1996] ECR I-5403.

ECR I-2323 at paragraph 42, that the criteria and/or thresholds mentioned in Article 4(2) are designed to facilitate examination of the actual characteristics of any given project in order to determine whether it is subject to the requirement of assessment, not to exempt in advance from that obligation certain whole classes of projects listed in Annex II which may be envisaged as taking place on the territory of a Member State.

52. In a situation such as the present, it must be accepted that the Member State concerned was entitled to fix criteria relating to the size of the dykes in order to establish which dyke projects had to undergo an impact assessment. The question whether, in laying down such criteria, the Member State went beyond the limits of its discretion cannot be determined in relation to the characteristics of a single project. It depends on an overall assessment of the characteristics of projects of that nature which could be envisaged in the Member State.

53. Thus a Member State which established criteria or thresholds at a level such that in practice, all projects relating to dykes would be exempted in advance from the requirement of an impact assessment would exceed the limits of its discretion under Articles 2(1) and 4(2) of the directive unless all projects excluded could, when viewed as a whole, be regarded as not being likely to have significant effects on the environment.

...

59. The fact that in this case the Member States have a discretion under Articles 2(1) and 4(2) of the directive does not preclude judicial review of the question whether the national authorities exceeded their discretion.

60. Consequently where, pursuant to national law, a court must or may raise of its own motion pleas in law based on a binding national rule which were not put forward by the parties, it must, for matters within its jurisdiction, examine of its own motion whether the legislative or administrative authorities of the Member States remained within the limits of their discretion under Articles 2(1) and 4(2) of the directive, and take account thereof when examining the action for annulment.

61. If that discretion has been exceeded and consequently the national provisions must be set aside in that respect, it is for the authorities of the Member State, according to their respective powers, to take all the general or particular measures necessary to ensure that projects are examined in order to determine whether they are likely to have significant effects on the environment and, if so, to ensure that they are subject to an impact assessment.

In this part of its judgment, the Court of Justice neatly side-stepped the issue of whether the EIA Directive creates rights for individuals which may be enforced in their national courts, and instead imposes an onus on these courts to raise the issue and decide whether a national authority has exceeded its discretion in excluding a class of project or, indeed, an individual project from the scope of the Directive.

This was a fairly straightforward case of a Member State exceeding the limits of its discretion because the Netherlands had in effect pre-empted all future decisions about the application of the EIA Directive in the case of at least one category of project. A more complex scenario formed the subject of a case brought by the European Commission against Ireland for its apparent failure to transpose the Directive correctly. Unlike *Kraaijeveld* this case was not concerned with the setting of thresholds, but rather with their application, which the European Commission regarded as contrary to the Directive because incremental and cumulative effects of development were not taken into account. In the course of its judgment the Court familiarised itself with the damaged ecological condition of areas of rural Ireland including Dunragh Loughs and Pettigo Plateau (a vast blanket bog), the Burren (an extensive area of limestone pavement in County Clare) and Ballyduff-Clonfinane Bog in County Tipperary, and discussed the detrimental effects of applying absolute and quantitative thresholds in relation to common agricultural and forestry practices, such as the cultivation of land, planting of forests and peat cutting. For example Ireland had set a threshold of 100 hectares for projects for the conversion of uncultivated land or semi-natural areas for intensive agricultural purposes, without reference to either the conservation status of the land, or the effect of other, related, projects. In giving its judgment on this case, the Court of Justice should be credited with emphasising the importance of the sensitivity of the land being developed when deciding whether a project, or several projects when viewed together, are likely to have significant effects on an environment.

### Case C-392/96 *Commission* v. *Ireland* [1996] ECR I-5901

64. [The Court repeated its statement in paragraph 50 of the *Kraaijeveld* judgment]

65. Thus, a Member State which established criteria or thresholds taking account only of the size of projects, without also taking their nature and location into consideration, would exceed the limits of its discretion under Articles 2(1) and 4(2) of the Directive.

66. Even a small-scale project can have significant effects on the environment if it is a location where the environmental factors set out in Article 3 of the Directive, such as fauna and flora, soil, water, climate or cultural heritage, are sensitive to the slightest alteration.

67. Similarly, a project is likely to have significant effects where, by reason of its nature, there is a risk that it will cause a substantial or irreversible change in those environmental factors, irrespective of its size.

68. In order to demonstrate that Ireland has failed to fulfil its obligations in this regard, the Commission has put forward several convincing examples of projects which, whilst considered solely in relation to their size, may none the less have significant effects on the environment by reason of their nature or location.

69. The most significant example is afforestation because, when carried out in areas of active blanket bog, it entails, by its nature and location, the destruction of the bog ecosystem and the irreversible loss of biotopes that are original, rare and of great scientific interest. In itself, it may also cause the acidification or eutrophication of waters.

70. It was however necessary, and possible, to take account of factors such as the nature or location of projects, for example by setting a number of thresholds corresponding to varying project sizes and applicable by reference to the nature or location of the project.

71. Ireland's explanation that other environmental protection legislation, such as the Habitats Regulations, made it unnecessary to assess afforestation, land reclamation or peat extraction projects carried out in environmentally sensitive locations must be dismissed. Nothing in the Directive excludes from its scope regions or areas which are protected under other Community provision from other aspects.

72. It follows that, by setting, for the classes of projects covered [discussed above], thresholds which take account only of the size of projects, to the exclusion of their nature or location, Ireland has exceeded the limits of its discretion under Articles 2(1) and 4(2) of the Directive.

73. As regards the cumulative effect of projects, it is to be remembered that the criteria and/or thresholds mentioned in Article 4(2) are designed to facilitate the examination of the actual characteristics exhibited by a given project in order to determine whether it is subject to the requirement to carry out an assessment, and not to exempt in advance from that obligation certain whole categories of projects listed in Annex II which may be envisaged on the territory of a Member State [the Court cites its judgment in *Kraaijeveld* and related case law].

74. The question whether, in laying down such criteria and/or thresholds, a Member State goes beyond the limits of its discretion cannot be determined in relation to the characteristics of a single project, but depends on an overall assessment of the characteristics of projects of that nature which could be envisaged in the Member State concerned.

75. So, a Member State which established criteria and/or thresholds at a level such that, in practice, all projects of a certain type would be exempted in advance from the requirement of an impact assessment would exceed the limits of its discretion under Articles 2(1) and 4(2) of the Directive unless all the projects excluded could, when viewed as a whole, be regarded as not being likely to have significant effects on the environment. [The Court then referred to para. 53 of its judgment in *Kraaijeveld*.]

76. That would also be the case where a Member State merely set a criterion of project size and did not also ensure that the objective of the legislation would not be circumscribed by the splitting of projects. Not taking account of the cumulative effect of projects means in practice that all projects of a certain type may escape the obligation to carry out an assessment when, taken together, they are likely to have significant effects on the environment within the meaning of Article 2(1) of the Directive.

77. In order to demonstrate that Ireland has failed to fulfil its obligations in this regard, the Commission has also provided various examples of the effects of the Irish legislation as drafted.

78. Ireland has not denied that no project for the extraction of peat, covered by … Annex II to the Directive, has been the subject of an impact assessment, although small-scale peat extraction has been mechanised, industrialised and considerably intensified, resulting in the unremitting loss of areas of bog of nature conservation importance.

79. As regards initial afforestation, covered by … Annex II to the Directive, such projects, encouraged by the grant of aid, may be implemented in proximity to one another without any impact assessment at all being carried out, if they are conducted by different developers who all keep within the threshold of 70 ha over three years.

80. The Commission has also cited the example of land reclamation projects, covered by ... Annex II to the Directive, whose cumulative effect is not taken into account by the Irish legislation. Nor has it been disputed that much land clearance has taken place in the Burren without a single impact assessment being carried out, although it is an area of unquestionable interest. Limestone pavement, which is characteristic of the area, has been destroyed, as have vegetation and archaeological remains, giving way to pasture. Considered together, those interventions were likely to have significant environmental effects.

81. As regards sheep farming in particular, the Commission has proved that, again encouraged by the grant of aid, this has grown in an unrestrained fashion, which is a development which may have adverse environmental consequences. However, it has not demonstrated that sheep farming as practised in Ireland constitutes a project within the meaning of ... the Directive.

82. It follows from all the foregoing that, by settling thresholds for the classes of projects covered by ... Annex II to the Directive without also ensuring that the objective of the legislation will not be circumvented by the splitting of projects, Ireland has exceeded the limits of its discretion under Articles 2(1) and 4(2) of the Directive.

The Court appears to be seeking to align the rules of environmental assessment more closely to ecological conditions and impacts upon these 'on the ground'. The judgment is recognition that loss or damage to a part of the environment does not take place only in respect of a defined area, but that harmful effects may be combined with others and thereby exacerbated.

## (ii) Scoping and the gathering of information

One of the main rationales for environmental assessment is the collection and dissemination of information about the likely effects of a proposed project on the environment. As we have mentioned, there is an onus on the developer to provide the bulk of this information in the form of an environmental statement. This is not a straightforward process. As Wilkins notes, 'setting boundaries is a crucial step in the EIA process. Too narrow a scope will leave out important issues, while too broad a scope may make an assessment either superficial or too difficult to manage and incomprehensible.'[35] The developer may be guided in setting the boundaries for the assessment by the consenting authority (most likely the local planning authority) issuing a 'scoping opinion' to the developer, if requested.[36] Such opinions outline the main likely effects of the development and therefore the scale and range of the assessment, and are based on consultation with the developer and other interested authorities or agencies. This potentially opens up an important exchange between the planning authority, the developer and other official bodies. At present there is no

---

[35] Hugh Wilkins, 'The Need for Subjectivity in Environmental Law' (2003) 23 *EIA Review* 401, p. 405.     [36] Article 5(2) EIA Directive.

opportunity for the public to contribute to this process by commenting on the content or adequacy of the opinion. Rather this aspect of the process is decidedly expert-led.

Following the scoping exercise, the developer must then compile an environmental statement, containing at the very least a description of the proposed development, the measures envisaged to mitigate ('avoid, reduce, and, if possible, remedy') significant adverse effects, the data used to ascertain this information, and an outline of the main alternatives considered, all of which should be accompanied by a non-technical summary of these descriptions.[37] The description of the likely significant effects should cover all 'direct effects and any indirect, secondary, cumulative, short, medium and long-term, permanent and temporary, positive and negative effects of the project'.[38] In practice this often considerable body of environmental information is collected and compiled by an environmental consultant, often on the basis of information held by authorities who are under an obligation under the terms of the Directive to give relevant information to the developer.

In cases in which a developer applies for outline planning permission (with detailed matters reserved for subsequent approval), the adequacy of any information provided in an environmental statement (if one is provided at all[39]) is for the decision maker to assess, rather than the court as a matter of primary fact. In one such case, which formed the subject of two rounds of litigation (*Tew 1* and *Tew 2*[40]), a developer provided only an 'illustrative masterplan' of a proposed business park which was to be developed in several phases. Once it had been decided that there had been a failure to provide the level of information required by the 1988 EIA Regulations[41] – in particular, there was insufficient information about mitigating measures – the developer set about revising the application, which this time was accompanied by an environmental statement. The Council's grant of outline permission was again challenged on the grounds that although the revised application detailed the scale and size of the projects, the 'details' of the project (landscaping, design, appearance of the buildings) were reserved matters. In *Tew 2* the judge, Sullivan J, considered that judgments about the adequacy of environmental information are solely for the planning authority to make. As well as demonstrating judicial deference to decision makers (identified in the context of

---

[37] Article 5(3) EIA Directive, as elaborated by Annex IV of the Directive. On the methods employed to ascertain this information, see Holder, *Environmental Assessment*, pp. 39–42.

[38] Annex IV.

[39] For example, in *R* v. *London Borough of Hammersmith and Fulham ex parte CPRE London Branch* [2000] Env LR 532, the planning authority's failure to require an environmental statement at all for a 40-acre urban regeneration project was unsuccessfully challenged by the CPRE.

[40] *R* v. *Rochdale Metropolitan Borough Council ex parte Tew (Tew 1)* [2000] Env LR 1 and *R* v. *Rochdale Metropolitan Borough Council ex parte Milne (Tew 2)* [2001] Env LR 22.

[41] Town and Country Planning (Assessment of Environmental Effects) Regulations 1988 (SI 1988 No. 1199), now superseded by Town and Country Planning (Environmental Impact Assessment) (England and Wales) Regulations 1999 (SI 1999 No. 293).

environmental assessment rules by John Alder many years previously – see above, p. 556), this case also provides a good example of a residual concern about environmental assessment (and environmental regulation more generally) obstructing economic progress. Sullivan J commented that such urban development projects have been placed in a 'legal straitjacket' by environmental assessment procedures.[42]

After an inordinately long wait, the European Court of Justice has now ruled on this matter in *Barker*,[43] a case which arose in the course of proceedings between Ms Barker and the London Borough of Bromley concerning the grant of planning permission to develop a large leisure complex (including cinemas, restaurants and cafes, a car park and exhibition and 'leisure areas') in Crystal Palace Park, London, without an environmental impact assessment having been carried out. Outline planning permission had been granted, reserving certain matters for subsequent approval before any construction work could begin. Although these reserved matters formed important features of the development, they were not subject to any environmental assessment procedure, the Council having taken advice that as a matter of domestic law an assessment could be carried out only at the initial outline planning permission stage. A question arose about the compatibility with Community law of the national rules on this point. The Court first reiterated the definition of 'development consent' as the decision of the competent authority which entitles the developer to commence with the work needed to carry out the project (para. 39) (following earlier case law, for example case C-201/02 *Wells*[44] (discussed below, pp. 588-9)). It then considered whether Articles 2(1) and 4(2) of the Directive require an assessment to be carried out if, following a grant of outline planning permission, it appears at the time of approval of reserved matters that the project is likely to have significant effects on the environment.

### Case C-290/03 *R (Barker)* v. *London Borough of Bromley*, 4 May 2006

46. … it is [therefore] the task of the national court to verify whether the outline planning permission and decision approving reserved matters which are at issue in the main proceedings constitute, as a whole, a 'development consent' for the purposes of Directive 85/337 (see in this connection, the judgment delivered today in Case C-508/03 *Commission* v. *UK*, paragraphs 101 and 102).

47. Second, as the Court explained in Wells, at paragraph 52, where national law provides for a consent procedure comprising more than one stage, one involving a principal decision and the other involving an implementing decision which cannot extend beyond the parameters set by the principal decision, the effects which a project may have on the environment must be identified and assessed at the time of the procedure relating to

---

[42] At para. 91.     [43] Case C-290/03 *R (Barker)* v. *London Borough of Bromley*, 4 May 2006.
[44] [2004] ECR I-723.

the principal decision. It is only if those effects are not identifiable until the time of the procedure relating to the implementing decision that the assessment should be carried out in the course of that procedure.

48. If the national court therefore concludes that the procedure laid down by the rules at issue in the main proceedings is a consent procedure comprising more than one stage, one involving a principal decision and the other involving an implementing decision which cannot extend beyond the parameters set by the principal decision, it follows that the competent authority is, in some circumstances, obliged to carry out an environmental impact assessment in respect of a project even after the grant of outline planning permission, when the reserved matters are subsequently approved (see, in this regard, Case 508/03 *Commission* v. *UK*, paragraphs 103 to 106). This assessment must be of a comprehensive nature, so as to relate to all the aspects of the project which have not yet been assessed or which require a fresh assessment.

49. ... Articles 2(1) and 4(2) are to be interpreted as requiring an environmental impact assessment to be carried out if, in the case of grant of consent comprising more than one stage, it becomes apparent, in the course of the second stage, that the project is likely to have significant effects on the environment by virtue inter alia of its nature, size or location.

This is a case carrying great political and legal weight since the facts also formed the subject of enforcement proceedings brought by the European Commission against the UK government, on which a judgment was delivered by the Court of Justice on the same day (Case C-508/03 *Commission* v. *United Kingdom*). The Court decided in that case that the national rules which provided that an environmental impact assessment may be carried out only at the initial outline planning permission stage, and not at the later reserved matters stage, are contrary to Articles 2(1) and 4(2) of the Directive. The case also reaches far into current planning practice, and in particular means that developers should be unable to circumvent environmental assessment rules by providing a detailed description of a project at the later stages of planning procedures.

### (iii) Consultation and participation

We have already discussed the participatory ideal represented by environmental assessment generally (pp. 557–60), and specifically by the EIA Directive (pp. 557–8). However, until fairly recently, a more simplistic view of environmental assessment as an information-gathering tool prevailed. This was expressed in the Directive in the form of quite limited rights for the public to be consulted and to make representations based on information provided, most typically by the developer. The 2003 Participation Directive,[45] which seeks to give effect to the Aarhus Convention, has made important changes to this right so that the aim is now to give the public 'early and effective opportunities to participate

---

[45] Directive 2003/35/EC.

in the environmental decision-making procedures referred to in Article 2(2) [of the EIA Directive]' and, further, that the public 'shall, for that purpose, be entitled to express comments and opinions when all options are open to the competent authority or authorities before the decision on the request for development consent is taken' (Art. 6(4) EIA Directive as amended). A nod to Member State autonomy is made in this regard since the detailed arrangements for informing the public (for example by bill-posting within a certain radius or publication in local newspapers) and for consulting the public concerned (for example by written submissions or by way of a public inquiry) are to be determined by the Member States (Art. 6(5)). Roughly parallel provisions apply in the case of projects likely to have transboundary effects (Art. 7).

The move towards greater respect for the role of the public in the environmental assessment process has been reflected in a similar shift in judicial attitudes. The early case law on environmental assessment in the United Kingdom revealed a failure on the part of the judiciary to appreciate the participatory aspects of the EIA Directive. For example in *ex parte Beebee*,[46] the facts of which are discussed more fully in Chapter 15 (pp. 622–4), the applicants, who represented the British Herpetological Society, applied for judicial review of the Council's decision to grant itself planning permission for a housing development on a site important for nature conservation, on the grounds that the authority had failed to consider whether an environmental assessment should have been carried out. The authority had, however, considered some relevant information on the environmental effects of the development, some of which had been provided by the applicants. Schiemann J refused to revoke the planning permission (though the Secretary of State later did) because 'the substance of all the environmental information which was likely to emerge by going through the formal process envisaged by the [implementing] Regulation had already emerged and was apparently present in the council's mind' (p. 299). Reasoning along these lines also characterises the judgments in *Twyford Down*[47] and *ex parte Velcourt*[48] suggesting that the judiciary strongly adhered to an information theory of environmental assessment (that it exists primarily as a means of conveying information to the public), rather than seeing it as a means by which participants might contribute to the decision-making process and thus help to inculcate changes in legal and administrative culture.

A sharp departure from this limiting approach to the participatory requirements of the Directive was made in *Berkeley (No. 1)*[49] which raised the issue of whether the gathering of a body of environmental information is capable of fulfilling the requirement to conduct a formal environmental assessment

---

[46] *R* v. *Poole Borough Council ex parte Beebee* (1991) 3 JEL 293.

[47] *Twyford Parish Council* v. *Secretary of State for Transport* (1992) 4 JEL 273.

[48] *Wychavon District Council* v. *Secretary of State for the Environment ex parte Velcourt Ltd* (1994) 6 JEL 352, p. 357.

[49] *Berkeley* v. *Secretary of State for the Environment and Fulham Football Ground* (*Berkeley (No. 1)*) [1998] 3 PLR 39.

process as a matter of national and Community law. This question arose in the context of proceedings challenging the Secretary of State's grant of planning permission to Fulham Football Club for new stands, together with the building of parking areas, access roads, and a new riverside wall and walkway with some encroachment onto the River Thames. The effects of these developments on the ecology of the river (the damage to the habitats of plants, invertebrates, fish and birds) were to be offset by the provision of a wetland shelf planted with reeds along the foreshore. The Secretary of State accepted that there had been a failure to comply with the requirements of the 1988 Regulations[50] (the project was an urban development project which was likely to have significant effects on the environment by virtue of its sensitive location) but considered that even if a formal environmental assessment had been carried out this would have made no difference to the outcome because all the relevant environmental matters had been considered in the course of a public inquiry. The Court of Appeal agreed with this opinion. As Pill LJ stated, 'a vast amount of information was available and available in comprehensible form',[51] which effectively downplays the importance of the procedural requirements of the Directive. In the House of Lords, however, Lord Hoffmann (giving the judgment) appeared highly influenced by the idea that public participation can make a difference to the outcome of a decision. On this point it is useful to compare the judgments of Thorpe LJ (who implicitly adheres to an 'information theory' understanding of the utility of environmental assessment) and Lord Hoffmann who instead advances more of a 'culture theory' approach (above, pp. 522–3).

### *Berkeley v. Secretary of State for the Environment and Fulham Football Ground (Berkeley (No. 1))* [1998] 3 PLR 39, para. 54 (CA)

Thorpe LJ:

On the facts of the case I am left with the clear conviction that the procedures adopted, though flawed, were thorough and effective to enable the [Planning] Inspector to make a comprehensive judgment on all the environmental issues affecting the Thames and particularly the likely adverse impact of the slight expansion of the proposed development beyond its existing boundary.

### *Berkeley v. Secretary of State for the Environment and Fulham Football Ground (Berkeley (No. 1))* [2001] AC 603, p. 615 (HL)

Lord Hoffmann:

The Directive requires not merely that the planning authority should have the necessary information, but that it should have been obtained by means of a particular procedure, namely that of an EIA. And an essential element in that procedure is what the Regulations [the Town

---

[50] SI 1988 No. 1199.  [51] [1998] Env LR 741, p. 757.

and Country Planning (Assessment of Environmental Effects) Regulations 1988] call the 'environmental statement' by the developer should have been made available to the public and that the public should have been 'given the opportunity to express an opinion' in accordance with Article 6(2) of the Directive. As Advocate General Elmer said in *Commission of the European Communities* v. *Federal Republic of Germany* (Case 431/92) [1995] ECR I-2189, 2208–9, para. 35:

> It must be emphasised that the provisions of the Directive are essentially of a procedural nature. By the inclusion of information on the environment in the consent procedure it is ensured that the environmental impact of the project shall be included in the public debate and that the decision as to whether consent is to be given shall be adopted on an appropriate basis.

The directly enforceable right of the citizen which is accorded by the Directive is not merely a right to a fully informed decision on the substantive issue. It must have been adopted on an appropriate basis and that requires the inclusive and democratic procedure prescribed by the Directive in which the public, however misguided or wrongheaded its views may be, is given an opportunity to express its opinion on the environmental issues.

…

A court is therefore not entitled retrospectively to dispense with the requirement of an EIA on the ground that the outcome would have been the same or that the local planning authority or Secretary of State had all the information necessary to enable them to reach a proper decision on the environmental issues.

…

… nothing less than substantial compliance with the Directive could enable the planning permission in this case to be upheld.

As well as seeking to engage the public in decision making, as upheld by Lord Hoffmann in *Berkeley (No. 1)*,[52] the Directive also provides for a further dimension to participation in the decision making process by requiring the local authority to consult with authorities with special environmental responsibilities and to give them an opportunity to express their opinion on the information supplied by the developer and on the request for development consent.[53] Finally, note that the model of environmental assessment provided for in the EIA Directive effectively stops with the decision whether or not to grant development consent because no post-assessment monitoring is required. The relationships and pathways of information between developer, authority and agencies opened up by the earlier stages of the assessment process are abruptly finalised at this stage, an issue we discuss further below, pp. 604–7.

---

[52] This remains an important statement of principle, but note that in some later cases the courts have taken a harder look at the trade-offs of enforcing rigorous procedural requirements, for example *Jones* v. *Mansfield District Council* [2004] Env LR 21, especially the comments of Carnwath LJ, paras. 56–61.    [53] Article 6(1).

## (iv) Problems of implementation: the case of 'revived' mining permissions

In this account of environmental assessment we have hitherto explored environmental assessment as an integral part of the town and country planning system. However, an environmental assessment is, or should be, applied to many other regimes governing environmental decision making. One such regime (ROMPS – the review of old mineral permissions) is designed to regulate the revival of dormant permissions for mining or quarrying by registering the existence of old planning permissions and attaching conditions. The regime, introduced in 1991,[54] was designed to flush out plans to mine or quarry (the commencement or resumption of which sometimes came as an unpleasant surprise to people who had bought homes in the area many years after the permission had been granted) and thereby protect the local environment. However, because the granting of the original permission almost inevitably predated the implementation of the EIA Directive, often by many years, environmental assessment procedures were not carried out at the point at which conditions were attached which permitted the resumption of activities on a particular site.[55] This is a typical example of the problems experienced in the UK in implementing the Directive,[56] indicating some official resistance to the purpose or spirit of the Directive and the hampering of public participation requirements, and, finally, resulting in the need for legislation to fill the implementation gap.

At the core of a series of revived permission cases was the correct interpretation of 'development consent' which is the trigger for the application of the EU's environmental assessment regime (Art. 2 of the EIA Directive requires that 'before development is given, projects likely to have significant effects on the environment by virtue, inter alia, of their nature, size or location are made subject to a requirement for development consent and an assessment with regard to their effects' (see above, p. 573)). The particular difficulty was whether the environmental assessment regime 'bit' at the point at which permissions were reviewed and possibly conditions attached, thus allowing the mining to proceed. The underlying issue was whether environmental considerations should inform each stage of the development consent process and thus reflect the practical reality that decision making reaches over several stages, each requiring different standards of environmental information, and involving varying levels of uncertainty about the likely significant effects of development and the likely effectiveness of mitigating measures.

---

[54] Section 22 and Sch. 2 Planning and Compensation Act 1991.

[55] See Council for National Parks and Friends of the Peak District, *Old Permissions and National Parks* (2004).

[56] Other examples of non-implementation or faulty implementation include environmental assessment of forestry projects, assessment of development on crown estates land, and assessment in cases in which development is granted retrospective planning permission. In each of these examples, legislation was, tardily, introduced in order to bring environmental assessment into a broader range of developmental activity than was originally thought to be needed. On each of these examples, see further Holder, *Environmental Assessment*.

In *ex parte Brown and Cartwright*,[57] Lord Hoffmann considered that the nature of the regime was sufficient to bring it within the EC concept of 'development consent' as defined by the EIA Directive – as a decision of the competent authority or authorities which entitles the developer to proceed with the project. Lord Hoffmann's judgment relied more on the destructive and disruptive potential of mining work than a concern with rights of participation under the Directive. However, in *ex parte Huddleston* (see below) it became clear that, without an environmental assessment process being conducted, the practical effect of the revival of a dormant planning permission was to circumvent rights of participation in the decision whether quarrying should proceed. In this case the applicant had lived for eighteen years in a house near the quarry. One discerns a human rights dimension to protecting individual rights granted by the Directive in Brooke LJ's judgment, regardless of the ambiguous position in EC law regarding the imposition on a private entity of a duty contained in an unimplemented Directive.

### *R* v. *Durham County Council ex parte Huddleston* [2000] 1 WLR 1484, para. 43

In my judgment, Mr Huddleston is entitled to say to the court: 'I, an individual citizen, should have had a valuable opportunity to take part in an informed consultation in relation to an extraction project which will detrimentally affect my home and the environment in which I live. Because the state has failed to comply with its obligations under the Directive, I am entitled to ask the court to give direct effect to the Directive. It is a matter of indifference to me that it was a different emanation of the state that created my dilemma when it enacted the provisions as to deemed consent (without a prior environmental impact assessment) for conditions relating to dormant old mining permissions that are contained in paragraph 2(6)(b) of Schedule 2 to the 1991 [Planning and Compensation] Act. The state has failed to afford me my rights, and I am entitled to ask for an order which will give the 1985 Directive direct effect.'

Brooke LJ had read the non-technical summary of an environmental statement which had been prepared for the mining company several months *after* permission was deemed to have been granted subject to conditions. In his view, 'It is sufficient to say that this summary contains information which would have enabled Mr Huddleston, whose amenities (both in his home and in the environment close to his home) would be detrimentally affected by the proposed quarrying, to have taken a much more informed part in the consultation process, as was his right if the Directive had been effectively implemented.'[58]

Delena Wells faced similar difficulties to Brown and Huddleston. Operators of a quarry had obtained planning permission to work it in 1947 but as this permission was dormant new conditions were required before operations could be

---

[57] [1992] 2 WLR 452.
[58] *R* v. *Durhan County Council ex parte Huddleston* [2001] 1 WLR 1484, para. 39.

resumed. The Court of Justice was asked whether the determination of planning conditions constitutes development consent within the meaning of the EIA Directive. A complication was that the planning conditions for the quarry were determined in two stages: first, the Secretary of State's decision to impose conditions on the planning permission (thus permitting extraction at the quarry); and second, the mineral planning authority's approval of certain reserved matters such as the monitoring of noise and blasting on the site. Hence a further question was which of these decisions properly constituted development consent. The Court of Justice decided that the decision determining new conditions and the decision approving reserved matters for the working of the quarry amounted to development consent and thus required an environmental assessment to be carried out.[59] The Court elaborated that, where a consent procedure comprises several stages, assessment must in principle be carried out as soon as it is possible to identify and assess all the effects which the project may have on the environment.[60] This interpretation of the Directive follows Advocate General Leger's opinion that although the national law of each Member State establishes the moment from which the developer is granted the right to proceed with the project, development consent is not a national concept. The Advocate General appeared influenced by the premise that the resumption of extraction of minerals at the quarry was likely to have significant effects on the environment, which called for a purposive reading of the Directive in line with previous case law of the Court giving the Directive a broad scope (notably, *Kraaijeveld*, discussed above, pp. 576–8).

The Court's judgment was also shaped by (understandable) concerns about the effectiveness and enforceability of the EIA Directive – it has been notoriously difficult to implement – stating that the Directive would be undermined by regarding the adoption of decisions which replace the terms and substance of prior consent, such as the old mining permission, as mere modifications of an existing consent. The Court related this finding to the enforceable nature of participatory rights, confirming the Advocate General's opinion that the provisions of the Directive entitling individuals to express their opinion of the likely significance of a project are sufficiently precise and enforceable as a matter of the principle of direct effect. Furthermore the Court clarified that the limits it had laid down previously on the (horizontal) direct effect of directives do not apply when there are 'mere' adverse repercussions for third parties (apparently including the halting of mining operations awaiting the results of an environmental assessment, as in this case), rather than obligations directly applied (paras. 56–7).

Amending legislation was adopted in 2000 which had the effect that old mineral permissions are suspended where the applicant for new conditions fails to supply an environmental statement or any other information.[61] This

---

[59] Case C-201/02 *R (Delena Wells)* v. *Secretary of State for Transport, Local Government and the Regions* [2004] Env LR 27, para. 47.     [60] *Ibid.*, para. 54.

[61] Town and Country Planning (Environmental Impact Assessment) (Amendment) Regulations 2000 (SI 2000 No. 2867).

instrument applied to applications made *after* 2000, but the *Wells* judgment lends strong support to an argument that a planning authority should also be able to require an environmental statement for applications made before that date.

### (v) The decision: what difference does environmental assessment make?

The positive idea of environmental assessment is that it initiates a process of 'rethinking'[62] aimed at achieving equal consideration of environmental, social and economic issues in decision making, with the expectation that decisions will be reoriented towards outcomes which favour environmental protection. In reality, it is notoriously difficult to establish the precise effect of the environmental assessment process on the outcome of decision making because the environmental information gathered during the process generally forms just one consideration to be taken into account, amongst many other factors. In most cases the body of *environmental* information carries no greater weight than these factors (note, though, that the form of environmental assessment provided for in the Habitats Directive has specific, substantive consequences for decision making, as we discuss further in Chapter 15, pp. 649–50). In addition, the development planning process invokes multiple sources of environmental information – from environmental assessment procedures, but also from representations made to planning authorities, from planning inquiries, and as the result of consultation with interested bodies and agencies. This means that whilst environmental assessment contributes to a formal consolidation of environmental information in the case of some types of development, this category of information might well be superseded by that obtained from other procedures. Research conducted on the effect of environmental assessment procedures on local authority decisions in the UK suggests that the implementation of the EIA Directive has had a gradual rather than revolutionary effect on decision making. Its main benefits have been the enhanced provision of environmental information and, to a lesser extent, assistance in setting conditions and in modifying proposals. It is equally clear that these benefits are not occurring in all cases and that better integration of environmental considerations into project planning needs to be realised.[63]

The uncertain effect of the introduction of formal environmental assessment procedures is a consequence of a lack of prescription in the EIA Directive about the effects of a finding that a project will have negative effects on the environment. With deceptive simplicity, Art. 8 of the EIA Directive requires that 'the results of consultations and the information gathered pursuant to Articles 5, 6 and 7 must be taken into consideration in the development consent procedure'. Article 9, as amended by the 2003 Participation Directive, sets out the procedures to be followed once a decision has been arrived at, and

---

[62] Staeck, Malek and Heinelt, 'The Environmental Impact Assessment Directive', p. 33.

[63] Chris Wood and Carys Jones, 'The Effect of Environmental Assessment on UK Local Planning Authority Decisions' (1997) 34 *Urban Studies* 1237.

thereby narrows the opportunity for the consenting authority to overlook the results of participation. For example, as well as making available to the public the content of the decision and any conditions attached to this, it must also give the main reasons and considerations on which the decision is based, including information about the public participation process, and a description of the main mitigating measures to be taken by the developer (Art. 9(1)).

The 2003 Participation Directive also inserted the following important provision into the text of the EIA Directive, the full implications of which are not yet apparent.

Article 10a

Member States shall ensure that, in accordance with the relevant national legal system, members of the public concerned:

(a) having a sufficient interest, or alternatively,
(b) maintaining the impairment of a right, where administrative procedural law of a Member State requires this as a precondition,

have access to a review procedure before a court of law or another independent and impartial body established by law to challenge the substantive or procedural legality of decisions, acts or omissions subject to the public participation provisions of this Directive.

Member States shall determine at what stage the decisions, acts or omissions may be challenged.

What constitutes a sufficient interest and impairment of a right shall be determined by the Member States, consistently with the objective of giving the public concerned wide access to justice. To this end, the interest of any non-governmental organisation meeting the requirements referred to in Article 1(2), shall be deemed sufficient for the purpose of subparagraph (a) of this Article. Such organisations shall also be deemed to have rights capable of being impaired for the purpose of subparagraph (b) of this Article.

The provisions of this Article shall not exclude the possibility of a preliminary review procedure before an administrative authority and shall not aVect the requirement of exhaustion of administrative review procedures prior to recourse to judicial review procedures, where such a requirement exists under national law. Any such procedure shall be fair, equitable, timely and not prohibitively expensive.

In order to further the effectiveness of the provisions of this article, Member States shall ensure that practical information is made available to the public on access to administrative and judicial review procedures.

What is clear at this stage is that by providing minimum standards of review before a court of law or 'another independent and impartial body', Art. 10a makes a significant contribution to the Directive, which was previously silent on remedies. However, as with other key provisions in the Directive, Art. 10a imbues Member States with a great deal of discretion about the design and organisation of review procedures at national level.[64] Perhaps the most important change is that this provision makes more likely the challenge of the *substantive* legality of decisions, as well as their procedural legality, which is the current position. Whilst it probably does not *require* any change, this might open up the possibility of a closer examination of the merits of a decision, for example on the basis that alternative options have not been considered fully, or that the proposed mitigating measures are inadequate.

An early indication of how a more substantive review of decisions which have been informed by the environmental assessment process may work is the Secretary of State's decision to refuse consent for the construction of a new deep water terminal at Dibden Bay in Hampshire (the Secretary of State is able to revisit the merits of a decision). This decision was based upon a planning inspector's report on a public inquiry which first considered the adequacy of the environmental statement prepared by the developer. In terms of an 'appropriate assessment' undertaken by the developer under conservation law (see further Chapter 15, pp. 649–61), the Inspector criticised the 'functional approach' towards assessing environmental impact. He considered the developer's assessment fundamentally flawed in that it treated compensatory measures as mitigation and wrongly relied on proposed habitat creation schemes outside existing protected areas in concluding that the development would not adversely affect their integrity in conservation terms.[65] The inspector's negative view of the adequacy of the developer's environmental statement was clearly influential in this case.

A quite different approach was taken by the Privy Council in a case concerned with the construction of the Chalillo Dam in Belize[66] which will cause the loss of a biologically rich floodplain. The environmental alliance challenged the decision to build the dam as unlawful mainly because the environmental statement produced by the developer was considered to be inadequate – it contained an important error about the geological state of the river bed on which the dam was to be built. The majority judgment of the Privy Council (given by Lord Hoffmann) detailed other deficiencies in the statement but, quite remarkably, decided that this did not mean that the environmental assessment process necessarily failed to comply with the law relating to environmental assessment in Belize. The Privy Council concluded that the Department of Environment's decision whether or not to consent to the project constituted a political judgment about the 'public interest', and was therefore not reviewable (para. 82). In reaching this judgment the majority appeared to be persuaded by the fact that

[64]  See Aine Ryall, 'Access to Justice and the EIA Directive: The Implications of the Aarhus Convention' in Holder and McGillivray (eds.), *Taking Stock of Environmental Assessment.*
[65]  Dibden Bay, Decision Letter, 20 April 2004, para. 17.
[66]  *Belize Alliance of Conservation Non-Governmental Organisations* v. *Department of the Environment and the Belize Electric Company Ltd* [2004] Env LR 38. We further discuss this case in relation to the application for an interim injunction in Ch. 3, pp. 116–18.

the Department of the Environment in Belize had considered representations other than those made by the developer before arriving at the decision. In direct contrast, in his punchy dissenting judgment Lord Walker paid more attention to the deficiencies of the environmental statement and assessment procedures, including the lack of public consultation:

> Belize has enacted comprehensive legislation on environmental protection and direct foreign investment, if it has serious environmental implications, must comply with that legislation. The rule of law must not be sacrificed to foreign investment, however desirable … it is no answer to the erroneous geology in the EIA to say that the dam design would not necessarily have been different. The people of Belize are entitled to be properly informed about any proposals for alterations in the dam design before the project is approved and before work continues with its construction.[67]

The majority and dissenting judges in this case expressed very different views about what should be the practical effect of an inadequate environmental assessment process. Evaluating what difference environmental assessment makes is therefore far from a simple judgment. Different criteria have been used to judge the efficacy or otherwise of environmental assessment, but these are mainly along the lines of the extent to which it provides a means of challenging the developmental orthodoxy.[68] Cashman marks the EIA Directive's 'score card' in this respect, but he also implicitly suggests opening up more areas in which environmental assessment might be applied, such as the promotion of aesthetic standards.

### Liam Cashman, 'Environmental Impact Assessment: A Major Instrument for Achieving Integration' in Marco Onida (ed.), *Europe and the Environment: Legal Essays in Honour of Ludwig Krämer* (Europa Law Publishing, 2004), pp. 86–90

Measured against the pressures that impinge on the environment, the Directive's influence has been limited. In relation to its first phase of implementation [prior to its revision by Directive 97/11/EC], it has been referred to in terms of unfulfilled expectations. These unfulfilled expectations concern a failure to carry out EIA in the first place, as well as the limited effectiveness of the EIA process in avoiding environmental harm or promoting environmental protection and improvement.

For major infrastructure projects, such as motorways, project assessment has become routine, but for other important categories, such as the urban development one, its use tends to be exceptional. It has not, for example, acted as a meaningful check in those parts of the Community where urban sprawl occurs. Nor has it made any significant impression on continued agricultural intensification, despite [the EIA] Directive featuring several agricultural project categories and despite strong evidence of related environmental degradation, such as nutrient enrichment of water-bodies and widespread impairment of biodiversity.

---

[67] Paras. 118–20.     [68] See also Wood and Jones, 'The Effect of Environmental Assessment'.

This may reflect a tendency to exclusively associate the need for assessment with large-scale infrastructure and industrial projects, despite the fact that the Court has confirmed that project assessment is potentially relevant for small-scale, non-industrial projects. It may also reflect a perception that impact assessment is intended for particular types of negative environmental impact, especially air and water pollution and habitat loss.

However, there are strong arguments for using assessment as a tool for achieving enhanced environmental benefits in circumstances where a project is not intrinsically harmful, for example as a tool for architects and planners to create improved urban neighbourhoods. Furthermore, impact assessment is a tool that is not only relevant for impact on the natural environment, but also for impacts on the historic built or cultural environment. This has been noted by the European Parliament. Furthermore, while at European Union level the importance of architectural quality has been acknowledged as a means of integrating new buildings and structures into the existing environment, EIA is rarely used as a methodological tool for promoting high aesthetic and resource-use standards in residential developments.

...

To the extent that impact assessments have been undertaken over the past fifteen years, it is unfortunate that empirical evidence of the benefits that have resulted is lacking. The implementation reviews carried out under [the EIA] Directive have undoubtedly served a useful purpose, but there is a dearth of case-studies examining the outcomes of assessment. In the author's experience, project-related EIA is often effective in mitigating environmental harm, by pinpointing likely problems and identifying and promoting better design solutions. However, its potential is undermined by factors such as an inherent developer-bias (information provided by the developer leads the process and may sometimes be uncritically accepted), a lack of participation by environmental authorities in the consultation phase and an inability or unwillingness of decision makers to ensure quality-control. Moreover, EIA is commonly of no or limited assistance in ensuring that a project is optimally located. This can reflect a context of generally poor spatial planning (*i.e.* spatial planning that fails to steer damaging development away from sensitive or inappropriate locations) or the absence of any rigour in dealing with the aspect of project alternatives. In practice, the decision at project-level may be little more than a ratification of a prior political or plan-led choice.

...

For the foreseeable future, there will continue to be processes at societal level that will not necessarily undergo assessment. Except possibly in relation to Natura 2000,[69] ministers for finance will not, for the present, have to submit their budgets to prior environmental assessment. Fiscal or subsidy schemes including state aids, which act as critical determinants of certain environmental impacts, such as climate change, may continue to be formulated in the absence of proper environmental analysis. Even if these gaps are legislatively closed, volatile social and market forces are always likely to limit the role of assessment in directing change.

Nonetheless, several factors – stress on natural resources, the recognition of global environmental problems, the ever-increasing integration of the world's economies, the steps

---

[69] See Ch. 15, pp. 665–7.

towards forms of global environmental regulation and the growth and dissemination of expertise in assessment – suggest that, at all levels of administration, the status and importance of environmental assessment is likely to grow.

The debate about the extent to which environmental assessment works to secure environmental protection tends to focus upon the possible substantive effects of the process, as opposed to its 'merely' procedural aspects. We opened this chapter by stressing the procedural nature of environmental assessment; for example we stated clearly that even an environmentally 'corrupt' development may be given the go-ahead after having been subject to an environmental assessment process. What is important is that the procedures are complied with. In other words, environmental assessment is a 'tool not a [substantive] rule'.[70] But this is far from the whole story. The procedural control exercised by environmental assessment, especially the involvement of the public, has the potential to shape the substantive outcome of the final decision whether or not to grant development consent because there is a fine line between procedural due process (affecting the propriety of the procedure involved in reaching a decision) and substantive due process (affecting the quality of the decision reached).[71] Some environmental assessment regimes do instill the environmental assessment process with a stronger substantive core. The form of environmental assessment mandated in the Habitats Directive is one such example (Chapter 15, pp. 649–55). In the case of a negative assessment of the environmental effects of a plan or project, Art. 6 of the Habitats Directive provides that the plan or project can only proceed for certain, prescribed, reasons, and if compensatory measures are taken. In this case, environmental assessment operates as a procedural safeguard with some substantive impact. This is also the case with the form of environmental assessment envisaged in the Water Framework Directive.[72] The European Commission, perhaps recognising the inherent limitations of environmental assessment, has also been exploring the means by which a more substantive element may be introduced into the Member States' environmental assessment regimes by obliging authorities to refuse consent for a project that is likely to have negative impacts on the environment,[73] although no real progress has been made in this direction. A sense of how this might work in practice is seen in Portuguese law in an unusual example of 'overcompliance' with the requirements of the EIA Directive, in which the environmental assessment process has considerable legal force. Interestingly, Alexandra Aragao sets out how this can be a two-edged sword in environmental terms.

---

[70] Jonathan Wiener, lecture on 'Better Regulation', 25 May 2006, UCL.

[71] See further discussion in Holder, *Environmental Assessment*, pp. 237–43.

[72] See William Howarth, 'Substance and Procedure under the Strategic Environmental Assessment Directive and the Water Framework Directive' in Holder and Campbell-Holt (eds.), *Taking Stock of Environmental Assessment*.

[73] Internal note accompanying European Commission, *Five Years Report to the Parliament and the Council on the Effectiveness of the EIA Directive* (CEC, 1992).

### Alexandra Aragao, 'The Impact of EC Environmental Law on Portuguese Law' in Richard Macrory (ed.), *Reflections on Thirty Years of EU Environmental Law: A High Level of Protection?* (Europa, 2006), p. 507

Binding effects

When the EIA concludes that the project could be detrimental to the environment, the final statement on the environmental impact of the project [issued by the Minister of the Environment] has binding effects both on the developer and on other public authorities. In this case, the project may not be authorised or executed. If 'development consent' is in fact subsequently granted, then this act would be void, producing no effects, and could be declared so at any time and upon application by anyone.

On the contrary, if the EIA comes to the opposite conclusion (the irrelevance of the environmental impacts of the project), the Minister's statement neither compels the developer to go on with the project nor forbids a rejection of the project by the competent authorities for non-environmental reasons.

This solution shows how the national legislature has clearly decided, for political reasons, to go beyond the European system of legislation that is *'compulsory but not binding'*, in providing a more stringent statute and stronger effects for a negative EIA.

We will not question why the legislator took this option. It could have been due to a genuine commitment to the environment, or just to prevent domestic conflicts over locally unwanted land uses (lulu), or even for other reasons that are less clear. What matters now is that this regime has been in force in Portugal since May 2000 and is considered to be, by the scientific community as well as by the local NGOs, a stringent and pro-environmental regime.

Yet, in January 2004, the Ministries of the Economy and the Environment issued a very questionable Ministerial Order increasing the strength of the Minister's statement in the cases of favourable EIA.

Now, projects for producing energy from renewable sources (wind, water, biomass, biogas, waves and photovoltaic, with the exception of waste incineration) that receive a favourable EIA statement are in practice automatically authorised even if they are to be developed within nature conservation areas.

In fact, the Institute for Nature Conservation [the authority belonging to the structure of the Ministry of the Environment, responsible for the management of nature conservation areas] is obliged to give a favourable opinion to the pursuit of whatever energy project that is to be developed within the areas under its jurisdiction (*Special Protection Areas* for birds, *Special Areas of Conservation* for habitats and species, and *Nature 2000* sites).

But does this not give too much weight to the EIA decision in cases where the law (on nature conservation) is used to request the intervention of an authority with specific competence in the field of nature conservation?

Besides, as it has been designed in Portuguese law, the EIA is not an instrument suited to nature conservation. One can say that the EIA law even presents some significant breaches of nature conservation.

In terms of making a difference to decision making, the inherent limitation of one-off, or project-based, assessment is that frequently decisions at this level have been taken in the context of far broader policy frameworks which might have been set with little or no reference to environmental criteria. For example a motorway development is almost bound to have been decided by reference to regional, national and European transport policy. The extension of environmental impact assessment to allow for the impacts of different policy judgments to be evaluated is recognition of this flaw.

## 4 Extending EIA: Strategic Environmental Assessment

Environmental impact assessment has long been an important part of the planning system (even well before the adoption of the EIA Directive). Strategic forms of environmental assessment now stretch well beyond the formal boundaries of the town and country planning system, as set by the definition of 'development', and, in keeping with the new system of integrated spatial planning, permit a broader assessment of policy objectives and their likely impact on the environment. Strategic forms of assessment are also applied to legislation (regulatory impact), economic policies, budgets and sectoral policies, plans and programmes on, for example, agriculture, transport, waste and international aid. This remarkable expansion of the content of environmental assessment is a mark of the ability of the instrument to accommodate a range of issues and to feed into decision making at different, and often inter-related, levels. It also suggests a deeper level of integration and policy coordination than could ever be the case with project-based assessment. A great many (and sometimes inflated) claims have been made for strategic environmental assessment. The following presents just a few.

### Riki Therivel, *Strategic Environmental Assessment in Action* (Earthscan, 2004), pp. 14–16

#### Advantages of SEA
Why is SEA needed? What is its 'value added' over project EIA or other systems of environmental management, footprinting or standards?

First, SEA gets in earlier. Strategic actions lead to and shape projects so appraising the strategic actions offers the chance to influence the *kinds* of projects that are going to happen, not just the details after projects are already being considered.

Second, SEA deals with impacts that are difficult to consider at project level. It deals with cumulative and synergistic impacts of multiple projects, for instance the traffic implications of the redevelopment of an entire area. This is very difficult to address on a project-by-project level … Similarly, SEA can deal with larger-scale environmental impacts such as those on biodiversity or global warming more effectively than can individual EIAs.

SEA promotes a better consideration of alternatives. By the time most projects are proposed, many alternatives have already been closed off because of higher-level decisions.

For instance, renewable energy developments are unlikely to get built in a region whose energy strategy promotes gas-fired power stations. SEA affects the decision-making process at a stage where more alternatives are available for consideration, including reducing demand (reducing the need to travel, promoting accessibility rather than mobility) ...

SEA incorporates environmental and sustainability considerations in strategic decision making. Using the example above, SEA would inform decision-makers about the environmental and sustainability implications of energy efficiency versus renewable energy versus fossil fuel power generation. These implications could then be considered alongside financial, technical, political and other concerns. SEA thus adds an additional dimension to the decision-making process. SEA facilitates – in theory, even if not in practice – public participation in strategic decision-making. Traditionally, strategic actions have been developed with limited public input. At minimum, SEA provides one opportunity for the public to comment on a strategic action before it is formally agreed. At best, it allows the public to be actively involved throughout the strategic decision-making process.

All of these factors make the decision-making process more transparent and robust. SEA helps to ensure that the strategic action will be implemented effectively and that no unintended impacts will result from the strategic action. It also helps the strategic action to be approved more quickly by an inspector or auditors. As a side effect, SEA helps decision-makers to better understand their plan, feel more confident about it, and learn about sustainability.

Finally, because of tiering, SEA has the potential to promote more streamlined decision-making, where decisions taken at one planning stage (using SEA at that stage) may not need to be revisited at subsequent stages of decision-making (and their SEA or EIA). It could obviate, for instance, the need for lengthy project-level inquiries that consider strategic-level issues, though in practice it is rarely possible to fully separate the strategic and project levels.

Therivel balances this campaign for strategic environmental assessment with a review of its drawbacks – it takes time and resources, mechanisms for public consultation are difficult to set up and, in the end, such assessments are only one input into the decision. However, she remains convinced by their utility: 'there are also times when, in the midst of filling in an SEA matrix, the decision-maker comes up with a new, elegant approach to a problem. Or [where] a doubtful politician is convinced to take a more sustainable option because of the findings of an SEA' (p. 18). If anything, Therivel understates the potentially radical and transformative, even destabilising, potential of SEA through the changes that it is capable of forcing in the way governments, administrations and corporations create and carry out their policies (a point made by Susan Owens and Richard Cowell, above, p. 563). This quality of strategic forms of environmental assessment also explains the reluctance on the part of some Member States in the European Union to adopt a mandatory and extensive form of SEA.

## (a) SEA directive

An early form of strategic environmental assessment was developed in the United States under NEPA 1969 (discussed above, pp. 567–8). This required Federal agencies to make a detailed assessment of the environmental implications of any action (be that a development project or policy) likely to affect significantly the quality of the environment. Clearly influenced by this, the European Commission drafted a similar instrument in 1980, but strong resistance by some Member States meant that this plan for a strategic form of environmental assessment was abandoned in favour of the (slightly) less controversial, and strongly project-based, form of environmental assessment, the EIA Directive, discussed above.

The idea of a policy-oriented instrument was revisited in the 1990s, and a weakened version was adopted by the Union as Directive 2001/42/EC on the assessment of the effects of certain plans and programmes on the environment in 2001 (implemented in England and Wales via the Environmental Assessment of Plans and Programmes Regulations 2004[74]). The structure of the SEA Directive (requiring screening,[75] the compilation of an 'environmental report',[76] consultation based on this document,[77] and taking into account the resulting information when preparing a plan or programme and before its adoption or submission to the legislative process[78]) mirrors that of the EIA Directive. The SEA Directive is expressly designed to provide a framework for the future development consent of projects listed in the EIA Directive, as described in Art. 3. Crucially, the SEA Directive applies to the preparation of plans and programmes, *not* policy decisions. A useful definition of these terms is provided by Wood and Djeddour: 'a policy may ... be considered as the inspiration and guidance for action, a plan as a set of coordinated and timed objectives for the implementation of the policy, and a programme as a set of projects in a particular area'.[79]

### Directive 2001/42/EC on the assessment of the effects of certain plans and programmes on the environment OJ 2001 L 197/30

Whereas:

4. Environmental assessment is an important tool for integrating environmental considerations into the preparation and adoption of certain plans and programmes which are likely to have significant effects on the environment in the Member States, because it ensures that such effects of implementing plans and programmes are taken into account during their preparation and before their adoption.

---

[74] SI 2004 No. 1633.
[75] Articles 3 and 4 (in conjunction with Annex II), criteria for determining likely significant effects.    [76] Article 5, coupled with Annex I.    [77] Articles 6 and 7.    [78] Articles 8 and 9.
[79] Chris Wood and Mohamed Djeddour, 'Strategic Environmental Assessment: EA of Policies, Plans and Programmes' (1991) 10 *The Impact Assessment Bulletin* 3, p. 3.

5. The adoption of environmental assessment procedures at the planning and programming level should benefit undertakings by providing a more consistent framework in which to operate by the inclusion of the relevant environmental information into decision-making. The inclusion of a wider set of factors in decision-making should contribute to more sustainable and effective solutions.

...

### Article 1 – Objectives

The objective of this Directive is to provide for a high level of protection of the environment and to contribute to the integration of environmental considerations into the preparation and adoption of plans and programmes with a view to promoting sustainable development, by ensuring that, in accordance with this Directive, an environmental assessment is carried out of certain plans and programmes which are likely to have significant effects on the environment.

### Article 3 – Scope

1. An environmental assessment, in accordance with Articles 4 to 9, shall be carried out for plans and programmes referred to in paragraphs 2 to 4 which are likely to have significant environmental effects.

2. Subject to paragraph 3, an environmental assessment shall be carried out for all plans and programmes,

    (a) which are prepared for agriculture, forestry, fisheries, energy, industry, transport, waste management, telecommunications, tourism, town and country planning or land use and which set the framework for future development consent of projects listed in Annexes I and II to Directive 85/337/EEC, or

    (b) which, in view of the likely effect on sites have been determined to require an assessment pursuant to Article 6 or 7 of Directive 92/43/EEC [the Habitats Directive[80]]

3. Plans and programmes referred to in paragraph 2 which determine the use of small areas at local level and minor modifications to plans and programmes referred to in paragraph 2 shall require an environmental assessment only where the Member States determine that they are likely to have significant environmental effects.

4. Member States shall determine whether plans and programmes, other than those referred to in paragraph 2, which set the framework for future development consent of projects, are likely to have significant environmental effects.

The form of strategic environmental assessment advanced in this Directive remains closely related to project-based forms of assessment. In fact, in some cases it is difficult to pinpoint exactly where strategic environmental assessment ends and environmental impact assessment begins. For example the assessment carried out to evaluate the environmental effects of granting licences for renewable energy projects (discussed in Chapter 17, pp. 723–9) was ostensibly a strategic environmental assessment, but it inevitably considered in some detail the suitability of particular sites.

---

[80] See Ch. 15, pp. 634–6.

One important distinction between the EIA and the SEA Directives is the requirement in the latter that 'Member States shall monitor the significant environmental effects of the implementation of plans and programmes in order, inter alia, to identify at an early stage unforeseen adverse effects and to be able to undertake appropriate remedial action.'[81] The imposition of post-assessment monitoring might be explained by the fact that this Directive generally imposes obligations on public authorities, who are likely to have easier access to the sources of this type of information (we discuss post-assessment monitoring further below, pp. 604–7). The EU appears to remain reluctant to oblige private bodies, more likely to be subject to the terms of the EIA Directive, to do the same.

## (b) Sustainability analysis

Strategic environmental assessment represents a conceptual and practical progression from environmental impact assessment, particularly in terms of thinking about and instituting the integration of policy areas as a necessity of sustainable development. A further development of environmental assessment is now firmly on the political agenda in the European Union in the form of 'sustainability analysis', currently applied inwardly, to the European Commission's own policy making procedures, but also likely to be projected onto Member State policy making apparatus in the near future (see typology of environmental assessment in Table 14.1). This amended and expanded form of assessment amalgamates the Commission's existing sectoral assessment procedures (business impact assessment, gender assessment, regulatory impact assessment and, of course, environmental assessment) and requires an assessment of the environmental, social and economic impacts of all major policy initiatives or legislative proposals.

The Commission's expansion of environmental assessment into 'sustainability analysis' is an attempt to create an integrated policy and legislative appraisal procedure which allows for broad and cross-sectoral consideration of alternative policy choices by regulating decision making processes in line with the demands of sustainable development. To some limited extent the Commission's action should be lauded. The difficulty lies in the political reality that different weights are granted to environmental, social and economic factors in any policy making process, but particularly in the European Commission where the dominant policy blocks (or Directorates-General) of agriculture, transport, the internal market and competition hold sway in most examples of decision making. The explicit consequence of merging existing assessments into a single 'sustainability' instrument, allowing for the overall consideration and assessment of impacts, is the identification of trade-offs

---

[81] Article 10.

**Table 14.1** Types of Environmental Assessment

| Instrument | EIA | SEA | Sustainability analysis |
|---|---|---|---|
| Legal framework | EIA Directive 85/337/EEC as amended | SEA Directive 2001/42/EC | Exists as a matter of policy, e.g. EU Commission internal policy making practices |
| Function | Assessment of major developments<br><br>Identification of mitigating measures | Assessment of cumulative effects and synergistic and long-term effects | Assessment of policy and legislation according to sustainability criteria |
| Example | Kentish Flats wind farm project[82] | Offshore wind farm SEA (Round 2 licences) – though note fundamentally site-based[83] | EU Commission internal policy making practices |
| Advantages | – range of information sources<br>– cultural change | – integrationist<br>– proactive / forward planning;<br>– public interest;<br>– addresses sources of environmental damage and capable of carrying capacity concerns | – integrates environmental impact considerations at the outset of policy/legislation formation |
| Drawbacks | – reactive – triggered by project proposal;<br>– restricted appreciation of alternatives, cumulative effects and carrying capacity and integrity of natural system | – problems with effective participation;<br>– information complexity | – problem of 'trade-offs' with social and economic criteria;<br>and marginalisation of environmental protection considerations as against the 'heavy-weights' of trade, agriculture and competition |

---

[82] See pp. 563–7.      [83] See Ch. 17, pp. 723–9.

between competing objectives. Whilst such an exercise might be considered an inherent part of sustainable development, here it creates the conditions for the marginalisation of an integrated, but diluted, environmental policy. This concern is borne out by the methodological principles guiding the Commission's internal impact assessment procedure:

> The economic, social and environmental impacts identified for the proposed option should be analysed and presented in a format that facilitates a better understanding of the trade-offs between competing economic, social, and environmental objectives. To show the different impacts, make comparisons easier and identify trade-offs and win-win situations in a transparent way, it is desirable to quantify the impacts in physical and, where appropriate, monetary terms (in addition to a qualitative appraisal).[84]

In general the methods of assessment currently advocated by the Commission are largely reductionist and simplistic, with greater emphasis placed upon cost benefit analysis and other examples of economist methodology than upon techniques more sensitive to the unique quality of environmental values. (We review this debate in Chapter 1, pp. 37–40.) The Directorate-General responsible for environmental policy even adheres to this approach to identifying and valuing impacts in its guide to impact assessment, distributed throughout the Commission to ensure adequate account is taken of environmental impacts in the new cross-policy impact assessment procedure:

> Quantifying the effects that a policy proposal has on the environment is extremely useful and effective. Giving figures or values to the impacts, perhaps in monetary terms, means that they can be more easily compared with economic benefits for instance. The Commission should be provided with a clear idea of the scale of the implications of any policy. For example, the policy proposal may bring 500,000 extra tourists to a region of the Community but at a cost of a 20% worsening of air quality in those urban areas which is likely to cause 6,000 early deaths a year. By being as precise as possible about the effects, the Commission will have the best possible information on which to take the decision … For the more strategic policies, the impacts will probably need to be expressed in qualitative ways rather than quantitative ways since meaningful figures (e.g. a 15% loss of a specific habitat across the Community) are unlikely to be possible.[85]

The methodologies advanced for the impact assessment procedure appear likely to give weight to economic factors, by fitting environmental values into crude economic models (such as cost benefit analysis) and adopting economic language, objectives and methods, all of which may have the effect of excluding alternative values and policy choices. More specifically, this methodological approach is quite out of kilter with the drive to encourage meaningful lay

---

[84] European Commission, *Communication from the Commission on Impact Assessment* COM (2002) 272 final.     [85] European Commission, *Communication on Impact Assessment*, p. 20.

participation in decision making in the European Union – consultation, such as it is, takes place after the environmental assessment report is complete.

Finally we should note that this move on the part of the European Commission (and its attendant drawbacks) is not novel. In the United Kingdom, 'sustainability appraisal' now forms part of the extended planning system introduced by the Planning and Compensation Act 2004, discussed in the last chapter (pp. 522–9). A particularly interesting application of this form of assessment was the sustainability impact assessment study of the international trade policy which constituted the World Trade Organisation's (WTO's) Round in Doha. The study assessed the significance of the likely impacts of a list of measures involved in the Round such as changes to agreement on agriculture, measures relating to technical barriers to trade, clarification of the relationship between WTO trade rules and trade measures taken pursuant to multi-lateral environmental agreements and other environmental policy initiatives and so on. Each measure was assessed in terms of its social, economic and environmental impact for the European Union and for developing and least-developed countries. The report also suggested 'flanking' measures designed to mitigate or enhance negative or positive impacts.[86] Recent research is more critical of the extent to which the Commission's new impact assessment regime functions as an effective instrument for the implementation of the EU's commitment to promoting sustainability 'externally' in the developing world, in particular claiming that current strategies such as impact assessment provide opportunities for 'information exchange' between Directorates-General, networks and groups, but that the results of such assessment are not feeding sufficiently into high-level policy making strategies, such as the Sustainable Development Strategy.[87]

## 5 Future evolutionary paths

Environmental assessment has undergone rapid development, mainly in terms of its expansion to include a broad range of policy concerns in strategic forms of assessment. It remains capable of further development, particularly in terms of providing a better fit with the complexity of more integrated, and complex, forms of environmental decision making than existed (or were capable of being understood) in the early days of the development of environmental assessment.

### (a) Post-assessment monitoring: 'living assessments'[88]

In introducing the idea of environmental assessment, we, like many others, have focussed upon environmental assessment as a pre-emptive, anticipatory

---

[86] Colin Kirkpatrick and Norman Lee, *WTO New Round, Sustainability Impact Assessment Study, Phase Two Report* (University of Manchester Press, 1999).

[87] Camilla Adelle, Julia Hertin and Andrew Jordan, 'Sustainable Development "Outside" the European Union: What Role for Impact Assessment?' (2006) 16 *European Environment* 57, p. 69.

[88] This apt phrase was coined by a consultant working on an environmental assessment of the Solway Firth wind farm project, discussed in Ch. 17, pp. 730–5.

mechanism, deployed *prior* to a decision whether or not to grant authorisation for an activity or project (pp. 556–7), and relying on a degree of 'clairvoyance'.[89] However, this is to present the decision making process in very narrow terms and to neglect the increasing occurrence and usefulness of post-assessment monitoring or follow up. Making environmental assessment an 'on-going investigation and management of impacts, rather than a one-time prediction during the pre-decision stages',[90] encourages the creation of feedback loops which may help organisations and administrations, and even lawyers, learn about the way in which particular projects or policies may damage the environment in the future. Jos Arts and Angus Morrison-Saunders argue that this development fits well with the reality of decision making in the planning system, as one of the main contexts in which environmental assessment takes place, by recognising that as a process eliciting multiple sources of information and engaging multiple actors and interests it is far removed from the rational picture of decision making drawn from law and policy in the area (the standard view of deliberation based upon material considerations and representations, leading inexorably to *the* decision). In practice, planning is altogether a more complex and mediated social and legal experience in which decision making is shaped by changes in, for example, the physical environment of an area, political priorities, regulations or policies, societal views and scientific knowledge, as well as by negotiations, persuasion and bargaining.[91] They affirm that environmental assessment is now firmly embedded in the planning system. Their account also goes beyond a generally accepted version of events – that environmental assessment has brought about important changes (a process of 'greening') in planning[92] – by suggesting that more collaborative understandings of planning (discussed in the last chapter, pp. 530–45) are capable of having equally important effects on the structure and content of environmental assessment, particularly in terms of encouraging post-assessment procedures.

A further important role for post-assessment monitoring or 'living assessment' is that it provides a way of checking up on developers' claims about the likely impact of a project, and also the reality of claims about mitigating measures which are in some cases extravagantly described in environmental statements, and tend to provide the basis for conditions attached to the grant of development consent. Combined with greater access to data contained in environmental statements, perhaps through the digitalisation of this type of information, as we discuss further below, this suggests a potentially powerful use for environmental assessment as a (public) enforcement mechanism. Such a role might even cause us to redefine the regulatory territory occupied by environmental assessment – from a predominantly procedural instrument, to one having more substantive effects.

[89] Karkkainen, 'Toward a Smarter NEPA', p. 907.
[90] Jos Arts and Angus Morrison-Saunders, 'Theoretical Perspectives on EIA and Follow-Up' in Angus Morrison-Saunders and Jos Arts (eds.), Assessing Impact: Handbook of EIA and SEA Follow-up (Earthscan, 2004), pp. 24–5.    [91] Ibid., p. 30.    [92] See further Ch. 12, pp. 494–502.

The practice of carrying out post-assessment monitoring might also carve out a place for environmental assessment in on-going 'ecosystem governance' or management. Karkkainen gives an example of the apparently successful integration of environmental assessment procedures into ecosystem governance, notwithstanding the apparently poor fit between the standard environmental impact assessment paradigm of case-by-case analysis on an agency- and project-specific basis (as mandated by NEPA), and ecosystem governance which aims at continuous reassessment and readjustment of policies and practices and the partnership of a range of agencies. Whilst this is familiar ground to lawyers in the United States, such an approach might encourage embedding environmental assessment within existing environmental management and audit systems in the European Union.

### Bradley C. Karkkainen, 'Toward a Smarter NEPA: Monitoring and Managing Government's Environmental Performance' (2002) 102 *Columbia Law Review* 903, p. 967

A leading example comes from South Florida where a major regional effort is underway to restore the ecological health of the Everglades and associated ecosystems …

The Everglades is a unique and irreplaceable wetland complex that includes the Everglades National Park, the Big Cypress Preserve, and the Loxahatchee National Wildlife Refuge. It is one of the most biodiverse regions in the nation, providing habitat for numerous bird and animal species. But the Everglades ecosystem was slowly dying as a result of large scale water diversions that date back to the 1940s, when the Army Corps of Engineers undertook a massive infrastructure project that rerouted the Everglades' natural hydrological flow in order to 'reclaim' wetlands in the north Everglades, control flooding, provide public drinking water supplies, and generally promote both urban and agricultural development in South Florida. The south Everglades, meanwhile, not only was starved of its water, but also began to choke on nonpoint nutrient pollution, much of it generated by the large sugar plantations operating in the 'reclaimed' lands to the north.

Eventually it became apparent that conventional 'inside-the-fenceposts' management could not restore the hydrology and water quality that would be needed to save the dying wetlands …

The centrepiece of the restoration effort is another massive, federally funded infrastructure project, once again aimed at restructuring the hydrological system – but this time in an attempt to mimic prediversion water flows to the south Everglades, while nonetheless maintaining the flow and quality of public drinking water supplies. Unfortunately, however, little detailed historical data is available on prediversion water flows, and in any event, ecological conditions have changed radically over the course of fifty years of water diversions, so that perfect replication of prediversion conditions would be impossible even if such data were available. Nor is anyone certain how various combinations of seasonal and annual water flows will affect the complex and varied mosaic of habitats that comprise the Everglades as it exists today. The project, in short, is a gigantic series of ecological experiments – albeit necessary experiments. If we do nothing the Everglades will surely die;

yet even with the best science, we are incapable of ascertaining a precise formula to guarantee a cure.

The new infrastructure plan was developed in the Central and Southern Florida Project comprehensive Review Study ('Everglades Restudy'), prepared by the Army Corps of Engineers and the South Florida Water Management District. The NEPA-mandated Final Environmental Impact Statement associated with this project does not appear as a separate document, but instead is integrated into the planning document itself, reflecting a merger of environmental impact analysis into the agency's decision making process. Rather than attempting to evaluate, in typically comprehensive fashion, the many highly uncertain ecological effects of the project, the Statement is refreshingly candid in acknowledging uncertainties, establishing the need and framework for future monitoring, and outlining a range of adaptive measures that will be integral to ongoing management efforts over the life of the project. In this case, then, the NEPA-mandated Environmental Impact Statement is effectively integrated into a larger ecosystem management framework. Because it will be necessary to manage adaptively, provision is made for the post-decision monitoring and adaptive adjustment that NEPA alone fails to provide. In the process, the EIS is reconceptualised as a more modest but nonetheless useful analytical exercise; it is one in a series of points at which to take stock of the expected environmental consequences, rather than the sole source of 'fully informed' decision making.

### (b) Digitalisation and freedom of access to information

Currently the environmental statements prepared by developers seeking to gain development consent for their proposals represent no more than fragments of environmental knowledge, as the following account (from the United States) suggests:

In a metropolitan area or major natural resource area, there may have been hundreds of Federal and state impact studies conducted since 1970 [post NEPA 1969]. These stand-alone reports consist of a diverse range of secondary data and new information created for the particular study. When the review is completed, the report is archived. This approach is not designed to promote community learning over time, wherein each new statement contributes new transactional updates to a shared knowledge base. This one-stop approach of the impact statement is highly wasteful of scarce environmental information expenditures, and the lack of a managed information framework condones the mediocre predictive quality that typifies many analyses.[93]

Daniel Farber has argued consistently for the consolidation, digitalisation and accessibility of this body of information in order that researchers, protestors and local residents interested in the environmental impacts of projects affecting a particular species or habitat or local area can easily access an archive of environmental statements on these subjects.[94] He offers a 'social learning' argument

---

[93] John Felleman, *Deep Information: The Role of Information Policy in Environmental Sustainability* (Ablex Publishing, 1997), p. 175, cited by Farber, 'Bringing Environmental Assessment into the Digital Age'.    [94] Farber, 'Bringing Environmental Assessment into the Digital Age'.

in favour of freedom of access to environmental information elicited in the environmental assessment process on the ground that society urgently needs better information about the present condition of the environment and that if this is not forthcoming we will never be capable of discovering problems or monitoring the effectiveness of our current efforts, which are prerequisites of learning to do better. Making developers' environmental statements (or reports as they are referred to in the United States) readily accessible and searchable might further contribute to the development of 'best practice' standards based upon the diverse approaches taken by different agencies. Farber likens this to the development of the common law: 'the environmental assessment process, like the common law, consists of a series of individual decisions that may cumulatively establish the contours of accepted practice. Just as the publication of opinions accelerated the development of the common law, so making environmental assessments available on line will help build a body of known "precedents" for reviewing environmental impacts.'

The vision of freely available information detailing predicted impacts, as well as the actual impacts, in the form of data from post-assessment monitoring, and perhaps integrated with GIS (geographical information systems), is a very powerful one, giving individuals and organisations the means to get to know their local environment better, as well as the threats to it. But Farber also recognises the strength of the resistance to this, mainly because of the opportunities it offers to check compliance with commitments about mitigating measures made in developers' environmental statements and adherence to conditions attached to development consent based upon predictions made in the course of the assessment process. The message is that the technology exists to build a database of environmental statements, but that the political will is currently lacking.

## 6 Conclusions

As originally conceived, environmental impact assessment was a modernist instrument, representing a synoptic, one-off and simplistic (albeit integrated) view of the environment and the sum of human impacts upon it. It was adopted in both the United States and the EU as an important part of progressive environmental policy programmes and was accompanied by much optimism that the prior assessment of environmental effects could deliver not just better procedures, but also better *decisions*, in favour of environmental protection. It was also imbued with expectations about the positive contribution of public participation to decision making, although the reality of environmental assessment procedures was quite different, with great emphasis being placed upon quantitative methodologies and models for predicting future effects of development. A reassessment of environmental assessment has since taken place, highly influenced by a broader debate about the inevitably limited and flawed nature of 'technocentric' decision making procedures, in the planning system and beyond. There is now a greater appreciation of the complex, 'looped', nature of decision making as a whole, which has had implications for the way in which environmental assessment (and its success as an environmental protection mechanism) is conceived. In particular the exposure of the fallibility of *ex ante* predictions suggests the utility of post-assessment monitoring.

The development of strategic environmental assessment is similarly a mark of recognition of the complexity of decision making, especially the idea that development consent is never a discrete choice but takes place in a pre-established policy framework. Whilst strategic environmental assessment is capable of making important inroads into the policy making process by requiring environmental consequences of decisions to be considered at a high level of abstraction, the potential radicalism of the instrument has been reined in, as witnessed by the weakness of the SEA Directive in many key respects, but particularly its application to plans and programmes, not policy.

There remains considerable potential for environmental assessment to be recreated, or 'retooled' as Karkkainen puts it,[95] to produce a more flexible and responsive decision making tool, which relates to each stage of a decision and extends beyond the point of consent to reflect more accurately and accommodate the uncertainties and complexities of trying to predict 'cause and effect' in the environment, possibly as part of on-going environmental management systems. Already, a key shift in environmental assessment has been from a reliance on technocentric methodologies to a greater emphasis upon participatory democracy, to the extent that environmental assessment has recently been championed by some members of the judiciary as a form of 'local democracy',[96] suggesting the need to put to rest the long-held view that legal culture is fundamentally in opposition to the central tenets of environmental assessment.

## 7 Further reading

In this area, the literature from the United States leads the field. Academics and practitioners are well ahead of the game because of the longer history of environmental assessment. Daniel Mandelker's *NEPA Treatise* (Thompson West, loose-leaf, latest update 2006) is a huge and on-going work with coverage of environmental assessment in the USA, the UK and Canada. Bradley Karkkainen's 'Toward a Smarter NEPA: Monitoring and Managing Government's Environmental Performance' (2002) 102 *Columbia Law Review* 903 gives a very complete account of the various 'pathologies' of assessment in the United States.

In the United Kingdom, the most comprehensive and step-by-step guide to the law relating to environmental assessment is Stephen Tromans and Karl Fuller's *Environmental Impact Assessment: Law and Practice* (Butterworths, 2003). William Sheate's *Environmental Impact Assessment: Law and Policy* (Cameron May, 1996) is more broad ranging, paying greater attention to the role of policy in environmental assessment. Holder's

---

[95] 'Toward a Smarter NEPA', p. 903.

[96] See, for example, *Richardson v. North Yorkshire County Council and Secretary of State* [2003] EWCA Civ 1860 (CA) in which Richard J aligned the EIA regime with the workings of local democracy (para. 4).

*Environmental Assessment: The Regulation of Decision Making* (Oxford University Press, 2004) is a more selective and theoretical look at environmental assessment procedures, using case studies to highlight particular features of the process – prediction, significance, participation and decision making.

A sound introduction to environmental impact assessment (though not from a legal point of view) is given by John Glasson, Riki Therivel and Andrew Chadwick in their *Introduction to Environmental Impact Assessment* (Routledge, 3rd edn, 2005). This contains a very useful section on case studies – 'EIA in Practice'. More specifically on strategic environmental assessment is Riki Therivel's *Strategic Environmental Assessment in Action* (Earthscan, 2004) which is above all a practical guide to the methodologies, succeeding in making these transparent and apparently 'do-able'. This book also draws on case studies, including interesting accounts of the strategic environmental assessments conducted of British farming strategy, regional economic strategy and local development plans. This would be perfect for students grappling with the more abstract nature of SEA procedures. We have already referred to the conceptually advanced and theorised account of the argument for post-assessment monitoring by Angus Morrison-Saunders and Jos Arts (p. 605). This heads a wide-ranging edited collection by the same authors, *Assessing Impact: Handbook of EIA and SEA Follow-up* (Earthscan, 2004) which, again, gives lots of examples of practice in this still-emerging field of environmental assessment.

On a more legal theme, in addition to those articles already mentioned in the course of this chapter, Aine Ryall's *Effective Judicial Protection and the Environmental Impact Assessment Directive in Ireland* (Hart, 2007) takes a close look at public participation. In Jane Holder and Donald McGillivray's edited collection, *Taking Stock of Environmental Assessment: Law, Policy and Practice* (Routledge Cavendish, 2007), experts in the field critically review the development and aspects of the current state of environmental assessment in Europe and the United States.

**15**

# Nature Conservation and Biodiversity: the Technique of Designation

## 1 Introduction

In this Part, on the legal mechanisms for controlling land use and development, we have traced the roots of a division between controls over urban and country areas to the post-war land settlement (see especially pp. 479–87). We explained that the reason for the exclusion of agricultural and forestry activities from the scope of the Town and Country Planning Act (TCPA) 1947 (the title of the Act being something of a misnomer) was the assumption that there would be no conflict between the production of food and wood, and the protection of the environment.[1] This has clearly proved not to be the case. In this and the next chapter, we focus upon the current state of law seeking to secure the conservation of nature, applying mainly to the countryside and developed primarily in response to what William Adams calls the 'industrialisation of agriculture'. The consequences for nature of this phenomenon, in particular the fragmentation of natural areas, are described below. In the following passage, Adams also introduces the (imperfect) idea of designating areas of land for special protection, which constitutes the main legal technique in nature conservation law and policy.[2]

### William M. Adams, *Future Nature: A Vision for Conservation* (Earthscan, 2003), pp. 117–18

The industrialisation of agriculture ... has everywhere tended to produce landscapes that are limited in their diversity. In parts of the country where agricultural intensification has

---

[1] Wendy Le-Las, 'Sustaining Biodiversity: The Contribution of the Planning System in Controlling Development' in Nicholas Herbert-Young (ed.), *Law, Policy and Development in the Rural Environment* (University of Wales Press, 1999), p. 80, citing Marion Shoard, *The Theft of the Countryside* (Temple Smith, 1980), p. 101. Richard Macrory and William Sheate describe the exclusion from the scope of planning controls governed by the TCPA of use of land for agricultural and forestry purposes as the *Leitmotif* of the British planning system in 'Agriculture and the European Community Environmental Assessment Directive: Lessons for Community Policy Making' (1989) 28 *Journal of Common Market Studies* 68, p. 78.

[2] Note that the protection of species is an indirect control mechanism relating to land, i.e. the need to avoid 'disturbance' to a particular species may have beneficial consequences for conservation interests, as discussed by Stuart Bell and Donald McGillivray, *Environmental Law* (Oxford University Press, 6th edn, 2005), pp. 840–7.

wrought extensive changes, such as the prairies of East Anglia, the vast bulk of land is of limited diversity and conservation interest because of the clearances of hedges and trees, 'improvement' of grassland and wetlands, constant cultivation and application of pesticides of various kinds. Within this landscape, habitats are fragmented and protected areas of all kinds are isolated. However, even here, fragments of semi-natural habitat and landscape features do remain, and provide some kind of link between protected areas. The best surviving fragments are often places left out of the planning of high-tech farmers and incoming urban migrants, existing on the margins of their properties. Such places include grasslands in churchyards and on road verges, and hedgerows, copses and small patches of unimproved land on farms. The network is skeletal in such areas, but in other parts of the UK where economic restructuring has proceeded less far (for example in Wales or Northern Ireland), the matrix of habitats in the 'wider countryside' is far richer, and designated sites are less isolated.

The density and ecology of this mosaic of landscape features is of great significance to the effectiveness of the protected areas that exist within the landscape, but perhaps more importantly it determines what wildlife the landscape as a whole can sustain, and it is also critical to the visual appearance of the landscape. Established protected areas are important, but conservation must move vigorously to address the management of the wider mosaic of habitats and landscapes within the countryside. The traditional concern for individual protected areas must be transformed to a concern for whole landscapes. We need, in the words of Roger Disilvestro, to begin 'formulating a remedy to fragmentation'.[3]

The process of remedying fragmentation is one of the themes of this and especially the next chapter. Notwithstanding the many faults that exist with an enclave approach to conservation, its continuing centrality in conservation law and policy means that in this chapter we closely examine the legal technique of designating land for special protection, specifically the regime for sites of special scientific interest (SSSIs) provided for by Part II of the Wildlife and Countryside Act 1981, as amended by the Countryside and Rights of Way Act 2000. In doing so, we identify and account for a major shift in the regulatory form for habitat protection from a predominantly voluntary approach (through various management agreements between conservation agencies and landowners), to the adoption of what amounts to a licensing regime for the authorisation of activities that are potentially harmful to the conservation interests of a designated site. Management agreements are still used, but with the important difference that the conservation agencies seek to secure positive environmental works or 'gains' in return for payments, rather than in the negative sense of payments for profit forgone. The demise of voluntarism that the 2000 Act brought about represents a 'contraflow' against the major trend in current environmental law and policy of encouraging environmental protection through the use of contracts or agreements. In terms of our portrayal of the relationship between law

---

[3] Roger L. Disilvestro, *Reclaiming the Last Wild Places: A New Agenda for Biodiversity* (Wiley, 1993), p. 207.

and policy, the radical changes brought about by the 2000 Act represent the law catching up with the policy and the practice of conservation agencies seeking to secure positive management of protected sites.[4] In this context we refer to arguments that the general policy move towards positive management of agricultural land is creating a new form of environmental property right.

In outlining this progression we represent the strong influence of the European Community (EC) in providing protection for certain habitat types. We focus on the two main European designations – special protection areas (SPAs or 'European sites') and special areas of conservation (SACs), provided for by the Birds Directive and Habitats Directive respectively.[5] The latter Directive in particular has impinged directly on the planning system because it established procedural safeguards in the case of a development to be located on a European site, for example the need to conduct an 'appropriate assessment' and, in the event of a 'negative assessment', to consider alternative solutions and compensatory measures. More fundamentally, it also introduced substantive requirements that such a project should only be granted development consent for particular reasons, thus limiting the decision making ability of local planning authorities and the Secretary of State. The influence of these measures in the planning system has been such that there is now debate at a more general level about the integration of conservation interests. The accommodation of conservation interests in planning decisions commonly takes several forms, including an undertaking by the developer to create new habitats, move threatened species or restock damaged areas.[6] But, as case law shows, even against the background of the 'reconciliatory potential of sustainability',[7] there is still considerable potential for a clash of nature conservation and development interests.

Following from the analysis of procedural safeguards for European sites, we point out that, as a regulatory mechanism, environmental assessment has the potential to operate as a point of convergence between planning law and policy and nature conservation because an assessment of the likely effects of a project or plan on the local environment is required both as a matter of the planning system (environmental impact assessment) and as part of the protection scheme established by the Habitats Directive (in the form of an 'appropriate assessment').[8] Below (pp. 563–7), we critically analyse an example of this type

---

[4] See National Parks and Access to the Countryside Act 1949, of which s. 16(3)(a) provided the Nature Conservancy Council with a power to enter into an agreement with an owner, lessee or occupier providing for the management of land and the carrying out of work.

[5] Directive 79/409/EEC on the conservation of wild birds OJ 1979 L 103/1 and Directive 92/43/EEC on the conservation of natural habitats and of wild fauna and flora OJ 1992 L 206/7.

[6] Such undertakings may form the subject of planning conditions; more extensive undertakings generally take the form of planning contributions. See Ch. 13, pp. 510–11.

[7] Susan Owens and Richard Cowell, *Land and Limits: Interpreting Sustainability in the Planning System* (Routledge, 2003), p. 103.

[8] As transposed by the Conservation (Natural Habitats, &c.) Regulations 1994 (SI 1994, No. 2716).

of assessment in the case of a proposed wind farm at Walland Marsh, Kent, and in Chapter 17 we consider the environmental impact assessments carried out for other wind farms.[9] Despite the obvious potential for convergence, the precise relationship between the two forms of assessment remains unclear, particularly in terms of the varying obligations to consider alternatives, as we also discuss in Chapter 17, pp. 740–1.

## 2 Designation

Designation of a parcel of land for a particular purpose means that within the boundaries of that specific area special rules apply, overriding the exercise of normal property rights. It can be a very powerful legal tool having significant effects on the social world both within and outside the designated area. An enclave approach to nature conservation may, however, be counterproductive: the manager of land nearby may rationalise destroying similar features of interest on the undesignated land, on the ground that it could have been designated but was not.[10] Designation of land clearly involves the drawing of a boundary, an exercise which is particularly problematic when a site's special characteristics rely upon a less easily defined 'buffer zone'.[11] The process of designation draws heavily upon scientific evaluations of the ecological condition of land and predictions about the likely effect of designating or not designating an area. The process is not immune from political considerations, as suggested by the allegation of 'quota-filling' in at least one case (see below, pp. 643–4) and by references to 'electorally sensitive areas' in describing Environmentally Sensitive Areas (ESAs, Chapter 16, pp. 683–4). In addition, the designation of land is likely to have profound economic implications, a factor which has been used to explain the exclusion of areas earmarked for development from a surrounding protected site.[12] In recognition of the complex mix of political and economic influences and scientific information in decisions whether or not to designate areas of land for special protection, the Habitats Directive provides procedures

---

[9]  Robin Rigg in the Solway Firth, pp. 730–5, and the proposed wind farm on the Isle of Lewis, pp. 735–42. We also consider the strategic environmental assessment process for 'Round 2' wind farm licences, pp. 723–30.

[10]  This is borne out by research conducted by Sue Elworthy on nitrate-sensitive areas, discussed in *Farming for Drinking Water* (Ashgate, 1994).

[11]  In *Sweet* v. *Secretary of State for the Environment and Nature Conservancy Council* [1989] JPEL 927, concerning the designation of an SSSI, it was held that it is possible to designate a penumbra of land that does not have the same scientific interest as the core area provided it belongs to the same environmental unit. What was not clear is whether surrounding 'buffer zone' land may be designated. The Countryside and Rights of Way Act has provided that 'if land adjacent to a site of special scientific interest were combined with the site of special scientific interest, the combined area of land would be of special interest', and that fact could be notified (s. 28B Wildlife and Countryside Act 1981). The 2000 Act was a lost opportunity to clarify the legitimacy of designating land that merely 'protects' designated land.

[12]  See, for example, Case C-44/95 *R* v. *Secretary of State for the Environment ex parte Royal Society for the Protection of Birds (Lappel Bank)* [1996] ECR I-3805 (discussed pp. 630–2) and *WWF-UK and RSPB* v. *Secretary of State for Scotland* [1999] Env LR 632 (discussed p. 651).

for the exchange and review of scientific information and the resolution of differences of opinion (see pp. 636–40).

Designation may be an inherently problematic exercise, but pragmatically it is useful in a variety of contexts. For example, when drawing up local development plans, planners may be made aware that a designated area is inappropriate for industrial development. As we explained in Chapter 13 the designation of land for special protection is a 'material consideration'; an individual planning application may fail, or have conditions attached, in order to maintain the scenic or biological integrity of an area. Importantly, as we discuss further below, the planning system does not provide absolute protection for conservation sites. This may be viewed as the fatal weakness at the heart of nature conservation law in Britain. William Adams has elaborated on the nature of designation along these lines.

### Adams, *Future Nature*, pp. 116–17

Reconnecting the landscape

...

Whatever their limitations, there is no doubt that protected areas will remain at the heart of conservation action in the UK. This is not only because we have invested far too much effort in entrenching the idea of protected areas into legislation, into the bureaucratic structure of government, and into the minds of landowners and naturalists to be able to abandon it, but also because it is difficult to see how else to deal with the accumulated biological and cultural values of the pieces of nature that have endured over generations in our changing land. The advantages of an approach involving protected areas are numerous. Protected area designation recognises that some places are more important than others for conservation (whether that judgement is made in terms of biodiversity, landscape, or heritage), and they allow resources to be prioritised. Protected areas are an established concept, powerful in political debate and appealing to the general public.

However, protected areas also have disadvantages. A conservation strategy based on protected areas can make a holistic approach to conservation more difficult, encouraging the view that conservation is a sector or a land use. Their existence can also imply that the needs of conservation have been met, making it harder to achieve integrated policies that cut across economic sectors and make a difference to national policies. Protected areas tend to be treated as separate entities from surrounding land, soaking up available conservation resources. Protected area boundaries are often arbitrary lines on maps, created by accidents of land tenure and the financial circumstances of conservation organisation, irrelevant to natural processes and environmental problems (pollution, for example). Furthermore, once a protected area is established, government agencies and the general public begin to think that they have a free licence to do whatever they like outside of its boundaries, which makes semi-natural habitat even more isolated and fragmented.

Protected areas are a necessary part of a future conservation strategy but they are not sufficient. An editorial in the journal *Conservation Biology* in 1992 called for conservation biologists to expand beyond their own 'reserve mentality'. The reasoning was partly pragmatic, reflecting a view that protected areas of all kinds are likely to become harder to acquire, but it was also argued that many species do not need special protection areas, but 'can coexist with reasonable amounts of intelligently managed commodity production and recreation'.[13] In their book *Conservation for the Twenty-First Century,* David Western and his collaborators suggest that one of the ways to make protected areas more effective is to integrate conservation into wider land use.[14]

Adams' idea of moving conservation out beyond the boundaries of protected areas, and of starting to conceive of conservation of the whole landscape, is well supported by biological research on islands. This has found that the number of breeding species is determined by rates of immigration and extinction which are controlled by the isolation and size of the island. Put simply: 'large islands close to a continental source tend to have more species than small isolated islands'.[15] When applied to mainland habitats, the theory similarly holds that isolation and the size of habitat fragments are important influences on the probability of extinction. In conclusion, in order to tackle the fragmentation of habitats and the degradation of landscape, we need to look beyond the boundaries of protected areas to the characteristics of the land around them, and to create large habitats of functionally linked systems of protected areas.[16] This idea has informed the compilation of biodiversity action plans (Chapter 16, pp. 671–3) and some of the more recent agri-environmental measures in the Common Agricultural Policy (CAP) (pp. 682–5).

As well as there being good biological reasons against designation, some consider this legal technique to reflect the artificial separation of humans and nature, reaching back to the Enlightenment. Peter Taylor considers the psychological aspects of designation or 'nature in reservations' from this perspective, and the implications of this for wildlife. The following passage foreshadows many of the issues discussed in the next chapter, including habitat creation and agricultural reform.

### Peter Taylor, *Beyond Conservation: A Wildland Strategy* (Earthscan, 2005), pp. 2–4

#### Nature in Reservations
Whatever the new-found strength of the conservation organisations, 'nature' as such is still marginalised. It exists as much in 'reservations' of the mind as in physical reservations in the countryside. It is still a minority interest, a hobby even, rather than an appreciation

---

[13] Peter F. Brussard, Dennis D. Murphy and Reed F. Noss, 'Strategy and Tactics for Conserving Biological Diversity in the United States' (1992) 6 *Conservation Biology* 157, p. 158.

[14] Oxford University Press, 1989, p. 313.

[15] Described by William M. Adams, *Future Nature: A Vision for Conservation* (Earthscan, 2003), pp. 118–19.    [16] *Ibid.,* p. 121.

of the underlying reality of our existence – indeed, that which has given birth to all existence! In some sense, I believe, the whole nature conservation endeavour has been a category mistake, born of a false separation between what it is to be human and what it is to be natural. Having thus separated ourselves, we have lost touch with nature's processes both outside of ourselves and, more crucially, within ourselves. We think we know what nature is, and hence how we might conserve it – but afflicted by our separation, we see through the distortions of denial, and only now are we realising how much has been delusion.

…

Virtually all of our nature reserves are unnaturally denuded of large herbivores, natural grazing regimes and big predators. They are too small to accommodate natural processes of fire, storm damage and climate shifts. Many are grazed by domestic stock and therefore managed according to human agendas of preference and interference with natural processes of succession. Furthermore, much of the food chain is underpinned by 'alien' introductions, such as muntjac, rabbit, brown rat, pheasant and red-legged partridge. These reserves are themselves surrounded by ever-intensifying agriculture. Where 50 years ago there might have been a gradient of naturalness, with the reserves providing a nucleus, the boundaries have become steadily sharper, even in the relatively wild uplands where intensive grazing regimes have drastically altered vegetation patterns.

As a consequence, the land in-between nature reserves has become sterile, with huge swathes of species-poor acid grassland dominating the uplands, monocultural rye-grass replacing the ancient flower-rich hay meadows, even within national parks; and arable eastern England witnessing massive declines in once-common farmland species of birds, butterflies, moths, small mammals and amphibians. Ponds, hedges, river margins and woodland have been reduced to 'weeds' eradicated, and a great divide created between an eastern arable and a western pastoral Britain.

In response, conservationists have evolved a dual strategy of attempting to modify mainstream agriculture and make it less intensive on one hand, and creating new habitats such as reedbed, coastal marsh and heathland on the other. In my view, there is little chance that agriculture will be open to sufficient reform to do more than stem the tide of current losses, whilst the current strategy of habitat creation suffers from a lack of overall strategy, agreed goals or understanding of what is at stake. The key conservation organisations are open to cooperation but still pursue their own visions and values many of which are rooted in the status quo. Much of what conservation strives to protect or to restore is already the product of human management rather than natural processes. In this case, 'target' species and habitats are the main focus of action, with some species, such as domestic herbivores and even beavers, being brought in as 'management tools'.

The cultural underpinnings of the designation of land have also been viewed from a feminist perspective, with the allocation of land for nature reserves – 'the setting aside of places for "nature"' – being seen as 'symptomatic of a deep malaise which sees and experiences "nature" as "other"',[17] just as is the case with

---

[17] Sue Elworthy, 'National Nature Reserves: Nature as "Other" Confined' (working paper).

women. Sue Elworthy, for example, sees similarities between delineating areas of land for nature and marking out domestic space as the ' "proper" place for women'.[18]

## (a) Sites of Special Scientific Interest

By far the most important type of designation is the SSSI regime, described as providing the 'bedrock' of nature conservation in the United Kingdom, including providing the main mechanism by which European sites may be protected (below, pp. 627–68), and thus in principle fulfilling the United Kingdom's obligations under EC law. The concept of this category of designation first appears in the Huxley Report on Conservation of Nature in England and Wales, which used the label 'sites of special scientific *importance*'.[19] Although this was replaced with 'interest', the idea of importance has informed the selection of such sites.

### Nature Conservancy Council (NCC), *Guidelines for Selection of Biological SSSIs* (NCC, 1989), p. 5

In deciding what is 'special', we seek to identify the most important areas for the range of habitats and diversity of wildlife occurring naturally in Britain. The wider environment outside SSSIs also contains a great deal of wildlife interest, though in some areas much of it has been lost through intensive agriculture, coniferous afforestation and building. The more that the wider environment becomes impoverished in its wildlife, the sharper is the distinction between what is 'special' and what is not. And the more that natural and semi-natural habitats decline through human impact, the more important do the remaining areas become. Thus we keep the total number and extent of SSSIs under current review, and our judgement is assisted by our growing knowledge of the status and distribution of habitats, with their associated animals and plants.

Part II of the Wildlife and Countryside Act 1981 established a specific system of protection for SSSIs (areas provided for in the National Parks and Access to the Countryside Act 1949 because of their features of special interest): s. 28 of the 1981 Act imposes a duty on the NCC (now Natural England, formerly English Nature, Scottish Natural Heritage and the Countryside Council for Wales[20]) to

---

[18] *Ibid.*
[19] Wildlife Conservation Special Committee (England and Wales), *Conservation of Nature in England and Wales*, Cmd 7122 (1947). See further Ch. 12, pp. 484–5.
[20] The institutional structure of conservation bodies is complex: the NCC was organised on a Great Britain basis until it was split into three national bodies by the Environmental Protection Act 1990. In Wales and Scotland, the Countryside Council for Wales and Scottish Natural Heritage combine nature conservation functions with amenity functions. English Nature is 'just' concerned with conservation, its statutory remit being set by s. 130 Environmental Protection Act 1990. The Countryside Agency deals with amenity and recreation issues. The Natural Environment and Rural Communities Act 2006 creates an integrated agency ('Natural England') bringing together English Nature, the Countryside

notify the local planning authority, every owner and occupier of the land, and the Secretary of State that it is of the opinion that an area of land 'is of special interest by reason of any of its flora and fauna, or geological or physiographical features'.

The NCC acknowledged that the determination of special interest prior to notifying a site is a complex process. The following description of the process recalls the discussion in Chapter 1 of the expert/rationalist approach to valuing nature, as opposed to more subjective, 'alternative', ways of viewing the world, and captures this tension (*and* common ground between the various viewpoints) within a decision making process informed predominantly by scientists and with little expression of the now commonplace role for 'public participation' other than a reference to the weight of the - 'collective interest'. It is also striking that this fundamental part of the regime, the determination of sites, is not really governed by law, the formulation in s. 28 of the 1981 Act offering very little by way of guidance, and conferring considerable discretion on the conservation agencies. This might be compared with the complex, and politically sensitive, procedure for designating special areas of conservation (SACs), set out in the Habitats Directive (below, pp. 636–47).

### NCC, *Guidelines for Selection of Biological SSSIs*, paras. 3.2–3.3

3.2 The determination of special interest requires first the descriptive recording of the biological attributes and controlling physical environmental features of an area and then the application to these of agreed criteria of nature conservation value. The descriptive part of the process can, within the limitations of available resources and expertise for field survey, be made reasonably objective, or, at least standardised. The evaluation part involves integrating and balancing the views not only of widely differing interests in the phenomena of nature but also many different individuals within each interest …

3.3. The complexity in evaluation lies not only in differences in values and needs between separate interests, but also in the diversity of viewpoints within any one interest. And in nature itself, there is such an enormous variety to be considered – a vast array of habitats, communities and species which need assessing in different ways by virtue of the widely varying environmental patterns which control their existence. Nor do nature conservation values necessarily remain static: as certain features become ever rarer through human impacts, so the value of the remaining examples increases. And, as more people become interested in a particular aspect of nature, so their view increasingly weights the collective interest. The values that people place upon nature are fundamentally subjective and we can only try to synthesise them into a corporate view. The second part of the determination

Agency and most of the functions of the Rural Development Service but *not* the Forestry Commission. The Act also extends the functions of the Joint Nature Conservation Committee which was introduced on the break-up of the NCC. For a fuller discussion of the institutional make-up and statutory responsibilities of these bodies, see Bell and McGillivray, *Environmental Law*, pp. 805–6.

process must therefore inevitably remain a matter of best judgements. It is, nevertheless, important to rationalise and systematise the evaluation and selection of SSSIs and to impose as much rigour and consistency as possible on the whole process. Because nature conservation values are dynamic and still evolving, periodic review of this process is necessary, to ensure that it continues to meet the needs of society.

The SSSI regime was for a long time based on compensation payments made to landowners or occupiers for profit forgone following notification of the site as an SSSI by one of the UK conservation bodies.[21] The notification sent by the conservation agency to an owner or occupier of a site contained a list of all operations which, in the agency's view, could damage the site. Notice had to be given in writing by the occupier or owner of any such operations at least four months before they were carried out. During that period, the conservation agency could give consent to the operation, refuse it, or invite the owner or occupier to consider modifications which might avoid damaging the wildlife or site. Under s. 15 of the Countryside Act 1968, the conservation body was able to offer the owner or occupier a payment in return for signing up to a management agreement that restricted the operations that could be carried out. The following list, taken from a 'menu' of potentially damaging operations used by the nature conservancy agencies when drawing up management agreements, indicates the potential breadth of control over 'normal' agricultural practices: 'cultivation, including ploughing, rotovating, harrowing and re-seeding, changes in the grazing regime, application of manure, fertilisers and lime, and the application of pesticides'.[22]

Significantly, the notification of land as an SSSI did not guarantee its absolute protection: owners could legally carry out damaging activities if they had given notice to a conservation agency and the four-month period, available to the agencies to negotiate a management agreement, had expired. Famously, this led Lord Mustill to describe the SSSI regime as fundamentally flawed: 'it needs only a moment to see that this regime is toothless, for it demands no more from the owner or occupier of an SSSI than a little patience ... the owner will within months be free to disregard the notification and carry out the proscribed operations'.[23] Even if the owners or occupiers agreed to enter into a voluntary agreement, it was most likely that any agreement reached was of a negative

---

[21]  This derives from s. 16(3)(c) National Parks and Access to the Countryside Act 1949 which provided that agreements entered into between the NCC and the owner 'may contain ... the making of payments by the Conservancy, and in particular for the payment by them of compensation for the effect of the restrictions ... that may be expedient'.

[22]  NCC, *Site Management Plans for Conservation: A Working Guide* (NCC, 1991). Note that in *Sweet*, a very broad interpretation was given to the meaning of 'operations' for the purposes of s. 28 Wildlife and Countryside Act 1981.

[23]  *Southern Water Authority* v. *Nature Conservancy Council* [1992] 1 WLR 775, at p. 778.

nature, to prevent them carrying out a potentially damaging operation, rather than including more positive commitments to manage the land in some environmentally advantageous manner (even though a legal base for this existed).[24] This meant that management agreements were not often used to guard against the general neglect of a site, which in some respects may be more damaging than more dramatic, one-off, damaging operations. This negative aspect of the designation system also left the conservation agencies open to having to pay very large sums in compensation to landowners and occupiers and gave landowners considerable bargaining power, even to the extent of opening up the system to abuse. A blatant example of this potential was the case in which a landowner was awarded £500,000 because SSSI notification prevented him from planting trees at Glen Lochy – such 'compensation' payments (with interest) exceeding the cost of his estate.[25] Such an approach, depending upon the persuasive force of economic rewards as part of management agreements, in practice subverts the principle of environmental policy that the 'polluter pays', and emphasises that, for the purposes of controlling environmental damage, agriculture and forestry remain a special case.

Hitherto, the main approach to the designation of land as an SSSI was clearly one of voluntariness, rather than compulsion. This approach, or ethos, has its roots in the post-war land settlement, which divided agricultural land use from 'town and country planning', and so excluded agricultural activities from the purview of the system of development control in the Town and Country Planning Act 1947, which thus ensured security of land use for agriculture and unhampered agricultural development. As we discussed in Chapter 12 (pp. 479–87), several official reports were highly influential in bringing about this exclusion. The Scott Report 1943 decided that farming was essential for the whole country – for food production, and for aesthetic and social reasons – and described farmers as the 'nation's landscape gardeners' and 'guardians of the countryside'. The Huxley Report 1947 (which led to the National Parks and Access to the Countryside Act 1949) and Ritchie Report 1949 on Scottish Nature Reserves were similarly instrumental in the portrayal of agricultural interests as benign and even facilitating conservation. The voluntary approach also determined the cooperative regulatory style of the NCC. The following passage, taken from the NCC's guidelines for selecting SSSIs, highlights this approach and also the Council's awareness of the need for positive measures, suggesting an important link between cooperation between the parties to an agreement and the carrying out of positive works as provided for originally by the 1949 Act (in relation to National Nature Reserves) and further encouraged as a matter of policy.

---

[24] Section 16(3)(a) National Parks and Access to the Countryside Act 1949.
[25] *Cameron* v. *NCC* (1991) SLT 85. Note, however, that there has generally been a greater use of management agreements for positive works in Scotland.

### NCC, *Guidelines for Selection of Biological SSSIs*, pp. 5–6

The NCC's approach to the conservation of SSSIs is based on cooperation with owners and occupiers in the appropriate management of the land to maintain its special interest. It is not our policy to seek to exclude all agriculture and forestry;[26] indeed the continuation of the current land-use is often essential to maintain the habitat for wildlife. For example, the interest of chalk downland depends on grazing, of hay meadows on mowing, and of much ancient woodland on coppicing. However, some forms of agriculture and afforestation are incompatible with the conservation of SSSIs. In these cases, the NCC is normally prepared to offer landowners and occupiers compensation, calculated on the basis of profit forgone, through a management agreement if they give up their proposals; where an agricultural grant application is refused because of our objection, this is a statutory obligation. The NCC also offers management agreements and grants for positive management of SSSIs, and these can encourage local employment.

Apart from the fundamentally voluntary nature of the system, there were a number of other problems with the system of SSSIs. Damage could be caused by third parties who were not covered by SSSI procedures. As a result, a water authority which carried out drainage works described as an act of 'ecological vandalism' by the House of Lords, whilst *temporarily* working on an SSSI, did not commit an offence under s. 28 of the 1981 Act even though the company knew that its operations were 'potentially damaging'.[27] Nor could SSSIs be isolated from the effects of development on adjacent or nearby land. Most importantly, a grant of planning permission constituted (and still does) a defence to the criminal offence of carrying out a potentially damaging operation;[28] local and private Acts of Parliament and Statutory Orders may also allow developments to proceed which damage the site.

Several of the limitations of the SSSI system and its interplay with the planning system may be seen in *R* v. *Poole Borough Council, ex parte Beebee*,[29] which arose because the Council granted itself planning permission for a housing development on land forming part of Canford Heath and included in an SSSI. The NCC had objected to the development proposals and had requested that the Secretary of State call it in to be determined. This was refused. The applicants applied for judicial review on the ground, *inter alia*, that the Council had not taken into account a relevant consideration, namely the fact that the site in question was part of an SSSI.

[26] Note this refers to management agreements, not exclusion from the town and country planning system.

[27] *Southern Water Authority*, in which the House of Lords decided that for the purposes of s. 28 Wildlife and Countryside Act 1981, someone is an occupier only if they have some form of stable relationship with the land.

[28] Section 28(7) 1981 Act. Following the reform of the Act by the Countryside and Rights of Way Act 2000 (see below, pp. 625–6), this provision is now found at s. 28P(4).

[29] *R* v. *Poole Borough Council, ex parte Beebee* (1991) 3 *Journal of Environmental Law* 293, pp. 297–8.

The case highlights that at the time that it was heard planning permission could be granted in the normal way even though the development was to take place on land designated as an SSSI and, more fundamentally, that notification of an SSSI did not 'raise any presumption against development'.[30] It shows also that the nature of the 'material considerations' formulation in s. 70(2) of the Town and Country Planning Act 1990 (Chapter 13, p. 515) means that it is very difficult to challenge the weight given to various considerations by the local planning authority, including the consideration that the land is an SSSI. The strongly procedural rather than substantive nature of the environmental assessment process is also illustrated by this case, as we discussed in the previous chapter (p. 584). Schiemann J considered that the information which would have come to light during the formal environmental assessment process was already in the local planning authority's possession, thus effectively ignoring the contribution that expert opinion and public participation (elements of a formal environmental assessment process) might make to gathering and evaluating information about the environmental effects of the development.

### R v. Poole Borough Council, ex parte Beebee (1991) 3 *Journal of Environmental Law* 293, pp. 297–8

SCHIEMANN J.

First, the Council did not take into account a relevant consideration, namely the fact that the subject sites were part of an SSSI. That was the first submission. It is common ground that the subject sites were part of an SSSI and that this was a relevant consideration. Further, it is common ground that the Council knew that the NCC wished to extend the boundary of the existing SSSI so as to include the subject sites, and apparently took that factor into account.

The wording of the officer's report with its references to 'intention to extend the boundaries of the SSSI' and 'proposed SSSI boundary' was unfortunate and supports the applicants' contention that the Council may well have proceeded on the basis that the subject sites were not as yet within an SSSI. Hence [Counsel for the applicant's submission] that the Council had failed to take into consideration a relevant consideration, namely that the subject sites were within an SSSI. I regard that submission as justified.

However, although in general, once the submission has been accepted that the decision maker failed to take into account a relevant consideration, the decision would be quashed, I don't think that that result should follow in the instant case. My reason for so holding is that in my judgment the officer preparing the report, and the Council, did take into account the substance of what they were required to take into account.

…

… The purpose of the … regime, so far as presently relevant, is to ensure that the planning authority, prior to granting any planning permission, is appraised of the fact that the

---

[30] J. D. C. Harte, 'Sites of Scientific Interest in England and Wales' (1991) 3 *Journal of Environmental Law* 297, p. 301.

NCC regard the site as one of special scientific interest. In the present case there is no doubt that the planning authority were perfectly aware of this fact and were aware of the reasons for it. The fact that the planning authority might not have been aware that the site had been formally notified under the new regime did not deprive them of knowledge of any material underlying fact.

Schiemann J then considered the other grounds, including that an environmental impact assessment had not been conducted.

Having looked at all the evidence, I am not persuaded that the committee here were misled at all. Planning circulars and structure plans are full of broad statements with many presumptions, many of which are mutually irreconcilable so that in a particular case one must give way to another. Neither the instant report nor the planning circulars are to be read as though they were taxation statutes to be carefully construed. The local authority officers who draft these reports are not by training or inclination in general endowed with the skill of Parliamentary draftsmen. It seems to me that [Counsel for the respondents] was absolutely right when he said … that there was a balance to be struck. There were strong policy/historical arguments in favour of a grant and strong conservation reasons against the grant. That was the matter with which the committee grappled at some length and came down in the favour of adhering to their earlier policy, notwithstanding the fact that they knew that the NCC were anxious that this site should be preserved for perfectly good ecological reasons.

In my judgment, when one looks at the evidence as a whole rather than the odd isolated phrase in one or another of the documents before the Council, there was no reason to suppose that the Council took into account any significant matter which they should not have taken into account, or that they failed to take into account any significant matter which they ought to have taken into account; or that they committed some other error which should lead to this permission being quashed. Some of the criticisms made by [Counsel for the applicants] of this phrase or that do have force. But at the end of the day the court has to sit back, as it were, and ask itself whether there was anything which vitiated the decision-making processes and which would make it desirable for the Council to look at this matter again.

In my judgment, there was not, and this application is dismissed.

In this case, the conservation interests of the site were trumped by the economic and social desirability of the housing development. In such circumstances, the grant of planning permission constitutes a defence to the offence of causing loss or damage to the SSSI. Schiemann J adopted a seemingly relaxed approach to the damage likely to be done to the SSSI in line with the relatively weak protection granted to such sites as a matter of law and policy at that time. It is important to note that, in this case, had the SSSI designation been used as a means to protect a European site, a higher level of protection would have been accorded to the site, and thus might have more effectively hampered the developer's progress, as we discuss further below, pp. 640–61.

These features of the SSSI regime – its voluntary nature, the existence of legal loopholes, and the provision for the legal destruction of sites by 'operations' for which planning permission has been granted – meant that the designation of a site did not necessarily mean that it would be safeguarded. A report by the National Audit Office in 1994 highlighted the ineffectiveness of the regime: one-fifth of SSSIs had suffered damage, in many cases leading to the denotification of the site.[31] These statistics were highly influential in the reform of the system by the Countryside and Rights of Way Act 2000, the better protection of SSSIs having been presented as a pre-election promise in 1997.

### (b) The demise of voluntary controls

Above, we described the SSSI regime as an extreme example of voluntarism which has more generally pervaded the legal control of activities in the countryside. The Countryside and Rights of Way Act 2000 overhauled the SSSI system,[32] including fundamental changes to its voluntary premise. In addition to clearing up some of the inadequacies of the existing regime,[33] the main point is that the 2000 Act introduced what amounts to a licensing regime by granting the appropriate conservation agency the power *indefinitely* to refuse consent for activities ('operations') deemed to be potentially damaging to SSSIs.[34] This power relies upon an obligation upon owners and occupiers of land to notify the conservation agency of a proposal to carry out any such activities. A potentially damaging operation may be carried out with the agency's consent, or if the operation is carried out within the terms of a management agreement.[35] It may also be carried out in accordance with a 'management scheme', which is a variant of a management agreement, served upon an owner or occupier of land, but following consultation with them,[36] and with the emphasis very much upon positive site management, in policy, if not explicitly in law.[37] A mandatory

---

[31] National Audit Office, *Protecting and Managing SSSIs* (HMSO, 1994).

[32] Section 75 and Sch. 9 of the Countryside and Rights of Way Act 2000 replaced the original s. 28 of the Wildlife and Countryside Act 1981 with a new s. 28 together with ss. 28A to 28N and 28P to 28R.

[33] For example, s. 28P(6) Wildlife and Countryside Act 1981, inserted by Sch. 9 of the Countryside and Rights of Way Act 2000, adds a category of 'general offence' to those offences carried out by owner, occupier or statutory undertakers.

[34] Section 28E Wildlife and Countryside Act 1981.

[35] Made under s. 16 National Parks and Access to the Countryside Act 1949 or s. 15 Countryside Act 1968.

[36] Section 28J(2) of the 1981 Act states 'A management scheme is a scheme for (a) conserving the flora, fauna, or geological or physiographical features by reason of which the land (or the part of it to which the scheme relates) is of special interest; or (b) restoring them; or (c) both.' Compare this formulation with the original premise for such management agreements – s. 15 of the National Parks and Access to the Countryside Act 1949 which refers to the making of payments to compensate landowners for the effect of any restrictions made with respect to their land (see further Ch. 12, p. 486).

[37] See DEFRA, *SSSIs: Encouraging Positive Partnerships* (DEFRA, 2003).

element is introduced by the ability of the conservation agency to serve a notice requiring the owner or occupier to carry out work on the land in accordance with the management scheme.[38] The regime is also backed up by more stringent penalties.[39] This, and the general bolstering of the SSSI regime through strengthening of the position of the various conservation agencies, makes the designation of land a crucial decision for owners and occupiers.[40] In summary, the 2000 Act has embedded a strengthened form of management by agreement within a traditional licensing regime, demonstrating the potential effectiveness of a combination of diverse regulatory methods. These changes are described by Bell and McGillivray as 'more regulatory and increasingly legalistic', though they are careful to differentiate the regime from a standard 'command and control' model.[41]

Above, we discussed the fact that, prior to the reforms brought by the Countryside and Rights of Way Act 2000 the payment of compensation for profit forgone meant that the negotiation of management agreements between owners and occupiers was a weak, and easily exploited, part of the regime (pp. 620–2). In contrast, the positive nature of commitments made under schemes for the management of SSSIs, and the condition that these be fulfilled before payments are made, is now a central feature of conservation law and policy. Effectively contracts in terms of their legal form, management agreements or schemes are considered means by which the active maintenance and enhancement of the environment may be achieved, akin to the 'purchase of environmental "goods"'.[42] Under the 2000 Act, the strengthened position of the conservation agencies in drawing up and serving notice of such schemes has altered the respective roles of the owner/occupier and conservation agency in determining the nature of activities upon privately owned land. This raises the prospect of a new form of 'environmental' property right, in which the responsibilities of ownership, towards conservation interests, come to the fore as a modern form of land stewardship. We further discuss this idea and its implications for conceptions of property in the context of the reform of the CAP (Chapter 16, pp. 685–7).

Although undeniably significant in terms of legal practice and property theory, the reform of the SSSI regime left intact the defence that a damaging operation is authorised by a grant of planning permission,[43] a fundamental limitation in the scope of the 1981 Act, and one which is not replicated in the case of sites designated under EC law for their conservation value; instead certain procedural safeguards are triggered in the event of a development being proposed on such sites, as discussed below (pp. 647–65).

---

[38] Section 28K 1981 Act.    [39] Section 28P 1981 Act.

[40] See, for example, *R (Aggregate Industries)* v. *English Nature* [2002] EWHC 908, in which the applicants unsuccessfully sought to challenge the notification of their land as an SSSI on the ground that it was incompatible with human rights law.

[41] Bell and McGillivray, *Environmental Law*, p. 809.

[42] DEFRA, *CAP: Implementation Consultation* (DEFRA, 2004), p. 11. For more on CAP reform, see Chapter 16, pp. 682–5.    [43] Section 28(P)(4) 1981 Act, as amended.

## 3 European sites

The system of countryside designation outlined above has been developed
further to comply with EC law, specifically the two key Directives, the Birds
Directive and the Habitats Directive. As at national law, these Directives apply
a system of designation, followed by a process for the protection of those designated areas.

### (a) Special protection areas

Directive 79/409/EEC on the conservation of wild birds[44] was the first EC foray
into nature conservation law. The Birds Directive arose from public concern
over the customary annual hunting of migratory birds in southern Europe
and northern Africa, and from scientific research conducted by the European
Commission which indicated that the number of species of European birds was
falling. It was also designed to implement the international obligations of the
Member States under the Ramsar Convention 1971.[45] The main legal technique
employed by the Directive to protect bird habitats such as wetland areas is
the designation of land for special protection.[46] This reliance on designation is
not surprising given that the drafting of the Directive was greatly informed by
the British experience of demarcating areas for conservation at that time (the
Royal Society for the Protection of Birds (RSPB) provided a strong delegation
of experts). The Directive was a highly influential piece of legislation, affecting
for the first time the Member States' use of their land, and setting the tone for a
bold and absolute approach to nature and wildlife protection through the protection of land:[47] it permitted no derogations from the Member States' duty to
protect an area once it had been designated for conservation.

The key parts of the Directive with respect to the designation and protection
of birds' habitats are Arts. 2, 3 and 4. Note also the references in the preamble
to birds constituting a 'common heritage' (as well as a classic transfrontier
problem), and also the avowed importance of the Directive to the operation of
the common market (there being no specific legal base for environmental and
conservation legislation when the Directive was adopted[48]).

---

[44]  OJ 1979 L 103/1.

[45]  The Convention on Wetlands of International Importance Especially as Waterfowl Habitat
(1971) 11 ILM 963.

[46]  Note that Art. 5 requires Member States to set up a system of protection for all species of
birds, prohibiting the deliberate killing or capture, deliberate destruction of nests and eggs or
the removal of nests and eggs, deliberate disturbance and the keeping of species the hunting
and capture of which is prohibited. Articles 6–9 then provide the legal base for derogations
from this prohibition in the case of the hunting and sale of birds.

[47]  Note, in contrast, the Directive permitted compromises in terms of the protection of wild
birds, allowing for the granting of licences for their capture, sale and killing (Arts. 6–10).

[48]  Hence the reliance upon Art. 235 EEC (now Art. 308 EC). See Ch. 4 on the use of this
provision and insertion into the EC Treaty of a Title on the Environment, providing a legal
base for such future measures (pp. 158–64), and on the transfrontier argument in favour of
legal action, *ibid.*

## Directive 79/409/EEC on the conservation of wild birds OJ 1979 L 103/1

...

Whereas a large number of species of wild birds naturally occurring in the European territory of the Member States are declining, very rapidly in some cases; whereas this decline represents a serious threat to the conservation of the natural environment, particularly because of the biological balances threatened thereby;

Whereas the species of wild birds naturally occurring in the European territory of the Member States are mainly migratory species; whereas such species constitute a common heritage and whereas effective bird protection is typically a trans-frontier environment problem entailing common responsibilities;

...

Whereas the conservation of the species of wild birds naturally occurring in the European territory of the Member States is necessary to attain, within the operation of the common market, the Community's objectives regarding the improvement of living conditions, a harmonious development of economic activities throughout the Community and a continuous and balanced expansion, but the necessary powers to act have not been provided for in the Treaty;

### Article 1

1. This Directive relates to the conservation of all species of naturally occurring birds in the wild state in the European territory of the Member States to which the Treaty applies. It covers the protection, management and control of these species and lays down rules for their exploitation.

2. It shall apply to birds, their eggs, nests and habitats.

### Article 2

Member States shall take the requisite measures to maintain the population of the species referred to in Article 1 at a level which corresponds in particular to ecological, scientific, and cultural requirements, while taking account of economic and recreational requirements, or to adapt the population of these species to that level.

### Article 3

1. In the light of the requirements referred to in Article 2, Member States shall take the requisite measures to preserve, maintain or re-establish a sufficient diversity and area of habitats for all the species of birds referred to in Article 1.

2. The preservation, maintenance and re-establishment of biotopes[49] and habitats shall include primarily the following measures:
(a) the creation of protected areas;
(b) upkeep and management in accordance with the ecological needs of habitats inside and outside the protected zones;

---

[49] A small area which supports its own community, e.g. the bark of a tree.

(c) re-establishment of destroyed biotopes;

(d) creation of biotopes.

### Article 4

1. The species mentioned in Annex I are to be the subject of special conservation measures concerning their habitat in order to ensure their survival and reproduction in their area of distribution.

In this connection, account shall be taken of:

(a) species in danger of extinction;

(b) species vulnerable to specific changes in their habitat;

(c) species considered rare because of small populations or restricted local distribution;

(d) other species requiring particular attention for reason of the specific nature of their habitat.

Trends and variations in population levels shall be taken into account as a background for evaluations.

2. Member States shall classify in particular the most suitable territories in number and size as special protection areas for the conservation of these species, taking into account their protection requirements in the geographical sea and land area where this Directive applies.

3. Member States shall take similar measures for regularly occurring migratory species not listed in Annex I, bearing in mind their need for protection in the geographical sea and land area where this Directive applies, as regards their breeding, moulting and wintering areas and staging posts along their migration routes. To this end, Member States shall pay particular attention to the protection of wetlands and particularly to wetlands of international importance.

4. In respect of the protection areas referred to in paragraphs 1 and 2 above, Member States shall take appropriate steps to avoid pollution or deterioration of habitats or any disturbances affecting the birds, in so far as these would be significant having regard to the objectives of this Article. Outside these protection areas, Member States shall also strive to avoid pollution or deterioration of habitats.[50]

In summary, the Directive requires that Member States must preserve, maintain or re-establish a sufficient diversity and area of habitats ('protected areas') so that general bird populations are maintained. With respect to endangered bird species (listed in Annex I of the Directive) and regularly occurring migratory birds (not listed in Annex I), the 'most suitable' land and sea territories for these birds must be classified as 'special protection areas' (SPAs) (Art. 4(2)). Although the phraseology of this subsection suggests some discretion on the part of the Member State, the extent of this has been successfully curtailed by the European Court of Justice in the course of a run

---

[50] Note that Art. 7 of the Habitats Directive replaces this obligation by those (less stringent requirements) contained in Art. 6 of the Habitats Directive, as discussed below, pp. 661–8.

of significant cases. Most notably, in Case C-355/90 *Commission* v. *Spain (Santoña Marshes),*[51] the Court of Justice confirmed that the obligation to designate land as an SPA must be based solely on objective, ornithological, criteria. In relation to this, a controversial issue has been the correct reading of Art. 2 of the Birds Directive in the interpretation of these duties upon Member States. Article 2 requires Member States to take the requisite measures in relation to naturally occurring wild birds, 'while taking account of economic and recreational requirements'. Article 3, which deals with *general* conservation measures, expressly provides for account to be taken of these economic and social requirements. In contrast, Art. 4, which sets out the process for designating *special* conservation areas to protect those particularly endangered bird species listed in Annex I to the Directive and regularly occurring migratory birds not listed in the Annex, fails to mention the relevance of Art. 2 and makes no reference to economic or recreational requirements.

The issue of the correct interpretation of Art. 2 of the Birds Directive was raised in Case C-44/95 *Lappel Bank,* following a reference from the House of Lords to the Court of Justice for a preliminary ruling (the Court of Appeal having been split on the issue of whether or not economic and recreational factors can be taken into account at the stage of designating land as an SPA).[52] The RSPB challenged the Secretary of State's decision to exclude from the Medway estuary and marshes special protection area, on economic grounds, an area of about 22 hectares known as Lappel Bank. Although Lappel Bank shared many of the ornithological qualities of the area, as a whole it did not support any of the species referred to in Art. 4(1) of the Birds Directive. Nevertheless, the RSPB argued that, as an important component of the overall estuarine ecosystem, the loss of the wetland area of Lappel Bank would result in a reduction of the bird populations of the broader Medway estuary and marshes. It is important to note that there were some good economic reasons for the expansion of the port of Sheerness, such as a much-needed boost to local employment. Unfortunately, because of the location of the port, its further development was bound to affect the surrounding wetlands, essential to migratory birds for feeding, resting and breeding.

### Case C-44/95 *R* v. *Secretary of State for the Environment ex parte Royal Society for the Protection of Birds (Lappel Bank)* [1996] ECR I-3805

#### The first question

17. The point of this question is whether Article 4(1) or (2) of the Birds Directive [see above, p. 629] is to be interpreted as meaning that a Member State is authorised to take account of the economic requirements mentioned in Article 2 thereof when designating an SPA and defining its boundaries.

---

[51] [1993] ECR I-4221.     [52] UK proceedings reported at (1995) 7(2) JEL 245.

18. As a preliminary point, it must be borne in mind that, according to the ninth recital in the preamble to the Birds Directive, 'the preservation, maintenance or restoration of a sufficient diversity and area of habitats is essential to the conservation of all species of birds [covered by the Directive]', that 'certain species of birds should be the subject of special conservation measures concerning their habitats in order to ensure their survival and reproduction in their area of distribution', and, finally, that 'such measures must also take account of migratory species'.

19. That recital is formally reflected in Articles 3 and 4 of the Directive. In paragraph 23 of its judgment in Case C-355/90 *Commission* v. *Spain* [1993] ECR I-4221 (hereinafter *'Santoña Marshes'*) the Court pointed out that the first of those provisions imposes obligations of a general character, namely the obligation to ensure a sufficient diversity and area of habitats for all the birds referred to in the Directive, while the second contains specific obligations with regard to the species of birds listed in Annex I and the migratory species not listed in that Annex.

20. According to the United Kingdom Government and the Port of Sheerness Limited, Article 4 cannot be considered in isolation from Article 3. They state that Article 4 provides, in relation to certain species of particular interest, for the specific application of the general obligation imposed by Article 3. Since the latter provision allows account to be taken of economic requirements, the same should apply to Article 4(1) and (2).

21. The French Government reaches the same conclusion, observing that, when an SPA is created, the Member States take account of all the criteria mentioned in Article 2 of the Birds Directive, which is general in scope, and, therefore, *inter alia*, of economic requirements.

22. Those arguments cannot be upheld.

23. It must be noted first that Article 4 of the Birds Directive lays down a protection regime which is specifically targeted and reinforced both for the species listed in Annex I and for migratory species, an approach justified by the fact that they are, respectively, the most endangered species and the species constituting a common heritage of the Community (see Case C-169/89 *Van den Burg* [1990] ECR I-2143, paragraph 11).

24. Whilst Article 3 of the Birds Directive provides for account to be taken of the requirements mentioned in Article 2 for the implementation of general conservation measures, including the creation of protection areas, Article 4 makes no such reference for the implementation of special conservation measures, in particular the creation of SPAs.

25. Consequently, having regard to the aim of special protection pursued by Article 4 and the fact that, according to settled case-law (see in particular Case C-435/92 *APAS* v. *Préfets de Maine-et-Loire and de la Loire Atlantique* [1994] ECR I-67, paragraph 20), Article 2 does not constitute an autonomous derogation from the general system of protection established by the Directive, it must be held (see paragraphs 17 and 18 of *Santoña Marshes*) – that the ecological requirements laid down by the former provision do not have to be balanced against the interests listed in the latter, in particular economic requirements.

26. It is the criteria laid down in paragraphs (1) and (2) of Article 4 which are to guide the Member States in designating and defining the boundaries of SPAs. It is clear from

paragraphs 26 and 27 of *Santoña Marshes* that, notwithstanding the divergences between the various language versions of the last sub-paragraph of Article 4(1), the criteria in question are ornithological criteria.

27. In view of the foregoing, the answer to the first question must be that Article 4(1) or (2) of the Birds Directive is to be interpreted as meaning that a Member State is not authorised to take account of the economic requirements mentioned in Article 2 thereof when designating an SPA and defining its boundaries.

This forthright judgment was based on the Court's earlier assertion in Case 240/83 *ADBHU*[53] that environmental protection is an 'essential objective' of the Community, and builds upon its previous case law in this area (notably *Santoña Marshes*),[54] applying this to the difficult situation in *Lappel Bank* – the exclusion of a relatively small area from the overall designation of an area as an SPA. The case was pursued through the courts by the RSPB because of its importance as a test case – the situation in Lappel Bank was replicated in eighteen sites around the country. The judgment failed to save Lappel Bank itself (it has been described as a 'paper triumph'[55]): at the time the judgment was heard, the land was being developed as a huge hold for imported cars (partly in response to the demand for improved European transport links for moving goods). The RSPB had been unable to secure interim protection of the site in national law for financial reasons. The loss of this site also shows up the limited strength of interim measures for conservation reasons as a matter of European Community law.[56]

In Case 3/96 *Commission* v. *Netherlands*,[57] the Court elaborated and further narrowed the 'margin of discretion' available to Member States when designating land as an SPA and the type of information which would meet the description of objective, ornithological criteria (see generally our discussion of scientific evidence in environmental law, in Chapter 1, pp. 12–34).

### Case C-3/96 *Commission* v. *Netherlands* [1998] ECR I-3031, paras. 60–70

60. ... while the Member States have a certain margin of discretion in the choice of SPAs, the classification of those areas is nevertheless subject to certain ornithological criteria determined by the Directive (see Case C-355/90 *Commission* v. *Spain*), paragraph 26.

61. It follows that the Member States' margin of discretion in choosing the most suitable territories for classification as SPAs does not concern the appropriateness of classifying

---

[53] Case 240/83 *Procureur de la République* v. *Association de Défense Des Brûleurs D'huiles Usagées* [1985] ECR 531. See further Ch. 4, pp. 161–2.     [54] [1994] ECR I-67.

[55] Owens and Cowell, *Land and Limits*, p. 119.

[56] See discussion in case note, Jane Holder (1997) 34 *Common Market Law Review* 1469.

[57] [1998] ECR I-3031.

as SPAs the territories which appear the most suitable according to ornithological criteria, but only the application of those criteria for identifying the most suitable territories for conservation of the species listed in Annex I to the Directive.

62. Consequently, Member States are obliged to classify as SPAs all the sites which, applying ornithological criteria, appear to be the most suitable for conservation of the species in question.

63. Thus where it appears that a Member State has classified as SPAs sites the number and total area of which are manifestly less than the number and total area of the sites considered to be the most suitable for conservation of the species in question, it will be possible to find that the Member State has failed to fulfil its obligation under Article 4(1) of the Directive.

...

68. In this connection, it must be pointed out that IBA 89 [International Birds Areas in the European Community 1989] draws up an inventory of areas which are of great importance for the conservation of wild birds in the Community. That inventory was prepared for the competent directorate general of the Commission by the Eurogroup for the Conservation of Birds and Habitats in conjunction with the International Council of Bird Protection and in cooperation with Commission experts.

69. In the circumstances, IBA 89 has proved to be the only document containing scientific evidence making it possible to assess whether the defendant State has fulfilled its obligation to classify as SPAs the most suitable territories in number and area for conservation of the protected species. The situation would be different if the Kingdom of the Netherlands had produced scientific evidence in particular to show that the obligation in question could be fulfilled by classifying as SPAs territories whose number and total area were less than those resulting from IBA 89.

70. It follows that that inventory, although not legally binding on the Member States concerned, can, by reason of its acknowledged scientific value in the present case, be used by the Court as a reason for assessing the extent to which the Kingdom of the Netherlands has complied with its obligation to classify SPAs.

...

71. Since it thus appears that the Netherlands has classified as SPAs territories whose number and total area are clearly smaller than the number and total area of the territories suitable, according to IBA 89, for classification as SPAs, the requirements of Article 4(1) of the Directive cannot be regarded as satisfied.

Prior to the adoption of the Habitats Directive (Art. 7 of which fundamentally alters the level of protection accorded by the Birds Directive, on which see below, pp. 647–67), Member States were obliged by Art. 4(4) of the Directive to 'take appropriate steps to avoid pollution or deterioration of habitats or any disturbances affecting the birds' in areas designated as SPAs. Outside these areas, there is a residual (negative) duty on Member States to 'strive to avoid pollution or deterioration of habitats'. A hierarchy of protection is therefore established by the Directive, making particularly important the initial compilation (and frequent amendment) of the accompanying Annex I (of endangered birds).[58] A coordinating role is envisaged for the European Commission, so that it can oversee the creation of Natura 2000 – a coherent ecological network which meets the protection requirements of these species in the geographical sea and land area where this Directive applies.

In line with its judgments on the initial classification of land as an SPA, the Court of Justice reinforced the absolute nature of protection granted to such sites by the Directive once they have been designated, with exceptions carved out by the Court only for reasons of public health and public safety, or when some positive environmental benefits are thought likely to ensue.[59] The high level of protection conferred upon SPAs by the Birds Directive, and reinforced by the European Court of Justice, imposed a strain on those Member States eager to develop economically, particularly in response to the European Community's ambitious programme of creating transport links to facilitate the internal market (as with *Lappel Bank*).[60] As mentioned, this level of protection has now been significantly compromised by the amendment of the Birds Directive by the Habitats Directive, resulting in interesting questions about the proper inter-relation of the two Directives (as discussed below, p. 665).

### (b)  Special areas of conservation

Directive 92/43/EEC on the conservation of natural habitats and of wild fauna and flora (the 'Habitats Directive')[61] uses the same legal technique as the Birds Directive – the designation of land, in this case 'special areas of conservation'. Also in keeping with the general approach adopted in the Birds Directive, the emphasis of the system of land protection under the Habitats Directive is still very firmly on 'important' or 'special' sites; a hierarchical system of protection operates, with priority natural habitat types and species at its apex, rather than the aim being to secure a general standard of protection for areas of land which may develop these characteristics in the future. Notwithstanding these similarities, the Habitats Directive represents a significant conceptual shift from the Birds Directive because it aims to conserve biodiversity, in recognition that species and habitats are closely connected and dependent upon each other. The Habitats Directive thus advances a more holistic and integrated approach to

---

[58]  There were only 74 species listed under Annex I in the original Directive. This has been steadily increased to 144 by amending legislation.

[59]  Case C-57/89 *Commission* v. *Germany (Leybucht Dykes)* [1991] ECR I-883.

[60]  A further strain on conservation interests was German unification and the accompanying rapid construction of motorways between East and West, some of which dissected important habitats (on these, see discussion of Commission Opinions issued under the Habitats Directive).     [61]  OJ 1992 L 206/7.

nature conservation than the Birds Directive. However, whilst its provisions on land designation (primarily Arts. 3 and 4) offer broad coverage – the protection of fauna, flora and habitats rather than a single species – Art. 6 of the Habitats Directive permits a lesser standard of protection for conservation sites than that originally conferred upon birds' habitats under the Birds Directive, as we discuss further below (pp. 647–67).

The Habitats Directive represents the European Community's attempt to fulfil its obligations in international law arising from the Biodiversity Convention 1992.[62] The Directive is in many ways a product of the discourse on sustainable development which shaped the Convention, including within its provisions many of the limitations and compromises that make up the concept of sustainable development, in particular ideas about compensation for the loss of habitats and species. This influence is made clear by the preamble and Art. 2 of the Directive (which may usefully be compared with the equivalent provision in Art. 2 of the Birds Directive, above, p. 628).

### Directive 92/43/EEC on the conservation of natural habitats and of wild fauna and flora OJ 1992 L 206/7

...

Whereas, the main aim of this Directive being to promote the maintenance of biodiversity, taking account of economic, social, cultural and regional requirements, this Directive makes a contribution to the general objectives of sustainable development; whereas the maintenance of such biodiversity may in certain cases require the maintenance, or indeed the encouragement, of human activities.

...

#### Article 2

1. The aim of this Directive shall be to contribute towards ensuring biodiversity through the conservation of natural habitats and of wild fauna and flora in the European territory of the Member States to which the Treaty applies.

2. Measures taken pursuant to this Directive shall be designed to maintain or restore, at favourable conservation status, natural habitats and species of wild fauna and flora of Community interest.

3. Measures taken pursuant to this Directive shall take account of economic, social and cultural requirements and regional and local characteristics.

Article 2 effectively forecloses the argument (expressed in relation to Art. 2 of the Birds Directive) that the Directive was *drafted* 'taking account' of social and economic factors and therefore that these should not influence either the initial designation of sites, or their protection thereafter. It also creates an opportunity

---

[62] See further below, p. 672.

for the type of challenges made by companies and individuals whose economic interests are adversely affected by the designation of land as an SAC, such as in *First Corporate Shipping*,[63] discussed below, pp. 639–43.

## (i) The designation process

In terms of its use of designation as a legal technique, the Habitats Directive seeks to establish 'a coherent European ecological network'[64] of conservation sites throughout Europe, containing specific natural habitat types (listed in Annex I to the Directive) and species (listed in Annex II). The areas of land designated for their special character under the Habitats Directive (SACs) form the basis of the network. This network also includes the special protection areas (SPAs) designated under the Birds Directive; the whole network being referred to as Natura 2000.[65] The aim of establishing the ecological network is to enable the natural habitat types and the species' habitats 'to be maintained or, where appropriate, restored at a favourable conservation status in their natural range'.[66] The ambitious concept of Natura 2000 clearly requires the close involvement of the Commission, operating in its supra-national capacity, to provide an overview of the distribution of sites, and to govern a decision making framework which is capable of overcoming Member State resistance to the restrictions which inevitably flow from the designation of land for conservation reasons, whilst also being sensitive to the position of those Member States 'overburdened' by priority natural habitat types and species.[67]

The decision making process for designating SACs is also remarkably sensitive to ecological conditions and patterns, perhaps reflecting advances made in ecological thinking on the part of the European Community. For example the attempt to join together important conservation sites to create Natura 2000 is recognition of the natural distribution of habitat types and the movement and migration of species through these habitats – the idea being that this will constitute less a patchwork (as was always going to be the case with SPAs designated under the Birds Directive) and more a *blanket* of protected sites. The creation of the network, securing the diversity and distribution of natural habitat types throughout Europe also means that there is less risk of the loss or damage of a habitat type or species arising from conditions peculiar to a particular region. The Directive further takes into account the behaviour of species, for example it requires that the boundaries of sites should correspond to the area in which

---

[63] Case C-371/98 *R* v. *Secretary of State for the Environment, Transport and the Regions, ex parte First Corporate Shipping Ltd* [2000] ECR I-9235.

[64] Article 3(1) Habitats Directive.       [65] *Ibid.*, Article 3(1).

[66] Article 3(1). Note that the conservation status of a natural habitat or species is defined in Art. 1 of the Habitats Directive, but that it basically refers to the long-term natural distribution and long-term survival of the habitat or species.

[67] Note that Member States whose sites hosting one or more natural habitat types and priority species represent more than 5 per cent of their national territory may, in agreement with the Commission, request that the criteria listed in Annex III (Stage 2) be applied more flexibly in selecting all the sites of Community importance in their territory (Art. 4(2)).

animals range in order to feed and reproduce,[68] and encourages the protection of ecological features such as 'green corridors' (hedgerows, rivers, ditches) or 'stepping stones' (small woods, ponds) to help the migration, dispersal and genetic exchange of wild species.[69]

The process of selecting sites begins with Member States choosing sites on the basis of the habitats and species present in a particular area (Stage 1),[70] using criteria set out in Annex III of the Directive. These include the degree of representativeness of the site, the area of the site compared to the total land area of the Member State, the density of a species population at a site, and the isolation of that population. The Member States' lists are then sent to the Commission.[71] There follows a further process of selection, or more accurately 'moderation' (Stage 2), conducted by the European Commission but with the involvement of the Member States. Firstly, the Commission collates lists of all the sites identified by the Member States in Stage 1 as containing natural habitat types in danger of disappearing and/or endangered species, referred to as 'priority' habitats. Such habitats are indicated by an asterisk in Annex I to the Directive, and include, for example, sphagnum bogs, limestone pavements and Caledonian forests. Priority animal and plant species (listed in Annex II and marked with an asterisk) include wolves and lynx, and various orchids (but not birds[72]). Those sites defined as hosting priority habitats and/or species are referred to as 'sites of Community importance'.[73] For 'non-priority' or threatened sites, an assessment of their status as 'sites of Community importance' is made by reference to their contribution to maintaining or establishing a natural habitat or species and/or to the coherence of Natura 2000, with the European Commission applying another set of criteria set out in Annex III of the Directive: the relative value of the site at national level, the geographical importance of the site for migratory species, the total area of the site, the number and type of habitat and species present on the site which are listed in the Directive, and the global ecological value of the site, 'as regards both the characteristic or unique aspect of its features and the way they are combined'. Both sets of criteria (Stage 1 and Stage 2) are designed to steer decision making, but also leave considerable scope for value judgments to be made, often with a political or economic flavour, as illustrated by the *First Corporate Shipping* and *Newsum No. 2*[74] cases, discussed below (pp. 639–47).

---

[68] Article 4(1).    [69] Article 10. On field margins, see Ch. 16, pp. 687–9.    [70] Article 4(1).

[71] Note, Art. 5 sets out procedures to be followed in 'exceptional cases' in which the Commission considers that a national list submitted to it by a Member State omits a site hosting a 'priority' natural habitat type or 'priority' species (i.e. endangered habitats or species) – bilateral consultation is to take place so that scientific data can be compared. The Council takes the final decision in the event of a serious difference of opinion.

[72] On the implications of this anomaly, see p. 665.

[73] This means a site which, in the biogeographic region or regions to which it belongs, contributes significantly to a natural habitat type or species listed in the Directive and to the coherence of Natura 2000 and/or significantly contributes to the maintenance of biological diversity within the biogeographic region or regions concerned (Art. 1).

[74] *R (on the application of Newsum and Others)* v. *Welsh Assembly (No. 2)* [2005] EWHC 538 (Admin).

A final list of sites to be designated as SACs is then adopted by the Commission, possibly following a politically sensitive, and complex, decision making procedure invoking the 'assistance' of a committee of representatives of the Member States.[75] The final stage rests with the Member States. They must designate all 'sites of Community importance' in their territory as SACs within six years at most, 'establishing priorities in the light of the importance of the sites for the maintenance or restoration, at a favourable conservation status, of a natural habitat type in Annex I or a species in Annex II and for the coherence of Natura 2000, and in the light of the threats of degradation or destruction to which those sites are exposed'.[76] All SACs should have been finally designated by 2004, but the selection process has been subject to many delays at both Member State and Commission level.

A vital part of the designation process is scientific information (described in the Directive as 'relevant and reliable'[77]) because this underpins both the compilation of the lists of natural habitat types and species in Annex I and II of the Directive (and determines their review and amendment[78]) at the European Union level, and the initial selection of sites hosting these habitat types and species at the national level. The provision made in the Directive for procedures by which resolution or compromise can be reached[79] suggests that differences of opinion in the scientific information relied upon by the Commission and Member States were envisaged. The Directive aims also to encourage research and scientific work in this area by establishing a system for the exchange of information between Member States and the Commission.[80] There is an obligation on Member States to carry out surveillance of the conservation status of natural habitats and species,[81] especially those considered to be endangered or 'priority', and to report on the impact of the conservation measures in the Directive.[82] In relation to the use of scientific information and evidence, a precautionary approach is explicitly pursued in at least one aspect of the Directive: once a site is considered to be 'of Community importance' it benefits from protection under Art. 6 of the Directive, in advance of its adoption as an SAC by a Member State. The Court of Justice also appears to have taken a precautionary approach when considering when Member States are required to carry out an 'appropriate assessment' of proposed development (below, pp. 652–4).[83] An apparently unexplored issue is the influence of the precautionary principle when the lists of endangered habitat types and species are being drawn up or amended.

---

[75] See Art. 21 for the voting procedures to be followed in the event of a difference of opinion between the Commission and the Committee – with the Council having the 'final say'.

[76] Article 4(4).     [77] Article 5.     [78] See Art. 19.

[79] See the 'conflict resolution' procedures set out in Arts. 5 and Art. 21.

[80] Article 17.     [81] Article 11.     [82] Article 17.

[83] Case C-127/02 *Landelijke Vereniging tot Behoud van de Waddenzee* v. *Staatssecretaris van Landbouw Natuurbeheer en Visserij* [2005] 2 CMLR 31, discussed further below, pp. 652–4.

### (ii) Economic and political influences

As discussed above, the Habitats Directive sets out criteria to be applied in decisions about the selection of sites for special protection at the European Union and national level. Such criteria are exclusively ornithological or ecological, though admittedly with some flexibility in their application in certain cases. However, as with the designation of SPAs under the Birds Directive, questions have been raised about the role of economic factors in influencing judgments about the suitability of sites to be designated as SACs at the national level. Similarly to *Lappel Bank*, *First Corporate Shipping* raises this issue and also involves port development. But the case presents a quite different legal scenario from that in *Lappel Bank* – the Secretary of State's decision to *include* within the United Kingdom's list of candidate SACs a wetlands area in the Severn Estuary was challenged by a company seeking to expand its operations.

### Case C-371/98 *R v. Secretary of State for the Environment, Transport and the Regions, ex parte First Corporate Shipping Ltd* [2000] ECR I-9235

#### The Judgment

…

#### The main proceedings and the question referred for a preliminary ruling

7. FCS [First Corporate Shipping Ltd] is the statutory port authority for the port of Bristol, on the Severn Estuary, and owns considerable land in the neighbourhood of the port. Since acquiring the port, FCS has invested, in partnership with other undertakings, nearly £220 million in capital in developing its facilities. It employs 495 permanent full-time employees. The number of workers employed at the port, including FCS's own employees, is between 3000 and 5000.

8. The Secretary of State indicated that he was minded to propose the Severn Estuary to the Commission as a site eligible for designation as an SAC under Article 4(1) of the Habitats Directive, most of the intertidal part of the estuary having already been classified as a special protection area under [the Birds Directive]. FCS thereupon applied to the Queen's Bench Division (Divisional Court) of the High Court of Justice of England and Wales for leave to apply for judicial review.

9. FCS submitted before that court that Article 2(3) of the Habitats Directive obliged the Secretary of State to take account of economic, social and cultural requirements when deciding which sites should be proposed to the Commission pursuant to Article 4(1) of that directive.

10. The Secretary of State contended that, in the light of the Court's reasoning in [*Lappel Bank*], he could not take economic, social and cultural requirements into account when deciding which sites should be proposed to the Commission pursuant to Article 4(1) of the Habitats Directive.

11. In those circumstances, the High Court of Justice stayed proceedings and referred the following question to the Court for a preliminary ruling:

    'Is a Member State entitled or obliged to take account of the considerations laid down in Article 2(3) of Council Directive 92/43/EEC on the conservation of natural habitats and of wild fauna and flora (OJ 1992 L 206, p. 7), namely, economic, social and cultural requirements and regional and local characteristics, when deciding which sites to propose to the Commission pursuant to Article 4(1) of that Directive and/or in defining the boundaries of such sites?'

**The question referred for a preliminary ruling**

12. It should be noted that the question of interpretation referred for a preliminary ruling relates only to Stage 1 of the procedure for classifying natural sites as SACs laid down by Article 4(1) of the Habitats Directive.

13. Under that provision, on the basis of the criteria set out in Annex III (Stage 1) together with relevant scientific information, each Member State is to propose and transmit to the Commission a list of sites, indicating which natural habitat types in Annex I and native species in Annex II are to be found there.

14. Annex III to the Habitats Directive, which deals with the criteria for selecting sites eligible for identification as sites of Community importance and designation as SACs, sets out, as regards Stage 1, criteria for the assessment at national level of the relative importance of sites for each natural habitat type in Annex I and each species in Annex II.

15. Those assessment criteria are defined exclusively in relation to the objective of conserving the natural habitats or the wild fauna and flora listed in Annexes I and II respectively.

16. It follows that Article 4(1) of the Habitats Directive does not as such provide for requirements other than those relating to the conservation of natural habitats and of wild fauna and flora to be taken into account when choosing, and defining the boundaries of, the sites to be proposed to the Commission as eligible for identification as sites of Community importance.

17. FCS submits that identifying and defining the boundaries of the sites to be notified to the Commission with a view to designation as SACs, as required by Article 4(1) of the Habitats Directive, constitute a measure taken pursuant to the directive within the meaning of Article 2(3). It follows that Article 2(3) imposes an obligation on a Member State to take account of economic, social and cultural requirements and regional and local characteristics when it applies the criteria in Annex III to the directive when drawing up the list of sites to be transmitted to the Commission.

18. According to the Finnish Government, it is open to a Member State, when proposing its list of sites to the Commission, to take account of economic, social and cultural requirements and regional and local characteristics, provided that it does not compromise realisation of the Habitats Directive's nature protection objectives. The Government observes

that there may, for example, be such a large number of sites eligible to be considered of Community importance within the territory of a Member State that that State is entitled to exclude some of them from its list of proposed sites without jeopardising realisation of those objectives.

19. It should be noted that the first subparagraph of Article 3(1) of the Habitats Directive provides for the setting up of a coherent European ecological network of SACs to be known as 'Natura 2000', composed of sites hosting the natural habitat types listed in Annex I and habitats of the species listed in Annex II, to enable them to be maintained or, where appropriate, restored at a favourable conservation status in their natural range.

20. Moreover, Article 4 of the Habitats Directive sets out the procedure for classifying natural sites as SACs, divided into several stages with corresponding legal effects, which is intended in particular to enable the Natura 2000 network to be realised, as provided for by Article 3(2) of the directive.

21. In particular, the first subparagraph of Article 4(2) prescribes that the Commission is to establish, on the basis of the lists drawn up by the Member States and in agreement with each Member State, a draft list of sites of Community importance.

22. To produce a draft list of sites of Community importance, capable of leading to the creation of a coherent European ecological network of SACs, the Commission must have available an exhaustive list of the sites which, at national level, have an ecological interest which is relevant from the point of view of the Habitats Directive's objective of conservation of natural habitats and wild fauna and flora. To that end, that list is drawn up on the basis of the criteria laid down in Annex III (Stage 1) to the directive.

23. Only in that way is it possible to realise the objective, in the first subparagraph of Article 3(1) of the Habitats Directive, of maintaining or restoring the natural habitat types and the species' habitats concerned at a favourable conservation status in their natural range, which may lie across one or more frontiers inside the Community. It follows from Article 1(e) and (i), read in conjunction with Article 2(1), of the directive that the favourable conservation status of a natural habitat or a species must be assessed in relation to the entire European territory of the Member States to which the Treaty applies. Having regard to the fact that, when a Member State draws up the national list of sites, it is not in a position to have precise detailed knowledge of the situation of habitats in the other Member States, it cannot of its own accord, whether because of economic, social or cultural requirements or because of regional or local characteristics, delete sites which at national level have an ecological interest relevant from the point of view of the objective of conservation without jeopardising the realisation of that objective at Community level.

24. In particular, if the Member States could take account of economic, social and cultural requirements and regional and local characteristics when selecting and defining the boundaries of the sites to be included in the list which, pursuant to Article 4(1) of the Habitats Directive, they must draw up and transmit to the Commission, the Commission

could not be sure of having available an exhaustive list of sites eligible as SACs, with the risk that the objective of bringing them together into a coherent European ecological network might not be achieved.

25. The answer to the national court's question must therefore be that, on a proper construction of Article 4(1) of the Habitats Directive, a Member State may not take account of economic, social and cultural requirements or regional and local characteristics, as mentioned in Article 2(3) of that directive, when selecting and defining the boundaries of the sites to be proposed to the Commission as eligible for identification as sites of Community importance.

The Court's judgment is based on the recognition that the creation of a supranational ecological network is reliant upon the Commission having a complete picture of the interconnection of habitats, particularly when these cross state boundaries, based upon an exhaustive list of sites eligible as SACs. Donald McGillivray has commented that in its judgment on this case, the Court of Justice usefully cast light on some of the murky details of the Habitats Directive that had hitherto received little scrutiny and that these 'reveal the widespread permeation of non-environmental considerations into nearly every stage of the Habitats Directive designation process';[84] that is, whilst the consideration of economic and social questions is impermissible at the first, national, stage of designation, it is implicitly expected at subsequent stages of drawing up the final lists. This describes also Advocate-General Leger's interpretation of the 'Stage 2', 'moderation' process for SACs, based on his reading of sustainable development. The Advocate-General's Opinion constitutes the first comment on sustainable development by the Court of Justice.

### Advocate General Leger's Opinion

The concept 'sustainable development' does not mean that the interests of the environment must necessarily and systematically prevail over the interests defended in the context of the other policies pursued by the Community in accordance with Article 3 of the EC Treaty ... On the contrary, it emphasises the necessary balance between various interests which sometimes clash, but which must be reconciled.

The concept originates in [the First Environmental Action Programme, which stated that Community policy] should henceforth be implemented in accordance with the principle of 'integration': Implementation of these proposals must not constitute a new common policy separate from the others. Rather, all Community activities aimed at promoting throughout the Community harmonious development of economic activities, accelerated raising of the standard of living and closer relations between Member States under Article 2 of the EEC Treaty must now take into consideration the protection of the environment.

---

[84] Donald McGillivray, 'Valuing Nature: Economic Value, Conservation Values and Sustainable Development' (2002) 14 *Journal of Environmental Law* 85, p. 90.

'Sustainable development', a fundamental concept of environment law, was taken up and defined in 1987 in the Brundtland Report. According to that report, sustainable development is development which meets the needs of the present without compromising the capacity of future generations to meet their needs. It states that the concept means that the conduct of the various policies must, at the very least, not endanger the natural systems which give us life, the atmosphere, water, earth and living creatures. The report stresses that it is necessary not to set development against the environment but on the contrary to let them evolve in coordinated fashion.

To reconcile these diverse interests in the context of 'sustainable development', the Treaty on European Union introduced the principle of 'integration' in Article 130r(2). That principle requires the Community legislature to conform with environmental protection requirements in the definition and implementation of other policies and actions. Integration of the environmental dimension is thus the basis of the strategy of sustainable development enshrined in both the Treaty on European Union and the Fifth Environment Programme, entitled 'Towards Sustainability' …

So it seems that the approach of the Commission and the Member States in the second stage of the procedure for designating SACs must, observing the objective of 'sustainable development' and the principle of 'integration', consist of assessing the interests concerned, ascertaining whether or not the maintenance of human activities in the area concerned may be reconciled with the objective of conservation or restoration of natural habitats and wild fauna and flora, and drawing the necessary consequences as regards setting up an SAC.

McGillivray sees these comments as problematic, particularly if this reading of sustainable development in relation to the Directive allows economic/social considerations to enter into the designation process, albeit after the national stage of listing. In his view, 'cases like *First Corporate Shipping* should, on the whole, not be concerned with balancing economic and ecological interests but about identifying sites that are of high conservation value in an EC context and designating them for this reason'.[85] Any 'balancing' should be reserved for the more transparent and accessible stage of permitting harmful developments within a protected area.

Notwithstanding the resolute tone of the Court of Justice's judgment in this case that economic considerations should be excluded from the national decision making process of designating an area of land as a special area of conservation, *First Corporate Shipping* did not lay this issue to rest. *Newsum No. 2*[86] is similarly concerned with a challenge to a decision to designate land as an SAC – in this case Halkyn Mountain in Wales – because it hosted a rare type of grassland and a colony of great crested newts (a protected species under the Habitats Directive, though not a priority species). The UK had been finally 'persuaded' by the

---

[85] *Ibid.*, p. 97.

[86] See previous proceedings on Newsum's attempt to translocate the newt colony which brought into question the meaning of 'overriding public interest' in the Habitats Regulations 1994: *Newsum* v. *Welsh Assembly* (*Newsum No. 1*) [2004] EWHC 50 (Admin).

Commission to select the site.[87] The claimants primarily argued that the existence of an extant planning permission to carry out minerals quarrying on part of the land should have been taken into account in the decision to designate the site. The case is interesting because of the political, rather than ecological, judgments that appear to have influenced the selection process at the *national* level because 'Wales was identified as a geographical gap' (para. 16) – or, as the applicant described it, this was a case of 'quota filling' (in an attempt to stave off infringement proceedings by the European Commission). The Court also held that the whole site was lawfully proposed (including a golf course!), even though the grassland and newts occupied only a small proportion of it, on the ground that it was acceptable to have a management regime that covered the whole of the area. Most importantly, the site in question was included in the Commission's list of sites of Community importance in 2004, shortly after which the Welsh Assembly designated all such sites in Wales, including Halkyn Mountain, as SACs in accordance with Art. 4(4) of the Habitats Directive and Regulation 8(1) of the Habitats Regulations.[88]

A key part of the claimants' argument before the High Court (as well as the Court of First Instance in their challenge to the Commission's decision) is that the consultation procedures were unfair and insufficient. Although the judgment on this point[89] is highly interesting in terms of considering the role of public participation in furthering, or *impeding*, environmental protection, in the following extract from the judgment we focus on the issues relating to the selection of European sites. These suggest the impossibility of securing neutrality in scientific information, quite apart from the question of the desirability of 'neutrality' in the first place.[90]

### R (on the application of Newsum and others) v. Welsh Assembly (No 2) [2005] EWHC 538 (Admin)

Mr Justice Richards:

78. The claimants point to the dramatic change in approach to Halkyn Mountain following the Kilkee [Stage 2 'moderation'] meeting in September 1999 and the pressure brought to bear upon the United Kingdom to list further candidate SACs. Halkyn Mountain had

---

[87] The United Kingdom did not meet its obligation to submit a list of candidate SACs to the Commission by 5 June 1995 in accordance with Art. 4(1) of the Habitats Directive and Regulation 7(4) of the Habitats Regulations. A list of 340 candidate SACs was submitted in June 1999 (which did not include Halkyn Mountain, the subject of these proceedings). At 'moderation' meetings in 1999, the UK was threatened with infraction proceedings because the list submitted was judged to provide insufficient representation of a relatively large number of habitats and species.

[88] This triggered a challenge before the Court of First Instance by the claimants to the Commission's decision to include the site on its final list: Case T-57/05, brought under Arts. 230 and 231 EC for annulment of that part of the Commission's decision that relates to Halkyn Mountain.     [89] Paras. 59–77.

[90] We discuss these issues in detail in Ch. 1, pp. 40–7.

previously been surveyed on a number of occasions but had never been considered to be of more than local interest. The area had not been notified as an SSSI. Two nearby areas were SSSIs, but they were small and their interest lay in features that are not material for present purposes. Within a period of about three months after the Kilkee meeting, however, Halkyn Mountain was being put forward as a possible SAC, as part of a move that saw the total number of proposed SACs in Wales more than double (from 40 to 86).

79. The claimants contend that nothing has been adduced to show that the scientific judgments underpinning the original list, i.e. excluding Halkyn Mountain, were wrong; and that the haste to produce a further list of candidate SACs which did include Halkyn Mountain was at the expense of a proper scientific justification. The Prosser/Wallace report, on which principal reliance was placed for the first decision, did not recommend that Halkyn Mountain should be a SAC. Nor is SAC status supported by the later evidence. Criticism is made of the reliance on calaminarian grassland and great crested newts as reasons for the inclusion of the site at all, and of the extent of the site put forward by reference to them. **It is pointed out that calaminarian grassland occurs only in small fragmented stands (on former mineral spoil areas) which, according to the 2002 survey, extend in total to 12 hectares out of the 610 hectares of the SAC. The ponds and surrounding habitat required by great crested newts also take up only a proportion of the total site.**

80. Against the background of that general theme, a number of specific issues are raised, namely that (i) the inclusion of Pen yr Henblas [Quarry] within the candidate SAC did not have proper regard to **the existing planning permission** or to the possibility of translocation of the great crested newts to another site; (ii) the decision to include Halkyn Mountain as a candidate SAC because of its great crested newt population was in any event unreasonable.

On the first issue, the claimants had sought to distinguish this case from *First Corporate Shipping*:

102. **It is true that the court in First Corporate Shipping was looking more broadly at economic requirements and the like rather than at the existence and potential impact of a particular planning permission. In my judgment, however, the reasoning of the court in that case is equally applicable to the claimants' arguments in the present case. It emphasises that the relevant assessment criteria are defined exclusively in relation to the conservation objective. If one focuses on the Annex III [of the Habitats Directive, see above, p. 637] criteria, as the court makes clear must be done, I see no room for excluding an otherwise appropriate site on the basis that the relevant habitats or species are liable to be affected by the implementation of existing consents. One of the purposes of the Directive is to confer protection upon sites that meet the Annex III criteria. Such protection includes a review of existing consents, to determine whether and on what conditions they can be implemented. It would turn the scheme of the Directive on its head if the existence of a consent could be relied on as a reason for not protecting a site in the first place.**

103. **I therefore consider that, if a site otherwise meets the criteria for inclusion as a candidate SAC, it cannot be lawful for a Member State to exclude it from the list of candidates on the ground that the habitats or species it contains will or may be affected by implementation of an existing planning permission or licence.**

104. It follows that the possibility or probability (not a certainty, despite the strong language used in [Counsel for the claimants'] submissions) that, but for SAC status, the existing planning permission would be implemented and that the colony of great crested newts would be lost or relocated was not a legally relevant consideration in determining whether to include Pen yr Henblas or Aberdo within the area of the candidate SAC. **The potential impact that implementation of existing consents might have on protected habitats or species may form part of the information to be provided to the Commission, but is not a good reason for deciding not to include a site as a candidate SAC. The defendant's decision cannot therefore be successfully impugned by reference to a failure to take such matters into account.**

Mr Justice Richards continued to describe the 'true position' as follows: the inclusion of a site on a list of candidate SACs begins a process capable of protecting the site. When the list is approved and the site becomes an actual SAC, as happened in this case, the existing planning permission becomes immediately subject to review in the light of the relevant conservation objectives (Regulations 10 and 48–57 of the Habitats Regulations 1994); in contrast the claimants' argument ran counter to the purpose and scheme of the Directive, as interpreted by the Court of Justice in *First Corporate Shipping*.

Both *First Corporate Shipping* and *Newsum No. 2* were concerned with the inclusion of an area on national lists of natural habitat types and species which were likely to form the basis of the European Commission's list of sites of Community importance. An earlier case, brought by WWF-UK and the RSPB against the Secretary of State for Scotland, challenged the drawing of a boundary of a proposed SAC[91] which had the effect of *excluding* the summit of Cairn Gorm, upon which planning permission had been granted for skiing development (including the building of a funicular railway). As the 'Save the Cairngorms Campaign' argued, 'the funicular site is virtually surrounded by land proposed for designation, and yet in ecological terms is very similar to the surrounding, soon to be protected, land'.[92] The petitioners' argument was that the grant of planning permission was unlawful because approval of the project was made possible by drawing inappropriate boundaries for the European conservation site. In the Court of Session, Lord Nimmo Smith rejected this on the basis of his interpretation of the Birds and Habitats Directives: specifically that these Directives require that a discretion be exercised in the determination of

---

[91]  *WWF-UK and RSPB* v. *Secretary of State for Scotland* [1999] Env LR 632 (Court of Session).
[92]  Save the Cairngorms Campaign, *Cairn Gorm: Potential for Conflict With Europe* (Cairngorms Campaign, 1997).

boundaries, as in other respects.[93] In his view, this means that so long as the criteria applied are ornithological or ecological, in line with European Court of Justice authority on this matter, then there was a discretion to be exercised in identifying the boundaries of the site, as an integral part of the process of identifying the site itself.

As Chris Hilson explains,[94] the growing number of legal disputes arising on the subject of the Member States' 'margin of discretion' in the designation of land for special protection is quite simply a product of a move away from 'old-style directives' which tended to use easily measured limit values (see Chapter 9, pp. 658–9), in favour of those pursuing a more mediated, coordinated approach to regulation, a hallmark of which is the conferral of 'localised discretion' upon Member States. In principle such an approach is more sensitive to local ecological conditions and local sources of information, but also, as *Newsum* demonstrates, may be open to political influences.

### (iii) The protection regime

Once land has been designated according to the procedure described above, Art. 6 of the Habitats Directive requires Member States to establish the necessary conservation measures for SACs (Arts. 6(1) and (2)), and also provides for procedural safeguards in the event that development is planned in such areas (and SPAs also[95]) (Arts. 6(3) and (4)).

#### Habitats Directive

##### Article 6

1. For special areas of conservation, Member States shall establish the necessary conservation measures involving, if need be, appropriate management plans specifically designed for the sites or integrated into other development plans, and appropriate statutory, administrative or contractual measures which correspond to the ecological requirements of the natural habitat types in Annex I and the species in Annex II present on the sites.

2. Member States shall take appropriate steps to avoid, in the special areas of conservation, the deterioration of natural habitats and the habitats of species as well as disturbance of the species for which the areas have been designated, in so far as such disturbance could be significant in relation to the objectives of this Directive.

3. Any plan or project not directly connected with or necessary to the management of the site but likely to have a significant effect thereon, either individually or in combination with other plans or projects, shall be subject to appropriate assessment of its implications for the site in view of the site's conservation objectives. In the light of the conclusions of the assessment of the implications for the site and subject to the provisions of

---

[93]  [1999] Env LR 632, p. 672.

[94]  Chris Hilson, 'Legality Review of Member State Discretion under Directives' in Takis Tridimas and Paulisa Nebbia (eds.), *European Union Law for the Twenty-First Century* (Hart, 2004), pp. 237–8.    [95] As a matter of Art. 7 Habitats Directive.

paragraph 4, the competent national authorities shall agree to the plan or project only having ascertained that it will not adversely affect the integrity of the site concerned and, if appropriate, after having obtained the opinion of the general public.

4. If, in spite of a negative assessment of the implications for the site and in the absence of alternative solutions, a plan or project must nevertheless be carried out for imperative reasons of overriding public interest, including those of a social or economic nature, the Member States shall take all compensatory measures necessary to ensure that the overall coherence of Natura 2000 is protected. It shall inform the Commission of the compensatory measures adopted.

Where the site concerned hosts a priority natural habitat type and/or a priority species [indicated by an asterisk in the Directive's annexes], the only considerations which may be raised are those relating to human health or public safety, to beneficial consequences of primary importance for the environment, or further to an opinion from the Commission, to other imperatives of overriding public interest.

In terms of the obligation in Arts. 6(1) and (2) that Member States establish the necessary conservation measures for natural habitat types and species listed in the Directive, the United Kingdom government chose (as with other areas of environmental law, such as environmental assessment[96]) to implement this through existing legal machinery and administrative structures, rather than introduce primary legislation.[97] In this case the existing regime was that for the conservation of SSSIs (above, pp. 618–27), but with some additions to secure the higher level of protection granted to European sites compared (at the time of the transposition of the Directive) with national SSSIs.[98] The SSSI regime therefore provides the foundation for protecting the European site network established by the Habitats Directive, as it was similarly used to implement the Birds Directive. In practice this means that before land can be designated as an SPA or an SAC by an order made by the Secretary of State, it must be notified as an SSSI to secure its legal protection under the Wildlife and Countryside Act 1981, as amended. The conservation agencies advise the Secretary of State which areas should be considered for designation and consult with any landowners and the local authorities. The system for protecting European sites in the United Kingdom originally echoed the SSSI system in favouring compensation and voluntary agreement rather than compulsion. A much stricter approach is now adhered to as a matter of policy, as set out in Planning Policy Statement 9.[99] Indeed, it is the case that stronger protection is seemingly granted

---

[96] See Ch. 14.

[97] The Directive was transposed into United Kingdom law by statutory instrument – the Conservation (Natural Habitats, &c) Regulations 1994 (the 'Habitats Regulations') SI 1994 No. 2716.

[98] For example Nature Conservation Orders made under s. 29 Wildlife and Countryside Act (WCA) 1981 (this section was repealed, in England, by the Countryside and Rights of Way Act 2000).    [99] See below, p. 676.

to *national* SSSIs because of the possibility of an indefinite ban on potentially damaging operations, discussed above,[100] whereas the Habitats Directive specifically envisages the compromising of 'ordinary' European sites for social or economic reasons, as we recount below.

### (iv) Threats: an 'appropriate assessment' and general prohibition on development

If a plan or project 'not directly connected with or necessary to the management of the site but likely to have a significant effect thereon, either individually or in combination with other plans or projects' is proposed, Art. 6(3) of the Habitats Directive triggers a series of procedural safeguards, the most important of which is that the plan or project 'shall be subject to appropriate assessment of its implications for the site in view of the site's conservation objectives'. This clearly mirrors the form of environmental assessment provided for by the Environmental Impact Assessment (EIA) Directive,[101] since it seeks to establish the 'implications' of a plan or project in a precautionary manner, is related to the likelihood of 'significant effects', and is a step preceding and providing a basis for other steps – in particular the approval or refusal of a plan or project. This similarity is borne out by guidance from the European Commission which advises that in most cases in which a project is considered likely to have a significant effect on a sensitive site for conservation reasons, 'it will often be appropriate to undertake an assessment that fulfils the requirements of Directive 85/337/EEC'.[102]

In such cases, an assessment under the EIA Directive will accommodate an assessment for the purposes of Art. 6(3) of the Habitats Directive. In cases in which an assessment for the purposes of Art. 6(3) does *not* take the form of an assessment under the EIA Directive, questions then arise as to what may be considered 'appropriate' in terms of its form, particularly given the brevity of Art. 6(3) on this point. The European Commission states, fairly obviously, that the assessment should be recorded, and then goes on to state that a corollary of this is that it should provide a reasoned basis for the subsequent decision, rather than a 'simple' positive or negative view of the project. A further question is raised about who should compile the assessment, particularly given the lack of guidance on this point in law and policy guidance. The preceding reference to 'Member States' in Art. 6(3) suggests that the relevant Secretary of State should undertake this. A problem arising from the similarities between environmental impact assessment, under the EIA Directive, and assessment for the purposes of the Habitats Directive is that the focus in the former on information provided by the developer as an environmental

---

[100] See s. 28E WCA 1981, and accompanying guidance, discussed p. 676.

[101] See Ch. 14. It also mirrors the conceptual premises of the Strategic Environmental Assessment (SEA) Directive, on which see also pp. 599–601.

[102] European Commission, *Managing Natura 2000 Sites: The Provisions of Article 6 of the Habitats Directive 92/43/EEC* (CEC, 2000), para. 4.5.1.

statement may unduly influence the content of the 'appropriate assess-ment'.[103] This likelihood is illustrated by the appropriate assessment con-ducted to predict the likely effects of a proposed wind farm on Walland Marsh in Kent, presented below, pp. 655–61.

Notwithstanding the similarities outlined above, in strict terms the scope of an Art. 6(3) assessment under the Habitats Directive is narrower than an assessment under the EIA Directive because it is confined to the implications for the site in view of the site's *conservation* objectives. However, as the Commission notes, in reality the impacts of the plan or project on these objec-tives can only properly be assessed by reference to other environmental crite-ria (soil, water, landscape, etc.) as set out in the EIA Directive.[104] A key difference between these two forms of environmental assessment lies in the opportunities made for public participation: the Habitats Directive does not indicate when the opinion of the public should be sought as part of the assess-ment process, whereas consultation has become an important feature of the EIA Directive.[105] This suggests that it is only where the assessment required by Art. 6(3) takes the form of an assessment under the EIA Directive that public consultation is necessary. That said, the European Commission's guidance in *Managing Natura 2000 Sites* more than hints at the implications of the Aarhus Convention on this position because the Convention emphasises the impor-tance of public consultation in relation to environmental decision making more generally.[106]

Further on the content of an appropriate assessment, although Art. 6(3) does not itself look beyond the plan or project proposed to address alternative solu-tions and mitigation measures, these factors may contribute to the judgment on whether the plan or project will *not* adversely affect the integrity of the site. This is the core consideration of the Directive because Art. 6(3) contains a general prohibition on development unless the competent national authorities have ascertained that it will not adversely affect the integrity of the site concerned (if appropriate, after having obtained the opinion of the general public). Although the concept of the 'integrity of the site' is clearly pivotal in this respect, the Habitats Directive fails to offer a definition. Looking to guidance from the Commission, this is taken to mean the coherence of its ecological structure and function – across its whole area – that enables it to sustain the habitat and the

---

[103] We discuss the partisan nature of information in developers' environmental statements in Ch. 14, pp. 563–7. The practical effects of this may be seen in the case of the proposed wind farm on the Isle of Lewis in which there is doubt on the part of the RSPB as to whether the developer's 'appropriate assessment' will suffice, or whether the Scottish Executive must separately and independently evaluate the likely effects of the project on the environment.

[104] Article 3 EIA Directive. On this point, see European Commission, *Managing Natura 2000 Sites*, para. 4.5.2.

[105] The participatory elements of EIA were recently enhanced by Directive 2003/35/EC providing for public participation in respect of the drawing up of certain plans and programmes relating to the environment and amending with regard to participation and access to justice Directives 85/337/EEC and 96/61/EC OJ 2003 L 156/17. See further pp. 590–2.

[106] European Commission, *Managing Natura 2000 Sites*, para. 4.6.2.

levels of populations of species for which it was classified.[107] The Commission makes clear that the decision whether a site is adversely affected should focus on and be limited to the site's conservation objectives.[108]

The neutrality of this requirement apparently came under strain in *WWF-UK and RSPB* v. *Secretary of State for Scotland*,[109] concerning the exclusion of the summit of Cairn Gorm from a proposed SAC which surrounded it (as discussed above, pp. 646–7). WWF-UK and RSPB (Scotland) alleged that Scottish Natural Heritage and the Highland Council had failed to carry out a proper assessment of the implications of the funicular project, and associated skiing developments, for European conservation sites. The question before the Court was whether an assessment on the effects of the project entailed the need for an *absolute guarantee* that the integrity of the site would not be affected by the proposed development. The applicants argued that the *draft* nature of the plans for controlling visitors (in particular the 'closed system' which prevented them from exploring the summit by keeping them within the confines of the 'interpretation' centre *cum* restaurant) meant that such an assurance could not be given, and therefore planning permission should not have been granted. In contrast, Lord Nimmo Smith accepted the developer's assurances that the proposed planning agreement and visitor management plan imposed real controls; the funicular could not be brought into use until the visitor plan had been finalised and implemented, thus giving Scottish Natural Heritage a 'stranglehold' over the commercial enterprise. The Judge also made clear the potential for reviewing Highland Council's interpretation of the efficacy of this guarantee: 'The question whether the way in which the development would be operated would prevent adverse effects was a question of fact for the authority carrying out the assessment. It was speculation to suggest that controls would not be used' (p. 699). He further stated, pragmatically, that there need not be an absolute guarantee that the integrity of the site will not be adversely affected because: 'there never can be an absolute guarantee about what will happen in the future, and the most that can be expected of a planning authority ... is to identify the potential risks, so far as they may be reasonably foreseeable in light of such information as can reasonably be obtained, and to put in place a legally enforceable framework with a view to preventing these risks from materialising' (p. 700).

Fortunately, the European Court of Justice has since taken a far more precautionary approach to this question. In Case C-127/02 *Waddenzee (Cockle Fishers)*,[110] the threat to the special protection area on the Wadden Sea coast (designated under Art. 4 of the Birds Directive (see above, p. 629)) was in the form of a mechanical form of fishing using hydraulic suction to dredge for cockles and mussels, which, as well as taking food away from the birds in the area, was also considered by the Netherlands Association for the Protection of

---

[107] *Ibid.* para. 1.6.3.     [108] *Ibid.*     [109] [1999] Env LR 632 (Court of Session).

[110] Case C-127/02 *Landelijke Vereniging tot Behoud van de Waddenzee* v. *Staatssecretaris van Landbouw Natuurbeheer en Visserij (Cockle Fishers)* [2005] 2 CMLR 31.

Birds to seriously damage the geomorphology and fauna and flora of the seabed. The Court concluded that a risk to the integrity of a such a site exists if it cannot be excluded on the basis of 'objective information' that the plan or project will have significant effects on the site concerned. Of particular interest is that the Court read Art. 6(3) in conjunction with the EIA Directive and the precautionary principle.[111]

### Case C-127/02 *Landelijke Vereniging tot Behoud van de Waddenzee* v. *Staatssecretaris van Landbouw Natuurbeheer en Visserij* (*Cockle Fishers*) [2005] 2 CMLR 31

39. According to the first sentence of Article 6(3) of the Habitats Directive, any plan or project not directly connected with or necessary to the management of the site but likely to have a significant effect thereon, either individually or in combination with other plans or projects, is to be subject to appropriate assessment of its implications for the site in view of the site's conservation objectives.

40. The requirement for an appropriate assessment of the implications of a plan or project is thus conditional on its being likely to have a significant effect on the site.

41. Therefore, the triggering of the environmental protection mechanism provided for in Article 6(3) of the Habitats Directive does not presume – as is, moreover, clear from the guidelines for interpreting that article drawn up by the Commission, entitled 'Managing Natura 2000 Sites: The provisions of Article 6 of the "Habitats" Directive (92/43/EEC)' – that the plan or project considered definitely has significant effects on the site concerned but follows from the mere probability that such an effect attaches to that plan or project.

42. As regards Article 2(1) of Directive 85/337, the text of which is essentially similar to Article 6(3) of the Habitats Directive, provides that 'Member States shall adopt all measures necessary to ensure that, before consent is given, projects likely to have significant effects on the environment … are made subject to an assessment with regard to their effects', the Court has held that these are projects which are likely to have significant effects on the environment.

43. It follows that the first sentence of Article 6(3) of the Habitats Directive subordinates the requirement for an appropriate assessment of the implications of a plan or project to the condition that there be a probability or a risk that the latter will have significant effects on the site concerned.

44. In the light, in particular, of the precautionary principle, which is one of the foundations of the high level of protection pursued by Community policy on the environment, in accordance with the first subparagraph of Article 174(2) EC, and by reference to which the Habitats

---

[111] Compare this judgment with the earlier restrictive approach in *North Uist Fisheries Ltd* v. *Secretary of State for Scotland* (1992) JEL 24: in the context of a nature conservation order made under s. 29 of the Wildlife and Countryside Act 1981 (now repealed), the national court interpreted the prohibition upon persons carrying out operations likely to destroy the natural history interest of an area, the meaning of 'likely' being understood as 'probable', rather than as a bare possibility.

Directive must be interpreted, such a risk exists if it cannot be excluded on the basis of objective information that the plan or project will have significant effects on the site concerned.[112] Such an interpretation of the condition to which the assessment of the implications of a plan or project for a specific site is subject, which implies that in case of doubt as to the absence of significant effects such an assessment must be carried out, makes it possible to ensure effectively that plans or projects which adversely affect the integrity of the site concerned are not authorised, and thereby contributes to achieving, in accordance with the third recital in the preamble to the Habitats Directive and Article 2(1) thereof, its main aim, namely, ensuring biodiversity through the conservation of natural habitats and of wild fauna and flora.

45. In the light of the foregoing, the answer to [the Question referred] must be that the first sentence of Article 6(3) of the Habitats Directive must be interpreted as meaning that any plan or project not directly connected with or necessary to the management of the site is to be subject to an appropriate assessment of its implications for the site in view of the site's conservation objectives if it cannot be excluded, on the basis of objective information, that it will have a significant effect on that site, either individually or in combination with other plans or projects.

Reinforcing this precautionary approach, the (full) Court also held that Member States breach EC law if they subsequently *allow development* when there is 'reasonable scientific doubt' about its effects on the integrity of a site protected under EC law (para. 61).

Ellen Stokes[113] considers this to be a very significant case, suggesting an evolution in the Court's reading of the precautionary principle from an approach rooted in scientifically established risk (as in *Pfizer*[114]) to one which is based on whether there is a probability or a risk the plan or project will have significant effects on a site. Such a shift in approach was no doubt informed by Advocate-General Kokott's Opinion in this case, in which she considered any damage to the conservation objectives of a site was reason enough for the competent authorities to apply Art. 6(3) and require an appropriate assessment to be conducted. On this point she stated:

If adverse effects resulting from plans and projects were accepted on the grounds that they merely rendered the attainment of these objectives difficult but not impossible or unlikely, the species numbers and habitat areas covered by Natura 2000 would be eroded by them. It would not even be possible to foresee the extent of this erosion with any degree of accuracy because no appropriate assessment would be carried out. These losses would not be offset because Article 6(4) of the Habitats Directive would not apply. Thus in principle any adverse effect on the conservation objectives must be regarded as a significant adverse effect on the integrity of the site concerned (paras. 84-5).

---

[112] See, by analogy, *inter alia*, Case C-180/96 *United Kingdom* v. *Commission* [1998] ECR I-2265, paras. 50, 105 and 107.

[113] 'Liberalising the Threshold of Precaution' (2005) 7 *Environmental Law Review* 206.

[114] See Ch. 1, pp. 18–31.

The geographical scope of the integrity test has also been questioned, that is whether the impact of the 'plan or project' should be judged solely by reference to the effects on a species in an SPA, or rather in terms of the European population of the species. The latter test was advanced by the Secretary of State to justify his decision to issue licences for shooting barnacle geese on two farms on Islay (an island off the west coast of Scotland) when this was challenged by the RSPB. The implication of this justification was that even serious 'disturbance' of a species in a particular SPA may be acceptable if it does not significantly affect the wider population of the species over its natural range. The Outer House originally dismissed the petition by the RSPB holding that the Secretary of State had correctly approached the granting of the licence against the background of the general effect on the species' population as a whole, and accepted, that although the shooting would have a disturbing effect on the sites themselves, the Secretary of State was not required to consider the local impact *at all*. The Inner House decided quite differently, following a purposive reading of the Habitats Directive and having considered the practical difficulties involved in assessing the effect of the cull on the species across their natural range. Underlying the judgment is an understanding of the need to protect individual sites as vital components of the wider Natura 2000 ecological network.

### *Royal Society for the Protection of Birds* v. *Secretary of State for Scotland* [2001] Env LR 19

31. The Community initiative for the conservation of vulnerable species of birds, by giving special protection to the most suitable territories would be undermined if the effects of any disturbance on the local population in these territories were not taken into account. Indeed, taken to its logical conclusion, the respondents' approach would mean that … any disturbance whatever of a species on a special protection area would be permissible provided only that it could not affect the viability of the species over its natural range. But, as the *German Dykes* case shows,[115] Member States are under a legal obligation to classify these particular sites and, even for substantial economic reasons, they cannot impair them by subsequently reducing their area. Moreover, the scope for development which would affect the integrity of such sites is strictly limited by the provisions of Article 6(3) and (4) of the Habitats Directive. The respondents' contention that under Article 6(2) the significance of any disturbance is to be judged only by reference to the viability of the species over its natural range is therefore inconsistent with the concern for the integrity of the individual sites which is demonstrated by the *German Dykes* case and by the other paragraphs of Article 6. Furthermore, even assuming that in this particular case the Scottish Ministers are in a position to estimate the significance of any disturbance by reference to the viability of the geese over their natural range, there might be situations where the natural range of the species covered the territories of several Member States and where, as a result, such a test would be difficult, if not impossible, for the authorities of any individual Member State to apply. Indeed, as the third recital and Article 4(3) of the Wild Birds Directive[116] and Articles 3 and 4 of the Habitats Directive[117] show, the responsibility for

---

[115] *Leybucht Dykes.*    [116] See p. 629.    [117] Discussed pp. 636–7.

making such judgements is not vested exclusively in the individual Member States. This is not to deny that, where the Scottish Ministers can in fact conclude that a disturbance on a special protection area could affect the viability of a species over its natural range, they must take appropriate steps to avoid it. Both the local and wider effects are relevant.

### (v) Walland Marsh wind farm: an 'inappropriate assessment'?

In order to transpose Art. 6(4) of the Habitats Directive, Regulation 48(1) of the Habitats Regulations 1994 requires that an appropriate assessment be conducted in circumstances in which a plan or project is likely to have a significant effect on the conservation interest of a European site. An example of this assessment is provided by the case of a proposed wind farm development on Walland Marsh in Kent, 'a precious corner of England'.[118] Although the proposed development is not in any such European protected site (or possible future extensions of such sites), it is located nearby and therefore had to be assessed because of its likely impact on the designated sites.

The appropriate assessment conducted for this project raises a raft of issues. The first (as discussed above, pp. 650–3) is when is an appropriate assessment required? The Habitats Directive refers to the need for such an exercise when a plan or project is likely to have a significant effect on the site 'either individually or in combination with other plans or projects'.[119] The difficulty is that 'significant' is open to different interpretations and no thresholds are given. This is quite unlike the EIA Directive which provides both quantitative exclusionary thresholds and qualitative indicative criteria[120] (such as the sensitivity of the land in terms of its conservation interest) in order to determine the point at which significant effects are likely to ensue. In this case the developer (Npower Renewables Ltd) and the planning inspector, who held an inquiry into the proposal, were of the opinion that an 'appropriate assessment' was not required (in line with the *developer's* conclusion that the proposals would *not* have an adverse effect on the integrity of any existing or possible future protected sites[121]). In contrast, English Nature and the Department of Trade and Industry considered such an assessment was necessary. A second issue is the adequacy of the assessment on this development compiled by the Secretary of State (but with much of the information provided by the developer), because of the limited nature of the document (it runs to seven pages), particularly the incomplete analysis of various 'habitat enhancement measures' and a management plan, both of which proved central to the Secretary of State's decision to authorise the construction of the wind farm. The following extract is taken from the assessment. Note

[118] As writes Simon Jenkins, 'Better to Have Nuclear Power than a Blot on the Landscape – Romney Marsh is to be Sacrificed in Pursuit of Renewable Energy', *Guardian,* 28.10.05.
[119] Article 6(4).    [120] See Ch. 14.
[121] This is clearly the wrong test – the correct test is the likelihood of a significant effect on the site (Art. 6(3) first sentence). The test whether the plan or project will adversely affect the integrity of the site concerned is to be concluded *on the basis* of the appropriate assessment, not as a precursor to it.

particularly the clear setting out of the conservation objectives for the site, in the light of which the assessment must be conducted according to the terms of Art. 6(3), and the references made to the consultation process for this assessment (which amounted to little more than the Secretary of State relying on information provided in the course of an (earlier) public planning inquiry).

### Department of Trade and Industry (DTI), *Appropriate Assessment of Proposed Wind Farm's Effects on the Dungeness to Pett Levels Special Protection Area and Proposed Ramsar Site, Little Cheyne Court Site of Special Scientific Interest and Walland Marsh Site of Special Scientific Interest Prepared under Regulation 48(1) of the Conservation (Natural Habitats, &c) Regulations 1994 ('Habitats Regulations')* (DTI, October 2005)

#### Introduction

Npower Renewables Limited ('NRL') applied on 15 November 2002 for the Secretary of State for Trade and Industry's (SoS) consent under section 36 of the Electricity Act 1989[122] to construct and operate a 26 turbine wind farm with a capacity of up to 78 megawatts at Little Cheyne Court, Walland Marsh, Kent ('the Development'). In accordance with the Electricity Works (Environmental Impact Assessment) (England and Wales) Regulations 2000 NRL also submitted on 15 November 2002 a document entitled 'Environmental Statement' ('the ES'). The document describes the Development and gives an analysis of its environmental effects. The ES was advertised and placed in the public domain and an opportunity given to those who wished to comment on it to do so. NRL supplemented this document in July 2004 with further documents entitled 'Wintering Bird Studies 2002/03' and 'Wintering Bird Studies 2003/04' ('the further Bird Studies'), these too were placed in the public domain. A public inquiry into the application for consent was held between 12 October 2004 and 14 January 2005 at which consideration was given to a report, dated September 2004, entitled 'Report to inform an appropriate assessment for the proposed Little Cheyne wind farm' ('the AA Report') prepared for NRL by Ecology Consulting.

The SoS has concluded that an Appropriate Assessment is required by virtue of regulation 48 of the Conservation (Natural Habitats,&c.) Regulations 1994 ('the 1994 Regulations'). The remainder of this document therefore comprises the Appropriate Assessment which takes into account the Conclusions and advice given by the Public Inquiry Inspector.

...

#### Appropriate Assessment

The AA Report addresses the nature conservation issues raised by the development in relation to the Dungeness to Pett Level SPA, possible extensions to that SPA, and the possible Ramsar site.[123] The AA Report provides baseline data and analysis, and draws on information presented in the ES and the further Bird Studies and focuses on the key species identified

---

[122] On the consent system for wind farms, see Ch. 16.

[123] A Ramsar site is a wetland of international importance designated under the Ramsar Convention on Wetlands of International Importance.

by EN [English Nature] as likely to be qualifying features of a possible extended SPA and new Ramsar site.

The AA Report begins by outlining the relationship of the application site to the nearby Cheyne Court and Walland Marsh SSSIs, and to the Scotney gravel pits which are currently under consideration by EN as a possible SSSI.

…

Under the 1994 Regulations the first test is whether the development is likely to have a significant effect on any of the populations of importance for which the site has been notified. If it would, then an appropriate assessment needs to be carried out to determine whether the development would threaten the ecological integrity of the SPA, in light of its conservation objectives. This is the second test.

There are no published nature conservation objectives for the possible SPA although EN has advised that they are likely to be along similar lines to those of the existing SPA but including the updated list of qualifying features. The existing objectives are:

> To maintain, in favourable condition, the habitats for the populations of Annex 1 species of European importance, ie Bewick's swan, common tern, Mediterranean gull, with particular reference to:
> * standing water
> * shingle
> * marshy grassland
> * arable
>
> To maintain, in favourable condition, the habitats for the populations of migratory bird species of European importance, ie shoveler with particular reference to:
> * standing water
> * marshy grassland

The provisional qualifying interests for the Dungeness to Pett Levels SPA, including the extension that EN may propose to the Secretary of State for the Environment, Food and Rural Affairs, are:

> Species qualifying under Article 4.1 (ie species listed in Annex 1 of the EU Birds Directive occurring in at least nationally important numbers):
> * Breeding common tern, little tern and Mediterranean gull.
> * Passage aquatic warbler.
> * Wintering bittern, Bewick's swan, hen harrier and golden plover.
>
> Species qualifying under Article 4.2 (ie migratory species occurring in internationally important numbers and assemblages in excess of 20,000 individuals):
> * Wintering shoveler.
> * An internationally important assemblage of over 20,000 waterfowl in the non-breeding season, including great crested grebe, cormorant, Bewick's swan, European white-fronted goose, wigeon, gadwall, shoveler, pochard, golden plover, lapwing, sanderling and whimbrel.

The provisional avian qualifying interests for the possible Dungeness to Pett Level Ramsar site are:

- Criterion 5: an internationally important assemblage of over 20,000 waterfowl in the non-breeding season.
- Criterion 6: internationally important wintering numbers of mute swan and shoveler.

…

### Breeding species

The proposed wind farm would have no likely significant effect on any of the SPA breeding species (*common tern, little tern, Mediterranean gull*) and there would therefore be no threat to the integrity of these populations.

### Passage species

There would be no likely significant effect on the passage species (*whimbrel and aquatic warbler*) and no threat to the integrity of their populations.

### Wintering species

Species occurring in internationally important numbers

*Shoveler:* Being a wetland species, the large majority of the records were from the Cheyne Court SSSI. The only other parts of the study area in which it was regularly recorded were Scotney gravel pits and Little Cheyne reservoir, although numbers there were much lower. The mean peak count within the wind farm potential impact zone (600 metres) was only 16 birds, with all these recorded on the Little Cheyne reservoir. Over-flying rates through the wind farm site were very low indeed (averaging only 0.03 per hour) and only 13% of flights were at rotor height. The risk of collision would be of negligible magnitude and not significant; only 0.02 per year, equivalent to only 0.008% on the background mortality. With low numbers in the potential disturbance zone any effect on this species would be of negligible magnitude and not significant.

EU Birds Directive Annex 1 species occurring in nationally important numbers

*Bittern:* The only place that it has been recorded within the wintering bird study area is the Cheyne Court SSSI. None has been recorded over-flying the wind farm site and none within the potential disturbance zone. No effects would be likely for this species as it makes negligible use of the Little Cheyne Court area.

The Assessment continues to detail the likely effects on further groups of bird species.

Mitigation measures

The AA report then considers various mitigation measures. The principal one has been to locate the turbines away from the main areas of wintering bird interest. However, it is also proposed to implement a Habitat Management Plan. While no significant ornithological or other ecological effects are predicted to occur, the Plan seeks to ensure that this position is maintained throughout the lifetime of the wind farm. The Management Agreement[124] would ensure secure feeding areas outside the wind farm so that in each winter season crops of rape would always be present in about 30% of the area and cereals in another 30%. The deliberate scaring of swans and geese from that zone would be discontinued. A secondary measure would be the discouragement of swans from certain areas by an undertaking not to plant rape in fields on the eastern side of the wind farm closest to the birds' preferred feeding area. Local conservation gains would derive from provision of headland grassland strips (ensuring a net gain in ditch margin habitat), ditch re-profiling, deepening of dry ditches, clearance of reeds from certain ditches, a programme for the control of mink, and monitoring of effects of the habitat creation and enhancement programme.

...

Conclusion

The SoS accepts that there are limitations as to the accuracy of modelling exercises but is of the view that taken together with the other measures he is confident that there should not be a significant increase in bird mortality passing through the site of the Development.

The SoS therefore concludes from this Appropriate Assessment that though some very minor effects of negligible magnitude might occur on some of the SPA/possible SPA/Ramsar populations, none would threaten the ecological integrity of the sites. This is particularly the case, as it should be, on the basis of the whole project including the habitat enhancement measures that form an integral part of the Development.

This body of information, referred to as an 'appropriate assessment' by the Secretary of State, was issued as an appendix to the decision letter that stated that the Secretary of State had approved the development. This meant that organisations such as English Nature were unable to comment on the assessment prior to its publication. As mentioned above, a planning inquiry preceded the Secretary of State's decision,[125] conducted by a planning inspector, Mr Richardson. The inspector's report on this inquiry contributed to the decision to authorise the development (the Secretary of State follows planning inspectors' recommendations in the majority of cases). The report contained a fuller assessment of the conservation interests at stake than the 'appropriate assessment' published afterwards, and which appears to be little more than a summary of the evidence elicited in the course of the inquiry. In his report, the inspector notably remarked upon the trustworthiness of the developer's evidence (based on a 'scientific approach'), when compared to the 'assertion

---

[124] On management agreements, see above, pp. 620–6.
[125] Following objections from the relevant planning authorities – Kent County Council and Shepway District Council – to the application, the Secretary of State was obliged to cause a public inquiry to be held under Sch. 8 Electricity Act 1989.

and supposition without a valid scientific underpinning'[126] which made up the evidence of English Nature and the RSPB. English Nature have since described the nature of their evidence as 'precautionary' in terms of the potential effects of the wind farm on bird populations in the area.[127] Mr Richardson also highlighted the existence of a habitat management plan drawn up by the developers.[128] As discussed, there are limitations on the circumstances in which development can be permitted on a designated site. The inspector strongly recommended that the proposed development be granted development consent, having concluded (on the basis of the developer's evidence) that the proposed development would *not* adversely affect the integrity of the Dungeness to Pett Levels SPA or its proposed extensions by reducing the level of the population of sensitive bird species present.

### Report to the Secretary of State for Trade and Industry by C. A. Richardson (Planning Inspector), GDBC/003/0001C (May 2005)

179. Npower Renewables Ltd contend that a proper application of European and domestic policy indicates that this scheme is not ecologically unacceptable. The proposed development would not result in a likely significant effect on any existing or possible international or European site. Even if it did, the proposal would not threaten the ecological integrity of the SPA or any new/extended site designated by the Secretary of State. This is primarily because of the geographic separation between the wind farm site and the important areas for birds – the wind farm having been located outside any areas of high bird activity and outside the main areas used by the possible SPA/possible Ramsar site populations. The Habitat Management Plan, welcomed by EN/RSPB, provides additional comfort throughout the life of the project. Should different conclusions be reached, the proposal should still be consented given the absence of alternative solutions and imperative reasons of overriding public interest.[129]

In October 2005, the Secretary of State concurred with this conclusion, stating that the proposed development passes the 'Integrity Test' set out in Art. 6(3) of the Habitats Directive: 'though some effects might occur on the constituent

---

[126] Report to the Secretary of State for Trade and Industry by C. A. Richardson (Planning Inspector) GDBC/003/0001C (May 2005), para. 180.

[127] Pers. comm., Brian Banks, English Nature (Kent), 8.2.06.

[128] The Secretary of State noted that the Applicant, English Nature and the Royal Society for the Protection of Birds entered into a management agreement establishing a management group which provides for a crop management programme, ecological management, creation and enhancement of conservation headland grassland strips, monitoring of birds during construction and operation, and an environmental officer to coordinate the measures and report back to the management group, and for the costs of the measures to be funded by the Applicant.     [129] On the alternative solutions and overriding public interest tests, see pp. 661–5.

features of the European Sites, none would be so serious so as to threaten the ecological integrity of the Sites'.[130] Authorisation was then granted, subject to various planning conditions and having regard to the management plan. This meant that there was no need for the Secretary of State to consider further whether there were any 'alternative solutions' to the proposed wind farm or whether it was required on the basis of there being an overriding public interest in the development of the wind farm, capable of overcoming the conservation interests represented in the protected sites, although, as we discuss further below (pp. 663–4), the inspector did consider these issues.

### (vi) The general prohibition on development and derogations

The appropriate assessment of the impacts of a plan or project on a European site should enable the competent national authorities to arrive at conclusions about the effects of these on the integrity of the site. If the conclusions are positive in the sense that there is a high degree of certainty that the plan or project will not affect the site, then authorisation may be granted (as was the case with the Walland Marsh wind farm, discussed above). Where a negative conclusion is reached or where there is some doubt, 'the precautionary principle should be applied',[131] and the procedures and conditions in Art. 6(4) apply.[132] Article 6(4) contains a derogation from the general prohibition contained in Art. 6(3) that development must not be authorised unless it has been ascertained that this will not adversely affect the integrity of the site. As a derogation, the European Commission has stated that it should be interpreted strictly, and be limited to those circumstances in which the conditions provided for in Art. 6(4) are complied with.[133]

The first condition is that the competent authorities must examine whether it is possible to adopt 'alternative solutions' which better respect the integrity of the site. Ideally, these should have been identified in the course of the appropriate assessment conducted under Art. 6(3). It is important in this context that there is an apparent discrepancy about the scope of alternatives under Art. 6(3) of the Habitats Directive ('alternative solutions') and the EIA Directive which, by implication, is concerned with alternative *sites*. The practical effect of these different requirements formed the subject of a (pre-emptive) complaint to the European Commission by RSPB (Scotland) alleging the infringement of EC law on this point by the Scottish Executive (see Chapter 17, pp. 740–1) with respect to a proposed wind farm on the Isle of Lewis. In its complaint, the RSPB raised the question of the geographical scope of alternative solutions (should the search for an alternative to the proposed wind farm be restricted to the Western Isles, or may it extend throughout Europe?) and, indeed, the very meaning of

---

[130]  Letter to Npower Renewables Ltd from Jim Campbell, Energy Resources Development Unit, Department of Trade and Industry, 18 October 2005.

[131]  European Commission, *Managing Natura 2000 Sites*, para. 5.2.     [132]  See p. 648.

[133]  European Commission, *Managing Natura 2000 Sites*, para. 5.2.

'solutions', beyond a consideration of other sites, so as possibly to encompass matters of energy conservation and alternative sources of energy.

The second condition is that development can only go ahead for 'imperative reasons of overriding public interest' capable of overcoming the conservation interests represented by the Directive. Importantly, such reasons may include 'those of a social or economic nature', echoing the provisions of Art. 2 of the Directive (see above, p. 635). The Commission has provided the following elaboration on this point:

### European Commission, *Managing Natura 2000 Sites: The Provisions of Article 6 of the Habitats Directive 92/43/EEC* (CEC, 2000), para. 5.3.2

It is reasonable to consider that the 'imperative reasons of overriding public interest, including those of a social or economic nature' refer to situations where plans or projects envisaged prove to be indispensable:
- within the framework of actions or policies aiming to protect fundamental values for citizen's lives (health, safety, environment);
- within the framework of fundamental policies for the State and society;
- within the framework of carrying out activities of an economic or social nature, fulfilling specific obligations of public service.

The Commission also sets out that the public interest can only be overriding if it is a long-term interest, and rules out the possibility that projects that lie *entirely* in the interests of companies or individuals could be covered by this formulation.

The 'overriding public interest' test is designed to allow for the proportionate, and principled, derogation of Member States from the conservationist principles of the Directive. However, it has been interpreted before the courts in such a way that permits political judgments weighted in favour of developmental interests to enter decision making procedures. This assertion is drawn from the High Court judgment in *Newsum No. 1*,[134] concerning whether the existence of a (renewed) planning permission for working the Pen yr Henblas Quarry[135] constituted a matter of public interest. The Welsh Assembly had refused a licence for the translocation of a population of great crested newts which had colonised a pond created by the working of the quarry, thereby raising the prospect of the claimants becoming criminally liable for any disturbance caused to the newts in the course of their lawful working of the quarry

---

[134] *Newsum and Others* v. *Welsh Assembly Government* (*Newsum No. 1*) [2004] EWHC 50 (Admin) (overturned by the Court of Appeal, [2005] Env LR 16). Broadly on this point, see also Case C-434/01 *Commission* v. *United Kingdom* [2003] ECR I-3239. Note that *Newsum No. 1* is primarily concerned with Art. 16 on species protection. This mirrors the provisions in Art. 6 Habitats Directive and as such raises similar issues about the 'overriding public interest' test.     [135] The subject also of *Newsum No. 2*, above, pp. 644–6.

(described by the judge hearing the case as a 'Catch 22 situation'). In interpreting the meaning of 'overriding public interest', the Assembly focused narrowly on the economic benefit of quarrying at the site, finding that there was sufficient production capacity and reserves elsewhere to meet local and regional demand, and insufficient 'environmental capacity' to accommodate another working quarry in the area. In contrast, the existence of a valid planning permission was relied upon by the claimants as strongly suggesting that there was no satisfactory alternative to issuing a licence for moving the newts, since the working of the quarry for minerals would destroy the current habitat and damage the newt population. The claimants argued that it was overwhelmingly in the public interest that a licence be granted to secure their 'rescue' (the 'overriding public interest is to preserve and enhance the relevant species and biodiversity generally' (para. 42)). Pitchford J upheld this broad reading of the test, finding that the Assembly should have concerned itself with the claim that the translocation exercise was of overriding public interest of beneficial consequences for the environment; its failure to do so meant that it had failed to take account of a material consideration (para. 62). Although it might be considered desirable for the 'public interest' to be drawn so broadly, so as to include the protection of rare species, in this case this served to facilitate the resumption of damaging works on the site. A more principled stance was suggested in this case by the defendant Assembly that the consideration of a 'satisfactory alternative' should be based on alternatives to the development proposal, not on the assumption that the proposal will go ahead and that there is therefore no alternative to undertaking the translocation of the species.

Returning to the proposed wind farm on Walland Marsh, discussed above, pp. 655–61, the inspector holding the public planning inquiry on the application for development consent made a robust assertion that there were no alternatives to the proposed project and that it complied with the overriding public interest test.

### Report to the Secretary of State for Trade and Industry by C. A. Richardson, GDBC/003/0001C (May 2005), paras. 174-5

174. Npower Renewables Ltd acknowledges the possibility that the Secretary of State might take a different view on appropriate assessment and therefore, under regulation 49 of the Habitat Regulations 1994, the applicants are required to go on to consider overriding public interest and the absence of alternative solutions. Firstly, as regards alternative solutions, NRL has set out its site selection process based amongst other matters, on wind speed, land designations and proximity to dwellings. Despite a fog of vague suggestion, no firm alternatives have been identified by other parties. In view of the Kent sub-regional target and the lack of progress made so far, the role of onshore wind as a key plank of renewables delivery, and Government policy that meeting targets does not provide a reason for resisting other schemes, the concept of alternatives is not one that can be applied here.

175. Turning to imperative reasons of overriding public interest, this scheme is clearly in the public interest and comes forward in response to an urgent need arising from climate change. The only issue is whether the reasons are overriding. The EC Directive on Renewable Energy[136] post-dates the Wild Birds Directive and the Habitats Directive by just over two decades and just under one decade respectively and imposes an imperative and here over-riding element. In contrast, the EN/RSPB approach is a blinkered and timid do-nothing response to the imperatives of climate change. This is a situation where the do-nothing approach is far more damaging than the risk of the adverse effect alleged by EN/RSPB. If consent is refused on ecological grounds the energy sector will take note and the already constrained supply of renewable energy sites will be further restricted.

The inspector's assertion that there existed in this case reasons of overriding public interest was based on the adoption of the EC Directive on Renewable Energy. This suggests (erroneously) the operation of a type of implied repeal by which the objectives of the most recent piece of legislation take precedence over those expressed in earlier instruments in the event of a clash of objectives. Note also that decisions about the fulfilment of these tests are properly to be made by the Secretary of State, not the applicant developer, as asserted here.

The final condition set out in Art. 6(4) of the Habitats Directive when a plan or project must be 'carried out for imperative reasons' is the need on the part of the Member State to take all compensatory measures necessary to ensure that the overall coherence of Natura 2000 is protected. This might take the form of recreating a habitat, for example a wetland, on a new or larger site, or 'improving' a habitat on part of the site to be damaged or on another Natura 2000 site.[137] This suggests a functionalist approach to conservation, based upon the reality that plans and projects will be authorised for social and/or economic reasons, but that some compensation of an ecological nature should be forthcoming when this occurs. Such an approach is in line with a weak version of sustainable development which holds that the overall 'stock' of environmental capital should be maintained, even if over time this is banked, traded or transferred.[138] Importantly, no mention of compensation is made in the paragraphs preceding Art. 6(4) of the Habitats Directive which only bites when a decision has been taken that the plan or project 'must nevertheless be carried out', even when there are negative implications for the site. This is deliberate, ensuring that the offer of compensatory measures does not affect the initial judgment about whether the plan or project will or will not adversely affect the integrity of the site. As described by the Commission, compensatory measures should

---

[136] Directive 2001/77 OJ 2001 L 283/33.

[137] European Commission, *Managing Natura 2000 Sites*, para. 5.4.2.

[138] On conservation banking, see J. B. Ruhl, Alan Glen and David Hartman, 'A Practical Guide to Habitat Conservation Banking Law and Policy' (2005) *Natural Resources and Environment* 26. In a nutshell, a conservation bank is an area of habitat that has been conserved and managed for the conservation of identified natural resource values, the benefits of which are used to offset negative impacts to the resource occurring on other areas from land use activities.

constitute the 'last resort'.[139] The compensation for the loss or damage of protected sites and species raises many difficult issues, beyond the protection of European sites. Accordingly, we discuss compensation (and mitigation) in the context of planning decisions relating to nature conservation interests (Chapter 16, pp. 677–80).

Article 6(4) establishes a two-tier system of protection. 'Ordinary' SACs may be overridden on social or economic grounds, but priority SACs may only be overridden on grounds of human health or public safety, or for certain environmental reasons ('beneficial consequences of primary importance for the environment'). These justifications are a partial codification of the Court of Justice's judgment in *Leybucht Dykes*[140] which defined and curtailed the reasons for damaging or destroying an SPA designated under the Birds Directive; but the Habitats Directive weakens this judgment by applying it only to *priority* habitats or species. Finally, a priority SAC may be overridden following an Opinion (a non-binding legal act) issued by the Commission, for other imperative reasons of overriding public interest. This last category is famously open-ended, as borne out by the Commission's opinions which justify the loss or damaging of priority sites on 'overriding' economic grounds, such as providing transport links between East and West in the newly unified Germany.[141]

In summary, the protection accorded to SACs by the Habitats Directive is not absolute. The *express* objective of Art. 6 of the Directive is to negotiate an accommodation between economic development and nature conservation, by putting in place procedural safeguards, such as the carrying out of an environmental assessment of sorts to establish the extent of the damage likely and requiring compensation for any ecological losses incurred, the latter being typical of a weak sustainability approach (discussed in Chapter 6, pp. 232–7).

### (c) Natura 2000: the inter-relation of the Birds and Habitats Directives

The imperfect protection offered to SACs by the Habitats Directive, discussed above, was extended to SPAs designated under the Birds Directive,[142] but with the serious anomaly that no birds species are listed as priority species. This has important consequences in terms of the nature of justifications for the loss or damaging of birds' habitats (as discussed above, pp. 661–5). In *Lappel Bank* (pp. 630–2) the House of Lords referred to the European Court of Justice

---

[139] European Commission, *Managing Natura 2000 Sites*, para. 5.4.1.

[140] Case C-57/89 *Commission* v. *Germany* [1991] ECR I-883.

[141] See Opinion on the planned A20 motorway in Germany which will intersect the Trebel and Recknitz Valley OJ 1995 C 178/3 and Opinion on the intersection of the Peene Valley by the planned A20 motorway OJ 1996 L 6/14. For a review of these, see Andre Nolkaemper, 'Habitat Protection in European Community Law: Evolving Conceptions of a Balance of Interests' (1997) 9 *Journal of Environmental Law* 271.

[142] Article 7 Habitats Directive. See further Woulter P. J. Wils, 'The Bird Directive 15 Years Later: A Survey of the Case Law and a Comparison with the Habitats Directive' (1994) 6 *Journal of Environmental Law* 219.

questions about the effect of the Habitats Directive on the protection accorded to SPAs, designated under the Birds Directive. The Court made very clear that, even following amendment of the Birds Directive by the Habitats Directive (in terms of incorporating the protection regime set out in Art. 6 into the Birds Directive), Member States, when designating an SPA and designating its boundaries under Art. 4(1) or (2) of the Birds Directive, are unable to take account of economic requirements as constituting a general interest superior to that presented by the ecological objectives of the Birds Directive (in line with Case C-57/89 *Commission* v. *Germany (Leybucht Dykes)*). Similarly, the Court clarified that in the same circumstances economic considerations cannot be invoked as 'overriding public interests' of the kind referred to in Art. 6(4) of the Birds Directive.

By this judgment, the Court of Justice preserved the protection granted by the Birds Directive at the stage of designation of a site as an SPA. At a later stage, when such a site is under threat, the less stringent provisions of Art. 6 of the Habitats Directive, however, expressly apply. The autonomy of the Birds Directive was nevertheless also strictly upheld by the Court in its judgment in Case C-374/98 *Commission* v. *France (Basses Corbière)*.[143] This was brought on the ground that the Basses Corbière site should have been designated an SPA under the Birds Directive because of the presence of Bonnelli's eagle (this legislation was delayed due to 'fierce local controversy'[144]) and, as such, conservation measures should have been taken to prevent the working of limestone quarries in the area. The question of whether the French could in these circumstances appeal to the lesser standard of protection (when compared to the Birds Directive) under Art. 6(4) of the Habitats Directive raises the possibility that a Member State could benefit from its failure to give effect to Community law on time. The Court, however, confirmed that, even after the date by which the Habitats Directive should have been transposed into national law, areas which had not been classified under the Birds Directive but should have been so classified cannot take advantage of the more lenient protection regime established by the Habitats Directive.[145]

In the case of a site already designated as an SPA (under the Birds Directive), it is clear that the Habitats Directive alters the standard of its protection. But uncertainty existed about the nature of the changes made by this amendment, as seen in *RSPB* v. *Secretary of State for Scotland*,[146] concerning the 'disturbance' to barnacle geese on Islay by shooting. In this case, the RSPB successfully argued that Art. 6(2)[147] of the Habitats Directive imported into the Birds Directive the need to take appropriate steps in SPAs to avoid disturbance of the bird species for which the area had been classified, in so far as such disturbance could be significant in relation to the objectives of 'this Directive' – taken to mean the Habitats Directive (paras. 11–18), rather than the Birds Directive as argued by the Secretary of State. This is an important distinction because it encourages

---

[143] [2000] ECR I-10799.    [144] *Ibid.*, Para. 11.    [145] *Ibid.*, Para. 47.
[146] [2001] Env LR 19. See discussion of the geographical extent of the integrity test under Art. 6(3) Habitats Directive, above, p. 661.    [147] See p. 647.

greater consideration of the loss of species on individual SPAs, which together make up the ecological network of Natura 2000 which forms the main objective of the Habitats Directive.

In summary, the Habitats Directive and Birds Directive employ the same main legal technique – the designation of land for special protection.[148] Despite this important similarity, they are derived from quite different philosophical approaches to conservation. The Birds Directive reflects a strong sustainability approach in the sense that its (unamended) provisions gave absolute protection to the sites designated under its terms, and failed to justify the loss or damage of these.[149] In contrast, the Habitats Directive advances what might be called a weak sustainability approach on the basis that it expressly envisages and permits the loss or compromise of protected sites for several reasons, including those of an economic or social nature. That important distinction apart, the *breadth* of protection granted by the Habitats Directive far exceeds the Birds Directive, and as such it adopts a more holistic approach to nature conservation. The protection regime set out in the Habitats Directive now supplants that of the Birds Directive, which has resulted in some tensions and difficulties of interpretation.

Nicolas de Sadeleer provides a useful evaluation of the inherent limitations of the technique of designation of land for special protection, as advanced in both the Birds and Habitats Directives.

### Nicolas de Sadeleer, 'Habitat Conservation in EC Law: From Nature Sanctuaries to Ecological Networks' (2005) 5 *Yearbook of European Environmental Law*, pp. 251–2

Species whose habitats are not conserved are condemned to disappear. In this context the linchpin of the Birds and Habitats Directives is the Natura 2000 network. … [H]owever there have been considerable delays in the establishment of this network, which is all the more unjustifiable at a time when the deterioration of many ecosystems has never been so marked. Nonetheless, over these past years the Commission has not spared any effort in taking court action against recalcitrant States and cutting their subsidies. A difference has also been noted between the ECJ's relatively strict interpretation of the texts and the European Commission's apparently more lax view of the granting of derogations for infrastructure projects in protected areas. Moreover the legal machinery put in place to ensure the conservation of natural habitats is highly complex and understood by only a select elite of environmental law specialists …

However, even if the rules discussed above were to be correctly and quickly applied, they would probably still not be able to halt the diminution of biological diversity in Europe.

… as the Natura 2000 network will cover little more than a fraction of the most spectacular natural and semi-natural areas of the European continent, it is therefore up to the Member States to make substantial efforts at conservation both in the areas forming part of the Natura 2000 network and outwith these areas.

---

[148] Note that both Directives also have species protection elements.
[149] On weak and strong sustainability more generally, see Ch. 6.

## 4 Conclusions

In this chapter we have discussed the well-worn legal technique of designating particular pockets of land for nature conservation. From beginnings characterised by voluntariness and resistance, designation has become a powerful legal tool, capable of providing considerable environmental benefits.

Notwithstanding these benefits, designation is inadequate when used as the sole tool of nature conservation. It implies fragmentation, first, of legal controls: one result of many years of legal protection by designation is a plethora of appellations for land thought to require special treatment, many of which might be applied simultaneously to an individual piece of land.[150] More importantly, it also implies fragmentation of the environment for which protection is sought. The rigid distinction between protected and unprotected areas – 'between land designated because it is thought to be particularly vulnerable, and that left to drift on the stormy seas of economic change, to endure or thrive as it may'[151] – condemns much of that unprotected land, and fundamentally fails to recognise the profound inter-relationship between different elements of biodiversity. It also runs counter to the more general drive towards policy integration, and we increasingly expect conservation concerns to be taken more fully into account in other areas of decision making, most notably in the planning system.

The fragmented approach is deeply entrenched in law and policy, and will be difficult to overcome. Increasingly, however, conservation law recognises individuals' duties to land *regardless* of its special qualities. We turn in the next chapter to the important subject of nature conservation *beyond* designated areas, and the move towards the 'integration' of nature conservation in other legal and policy fields of activity. Importantly, a fully integrated approach must also take account of the conservation of marine areas, the law and policy on which has lagged behind those of the conservation of land (even though 50 per cent of UK species are found in the marine environment).[152] For example a significant gap in conservation law and policy has been the limited regulation of activities such as dredging the seabed for aggregates.[153] Some attention is now being paid to this area, the result of many years of lobbying and various failed private Bills, and because of the current policy emphasis on offshore wind farms (see Chapter 17) and the damaging effects of fishing practices (as recently highlighted by the Royal Commission on Environmental Pollution[154]). A Marine Bill is now providing a

---

[150] See first edition of this book, in which Loch Druidibeg in South Uist was a case study for designation as a legal technique – a 4-mile area, it was subject to a plethora of designations: Ramsar site, National Nature Reserve (UK), SPA (Bird Directive), candidate SAC (Habitats Directive), SSSI, Biosphere reserve (UNESCO), and several agricultural designations including an Environmentally Sensitive Area.

[151] Adams, *Future Nature*, p. 115. See Adams' excellent discussion of this divide in Ch. 8.

[152] See Memorandum submitted by the RSPB to the House of Commons Select Committee on Environment, Food and Rural Affairs (2004).

[153] See Owens and Cowell, *Land and Limits*, p. 105, on this point.

[154] Royal Commission on Environmental Pollution, Twenty-fifth Report, *Turning the Tide: Addressing the Impact of Fisheries on the Marine Environment*, Cm 6392 (2004).

vehicle for new institutional arrangements and the integration of conservation and fisheries policy. Most notably, the Bill aims to introduce a system of 'marine spatial planning'[155] to set out priorities and environmental standards for different marine areas and to streamline consents to develop or operate in the marine environment, both of which are obviously important for offshore renewables developments, as we discuss in Chapter 17.

## 5 Further reading

Stuart Bell and Donald McGillivray provide a useful overview of nature conservation law in *Environmental Law* (Oxford University Press, 6th edn, 2005). Although much of what is described as 'conservation law' applies to the United Kingdom as a whole, Colin Reid's work (*Nature Conservation Law* (Green and Son, 2002)) tends to provide a much-needed Scottish perspective. On the history of designation as a legal mechanism, see Kathryn Last, 'Mechanisms for Environmental Protection – A Study of Habitat Conservation' in Andrea Ross (ed.), *Environment and Regulation* (Edinburgh University Press, 2000). In this chapter we have focussed upon the designation of land for special protection as the main legal technique for nature conservation. A quite different technique of buying land is the subject of Sally Fairfax *et al.*'s well-researched and interesting *Buying Nature: The Limits of Land Acquisition as a Conservation Strategy, 1780–2004* (MIT, 2005).

The classic 'protest' work on the countryside is Marion Shoard's *This Land is Our Land: The Struggle for Britain's Countryside* (Gaia Books, 1997) which places nature conservation in a historical context and in a much broader political landscape of property rights. On a particular protest, Barbara Bryant's *Twyford Down: Roads, Campaigning and Environmental Law* (Spon, 1996) is an insightful and readable record of the campaign to save Twyford Down, an area of great conservation value near Winchester in southern England, from damage from roadbuilding.

Further, and broader, readings on nature conservation are provided at the end of Chapter 16.

---

[155] On spatial planning generally, see Ch. 13.

# 16

# Nature Conservation and Biodiversity: Beyond Designation

## 1 Introduction

The last chapter focussed on the 'cores' of nature conservation – the areas of land designated for their special characteristics, and protected (up to a point) by law and policy. Now of equal concern is the conservation state of the land *in-between* the protected sites. The main influence moving law and policy away from the demarcation of areas of land for protection because of their special features is the concept of biological diversity, or biodiversity. The value of biodiversity in general is now better understood than when the legal regime for the designation of land for special protection was first developed,[1] and there is also greater recognition of the deterioration in biodiversity in undesignated areas, from agricultural intensification, house and road building, and other factors such as tourism. There is also a more general concern about the effects of climate change, in particular the ability of isolated areas to adapt, which has made the connections *between* designated areas more important.[2]

'Biodiversity Action Plans' ((BAPs) – pp. 671–3) are now an important, proactive, feature of nature conservation, looking beyond protected areas. The trend of integrating previously separate land use controls, influenced by the general concern with biodiversity, has been directed by European Community (EC) law, particularly the Habitats Directive. The integration of planning and nature conservation decisions (pp. 673–80) parallels that seen in the context of pollution controls (Chapter 9) and in planning with the onset of an integrated form of spatial planning (Chapter 13, pp. 622–30).

In the last chapter we looked closely at the positive contribution of the EC to nature conservation; it has also contributed in a less positive sense, primarily through the adverse impact on biodiversity of the Common Agricultural Policy (CAP). This is despite attempts to bring about fundamental reform of agricultural practices as part of the Agenda 2000 reforms, mainly by revising the consequences of designating land. Again, we focus here upon the legal technique of

---

[1] See Ch. 12, pp. 486–7, on the designation of national nature reserves under the National Parks and Access to the Countryside Act 1949.

[2] See, on this point and for general discussion, 'The Land In-between: Wilding Agriculture' by Peter Taylor, *Beyond Conservation* (Earthscan, 2005), Ch. 10.

designating areas for particular purposes, in this case agricultural land, but also note a move away from an exclusively enclave approach to conservation in such areas. We specifically consider the use of management or 'stewardship' schemes designed to encourage the creation of field margins as havens for wildlife in return for payments (pp. 687–9) and, in stark contrast, the introduction of a licensing system for the protection of hedgerows (pp. 689–90). This gives us the opportunity to contrast different legal approaches to the problem of regulating agricultural activities on private land.

## 2  Biodiversity action plans

Biodiversity has become the governing concept of conservation law and policy, to the extent that it has become synonymous with nature conservation. Nicolas de Sadeleer introduces the term:

### Nicolas de Sadeleer, 'EC Law and Biodiversity' in Richard Macrory (ed.), *Reflections on 30 Years of EU Environmental Law: A High Level of Protection?* (Europa, 2006), pp. 351-2

The term biodiversity was itself not coined until the 1980s, when it was popularised by the eminent Harvard biologist Wilson.[3] The most tangible manifestations of biodiversity are the species of plants, animals and micro-organisms that surround us. Yet biodiversity means more than just species diversity. At the micro level it includes the genetic material that makes up the species, whilst at the macro level it covers natural communities, ecosystems and landscapes. Biodiversity essentially relates to the full array of life on Earth.

In an apparently continuous progression, biodiversity emerged over the course of the geological eras, wending its way through both biological evolution and periods of mass extinction. Such diversification of the living world is made possible by the genetic adaptation of species to environmental changes, whether natural or man-made. Communities themselves evolve on the basis of fluctuations in their environment, according to complex historical processes that explain the present state of the biosphere. The first living beings appeared in the oceans in the form of primitive bacteria roughly 3.5 billion years ago, which subsequently diversified into the multitude of organisms of every shape and all sizes which is nowadays classified under five kingdoms (animal, plant, fungi, bacteria and protists), each of which is divided into systematic sub-classification which emerged following the branching out of particular species. Mankind has at present still a long way to go before acquiring a complete knowledge of the species that populate the Earth. Whilst about 1,320,000 animal species have been catalogued, scientists estimate the total number of species on Earth at more than ten million. This biodiversity is not, however, distributed evenly across the planet. Generally speaking, on the continents, it increases from the poles toward the equator, whilst in the oceans the increase is much less pronounced, and sometimes operates in reverse. Such an unequal distribution can be explained by climatic, historic and geomorphological factors.

---

[3]  Edward O. Wilson and Francis Petter (eds.), *Biodiversity* (National Academy Press, 1988).

> Biodiversity today is passing through a period of major crisis. Most natural or semi-natural, continental and coastal ecosystems are now subject to significant modifications as a result of human activity. Scientists expect that these disruptions will cause an unprecedented drop in the wealth of specific and genetic diversity.

The major international law response to the loss of biodiversity is the Biodiversity Convention 1992,[4] Art. 2 of which defines biodiversity as 'The variability among living organisms from all sources including, *inter alia*, terrestrial, marine, and other aquatic ecosystems and the ecological complexes of which they are a part; this includes diversity within species, between species and of ecosystems.' The Convention first confirms the sovereign right of States 'to exploit their own resources pursuant to their own environmental policies' whilst conferring responsibility to ensure that activities within their jurisdiction or control do not cause damage to the environment of other States or of areas beyond the limits of national jurisdiction (Art. 3). There follows a list of actions for governments to pursue in order to conserve biodiversity and to ensure the sustainable use and exploitation of species and habitats, including the drawing-up of national strategies, plans or programmes to secure biodiversity and the integration of these into other cross-sectoral plans, programmes and policies (Art. 6). Foreshadowing similar provisions in the Habitats Directive (discussed above, p. 649), the Convention requires States to introduce 'appropriate procedures requiring environmental impact assessment of [their] proposed projects that are likely to have significant adverse effects on biological diversity with a view to avoiding or minimising such effects and, where appropriate, allow for public participation in such procedures', and 'introduce appropriate arrangements to ensure that the environmental consequences of [their] programmes and policies that are likely to have significant adverse impacts on biological diversity are duly taken into account' (Art. 14). More controversially, the Convention also contains provisions on the handling of biotechnology and the distribution of its benefits (Art. 169).

The most marked response to the Convention in the United Kingdom has been *Biodiversity: The UK Action Plan* (1994). This sets county-wide objectives and targets to guide the work of the government and its agencies over the course of twenty years. This framework for action has led to plans for 391 species of plants and animals (for example the Red Squirrel Conservation Implementation Plan 2004/05[5]) and 45 habitats, and a further 162 Local BAPs (we include a Local BAP on field margins below, pp. 688–9). The local plans are generally organised along county, or district, boundaries, but there are also plans covering national parks. These are expected to help achieve the national targets and to identify and 'deliver

---

[4] 31 ILM 822. See also Convention on International Trade in Endangered Species 1973 993 UNTS 243.

[5] As drawn up by the Joint Nature Conservation Committee; for further details of this and other BAPs (for brown hare, dormouse, otter and water vole), see www.incc.gov.uk.

targets' for biodiversity for locally distinct wildlife. A key part of the plans at local level is the encouragement of partnerships with a range of cross-sectoral organisations and public participation in developing conservation strategies. Most importantly in terms of the themes of this part of the book, the plans are a sign of recognition that site protection properly forms just one part of conservation efforts, rather than providing its foundations. The UK Government's *Biodiversity Action Plan* states as much in acknowledging that many plants and animals 'are not generally amenable to site based conservation initiatives but instead require the retention of such features of the wider countryside as hedges and copses, ponds and flushes'.[6] These various action plans were placed on a statutory footing by the Countryside and Rights of Way Act (CROW) 2000.[7] The Natural Environment and Rural Communities Act 2006 introduces instead for the first time in England and Wales a general biodiversity duty for all public bodies, although this now falls short of the specific duty for ministers and government departments to have particular regard to the Biodiversity Convention 1992, in keeping with the similar duty which has existed in Scottish law since 2004,[8] as proposed in the preceding Bill.

The concept of biodiversity has notably broadened the focus of conservation law and policy from protecting rare and endangered habitats and species to maintaining the variability and population of species on a number of different levels and across the full range of life forms. As Kate Cook describes this shift, 'biodiversity brings the whole of the natural world into the legal arena, at both macro and micro level'.[9] Although the Convention advocates the use of the legal technique of designation, requiring that States must establish a system of protected areas where special measures – regulation or management – are taken to conserve biodiversity,[10] in general the focus on biodiversity encourages a move *away* from an enclave approach such as this and towards the greater integration of conservation issues in other policy areas such as planning and agriculture, as we discuss further below.

## 3 Integrating conservation in planning

In 1992 Linda Warren described conservation as 'a secondary consideration',[11] citing the involvement of voluntary groups in its development, and the primacy of agricultural interests in the case of conflicts of interest as reasons

---

[6] UK Government, *The UK Biodiversity Action Plan* (UK Government, 1994), para. 4.25, quoted in Susan Owens and Richard Cowell, *Land and Limits: Interpreting Sustainability in the Planning System* (Routledge, 2003), p. 107.

[7] Section 74 CROW 2000. Now repealed by the Natural Environment and Rural Communities Act 2006.          [8] Section 1 Nature Conservation (Scotland) Act 2004.

[9] Kate Cook, *Wildlife Law: Conservation and Biodiversity* (Cameron May, 2004), p. 19.

[10] Article 8 Biodiversity Convention 1992.

[11] Linda Warren. 'Conservation – A Secondary Consideration' (1992) in Robin Churchill, Lynda Warren and John Gibson, *Journal of Law and Society*, 'Special Issue on Law, Policy and the Environment'.

for its lack of status in policy terms, particularly when planning decisions were being made. This description was supported by research on the limited performance of local authorities in 'delivering' nature conservation through the planning system.[12] Government recognition of the need for 'a broader and more integrated approach to conservation',[13] influenced a great deal by European law and policy (see Chapter 15), led to a warmer reception for conservation interests in planning. This has been further enhanced by the integrated nature of planning reforms brought about by the Planning and Compulsory Purchase Act 2004 which provides a more formal framework for the inclusion and consideration of biodiversity action plans than hitherto. However, in general the emphasis of the protective mechanisms for conservation in the planning system remains on designated sites. For example, the protection of European sites (see Chapter 15) and sites protected under international designations such as Ramsar sites[14] is advanced by a combination of the provisions of the Habitats Regulations 1994 and s. 28 of the Wildlife and Countryside Act 1981, as amended by the Countryside and Rights of Way Act 2000. European sites are notified as Sites of Special Scientific Interest (SSSIs) under s. 28 of the 1981 Act and planning authorities will therefore be aware of their presence in areas subject to proposals for development. Planning authorities are required to consult English Nature[15] before granting planning permission for development likely to damage an SSSI, even if the development is not located in the SSSI.[16]

The recent association of planning with the aims of conservation and the means by which designated land is protected is apparent in Regulation 49 of the Habitats Regulations 1994, which restricts the granting of planning permission for development which is likely to significantly affect a European site by requiring that an appropriate assessment of the implications of the development for the site's conservation objectives is first carried out. This implements the requirement contained in Art. 6(3) of the Habitats Directive (Chapter 15, pp. 647–9) that competent national authorities consider the effect of development on a European site when deciding whether or not to grant planning permission. The decision whether an appropriate assessment is necessary is to be made on a precautionary basis, in line with the *Waddenzee (Cockle Fishers)*

---

[12] Robert Marshall and Catherine Smith, 'Planning for Nature Conservation: The Role and Performance of English District Local Authorities in the 1990s' (1999) 42 JEPM 691.

[13] Department of the Environment, Transport and the Regions, *Sites of Scientific Interest: Better Protection and Management, A Consultation Document for England and Wales* (DETR, 1998).

[14] A Ramsar site is a wetland of international importance designated under the Ramsar Convention on Wetlands of International Importance.

[15] See Ch. 15, p. 618, for explanation of English Nature's role and remit.

[16] See Art. 10 and para. (u) of the Table in Town and Country Planning (General Development Procedure) Order 1995 SI 1995 No. 419, and s. 28I 1981 Act.

judgment.[17] The local planning authority may only grant planning permission having ascertained that it will not affect the integrity of any European site. Where an authority proposing to allow development cannot ascertain that it will not adversely affect a European site, they must notify the Secretary of State in order that the application may be 'called-in'.[18] Under such circumstances, the authority must also satisfy themselves that there are no 'alternative solutions',[19] thus implementing Art. 6(4) of the Habitats Directive. The hierarchy of protection established in Art. 6 of the Habitats Directive is reproduced in the implementing Regulations.[20] For a 'standard' European site, and if the authority is satisfied that there are reasons of overriding public interest, including social and economic reasons,[21] the authority may agree to the development notwithstanding that it will have adverse effects on the site's conservation interests. In the case of a 'priority' site (as marked in Annex I of the Directive), the authority can only grant planning permission for reasons relating to human health, or for further reasons following an Opinion from the European Commission.[22] This hierarchy permits the fulfillment of objectives other than nature conservation in the planning system.

In the case of the protection by the planning system of conservation interests *outside* specifically designated areas, progress has been slower – by 2000 fewer than 20 per cent of English planning authorities had used BAPs to inform their development plan policy and only a small proportion of development plans contained effective policies to encourage positive management in the wider countryside. Owens and Cowell consider such figures indicate that a holistic approach to nature conservation is difficult to integrate with conventional planning processes.[23] However, the most recent policy guidance provides a relatively strict line on the protection of conservation interests in the face of developmental pressures, even in the case of land lying outside designated areas, particularly when compared to previous versions of such guidance which warned that planning authorities should take care 'to avoid unnecessary constraints on development'.[24]

---

[17] Case C-127/02 *Landelijke Vereniging tot Behoud van de Waddenzee* v. *Staatssecretaris van Landbouw Natuurbeheer en Visserij* [2005] 2 CMLR 31, see Ch. 15, pp. 652–3. Further on this point, see Joint Government Circular, Office of the Deputy Prime Minister (ODPM), Circular 06/2005, Department of the Environment, Food and Rural Affairs (DEFRA), Circular 01/05, *To Accompany Planning Policy Statement 9: Biodiversity and Geological Conservation – Statutory Obligations and their Impact within the Planning System* (ODPM, DEFRA, 2005), para. 13.

[18] Regulation 49. For a diagrammatic representation of these procedural safeguards, see Joint Government Circular on *PPS 9: Biodiversity and Geological Conservation*, p. 7.

[19] Regulation 49(1).

[20] Regulation 49(1). On this hierarchy, see p. 665.

[21] On the overriding public interest test, see Ch. 15, pp. 661–5.

[22] Regulation 49(2) and (3).     [23] Owens and Cowell, *Land and Limits*, pp. 118–19.

[24] Department of the Environment, Planning Policy Guidance Note 9, *Nature Conservation* (HMSO, 1994).

### ODPM (now succeeded by the Department for Communities and Local Government), Planning Policy Statement 9, *Biodiversity and Geological Conservation* (HMSO, 2005) (emphasis added)

KEY PRINCIPLES

1. Regional planning bodies and local planning authorities should adhere to the following key principles to ensure that the potential impacts of planning decisions on biodiversity and geological conservation are fully considered.

(i) Development plan policies and planning decisions should be based upon up-to-date information about the environmental characteristics of their areas. These characteristics should include the relevant biodiversity and geological resources of the area. In reviewing environmental characteristics local authorities should assess the potential to sustain and enhance those resources.

(ii) Plan policies and planning decisions should aim to maintain, and enhance, restore or add to biodiversity and geological conservation interests. In taking decisions, local planning authorities should ensure that appropriate weight is attached to designated sites of international, national and local importance; protected species; and to biodiversity and geological interests within the wider environment.

(iii) Plan policies on the form and location of development should take a strategic approach to the conservation, enhancement and restoration of biodiversity and geology, and recognise the contributions that sites, areas and features, both individually and in combination, make to conserving these resources.

(iv) Plan policies should promote opportunities for the incorporation of beneficial biodiversity and geological features within the design of development.

(v) Development proposals where the principal objective is to conserve or enhance biodiversity and geological conservation interests should be permitted.

(vi) The aim of planning decisions should be to prevent harm to biodiversity and geological conservation interests. Where granting planning permission would result in significant harm to those interests, local planning authorities will need to be satisfied that the development cannot reasonably be located on any alternative sites that would result in less or no harm. In the absence of any such alternatives, local planning authorities should ensure that, before planning permission is granted, adequate mitigation measures are put in place. *Where a planning decision would result in significant harm to biodiversity and geological interests which cannot be prevented or adequately mitigated against, appropriate compensation measures should be sought. If that significant harm cannot be prevented, adequately mitigated against, or compensated for, then planning permission should be refused.*

The last principle indicates that a higher standard of protection should be pursued for conservation interests *in the wider environment* than for European sites designated under the Habitats Directive: the Directive permits the development of special protection areas (SPAs) and special areas of conservation (SACs) for certain reasons, including those of a social or economic nature, and where there are no alternative solutions to the proposed plan or project (see above, pp. 661–5). This discrepancy will have little effect in practice because European sites are also designated as SSSIs in order to give them legal effect in the UK, as discussed above, Chapter 15.

### ODPM, *Biodiversity and Geological Conservation* (emphasis added)

#### Sites of Special Scientific Interest (SSSIs)

8. *Where a proposed development on land within or outside an SSSI is likely to have an adverse effect on an SSSI (either individually or in combination with other developments), planning permission should not normally be granted.* Where an adverse effect on the site's notified special interest features is likely, an exception should only be made where the benefits of the development, at this site, clearly outweigh both the impacts that it is likely to have on the features of the site that make it of special scientific interest and any broader impacts on the national network of SSSIs. Local authorities should use conditions and/or planning obligations to mitigate the harmful aspects of the development and, where possible, to ensure the conservation and enhancement of the site's biodiversity or geological interest.

These policy statements send an important signal to decision makers about the protection of conservation interests in planning decisions, but fail to provide a firm ground for challenging decisions, at least so long as the relevant policy has been taken into account by the local planning authority or Secretary of State. The statement on the protection of SSSIs also represents the sharp end of the relationship between law and policy because, whatever the standard of protection advanced in policy guidance, under the Wildlife and Countryside Act 1981 a grant of planning permission continues to constitute a defence to the criminal offence of carrying out a potentially damaging operation on such a site.[25]

### (a) Environmental 'compensation'

In the event that a plan or project having an adverse affect on the integrity of a protected site is granted planning permission (for reasons of overriding public interest), Regulation 53 of the Habitats Regulations requires the Secretary of State to ensure that any necessary compensatory measures are taken to ensure the overall coherence of Natura 2000. Such measures may include the creation or replacement of habitats, possibly including the translocation or introduction of species. These provisions for environmental compensation can be located within the sustainable development discourse, particularly in terms of the potential which exists for reconciling development with environmental protection, as Cowell identifies.

---

[25] Section 28P(4). See further above, pp. 625–7.

### Richard Cowell, 'Stretching the Limits: Environmental Compensation, Habitat Creation and Sustainable Development' (1997) 22 *Transactions of the Institute of British Geographers* 292, pp. 292–3

From roots in urban nature conservation and the restoration of mining land, the idea and practice of habitat conservation have grown in prominence ... The 'art' of environmental restoration has aesthetic, technical and political dimensions. It can act to reconcile environmental concerns with economic development – a purpose which increasingly connects it with political projects of sustainable development.

While sustainable development is something of a conceptual chameleon, a number of principles have become common to a breadth of approaches. The reversibility of environmental change is widely regarded as a central consideration; the basic argument is that serious and irreversible environmental changes should be avoided so as not to jeopardise human survival or the welfare of future generations. This issue is highlighted by economistic interpretations of sustainable development which emphasise maintaining 'stocks' of 'natural capital'. The contention here is that it is insufficiently precautionary for economic growth to continue as though 'natural capital' (biophysical system, resources, amenity) can be readily substituted by 'human capital' (labour and knowledge) or 'human-made capital' (such as built infrastructure and machines). Because environmental systems have distinct properties that are vital, unique and poorly understood, maintaining these systems should be a central goal of policy.

Interpreting sustainability in this way appears to challenge current patterns of economic growth by prioritising the maintenance of the environmental resource base. This does not mean the end of growth but concentrates attention on mechanisms by which social activities may be reconciled with maintaining the 'capacity' of the environment to continue to deliver benefit streams. Alongside technological, economic, cultural and regulatory changes, a key mechanism is 'environmental compensation'. Development which erodes natural capital can still proceed where losses could be restored or 'reversed' by environmental compensation – positive environmental measures of comparable worth – to maintain the overall 'stock'. Whether environmental degradation can be fully compensated in this way is a pivotal concern and affects the elasticity of environmental constraints.

...

An important conclusion is that the use of habitat creation as a form of environmental compensation has tended to accommodate those interests well-represented in the planning system, particularly major developers. Wider issues are at stake, however, as the metaphor of maintaining environmental capital becomes bound into social practices: the tendency to reinforce technocratic, managerialist approaches to sustainable development and the separation of important issues about the economic, social and environmental desirability of different development patterns from public debate.

But this is a highly controversial area of conservation law and planning. In ethical terms, the main problem is with the process of attributing values to the essential natural qualities of a place. This practical expression of the intrinsic/instrumental debate, introduced in Chapter 1, pp. 47–57, is colourfully discussed by Susan Owens and Richard Cowell in an account which also highlights alternative (and sometimes inconsistent) ways of viewing the (natural) world.

### Susan Owens and Richard Cowell, *Land and Limits: Interpreting Sustainability in the Planning System* (Routledge, 2003), p. 121

Compensation … is far from being a technical issue, however: rather, the question of compensation focuses attention once more on what is 'critical' and on the reasons for valuing particular habitats in the first place. If, for example, natural or semi-natural systems are deemed to have intrinsic value because of the processes that have produced them, rather than merely instrumental value by virtue of the 'services' they provide, then by definition they are not replaceable. The notion of 'maintaining environmental capital' through habitat creation then becomes contentious – a clear case in which conflict is underlain by profoundly different contentions. There are other difficulties too: regarding a particular site as compensatable risks severing systemic ecological links and reinforces the concept of protection as tied to discrete parcels of land. Indeed the 'integrity' of a site or system has proved something of a weasel word, around which reductionist and holistic views of ecological value have come into collision. To take one high-profile example, the Cardiff Bay Development Corporation spent more than £9 million in creating a wetland nature reserve as part of a package of compensatory measures to offset the loss of the Taff/Ely Estuary SSSI, where an amenity barrage would destroy a bird feeding habitat. While promoters of the new reserve defended it as 'a major asset' from which 'economic benefits would flow', environmentalists' scepticism about a 'glorified duckpond' reflected their view that what had been traded off was an integral part of a wider ecological system. On the other hand, Scottish Power's enhancement of 10 square kilometres of hunting habitat for a pair of golden eagles 'to ensure that the birds have a net increase in prey should they choose to avoid the [Beinn an Tuirc] wind farm' in mid-Kintyre, Scotland, seems to have been broadly welcomed by the RSPB.

A further problem is that decisions about whether environmental contributions are capable of overcoming planning objections to development are often taken without public participation, with the opportunity for negotiation only between developer and planning authority. Greater transparency has been sought through reforms which now require planning 'contributions' such as habitat recreation to be determined in advance and set out in development plans.[26]

There are clearly considerable ethical concerns about the 'art' of environmental compensation. There are equally many ecological problems, including the difficulty of achieving equivalence, or 'like-for-like' habitat, so that, for example, an SSSI is unlikely ever to be fully replicated because it is almost impossible to recreate the subtlety, complexity and biodiversity of an ecosystem

---

[26] Section 46 Planning and Compulsory Purchase Act 2004. See further Ch. 13, pp. 510–11.

that has evolved over time.[27] This underlines that the establishment and evolution of compensatory habitats (as well as long-term monitoring of these) is entirely out of synch with the shorter timescales of most planning decisions.

The creation of ersatz habitats as compensation for the loss of the conservation interest of sites frequently involves the translocation of species. In *Newsum No. 1*,[28] for example, the applicants sought a licence from the Welsh Assembly to 'rescue' a population of great crested newts which had colonised pools in a quarry, prior to the resumption of works on the site. The applicants presented this exercise as a wholly positive and compensatory measure. On approving the applicant's challenge to the Assembly's refusal to grant the licence, Pitchford J similarly saw protection of the species and its translocation as one and the same. In practice, though, there is a very high failure rate for translocated species, mainly because of the frequent failure to reinstate the necessary functions of the ecosystem relied upon by the species.[29] It is also the case that resident species on the recipient sites may also suffer from the process because of the introduction of unfamiliar pathogens and parasites by the incomers. More specifically on the translocation of great crested newts, researchers have found that newly created ponds were generally smaller than those lost to development and, of the ponds that were retained as mitigation for any losses, less than half were managed or enhanced.[30]

The recent emphasis in law and policy on environmental compensation may be understood as an undesirable effect of conservation interests being attributed greater weight in the planning system. According to Cowell, this has produced tensions in the government's approach to sustainability – between commitments to protecting environmental quality and avoiding constraints on development. The burden of ameliorating these tensions inevitably falls upon environmental compensation as a means of recognising environmental standards whilst also overcoming planning objections to ecologically undesirable development.[31]

## 4 Changing agricultural practices

We opened Chapter 15 by commenting that the industrialisation and intensification of agriculture have had seriously deleterious effects on biodiversity, and that one of the reasons for this has been its operation outside the

---

[27] Oliver Gilbert and Penny Anderson, *Habitat Creation and Repair* (Oxford University Press, 2005), p. 236.

[28] *Newsum* v. *Welsh Assembly* [2004] EWHC 50 (Admin). See Ch. 15, pp. 644–6.

[29] J. M. Bullock *et al.*, *A Review of Information, Policy and Legislation on Species Translocations, Report to the Joint Nature Conservation Committee* (Institute of Terrestrial Ecology, 1995).

[30] P. Edgar and R. A. Griffiths, *An Evaluation of the Effectiveness of Great Crested Newt* Tritus cristatus *Mitigating Projects in England 1990–2001* (English Nature, 2004).

[31] Richard Cowell, 'Stretching the Limits: Environmental Compensation, Habitat Creation and Sustainable Development' (1997) 22 *Transactions of the Institute of British Geographers* 292, p. 297.

development consent system because of an unduly restrictive definition of 'development' in a series of Town and Country Planning Acts (see Chapter 13, pp. 513–14). In addition the traditional focus of nature conservation has been the protection of areas that host species of national and, latterly, European value. The Habitats Directive, for example, secures protection for only a small proportion of Europe's natural heritage. It does not offer protection to the relatively large areas of land not designated for special protection, but which may nevertheless provide important habitats for a diversity of species.

In its *Environmental Planning* report,[32] the Royal Commission on Environmental Pollution considered the case for extending the scope of the town and country planning system so as to embrace agricultural activities and development, as we discussed in Chapter 13, pp. 506–7. Although the Commission's recommendations fell short of advocating this, a specific recommendation was that each agricultural holding receiving public subsidy should be required to prepare a farm plan containing actions to improve the environment, which could then be monitored. This recommendation now forms the basis of the Environmental Stewardship Scheme within which Farm Environment Plans bring together in one document information for the purposes of grant schemes, production subsidies and voluntary and mandatory measures, thereby integrating the administration of conservation and agricultural regimes.

A further example of the integration of agricultural and conservation interests that has (finally) been realised is the new consent procedure for the conversion of uncultivated land or semi-natural land (typically, meadows, downland, grassland and moorland) to land for intensive agriculture, based upon environmental impact assessment. This has been a long time in coming. Although listed in Annex II of the EIA Directive adopted in 1985, this category of project fell outside the scope of the implementing regulations[33] because these were based upon the existing narrow categories of 'development' requiring planning permission, which exclude certain agriculture and forestry projects. After lengthy negotiations with the European Commission about the inadequacy of the implementing provisions for the EIA Directive, the United Kingdom government eventually conceded in 1992 that environmental impact assessment procedures should apply to the conversion of semi-natural and uncultivated areas to intensive agriculture,[34] but separate sets of regulations for this were not issued until 2001 (2002 in the case of Scotland).[35] The new regime, administered by the DEFRA, the Welsh Assembly, and the Scottish Executive,

[32] Royal Commission on Environmental Pollution, Twenty-third Report, *Environmental Planning*, Cm 5459 (2002).
[33] Town and Country Planning (Assessment of Environmental Effects) Regulations 1988 (SI 1988 No. 1199).    [34] HC Written answers, 16.12.1992, Cols. 319–20.
[35] Environmental Impact Assessment (Uncultivated Land and Semi-Natural Areas) (England) Regulations 2001 (SI 2001 No. 3966); Environmental Impact Assessment (Uncultivated Land and Semi-Natural Areas) Regulations (Northern Ireland) 2001 (SI 2001 No. 435) and Environmental Impact Assessment (Uncultivated Land and Semi-Natural Areas) (Scotland) Regulations 2002 (SI 2002 No. 6).

requires an environmental impact assessment to be prepared before land is brought into intensive agricultural use if this is likely to cause significant environmental effects. Where it is considered likely to do so, the land manager must prepare an environmental statement assessing the implications of the project and containing sufficient information to allow a reasonable decision on whether the project should proceed. The consenting authority will decide this having consulted a range of conservation agencies including Natural England (which supersedes English Nature), Scottish Natural Heritage or the Countryside Council for Wales, and taking into account the existence of habitats and particular species covered by the UK BAP and whether the land is designated for special protection, for example as a Natura 2000 site. Although not provided for in the scheme, the Royal Commission on Environmental Pollution has additionally urged that the consenting bodies 'should not hesitate to refuse schemes that would cause significant environmental damage, nor miss such schemes at the initial screening stage',[36] and that the efficacy of the regime should be subject to review.

As with this consent regime, many of the more far-reaching changes to agricultural practices have a European heritage,[37] particularly those designed to temper the more environmentally damaging effects of the CAP.

## (a) The 'reform' of the CAP – Agenda 2000

Subsidies for the production of food formed the basis of the European Union's (EU's) CAP for more than half a century. The resulting intensification of farming – involving the over-application of fertilisers, drainage and irrigation, the restructuring of farms to accommodate large-scale machinery, and a reduction in the number of species and varieties used (including by recourse to genetically modified organisms) – has directly and indirectly led to the damage and loss of important habitats and species. Peter Taylor describes the EU's agricultural policy as 'the engine of destruction, having subsidised food production to the detriment of the environment'.[38] Joanne Scott further relates this gross overproduction (creating 'lakes' and 'mountains' of stored foods) through price support to the EU's rural development policy which primarily sought to support regions 'lagging' behind the rest of the Union in purely economic terms.[39]

Slowly, recognition of the unsustainable nature of a production-led system, and the need to integrate environmental concerns (especially biodiversity) into all areas of EU policy, including agriculture, encouraged the reform of the CAP. A further important influence was the environmental condition

---

[36] *Environmental Planning*, para. 9.49.

[37] For a further example, see case study on Nitrate Vulnerable Zones in first edition of this book, Ch. 9.      [38] Taylor, *Beyond Conservation*, p. 187.

[39] Joanne Scott, *Development Dilemmas in the European Community: Rethinking Regional Development Policy* (Open University Press, 1995), pp. 108–11.

of the new Member States in central and eastern Europe, in which biological diversity has been better maintained through traditional farming approaches. There was a perceived need to help small farmers resist intensive methods in the face of Europe-wide competition.[40] A more cynical view is that the reform of agricultural policy, particularly in favour of organic food production, allows the EU to 'green box', or remove its goods from the purview of world trade rules, thus justifying continuing to provide European farmers with income support.[41]

At first the reorientation of the CAP took the form of financially rewarding positive environmental measures in areas designated as Environmentally Sensitive Areas[42] (areas of particularly high landscape, wildlife or historic value) under the terms of Directive 797/85/EEC on improving the efficiency of agricultural structures. At the time of its adoption, the European Commission commented that 'the Directive may not be used to encourage conservation per se, but is to be used for the encouragement of farming which, in turn, will have a positive effect on the conservation of the countryside'.[43] The key provision (Art. 19) authorised Member States to establish national schemes for the 'introduction or continued use of agricultural production practices compatible with the requirements of conserving the natural habitat ensuring an adequate income for farmers'. In the English Environmentally Sensitive Areas scheme, farmers agreed to carry out their farming within a system of constraints in return for an annual payment. The scheme was rather more purposefully taken up in Scotland, where greater emphasis was placed on positive conservation measures rather than the imposition of restrictions and, prior to receiving payments, farmers were required to prepare and agree a farm management plan.

An explicit agri-environment Directive[44] was adopted as the environmental accompaniment to the extensive package of ('McSharry') reforms to the CAP adopted in 1992. The aim of this was to encourage farming practices compatible with the protection of the environment and the upkeep of the landscape and natural resources through financial support for such practices, including long-term set-aside of land (taking land out of arable production in favour of being left fallow or used for non-intensive grazing), reducing the application of fertilisers and chemicals, managing abandoned land, reducing livestock density,

[40] European Environmental Advisory Councils, *Statement on a Sustainable Agricultural Policy* (2002), issued by a number of official but independent advisory councils (www.EEAC-network.org). See E. M. Bignal and D. J. McCracken, 'The Nature Conservation Value of European Traditional Farming Systems' (2000) 8 *Environmental Reviews* 149, and see further P. F. Donald *et al.*, 'The Common Agricultural Policy, EU Enlargement and the Conservation of Europe's Farmland Birds' (2002) 89 *Agriculture, Ecosystems and the Environment* 167–82.     [41] Taylor, *Beyond Conservation*, p. 188.

[42] Article 19 Directive 797/85/EEC on improving the efficiency of agricultural structures OJ 1985 L 93/3.     [43] Commission Press Release.

[44] Directive 2078/92/EEC on agricultural production methods compatible with the requirements of the protection of the environment OJ 1992 L 215/85.

and favouring organic methods of farming. Although this instrument, along with other reforms, was described as marking a decisive turning point, away from the traditional rationality of the CAP, the actual success of some of its elements, such as the set-aside scheme, has been more limited than expected, and described as 'minimal' when set against the damage done by the CAP.[45] On the positive side, the agri-environment Directive undeniably encouraged a broader approach to environmental stewardship on farms by expanding the financial rewards for good environmental management beyond the scope of designated areas.

A further attempt at reforming the CAP (Agenda 2000) has sought to bring about the final decoupling of payments from food production. Under Regulation 1782/2003/EC,[46] direct payments to farmers are now made conditional upon achieving a range of EU standards – including environmental, food safety, animal health and welfare standards – that is 'cross-compliance' with other measures. The key premises of this change are set out in the preamble to the Regulation:

### Regulation 1782/2003/EC establishing common rules for direct support schemes under the common agricultural policy OJ 2003 L 270/1, Preamble

(2) The full payment of direct aid should be linked to compliance with rules relating to agricultural land, agricultural production and activity. Those rules should serve to incorporate in the common market organisations basic standards for the environment, food safety, animal health and welfare and good agricultural and environmental condition. If those basic standards are not met, Member States should withdraw direct aid in whole or in part on the basis of criteria which are proportionate, objective and graduated. Such withdrawal should be without prejudice to sanctions laid down now or in the future under other provisions of Community or national law.

(3) In order to avoid the abandonment of agricultural land and ensure that it is maintained in good agricultural and environmental condition, standards should be established which may or may not have a basis in provisions of the Member States. It is therefore appropriate to establish a Community framework within which Member States may adopt standards taking account of the specific characteristics of the areas concerned, including soil and climatic conditions and existing farming systems (land use, crop rotation, farming practices) and farm structures.

(4) Since permanent pasture has a positive environmental effect, it is appropriate to adopt measures to encourage the maintenance of existing permanent pasture to avoid a massive conversion into arable land.

In England, the primary vehicles for implementing the Agenda 2000 reforms in favour of positive management are the Environmental Stewardship Scheme

---

[45] Scott, *Development Dilemmas*, pp. 115–22.

[46] Establishing common rules for direct support schemes under the common agricultural policy OJ 2003 L 270/1.

(previously, the Countryside Stewardship Scheme[47]), administered by DEFRA, and, in the case of land designated as an SSSI, the wildlife enhancement scheme, administered by Natural England (formerly English Nature). In Wales, the integration of environmental considerations in agriculture is advanced by the Tir Gofal scheme which is similarly based on payments for works of environmental benefit. The Environmental Stewardship Scheme, even when entering at the lowest level,[48] may require substantial changes in husbandry and agricultural practices, such that some farmers are unwilling or unable to sign up to the schemes. However, it is also the case that the general environmental awareness that the schemes foster, as well as the knowledge shared between farmers about the requirements (and benefits) of the schemes, have led to improvements being made by farmers working towards 'environmental stewardship' even when they have not signed up to a specific scheme. Even taking into account this important 'reach' of environmental schemes, they still remain far overshadowed by support linked to crop and livestock production.[49]

### (b) An ethic of stewardship?

As with the reform of the SSSI regime (discussed above, pp. 625–7), payments for positive management involve a fundamental shift towards recognising the duties of property ownership as well as its benefits. Christopher Rodger's thesis is that a new form of environmental property right is emerging as a result of these changes.

### Christopher Rodgers, 'Agenda 2000, Land Use and the Environment: Towards a Theory of "Environmental" Property Rights' in Jane Holder and Carolyn Harrison (eds.), *Law and Geography* (Oxford University Press, 2002), pp. 255–6

Legal rules requiring positive land management, whether imposed within a contractual framework or through the administrative arrangements for producer support, cannot be satisfactorily classified simply as property-limitation rules. Their primary focus is the requirement of positive land management in accordance with an established normative standard. They are therefore a species of property-duty rule. Harris's classification of property rights recognises the distinction between property-liability rules and property-duty rules, but locates property-duty rules in the imposition of obligations on the owner of the assets which have nothing to do with the exercise of any ownership privileges over the asset in question (in our case land).[50]

...

---

[47] Countryside Stewardship Regulations 2000 (SI 2000 No. 3048).
[48] Payments are graded according to the level of stewardship reached – entry level, organic level and higher level.
[49] Royal Commission on Environmental Pollution, *Environmental Planning*, para. 9.31.
[50] James W. Harris, *Property and Justice* (Oxford University Press, 1996), p. 37.

Environmental rules of this kind do not fit within the paradigm: they are a new species of property rule that imposes positive obligations specifically as an attribute of the exercise of ownership privileges. They do not abrogate property rights as such, rather they impose positive obligations that impact *on the way in which* ownership privileges and powers are exercised. A farmer is perfectly entitled to adopt the system of farming he wishes on his land, whether intensive arable, dairy, or livestock farming. This is a privilege of ownership and remains so. Having made his choice, however, the law requires him to manage his land in accordance with the dictates of good agricultural practice, in so far as they apply to the land use he has chosen. And he may be offered a management agreement with incentive payments if the requirements of environmental protection indicate that something beyond this base line of sound management is required to deliver the policy goal sought.

Coyle and Morrow similarly understand such reforms, producing curbs on property rights (albeit that these are compensated in monetary terms), as 'articulating moral limits to ownership of resources arising from an ethic of stewardship'.[51] They continue: 'in this case, individual rights to property must be understood primarily in terms of responsibilities: responsibilities, rather than rights, would form the basic counters in our understanding of property, though the responsibilities would not be owed primarily, or wholly, to identifiable communities' (p. 169), but to a more amorphous conception of 'the environment'. This analysis is based in part on more general support for a move away from a rights-based notion of property.

### Sean Coyle and Karen Morrow, *The Philosophical Foundations of Environmental Law* (Hart, 2004), pp. 167-8

When a society's conception of property rights is heavily conditioned by perspectives which emphasise the controls and limitations placed upon the scope of those rights for the benefit of collective interests, various theoretical perspectives become available to explain the formal characteristics of the institution of property in ways which stress the collective controls as the primary terms in which an understanding of property must be sought rather than the individual entitlements. In a recent essay, Kevin and Susan Gray argue that there is some judicial support for a move away from a rights-based notion of property in favour of one based on responsibility. 'The crucial variable', they write,

> has now become the degree to which the courts are prepared to hold that the proprietary utilities available to a land-holder are inherently curtailed by a community-directed obligation to conserve and promote fragile features of the environment.[52]

---

[51] Sean Coyle and Karen Morrow, *The Philosophical Foundations of Environmental Law* (Hart, 2004), p. 169.

[52] Kevin Gray and Susan F. Gray, 'The Idea of Property in Land' in Susan Bright and John Dewar (eds.), *Land Law: Themes and Perspectives* (Oxford University Press, 1998), p. 49.

According to this conception,

> Property becomes ... an allocative mechanism for promoting the efficient or ecologically prudent utilisation of [scarce] resources. So analysed, this community-oriented [*sic*] approach to property in land plays a quite obviously pivotal role in the advancement of our environmental welfare.[53]

Here, the collective interests which affect individual rights to property are treated neither as necessary incidents of the concept of 'right' (or 'property'), nor as a mere collection of legislated restrictions which alter the scope of existing rights. Inherent curtailment, in the sense wielded above, suggests a collection of principles which affect the scope of property rights by constituting the moral/political framework within which claims of rights are expressed and understood. Such a conceptual framework is neither historically inevitable nor incontestable, but it is capable of redrawing the terms in which property rights are conceived. In stressing responsibilities and obligations as the fundamental terms within which property rights must be understood, the Grays' proposal removes some central determinants of property rights from the capitalist system of free-market exchange and, at the same time, from unalloyed utilitarian calculations about the extent to which individual property rights collide with broader social welfare goals. Both kinds of allocative mechanism can, of course, continue to affect various aspects of property ownership; but certain, central aspects of ownership will, on this view, be isolated from and immune to manipulation through these channels.

Notwithstanding the argument that property may be freed from influence from the free market in such circumstances, the policy and schemes for encouraging the provision of nature conservation have been critiqued as an application of quasi-market principles, by which the farmer performs the role of provider and the government or conservation agency acts as the purchaser. In explaining the reform of agricultural assistance according to market principles, Iain Fraser warns of the creation of a fragmented environmental landscape: 'the combining of environmental output and rural amenity use could give rise to a theme park mentality and a lack of sound ecological reasoning behind agri-environmental policy motivation'.[54] There are also residual doubts about the extent to which birds and plants prosper under agri-environmental schemes because, even with considerably reduced applications, levels of fertilisers might still be too high, and seed sources too scarce, to encourage the development of more species-rich vegetation.[55]

## (c) The story of field margins

The creation of 'buffer strips' at the margins of fields is a highly visible effect of the CAP reforms, permitting 'set-aside' land (land taken out of production) to

---

[53] *Ibid.* at p. 41.
[54] Iain Fraser, 'Quasi-Markets in the Provision of Nature Conservation in Agri-Environmental Policy' (1996) 6 *European Environment* 95, p. 99.
[55] David Kleijn *et al.*, 'Agri-Environmental Schemes do not Effectively Protect Biodiversity in Dutch Agricultural Landscapes' (2001) 413 *Nature* 723.

take the form of strips at least 5m wide for 'duly justified environmental reasons',[56] and providing for farmers to receive payments for this. Leaving land fallow has long been an important part of the EU's agricultural policy in an attempt, primarily, to reduce surpluses, but also to reduce the use of artificial fertilisers and pesticides, reduce soil erosion and compaction and the pollution of watercourses, and provide habitats to encourage farmland biodiversity.[57] The idea behind making strips of set-aside land at field margins is to buffer sensitive habitats such as ditches, SSSIs, woodland and hedges from agricultural land still in production.

Encouraging farmers to create wide field margins is just one component of the current Environmental Stewardship Scheme,[58] introduced to implement the CAP reforms.[59] The Scheme ('Look After your Land and be Rewarded'[60]) pays farmers, through management agreements, for the effective environmental management of their land. Farmers are required to prepare a Farm Environmental Record which identifies the areas of land to benefit from positive management, as agreed with the local Rural Development Service, an agency of DEFRA. Payments may be claimed after the completion of any of the work agreed upon. Other so-called 'management options' included in agreements are hedgerow management (discussed further below), creating beetle banks, reducing soil erosion through careful management of maize crops, and encouraging a range of crop types (for example sowing wild bird seed mix or pollen and nectar mix in grassland areas). In at least one case, the creation of wide field margins for wildlife also forms the basis of a local BAP (discussed above, pp. 671–3), suggesting the combining of techniques for reforming agricultural practices and encouraging biodiversity.

### Leicestershire and Rutland Wildlife Trust, *Biodiversity Action Plan – Field Margins* (2003–5)

Arable field margins act as a buffer zone between the field boundary and the crop or road, and form important wildlife corridors between species rich areas. In Leicestershire and Rutland, field margins are a key habitat for a number of Red Data Book species,[61] including many farmland birds, arable plants and insects. The structural condition of a field margin is extremely important for biodiversity along with the presence of associated features such as hedgerows, ditches, walls or watercourses.

---

[56] Article 54(4) Regulation 1782/2003/EC.

[57] Set-aside formed an important part of the McSharry set of agricultural reforms in 1992, on which see above, pp. 683–4.

[58] This replaces several existing schemes, for example Countryside Stewardship, Environmentally Sensitive Areas, and Organic Farming Schemes.

[59] Under the provisions of Regulation 1782/2003/EC.

[60] Title of on-line brochure for Environmental Stewardship Scheme (DEFRA).

[61] These are lists of species whose continued existence is threatened.

### Some characteristic species

Arable weeds are one of the most threatened categories of plant in the UK. Species like the Cornflower (*Centaura cyanus*) disappeared from Leicestershire and Rutland long ago. Other once common plants, including Corn Marigold (*Chrysanthemum segetum*), Shepherd's Needle (*Scandix pecten-veneris*) and even Common Poppy (*Papaver rhoeas*) are becoming increasingly rare. Seeds from arable weeds, such as Fat Hen (*Chenopodium album*), are an important food source for many species of farmland bird, while species such as Grey Partridge (*Perdix perdix*), Corn Bunting (*Emberiza calandra*) and Skylark (*Alauda arvensis*) benefit from sympathetic management of arable field margins. Characteristic butterfly species include Small Skipper, Gatekeeper and Ringlet.

### Most important factors affecting the habitat
- Ploughing/cultivation right up to the base of the field margin;
- Spray drift of fertilisers and pesticides
- Over-management to keep field margins 'neat and tidy'

### Proposed action with lead agencies
- Continue to promote the use of agri-environment schemes which target arable field margins;
- Continue to promote and advise farmers and landowners on field margin management;
- Target creation of 6m field margins to areas of high biodiversity (e.g. land adjacent to Wildlife Sites, water courses, ancient woodland and SSSIs) to protect from effects of agricultural sprays and fertiliser applications;
- Promote the use of cultivation options in agri-environment schemes to manage field margins to benefit arable weed species.

The key point to note is that the payments for creating wide field margins may be made in respect of *any* land, not just that designated for special protection.

## (d) Protecting hedgerows

Hedgerows have fallen victim to many modern agricultural practices – the use of mechanised pruning equipment, the consolidation of fields in favour of acres of 'monocrops', and the over-application of artificial fertilisers. These examples of 'technological' farming were positively encouraged by the Ministry of Agriculture, Fisheries and Food which until 1992 gave grant aid to farmers to remove their hedges. The grubbing up and general neglect of hedgerows has caused a loss of plant and animal species as well as making the resultant large fields vulnerable to wind erosion of the fertile top soil. Although official reports described the loss of hedgerows as a serious problem from the 1970s, the law lagged behind the reality of this. But as farming came to be seen as increasingly problematic in conservation terms and the loss of hedgerows was seen as emblematic of this, different legal techniques were developed to stem their loss and damage. In line with a 'quasi-market' approach to nature conservation, the

Hedgerow Incentive Scheme was introduced in 1992. This voluntary scheme administered by the Countryside Commission in England (a similar scheme – the Hedgerow Renovation Scheme – exists in Wales) offers financial incentives for the restoration of hedgerows. An element of cross-compliance is included because all hedges on a farm fall within the scheme, not just those identified for special protection.[62]

In marked contrast, the Hedgerow Regulations 1997[63] introduced a licensing system whereby the *removal* of countryside hedgerows (rather than slow dieback which is typical of hedgerow loss from chemical and fertiliser use) is prohibited unless certain procedures are followed and the consent of the local planning authority is obtained, thus separating arrangements for the protection of hedgerows from aid for their management. The legislative motivation for this instrument came from the government's commitments to secure biodiversity and protect the rural landscape.[64] In terms of procedure, owners must give notice to the authority that they wish to remove a hedgerow. Should the authority decide, according to criteria set out in the regulations, that the threatened hedgerow is 'important', it may issue a hedgerow retention notice stating that the works should not be carried out. 'Important' hedgerows are those considered in the Regulations to have existed for thirty years or more and which satisfy at least two sets of criteria. The first set relates to archaeological and historical matters, for example if the hedgerow marks the boundary of at least one historic parish or township existing before 1850. The second set relates to wildlife and landscape considerations and includes lists of woodland species (bluebell, oxlip, toothwort, etc.), woody species (rowan, alder, wild cotoneaster, etc.), endangered or vulnerable animals and bird species, and various hedgerow features. The whole system is reinforced by criminal sanctions and the requirement that hedgerows removed in contravention of the Regulations must be restored.

At the time they were laid down, the Hedgerow Regulations represented a new direction for conservation law. The legal regime – of notification, licence and sanction – is the familiar 'command and control' model pursued for development control and pollution control, but was in this case invoked for the purposes of protecting hedgerows as part of the rural landscape. In this case, this model usurps the tradition of governing the countryside via 'management' by farmers, backed up by voluntary systems of financial incentives, grants and subsidies.

---

[62]  Fraser, 'Quasi-Markets in the Provision of Nature Conservation', p. 97.

[63]  SI 1997 No. 1160. This set of Regulations was introduced following the failure of several private members' Bills to introduce specific regimes for their protection. Powers to make regulations to protect hedgerows were granted by s. 97 Environment Act 1995.

[64]  UK Government, *The UK's Biodiversity Action Plan* (UK Government, 2004) included an action plan for the protection of ancient or species-rich hedgerows. See further Jane Holder, 'Law and Landscape: The Legal Construction and Protection of Hedgerows' (1999) 62 *Modern Law Review* 100.

The system for the protection of hedgerows established by the 1997 Regulations provided a template for the reform of the SSSI regime (Chapter 15, pp. 625–6). However, as with some other licensing regimes,[65] it is blunt and unresponsive. The working of the Regulations relies upon a scientific assessment of the number and the type of species present in a measured stretch of hedgerow, with little recognition of less tangible attributes such as typicalness, local distinctiveness and setting. The adoption of quantitative criteria such as these form part of the more general incorporation of economic valuing techniques in environmental law. In these circumstances, the management agreement, allowing for some degree of negotiation between parties and variability according to local conditions, might be a more appropriate mechanism for protecting this aspect of the landscape.

## 5 Conclusions

In the previous chapter we examined nature conservation law by focussing on the designation of particular parcels of land deemed worthy of special protection. We explained that this approach has many strengths, but a number of inherent flaws. The relatively recent recognition of the complexity and necessity of *biodiversity* protection has encouraged efforts to move beyond this fragmented approach to conservation, and towards greater integration of nature conservation considerations into other areas of decision making.

The systems of town planning and countryside protection have traditionally operated in relief: the planning system aims at blanket coverage – all 'development' requires planning permission unless specifically exempted – whereas the system of countryside designation has traditionally demarcated only particular areas for special protection, in celebration of the 'specialness' or rarefaction of certain sites or species according to scientific criteria. This partial approach to conservation led to well-founded criticism: the Wildlife and Countryside Act 1981, for example, was criticised in its passage through Parliament for doing nothing for the basic fabric of the countryside, the 'everyday things such as ponds, hedges, hedgerow trees and small woodlands'.[66] A more holistic approach to the control of land use and development may now be seen in the *general* requirement that nature conservation objectives be taken into account in all planning activities and decisions affecting rural land use and in urban areas where there is wildlife of local importance. The integration of planning controls and countryside protection regimes arises from a recognition that planning performs an important role in *preventing* environmental harm and that this function may have a far wider application than town planning.

---

[65] See Ch. 9.
[66] Hansard HL, December 1980, Col. 994, as quoted by Cook, *Wildlife Law*, p. 183.

Increasingly, the focus of conservation law is upon recognition of individuals' (especially farmers') duties to land, regardless of its special qualities. The concept of stewardship, now appropriated to describe various agri-environmental schemes, is in some respects the practical fulfilment of Leopold's idea of humans absorbed into a 'community with the land'.[67] This infiltration of matters of conservation into agricultural policy and practice may yet provide a strong example of policy integration and, more importantly, may create the conditions for the establishment of a genuine, ecological network, based upon but also exceeding in coverage the special sites making up Natura 2000.

## 6 Further reading

The readings outlined in Chapter 15 are highly relevant here. More specifically on biodiversity, Kate Cook's *Wildlife Law: Conservation and Biodiversity* (Cameron May, 2004) draws together diverse laws in this area with an emphasis upon UK legal practice (her experiences as a civil servant and working for non-governmental organisations giving her a particularly interesting perspective on law and policy – she mentions suing her former colleagues!). This is an accessible, punchy and well-written account which also includes a chapter devoted to protection of the countryside *outside* designated sites.

On agriculture and environmental law the collections edited by William Howarth and Christopher Rodgers – *Agriculture, Conservation and Land Use* (University of Wales Press, 1992) – and by Christopher Rodgers – *Nature Conservation and Countryside Law* (University of Wales Press, 1996) – are important contributions to the field, allowing one to track the progression of particular issues over time, such as the set-aside regime. On the theme of conflict in the countryside, Graham Harvey's *The Killing of the Countryside* (Vintage, 1997) is a detailed and descriptive attack on current agricultural methods and their impact on nature. The collection of essays in *Town and Country* (edited by Anthony Barnett and Roger Scruton) (Jonathan Cape, 1998) contains a wide-ranging set of reflections on food production, conservation, hunting and development. For an accessible account of the making of the British countryside (from the Ice Age to modern farming) and an introduction to some of the main issues facing conservationists, illustrated with sketches of good countryside practice, see David Bellamy, *Conflicts in the Countryside: The New Battle for Britain* (Shaws, 2005).

In the United States, the conservation debate has long been raging. This is headed by Bill McKibben's *The End of Nature* (Penguin, 1990) which is a searing essay on the damage caused by 'progress'. The role of government and big business ('Bush and the Kyoto Killers') is accessibly explored by Robert Kennedy, *Crimes Against Nature* (Penguin, 2004). More specifically on nature conservation, Eric Freyfogle's *Why Conservation is Failing and How it Can Regain Ground* (Yale University Press, 2006) sets out to account for the failings of the conservation movement, in the course of which he seeks to reassert Aldo Leopold's land ethic.

In this and the preceding chapter we have tried to illuminate conservation law and policy with the arguments of theorists, some of whom have a radical take on bringing

---

[67] Aldo Leopold, *A Sand County Almanac* (Ballantine Books, 1968). See further Ch. 1, pp. 48–50.

nature and society together. David Delaney's wide-ranging and hugely stimulating work *Law and Nature* (Cambridge University Press, 2003) contains chapters on 'Law and Wilderness' (including metaphoric wilderness) and 'Law and Endangered Species', neither of which fall into the 'transcendentalist man in the wilderness' (or 'eco-la la') trap represented by some other works. Cormac Cullinan's much-debated *Wild Law: A Manifesto for Earth Justice* (Green Books, 2002) is far broader than conservation law, but his arguments about earth's rights should be central to thinking about conservation. Finally, William M. Adams' wonderful *Against Extinction: The Story of Conservation* (Earthscan, 2004) is far more than a historical account; it provides at times a searing critique of the use of designation (particularly when discussed in relation to colonialism – 'Parks for the Colonies').

**17**

# Wind Farm Development and Environmental Conflicts

## 1 Introduction

In this chapter we present a case study on wind farm development, reinforcing an idea of the planning system as a potential medium for sustainability. In discussing the law and policy relating to wind farms, we highlight the difficulties from a planning perspective of securing the support of local people and local planning authorities for this category of development – the frequently vociferous local opposition to such developments being at odds with central planning guidance in support of wind farm projects. This issue suggests the limits of the possible positive contribution of public participation to environmental protection. It is also a good example of the central difficulty facing environmentalism – tempering individual preferences or freedom for the common good (or encouraging communitarianism over individualism). Patsy Healey presents this as a central problem of modernity: 'The challenge for public life in our present times is how to reconcile the individualisation of cultural identity with recognition of commonality between individuals with different frames of reference, as well as different interests, in ways which do not trap us in modes of thought and practice which suppress our individual capacity to flourish.'[1] The general nature of the problem suggests that the legal and policy methods aimed at securing support for wind farm development may well be applied beyond this type of development. Although in many ways a typical environmental problem, the case of wind farm development also appears to move us beyond a simplistic development/ conservation binary (or the idea that all development will necessarily involve environmental costs) so often invoked in environmental debate because, it is hoped, the generation of renewable forms of energy will help avoid some of the effects of climate change. That said, the nature of the environmental benefits of wind power is also highly complex. As Dave Toke and Peter Strachan state, 'Wind power has emerged as both a solution to environmental problems and as an environmental problem in itself in the UK.'[2]

---

[1] Patsy Healey, *Collaborative Planning: Shaping Places in Fragmented Societies* (Macmillan, 1997), p. 44. On collaborative planning, see Ch. 13, pp. 530–6.

[2] David Toke and Peter Strachan, 'Ecological Modernisation and Wind Power in the UK' (2006) 16 *European Environment* 155, p. 155.

The following article, published in the newsletter of the Environmental Law Foundation (ELF), provides an overview of many of the legal and environmental issues raised by this form of energy (in this case *on*shore farms), from a local perspective. As an organisation set up with two main aims – to refer protesters to sources of legal advice *and* to campaign for environmental justice – ELF is faced with a very real dilemma, and one which is by now familiar to environmentalists: should priority be given to global environmental security over local environmental quality? Note also that the objections to wind farm development detailed in this article are not based only on aesthetic grounds, and are thus not easily dismissed as 'subjective'.[3]

### Simon Jackson, 'Wind Power: The Legal and Environmental Issues' (2005) *ELFline*, p. 4

At first sight the environmental benefits of generating energy from wind farms would seem to be overwhelming, and the gut reaction of anyone who is concerned with global warming would be to welcome unreservedly any announcement of a policy to support the rapid expansion of wind farms in the United Kingdom.

Pursuant to that policy objective, the Welsh Assembly has announced that it wishes to see 800 megawatts of energy provided by onshore wind energy developments in selected areas of Wales. In its Planning Policy Wales document and the accompanying Technical Advice Note it encourages planning authorities within those selected areas to promote and support wind power schemes.

As a result of this policy, ten applications have been made for the development of wind farms in the Denbighshire Moors area of North Wales. If all these were granted then over two hundred separate wind turbines would be erected, some of them up to 105 metres in height.

Faced with the potential development of multiple wind farms, those who live in the vicinity of those developments are beginning to see the issue from a different perspective, and realising that there are environmental and economic costs of wind farm development that have to be weighed against the benefits.

A group of local residents from the North Wales area contacted ELF and subsequently met with a lawyer through ELF's Advice and Referral Service. There were a variety of issues causing concern.

First is the noise generated by active turbines. The concerns here are twofold. Turbines can be constructed within 500 metres of a residential property and when operating produce substantial amounts of noise. A case has been brought for statutory noise nuisance in

---

[3] The tendency has been to portray opponents' arguments in this way, for example Dorothy W. Bisbee, 'NEPA Review of Offshore Wind Farms: Ensuring Emission Reduction Benefits Outweigh Visual Impacts' (2004) 31 *Boston College Environmental Affairs Law Review* 349: 'Local aesthetic preferences must not be permitted to overshadow broad regional benefits.' Admittedly, many of the objections raised in the ELF article do *not* apply to offshore wind farms, but certainly environmental effects of this category of project extend beyond the visual. On the environmental effects of offshore development, see further below, pp. 719–35.

respect of a wind farm in South Lakeland. This case did not succeed, on the ground that the complainant was unusually sensitive, and that objective evidence of a nuisance was lacking. However each case has to be judged on its own merits, and it may be in the future that a case in nuisance, either statutory or at common law, could be established.

There are also concerns about low frequency noise. This is considered to be noise between 100 and 150 Hz. There are concerns that sufficiently high levels of low frequency noise can cause long term health problems such as nausea, headaches and anxiety. Whilst the industry points to research suggesting no proven case, others are less sure.

The second area of concern is the visual impact of wind farms. This is an issue both for those who live near wind farms and for those who come to areas such as the Denbighshire Hills which have high environmental and amenity value. The significance of this issue is increased by the cumulative effect that numerous wind farms would have together. So in Denbighshire one farm might not affect visual amenity to a significant degree, whereas ten would.

The third issue causing concern is the hydrological implications of turbine construction. A photograph supplied by the North Wales group shows a member standing in the huge crater produced for the foundations of one turbine. Multiply this by up to 25 turbines per site and it is easy to see that the natural drainage of the surrounding land could be seriously affected. Many country properties rely on springs for water supply, and if these are interfered with there may be no alternative source of supply.

Local residents are clearly getting organised[4] and invoking laws from different areas to oppose such developments. The above account of local opposition to wind power in Wales additionally highlights the social impact of renewable energy sources which, Peter Strachan and David Lal argue,[5] has been neglected in policy making. Drawing on mainly Scottish sources (although their analysis is more broadly applicable), they consider the main emphasis of policy has hitherto been on a 'first strand' of thinking on the science and technological aspect of wind energy. An equally important 'second strand' has focussed on evaluating the national 'technology-push' and 'demand-pull' policies put in place to support sustainable energy production. The technology-push policies refer to initiatives such as research and development programmes, in which the government has invested some £250 million for the period 2002–6, while demand-pull policies are associated with a variety of market and regulatory mechanisms established by government. The primary intention of the government, they note, appears to be based around the notion of creating an opportunity for British businesses to become 'world-leaders' in the international

---

[4] As are the non-governmental organisations, e.g. the YES2WIND group, established by Friends of the Earth and Greenpeace, allowing for on-line registration of support of wind energy sources. The British Wind Energy Association has organised an energetic wind power campaign called 'Embrace'. In Scotland, anti-wind energy campaigners have set up an umbrella group, 'Views of Scotland', to provide support to new protesters.

[5] Peter Strachan and David Lal, 'Wind Energy Policy, Planning and Management Practice in the UK: Hot Air or a Gathering Storm?' (2004) 38 *Regional Studies* 551, pp. 553–4.

renewables sector just as the USA, Denmark, Germany and Spain have done during the last twenty-five years. Strachan and Lal continue:

> we recommend that more attention be given to a third strand – that of the social impacts (including public opposition and the perceived environmental impacts) associated with wind farm developments ... In the UK, battle lines are now being drawn between a pro- and anti-wind lobby. The UK public debate on wind power expansion has gained momentum during the last two years, to the extent that it is now beginning to challenge the efficacy of the UK Government and Scottish Executive's renewable strategies, with the limitations of wind energy being glossed-over by a pro-wind lobby.
>
> ...
>
> This expansion in wind power, however, has not been supported by any sort of governmental awareness raising campaign to educate the Scottish populace to the benefits of a sustainable energy system based on wind power. Thus, the Government's strategy to date is seen as being top-down, rather than both top-down and bottom-up, as has been the case in Denmark. (p. 545)

Taking this appeal as a cue, in this chapter we first outline the nature of the conflict between central government policy on renewable energy development and local opinion. Largely because of local resistance to renewable energy developments on the grounds of changes to the landscape, there has been a marked shift in favour of offshore wind farms. We focus on the licensing regime for this type of wind farm and examine in detail the Robin Rigg wind farm located in the Solway Firth. As part of the licensing system, we consider the use of environmental assessment as a mechanism for predicting the likely environmental effects of these projects on conservation interests, as well as more strategically establishing a framework for decisions about their location. In this context, the limitations of environmental assessment become apparent, not least because many of the effects of wind farm installations on wildlife are still uncertain. In addition, environmental statements may be contested, as in the case of the proposed wind farm on the Isle of Lewis. We also consider the role of financial incentives as a means of stemming adverse public opinion.

Throughout this chapter we consider the evolution of policy, particularly the move towards giving significant weight to '*the wider environmental and economic benefits of all proposals for renewable energy projects* [emphasis added]'[6] as a result of consultation, examination by official committees and commissions, and legal debate. This policy constitutes a material consideration in decision making, whether by the local planning authority, or by the Secretary of State on appeal.[7] The main lesson learnt is that policy change such as this may be the *consequence* of legal practice and legal obligations, rather than the precursor to a specific legal measure, as policy is more commonly portrayed.

---

[6] Office of the Deputy Prime Minister (ODPM), Planning Policy Statement 22, *Renewable Energy* (HMSO, 2005), para. 1(iv); see further pp. 705–9.

[7] Under s. 36 Electricity Act 1989 consent is required from the Secretary of State for Trade and Industry (or the Scottish Executive) for any new electricity plant generating over 50 Mega

## 2 Planning policy conflicts

As we discussed in Chapter 13, the location of development, combining environmental, social and spatial factors, is the central and perennial problem facing planners; the utilitarian 'Where do things belong?' question being described as the primary calculus of land use planning.[8] With wind farm development, the problem of location is exacerbated due to physical constraints (the need for windy conditions, leading to farms in highland, exposed, coastal and remote areas – exactly those areas which are important for wildlife) but also uncertainty about the effect of wind farms upon wildlife. In addition to the physical constraints, there is a further issue about whether the siting of wind farms is politically and economically motivated, with the preponderance of farms planned for the north-west of the country, rather than the south-east (the exception, the identification of the Thames Estuary as an area earmarked for such development,[9] serving to emphasise this tendency).

In Chapter 13 we also discussed the slow movement towards integrated spatial planning, the main motivation for which was to reduce the occurrence of serious conflicts between key policy areas, such as transport, energy, and water resources, in line with the demands of sustainable development. In the case of renewable energy developments, policy conflicts are not so much sectoral in nature,[10] but exist on different scales, as between central and local government, precisely because of the locational issues involved. In this respect, superimposed upon the primary distinction identified in decision making between expert and lay opinion (see especially Chapter 1) is the criterion of *scale* in terms of both environmental politics and environmental effects; decisions having global effect may be made at

Footnote 7 (*cont.*)

Watts (MW). Applications for plants below this threshold are to be decided by the local planning authority under the Town and Country Planning regime (see Ch. 13). Consent from the Secretary of State is also required for electricity lines (s. 37 1989 Act). In cases in which the local authority objects to an application made under either s. 36 or s. 37 of the 1989 Act, the Secretary of State will call a public inquiry (Sch. 8 1989 Act) and will decide whether or not to grant consent for the development on the basis of the report of the inspector who held the inquiry. In addition, such applications must be accompanied by an environmental impact assessment (EIA) under the Town and Country Planning (Assessment of Environmental Effects) Regulations 1999 (SI 1999 No. 293) (the EIA Regulations 1999) Sch. 2 (3) (h) (i) in cases in which the development involves the installation of more than 2 turbines; or the hub height of any turbine or height of any other structure exceeds 15 metres. Note the rules relating to licensing *offshore* wind farms, below, pp. 719–35.

[8] Nick Blomley, 'Enclosure, Common-rights and the Property of the Poor' (2007) *Journal of Law and Society*, 'Special Issue on Commons' (forthcoming).

[9] See Department of Trade and Industry's strategic environmental assessment on the granting of licenses for offshore wind farms, pp. 723–9.

[10] The case of *offshore* wind farms is quite different, with the potential for sharp policy conflicts between different sectors (fisheries, navigation, conservation), see Karen Scott, 'Tilting at Offshore Windmills: Regulating Wind Farm Development Within the Renewable Energy Zone' (2006) 18 *Journal of Environmental Law* 89. She discusses this point in the context of a critique of the current lack of any system of integrated spatial planning for marine areas (p. 116), resulting in a lack of cumulative assessment of environmental impact of development in these areas – see further below, pp. 722–3.

the local level, where the immediate effects of the development are felt most keenly, rather than the potentially more serious deleterious effects that are felt on a global scale. Mark Stallworthy explains the implications of this: 'the planning system operates in an area where national and regional policy targets are increasingly being promulgated, for instance ... as to air quality and transport planning, as well as waste treatment and disposal. Central demands will often come into conflict with local community perspectives, which are in turn likely to put planning decision making procedures under extreme pressure.'[11]

## (a) Central government policy

In general there has been a slow gathering of momentum in support of renewable energy in policy in the United Kingdom. The starting point is a growing body of scientific evidence that continued increases in atmospheric concentrations of certain 'greenhouse gases'[12] will exert a warming effect on the earth and contribute to global climate change.[13] In response and after lengthy negotiations at the international level, the United Nations (UN) Framework Convention on Climate Change[14] was signed by 155 states and the European Community in 1992. As a result of this and other UN initiatives, the European Commission has pushed a European renewable energy agenda, in an attempt to create a European wind energy market.[15]

In the United Kingdom, wind farm development was quickly identified as a means of achieving reductions in the production of greenhouse gases.[16] This was bolstered by the ability on the part of the Secretary of State to require newly privatised electricity companies to secure a proportion of their supplies from renewable sources, the 'Non Fossil Fuel Obligation' (NFFO).[17] With other

[11] Mark Stallworthy, *Sustainability, Land Use and Environment: A Legal Analysis* (Cavendish, 2002), p. 213. In this context, see Philip Smith and Raphael Heath, 'Local Roadblocks to Global Thinking' (1998) *Planning* 20.

[12] Including carbon dioxide, methane, nitrous oxide, hydrofluorocarbons, perfluorocarbons and sulphur hexafluoride.

[13] See Intergovernmental Panel on Climate Change (IPCC), 'Climate Change 2001: The Scientific Basis' in its *Third Assessment Report: Climate Change 2001* (IPCC, 2001). See the general account of law relating to climate change in Philippe Sands, *Principles of International Environmental Law* (Cambridge University Press, 2003), pp. 357–81.

[14] 31 ILM 849 (1992).

[15] European Commission, *White Paper for a Community Strategy and Action Plan – Energy for the Future: Renewable Sources of Energy* COM(97) 599 final, culminating in Directive 2001/77/EC on the promotion of electricity from renewable sources in the internal electricity market OJ 2001 L 283/33.

[16] See Neil Douglas and Gurudeo Saluja, 'Planning's Role in Wind Energy Development' (1995) *Town and Country Planning* 50.

[17] The NFFO was introduced as part of the programme for the privatisation of the electricity industry. Originally applying only to the nuclear industry, the Obligation was revised to include renewable sources, and required that electricity companies purchase a minimum of electricity generated by renewable sources. Under a new system, green electricity certificates (Renewable Obligation Certificates (ROCs)) are given to wind power developers to sell to electricity suppliers who must supply a set quantity of electricity from renewable sources.

financial incentives, this made renewable energy schemes not just viable, but also potentially highly profitable.[18]

Initially and informally, government policy was that planning permission for onshore projects should be granted unless demonstrable harm would be caused to interests of acknowledged importance.[19] However, the government failed to clarify whether this presumption would apply to certain areas designated for special protection,[20] fuelling concerns of the Countryside Commission and other amenity groups that wind farm development would take place in these areas. In 1993, Planning Policy Guidance Note (PPG) 22 on *Renewable Energy*[21] was issued in part to clarify this issue and the more general one of whether there existed a policy presumption in favour of this type of development; in the event the guidance further contributed to the uncertainty. Although the guidance note clearly rejected the tacit presumption in favour of wind energy development, it instead required that 'The Government's policies for developing renewable energy sources must be weighed carefully with its continuing commitment to policies for protecting the environment' (para. 21). The difficulty was that the guidance gave no indication of how the balance between these conflicting policies should be struck. As Alasdair Cooper commented, 'A local authority is expected to weigh the advantages of the proposal, which will offer a small contribution to the national objective and be of imperceptible benefit locally, against local impacts that will be all too apparent.'[22] This differed notably from the housing or minerals sectors in which planning authorities could gauge the size of contribution to the national need which should be found within their area.[23]

The effect of the ambiguity on this point in PPG 22 became clear in the course of several legal disputes.[24] Most notably, in *West Coast Wind Farms Ltd* v. *Secretary of State and North Devon DC*,[25] the Court of Appeal was called upon to decide whether a policy presumption in favour of wind farm developments could be considered to flow from the 'policy aim' contained in the guidance. The case was brought by developers seeking to challenge the Secretary of

Footnote 17 (*cont.*)

The suppliers are penalised for every kWh of green electricity that they fail to supply towards meeting their target. See explanation by David Toke, 'Will the Government Catch the Wind?' (2005) *Political Quarterly* 48, p. 49.

[18] See further Guy Roots, 'Tilting at Windmills, Development Control and Renewable Energy' [1993] *Journal of Planning and Environmental Law* 515.

[19] Statement of the Planning Minister in response to a Parliamentary question by the Chairman of the Countryside Commission, as described by Roots, 'Tilting at Windmills'.

[20] On the designation of land for special protection, see Ch. 15.

[21] In Scotland advice was contained in National Planning Policy Guidelines 6 on *Renewable Energy* and Planning Advice Note 45: *Renewable Energy Technology*.

[22] Alasdair Cooper, 'PPG 22 – An Obstacle to Wind Power Development' [1998] *Journal of Planning and Environmental Law* 423, p. 433.    [23] *Ibid.*, at p. 433.

[24] See *International Wind Development UK Ltd* v. *Secretary of State for the Environment* [1997] JPL B153; *National Wind Power Ltd* v. *Secretary of State for the Environment, Transport and the Regions* [1999] NPC 128; and *Campaign for the Protection of Rural Wales* v. *Secretary of State for Wales* [2002] JPL 1304.

[25] *West Coast Wind Farms Ltd* v. *Secretary of State and North Devon DC* [1996] JPL 767.

State's refusal to permit them to build two wind farms, a decision similarly arrived at by both the local council and the planning inspector who held an inquiry into the proposed developments. The developer had complained that in weighing the environmental factors with the need for the development of renewable energy sources as expressed in the policy documents, the inspector had misunderstood government policy and insufficient weight had been given to the need expressed in the document PPG 22. In particular, in his report the inspector approved the arguments that alternative sites existed with potential for wind energy development and that wind power is only one of several renewable energy sources, concluding:

> whilst the greatest importance should be attached to the need to reduce $CO_2$ emissions and their adverse effects on global warming, these proposals are but two amongst many measures which would help in achieving that national policy aim. Accordingly, I do not accept that there is a national or local need for these particular proposals which could not be met elsewhere and which would merit their being afforded the greatest weight.[26]

Pill LJ concluded that the inspector had properly conducted the balancing exercise which planning policies for renewable energies required and, having rejected the appellant's argument for special 'presumptive' status for the proposals, had reached a conclusion he was entitled to reach on the basis of policy and on the facts of the case. The appellants therefore failed to convince the Court of Appeal that the government's policy guidance amounted to a presumption in favour of renewable energy developments, even if such developments were undoubtedly a policy aim of the government. Although renewable sources of energy might be 'needed' in a general sense, each application still had to be decided on its merits. The inspector was therefore entitled to give greater weight to local issues in this case. The Court also upheld the inspector's rather vague assessment of the existence of alternative sites and sources of renewable energy, on the basis that he was 'stating the obvious'. This had the effect of further diluting the appellant's arguments about the need for their, particular, proposed wind farms. This part of the judgment is particularly problematic from an environmental protection point of view. As Alasdair Cooper stated: 'This decision gives weight to planning authorities refusing planning permission with the justification that the individual development will not significantly alter the nation's overall reliance on fossil fuels. The fact that there are alternative sites can be used as a reason for non-development. This argument could effectively be used with most energy developments.'[27]

*West Coast Wind Farms* showed up the unworkable nature of the government's policy on renewables at this time, mainly because of a lack of clear criteria by which a balance could be struck between local environmental quality and achieving reductions in greenhouse gases for broader environmental protection purposes. For this reason PPG 22 was considered to be a failure in

---

[26] Paras. 74 and 75.     [27] Cooper, 'PPG 22', p. 423.

terms of facilitating the achievement of the government's renewable energy objectives,[28] and not only by the renewables industry – the Royal Commission on Environmental Pollution (RCEP) forcefully recommended its revision in its report on *Environmental Planning*.[29] As Pill LJ suggested in his judgment in *West Coast Wind Farms*, it was open to the Secretary of State to create a clear presumption in favour of renewable energy development if he considered that the achievement of the government's targets for reducing carbon dioxide required it. This course of action was eventually taken, following a further round of official reports and several important legal events.

In particular, further impetus to the formation of policy giving stronger support to renewable energy sources was given by the adoption of a Protocol to the Framework Convention on Climate Change in Kyoto in 1997,[30] committing the contracting states to specific targets for reducing greenhouse gases. States within the European Union undertook to reduce their production of these gases in the period 2008–12. However, a tranche of official reports warned that the planning system was impeding progress towards reaching these targets. An initial warning of the 'retarding influence'[31] of the planning system upon wind farm development came from the government's own Performance and Innovation Unit:[32] 'The business of obtaining planning permission for renewable investments, particularly onshore wind in England and Wales, remains costly and time-consuming … Unless success rates increase, targets will not be met.'[33] The House of Lords Environmental Audit Committee took up the point. The Committee noted that in Wales, resistance has tended to come from the National Assembly rather than at the local level, but this remains an interesting departure from the usual pattern of policy conflict between central and local levels.

### House of Lords Environmental Audit Committee, Fifth Report of Session 2001-2, *A Sustainable Energy Strategy? Renewables and the Performance and Innovation Unit Review* HC 582-1

#### What are the barriers to progress?

#### Planning

58. **Obtaining planning permission remains a major obstacle to the increased deployment of renewables.** On-shore wind power offers the greatest potential in the short to medium term, but it has also proved to be the most controversial, with many objections being lodged by local groups and environmental organisations. The success rate of planning permission in England and Wales has to date been only in the order of 26 per cent. Various organisations indicated that there was a particular problem in Wales, where the

---

[28] E.g. *ibid*.    [29] RCEP, *Environmental Planning*, para. 8.72.    [30] 37 ILM 22 (1998).

[31] Glen Plant, 'Offshore Wind Energy Development: The Challenges for English Law' [2003] *Journal of Planning and Environmental Law* 939, p. 941.

[32] The Performance and Innovation Unit (PIU) is part of the Prime Minister's strategy unit, providing advice and policy analysis.

[33] Quoted in RCEP, *Environmental Planning*, para. 8.60.

potential for wind energy is great, but where many applications have been called in by the National Assembly for Wales despite approval at local level. The length of the procedure can be inordinately long, as highlighted in one recent project where planning permission was finally rejected after some 8 years.

The RCEP concurred: 'planning applications have met with so much resistance in numerous localities that the development of wind energy on land in the UK is, in effect, stalled'.[34]

To some extent, United Kingdom policy has now moved beyond the Kyoto Protocol commitments, in recognition that, even if fully implemented, the Protocol will only have a marginal attenuating effect on the growth in $CO_2$ emissions. In its Energy White Paper 2003,[35] the government aims to cut carbon dioxide emissions by 20 per cent by 2010 and by 60 per cent by 2050. It seeks to do this in large part by increasing the generation of energy from renewable sources – to a level of 10 per cent of all generation by 2010, increasing to 15.4 per cent by 2015–16 and 20 per cent by 2020.[36] The Scottish Executive more ambitiously aims at a 40 per cent target of renewable electricity supply by 2020. In keeping with this approach, a more favourable planning policy towards renewable energy developments now exists. Planning Policy Statement (PPS) 1 (which, as we discussed in Chapter 13, sets out 'the overarching planning policies on the delivery of sustainable development through the planning system'[37]) defines the development of renewable energy resources as a key principle which should be applied to ensure that development plans and decisions taken on planning applications contribute to the delivery of sustainable development.

### Office of the Deputy Prime Minister (now succeeded by the Department of Communities and Local Government (DCLG)), Planning Policy Statement 1, *Delivering Sustainable Development* (HMSO, 2005), p. 6

KEY PRINCIPLES

13 ...

(ii) Regional planning bodies and local planning authorities should ensure that development plans contribute to global sustainability by addressing the causes and potential impacts of climate change[38] – through policies which reduce energy use, reduce emissions (for example,

---

[34] *Ibid.*

[35] UK Government Energy White Paper, O*ur Energy Future – Creating a Low Carbon Economy*, Cm 5761 (2003).

[36] Reaching these targets will require a huge building programme: approximately 10,000 MW of renewable energy will have to be installed by 2010, requiring an annual 'build rate' of 1,250 MW. To date, approximately 552 MW of renewable energy has been installed, leaving a considerable shortfall. On this point, see Strachan and Lal, 'Wind Energy Policy', p. 558.

[37] ODPM, Planning Policy Statement 1, *Delivering Sustainable Development* (ODPM, 2005), p. 1. On the legal status of PPSs, see Ch. 13, pp. 511–13.

[38] Further guidance can be found in ODPM, 'The Planning Response to Climate Change – Advice on Better Practice' (ODPM, 2004).

by encouraging patterns of development which reduce the need to travel by private car, or reduce the impact of moving freight), promote the development of renewable energy resources, and take climate change impacts into account in the location and design of development.

...

20. Development plan policies should take account of environmental issues such as:
    - mitigation of the effects of, and adaptation to, climate change through the reduction of greenhouse gas emissions and the use of renewable energy; ...

**Prudent use of Natural Resources**

21. The prudent use of resources means ensuring that we use them widely and efficiently, in a way that respects the needs of future generations. This means enabling more sustainable consumption and production and using non-renewable resources in ways that do not endanger the resource or cause serious damage or pollution ...

22. Development plan policies should seek to minimise the need to consume new resources over the lifetime of the development by making more efficient use or reuse of existing resources, rather than making new demands on the environment; and should seek to promote and encourage, rather than restrict, the use of renewable resources (for example by the development of renewable energy). Regional planning authorities and local authorities should promote resource and energy efficient buildings; community heating schemes, the use of combined heat and power, small scale renewable and low carbon energy schemes in developments; the sustainable use of water resources; and the use of sustainable drainage systems in the management of run-off.

This clear statement of support for renewable energy in policy was reinforced by PPS 22 on *Renewable Energy*, which replaces PPG 22, discussed above. The general policy approach now is to ensure that local authorities *facilitate* renewable energy development. The main means of securing this is by imposing an obligation on decision makers to give the fact that a proposed development is a renewable energy development *significant weight* in every case (see 'Key Principles', point 1(iv) below (p. 706)), thus disregarding the usual approach of considering each case on its own facts and in accordance with the development plan unless material considerations indicate otherwise.[39] This policy statement falls short of a *presumption* in favour of renewables development, but it is a strong enough revision of the 'case-by-case' approach to suggest that *West Coast Wind Farm* (discussed above, pp. 700–2) could now be decided differently, in all probability in favour of the developer. As we indicated above, this introduction of a clear requirement to give significant weight to the wider economic and environmental benefits of renewable energy was driven by legal obligations (such as the Kyoto Protocol), rather than vice versa. This differs from the usual portrayal of policy as the precursor to legal change.

[39] Section 38 Planning and Compensation Act 2004. See further p. 515. See interpretation of these provisions by Jeremy Pike, 'PPS1 and the Government's New Planning Policy Documents' (2005) 7 *Environmental Law Review* 273.

PPS 22 is framed according to the planning reforms brought about by the Planning and Compensation Act 2004. As we explained in Chapter 13 (pp. 522–9), the 2004 Act introduces a system of integrated spatial planning, based upon conformity between regional spatial strategies (compiled initially by the Secretary of State, and by regional planning boards thereafter) and local development documents which are the responsibility of local planning authorities. The general idea is that these plans take into consideration spatial issues, including but not restricted to land use, and encompass policies on transport, energy and waste. PPS 22 states that these regional and local plans should incorporate policies in order to promote renewable energy development and not to restrict them. Several novel approaches are used to achieve this. First, the specific targets for renewable energy, set out in the government's Energy White Paper (see pp. 705–8), are to be indicated in regional spatial strategies. At the local level, development documents must conform to these targets, for example by disaggregating regional targets into subregional targets and showing how local planning policies might contribute to reaching these. Local authorities may also include in their plans policies that require a certain percentage of energy to be used in new developments to come from on-site renewable sources. Note also the policy relating to new renewable energy developments in areas of international importance for landscape and nature conservation and wildlife. This basically provides a statement of law on development in protected sites, and requires that an 'appropriate assessment' of the effects of the development is conducted, in line with the requirements of the EC Birds and Habitats Directives (see Chapter 15, pp. 649–55). We discuss some of the consequences which flow from this form of assessment in the context of the proposed wind farm on the Isle of Lewis (below, pp. 735–42). In the case of nationally designated sites, a balancing exercise must be carried out in order to ensure that any significant adverse effects on the qualities for which the area has been designated are clearly outweighed by the environmental, social and economic benefits of the renewable energy project.

### ODPM, PPS 22, *Renewable Energy* (ODPM, 2004), pp. 6–11 (emphasis added)

The Government's Objectives

…

Increased development of renewable energy resources is vital to facilitating the delivery of the Government's commitments on both climate change and renewable energy. Positive planning which facilitates renewable energy developments can contribute to all four elements of the Government's sustainable development strategy:

- social progress which recognises the needs of everyone – by contributing to the nation's energy needs, ensuring all homes are adequately and affordably heated; and providing new sources of energy in remote areas;

- effective protection of the environment – by reductions in emissions of greenhouse gases and thereby reducing the potential for the environment to be affected by climate change;
- prudent use of natural resources – by reducing the nation's reliance on everdiminishing supplies of fossil fuels; and,
- maintenance of high and stable levels of economic growth and employment – through the creation of jobs directly related to renewable energy developments, but also in the development of new technologies. In rural areas, renewable energy projects have the potential to play an increasingly important role in the diversification of rural economies.

### National Planning Policies

### Key Principles
1. Regional planning bodies and local planning authorities should adhere to the following key principles in their approach to planning for renewable energy:

(i)  Renewable energy developments should be capable of being accommodated throughout England in locations where the technology is viable and environmental, economic, and social impacts can be addressed satisfactorily.

(ii) Regional spatial strategies and local development documents should contain policies designed to promote and encourage, rather than restrict, the development of renewable energy resources. Regional planning bodies and local planning authorities should recognise the full range of renewable energy sources, their differing characteristics, locational requirements and the potential for exploiting them subject to appropriate environmental safeguards.

(iii)  At the local level, planning authorities should set out the criteria that will be applied in assessing applications for planning permission for renewable energy projects. Planning policies that rule out or place constraints on the development of all, or specific types of, renewable energy technologies should not be included in regional spatial strategies or local development documents without sufficient reasoned justification. The Government may intervene in the plan making process where it considers that the constraints being proposed by local authorities are too great or have been poorly justified.

(iv)  *The wider environmental and economic benefits of all proposals for renewable energy projects, whatever their scale, are material considerations that should be given significant weight in determining whether proposals should be granted planning permission.* [Our emphasis]

(v) Regional planning bodies and local planning authorities should not make assumptions about the technical and commercial feasibility of renewable energy projects (e.g. identifying generalised locations for development based on mean wind speeds). Technological change can mean that sites currently excluded as locations for particular types of renewable energy development may in future be suitable.

(vi) Small-scale projects can provide a limited but valuable contribution to overall outputs of renewable energy and to meeting energy needs both locally and nationally. Planning authorities should not therefore reject planning applications simply because the level of output is small.

(vii) Local planning authorities, regional stakeholders and Local Strategic Partnerships should foster community involvement in renewable energy projects and seek to promote knowledge of and greater acceptance by the public of prospective renewable energy developments that are appropriately located. Developers of renewable energy projects should engage in active consultation and discussion with local communities at an early stage in the planning process, and before any planning application is formally submitted.

(viii) Development proposals should demonstrate any environmental, economic and social benefits as well as how any environmental and social impacts have been minimised through careful consideration of location, scale, design and other measures.

**Regional Targets**

2. The Energy White Paper indicated that the Government would be looking to work with regional and local bodies to deliver the Government's objectives, including establishing regional targets for renewable energy generation. The Regional Spatial Strategy should include the target for renewable energy capacity in the region, derived from assessments of the region's renewable energy resource potential, and taking into account the regional environmental, economic and social impacts (either positive or negative) that may result from exploitation of that resource potential.

...

**Locational Considerations**

*International Designated Sites*

9. Planning permission for renewable energy developments likely to have an adverse effect on a site of international importance for nature and heritage conservation (Special Protection Areas, Special Areas of Conservation, RAMSAR Sites and World Heritage Sites) should only be granted once an assessment has shown that the integrity of the site would not be adversely affected.

10. If the renewable energy development would have an adverse effect on the integrity of an internationally designated nature conservation site, planning permission should only be granted where there is no alternative solution and there are imperative reasons of overriding public interest, including those of a social or economic nature.[40]

*National Designations*

11. In sites with nationally recognised designations (Sites of Special Scientific Interest, National Nature Reserves, National Parks, Areas of Outstanding Natural Beauty, Heritage

---

[40] The Conservation (Natural Habitats &c) Regulations 1994 set out the legal requirements to be met in respect of European nature conservation sites and protected species where it is intended to grant planning permission for a project. Further guidance is currently provided in PPS9. See also ODPM Circular 01/2005, *Biodiversity and Geological Conservation – Statutory Obligations and their Impact Within the Planning System*, which provides administrative guidance on the legislative framework at both international and national levels for the protection of sites and species.

Coasts, Scheduled Monuments, Conservation Areas, Listed Buildings, Registered Historic Battlefields and Registered Parks and Gardens) planning permission for renewable energy projects should only be granted where it can be demonstrated that the objectives of designation of the area will not be compromised by the development, and any significant adverse effects on the qualities for which the area has been designated are clearly outweighed by the environmental, social and economic benefits.

12. Regional planning bodies and local planning authorities should set out in regional spatial strategies and local development documents the criteria based policies which set out the circumstances in which particular types and sizes of renewable energy developments will be acceptable in nationally designated areas. Care should be taken to identify the scale of renewable energy developments that may be acceptable in particular areas. Small-scale developments should be permitted within areas such as National Parks, Areas of Outstanding Natural Beauty and Heritage Coasts provided that there is no significant environmental detriment to the area concerned.

These policy statements demonstrate the strength of the government's commitment to renewable energy as a means of reaching its targets under the Kyoto Protocol, but they have not won universal approval. As Toke and Strachan put it, the statements underline how 'the government has adopted a "top-down" approach to problem solving ... seeking to gain adherence to its policy by issuing instructions from the centre rather than encouraging activism in support of wind power at the local level'.[41] A particularly terse submission from the Countryside Agency on the draft PPS 22 pointed out the narrow conception of 'the environment', which underlies the policy statement: 'the protection of the environment is not restricted solely to the reduction of greenhouse gases. It also includes the protection of fine landscapes.'[42] To this end, the Agency recommended a policy presumption *against* commercial wind energy developments in designated areas, on the ground that 'major development[s]' such as these are incompatible with the objectives of designation for nature conservation. In contrast, others suggest that the policy could go further to facilitate small-scale wind farm schemes, for example by relaxing the requirement to carry out an environmental impact assessment in these cases.[43] In any event, it is to be expected that the policy of according greater weight to the wider environmental and economic benefits of renewable energy projects, coupled with the incorporation of regional targets in local development plans, will reduce the scope for local authorities to refuse planning permission for onshore wind

[41] Toke and Strachan, 'Ecological Modernisation and Wind Power in the UK', p. 161.
[42] Countryside Agency, *Draft Planning Policy Statement 22: Renewable Energy*, available at www.countryside.gov.uk/Images/PPS22Response_tcm2–16754.pdf.
[43] Schedule 2 of the Town and Country Planning (Environmental Impact Assessment) (England and Wales) Regulations 1999 (SI 1999 No. 293) requires assessment of developments of more than two turbines or whose hub height exceeds 15m, whereas Circular 2/99 states that an environmental impact assessment is only likely to be required for commercial developments of five or more turbines.

farms solely on the basis of local opposition.[44] However, since it is most unlikely that local resistance will be abated entirely, other policy strategies have been advanced, as we discuss below.

### (b) Overcoming local resistance

We have explained that a considerable hurdle to the renewable energy sector has been securing planning permission at the local level,[45] or local opposition, frequently cast as 'nimbyism'. Returning to the pervasive idea of a necessary correlation between democratic and broad-based participation in decision making and environmental protection (see especially Chapter 13, pp. 530–42), we have seen in law and policy the expression of Habermasian deliberative theory about the need for *moral reasoning and emotive–aesthetic reasoning* to inform decision making – to permeate apparently objective and instrumental or technicist reasoning.[46] In Chapter 13, we traced the influence of such ideas in planning, the effect of which has been enhanced and extended opportunities for public participation in this area, creating at the very least the conditions for more collaborative decision making about land use (on collaborative planning, see pp. 531–5). We have understood such developments to be a welcome reaction to the long-standing priority given to expert opinion ('rationalism') over local, community and lay knowledge ('populism'). As one aspect of this, we presented the case for the extension of rights of appeal to local protesters in planning cases (Chapter 13, pp. 519–21). Such developments seem particularly justified in cases in which local communities seek to challenge the *private* development of *public* or common land (school playing fields, beaches, greens) for economic gain, even if the effects on the environment or human health are uncertain, as is still the case with telecommunication masts (see Chapter 13, pp. 542–5). But one effect of strengthening the role of local communities in the planning system is that the renewables programme may be stalled, by prioritising local interests over a broader public and environmental interest in generating energy from renewable sources. This is borne out by statistics on approval rates for planning applications for wind farm developments: since 1998 only a quarter of wind farm proposals in England have been accepted by local authorities. In contrast, a high proportion of the applications taken to appeal are approved by the Secretary of State, bringing the *overall* acceptance rate to 60 per cent.[47] In Scotland, the success

---

[44] Note, however, that in Scotland the number of local authorities refusing development consent is increasing, even with more permissive policy guidance in place (Ben McGuire, Scottish Executive, pers. comm., 14 December 2005).

[45] Ministry of Defence (MoD) objections (on the grounds that wind farms interfere with radar) have also been significant. The MoD has now revised its rules on the proximity of wind farms to its radar stations, opening up many more sites for this sort of development.

[46] See ODPM, PPS1, *Creating Sustainable Communities* (2004) (passage included in Ch. 13, pp. 535–6) and ss. 6 and 18 Planning and Compensation Act 2004 which require the production of statements of community involvement – see further Ch. 13, pp. 536–8.

rate of planning applications is approximately two-thirds in the first instance, a difference attributed to stronger support for renewable development projects in planning guidance, and lower population densities.[48] One difficulty is that because the renewables market is potentially so lucrative and is currently being shaped by a small number of private consortia making multiple applications to develop land and offshore sites for wind farms (at the end of 2004, just four companies owned over 70 per cent of UK wind power capacity[49]), the line between public (environmental) and private interests involved in this form of development has become blurred. The inevitable consequence of developers being viewed as 'outsiders who parachute into localities to take resources while offering little in return'[50] is local political controversy over the location and size of wind farms. In such cases, local groups consider themselves to be the passive recipients of technologies (even renewable technologies), rather than actively involved citizens, collaboratively planning their own local and sustainable environments and adjusting their energy consumption accordingly – the original, 'dark green' dream of small-scale renewable energy schemes.[51] The loss of this ideal presents a surprisingly similar dynamic to that described by Mark Sagoff in relation to biotechnology in agriculture.[52]

In the context of seeking to secure development consent for wind energy projects, we therefore see that one consequence of giving a stronger voice to local and collective concerns is more effective challenges to wind farm proposals. In more general terms, the whole structure of decision making over land use grants a great deal of discretion to local government, accountable and responsive to an increasingly well-organised local electorate, but with the final decision resting with the Secretary of State in the case of an appeal against the refusal of planning permission by a developer, or the 'call-in' of an application.[53] This state of affairs invariably leads to legal disputes. Conferring rights of appeal upon third parties would further allow neighbours and interested groups to challenge planning permission granted to such projects (see Chapter 13, pp. 519–21). Interestingly, just at the point at which government policy is more clearly in support of renewable energy projects, the policy of strengthening local communities' involvement in planning decisions creates the conditions for a serious conflict.

The nature of this conflict has been the subject of various interpretations. David Toke, for example, describes the local inhibition on renewable energy development as having more general and destabilising political effects.

---

[47] Toke, 'Will the Government Catch the Wind?', p. 48.

[48] RCEP, *Environmental Planning*, para. 8.71. The Commission recommends the need for similarly supportive policy guidance in England.

[49] Toke and Strachan, 'Ecological Modernisation and Wind Power in the UK', p. 160.

[50] Toke, 'Will the Government Catch the Wind?', p. 48.

[51] Toke and Strachan, 'Ecological Modernisation and Wind Power in the UK', p. 159.

[52] Mark Sagoff, 'Biotechnology and Agriculture: The Common Wisdom and its Critics' (2001) 9 *Indiana Journal of Global Legal Studies* 13. See Ch. 2, pp. 74–6.

[53] See 'Elements of the planning system', Ch. 13, pp. 510–22.

## David Toke, 'Will the Government Catch the Wind?' (2005)
*Political Quarterly* 48, p. 50

The determination of the government to continue a planning strategy that is broadly favourable towards onshore wind power is being tested by the continuing onslaught of anti-windfarm campaigns. Anti-windfarm campaigners hope they can turn around the government's policy much in the same way as the Conservative government bowed to pressure for planning restrictions on wind power in 1994. Early in 1994, a campaign against a proposed windfarm at Hebden Bridge in Yorkshire, in so-called Bronte country, gained the support of many writers and artists. This led to a governmental promise to curb the number of windfarms.

...

Anti-windfarm campaigners are hoping to depict windfarms, once again, as a threat to the national heritage.

This description of events suggests a concerted and successful campaign against a particular wind farm development in an attempt to destabilise the government's entire policy of supporting renewable energy developments. This is reminiscent of the altering of transport policy in the wake of high-profile 'anti-roads' campaigns (for example Twyford Down, Newbury) in the early 1990s. However, an interesting gap has been identified between widespread *public* support for wind farms and campaigns against *individual* sites by local residents and amenity groups.[54] In many respects, this more subtle analysis of nimbyism is a modern example of Mark Sagoff's classic theory of environmental action by individuals, who may act as both citizens and as consumers: 'As a *citizen*, I am concerned with the public interest, rather than my own interest; with the good of the community rather than simply the well-being of my family ... In my role as a *consumer* ... I concern myself with personal or self-regarding wants and interests; I pursue the goals I have as an individual.'[55] A good example of the potential for conflict between the roles of citizen and consumer arose from Strachan and Lal's research on local protests against wind farms in Scotland. The following quote was made by the Chairman of the Buchan Wind Farm Action Group about the proposed siting of a wind farm consisting of forty-two wind turbines on farmland near Peterhead: 'We're not against wind farms in principle, we simply believe that in this case the location is wrong ... The plans indicate some of the turbines will be within a few hundred metres of people's homes and that is not acceptable ... the visual impact of the structures will ruin (the residents') lives' (*Aberdeen Press and Journal*, 2001).[56]

---

[54] Derek Bell, Tim Gray and Claire Haggett, 'The "Social Gap" in Wind Farm Siting Decisions: Explanations and Policy Responses' (2005) 14 *Environmental Politics* 460.

[55] Mark Sagoff, *The Economy of the Earth: Philosophy, Law and the Environment* (Cambridge University Press, 1988), p. 8.    [56] Strachan and Lal, 'Wind Energy Policy', p. 561.

In the light of cases such as this, one should perhaps be careful about suggesting general disapproval of 'consumer' objections to wind farm development. Objections might well be based on more complex concerns than self-interest. Advancing this approach in an influential article, Derek Bell, Tim Gray and Clare Haggett recommend specific strategies for policy makers to adopt, in an attempt to bridge the gap between the consumer–citizen roles that individuals play. They first offer a theoretical framework for their findings.

### Derek Bell, Tim Gray and Claire Haggett, 'The "Social Gap" in Wind Farm Siting Decisions: Explanations and Policy Responses' (2005) 14 *Environmental Politics* 460, pp. 460–74

If approximately 80% of the public support wind energy, why is only a quarter of contracted wind power capacity actually commissioned? One common answer is that this is an example of the 'not in my backyard' (Nimby) syndrome: yes, wind power is a good idea as long as it is not in my backyard. On this account, there is a gap between an attitude motivated by concern for the 'common good' and behaviour motivated by 'self-interest'. As a result of this gap, people who favour wind power in general oppose particular developments proposed for their area. However, the Nimby concept has rightly been criticised on the grounds that it fails to reflect the complexity of human motives and their interaction with social and political institutions ... we consider the role of politics and policy in generating – and potentially bridging – the gap between public support for wind energy and successfully building wind energy capacity.

...

**Theoretical framework: Two Gaps and Three Explanations**

We begin by distinguishing two gaps, which we will call a social gap and an individual gap. The social gap is the gap between the *high* public support for wind energy expressed in opinion surveys and the *low* success rate achieved in planning applications for wind power developments. The individual gap is the gap that exists when an individual person has a *positive* attitude to wind power in general but *actively opposes* a particular wind power development. Our primary interest is in the social gap – as we know it exists and that it needs to be bridged if the potential contribution of wind power is to be realised. Our interest in the individual gap is derivative – if the individual gap causes the social gap, we need to understand its nature and how it might be bridged.

*The 'Democratic Deficit' Explanation*

The first explanation regards the social gap as the product of a 'democratic deficit'. The claim is that while opinion polls show that a majority of people are in favour of wind power, particular wind power development decisions are controlled by the minority who oppose wind power. The outcome of the permitting process does not reflect the will of the majority. The 'democratic deficit' explanation does not depend on any individual 'suffering' from an individual gap. The key question for the 'democratic deficit' explanation is why opponents of wind power are able to dominate the permitting process.

Wolsink[57] suggests that people generally do not come forward with positive responses to planners' agendas. In part, this may be a product of the design of the planning process whereby initial decisions are made by developers, announced to the public and then defended against public criticism. The role of the public on this 'decide-announce-defend' model of decision making is to provide criticism rather than support. As Kahn puts it, 'siting reviews are open forums where criticism is not only accommodated, it is solicited'.[58]

...

*The 'Qualified Support' Explanation*

The second explanation of the social gap is that the failure of particular wind developments reflects a general principle of qualified support for wind energy. Most of the people who support wind energy do not support it without qualification. They believe that wind energy is a good idea but they also believe that there are general limits and controls that should be placed on its development. Typically these might include qualifications regarding the impact of developments on landscape, the environment, animals (e.g. birds, fish) and humans. If there are many people who adopt a qualified general principle of support for wind energy, they may be responsible (or partly responsible) for the social gap. Many public opinion surveys merely ask if people support wind energy in general. They do not give respondents the opportunity to enter qualifications. People who are qualified supporters of wind energy may appear to be making an exception to their general principle in a particular case that has a direct effect on them when in fact they are following their general principle (of qualified support) in that particular case.

*The 'Self Interest' Explanation*

The third explanation of the social gap is that people support wind energy in general but actively oppose any developments in their own area for self-interested reasons ... The Nimby explanation is both very popular and very widely criticised. For our purposes, the very important point is that the Nimby concept properly understood offers a very specific account of the social gap as the product of a particular kind of collective action problem. In a multi-person prisoner's dilemma it is collectively rational for the public good (wind energy) to be produced but it is individually rational for each individual to 'free ride' on the contributions of others (not have a wind farm in their area). The individual's contribution to the public good (a few megawatts of wind energy from the local wind farm) is negligible, while the cost of making that contribution may be considerable (e.g. lower utility resulting from their favourite walk being 'spoiled'). Every individual makes the same individual calculation and chooses to 'free-ride' (not have a wind farm in their area). Therefore, the public good is not provided (wind developments fail).

The authors then match these various explanations for the experience of a social gap in support for wind farms with possible policy responses.

---

[57] Maarten Wolsink, 'Wind Power and the NIMBY-Myth: Institutional Capacity and the Limited Significance of Public Support' (2000) 21 *Renewable Energy* 49, p. 58.

[58] Robert Kahn, 'Siting Struggles: The Unique Challenge of Permitting Renewable Energy Power Plants' (2000) 13 *Electricity Journal* 21, p. 26.

*The Significance for Policy of a Democratic Deficit*

...

The obvious solution is to change the decision-making process. The most straightforward way of doing that might be to require a direct public vote on wind farm developments. However the problem of specifying the relevant constituency will arise again. Moreover, it is not clear that a direct public vote would solve the problem. It is true that voting is likely to be less demanding than writing a letter to your local authority, so wind energy supporters might be more likely to become active participants in the decision-making process. It is also likely that a voting procedure would not solicit opposition in the same way as the 'decide-announce-defend' model inherent in the current planning process. However, it is not clear that voting would actually overcome the problem of apathy or inactivity among supporters ...

...

An alternative to a public vote that tries to overcome the democratic deficit by giving power to the people might be a top-down decision based on an independent survey of a representative sample of the demos. In some respects, this may be a better reflection of people's attitudes than a public vote. However it is an expensive and undemocratic option. A public opinion survey may overcome one democratic deficit that allows minority opposition to block developments, only to create another by explicitly excluding anyone not included in the sample survey from the decision-making process. A 'middle way' would retain the planning process as it is but support independent public surveys which could be used by planning authorities to inform and justify their decisions. In this way, survey support for a development might help to offset the bias toward opposition that is built into the existing planning system.

One final option is to change the underlying character of the planning process from confrontation to collaboration. A collaborative approach is grounded in the claim that 'deliberative' rather than 'technical' rationality should be the basis for environmental decision making. Collaborative planning shifts the emphasis from competitive interest bargaining to consensus building; it recognises and includes all stakeholders; and seeks to identify diverse interests and the mechanisms of power that may work to subordinate some of them. The aim is public participation rather than public consultation; it does not aim to 'educate' but to create opportunities for discussion. A collaborative process might overcome the democratic deficit by encouraging (some of) the 'silent majority' to participate in decision making.

...

*The Significance for Policy of Qualified Support*
The second explanation of the social gap is that the failure of particular wind developments reflects a general principle of qualified support for wind energy. There are two basic kinds of responses to this 'problem'. First, we might try to change people's minds so that their support becomes unqualified or, at least, the qualifications on their support are reduced or modified. Second, we might change key features of (particular) wind energy developments so that they meet the criteria for support.

The authors go on to discuss various policy strategies for improving knowledge in both of these cases. They acknowledge that 'any information provided by the developers or "independent" experts will be evaluated and understood in the context of each individual's existing "web of beliefs"', influenced by their education, experience, local knowledge and tacit or 'practical knowledge'.[59]

The implications for policy of Bell, Grey and Haggett's third explanation for the social gap – self-interest – are particularly important in terms of analysing the use of financial contributions as compensation for the effects of development, for example the change of a valued landscape. But first they consider a more authoritarian, but apparently discredited, 'solution'.

### The Significance for Policy of Self-interest

The third explanation of the social gap is that people support wind energy in general but actively oppose any developments in their own area for self-interested reasons. There are three important ways of responding to Nimbyism. The classic response to collective action problems of this kind is to propose an authoritarian solution. A good example of this kind of response is the so-called 'Nimby Bill' in the Netherlands:

> [The Nimby Bill] gives the national and provincial government the authority to impose concrete land uses to be taken up by the municipality in its zoning scheme. The instrument was intended to force decisions on locations for waste facilities and manure processing installations, or other unpopular facilities, like asylum seekers' centres, or wind farms.[60]

However, Bruekers and Wolsink note that '[A] first and only attempt to ever apply the Nimby instrument failed [in 2000]. Authoritarian "solutions" may be more likely to promote opposition than overcome it. Attempting to exclude people from the decision-making process is likely to alienate them and increase levels of opposition.'

...

The second response is to appeal to people's 'better nature' or to try to promote a more effective sense of 'environmental citizenship'.[61] In our opinion, the promotion of environmental citizenship is an essential part of a successful environmental policy but it is far from clear how environmental citizenship can be promoted effectively. In the context of wind energy developments, it is difficult to see how Nimbys are likely to be converted by any kind of targeted education programme. The promotion of environmental citizenship seems much more likely to be dependent upon cultural changes that will occur only over long periods of time and through the development of the right kinds of 'green' social, cultural and (ultimately) physical infrastructure.

The third response to Nimbyism takes most seriously the Nimby's motives. If Nimbys are motivated by self-interest, the best response might be to find ways of increasing the personal benefits that they will receive from a wind energy development. Two versions of this approach might be distinguished. The first version offers financial compensation to

---

[59] Bell *et al.*, 'The "Social Gap"', at p. 469.

[60] Sylvia Breukers and Maarten Wolsink, 'Institutional Capacity in Policy Processes for Wind Energy in the Netherlands', paper presented at European Consortium for Political Research General Conference, Marburg, September 2003.

[61] Andrew Dobson, *Citizenship and the Environment* (Oxford University Press, 2003).

offset the costs of the development to the Nimby. This strategy might provide a way of overcoming Nimby opposition or 'co-opting nascent Nimby opposition'.[62] Moreover, even principled opponents of particular wind developments might be 'co-opted' by sufficient financial incentives. Their opposition to a development may not be grounded in self-interest but they might be tempted *not* to oppose the same development if they stand to gain financially from it.

...

The second 'personal benefits' approach allows the Nimby to buy shares in a community- (or privately) owned wind energy development project so that they have a financial stake in its success. Community-owned wind farms are widely advocated because of the success of the Danish model [including cooperative shareholding and the existence of local networks of voluntary activists and professional agents of the wind industry].[63] However, it may be important to distinguish the economic from the social and political effects of community ownership. The benefits of community ownership may have as much to do with local involvement in the development process as they do with the potential profits of ownership. For example, reduced opposition to community wind farms might be due more to local control over the siting process – including local accommodation to the concerns of qualified supporters of wind energy and the personal concerns of Nimbys – than to the financial incentives offered by share ownership. If it is control rather than money that reduces opposition to community wind farms, private developers should not expect to overcome local opposition by selling (or giving) shares in wind farms to local people but they might reduce opposition by involving local people in the planning, development and management of wind farms.

The authors seem to suggest that policy makers reach into the psyches of those resisting this form of development, particularly to discover whether financial incentives might be effective in advancing particular wind energy projects – 'Can qualified supporters of wind energy be "bought" at an "affordable price"? Is it money that matters to opponents of wind energy or is it control over the character of developments?'[64] Certainly wind farm developers routinely make offers of payments to the local communities at the planning stage, and even afterwards, as illustrated in the case of the Lewis wind farm development, discussed below (pp. 735–42). Perhaps more controversial are compensation packages which aim to overcome resistance to a development on conservation grounds by offering to create 'new' habitats or restock damaged areas. We discuss the law and policy relating to this issue in Chapter 16 (pp. 677–80).

It has also been suggested that participatory 'experiments' such as citizens' juries or panels might perform an educational role, thus mutually reinforcing the key policy objectives of supporting renewables and strengthening community involvement in planning decisions.

---

[62] Kahn, 'Siting Struggles', p. 28.
[63] David Toke and David Elliot, 'A Fresh Start for UK Wind Power?' (2000) *International Journal of Ambient Energy* 21, pp. 67–76.    [64] Bell *et al.*, 'The "Social Gap"', at p. 474.

### House of Lords Environmental Audit Committee, *A Sustainable Energy Strategy?*

59. More generally, the ambivalence displayed towards renewable energy, particularly wind farms, even by environmental groups, exemplifies the need for the government to do much more to raise awareness and prompt real debate among the members of the public. We have ourselves consistently highlighted this issue in previous reports. Public attitudes define the limits of what is politically possible. The success of European nations, such as Denmark, Germany and Switzerland, in achieving greater levels of sustainability, whether it is in waste minimisation, recycling, energy efficiency or the promotion of renewables, reflects not only effective policy making and implementation but also the higher priority which ordinary members of the public accord to environmental objectives. Indeed, the PIU recognised the importance of such considerations in their Energy Review, and recognised that the Government should involve the wider public in energy debate – perhaps through novel approaches such as the use of Citizen's Panels. We see little evidence of this occurring. The Government, together with local authorities, needs to launch a sustained and hard-hitting campaign to raise the level of public awareness and understanding of these issues.

A more radical option is the common ownership of renewable energy projects. This approach extends beyond policies of inclusion and educational strategies in decision making, seeking instead local acceptance of renewable forms of energy through 'political sustainability'. Indeed, returning to Strachan and Lal's typology for the development of renewable sources of energy,[65] this might be considered to constitute a fourth strand of thinking.

### Toke, 'Will the Government Catch the Wind?', p. 48

In Denmark and Germany the wind industry readily acknowledges how widespread farmer ownership of wind power, cooperative shareholding, and the existence of local networks of voluntary activists and professional agents of the wind industry have generated a long term political sustainability for wind power programmes. If local farmers and local people are the main movers and owners of windfarms then they will usually be more effective in mobilising local opinion in favour of planning applications for windfarms. By contrast, in the UK very little wind power capacity is locally owned. The large majority of the dominant corporate wind power developers seem to have taken the view that community-orientated planning strategies are expensive in the short term, and that a relatively high planning permission rejection rate can be absorbed in the income stream by the successful projects.

---

[65] Strachan and Lal, 'Wind Power Policy', describe the first strand of thinking as being concerned with scientific and technological issues, the second with the policies and strategies supporting sustainable energy production, and the third with social impacts of renewables development, including local public opposition to wind farms.

A similar approach, begun in the 1970s in the United States and now gaining in favour, involves changing the siting of wind farms from sensitive rural areas to urban (and suburban) locations as a way of giving responsibility for small-scale energy production and conservation to individuals and communities. In addition to energy efficiency gains (producing energy near to where it will be used means less energy is lost during the often long journey from its source), this relocation of sources of renewable energy is part of a powerful political agenda built upon the ideal of local self-sufficiency – decentralised, or 'distributed', power and individual responsibility for energy use and conservation. The basic idea is that 'if every apartment building, every suburban home, had a wind generator on its roof, every tenant, every homeowner, would have a personal stake in renewable energy',[66] in marked contrast to wind farms being owned by a few big companies and their shareholders.

Supporting widespread community or cooperative shareholding in wind farms would clearly work against the government's current 'technology-push' support programme for 'big business', aimed at securing considerable economic advantages for British companies. It would also considerably alter the structure of the renewables market in favour of small producers and hence the physical scale of wind farms, with an attendant need to bring the law on the environmental assessment of such developments into line with current policy. At present, the EIA Regulations 1999[67] require an environmental impact assessment for developments of two or more turbines, or where the hub height exceeds 15 metres and where the project is likely to have a significant effect on the environment, whereas current *policy* guidance states that assessment is only likely to be required for commercial developments of five turbines or more.[68] In reviewing this discrepancy, Marcus Beddoe and Andrew Chamberlain[69] argue that setting the threshold for assessment in this way would encourage the development of more small-scale wind energy schemes, without the costs of preparing an environmental statement, which can often render the project financially unviable. They suggest a procedural safeguard that such small-scale projects should only be excluded from the assessment process if they meet predefined criteria such as on noise levels at residential properties and the avoidance of sites in designated landscape areas.

Although some financial incentives are now available with some interesting results (such as linking renewable energy schemes with energy efficiency programmes),[70] a community-led approach is not widespread. Rather, one sees

---

[66] Josh Weil, 'A New Spin on Wind' (2005) *Orion* (Nov./Dec.) 60. This idea has particular relevance in developing countries, as described by Eric Hoffner of Green Empowerment, a charity which provides renewable energy and water systems (see (2005) *Orion* (Nov./Dec.) 78).     [67] SI 1999 No. 293.

[68] Circular 2/99 *Environmental Impact Assessment* (Department of the Environment, Transport and the Regions (DETR), 1999), para. A15. On thresholds for EIA, see Ch. 14, pp. 000.

[69] Marcus Beddoe and Andrew Chamberlain, 'Avoiding Confrontation – Securing Planning Permission for On-Shore Wind Energy Developments in England: Comments from a Wind Energy Developer' (2003) 18 *Planning Practice and Research* 3, p. 15.

[70] See Matt Ross, 'Power to the People' (2002) *Regeneration and Renewal* 16, on community-led energy projects.

a marked policy towards offshore locations, a geographical shift which renders landscape issues less of a concern (though not nugatory) for 'local' residents, as we discuss further below.

## 3 Offshore wind farm development

In 2001 the government announced its intention to expand its interest in wind power to offshore wind farm developments, ostensibly in an attempt to meet its renewables obligations, but also possibly because of a decline in the United Kingdom's indigenous supplies of oil, gas and coal, and nuclear fuels.[71] A first 'round'[72] of site leases was awarded by the Crown Estate Commissioners[73] in 2001, amounting to around 500 turbines around the country (including North Hoyle, Scrobie Sands and the Kentish Flats) producing 1 per cent of the United Kingdom's electricity supply. A second round of leases ('Wind R 2') has been approved for fifteen offshore sites (three outside territorial waters) with the aim of producing a further 7 per cent of the country's electricity supply. This round has been designed to 'provide a framework for the rapid and successful expansion'[74] of the wind power industry, prompting the question whether granting site leases in this manner pre-empts the granting of development consent (discussed below, pp. 721–3). In general there are fewer obstacles to the development of offshore farms, both in terms of local opposition, as mentioned above, and because of legal controls which obviate the need for a great degree of local planning authority involvement (the main control for offshore projects within territorial waters being a consent from the Secretary of State for Trade and Industry under s. 36 of the Electricity Act 1989[75]). The result is possibly 'a less torrid passage through the planning consultation process compared to many onshore projects'.[76] In addition, with most onshore sites now earmarked for development, it was considered necessary for the expansion of the wind power industry (the 'technology-push' described above) to move offshore, and, increasingly, beyond the (twelve-mile) limit of territorial waters. This last category of development

---

[71] See Sarah Hills, Joseph Griffiths and Clare Costello, 'The UK Energy Act 2004 – Changes Blowing in the Wind' (2004) 5 *International Energy Law and Taxation Review* 124, p. 125. On declining fossil fuel and nuclear fuel supplies, they note that one wind farm is planned on the remains of the disused North Sea platform in the Moray Firth.

[72] Akin to the rounds or tranches of exploration licences granted to the petroleum industry.

[73] For detailed discussion of the role and suitability of the Crown Estate Commissioners, see Plant, 'Offshore Wind Energy Development'.

[74] Department of Trade and Industry (DTI) General Question and Answer Briefing note, 'Offshore Windfarms Round 2', www.dti.gov.uk/energy/renewables/technologies/offshore-wind.shtml (note this website is no longer available).

[75] Note also a range of other consents required: a licence from the Department for Environment, Food and Rural Affairs (DEFRA) under s. 5 of the Food and Environmental Protection Act 1985 for the placing of structures on the sea bed and for the protection of the marine environment; planning permission under s. 57 Town and Country Planning Act 1990 may also be needed if cables and National Grid connections are to be placed above the mean low water mark; and consent under s. 34 Coast Protection Act 1949.

[76] Toke, 'Will the Government Catch the Wind?', pp. 49–50.

carries certain advantages, including that they can be built on a larger scale and are less likely to have a negative impact on inland and coastal marine life and water-based recreational activities.[77]

This is not to say that offshore projects are without difficulties: the construction costs are considerably higher than for more accessible onshore sites, the harsher environment requires more stringent requirements in the design of the turbines,[78] and developers must accommodate wide-ranging national and international marine interests such as the exercise of rights of navigation and fishing.[79] There is also growing concern about the effects of offshore wind farms on wildlife in the vicinity, particularly birds, as acknowledged in the following guidance to developers about the compatibility of wind farm development and conservation interests.

### DEFRA, *Nature Conservation Guidance on Offshore Windfarm Development: A Guidance Note on the Implications of the EC Wild Birds and Habitats Directives for Developers Undertaking Offshore Windfarm Development* (DEFRA, 2005), pp. 14–16

A range of birds could potentially be affected by offshore windfarms. This includes sea birds which feed and roost in offshore areas, such as divers, grebes, gannets, seaducks, auks, gulls and terns. It also includes a wider range of species that may move through the area of a windfarm, whether as part of local movements on a daily basis, or during national or international migration. Such species include the sea birds listed above, as well as other wildfowl, waders and migrant songbirds.

...

#### 2.2.1 The Types of Impacts
The potential impacts of offshore windfarms on birds can be divided into five categories: ...

- Habitat loss refers to the direct loss of seabed resulting from the placement of the turbine foundations and any scour protection, along with any associated losses or changes to benthos due to scour or smothering.
- Loss of food resources (i.e. fish stocks or invertebrates) can result from damage, disturbance, or scouring of the sites during the development's construction or maintenance phases.
- Displacement is used here to describe the potential for birds to avoid turbines, or the entire area of a windfarm, due to their reluctance to feed adjacent to large structures because of a perception of threat. This is likely to vary greatly depending on species, and perhaps also on issues such as the size and spacing of turbines and noise caused by the rotors and lighting. Displacement is likely to be increased by maintenance activities requiring the use of boats and helicopters.

---

[77] Hills, Griffiths and Costello, 'The UK Energy Act', p. 125.
[78] On these factors, see M. Challis, 'Offshore Wind – Planning for the New Era' (2001) 8 *International Energy Law and Taxation Review* 180.
[79] These interests are described in detail by Plant, 'Offshore Wind Energy Development', pp. 943–4.

- Barrier effects result from birds changing their flight lines in response to the perceived barrier presented by a row of turbines. This relates to regular local movements, for example between feeding and roosting areas, as well as migratory flight paths. The barrier effect could result in birds undertaking longer flights to avoid windfarms, thus resulting in increased energy expenditure and reduced time for other essential activities. If birds are prevented from reaching feeding grounds because of the barrier caused by the turbines, sterilisation of the feeding grounds could result.
- Collision mortality as a result of birds striking turbine towers, nacelles or rotors may be a significant issue where large numbers of birds make regular flights through the windfarm area, especially during conditions of poor visibility or when birds panic in response to disturbance.

The guidance also notes the likely impacts of offshore wind farm development on marine mammals, fish and shellfish, subtidal benthos (sea bed habitats), intertidal habitats, terrestrial and coastal habitats and on coastal sedimentary processes, and lists measures to be taken to mitigate or compensate for these impacts.[80]

## (a) The new licensing regime

Government policy to implement the targets set out in the Energy White Paper 2003 (see above, pp. 705–8) is now reflected in the Energy Act 2004, a large part of which is devoted to facilitating renewable energy developments – wave and tidal, as well as wind – in particular by providing a legal framework for such development beyond territorial waters.[81] The Act effectively fills in the 'legislative deficit' that has hitherto precluded renewable energy developments in the 200 nautical mile (NM) zone beyond territorial waters, deemed necessary in the light of the rapid (technological and geographic) expansion of the industry.[82] At the core of the 2004 Act are provisions which allow the Crown Estate to grant licences for wind farm development in specified statutory zones outside territorial waters, to be known as 'renewable energy zones', in much the same way as it currently leases sites within territorial waters.[83] It does so by extending the current licensing regime for offshore wind farms[84] within territorial waters (a consent required from the Secretary of State for the purposes of s. 36 of the Electricity Act 1989) to those planned in the renewable energy zones.[85] The problem of

---

[80] On mitigation and compensation of environmental effects, see Ch. 16, pp. 677–80. See also Royal Society for the Protection of Birds, *Windfarms and Birds* (2004).

[81] On the policy and legal history of the Energy Act 2004, see DTI, *Future Offshore: A Strategic Framework for the Offshore Wind Industry* (DTI, 2002). See comment by Glen Plant, 'Offshore Renewable Energy Development and the Energy Bill' [2004] JPL 868. See, as a precursor to this, Plant, 'Offshore Wind Energy Development'. A very complete account of the Act is to be found in Scott, 'Tilting at Offshore Windmills'.

[82] See Plant, 'Offshore Renewable Energy Development and the Energy Bill', p. 869.

[83] Section 84 Energy Act 2004.

[84] The position for onshore wind farms is discussed above, pp. 697–8.

[85] Section 93 Energy Act 2004.

decommissioning offshore renewables projects is tackled by requiring a (hopefully stringent) decommissioning programme to be approved in advance of the licence being granted.[86] The 2004 Act additionally provides legal protection for developers from those asserting navigation rights in the sea area around the proposed wind farm,[87] and seeks to secure the safety of installations by establishing safety zones[88] and civil aviation regulations. In summary, the Act provides a legal framework for the further expansion of the industry, and thus security for (large, invariably multinational) investors. A set of implementing regulations and guidance has yet to be adopted, for example concerning environmental assessment of offshore wind farm development in the renewable energy zones (discussed further below, pp. 723–9). This is the current position in England and Wales. Different procedures apply in Scotland and Northern Ireland, as we discuss in the context of the Robin Rigg and Isle of Lewis wind farms, below (pp. 730–42).

Karen Scott's wide-ranging and thoughtful critique of this new legislative framework focusses on the fact that it does not form part of a wider system of strategic planning for marine areas (to parallel the onset of spatial planning on land (discussed in Chapter 13, pp. 522–30)). Scott also makes several points relating to environmental assessment which we take up immediately below. Implicit in her analysis is the idea that the legislative framework was put in place quite hastily, most probably to accommodate (and further) the interests of the developing industry in offshore renewable energy.

### Karen Scott, 'Tilting at Offshore Windmills: Regulating Wind Farm Development Within the Renewable Energy Zone' (2006) 18 *Journal of Environmental Law* 89, pp. 117–18

Whilst the threats posed by climate change create a very real urgency in taking action to promote and foster the development of renewable energy sources, it is regrettable that the legislative framework facilitating offshore development has been adopted prior to the formulation of a marine conservation strategy based on ecosystem management, spatial planning and the creation of a coherent ecological network of protected areas … the 2004 Energy Act fails to impose a duty on the Secretary of State to expressly consider the environmental implications of a wind farm development, and although such obligations exist under other Acts and statutory instruments, there is growing consensus that these provisions not only inadequately protect the marine environment but also fail to meet many of the UK's international conservation commitments. Although the government commissioned a strategic environmental assessment of the three locations deemed suitable for offshore exploitation, this is no substitute for spatial planning. The UK SEA gave only cursory consideration to other potential users of the strategic areas and made no real attempt to assess the impact that other industries have on the environment within these regions, or to predict their cumulative impact in the event of

---

[86]  Sections 105–13 Energy Act 2004.
[87]  Section 99 Energy Act 2004. This provision renders unnecessary the 'second route' to authorisation for such developments, including obtaining Orders under s. 3 Transport and Works Act 1992.    [88] Section 95 Energy Act 2004.

offshore development. Moreover, whilst the UK SEA noted the existence of SPAs (special protection areas), SACs (special areas of conservation) and Ramsar Sites [see Chapter 15 on these
designations] within each of the three strategic areas, the government has acknowledged that
neither Directive 79/409/EEC nor 92/43/EEC has been fully implemented within UK waters.
Furthermore the House of Commons Marine Environment Report notes that there are a number
of species and habitats that may need to be protected within UK waters, but which do not fall
within the scope of either directive. Although this lacuna could be – and indeed should be –
remedied by the creation of a network of protected areas under the auspices of OSPAR and/or
the North Sea Conferences, both schemes are at a preliminary stage in their development, and
it is likely to be some years before such a network is established ... In conclusion, although
the 2004 Energy Act establishes a workable framework for the construction and operation of
wind farms within UK waters, it is disappointing that the UK government did not view the creation of an offshore renewable energy industry as an opportunity to develop and apply the
new marine conservation strategies which are in the process of being recommended by bodies
established by the government for this very purpose.

## (b) Invoking environmental assessment

The potential range and significance of impacts associated with offshore wind
farm development means that environmental assessment has a key role to play
in the licensing system and the prior identification of suitable areas for this type
of development. For example, the government's policy of expanding wind
energy to three offshore locations ('strategic areas') – the North West (Liverpool
Bay), the Greater Wash, and Thames Estuary – as set out in its consultation document *Future Offshore* (2002),[89] was made subject to a strategic environmental
assessment exercise, in advance of the EC's SEA Directive coming into force.[90]

### *Offshore Wind Energy Generation: Phase 1 Proposals and Environmental Report* (BMT Cordah Ltd, Environmental Management Consultants) for consideration by the Department of Trade and Industry (2003), pp. 1–24

**Non-technical summary**

**Description of the environmental situation**

...

Each Strategic Area is important in terms of its marine wildlife, particularly waterfowl,
seabirds, harbour porpoise, seals and commercial fish species spawning and/or nursery
areas. Large tracts of the coastline and inshore areas have been or are proposed to be
designated under the Habitats Directive for their intertidal areas (which in turn often support
large populations of birdlife), seal haul out locations, shallow subtidal sandbanks and
biogenic reefs ... Offshore areas of potential reef and shallow subtidal sandbank occur in all

---

[89] *Future Offshore: A Strategic Framework for the Offshore Wind Industry* (DTI, 2002).
[90] Directive 2001/42/EC on the assessment of the effects of certain plans and programmes
on the environment OJ 2001 L 197/30. See further Ch. 14, pp. 567–97.

three Strategic Areas, particularly in the Greater Wash. English Nature is deliberating, also, on potential sites for conservation designation within the 12nm limit of territorial waters. Similarly, coastal areas have also been designated, as Special Protection Areas under the Birds Directive, because of their bird interests and potential future offshore areas are currently being considered for designation as well. Cetaceans, sharks and rays are known to be, or believed to be, present in each of the Strategic Areas. Along the coast of each Strategic Area are a number of Special Protection Areas (Birds Directive).

Economically, each Strategic Area is significant because of the presence of large ports and the associated shipping, including fishing, activity. Commercial fisheries include several whitehead species as well as shellfish (molluscs and crustaceans). Fishing activities range from nearshore fishing for crab and lobster to large-scale offshore, commercial operations.

...

There are differences in seascape character and value between the three Areas. Liverpool Bay has the most diverse range of seascapes. The seascapes within each of the Greater Wash and Thames Estuary Areas are relatively uniform. In the Greater Wash they are predominantly rural, but lack sufficient 'character' elements to warrant landscape designations. Many of the seascapes in the Thames estuary are characterised by industrial and high-density settlement features and, also, 'insufficient character' elements warranting landscape designations. [The SEA Report then maps the different 'seascape sensitivity' of the areas.]

### Summary of potential significant impacts

The medium and significant risks of environmental impact on the various environmental factors have been tabulated [not included].

A risk based analysis has shown that the main concerns for offshore windfarm development are the potential effects on:

- sediment transport processes;
- conservation sites, biodiversity of habitats and species;
- collision risk, displacement, disturbance and barrier effects on birds;
- collision and subsequent loss of inventory from cargo vessels; and
- collision and loss of life from passenger ferries.

Positive impacts are:

- potential fisheries and biodiversity recovery areas should they offer refugia from other activities;
- job creation during construction and operational phases;
- contribution to reduction in greenhouse gases and other atmospheric emissions;
- improved balance of payments; and
- increased energy security.

In addition, a separate analysis of the seascape issues suggests that developments less than a certain distance from the coast (within 8 to 13 km) will probably have significant visual impact. The distance will vary according to the nature of the seascape in the range of 8 km to 13 km.

...

### Summary of potential cumulative impacts

The assessments of the potential risk of significant cumulative impact have been summarised and tabulated in [the main report] and the main points highlighted below:

There is a potential risk of cumulative impacts on:

- macro-scale effects on physical processes including sediment transport;
- seascape if development concentrates within medium or high areas of visual sensitivity;
- exclusion of marine animals due to noise disturbance from seismic and operational activities;
- specific bird species such as common scoters, red-throated divers and terns; and
- elasmobranchs remain unknown because of lack of data on how these receptors react to physical and environmental changes induced by windfarms.

These statements hold for all Strategic Areas.

### Comparative analysis of development scenarios

#### Liverpool Bay

...

Overall, the greater amount of constraint and sensitivities occur in the southern part of the Strategic Area, particularly the presence of bird interests, marine habitats of conservation interest, seascape, fisheries and marine traffic. Seascape constraints in the north of the area are significant as a consequence of topography and amount of surrounding coastline including the Isle of Man. Conversely, industrialisation and population density is greater in the south, which in isolation would be thought to offer good siting potential, and a local market.

It is therefore considered appropriate for the greater proportion of future windfarm development to concentrate in the offshore portion of the Strategic Area, most likely with a focus on fewer large windfarms. Locating offshore would limit concerns about visual impacts and birds. Some development, probably of smaller windfarms, could be accommodated within the remainder of the Strategic Area but would be subject to greater levels of constraint and hence potential opposition from one or more interested party, statutory or otherwise.

...

#### Greater Wash

...

The Greater Wash Strategic Area is the largest of the three under consideration and offers the greatest potential capacity for windfarm development. Inshore areas, particularly along the southern part of the area from the Wash and along the north Norfolk Coast, carry the greatest amount of constraint and sensitivity, particularly with respect to visual, marine mammals, inshore fisheries, birds and offshore SAC/SPA (Special Area of Conservation / Special Protection Area[91]) habitats.

...

---

[91] For explanation of these forms of designation, see Ch. 15, pp. 627–36.

### Thames Estuary

...

This Strategic Area has fewer environmental constraints than the other Strategic Areas, though coastally, several estuaries and marshes are important bird habitats. Seagrass beds are also present along the Essex coast at Maplin sands. Commercial activities and recreational navigation are other main constraints ... In general, avoidance of coastal sensitivities, including conservation interests and visual impacts, favours offshore development.

For each Strategic Area, the likely energy outputs were assessed and graded against the potential significant environmental impacts for each Area. The broad conclusions of the exercise are as follows:

Conclusions of the Environmental Report

...

In order to assist windfarm development with minimal environmental disturbance, it is suggested that the following strategic approach is adopted:

- in all Strategic Areas, avoid the majority of development within the nearshore zone of high visual sensitivity;
- where development might occur in nearshore areas, preferentially select low constraint areas and consider small scale development;
- avoid development in shallow water where common scoter and red throated diver and other species (including marine animals) are known to congregate (particularly in Liverpool Bay and Greater Wash), pending the outcome of monitoring studies;
- address the uncertainties of large scale impacts at a strategic level, particularly cumulative and those impacts that apply equally to developments irrespective of their location;
- consideration of the potential for adverse environmental impacts of offshore wind energy to compromise development efforts should take into account the economic benefits and more importantly, the indisputable benefit of generating energy using the renewable resource of offshore wind.

The rigour of this strategic environmental assessment exercise may be questioned.[92] Its subject matter strays beyond the scope of the SEA Directive by taking into account the likely environmental effects of wind farm development on employment and recreation in each of the strategic areas (albeit that these factors are highlighted as important elements of the government's sustainable development strategy in PPS1[93]) and by predicting the likely sources of 'opposition' to individual projects.

But the more serious flaw is that the assessment presupposes that the development of wind farms will take place by analysing *where* they should be located, rather than whether such development should go ahead in the first place.

---

[92] Glen Plant, 'Offshore Renewable Energy Development and the Energy Bill', p. 869.
[93] See PPS 1, above, pp. 703–4.

On this point, it is particularly telling that the consideration of alternatives is restricted to alternative sites, rather than a more thorough assessment of alternative policy options, such as energy conservation programmes or the development of other forms of renewable energy. This highlights a key difficulty in carrying out a strategic exercise such as this: it must be sufficiently abstract to assess a range of policy options or plans, whilst also being detailed enough to provide a framework for development (the *raison d'être* of the SEA Directive[94]). The Countryside Council for Wales, for example, critically stated that the environmental report gave no indication of the 'carrying capacity' of each of the strategic areas available, other than the physical seabed space available. However, maintaining a balance between 'strategic' elements of the report and site-specific information is particularly difficult in a case such as this in which the given objective of the assessment was to inform decision making about the suitability or otherwise of specific areas for wind farm development, rather than the desirability of offshore wind energy development per se. The strategic environmental assessment process appears to use methods better suited to project-based environmental assessment (EIA) procedures (as discussed below in the case of the Robin Rigg wind farm on the Solway Firth, pp. 730–5), such as identifying the potential impacts of wind farm installations in specific areas, although in this case without the baseline data from which the significance of the likely impacts of specific projects may be extrapolated. This geographical specificity gives the strategic environmental assessment the appearance of a 'bundle of EIAs', and leads to concerns about how the information in the environmental report might influence the licensing process, in particular whether the granting of ('Round 2') leases might pre-judge decisions about development consent, possibly supplanting local decision making and circumventing local public participation and, importantly, 'opposition'. This is likely to be a problem where, as in this case, the policy making body (the Department of Trade and Industry) also decides applications for development consent. Instead, site-specific decisions about development consent should more properly be based on the findings of project-based environmental impact assessment procedures,[95] and informed by robust participation at the local level. In summary the danger is that an over-detailed and prescriptive strategic environmental assessment exercise might act as a substitute for decision making procedures at the local level.

The environmental report, the non-technical summary of which is extracted above, is just one product of a process of information gathering and consultation of different groups and stakeholders, some of which were brought together expressly for this reason, such as the DTI Renewables Advisory Board and SEA

---

[94] Notably, the SEA Directive requires analysis of the environmental effects of plans and programmes, not *policy* as in earlier versions of the Directive. See further on SEA, Ch. 14, pp. 597–604.

[95] DTI, *R2 Offshore Wind Energy SEA Consultation Report Responses*, www.offshore-sea.org.uk/consultations/Wind-R2/Wind-responses.pdf.

Steering Group. Although various groups were engaged in the consultation exercise, there was a lack of lay, public participation, possibly because local groups tend to be formed in response to a specific 'threat' of development in a particular area, rather than more 'strategic' exercises such as this. Notably, the Energy Act 2004 fails to provide for public participation in decision making, for example by requiring statements of community involvement, as introduced in the town and country planning system by the Planning and Compulsory Purchase Act 2004 (on which, see Chapter 13, pp. 536–8).

The results of *consultation* as part of the strategic environmental assessment process are published alongside the environmental report. Many of the responses come from key groups and agencies such as the Marine Conservation Society and the Countryside Agency. The consultation exercise also gave wind farm developers the opportunity to advance their views, for example that the framework being proposed appeared to discourage development *outside* the proposed regions and that, as a result, the DTI should publish a timetable for future rounds of leases and strategic environmental assessment procedures for other areas.

The consultation exercise has had some material effects: analysis of the responses led the DTI to exclude from development a coastal strip with a width of 8 km, extending to 13 km in areas of particular sensitivity. In addition certain shallow water regions were excluded from the North West strategic area, in recognition of the potentially higher sensitivity of shallow coastal waters to wind farm development – in particular, disturbance to birds. Developers are now able to tender for any sites within the boundaries of the strategic areas other than in the excluded regions. This lends a de facto policy presumption in favour of development in the strategic areas which are *not* the subject of the above exclusions.

A final point is that, although documents such as this are designed to present information in a neutral fashion, in effect this environmental report reinforces policy about giving greater weight to the 'economic benefits' and 'indisputable benefit of generating energy using the renewable resource of offshore wind' as opposed to any 'adverse [local] environmental impacts' to flow from this, and guards against compromising 'development efforts'.[96]

In addition to strategic assessments such as this example, at the project level specific applications for offshore wind farms must be accompanied by an environmental impact assessment under the Electricity (EIA) Regulations.[97] An example of such an environmental impact assessment is given below, in the case of the Robin Rigg offshore wind farm in the Solway Firth (see pp. 730–5).

---

[96] *Offshore Wind Energy Generation: Phase 1 Proposals and Environmental Report* (BMT Cordah Ltd, Environmental Management Consultants) for consideration by the Department of Trade and Industry (2003), pp. 1–24, p. 24.

[97] Electricity Works (Environmental Impact Assessment) (England and Wales) SI 2000 No. 1927 and, in Scotland, the Electricity Works (Environmental Impact Assessment) (Scotland) Regulations 2000, SI 2000 No. 320. These transpose the EIA Directive (Directive 85/337/EEC, as amended by Directive 97/11/EC) requiring that an environmental impact assessment be carried out for 'installations for the harnessing of wind power for energy production (wind farms)' likely to have a significant effect on the environment.

Although it is not yet entirely clear whether an environmental impact assessment will be required of developments in renewable energy zones, it is most likely that the scope of these Regulations will be extended to include such developments.

A further environmental assessment must be carried out in accordance with the Habitats Regulations 1994, which aim to transpose the EC Birds and Habitats Directives (see Chapter 15). Regulation 48(1)(a) of the Habitats Regulations requires that 'a competent authority, before deciding to undertake, or give consent, permission or other authorisation for, a plan or project which is likely to have a significant effect on a European site[98] in Great Britain ... shall make an *appropriate assessment* of the implications for the site in view of that site's conservation objectives'. Unlike environmental assessment under the Electricity (EIA) Regulations 2000, the aim of which is to provide information about the likely effects of development and alternatives (either in terms of the design or location of the project, or alternatives to the project itself), the scheme of the Habitats Directive is such that certain substantive consequences flow from undertaking such an assessment. As we discuss in more detail in Chapter 15 (pp. 661–5), most importantly, development consent must not be granted in the case of a negative assessment, unless there are no alternatives. In such circumstances, the plan or project may only be carried out 'for imperative reasons of overriding public interest', and compensatory measures must be taken to ensure the overall coherence of Natura 2000, the network of European conservation sites.[99] In cases in which a site hosts a 'priority natural habitat type and/or a priority species', the only considerations which may be raised are those relating to 'human health or public safety, to beneficial consequences of primary importance for the environment, or, following an opinion from the European Commission, to other imperatives of overriding public interest'.[100] The uncertainties involved in the designation of such sites, and the extent of the onus on the developer to seek alternatives, or compensate for any damage, has led Glen Plant to offer the following advice: 'Bearing in mind that the locations and sizes of European marine sites might change over time (not least as climate change increasingly affects wildlife populations and habitats), developers are well-advised to avoid prospective as well as identified European marine sites.'[101] The geographical scope of the Habitats Regulations is likely to be extended to offshore areas beyond territorial waters,[102] so that an 'appropriate assessment' of the environmental effects of offshore projects beyond territorial waters will also be required.[103]

---

[98] Namely a special protection area or special area of conservation. See Ch. 15, pp. 627–36, for further explanation.

[99] Regulation 49 Habitats Regulations 1994, implementing Art. 6(4) of the Habitats Directive.

[100] Following the second paragraph of Art. 6(4) of the Habitats Directive. See further on these points, Ch. 15, p. 665.        [101] Plant, 'Offshore Wind Energy Development', p. 952.

[102] By the Offshore Marine Conservation (Marine Habitats &c) Regulations (still in draft at the time of writing).

[103] Note the High Court decision *R* v. *Secretary of State for Trade and Industry ex parte Greenpeace* [2000] 2 CMLR 94, in which a declaration was granted to the effect that the Habitats Directive applied to the United Kingdom continental shelf (UKCS) and that the Secretary of State was

### (c) Robin Rigg in the Solway Firth

The Robin Rigg offshore wind farm[104] in the Solway Firth formed part of the 'Round 1' tranche of installations awarded site leases by the Crown Estate. Its location in Scotland meant that development consent was to be decided by the Scottish Executive. But other aspects of the development, for example permissions to run cables from the site to the Cumbrian coast, were decided by the English planning authorities. The border location of the project means that it holds particular cultural and historical significance, as well as being an important estuary for wildlife; 'The Solway' has been described as 'one of the last unspoiled estuaries in the United Kingdom'.[105] The following captures the 'sense of place' of the Solway Firth in a more poetic and sophisticated way than that attempted in legal documents such as environmental statements.

### David Hayes, 'Ozymandias on the Solway' in Anthony Barnett and Roger Scruton (eds.), *Town and Country* (Jonathan Cape, 1998), pp. 46–7

This too is the last of England. The Solway estuary west of Carlisle is a desolate place of salt marshes, migratory birds, industrial relics and imperial ambitions. The Roman wall reached its limit at Maia (Bowness today), part of a defensive system that stretched forty miles down the coast. African legionnaires were here a millennium before the Normans. The Brythonic (Welsh) kingdoms of Rheged and Strathclyde straddled both sides of this narrow firth. Norse settlers from Ireland and the Isle of Man spread through the region. The expansion of Northumbria led to new forms of cultural synthesis, as the Anglo-Scandinavian stone crosses at Gosforth and Dearham indicate. The Scots held sway when the Domesday Book was being compiled elsewhere, and contested the areas for two centuries after the arrival of the Normans. In the nineteenth century, a canal and railway built by Irish labour attempted to link Carlisle with the sea. The past of this 'corner of a corner of England', to adapt Hilaire Belloc, 'is infinite and can never be exhausted'.[106]

...

   The Solway (from sulwath or muddy ford in Norse) is now part of England's far north, remote from and unconsidered by what are significantly called its 'home counties'. The basic components of the landscape – water, farming plain, village settlement, the view of higher ground – are hardly unique. This is very much countryside, even if it would not normally be considered as 'the' countryside. In this, the Solway may be emblematic of those diverse

Footnote 103 (*cont.*)
> under a duty to consider and apply the provisions of the Directive when proposing to grant exploration licences in relation to the UKCS and to superjacent waters up to a 200 nautical mile limit. Although there was no specific definition of the phrase 'the European Territory of the Member States' within the terms of the Directive, it was possible for a directive or regulation to apply beyond the territorial waters of the Member States. This point is confirmed by the ECJ in Case C-6/04 *Commission* v. *UK*, paras. 115–20.

[104] The Solway Firth was originally the site for two wind farms, one of which – Robin Rigg – was at a more advanced stage of development. For all practical purposes, e.g. for environmental assessment, the projects are treated as one and referred to collectively as Robin Rigg.

[105] Solway Rural Initiative.

[106] Cf. Patrick Wright, *The Village that Died for England* (Cape, 1996), p. xv.

components of England – some (Cornwall, East Anglia, the North-East) quite sharply defined, others (the West Country, the North West) perhaps less so, yet which all themselves subsume numerous odd corners seeming to escape easy categorisation. For the regional status of the Solway is ambiguous – a northern extension of the Lake District, a western promontory of the Borders, and eastern territory of the Irish Sea, yet not quite belonging to any. This too is the work of history. Many ambitions of power lie buried here. The Roman wall has been recycled into churches and farms, the anchorage at Skinburness (from which a large English fleet sailed north in 1296) was reclaimed by the sea, the ruined harbour at Port Carlisle is lonely evidence of industrial failure, the massive toxic weapons dump at Beaufort's Dyke is a sunken monument to military vanity.

These cultural and environmental features of the area help to explain why the development aroused so much local concern: Dumfries and Galloway Council, Dalbeattie County Council and Scottish Natural Heritage all opposed the application. However, the sixty-turbine development was finally authorised by the Scottish Executive in 2003, in line with its plan to generate 40 per cent of Scottish electricity from renewable sources by 2020. The relevant planning policy, contained in National Planning Policy Guidance 6, *Renewable Energy*, is broadly equivalent to the key statement of policy in PPS 22. NPPG 6 states that, in deciding whether to authorise renewable energy development, 'the wider environmental and economic benefits of such developments should be a significant consideration, particularly where the impact on the local environment is not likely to be significant'.[107] The developers (originally Offshore Energy Resources Ltd, now Powergen Renewables) also sponsored a Private Bill in the  Scottish Parliament to change navigation and fishing rights in the area,[108] which was granted assent in 2003. The authorisation was made conditional upon a 'positive' environmental impact assessment. The following extract from the Environmental Statement which accompanied the application for development consent was compiled to fulfil the Electricity Works (Environmental Impact Assessment) (Scotland) Regulations 2000.[109] It is notable that the statement provides arguments *in favour of* the project.

---

[107] NPPG 6, *Renewable Energy* (Scottish Executive, 2000), para. 24; see generally paras. 13–25. Note in particular the presumption in para. 19 that renewable energy projects should be permitted unless certain circumstances can be demonstrated, e.g. they would be significantly detrimental to the landscape character of National Scenic Areas and National Parks. However, although more permissive (especially when compared to policy pre-2000), the policy guidance is still considered to be open to interpretation and capable of forming a platform for objections: 'it leaves scope for planning authorities to legitimately – or illegitimately – block these developments … and the anti-wind campaign is growing' (Ben McGuire, Scottish Executive, pers. comm., 14 December 2005).

[108] Robin Rigg Windfarm (Navigation and Fishing) (Scotland) Act, introduced in Parliament 27 June 2002. Assent was given to the Robin Rigg Act in 2003. The Private Bill was made under ss. 28 and 29 Scotland Act 1998 and the Private Legislation Procedures Scotland Act 1936, as amended.

[109] SI 2000 No. 320. The Statement was also prepared in support of an application under s. 57 Town and Country Planning Act 1990 and s. 37 of the Electricity Act 1989 for the on-land grid connection in England.

### *Environmental Statement: Offshore Wind Farm at Robin Rigg,* Non-Technical Summary, produced by Natural Power Consultants Ltd (2001)

**1. Introduction** [gives details of authorisations applied for]

**2. Site Location**

The main part of the development including turbines, foundations and the offshore substation would be located in the central part of the Solway Firth immediately to the north of the English/Scottish border which roughly bisects the Firth. The centre of the turbine layout site would lie some 11 km south of the Scottish coast at Balcary Point in Dumfries and Galloway and 13.5 km from the English coast at Maryport in Cumbria …

**3. The Need for and Benefits of the Proposal**

**3.1. Environmental Benefits**

Use of renewable energy plays an important part in the strategies to reduce the threat of climate change arising from atmospheric pollution, which is widely regarded as the most critical environmental problem of this century. The displacement of pollution from fossil fuel power stations also helps combat acid rain and conserves fossil fuel reserves.

The Environmental Statement then gives the UK's targets for reducing carbon dioxide emission levels and producing energy from renewable sources, and quantifies the net pollution '*savings*' made over the lifetime of the wind farm. It continues:

The wind farm at Robin Rigg is estimated to produce between 417 and 750 GWh of electricity per year depending on the final turbine selected for the site (2 MW to 3.6 MW machines). This would be sufficient to provide clean electricity to between 99,000 and 178,000 households. The renewable electricity produced would be equivalent to between 17% and 30% of the *total* new output needed to meet the 2010 Scottish renewables target. The proposed wind farm at Robin Rigg would therefore represent a very significant contribution to the UK renewables and $CO_2$ emissions reduction targets.

**3.2 Economic Benefits**

**Construction** – the investment value of the Robin Rigg wind farm through design, construction and commissioning would be at least £150 million. If the Robin Rigg wind farm project follows the pattern of onshore wind farms, upwards of £30 million would be invested into the economies of southwest Scotland and northwest England during construction. The works would also lead to a major investment in a local port or ports likely to include Silloth, Maryport, Workington or Barrow-in-Furness. This period of intensive use of port facilities is expected to last for two construction seasons. Up to 120 skilled and non-skilled workers would be employed for the construction period both onshore and offshore for the construction season(s). A number of these workers are likely to be sourced locally.

Site selection and design of the wind farm, including turbine type and size, cabling and navigation, are then discussed.

### 16. Summary findings of the Environmental Impact Assessment
In carrying out and presenting the results of the specialist assessments within the Environmental Statement, care has been taken to adopt a worst case approach, to ensure that environmental effects are not underestimated.

The report then discusses the likely effects of the project on hydrology, sediments and coastal processes, water quality, marine benthos, marine animals and fish, but predicts no likely adverse effects for any of these categories. In fact, it was suggested that the turbines would act as 'Fish Aggregation Devices' attracting fish to the new habitat and shelter created by the foundation structures placed in the seabed, and that 'some reef dwelling species may colonise the new structures, thereby increasing population sizes in the Firth' (p. 19). It was considered that this would have the additional effect of attracting birds, porpoise and dolphin to the area for hunting (p. 21). The consultants recommended three years' post-construction monitoring of effects on fish, in order 'to confirm the conclusions of the EIA' (p. 19). Given that concerns about the environmental effects of wind farms have focussed upon the impacts upon birdlife, we reproduce this part of the Statement below.

### 16.5. Birds
The area was considered to be of potential sensitivity for bird impacts, lying as it does some 7km south and west of an area designated under European law as a Special Protection Area for individual water fowl species and also for overall assemblages of overwintering birds. Therefore particular attention was given to finding out how much use these important bird species made of the sea above the Robin Rigg bank.

Boat based surveys have been carried out twice a month for 12 months (apart from a couple of missed surveys for bad weather) covering low and high tides, dawn and dusk; together with a number of aerial surveys to verify the boat counts. The survey area covered the wind farm area, a control area and a buffer zone which was expanded to study the feeding habits of the most common bird in the area, the Common Scoter. The results of the bird surveys were then integrated with the other surveys to ensure the whole picture was available for the assessment work. The assessment covered food sources, migration routes, roosting, breeding and moulting areas, flight patterns, collision risk, and changes in habitat due to storm conditions. It assessed the wind farm proposal and its surrounding area during construction, operation and decommissioning.

From the survey work key species were identified using the area around the wind farm, such as Common Scoter, Divers and migrant waterfowl. Using 12 months' data of numbers of these species crossing the wind farm area and the height at which they flew, a model of the annual number of birds likely to collide with wind turbines was created according to methodologies developed with Scottish Natural Heritage. In all cases collision rates were found to be significantly lower than natural death rates, and therefore the wind farm was not considered to represent a significant collision risk for these species.

In addition no significant disturbance impacts are predicted due to noise and visual presence of turbines. Disturbance would affect at most regionally important numbers of any species, and the wind farm area does not provide any particularly important ecological resource for these bird populations. The only two species to occur in the overall study area in nationally important areas are Red Throated Divers and Common Scoter. Displacement zones of more than 5km for Red Throated Divers and 3 km for Common Scoters would be needed to affect nationally important numbers, and given that the maximum distance displacement that has been demonstrated at existing wind farms is 800m, it can safely be concluded that disturbance to these species over such large distances would be very unlikely. This applies for construction, operation, and decommissioning.

A recommendation has been made for further ongoing survey work comprising monthly boat surveys until construction is started, twice-monthly during construction and monthly surveys for another three years post construction. These surveys would cover the same areas as the baseline work to ensure consistent survey results, and confirm the conclusions reached in the assessment.

The Statement continues by elaborating the expected socio-economic impacts of the development, such as local investment and tourism. On the latter issue, the report cites anecdotal evidence that wind farms attract tourists and visitors to an area, concluding that 'a significant effect does not imply a negative effect' (p. 30). As we discussed in relation to the environmental report of the strategic environmental assessment of Round 2 areas (p. 726), this category of information does not fall within the list of information to be included in environmental statements under Annex IV of the EIA Directive, as transposed by the Scottish Electricity Works Regulations 2000. Its inclusion has the effect of combining the public benefits arising from the project with considerable (private) financial rewards, in a manner favourable to the developer.[110] A further aspect of this is the use of the environmental statement to argue the case for the development ('The Need for and Benefits of the Proposal'), which is reinforced by the failure to consider any alternatives to the proposed development, in the sense either of alternative sites, or of a more wide-ranging analysis of other ways of producing (or conserving) electricity, as required by the Scottish Electricity Works Regulations 2000. More positively, the Statement envisages post-assessment monitoring, or a 'living environmental assessment',[111] although it should not be presumed that such monitoring will necessarily 'confirm the conclusions reached in the assessment'. A key point is that as a matter of law, no clear results flow from a finding that the consequences of development depart from predictions made in the developer's environmental statement, as we discuss further in Chapter 14, pp. 604–7.

The construction of the Robin Rigg wind farm is currently postponed following difficulties with procuring the turbines, and there are some doubts

---

[110] This aspect of environmental assessment is discussed in theoretical terms in Ch. 14, pp. 563–7.

[111] Ian Johnson, Powergen Renewables, pers. comm., 15 October 2005.

about whether the project will proceed. However, in terms of obtaining development consent, the various concerns about the effects on birdlife and the seascape were overcome, mainly by avoiding development in protected areas within the Solway Firth. In contrast, the proposed wind farm development off the Isle of Lewis is generating controversy and has become the subject of legal action for precisely this reason.

## 4 Conservation objections

We explained that, initially, local concerns about wind farms tended to be concentrated upon their impacts on the landscape. Such concerns were easily dismissed as 'subjective' and, given the far more serious consequences of climate change for the landscape, short-sighted.[112] The policy in favour of renewable energy generation was then refocussed upon large, offshore wind farms which generally attract less public attention, and tend to generate more electricity. However, the location of wind farms in areas designated for their conservation value has now mobilised conservation groups because of the possible disturbance and killing of birds and other wildlife,[113] as seen particularly in the case of the proposed wind farm on the Isle of Lewis in the Hebrides.

This proposal by Amec and British Energy (Lewis Wind Power Ltd) involves the construction of 190 wind turbines on the Island. The project is controversial because the turbines would be spread across two special protection areas (the Lewis Peatlands SPA and the Ness and Barvas SPA) and the Lewis Peatlands Ramsar site (protected under the Ramsar Convention on Wetlands of International Importance), so designated because of the importance of these habitat areas for a range of birds dependent upon diverse environmental conditions – golden eagles, merlins, black-throated divers, red-throated divers, dunlins and greenshanks.[114] The effects of the development on the hydrology of the area, as well as further indirect effects from road and pylon building, may also extend to a special area of conservation (Lewis Peatlands SAC) located within the main SPA site (for discussion of these designations, see Chapter 15, pp. 627–36). Because of the designation of parts of the site (and nearby land) as 'European sites' (SPAs and SACs), certain procedural safeguards apply when development is proposed on the sites. If the development is thought likely to create a 'significant and adverse impact' on the site under the Habitats Regulations 1994[115] (implementing Art. 6(4) of the Habitats Directive (discussed

---

[112] Countryside Commission, *Climate Change, Acidification and Ozone: Potential Impacts on the English Countryside* (Countryside Commission, 1995). For comment on the irony of landscape impacts, given that climate change is likely to produce far-reaching effects, see Paul Burall, 'NIMBYs and Renewable Energy' (2002) *Town and Country Planning* 311, p. 312.

[113] Mark Townsend, 'Wind Farms Threaten the Red Kite', *Observer*, 25 January 2005.

[114] See RSPB briefing note 'RSPB Lodges Official Objection to World's Largest Onshore Wind Farm'.

[115] The Conservation (Natural Habitats &c.) Regulations 1994 (SI 1994 No. 2716), Regulation 49.

in Chapter 15, pp. 648 and 661), and there are no viable alternatives, the Scottish Executive may only authorise it for 'imperative reasons of overriding public interest'. The building of such a large wind farm ('the world's largest onshore wind farm'[116]) on boggy peatland would be a great engineering feat, requiring extensive drainage operations and the building of large concrete foundations. But it also presents the likelihood of serious and enduring adverse effects on the nature conservation interests of the Island, some of which are detailed in the developer's environmental statement which accompanied the application for development consent for the wind farm and associated infrastructure made under s. 36 of the Electricity Act 1989 and submitted to the Scottish Executive in November 2004. Note that the non-technical summary from this statement, extracted below, adopts the language of environmental impact assessment ('significance', 'impact', 'fragility') in describing the *socio-economic* impacts of the project but with a positive spin. It greatly emphasises the financial compensation for the local community, seemingly implementing the advice to policy makers about appealing to people's self-interest, discussed above (pp. 713–17).[117]

### Lewis Wind Power Ltd, *Environmental Statement,* Non-Technical Summary, October 2004, Summary of Findings, pp. 8–9

The EIA process requires a number of surveys and studies to be undertaken. These studies have been carried out following consultation with the Scottish Executive, Comhairle nan Eilean Siar (Western Isles Council), Scottish Natural Heritage (SNH) and others.

Lewis Wind Power's interpretation of the main findings of the EIA is presented below. The main findings presented are those that have a substantial impact on the environment or economy of Lewis.

#### Socio-economics

The construction and operation phases of the Lewis Wind Farm are predicted to have a significant impact on the fragile economy of the Western Isles, particularly in terms of job creation. There are also predicted benefits to the wider Scottish economy.

[The Statement estimates the number of jobs that would be created]

...

#### Habitats

The construction and operation of the proposed wind farm is predicted to result in the loss, disturbance and change to 788 hectares (1947 acres) of land, of this 577 hectares (1426 acres) are within the Lewis Peatlands Special Protected Area (SPA). The SPA is protected for its bird interest. This accounts for less than 1% of the total area of the SPA and is not considered significant in relation to the function of the SPA. No impacts are predicted for Lewis Peatlands candidate Special Area of Conservation (cSAC) or Loch Scarrasdale Site

---

[116] See RSPB briefing note 'RSPB Lodges Official Objection'.

[117] Picking up on the willingness of developers to make such contributions, the Highland Council has prepared a draft toolkit for community councils, 'Can Your Community Benefit from Renewable Energy Developments?'

of Special Scientific Interest (SSSI). The roads and access tracks crossing the blanket bog and other habitats could cause a potential impact. These structures may act to restrict the movement of species from one area to another and potentially make them less viable. The layout has been designed around sensitive habitats, avoiding them wherever possible. To alleviate the remaining impacts significant schemes would be put in place to restore areas of plantation forests back to native blanket bog and restore areas of peatlands to better conditions.

### Ornithology

This assessment draws largely on a precautionary approach due to the uncertainty surrounding the prediction of impacts. This precautionary approach predicts that the proposal has the potential to have effects on important bird species of the Lewis Peatlands SPA including dunlin, golden plover, greenshank, golden eagle and merlin. The Scottish Executive will make their own assessment of the impacts and the significance of effect on the Lewis Peatlands SPA. The Lewis Wind Farm proposal includes measures to reduce the impacts of habitat loss and the displacement of upland waders. An example of this is through the restoration of former peat cuttings and felling of areas of recent coniferous planting. LWP would be willing to consider enhancing habitats in the wider geographical area, should this be necessary.

### Landscape Impacts

The impacts on the landscape would be significant; the landscape of northern Lewis with its flat plateaus and slightly undulating hills of blanket bog not being able to hide the wind turbines. The wind turbines would only be seen from the tops of the highest peaks in the South Lewis, Harris and North Uist National Scenic Area. The wind farm would be visible from the historic garden and designed landscape of Lewis Castle, but only from high ground within the castle grounds.

### Rivers

If the construction of a wind farm is not properly managed, there is the potential to pollute the rivers and streams of the area. Excavation could cause sediment to enter watercourses or change habitats, which could alter the response of the catchment to rainfall or cause peat to dry out. All construction operations would follow Best Practice and Scottish Environmental Protection Agency guidelines to protect the watercourses, therefore the risk of pollution would be low.

The environmental statement continues to discuss the potential impacts on archaeology and cultural heritage, fisheries and fauna, and the need to balance the carbon emissions from the peat on which the wind farm is to be built.

RSPB Scotland commissioned independent research to evaluate the extent to which this statement correctly and adequately assessed the potential impacts of the development.[118] The resulting report by Richard Lindsay states that the developer's environmental statement considerably undercalculates the scope of

---

[118] RSPB, *Lewis Wind Farm Proposals: Observations on the Official Environmental Impact Statement* (2005), compiled by Richard Lindsay, p. 54.

impact, including the number of bird deaths which are likely to ensue, and includes a number of inaccuracies, including incorrectly defining the legal status of land designations. Most importantly it asserts a fundamental problem with the developer's 'deconstructivist' approach to assessing environmental effects, by which a system is broken down into its constituent parts and assumptions are made about the way in which these various parts will react to the construction of the wind farm. Instead, looking at the way the entire system works, Richard Lindsay reports that the effect of the large-scale drainage and construction work on the hydrological condition of the peatlands bog will seriously compromise the *wider* ecological state of the area, including the Special Area of Conservation. For example, the Lewis Wind Farm Environmental Statement acknowledges the existence of a blanket mire ecosystem in the peat bog in terms of its structure and classification, but shows little understanding of its broader *functional* significance. This raises an important issue about the correct 'unit' for the purpose of carrying out the environmental assessment and as a matter of decision making, namely whether this should conform to objective legal boundaries (of the specific development site boundaries), or rather be guided by the ecological conditions on the site (in this case the fact that peatland systems react as whole hydrological entities, so that the fact that even individual turbine excavations have the potential to result in widespread impact in the form of draining the peatland is highly important). The European Commission in its guidance on conducting environmental impact assessments recommends adopting the latter, broader and more integrated, approach to assessment:

> Indirect and cumulative impacts and impact interactions may well extend beyond the geographical site boundaries of the project. Determining the geographical boundaries will therefore be a key factor in ensuring the impacts associated with a project are assessed comprehensively wherever possible … Additional data may need to be gathered to cover wider spatial boundaries, taking into account the potential for impacts to affect areas further away from the site than if just direct impacts were considered. Consideration should be given to the distance that an impact can travel, and any interaction networks.[119]

Following such guidance, the review of the developer's environmental statement for the RSPB takes greater account of indirect effects than the developer's statement itself. This adoption of a fundamentally different approach to studying the environmental effects of development makes clear that the methodological approach used in such studies is contestable, and therefore that the resulting information, presented in environmental statements as fact, may be subject to varying interpretations. As a consequence, RSPB Scotland lodged an objection letter with the Scottish Executive in February 2005.

---

[119] European Commission, *Guidelines for the Assessment of Indirect and Cumulative Impacts as well as Impact Interactions* (1999).

The RSPB wishes to register its OBJECTION to this proposal as set out in detail in Annex 1.[120]

...

The Lewis Wind Farm proposals will result in the loss of and disturbance to wildlife habitats which are of local, national and international importance. Impacts, as identified by the ES, include:

- The loss of at least 20 red-throated divers due to collision with turbines during the lifetime of the development (although we believe this figure to be inaccurate due to a basic spreadsheet error and should in fact be 75–150 divers due to collision);
- The loss of at least 50 golden eagles due to collision with turbines and the displacement of one breeding pair for the lifetime of the development;
- The loss of 50 merlin due to collision with turbines and the displacement of 5 breeding pairs for the lifetime of the development;
- The loss of 350 pairs of golden plover (1.5% of the GB and Ireland population) due to displacement;
- The loss of 314 pairs of dunlin (4% of the GB and Ireland population and 3% of the entire temperate population of *schinzii* dunlin) due to habitat loss and displacement impacts;

Notwithstanding the enormity of these statistics we believe many of the impacts in the ES to be underestimated, in particular those relating to habitat. In order to evaluate more closely the information provided on habitat and hydrology we have commissioned an independent review of the data by a recognised expert [i.e. the *Lewis Wind Farm Proposals: Observations on the Official Environmental Impact Statement* (2005), compiled by Richard Lindsay] ... The conclusions from this work indicate that the level of habitat impacts may be thirty times greater than those predicted in the ES.

From the information currently available Scottish Ministers should reject this application on the basis that:

- It cannot be ascertained that the integrity of the Lewis Peatlands cSAC, the Lewis Peatlands SPA and Ramsar site, and the Ness and Barvas SPA will not be adversely affected;
- It has not been shown that there are no alternative solutions;
- It has not been shown that there are imperative reasons of overriding public interest; and
- The ES does not provide suitable mitigation or compensation proposals.

Should Scottish Ministers not be minded to refuse this application immediately we request that a Public Local Inquiry be held to consider the application in detail.

In June 2005, Comhairle nan Eilean Siar (Western Isles Council) voted in favour of the wind farm proposal and recommended approval of the scheme to the Scottish Executive which makes the final decision. The Executive may decide to

---

[120] Not included, see full objection report at www.rspb.org.uk/images/lewis.

call a public inquiry beforehand, although it is under no obligation to do so in cases such as this when the local authority approves the development.[121]

Should the Executive grant development consent, there remains the possibility of invoking the protection granted to SPAs and SACs under EC law should the 'appropriate assessment', compiled for the purposes of Art. 6(4) Habitats Directive,[122] conclude that the project will adversely affect the integrity of the site. Lewis Wind Power has stated that it intends to produce such a document.[123] A difficulty is that it is unclear whether the developer's assessment will suffice in this respect, or whether the Executive must separately and independently evaluate the likely effects of the wind farm on the peatland environment. The second issue is whether feasible alternatives exist. On this point, RSPB Scotland have lodged a pre-emptive complaint with the European Commission[124] alleging that the approach taken by the Executive about the existence of alternatives is contrary to EC law. They argue that the Executive has merely accepted the information provided by the developer under the Electricity Works Regulations 2000, focussing upon alternative *sites* in the Western Isles, rather than themselves carrying out a broader assessment of alternative *solutions* as required by the Habitats Regulations. The complaint begins by giving details of the nature conservation interest of the site and the relevant planning procedures, including the restricted nature of advice on alternatives seemingly adopted by the Comhairle. It then sets out the reason for the complaint. The complaint raises the issue of the geographical scope of the requirement to consider alternatives – that is, whether this should extend to *sites* beyond the Western Isles, not least given that the aim of the project is ultimately to provide power to the *national* grid. There is additionally the requirement to consider alternative *solutions*.

### Complaint to the Commission of the Europe Communities Concerning Failure to Comply with Community Law, Pursuant to Article 226 of the EC Treaty

### Complaint by the Royal Society for the Protection of Birds against the United Kingdom Government in respect of a potential failure by UK authorities to protect the Lewis Peatlands SPA, Ness and Barvas SPA and Lewis Peatlands SAC

#### 8.5 Failure to comply with Article 6(4) Habitats Directive

8.5.1 We believe the advice from the Scottish Executive to restrict the consideration of alternative solutions to the Western Isles constitutes a failure to comply with the requirements of Article 6(4) of the Habitats Directive. Furthermore, given that this is the advice apparently being provided by the competent authority to developers, we

---

[121] Section 37 Electricity Act 1989, see above, pp. 697–8.
[122] As transposed by Regulation 48 Habitats Regulations 1994.
[123] Anne McCall, RSPB (Scotland), pers. comm., 9 December 2005.    [124] See Ch. 15, pp. 661–2.

are concerned that this is a clear indication of the approach being taken by the competent authority in its own deliberations.

### 8.6 Alternative Solutions

...

8.7.1. The consideration of alternative solutions by the developer is restricted to alternative locations for a large-scale wind farm development in the Western Isles. Within the Western Isles the Environmental Statement makes no mention of two other large-scale proposals on the Western Isles, Pairc and Eishken; the former has yet to be submitted as an application, the latter is for 133 turbines and was considered alongside the Lewis Wind Power proposal by the Council.

8.7.2. Beyond the boundaries of the Western Isles there is clearly a huge interest in the potential for wind farm developments in Scotland. There are currently around 250 wind farm sites which are constructed, consented or have been submitted for planning consent. Of these, there are a number of large-scale proposals which will not impact on Natura sites. In terms of renewable energy capacity the Scottish Executive has published a study which concludes that Scotland's onshore wind farm capacity, avoiding a wide range of designated sites, low-flying zones, scenic areas etc. is in the region of 11.5GW ... The second study indicates that to achieve the target of generating 40% of our electricity from renewable sources we need 6GW of installed capacity, of which just under 50% has already been constructed, consented or applied for.

Given the progress already made in Scotland to meet renewable energy targets by 2010, there is also utility in considering a 'do-nothing' option, as required by the SEA Directive.[125]

Should it be decided that no alternatives to this project exist, such an action would then turn on interpretations of the 'imperative reasons of overriding public interest' test (contained in Art. 6(4) as discussed in Chapter 15, pp. 661–5). The lack of bird species listed as 'priority' species under the Habitats Directive is crucial here; in this case the project may be carried out for such reasons, 'including those of a social or economic nature'. Acceptance of the argument that the project would be likely to affect indirectly an SAC (as Richard Lindsay argues in his report for the RSPB), and that this might affect priority habitat types or priority species, would restrict the reasons of overriding public interest to considerations relating to human health or public safety, and to beneficial consequences of primary importance for the environment, or other reasons considered by the European Commission to override the conservation interest of the site (as discussed in Chapter 15, p. 665).

---

[125] Annex I(b) states that information shall be provided by the developer on, *inter alia*, 'the relevant aspects of the current state of the environment and the likely evolution thereof without implementation of the plan or programme'. Although there is no equivalent in the EIA Directive, Commission guidance on the Habitats Directive does call for a 'zero-option' to be considered too (European Commission, *Managing Natura 2000 Sites* (2000), para. 5.3.1).

In summary, this proposal has been highly controversial and divisive, with various environmental groups and local groups holding opposing views on the need for the project and its likely effects. As well as confirming the desirability of taking wind farm development offshore, the Lewis case has highlighted the difficulty of drawing physical boundaries for the purpose of carrying out environmental impact assessment. It reveals also continuing uncertainties about the meaning and adequacy of an 'appropriate assessment' (and relationship with the environmental assessment),[126] and the extent of the procedural requirement to consider alternatives to the proposed project.

## 5 Conclusions

The case of wind farm development illustrates the close inter-relationship between law and policy, the permeability of these categories, and the great potential for inconsistencies and clashes between them. In simple terms, the Energy Act 2004 was enacted to provide the legal machinery to carry out the government's policy on the rapid expansion of the renewables industry, particularly the offshore sector. The basic regulatory mechanism is the licence. Within the licensing process, environmental assessment has an increasingly important role in terms of informing decision makers about the general suitability of areas for wind farms from an environmental perspective, and the authorisation of individual projects. However, environmental assessment is also capable of being used by developers, consultants and the government to advance a particular policy, or project. We see this aspect of the procedure in the encouragement to 'take into account the economic benefits and more importantly, the indisputable benefit of generating energy using the renewable resource of offshore wind' in the strategic environmental assessment for Round 2 offshore projects. Such wording recalls the government's policy statement in PPS 22 on renewable energy that significant weight should be given to 'the wider environmental and economic benefits of all proposals for renewable energy projects', which is likely to be interpreted by developers as a legal test, to be upheld by the courts in the event of an unsuccessful application for development consent. It is also evident in the presentation of information about the socio-economic benefits likely to flow from the construction of the Robin Rigg wind farm in the Solway Firth. These examples underline the potential role of the environmental statement as a political tool in decision making, as well as as a legal document, and offer practical illustrations of the theoretical arguments advanced about environmental assessment in Chapter 14. The case of the proposed wind farm on the Isle of Lewis also points to the fact that the data and methodology of environmental statements can be contested and subject to varying interpretations. Further, in terms of regulatory mechanisms, the Energy Act 2004 also uses the technique of designation (discussed in Chapter 15): the Act permits sea areas to be

---

[126] We discuss this aspect further in Ch. 15, pp. 649–55.

designated as 'renewable energy zones' as a means of marking out suitable areas for wind farm development. In each of these cases, law and policy are mutually reinforcing. But there is also the potential for conflict between law and policy in this area, since the legal protection granted to 'European sites' as a matter of EC law has the potential to skew pro-wind energy policy, as seen in the case of the project on the Isle of Lewis.

The RCEP has commented upon the difficult nature of the balance to be struck by law and policy makers in such cases:

> Mechanisms are needed to ensure that legitimate societal needs can be met in the face of preferences opposing the developments implied by those needs. The town and country planning system is intended to be such a mechanism but such developments must be essential parts of comprehensive and generally accepted policies, they must stem from transparent assessments of needs and environmental capacity, and there must be more imagination in countering any adverse effects on particular areas.[127]

The Royal Commission is right to highlight the difficulty of reaching 'transparent assessments of needs' in an energy debate apparently governed and obscured by a few big electricity companies. The call more imaginatively to counter the adverse effects of wind farm development in local areas, whether by environmental or by monetary forms of compensation, is more problematic, for the reasons discussed above, and in Chapter 16 (pp. 677–80). Not envisaged by the Royal Commission, and far outside the current policy frame, is radical change in the ownership of wind farms in favour of small-scale community, or 'distributed', energy producing schemes. Such schemes, with financial support and a facilitative legal framework, would extend far beyond the current vogue in policy for public participation, or 'community involvement' in decision making, by giving responsibility for and crucially some of the benefits from energy production and conservation to individuals and communities, and possibly encouraging more far-reaching environmental and political sustainability.

## 6 Further reading

For a general account of the law relating to climate change, see Philippe Sands, *Principles of International Environmental Law* (Cambridge University Press, 2003) pp. 357–81. For a more detailed legal context for the two Scottish cases of wind farm development, see Jeremy Rowan-Robinson and Donna W. McKenzie Skene (eds.), *Countryside Law in Scotland* (T. & T. Clark, 2000) (although note the chapter on Habitat Protection predates many of the changes brought about to the SSSI system by the Nature Conservation (Scotland) Act 2000). A historical account of land use in Scotland is given by Donald Mackay's *Scotland's Rural Land Use Agencies* (Scottish Cultural Press, 1995), and a more general perspective is lent by Roger Croft (ed.), *Scotland's Environment: The Future* (Tuckwell Press, 2000). For a policy and legal

---

[127] *Environmental Planning*, para. 8.73.

background to landscape issues in wind farm projects, see IUCN (World Conservation Union), *Landscape Conservation Law: Present Trends and Perspectives in International and Comparative Law* (IUCN, 2000).

We highly recommend Karen Scott's article, 'Tilting at Offshore Windmills: Regulating Wind Farm Development Within the Renewable Energy Zone' (2006) 18 *Journal of Environmental Law* 89, which gives a remarkably thorough account of the state of the regulatory apparatus in this area. An interesting theoretical approach to the UK's wind power law and policy is taken up by Dave Toke and Peter Strachan in 'Ecological Modernisation and Wind Power in the UK' (2006) 16 *European Environment* 155, in which they align the government's policy with a 'weak' ecological agenda, and argue that advancing wind power is not enough – strategies to decentralise decision making and encourage community ownership must also be put in place.

For an insight into the commercial exploitation of wind power, see the websites of the British Wind Energy Association (www.bwea.com) and the European Wind Energy Association (www.ewea.org). For research initiatives into the environmental impacts of offshore wind power, see www.offshorewindfarms.co.uk, the website for Collaborative Offshore Wind Research Into the Environment (COWRIE), a joint venture between the Crown Estate, the DTI and the British Wind Energy Association.

# Index